WAR

EDITORIAL CONSULTANT **SAUL DAVID**

WAR

FROM ANCIENT EGYPT TO IRAQ

**LONDON, NEW YORK, MELBOURNE,
MUNICH, AND DELHI**

DORLING KINDERSLEY

Senior Art Editor Gadi Farfour   **Senior Editor** Alison Sturgeon
Designers Richard Horsford, Dean Morris   **Project Editors** Tarda Davison-Aitkins
Elizabeth O'Neill, Amy Orsborne   Ferdie McDonald, Andrew Szudek
Cartography Encompass Graphics Ltd,   **Editor** Patrick Newman
Paul Eames, Simon Mumford, David Roberts   **Editorial Assistant** Manisha Thakkar
Picture Research Sarah and Roland Smithies   **Production Editor** Tony Phipps
Creative Retouching Miranda Benzies   **Production Controller** Rita Sinha
Creative Technical Support Adam   **Managing Editors** Camilla Hallinan
Brackenbury, John Goldsmid   and Debra Wolter
Managing Art Editor Karen Self   **Associate Publisher** Liz Wheeler
Art Director Bryn Walls   **Reference Publisher** Jonathan Metcalf

TOUCAN BOOKS LTD

Senior Designer Mark Scribbins   **Senior Editor** Hannah Bowen
Designers Nick Avery, Phil Fitzgerald,   **Editors** Natasha Kahn, Donald Sommerville
Thomas Keenes   Anna Southgate
Assistant Abigail Keen   **Managing Director** Ellen Dupont

AMBER BOOKS

Design Manager Mark Batley   **Managing Editor** James Bennett
Designers Joe Conneally, Rick Fawcett   **Editors** Jacqueline Jackson, Cécile Landau
Nicola Hibberd, Brian Rust   Anne McDowall, Constance Novis
Picture Research Terry Forshaw   **Publishing Manager** Charles Catton

EDITORIAL CONSULTANT
Saul David

CONSULTANTS
Lindsay Allen, Roger Collins, Adrian Gilbert (Directory),
Richard Overy, David Parrott, Brendan Simms

CONTRIBUTORS
R.G. Grant with Simon Adams and Michael Kerrigan

DIRECTORY CONTRIBUTORS
Martin J. Dougherty, Michael E. Haskew, Hunter Keeter,
Chris McNab, David Porter, Robert S. Rice

PHOTOGRAPHY
Gary Ombler, Graham Rae

First published in Great Britain in 2009 by Dorling Kindersley Limited
80 Strand, London WC2R 0RL

A Penguin Company

Discover more at
www.dk.com

CONTENTS

WAR IN THE ANCIENT WORLD
3000 BCE – 500 CE   10

2

WAR IN THE MEDIEVAL WORLD
500 – 1500 — 56

3

EARLY MODERN WARFARE
1500 – 1750 — 108

4

THE AGE OF REVOLUTION
1750 – 1830

5

THE DAWN OF MECHANIZED WARFARE
1830 – 1914

6
ERA OF THE WORLD WARS
1914–1945

7
CONFLICTS AFTER WORLD WAR II
1945–PRESENT

DIRECTORY 352

**A comprehensive directory of wars,
battles, and military statistics from
ancient to modern times.**

Foreword

It is well that war is so terrible – we would grow too fond of it", wrote the great Confederate general Robert E. Lee in 1862, thus neatly encapsulating the two conflicting emotions that war has always stirred in the human breast: repulsion and fascination.

War has always been with us as a violent method of resolving disputes. The earliest communities fought each other for control of food and land. But war in its strictest definition is the state of armed conflict between nations or states, or between groups within the same state (otherwise known as civil war). The first recorded wars between organized armies were fought by the city-states of Sumer in the third millennium BCE. Since then, states have habitually used war as a means of achieving their political ends when all peaceful options have been exhausted. War, according to the Prussian military theorist Clausewitz, "is nothing but the continuation of politics by other means".

Scarcely a generation passes in any nation without some exposure to war. Between 1500 BCE and 1860 CE there were in the known world, on average, thirteen years of war to every one year of peace. Virtually all frontiers between nations, races, and religions have been established by wars, and most previous civilizations and empires have expired because of them. The history of the world is primarily the history of war.

The carnage of the 20th century – two world wars and numerous instances of genocide – and the advent of nuclear weapons have made conflict between the major powers both undesirable and unthinkable. Yet for some combatants war has always had its attraction. "Comradeship", wrote a US veteran of World War II, "reaches its peak in battle." In truth, war brings out the best and worst of people. It mobilizes our resources of love, compassion, courage, and self-sacrifice, but also our capacity for hate, xenophobia, brutality, and revenge.

One of the strengths of this impeccably researched, well-written and beautifully illustrated volume is that it covers more than 5,000 years of warfare – from the Sumerians to the modern day – in such a multi-faceted way. It shows how armies were organized, and equipped; how battles, campaigns, and wars were won and lost; and how technology has gradually changed the face of battle from brutal hand-to-hand encounters with axes and swords to the use of impersonal computer-guided weaponry today. It also looks at war from the perspective of politicians, generals, ordinary soldiers, and civilians. And it charts the attempts – not always successful – to regulate war and make it less brutal.

Is there such a thing as a "just" war? Thomas Aquinas thought so, and those who fought for the Allies in World War II would surely agree. Wars are sometimes a necessary evil – to topple dictators, curb aggression, and protect the weak. If a nation is unwilling to fight in what it believes is a just cause, it will not deter others from going to war.

SAUL DAVID, 2009

1

WAR IN THE ANCIENT WORLD

3000 BCE – 500 CE

**Mesopotamia, Egypt, and China saw the
development of complex urban civilizations,
whose rulers protected and increased their
wealth by conquest and exacting tribute.
Their example was followed by the later
empires of the Persians, Greeks, and Romans.**

EGYPTIAN BRONZE SPEARHEAD, 2ND MILLENNIUM BCE

WAR IN THE ANCIENT WORLD
3000 BCE – 500 CE

Whether or not humans should be regarded as warlike by nature, there is substantial archeological evidence of organized combat in prehistoric times. Fighting between different groups of people was frequent in societies of hunter-gatherers and Stone Age farmers. If some encounters seemed designed to minimize casualties – two bands of villagers hurling missiles at one another from a distance – there is also evidence of genocidal warfare, aimed at the extermination of another people to take over its land and resources.

Warring states and empires

As more complex societies developed, they provided the resources for larger-scale armies to be deployed in sustained warfare. Wherever early civilizations emerged – in Mesopotamia, Egypt, China, northern India, or Central America – military success was the basis of imperial power. Triumph in war built up the ruler's prestige as well as his wealth in plunder, land, and slaves. By 3000 BCE the weapons that would remain in use for millennia had already been developed: bows, slingshots, javelins, spears, clubs, knives, and swords, along with shields and armour. Metals such as bronze and iron largely supplanted stone. Early wars were fought exclusively on foot, but in Eurasia and Africa in the 2nd millennium BCE

Greek hoplites

In their disciplined phalanxes protected by a wall of shields, Greek hoplites were a formidable infantry force. They wore well-made bronze armour and helmets and their main weapon was the long, stabbing spear.

many elite warriors rode in chariots, and in the following millennium soldiers also began to fight on horseback. Rulers such as the pharaohs of New Kingdom Egypt and the kings of Assyria maintained substantial standing armies and campaigned over long distances. They also developed the science of siege warfare, with effective machines for battering down or storming city walls.

From the 6th century BCE Greek city-states such as Athens and Sparta fielded armies in which every citizen over a certain age was obliged to serve. The soldiers fought in dense spear-armed infantry formations known as phalanxes. In the eastern Mediterranean naval warfare developed as the Phoenicians and Greeks built fleets of oared galleys, with rams for sinking their opponents. By combining an elite cavalry force with an infantry phalanx, the Macedonian Alexander the Great conquered the mighty Persian empire and extended Macedonian-Greek rule from Egypt to India.

The might of Rome

The subsequent rise of Rome as a major power was initially built on the Greek citizen-soldier concept, although the Roman army was transformed into a

Scythian horseman

It was among the nomadic societies of Central Asia that horses were first domesticated and where they were first ridden in battle.

permanent force of professional soldiers during the 1st century BCE. The Romans extended their rule over a wide-ranging empire through military skill and ruthless willpower. The superior flexibility of their legion infantry, armed with sword and javelin, rendered the phalanx obsolete. However, in a long series of wars, they failed to establish supremacy over Persia, where mounted archers formed a principal element of the armies of the Parthian and Sasanid dynasties.

The fall of empires

The larger empires proved, in the long run, difficult to sustain. Varieties of catapult and crossbow – especially highly developed in China – gave imperial armies a technological edge, as did their engineering skills. But the empires of Rome and Han China could never guarantee their frontiers against incursions by tribal warbands and nomadic peoples. Indeed, both empires often lost to steppe horsemen in battle, although they had considerable success in drawing these so-called "barbarians" into their service. The ancient empires also suffered from the tendency of their armies to fragment into independent sources of power, leading to destructive civil wars between rival generals or regional warlords. If warfare created empires, it also undid them.

c.3000–2500 BCE
The city-states of Sumer in Mesopotamia leave the earliest evidence of organized armies.

» Sumerian ceremonial gold helmet

c.2300 BCE
Sargon of Akkade builds an empire by conquest in Mesopotamia.

c.1760 BCE
Babylon creates an empire in Mesopotamia under Hammurabi.

c.1700 BCE
War chariots drawn by horses are introduced into the Middle East by the steppe pastoralists of Central Asia.

1570 BCE
In Egypt, New Kingdom emerges. Pharaohs such as Thutmosis III (reigned 1479–1425) and Ramesses II (reigned 1279–1213) fight campaigns of conquest.

c.900 BCE
The rule of the warlike Assyrians extends over most of Mesopotamia and Lebanon.

770–475 BCE
In China the Spring and Autumn period of the Zhou dynasty sees conflict between feudal lords, with battles often fought with massed chariots.

c.700–500 BCE
Phoenicians and Greeks develop specialist oared warships – penteconters, biremes, and triremes – some armed with rams.

668–627 BCE
Under Ashurbanipal, the Assyrian empire reaches its greatest extent.

605 BCE
The Assyrian empire is destroyed and the Neo-Babylonian empire flourishes in its place.

559–539 BCE
Cyrus the Great founds the Achaemenid empire in Persia and conquers Babylon.

» Greek bronze helmet of the 5th century BCE

c.500 BCE
The city of Rome begins to extend its control over the neighbouring Latin-speaking tribes, becoming a local power centre.

490 BCE
Greek hoplites repel a Persian seaborne invasion at the battle of Marathon.

480–479 BCE
A large-scale invasion of Greece by Persian emperor Xerxes is defeated by an alliance of Greek city-states led by Athens and Sparta.

475 BCE
The Warring States period in China begins; the civil conflict lasts until 221 BCE. Warfare is on a large scale, with widespread use of crossbows and heavy siege weapons.

« Model of Greek trireme

431–404 BCE
Peloponnesian War pits Athens and its allies in a land and sea war against the Peloponnesian League led by Sparta. Athens is ultimately defeated after a disastrous expedition against Syracuse in Sicily (415–413).

397 BCE
For a campaign against the Carthaginians, Dionysios I, tyrant of Syracuse in Sicily, creates the first siege train in Europe with torsion catapults and a proto-crossbow, the *oxybeles*.

390 BCE
Rome is sacked by the Gauls. This defeat is followed by the reform of the Roman army. The legions, a citizen militia, abandon the infantry phalanx for more flexible tactics.

359–336 BCE
Philip II rules the kingdom of Macedon, transforming it into a major military power and imposing his leadership on the smaller Greek city-states.

343–341 BCE
The Romans fight mountain peoples of southern Italy in the First Samnite War. Rome makes substantial territorial gains.

334–330 BCE
Alexander of Macedon conquers the Persian empire, including Egypt and Mesopotamia, with victories at Issus in 333 and Gaugamela in 331.

« Alexander of Macedon, known as "the Great"

327–304 BCE
Second Samnite War. After initial setbacks, Rome defeats the Samnites and Etruscans.

326 BCE
Alexander invades India and fights King Porus at the battle of Hydaspes. Porus's use of war elephants impresses the Macedonians, who later imitate it.

323 BCE
Death of Alexander triggers a struggle for the succession among his generals. The fighting continues until 276, by which time the Ptolemys rule in Egypt, the Seleucids in Persia, and the Antigonids in Macedonia and Greece.

« Seleucus I, one of Alexander's successors

298 BCE
Mauryan ruler Chandragupta dies, having founded an empire in northern India.

298–290 BCE
Rome is victorious in the Third Samnite war.

« Samnite warriors of the 4th century BCE

280–275 BCE
Rome fights a war against King Pyrrhus of Epirus. Pyrrhus fails to prevent Rome taking control of the Greek cities of southern Italy.

265–262 BCE
Mauryan emperor Ashoka campaigns against Kalinga in India; he renounces war.

ꚜ Mauryan cavalryman in ceremonial dress

264–241 BCE
First Punic War. Massive naval battles between the Roman and Carthaginian fleets. Rome wins control of Sicily.

260 BCE
In China around one million men fight at Changping, a Qin victory over Zhao in the period of the Warring States.

13

250 BCE	200 BCE	150 BCE	100 BCE	50 BCE	1 CE

200 BCE
Steppe nomad horsemen, the Xiongnu, invade China. The Han, rulers of China since 202 BCE, survive through military action and diplomacy.

91–88 BCE
In the Social War, Rome is threatened by a rebellion of its Italian allies. Sulla is one of the generals who suppress the rebellion.

49–45 BCE
Caesar and Pompey fight a war for control of the Roman Republic. In 48 Pompey is defeated at Pharsalus.

« Chinese emperor Shi Huangdi's terracotta army

» Gnaeus Pompeius (Pompey the Great)

149–146 BCE
Third Punic War. The Romans send an expedition to destroy the city of Carthage.

119 BCE
Han China launches a major offensive into the Mongolian territory of Xiongnu nomads.

88–82 BCE
Civil war between legions loyal to Sulla and those supporting Marius. Sulla wins and is dictator of the Roman Republic for two years.

73–70 BCE
Spartacus leads a slave uprising in Italy.

9 CE
Germanic tribes under Arminius massacre Roman legions under Varus at the battle of the Teutoburg Forest.

« Coin of Julius Caesar

221 BCE
Qin Shi Huangdi declares himself first emperor of a unified China. Qin dynasty rules only until 206 BCE.

218 BCE
Carthaginian leader Hannibal invades Italy across the Alps, precipitating the Second Punic War.

197 BCE
Roman army defeats Philip V of Macedon at Cynoscephalae.

192–189 BCE
The Romans wage war on Seleucid King Antiochus III in Syria, winning a notable victory at Magnesia.

112–106 BCE
Rome fights a war against King Jugurtha of Numidia in North Africa. The war advances the transformation of the legions into a professional standing army.

111 BCE
The armies of Han China invade and conquer Vietnam.

44 BCE
Assassination of Julius Caesar in Rome triggers a new round of civil wars.

42 BCE
Caesar's assassins Brutus and Cassius are defeated by Mark Antony and Octavian at Philippi. Rome is ruled by a triumvirate.

14–16 CE
Germanicus, nephew of Emperor Tiberius, leads punitive campaigns against Arminius that end with heavy losses on both sides.

43 CE
The armies of Han China crush nationalist uprising in Vietnam led by the Trung sisters.

216 BCE
Hannibal inflicts a defeat on the Romans at Cannae.

202 BCE
Roman forces invading North Africa defeat Carthaginians at the battle of Zama. Carthage surrenders the following year, ending the Second Punic War.

168 BCE
Roman legions again defeat the Macedonians at Pydna. This gives Rome effective control of Greece.

32–30 BCE
Octavian fights a war with Antony and the Egyptian ruler Cleopatra. After a naval defeat at Actium in 31, Antony and Cleopatra flee to Egypt, where both commit suicide.

43–47 CE
During the reign of Emperor Claudius, the Romans invade Britain and gain control of southern England despite the opposition of Caratacus.

» Vercingetorix, Gallic chieftain defeated by Julius Caesar

« War elephant, adopted by the Greeks and Carthaginians by the 3rd century BCE

58–50 BCE
The Gallic Wars. Julius Caesar campaigns in Gaul, invading Britain on two occasions and defeating the Gallic leader Vercingetorix at Alesia.

27 BCE
Octavian is given the title Augustus and granted imperial powers by the Roman senate. Under his rule (to 14 CE) the Roman legions take on a permanent structure.

» Battle of Actium, key victory in Octavian's rise to power

109 BCE
Han China conquers northern Korea, destroying the state of Wiman Joseon.

105–101 BCE
Rome fights a war against the "barbarian" Cimbri and Teutones. Roman general Marius defeats the Teutones at Aquae Sextiae in 102.

53 BCE
The Parthians defeat a Roman army at Carrhae; Crassus, the Roman commander, is killed.

60–61 CE
In Britain the Iceni tribe led by Boudicca revolt against Roman rule. The uprising is suppressed.

c.100 CE
The Moche civilization emerges in the Andes, South America. Its soldiers fight with clubs, maces, slingshots, and javelins.

208 CE
Han general Cao Cao fights the battle of the Red Cliffs (Chibi) against his rivals Sun Quan and Liu Bei.

« Cao Cao on the eve of his defeat at Red Cliffs

312 CE
Constantine defeats Maxentius at battle of the Milvian Bridge outside Rome to become emperor in the West.

319 CE
Chandragupta I founds the Gupta empire in northern India.

410 CE
Gothic Roman army auxiliaries, led by Alaric, sack Rome.

434–453 CE
Attila is ruler of the Huns, steppe horsemen from Central Asia. He leads them on aggressive campaigns, including incursions into the Roman empire from 441.

66–73 CE
A Jewish rebellion in Judaea is suppressed by a Roman army under Titus. Jerusalem falls in 70 and the rebels' final stronghold, the fortress of Masada, is captured in 73.

101–106 CE
Roman emperor Trajan fights two Dacian Wars, incorporating Dacia into the Roman empire. The campaigns are recorded on Trajan's Column in Rome.

≫ Roman legionaries make camp (from Trajan's Column)

226 CE
The Persian Sasanids under Ardashir I defeat the Parthians.

244 CE
Roman emperor Gordian III is defeated by the Sasanids and dies in Mesopotamia.

324 CE
Constantine defeats his co-emperor Licinius to become ruler of the whole Roman empire.

c.154 CE
Construction of the Antonine Wall – named for Roman emperor Antoninus Pius – across the middle of Scotland.

251 CE
Roman emperor Decius is defeated and killed by the Goths at Forum Trebonii.

260 CE
Roman emperor Valerian is defeated and captured by the Sasanid king Shapur I at Edessa.

69 CE
Year of the Four Emperors: Rome is again plunged into civil war as legions support different candidates for the imperial throne. Vespasian wins the struggle.

161–166 CE
Romans fight the Parthians for control of Armenia.

166–180 CE
Roman emperor Marcus Aurelius campaigns against Germanic tribes threatening Rome's Danube frontier.

375 CE
Death of Samudragupta, ruler of the Gupta empire, who has conquered much of India through his victories over 21 kings.

⌃ Attila the Hun

455 CE
Vandals sack Rome.

476 CE
Emperor Romulus Augustus is deposed by Germanic general Odoacer. The end of the Roman empire in the West.

≫ Roman legionary's short sword and scabbard

113–117 CE
Trajan campaigns successfully against the Parthians in Mesopotamia.

117–138 CE .
Hadrian is Roman emperor. From 122 Hadrian's Wall is built to mark the northern boundary of Roman Britain.

184 CE
The Yellow Turban peasant revolt led by Zhang Jiao devastates Han China.

190 CE
In China warlords begin competing for control of the disintegrating Han empire.

⌃ Two of Rome's quartet of rulers, the tetrarchs

378 CE
Valens, Roman emperor in the East, is defeated and killed by the Goths at the battle of Adrianople.

493 CE
Odoacer is defeated by the Ostrogoth Theodoric, who rules the kingdom of Italy until his death in 526.

132–135 CE
Simon bar Kokhba leads another Jewish revolt against Roman rule in Judaea. The revolt is crushed with great severity; most Jews in Judaea are killed, enslaved, or exiled.

193 CE
Rome enters a new period of civil wars and violent changes of emperor after a century of firm government and security.

284 CE
Diocletian becomes Roman emperor. He stabilizes the empire, creating the Tetrarchy (rule of four people), with two emperors and two junior co-emperors.

394 CE
Emperor Theodosius wins a victory over the usurper Eugenius at Frigidus thanks to his Vandal general Stilicho.

≫ Stilicho, a powerful Romanized Vandal

EGYPT AND MESOPOTAMIA

1 Empire of Sargon of Akkade
Dates c.2300–2215 BCE
Location Mesopotamia to the Mediterranean

2 Egypt under Ramesses II
Dates 1279–1213 BCE
Location Egypt, Palestine, and Syria

Wars in Sumer and Egypt

The valleys of the Euphrates and Tigris rivers in Mesopotamia and the Nile in Egypt were the birthplaces of hierarchical societies, with powerful rulers who used warfare to found empires at the expense of weaker neighbours. War brought a rich reward in plunder and slaves, as well as glory to the victorious leader.

BEFORE

The first farming communities in the Nile Valley, Mesopotamia, and the eastern Mediterranean fought one another for cattle and women. They also warred with hunter-gatherers and nomadic pastoralists who preyed upon their settled societies.

WALLED TOWNS
As societies became larger and more complex, warfare similarly increased in sophistication. The earliest evidence of defensive fortifications was

59 The number of bodies found by archeologists at Jebel Sahaba in Egypt. Many had been killed by arrows and were probably victims of warfare conducted some 13,500 years ago.

found at the ancient town of Jericho near the river Jordan, where walls were built around 8000 BCE. In the first half of the third millennium BCE **the first cities emerged in Mesopotamia and Egypt**, as well as in the Indus Valley and China. They created territorial states that were won and held by armed force.

Ancient arrowheads
The Ancient Egyptians typically tipped their arrows and spears with flint, copper, or bronze. Shapes varied from barbed, which were hard to extract from a wound, to leaf-shaped.

The first recorded wars between organized armies were fought by the city-states of Sumer in southern Mesopotamia in around 3000–2500 BCE. Even the largest of these states was only capable of fielding a small army for a short campaign. The bulk of their forces consisted of helmeted foot soldiers armed with spears. There were also trundling solid-wheeled carts drawn by asses that carried aristocratic warriors or archers to the battlefield.

Conflicts between city-states were motivated by disputes over territory and scarce water supplies. A number of inscriptions, including one on a monument known as the Stele of the Vultures, record wars fought between the aggressive city of Lagash and its neighbour, Umma, around 2500 BCE. The stele shows Lagash's ruler, Eannatum, advancing at the head of his troops, who have adopted a tight-packed infantry formation. According to the accompanying inscription, Eannatum was wounded by an arrow in the fighting but triumphed over Umma.

There is no mistaking Lagash's joy in the slaughter of war, for the stele depicts carrion birds feasting on the entrails of the enemy dead. Yet it is doubtful that these early Sumerian wars took a heavy toll, even on the lives of the defeated. Another inscription records that on a later occasion, Umma, again defeated in battle, lost 60 carts and their crews – probably 120 men, given one driver and one warrior per vehicle. These casualties seem to have been regarded as heavy. On the other hand, the deaths of foot soldiers are unrecorded and these may have been far more numerous.

The Akkadian empire
The rulers of Lagash were not unambitious – there is a record of a military expedition to distant Elam in present-day western Iran – but it was not until the campaigns of Sargon of Akkade around 2300 BCE that empire-

Egyptian sword
This double-edged copper sword was crafted for an elite soldier during the New Kingdom era in Ancient Egypt. It was a thrusting weapon, worn on a belt around the warrior's waist.

building became the impulse behind war-making. Sargon seized power in Kish, a Mesopotamian city well to the north of Lagash, and then founded his own power base at Akkade. From there he imposed his rule on the other Mesopotamian city-states as far south as the Persian Gulf, and then continued his career of conquest northwest to the Mediterranean coast of Syria and eastern Anatolia, and east to Elam. If his inscriptions are to be believed, Sargon maintained a standing army of 5,400 soldiers and won 34 battles during a reign that lasted over 40 years.

Sargon's empire outlived him by more than a century. Its last great leader, Naram-Sin, ruled from the Taurus Mountains in the north to the south of the Persian Gulf. The Akkadian empire founded a tradition for others to follow. Around 1760 BCE Hammurabi, ruler of Babylon, defeated the Elamites and then subjugated the cities of Mesopotamia to create an empire from Syria to the Persian Gulf.

Territorial pharaohs
Another centre for the development of imperial warfare was Egypt. In the Middle Kingdom era (about 2040 to 1785 BCE) Egyptian pharaohs campaigned southward into Nubia and built strings of fortresses to define and defend their conquests. Their weaponry included bows, spears, maces, and throwing sticks made of wood, stone, copper, and bronze. The Middle Kingdom ended in a troubled period when Egypt was dominated by the Asiatic Hyksos, but after this the pharaohs of

Stele of Sargon of Akkade
Naram-Sin, ruler of the Akkadian empire, is represented as a god trampling mercilessly upon the bodies of his fallen enemies and revered by his soldiers.

the New Kingdom, dated from 1570 BCE, resumed and extended the Egyptian tradition of imperial conquest. Their campaigns exhibited the very latest development in military technology: the horse-drawn two-wheeled war chariot.

The civilizations of west Asia and the eastern Mediterranean almost certainly learned the use of war chariots from nomadic pastoralists who occasionally irrupted from the steppe into the lands of settled agriculture and cities. It was probably from the same source that they adopted the composite bow as a more powerful alternative to the simple self-bow. The 17 campaigns of pharaoh Thutmosis III (reigned 1479–1425 BCE) recorded by his royal scribes ranged from as far south as the fourth cataract of the Nile in Nubia to Syria and the Euphrates in the north.

Ramesses II, in a long reign from 1279 to 1213 BCE, battled with a rival power, the Hittites, for control of Palestine and Syria – the Hittites expanding to the south from their native lands in Anatolia.

The common soldiers of the Egyptian New Kingdom were a mixture of volunteers and conscripts, some of them long-serving

professional soldiers rewarded for their services with a grant of land. New recruits were trained in fighting technique, drill, and manoeuvres at "boot camps", where beatings to instill discipline were common. The corps of bowmen was an elite, the use of the composite bow in particular requiring exceptional skill. Archery was practised from childhood. The aristocracy and the pharaoh himself rode in chariots that were armed with a bow or mace. The soldiers were supported by administrative staff that kept records, organized supplies of

Unknown Akkadian ruler
This copper head was unearthed during excavations at Nineveh. It was made at the time of Sargon of Akkade, and is often given that name.

in some detail. Around 1460 BCE Thutmosis III led a punitive expedition against the rebellious princedoms in Palestine. Marching 20km (12½ miles) a day across desert and mountain terrain, the Egyptians emerged in front of the city of Megiddo in superior force, catching their enemies unprepared. The battle that followed later was a swift rout, the enemy bolting to seek safety behind the city walls while the rampant Egyptians plundered their abandoned camp. Megiddo surrendered after a seven-month siege.

AFTER

By the 12th century BCE the Hittite empire had collapsed and Egyptian power was on the wane. Mesopotamia too had entered a period of fragmentation and instability.

RISE OF ASSYRIA
Egypt underwent **political disintegration that destroyed its unity** and left it prey to invaders. The country was conquered by the Kushites in the 8th century, the Assyrians in the 7th century, and the Persians in the 6th century BCE.

In Mesopotamia the Babylonian empire founded by Hammurabi was overrun by the Hittites around 1530 BCE. **Babylon ceased to be a major military force.** It was overtaken by Assyria, a city-state on the northern Tigris that, by the 13th century BCE, had developed into a major power. From the reign of Tiglath-Pileser III (745–727 BCE) to that of Ashurbanipal (669–627 BCE), Assyria would establish its Mesopotamian-based rule **18–19 »** over a large area.

ASHURBANIPAL

"Bring forth weapons! Send forth the army to destroy the rebellious lands!"

ATTRIBUTED TO PHARAOH RAMESSES III, FROM THE TEMPLE OF MEDINET HABU

food and weaponry for their campaigns, and ensured wells were dug along lines of march. Wall paintings depicting battles of the period show medical personnel attending to the wounded. Egyptian warfare had religious sanction from the god Amun and was fought with the ruthlessness of a crusade. Soldiers were known to collect body parts from slain enemies while prisoners were sometimes impaled or burned alive. The luckier among the defeated were carried off into slavery.

Egyptian campaigns
Because of the records the Egyptians kept of their campaigns, it is possible to reconstruct a few military actions

A more tightly contested battle was fought between the armies of Ramesses II and Hittite ruler Muwatalli at Kadesh around 1275 BCE in the course of a war for control of Lebanon and Syria. Both sides were able to deploy large numbers of chariots – possibly 2,000 of the lighter two-man Egyptian vehicles were involved and 3,500 heavier three-man Hittite chariots. The Hittites achieved surprise, attacking the Egyptians while their forces were divided. But the massed Hittite chariots were halted on the brink of victory by a bold counter-attack, led by the pharaoh himself, in which the manoeuvrability of the Egyptian chariots and the skill of their archers with the composite bow carried

the day. This battle was followed by the first recorded peace treaty, a settlement that reflected the even balance between Hittite and Egyptian forces.

The later history of the Egyptian New Kingdom is dominated by defensive wars. Ramesses III, ruling from 1186 to 1154 BCE, had to fight off incursions by Libyans and waves of invasion by raiders known as the "Sea Peoples". The occasion for the first recorded "naval battle" in 1176 BCE was fought in the mouth of the Nile Delta between these raiders travelling by sea and a flotilla of Egyptian river vessels packed with soldiers. By then, however, the power of Egypt and its armies was falling into steep decline.

TECHNOLOGY

EGYPTIAN WAR CHARIOT

Built of wood and leather, the Egyptian war chariot was a lightweight vehicle that was designed for maximum speed and manoeuvrability. It was pulled by a team of two horses and, with widely spaced spoked wheels and the axle well to the rear, could execute very tight turns. The two-man crew consisted of a driver and a warrior who shot arrows or threw javelins. The charioteers were supported by armed runners who sprinted alongside the vehicles on the battlefield. The chariot warriors

were wealthy aristocrats and would sometimes embellish their vehicles with precious metals. Even without this extra expense, chariots were costly to build and maintain. Whereas the Hittites used their heavier three-man chariots as a shock force in massed charges, the Egyptians seem to have used their chariots in a looser harassing and skirmishing role in support of the infantry. They also used them to rescue the wounded.

CASKET DETAIL OF TUTANKHAMUN RIDING A WAR CHARIOT

« BEFORE

Assyria was originally a relatively small Mesopotamian kingdom that ruled the area around the cities of Ashur and Nineveh on the Tigris river. Its slow rise to supremacy began in the 14th century BCE.

ESTABLISHED TRADITION

In its early history, Ashur was subject to conquest by more powerful Mesopotamian states. It was part of the **empires of Sargon of Akkade and of the Babylonian Hammurabi « 16–17**. The Assyrians had, however, a tradition of war-making, carrying out expeditions

28	The number of campaigns carried out by King Tiglath-Pileser I (1115–1077 BCE) against the Aramaeans, according to an ancient Assyrian inscription.

to subdue the neighbouring mountain peoples who raided their territory. Their soldiers were part-timers, who could only campaign for short periods before returning to work in the fields.

ASSYRIAN EXPANSIONISM

From the reign of Ashur-uballit I (1365–1330 BCE) Assyrian military and diplomatic action became more expansive. Once subsidiary to Babylon, the Assyrians became its rulers after their king, Tikulti-ninurta I, sacked the city in 1235 BCE. **Assyrian power continued to wax and wane, subject to Babylonian resurgences** and incursions by peoples from outside Mesopotamia. An early peak was reached under Tiglath-Pileser I (1115–1077 BCE), but by the end of his reign the Assyrians were again under pressure, this time from invading Aramaeans. It was not until the late 10th century BCE that the Assyrian drive for empire resumed with renewed vigour.

Assyrian Conquests

The Assyrians created a powerful, brutal army as a tool for campaigns of conquest and sustained their empire through the exploitation of the conquered. Rulers such as Tiglath-Pileser III and Ashurbanipal were particularly fearsome military leaders with a clear-headed sense of the efficacy of terror.

The beginning of the rise of Assyria to imperial power is usually dated back to the reign of Adad-nerari II, who came to the throne in 911 BCE. By the time Ashur-nasir-pal II had become Assyrian ruler, from 883–859 BCE, the empire encompassed most of Mesopotamia and Lebanon. But it was only with the reign of Tiglath-Pileser III, from 745–727 BCE, that what is often referred to as the Neo-Assyrian empire achieved its mature form. Not only were the frontiers of the empire extended south and east to include southern Mesopotamia, Palestine, and part of eastern Anatolia, but the

Assyrian army was reorganized into a fighting machine of unprecedented efficiency and ruthlessness.

Instead of levies raised for short-term service, Tiglath-Pileser III preferred to form a standing army. The majority of the foot soldiers, who necessarily made up the numerical bulk of the army, were a mix of Assyrians and foreigners – mercenaries employed for their specialist military skills, contingents supplied by tributary states of the empire, and prisoners captured in the wars of conquest. They were equipped with bows, spears, shields, and armour by the

Scythian warrior in action
The Scythians were among the steppe nomads who taught the Assyrians to ride horses into combat. This figure shows how Scythians were later imagined.

The elite of the army were the native Assyrians who formed the corps of charioteers and, with the passage of time, the cavalry. The Assyrians developed heavy four-horse chariots with a four-man crew, probably two elite warriors and their shield-bearers, the latter also responsible for driving the vehicle. Used en masse, these chariots constituted a formidable shock force on the battlefield. The advantages of cavalry were something the Assyrians probably learned from their contact with nomadic horsemen such as the Scythians, who fought as skirmishers using the composite bow fired from horseback. More usefully to the Assyrians, however, was their later development of heavy

> ## "The warriors I cut down
> with the sword … Their
> ## corpses I hung on stakes."
> TEXT FROM SENNACHERIB'S PRISM, C.689 BCE

efficient Assyrian supply system. The Assyrians gave pride of place to missile weapons – in particular, powerful composite bows and slingshots. Each archer was accompanied by a spearman who held a large wicker shield to defend the bowman against enemy missiles and who would also protect him against close-quarters attack.

Assyrian territory

At its greatest extent, the Assyrian empire included all of Mesopotamia, southwestern Anatolia, western Iran, and the entire eastern seaboard of the Mediterranean. In the 7th century BCE its armies penetrated deep into Egypt.

Key

- Assyria under Ashur-dan II (934–912 BCE)
- Territory added by death of Shalmaneser III (824 BCE)
- Territory added by death of Sargon II (705 BCE)
- Territory added by death of Ashurbanipal (627 BCE)
- Greatest extent of Neo-Babylonian empire (625–539 BCE)
- ✗ Major battle or siege

**Map labels:**
PHRYGIA · Gordium · LYDIA · Sardis · Anatolia · Holys · Taurus Mountains · CILICIA · Carchemish 605 BCE: Defeat of Assyrian and Egyptian armies by combined forces of Babylonia and Media · Harran 608 BCE: destroyed by Babylonians · SCYTHIANS · Toprakkale · Lake Van · Tushpa · KINGDOM OF URARTU · Khorsabad · Lake Urmia · MANNEA · Nineveh 612 BCE: Assyrian capital destroyed by Babylonians · Nimrud · ASSYRIA · Ashur 614 BCE: destroyed by Babylonians · MEDIA · Ecbatana · Mesopotamia · Euphrates · Diyala River 693 BCE · Tigris · ELAM · Cyprus · Mediterranean Sea · Byblos · Syria · Sidon · Tyre · Damascus · Syrian Desert · Megiddo 605 BCE · ISRAEL · Jerusalem 587 BCE: destroyed by Babylonians · Gaza · Qarqar 853 BCE · Lachish 701 BCE · Babylon 689 BCE: Babylon is destroyed by Sennacherib. Rebuilt by his successor Esarhaddon and by Babylonian king, Nebuchadnezzar II, (605–562 BCE) · BABYLONIA · Uruk · Ur · 648–47 BCE: Ashurbanipal destroys kingdom of Elam for its support of Babylonians; lands are sown with salt · EGYPT · Memphis 671 BCE: captured by Esarhaddon · 669 BCE: Egypt is conquered by Assyrian king, Esarhaddon, and ruled through native princes · Sinai · Nile · Arabian Peninsula · Red Sea · Thebes 663 BCE: destroyed by Assyrian king, Ashurbanipal

0   400km
0   400 miles

The siege of Lachish
This artist's impression of the siege of the Judaean city of Lachish by Assyrian forces in 701 BCE is based on contemporary reliefs at Nineveh. Bowmen back up the wheeled rams.

Assyrian bowman

An Assyrian archer draws his bow, protected by his shield-bearer. Invented by steppe nomads, the composite bow was made from several pieces of wood.

cavalry – armoured riders with spears who practised the cavalry charge and eventually supplanted the charioteers.

The Assyrian state was designed for the conquest of foreign lands. Roads were built to allow the easy movement of armies and a post system was created for rapid and effective military communications. Conquest itself fed the military machine, giving control of strategic resources – iron from Anatolia for weapons, horses for the chariots, and cavalry from western Iran – and generating a supply of manpower and of wealth in the form of tribute or plunder. Domination was maintained by the exercise of terror against those who dared to rebel. The Assyrians practised the deportation of peoples who opposed them. Whether in combat or its aftermath, they readily practised massacre and despoliation.

The pressures of empire

But the strains of maintaining a large empire with restive subject peoples were eventually to prove too much for Assyria. During the 7th century BCE strategic overreach set in: the Assyrian empire reached its greatest extent and catastrophically imploded. Under Ashurbanipal (reigned 668–627 BCE) Assyrian armies campaigned deep into southern Egypt, destroying the city of Thebes in 663. The Elamites, enemies of the Assyrians in present-day western Iran, were ruthlessly conquered between 642 and 639, their cities looted and laid waste, their population deported. In the terrifying words of Ashurbanipal celebrating the defeat of Elam: "I left his fields empty of the voice of mankind."

Yet even during Ashurbanipal's reign the pressures on Assyria were growing. There were just too many enemies. A Babylonian, Nabopolassar, made himself ruler of Babylon in 617 and initiated a series of campaigns that sapped Assyrian strength. He allied himself with the Medes and with the steppe hordes, capturing and sacking Nineveh, the capital of the Neo-Assyrian empire, in 612 BCE. The remnants of the Assyrian army continued the war in alliance with Egypt, but the crushing Chaldean victory at Carchemish in 605 completed the destruction of Assyria.

AFTER »»

After the defeat of the Assyrians the Neo-Babylonian empire flourished, until the rise of a new people who would create an even mightier empire: the Persians.

NABOPOLASSAR AND NEBUCHADNEZZAR

The Neo-Babylonian empire was founded by Nabopolassar, victor over the Assyrians, and his son, Nebuchadnezzar, who succeeded him in 605 BCE. **Nebuchadnezzar is remembered for destroying Jerusalem in 597 BCE**, and for exiling the Jews of Judaea into "Babylonian captivity".

CYRUS THE GREAT

GREAT CYRUS

From Anshan, in the old kingdom of Elam, came a new leader who swept through the Babylonian empire, **conquering lands from the kingdom of Croesus in Anatolia to Central Asia in the space of 30 years (c.559–530 BCE)**. In the new imperial heartland of Cyrus the Great, Parsa (western Iran), lived tribes who become known to the world as the Persians. **Cyrus built a grand columned palace around great gardens at Pasargadae**. His son, Cambyses, conquered Egypt in 525 BCE.

« BEFORE

The origins of Ancient Greek civilization are in many ways obscure, but the Greeks themselves confidently traced their history back to the era of the Trojan War.

THE POWER OF GREECE

The poet Homer's epic poem, the *Iliad*, probably created in the 8th century BCE, tells the story of the Greek siege of the city of Troy. **Historians have surmised that, although mythologized, the *Iliad* refers to a real event**, probably a war between the Mycenaeans, who flourished in Greece from c.1500 to 1200 BCE, and the Anatolian Hittites. The site of Troy has been tentatively identified in the west of modern-day Turkey. The Mycenaeans fought with bronze weapons and chariots, in the manner of their time. Homer describes a style of warfare in which single combat between elite warriors was common, but also the use of missile weapons and group combat with spear and shield.
The disappearance of Mycenaean civilization in the 12th century BCE was followed by a period of disruption, which is often referred to as the Greek Dark Ages. Out of this obscurity **Greek city-states such as Athens, Thebes, and Sparta began to re-emerge** around the 8th century BCE.

SIEGE OF TROY

PERSIAN DOMINANCE

By the 6th century BCE the Persians could claim with much justification to come from the heart of civilization, compared with the Greeks who lived on its periphery. The empire founded by the Achaemenid ruler, **Cyrus the Great, between 559 and 530 BCE** **« 18–19** controlled Mesopotamia and was later extended by his son, Cambyses, to include Egypt, thus combining two major centres of early civilization.

The Greco-Persian Wars

The campaigns fought by the city-states of Greece against the invading Persian empire, first in 490 BCE and then in 480–479 BCE, are classics of military history. At Marathon, Thermopylae, and Salamis, Greek forces demonstrated their skill and courage against superior opposition.

The great Persian king, Darius I, whose long reign lasted from 521–486 BCE, had many Greek city-states within his domains. His predecessors had conquered Anatolia and had gained control of the Ionian Greeks who lived on the eastern side of the Aegean. At the start of the 5th century BCE the Ionian cities rose in revolt against Persian rule. Darius sent an army and a navy – the ships supplied by another of his subject peoples, the Phoenicians – to crush the revolt. The Ionians received some support from Athens and Eretria but they were still humbled. In 494 BCE the ringleader among the Ionian cities, Miletus, was destroyed by the Persians and its population deported to Central Asia. Carried forward by the momentum of this campaign, the Persians decided to extend their empire so it would cover the Aegean islands and mainland Greece. When Athens and Sparta rejected a demand for formal submission to Persian authority, Darius mounted a seaborne expedition to bring the city-states to heel.

Greek resistance

At this time Athens and Sparta were exceptional societies. Over the previous century Athens had evolved its own democratic system of government and

Persian soldiers at Susa
This frieze from the palace of the Persian king, Darius I, at Susa depicts soldiers on parade. They may be members of Darius's imperial guard, the Immortals, the elite infantry that formed the core of the Persian army.

Greco-Persian wars
At the beginning of the 5th century BCE Greeks revolted against the expanding Persian empire. In the face of strong opposition, they continued to fight the Persians in the Mediterranean until 480 BCE.

Key
- Persian empire
- Greek opponents of Persia
- Route of Xerxes's army 480 BCE
- Route of Xerxes's fleet 480 BCE
- ⚔ Greek victory
- ⚔ Persian victory
- ⚔ Inconclusive battle
- Persian Royal Road

Map labels: 480 BCE: Persians dig canal for fleet to cross Athos Peninsula, thus avoiding danger of storms; 492 BCE: Persian fleet is dispersed by violent storm and invasion is called off; Black Sea; Sea of Marmara; THRACE; Pella; MACEDONIA; Xerxes Canal; Lemnos; Abydus; PERSIAN EMPIRE; Larissa; *Greece*; Aegean Sea; Lesbos; Artemisium 480 BCE; Thermopylae 480 BCE; Plataea 479 BCE; Delphi; Chios; Ephesus; Sardis 498 BCE; IONIA; Marathon 490 BCE; Corinth; Athens; Mycale 479 BCE; Salamis 480 BCE; *Peloponnese*; Lade 494 BCE; Miletus 494 BCE; Sparta; Rhodes

its citizens were expected to perform military service when required, turning out with their own weaponry and armour. Sparta was a militarized society in which male citizens were raised as soldiers and lived in barracks from the age of 20. On land both Spartans and Athenians fought chiefly as armoured infantry, or hoplites. Each carrying a stabbing spear and a shield, the hoplites fought in a tight formation known as a phalanx (see p.23).
Although the Greeks did also employ auxiliaries equipped with bows and slingshots as skirmishers, the focus on the tight-knit phalanx of citizen-soldiers made their armies contrast starkly with the forces of the Persian empire. Bowmen were a vital element in their style of warfare, which gave missiles primacy over close combat, as were cavalry and chariots. Persian armies were large and well organized, operating under professional generals, and their campaigns were well planned with due attention to logistics.

Hoplite axe and sword
Weapons carried by the Greek infantry included axes and the short, curved "kopis" swords.

The Persian force that landed at Marathon, 40km (25 miles) from Athens, in August 490 BCE was small by imperial standards; roughly 20,000 men were put ashore, along with some horses for the cavalry. The Athenians appealed to Sparta for support, but the Spartans claimed to be unable to dispatch soldiers immediately for religious reasons. Rather than wait for Sparta to finish its religious festival, Athens sent its hoplites to challenge the Persians while they were still on the beach. The Greeks were outnumbered by at least two to one, but they formed up in phalanxes and attacked. The onrush of the Athenian infantry turned the battle into a close-quarters melee in which Persian archery and horses could play no effective part. The shocked invaders extricated themselves with difficulty and at heavy cost in lives.

of triremes. These fast, manoeuvrable galleys, armed with a ram at the prow and rowed by 170 oarsmen, were to prove crucial to the outcome of the war.

The 200,000-strong Persian army crossed the Hellespont in spring 480 BCE, led by Xerxes in person. It marched south down the coast towards Athens, with a fleet of more than 1,000 war galleys and supply ships following offshore. The Athenians persuaded their allies to advance north to meet the invaders. The Greek fleet fought an indecisive battle with the Persians off Cape Artemisium, while a force of 7,000 hoplites and skirmishers commanded by the Spartan ruler Leonidas took up a strong defensive position in a narrow pass at Thermopylae. There, they fought a holding action for three days, the restricted battlefield preventing the Persians exploiting their vast superiority in numbers. Eventually, the Persians found a path through the mountains that brought them down on the rear of the Greek position. Leonidas and the cream of his hoplites fought on heroically until they were annihilated.

Destruction of Athens

As the Persians continued their advance, Athens was evacuated, its population carried to the safety of the island of Salamis, where the Greek fleet was now stationed. The Persian army sacked and then occupied Athens, as the Greek army withdrew further to the south so that it could defend the Peloponnese. The Spartans were keen to pull back the fleet as well, but Themistocles was insistent that the triremes stand and fight. The Greek fleet was heavily outnumbered – probably 300 warships to at least 700 in the Persian fleet – but Xerxes threw away much of this numerical advantage by dispersing his superior naval forces, and placing blocking squadrons to

Corinthian helmet
Greek hoplites wore bronze helmets, like this one, which gave protection to the face and neck. They also provided an opportunity for display with their fine horsehair crests.

When Xerxes I ascended the Persian throne in 485 BCE, he inherited the task of punishing the presumptuous Greek cities. This time there was to be no hastily organized seaborne expedition, but a well-planned, full-scale land invasion with naval support. The preparation of the invasion route by Xerxes's engineers was astonishingly thorough. They built two pontoon bridges across the narrow but treacherous straits of the Hellespont (the Dardanelles) so that the massive army could march from Asia into Europe. They also dug a canal cutting across an isthmus by Mount Athos in Macedonia, so the Persian fleet that was accompanying the army on its journey would not have to sail around a notoriously dangerous promontory.

Meticulous plans
The Persian preparations took four years, giving Athens and Sparta plenty of time to look to their defences. Most of the city-states in northern Greece gave their allegiance to Persia, but the city-states of the Peloponnese allied themselves with the Athenians and Spartans. Themistocles, a political leader in Athens, persuaded his fellow citizens to devote the wealth from a newly discovered silver mine to building a large fleet

Bronze-sheathed ram

Mast and sail not carried into battle

Stempost in form of a fishtail

Three banks of oars

A Greek trireme
The trireme was a light, quick, manoeuvrable warship designed to sink enemy ships by ramming.

AFTER ➤➤

After defeating Xerxes's invasion force the Greeks launched a counter-offensive, but the city-states were often as keen to fight one another as to attack the Persians.

FREEDOM FROM PERSIA
The offensive against Persia was led by Athens, which formed the Delian League of city-states to prosecute the war. **The main goal was to free the Aegean islands and the Ionian Greek cities of Anatolia from Persian rule.** Athenian-led forces also campaigned at length in Cyprus, and in 460 BCE Athenian triremes were sent to Egypt to support an anti-Persian rebellion. The Egyptian expedition was a disaster, but in general Athens was successful in extending its own power and weakening Persian influence in Anatolia and the Aegean.

PERSIA TAKES CONTROL
By 450 BCE the Greek city-states were fighting among themselves, as Sparta led a reaction against the increasingly dominant position of Athens. During the later stages of the **Peloponnesian War of 431–404 BCE 22–23 ➤➤**, Sparta allied itself with the Persians against Athens; in the Corinthian War of 395–387 BCE, Athens allied itself with Persia against Sparta. As a result of its participation in these wars of Greek against Greek, Persia regained control of the Ionian cities and part of the Aegean.

10 THOUSAND **Greek hoplites and auxiliaries took part in the battle of Marathon.**

6 THOUSAND **Persian soldiers were killed in the battle of Marathon.**

intercept a wrongly anticipated Greek withdrawal. When battle was finally joined off Salamis, the reduced Persian fleet was routed, smashed by the rams of the rapidly manoeuvring triremes with their skilful teams of oarsmen. Xerxes abandoned all hope of victory that year and withdrew northwards to winter his quarters.

Called away for other imperial duties, Xerxes left for the east with part of his army, leaving his general, Mardonius, to continue the campaign the following year with the remainder. The Greek allies, after many hours of bickering among themselves, gathered all their manpower resources to field an army probably numbering 80,000, not greatly inferior to the force available to Mardonius. At Plataea in July 479 BCE, the two armies clashed in a confused battle that the Greeks were able to win because of the superior fighting qualities of the hoplite infantry. Mardonius was killed along with many thousands of his soldiers. At the same time, a seaborne raid destroyed the remnants of the Persian fleet beached at Mycale. Persia's invasion of Greece had failed.

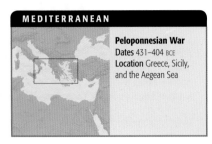

The Peloponnesian War

Between 431 and 404 BCE a war was fought between rival alliances of Greek city-states led by Athens and Sparta. Partly because the two cities had contrasting strengths – Sparta more powerful on land and Athens more dominant at sea – the conflict was for many years indecisive. It ended with humiliation for Athens.

BEFORE

The origins of the Peloponnesian War lay in the growing wealth and power of Athens and the fear and resentment that this engendered in other Greek city-states.

THE GOLDEN AGE

After the defeat of the **Persian invasion of Greece in 480–479 BCE ‹‹ 20–21**, Athens assumed leadership of an alliance of city-states around the Aegean, the Delian League. The original purpose of the league was to fight the invasion of the Persians, but it turned into an informal Athenian empire with the other league members providing troops and tribute for Athens to use as it wished. Cities that rebelled were ruthlessly crushed by Athenian military action. The wealth extracted from the league during this period underpinned the Golden Age of Athens under the leadership of Pericles, and the Athenian statesman believed that the interests of the city lay in developing trade around the Mediterranean. **The Spartans, traditionally acknowledged as the leading military power in Greece, were affronted by the rise of Athens** and turned the Peloponnesian League of city-states, which they led, into a counter-balance to Athenian power.

PERICLES

The fragmentation of the Greek world into independent city-states presented many opportunities for conflict – disputes over allegiance, territorial boundaries, and affronts to honour. Around 460 BCE a clutch of such issues brought a drift to war. Relations between Athens and Sparta were embittered by an exchange of insults over the Athenians' role in helping the Spartans suppress an uprising of helots (serfs or slaves). The

100 PER CENT of Spartan males aged 20 to 54 were sent to the battle of Mantinea in 418 BCE.

30 THOUSAND men took part in the naval battle of Arginusae, in 406 BCE.

city-state of Megara revolted against its overlord, Corinth, a member of the Spartan-led Peloponnesian League; Athens backed Megara. Thebes aspired to leadership of the cities of Boetia, a role denied it by Athens; the Spartans backed Theban aspirations. After a series of skirmishes and campaigns, the Athenians and Spartans agreed a Thirty Years' Peace in 445 BCE. It lasted less than half that time.

The road to war

In 435 BCE Corinth faced a revolt by its colony Corcyra (Corfu). The Athenians backed the Corcyrians and sent a force of triremes to prevent the Corinthians from re-imposing their rule. Corinth appealed to the Peloponnesian League

for support and in 432 Sparta declared war on Athens. Fighting began the following year. Pericles devised a strategy based upon the naval power of Athens and its Delian League allies. Withdrawing within the walls of their city, the Athenians would survive sustained by supplies brought in by sea, while using their fleet to raid the shipping and coasts of the Peloponnesian League states. Five times the Spartans rampaged through the territory around Athens, but without decisive effect. The Athenians made good use of their naval strength by establishing a base at the town of Pylos on the Peloponnesian coast, from which they raided Spartan territory and encouraged revolt among the Spartan helots. When the Spartans attacked the Pylos garrison in 425 BCE they were outmanoeuvred by Athenian sea and land forces and defeated. The Athenians, on the other hand, were beaten badly by Sparta's allies, the Theban-led Boeotians, at Delium in 424 BCE, a reminder of their weakness on land.

Maximum facial protection
This example of an early Greek helmet follows the shape of the skull, and is made from a single piece of bronze.

The warfare was characterized by the similarity between the opposing sides, which fought with essentially the same equipment and tactics. The core of the rival armies was the heavy infantry hoplite, a citizen-soldier fighting in a tight-knit formation, the phalanx (see TACTICS). The hoplites were supported by large numbers of skirmishers, the peltasts, men of lower social status who used missile weapons – bows, slingshots, and javelins. Once on enemy territory, any army would plunder and lay waste at will. Campaigns were short because part-time soldiers needed to return to their farms. A fleet was far more expensive to maintain than an army, and made heavy demands on manpower. A trireme required a crew of 200, most of them experienced oarsmen, although they were typically lower class citizens rather than hoplites. The naval dominance of Athens depended on its superior financial resources and its skilled population of seafarers

GREEK PHALANX

The armoured Greek hoplite infantry fought in a tight formation called a phalanx. Carrying shields and spears wielded overarm, the hoplites usually advanced close enough together for each man's right flank to be protected by the shield of the comrade to his left. The formation was typically eight rows deep. When phalanx met phalanx, opposing hoplites stabbed at one another from behind their shield wall or clashed shield to shield (known as "othismos") in a shoving match. Most casualties occurred when a phalanx broke up, exposing the hoplites to piecemeal slaughter.

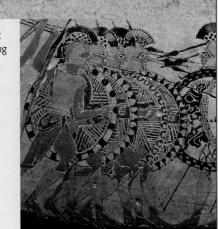

and boat-builders. As on land, there were no adequate supply arrangements, triremes beaching regularly to forage or buy food from coastal towns. Sea battles were ramming contests decided by dexterity of manoeuvre.

Athens defeated

The first round of the Peloponnesian War came to an end in 422 BCE, after the chief war leaders on the opposing sides, the Spartan general, Brasidas, and the Athenian demagogue, Cleon, were both killed while campaigning in Thrace. Despite a resultant peace agreement made the following year, skirmishes continued uninterrupted and a full-scale battle was fought at Mantinea, north of Sparta, in 418 BCE – a Spartan victory that confirmed the supremacy of their hoplites. At this point the Athenians extended the war into a new theatre, with disastrous consequences. In 415 they sent an expedition to Sicily, seeking to defeat the dominant city of Syracuse and bring the island into their empire. Supported by a relatively small Spartan force under Gylippus, the Syracusans resisted an Athenian siege for two years. Athens poured in more troops, but by 413 it was they who were trapped, their fleet blockaded in Syracuse harbour. After a failed breakout attempt ended in the destruction of the majority of their warships, the Athenians vainly tried to escape overland. Harassed by cavalry and light troops with bows and javelins, the remnants of the expeditionary force surrendered, ending their lives as slaves labouring in Sicilian stone quarries.

This comprehensive Athenian disaster encouraged the Spartans. They made an alliance with Persia, which provided funding to build a fleet that could compete for naval supremacy. Athens was in trouble, riven by political disputes and unable to make good the loss of experienced oarsmen and sailors at Syracuse. The Athenians achieved a last naval victory at the battle of Arginusae in 406 BCE, but Sparta was more readily able to make good its heavy losses than Athens its relatively light number. Athens was utterly dependent for food supplies on grain imported from the Black Sea and the war came finally to focus on Spartan efforts to sever that lifeline by winning control of the Hellespont (the Dardanelles). Under Lysander, the Spartan fleet seized the straits and, at the battle of Aegospotami, crushed an Athenian fleet sent to win them back. Athens surrendered in 404 BCE.

> # "So many cities depopulated … Never before had there been so much killing."
>
> THUCYDIDES, "THE PELOPONNESIAN WAR", BOOK I, 23, 411 BCE

The Spartan victory in the Peloponnesian War did not bring peace or unity to the Greek city-states. Weakened by civil strife, they fell under the rule of Macedonia.

WAR RESUMES

Ten years after the end of the Peloponnesian War, a new conflict broke out. **The Corinthian War set Sparta against Corinth, Athens, Thebes, and Argos**. These allies were dependent upon the support of Persia, which re-imposed its rule on the Ionian cities of Anatolia.

AN UNEASY PEACE

The Corinthian War ended in a compromise in 387 BCE. Thebes aspired to leadership in its own region, Boeotia, but this was resisted by Sparta. Inspired by General Epaminondas, the Thebans defeated the Spartans at Leuctra in 371 BCE. In reaction to the threat of Theban hegemony, Athens aligned itself with Sparta. Epaminondas scored another victory over Sparta, Athens, and their allies at Mantinea in 362 BCE, but he was killed in the battle, preventing Thebes profiting from its triumph.

The Greek city-states were exhausted. **When Philip II of Macedon invaded Greece in 338 BCE, he defeated the combined armies of Athens and Thebes** and united the country by force, organizing the city-states into the Macedonian-led League of Corinth.

SPARTAN SHIELD

Ancient Athens
The Parthenon and other glories of Athens built in the 5th century BCE were paid for with the proceeds of empire. The Peloponnesian War broke out in the middle of the city's cultural "Golden Age".

« **BEFORE**

King Philip II of Macedon made his country the leading power in Greece and created the army with which his son, Alexander, would conquer a great empire.

GREEK HERITAGE
When Philip became king in 359 BCE, Macedonia was a relatively backward state. As a young man he had lived in Thebes, where he had witnessed a change in Greek warfare; professional soldiers were replacing the part-time citizen hoplites, and cavalry and skirmishers were playing an increasingly important role. Combining

5.4 MILLION The size of Alexander's empire in square kilometres (2,100,000 square miles).

Macedonia's horse-riding aristocracy with an infantry phalanx armed with the two-handed sarissa spear, **Philip formed a standing army that defeated Athens and Thebes** at the battle of Chaeronea in 338 BCE. He assumed leadership of the Greek cities grouped in the League of Corinth and began preparations for an invasion of the Persian empire. In 336 Philip was assassinated and succeeded by his son.

Conquests of Alexander

Alexander of Macedon was a military leader endowed with skill, daring, and ambition. Only 32 years old when he died, he created an empire that stretched from Greece and Egypt to northern India. His heroic campaigns of conquest influenced imitators as distant as Napoleon and Hitler.

By the time Alexander inherited the Macedonian throne from his assassinated father, Philip II, in 336 BCE, he was already an experienced fighting commander. Aged 18 he had led the Macedonian cavalry charge at the battle of Chaeronea. His initial moves as king were decisive and ruthless, killing his main rival for power in Macedonia and crushing a rebellion by the city of Thebes. In 334 he was ready to carry out his father's project for an invasion of the Persian empire.

The army that Alexander led across the Hellespont into Persian-ruled Asia Minor was a hybrid force. The cavalry (the Companions), whom Alexander led in person into battle, were Macedonians. The armoured infantry was Macedonian and Greek. Thessaly provided light cavalry, Thrace

javelin-throwers, and Crete archers. There was also a train of siege engines. The first victory of his campaign was won at Granicus in western Anatolia, against a Persian satrap whose army contained a large contingent of Greek mercenaries. Alexander then proceeded to liberate the Greek cities of the region from Persian rule – even if they did not want liberation, which some did not.

An underestimated threat
In Persepolis the Persian king, Darius III, at first perceived only an irritating local disturbance on the western edge of his vast empire. He launched a naval counter-offensive in the Aegean and plotted to raise Athens and other Greek cities in revolt against Alexander.

Persian capital Persepolis
The ceremonial capital of the Achaemenid Persian empire, Persepolis was occupied by Alexander's Macedonians in 330 BCE. It was heavily damaged by fire at that time, whether deliberately or accidentally is not certain. Its ruins testify to its ancient glory.

Through the following year Alexander practised siege warfare, overcoming the resistance of the coastal cities of Tyre and Gaza and punishing their inhabitants with enslavement or massacre for the trouble they had caused. In Egypt he was diplomatically welcomed as a liberator from Persian oppression, and one oracle (at the Siwah oasis) addressed him as a "son of Zeus". He founded the city of Alexandria as a future capital for his Egyptian realm.

Instead of waiting to be attacked, Alexander preferred to take the offensive and in the spring of 331 he marched out of Egypt towards Persia. Darius awaited him on the far side of the Tigris in Gaugamela. Recruited mostly from Persia's central and eastern domains, this was a predominantly Asiatic army, with Indian war elephants, Scythian horsemen, and chariots. Alexander devised a battleplan that would allow the shock effect of his Companion cavalry to negate the numerical advantage of the Persian host. Most of his troops were committed to a desperate holding action while he

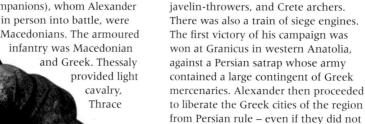

"**Heaven** cannot brook two suns, nor earth **two masters**."
ATTRIBUTED TO ALEXANDER BEFORE THE BATTLE OF GAUGAMELA, 331 BCE

When this plan failed and Alexander headed eastwards across Anatolia in 333, Darius advanced to meet him with a large army. Alexander's instinct was to seek out, engage, and destroy his enemy's army, whatever the odds. The two forces met late in the year at Issus (see p.26) near the Syrian-Turkish border. The battle ended in a shock defeat for the Persian king, leaving the eastern Mediterranean open to Macedonian conquest.

The face of Alexander
Alexander took great care to control his public image. The sculptor Lysippos was engaged to create an idealized image of the conqueror that was then imitated by all subsequent artists.

led the cavalry and elite infantry units in a thrust through the Persian centre where Darius himself was positioned. The emperor fled and Alexander turned his cavalry back to overwhelm the army abandoned by its leader.

Consolidating the empire
The victory at Gaugamela and Darius's subsequent murder by his own satraps opened the way for Alexander to claim the succession to the Persian imperial throne. Three years of campaigning were required to establish his control over the satrapies of Bactria and Sogdiana further to the east. Just as he had adopted local symbols of power in Egypt, Alexander now took on some

Spring 326 BCE: Leading an army of some 80,000 troops and 30,000 camp-followers, Alexander crosses Indus and marches on Taxila

Spring 333 BCE: Over 30 cities in Lycia surrender to Alexander

Spring 328 BCE: Capture of Sogdian Rock

Nov 331 BCE: Surrender of Babylon

Jun 323 BCE: Alexander dies in Babylon

Sep–Nov 332 BCE: Siege of key Persian fortress of Gaza. Alexander wounded by catapult bolt

Feb 331 BCE: Alexander visits oracle of Ammon at Siwa

30 Jan 330 BCE: Alexander reaches Persepolis

Sep 326 BCE: At Hyphasis river, Greek troops refuse to go any further. Army turns back

EGYPT

Key
- Empire of Alexander
- Dependent regions
- → Route of Alexander
- ✗ Major battle

Alexander's territory

Alexander's great desire was to wage war on behalf of all Greeks. In only ten years after succeeding Philip II, his father, Alexander's army conquered much of Asia, as well as parts of northern India, North Africa, and Europe.

of the customs and dress of the Persian court. In 327 he married a 16-year-old Bactrian princess, Roxanne, as a way of reconciling that restive region of his empire to his rule.

The expedition that Alexander led into India in 326 probably appeared the best means at his disposal to restore

fraying bonds between the Macedonian band of brothers. He won a gruelling battle against the rampaging chariots and war elephants of King Porus at the Hydaspes (see pp.54–55), but his soldiers were becoming exhausted and set a limit to his conquests by insisting on turning back at the Beas river in the Punjab. Alexander's army marauded down the Indus to the sea. Then he marched across the Gedrosian desert,

in present-day Iran, back to Persia, a mistake that cost thousands their lives to dehydration and exhaustion.

Alexander was still full of plans for further expeditions and campaigns, but his health had suffered due to his battle wounds and from the strains of years of campaigning. In 323, a month short of his 33rd birthday, he died in Babylon – rumour said of poisoning, but it was probably of a fever.

AFTER »

When Alexander died his plans for expanding his empire were halted. Nonetheless, his conquests left a long-term legacy of political and cultural changes.

CULTURAL INTEGRATION

Later commentators viewed Alexander's conquests as a means of extending Greek civilization throughout the world. He envisaged integrating his empire ethnically – for example, by marrying his Macedonian officers to Persian wives and training young Persians to fight as hoplites – while at the same time imposing Greek culture and values.

AFTER ALEXANDER

After Alexander's death his **generals fought over his inheritance 28–29 »**. Ptolemy took Egypt, Seleucus gained Syria and Iran, and Antigonus controlled Anatolia, but they

17 Length of the Macedonian sarissa spear in metres, equivalent to 23 feet.

all lacked his vision. They abandoned his projects for integrating Persians and other ethnic groups into the upper ranks of the empire, ruling as Macedonians over conquered peoples. However, the influence of Hellenic culture and the Greek language was extended deep into Asia; for example, Indian sculptures of Buddha reflected Greek representations of Apollo. **Alexandria, the city Alexander founded in Egypt, grew to be one of the greatest cities in the ancient world**, a major centre of Greek art and learning, as well as of trade and government.

The battle of Issus
This Roman mosaic representation of the battle of Issus was probably copied from a 4th-century BCE wall painting. Alexander (left) and Darius (right) lock eyes across a battlefield dominated by *sarissa* spears.

Issus

Fought in November 333 BCE, the battle of Issus was the second of Alexander the Great's three victories in his campaign against Persian king Darius III. Alexander's 50,000-strong army was outnumbered by two or three to one. It was a triumph of the attacking spirit of the Macedonian cavalry and the inspirational leadership of Alexander, a warrior who always led from the front.

The battle took place near the modern Turkish border on the strategically crucial route to the Levant coast. Advancing south into Persian territory, Alexander's forces were surprised to find Darius's army behind them. Keen to face the enemy, they turned and marched north to give battle. The Persians took up a defensive position behind a steep-banked stream. Against a numerically superior enemy, it was important for Alexander not to be outflanked. He stretched his line thinly across a 2.6-km (1.6-mile) front from the Mediterranean shore on the east (his left) to the foothills of the mountains inland. When the Persians sent men into the mountains to bring them down in the Macedonians' rear, Alexander dispatched his Thracian skirmishers, skilled in the use of the javelin, to block their path.

Order of battle

On the left of Alexander's line were his Thessalian horsemen, unarmoured light cavalry. The infantry phalanx in the centre consisted primarily of Macedonians armed with the long, two-handed pike known as the *sarissa*. Because of the stretching of the line, the phalanx was far shallower than the usual 16 ranks. Alexander's armoured Macedonian horsemen, the Companion cavalry, held pride of place on the right of the line, supported by Greek

hypaspists – elite hoplite infantry. Like Alexander's army, the Persian forces were ethnically diverse, including Greek mercenaries forming a phalanx alongside Persian infantry in the centre. Whereas Alexander, on horseback with spear and sword, led the Companion cavalry, Darius commanded from behind the front line, positioned in a chariot among his elite imperial guard.

Macedonian triumph

Alexander ordered a general advance. The tight formation of the Macedonian infantry phalanx lost cohesion moving forward over rough ground and crossing the stream. Darius's infantry were able to penetrate gaps in the bristling barrier of spears and to cut and stab at men in the exposed core of the phalanx. But on the left the Thessalian horsemen performed well against the strongest concentration of Darius's cavalry, while on the right Alexander led a charge of the Companion cavalry that swept all before it. Wheeling in from the flank, Alexander's horsemen bore down upon the rear of the enemy infantry who were driven onto the anvil of the Macedonian phalanx. Darius and his entourage fled the battlefield to avoid capture. Much of the infantry was trapped and cut down where it stood, while large numbers of fleeing cavalry and skirmishers were pursued and massacred.

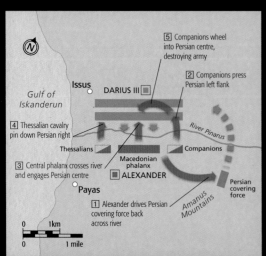

LOCATION
Plain on the Gulf of Iskanderun, present-day Turkey

DATE
November 333 BCE

FORCES
Persians: 110,000;
Macedonians: 35,000

CASUALTIES
Persians: 50,000 (allegedly);
Macedonians: 450

KEY
- Persian forces
- Macedonian infantry
- Macedonian cavalry

Map labels:
- 5 Companions wheel into Persian centre, destroying army
- 2 Companions press Persian left flank
- Issus
- DARIUS III
- Gulf of Iskanderun
- 4 Thessalian cavalry pin down Persian right
- River Pinarus
- Thessalians
- Companions
- Macedonian phalanx
- 3 Central phalanx crosses river and engages Persian centre
- ALEXANDER
- Payas
- Persian covering force
- 1 Alexander drives Persian covering force back across river
- Amanus Mountains
- 0 1km
- 0 1 mile

Alexander Sarcophagus
This detail of the Alexander Sarcophagus, made in Sidon (southern Lebanon) in the 4th century BCE, shows Alexander leading his Companion cavalry. A Persian soldier lies trampled underfoot.

« BEFORE

Alexander of Macedon's great empire « 24–25 stretched from Greece to India and included both Persia and Egypt. When he died in 323 BCE, there was no obvious heir.

STOPGAP SOLUTIONS
Alexander's wife, Roxanne – resented by his Macedonian followers because she was Bactrian – was pregnant. Otherwise the only candidate from Alexander's family was a feeble bastard half-brother, Arrhidaeus. Neither would be able to rule except as **puppets of the generals**. Alexander's second-in-command, **Perdiccas, appointed himself regent**. Alexander had adopted the **Persian system of satrapies** to rule his empire. The Macedonian generals continued this system, authorizing various of their number to **run different parts of the empire as satraps**, while the ageing Antipater became **viceroy of Macedonia**.

EASTERN MEDITERRANEAN

Wars of the Diadochi
Dates 322–281 BCE
Location Chiefly Asia Minor, Syria, Greece, and Macedonia, although a few battles were fought as far east as Persia

Alexander's Successors

For 50 years after his death, Alexander the Great's successors, known in Greek as the _Diadochi_, fought over his inheritance. Using the plundered wealth of imperial conquest to fund their wars, they founded three major dynasties: the Ptolemies in Egypt, the Seleucids in Asia, and the Antigonids in Macedonia.

Asked on his deathbed to whom he left his empire, Alexander is said to have replied: "To the strongest." Alexander's generals hardly needed this invitation to a power struggle after his death. Macedonian aristocrats were hard-fighting, hard-drinking men, and naturally quarrelsome.

At first all assumed that one man would end up controlling the whole empire, and several believed their chances were good. Ptolemy gained appointment as satrap of Egypt and carried off the body of Alexander with him. Embalmed and displayed, the corpse became a great tourist attraction and brought Ptolemy much prestige. Based in Anatolia, Antigonus One-Eye, a bluff old warrior of limitless energy, also set about staking a claim to the succession.

The settlement sketched in Babylon on Alexander's death swiftly unraveled. Perdiccas, self-appointed regent of the empire, tried in vain to assert his authority over Ptolemy and Antigonus. He invaded Egypt but his troops were

Ruins of Apamea in Syria
Apamea was one of many Hellenistic cities in Asia founded or enlarged by Seleucus I. Vast stables were built here to house his war elephants and cavalry horses. The city continued to flourish throughout the Roman era.

> "He added, and these were **his last words**, that **all of his leading friends** would **stage a vast contest** in honour of his funeral."
>
> ALEXANDER'S LAST WORDS ACCORDING TO DIODORUS SICULUS, 1ST CENTURY BCE

Macedonian rivals

The coins bear the heads of Pompey I (left), Seleucus I (centre), and Demetrius Poliorcetes, son of Antigonus (right), the three principal generals who fought to inherit the vast empire created by Alexander the Great.

Macedonian rule. The successors' armies were primarily composed of Macedonians and Greeks, mercenaries who readily deserted any leader who seemed to be losing or lacked the money to pay them. They naturally continued Alexander's style of warfare, with battles conducted by an infantry phalanx armed with long pikes, supported by cavalry and skirmishers with missile weapons. Their armies were much larger than any Alexander led, and they employed war elephants, introduced after contact with India.

Clash of the pretenders

At first Antigonus looked the likely winner. He gained control of most of the empire in Asia and built a fleet in Phoenician shipyards to extend his dominance on land to the sea. Ptolemy beat off an attack on Egypt led by Antigonus's son, Demetrius, in 312 BCE but the Antigonid navy defeated Ptolemy's warships off Cyprus in 306 and laid siege to the independent Greek island city of Rhodes. With Ptolemy's aid the Rhodeans held out, despite Antigonus's deployment of the latest siege engines, including giant catapults and siege towers. In gratitude, Rhodes named the Egyptian ruler Ptolemy Soter ("Saviour"). This setback did not prevent the Antigonids invading Greece and threatening Macedonia.

lost in the Nile Delta, many becoming food for crocodiles; the regent himself was murdered by his discontented followers. In Macedonia Alexander's son and half-brother met violent deaths. Arrhidaeus was murdered by Alexander's mother, Olympias. She was then herself killed, along with Alexander's son and wife, after Cassander, son of the now deceased viceroy Antipater, seized control of Macedonia. This welter of blood set the tone for all that was to follow.

Macedonian generals competed with scant regard for the inhabitants of the lands they fought over. The only subjects whose support they actively sought were those of the Greek cities, which were also the most troublesome source of intermittent rebellion against

By the usual logic of multi-sided power struggles, the success of Antigonus and Demetrius drove the other Diodachi to combine. In 301 BCE Cassander and Ptolemy were joined by Lysimachus, ruler of Thrace, and Seleucus, satrap of Babylonia, in an anti-Antigonid alliance. They decided to defend Macedonia indirectly, by an offensive in Asia that Antigonus and Demetrius could not ignore. While Ptolemy snapped up Palestine and Syria, Cassander, Lysimachus, and Seleucus marched into Anatolia. Battle was joined at Ipsos. Antigonus and Demetrius had slightly the larger army, but Seleucus had brought almost 500 elephants with him from the East, the fruit of a treaty with the Indian Mauryan empire (see pp.54–55). Demetrius led the cavalry

150,000 The approximate number of soldiers who took part in the battle of Ipsos in 301 BCE. The Antigonids had some 80,000 men, the alliance that opposed them a slightly smaller army of 70,000.

charge on the Antigonid right and swept all before him, but Seleucus used his elephants to block Demetrius's horsemen from coming to the aid of the Antigonid infantry, which wilted under a rain of arrows. Many of the foot soldiers decided it was a good moment to change sides, and the 80-year-old Antigonus was killed by a javelin.

The great victor of Ipsos was Seleucus. He emerged in control of most of the empire in Asia, which he shared with his son, Antiochus. The successors might now reasonably have settled for kingship in their respective regions. This was indeed the policy of Ptolemy, who in 283 achieved the rare feat of dying in his own bed of natural causes, handing Egypt on to his son. But elsewhere bloody feuds continued. Lysimachus succeeded in making himself king of Macedon, but was killed by Seleucus in 281 at the battle of Corupedium. Seleucus did not live to enjoy his victory, however, being assassinated the moment he set foot in Macedon to claim the throne. Ironically, it was the defeated Antigonids who ended up as rulers of Macedon. Demetrius had died as a prisoner of Seleucus, but from 276 his son, Antigonus Gonatus, won control of Macedon and most of Greece.

AFTER »

The empire had been carved up into three main successor states, which remained mutually hostile. Alongside them, other smaller dynasties arose, especially in Asia.

OTHER HELLENISTIC DYNASTIES

Hellenistic cities kept alive the heritage of Alexander across Asia. Far to the east on the River Oxus, a **Greco-Bactrian kingdom** flourished in c.245–125 BCE. Finds at **Ai Khanoum** have revealed a fascinating blend of Greek and Persian artistic styles and religious beliefs. A comparable **fusion of Eastern and Western cultures** is found at the hilltop

NEMRUT DAG SHRINE

shrine of **Nemrut Dag**, built in the 1st century CE by the ruler of Commagene in present-day Turkey.

CONTINUING CONFLICT

The Ptolemies and Seleucids disputed control of Syria through the 3rd century BCE. At the **battle of Raphia in 217**, the Seleucid army of Antiochus III was defeated by Egyptian ruler Ptolemy IV. Antigonid Philip V of Macedon came to the aid of Antiochus, and their combined power was sufficient to push Egypt back on the defensive.

But none of the three states was a match for the rising power of Rome. Philip V allied with the **Carthaginian Hannibal against the Romans 32–33 »**. After the **Carthaginian defeat in 201**, Philip was the target for Roman vengeance. The Roman legions cut apart the Macedonian phalanx at **Cynoscephalae in 197**. Antiochus was **defeated by the Romans at Magnesia** in 190 BCE. Seleucid power shrank to nothing, eroded by Rome in the west and the Parthians in the east. The Antigonid dynasty came to an end after a **final defeat by Rome at Pydna** in 168. Ptolemaic Egypt survived until 30 BCE, when the **last of the Ptolemies, Cleopatra VII**, died and **Egypt became a province of the Roman empire 38–39 »**.

STATUE OF ROMAN LEGIONARY

WAR ELEPHANTS

First used in south Asia, war elephants served as elevated command posts, platforms for soldiers armed with bows and javelins, and chargers to trample infantry underfoot. They were effective against cavalry, because horses disliked their smell. The Seleucids used Indian elephants, while the Ptolemies deployed smaller, African forest elephants. Although they inspired terror, elephants were themselves easily panicked, running amok and causing havoc among their own troops.

GREEK TERRACOTTA FIGURINE OF A WAR ELEPHANT

Samnite warriors
This 4th-century BCE tomb fresco from southern Italy shows Samnite tribal warriors in their distinctive armour and plumed helmets. The Samnites fought both as enemies and allies of Rome.

The **Rise** of Rome

The Roman Republic was not a likely contender for imperial power in the 4th century BCE. Yet its relentless fighting spirit and refusal to accept defeat enabled Rome to subject Samnite tribes and Greek colonies to its rule. Control of southern Italy would prove a springboard for wider empire.

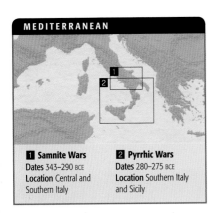

MEDITERRANEAN

1 **Samnite Wars**
Dates 343–290 BCE
Location Central and Southern Italy

2 **Pyrrhic Wars**
Dates 280–275 BCE
Location Southern Italy and Sicily

BEFORE

The origins of Rome, dated by the Romans themselves to 753 BCE, are shrouded in legend. The growth of the city into a significant regional power took centuries.

ROME'S FIRST VICTORIES
The **dominant people in Italy** during the early years of Rome were **the Etruscans**. Rome was merely one of many small Latin communities of central Italy whose warrior bands fought one another over land or livestock.

By the 5th century BCE, **under the influence of the Greeks**, who had founded cities in southern Italy, the Romans had adopted a new style of warfare. Their **citizen militia** fought as **armoured hoplites** with thrusting spear and shield **in an infantry phalanx ‹‹ 22–23**. By the early 4th century they had established their independence of the Etruscans and their **dominance over other Latin cities**. With their allies they would now have to face more formidable enemies, including the **Greeks**, who had flourishing **colonies in southern Italy**.

In 387 or 390 BCE – the date is disputed – a Roman army was defeated at the Allia river by the Gauls, fierce warriors who had invaded northern and central Italy. Rome was occupied and the Gauls left only after being paid a large sum in gold. This humiliation revealed the defects not only of Rome's city walls but also its battle tactics, modeled upon the Greek phalanx. In the course of the 4th century military reforms produced a more flexible and effective army that would win the Romans a far-flung empire.

The Roman army was a militia of part-time soldiers, structured according to the social status and age of the citizens

Etruscan soldier
Etruscan infantry wore bronze helmets and armour of bronze plates, and carried a round shield and a spear. They were overcome by the more warlike Romans.

Roman aggression
From around 343 to 275 BCE the Roman legions fought a series of wars that established Rome's domination over southern Italy. The fiercest of their enemies at first were the Samnites of the

Rome's next targets were the Greek colonies of southern Italy. In 281 BCE the Romans attacked Tarentum (modern-day Taranto). The city appealed for help to one of the most experienced war leaders in the Greek world, King Pyrrhus of Epirus. The army with which he arrived in Italy was typical of the post-Alexander era in the eastern Mediterranean. Most of his troops were spear-wielding infantry, but he also had light and heavy cavalry, several thousand archers, and a score of war elephants. At Heraclea and Asculum in 280–279, Pyrrhus twice defeated the Roman legions through the impact of his elephants and cavalry. Yet the battles were won at such a heavy price – Pyrrhus is alleged to have said, "One more such victory and I am lost." After a final drawn battle at Beneventum in 275, Pyrrhus went home, allowing Rome to complete its domination of southern Italy. The Roman legions had successfully stood up to one of the most advanced professional armies of the day.

> ## "The Romans fought **fiercely** … **reckless of their lives**."
> **PLUTARCH ON THE BATTLE OF ASCULUM IN HIS "LIFE OF PYRRHUS"**

in its ranks. Since citizen-soldiers had to supply their own equipment, the richest formed the cavalry, being able to afford a horse, and the poorest served as lightly armed skirmishers, with the armoured heavy infantry in between. Two annually elected magistrates – the consuls – shared overall command. That such an amateur arrangement should have proved an empire-winning force was partly due to weapons and tactics. Instead of the

Apennine mountains, who often fought in alliance with other peoples resisting Roman expansion, such as the Gauls and the Umbrians. There were three Samnite Wars: in 343–341, 327–304, and in 298–290.

The Romans were not always victorious. At the battle of the Caudine Forks in 321, a Roman army was ambushed in mountain terrain and forced to surrender as Samnite warriors rained missiles down upon the trapped legionaries from impregnable heights. Typically, having accepted humiliating peace terms to secure the soldiers' release, the Romans then refused to carry out the terms once the men were freed. Rome was sometimes beaten on the battlefield but it never accepted defeat. A hard-fought victory over Samnites and Gauls at Sentinum in 295 opened the way for the Roman pacification of the mountain tribes. The Samnites eventually took a place as allied auxiliaries of the Roman legions.

13,000 According to one estimate, the number of Pyrrhus's soldiers killed fighting the Romans at Heraclea in 280 BCE, the first of the Greek king's "Pyrrhic victories" – battles won at devastating cost.

hoplite thrusting spear, the heavy infantry were equipped with a throwing spear and a sword for close combat. The legions into which troops were organized, each 4,500–5,000 strong, were subdivided into maniples of 120 men, which could manoeuvre independently on the battlefield. The soldiers accepted rigorous discipline and training, forming a tight-knit, highly committed force. The legions were supported by auxiliaries recruited from Rome's subordinate Italian allies.

Pyrrhus
The king of Epirus in Greece, Pyrrhus was an experienced campaigner who often led from the front. In support of Greek colonies, he fought against the Carthaginians in Sicily as well as the Romans in Italy.

AFTER

The expansion of Rome took on an unstoppable momentum in the century after victory in the war with Pyrrhus.

A MEDITERRANEAN EMPIRE
Roman control of southern Italy brought conflict with the **Carthaginians in Sicily**. In 264 BCE this led to the first of **the Punic Wars 32–33 ››**. **The Second Punic War of 218–201** ended with Rome dominating the whole of the western Mediterranean. In the 2nd century BCE **victories over the Antigonid rulers of Macedonia** and the **Seleucids in Syria ‹‹ 28–29** extended Roman rule into the eastern Mediterranean.

The creation of such an **extensive empire** put pressure on the existing Roman military system. An army of part-time citizen-soldiers was ill-suited to **lengthy overseas campaigns** and providing garrisons in far-flung territories. The **legions** would eventually have to become a **full-time professional force 42–43 ››**.

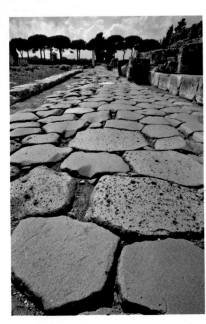

The Appian Way
The Romans began building the first of their famed military roads, the Via Appia, during the second Samnite War in 312 BCE. The road allowed legionaries to be moved swiftly south from Rome.

« BEFORE

The destructive series of wars between Rome and Carthage began as a relatively minor conflict on the island of Sicily, which lay between the two states.

THE PATH TO WAR

Sited on the coast of North Africa in modern-day Tunisia, Carthage was a colony founded by Phoenicians from the Levant around 800 BCE. The Phoenicians were seafarers and Carthage grew rich on maritime trade. By the 3rd century BCE its **naval power** allowed it to **dominate much of the western Mediterranean**. It had a strong presence in Sicily, where its main enemy

CARTHAGINIAN GOLD COIN

was the **Greek city of Syracuse**. At the same time, Rome was extending its power southward through Italy. Between 280 and 275 BCE **King Pyrrhus of Epirus**, intervening in defence of the Greek cities in the area, **fought both the Carthaginians in Sicily and the Romans in southern Italy << 30–31**. After Pyrrhus left, Roman forces pushed down to the toe of Italy. Their anxiety about the Carthaginian presence in Sicily led them to **cross the straits of Messina in 264** to lend support to **the Mamertines**, a band of mercenary soldiers in conflict with both Syracuse and Carthage. This intervention escalated into **a full-scale war for possession of Sicily.**

The Punic Wars

In the 3rd century BCE the rivalry between the Romans and Carthaginians developed into a life-or-death struggle. An invasion of Italy by the Carthaginian general, Hannibal, brought the city of Rome to the brink of disaster, but the Punic Wars ended in the total destruction of Carthage.

The First Punic War, from 264 to 241 BCE, began as a land conflict in Sicily. The Carthaginians were dependent upon supply and reinforcement by sea from North Africa. Rome was not a naval power, but in 261 BCE decided to create a fleet from scratch, as the only means of driving the Carthaginians out of the island. What followed was, in terms of the numbers of ships and men committed, by far the largest naval war fought in the ancient world.

Building a navy

Taking Carthaginian warships as their models, the Romans managed to build 100 quinqueremes and 20 triremes in 60 days. A quinquereme was a hefty vessel, rowed by 300 oarsmen and capable of carrying 120 soldiers. The Romans could not match the skilled Carthaginian seamen in manoeuvre, but their legionary marines were a formidable boarding force. Rome won a series of victories from Mylae in 260 to Tyndarus in 257 BCE. In 256 the Romans prepared a seaborne invasion of North Africa. The Carthaginians intercepted the invasion fleet off the Sicilian coast at Cape Ecnomus, but in the battle that ensued lost almost 100 ships captured

680 **The number of ships engaged in the battle of Cape Ecnomus in 256 BCE, according to Greek historian Polybius. If the estimate of 286,000 men on board is correct, this puts it among the largest naval battles in history.**

or sunk. This disaster left them incapable of preventing a Roman landing in Africa. In 255 Rome seemed on the brink of winning the war, but severe setbacks followed. The Roman expeditionary force in Africa was routed and almost annihilated after a devastating charge by Carthaginian massed elephants at Tunis. At sea hundreds of Roman warships were lost in storms. The costs of the prolonged war threatened to exhaust Rome's resources. After the

Roman warships

This relief of Roman war galleys shows vessels with double banks of oars packed with soldiers. Roman naval tactics centred on the boarding of enemy ships.

failed African expedition, fighting was once more concentrated in Sicily. Carthaginian forces, under general Hamilcar Barca from 247, adopted a purely defensive strategy, resisting sieges and engaging in raids and skirmishes. Their position grew increasingly precarious. In 241 a desperate effort to resupply the remaining Carthaginian-held cities in Sicily was thwarted when a grain fleet from Africa was intercepted by a Roman fleet at the Aegates Islands. The Romans sank or captured 120 of the heavily laden ships. Carthage agreed to abandon Sicily and pay a large indemnity in return for peace.

The second war

For a long time the Carthaginians were in no state to resume war with Rome. The desire for revenge was passed down a generation, Carthaginian general, Hannibal, inheriting it from his father, Hamilcar Barca. Spain, where both Rome and Carthage were expanding their influence, provided the flashpoint for renewed war. In 219 Hannibal seized the Spanish city of Saguntum in defiance of Rome. The following year he led an army from Spain through southern Gaul and across the Alps into Italy.

Hannibal's army – including Spanish tribesmen, Libyan infantry, Numidian horsemen, and Gallic warriors recruited en route – descended into Italy from the Alpine passes with a few surviving war elephants and struck towards Rome. A Roman army sent to meet them was ambushed and destroyed at Lake Trasimene. Fabius, appointed "dictator" to lead the Roman war effort under now desperate circumstances, adopted a strategy that won him the nickname

Key

▬	Roman territory 264 BCE
▬	Roman gains by 238 BCE
▬	Roman gains by 200 BCE
—	Carthaginian empire 264 BCE
—	Carthaginian territory 200 BCE
—	Hannibal's campaign (219–202 BCE)
—	Campaigns of Scipio Africanus (210–206 BCE and 204–202 BCE)
✕	Roman victory
✕	Carthaginian victory

218 BCE: Hannibal crosses Alps with 26,000 infantry, 9,000 cavalry, and 15 war elephants

219 BCE: Hannibal takes Saguntum; Rome declares war

202 BCE: Hannibal returns to North Africa to defend Carthage but is defeated by Scipio Africanus

149–146 BCE: Third Punic War; Carthage besieged and then destroyed by Roman army

ATLANTIC OCEAN

Iberian Peninsula

Pyrenees

Tolosa

Narbo

Massalia

Rhodae

Emporiae

Tarraco

Dertosa

Saguntum

Numantia

Ilipa 206 BCE

Baecula 208 BCE

209 BCE

Gades

Tingis

Malaca

Carthago Nova

Rusaddir

Cartenna

Iol

Saldae

Atlas Mountains

AFRICA

Sahara

Alps

Placentia

Trebia 218 BCE

Pisae

Lake Trasimene 217 BCE

Ariminum

Metaurus 207 BCE

Perusia

Rome

Ostia

Olbia

Capua

Cannae 216 BCE

Tarentum

Thurii

Croton

Corsica to Rome 238 BCE

Aleria

Sardinia

Tyrrhenian Sea

Carales

Aegates

Mylae 260 BCE

Messina

Lilybaeum

Ecnomus 256 BCE

Syracuse

Sicily

Utica

204 BCE

Carthage

Zama 202 BCE

Hadrumetum

203 BCE

Mediterranean Sea

Baleares

Leptis Magna

Charax

N

0   400km

0   400 miles

Rome's wars with Carthage

The first war was decided in Sicily and on the waters surrounding the island. The second spread from the Iberian Peninsula to the mainland of Italy, and finally to the North African heartland of Carthage.

"Cunctator" ("delayer"), avoiding pitched battle with Hannibal's superior forces. This did not satisfy the Romans' bellicosity. In 216 Fabius was dismissed and the Romans and their allies confronted Hannibal at Cannae. The outmanoeuvred Romans were encircled and systematically butchered – as many as 48,000 men may have been killed.

A protracted struggle

Despite these losses Rome refused to sue for peace and resumed Fabian delaying tactics. Hannibal maintained his army in southern Italy year after year, living off the land, but had no clear strategy for bringing the war to a successful conclusion. Some cities took the opportunity to rebel against Roman domination, among them Syracuse in 213. The Romans retook the city in 211 after a long siege, despite the inventor Archimedes providing the Syracusans with ingenious defensive devices, such as a ship-lifting claw and an incendiary

> ## " ... no other nation ... would not have succumbed beneath such a weight of calamity."
>
> ROMAN HISTORIAN LIVY ON ROME'S REACTION TO THE DEFEAT AT CANNAE

heat ray. Few reinforcements reached Hannibal from Carthage. When his brother, Hasdrubal, led another army from Spain over the Alps in 207, he was defeated and killed by the Romans at the battle of the Metaurus. When Hannibal finally returned to Carthage in 202, he had been in Italy for a total of 16 years.

Roman general Scipio, a survivor of Cannae, had executed a triumphant campaign in Spain from 210 to 206, scoring a series of victories over the Carthaginians. After returning to Italy, in 204 he mounted an invasion of North Africa

from Sicily. At first the Carthaginians sued for peace, but Hannibal's return with his army stiffened their resolve and peace negotiations broke down. In 202 Hannibal faced Scipio's army at Zama. Scipio's forces were strengthened by the defection of the Numidian cavalry from the Carthaginian side. The battle was close-fought but ended in total victory for Rome. Carthage admitted defeat and was stripped of its navy and its remaining colonial possessions around the western Mediterranean. Scipio had earned the cognomen (nickname) "Africanus" by which he is known to history.

AFTER

After the defeat at Zama, Carthage was stripped of its military power, but Rome's thirst for vengeance would not be satisfied until its rival had been utterly destroyed.

DESTRUCTION OF CARTHAGE
The most prominent advocate of renewed military action was the Roman orator, **Cato the Elder**, who ended every speech with the statement: **"Carthage must be destroyed!"** In 149 BCE the Romans sent an army to **besiege the city**, accusing the Carthaginians of breaking their treaty with Rome. The siege went badly until the arrival of **Scipio Aemilianus**, adoptive grandson of Scipio Africanus. The city was first **blockaded to near-starvation** and then, in 146 BCE, **taken by assault**. The Carthaginians fought desperately, a final core of resisters burning themselves to death in a temple. All surviving Carthaginians were marched off into slavery. The Romans then **razed the city**, leaving not a single building standing.

Battle of Zama

This is a fanciful Renaissance representation of the final battle of the Second Punic War, Scipio's victory over Hannibal in 202 BCE. Carthage's African forest elephants could not have carried quite such a load of soldiers.

EUROPE

1 Caesar's Gallic Wars
Dates 58–51 BCE
Location France, Switzerland, and Belgium

2 Caesar's invasions of Britain
Dates 55, 54 BCE
Location Southeast England

The Gallic Wars

Between 58 and 51 BCE Roman general, Julius Caesar, defeated the tribes of Gaul in a series of campaigns that combined military efficiency with subtle diplomacy and ruthless massacre. Caesar exploited the divisions between his enemies and extended the frontiers of empire by piecemeal conquests.

BEFORE

By the end of the 2nd century BCE Rome had established a Mediterranean empire but was still vulnerable to attack by tribal peoples from the north.

NEW ENEMIES AND A NEW ARMY
From 113 BCE Rome found itself at war with the **Cimbri and Teutones**, Germanic tribes migrating from the Baltic to invade the territory of the Romans and their allies in Gaul. The

80,000 The number of Roman soldiers who died fighting the Cimbri at Arausio (modern-day Orange, France) in 105 BCE.

Roman legions suffered heavy defeats, experiencing their worst casualties since **the Punic Wars << 32–33**. The tide was turned under **Gaius Marius**, who **defeated the Teutones at Aquae Sextiae** (modern-day Aix-en-Provence in southern France) in 102 BCE.

To strengthen the Roman forces for that campaign and for a **war against the Berber Jugurtha in North Africa**, Gaius Marius recruited volunteers from among the poorest Roman citizens into the legions. Formerly a citizen militia, the Roman army mutated into a **professional force of full-time career soldiers**. Military leaders also began to vie for political power: Marius and his rival general, Sulla, twice **fought civil wars for control of Rome**, in 88–87 and again in 83–82 BCE.

Celtic decorated knife and sheath
The Celts of Gaul and Britain had a love of elaborate decoration, as seen on the handle and sheath of this dagger found in London's river Thames. The blade is made of iron.

I n 59 BCE Julius Caesar, a member of the aristocracy with a modestly successful military record, served as a Roman consul. This one-year appointment was traditionally followed by a posting to govern a province. Since Caesar was a close ally of Rome's most successful general, Pompey, and its richest citizen, Crassus, he was given control of the extensive area of Cisalpine Gaul (northern Italy), Transalpine Gaul (Provence), and Illyricum (the Balkans) for five years instead of the usual one-year term. It was an opportunity for Caesar to win military glory – important for a politically ambitious man – and to find plunder to pay off his considerable debts.

A warlike people
Cisalpine Gaul and Illyricum were peaceful, but in Transalpine Gaul Caesar found ample scope for war-making. Among the Celtic tribes known to the Romans as the Gauls, warfare was endemic. The tribes had traditionally been led by warrior chieftains who raided their neighbours and distributed the proceeds to reward their warband. Although Gallic societies were evolving away from this primitive model, tribes formed alliances against one another and in order to defend against pressure from outsiders such as Germanic people from east of the Rhine. From the Gauls' point of view, the Roman presence fitted quite easily into this world. They were happy to enter into temporary alliances with

Rome, calling for military support when they needed it and joining the Romans in attacks on rival tribes. But they did not expect that they would be reduced to a permanently subservient status.

Gaul, Germany, and Britain
Caesar's first wars in Gaul after taking up command in 58 BCE were fought in alliance with the Aedui, tribes that lived between the Saone and Loire rivers. The first enemy was the Helvetii, a people from Switzerland who set out to migrate to western Gaul. Caesar fought and defeated them, forcing those that survived to return to their homeland. Then the Aedui asked for protection against the Germanic warrior, Ariovistus; Caesar's legions confronted him in the Vosges and drove him back across the Rhine. These defensive campaigns were followed by a series of much bolder operations that extended the boundaries of Roman domination. On the pretext again of an attack on a Celtic ally, Caesar invaded the territory of the Belgic tribes to the northeast in 57 BCE. The following year he defeated the Veneti in Brittany. In 55 BCE he ventured beyond the borders of Gaul, bridging the Rhine for a foray into Germany and taking two legions across the English Channel on board 80 transport ships. This landing in Britain was repeated the following year on a larger scale, the Romans advancing as far north as the river Thames, although Caesar left no permanent presence.

Coin of Julius Caesar
Born into the Roman aristocracy in 100 BCE, Julius Caesar was a towering political figure as well as a great general.

By 54 BCE Caesar had expanded the Roman-ruled area of Gaul from southern France to the Atlantic, Channel, and North Sea coasts. Publicized by Caesar himself in his written accounts of his wars, these successes greatly enhanced his reputation. His term as provincial governor was extended from five to ten years. The campaigns had enabled him to improve the training and combat experience of his legions and weld them into an army loyal to himself, rather than to the Republic. The legions were not invulnerable: during the campaign against the Belgic tribes in 57 BCE they were nearly defeated by a surprise

Gallic hero
Vercingetorix, a chieftain of the Arverni, led the most extensive resistance to the Roman conquest of Gaul. He is celebrated by this statue in his native Auvergne.

attack while making camp near the river Sambre. All legionaries by this period fought as heavy infantry, with skirmishers and cavalry provided by various auxiliaries – Gauls and Germans, along with other peoples from as far afield as Crete and North Africa. The Romans were superior to their Gallic enemies in discipline, logistics, and engineering skills – fortification and bridge-building – but in a face-to-face fight, a Gallic warrior was still a formidable opponent. Widespread resentment against the Romans began to show itself in the winter

of 54–53 BCE. The Belgic tribes revolted and a Roman column was ambushed and annihilated. Another garrison had to be rescued by a relief column. The following winter Vercingetorix, who had established himself as leader of the Arverni, succeeded in uniting the tribes of western and central Gaul in an uprising against the Romans. Caesar went on the offensive, but Vercingetorix cleverly avoided pitched battle. His plan was to let the Romans exhaust themselves in long sieges of fortified hill towns, while depriving them of supplies through a scorched earth policy and harassing them with his cavalry. Caesar succeeded in taking the town of Avaricum after a 25-day siege – almost the entire population was massacred when the town fell – but Gergovia, near modern-day Clermont-Ferrand, was successfully defended against the legions.

Showdown at Alesia
For a while the Gallic and Roman armies skirmished and shadowed one another. Finally, Vercingetorix installed his army at the fortified hill town of Alesia, where he was besieged. Some

Caesar's victory at Alesia guaranteed Roman rule in Gaul, which was to last for the following 500 years. Roman troops returned to occupy Britain in 43 CE.

GROWING RIVALRY
The prestige that accrued to Caesar through his campaigns in Gaul were **a threat** to the position of **his rival general, Pompey, in Rome**. Caesar was not allowed the celebration of a triumph and, in 50 BCE, was ordered to disband his army. Instead, **he marched on Rome and civil war followed 38–39 ›››**.

CAVALRY TRAINING HELMET, ROMAN BRITAIN

THE PRICE OF REBELLION
Caesar's **triumph for his Gallic victories** finally took place in Rome in 46 BCE. At the triumph, Vercingetorix, held prisoner since Alesia, was first displayed to the Roman public, then **executed by strangulation**.

> " I did not undertake the war … for private ends, **but in the cause of national liberty**. And since I must now accept my fate, **I place myself at your disposal**."
>
> VERCINGETORIX BEFORE SURRENDERING AT ALESIA, ACCORDING TO CAESAR'S "GALLIC WARS", 52 BCE

of his cavalry broke through the Roman lines and rode off to call on the allied tribes to send reinforcements. Once Caesar's legionaries had completed the fortifications around the town, it was under total blockade and the Gauls began to starve. They attempted to send away their women and children but the Romans would not allow it. When a Gallic relief force arrived, there was bitter fighting. The Romans found

themselves attacked from both sides as Vercingetorix's warriors coordinated attempted breakouts with attacks on the Roman fortifications and lines by his allies outside. There was a moment when the legionaries were almost overrun, but they held and the relief force was eventually driven off. Vercingetorix had no choice but to surrender, riding into Caesar's camp and laying down his arms at his feet.

KEY MOMENT

THE FORTIFICATIONS AT ALESIA

During the siege of Alesia in 52 BCE, Caesar set his legionaries to build two lines of fortifications around the hill town – one to keep Vercingetorix's Gallic army in and the other to defend the Roman besiegers against an attack from the rear by a relief force. Totalling 35km (22 miles) in length, the fortifications consisted of a series of ditches and an earth and timber rampart, with a tower every 25m (80ft) as well as 23 forts.

RECONSTRUCTION OF CAESAR'S FORTIFICATIONS

Engineering

Military engineers have always been at the forefront of technology. Their skills range from map-making and constructing fortifications, to bridging rivers, building strategic roads, and blowing up enemy installations. At the same time they are fighting men whose lives are in constant danger.

Military engineering has been a feature of organized warfare since earliest times, and was already sophisticated when the Assyrians ruled the Fertile Crescent (see pp.18–19). Even when technological levels were low, engineers were put to use on fortifications, such as those of the first walled cities of the Middle East and the Maori village strongholds of New Zealand.

The greater resources of larger states and empires increased the scope of their military engineering. The army of the Achaemenid empire of Persia (see pp.22–23) built military roads, pontoon bridges, and canals, but the ancient Romans (see pp.30–47) seem to have been the first to employ professional engineers as specialists in their army. Since Roman times, their work has been both defensive and offensive; a mixture of building an army's defences and breaking those of the enemy.

Construction engineering

Many military construction projects – strategic roads and railroads, water supply systems, and facilities such as barracks – are all but indistinguishable from civilian projects. Indeed, they have often had civil as well as military uses. For example, US Army engineers carried out the mapping of the American West in the 19th century, and the US Army Corps of Engineers is responsible for flood defences today.

The key permanent works of military engineers, however, have always been fortifications. These range from border defences such as the Great Wall of China and Hadrian's Wall through medieval stone castles and walled cities to the many elaborate 16th- to 18th-century star-shaped forts of the style associated with French engineer the Marquis de Vauban. Fortifications of the 20th century include the Maginot Line – built

Versatile siege weapon
Roman engineers used ballistas to fire bolts and stones at troops and walls up to 450m (500yd) away. At short range on a low trajectory, ballistas were highly accurate.

in the 1930s along France's border with Germany – and the German-built Atlantic Wall in France, which the Allied forces encountered in 1944.

As well as permanent structures, engineers have long been responsible for field fortifications, siege works, and camps set up in haste. A daily task for Roman engineers was to march ahead of the army to construct a camp, surrounded by a ditch and a rampart, for each night's rest. In modern times, field fortifications (traditionally a trench or palisade) have been further defended by barbed wire, minefields, and anti-tank traps. In World War I (see pp.266–77), these evolved into elaborate defensive systems in which soldiers lived for months on end.

By clearing obstacles, improvising roads, bridging rivers, and creating

Roman engineers at work
A spiral bas relief on Trajan's Column, erected in Rome in 113 CE, commemorates the emperor's victory in the Dacian Wars, and has scenes of soldiers engaged in construction, such as making bridges or siege ramps.

Building a Bailey bridge in World War II

The Bailey bridge was designed to be quickly and easily transported and put together with the help of ordinary troops. Here, US troops are bridging a river in Italy.

temporary bases, engineers have also historically had a vital function in enabling troops to advance or retreat at speed. Just as Roman engineers built bridges out of boats, in World War II (see pp.288–305) the Allied armies made Bailey bridges from prefabricated steel segments that they carried with them on trucks and put up across rivers. To the same end, engineers have built airstrips on Pacific islands – a speciality of the US Navy Seabees (Construction Battalions, hence "CBs") in World War II – and carved out helicopter landing zones and fire-bases in the Vietnamese jungle (see pp.322–23). More recently they have built a pipeline, served by 20 pump stations, from Kuwait into Iraq to protect the coalition forces' fuel supply during Operation Iraqi Freedom (see pp.348–49) and set up outposts for NATO troops in the hostile terrain of Afghanistan (see pp.340–41).

Combat engineering

Through much of recorded history, combat engineers – better known as sappers, or pioneers – have above all been identified with siege warfare. Just as construction engineers specialize in building fortifications, sappers are the men tasked with overcoming them.

Roman combat engineers built and operated siege engines such as stone- and bolt-throwing *ballistas* (catapults) to batter enemy defences. They also built huge, iron-tipped battering rams and mobile towers, and constructed earth and timber ramps so that these machines could be rolled up to the level of the elevated fortifications. Roman sappers also tunnelled under enemy walls so that they would partially collapse and open breaches for an assault.

The siege role of combat engineers did not fundamentally change until the gunpowder age. When cannon were first introduced into warfare, with devastating effect on stone-walled castles, they were at first the responsibility of engineers, just as catapults had been. However, the creation of independent artillery services took this burden off engineers.

Tunnelling under enemy walls long continued to be a vital part of siege warfare, but in the gunpowder age a small bomb called a petard was usually placed at the end of the completed tunnel and exploded to make the breach.

Like tunnelling, digging complex trench systems to approach the walls in preparation for an assault was an art brought to a high pitch by engineers of the 17th and 18th centuries. These techniques were required afresh in the trenches of World War I. On the Western Front engineers tunnelled under enemy lines to place mines, and laboured to build miles of front line, support, and communication trenches. Vast explosions were set off under German lines at the Somme, and at Messines Ridge in 1917, where 10,000 German troops were killed by the almost simultaneous detonation of 19 huge mines.

Hazardous occupation

Military engineers have always risked their own lives in the course of carrying out their often highly dangerous duties. They can suffer high casualty rates, either because they are operating in exposed positions in advance or to the rear of the main body of the army in mobile warfare, or because of their offensive role in siege warfare. Mining under walls is a dangerous activity, as is racing forward under enemy fire to place charges against the gates of a fortress, as British sappers did during the two-month siege of Delhi in 1857 in the Indian Mutiny.

Modern combat engineers, in the same spirit, are trained to carry out small-unit raids to lay charges against enemy targets. In World War II, sappers were tasked with blowing up German defensive positions overlooking the Normandy beaches on D-Day, as well as with clearing obstacles planted by the enemy on the beaches. Mine-clearing became one of most dangerous tasks carried out by engineers in World War II. Today, in Iraq and Afghanistan, an equally dangerous task is dealing with booby-traps and roadside bombs – two common killers in modern guerilla wars.

Royal Engineers insignia

The British Royal Engineers can trace their origins to the Norman Conquest of 1066.

Preparing the ground

US troops getting ready to invade Iraq from Kuwait in 2003 take cover while a Kuwaiti engineer uses a bulldozer to widen a ditch-crossing for them at an abandoned UN checkpoint on the Kuwait-Iraq border.

TIMELINE

- **701 BCE** Assyrian engineers mine walls and build ramps during the siege of Lachish in Palestine.

- **480 BCE** Persian engineers prepare for an invasion of Greece by digging a canal across the Mount Athos isthmus and making pontoon bridges across the Hellespont.

- **52 BCE** At the siege of Alesia in Gaul, the Romans build fortification lines totalling 39km (24 miles).

- **73 BCE** The Romans build a mountainside siege ramp to assault the Jewish fortress of Masada.

- **122 CE** Work begins on building Hadrian's Wall, marking the limit of the Roman empire in Britain.

- **c.1500** The introduction of the star fort, or *trace italienne*, adapts fortification and siege warfare in Europe to the gunpowder era.

- **1678** Vauban is appointed General Commissioner for Fortifications by Louis XIV of France. He takes the art of fortification and siegecraft to new levels.

VAUBAN'S FORT DE LA PRÉE ON THE ÎLE DE RÉ

- **1802** The US Army Corps of Engineers is created.

- **1812** Napoleon's army retreating from Moscow is saved from annihilation when engineers improvise a bridge across the freezing Berezina river.

- **1862** The Union side in the American Civil War creates a Military Railroad Construction Corps.

- **1864** Union engineers construct a 660-m (2,170-ft) pontoon bridge across the James river, the longest floating bridge in military history.

- **1914-18** European armies in World War I build a vast system of field fortifications on the Western Front, from the English Channel to Switzerland.

- **1930** France begins construction of the Maginot Line, a fortification along its border with Germany.

- **1942** The US Navy founds Construction Battalions – the Seabees.

- **1943** The Allies introduce the Bailey bridge during operations in Italy. Each can take the weight of a line of tanks.

- **1944** On D-Day Allied combat engineers land on Normandy beaches to attack the Atlantic Wall fortifications, and construction engineers build an artificial Mulberry harbour to help with troop landings.

WORLD WAR II SEABEES RECRUITMENT POSTER

- **1967** US Army engineers use the Rome Plow, an armoured bulldozer, to clear areas of dense jungle in the Vietnam War.

- **2003** US Army combat engineers build a record 354-km (220-mile) fuel pipeline to supply coalition troops in Operation Iraqi Freedom.

Roman Civil War

Between 49 and 30 BCE a series of armed struggles determined who would rule the Roman world as it mutated from republic into empire. Legion fought legion, loyal to their generals rather than the state. The eventual victor was Octavian, who would later be known as the Emperor Augustus.

Cleopatra

Although often represented as the Egyptian goddess Isis, Cleopatra was a Macedonian descendant of Alexander's general, Ptolemy. She had liaisons with both Julius Caesar and Mark Antony.

In 56 BCE Julius Caesar, then building his reputation as a general in the Gallic Wars (see pp.34–35), held meetings with Crassus and Pompey in northern Italy. The Triumvirate, the political alliance the three had formed, was under strain, but an agreement was reached. Caesar was confirmed in his command in Gaul for a further five years, Crassus was given control of the rich province of Syria, and Pompey remained in Rome while serving as absentee governor of Hispania. This arrangement ended when Crassus was ignominiously defeated by a Parthian army at Carrhae in 53 BCE. Both Crassus and his son were killed.

Caesar was at first distracted by the crisis of Vercingetorix's uprising in Gaul, but once the Gauls had been pacified the issue of his relationship with Pompey had to be resolved.

Originally the junior partner in the Triumvirate, Caesar had earned fame and wealth through his Gallic campaigns – wealth he used liberally to ensure the personal loyalty of his legions.

After some initial hesitation, Pompey threw in his lot with the anti-Caesar faction in the Roman Senate, which demanded that Caesar leave his army in Gaul and return to Rome. Instead, on 10 January 49 BCE, Caesar led his legionaries across the Rubicon, the river that marked the border between Cisalpine Gaul and Italy proper. Within weeks he occupied a largely unresisting Italy and forced Pompey to flee across the Adriatic. Instead of pursuing him, Caesar headed west, securing control of Hispania. Returning to Rome, he had himself declared dictator.

The defeat of Pompey

Pompey had meanwhile established himself in Macedonia, where he assembled an impressive army drawn from Rome's eastern provinces. He also had a powerful war fleet. In January 48 BCE Caesar nonetheless succeeded in transporting seven legions across the Adriatic, joined later by four more legions under his follower, Mark Antony. Outside the port of Dyrrachium, in present-day Albania, they were confronted by Pompey's numerically superior army. Short of food and water, Caesar's legions were in a precarious

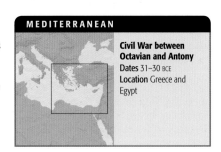

MEDITERRANEAN

Civil War between Octavian and Antony
Dates 31–30 BCE
Location Greece and Egypt

by sea to seek refuge in Egypt. Seeking to avoid offence to the victorious Caesar, Egyptian ruler, Ptolemy XII, had Pompey killed the moment he stepped ashore.

Caesar assassinated

Pompey's death did not end the civil war. While Caesar enjoyed an affair with Ptolemy's sister, Cleopatra, and supported her claim to the Egyptian throne, Pompeian forces rallied. After some brisk campaigning in Asia, Caesar had to fight battles at Thapsus in North Africa in 46 and Munda in Spain in 45 BCE before his victory over Pompey's faction was complete. It proved nonetheless short-lived. Returning to Rome Caesar was declared dictator-for-life. Shortly after, on 15 March 44, he was assassinated by a conspiracy of Roman senators, led by Marcus Junius Brutus and Gaius Cassius Longinus, claiming to defend freedom and the Republic. Ironically, his body fell at the foot of a statue of Pompey.

> **"Absolute power** is what both **Pompey and Caesar** have sought. Both want to be **kings."**
>
> CICERO IN A LETTER TO HIS FRIEND ATTICUS, 49 BCE

position. The two sides engaged in a cagey contest, constructing fortifications and counter-fortifications and fighting some costly skirmishes, before Caesar skilfully disengaged and marched into Greece, shadowed by Pompey. The armies met again on a plain outside Pharsalus. Outnumbered two to one, Caesar nevertheless accepted a challenge to give battle. By aggressive use of his infantry cohorts he first drove off Pompey's large cavalry force and then smashed his infantry formation. Pompey escaped the debacle and fled

Caesar's death opened a new round of civil strife. Brutus and Cassius fled Rome and power was assumed by a Second Triumvirate: Mark Antony, an experienced officer who had served under Caesar in Gaul as well as in the civil war; Caesar's chosen heir, Octavian, an inexperienced boy of 19; and Lepidus, a cavalry commander. They did not control the eastern provinces from Greece to Syria, however, which remained in the hands of the Republican forces. Brutus and Cassius took up a strong defensive

« **BEFORE**

In the 1st century BCE the Roman Republic was racked by violent social conflicts in Italy and by power struggles within the ruling elite.

REVOLT AND CIVIL WAR

The generals **Publius Cornelius Sulla** and **Gaius Marius** led the suppression of **a revolt by some of Rome's Italian allies**, known as the **Social War**, from 91 to 88 BCE. At the end of the war Sulla led his army into Rome to expel Marius. The dispute was not resolved until 82 BCE, when **Sulla defeated a Marian army** outside Rome. Sulla ruled for two years as dictator before retiring.

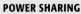

POMPEY THE GREAT

POWER SHARING

From 73–71 BCE an army of escaped slaves led by the **former gladiator Spartacus** waged guerrilla war in southern Italy. This uprising was brutally crushed by the wealthy **Marcus Licinius Crassus**, aided by **Pompey**. The latter went on to carry out successful campaigns to **suppress piracy** and extend Rome's empire in the eastern Mediterranean, earning the appellation **"the Great"**. In 60 BCE he formed an alliance with Crassus and the ambitious **Julius Caesar** « 34–35 to dominate Roman politics. This is known as the **First Triumvirate**.

position near Philippi in eastern Macedonia, where they confronted an army of similar size – probably around 100,000 men – led by Antony and Octavian. Two battles were fought at Philippi in October 42 BCE. In the first Brutus's forces overran Octavian's camp in a surprise assault that found the young triumvir absent from his post. At the same time, Antony successfully attacked Cassius's fortified position. Wrongly believing Brutus also to have been defeated, Cassius fell upon his sword. The Republicans were not defeated, but their morale was wavering and after a three-week stand-off Brutus felt obliged to give battle again. Rival legions clashed in a vicious close-quarters fight that Octavian and Antony won. Left with inadequate forces to continue the war, Brutus too committed suicide.

After this victory Octavian returned to govern in Rome while Antony campaigned in the east. Both met with serious challenges. Sextus Pompeius, a son of Pompey the Great, had seized Sicily, deploying a war fleet to hold off Octavian's legions. Octavian tasked his general, Marcus Vipsanius Agrippa, with building and equipping a fleet to take on Sextus Pompeius. Agrippa destroyed most of the rebel warships at Naulochus in 36 BCE, allowing Octavian to retake Sicily. Meanwhile, Antony undertook an overambitious invasion of Parthia, successor power to the Seleucids in the

The first emperor
Octavian was Julius Caesar's great-nephew and his political heir. Victor in the civil war, he discreetly assumed the powers of an emperor, ending the Republican system of government in Rome.

East, losing large numbers of troops in the process. Starved of reinforcements by Octavian, he fell back on the support of Cleopatra of Egypt, establishing himself with her in Alexandria.

Octavian's final moves

By 35 BCE the Triumvirate was at an end. Lepidus had been ousted by Octavian, who then mounted a propaganda campaign against Antony and his allegedly scandalous behaviour in the east. In 32 BCE the Roman Senate was persuaded to declare war on Antony and Cleopatra. Antony planned an amphibious invasion of Italy, exploiting the strength of the Egyptian fleet, but only made it as far as Actium on Greece's Ionian coast. The fleet that Agrippa had created was even stronger and allowed Octavian both to ferry an army across to Greece and to subject Antony and Cleopatra to a naval blockade. Octavian installed himself in a fortified position and refused to give battle, waiting while his opponents' forces withered through malnutrition and disease. In desperation Antony led a naval breakout in September 31 BCE, but most of his fleet was trapped and destroyed. Antony and Cleopatra escaped back to Egypt, where they were pursued by Octavian. Deserted by a large part of his army as the Romans approached Alexandria, Antony took his own life, an example soon followed by Cleopatra. Octavian was left in sole command of the Roman empire.

Victorious in the civil war, Octavian was able to establish his personal rule over the Roman empire, while maintaining a façade of Republican institutions.

A NEW ROME
The defeat and death of Cleopatra in 30 BCE brought Ptolemaic rule in Egypt to an end. Octavian ordered her heir, Julius Caesar's son Caesarion, to be strangled, and **Egypt** became a **province of the Roman empire**.

In 27 BCE the Roman Senate authorized Octavian's extensive powers over the empire and gave him the title **Augustus**, by which he is generally known. In practice, his power depended not on the Senate, but on the **support of the full-time professional soldiers of the Roman army 42–43** ≫. He stabilized this

CAESAR The family name of Julius Caesar evolved into an imperial title. It survived into modern times as the German Kaiser and the Russian Tsar.

force, establishing fixed terms of service and turning the legions into permanent formations, each with its own traditions and identity.

Augustus died in 14 CE. He selected his own heir, his stepson, Tiberius. The **lack of a formal system of succession**, whether hereditary or elective, left plentiful scope for **future power struggles**. Nonetheless, the empire was to prove remarkably durable.

Battle of Actium
Attempting to sail out of Actium, Antony and Cleopatra's fleet encountered Octavian's warships commanded by Agrippa. Antony and Cleopatra escaped, but lost at least 150 ships in the battle.

A Distant Posting

Flavius Cerialis was an officer in the Roman army in 100 CE, stationed in a rainswept fort at the northern extremity of the empire. Details of his life and the lives of his men have been revealed through hundreds of letters and notes, written in ink on postcard-size wooden tablets that have survived to the present day.

Formal greeting from Niger and Brocchus

Vindolanda was a Roman fort in northern England. Built before the construction of Hadrian's Wall, it was a distant outpost of the Roman world, providing a base for troops policing the border between the province of Britannia and unconquered Caledonia to the north.

Frontier guard

From 97 CE the fort's garrison consisted of two cohorts of Batavian troops, plus a wing of cavalry from Spain. Flavius Cerialis was the prefect commanding IX Batavorum, a body of some 500 men. The Batavians were auxiliaries – troops drawn from the subject peoples of the empire. They were a tough Germanic people whose homeland was in the area of the present-day Netherlands. Their fighting qualities were much admired by the Romans and they had served in the invasion and conquest of Britain from 43 CE. It was standard practice for provinces to be garrisoned by men from elsewhere in the empire. The likelihood of revolts was much greater when soldiers were stationed among their fellow countrymen in

Roman legionaries
This frieze is from Tropaeum Traiani in Romania on the empire's Eastern European frontier. Most Roman troops were stationed on the borders.

their province of origin. The Vindolanda tablets include disparaging references by the Batavian soldiers to the local people, referred to derisively as *Brittunculi* ("little Britons").

Like the soldiers under his command, Flavius was Batavian, but unlike them he was a Roman citizen. He must have been wealthy, for he enjoyed equestrian status, an aristocratic rank that was only open to men who could satisfy a strict property qualification. His wife, Sulpicia Lepidina, lived with him in his quarters at the fort. One of the letters is an invitation for Sulpicia to come to a birthday party thrown by the wife of Aelius Brocchus, an officer in the nearby fort of Briga.

Home comforts

The fort under Flavius's command was largely self-sufficient. It had its own shield-maker, brewed its own beer, and made and repaired its own shoes. In around 100 CE its soldiers built their own bathhouse. Accommodation for the commander was comfortable, but the soldiers slept in dormitories, probably under woollen blankets on mattresses on the floor. Although

Vindolanda tablet
This letter, found by archeologists excavating an ancient rubbish heap at Vindolanda fort, is addressed to Flavius Cerialis by fellow officers Niger and Brocchus. It wishes Flavius success in meeting the governor of Britannia.

clothing was issued from central stores, the troops received extra items sent in parcels from their families at home. Similarly, food was in plentiful supply with grain and bacon prominent among items sourced locally, but luxuries were imported to liven up the diet. Flavius expected to have olives, spices, and wine on his table, and even ordinary soldiers managed to procure pepper and oysters.

Garrison life had many features that would be familiar to soldiers today: morning parades, guard duty, drill, patrols, and clerical work compiling official reports. The messages on the wooden tablets include requests for leave, presumably very desirable from what must have been at times a grim posting – especially in the frequent bad weather. Officers were naturally interested in personal advancement, hoping for a recommendation from one of their superiors that might bring promotion or, in Flavius's case, angling for a meeting with the provincial governor. The eventual fate of Flavius Cerialis is unknown, although his colleague, Brocchus, was later recorded as commander of a cavalry unit in the Eastern European province of Pannonia, another distant posting.

Hadrian's Wall today
Roman legionaries and auxiliaries stationed on the northernmost frontier of the empire probably faced slightly milder winters than those of modern times. Even so, there would have been frequent rain and snow.

> **"** I have sent … **pairs of socks** from Sattua, **two pairs of sandals** and **two pairs of underpants** … Greet … all your messmates. **"**

FROM A LETTER WRITTEN TO A SOLDIER SERVING UNDER FLAVIUS CERIALIS AT VINDOLANDA, C.100 CE

The tablets are thin pieces of wood, with messages written on them in ink. About the size of a modern-day postcard, they are usually less than 1mm thick and folded to protect the contents. The name of the addressee is written on the other side.

The Roman Empire

The period between the beginning of the reign of Augustus in 27 BCE and the end of the reign of Marcus Aurelius in 180 CE is often called the *Pax Romana* – Roman peace. Apart from suppressing scattered internal rebellions, the legions garrisoning the empire fought wars only at or beyond its frontiers.

The last phase of expansion of the Roman empire occurred in the period between the reign of Augustus (27 BCE–14 CE) and the end of the reign of Emperor Trajan in 117 CE. The Romans were tempted to cross the long land frontiers of their provinces in Western and Southern Europe and to press further into Asia from their provinces in the eastern Mediterranean. They also traversed the English Channel to occupy much of Great Britain.

Although the Roman legions were a formidable fighting force, the campaigns that they were engaged in were far from supplying the empire with an unbroken string of successes. The battles they fought often revealed their vulnerability when faced with enemies employing very different tactics on what was to the Romans alien terrain.

An early reminder of the limits of Roman power was provided by a defeat at the hands of the Germanic tribes led by Arminius, a chieftain of the Cherusci, who lived in the area of present-day Hanover. Arminius was commanding a body of auxiliaries fighting for the Romans, while secretly forming a tribal alliance to oppose them. At the Teutoburg Forest in 9 CE, three legions under Publius Quinctilius Varus were ambushed by Arminius's forces and massacred. The Romans had their revenge through punitive expeditions led by Germanicus between 14 and 16 CE, but the tribes across the Rhine were never subdued as the Gauls had been.

Romans in Britain
The conquest of Britain began under Emperor Claudius in 43 CE. Rome had exercised an influence over Britain's Celtic peoples ever since Julius Caesar's

Cavalryman's helmet
Roman cavalry helmets often had a hair pattern on the bowl. In the 1st century CE cavalry made up a small part of a legion – typically 120 men out of 5,000. Auxiliaries provided most of the army's horsemen.

"**The Romans** owed the conquest of the world to no other cause than **continual military training**."
PUBLIUS FLAVIUS VEGETIUS, FROM HIS BOOK "DE RE MILITARI", 4TH CENTURY CE

BEFORE «

The key to the power of the Roman empire was a stable, well-drilled professional army. Emperor Augustus (27 BCE–14 CE) planned the final phase of its development.

ARMY REFORMS
Coming to power through civil war « 38–39, Augustus knew that the army was the foundation of his rule. He made the legions permanent formations with names and numbers. All legionaries had to be Roman citizens and he established a fixed term of service for soldiers, eventually set at 25 years. Completion

130,000 The number of legionaries in the army of Augustus. Auxiliaries equalled this number, giving a total army strength of around 260,000.

of service was rewarded with a grant of land. Non-citizen allies of Rome provided **auxiliaries to fight alongside the legionaries**. Almost all legionaries were stationed at permanent forts around the margins of the empire. The Praetorian Guard was often the force that made or unmade emperors in power struggles.

two expeditions across the Channel almost a century earlier. There were puppet kingdoms that paid tribute to Rome, and Roman support for an ousted allied king provided an easy pretext for military occupation. Four legions ferried across from Boulogne sufficed to overcome initial resistance in the southeast, but Caratacus, a chieftain of the Catuvellauni tribe, escaped to continue the fight further west. By 47 CE the whole of southern England was under Roman rule, although resistance in Wales continued despite the eventual capture and execution of Caratacus. The Romans were distracted from warfare in Wales in 60 CE by a major revolt in eastern England, led by Boudicca of the Iceni tribe. After this had been suppressed, it took another 16 years for all of Wales to be brought to heel.

Conquest to the north proved more problematic. The Romans advanced into Caledonia (modern-day Scotland) and won a victory at Mons Graupius in 84 CE, but the tribes of the region escaped their long-term rule. When Hadrian's Wall was built as a defensive perimeter to the British province in 122 CE, it was much further south than the previous wall that they built in Scotland. In 142 the Antonine Wall, built along the line of the Clyde and the Forth rivers in central Scotland, was the Roman empire's most northern frontier in Britain; it took 12 years to build, but was held for only 20 years.

Extending the empire
Rome's preoccupation with maintaining and extending its imperial frontiers was occasionally disrupted by disturbances within the empire. In 66 CE the province of Judaea rose in revolt. Vespasian, an experienced military commander who had taken part in the invasion of Britain in 43, was sent to suppress the revolt, but his campaign was interrupted by an outbreak of civil war that followed the death of Emperor Nero in 68. After legion once more fought legion, as in the days of Caesar and Pompey, Vespasian emerged as emperor. He appointed his son, Titus, to continue the war in Judaea. In 70 CE Jerusalem was taken by the Roman army after a long siege, its temple was destroyed and the revolt effectively ended. A small Jewish group held out in the hill fortress of Masada until 73 CE. The taking of Jerusalem and Masada were both classic examples of Roman siege warfare, with the use of rams, ballistas, and siege towers. At Masada, on the coast of the Dead Sea, the building of an immense ramp was required to bring the siege engines up the mountainside. In neither case did the city's defenders stand a chance in the face of the Roman forces; at Masada the population finally committed suicide to avoid capture.

In 98 CE the Roman empire came under the rule of an exceptional military leader,

Trajan's Column
Erected in Rome in 113 to celebrate victory in the Dacian Wars, Trajan's Column depicts military life. Here, auxiliaries, with their distinctive oval shields, slaughter Dacians.

Dagger and scabbard
Worn on the opposite side of a legionary's belt from his sword, the dagger, or *pugio*, was a useful secondary weapon.

Mesopotamia who fought chiefly as mounted archers, had inflicted a notorious defeat on the Romans at Carrhae in 53 BCE and remained a potential threat to Rome's eastern provinces. On the pretext of a disagreement over Armenia, but out of a desire above all for military glory, Trajan invaded Parthian territory in force, overrunning Mesopotamia, reaching the Persian Gulf, and capturing the Parthian capital, Ctesiphon. When Trajan died of natural causes in 117, the Roman empire had reached its greatest extent.

Trajan's gains in Mesopotamia could not be sustained. Under his far less warlike successors, Hadrian and Antoninus, the legions pulled back to defensible borders. Marcus Aurelius (ruled 161–180) fought many wars, but they were mostly defensive actions against renewed pressure on the borders from Germanic and Parthian aggression.

Roman empire under Hadrian
This map shows the Roman empire in 120 CE during the reign of Emperor Hadrian (reigned 117–138 CE). Hadrian gave up the territory gained by his predecessor, Trajan, in his wars against the Parthians.

Gladius and scabbard
The Roman legionary's short sword, the *gladius*, was equally suitable for slashing and thrusting. The shaped handgrip was made of bone, with a wooden pommel.

the Spanish-born Emperor Trajan. He indirectly owed his rise to power to King Decebalus of Dacia (roughly modern-day Romania) who had refused to be cowed by Roman military campaigns under Emperor Domitian. The subsequent fall of the humiliated Domitian allowed Trajan to emerge as emperor, and dealing with Dacia in order to reassert Roman authority in the region was thus the first item on his agenda. Trajan fought two campaigns in Dacia. The first in 101–102 was followed by a peace that left Decebalus on the throne as a

6.5 MILLION
The area covered by the expansionist Roman empire in square kilometres (2.5 million sq miles) after Trajan's conquest of Dacia in 106 BCE.

puppet ruler. When the Romans left, Decebalus rebuilt his army and began to show signs of causing trouble again, so in 105–106 Trajan returned, assaulted and laid waste the Dacian capital, Sarmizegethusa, and absorbed Dacia into the Roman empire. Trajan's Column, erected to mark this triumph, records exceptional feats of engineering, such as bridge building, accomplished by the legions, as well as the defeat and enslavement of the Dacians.

In 114, when Trajan was over 60 years old, he embarked upon another remarkable military venture in the east. The Parthians, rulers of Persia and

Lance and pilum
The *pilum*, or javelin (right), was a standard legionary weapon. Legionaries threw their javelins before advancing to engage with the sword. Roman cavalry, whether they were legionaries or auxiliaries, carried lances.

AFTER »

By the end of the 2nd century CE the great age of Roman expansion was at an end. The empire was subjected to mounting internal and external strains.

STABILITY RESTORED
In the 3rd century CE the Roman empire almost disintegrated. Barbarian invaders overran the frontiers as rival claimants battled for the imperial throne. **The empire was saved from collapse by the Emperor Aurelian** (reigned 270–275) who restored unity, defeated the Goths, and endowed Rome with defensive walls.

ROME'S FOUR RULERS
In 293 Emperor Diocletian devised a tetrarchy, four co-rulers, to defend the over-large empire. Two senior emperors (with the title Augustus) reigned together, each assisted by a junior emperor (with the title Caesar). **The four rulers acted as military commanders, based near vulnerable frontiers rather than in Rome**. This system allowed the empire to reassert its military strength, with, in particular, a rare victory over the Sasanids, the successors to the Parthians in Persia. The tetrarchy collapsed after Diocletian's abdication in 305. This led to another period of civil war as claimants to the title of Augustus proliferated.

STATUE OF TWO TETRARCHS

Key
- Roman empire c.120 CE
- LYCIA Province in reign of Hadrian
- Legion headquarters
- Fortified frontier
- Frontier 120 CE
- Approximate frontier 120 CE

BATTLE BETWEEN ROMANS AND GERMANIC TRIBES
In the first two centuries CE, the Roman empire was constantly threatened by Germanic tribes from beyond the Rhine and the Danube. Emperor Marcus Aurelius spent much of his reign (161–180 CE) campaigning against the Quadi, Marcomanni, and other tribes along the Danube frontier. This relief decorating a marble sarcophagus in Rome shows the helmeted Roman legionaries getting the better of their Germanic foes.

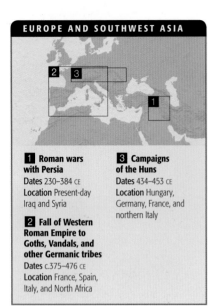

1 Roman wars with Persia
Dates 230–384 CE
Location Present-day Iraq and Syria

2 Fall of Western Roman Empire to Goths, Vandals, and other Germanic tribes
Dates c.375–476 CE
Location France, Spain, Italy, and North Africa

3 Campaigns of the Huns
Dates 434–453 CE
Location Hungary, Germany, France, and northern Italy

BEFORE

The Roman empire survived near-disintegration in the 3rd century CE, but it remained divided, prone to civil strife, and under severe pressure from its neighbours.

DECLINE OF ROME
In 324, after winning a long series of wars against imperial rivals, **Constantine I established himself as sole emperor**, but his death was followed by a further collapse into civil war. The eastern and western halves of the empire were

11 The number of Roman emperors assassinated in the half century between 235 and 284 CE.

increasingly divided. The wealth and power lay in the east, where Constantine created an alternative capital at Byzantium (Constantinople).

BORDER CONTROL
The western empire was under constant pressure from tribes beyond the Rhine and Danube, who raided across the frontier and sometimes settled within Rome's borders. **The eastern empire had a dangerous neighbour in the Sasanids**, a dynasty that took over control of Persia from the Parthians in 224. Successive Roman emperors had much the worse of fighting with the Persians.

EMPEROR VALERIAN KNEELING BEFORE PERSIAN KING SHAPUR I

The Late Roman Empire

In the final period of the Roman empire in the west, from around 350 CE, Germanic tribes increasingly dominated warfare in Europe, whether as enemies or as allies and auxiliaries of Rome. By the time Attila the Hun ravaged Gaul and northern Italy in the 450s, the western empire was disintegrating.

The career of Emperor Julian, known as the Apostate, reveals much about the state of the Roman empire in the 4th century CE. A nephew of Emperor Constantine I, he narrowly survived with his life in the round of massacres and usurpations that followed Constantine's death in 337. When Constantius II emerged as victor in this vicious power struggle, he appointed Julian his subordinate co-emperor in the west while he fought Sasanid Persia in the east. But when Constantius ran into trouble fighting the Persians and called for Julian to bring his army to the east, the Gallic legions refused to go and instead proclaimed Julian emperor. A civil war was avoided because Constantius died of a fever in 361.

Now sole emperor, Julian led a large army deep into Sasanid territory in 363. The expedition was a disaster. Julian was killed in a skirmish and the Romans had to accept humiliating peace terms. This was an empire in which emperors were elected by armies and mostly lived as military commanders; in which the need to campaign simultaneously on different frontiers led to divisions of authority; and in which resources were stretched to cope with the military problems posed by external pressures.

Rome's faltering army
The Roman army that faced these pressures in the 4th and 5th centuries CE was significantly different from the army that had enforced the Roman Peace (*Pax Romana*) of the 1st and 2nd centuries. It was divided into border forces – permanent garrisons for the forts and fortifications around the frontiers – and mobile field armies

aristocracy of Roman senators, but by the end of the 3rd century they were career soldiers, drawn from anywhere in the empire. These senior officers made and unmade emperors.

Shortages of material resources showed in a decline in the quality of equipment, and shortages of manpower were even more evident. The volunteers who came from the poorer strata of Roman citizens no longer dominated the ranks. The legions were staffed mostly by conscripts, although the border forces included a large number

"So many murders ... the dead could not be numbered."
CALLINICUS, DESCRIBING THE INVASION OF ITALY BY THE HUNS, C.450 CE

stationed deeper inside the empire. The field armies could be a reserve to respond to military emergencies wherever these occurred, but they were also power bases for their commanders who needed to uphold their slice of authority inside the empire. The senior officers who commanded the armies had previously been drawn from the

of hereditary soldiers – the children of career legionaries settled in the area where they served. The army had long ceased to be ethnically Roman, but was recruited from across the multi-racial empire, including from "barbarian" tribes who had been permitted to settle within the empire's frontiers. The employment of non-citizens as

The Vandal general
The Roman general, Stilicho, had a Vandal father and a Roman mother. He served faithfully as a defender of the failing Roman empire until his execution in 408, a victim of political intrigue.

auxiliaries – for example, from allies of Rome beyond the frontiers – was a long-established tradition, but increasingly tribal warbands served alongside the legions under their own chieftains as allies or "federated" people. The prominence of "barbarian" soldiers in the Roman army was to be crucial to the development of events as the western empire declined.

Roman forces became more varied. Although armoured legion infantry remained central, there was a growing emphasis on missile weapons, with specialist artillery units and bodies of bowmen. Cavalry had an increasing impact on the battlefield. The Romans deployed heavily armoured horses and riders in imitation of the Persian cataphracts, as well as lighter cavalry with spears and mounted archers. These developments were doubtless a response to the occasional setbacks the Romans suffered at the hands of enemies who were practised in missile and cavalry warfare, such as the Goths who defeated Valens at Adrianople in 378.

Weak political leadership
The mounting problems of the Roman empire did not, however, stem from such defeats – pitched battles were rare in any case. The issue, especially in the western empire, was a failure of political organization and resources. The Romans were unfortunate to confront at this point in their history a major movement of the Germanic peoples. During the second half of the 4th century Ostrogoths and Visigoths, Vandals, Burgundians, and Lombards, Franks, Alemanni, and Saxons were all driven westward or southward by pressure from nomadic steppe horsemen, chiefly the Huns, who attacked them from the east. Although the Roman empire continued to apply long-established processes by which such people were settled, Romanized,

and taken into the armed forces as auxiliaries and allies, the tide was too powerful to be controlled.

The battle of Frigidus in 394 and its aftermath show a failing system in action. The battle was fought between forces loyal to Emperor Theodosius, ruling from the eastern empire, and a usurper in the west. Theodosius's forces were commanded by Stilicho, the son of a Vandal father and a Roman mother. The other side was commanded by Arbogast, a Frank. Both were generals in the Roman army. Stilicho's

Attila the Hun

The Huns were steppe horsemen who fought mostly as mounted archers. Under Attila, their fearsome leader from 434 to 453, they raided and pillaged the Roman empire for a decade.

forces included a large contingent of Visigoths, led by their chieftain, Alaric. Stilicho defeated the usurper, but soon found himself engaged in a prolonged struggle against Alaric's rampaging followers, transformed from allies into enemies. In 410, after Stilicho's death, the Visigoths sacked Rome, the first time the city had fallen to hostile forces in almost eight centuries. Yet only a few years later, the Romans were again appealing to the Visigoths as allies to help fight the Vandals, another Germanic people.

The incursions of the Huns into Roman territory between 441 and 452,

under the leadership of the dreaded Attila, revealed an empire that had lost coherence and control. The Romans succeeded in checking Attila at a battle near Châlons in 451 but only his death in 453, not in battle, brought the Huns' forays to an end. By then the Roman empire in the west was falling apart.

AFTER

The collapse of the Roman empire in the west was followed by the creation of new kingdoms, mostly by Germanic chieftains. The Roman empire continued in the east.

COLLAPSE IN THE WEST

The fall of the western Roman empire is traditionally dated to 476, when Emperor Romulus Augustus was deposed by the commander of Rome's Germanic allies in Italy, Odoacer. But Odoacer did not claim the imperial title, which was held by Emperor Zeno at Constantinople.

FRANKISH AXE

FILLING THE VOID

Germanic kingdoms were established as the empire fell. In Gaul the Franks established a powerful state under Clovis. The Visigoths ruled Spain, from which they had evicted the Vandals who themselves established a kingdom in North Africa. In Italy Odoacer was defeated by the Ostrogoths under Theodoric in 493, Theodoric then ruling as theoretically a viceroy of the eastern emperor in Constantinople.

Under Emperor Justinian in the 6th century, there was a determined, but failed, effort to restore imperial control over Italy and the rest of the western Mediterranean 62–63 ❯❯. Nor was the memory of the empire lost in Western Europe – the Frankish ruler, Charlemagne, was to claim the imperial title in Rome in 800 68–69 ❯❯.

The Warring States Period

Warfare in ancient China was refined through centuries of civil conflict. Feudal domains that flourished in the absence of a strong central authority competed for territory, expanding the resources devoted to war until the climactic battles of the 3rd century BCE led to unification under Emperor Qin.

« **BEFORE**

The beginnings of warfare in ancient China saw peasant soldiers armed with bronze or stone weapons under the command of aristocratic warriors in chariots.

EARLY DYNASTIES

The first dynasty in China was the Shang, ruling around the Yellow river valley from 1600 to 1050 BCE. **The Shang was succeeded by the Zhou,** which introduced the use of iron weapons. The Zhou supported a substantial standing army that campaigned against the "barbarians" around the borders of the realm. The Zhou dynasty officially lasted until 256 BCE, but in reality **central authority disintegrated in the course of the 8th century BCE**, initiating a long and complex period of wars between competing Chinese states. This is known as the Spring and Autumn Period. Beginning around 770 BCE, **it was a long prelude to the Warring States Period**, the start date of which historians conventionally give as 475 BCE.

The rulers of the Zhou dynasty created a feudal system in which power was devolved to regional lords, who depended on the allegiance of their own vassals controlling smaller areas. Conflict was inevitable in such an unstable system. In the Spring and Autumn Period the southerly state of Chu, centred on the Yangtze river, emerged as one of the most powerful players, competing with Yellow river states that included Jin, Qi, and Qin. There were many conflicts within and between these loosely structured states. Battles involved the offensive use of chariots – which in earlier times were

Ancient Chinese bronze sword

Dating from the 4th century BCE, this sword shows the persistence of bronze weapons into the Iron Age of the Zhou dynasty. Such weapons were mass produced.

EAST ASIA

China in the Warring States Period
Dates 475–221 BCE
Location Central and eastern China

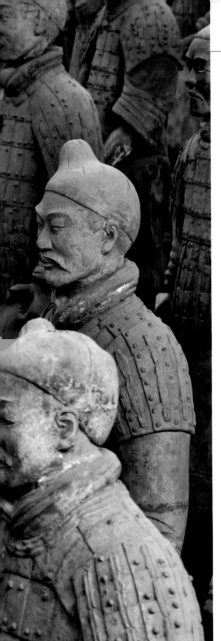

Peasant soldiers from the terracotta army
The terracotta figures buried with Emperor Qin Shi Huangdi in 210 BCE give a faithful impression of the mass of conscript peasant infantrymen who made up the bulk of any ancient Chinese army.

states developed increasingly efficient central administrations that could conscript hundreds of thousands of peasant infantrymen and equip them with mass-produced iron weapons.

Heavy siege crossbows came into widespread use, as did small crossbows carried by skirmishing infantrymen pushed out in front of the line of battle.

450,000 According to ancient Chinese sources, the number of Zhao soldiers who died at the battle of Changping in 260 BCE.

Chariots were still used – crewed by three men and pulled by four horses – but cavalry took over as a shock force. The Chinese learned about mounted warfare from fighting the nomads on their frontiers. Wuling, ruler of Zhao, created the first fully-fledged Chinese cavalry around 300 BCE, ordering his elite soldiers to abandon traditional robes for trousers. He used both mounted archers and heavy cavalry. But the core of any Chinese army was still the conscript peasant infantry, mostly armoured for fighting in close formation with long halberds and pikes.

The art of war
Constant warfare in China led to the sophisticated discussion of strategy and tactics. This was the period when the great military thinker known as Sun-tzu wrote his famous work, *The Art of War*. Written around 400 BCE, it is generally considered to be the world's first treatise on the theory and practice of warfare. In it he recommends the use of

> **"**An army avoids strength and attacks **weakness."**

SUN-TZU, "THE ART OF WAR", 4TH CENTURY BCE

Massive state armies
The Warring States Period proper emerged through the reorganization and consolidation of the larger Chinese states – inevitably a gradual process. Jin, probably the most powerful state by 475 BCE, broke up into three: Han, Zhao, and Wei. The four other states that eventually dominated the contest for power in China were Chu, Yan, Qi, and Qin. These seven

probably employed only as mobile command platforms. The chariots were sometimes massed in large formations, with Jin reportedly fielding 700 of them in the defeat of Chu at Chengpu in 632 BCE. But armies can rarely have been large, given the limited resources of the fragmented feudal territories.

deception, and avoiding battle on the enemy's terms. He also stresses the importance of intelligence, and highlights the impact of morale on the outcome of conflict.

Sun-tzu's theories were successfully put into practice by the Qi general, Sun Bin, when he defeated the superior forces of Wei, first at Guiling in 354 BCE, then again at Maling in 342 BCE. On each occasion, remarkably, Sun Bin relieved the enemy's pressure on an

IMPERIAL RULE
After the death of the first emperor, Qin Shi Huangdi, in 210 BCE, China looked set to return to the civil conflict of the Warring States Period. The successor to the throne, Qin Er Shi, was weak and incompetent, and **rebellions soon broke out**. A serious bid for power was made by Xiang Lang of Chu, who was contested by Liu Bang, a general controlling Han. **Liu Bang won the contest** and, as Emperor Gao, founded the Han dynasty, **reconsolidating imperial authority in China**: a state of affairs that would last another 400 or so years.

CONFUCIAN GOD OF WAR

REPELLING THE HORSEMEN
The Han empire established by Gao was threatened by the Xiongnu, nomadic horsemen who were based in the northern steppes. To keep the horsemen out, **the Han reinforced the Great Wall** that Emperor Qin had built. Moreover, Han armies were sent through the wall to attack the horsemen in their home territory in an attempt to defeat them before they could get anywhere near the Great Wall. The combined measures succeeded, the Xiongnu were beaten, and **eventually the horsemen were reduced to mere tributary status**.

HAN EXPANSION
Under the leadership of Emperor Wu (141–87 BCE), marauding **Han armies penetrated south** as far as the Mekong River in Vietnam, **west into Central Asia, and into northern Korea**.

ally not by marching to confront the Wei army directly, but by making a feinting move towards the Wei capital. When the Wei army then of necessity

Bronze chariot decoration
This gold-inlaid bull's head adorned a chariot shaft in the Warring States Period. Chariots were owned by elite warriors with a taste for ostentatious display.

moved to defend its capital, Sun Bin succeeded in luring it onto terrain where it could then be surrounded and destroyed by his own waiting forces.

Despite such tactical subtleties, victory in the great Chinese power struggle eventually went to the state that could mobilize the maximum resources for warfare – men, weapons, food, and other supplies – with the greatest efficiency. The victor in this early version of total war was Qin.

The mighty Qin
A state in western China, Qin underwent political and social reforms that, by the 3rd century BCE, gave it a powerful centralized government that had crushed the residual independence of the old feudal aristocracy. Government officials and military commanders were appointed on merit, and the population was mobilized for public works and war. Being close to the nomadic horsemen of the north, Qin also had access to a supply of good horses, a crucial edge as cavalry grew in importance.

Through the first half of the 3rd century BCE, Qin's aggression forced the other states to form alliances and mobilize their own resources. Zhao, for example, conscripted all men over the age of 15. There were epic battles, as at Changping in 260 BCE, where a Zhao army was encircled and massacred in a long encounter that may have involved a million men. Under the rule of King Ying Zheng from 246 BCE, Qin crushed all its enemies, although the campaigns against the Chu tested it to the limits. Finally, though, in 221 BCE Ying Zheng declared himself the first emperor of a unified China as Qin Shi Huangdi.

The Three Kingdoms

Beginning with the Yellow Turban peasant revolt of 184 CE, the authority of the Chinese Han emperors was fatally weakened and a struggle developed for the succession between rival warlords. The failure of anyone to win total power left China divided into three warring kingdoms.

« BEFORE

The Han dynasty (206 BCE–220 CE) ruled China for more than four centuries. It was a period of military and economic growth, and cultural achievements.

A MIGHTY EMPIRE
The Han empire probably had the world's most powerful armed forces in its day. In the 1st century CE its armies campaigned **as far south as Vietnam**, where a revolt led by the sisters, Trung Trac and Trung Ni, was crushed in 43 CE, and **as far west as Central Asia**. In 96 CE the imperial general, Ban Chao, led a Chinese military

50 MILLION The **size of the Chinese population according to a census in the late Han dynasty.**

expedition to the Caspian Sea at the heart of the **Parthian empire**. The **Silk Road**, the great trade route that carried Chinese silks to Rome and the Mediterranean world, ran through Parthian territory. The Romans fought regular wars with the Parthians, **Emperor Trajan « 42–43** invading their empire in 114, but **no direct contact between the Han empire and the Roman empire** is recorded.

In the course of the 2nd century CE **the Han empire went into decline**, undermined by the attacks of steppe nomads, corrupt officials, and the excessive privileges of landowners.

Key

.... Approximate frontiers c.250 CE
DI Nomadic people
⚔ Battle

XIONGNU   WUHUAN
Gobi   Yellow River   XIANBEI
DI   Bo Hai
WEI
220–640 CE   Yellow
Chang'an   Luoyang   Sea
QIANG
Jiankang
Chengdu   ⚔ Red Cliffs
208 CE
Yangtze
SHU   WU
221–263 CE   222–277 CE
Taiwan

South
China
Sea   Hainan

0   500km
0   500 miles

The Yellow Turban rebellion was a response to the poverty, injustice, and famine suffered by China's peasant population. These conditions made them responsive to the teachings of Zhang Giao, who proposed a mix of religious and magical beliefs as a solution to the people's sufferings. The movement attracted hundreds of thousands of followers, who wrapped yellow scarves around their heads to mark their allegiance. Marshalled into mass armies, they inflicted a number of severe defeats on the empire's professional forces. It took the Han generals close to one year to bring the revolt under control.

Pacification was not, however, enough to restore the stability of the increasingly fractious imperial dynasty. Following the death of Emperor Ling in 189, power within the imperial palace was seized by Dong Zhuo, an exceptionally brutal military commander. His authority was immediately contested by other generals leading armies in the provinces and chaos ensued. Dong Zhuo was soon assassinated and Cao Cao, who had led cavalry forces in the suppression of the Yellow Turbans, took control of the imperial government. Like Dong Zhuo, he was unable to win the allegiance of provincial warlords and the power struggle continued.

Historic battles

Later known as the Prince of Wei (and posthumously as Emperor Wu), Cao Cao fought in two battles that are classics of Chinese military history because of the odds facing the victors. The first, at Guandu on the Yellow river in 200 CE, saw Cao Cao at the head of an army of 20,000

China divided

The northern kingdom of Wei was centred on the Yellow river, the traditional heartland of Chinese culture. Shu and Wu controlled the Yangtze.

Crossbow trigger
This bronze trigger is all that remains of a crossbow used by a soldier from Wei, one of the Three Kingdoms. The piece is dated to the year 242 CE.

men confronting the 100,000 troops of his rival, Yuan Shao. There was a stand-off between the two armies, Yuan Shao hesitating to attack an enemy dug into a strong defensive position. As the months passed, the outcome turned on who could keep his men and horses supplied with food and fodder. With the larger army, Yuan Shao had the bigger problem. Cao Cao sent out detachments of troops to harass his enemy's supply lines and destroy grain stores. Many of Yuan Shao's malnourished troops surrendered and Cao Cao then vanquished the weakened foe.

Eight years later it was Cao Cao's turn to be worsted in a battle won by the numerically inferior side. Two southern warlords, Liu Bei and Sun Quan, formed an alliance to resist Cao Cao's increasingly successful efforts to unify China. The warlords depended upon their control of the Yangtze river – they were organized to fight on water while Cao Cao's forces were entirely land-based. But marching south to attack them with a large army, Cao Cao captured the river port of Jiangling and with it enough boats to sail his troops down the Yangtze. At a point known variously as Chibi or the Red Cliffs, they encountered the warlords' forces commanded by general Zhou Yu. Cao Cao's northern soldiers had travelled a vast distance into an

800,000 **According to ancient sources, the number of soldiers with Cao Cao at Red Cliffs; historians now estimate 220,000 took part.**

alien environment. They were exhausted and disease raged in the ranks. Above all they were inexperienced in fighting on water. Cao Cao lashed his boats together to make a stable platform for his soldiers. Zhou Yu prepared fireships and sent them to drift down on to destroy Cao Cao's fleet that had become immobilized. The resulting conflagration was enough to persuade Cao Cao to lead his weary forces back north by land, a withdrawal that under constant harassment turned into a rout.

Cao Cao on the Yangtze
This illustration from the 14th-century epic the *Romance of the Three Kingdoms*, shows the Wei commander on the eve of the battle of the Red Cliffs, fought in 208 CE.

The nature of Chinese armies and their equipment in the time of Cao Cao and the subsequent Three Kingdoms wars is far from certain, since much of our information comes from texts, such as the *Romance of the Three Kingdoms*, that seem closer to legend than history, but

16 MILLION
The number of Chinese citizens according to a census from the early Jin dynasty (265–316 CE).

archeologists have confirmed much that was divined from written sources. Armies were large by any standards, sometimes numbering in hundreds of thousands, but almost certainly short of the 800,000 attributed by the ancient chroniclers to Cao Cao at the Red Cliffs. They were equipped with iron and steel weapons and armour; horses were armoured as well as the men. Crossbows were an important element, used both as hand-held infantry weapons and in larger versions as field artillery. There were even rapid-fire crossbows, known as *zhuge nu*, that fired bolts stored in a magazine by the simple operation of a lever – precursors of modern repeater rifles. Warfare included sieges for which various siege engines had been developed – mobile towers, battering rams, and torsion catapults. Incendiary devices had an important place in the Chinese armoury – the fireships used at the battle of the Red Cliffs were packed with dry reeds and wax, but many other substances were available for placing on the tips of arrows or coating projectiles hurled by catapults.

Cavalry formed the aristocratic elite of Chinese forces, although large numbers of steppe horsemen were also recruited as auxiliaries. River warfare employed much the same weaponry as was used on land, the warships being propelled by oar and sail.

Waging war in China
After the defeat at the Red Cliffs, Cao Cao had to content himself with regional power. Cao's domains came to be known as Cao Wei, while Liu Be's power base was called Shu Han, and Sun Quan ruled Dong Wu. Although these are known as the Three Kingdoms, they were not ruled by kings but by claimants to the title of emperor, for the last nominal Han dynasty emperor was deposed after the death of Cao Cao in 220. The Three Kingdoms were destined to fight one another, because each aspired to rule the whole of China.

The wars of the Three Kingdoms devastated the Chinese economy and led to depopulation, leaving the country exposed to the incursions of steppe nomads.

FURTHER FRAGMENTATION
In a process similar to that experienced by the contemporary Roman empire, steppe tribesmen collectively known as **the Wu Hu had begun migrating into lands within the boundaries of the Han empire**. The much weaker Jin dynasty established in 264 could not cope with the tide of "barbarian" horsemen, who took control of northern China in the 4th century as **the country split into the "Sixteen Kingdoms"**. Many Han Chinese migrated to the south, into the area around the Yangtze.

ONE NATION AGAIN
China was not reunited until 581, when the short-lived Sui dynasty established control over both the north and the south. **The Tang dynasty in 618 marked the beginning of a golden age of Chinese civilization.**

Arrow and spear heads
Chinese arrows, whether fired from crossbows or from field artillery, were frequently tipped with iron and steel. They would also be coated with flammable materials to set fire to vessels.

The northern state of Cao Wei was by far the strongest of the Three Kingdoms, but its power was balanced by an alliance between the southern kingdoms of Shu Han and Dong Wu. The most famous general of the Three Kingdoms period was Zhuge Liang, who led the armies of Shu. He mounted a series of campaigns against the Wei from 228. Known as the Northern Expeditions, these campaigns were resisted and eventually defeated by the cautious Wei commander, Sima Yi, who avoided battle and kept his forces safe in fortified positions until Zhuge Liang was forced to withdraw through exhaustion and shortage of supplies.

After Zhuge's death in 234, Shu went into decline. The descendants of Sima Yi conquered Shu in 263 and the following year established the Jin dynasty, which ruled all of China except Wu. Remembering the fate of Cao Cao at the Red Cliffs, the Jin prepared for the conquest of Wu by building their own fleet and by training large numbers of soldiers as marines, in order to win control of the Yangtze river. In 280 Wu was overwhelmed by the Jin armies, bringing the era of the Three Kingdoms to a close.

1 SUMERIAN CEREMONIAL HELMET (C.2600 BCE)

2 CHALCIDIAN HELMET (ANCIENT GREECE)

3 LEGIONARY'S HELMET (ANCIENT ROME)

6 GERMAN SALLET (15TH CENTURY)

5 ITALIAN HOUNSKULL BASINET (LATE 14TH CENTURY)

7 OTTOMAN CAVALRY HELMET (16TH CENTURY)

12 BRITISH HEAVY CAVALRY HELMET (19TH CENTURY)

13 PRUSSIAN PICKELHAUBE (19TH CENTURY)

Helmets

Ideally, helmets need to be made of light but strong material. Increasing the degree of protection they afford has usually been at the expense of comfort, mobility, and all-round vision. As well as protection, helmets offer a chance for display, although purely functional designs have predominated since World War I.

1 This **Sumerian helmet** is 4,500 years old; made of gold, it was probably worn in ceremonies in the ancient city of Ur. **2** The **Chalcidian helmet**, worn by Ancient Greek hoplite infantry, was made of bronze and topped by a horsehair crest. **3** The **Roman legionary's iron helmet** is in the Imperial Gallic style of the late 1st century CE. **4** This **Viking helmet** belonged to a 9th century Swedish warrior; it protected his face with a spectacle visor and nose guard. **5** The **medieval knight's basinet**, from the late 14th century, protected the face with a hounskull ("dog-face") hinged visor and the neck with a mail aventail. **6** The **sallet**, developed in Italy, was worn by foot soldiers across much of Europe in the 15th century. **7** The *chichak* **helmet** was worn by Ottoman cavalry in the 16th century. **8** The **close helmet** of the 16th-century knight offered good protection but was also an elaborate display of the wearer's wealth. **9** The **morion open helmet** was worn by the Spanish infantry of the 16th

century. **10** The **"lobster-tail" helmet** of an English Civil War cavalryman evolved from the Ottoman *chichak*. **11** The **Japanese samurai helmet** *(kabuto)* comprised a bowl *(hachi)* and neck protection *(shikoro)*, often elaborately decorated. **12** The **British heavy cavalry helmet** of the Napoleonic period was primarily decorative rather than functional. **13** The **Prussian** *Pickelhaube*, topped with a spike for the infantry and a ball for the artillery, was adopted in 1842. The leather helmet proved inadequate as protection in World War I. **14** The **German** *Stahlhelm* **steel infantry helmet**, with its distinctive "coal scuttle" shape, was introduced in 1916 during World War I trench warfare. **15** This **World War I British tankman's helmet** incorporated chain mail for defence against splinters of metal. **16** The **M4 flak helmet**, made of steel covered with green cloth, was worn by US bomber crews in 1944–45. **17** This **British infantry helmet**, typical of late 20th-century head protection, is made of synthetic Kevlar.

4 VIKING HELMET
(9TH CENTURY)

8 GERMAN CLOSE HELMET
(16TH CENTURY)

9 SPANISH MORION
(16TH CENTURY)

10 ENGLISH LOBSTER-TAIL
HELMET (17TH CENTURY)

11 JAPANESE SAMURAI HELMET
(16TH CENTURY ONWARDS)

14 GERMAN INFANTRY HELMET
(WORLD WAR I)

15 BRITISH TANKMAN'S HELMET
(WORLD WAR I)

16 AMERICAN FLAK HELMET
(WORLD WAR II)

17 BRITISH INFANTRY
HELMET (C.2002)

Stupa of Ashoka
The Mauryan emperor, Ashoka, built this Buddhist stupa at Sanchi in Madhaya Pradesh. Ashoka may have converted to Buddhism in reaction to the horrors of war.

« BEFORE

The Mauryan Empire

The wars of the Mauryan emperor Chandragupta and his successors demonstrated the military sophistication of the largest Indian states in the 4th and 3rd centuries BCE. With their full-time soldiers, Indian armies were expensive to maintain but were effective instruments of conquest and domination.

Ancient Indian civilizations developed in the swathe of territory across the north of the subcontinent from the Indus valley in the west to the Ganges in the east.

THE MAHABHARATA

Evidence for warfare in ancient India comes mostly from the **Sanskrit epic, the _Mahabharata_**. This recounts the **18-day battle of Kurukshetra between the rival clans of the Pandavas and the Kauravas**. The _Mahabharata_ is legend rather than history, but it sketches a style of warfare that was probably true to life. Both sides assembled and supplied large armies, both fought in horse-drawn chariots, and both employed war elephants. **The chief weapons were the bow, the javelin, and the mace.**

In 326 BCE the Macedonian conqueror, Alexander the Great (see pp.24–25), led an army through the Hindu Kush into northern India. He was confronted by the army of a king whom the invaders called Porus, the ruler of a powerful state in the Punjab. The size of Porus's army seems to have been impressive; accounts that have survived, written much later, suggest 20,000–30,000 infantry, 300 chariots, and possibly 200 war elephants deployed in the van.

Porus was defeated by Alexander at the battle of Hydaspes, unable to cope with the devastating flexibility of the Macedonian cavalry and the discipline of the infantry phalanx. Both sides were to be influenced by this collision of cultures. Alexander's successors adopted the elephant, while in India a young man called Chandragupta Maurya was inspired to regenerate Indian military power and to emulate Alexander's campaigns of conquest.

Chandragupta's origins are obscure and so is his precise relationship with Alexander (it is unclear whether the two men actually met), but by around 321 BCE he had established himself as the ruler of the kingdom of Magadha, seizing power from the Nanda dynasty in a series of well-orchestrated military campaigns. This was a startling achievement given the sophisticated nature of the Nanda state's armed forces. Chandragupta may have

Mauryan empire
Dates 321–181 BCE
Location Northern and central India

employed a form of guerrilla warfare, for some sources suggest that outlying areas were progressively taken under the rebels' control until a tightening noose closed around the Nanda capital.

War with the Seleucid Empire
Chandragupta's authority was initially concentrated in the east of the Indian subcontinent, in Bihar and Bengal, but soon he pressed westward, filling the power vacuum left by Alexander's rampaging campaign and subsequent withdrawal. By 305 the Indus river had become the border between Chandragupta's realm and the territory claimed by Alexander's former general, Seleucus Nicator. Between 305 and 303 the Mauryans and the Seleucids fought a war for the control of Gandhara, a wealthy region covering what is now Kashmir, northern Pakistan, and eastern Afghanistan. Although there is no historical record of the fighting, Chandragupta must have won the war, since Gandhara passed into Mauryan hands. In the peace treaty that ended the conflict, Chandragupta agreed to provide 500 elephants for Seleucus's army as a sign of good faith – an impressive number of animals, but small compensation for the loss of such valuable lands.

At this time Chandragupta ruled from the Ganges plain across to the Indus and the northwestern borderlands of the subcontinent, as well as part of central India. This formidable empire was visited by a Greek envoy of Seleucus, called Megasthenes, who wrote an account of what he saw on his trip. According to Megasthenes,

Mauryan imperial legacy
This coin features Chandragupta I, ruler of India in the 4th century CE. He took the name of the founder of the Mauryan Empire six centuries earlier.

warriors were one of the seven castes into which Mauryan society was divided. These were full-time, highly trained professional soldiers – men who "practise nothing but warlike exercises" and "receive high pay from the state" in war and peace alike. The money they received was sufficient for them to pay for servants, grooms for their horses, charioteers, and men "to keep their weapons bright and manage the elephants". Megasthenes emphasized the warriors' high morale, twice describing them as being of "good cheer". Indian warfare was dominated by the use of missile weapons; Megasthenes states that close-quarters battle "rarely happens between Indians". Their bow, the standard infantry weapon, was "equal in length to the man who carries it" and shot a long, heavy arrow that could penetrate any armour. Foot soldiers also carried a broad, two-handed sword and a long, narrow ox-hide shield. The horsemen were light cavalry skirmishers, riding bareback and throwing javelins. War elephants were crewed by a mahout (elephant driver) and four soldiers who shot arrows and threw javelins from atop the animal's back. The elephant's main military use, however, was less as a weapons platform than as a weapon in itself; it was used to trample enemy infantry and gore them with its tusks.

Chandragupta died around 298 BCE. The resources provided by his conquered territories no doubt facilitated further expansion of the Mauryan empire under his successors. Bindusar, who ruled until 272 BCE, pressed further south along the west coast of India as far as Mysore, but it was Bindusar's son, Ashoka, who took the Mauryan empire to its furthest limits.

Reign of Ashoka
Although the details of his life are poorly documented, Ashoka appears to have been a formidable warrior from an early age and to have won a vicious armed struggle for the succession against his brothers in the four years

One legacy of the Mauryan empire was an idea of the potential unity of India. In practice, the subcontinent was disunited and exposed to invasions from the north.

THE GUPTA EMPIRE
A variety of states flourished in the aftermath of the Mauryan empire, including an **Indo-Greek kingdom (an offshoot of Alexander the Great's conquests)** ruled in the 2nd century BCE by Menander Soter in the area of modern-day Pakistan and northern India. The most ambitious attempt to recreate the Mauryan empire was made by a dynasty that came to power in the 4th century CE, and whose first emperor adopted the name **Chandragupta – from which the dynastic name "Gupta" was then derived**.

GUPTA-ERA BUDDHA

Between about 319 and 415, under Chandragupta I, Samudragupta, and Chandragupta II, the Gupta empire expanded to claim suzerainty over a substantial area of the Indian subcontinent. One boastful Gupta inscription refers to **Samudragupta's victories over 21 kings**. However, historians have cast doubt on Gupta claims to have ruled distant parts of India that may in reality have only owed them some vague allegiance.

NOMADIC INCURSIONS
In the 5th century the **Guptas came under increasing pressure from the White Huns** – steppe nomads from Central Asia who wore down the empire's defences and eventually destroyed it, laying waste the cities and monasteries of the Ganges plain. But the Indian warrior tradition was far from exhausted, **reviving from the 8th century in the Rajput kingdoms of northern India**.

after his father's death. His most famous campaigns as ruler were fought around 265–262 BCE against the kingdom of Kalinga on the east coast of India. Ashoka's first invasion of Kalingan territory was repulsed, leading him to assemble overwhelming forces for a second campaign. The Kalingans again resisted, but they were overcome after a savage battle by the Daya river. According to an inscription attributed to Ashoka himself, 100,000 Kalingans were killed and 150,000 were deported (presumably as slaves) and many more died as a result of the devastation wrought by the war and its aftermath. The same inscription states that Ashoka later experienced an extreme revulsion against the brutality of conquest. This led him to convert to Buddhism.

A peaceful Buddhist state
Ashoka appears to have broadly followed Buddhist precepts in the benevolent later years of his reign, which ended peacefully in 234 BCE. There is no suggestion that he disbanded his army or abandoned the use of force, but any sensitivity to the sufferings of a defeated enemy and the human cost of war is so rare in the pre-modern world that Ashoka undoubtedly deserves his reputation as an exceptionally humane individual.

The Mauryan empire united more of the Indian subcontinent than any state until the Moguls in the 16th century CE, leaving out only

the southernmost area of the great peninsula and Sri Lanka. Yet the empire outlived Ashoka for only 50 years. The last Mauryan emperor, Brihadratha, was overthrown in a coup in 185 BCE and the various component parts of the empire went their independent ways.

Mounted Mauryan warrior with bhuj
This carving shows a Mauryan warrior carrying a rare kind of axe called a *bhuj*. A cross between a sword and an axe, the weapon is native to northwestern India.

"When an independent country is conquered, the slaughter of the people is grievous ..."
EDICT OF ASHOKA, REFERRING TO THE CONQUEST OF KALINGA

2

WAR IN THE MEDIEVAL WORLD

500 – 1500

Many wars were fought in the name of the religions of Islam and Christianity. Weak, quarrelsome states were prey to conquest by nomads such as the Mongols, who created the greatest empire the world had ever seen.

FRENCH POLEAXE, 1475

WAR IN THE MEDIEVAL WORLD
500 – 1500

During the period 500–1500 CE, centralized states in Europe and Asia were often weak and vulnerable both to nomadic invaders and to dissident warlords with local power bases. Neither technology nor organization gave any great advantage to central authority or settled civilizations. War was endemic in many regions, especially in Western Europe, and organized warfare often degenerated into plunder and piracy. As people sought refuge from insecurity inside castles and behind town walls, siege warfare and the building of strong fortifications became the cornerstone to military success.

At the beginning of the period the rulers of the Byzantine empire made a determined effort to restore the Mediterranean empire of Rome to its full glory, but failed in the West where Christianized Germanic kingdoms were established. Both Byzantium and Sasanid Persia were then confronted with the armed expansion of Islam. Arab armies inspired by the new Muslim faith conquered vast territories from Spain to India.

Western Europe was vulnerable to invaders and raiders – Vikings and Magyars, as well as Arabs – but the region experienced a military resurgence from the 11th century. Almost constant warfare between West European Christian states stimulated the development of new military tactics, while the Crusades founded short-lived Christian states in the eastern Mediterranean and drove back Islam in Spain.

A Viking shield
Colourful shields were an important part of the seafaring Vikings' battlefield equipment. They were usually made of wood that was covered with leather and painted. The principal Viking weapons were spears, swords, and axes.

Nomads and knights
In China the Tang dynasty was able to restore imperial rule in the early medieval period. Subsequent dynasties, such as the Song, which ruled in the south, often had to pay off various nomadic tribes as insurance against attack from the north. Whether Turks, Mongols, Jurchens, or Tartars, the nomadic horsemen of the steppes were formidable warriors, armed with composite bows, skilled in manoeuvre, and ruthless to the defeated. Under charismatic leaders such as Genghis Khan and Timur, their warlike qualities made them at different times conquerors of China, Persia, the Middle East, Russia, and eventually the Byzantine empire. In order to make their conquests permanent, they adopted many of the skills and customs of the settled civilizations.

Mace from China
This decorated iron mace would have been used by a Mongol warrior on horseback.

In medieval warfare, high status was generally identified with fighting on horseback. This was especially true of armoured cavalry, from the cataphracts of the Byzantine empire and the Persian Sasanids to the knights of Western Europe. The spread of the stirrup, improved metalworking for armour and swords, and the breeding of bigger horses all contributed to the evolution of the medieval knight. High-status warriors, whether European knights or Japanese samurai, adopted chivalric codes of honour and viewed warfare as first and foremost a means of demonstrating personal prowess. Infantry were mostly of low status and consigned to an auxiliary battlefield role rather than the central place they had held in Ancient Greece or Rome. Nonetheless, in European warfare properly organized foot soldiers, especially when armed with longbows or crossbows, and later with pikes, became increasingly influential from the 14th century onwards.

Technical advances
Technological progress was fitful and often less important than fresh tactics – the longbow, for example, was a rather primitive weapon in itself but surprisingly effective when deployed en masse by the English in the Hundred Years War. Gunpowder weapons developed first in China, where they were in extensive use by the 14th century, yet marginal in their overall impact. It was in Europe around 1450 that cannon started to change the face of war, ending the reign of stone castles by battering down their walls.

Throughout this time a wholly separate tradition of warfare was maintained in the Americas, in the absence of both the wheel and the horse. Metalworking was rare and weapons were generally edged or tipped with stone. This did not prevent the creation of large empires, with both the Incas in Peru and the Aztecs in Mexico extending military domination over substantial areas.

500	565	620	675	730	785

502–506
The Byzantine (Eastern Roman) empire fights a war with the Persian Sasanid empire. Further wars are fought in 526–532, 539–543, and 572–590.

568
The Lombards and other Germanic ethnic groups cross the Alps and conquer northern Italy.

577
Victory over the Britons at the battle of Deorham in the southwest gives the Saxons control of much of England.

627
Byzantine emperor Heraclius defeats Sasanid emperor Khosroe II at Nineveh in the war against the Persians.

732
At the battle of Tours (or Poitiers) the Franks under Charles Martel turn back a Muslim raiding force advancing north from Spain.

793
Viking raiders from Scandinavia sack the monastery of Lindisfarne on the coast of Northumbria in northern England.

524
During their successful conquest of the Burgundian kingdom, the Franks defeat King Sigismund at the battle of Vézeronce.

632–34
Under Caliph Abu Bakr, leader of newly established Islam, Arabia is brought under Muslim control and Arab armies invade the Sasanid and Byzantine empires.

800
Charlemagne is crowned Holy Roman Emperor by the pope in Rome.

⌄ Emperor Charlemagne

⌃ The battle of Karbala, Iraq, in 680

680
The Prophet Muhammad's grandson, Husain ibn Ali, his family, and 54 of his followers are massacred at Karbala by the army of Umayyad caliph Yazid I.

598
Initiating the Goguryeo-Sui wars, the Chinese Sui dynasty emperor Wendi attacks the Korean kingdom of Goguryo, but is repulsed.

751
The Turkish peoples of Central Asia come under Muslim influence after Muslim Abbasids defeat Tang Chinese at the battle of Talas.

641
Arab armies conquer the Sasanid empire and invade Byzantine-ruled Egypt.

663
Forces from Japan and from Tang dynasty China clash in Korea at Baekgang.

687
In Merovingian Gaul, the battle of Tertry makes Pepin the effective ruler of the Franks.

⌃ Justinian I (reigned 527–565)

533–54
Justinian I, known as "the Great", attempts to restore Roman rule in the western Mediterranean. His general Belisarius defeats the Vandals in North Africa and the Ostrogoths in Italy.

614–18
Persian Sasanid emperor Khosroe II conquers Jerusalem and goes on to invade Anatolia during the ongoing conflict with the Byzantine empire.

674–677
An Arab siege of Constantinople fails; the Byzantines possibly use the first ever incendiary weapon, "Greek fire".

711
A Muslim army crosses from North Africa and invades Spain, conquering the Visigothic kingdom.

772
Charlemagne, ruler of the Franks, begins a series of campaigns against the Saxons and the Lombards.

806
Muslim caliph Harun al-Rashid campaigns in Anatolia and forces the Byzantine empire to pay tribute.

⌄ Cataphract (heavy cavalryman) of the Sasanid dynasty (226–640 CE)

718
In a siege of Constantinople, the Arabs fail for a second time to take the city.

722
In Spain Muslim forces are rebuffed at Covadonga in the northern region of Asturias.

⌄ 8th-century Frankish axe

840	895	950	1005	1060	1115

840–860
Viking longships make numerous raids around the coast of Europe from Ireland to France and southern Spain.

906
Magyar horsemen from the Hungarian plain overrun Moravia and invade Saxony and Bavaria.

1013
Danish king Sweyn Forkbeard invades England, defeating Anglo-Saxon King Aethelred II.

⌃ An Anglo-Saxon seax sword

⌃ The battle of Hastings, 1066, depicted in the Bayeux Tapestry

911
In France the duchy of Normandy is founded by settled Norsemen led by Rollo.

955
Otto I, Saxon king of Germany, defeats the Magyars at the battle of Lechfeld.

980
A new wave of Viking invasions begins in England.

1016
Cnut, King Sweyn's successor as king of Denmark, defeats Edmund Ironside at Ashingdon and becomes ruler of England.

1066
In England, King Harold II defeats Harald Hardrada at Stamford Bridge, but is defeated by William of Normandy at Hastings. Harold is killed in the battle.

1118
King Alfonso I of Aragón defeats the Almoravids and captures the city of Zaragoza in Spain.

865
A Danish Viking army lands in England and begins campaigns of conquest.

878
Alfred the Great, king of Wessex, defeats the Danes at the battle of Edington.

929
In Spain Abd ar-Rahman proclaims himself caliph of Córdoba and campaigns against the Christian kingdom of León.

1071
The Seljuk Turks led by Arp Aslan inflict a crushing defeat upon the Byzantine emperor Romanus IV at the battle of Manzikert.

⌄ Turkish Seljuk warriors

885
A Viking army lays siege to Paris, but fails to take the city.

938
Ngo Quyen defeats the Chinese and establishes an independent kingdom in northern Vietnam.

⌃ Mahmud of Ghazni, far right (971–1030)

999
In Central Asia, Mahmud of Ghazni defeats the Saminids.

1000
Olag Trygvasson, king of Norway, dies at the battle of Svold, defeated by Sweyn Forkbeard, king of Denmark.

1028
King Cnut conquers Norway, adding it to his realms of England and Denmark.

1126–27
Jurchen steppe warriors take the Song Chinese capital Kaifeng, despite the use of gunpowder "thunderclap bombs" to defend the city.

⌄ Viking longship

1000–30
Mahmud of Ghazni fights 17 military campaigns in India, establishing the Ghaznavid empire, which stretches from Samarkand to the Ganges.

1095–99
The First Crusade. Knights from Western Europe march across Anatolia and capture Antioch and Jerusalem.

1129
The Knights Templar, established in Jerusalem, is officially recognized by the Church as a monastic order dedicated to fighting for the Christian faith.

« A crusader's helmet

1051–63
Minamoto Yoshiie, fighting in the Nine Years War in Japan, establishes the ideal of the samurai warrior.

1160
In Japan the Heiji Rebellion pits the Taira samurai clan against the Minamoto clan; the Taira are victorious and form the first samurai-dominated government.

| **1170** | **1225** | **1280** | **1335** | **1390** | **1445** | |

1176
At the battle of Legnano in northern Italy, Emperor Frederick Barbarossa is defeated by the forces of the Lombard League.

⌄ Invasion of Japan by Kublai Khan

1281
After an initial raid in 1274, Kublai Khan launches a seaborne invasion of Japan from Korea; it is repelled by Japanese resistance and a typhoon (*kamikaze* or "divine wind").

1415
English king Henry V defeats a much stronger French army at Agincourt, France.

1449
Oirat steppe horsemen wipe out a Chinese army and besiege Beijing; the experience pushes the Chinese empire to strengthen and extend the Great Wall.

⌃ Mongol leader Kublai Khan

1180–85
The Gempei War in Japan. The Minamoto clan defeats the Taira and subsequently establishes the shogunate.

1241
A Mongol army ravages Poland and Hungary, defeating Christian knights at the battle of Liegnitz.

1337
Taking the Byzantine city of Nicomedia (Izmit), the Ottomans extend their rule over most of Anatolia. ■ Start of the Hundred Years War between England and France.

1187
Saladin, the Kurdish ruler of Egypt, defeats the Christians at the battle of Hattin and occupies Jerusalem and Acre, triggering the Third Crusade.

1250
In Egypt, a crusade led by Louis IX of France ends in disaster when the army is defeated and the king taken prisoner. ■ Mameluk slave soldiers take power in Egypt.

1346
English king Edward III defeats French king Philip VI at Crécy. Longbows are crucial to the victory. The English also deploy small cannon.

1420–34
Led initially by Jan Zizka, the Hussite "heretics" in Bohemia resist a crusade by the forces of Emperor Sigismund, using cannon and handguns.

1189–92
Third Crusade. The crusaders retake Acre but fail to reach Jerusalem. English king Richard the Lionheart signs a treaty with Saladin, by which Christian pilgrims are allowed to visit Jerusalem.

1282–1302
War of the Sicilian Vespers. Charles of Anjou and the kingdom of Aragon fight for control of Sicily.

1298
In the Anglo-Scottish Wars, English king Edward I defeats the Scots under William Wallace at Falkirk.

⌄ Edward I of England

1369
Turkish military leader Timur (Tamerlane) establishes his capital at Samarkand; in campaigns through the rest of the century he conquers Asia from Persia and Syria to northern India.

1429
Inspired by Joan of Arc, the French turn the tide against the English at the siege of Orleans.

1430
Joan of Arc is captured by the English and burned at the stake as a "witch".

⌃ Fall of Constantinople, 1453

1453
Ottoman forces under Mehmed II overcome a much smaller Christian force and take Constantinople.

1211
Mongol leader Genghis Khan, having unified the steppe tribes, invades northern China. Start of the Mongol conquests.

1265
Charles of Anjou is declared king of Sicily by Pope Clement IV. Unpopular French rule leads to the War of the Sicilian Vespers.

⌄ Charles of Anjou sails to Sicily in 1265

c.1486
German emperor Maximilian I pays for the creation of mostly pike-armed mercenary bands, the *landsknechts*.

1492
Columbus's first voyage to the Caribbean paves the way for the European conquest of the New World.

1314
English king Edward II is defeated by the Scots under Robert Bruce at Bannockburn, re-establishing Scottish independence.

1325
In Central America the Aztecs found a capital at the lake city of Tenochtitlán.

1370–80
Led by Bertrand du Guesclin, the French regain much of the territory lost to the English in the Hundred Years War.

⌃ Joan of Arc, French heroine and martyr

1435
French king Charles VII hires Jean and Gaspard Bureau to organize artillery for his war against the English.

1494
Charles VIII of France invades Italy, beginning more than half a century of Italian Wars.

1498
Vasco da Gama's voyage to India opens up Asia to trade and colonization by European powers.

The Rise of Byzantium

For centuries the Byzantine empire remained true to its origins, a redoubt of Roman civilization in the east. However, most of its dealings – in war as in peace – were with Asia and its peoples: this left its mark on the military culture of Byzantium, informing both weaponry and tactics.

The Arabs called them the "Rum". Their city may have been founded by the Greeks, it may have looked eastward into Asia; but the Byzantines always saw themselves as Romans. Their empire perpetuated that of Rome, even if its western states – and its nominal capital – had been routed by barbarians. This applied in the military sphere too: the old legionary structures were kept, as were the old Roman values of order, discipline, and logistical efficiency.

For a while, in the 6th century, it seemed possible the lost territories might be recovered. The emperor Justinian I (527–65), famous for his codification of Roman law, laid out plans for a more ambitious project: the *renovatio imperii*, or "renewal of the empire".

Into Africa

That this could be more than an empty dream owed much to the daring and skill of Justinian's military commander, Belisarius. Born around 505, he is believed to have been of Greek or Thracian ancestry. In 528, having risen through the ranks of the Byzantine army, Justinian made him his commander in the Iberian war (fought not in the Iberian Peninsula but in the little Caucasian kingdom of Iberia). Byzantium had been locked in conflict with Persia's Sasanid rulers over

MEDITERRANEAN AND WEST ASIA

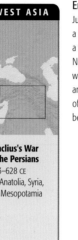

1 Justinian's war against the Vandals
Dates 533–534 CE
Location North Africa

2 Reconquest of Italy
Dates 535–554 CE
Location Italy and Sicily

3 Heraclius's War against the Persians
Dates 613–628 CE
Location Anatolia, Syria, Palestine, Mesopotamia

this country for some years, but the hostilities had now turned into open war. Belisarius triumphed at Dara in 530, but after a stalemate at Callinicum the following year, the Byzantines and Persians agreed an inconclusive peace. Justinian still felt strong enough to embark upon a new campaign in a different theatre and sent Belisarius out to conquer the Vandal kingdom in what for centuries had been the Roman province of Africa.

Though now established in eastern Algeria and Tunisia, the Vandals were of Germanic origin. In 429, with Rome's

25 **The percentage pay cut imposed on Byzantine troops in 588, prompting a mutiny – which invited an opportunistic attack by Persia and hence an expensive war.**

Empire rebuilder
Justinian I (far right) was a Byzantine emperor in a truly "Roman" mould. Nicknamed "the emperor who never sleeps", his armies recaptured much of the territory that had been lost to the Barbarians.

« BEFORE

Byzantium – beside the river Bosphorus where the city of Istanbul now stands – was founded as a colony by Greek traders in 667 BCE.

CONSTANTINE'S CAPITAL

Byzantium was an important trading centre, pivotally placed between Greece and the Mediterranean on one side and the rich cities of western Asia on the other. **The conquests of Alexander « 24–25** brought the Middle East into the Greek cultural sphere. It remained so after the **Roman conquest of the 2nd century** BCE **« 30–31**. By the 4th century CE the economic base of the

CONSTANTINE I

Roman empire had moved to the east. The first Christian emperor, Constantine I, built his city here, naming it "Constantinople" after himself. His successor, Emperor Theodosius II (408–450), bolstered the capital's defences, building what became known as the **Theodosian Wall**.

A NEW EMPIRE

Constantinople would soon overtake Rome in importance, but when the western empire **fell to the barbarians in the 5th century « 46–47**, Constantine's city was left the **unrivalled centre** of a primarily Asian "Roman" empire.

Sasanid sword
Persia's Sasanid rulers were immensely proud of their warlike traditions. A sword like this one was not just a weapon but a status symbol – often elaborately decorated with silver.

western empire in turmoil, they had swept southwards through Spain before crossing the Straits of Gibraltar. Sacking Roman Carthage, the Vandals soon set up their own capital there. Confined to the coastal plain, the new Vandal kingdom was insignificant in terms of territory. However, it made the perfect base for onslaughts across the Mediterranean: in 455 the Vandals had sacked Rome itself, and they continued to torment the eastern empire. In 533 Justinian dispatched his invasion-fleet. Belisarius's army was small: he had some 15,000 troops at

his disposal, of which 10,000 were infantry and the rest cavalry. Victory came swiftly at the battle of Ad Decimum. Fortune favoured the Byzantines – the city of Carthage was captured and Africa recovered.

Power struggle

In 535, exhilarated by this success, Justinian sent Belisarius to reclaim the Italian "homeland", at this time under the occupation of the Ostrogoths. By 536 Rome had been secured. However, the war for the rest of Italy was not to be so easy: in the following years, the balance of power in the peninsula shifted back and forth through a gruelling series of pitched battles and city-sieges. In 540 Belisarius recaptured the Ostrogoth base, Ravenna, making it the capital of a re-established western empire.

However, these gains were hard to hold. The Goths were not beaten and by the early 550s were resurgent in Italy. Problems were mounting for the empire: in 568 Italy was invaded from the north by the Germanic Lombards, while in 577 the Slavs and Avars invaded the Balkans from the north and east.

In Asia, meanwhile, the war with Persia had resumed in 572. It would continue intermittently for 50 years, shaping the Byzantine war machine. Persia's strength in cavalry had to be countered. The Sasanids could deploy thousands of cataphracts, armoured horsemen who charged with lances raised, smashing into the enemy with a force that even the toughest, most disciplined infantrymen could not withstand. After the shock of the first impact came the terrifying confusion as the units of cataphracts drew their bows and showered arrows all around.

Fighting back

The Byzantines saw no alternative but to match the Persian threat directly. They assembled cataphract units of their own, reinforcing them with light and heavy infantry. The Byzantines were short of people. Most of their soldiers were *foederati*, recruited from the many barbarian peoples who were bound by treaty to the Byzantine cause; others were mercenaries. But all served the empire well. The Persians were kept at bay and at last, in 627, the armies of Emperor Heraclius scored a daring victory over the Sasanids at Nineveh,

Military horsepower
Cataphracts used the movement of their horses to their advantage, gleaning extra power from the animal – a rider's lance was usually chained to the horse's neck and hind leg, using momentum to strengthen a lunge.

Iraq. But the relief this brought was a cruel illusion. The exhausted imperial armies had succeeded only in clearing the way for invasion by the Arabs.

That Constantinople held out for the next 500 years against more Arab assaults is testimony to the empire's naval power, and to the potency of "Greek Fire", the great Byzantine secret weapon. Believed to have been a blend of burning oil and tar propelled by a pump – a sort of medieval flame-thrower – it played havoc with the enemy in an age of wooden ships.

Decades of war in western Asia had left both Byzantium and Persia drained. Neither was able to hold up the expansion of the Arabs through the 7th century.

BELEAGUERED BYZANTIUM
The decline of the Byzantine empire from this time on was inexorable, and it was permanently on the defensive. But long after the bulk of its land-territories had gone, it remained an important naval power. In between attacks by the Arabs came assaults by many different enemies, from **the Varangians (Ukrainian-based Vikings) 70–71 »** to the Bulgars. Wars with these groups in the 9th, 10th, and 11th centuries saw Constantinople under threat, while the states in Italy and Sicily were taken by the Normans in the 11th century.

In 1204 **Constantinople was sacked** by the armies of the **Fourth Crusade 76–77 »**. It fell to **the Ottoman Turks 106–07 »** in 1453, and became their capital for almost 600 years.

The Ascent of Islam

**The 7th century saw the birth of Islam, and with it an extraordinary campaign of conquest.
In the space of a few generations, much of the known world was brought under Muslim rule.
The consequences of this metamorphosis have lasted into modern times.**

BEFORE

In 610 the prophet Muhammad retreated into the desert and received the first of a series of revelations that were to lead to the proclamation of Islam.

A LAND UNDISTURBED
Arabia was a place apart, remote and inhospitable: its people were **nomadic herders** and **desert traders**. While the very northernmost areas appear to have been occupied, **first by the Persians ≪ 20–21** and then by **the Romans ≪ 42–43**, the main part of the peninsula remained largely undisturbed.

THE KA'ABA, MECCA, CENTRE OF THE MUSLIM WORLD

A MISSION
A warlike attitude was forced on Muhammad from the beginning: the rulers of his native Mecca saw his message as destabilizing and he and his followers eventually had to leave. After the *hijrah* – the move to Medina in 622 – they had to fight for their survival. Inspired by their sense of mission, they triumphed at **the battle of Badr in 624**. Though defeated and almost destroyed at Uhud in 625, Muhammad and his followers recovered to win **the battle of the**

JIHAD An Arabic word meaning "struggle". *Jihad* could mean a literal war for Islam or an inner battle for personal renewal.

Trench in 627. Three years later they captured Mecca. By the time the prophet died in 632, his followers had grown accustomed to the idea that believers had to fight to make the truth prevail. His successor, the first caliph, Abu Bakr, **brought all the Arab tribes under Islamic rule**.

When, in 632, the prophet Muhammad died, he left behind not just a new religion but a cause for which his followers were prepared to fight and die. Till then a collection of warring tribes, the Arabs had found a shared ideal, an identity in which they could unite. Within a century, the prophet's message had been carried over an area reaching from northern Spain to Central Asia.

Arab horsepower
The Arab warriors had no heavy weaponry or armour: they relied principally on their swords, which were straight and double-edged and carried in wooden scabbards. Their main weapons, though, were speed and surprise, as well as a passionate commitment to their beliefs.

The Arabs had also been equipped for war by their way of life. Nomadic pastoralists, they had grown up tough, with superlative riding skills. They had the finest horses in the world: fast, resilient, and intelligent, but also docile. The Arabian camel,

Brass alam
This ornate alam (or standard) honours the martyrdom of Husain ibn Ali, who was killed at the battle of Karbala in 680. He is mourned each year in Muharram, the first month of the Islamic calendar.

or dromedary, was used as a beast of burden rather than a mount, but it was far quicker and more versatile than any wheeled cart.

Out of the desert
Abu Bakr's challenge as first caliph was bringing together all the Arab tribes. Only under his successor, Umar ibn al-Khattab, from 634–44, did the campaign of conquest begin in earnest. It did so with explosive violence – Umar's armies pouring out of the Arabian Peninsula to attack the southern borders of the Byzantine empire. In 636 Islam smashed a Byzantine force at Yarmük, now on the border between Syria and Jordan. Two years later Jerusalem was taken.

The Arabs had conquered Syria, Palestine, and Egypt by 641; they had also defeated the Sasanids. As yet, they were too few in number to take far-reaching areas of the Persian empire, but they quickly made new converts and consolidated their position.

In the following decades, the empire-building effort was hampered by internal divisions. At Karbala in Iraq in 680, the army of Umayyad Caliph Yazid I overcame that of Husain ibn Ali, the prophet's grandson. The massacre that ensued left a legacy of

bitterness, and caused the split between the rival Islamic traditions of Sunni and Shi'a which continues to this day. Even so, Iran was secured and Afghanistan taken, while an advance-guard poured across the Hindu Kush into what is now Pakistan. In the west, Tripoli was taken and ships seized the island of Cyprus.

Muawiyyah I's Umayyad dynasty, with its capital at Damascus, imposed a degree of unity and order on the Arab

10 MILLION The area, in square kilometres, of the Arab empire by the 8th century CE; all ruled by the Umayyads.

world. That world was still growing: in the early years of the 8th century, Arab armies advanced westwards from Libya across the Maghreb. In 711 the first raiding party of Arabs and Islamicized Berbers crossed the Straits of Gibraltar into Spain: Tariq ibn-Ziyad's warriors crushed the defenders sent to fight them. By 718 virtually the whole of the Iberian Peninsula lay in Muslim hands.

Battle of Karbala
Completely surrounded and hopelessly outnumbered, Husain ibn Ali, his half-brother, Abbas, and their supporters fought heroically to the death.

AFTER

The Arab attempt to conquer Europe was thwarted at the battle of Poitiers in 732. However, the Islamic hold on the Middle East remains strong to this day.

RESISTANCE
The Moors, as the Arabs were also known, would gradually be pushed southward through Spain during **the Reconquista 98–99 ≫**. Even so, the Islamic kingdom of al-Andalus was to flourish for several centuries.

A LASTING LEGACY
The long-term consequences of some of these events can be traced in the modern era. The split between Sunni and Shi'a underlay the bitter conflict between **Iraq and Iran** in the 1980s **342–43 ≫** and added additional complexity to the **occupation of Iraq 348–49 ≫**. The collision between the Islamic East and the West also occurred in the war between **NATO forces and the Taliban in Afghanistan 340–41 ≫**.

The Islamic world
In just a few generations, the Arabs extended their empire across much of the known world, from the Atlantic to the Indus and beyond.

Key
- Muslim lands by 634
- Muslim lands by 656
- Muslim lands by 756
- Abbasid caliphate at its greatest extent c.800
- Muslim raid with date
- Muslim victory
- Muslim defeat

BATTLE OF KARBALA
This 19th-century painting shows Husain ibn Ali (on horseback, left), the grandson of the prophet Muhammad, during the battle of Karbala in 680 CE. The encounter was sparked by Husain's refusal to swear allegiance to Yazid, who wanted the blessing of the family of the Holy Prophet to legitimize his rule. Husain was protected by a handful of relatives, many of them women and children, and was slain during the confrontation.

« BEFORE

Under King Clovis I (c.481–c.511), the Franks made themselves the masters of what had been Roman Gaul. He and his successors are known as the Merovingian Dynasty.

FRANKISH LAW

The Franks were a Germanic-speaking people, one of a number that, in the 5th century, had spilled across the frontiers of the western **Roman empire « 46–47**. Under Frankish law, land – like other possessions – had to be **shared out equally** among a man's sons. Equitable, perhaps, but where kingship was concerned, a **recipe for war**. A cycle of civil conflict developed in which individual rulers **reunited the Frankish realms** by force of arms, only to divide them up again among their sons.

FRANKISH HELMET

A WEAKENED MONARCHY

The authority of the Merovingian kings became undermined by a rise in aristocratic factionalism. The position **"Mayor of the Palace"** – the official charged with ensuring the smooth running of the royal household – grew in importance. From 687 it was monopolized by the Arnulfing family.

Frankish Expansion

From the 8th century, the Franks extended their dominion over much of Western and Central Europe. For all its internal dynastic conflicts, the Frankish empire brought a degree of stability to Europe that had not been seen since Roman times, and it became a bulwark against Muslim expansion from the south.

B y the 8th century, the authority of the Merovingians was greatly reduced. Power had passed to the aristocracy and to the "Mayors of the Palace", but even here dissension was rife. In Austrasia Pepin II had been "Dux" (duke or leader) since 680. An invitation to intervene in a dispute between aristocratic factions in Neustria in 687 saw Pepin dominating the realm until his death in 714. This precipitated a crisis. Lacking surviving sons, Pepin's widow, Plectrude, tried to secure the Mayor's office for an eight-year-old grandson, Theudoald, but Neustrian nobles elevated their own candidate, Ragenfred, to Mayor. Then in 715 they elected a new king, Chilperic II.

Franks fight Franks

The Neustrians invaded Austrasia and, as Plectrude was agreeing terms with them, an illegitimate son of Pepin's, Charles, whom she had been keeping in captivity, escaped. He attacked the

> ## "The men of the north stood motionless as a wall."
> **CHRONICLER ISIDORE PACENSIS ON THE FRANKISH STAND AT POITIERS, 754**

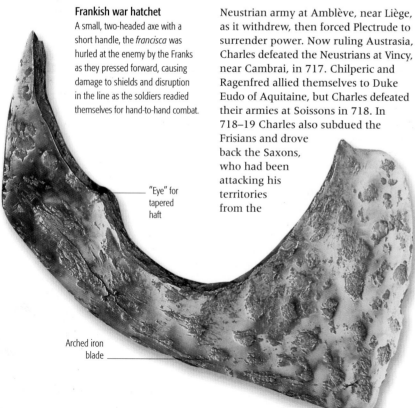

Frankish war hatchet
A small, two-headed axe with a short handle, the *francisca* was hurled at the enemy by the Franks as they pressed forward, causing damage to shields and disruption in the line as the soldiers readied themselves for hand-to-hand combat.

"Eye" for tapered haft

Arched iron blade

ETSYRIAM SOBAL· ET CONYERTIT
IOAB· ET PERCYSSIT EDOM INVAL
LESALINARYM·XII MILIA·

Neustrian army at Amblève, near Liège, as it withdrew, then forced Plectrude to surrender power. Now ruling Austrasia, Charles defeated the Neustrians at Vincy, near Cambrai, in 717. Chilperic and Ragenfred allied themselves to Duke Eudo of Aquitaine, but Charles defeated their armies at Soissons in 718. In 718–19 Charles also subdued the Frisians and drove back the Saxons, who had been attacking his territories from the

east. On the death of Chilperic II, Charles secured the election of a Merovingian king of his choosing, but it took him until 730 to bring western Neustria completely under control.

Muslim Arabs and Berbers had been raiding Aquitaine and Provence from Spain since 721. In 732 Duke Eudo of Aquitaine was unable to resist a raid led by 'Abd ar-Rahman, the governor of al-Andalus, Islamic Spain, and called upon Charles for assistance. He won a decisive victory over the Muslims at the battle of Poitiers in 732 and, when Eudo died in 735, seized control of his duchy.

From 734 Charles ruled without a king to legitimize his decisions. At his death in 741, he bequeathed authority to his sons. One, Carloman, retired to a monastery in 747; the other, Pepin, in 751 deposed the last Merovingian and had himself crowned King Pepin III, the first of the Carolingian line. When he died in 768, his kingdom was divided between his two sons, Charles and

Riding to war in the 9th century
Joab leads his troops in this biblical battle-scene. Created for the *Psalterium Aureum* manuscript around 845, this contemporary illumination gives a colourful impression of how the Frankish cavalry would have looked.

Carloman. A struggle for power seemed inevitable, but Carloman died in 771 and his men accepted Charles as king.

The Saxon wars

In 772 Charles ("Charles the Great" or Charlemagne) led an army against the Saxons, whose incessant raids were still causing problems in the northeast. His attention was diverted to Italy in 773 where the Lombard king, Desiderius, was supporting dissident Franks and putting pressure on the papacy. Charles besieged Pavia, the capital of Lombardy, until Desiderius surrendered in June 774. Then, with papal support, Charles persuaded the Lombard dukes to name him as their new king. Meanwhile, the Saxons took advantage of his absence

The birth of Europe

Though beset by Muslims to the south and by pagan Slavs on its eastern frontier, the empire under Charlemagne grew strong and powerful in its unique alliance of Church and State.

in Italy to rise up once again, launching a series of attacks into the northern part of Hesse. Charlemagne responded with another campaign against them. Up to now, these campaigns had been punitive expeditions to keep the enemy at bay. But this began to seem unrealistic. At the royal assembly held in Quierzy, Picardy, in January 775, Charlemagne announced his plans for an invasion – subjugating the Saxons once and for all.

That summer's campaign was brutally successful. Although an advance force was defeated at the river Weser by

> **IRMINSUL** A wooden column or tree trunk on which Saxon religious worship was centred. It appears to have been seen as a pillar that propped up the sky.

Widukind, Charlemagne's main army conquered huge territories, destroying the symbols of the Saxons' pagan religion wherever he went.

Setbacks and successes

Once again Charlemagne had shown his strength over the Saxons, yet once again it all seemed set to unravel, as a revolt in the early part of 776 compelled him to march south in haste to restore his rule in northern Italy. Hardly was his back turned than the Saxons rose up in rebellion. Within a few weeks, however, Charlemagne reappeared and crushed the Lombard revolt, robbing the Saxons of their spirit. This time, they accepted his authority. He promptly reinforced it by building a fortified city named after himself: "Karlsburg" (now Paderborn) was an urban centre and a statement.

Key
- Frankish kingdom 751
- Conquests of Pepin (751–768)
- Conquests of Charlemagne (771–814)
- Regions recognizing Charlemagne as overlord, at least nominally
- Papal states (part of Holy Roman Empire)
- — Frontiers c.814
- ⚔ Battle

Charlemagne was not always able to make his authority felt so easily, however. An invasion of Muslim Spain in 778 was repulsed and ended in disgrace with his rearguard mauled by a force of Basques in the Pyrenees. Even so, he later established a secure foothold to the south of the mountain range with the capture of Barcelona in 801. Meanwhile, he had been fighting on other fronts, his invasion of Bavaria in 777 bringing him into confrontation with the Avars – steppe nomads who

Belt buckle
The Frankish sphere of influence extended beyond the borders of the empire. This buckle for a sword belt was found in Oslo, southern Norway.

dominated the Danube Valley, but whose empire was disintegrating. Yet again, however, the Saxons exploited his absences to rise up against his rule. A renewed revolt surfaced in the year 778, and though Charlemagne suppressed the uprising, it was clear that the Saxons were never simply going to acquiesce to Frankish rule. It took until 782 for the king and his Franks to re-establish their hold: a vengeful Charlemagne supposedly conducted mass-executions during the Massacre of Verden. An effort was made to stamp out pagan practices among the Saxons to ease their absorption into the Frankish state. Not until 804, after the deportation of a number of Saxons into Francia, were they finally pacified.

Fighting a new enemy

By the time Charlemagne was crowned as *Imperator* in 800, there were signs of "overstretch". Charlemagne's conquest of the Saxons had brought his empire up against the frontier of the Danes in southern Jutland. King Godfred was sending fleets to attack the northern Frankish coast. Charlemagne at first had no answer to this problem, but after Godfred was succeeded by his nephew, Hemming, in 810, the emperor was able to push him into a peace treaty through a combination of diplomatic persuasion and military force.

AFTER

> Charlemagne died in 814. Fortunately, the customary succession-struggle was avoided because he had just one surviving son, Louis the Pious, who reigned from 814.

THE SAXON SITUATION
Difficult as it had been to bring it about, the **conquest of the Saxons** was enduring. Under Charlemagne's successors they were successfully absorbed into the Frankish state as **tributaries**. The **Dukes of Saxony** eventually became kings and, from the time of Otto I (**"the Great"**) – crowned in 962 – emperors in their own right.

> **OTTONIAN** The Germanic dynasty in power as great Saxon rulers between 919 and 1024. Though descendants of the Duke of Saxony, Henry I ("the Fowler"), they were named after their first emperor, Otto the Great (912–73).

This **strongly Germanic** eastern section of the empire would, in time, part company with the western region, which had once been **Roman Gaul**. The division, agreed among Louis the Pious's sons at the **Treaty of Verdun** in 843, eventually became permanent. Even so, the Frankish heritage of this western realm was commemorated in the name of **"France"**.

REBELLIONS AND RAIDS
In the meantime, troubles continued along the Frankish empire's frontiers, with unrest among the **Slavs and Danes** on the one hand and the **Basques and Bretons** on the other. Carolingian rulers of the 9th century also faced increasing problems from **Viking raids 70–71 ≫**.

KING OF THE FRANKS (747–814)

CHARLEMAGNE

The great-grandson of Pepin II, *Carolus Magnus*, or "Charles the Great" was born in 748 and succeeded his father, Pepin III, as king in 768. His realms included much of modern-day France and the southern and western parts of Germany, as well as north and central Italy. On Christmas Day 800, Pope Leo III crowned him emperor.

Charlemagne consolidated and enlarged his empire through a number of campaigns against his enemies, who ranged from the Byzantines to the Danes, and from the Slavs to the Saxons. His remarkable efforts to make his court a centre of great learning and to raise the educational levels of the clergy within his territories led to a golden age in learning and the arts, referred to today as the "Carolingian Renaissance".

Viking Raids and the Norman Conquest

From the end of the 8th century for almost 100 years, Scandinavian shipborne attackers looted the coastal peoples of Europe and North Africa. Over time the Vikings settled down to a life of trade, but though their raiding days were behind them, they were just as formidable in war.

BEFORE

With tillable land scarce in Scandinavia, those without suffered. No land meant no livelihood – and more prosperous societies were there for the taking.

ENVIRONMENTAL FACTORS

The peoples of Scandinavia lived as farmers, keeping cattle, sheep, and pigs, and growing crops, but land was at a premium. Much of the interior was mountainous, so people clustered around the coasts and **the pressure on arable areas was intense.** Landless men without prospects at home set out to prey on other, more successful, civilizations. To the extent that, initially at least, they were impelled by environmental factors, the Vikings can be compared with **earlier raiders like the Huns ≪ 46–47**.

On 8 June 793 the great monastery on Lindisfarne, an island off England's Northumbrian coast, was sacked and pillaged in the first known Viking raid. As the monk Alcuin of York reported: "Never before has such an atrocity been seen in Britain as we have now suffered at the hands of a pagan people … The Church of St Cuthbert has been spattered with the blood of the priests of God, stripped of all its furnishings, exposed to the plunderings of the pagans." Unfortunately, such terrible, nightmarish scenes were to recur only too frequently as Viking raids became a fact of life.

Seafaring adventurers

Monastic houses were a favourite target – they had rich treasures, isolated settings, and helpless inhabitants – but ordinary towns and villages also fell prey to the brutal invaders. Danish Vikings sailed back and forth across the North Sea to eastern England. Vikings from Norway, though, took a more westerly course, stopping off at the islands of Orkney and Shetland en route for Ireland with its ancient monasteries. Vikings established bases

Viking vessel

Streamlined for speed, the longship was fast enough for its crew to be able to rely upon the advantage of surprise. Typically, it would lurk beyond the horizon, dashing for the coast once darkness fell. Some were "dragon ships", with dragon-shaped prows – a terrifying sight for unsuspecting quarry.

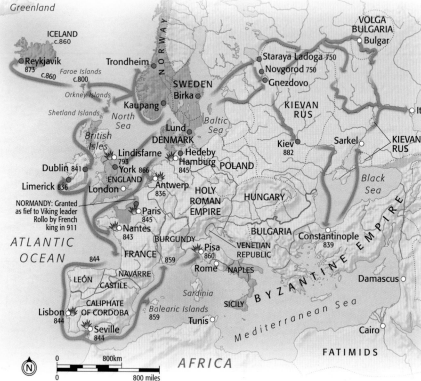

Far and wide
Whether raiding or trading, by sea or by river, the Vikings reached much of medieval Europe and Asia – and even ventured across the Atlantic.

Key
▨	Area settled by Vikings
▨	Duchy of Normandy c.1100
▨	Norman conquests by 1100
—	Frontiers c.1100
⋯	Approximate frontiers c.1100
→	Viking voyage, trade route, or raid
●	Viking settlement
❉	Town sacked by Vikings
844	Date of voyage, raid, or sacking

at Dublin and along the rivers Seine and Loire in France where they could wait out the winter, ready to resume raiding with the onset of spring.

The Vikings were skilled seafarers. While some headed westward across the Atlantic, setting up colonies in Iceland, Greenland, and ultimately North America, others explored the warmer waters of the south. The 9th century saw raids along the coasts of Spain, Morocco, and even the Canary Islands. Swedish Vikings, meanwhile, had ventured to the Black Sea.

Ambitious incursions

In 860 Vikings raided Constantinople. However, they primarily came to the Byzantine metropolis in peace in order to find a market for the slaves they had captured on their journey south. In fact, they brought so many Eastern

European captives to the city for sale that the Greek word *sklabos* (Slav) was adopted as the general word for "slave". Many Vikings hired themselves out to the Byzantines as mercenaries, forming an elite unit, the Varangian Guard. Increasingly, war-parties banded

> **BESERK** Sometimes a Viking, crazed by the excitement of battle, would tear off his "sark", or tunic, and fight barechested – hence the expression, going "beserk".

together for more ambitious raids. In 991 a fleet of over 90 longships appeared off the coast of Folkestone in southeast

Viking axe

A badge of wealth and status, a Viking's battle-axe was often ornate. These sharp-bladed weapons were deadly – one blow could kill instantly.

Inlaid blade

England. It landed an army of up to 3,000 men – including both Norwegian and Danish Vikings. Marching up to Maldon in Essex, a trail of destruction in their wake, they finally defeated an Anglo-Saxon militia force led by Ealdorman Byrhtnoth. The invaders soon withdrew on payment of a large ransom but not before the Anglo-Saxon leader was killed.

Warrior kingdoms

The Vikings were not just raiders, they were also highly formidable in larger-scale, static warfare – though they were always individualistic in

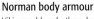

Norman body armour

Vikings seldom bothered with armour, but the Normans did. As the Bayeux Tapestry shows, the Normans wore chainmail *hauberks* that came down to the knees, with a split in the chain to facilitate riding.

their fighting style. Their battle-axes, swords, and circular, hide-covered wooden shields were items of immense prestige – often beautifully worked and richly adorned – while their owners had intimidatory war names (Erik Bloodaxe; Björn Ironside; Ragnar Hairy-Breeks) and had heroic poems composed about them by their bards.

Men who came as raiders began to stay as settlers, as the Anglo-Saxon Chronicle for 876 records: "In this year Halfdan shared out the lands of Northumbria, and they started to plough and make a living for themselves." The Vikings were beginning to behave more like conventional conquerors. In the late 9th century Olav Tryggvason made a kingdom out of Norway, while early in the 11th century King Cnut the Great joined Norway and Denmark with England to form a Nordic empire.

Norsemen to Normans

Meanwhile, Norwegian Vikings or Norsemen (the name "Normans" comes from Norsemen) had started to put down permanent roots in France, adopting the language, culture, and Christian religion. The Normans kept their longships but took up the French way of fighting, most obviously in their use of armour and heavy cavalry, as the events of 1066 would show.

On the 28 September that year, certain the English throne was his, William of Normandy (the Conqueror) launched a fleet of 700 ships, landing a formidable army on England's south coast. King Harold's English army had been forced to march from Yorkshire, where just days before it had fought off Harald Hardrada, the Norwegian king.

On 14 October, Harold ranged his troops at the top of Senlac Hill, near Hastings. William ordered his forces to feign retreat before Harold's Anglo-Saxon army. The ploy enticed the English down from their advantageous position to the boggy ground below, where they were at the mercy of William's cavalry. Even so, the struggle continued for hours, and might easily have ended differently had Harold not fatally fallen. By nightfall, victory for William was complete, and the English throne was his.

Another Norman was meanwhile establishing himself in Italy. In the 1030s Norman armies had gone to assist the

Byzantines, who had wanted to rid their westernmost possessions of Arab usurpers. Having arrived as mercenaries, the Normans came back as conquerors, wresting these vulnerable territories from Byzantine rule. It was Robert Guiscard who won what turned into an unseemly struggle of Norman warlords, and carved out a kingdom for himself in Sicily and southern Italy.

AFTER

As the generations passed, Scandinavia's peoples began to move away from the policy of plunder. Increasingly, they were drawn into European society.

PEACEFUL TRADERS

In time, as the **Scandinavians became Northern Europe's medieval merchant navy**, the dreaded "dragon ship" made way for the shorter, rounder *knarr*. The merchant navy followed the same routes as their raiding ancestors; now, though, they came peacefully as traders, transporting goods such as timber, weapons, ivory, and furs.

NORMAN EVOLUTION

The strong state the Normans had built in England fell apart in the "Anarchy" of the 12th century. The French House of Anjou took the throne as **the Plantagenet line 102–03 》**.

228,000 The number of coins – many of them Arab dirhams – found buried in Viking hoards, testimony to the value of Viking trade in the east.

During that time, the successors of Robert Guiscard had created a buoyant and prosperous multicultural kingdom in Sicily, in which Norman, Byzantine, and Arabic influences came together in a complex fusion.

> **"There was no village inhabited** between York and Durham.**"**
>
> SIMEON OF DURHAM ON THE HAVOC THE NORMANS WROUGHT, 11TH CENTURY

NORMAN MOTTE-AND-BAILEY CASTLE

The Normans built many "instant castles" on campaign by what was known as the motte-and-bailey method. First, a *motte*, or "mound of earth", was constructed (or an existing rise or outcrop used) with a wooden stronghold, or "keep", erected on top. A "curtain wall" was then placed around the motte, enclosing an open area, or "bailey", in which arms could be stored and horses grazed. These forts could be assembled almost overnight and later rebuilt in stone.

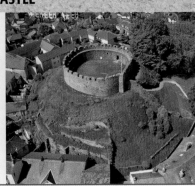

BEFORE ◀◀

The Turks originated in the remote steppes of Central Asia, and they were to have an important impact on the affairs of the West over many centuries.

NOMADIC MIGRATIONS

The many different Turkic peoples formed small and scattered **nomadic groups**. Their lifestyle was prone to instability, as competition for water and pasture could be intense. Historically, in **Central Asia**, such environmental stresses have prompted **mass-migrations** of the sort that saw **the Huns pushing westward into Europe ❮❮ 46–47** in ancient times.

30 The approximate number of Turkic languages still spoken today. There are six main branches within the Turkic language family.

UNREST IN THE MIDDLE EAST

Arab conquests ❮❮ 64–65 had transformed the Middle East and Persia, but by the beginning of the 9th century, **the first shockwaves** were subsiding. The **Abbasid dynasty** held nominal sovereignty over Islam's dominions, but **local warlords** were starting to assert themselves.

THE RISE OF THE GHULAM

The end of the first millennium brought a **new wave of migration**, propelling Islamicized Turks into the region, many of them enslaved by the region's rulers. **Skilled fighters**, with nothing invested in the rivalries and conflicts of the Middle East, these *ghulams* (slave-soldiers) served with unquestioning loyalty.

SOUTHWEST AND CENTRAL ASIA

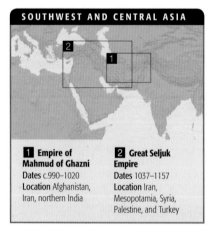

1 Empire of
Mahmud of Ghazni
Dates c.990–1020
Location Afghanistan,
Iran, northern India

2 Great Seljuk
Empire
Dates 1037–1157
Location Iran,
Mesopotamia, Syria,
Palestine, and Turkey

Seljuk mace head
Beautifully decorated with flowing foliage and fine calligraphy, this bronze mace head has raised fins to focus the impact of any blow. The mace is stereotypically seen as a Western weapon – in contrast to the Eastern scimitar – but the idea may well have reached Europe through the crusades.

The Rise of the Turks

The Turks who appeared in the Middle East during the 9th century were outsiders and slaves, but they were to exercise a powerful influence upon the region's history and, ultimately, upon that of Europe. Various Turkish empires were repeatedly to alarm Byzantium until, finally, they triggered the crusades.

The Arab invasions of the 7th and 8th centuries left an enduring legacy. Through much of the area they conquered, the Arabic influence – and Islam – still prevail today. Yet the Arab nobility itself was less secure. By the end of the 9th century, it had survived not only the wars surrounding the split between Sunni and Shi'a (over who was the rightful successor to the prophet Muhammad), but also the overthrow of Damascus' Umayyad dynasty by the Baghdad-based Abbasid caliphate (the caliphs saw themselves as the earthly enforcers of Allah's heavenly will). Whether now exhausted by centuries of conflict, or simply spread too thinly over such vast dominions, the Arab nobility was growing weaker and its authority increasingly ignored.

Soldiers of the Samanids

In Iran, especially, regional identities had been reasserting themselves and local families were once again coming to the fore. In the east, in the early 9th century, the Samanid dynasty had arisen among the Tajik peoples, establishing an empire that extended into Afghanistan, Uzbekistan, and present-day Pakistan. All this time nomadic Turks were drifting into the region from Central Asia: converted to Islam by the Samanids, many were recruited as slave-soldiers, or *ghulams*. Like the other nomadic peoples of the Central Asian steppe, the Turks were superlative horsemen and seasoned fighters, expert with the composite bow and with the sword. (They were armed with straight

Building alliances
Indian delegates are received at the court of Mahmud of Ghazni. Not just a conqueror but a diplomat, Mahmud was skilled in fashioning alliances and in making the enmities of others work to his advantage.

swords, rather than the curved scimitar of later times, and may also have carried spears or lances.)

The *ghulams* served the Samanids well: so much so that they became indispensable, and it was not long before leading families among them were wielding a great deal of power. By the 10th century, in Khurasan (an area including the east of Iran, the Bukhara region of Uzbekistan, and much of Afghanistan) the Simjurids had gone their own way, governing all but independently of their masters. In turn, this breakaway state was soon taken over by a rival *ghulam* dynasty, the Ghaznavids, their name deriving from the city of Ghazni, where their founder, Alpi Tigin, had made his headquarters in 962.

Meanwhile, to the west of the empire, the Abbasid caliphs of Baghdad had also recruited Turkic *ghulams* and were coming under mounting pressure from their supposed slaves. In the event, the caliphs managed to prevent a coup by the *ghulams* – but only by seeking the help (and by submitting to the bullying) of the Buyids, a dynasty of Iranian warlords

from Daylam, a mountainous region to the south of the Caspian Sea.

The Buyids deposed the caliph and ruled in their own right, but they in turn started to be undermined by warlords in the regions. In the end these territories were conquered by the Ghaznavids, who were very much in the ascendant now, especially during the reign of Mahmud of Ghazni (997–1030). At his death, the ruler left behind an empire extending from the Zagros Mountains (western Iran) to the river Indus (in Pakistan). Regular raiding east into India assured a steady flow of booty that underwrote a golden age of architecture, art, and culture. The Ghaznavids were to be overthrown in their turn by yet another influx of Turkic nomads newly arrived from the Central Asian steppe – the Seljuk Turks.

Seljuk and his successors

The Seljuk Turks gained their name because they had originally come together under the leadership of Seljuk, a charismatic warlord. They cannot be seen as a "people" or a "nation" in the normal sense. Towards the end of

> ## "[The Armenians saw] these **strange men**, who were armed with bows and had **flowing hair like women**."
> THE CHRONICLER, MATTHEW OF EDESSA, ON THE SELJUK TURKS' ADVANCE INTO ARMENIA, 1064

the 10th century, Seljuk, leader of the Kinik clan, had set himself up at the head of the Oghuz Confederation. This brought together a large number of nomadic communities who until then had been living in the Syr basin, an area of open grassland to the north and east of the Aral Sea. It was a loose and opportunistic alliance, formed for the purposes of conquest and plunder. It was big and powerful, however: Seljuk attracted hundreds of adherents.

Even so, the Seljuk Turks might have remained simply one more of many such raggle-taggle warbands roaming the western steppe had Seljuk himself not been impressed and inspired by the teachings of Muslim missionaries. All of his followers embraced Islam, and when his grandsons, Tugril Beg and Chagri, began their first raids on the northern frontier of the Ghaznavid empire, they did so with the justification that they were fighting in the prophet's name.

However, Mahmud of Ghazni's son, Mas'ud I, saw himself as the champion of Islam. He marched out to meet the interlopers with a mighty army, some 50,000 strong. As this formidable force marched northward, the Seljuks jabbed and harried, cutting off enemy supplies and preventing access to strategic wells.

And they were ready for a full-scale confrontation when the time came. The two armies clashed at Dandankan (now in eastern Turkmenistan), on 23 May 1040. Dehydrated, hungry, and demoralized, Mahmud's men were defeated before the order came to engage. The massacre that followed was a mere formality: though outnumbered by more than two to one, the Seljuks cut the Ghaznavids to ribbons.

Holy war

The Dandankan victory opened up a way to the west, heading over the Ghaznavid empire and beyond into Iraq. Tugril Beg seized Baghdad in 1055, taking the enfeebled Abbasid caliph under his "protection". The Seljuk Sultans (as they now referred to themselves) expected to rule jointly with the caliphs. The Great Seljuk empire was dedicated to the strictest principles of Sunni Islam and to the punishment of infidels of every kind.

To Arp Aslan, Tugril Beg's nephew and (on his uncle's death in 1063) his successor, that included both Christian Byzantium and the Shiite Fatimid

Masud's minaret

This magnificent minaret was built by the Ghaznavid Sultan, Masud III, in around 1100. Wooden cushions between the tiers of brick afforded some protection from earthquakes.

dynasty then ruling Egypt. He took Armenia from the Christians in 1064, and invaded the Byzantine empire four years later, occupying much of Anatolia (present-day Turkey). Arp Aslan then took Syria, invading Palestine, Egypt, and even Arabia itself in a bid to "liberate" the two holy sanctuaries of Mecca and Medina from Shiite rule. The closer these supposedly "pagan" Seljuk Turks came to Europe through

> **SULTAN** A Turkish king or emperor. The word was originally Arabic and meant "strength" or "authority". The Seljuks were the first to use it as a regal title.

their campaign of conquest, the more anxious Christendom became. When Arp Aslan then destroyed the Byzantine army at the battle of Manzikert in 1071 (present-day Malazgirt in Turkey), the West was in the grip of something close to panic.

Reaction

The Byzantine emperor, Romanus IV, had an army of up to 60,000 warriors at his disposal. Such vast numbers ought, in theory, to have made short work of the Turkish cavalry force that,

Warrior relief

Seljuk infantrymen prepare to enter into battle in this carved Turkish relief from the 13th century.

at most, numbered only 20,000 men. But Arp Aslan's warriors were battle-hardened. They were also bound to one another by ties of comradeship and loyalty that were simply lacking in the Byzantine army, as its members comprised a motley assortment of Frankish, Norman, Bulgarian, and German mercenaries.

The extent of disunity among the Byzantine troops became clear when, as evening approached after an initial and inconclusive round of fighting, the Byzantine leader gave the order to withdraw. A rational decision – but a communications breakdown brought disaster. Fearing that their commander had sensed defeat and was trying to

Malik Shah holds court

Arp Aslan's son, Malik Shah, succeeded him in 1072, advancing the work his father had begun at Manzikert by taking most of Anatolia from the Byzantines. He also furthered the cause of Sunni Islam during his reign.

save his own skin, the majority of the soldiers turned and fled the battlefield in abject rout. Arp Aslan's army streamed after them.

In the years that followed, Muslim Turks overran Anatolia, fundamentally transforming what had been a Christian land with a Hellenistic culture. Now the Middle East was Islamic, and the stage was set for one of the great showdown struggles of the medieval age.

AFTER

The rise of the Seljuk Turks caused great consternation in the Christian West. Always regarded with suspicion, Islam was now seen as a direct threat.

CHRISTIAN CRUSADES

The Seljuk **capture of Jerusalem** from the Fatimids in 1073 was of symbolic rather than strategic importance for the West, but for a fearful Christendom it seemed the final straw. Hence the eruption of support when, in 1095 at the Council of Clermont, **Pope Urban II** proclaimed the **First Crusade 74–75 »**.

CONTINUED DISTURBANCES

Meanwhile, the flow of nomadic invaders was set to continue, giving rise not just to the **Mongol invasions 80–81 »** and the wars of **Kublai Khan 84–85 »** but a second wave of Turks, the **Ottomans 106–07 »**. Slave-soldiers also continued to play a part in the history of war when the **Egyptian Mamelukes 76–77 »** seized power in Egypt in the 13th century.

THE SELJUK EMPIRE SPLITS

In 1092, following **Malik Shah's death**, one son, Kalij Arslan I, founded the "Sultanate of Rum" – so-called because its Anatolian territories had been taken from the Byzantines or Romans. His brothers established realms in Syria and Persia: the Seljuks were no longer the **monolithic menace** they once seemed to the crusaders.

Eye slit   Hinged visor

Crusader's "helm"
A flat-topped "pot helm", or casque, enclosed the crusader's whole head, protecting against enemy arrows and crossbow-bolts. The helmet's hinged visor and cheekbone-protectors form a cross.

«
BEFORE

The advent of the Seljuk Turks threw the entire Middle East into a state of turmoil, but the effects were felt throughout Christian Europe as well.

A POWER UNDER SIEGE
Islam had already made significant inroads into continental Europe, underlining what was already a widespread feeling that Christendom was

> **CRUSADE** From the Latin word *crux* meaning "cross", a military campaign on behalf of the Christian faith.

under siege. Despite suffering a setback against the Franks at Poitiers, **the Muslim Moors were well-established through much of Spain «« 64–65**. The Turkish win at Manzikert, though obviously a blow for Byzantium, **sent shockwaves through the Christian world at large «« 72–73**. Constantinople was clinging on, but its wider empire had inexorably been whittled away by the conquests first of the Arabs and then of the Seljuk Turks.

RECLAIMING THE HOLY SITES
The capture of Jerusalem by the Turks in 1073 was of no significance in itself (the city had already been in Islamic hands). However, when the Byzantines appealed to Pope Urban II for assistance, he found the idea of a military expedition or crusade to **recover the "Holy Places" for Christian pilgrims** the perfect rallying point for a wider attack on Islamic power.

The First Crusades

A detached Christendom united in the crusades, the wars to recover the "Holy Places" of Jerusalem held by Muslims for more than 400 years. Crusading quickly became both an organizing ideal and a way of warring life: tens of thousands of people across Europe set out to win salvation through soldiering.

At the Council of Clermont in 1095, Pope Urban II called on all Christians to join the fight for their holy faith, describing the plight of Christian Byzantium, its dominions overrun by a "godless" rabble that was an impending threat to the Western world. He finished his impassioned speech with the cry *"Deus hoc vult!"* (God wills this). His speech roused ardour with its promise of eternal salvation for those who enlisted; it also fired a greed for territories and plunder. Cheers erupted and in the weeks that followed this enthusiasm spread across Europe, among rich and poor. Thousands pinned crosses of red fabric to their tunics to show their allegiance to the cause of Christ: the "First Crusade" was as much a pilgrimage as an all-out war.

But this popularity posed problems. Though highly enthusiastic, the army that gathered in Constantinople for the assault on the Holy Land was disorganized, untrained, and very poorly provisioned.

The crusaders were mostly French, the pope having earlier argued with Germany's emperor, Henry IV. The French nobility

expected to fight as heavy cavalry themselves but had brought very large companies of infantrymen armed with swords, shields, and bows.

The excited mood was quickly sobered by the searing sun and rugged terrain of Anatolia's mountains – Seljuk Turk territory. Of the 100,000 soldiers who set out from Constantinople, only 40,000 reached Antioch in Syria. Those who did, in October 1097, found a city built – and fortified – on an intimidating scale. The crusaders settled down for a siege, although, marooned in hostile

territory, they were actually under a sort of siege themselves. Many had died of starvation and disease by the time Antioch fell on 2 June 1098.

The crusader kingdoms
It was a severely weakened army – only 12,000 in number now – that marched on to Jerusalem, and the prospect of another extended siege. In the event, it took the men only a few months to find their way through Jerusalem's defences. They celebrated with a spree of violence and destruction. The crusaders then had

Ways of the cross
Any crusade represented an enormous logistical challenge for a medieval army. From the Second crusade onwards, most voyaged to the Holy Land by sea. Louis IX sought to approach it from the south, through Egypt.

Key
- ▪ Western Christendom c.1096
- ▪ Orthodox Church c.1096
- ▪ Islamic lands c.1096
- — Frontiers of crusader states
- ➡ Routes of First Crusade
- ➡ Routes of Second Crusade
- ✕ Major battle or siege

KEY MOMENT
THE CAPTURE OF JERUSALEM, 1099

The Fatimid defenders had successfully resisted the crusaders' siege of Jerusalem for several weeks and looked capable of holding out indefinitely. But the Christians took their ships apart and used the ropes and wood to construct two enormous siege towers. The Muslims were unfamiliar with such equipment and were undecided how to proceed until, on 15 July, the first group of attackers managed to swarm across onto the city walls. Quickly overpowering the guards, they opened the gates and let their remaining comrades in to commence their orgy of bloodshed. More than 30,000 Jews and Muslims are believed to have been slaughtered in the following three days. "In the Temple and the Porch of Solomon," boasted Raymond of Aguiles, "men rode in blood up to their knees and bridle reins."

to secure their prize. They set up a series of states across Syria and Palestine, including the County of Edessa in Armenia, the Principality of Antioch in Syria, and the Kingdom of Jerusalem. A County of Tripoli (in what is now Lebanon) was added in 1104, with a "military order" of soldier-priests set up in 1120 to help protect the Holy Places. The priests were named the Knights Templar after the Temple of Jerusalem.

Though the Temple of Jerusalem and other monuments were now in Christian hands, the territory outside Jerusalem was less firmly held. Hence the formation of the Hospitallers. These people had long been caring for the sick in Jerusalem, but by the 1130s it was clear that pilgrims needed more hostile protection – the knights became their armed escorts. They too were militarized as the Order of the Knights Hospitallers, and would build the city's defenses.

As the fighting continued – mainly in the form of small-scale skirmishes and raids – the limitations of the Western

Symbol of the Knights Templar
The seal of the Knights Templar depicts two knights on one horse – legend has it that this is a sign of the order's early poverty.

way became apparent. A knight's heavy armour was an uncomfortable hindrance in the heat, and the wearer was easily outmanoeuvred by the swifter, more lightly armed Muslims. Arab cavalry wore no armour, relying on speed and agility, while the *ghulam* (armoured slave-soldiers) brought the battle to the enemy on their own terms.

Muslim fightback

The retaking of the County of Edessa by the Seljuks in 1145 came as a shock. Pope Eugenius III's call for a Second Crusade was largely ignored, until it was taken up by the popular French abbot, Bernard of Clairvaux; then France's King Louis VII and Conrad III of Germany followed. Conrad III's

contingent set off from Constantinople but suffered a shattering defeat at Dorylaeum, in southern Turkey, in 1147. What was left of his army met up with the French who, coming by sea, had now landed safely. But bickering between the new arrivals and the established crusaders compromised their mission: the siege of Damascus in 1148 broke down and the Second Crusade ended in disarray.

The Muslims now had the initiative; they were also fired by the spirit of *jihad*, reignited by their outrage at this second invasion by the West. Their struggle was renewed and at last, under the Kurdish leader, Salah al-Din or "Saladin".

Outmanoeuvred

The army of Ilghazi of Mardin trounced the crusaders at the battle of Ager Sanguinis ("The Field of Blood") in 1119. The heavily-armed Christians laboured in the heat and dust of the Middle East.

AFTER ⟫

The First Crusade was a success for the Christians but the Muslims were on the ascent. Further battles between the two would breed lasting suspicion.

A PERMANENT LEGACY
A breakdown of relations with Byzantium left the crusaders reliant on seaborne supplies, making the securing of coastal bridgeheads vital. Further expeditions were needed if the Christian presence in the Middle East was to be maintained.

Despite the best efforts of the Christians, the Muslims were in the ascendant. The West's military shortcomings were to be cruelly exposed at the **battle of Hattin 76–77** ⟫, allowing the Turks to retake Jerusalem in 1187.

After initial success, the crusading movement had **succeeded only in building rancour** between Christians and Muslims. The outright conflict, which was resolved only by the West's **victory at Lepanto 124–25** ⟫, was to leave a lasting legacy of distrust.

Expulsion of the Crusaders from the Holy Land

Saladin's recapture of Jerusalem in 1187 came as a shattering disappointment. The self-confidence of Christian Europe had been badly dented. Further crusades were mounted in the years that followed, but a series of humiliating failures left the West feeling defeated and demoralized.

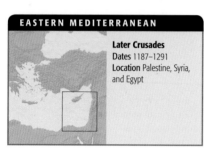

EASTERN MEDITERRANEAN

Later Crusades
Dates 1187–1291
Location Palestine, Syria, and Egypt

« BEFORE

The capture of Jerusalem in 1099 had been an undoubted triumph for the West. But the Holy Land was a long journey from Europe and Islamic opposition was growing.

NEW LEADERS EMERGE
The First Crusade had come to a climactic end with the **capture of Jerusalem in 1099** « 74–75. Most Christian believers felt that their mission had been accomplished, but their leaders knew that **without control of the hinterland, the Holy City was vulnerable.** Fighting continued and, as time went on, it grew harder to see how the Christian presence in the Middle East was to be maintained. To make matters worse, a **new generation of energetic Muslim leaders**, like the Emir of Syria, Nur ad-Din, and Saladin, were coming to the fore.

> After Saladin's capture of Jerusalem in 1187, Henry II imposed a "Saladin Tithe" in England to fund a crusade that, in the event, never took place.

ISLAM RESURGENT
Nur ad-Din had worked hard to unite Islam after the collapse of the Second Crusade, inspiring his followers with **a cold-blooded determination to drive out the infidels.** As far as Syria went, **he succeeded**. In 1157 he had confined the Knights Hospitallers to their fortress and destroyed the army that marched out from Jerusalem to relieve them. In 1162 he captured Raynald de Chatillon, Prince of Antioch (he was to hold him prisoner for 16 years).

Saladin was ultimately Nur ad-Din's rival (the two had came close to open war), and **shared Nur ad-Din's overriding aims**: Saladin was also a politician of rare talent and a general of genius.

An anthology of ancient Bedouin poetry by the 9th-century Arab poet, Abbu Tammam, records the words: "the sword is truer than what is told in books. In its edge is the separation between truth and falsehood." One man who carried this volume wherever he went was Salah al-Din, famous as a warrior yet a reader and thinker too. Born in Tikrit, Iraq, of Kurdish ancestry, he had risen in the service of Egypt's Fatimid caliphs; by 1131 he had set himself up as sultan, founding his own dynasty, the Ayyubids. The following years saw him extending that power as he cut a swathe through the crusader states, finally taking Jerusalem in 1187, but he always saw himself as fighting in the service of the truth.

Kings in conflict
An unusual figure by any standard, "Saladin" was a leader of extraordinary magnetism: he impressed his enemies as much as he inspired his followers. The Third Crusade, declared within a few weeks of Saladin's recapture of Jerusalem, is often referred to as the "Crusade of Kings"; it is so-called because it was led by kings Richard the Lionheart of England, Philip II of France, and Frederick I of Germany. Frederick I set off in 1188, months before his fellow monarchs, and drowned while crossing a river in Anatolia en route to the Holy Land. His successor, Leopold V of Austria, was unable to take charge effectively in the ensuing panic and a huge German army was practically wiped out. Leopold made it through, but with only a few thousand troops he could do little to help the crusader king, Guy of Jerusalem, who was bogged down in a stalemate with Saladin outside Acre.

The port city was important to the Christians, who could not anticipate holding on to Jerusalem (in the event of their retaking it) without some safe way of bringing in supplies. Not until 1191 did Philip and Richard arrive: the reinforcements they brought with them were decisive and Acre was taken.

Iron helmet

Protective sleeve

KING OF ENGLAND (1157–1199)

RICHARD I

By the time Richard I was 16 his father Henry II had entrusted the young king with the command of his own army, sent to crush a rebellion against his rule in France. His valour earned him a French nickname: *Coeur de Lion* or "Lionheart". He met his match in Saladin, however, and, for all his determination and dazzling generalship, his Third Crusade was at best only partially successful. To this day, Richard remains one of England's most celebrated kings.

Relations between Richard and Saladin were amicable at first but the situation deteriorated when – apparently certain that the Saracen leader was tricking him – the English king had 2,700 Muslim prisoners killed. Saladin reciprocated with mass executions of his Christian prisoners. But there was also rancour

Saracen armour
A suit of chain mail in the style of a Saracen warrior of the crusader period. Medieval armour was flexible and could be relatively light to wear, and provided good protection both from thrusts and slashing strokes.

Padding underneath the chain mail helped deflect arrows, while a kaftan on top allowed the wearer to be recognized – and prevented his metallic armour from overheating in the sun.

within the Christian camp. Unable to agree with Richard over how to proceed next, Leopold returned home; while Philip II had to leave following reports of unrest back in France.

The road to Arsuf
This left Richard alone at the head of the Third Crusade, he was undaunted, however, planning his mission in great detail. On 22 August 1191 he left Acre, marching his army south to where they could find food and water. Progress was slow: they were harried by Saladin's mounted archers, but Richard's bowmen maintained their own hail of arrows to keep the attackers at bay.

To their right, the cavalry were able to make progress relatively safely, while up ahead the baggage train lurched along, shielded by both the infantry and horses. Meanwhile, their ships tracked them down the coast to fend off any potential threat from the seaward side. Under Richard's leadership, his men remained calm as they inched along.

The king's aims, in fact, went further than keeping his army intact: he hoped that his apparently beleaguered situation would tempt the enemy into a full-scale charge. On 7 September, at Arsuf, north of Jaffa, the pressure from Saladin's forces became so unrelentingly intense that the Christian Knights Hospitallers could tolerate no more and, in their mounting frustration, broke first. Even now Richard remained in control of the

> "[Richard the Lionheart] was **courageous, energetic, and daring** in combat."

MUSLIM CHRONICLER BAHA AL-DIN, 12TH CENTURY

situation, his generalship turning certain defeat into triumph – albeit not the definitive victory he had desired. The result was inconclusive. Saladin and his army of Saracens had suffered a disastrous setback; Richard the Lionheart's reputation had been boosted, though it was difficult to see any tangible benefits from his victory. He himself was recalled to England soon after, having failed to win back the holy city of Jerusalem from the Saracens.

The Christians would have to keep fighting – and some were reaping huge rewards. When the Fourth Crusade was

20,000 **The number of knights taken by King Andrew II of Hungary on the Fifth Crusade. Each knight, in turn, had a party of foot soldiers. It is believed to have been the largest crusading army ever.**

called in 1199, Enrico Dandolo, the Venetian Doge, made sure that Venice, which provided much of the water-borne transport, earned a lot of money. And Genoa's rulers were little better in their profiteering. The Fourth Crusade was to have a hideous conclusion when the fleet diverted to Constantinople and its Christian troops sacked the city, killing many thousands as they burned and looted for three full days.

The final battles
The Fifth Crusade (1217–21) took a novel approach: the idea was to attack through Ayyubid Egypt. Bogged down and beaten, the Christians never reached the Holy Land. In 1228 the Sixth Crusade saw Germany's king Frederick II diplomatically negotiate the return of Jerusalem, though the concessions he made outraged his fellow Europeans. The Holy City was in any case retaken a few years later. The last great flowering

of the crusading ideal came with the Seventh Crusade, escorted by King Louis IX (St Louis) of France. Again, the idea was to attack from the west, through Egypt. Louis took with him an army of 15,000, including his mounted knights, his regular infantry, and crossbowmen. After a hopeful start, however, Louis's force was defeated by an army led by Baibars, the Mameluk sultan. The king and his entire company were taken prisoner and an enormous ransom was demanded for the restoration of the monarch.

In 1270, unfazed, Louis embarked on an Eighth Crusade, but only made it to Tunis, where he died. A Ninth Crusade led by England's Edward I began the following year, but Edward fared rather less well against the Mameluks.

A series of ignominious failures had left Europe exhausted, demoralized, and disenchanted with the crusading dream; yet it managed to find a new focus.

HERETICS EXECUTED IN FRANCE

GROWING INFLUENCE
Christendom's rulers launched "crusades" against the pagan Slavs on their eastern borders, as well as Orthodox Christians in the Balkans. **Cathars, Hussites, and other heretic groups were also targeted 94–95 ».** The "military orders" still prospered – in some cases they had gained great wealth and power – but the Knights Templar was finally disbanded in 1305. Meanwhile, Islam's influence grew; still the Turks came in from the eastern steppe.

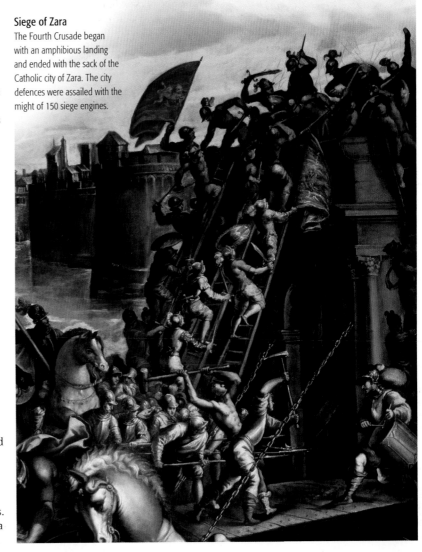

Siege of Zara
The Fourth Crusade began with an amphibious landing and ended with the sack of the Catholic city of Zara. The city defences were assailed with the might of 150 siege engines.

Warrior Saint

A true saint and a true soldier, King Louis IX of France personified the crusading movement in all its idealistic ardour, its heroism, and its haplessness. His piety could not be doubted, and his personal kindness was legendary, yet he burned with rage to see the Holy Places of Jerusalem in Islamic hands. Twice he led by example, setting out on crusades to fight the Muslims. But the Seventh Crusade was ultimately a disaster and the Eighth ended prematurely with his death.

By the time Louis IX ascended the throne of France, there had been no fewer than six crusades. Only the first had been an unqualified success. Perhaps it now took a visionary to continue to believe in the crusading ideal. A boy of 12 when he was crowned in 1226, he reigned with the guidance of his mother for the first few years, and retained a certain childlike innocence all his life.

In 1239 Louis spent a fortune buying what was believed to be a fragment of the "True Cross" – the cross on which Christ had been crucified – and the "Crown of Thorns" that Christ's tormentors had forced him to wear. To house these holy relics in Paris, he built the stunning Saint Chapelle. One of France's greatest Gothic churches, it was a riot of extravagant vaulting and stained glass. But if Louis liked grand gestures, he was also portrayed as a humble Christian: contemporary representations show him kneeling to wash the feet of his poorest subjects.

The young king

Louis' youth seemed an open invitation to France's power-hungry barons. But his tough and determined way with a series of rebels made it clear that – pious or not – he was no

Not peace but the sword
On a weapon fit for a crusading king, the stylized three-petalled *fleurs de lys* symbolize the French royal virtues of faith, wisdom, and chivalry, as well as the Holy Trinity.

weakling. He won a reputation for decisive leadership and physical courage. Things took a more worrying turn when one rebel, Hugh of Lusignan, allied himself with Henry III of England, but Louis defeated them at Taillebourg in western France in 1242.

Two Jerusalems

Two years later, as he recovered from a bout of malaria, Louis learned that Jerusalem was back in Muslim hands. Emperor Frederick II had negotiated its return in 1228, but now Egypt's Ayyubid rulers had retaken it. Louis' barons must have felt he was still delirious when he proclaimed a Seventh Crusade.

The visionary and the soldier came together in Louis' career as a crusader. His ultimate ambition was to build a "New Jerusalem" in France. The coming of this "heaven-on-earth" is prophesied in the New Testament Book of Revelation. Louis hoped that he and his people might show themselves worthy of the New Jerusalem by recapturing the old one.

Louis' first crusade

Once again, the dreamer proved determined: by 1248 Louis had assembled an army of 3,000 knights, 5,000 crossbowmen, and 7,000 foot soldiers. They sailed from the port of Aigues-Mortes in southern France, specially rebuilt for the purpose, via Cyprus, to Damietta, in the Nile Delta. Louis aimed to establish a bridgehead here before approaching Jerusalem and the Holy Land from the south.

Christian soldier

Contemporary chronicles see no conflict between Louis' pious humility and his kingly pride, nor between his roles as a believer and as a battler for Christ. To help finance his crusades, he confiscated money from the Jews.

Reliquary crown
This jewel-encrusted crown was presented by St Louis to a Dominican convent in Liège. It once contained relics of the "True Cross" and fragments of the bones of Christian martyrs. It is on display in the Louvre, Paris.

Archangel with holy scripture

The crusaders took Damietta in 1249, only to be caught out by the annual Nile flood. When they finally managed to make their move, in April 1250, their army was pinned down by the Sultan of Egypt's forces, and then almost annihilated at the battle of Fariskur. Despite leading with great distinction in the field, Louis's strategic planning left much to be desired. He was captured, along with his two brothers, and an enormous ransom had to be paid for his return. On his release, he spent time in the Holy Land, helping to refortify cities against Muslim attack.

Last crusade and death

Back in France, Louis' spirit was undimmed. In 1267 he called another crusade directed against the powerful new rulers of Egypt, the Mamelukes. This time, he started further to the west. In July 1270, he landed his army at Tunis and besieged the city, but, after drinking contaminated water, Louis fell sick and died on 25 August. Many of his soldiers suffered the same fate, and the crusade was abandoned. Yet, for all his failures, his idealism had been an inspiration to his contemporaries. He was canonized in 1297.

"I have warned you many times … The **armies that obey me** cover mountains and plains, they are **as numerous as the pebbles of the earth,** and they march upon you **grasping the swords of fate."**

LETTER FROM LOUIS IX TO THE AYYUBID SULTAN OF EGYPT AT THE START OF THE SEVENTH CRUSADE, 1248

French crusaders
French kings had a long tradition of crusading. Here, Louis' great-grandfather, Louis VII, is shown embarking from Cyprus on the Second Crusade in 1148.

Japan's Gempei Wars

With its feuding families, its warring samurai, and its epic scale, the story of the Gempei Wars (1180–85) has the ring of heroic myth. Yet the conflict convulsed Japan for five terrible years, leaving a lasting historical and cultural legacy. Moreover, it transformed the country's military institutions and attitudes.

Samurai warfare
Minamoto and Taira fight in a flurry of swirling banners and flashing *tachi* swords. Some ride into battle, lances levelled like Western knights, but most have dismounted and engage in single combat.

Simmering since the humiliation of the Heiji Rebellion three years before, the wrath of the Minamoto boiled over in 1180. Taira no Kiyomori, having first forced Emperor Takakura to abdicate, had installed his one-year-old grandson on the throne. The Minamoto figurehead, Prince Mochihito, was the half-brother of Takakura and was angry at being cheated out of the succession.

Taira no Kiyomori issued orders for Mochihoto's arrest. Minamoto Yorimasa and his samurai set off to spirit him to safety. The Taira caught up with them: Prince Mochihito was put to death, but Minamoto Yorimasa avoided capture

> ## "I put my neck to the sword. Its cut is but a **breath of wind**."
> **POEM COMPOSED BY THE SAMURAI SUKETOMO BEFORE COMMITTING "SEPPUKU"**

took fright, assuming it was a surprise attack: though superior in strength, the men were unnerved and fled. In 1181, at Sunomatagawa, the Minamoto did attempt a nocturnal ambush, but were detected in the darkness and defeated.

What strikes the reader of the *Heike Monogatari*, the great 13th-century epic account of the Gempei Wars, is how

Curved blade · Single edge

Samurai sword
The warrior's sword was his proudest possession, the symbol of his military prowess – and, potentially, the instrument of his ritual suicide if he were vanquished.

by disembowelling himself in the first known act of *seppuku*. From that time, this ritual suicide had its special place in the samurai code, enabling defeated warriors to die with honour.

1,300 The number of ships that are thought to have clashed at the battle of Dan-no-Ura in the Inland Sea. The Taira clan were crushingly defeated.

Death and drama
Minamoto Yoritomo now took up the leadership. He struggled to begin with but, at Fujigawa, luck came to his rescue. Hearing the rustling of birds' wings in the night, the Taira sentries

up-close and intimate the fighting was. Like the heroes of Homer's Trojan War, warriors make stirring speeches before battle and trade insults as they engage in single combat. This is all part of

the literary convention, affording an opportunity for building suspense. But it also reflects the realities of the time. There was no more noble calling than that of the soldier; samurai were schooled in their vocation as small boys.

Horsemanship was held in high regard – memorable descriptions abound in the *Heike Monogatari* – even though the samurai fought mainly on foot. Accomplishment in archery was essential; not just with the full-length *daikyu* but also with the shorter *hankyu* – both bows could be used on horseback. The

cult of the *katana*, or "samurai sword", was yet to be established, but the warrior still took great pride in his skill with the long, curved *tachi* sword and with the dagger.

Pride was all-important: the samurai followed the "Way of the Warrior", or *bushido*, which made an ethic of valour and heroic self-sacrifice in war. But the samurai who willingly gave up his life did so in the certain knowledge that he would be rewarded with both honour and everlasting fame. The desire of the individual fighter for such a dramatic and noble death helps explain why – serious and bloody as the Gempei Wars were – so much of the action now

BEFORE

Though his official status was divine, the tenno or emperor, of Japan was in medieval times a marginal figure. Real power rested with the nobility – and was hotly contested.

JAPANESE "CLANS"
By the 9th century dominant dynasties were emerging, their ascendancy embodied in the strength and prowess of the armies of **samurai warriors** they had assembled. These factions are known as **"clans"**, since they grew up around important families, though most of those fighting for them were not blood relations.

THE FADING FUJIWARA
The **Fujiwara clan** quickly established its presence, holding sway as *sesshos*, or "regents", and wielding the emperor's authority on his behalf. By the 12th century, however, its influence was ebbing fast and **other families were poised to take its place**.

CIVIL WAR IN JAPAN
Conflict, raging for generations between the powerful **Minamoto and Taira** clans, finally flared up into a full-blown civil war. The **Hogon Rebellion** of 1156 saw the Fujiwara themselves reduced to figureheads as the Minamoto and Taira fought over who should have power behind the scenes. Three years later, after the **Heiji Rebellion**, the Taira came out on top, and established Japan's **first samurai government**; the Minamoto, however, felt they still had absolutely **everything to fight for**.

Conflict across the islands
The focus of the fighting moved back and forth across Japan during the five years of the Gempei Wars (1180–85). Few communities were able to remain detached.

Key
Areas of control in early 1180s
- Minamoto Yoritomo
- Minamoto Yoshinaka
- Taira
- Northern Fujiwara
- Approximate frontiers
- Minamoto campaign
- Battle

Ceremonial Samurai armour
Iron plates, laced together and then lacquered over against rust, formed the basis for this high-ranking Samurai's armour. A tightly woven surcoat provided extra protection, while the curved helmet deflected blows.

seems "staged". An exchange of arrows by both sides was typically followed by a battle that unfolded as a series of highly formal single combats between warriors.

Changing times, changing fortunes

This ritualized way of making war could not be sustained. In the *Heike Monogatari*, the Minamoto drew the Taira into an engagement of this kind at Kurikara in 1183 – but only as a decoy – and the bulk of Minamoto Yoshinaka's army crept round to attack from the rear. Yoshinaka tied torches to the horns of frightened cattle, which were sent stampeding into the Taira. The Minamoto gained the advantage.

Despite this, in the following months, the Minamoto were split by a number of bitter power struggles. Yoritomo, loyally backed by his cousin, Yoshitsune, emerged the victor. Luckily for him, the Taira had been unable to regroup in time. At Ichi-no-Tani in 1184, the Minamoto went on the offensive, forcing the Taira to fall back on their home territory around the Inland Sea.

All at sea

In 1185 Yoritomo set out to take the Taira's main fortress at Yashima, off Shikoku. He had a party of men build fires in the hills inland to persuade the Taira that his army was approaching from that direction. The Taira took to their ships to make their escape, only to find the Minamoto sailing at them from the seaward side.

The battle of Yashima was more of a humiliation than a real defeat for the Taira, as most of them managed to make their way to safety. The

climactic engagement of the Gempei Wars came a few weeks later at Dan-no-Ura. This was technically a naval battle, though it was really more a land battle at sea. Warriors fired off showers of arrows as they came into range of one another, before boarding each other's vessels to continue fighting in hand-to-hand combat. It was a rigorous test of samurai strength, and one that Yoritomo's Minamoto won, decisively destroying the power of the Taira once and for all.

AFTER »

The Gempei Wars cast a long shadow over the subsequent history of Japan. Their impact was as much in the political and cultural spheres as in the military.

SHOGUN RULE

In 1192 Emperor Go-Toba gave Yoritomo the title of **shogun**, or "Supreme Commander". This was no more than an acknowledgement of what everybody knew: that **real power** in Japan resided with the Minamoto. Shogunates would, with only the briefest interruptions, remain in power until the second half of the 19th century. The Kamakura shoguns, named for their capital Kamakura, saw off the **Mongol invasion of the 13th century 85–87** ».

A WARRIOR TRADITION

Still more lasting, if less tangible, was the impact of the Gempei Wars on the **military culture of Japan**. Traditions and values established in medieval times were to resurface in the modern age. To an extraordinary extent, they still informed the military mind-set of 20th-century Japan, as became

BATTLE OF THE GENJI AND THE HEIKE CLANS

evident in the **war with Russia 254–55** », the **Sino-Japanese War 282–83** », and in the **Pacific theatre of World War II 302–03** ».

JAPANESE GENERAL (1159–1189)

MINAMOTO YOSHITSUNE

Yoshitsune was born in 1159, the year of the Heiji Rebellion. According to tradition, he was trained in the arts of war by Sojobo, mythical king of the *tengu* spirits of Mount Kurama. In 1180 he joined his cousins, Minamoto Yoritomo and Minamoto Noriyori, in raising an army to fight the Taira clan. Yoshitsune fought and killed a fourth cousin, the jealous Yoshinaka. He went on to win vital triumphs over the Taira but finally fell out with Yoritomo, who had him murdered in 1189.

« BEFORE

Tough, fierce nomads ranged the eastern steppe, warring over livestock and resources. From time to time they banded together to attack communities in the world beyond.

A NEW LEADER

The Mongol nomads lived on the move; however, this changed in the 12th century when the various tribal groups coalesced around a charismatic leader – the man known to history as **Genghis Khan**. He brought peace to the warring nomads and established a political and military body. He also revelled in his status as bogeyman: "All cities," he said, "should be razed so that the world may once again become a great steppe in which Mongol mothers shall suckle free and happy children."

A TIDE OF TERROR

Since ancient times a tide of warlike nomadic peoples had drifted westward out of Central Asia to bring terror to the civilizations of the Middle East and Europe. **The Huns**, headed by the fearsome Attila, had sent a shockwave through **the Roman world** « 46–47; the Seljuk Turks **had thrown Christendom into confusion** « 72–73; but the Mongols were surely the most terrifying yet – a fact made worse by Genghis Khan's voracious blood lust.

ATTILA THE HUN

The sack of Baghdad
Genghis Khan's grandson, Hulegu, took the Abbasid capital in 1258. The Mongols destroyed the city's dykes, trapping the caliph's army behind a sea of water. Those who did not drown were slaughtered in the ensuing battle.

Mongol Invasions

The Mongols were viewed with outright horror by civilized nations. They were happy to let their savage reputation go before them, but their strategic sophistication tells another story. The Mongols were fighters with flair and intelligence, who learned with every conquest.

Almost extinct in the modern world, the nomadic-pastoralist lifestyle was an unusual one and those people who lived it developed an extraordinarily specialized set of skills. Time after time, in both ancient and medieval history, these aptitudes had translated seamlessly from the open steppes of Central Asia to the field of war. Superlative horsemanship; skills with the bow and arrow and other weapons; all but unimaginable toughness and endurance: the Mongol people were equipped with all of these. For generations, though, they went to war only with one another, tribe against tribe – except when an enterprising warlord fostered a larger warband for an assault on a settled community reasonably close at hand. Thus it was from small beginnings that Genghis Khan and his sons created the biggest land empire ever seen, ranging all the way from the Pacific Ocean to Central Europe.

Order from chaos

In their scattered, ever-mobile tribal communities, the Mongols were not the most promising material for nation-building. Certainly, many of the tribal leaders resented Genghis Khan's rise to prominence. But, by coaxing some and forcing others, by giving a promise here and administering a little pressure there, Genghis Khan slowly fashioned the Mongols into a coherent people. By 1206, when he was about 40 years old, Genghis Khan could at last claim to be the *Khagan*, or "Great Khan", the undisputed ruler of the Mongols.

Mongol quiver
Mongols often carried two quivers of arrows – one easily accessible and one in reserve.

This freewheeling warrior of the steppe had already shown himself a cunning and calculating politician. Now he revealed his infallible instincts as a politician and administrator. He broke up the old hierarchies in Mongol society, marginalizing the traditional elite. Instead, he gave leadership positions to his most trusted friends – or to promising fighters plucked from the ranks. Having humbled the powerful, he won the gratitude of more vulnerable groups by outlawing the sale of wives and by excusing the poorest people from paying taxes. Genghis Khan divided his warriors up into groups of ten (*arbans*), a hundred (*zuuns*), 1,000 (*myangans*) and 10,000 (*tumens*) – taking care to cut across tribal lines of loyalty. That way he introduced a degree of regimentation to the anarchic warfare of the steppe. While he had no wish to tame his fighters' ferocity, he took careful steps to control it: rape and plunder without his sanction were strictly barred.

At a gallop

Genghis Khan hardly needed to train his men in archery and close-quarters fighting, however, he ensured that they practised daily to hone their skills. Manoeuvres on horseback were an essential part of herding and hunting life, but there was always scope to iron out imperfections. Rigid regimentation might have been alien to his approach, but discipline was not. Time after time, his horsemen caught out enemy forces when they appeared to break formation and flee in disorder – prompting mad pursuit – only to regroup at an instant's

122
The percentage of the Earth's land mass that was under Mongol rule at the height of their empire.

notice, wheel round, and fall upon their helpless enemy. (Western European cavalry forces were to adopt this trick in the centuries that followed.) Many of his warriors were to fight as armoured lancers; in fact, Genghis Khan himself developed particular mounted manoeuvres for these men,

drilling them tirelessly until they became second nature. Mongol soldiers travelled light: most had only layers of seasoned leather, sewn onto a fabric support, by way of armour, although the lancers' would be stiffened with plates of iron or bone. Agility in the saddle kept the soldiers safe for the most part; their diminutive horses possessed stamina and speed, and were able to travel considerable distances in a relatively short time. So much so that settled peoples who received news of Mongol attacks some distance away frequently underestimated just how quickly the brutal invaders would arrive.

A narrow escape

The Mongol army swept like a storm through East Asia, invading Xi Xia, the kingdom in northwestern China, in 1207. The Mongols sacked Beijing in 1215, before heading south into the heartland of the "Middle Kingdom". Moving west, their armies attacked the cities of the Central Asian Silk Road, and by 1222 they were making a diversion into northern India. The following year they ventured into the southern Russian steppe. By the time their enigmatic leader died in 1227, the empire of the Mongols extended from the Pacific Ocean in the east to the Caspian Sea in the west, and Khan's successors were menacing the Arab countries of the Middle East. The pace of the Mongols'

A Mongol's bow

Made of wood, horn, and sinew, with strings of animal hide, the composite bow melded maximum tension with minimum length. An adept archer could string a bow on horseback.

String-bridge

Bowstring

Gold-painted grip

Shaft

Key

- Empire of Genghis Khan
- Empires of Genghis Khan's successors c.1290
- Approximate frontiers c.1290
- Campaigns of Genghis Khan
- Campaigns of Genghis Khan's successors
- Mongol victory
- Mongol defeat

The Mongol empire

Genghis Khan set about building the most extensive land empire ever seen – an empire that had influence over approximately 100 million people. It survived long after his death, though it did break up into smaller khanates.

progress was dizzying, yet their military prowess depended on a great deal more than speed. Genghis Khan had never stopped learning – and never stopped improving his fighting force. Wherever he had gone, along with his other plunder, he had captured talent: weapons-makers, armourers, and, above all, engineers. This most nomadic of armies had become supreme in the most static form of warfare: the Mongols were renowned for their skill in siegecraft.

They could fill the deepest moats at speed with sandbags; their giant catapults (feats of engineering that could conveniently be taken apart for transporting on horseback, only to be reassembled quickly when needed) could hurl anything from flaming

naphtha to putrid animal carcasses over the highest battlements; and they had engines that could shoot dozens of fire-arrows at a time. They also had another weapon: sheer terror. When Samarkand in Uzbekistan fell after a siege in 1220, the Mongol leader had the inhabitants rounded up and led to a plain outside the city walls. The hapless people were then slaughtered and their

skulls arranged into a pyramid – a sign of victory and a warning to those who might have been tempted to resist.

The conquests continued under Genghis Khan's son, Ögedei. His forces invaded Russia in 1237, leaving a trail of devastation wherever they went. In

1240 Mongol troops sacked the city of Kiev after a gruesome siege. Ögedei's armies continued westward, separate warbands making exploratory forays into Poland and Hungary. On 9 April 1241, at Liegnitz, in Poland, a small subsidiary unit led by the Mongol general, Sübedei, smashed the Silesian army of Duke Henry II. Just two days later, Sübedei's main military force

"They are inhuman … **more like monsters than men**."

MATTHEW PARIS, 13TH-CENTURY CHRONICLER, ON THE MONGOLS

defeated the Hungarians at Mohi: the way to Western Europe, with all its riches, now lay wide open.

Then from the east came the news that Ögedei Khan had died. All the Mongol chiefs were called back for a conclave to elect his successor. By the time his successor, Gyyuk Khan, was in place, the Mongols were preoccupied with other campaigns in the eastern regions of their realm. Much the same happened later, in 1259, when Hulegu Khan's armies were ravaging the Middle East en route to Egypt: the region was reprieved by the death of his brother, Möngke Khan. Not, however, before Baghdad had been taken, Hulegu's Mongols literally outdoing themselves in wanton cruelty. Anything up to half a million people may have been slaughtered in the bloodletting that followed the Iraqi city's fall, as the world's most beautiful metropolis was razed to the ground.

AFTER »

The Mongols were nomads by nature, and never really took to the settled life; camping among their conquests, for the most part they remained outsiders.

ADVANCING EMPIRE

Only in China, conquered by Genghis Khan's grandson, Kublai Khan, did the nomadic Mongols put down real roots. Kublai Khan wholeheartedly embraced the civilized culture he found there – though his Mongol antecedents showed clearly in his **aggressive foreign policy 86–87** », most notably in his attempts to invade Japan.

In Russia the Mongol empire **endured in the shape of the "Golden Horde"**. This semi-independent arm of the empire lasted into the 16th century and for much of the time – after all the carnage of its creation – the Golden Horde enjoyed a great deal of **peace and prosperity**.

A MONGOL CASQUE (HELMET)

COPYCAT CONQUEROR

The West could consider itself extremely lucky to have escaped invasion, though it would have another scare in the 14th century when **Timur Lenk and his armies came rampaging out of the east 88–89** ». A Turkic Mongol by descent, Timur modelled himself on Genghis Khan and **sought conquest after conquest**: ultimately, India and western Asia bore the brunt and his reputation as a barbarous conqueror grew.

GENGHIS KHAN

Genghis Khan is a title that translates as "Very Mighty King". The man who earned himself this accolade was born Temujin in c.1162, the son of a minor chieftain. On his father's death, the young Temujin was ostracized and learned the hard way how to stand up for himself – by fighting. By 1206 he had won his title of Khan, forging a united people out of an array of squabbling tribes. He had also created a strong war-machine, as China, India, and others were to find out.

BATTLE OF BAGHDAD
The army of Hulegu Khan, a grandson of Genghis Khan, attacks the city of Baghdad in 1258, destroying what was then the centre of Islamic power. Hulegu's army, the largest ever fielded by the Mongols, was bolstered by Chinese, Turkish, Armenian, Persian, and Christian soldiers. In this near-contemporary manuscript, Chinese artillerymen break the city's defences. Estimates of the death toll range from 200,000 to 1,000,000.

BEFORE

To a Mongol warlord, China was one of the world's great prizes, a land of wealth and untold splendour. Genghis Khan had come here for booty, but had chosen not to linger.

RAIDING VISITORS

China had a long history of **nomadic incursions**: the Central Asian Hsiung Nu had made periodic incursions into the "Middle Kingdom" in ancient times. Next had come the Khitan, the Tanguts, and, in the 12th century, the Jurchen's **Jin empire occupied the north**.

SONG GENERAL YUE FEI

RETRENCHMENT

The advent of the Jin empire **forced the Song dynasty to transfer its capital** from northerly Kaifeng to Li'nan (present-day Hangzhou). The armies of this "Southern Song" managed to **hold back the Jurchen raiders** and so an uneasy equilibrium was maintained.

Genghis Khan's campaign had begun in China, but the northern region had borne the brunt. Not until the time of his grandson Kublai Khan did the Mongols establish a lasting presence further south.

In **Korea**, the three kingdoms of Koguryo, Silla, and Paekche had been **united as "Koryo"** by King Wang Kon of Koguryo in the 10th century.

The conquests and campaigns of Kublai Khan
Dates 1260–94
Location China, Korea, Japan, Vietnam, and Java

Mongol warrior
The mounted archers of the Mongol armies were out of their element in China's highly urbanized environment, but they quickly adapted to the new conditions.

The Wars of Kublai Khan

China posed a military and cultural challenge for the Mongols. Yet Kublai Khan was able to make himself a new kind of Mongol ruler here. He was just as warlike, though: he attacked neighbouring states, from Burma to Korea, and twice attempted to invade Japan.

Kublai Khan had come into contact with Chinese culture as a young man, while working as governor of the Mongols' southern territories. The Jin empire and Xi Xia were regions of China under nomad rule. The young Kublai was an ardent admirer of Chinese civilization, and covetous of Chinese wealth and technology, and so was keen to add the "Middle Kingdom" to the Mongol empire. He had been fighting against the Southern Song in China when he got news of his brother Möngke's death in 1259, and he faced a bitter struggle for succession with his younger brother, Ariq Böke. It was not until 1264 that Kublai Khan was able to return to his long-term plans. But his courage and determination to carve out a new Chinese empire for himself may well have been bolstered by this period of feuding.

While Kublai Khan had emerged the victor, he had lost a degree of support in the Mongol heartlands and an oppositional faction had grown up around his nephew, Kaidu. By 1271 he had committed himself so far to his project that he declared himself Huangdi, or "emperor" – the founder of a new Chinese "Yuan" dynasty.

This new title meant little, in that he did not yet control the majority of the areas to which he was laying claim, but it would have been full of significance for the Han Chinese. By appropriating it, Kublai Khan was sending out a powerful signal that he came, not merely as a conqueror, but as a new emperor. He underlined this by establishing his capital on Chinese soil, in Daidu (Beijing). How deep his self-reinvention as a Chinese ruler ran is difficult to know: many of his later reforms may be interpreted as attempts to recast traditional Chinese society along Mongol lines.

Stalemate at Xiangyang

Kublai Khan did not object to waging war on his adoptive country. He began by besieging Xiangyang in 1268, a strategically vital city as it controlled access to the Han river and hence to the Yangtze, and to the fertile plains of central China. Kublai Khan attacked with 100,000 mounted warriors, and he was equipped with trebuchets – catapults that could fling rocks across the river into the city. However, the Song defenders had widened the river at the vital point and padded their walls so that the missiles were

Chinese fire-lance

Contemporary chronicles agreed that the one Chinese weapon the Mongols feared was the fire-lance. It was used at close-quarters, and flames shot out from the gunpowder-packed canister at the end.

Defending Japan
Japanese samurai swarm onto the Mongol commander's vessel at Hakata Bay in 1281, seeing off the second of Kublai Khan's two failed invasion attempts.

CHINESE EMPEROR (1215–1294)

KUBLAI KHAN

Grandson of the great Genghis Khan, Kublai Khan was born in 1215. He became *Khagan*, or "Supreme Khan", in 1260 after the death of his elder brother, Möngke. A scholar of Chinese language and culture, renowned for his intelligence and enlightenment, in 1271 he established the Yuan dynasty. With his grandfather's gift for government and administration, Kublai Khan's new role as Chinese emperor meant his adopted country was all the stronger for his rule.

rendered harmless. Kublai Khan responded by building a fleet of ships to blockade the river. But the Song were able to hold out almost indefinitely. In the end, they held out for six years. The breakthrough came with the advent of counterweighted trebuchets – designed specifically for Kublai Khan. These new catapults could send 300-kg (661-lb) missiles a distance of 500m (1,640ft).

New departures
Xiangyang had been the Song dynasty's strongest fortress: once it fell, nothing could stop the Mongols from streaming through the heart of China. By 1276 most of China was in Mongol hands.

The Song's last stand came at the naval battle of Yamen in March 1279. Though outnumbered, the Yuan ships succeeded in enclosing the Song fleet in a narrow bay. The confined ships were tied

5,000 The number of ships said to have been constructed by Kublai Khan to prevent river-borne supplies reaching the Song at Xiangyang.

together in a line, so when the Yuan attacked, they were afforded a floating walkway to the central Song flagship.

Kublai Khan's success in conquering China was extraordinary. He contrived a miracle of organization and logistic

support, sustained it for the best part of ten years, and managed this over thousands of kilometres in an area that could hardly have been less suited to the traditional tactics of the Mongols.

Ill-prepared ventures
Subsequent invasions were rather less successful. In 1274 a seaborne assault of Japan at Hakata Bay on Kyushu was thwarted when a storm destroyed the Mongol fleet. Kublai Khan sent a second invasion fleet in 1281. Again, tradition has it, a typhoon dispersed the attackers' ships; modern experts have suggested that both fleets were too hastily built and inadequately prepared. Some even question whether the "divine winds" were anything more than the usual bad weather.

An invasion of Burma in 1277 fared much better. The country was quickly conquered and reduced to client status. But successive attacks on Vietnam were thwarted. In Korea, however, Kublai Khan used more guile, and lent discreet support to King Wonjong against his rivals: in return, he gained Korea's loyalty as a vassal state.

Kublai Khan enjoyed a successful reign and, by opening China up to change, transformed the whole country; but his Yuan dynasty was to last less than 100 years.

AN EMPIRE IN DECLINE
Kublai Khan showed open-mindedness in his military innovations, and his **reforms placed the empire on a stronger footing**, encouraging economic innovation and increasing social harmony with the help he gave the poor.

Kublai Khan died in 1294. He was followed by his grandson, Temur – but **his succession was as troublesome** as Kublai Khan's had been. Later Yuan emperors failed to reign successfully over such a vast empire.

DISASTERS AND DOWNFALL
A series of droughts and floods in the 1340s brought the agrarian economy to its knees. The government's inability to cope created anger and unrest. The **Red Turban Rebellion** broke out in the 1350s. Led by Zhu Yuangzhang, these Han Chinese rebels brought down the Yuan dynasty in 1368. Zhu Yuangzhang went on to found the Ming dynasty.

In Korea, meanwhile, the kings of Koryo were overthrown in a military coup in 1392 by General Yi Seongyi: his Choson dynasty was to remain in power until the last years of the 19th century.

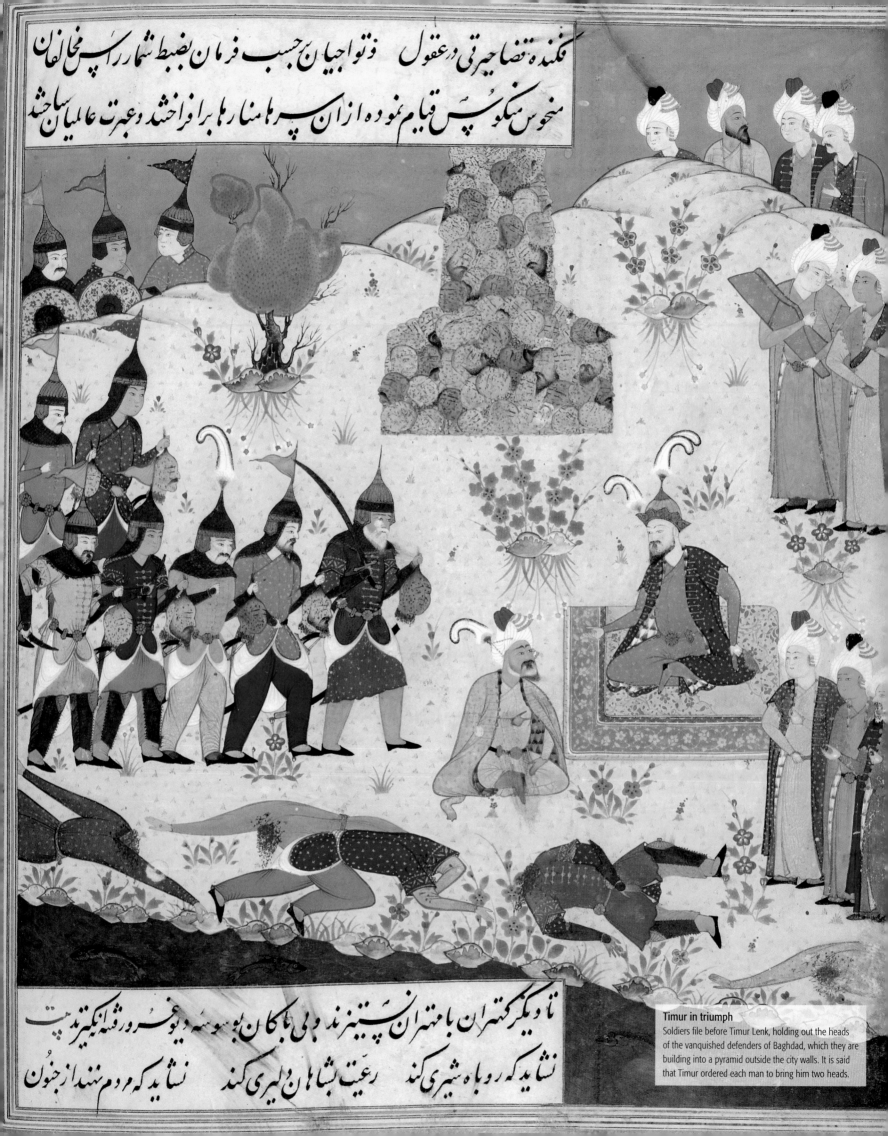

تا و یکصد کنهتران با مهتران نشینند این شینه زبند بی با کان بوسه و بغمر ورشه این کیرد پیش

نشاید که روبا به شیری کند رعیت بشاهان دلیری کند نشاید که مردم نهند از جنون

Timur in triumph

Soldiers file before Timur Lenk, holding out the heads of the vanquished defenders of Baghdad, which they are building into a pyramid outside the city walls. It is said that Timur ordered each man to bring him two heads.

The Conquests of Timur

For the settled civilizations of Western and Southern Asia, the threat from the Central Asian steppe was gaining momentum again. Even Christian Europe was unnerved. The more they demonized him, the better Timur Lenk liked it; he revelled in his self-styled status as a "second coming" of Genghis Khan.

CENTRAL AND SOUTHWEST ASIA

The conquests and campaigns of Timur
Dates 1379–1405
Location Uzbekistan, Afghanistan, Iran, Turkey, southern Russia, and northern India

BEFORE

To outward appearances, all was quiet on the Central Asian steppe by the 14th century, but warlords still jostled for advantage, setting their sights on greater things.

SETTING A PRECEDENT
In the 13th century Genghis Khan had emerged from nowhere with his Mongol warbands to establish the **biggest land empire the world had ever seen ‹‹ 82–83**. To the ambitious warlord, his story offered an alluring vision of what ruthlessness and courage might achieve.

A DUBIOUS HERITAGE
Transoxania, in present-day Uzbekistan, now belonged to the Khanate of Chagatai. Named for one of Genghis Khan's sons, the **territory was still ruled by his successors** – the Barlas – a Turkic-Mongolian group who prided themselves on their **illustrious line of descent**, though there is thought to be little merit to their claims.

Timur Lenk began his rise, in the best steppe tradition, as a raider and livestock-rustler. By his early 20s, he headed a warband 300 strong. His flair for fighting was already evident – as were his rigour and courage. Like his idol, Genghis Khan, however, he was a politician too. Deftly playing off the enmities and ambitions of men much more powerful than himself, Timur had made himself the leader of the Barlas clan by 1360; eight years later he was leader of the Chagatai Confederation. No one was in any doubt where the real power lay. Making Samarkand his headquarters, he vowed to transform it into one of the world's greatest cities.

But before he could do so, Timur had to make himself the master of the steppe: his campaigns of the 1370s took him east into the Altai region and north into the Golden Horde. Only when Central Asia had been secured did he direct his energies south and west. He began in 1381 by invading Iran, a land of small states once united under the Mongol Ilkhanids. First Herat, then other cities fell. Few offered their invaders any serious resistance.

Strategy of atrocity
Only afterwards, when Timur had left, did the region rise in rebellion. And only then was Timur's true nature displayed. Turning back to put down the revolt, he did so with a cruelty that was little short of frenzied. At Sabzevar he had 2,000 living prisoners heaped with mud and masonry, literally building them into the fabric of a tower. Yet there was method in his madness: he was using atrocity as an instrument of strategy.

> **28** The number of pyramids, each one comprising 1,500 skulls, that were counted by a chronicler of 1388 in a half-circuit of the walls of Isfahan, Iran, after Timur Lenk's sacking.

Wherever he went, he built pyramids of skulls – a warning to the world, and monument to his murderousness.

Pushing west through Azerbaijan into Christian Georgia, he forced the king to convert to Islam before heading south through Armenia and back into Iran. In 1387 he took Isfahan, but then rebels killed Timur's tax collectors. Again, he proved implacable in his anger.

Perpetual motion
Timur was always a nomad at heart, a raider rather than an empire-builder. He governed by fear, mounting punitive patrols at any sign of trouble. By 1393 he was back in Iran, crushing a rebellion with his customary cruelty. Attacks on Baghdad and Kurdistan were followed by raids on the Golden Horde, sacking and burning as he went. The impression is of a leader eaten up by an insane blood lust; but Timur was more rational than that. The sacking of southern Russia cut off one of the main commercial corridors between East and West. Trade had now to pass through his own territories further to the south.

Whatever horror he induced in the civilian populations of the countries he conquered, Timur inspired adulation and undying loyalty in his men. As his conquests continued, his army grew in size till it eventually numbered 200,000. A master-tactician, he loved ruses and feints; his troops would pretend to flee then suddenly regroup and attack.

Timur was a Muslim and frequently professed to be fighting for his faith – even if many thousands of his victims were Muslims too. In 1398 he led his army over the mountains of the Hindu Kush. From the Punjab to Delhi, they

sacked every city they passed and laid waste the land. It is said they killed as many as 100,000 civilians before they even reached the capital.

The Ottoman Turks also fell short of Timur's Islamic standards. In 1402 he marched against Sultan Bayezid I at Ankara. Bayezid's defeat gave Timur a dubious role as saviour of Christian Byzantium and the Turks' conquest of Constantinople was put back 50 years.

By 1404 Timur had achieved all he had set out to do. The Middle East was his; his sumptuous tomb stood pride of place in his capital, Samarkand. He was laid to rest in it the following year.

AFTER

To the great relief of his subject nations, Timur Lenk turned out to be an anomaly. His successors' Timurid dynasty quickly destroyed itself through infighting.

FOUNDING EMPIRES
One refugee from the Timurid dynasty's succession-struggle was the Muslim conqueror, Babur. In the early 16th century he invaded India and founded **the Mogul dynasty 120–21 ››**.

In the meantime, **the Ottoman Turks** were to recover from their defeat at the battle of Ankara to reassert their hold over Anatolia, taking Constantinople in 1453 and **widening their empire into Europe 106–07 ››**.

TIMUR HANDING HIS CROWN TO BABUR

A fitting memorial
Timur's magnificent mausoleum, Gur-e Amir, still stands in Samarkand. His body, embalmed with rose water, musk, and camphor, lies in an ornate coffin. A single block of jade marks his tomb.

> **"I am the scourge of God appointed to chastise you."**
> TIMUR LENK TO THE RULERS OF DAMASCUS, 1401

Decorated mace
Used in close combat, the mace was a heavy club that was common among the Mongols. These weapons were simple to make and could be as effective as swords.

Guelphs and Ghibellines

Italy witnessed mounting opposition between emperors and popes in the 12th and 13th centuries. The northern states banded together in the Lombard League, and the focus switched to the south after the "Sicilian Vespers" uprising. The Guelphs and the Ghibellines, two fluctuating alliances, fought these wars.

« **BEFORE**

In Western Europe during the Middle Ages, relations between the papacy and the emperors were strained at best – and their struggle for power would continue.

SETTING A STANDARD

When Charlemagne, king of the Franks, had himself crowned emperor by Pope Leo III in 800, he created a new model for the **relationship between Church and state in Europe ‹‹ 68–69**. German ruler, Otto I, ratified the contract when he went to St Peter's for his coronation as emperor.

HENRY IV

TROUBLED TIMES

The association between the two institutions was tested by the **"Investiture Contest"** of the 11th century. Emperor Henry IV was at odds with the papacy over rights and was excommunicated in 1076. He was compelled to make penance at Canossa, begging papal forgiveness.

The **Concordat of Worms** (1122) formally ended the power struggle between the emperors and the pope. Thereafter, while a semblance of **unity was restored**, relations remained uneasy and a tussle began over control of Italy.

Neatly resolving some political and institutional issues, the creation of the Holy Roman Empire of the German Nation was a masterstroke. However, this new union invited power struggles, and tensions were quick to show. The Hohenstaufen dynasty in Germany came to power in 1138 with the Emperor Conrad III determined to avoid a repeat of the humiliations visited on his predecessor, Henry IV. In 1155 Pope Adrian IV made Frederick I ("Barbarossa") emperor. After several incursions into northern Italy, he chose representatives from the region for an assembly, the Diet of Roncaglia (1158).

Victory at Legnano

In Italy prominent cities like Piacenza, Milan, Padua, Venice, and Bologna were trying to extract themselves from the intrusive local bishops. They found an ally in the pope, since the bishops were appointed by the emperor, not by Rome. Frederick served notice of the callous way with which he intended to rule when he launched an invasion, seizing Crema in 1159 and Milan in 1162. When Frederick's men played football with severed heads at Crema, the people responded by slaying captured soldiers. Pope Alexander III was outraged, and

"These are not men, rather they are devils, whose only wish is a battle!"

PROVENÇAL CAPTAIN ON THE MEN OF ROGER DI LAURIA'S FLEET, 8 JULY 1283

WESTERN MEDITERRANEAN

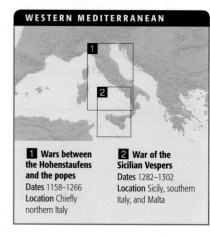

1 Wars between the Hohenstaufens and the popes
Dates 1158–1266
Location Chiefly northern Italy

2 War of the Sicilian Vespers
Dates 1282–1302
Location Sicily, southern Italy, and Malta

Battle of Benevento

Charles I defeats Frederick II's son, Manfred, in 1266, to secure Sicily and put an end to Italian Hohenstaufen rule. The importance of this victory to the Angevins finds testimony in this painting, made almost 200 years later.

sent out the army of the Commune of Rome, but it was severely mauled at Monte Porzio in 1167. Thwarted, the pope gave his support to the cities when they formed a defensive alliance, the Lombard League.

In 1174 Frederick's forces swept over the Alps again, besieging Alessandria. Its people fought frantically: even when the imperial sappers dug their way beneath the city walls, they beat the attackers off. The siege finally ended and the Lombard League was victorious.

Peace negotiations began but broke down in 1176. Battle was joined at Legnano. Frederick's army had more than 4,000 armoured knights; that of the Lombard League comprised mainly infantrymen. Their 1,000 or so knights were outnumbered: when the imperial cavalry charged, they fled. The infantry had dug in behind the defenses, however, forming a phalanx around the *carroccio* (ox wagon). They

Frederick II
Barbarossa's grandson, Frederick II, made further conquests into Italy in the 13th century.

18 The number of galleys captured by Roger di Lauria on 4 July 1299 at the battle of Cape Orlando.

presented their long spears like pikes and stood firm; behind, crossbowmen and archers wore down the enemy. The Lombard cavalry now regrouped, before charging back in to defeat the emperor.

Guelphs and Ghibellines

Frederick had to endure the humiliation of signing the Peace of Venice, a treaty with the Lombard League that had been brokered by the pope, but tension between the two sides continued. The situation was made worse by the fact that some Italian people supported the emperors: the cities and landowners in central Italy were more worried about the papacy's interference in their affairs than about any encroachments by the emperor from the north. This group came together as the "Ghibellines" – the name is supposed to have been a corruption of *Waiblingen*, the title

Troubled waters

Charles I voyages to Rome for his investiture as king of Sicily in 1265. Key battles in the War of the Sicilian Vespers would be fought at sea.

of a famous Hohenstaufen stronghold, and they were strong supporters of the emperor. The papal party christened themselves the "Guelphs" and took their name from the Hohenstaufen opposition – the Bavarian House of Welf. Conflict between the two factions continued for the rest of the 12th century and well into the 13th. In the 1230s the Lombard League (now part of the Guelph faction) suffered several defeats at the hands of Frederick II. The most severe of which came in 1237 at the battle of Cortenuova. Certain victory was snatched after the new emperor brought 8,000 Muslim archers from Apulia in the southern "toe" of Italy – a region where Arab influence was still strong.

The Sicilian Vespers

In 1262 Pope Urban IV conferred the throne of Naples and Sicily on Charles of Anjou. This was highly provocative, given the opposing claim of Manfred of Sicily, who was related by marriage to the Hohenstaufen family. Even so, Charles enforced his case, defeating Manfred's army at Benevento in 1266. Manfred himself was killed in the fighting.

Charles did not convince Sicilians of his right to rule. At Vespers (the evening service) in Palermo's Church of the Holy Spirit on Easter Monday 1282, this resentment erupted into rioting. In the weeks that followed, hundreds of people associated with the Angevins (the House of Anjou) were killed. Charles cracked down, and Manfred's heir (by virtue of their relationship by marriage), Peter III of Aragon, came into the conflict on the Sicilians' side. He landed with an army in Sicily and had himself crowned at Palermo. What had been a local insurrection was soon spiralling into a

full-blown war and spilling over onto the mainland of southern Italy. As their armies slugged it out, the pope added to the chaos by excommunicating Peter and inviting Philip III of France and his son, Charles of Valois, to invade his kingdom in the "Aragonese Crusade".

Battles at sea

Philip and Charles hoped to find allies in a nobility already known to be at odds with their king, Peter III. In the event, though, a full-scale French invasion was defeated, the people rising up in support

8,000 The number of French people believed to have been slaughtered in the course of the "Sicilian Vespers" insurrection of 1282.

of Peter and his lords. The French were stopped at sea as well, Peter III with an immense advantage – Roger di Lauria commanding his fleet.

The dashing Admiral di Lauria had already proved his worth, winning a great victory over the Angevins at the battle of Malta on 8 July 1283. Now his victory at the battle of Les Formigues, off the coast of Catalonia in 1285, was observed as a decisive reverse for the crusade. The admiral was disciplined and daring, and could trust the captains of his galleys to break formation, feign flight, and lead enemy vessels out of position in the knowledge that they could be commanded back to order at a moment's notice.

But when, on Peter's death in 1285, Pope Urban IV tried to restore Sicily to the Angevins, the conflict flared up all over again. While James, the elder of Peter's surviving sons, was happy to agree to the terms, the younger, Frederick III, was preparing to fight. Their father's admiral was again decisive. Fighting now for James, in favour of the treaty, Roger di Lauria defeated Frederick's fleet at the battle of Cape Orlando in 1299, and then again at Ponza, on 14 June 1300.

TECHNOLOGY

TREBUCHET

Catapults of various sorts had been used on the battlefield and in siege situations since ancient times. Roman *ballistae* worked like giant crossbows, shooting heavy bolts; other engines were used for hurling rocks. Such engines had relied on the torsion of twisted or ratcheted rope, and there were limits on how powerful they could be. But from the 12th century, engineers were employing the force of leverage, compounded by the use of counterweights. The arcing flight of the missiles thrown took them over ramparts. These new "trebuchets" could propel huge rocks over greater distances and with an accuracy never seen before.

AFTER

The struggle between popes and emperors had gone on for more than two centuries now, the conflict assuming a range of different guises at different times.

A CONTINUING CONFLICT

The papacy was never to be a **military power** in its own right. But the Church continued to be a **powerful influence in political affairs** – and a thorn in the side of successive emperors.

CARROCCIO An ox wagon carrying both the army's standard and an altar at which mass was said before battle. Heralds encircled it, sounding their trumpets throughout the fighting.

It was not until the 16th century that a resolution of sorts was finally attained when **Emperor Charles V triumphed over the power of the papacy during the Italian Wars 114–15 ≫**.

COMPETING CONCERNS

The Church was to have other preoccupations: with **the mounting threat of heresy in Europe 94–95 ≫**, and with the **Ottoman Turks in the east 106–07 ≫**.

Monument to a mercenary
A mercenary is loyal to whoever pays him. This statue in Venice depicts Bartolomeo Colleoni, a *condottiere* (contractor) who fought in the 15th-century wars between Milan and Venice – and served both sides at different times.

Mercenaries

Professional soldiers who fight for a living and pledge their loyalty to whoever pays them, mercenaries have been seen by many as no better than hired assassins. Throughout history, however, the recruitment of mercenaries has been an essential part of warfare, and it is a practice that continues in several parts of the world today.

In earliest times men fought for their families, for their homes, and out of loyalty to their chieftain in return for land. Conscription (compulsory military service), however, become the norm as large, centralized states emerged in Mesopotamia and Ancient Egypt (see pp.16–17). Sargon I of Akkad is the first king known to have conscripted an army, and in New Kingdom Egypt up to 10 per cent of males were forced by the pharaoh into military service. In both cases a soldier's time was spent as much working on engineering projects as it was fighting in battle.

Smaller states, however, were not equipped to raise and maintain large armies through conscription. Nor was conscription always viable, even for large empires, as large portions of the population could not always be removed from vital jobs to join the army. Hiring mercenaries was therefore an obvious recourse for states of all sizes, as mercenaries are both already trained and available as needed.

Nubian mercenaries in Egypt
This ancient Egyptian mural depicts Nubian mercenaries, who were soldiers with no stake in Egyptian society, and no loyalty to anyone except the pharaoh who paid them.

A noble trade

The mercenaries themselves usually came from warrior elites who saw the waging of war as the only fit occupation for a man of honour. Such groups came with weapons, skills, and a ready-made *esprit de corps* that could be placed at the service of a king. The cavalry of the Persian army (see pp.20–21), which from the 6th century BCE made Cyrus and his successors so feared, were Iranian warriors fighting as mercenaries. From the 3rd century BCE, Celtic warbands from Central Europe were in the service of both Egypt's Ptolemaic rulers and the kings of Asia Minor.

Such arrangements were often formalized over the longer term. After the first Vikings (see pp.70–71) found their way from Sweden down the Russian river system to the Black Sea in the 9th century, a number enlisted in the service of the rulers of Byzantium. By the 10th century there was a permanent Varangian Guard of these Viking mercenaries, several thousand strong. Likewise, Turkic warlords who drifted westward with their warriors out of the Central Asian steppe placed themselves and their warbands in the service of Islamic rulers – though the Sultans later found it more convenient to buy or capture boys as slaves, whose primary loyalty would be to them. Often, mercenaries were recruited because they could offer special skills. Sasanid Persia supplied its own armoured cataphracts, for example, but hired other cavalry and even elephant divisions from further afield.

Private armies

The Renaissance (14th–17th centuries) saw the rise of national armies, but also the emergence of free market economies and private enterprise in Europe. As a result, the creation of private armies became a lucrative business, organized by

Celtic mercenary's coin
Found in the port of Dover on the south coast of England, this Carthaginian coin was probably brought home by a Celtic mercenary.

German landsknecht mercenaries

A field captain on horseback talks to two *landsknechts* in this early 16th-century illustration. Going to war was a trade for generations of young men in the early-modern era.

generals-for-hire such as Italy's *condottieri*, or "contractors" (see pp.114–15), many of whom were veterans of the crusades (see pp.74–77). Soldiers from certain countries – Swiss pikemen, and German *landsknechts*, for instance – even came to specialize in mercenary war. More and bigger conflicts came in the wake of the Reformation, and mercenaries offered skills and disciplines that no group of conscripts could match.

Many men in this era came to depend on the mercenary life; it has been estimated, for example, that one-fifth of all Scottish males born in the 17th century went soldiering for foreign masters at some point in their lives.

Servants or masters?

Mercenaries have not always been the answer to their employers' problems – sometimes they have presented challenges of their own. Inevitably, their loyalty is only ever provisional. Around 240 BCE, after Carthage's defeat in the First Punic War (see pp.32–33), unpaid soldiers rose up against the city in what is known as the Mercenary War. Irish and German mercenaries mounted a similar revolt in 1828 at the end of the Argentina-Brazil War.

Mercenaries have often ended up holding the upper hand over their employers. *Condottieri* such as Braccio da Montone and Muzio Sforza became prominent figures in early 15th-century Italian politics. Brought in by the Nicaraguan government to help put down a rebellion in 1855, American mercenary leader William Walker made himself president within a year.

Accountability has always been a problem. Mercenaries have no stake in the countries they fight in, so there is

no particular incentive for them to be fair or humane. They have often seen plunder as a perk. The *landsknechts* became notorious for collecting not just their mercenary pay, but protection money from civilians too. Mercenaries have also committed terrible atrocities, such as their participation in the Massacre of Magdeburg during the Thirty Years War (see pp.142–43).

Modern-day mercenaries

Lack of accountability is part of the appeal of being and hiring a mercenary, and helps explain why mercenaries

endure in the modern era of national armies. Mercenaries are useful for unofficial engagements, such as the arm's-length involvement of the US in the Angolan Civil War in the late 20th century. They are also useful where sending official troops to fight is likely to be unpopular. This has been the case, for example, with the use of private military contractors (mainly Blackwater, now called Xe) by the US in Iraq. By 2009 there may have been as many as 100,000 private contractors in Iraq, in spite of considerable international pressure to ban their activities.

In 1989 the United Nations passed the International Convention Against the Recruitment, Use and Training of Mercenaries – a resolution that finally came into force in October 2001. The resolution bans the use of military contractors, who have since redefined themselves as security services offering armed guards to their employers. However, numerous countries have yet to sign the convention, including the US and the UK; as always, it is still cheaper to buy short-term services than to pay for an extended standing army. Until war itself is banned, it seems the mercenary soldier will always be with us.

Mercenaries in Angola

Portuguese mercenaries fought alongside soldiers of the National Liberation Front of Angola (FNLA) in the Angolan Civil War of 1975–2002. Angola was a Portuguese territory from the 16th century to 1975.

TIMELINE

- **6th century** BCE Iranian steppe nomads fight as mercenary cavalrymen for the kings of Persia.

- **3rd century** BCE Celtic mercenaries serve Egypt's Ptolemaic rulers and the kings of Asia Minor.

- **c.240** BCE The Mercenary War, an uprising of unpaid mercenaries against defeated Carthage at the end of the First Punic War.

- **c.800** Turkic *ghulam* slave-soldiers serve the Abbasid caliphs in the Middle East.

- **911** The first recorded mention of a Varangian Guard of Viking mercenaries in Byzantium.

- **1250** *Mamluk* slave-soldiers seize power in Egypt and establish a lasting dynasty.

- **1259** The first recorded mention of Gallowglass soldiers from Scotland's Highlands and Islands. They serve the Gaelic chiefs and Norman lords of Ireland for the next three centuries.

- **1476** Swiss pikemen attract attention across Europe with a spectacular victory over Charles the Bold's Burgundians at the battle of Grandson. Holy Roman Emperor Maximilian I founds the first *landsknecht* units at about this time.

- **1519** Spanish adventurer Hernán Cortés launches his invasion of Mexico. He will keep a share of any booty he brings back for the Spanish Crown.

- **1531** Francisco Pizarro campaigns against the Incas in Peru; like Cortés, his pay will be a share of the booty.

- **1534** *Landsknechts* employed by the Bishop of Münster against Anabaptist rebels go over to other side when he finds himself unable to pay them.

- **1631** The Massacre of Magdeburg: mercenaries slaughter an estimated 25,000 people, mostly civilians.

- **1817** The first recruitment of Nepalese Gurkha mercenaries by Britain's East India Company. The arrangement will later be formalized, with Gurkha regiments integrated into the British Army.

- **1831** The French Foreign Legion, an army of mercenaries of all nationalities, is founded in colonial Algeria.

- **1912** British and US mercenaries join the Nationalists in the Chinese Revolution.

- **1960–65** European mercenaries fight on all sides in the post-colonial Congo Crisis.

- **1975** The Angolan Civil War begins. Western governments fund mercenaries to help UNITA and FNLA rebels, after Cuba sends troops to support the government. Mercenaries are to play a similar role in the Mozambiquan Civil War (1977–92).

- **1995–2001** Foreign mercenaries directly employed by a South African private company, Executive Outcomes, support government forces in Sierra Leone's civil war.

- **2003** So-called military contractors take charge of support roles in Iraq, in the aftermath of the US-led invasion of the country and overthrow of Saddam Hussein. Most of these mercenaries are employed by a private company, Blackwater.

LANDSKNECHT'S BROADSWORD

Crusades in Europe

As the 12th century progressed, the medieval order came under increasing pressure. The authority of popes and kings began to wane. Home-grown heresies and popular resistance soon appeared as dangerous as the external, Islamic threat: the answer, once again, was to embark on a crusade.

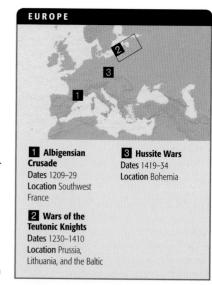

EUROPE

1 **Albigensian Crusade**
Dates 1209–29
Location Southwest France

2 **Wars of the Teutonic Knights**
Dates 1230–1410
Location Prussia, Lithuania, and the Baltic

3 **Hussite Wars**
Dates 1419–34
Location Bohemia

The Middle Ages are commonly described as an "Age of Faith". But the more fervently men and women believed in their religion and its ideals, the more susceptible they were to disillusionment. By the 12th century the wealth and power of the Church was giving rise to resentment. People saw it as being too close to the kings and nobles who exploited and oppressed them.

Some people, like the Cathars of the Languedoc in southwest France, rejected Christianity altogether. Theirs was a dualistic universe in which God and Satan were at war and love and power were locked in eternal opposition. The soul was immortal and belonged in heaven, the realm of God, of light. All that was material and earthly belonged to a darker, evil world – that of Satan or *Rex Mundi*, the "king of the world". Since Christ was "the Word made flesh", he

and his teachings were seen as evil too. The worldliness of the Church was obvious, and, far from being the "Bride of Christ", preached the Cathar, Arnald Hot, the Church was "espoused of the Devil and its doctrine diabolical".

Crusade against the Cathars

Such teachings found many followers, and as far as Pope Innocent III was concerned, this could not be ignored. The heretics were like the "Saracens", he said, and in 1209 he duly proclaimed a crusade against this enemy within.

From a military point of view, the "Albigensian Crusade" was a grotesquely one-sided affair: it took its name from the town of Albi, a hotbed of the heresy. Though local magnates like Count Raymond of Toulouse were involved, for the most part the "enemy" were defenceless peasants. All the ostentation of the medieval war machine – knights on horseback with huge processions of foot soldiers, including crossbowmen

10,000 The number of men who enlisted in the Albigensian Crusade against the Cathars of Languedoc in 1209.

and archers, as well as companies of mercenaries – were deployed against unarmed civilians. Sappers (military engineers) with siege-engines smashed through the walls of provincial cities.

There was no magnanimity towards the defeated. The crushing of heresy was sacred work. On 22 July 1209, crusaders sacked Béziers and killed 20,000 men, women, and children. More than 1,000 people were burned alive after taking refuge in a church. Though Pope Innocent II tried to rein in the carnage from about 1213, it had gained buoyant momentum and as many as a million people are thought to have died.

The Teutonic Knights

On Europe's eastern frontiers, the Baltic Slavs were recalcitrant under the shaky rule of the Polish kings. After recurrent invasions they remained obdurately unpacified – and pagan. When a call to defend the faith went out, the Teutonic Knights responded. A well-established

military order, they had been founded in Acre at the time of the Third Crusade. These German priests, like the Knights Hospitallers before them, had begun by tending the sick and wounded; in time they interpreted their duty more widely.

By 1198 the knights' role as fighting clerics had been acknowledged by the Church. Their function in the "Prussian Crusade" was not in doubt: from c.1230

◀◀ **BEFORE**

Christendom, now beleaguered both within and without, reverted back to the ideology and method of "Holy War" to resolve its problems and quash dissent.

IDEALISTIC RUSH
Pope Urban's call to Christians to join his crusade ◀◀ 74–75 had echoed down through the generations; it resonated on into the 13th century and beyond. Naturally, Europe's

HERESY An opinion or doctrine at variance with established religious beliefs. In the Middle Ages, the Christian church considered heresy a crime that could be punishable by death.

rulers – and their subjects – preferred to remember the **rush of idealism** that had originally inspired the wars with Islam rather than the **dismal failure of the more recent crusades** ◀◀ 76–77.

ENEMIES WITHIN
The Islamic threat had not vanished entirely, but Christian Europe faced new hazards at home. **Discontent with the Church was growing**; an increasingly educated public was tiring of its **tyrannical ways**. Those in power, however, saw this new threat in the same way as they saw the Islamic menace.

Battle of Muret
Simon de Montfort's crusaders take on the Albigensian army of Raymond of Toulouse, in 1213. De Montfort died besieging Raymond's stronghold in 1218.

they swept through Prussia and beyond into present-day Lithuania, Lativa, and Estonia. They fought as armoured cavalry, followed into the field by light cavalry and infantry. The pope had granted Prussia to the order as a "monastic state" – so, in theory, they were its rulers. But, in practice, this was untamed terrain and the knights struggled against opposing guerrilla factions. During the battle of Durbe in 1260, the knights allowed themselves to be surrounded by the Samogitians (pagan tribesmen from

Currency of the realm
The Teutonic Knights were able to carve out their own religious state in Prussia, and even issued their own currency, like this coin.

northwestern Lithuania) and suffered a damaging defeat that triggered a bloody uprising across Prussia.

Prussian resistance

This was not their first humiliation: to begin with the Teutonic Knights had campaigned not only against Prussian pagans but also against the Orthodox Christians of Russia. Attacking the city of Novgorod in 1240, they were defeated in 1242 by Prince Alexander Nevsky at the "Battle on the Ice". Here, they had been drawn out onto the frozen surface of Lake Peipus by Alexander's tactical retreat: the slipping charges of the heavily armoured knights were repelled by a resolute infantry, and those who did not fall through the thin ice became easy targets for archers.

From then on, the Teutonic Knights concentrated on Prussia, where they consolidated their position throughout the 14th century. Other states were growing in power, however: 1410 saw a showdown contest with the armies of Jagiellonian-ruled Lithuania and Poland.

During the battle of Grunwald (also named Tannenberg), more than 20,000 knights are believed to have faced up to 30,000 enemy cavalry, making this one of the biggest battles of medieval times. Both sides had thousands of infantrymen, crossbowmen, and archers. The knights also had field artillery, and viewing that as an advantage, they kept much of their cavalry in reserve. In the event, a downpour doused their gunpowder. When news came in that their general, Ulrich von Jungingen, had died morale collapsed and they fled in disarray.

Warfare reformed

Fighting with gunpowder may have had its disadvantages; nevertheless, this new technology offered a way forward – a fact that became evident in the Hussite Wars. Today, the teachings of Czech reformer and thinker, Jan Hus, are seen as paving the way for Martin Luther and the Reformation. But in his day, Hus was condemned as a heretic – and burned to death on July 6 1415. His followers rose in rebellion against the Bohemian Crown, which had the assistance of the Holy Roman Empire

of the German Nation – and of Pope Martin V, who proclaimed a crusade in 1420 "for the destruction of the Wycliffites, Hussites, and all other heretics in Bohemia". More crusades followed in 1421 and 1424. These campaigns proved inconclusive, thanks to the nerve and resourcefulness of the Hussite rebels – and the levelling effect of the hand-held cannons they used.

These cannons could hardly have been cruder: literally, they were little cannons held in the hand, their 20cm (8in) barrels mounted in wooden casing. The gunner cradled this in one hand, trying to keep it pointing in the direction of the enemy while he bent over to light the gunpowder charge with a spill or match. But accuracy or penetration-power mattered comparatively little, given that these weapons were being deployed against an enemy who came charging en masse, and who had no protection against flying shot – either through armour or through tactics. Mounted knights were losing their advantage over infantry. Gunpowder was democratizing war.

The Treaty of Thorn
Signed in 1412, this agreement brought peace between Poland, Lithuania, and the Teutonic Knights, but the reparations it called for would ruin the Teutonic state.

> ### AFTER

The crusading ideal was not yet dead as a philosophy, though it was constantly being reinterpreted in response to changing conditions and changing times.

CONTINUING CONFLICTS

In Spain the conflict between the Christians and the Muslims went on. **The Reconquista had been going on for centuries now and, though well advanced, had yet to be completed 98–99 ≫**. It was to last until 1492, each side taking and then retaking territories. The Teutonic Knights' war against Russian

8,000 The number of Teutonic Knights killed at the battle of Grunwald. A further 14,000 were captured or fled.

Orthodoxy had been a crusade against the cross. But soon **conflicts between fellow Christians** became the norm. The Reformation saw the **French Wars of Religion 134–35 ≫** and the cruel **Thirty Years War 142–43 ≫**.

But the method of war itself was undergoing change, and the religious conflicts of the following centuries were to provide the perfect testing-ground for ever more powerful, more accurate, and more sophisticated firearms.

TACTICAL REVOLUTION

The revolution in technology brought a revolution in tactics. Heavily armoured knights with lances gave way to **lighter cavalry armed with pistols** as well as swords. Infantrymen learned new drills for the coordinated loading, aiming, and firing of their matchlock and wheel-lock muskets. Artillery was also to play an increasingly important role, its presence in turn exerting a **powerful influence on tactics** in the field of war.

The fact that the Christians were fighting among themselves did not mean other threats had gone away. The Ottomans' rise changed the East; **in 1453 they took Constantinople 106–07 ≫**, and following centuries would see them **twice besiege Vienna 122–23 ≫**.

TACTICS

HUSSITE WAGENBURG

The *wagenburg*, or "wagon fort", was created by arranging carts to form a square enclosure, giving lightly armed infantry a way of resisting charging knights. Crucial to Hussite strategy, the idea of using wagons to create a wall was not new, but its use by the Hussites marked a real innovation. Set up discreetly and quickly, the *wagenburg* was consistently placed within firing range of the enemy. Inside, men with hand-cannons could safely open fire. The charging enemy found a solid wall of wagons, while the Hussites could keep up a steady barrage or sally forth among the horsemen with pikes or flails.

Anglo-Scottish Wars

The conflict between England and Scotland that began in the late 1200s continued intermittently for more than half a century. The period is known in Scotland as the Wars of Independence, yet the Scots were not fighting to gain their freedom, but rather to hold on to the independence they already had.

BRITISH ISLES

Anglo-Scottish Wars
Dates 1296–1328, 1332–57
Location Southern Scotland and northern England

John Balliol's coronation in 1292 was an uneasy compromise to the succession of King Alexander III of Scotland. Far from respecting Balliol's rule, Edward I of England insisted on his overlordship. Balliol looked to France for support, forging an alliance in 1295. Edward reacted furiously, invading Scotland. His army sacked Berwick-upon-Tweed before defeating the Scots at Dunbar, forcing John Balliol to abdicate. Edward carried off the Stone of Scone, on which the kings of Scotland had traditionally been crowned, and placed it in London's Westminster Abbey.

> **SCHILTRON Square or circular formation of infantry, with pikes presented outwards to create an impregnable wall of spikes to ward off enemy cavalry.**

Wallace's uprising

The following year, the Scots patriot William Wallace led a rebellion of minor nobles against the English. On 11 September 1297, they met the Earl of Surrey's army at Stirling Bridge over the river Forth. Three hundred Scottish knights were matched against ten times as many English cavalry, while some 10,000 Scots infantry faced up to more than 50,000 English.

The heroism of Wallace's victory has justly been acclaimed, but the battle was also a triumph of tactical cunning and discipline. The Scots waited on higher ground above the river until the English vanguard had crossed the narrow bridge, after which they surged downhill en masse. Seizing the bridge, the Scots set about the English army's advance-party, while Surrey and his remaining troops looked on helplessly from the other side of the river. Psychology did the rest: although Wallace's victory had by no means been complete, the demoralized Earl of Surrey ordered his men to retreat from the battle.

Enraged, Edward then led a second invasion, with 10,000 infantry and 2,000 knights. On 22 July 1298, he met Wallace at Falkirk, south of Stirling. Heavily outnumbered, the Scottish knights fled. Formed up in defensive schiltrons, however, the spearmen held firm, exacting heavy casualties on Edward's army.

In response, the English king brought up his reliable longbowmen: the Scots in their static schiltrons were

Fight to the death
Soldiers slug it out with bow and arrow, sword and axe, in this illustration from the Holkham Bible, written just a few years after the battle of Bannockburn.

sitting ducks. The arrows opened up gaping holes in their formations through which the English knights could charge. Hundreds died as Wallace's revolt met its bloody end.

The road to Bannockburn

Wallace escaped to France and did not return until 1303. He was caught and executed in 1305. The year after, the young Robert the Bruce killed his rival, John Comyn, in a quarrel and ascended the Scottish throne as Robert I. Comyn's family was not in a forgiving mood. Supported by Edward I, they surprised Robert at Methven, west of Perth, in 1306, almost wiping out his force. Robert was reduced to fighting a guerrilla war. In April 1307, his men rolled giant boulders down a steep hillside onto an unsuspecting English

« **BEFORE**

There was no such thing as "Britain" during the Middle Ages. Instead, there were two separate kingdoms – England and Scotland – and an autonomous principality, Wales.

ENGLAND'S PRE-EMINENCE
England had **size and wealth**, but the integrity of Scotland and Wales went unquestioned. English kings had enough difficulty keeping their **existing realm** together: their hold on the north was always shaky.

EDWARD I

THE INVASION OF WALES
Stronger than his predecessors, king Edward I invaded Wales in 1277 **to punish the defiance** of Prince Llewelyn. When the latter rebelled in 1282, Edward invaded again, smashing Welsh resistance and building a chain of castles to cement his rule. The power of the native-born princes was over, and **"Prince of Wales"** became a new title awarded to the English ruler's son and heir.

SCOTTISH SUCCESSION
The death of Alexander III's granddaughter in Scotland **sparked a crisis** in 1290. The king's sons had already died, so the succession lay open, with **14 claimants**, including Robert the Bruce, "the Competitor". Edward I judged the decision, demanding the **right of overlordship** – that of supreme lord or feudal superior – a "right" that was angrily rejected by the Scots. Robert had a son – also Robert the Bruce – as determined as his father that Scotland should be the kingdom of the Bruces.

army in Glen Trool, Galloway. Although not much of a "battle", Bruce took his triumphs where he could find them.

Edward I died in the summer of 1307. His son and successor, Edward II, was weak and indecisive, though he could still call upon a big and powerful army.

> **700** The number of villages in Northumberland that were burned to the ground by William Wallace and his army in the aftermath of his victory at Stirling Bridge in 1297.

Over 2,000 knights and some 14,000 infantrymen came north with him in 1314. They met Robert's army south of Stirling, in open country beside a stream – the Bannock Burn.

On 23 June, during their preliminary manoeuvres, an English knight spotted Robert the Bruce on his horse out in front of his own lines on open ground. He wore no armour and carried only a battle-axe. The knight charged, lance lowered for the kill. Refusing to flinch in sight of his watching soldiers, Robert calmly sidestepped and swung his axe, splitting the Englishman's helmet and skull wide open. The moment was an omen for the next day's battle.

Again, the Scots formed schiltrons. Yet, in the years since Falkirk, the troops had learned to advance without losing formation: the schiltron was no longer purely defensive. As the Scots advanced, their enemy was forced back. The English fled, many dying in the stampede across the Bannock Burn.

English bow and arrows
The continuing inability of the English mounted knights to deal with the schiltron of the Scottish infantry prompted a move towards mass deployment of longbowmen.

Diminishing returns

Bannockburn was Scotland's finest hour. Deposed in 1327, Edward II was succeeded by his son, Edward III. The king made common cause with the disgruntled "disinherited" faction (the Balliols and their supporters) against Robert the Bruce's young son, King David II. In 1332 John Balliol's son, Edward, defeated the Scottish army at Dupplin Moor near Perth. By July 1333 Berwick was under siege, and the English inflicted a shattering defeat at Halidon Hill. The town surrendered.

Dunstaffnage castle
As a stronghold of the Balliol cause, this 12th-century fortress outside Oban in the west of Scotland was besieged by Robert the Bruce in 1308 following the battle of the Pass of Brander.

AFTER

The capture of Berwick was a key turning point: the way was now open for the English, and the Scots could mount no credible defence against them.

AN ASSURED DEFEAT
The full-scale **conquest and occupation** of the country appeared inevitable. The Scots offered small-scale resistance with hit-and-run attacks and skirmishes, but knew they could not win a **head-on confrontation with the English**. Their strategy of harrying and hoping was to succeed beyond their wildest dreams. England's momentum in Scotland slowly ebbed away through the 1330s and beyond, with Edward increasingly preoccupied with his **hostilities with France 102–03 ≫**.

TREATY OF BERWICK
In 1357 David II signed the **Treaty of Berwick** with Edward III, agreeing that the English king should succeed him in Scotland on his death. The Scots as a nation never accepted this, however, appointing their own king, **Robert II**, when David died in 1371.

POLITICAL DEVELOPMENTS
The **Anglo-Scottish conflict** continued. Scotland remained its own kingdom, even after the devastating **defeat at Flodden** in 1513. A dynastic crisis forced the **"Union of the Crowns"** in 1603 – James VI becoming James I of England when Elizabeth I died childless. Full union of the two countries did not come until 1707.

« BEFORE

Medieval Spain was first conquered by the Moors in the 8th century, with many regions soon falling under the authority of the caliphate of Córdoba.

A MUSLIM ADVANCE

Since **the prophet Muhammad** first proclaimed his message in the 7th century, a series of Arab conquests had spread the **word of Islam** through much of the known world. Crossing the Straits of Gibraltar, the Moors (the Muslim inhabitants of North Africa) had **taken most of Spain « 64–65**. Their advance in Western Europe had been held by the Franks at the **battle of Poitiers « 68–69**, but this left almost all of the Iberian Peninsula in Moorish hands. Only in a tiny pocket, in the mountains of Asturias in the far north, did **Christian rulers** still hold sway.

A GLITTERING KINGDOM

Most of what we think of today as **Portugal and Spain** were under the control of the caliphate of Córdoba, proclaimed in 929 by Abd ar-Rahman III. The Moors referred to their Spanish kingdom as **al-Andalus**: centred on the south, in the region known today as Andalucía, it was a place of wealth

> **MOZARAB A Christian living in Moorish Spain who had adopted many aspects of Muslim culture. Mudejars, conversely, were Muslims living under Christian rule.**

and culture. **Toledo, the Visigothic capital** of the country, became a major centre under the Moors as well. After quarrels among the rulers of the al-Andalus, this region went its separate way, becoming an **independent kingdom** under the control of the caliphate.

The Spanish Reconquista

The identity of Spain was forged in fighting; the Reconquista – the "reconquest" of those territories taken by the Moors – was, for centuries, the guiding project of the nation. These wars became the stuff of legend for subsequent generations, but the reality was often messy and confused.

The Spanish Reconquista started as a fight for survival and became a power struggle, only gradually did it take on the character of a crusade. By the middle of the 8th century, the Moors had occupied almost the entire Iberian Peninsula. In 722, however, amid the mountains of Asturias to the north, the Muslims had been held by the local

88 The number of towers in the fortified walls encircling the Spanish city of Ávila.

Visigothic ruler, Pelayo, at the battle of Covadonga. Here, at least, the idea of a Christian Spain endured.

In the centuries that followed, the region of Asturias not only flourished but managed to extend its boundaries. In 910, indeed, it was divided into two. A new kingdom, Galicia, was established in the west, with a new state centred on León. Next to this, the kingdom of Castile was created: the two later united as the kingdom of Castile and León in the 11th century. To the east, following

Castillo de Loarre
From its perch in the Pyrenean foothills in Aragón, this 11th-century stronghold commanded what was then the border between Navarra and Muslim Zaragoza.

A boat departs for the crusades
Equipped for action and clad in armour, Spanish knights of the 13th century show their commitment to a strongly militarized version of the Christian faith.

Frankish incursions across the Pyrenees, the kingdoms of Navarra, Aragón, and Catalonia emerged. Although this was a patchwork of little states that warred as much with one another as with the Moors, all of northern Spain had now fallen into Christian hands.

War without end

Within these little kingdoms too, conflict was very much the norm, with local lords locked in endless small-scale turf wars. Combat was mostly between mounted knights: any local peasants who might have made up the infantry were usually needed on the land. At the same time, there were truces in fighting with the Muslims – some of them of long duration. The Moors had their own divisions, with inequalities between the Arab elite and the North African Berber rank-and-file leading at times to tension and, in some cases, open conflict.

The Reconquista was more messy and confusing than the later mythology would have us believe. The story of the renowned "El Cid" is case in point.

Rodrigo Díaz de Vivar (c.1045–99) was a truly formidable figure; but

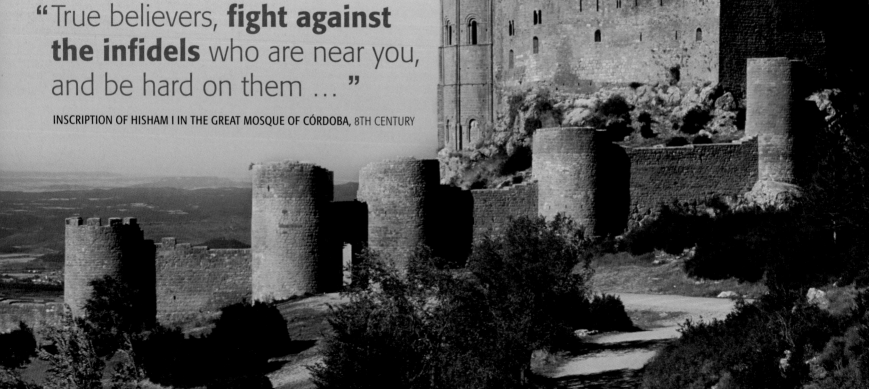

> " True believers, **fight against the infidels** who are near you, and be hard on them … "
>
> INSCRIPTION OF HISHAM I IN THE GREAT MOSQUE OF CÓRDOBA, 8TH CENTURY

FRANCE

to France
BÉARN
Toulouse
NAVARRA
Carcassonne
Santiago de
Compostela
Oviedo
GALICIA
León
Pamplona
Pyrenees
ANDORRA
Huesca
Burgos
Gîrona
Valladolid
Zaragoza
1118
CATALONIA
Lérida
Oporto
Douro
Ebro
Barcelona
Salamanca
Ávila
A
R
A
G
Ó
N
Teruel
Tarragona
Tortosa
1148
Coimbra
PORTUGAL
Alcántara
Tagus
Toledo
1085
Mallorca
Santarém
CASTILE
Valencia
1238
Palma
1229
Lisbon
1147
Sagrajas 1080
Badajoz
1230
Alarcos
1195
Calatrava
Cuarte
1096
Ibiza
Balearic
Islands
Alcacer
1217
Évora
Las Navas de
Tolosa 1212
Alicante
Ourique 1139
Seville
1248
Córdoba
1236
Murcia
1243
Silves
Algarve
Andalucía
Jaén 1246
Lorca
1243
Mediterranean Sea
Faro
1249
Jerez
1231
Antequera
Granada
1492
Almería
Cádiz
1262
Tarifa
1292
Málaga
Tangier
Ceuta 1415
ZAYYANIDS
to Portugal
WATTASIDS
AFRICA

N
0   200km
0   200 miles

Fortunes of war

The Reconquista only appears continuous and inexorable in retrospect: the frontier was porous; loyalties either side of it were divided. Very gradually, however, the Christian kingdoms extended their influence over southern Spain.

Key

Under Christian control by 1100
Under Christian control by 1180
Under Christian control by 1280
Under Christian control by 1492
Frontier of Almoravid Empire c.1115
Frontier of Almohad Empire c.1180
— Frontiers 1493
1230 Date of reconquest
⚔ Christian victory
⚔ Muslim victory

he was also a profoundly ambivalent one, as his very nickname shows. "Cid" is no Spanish word, but comes from the Arabic *sayyidi* ("chief" or "boss"). He was a warlord, loyal mainly to himself. Amidst the complicated realities of a rapidly changing situation, he found himself fighting on the Muslim side on more than one occasion.

Though real, religious oppositions sometimes paled into insignificance beside other enmities. It was not unusual for Muslim and Christian leaders to form alliances against rivals in their own camps. Even so, by slow degrees Christian kings were extending their sphere of influence: in 1074 Ferdinand I of León took Coimbra, now in Portugal, from the Moors.

Holy war

In 1077 Alfonso VI, king of Castile, announced that he was the "Emperor of all Spain". No longer content to tussle with his fellow kings, he saw himself – in aspiration, at least – as ruler of the peninsula as a whole. He captured Toledo, until then the centre of a rich and prestigious Muslim state.

Thrown into panic, the rulers of al-Andalus called on assistance from the Almoravids, who had recently taken power in North Africa. The Almoravids went on to beat Alfonso at the battle of Sagrajas in 1086. But their fight was only just beginning, as the elite of al-Andalus found out

to their consternation. A Berber movement, dedicated to both moral and spiritual renewal within Islam, the Almoravids disapproved of the easygoing attitudes they found in Moorish Spain, and now set about transforming it into their own kind of aggressively Islamic state.

The Almoravids started reversing the conquests of the Christians, but met their match in 1094 at Valencia. El Cid took the southeastern city after a siege of 20 months: he set up as ruler there, ostensibly in Alfonso's name. In many ways, El Cid was the last in a line whose attitude to the struggle with the Muslims remained opportunistic. But such pragmatism was becoming unacceptable. Even as the Almoravids were changing the tone of the conflict on the Muslim side, there was a clear shift on the side of the Christians too. The calling of the First Crusade in 1099 placed the conflict with the Moors in a new perspective, as a sacred struggle to reclaim Iberia for the creed of Christ.

On the offensive

It was a struggle the Christians seemed to be winning: in 1118 King Alfonso I of Aragón and Navarra took the city of Zaragoza. El Batallador ("The Battler") soon made deep inroads into the south, where Christian Mozarabs – happy under Moorish rule for many generations – were finding life a lot

El Cid's sword

An inscription claims that this weapon is Tizona, the legendary sword of El Cid. Metallurgical analysis has shown that the steel blade was forged in Córdoba in the 11th century.

less comfortable under the Almoravids. After one audacious raid, King Alfonso brought 10,000 of them back with him for resettlement along the Ebro in the far northwest.

In 1139 another Alfonso won a victory, defeating the Almoravids at Ourique, in what is now the south of Portugal. Here, Alfonso Henriques, son of Henry of Burgundy, who also claimed the title of Count of Portugal, led his considerably outnumbered Christian army to a victory. In the cold light of military history, this result, although unexpected, seems to have been the consequence of failing communication and disagreements on the Moorish side. Not unnaturally, the Christians were overjoyed at this most unexpected triumph and were quick to attribute it to divine agency.

It was in fact this triumph that brought the modern country into being. Alfonso declared – defying Castile and León – that he intended to reign over his conquered territory as Afonso I of Portugal. That country's capital, Lisbon, was liberated following a six-week siege by crusaders en route for the Holy Land: the local bishop promised them the right of rape and plunder in the city in return.

The Almoravids found themselves faced with another enemy in the 12th century. This time, they were Muslim. These were the Almohads, also Berbers, and also seeking Islamic renewal. Having already taken over the territories of the Almoravids in North Africa, establishing their capital at Marrakesh, they invaded al-Andalus in 1147. In doing so, they reversed what had been the gradual weakening in Moorish resistance to the Reconquista. Even so, the northern kingdoms scented victory and pressed hard to repel them. Begged by his officials in al-Andalus, Abu Yusuf Yaqub, the

30,000 The number of **Christian combatants killed at the battle of Alarcos, 1195, according to chroniclers of the day. Muslim losses were fewer than 500.**

The Reconquista substantially moulded early-modern Spain – very much for the worse, it might be argued. Religious and political conformity was rigidly enforced.

PURGING ISLAM

1469 saw the accession of the "Catholic Monarchs", Ferdinand and Isabella. Their marriage brought the kingdoms of **Navarra, Aragón, and Castile** together into a single Spain, so they were "catholic" in the sense of being universal. But they were also "Catholic" in the religious sense: indeed, the royal couple were fanatical in their faith and in their insistence that it should be practised throughout their territories. Under their authority, and that of their successors, the **Inquisition** sought to root out not only Christian heretics but anyone observing the rites of **Islam** (or, for that matter, of **Judaism**). The desire to purge society of **every trace** of its Islamic

FERDINAND AND ISABELLA, THE "CATHOLIC MONARCHS"

past led to an obsession with ideas of *limpieza* (racial and religious "cleanness" or "purity").

ACROSS THE OCEAN

The **final expulsion** of the Moors, as it happened, coincided with Columbus's discovery of America. The opening up of a **"New Spain"** in the colonial Americas was to be justified as a continuation of the Christianizing struggle of the Reconquista.

Almohad Caliph, came from Morocco and took personal command of the kingdom's armies. He inflicted a shattering defeat on Alfonso VIII in the battle of Alarcos, earning himself the title, by which he is still remembered, *al-Mansur* ("the Victor").

Final victory

The "Disaster of Alarcos" was followed by other reversals for Alfonso. But at the battle of Las Navas de Tolosa, he won his revenge. Leading his army stealthily over the mountains of Andalucía, he sprang a surprise attack upon the Almohads. The vast Muslim army – by all accounts up to 300,000 strong, although this amount is dubious – was all but exterminated in the brutal fighting. The Reconquista had acquired unstoppable momentum. Even so, the struggle was to continue for the best part of three centuries: it would not be until 1492 that the Moors were finally expelled from Granada.

The triumph of the longbow
Longbowmen and crossbowmen fire at point-blank range in this stylized 15th-century depiction of the battle. It was the longbowmen who determined the outcome – and changed military history for ever.

Crécy

The long and bloody story of the Hundred Years War was to have many more twists before it ended: the English victors in the battle at Crécy in northern France in August 1346 would go on to lose the war. But Crécy was still decisive: it was not just an army that was defeated that day, but the mounted knight, his military function, and – above all – his whole ethos, the code of chivalry he stood for.

The English were in good heart on crossing the sea to Normandy. Their landing had not been expected by the French. They all but sauntered into Caen, "liberating" large quantities of wine before continuing on their way. Longbowmen slipped off into wayside woods, returning with deer and other game. Edward III and his army were living the high life.

A demoralized army

The French, though at home and numerically much stronger, felt far less cheerful. Mobilized in haste, they were exhausted from their forced march north. Undersupplied, they were hungry and dehydrated. Even in Picardy's green countryside there was not enough water for their thousands of horses. Besides having no fewer than three commanders – Philip VI himself, blind King John of Bohemia, and Charles, Count of Alençon – the French army was top-heavy with knights and nobles. It felt paradoxically leaderless.

Edward's men were lined up along a ridge, with his longbowmen (up to 10,000-strong) under the command of his son – the Black Prince, Edward, Prince of Wales – grouped in wedges on either side. The French would have to attack uphill and brave the arrows as they advanced on the English centre.

An unsettling stillness fell upon the sultry summer's afternoon. Rooks descended in huge, chattering flocks, unnerving the soldiers as the sky grew ominously dark. Suddenly, lightning flashed, thunder clapped, and the heavens opened. Then, just as abruptly, the skies cleared, the downpour ceased, and the sun came out again. Now, though, it glinted on the armour of the English knights, dazzling the French.

A deadly rain

In the French front line stood Genoese crossbowmen, cruelly exposed: they had not had time to unpack their long shields, and their bowstrings were soggy from the rain. Dispirited, they broke as battle commenced and the first English and Welsh arrows hit home. As they ran, the French knights contemptuously cut them down.

The French cavalry charged, and the air again turned black – with showers of English and Welsh arrows. Panic and confusion gripped the French. "The archers shot so marvellously," recorded the 14th-century Flemish chronicler Jean le Bel, "that some of those on horseback, feeling these barbed arrows which did such wonders, would not advance, while others … capered hideously, and others turned their backs on the enemy." Chaos became carnage, the hill a heaving mass of screaming men and horses.

Nightfall ended the slaughter. The French had been trounced – and the mounted, armoured knight humbled by the low-born longbowman.

LOCATION
Picardy, northern France

DATE
26 August 1346

FORCES
French: 25,000–60,000;
English: 10,000–20,000

CASUALTIES
French: probably 4,000 dead;
English: 200 dead

KEY
■ French infantry
◢ French cavalry
■ Genoese crossbowmen
■ English, Welsh, and Irish infantry
■ English and Welsh longbowmen

The **Hundred Years War**

The insistence of England's kings that they had the right to reign over France as well sparked off a conflict which continued on and off for more than a century. Over that period, developments in military tactics and the advent of firearms technology gradually changed the face of medieval warfare.

« BEFORE

In the 1300s England and France were fluid concepts; kings and lords meant more than nation-states. The Plantagenet kings were rooted in English society *and* tied to France.

SOURED RELATIONS
Suspicion between England and France had existed since the **Norman Conquest of 1066 « 70–71**. William and his successors had been kings in England, with lands in Normandy and Aquitaine, but only vassals of the kings of France. They disliked deferring to the country's kings. Anglo-French relations were not helped by Louis VIII of France. He had aided mutinous English nobles in their attempt to **topple King John** in the first "Barons' War" of 1215–17.

EDWARD III

A WEAKENED KING
As Duke of Aquitaine, England's Edward II became exasperated with being an underling to successive kings of France: in 1324 his **anger boiled over in the War of Saint-Sardos**. Edward was defeated and found his position on both sides of the Channel weakened. His French queen, Isabella, was sent to negotiate on his behalf, and Edward of Windsor, the future Edward III, was **left in no doubt of his father's humiliation**.

CLAIMS TO THE THRONE
France's throne had been left vacant when **the Capetian line became extinct** with the death of Charles IV in 1328. His first cousin, Philip VI, succeeded him. However, England's Edward III was the late king's nephew – his mother, Isabella, had been Charles's sister. **His claims were not without merit**, even though they came through a **female line**.

NORTHWEST EUROPE

Hundred Years War
Dates 1337–1453
Location Chiefly northern France, also Flanders and Gascony

On 19 October 1337, Edward III wrote to Philip VI of France, upbraiding him as a usurper, "our enemy and adversary". However, declaring war was one thing, actually waging it another: Edward faced a frustrating struggle to fund his fight.

Not until 1340 was battle joined: on 24 June English and French fleets clashed at Sluys, off Flanders, whose independence Edward had promised to defend against French encroachments. The battle of Sluys was not so much a naval encounter as a land battle at sea. The French had chained their ships together to form a wall, but while this presented a solid front, it made their decks into a continuous battlefield. Longbowmen aboard the English vessels rained arrows on to the advancing French fleet, softening up any resistance before boarding parties were dispatched.

The French held out for eight bloody hours, but were eventually forced to capitulate – up to 18,000 soldiers and sailors were killed. Yet, despite the loss of their fleet, the French were by no means beaten.

An unequal struggle

Small-scale skirmishes and truces alternated until, in 1346, Edward III invaded France. He landed at Calais but, for the moment at least, ignored the port city. Instead, his soldiers advanced inland, burning and looting along the way. At Crécy they found a French army waiting.

Though the English were hugely outnumbered, there were other inequalities to be considered: Philip's 40,000 troops were largely untrained

2 The number of English knights believed to have been killed at the battle of Crécy. Fewer than 300 footsoldiers fell. But more than 1,500 French knights were killed and several thousand infantry.

and his nobles distracted by faction-fighting. Edward arrayed his men along a ridge in a "V-formation". His 5,000 spearmen were in the centre, his mounted knights (4,000 in all) on either side, and divided between the flanks, some 7,000 longbowmen. They were under the command of

Poleaxe
Three weapons in one, the poleaxe had a spike for thrusting, an axe-head for chopping, and a hammer for crushing: the shaft was protected by steel strips, or "langets".

— Axe-head

Edward III's son, Edward, Prince of Wales or the "Black Prince". Although the English had a few cannon – their first known appearance on the battlefield in Western history – they did not shape the battle. Instead, it was the innovative use of an ancient weapon

"We shall **claim and conquer** our heritage of France … "

LETTER FROM EDWARD III TO PHILIP VI OF FRANCE, 1337

– the longbow – deployed here en masse. On the Black Prince's signal, says chronicler Jean Froissart, "The English archers took one pace forward and poured out their arrows … so thickly and evenly that they fell like snow." The carnage was horrific, compounded by the heavy cannon fire that followed. What was most discouraging for the French was the fact that they never actually engaged their English enemy. Trained for close-quarters fighting, they were

held at a distance by Edward's archers: every time the French charged, a fresh blizzard of arrows cut them down.

Edward now turned his attention to Calais: its defences seemed just about impregnable, so he resigned himself to a lengthy siege. It took almost a year to starve the city into submission. Edward brought in settlers to make this crucial port an outpost of England. (It became an important centre for the wool trade.)

Siege and slaughter

The year 1347 saw the destructive power of humanity eclipsed by that of the Black Death. Up to a third of the population of Northern Europe may have been killed by the bubonic plague; serious hostilities had to be suspended for some years. By the 1350s, though, the English were ready to start fighting again. The Black Prince ravaged the country as he launched a *chevauchée* – a campaign of plunder and slaughter intended to demoralize the French and

deplete their resources. In 1356 the French, under Jean II, tried to make a stand at Poitiers; as at Crécy, their army massively outnumbered England's. Again, though, the longbow won the day, causing dreadful casualties among the French while the English went

Hostilities begin
During the naval battle of Sluys in 1340, the French fleet were tied together in a defensive wall – unable to move, they were at the mercy of the English. The triumph gave England control of the Channel for the rest of the war.

The siege of Orléans
The English used artillery, the French hand-cannon, but firepower lost out to inspiration. After six months of stalemate from 1428–29, Joan of Arc's counter-attacks lifted the Siege of Orleans in just nine days.

substantially unscathed. A truce of sorts was agreed, the fighting flaring up once more in the 1360s before subsiding from the 1380s onwards. When Henry V ascended the English throne in 1413, he looked across the Channel to a France divided by discord. His invasion of 1415 began disastrously, though: he lost half his men to the plague within weeks of landing in Normandy. The survivors set off for Calais but soon found themselves facing a huge French army at Agincourt.

More than 20,000 French soldiers faced fewer than 8,000 Englishmen. But while the battle was fought on open ground, woods hemmed the men in on either side, so the French soldiers could not fully exploit their advantage. The majority of their knights were preparing to fight on foot, while the rear ranks remained mounted: once the fighting started, they swept round to charge the English longbowmen on either flank. After their earlier defeats, the French were intent on neutralizing the threat of archers at the outset; but, forced back by the hail of arrows, they became snarled up in their own lines, leaving the entire French force in a state of confusion as the English advance began. It was Crécy and Poitiers again; another victory for the English longbow.

But the archer's ascendancy was of short duration. Gunpowder was playing a more important part in a conflict that was settling down into a series of sieges. However, it had a function in the field of battle too. Improved alloys allowed the manufacture of more powerful, stable cannons, which, in 1453, would deliver a deadly counterblast against the English archers at Castillon. Later that same year, Bordeaux was taken and the English army was at last expelled. Calais apart, France belonged to the French Crown.

So protracted a conflict could not help but have a lasting impact on both countries. Enmity between France and England continued for centuries afterwards.

FURTHER DIVISIONS
When Pope Julius II quarrelled with France in the 16th century, King Henry VIII of England took the pontiff's side. But the king's own falling-out with the Church did nothing to improve relations: rather, **the Reformation drove a further wedge** between Protestant England and Catholic France. Henry hoped to use the religious conflict to extend his French possessions. In the event, though, Mary I **lost the port of Calais in 1558**.

ENDURING ENMITY
The two countries clashed again during the **French Wars of Religion 134–35 ≫**, the **reign of Louis XIV 152–53 ≫**, and in **the War of the Spanish Succession 154–55 ≫**. Indeed, it was not until the second half of the 19th century that France and Britain were able to build an enduring friendship.

FRENCH SOLDIER (c.1412–1431)
JOAN OF ARC

A peasant's daughter, Joan of Arc was just 16 when, in 1428, she appeared out of nowhere, citing an order from God to drive the English out of France. She promised to lead her countrymen to victory over the invaders and, won round by her conviction, Charles VII had her kitted out with armour. The girl-soldier led the French to several important victories. In 1430, however, she was captured by the English. Still only 19, she was burned at the stake as a "witch", though she was later revered as a patriotic martyr and, eventually, canonized in 1920.

1 GERMAN BRONZE-AGE SWORD (1000 BCE)

4 SCOTTISH HIGHLAND
BROADSWORD (16TH CENTURY)

12 PERSIAN KILIJ
(19TH CENTURY)

7 EUROPEAN SWEPT-HILT
RAPIER (17TH CENTURY)

13 ENGLISH INFANTRY HANGER
(19TH CENTURY)

14 AMERICAN UNION INFANTRY
SWORD (1860)

2 VIKING SWORD
(1000 CE)

3 ITALIAN SWORD (15TH CENTURY)

5 JAPANESE KATANA (16TH CENTURY)

6 GERMAN DOUBLE-HANDED
BROADSWORD (1550)

8 SCOTTISH BROADSWORD (1750)

9 INDIAN KHANDA (19TH CENTURY)

Swords

A weapon, a personal talisman, a mark of rank, a status symbol: for centuries the sword was all these things. But even though it has become obsolete on the battlefield, the sword is still regarded by many to be the eternal accoutrement of the warrior.

10 INDIAN TULWAR (1801)

11 TURKISH SABRE (19TH CENTURY)

1 **This German Bronze-Age sword** dates from about 1000 BCE. It was designed for slashing and was often more effective than a spear. **2** **Viking swords** were made of iron. In use from the first millennium, iron was stronger than bronze and could be pattern-welded – blending separate bits of iron to form a stronger, longer whole. **3** **This medieval Italian sword** from the 15th century had its blade quenched in water for extra toughness; a crossguard helped protect the user's hand. **4** **This Highland "hand-and-a-half" sword** was developed in Scotland in the 16th century. It was light, yet powerful, and could be wielded with either one or two hands, hence its name. **5** **The** *katana* of the 16th century is the archetypal "Samurai Sword". **6** **This double-handed broadsword** was made to be wielded with both hands. It was not designed as a piercing weapon and has a blunt end.

7 **This European swept-hilt rapier** was a thrusting infantry weapon. The rapier was also the dueller's weapon of choice. **8** **The basket-hilted broadsword** is closely associated with the 18th-century Scottish Highlander. **9** **The** *khanda* was the sword of choice for India's Sikhs of the 19th century. **10** **The Indian** *tulwar* originated in Persia and was the typical sword of Mogul India. The curved blade is traditionally Indian. **11** **This Turkish sabre** from the Ottoman empire is inscribed with texts from the Koran. **12** **This Turkish-style** *kilij,* **or scimitar,** evolved from the sabres of the steppe warriors; the yelman, or flaring towards the tip, enhanced its cutting power. **13** **The hanger** was issued to English foot soldiers in the 19th century. It is a variation of a short hunting sword. **14** **This Model 1850 infantry sword** was worn, but not much used, by Union officers.

« BEFORE

The Byzantine empire had been under pressure for centuries, increasingly confined to the area immediately around its capital, Constantinople (present-day Istanbul).

MIXED FORTUNES

Originally the eastern part of the Roman empire, Byzantium went on to develop **its own identity**. After the fall of Rome in the 5th century, it became a superpower in itself, although it was predominantly eastward-looking in its **imperial ambitions « 62–63**.

By the **end of the first millennium**, the empire was on the retreat; the Seljuk Turks had overrun most of its **Middle Eastern territories « 72–73**. In 1204 Constantinople was **sacked by crusaders « 76–77**. Since then, the empire's fortunes had partially recovered.

CONSTANTINOPLE'S RESTORED CITY WALLS

EASTERN MEDITERRANEAN

Ottoman expansion
Dates 1300–1453
Location Turkey and the Balkans

TECHNOLOGY

GRENADES

The Byzantines made great efforts to defend Constantinople against the Turks. They did at least possess the useful secret of "Greek Fire" – thought to be a blend of burning oil and tar. At sea it was pumped from dispensers which could be aimed at enemy vessels. Moreover, it could also be used ashore: defenders used terracotta grenades which broke on impact, erupting into flames. The soldiers flung them from catapults or dropped them on the enemy from fortifications. The Byzantines also used them to flush out Mehmed's miners from the tunnels they had been instructed to dig beneath the city walls.

"GREEK FIRE" HAND GRENADES

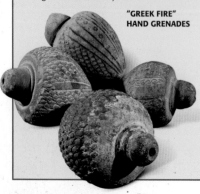

The **End** of the Byzantine Empire

By the middle of the 15th century the Ottoman Turks had all but completely encircled the Byzantine empire, occupying not just Anatolia but the Balkans and northern Greece. From 1451 Sultan Mehmed II started closing in on Constantinople: he laid siege to the city on 2 April 1453.

The Ottomans were named for Osman, a 14th-century Turkic warlord whose divinely ordained imperial destiny was said to have been revealed to him in a dream. Moving into Anatolia with his kinsfolk and clansmen, he offered their services as soldiers to the Byzantine empire and then built his own power base in what remained of the Seljuk state. He achieved this against the reluctance of the Byzantines; indeed, the mercenary bullied his masters into acquiescence.

Into Europe

Under Osman's son, Orkhan, the Ottomans extended their dominions across the Bosphorus and into Thrace. Successive sultans conquered Bulgaria and Macedonia. A coalition of Christian princes came together to face Murad I at the Amselfeld in Kosovo in 1389. A Serbian suicide-squad succeeded in assassinating Murad as the battle commenced, but Bayezid I took charge and won the day. His victory secured him Serbia and Bosnia.

Bayezid had been lucky – or so it seemed. The Christian knights had broken through the main mass of Ottoman infantry, foundering only at the last. It took a succession of these "narrow" defeats for them to realize that the Ottomans deliberately placed their softer, more expendable corps of conscripts in the front. European knights would have to fight their way through repeatedly and, exhausted, find themselves facing the enemy's elite soldiers: the janissaries. Fanatically loyal to each other, to the Ottoman empire, and to Islam, the janissaries were slave soldiers. Many of them, ironically, had originated from the empire's Christian territories. Recruited as boys, they grew up in the sultan's service. Highly disciplined and superbly trained, the majority of them knew no

Ottoman "turban" helmet
Beautifully crafted in steel in around 1500, this Ottoman helmet functioned not just as protective headgear, but also as a mark of rank.

other life. The Ottomans also deployed a growing range of artillery: cannon, first seen at Kosovo, were used increasingly from then on. Above all, the Ottomans were quicker and more ready to innovate than the Christians, who were still attached to the chivalric tradition. The news from Kosovo awoke the West to the danger represented by the Turks. Pope Boniface IX proclaimed a fresh crusade. Over 90,000 heeded the call: contingents came from Switzerland,

160,000 The number of Ottoman soldiers present at the siege of Constantinople in 1453. The defenders, only 5,000 strong, still held out for almost two months.

France, Germany, Hungary, Wallachia, and Poland; the Knights Hospitaller and Teutonic Knights also participated. Yet all these groups had their own leaders, and their divisions proved fatal to the cause. The Ottomans won a resounding victory at Nicopolis in 1396.

A major setback

Just as he prepared to close in on Constantinople, however, Bayezid met his own nemesis. In 1402 Timur Lenk appeared in Anatolia with his Mongol army. Taken by surprise, Bayezid marched his army across the country in the searing heat of summer. They reached Ankara, where Timur was waiting, in a state of near-exhaustion, only to find that the warlord had poisoned the wells and diverted the waters of the Çuluk Creek so that the Ottomans and their horses had no access to drinking water. Even so, they put up fierce resistance once battle was joined the next day, on 20 July, but

they ultimately suffered a shattering defeat. Bayezid was taken prisoner by Timur and died a year later, still captive.

It took the Turks decades to rebuild their forces. Christian Europe fought back – Hungary's Janos Hunyadi scored some spirited victories in the 1440s – but the European nations were still dogged by disunity, leaving them weak.

Under siege

Meanwhile, under Mehmed II, the siege of Constantinople began in April 1453. Mehmed II built his own fortress, Rumeli Hisar, which controlled access to the Black Sea. In a single night, more than 70 warships were shifted overland on rollers into Constantinople's inner harbour so that a sustained assault could be mounted from the water. Huge cannon were deployed around the city: the biggest could fire a 500kg (1,100lb) ball. While these big guns pounded the city walls above ground-level, Mehmed instructed miners to tunnel beneath. Despite tremendous resolve, on May 29, the city fell.

AFTER »

The fall of Constantinople brought the Byzantine empire to an end after 1,000 years, but – renamed Istanbul – it was to continue to play a historic role.

A NEW AGE FOR THE CITY

The **Ottoman empire** went from strength to strength. Eventually, along with southeastern Europe, it occupied much of the **old Arab Empire 122–23 »**. Constantinople was transformed, and the great church of Hagia Sophia became a **stunning mosque** as the sultans assumed the authority of the old caliphs as leaders of the **Islamic world**.

A LONG DECLINE

From the end of the 17th century, the Ottoman empire **stagnated** and then passed almost imperceptibly into a long decline. Even so, inertia carried this "Sick Man of Europe" on until the final collapse came after **World War I 266–67 »**.

The fall of Constantinople
That so small a force of defenders was able to hold out against the Ottomans for so long is testimony to the strength of this great city's fortifications.

3
EARLY MODERN WARFARE
1500 – 1750

As the major kingdoms of Europe grew more powerful, the Age of Discoveries opened up the world for conquest. The Americas were easily conquered, but Asia's empires – China, Mogul India, and the Ottoman Turks – were all more powerful than any European state.

INDIAN SPIKED MACE, EARLY 18TH CENTURY

EARLY MODERN WARFARE
1500 – 1750

During the era from 1500 to 1750 European land and naval forces transformed themselves into potential agents of world domination. This was apparent at sea early on, as sailing ships armed with cannon extended European power to the coasts of Africa and Asia, and made possible the conquest of substantial parts of the Americas. The Spanish conquistadors overthrew the great American land empires of the Aztecs and Incas in the 1520s and 1530s with what seemed remarkable ease. But these were Stone-Age societies, without horses or the wheel, and their populations were devastatingly vulnerable to Old World diseases. Elsewhere in the world, European armies at first enjoyed no clear technological or organizational superiority over Asian or African states.

In the 16th and 17th centuries Christian Europe was torn apart by religious and dynastic wars. It was also engaged in a desperate struggle to hold off pressure from the Muslim Ottoman empire in the Mediterranean and southeast Europe. Not only the Ottomans but the other great Muslim empires of the Moguls in India and the Safavids in Persia fielded impressive fighting forces, and the Moroccan army beat both African and European opponents. The conquest of Ming China by the Manchu in the mid-17th century involved military campaigns larger in scale than any contemporary European wars. Nor were armies outside Europe at all technologically backward. The Japanese, the Ottomans, and the Moroccans all made sophisticated use of muskets; the Chinese deployed cannon on a large scale; and the Koreans fought the Japanese in the 1590s with metal-armoured ships.

The changing battlefield

European armies began the period struggling to adapt their tactics to exploit increasingly effective gunpowder weapons and pike-wielding infantry. Although matchlock arquebuses and muskets were neither accurate nor quick-firing, they displaced bows from the battlefield. Various combinations of musketeers and pikemen were employed, with an increasing proportion of muskets as time went on. Commanders recognized the need for infantry to be disciplined and formal drill was introduced with musket and pike. Cavalry retained prestige and social status, but the armoured knight with lance gradually died out. Swords and firearms became the principal weapons of horsemen on the battlefield. These ranged from heavily armoured dragoons, who dismounted to fight with

The riches of South America

This gold mask was made by the Chimú people of Peru. The Chimú established the largest empire in South America before they were conquered by the Incas between 1465 and 1470.

Technological advances

This over-and-under flintlock pistol was made by Dutch gun-maker Andrew Dolep in the 17th century. By this time gunpowder weapons had become increasingly dominant on the battlefield.

carbines, to the light cavalry, who acted as scouts and skirmishers. Field artillery was introduced but, above all, guns revolutionized the design of fortifications. There were no more castles with high stone walls, but lower-lying star forts that allowed cannon to be used as an effective defensive weapon. European states typically relied on mercenary bands led by military entrepreneurs or on hastily trained levies. Recurrent problems with pay and supply meant armies, whether mercenary or not, were permanently disruptive, given to mutiny and plunder.

Through the second half of the 17th century, however, uniformed regular armies began to emerge, with higher levels of discipline, more dependable pay and supply, and a formal hierarchy of officers. Mercenaries were still important, but purchased from other states rather than from private entrepreneurs. The more efficient flintlock musket replaced the matchlock, and the bayonet took the place of the pike, so that all infantry could be musket-armed. At sea, meanwhile, European warships had evolved into huge three-masters armed with formidable arrays of cannon. The Dutch and English fought the first wars to be almost exclusively conducted at sea. These were motivated by disputes over colonial trade.

Efficient military machines

Through the first half of the 18th century European states continued to develop disciplined armies, with ever more effective field artillery. They were at the service of monarchs who enjoyed an impressive degree of centralized control over their realms. These rulers fought wars for limited dynastic objectives, characterized by lengthy sieges and generally indecisive battles, but their armies and navies would prove potent instruments for the more aggressive, expansionist age that followed.

1500	1510	1520	1530	1540	1555

1501–10
Shah Ismail unifies Persia in a series of military campaigns, founding the Safavid dynasty.

1512
In the Italian Wars, the French under Gaston de Foix defeat the Spanish-led Holy League at Ravenna, Italy, but de Foix is killed.

1514
Ottoman sultan Selim I defeats the Persian Safavids at Chaldiran and occupies the Safavid capital, Tabriz.

1520–21
The fall of the Aztec empire: forced to flee Tenochtitlán on the "Night of Sorrows", Cortés returns with Tlaxcalan allies and recaptures the city.

1556
Akbar the Great becomes ruler of the Mogul empire; his campaigns will greatly extend the area of India under Mogul control.

≫ Standard bearer of a band of Swiss mercenaries

1525
At the battle of Pavia in northern Italy, French king Francis I is defeated and taken prisoner by the forces of Habsburg emperor Charles V.

≫ Emperor Charles V (Charles I of Spain)

1543
Portuguese sailors arrive in Japan and introduce matchlock firearms into the country.

1562
Start of the French Wars of Religion between the Protestant Huguenot and the Catholic factions.

1515
In the Italian Wars, French king Francis I crosses the Alps with 50 bronze cannon and crushes an army of Swiss pikemen at Marignano.

1532–33
Spanish adventurer Francisco Pizarro, with a handful of followers, seizes control of the Inca empire in Peru.

1534
Spanish troops in Italy are re-organized into *tercios*. Spain's *tercios* go on to dominate European warfare for the next century.

≽ Portuguese merchants aboard ship in a Japanese harbour

1503
At the battle of Cerignola in the Italian Wars, the Spanish under Gonzalo de Córdoba defeat a French army consisting largely of Swiss mercenary pikemen. The Spanish demonstrate the effectiveness of infantry armed with arquebuses.

1526
Ottoman sultan Suleiman I defeats the Hungarians at the battle of Mohács. ■ Babur invades India and defeats the Sultan of Delhi at Panipat, heralding the start of the Mogul empire.

1529
Siege of Vienna fails, setting a limit to Ottoman expansion in Europe.

1545
At the battle of the Solent, a naval encounter between France and England, the English warship *Mary Rose* sinks off Portsmouth.

1565
Ottoman forces fail to take the island of Malta, resolutely defended under siege by the Knights of St John.

≫ Ottoman turban helmet

1509
In the Indian Ocean a Portuguese fleet destroys Egyptian galleys and Gujerati dhows at Diu, demonstrating the superiority of European sailing ships.

≫ Battle of Marignano

1519
Spanish soldier Hernán Cortés lands in Mexico with 600 men and marches to the Aztec capital, Tenochtitlán.

≫ Janissaries, the elite corps of the Ottoman army

1538
The Ottoman admiral Kheir-ed-Din (Barbarossa) defeats a large Christian fleet under Genoese admiral Andrea Doria at Preveza.

1550
Mongol leader Altan Khan crosses the Great Wall into Ming China and burns the suburbs of Beijing. China is also exposed to coastal raids by Japanese pirates.

1567
The Dutch Revolt against Spanish king Philip II begins the Eighty Years War. Philip sends the Duke of Alba to suppress the revolt.

1570	1585	1600	1615	1630	1645

1571
The Christian Holy League defeats the Ottomans at the naval battle of Lepanto, the last major battle fought by oared galleys.

⌄ St Bartholomew's Day Massacre in Paris

1588
King Philip II sends the Spanish Armada to cover an invasion of England. English warships and bad weather frustrate Spanish plans.

1600
Tokugawa Ieyasu defeats his rivals at Sekigahara, Japan. ■ In the Dutch Revolt Maurice of Nassau defeats Archduke Albrecht of Austria at Nieuwpoort, in present-day Belgium.

≫ Japanese Samurai helmet

1631
In the Thirty Years War, the population of the Lutheran city of Magdeburg is massacred by imperial forces. King Gustavus Adolphus of Sweden defeats an imperial army at Breitenfeld.

⌄ Gustavus Adolphus

1645
The English Parliament creates the New Model Army to fight against the Royalist forces in the British Civil Wars. ■ In China the Manchu overcome Ming loyalists at Yangzhou.

1618
The Thirty Years War begins with a revolt by Protestant nobles in Bohemia against the rule of their Catholic Habsburg king, Ferdinand.

1648
The Eighty Years War and the Thirty Years War end with the Peace of Westphalia.

1651
Defeat for the Royalists at the battle of Worcester ends the British Civil Wars.

1572
St Bartholomew's Day Massacre. Thousands of Huguenots are murdered following a plot to kill many of their leaders in Paris.

1603
Tokugawa Ieyasu establishes the Tokugawa shogunate, which rules Japan until 1868.

1619
Ferdinand is elected Holy Roman Emperor.

1632
Gustavus Adolphus defeats Wallenstein at Lützen, but is killed in the battle.

1634
Habsburg and Spanish forces defeat the Swedes at the battle of Nördlingen.

≪ 17th-century pikeman's breastplate and tassets

1578
King Sebastian of Portugal invades North Africa. He is killed and his army defeated at the battle of Alcazarquivir.

1592–93
Japanese leader Toyotomi Hideyoshi sends an army to invade Korea. The Japanese are defeated at sea by Korean admiral Yi Sun-sin.

⌄ Korean city of Busan besieged by Japanese, 1592

1607
A Dutch fleet attacks the Spanish war fleet anchored in Gibraltar Bay and completely destroys it.

1609
Spain and the rebel Dutch agree a 12-year truce.

1638
The Ottoman empire wins back control of Baghdad from Shah Abbas of Persia.

1652–54
The First Anglo-Dutch War, a series of naval battles in the English Channel and North Sea, sees the adoption of line-of-battle tactics for warships firing broadsides.

1580
In pursuit of his claim to the throne, Philip II of Spain invades and occupies Portugal.

1583
Toyotomi Hideyoshi establishes himself as the most powerful warlord in Japan with a decisive victory at Shiugatake.

1620
Ferdinand's Catholic imperial forces crush the Bohemian rebels at the battle of White Mountain outside Prague.

1625
King Christian IV of Denmark intervenes on the Protestant side in the Thirty Years War.

1611–13
Christian IV of Denmark fights Sweden in the War of Kalmar.

1614–15
Facing a rebellion against his rule in Japan, Tokugawa Ieyasu besieges and eventually defeats his enemies at Osaka.

1628
Dutch admiral Piet Heyn captures the Spanish treasure fleet in the Caribbean.

1629
A string of victories for Wallenstein, the Bohemian commander of the Catholic side, forces Denmark out of the Thirty Years War.

⌃ A British Civil War falconet cannon

1642
The first battle between Royalist and Parliamentary forces in the British Civil Wars is fought at Edgehill.

1644
The Ming dynasty falls in China and the Manchu seize Beijing.

1654
Russia and Sweden invade Poland. The losses for the Polish-Lithuanian Commonwealth are heavy.

1660

1662
The Ming loyalist Koxinga seizes control of Taiwan and holds it as an outpost of resistance to the Manchu Qing dynasty.

◢ Dutch ship of the line

1665–67
The Second Anglo-Dutch War. Inspired by Admiral Michiel de Ruyter, the Dutch end by humiliating the English with a raid on the Medway.

1674
In China the War of the Three Feudatories begins, as warlords in southern China rebel against the Kangxi emperor.

◢ The Kangxi emperor

1675

1676
Indian resistance to European settlement in New England is broken by the defeat of Wampanoag chief Metacomet in King Philip's War.

1681
Kangxi emperor defeats the warlords known as the Three Feudatories and gains control of all mainland China.

1683
The Ottomans besiege Vienna, but the city is relieved by a Christian army under Polish king Jan Sobieski. ■ China regains control of Taiwan.

1688
The War of the League of Augsburg begins. A coalition of the Holy Roman empire, the Dutch Republic, Spain, and Savoy opposes Louis XIV's France.

1689
Dutch prince William of Orange takes the English throne jointly with his wife Mary. England joins the League of Augsburg at war with France.

1690

1700
The Great Northern War begins. Charles XII of Sweden routs Russian tsar Peter the Great's forces at Narva.

◢ King Louis XIV of France

◢ A Vauban fortification

1703
Louis XIV's chief military engineer Sebastien Vauban is made a field marshal.

1704
An army led by England's Duke of Marlborough and Eugene of Savoy defeats the French at Blenheim.

1705

▲ The battle of Malplaquet

1709
French forces are defeated by the armies of Marlborough and Prince Eugene of Savoy at Malplaquet, France. Both sides suffer heavy losses.

1701
Louis XIV's grandson, Philip of Anjou, inherits the Spanish throne. The War of the Spanish Succession pits England, the Dutch United Provinces, the Holy Roman empire, and other states against France and Spain.

1713
The Peace of Utrecht brings the War of the Spanish Succession to an end.

1717–18
The Dzungars occupy Tibet and massacre a Chinese army sent to evict them.

1720

1720
A expedition sent by China's Kangxi emperor expels the Dzungars from Tibet.

1721
The Great Northern War ends with Russia replacing Sweden as the dominant power in the Baltic.

1722
An Afghan army under Mir Mahmud conquers Persia, ending the rule of the Safavid dynasty.

1723
Under King Frederick William I, Prussia begins reforms that give it one of the most effective armies in Europe.

▲ Prussian infantry sword

≫ Qianlong emperor's ceremonial robes

1735

1738–39
Nadir Shah, ruler of Persia, invades India, sacking Delhi and conquering the Punjab.

1740
The War of the Austrian Succession begins when Frederick II of Prussia invades Austrian-ruled Silesia.

▲ Battle of Fontenoy

1745
In the War of the Austrian Succession, France defeats a British and Hanoverian army at Fontenoy and occupies much of the Austrian Netherlands.

1745–46
The Jacobites under Charles Stuart invade England from Scotland, but withdraw and are slaughtered at Culloden.

1748
The Qianlong emperor sends troops to crush a rebellion in Lhasa, Tibet.

The Italian Wars

In the 1490s Italy became the base in which Western Europe's emerging powers – France, Spain, the Swiss, and the Italian city-states – fought for pre-eminence. Not until 1559 would an outcome be decided: Italy and France were ultimately the losers, swept aside by the rise of a Spanish superpower.

« BEFORE

A degree of peace had returned to the Italian peninsula after the turmoil of the 12th and 13th centuries, yet with no central authority it appeared to be there for the taking.

PREPARATIONS FOR WAR
In 1492 the Reconquista in Spain was over, with **the Muslims driven from their stronghold in Granada « 98–99**. The French monarchy was in search of further glory after having defeated England in the **Hundred Years War « 102–03**.

The **Swiss pikemen had won respect** with their dispatch of Charles the Bold's Burgundians in 1476. Many now needed work, and Charles VIII of France was only too happy to recruit them into his army.

He was keen to revive the **Angevin claim to the crown of Naples and Sicily « 90–91**. Pope Innocent VIII backed Charles, and Spain's King Ferdinand I agreed not to oppose him in return for a **free rein in the Pyrenean provinces** of Roussillon and Cerdagne. When, in 1494, King Ferrante I of Naples died, it seemed the moment Charles had been waiting for had come.

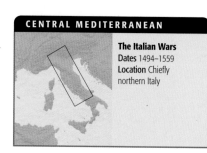
EMPEROR CHARLES V

When King Ferrante I of Naples died in January 1494, his son, Alfonso II, inherited the crown. Charles VIII saw this as an opportunity to advance his own Angevin claim on Naples by force. He was encouraged to do this by Duke Ludovico Sforza of Milan, whose right to hold his own duchy was disputed by the new king Alfonso. One of the characteristics of the Italian Wars was to be the ever-shifting tangle of enmities and alliances that

> **CONDOTTIERE (pl. *condottieri*)** Literally "contractor" in Italian. A freelance military commander with his own mercenary army. Some *condottieri* grew exceptionally powerful during the Italian Wars.

helped shape the unfolding action on the ground. The conflict began when Charles invaded Italy in October 1494: his forces, 25,000 strong, numbered 8,000 Swiss pikemen (Swiss soldiers of fortune who fought with spear-headed poles). Now sweeping southwards, Charles's soldiers encountered armies commanded by *condottieri*, mercenaries contracted to individual cities. Some attempted to fight back but Charles made short work of them, besieging cities and blasting at the walls and defences with huge cannon. His soldiers massacred the people inside – after decades of low-level tussling by *condottieri* armies, often more interested in taking prisoners for ransom than killing, Italy was getting a taste of "total war". Charles's army carved its cruel way south: by February 1495, he was on the throne of Naples.

Carrying the flag
Dressed far more elaborately than the typical Swiss pikeman, the standard bearer was crucial to the pike-square's sense of honour and identity.

Expelling the French
Ludovico now realized that Charles had his own designs on the Duchy of Milan. Pope Alexander VI added his authority to Ludovico's calls for an alliance against French aggression. The "League of Venice" was formed, its main purpose to force the French (namely Charles) into leaving Italy. Francesco II Gonzaga, a *condottiere* and also the Marquess of Mantua, was assigned to take command.

CENTRAL MEDITERRANEAN

The Italian Wars
Dates 1494–1559
Location Chiefly northern Italy

In July 1495, his Italians fought the French to a standstill at Fornovo. Forced to retreat back to the safety of France, Charles's army survived.

Charles's successor, Louis XII, invaded Lombardy in 1499 and took Milan. He deposed Duke Ludovico and continued south, agreeing with Ferdinand I of Spain to share the Kingdom of Naples. Soon, though, the two had fallen out. In April 1503, Louis's army was routed at Cerignola. Spanish commander, Gonzalo Fernández de Córdoba, found his army outnumbered four-to-one. But his men had firearms.

A pikeman's war
Named *El Gran Capitán* ("The Great Captain") by his associates, Gonzalo Fernández de Córdoba had the use of arquebuses (muzzle-loaded firearms) and heavy guns. He used them effectively in his *tercios*. Probably so-called because they combined pikes, arquebuses, and edged weapons equally, the *tercios* were Spain's answer to the Swiss pike-square. As cohesive and effective for defence in depth and aggressive attack as the Swiss square – thanks to a well-drilled elite of pikemen – the *tercio* could also make use of its arquebus firepower to provide additional impact.

Gaston de Foix's French force met the Spanish at the battle of Ravenna in 1512. With up to 8,000 *landsknechts* (German mercenaries) at its core, de Foix's army prevailed. The French never saw the benefit, however – the Swiss would soon invade Italy, taking Milan. The French returned the year after but were beaten at Novara, their *landsknechts* coming off decidedly the worse against the Swiss pikemen. In keeping with a feud between Swiss and *landsknechts*

Battle of Pavia
Francis I of France met his match at Pavia in 1525. His Swiss pikemen were unceremoniously put to flight. Some 10,000 of his soldiers are believed to have been killed in the battle, as against 1,500 on the Imperial side.

FRENCH KING (1494–1547)

FRANCIS I

Born in 1494 and crowned king in 1515, Francis I was driven by dynastic ambition. Well educated and a cultivated patron, Francis began his reign with the great military triumph at Marignano. But his dynastic rivalry with the emperor, Charles V, led him into a series of futile and ill-judged attempts to rule Italy. Defeated and captured at Pavia in 1525, he was forced to win his freedom by making huge concessions to Charles V. Repudiating his promises once back on French soil, he spent the rest of his reign carrying out further wasteful attempts to destabilize Charles's position, allying with the Ottoman sultan and scoring a diplomatic own goal in 1543 when he let the Ottoman fleet use the French port of Toulon. He died on 31 March 1547.

that went back several decades, the Swiss killed hundreds of the captured German *landsknechts*.

At Marignano in 1515, Louis's successor, Francis I, found the answer to the pike formations in artillery and

10,000 The population of Rome after the sacking of the city in 1527. A census just the year before had counted 55,000. Thousands of people had been killed, though many had fled to the countryside.

heavy cavalry. However, he first had to get his forces across the Alps. The best known passes were closely guarded and so Francis had new roads especially built across less frequented – and arduous – back routes. That done, he organized the transportation of his heavy artillery (up to 70 cannon). The fighting lasted 24 hours and cost up to 20,000 lives. The *landsknechts* did their work, as did Francis's cannon. The French emerged the victors and occupied northern Italy.

The prisoner of Pavia

In 1519 Francis was furious when Charles I of Spain became Emperor Charles V, as Francis had coveted that position for himself. He decided again on an invasion of Italy – but Francis's pikemen and cavalry were once again mauled by the *tercios* at Bicocca in 1522 and Sesia in 1524. A fresh invasion in 1525 was brought to a halt at Pavia. Francis's cannon tore great gaps in the Imperial lines but had to cease fire as the French cavalry surged forward. As both sides' *landsknechts* engaged, the Spanish arquebusiers could fire at will.

Battle of Marignano

The War of the League of Cambrai had broken out in 1508. Francis I suffered a series of reverses, but he transformed his fortunes with this victory at Marignano in 1515, where he was able to win back all the territories he had lost.

Francis, his horse killed beneath him, fought on but was captured. He was forced to agree to humiliating terms in the Treaty of Madrid in 1526.

Charles's troops soon fell apart. Funds to pay their wages ran out and, enraged, 30,000 men marched on Rome. Charles was noted for his Catholic piety, but the pro-French pope, Clement VII, was wary of Imperial power. Some of Charles V's 14,000 *landsknechts* had Lutheran sympathies, and this added a note of religious enmity to the sack of Rome. In May 1527 his German and Spanish troops inflicted an orgy of destruction in which the pope was forced to shelter, a virtual prisoner, in Castel Sant'Angelo.

AFTER

The struggle for power between France and Spain continued in the decades that followed, with ramifications reaching far and wide through Europe.

WARS OF RELIGION

Britain was soon drawn into the war between France and Spain: as allies of the Habsburgs, and hence of Spain, England routed France's Scottish allies at Flodden (in Northumberland) in 1513; **Henry VIII's navy fought France** in the Solent in 1545. Enriched by the profits of its American empire, meanwhile, Spain started to grow ever more powerful.

By the 17th century, Europe's two great Catholic powers began resisting the upsurge of Protestant power in Northern Europe. The **French Wars of Religion 134–35 ›**, the **Dutch Revolt 138–39 ›**, and the **growing enmity between Spain and England 140–41 ›** would bring the dangers more intensely into focus.

Italy itself now enjoyed a **welcome period of peace** and cultural flourishing under a largely **unchallenged Spanish hegemony**.

Spanish Conquests in the New World

The 16th century saw two mighty empires in the Americas overthrown by tiny groups of Spanish adventurers. The technology gap between these Old and New World cultures was crucial to these conquests, yet their sheer audacity still defies belief.

It was prophesied that the plumed serpent god, Quetzalcoatl, would one day appear from the eastern ocean in human form. When this happened, the destruction that the priests had been staving off with their animal and human sacrifices could be postponed no longer: Aztec civilization would meet its catastrophic end. When Hernán Cortés arrived from Spain in 1519, he was believed to be that serpent god. Yet the myth was of Spanish, rather than Mexican, origin; it was encouraged by Cortés in order to intimidate the people he was conquering.

That Cortés and his little band of men were able to subdue such an incredibly powerful empire was extraordinary. His courage, charisma, and ruthlessness are

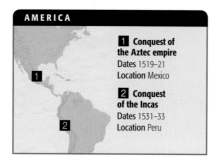

AMERICA

1 Conquest of the Aztec empire
Dates 1519–21
Location Mexico

2 Conquest of the Incas
Dates 1531–33
Location Peru

not in doubt. Nor is the cunning with which he exploited the existing enmities among the native peoples of Mesoamerica.

Alliances and atrocities

Cortés took Malinche, a Nahua woman whose people were hostile to the Aztecs, as his mistress and interpreter. With her help, he allied with the Tlaxcaltecas in what is now Tlaxcala in Mexico: they too felt threatened by the Aztecs. At Cholula, west of Puebla, Cortes and his men killed the male population, without doubt at the urging of the Tlaxcaltecas, who wanted to punish the Cholulans for submitting to Aztec rule. "We fought so hard," said Cortés, "in two hours more than 3,000 men were killed."

500 The number of Spaniards Cortés had with him in the battle of Tenochtitlán. Pizarro captured the Inca emperor, Atawallpa, with just 128 men.

This atrocity sent a message to Mexico's peoples. The scale of the slaughter the Spanish had been able to commit with their steel weapons and their firearms was scarcely imaginable to them. Hence the nervous adulation bestowed upon Cortés and his company upon arrival at the Aztec capital, Tenochtitlán, though ruler Moctezuma II seems to have taken Cortés's claims to be an "ambassador" at face value. The conquistador repaid his hospitality by taking him hostage. For six months Cortés ruled the empire with Moctezuma as his puppet. Then

The capture of Cuauhtémoc

In 1521, the defeated Aztec ruler was caught by Cortés and his men as he tried to slip away across Lake Tenochtitlán in a flat-bottomed pirogue or dugout canoe.

his lieutenant, Pedro de Alvarado, took fright at talk of a revolt and massacred the Aztec nobility. Cortés and his men had to fight their way out of the rebellion that ensued. Moctezuma was among those who died. Cortés was lucky to escape with 200 survivors.

Unequal struggles

In the months that followed, Cortés besieged Tenochtitlán, now stricken with the smallpox the conquistadors had unwittingly brought with them. Over 40 per cent of the native population died. Under Cuauhtémoc, the nephew of Moctezuma, the Aztecs resisted bravely. And they held a number of advantages, as Cortés and his men were aware. Frankly, Cortés acknowledged, they were daunted: "They had calculated

« **BEFORE**

The voyages of Christopher Columbus between 1492 and 1504 opened up a New World, but it soon became exploited by the Old one, and destruction followed discovery.

NEW WORLD COLONIES

Spain's colonization of Middle and South America's pagan cultures was ostensibly a Christianizing mission. But those **adventurers** who undertook the dirty work of conquest – the **conquistadors** – were tough, ruthless opportunists in search of booty. After all, these savages were ignorant of the **Gospel**; and they did moreover possess fabulous quantities of **gold**.

CHIMU MASK

IMPERIAL STRENGTH

Prior to the Europeans' incursions, the **Aztecs'** crushing of other Mesoamerican peoples led to the creation of their empire. They had **widened their dominions** through the Valley of Mexico in a series of conquests from the 15th century. Over the same period, the **Incas** had founded an even larger empire – over 3,500km (2,170 miles) across – conquering civilizations like the Chimu. On the eve of the Spanish conquest both empires were consolidating their power.

500 quetzal plumes make up this shimmering headdress. Each bird has two long tail plumes.

Moctezuma's feather headdress
Said to have belonged to Moctezuma II, this Aztec headdress is made from the tail feathers of the quetzal, consecrated to the plumed serpent Quetzalcoatl, Mesoamerican deity of death and resurrection.

Turquoise band

Gold trim

AFTER

In just a few years, and with only a tiny commitment of manpower, Spain had won a vast American empire. Its riches underwrote Spain's emergence as a superpower.

FURTHER CONQUESTS
Other **conquistadors** took other territories: Vasco Nuñez de Balboa in Panama; Francisco de Orellana in the Amazon; Pedro de Valdivia in Chile – such adventurers grew fabulously wealthy.

7,000 The number of tons of pure silver received by the Spanish Crown from a single mine – the Cerro Rico ("Rich Hill") at Potosí in Bolivia – between 1556 and 1783.

DEADLY DISEASES
The **cruelty of the colonists** was dwarfed in destructiveness by the ravages of the **infections they introduced**. In every region of the Americas, epidemiologists estimate that **90 per cent** of the population had been killed by disease within just 50 years of the arrival of the Europeans.

UNDER SUBJECTION
Mexico and Peru remained viceroyalties of "New Spain", despite the attempt of Tupac Amaru, a descendant of the Inca kings, to throw out the invaders in 1572.

that if 25,000 of them died for every one of us, they would finish with us first, for they were many and we were but few." The city's situation – on a series of islands in a shallow lake, connected to the mainland and to each other by narrow causeways – allowed defenders to focus their efforts more effectively. Even so, it was only a matter of time before the Spanish and their allies prevailed: Tenochtitlán fell on 13 August 1521.

European firepower and know-how had not been enough by themselves to overwhelm the Aztecs, but had given the Spanish attack an extra "edge".

Inca complacency
In the 1530s Francisco Pizarro took Peru against still more astounding odds. The Inca king, Atawallpa, had an army of 80,000 to Pizarro's 128 men. The latter did, of course, have weapons never before seen in

South America – arquebuses (muzzle-loaded firearms) and cannon, as well as steel-bladed swords. And they had horses, until then unknown on the continent. But in the end it was Inca complacency that allowed Pizarro's party to probe deep into the empire completely unscathed. Triumphant victor of a civil war that had wreaked the Inca empire for the last three years, and with his rival and half-brother captured, Atawallpa saw no reason to take a handful of "bandits and thieves" seriously. The two sides met, eventually, at the city of Cajamarca, in northern Peru. The conquistadors kept to their "Christian" commitment by bringing a priest out to preach to the Inca king. When Atawallpa brushed him aside, the Spanish had a pretext for

Aztec war club
The absence of iron was not too great a handicap to the Aztec warriors, who carried clubs of wood, studded with shards of obsidian (volcanic glass).

attacking, and opened up with cannon and arquebuses. Although their noise and smoke had far greater impact than their penetrative power, the cold steel of the conquistadors cut down the Inca troops, shocked into passivity.

In a few hours of one-sided fighting, Pizarro's men killed 7,000 Incas; then they seized Atawallpa. This proved so astonishing an outrage that the watching soldiers could barely believe it was happening. He was their divinity: now he was a prisoner; the Inca state had been decapitated. Holding Atawallpa captive in Cajamarca, the conquistadors demanded an enormous ransom, and then garroted the king anyway, setting another puppet, Manqo Qapac, in his place. Qapac quickly grew disenchanted and slipped away into the mountains. He led a belated fightback, but the Incas were finally defeated in 1536. Once again the courage of the Spanish conquistadors is as staggering as their unscrupulousness: holed up in Cuzco, they saw off a siege by some 40,000 of Qapac's men.

FRANCISCO PIZARRO

Like so many of the conquistadors, Pizarro originated from Extremadura – then the poorest part of Spain. His beginnings are obscure. He made his first (unsuccessful) foray into South America in 1524, faring better on his second, two years later, into Colombia and Ecuador, where he first heard of the wealth of the Incas. The success of his third expedition owed much to his qualities as leader. No strategist, but a formidable improviser, Pizarro always retained his composure, unfazed by the scale of his endeavour.

CONQUEST OF MEXICO
In this detail from a modern mural by Diego Rivera, Spanish soldiers under the command of Hernán Cortéz capture the Aztec city of Tenochtitlán in Mexico in 1521. Aided by a coalition of native people determined to overthrow the Aztecs, the Spanish, with horses, armour, modern weapons, and gunpowder, were the cutting edge of military power. The Aztecs, fighting on foot with clubs, bows, and spears, were overwhelmed within two years.

Mogul Conquests

Descendants of the great Mongol conqueror, Timur Lenk, the Muslim Mogul dynasty took pride in its Turko-Mongol origins and was celebrated for its civilization and culture. The Moguls lived up to their antecedents in the field of war, however, carving out an empire that ultimately extended across India.

Trigger | Barrel

Babur was just 12 years old when he was forced out of his home city of Samarkand in 1494 by the Uzbeks: at 15 he returned to besiege it, although without success. Leading his warband into Afghanistan, Babur took Kabul in 1504, making it his base for forays into the central Asian region of Transoxania. Towards the east the wealth of India beckoned. He made a series of invasions into Punjab and was soon asked by local nobles to assist them in overthrowing Ibrahim Lodhi's fearsome Afghan regime.

Before he did so, Babur took the time to furnish his army with the new gunpowder weapons and to train them in their use, meanwhile preserving the more traditional skills of steppe warfare. Not until the end of 1525 did he mount a full-scale invasion of Hindustan.

Victory at Panipat
Babur's army numbered only 10,000, but it brushed aside the Afghan force sent to intercept it. On 12 April 1526,

Sultan Ibrahim, with 100,000 men and 1,000 elephants, confronted the invaders at Panipat, north of Delhi. Unperturbed, Babur built an impromptu fortress on the open plain, lashing 700 carts together, with earthen ramparts, to safeguard his cannon and new matchlocks. He also dug trenches and felled trees to create barriers to left and

Mogul firepower
The era of the Moguls saw a gradual transformation of warfare in the subcontinent. Guns, like this 18th-century matchlock, would have a growing role.

was killed and Babur was left lord of Hindustan, soon occupying the cities of Delhi and Agra. Babur was to prove a humanitarian and civilized ruler, as

"What a **great day** it was for the vultures and the crows!"
MOGUL POET ON THE SIEGE OF CHITOR, 1568

right, leaving gaps through which his cavalry could charge. On 21 April, Ibrahim attacked, but his soldiers were brought up short at Babur's well-placed fortifications. As the Mogul cavalry approached from the wings to encircle the enemy, the bombardment began from behind the barrier, Babur's men firing at point-blank range into this close-packed mass. Unable either to advance or retreat, the Afghan army was pulverized – almost 16,000 soldiers fell. Many were trampled to death by their own elephants. Sultan Ibrahim

indeed were most of his successors. Babur had established a template: the use of modern firepower and field-fortifications alongside the traditional mounted archers of the steppe.

Shaping the empire
The Muslim Moguls are famed for their religious tolerance and their openness to India's aesthetic values. Babur's grandson, Akbar the Great, ascended the throne in 1556, allying himself with northwest India's Hindu princes, the Rajputs. The new emperor soon adopted Indian ways of waging war: from elephants to the *bagh nakh*, or "tiger claw" – a sequence of razor-sharp blades fitted to a haft or gauntlet, for slashing at close-quarters. Rajput nobles were recruited, along with their peasant troops: armies of up to half a million warriors were mobilized.

Akbar the Great spent almost all his reigning life at war. During the 1560s and 70s he asserted his power over his Rajput "allies" – most accepted, since Akbar gave them privileged offices of state. Those who resisted had to be cut down by force, as at the siege of Chitor in 1568; simultaneously, Akbar invaded the country's eastern states, including Orissa and Bengal, extending the empire across the

BEFORE

To the north, the subcontinent of India is protected by the formidable barrier of the Himalayas, but it has always been vulnerable to invasions and raids from the northwest, from the direction of Central Asia.

UNDER THREAT
By the 11th century there were regular raids by the armies of **the Ghaznavid empire ‹‹ 72–73**. Genghis Khan's Mongol horde swept through like a storm in the 1220s **‹‹ 82–83**; and in 1398 it was the turn of **Timur Lenk ‹‹ 88–89**, who sacked the city of Delhi.

FOUNDING A DYNASTY
Babur was a descendant of both Timur Lenk and **Genghis Khan**. Caught up in the Timurid dynasty's protracted succession struggles, he found himself **forced out of the Uzbek city of Samarkand** in the late 15th century. Babur built a power base first in Afghanistan, then in India, **establishing his own dynasty** in Delhi.

Spearsman

Padded armour

Mahout

Armoured elephant
Elephants could trample infantry, stampede horses, and demolish fortifications. "Where there are elephants, there is victory," one sage recorded.

Key

- Babur's domains 1525
- Babur's conquests 1526–39 before expulsion of the Moguls in 1539
- Mogul domains on death of Aurangzeb 1707
- Approximate frontier
- AGRA 1556 Region acquired by Moguls with date of acquisition
- Battle

whole of northern India. During this period Kabul was taken by Babur's old nemesis, the Uzbeks, under their formidable leader, Abd Allah Khan. Khan's death in 1598 brought the northwest security, and Akbar soon established a new frontier on the banks of India's Godavari River.

Under subsequent Mogul emperors like Jahangir (1605–27) and Shah Jahan (1627–58), these conquests were made

The siege of Chitor

Akbar's men storm the fort of Chitor in 1568. The Rajputs fought to the death; this fate seemed preferable to a dishonourable capture by the Mogul enemy.

Mogul expansion

Though based in the north – the historic centre of Islamic influence in India – the Mogul empire steadily expanded to take over the whole subcontinent, apart from the southern tip of the country and Sri Lanka.

safe. Emperor Aurangzeb pushed further into the south from 1658. A puritanical and single-minded Muslim, the Mogul empire reached its greatest extent under his authority, but it was less happy and more restive. Aurangzeb's death in 1707 saw his successors facing increasing difficulties and local unrest. In the end, the dynasty fell into decline, gradually losing its territories to others.

AFTER »

The Moguls had modernized Indian warfare, but had no answer to a changing political environment in which the power of Britain was playing an ever increasing role.

END OF AN ERA

As the 18th century went on, the Moguls were increasingly powerless to prevent the expansion of the **Maratha empire** from the south. The threat from the northwest was soon renewed, moreover: in 1739, at the **battle of Karnal**, Nasir Shah of

TIPU SULTAN'S TIGER

Iran defeated the Mogul army. His subsequent **sack of Delhi** was a massive humiliation. This was followed by a shattering defeat in 1764, at Buxar in Bihar, at the hands of the troops of **Britain's East India Company 176–77 »**.

India's Mogul empire was allowed to continue, but its reign was becoming a sham: revenue-raising and decision-making powers were claimed by the East India Company. In 1857, in the aftermath of the bloody **Indian Mutiny**, British rule continued and government reorganized, and India was incorporated into the ever-expanding **British empire**.

BEFORE

For centuries Constantinople had been regarded as the greatest city in the world. That it had fallen to the Ottomans sent shockwaves through Christendom.

EASTERN HOSTILITY

A string of hostile tribes had already emerged from the Central Asian steppe to threaten the West: **the Huns ‹‹ 46–47**, the **Seljuks ‹‹ 72–73**, the **Mongols ‹‹ 82–83**, and **the hordes of Timur ‹‹ 88–89**.

EMPIRE'S END

The Ottomans had seized territory in the eastern Balkans as early as the 14th century, when Sultan Murad I's forces had **defeated the Serbs** at the battle

OTTOMAN SULTAN MURAD I

of Kosovo in 1389. They had also brought the **Byzantine empire** to its end in 1453 with the **capture of Constantinople ‹‹ 106–07**.

ELITE TROOPS

JANISSARIES

The janissaries may have been slaves, but peasants in the Balkans knew that if their sons were taken they would be "made" for life. Some would try to pass their sons off as Christian so that they could be recruited into the sultan's special guard. From the Ottoman point of view, it made sense to have aliens who, far from their families, would bond the stronger with their comrades and "belong" completely to the corps. Conditions were restrictive and discipline ferocious, but the janissaries gained immense status and privilege. Their power was such that many sultans lived in fear of their "slave" soldiers.

Ottoman Expansion

From their base in Constantinople (present-day Istanbul), the Ottoman Turks pushed westwards, extending their influence by both land and sea. Though the Christian powers won significant victories, the Islamic forces were relentless. Not until the end of the 17th century would their advance be stayed.

The fall of Constantinople in 1453 brought the suspense of centuries to an end. But the West was now in the front line – and the Ottomans had shown their strength in the most ominous way; suddenly, they were a real and pressing threat.

The Ottoman Turks were a terrifying enemy. They had hundreds of thousands of warriors under arms – conscripts and mercenaries around a core of janissaries (elite troops). Recruitment fell to district officials, ensuring access to the whole population (more than 13 million) of an Islamic empire that occupied some

17 The number of days that the first siege of Vienna (1529), led by Suleiman the Magnificent, lasted.

59 The number of days that the second siege of Vienna (1683) lasted, with the Ottomans routed.

1,500,000 sq km (580,000 square miles). Town by town, soldiers were mobilized to correspond with quotas; so too were the engineers and labourers needed to construct bridges and dig trenches.

The janissaries were the nucleus of the sultan's army – not just a reliable elite but literally at the physical centre of his military operations. Conscripts provided a "cushion" at the fore, while at the rear came the tougher, more seasoned troops with their commander. Eventually, this idea was taken to such lengths that trenches were excavated and barriers erected at the heart of the army in the field. (The Mogul prince, Babur, followed this example at Panipat in 1526.) Big guns were placed there too, and were to feature increasingly in Turkish tactics. Mounted archers, or *sipahis*, acted as personal bodyguards to the sultan. The *akindshi*, a small group of cavalry, went before the principal army as scouts and raiders – pillaging, burning, and spreading panic.

A magnificent victory

The army demonstrated their might at Mohács in Hungary on 29 August 1526. Suleiman I ("the Magnificent") had a much bigger military force than that of the Hungarians led by Louis II, the Jagiellonian king. The Ottomans had at least 70,000 troops with 200 cannon, while Louis had fewer than

half that number of men with about 80 guns. This advantage was testimony to the organizational powers and logistical capacities of the Ottoman Turks, and helps explain their victory.

Suleiman's forces were also highly disciplined. Caught descending a steep escarpment above the river Danube, the army had to break into smaller groups as they came down. The Hungarians had hoped to apprehend these units as they reached the bottom, and – up to a point, at least – the idea worked. But Louis's soldiers started plundering the dead, allowing the janissaries to reach level ground and form up with their cannon. Up to half the Hungarian army lost their lives. The Ottomans went on to besiege Vienna in 1529. Far from

Battle of Mohács

Hungary, "the Shield of Christianity", had been the final buffer between the Ottoman empire and Central Europe. Its defeat at the battle of Mohács in 1526 opened the way to Vienna for the Ottomans.

home after months of campaigning, and at their logistical limits, the Ottomans attacked the city but were relatively easily repelled. The Austrians gave Suleiman the Magnificent his first defeat. However, the siege had been a rude awakening for the West.

One of the most striking aspects of the Ottomans' rise was their readiness to adapt. The high seas could hardly have seemed further from the Central Asian steppe, but they took to seafaring as though it were in their blood. Building

"Possessor of the kingdoms of the world, shadow of God over all peoples …"

DEDICATION ON SULEIMAN THE MAGNIFICENT'S MOSQUE IN ISTANBUL, 16TH CENTURY one of the great navies of the early-modern era, they delivered a series of checks to Portugal's colonial ambitions in the Indian Ocean in the 16th century.

Fighting back

In the 17th century the Ottomans extended their territories across North Africa. Freelance pirates, the Barbary corsairs (named for the Barbary coast in northern Africa), became an essential arm of Ottoman naval policy, harassing Christian shipping and raiding in the Mediterranean and beyond. (In 1631 they snatched 111 people in a slave-raid on the village of Baltimore in Ireland's County Cork.)

There were setbacks though: in 1565 the Ottoman army were thwarted at the siege of Malta; six years later saw the

Ottoman gains 1512–1639
Ottoman expansion into Europe and the Mediterranean meant that, in time, the empire stretched over three continents. It reached its greatest extent towards the end of the 17th century, whereafter came a gradual decline.

Key
- Ottoman empire and vassals 1512
- Ottoman empire and vassals 1639
- Austrian Habsburg possessions
- Spanish Habsburg possessions
- Frontiers c.1600
- Approximate frontiers
- Vassal frontiers
- Ottoman victory
- Ottoman defeat

defeat at Lepanto. But – testimony again to their organizational abilities – they quickly regrouped and returned to the offensive, occupying Crete in 1669.

By 1683 they were again advancing on Vienna, which they subjected to a 59-day siege. This time, Europe's Christian powers managed to co-operate. Together with the pope, Austria, Bavaria, Saxony, and Poland-Lithuania formed a "Holy League", raising a massive army that was more than 80,000 strong. John III Sobieski, king of Poland-Lithuania, led the decisive cavalry-charge down the

hillside – said to have been the biggest in history, with 20,000 horses. The Ottomans broke and fled.

The Holy League followed through with a series of victories in Hungary. In 1697, it inflicted an ultimately decisive defeat of the Ottomans at Zenta.

A bodyguard's halberd
Richly bound at the head with golden foil, its blade beautifully adorned with Koranic verses, this halberd was carried by one of Sultan's Mohammad III's bodyguards.

20 THOUSAND The number of Ottomans killed in the field at the battle of Zenta in 1697.

10 THOUSAND The number who died in the river Tisa, trying to escape the battle.

AFTER

All that was left for the Ottoman empire after its failure at the battle of Zenta was decline – but it was to be slow, and for a long time imperceptible.

POWER SHIFT
The Ottoman empire remained the **greatest power** in the eastern Mediterranean; its wider sphere of influence extended from Morocco to the Middle East. Already, though, **the Portuguese had gained control** of the trading centres of the Indian Ocean and Persian Gulf.

A WEAKENING HOLD
In Egypt and Algeria, local governors, or *beys*, began **asserting ever more autonomy** without quite breaking the link with Istanbul. The sultan's authority was weakening: the janissary corps, once his **greatest source of strength**, were becoming so powerful that they threatened the sultan's position. They were finally disbanded (amid violent resistance) in 1826.

The Ottomans' military might seemed spent. **Catherine II's Russia** inflicted catastrophic defeats 182–83 ≫, after which the **Greeks fought for their independence** 212–13 ≫. The empire was seen by other leaders as the "sick man of Europe" – a phrase that pertained to its **increasing loss of power** – and it **finally imploded in World War I** 270–71 ≫.

Lepanto

In 1571 the massed galleys of the Holy League faced a formidable Ottoman fleet in a decisive battle off the coast of Greece. Scores of ships were sunk, and thousands of lives were lost in this climactic confrontation of the Cross and the Crescent. The true strategic significance of the victory of the forces of Christendom has been disputed, but its symbolic impact could hardly have been greater.

In 1570 Ottoman forces had taken the island of Cyprus from the Venetian Republic, making the Ottomans masters of the eastern Mediterranean. With Christendom under threat, Pope Pius V summoned the Holy League, an alliance of Catholic powers against Islam. Its members included Spain (the most powerful of the Western states), Venice, Malta, Genoa, and Savoy, and its commander was Don John of Austria, the half-brother of King Philip II of Spain.

The opposing fleets

Don John mustered about 220 galleys and six galleasses (a hybrid vessel with the oars of a galley with the side-mounted cannon of a galleon) and the fleet was armed with more than 1,300 guns. Facing these on the Ottoman side were 205 galleys armed with some 740 guns, and a number of smaller ships. The fighting forces on both sides were large (some 30,000 soldiers each), the Ottomans equipped with composite bows and the Christians with muskets and arquebuses. But these arms were largely irrelevant to a battle that would be decided by close-quarters fighting with edged weapons, and the Ottoman commander, Ali Pasha, was confident that his fleet would win the encounter. As his main fleet engaged the enemy centre, his wings would close in, crescent-like, and attack the Christians' flanks. The Ottoman wings were commanded by two corsairs: Uluç Ali and the Alexandrian Chulouk Bey, or "Scirocco". Don John commanded the Christian centre, meeting the main body of Ali Pasha's fleet head on.

The battle unfolds

At the outset the Ottomans tried to spring their trap, closing in from the wings. But the initial impact of this manoeuvre was disrupted by the six Venetian galleases placed ahead of the main Christian galleys, whose size and firepower broke up the tightly-formed Ottoman line of battle. Despite this disruption Scirocco's ships on the right wing made some initial headway before being forced back and finding themselves hampered by coastal shoals. Uluç Ali's left wing was on the point of breaking through a gap that opened up on the Christian right when Don Juan de Cardona's reserve came up and blocked the Ottomans.

In the centre the battle raged, combatants leaping to board one another's vessels through the fog of smoke and the hail of lead and arrows, with whole ships erupting into flames as their powder magazines were hit. For a time Ali Pasha's fleet held firm against the onslaught but, pounded relentlessly through four hours' fierce fighting, eventually the flower of the Ottoman navy was all but destroyed.

MAP

GREECE

Gulf of Patras

1 Christian left forces Ottoman galleys back onto shoals

BARBARIGO 53 ships

3 Christian reserve covers centre and right

SCIROCCO 60 ships

4 Christian centre defeats Ottomans

RESERVE 37 ships

RESERVE 30 ships

DON JUAN 70 ships

ALI PASHA 80 ships

5 Ottoman left withdraws as centre collapses

2 Christian right is outmanoeuvred, leaving dangerous gap in the line

DORIA 60 ships

ULUÇ ALI 90 ships

0   5km
0   5 miles

KEY
- Ottoman ships
- Christian galleys
- Venetian galleases

LOCATION
Gulf of Patras, off modern-day Navpaktos, Greece

DATE
7 October 1571

FORCES
Ottomans: 88,000 (16,000 soldiers); Holy League: 84,000 (20,000 soldiers)

CASUALTIES
Ottomans: 15,000–20,000 killed; Holy League: 7,566 killed

A confused and bloody conflict
Ottoman ships (flying banners of the Crescent) and galleys of the Holy League engage at close quarters. Broadsides are exchanged as soldiers board each other's vessels to fight hand to hand.

Wars of the Sengoku Era

Unrest had been smouldering away for generations in Japan: local lords were at odds with one another and with the Kamakura shogunate. In the 16th century centralized authority broke down and wholesale violence erupted: the country became a battleground for the feuding clans.

BEFORE

15th-century Japan was at peace under the Kamakura shogunate. Nonetheless, bitter enmities were evident, as many lords and their samurai followers felt overlooked.

A TROUBLED PAST

Japan's military clans had plunged the country into a **civil war** in the 12th century **≪ 80–81**, before saving it from **Chinese invasion** in the 13th century **≪ 82–83**. The **Onin War** (1467–77) had brought another round of conflict as the *daimyo* (feudal lords) fought for supremacy.

ARMED AND DANGEROUS

The arrival of **Portuguese merchants** with firearms and gunpowder added a dangerous new ingredient to an already volatile mix.

The Europeans arrived in 1543, when a ship **en route to China** was caught in a storm and forced to put in on the island of Tanegashima. In spite of this, guns almost certainly found their way into Japan before this, brought by **Asian traders**.

PORTUGUESE TRADERS

The *daimyo* Oda Nobunaga, came to the fore in the 1550s in Owari, in the present-day Aichi Prefecture of southeastern Honshu. He was ready to extend his power by 1560, but the Yoshimoto and Matsudaira clans had other ideas. So, as Nobunaga headed towards Kyoto with 1,800 men, he heard that an army of over 20,000 was marching out to meet him. Unperturbed, he devised a dummy army, setting up a row of soldiers' hats and banners along a lengthy skyline to give the impression of a waiting force of many thousands. Meanwhile, his army discreetly made its way around to approach his enemies in the rear at Okehazama. His surprise attack sowed complete and utter panic and brought him an improbable victory.

Many of the defeated *daimyo* flocked to Nobunaga's banner. Among them was Matsudaira Motoyasu: born Matsudaira

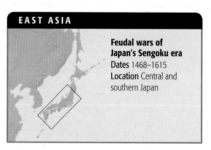

EAST ASIA

Feudal wars of Japan's Sengoku era
Dates 1468–1615
Location Central and southern Japan

Takechiyo, he would later find lasting fame as Tokugawa Ieyasu (the name he gave himself in 1567). Also destined for great things was Toyotomi Hideyoshi: he was now Nobunaga's sandal-bearer.

Opening fire

Though much reinforced by these new recruits, Nobunaga still faced enormous challenges – not least his rival, Takeda Shingen. A formidable warlord from

the nearby province of Kai, Shingen had hopes of uniting Honshu under his rule. But Nobunaga and Ieyasu were not to be deterred. They had set aside ancestral enmity to make common cause.

The inevitable collision with Shingen came in 1573, when his cavalry overran Ieyasu's army at Mikatagahara (Mikawa Province). Shingen died soon after the encounter, but his son and successor, Kutsuyori, was no less ambitious, and just as determined to dominate Japan.

When his much larger force met with Nobunaga's at Nagashino Castle, also in Mikawa Province, a repeat of the rout at Mikatagahara seemed likely. Instead, the impact of Kutsuyori's cavalry charge was checked by the disciplined stand of Nobunaga's men, and they were cut down in their thousands by his arquebusiers – men armed with muzzle-loaded firearms.

Siege of Osaka castle
Terrified civilians flee the fighting at the Toyotomi clan headquarters, under attack by the forces of Shogun Tokugawa Ieyasu, in 1615. Bloody and violent, the siege lasted for six months before the Toyotomi fell.

"The enemy's defeated host is as the maple leaves of autumn, floating on the water."

FROM A POEM BY THE SAMURAI SHIMAZU YOSHIHISA, 1578

Nagashino amounted to more than just a military triumph: symbolically, it marked Nobunaga out as a potential national leader. In hindsight, it was a victory, not just for Nobunaga, but also for modern ways of making war.

A unified Japan

Nobunaga died in 1582, forced to commit *sepukku* (ritual suicide) by one of his own generals, Akechi Mitsuhide, having allegedly insulted his mother. He was succeeded by his sandal-bearer, Toyotomi Hideyoshi, who had risen in his master's trust to become his most valued general. True to Nobunaga, Hideyoshi abandoned the campaign he had been waging in the east and

marched back to take on his lord's betrayer. Mitsuhide had the advantage at Yamazaki, in the present-day Kyoto Prefecture, but, the night before the battle, Hideyoshi sent out small parties to harass his men from the rear, unsettling them. In the next day's fighting, firearms once more proved decisive.

Hideyoshi's authority did not go uncontested within the Oda camp. Opposition united behind Nobutaka, Nobunaga's third son. The rebels included Tokugawa Ieyasu. But

Helmet with war fan
Plated with gold and covered with chain, this samurai helmet also has a detachable fan – both a signalling device and a defensive weapon.

JAPANESE DAIMYO (1543–1616)

TOKUGAWA IEYASU

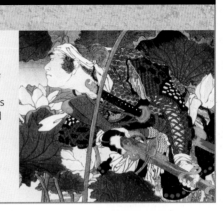

Born Matsudaira Takechiyo in 1543, the son of a small-time *daimyo*, Ieyasu was a self-made man. He renamed himself twice to boost his ascent to power: "Tokugawa Ieyasu" implied a connection to the famous Minamoto clan. Ruthless in his rise, he had a gift for making enemies: one story goes that a former ally, Sanada Yukimura, sided with the Toyotomi at the siege of Osaka; hiding in a lotus pond, he leaped out in an unsuccessful assassination bid.

Hideyoshi saw off the threat, defeating his enemies at Shizugatake, in the present-day Shiga Prefecture, in 1583. By 1585 he had secured his position as

24 The number of Takeda Kutsuyori's generals – his most trusted comrades – who took part in his cavalry charge at Nagashino. Only 16 survived the battle.

Japan's most powerful man: as regent to the emperor, he unified the country. He harboured ambitions of conquering China – and organized two invasions of Korea, although neither of these was ultimately to go as planned. Even so, by the time he died in 1598, Hideyoshi had brought order to Japan.

Ieyasu ascendant

Tokugawa Ieyasu had eventually made his peace with Hideyoshi, but he drew the line at respecting the succession of his son. Hideyori was only five, so was in no position to reign: fighting erupted over his regency. Hundreds of *daimyo* felt they had a stake in the outcome, but opposition coalesced around the figures of Ieyasu and Ishida Mitsunari, a loyal supporter of the Toyotomi. The former drew supporters from the east; the latter had his power base in the west. The showdown came on 21 October 1600, at the battle of Sekigahawa, (present-day Gifu Prefecture): over 150,000 warriors were involved. The fighting took place over a wide area, with small warrior-groups engaging in a series of running skirmishes. It resulted in a smashing victory for Ieyasu's army. Essentially static, given the need for laborious reloading, Ieyasu's arquebusiers had been peripheral. More crucial had been divisions in the Toyotomi camp

and the Tokugawa chief's back-channel diplomacy in the days preceding, which resulted in several key *daimyo* switching sides once fighting commenced. Ieyasu's victory was epoch-making, though unrest continued to simmer for several years. Only when the Toyotomi were finally cornered and destroyed at the siege of Osaka in 1615, could the wars of the Sengoku era be said to have reached their end.

AFTER

In 1603 Tokugawa Ieyasu was recognized as ruler of Japan by the emperor, Go-Yozei. The Tokugawa shogunate was to endure for 265 years (Ieyasu himself died in 1616).

MORE SETTLED TIMES
Japan benefited from the stability conferred by the **Tokugawa shogunate**, though it could be rough and ready in its maintenance of order. Thousands lost their lives during the **Shimabara Rebellion** of 1637–38, when Ieyasu's grandson, Iemitsu, clamped down on **Christian converts**.

FEAR OF THE WEST
The West was perceived by the shoguns as a threat: they effectively closed and barred Japan's doors, **restricting trade**. To shore up their authority at home, meanwhile, they **bore down on the samurai**, defining their privileges and **restricting their the use of firearms**.

SUSPENDED IN TIME
For **nearly three centuries**, the Tokugawa shoguns maintained Japan's isolation. But the country was poorly equipped when **Commodore Perry** and his American flotilla turned up in 1853, demanding **commercial access**. All the old structures – the shogunate, the **power of the samurai** – were soon swept away.

A SAMURAI'S WAKIZASHI SWORD

Siege of Busan
Faced with some 15,000 attackers and their alien weapons, the city's 8,000 defending troops stood no chance. The Japanese celebrated the capture of Busan in 1592 with an orgy of blood-letting.

Korea resists Invasion

Korea was to be the first overseas conquest for Toyotomi Hideyoshi's Japan – and a bridgehead for an invasion of China to the north. But, brave, resourceful, and resilient, the Koreans repulsed the invaders – not once, but twice – thus destroying Hideyoshi's imperial ambitions.

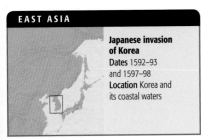

Japanese invasion of Korea
Dates 1592–93 and 1597–98
Location Korea and its coastal waters

BEFORE

Korea was a strong and stable kingdom in the 16th century. It was diplomatically close to neighbouring Ming China, and shared many of its values.

A UNITED KOREA
King Wang Kon of Koguryo had united Korea's "Three Kingdoms" (Koguryo, Paekche, and Silla) in the 10th century. China's Mongol ruler, **Kublai Khan**, had contrived the rise of **King Wongjong ≪ 86–87** but the country had managed to maintain a great deal of autonomy.

CHOSON RULE
The **Choson dynasty** had seized power in a coup in 1392: it was unabashed in its centralizing zeal. Attacking the **ancient privileges** of the country's aristocratic families, it built up its own authority at their expense. By the middle of the 16th century, however, its **stranglehold** on society was slowly weakening as rival factions started to emerge.

A TEMPTING TARGET
It was at precisely this time that Japan was being unified under **Toyotomi Hideyoshi ≪ 126–27**. Having turned his long-divided country into a **single nation-state**, he dreamed of **building an empire** overseas. Just a short hop from Kyushu – Japan's southernmost island – Korea was not just a prize in itself but a stepping-stone to a **possible conquest of Ming China**.

Toyotomi Hideyoshi was a visionary. While his contemporaries sparred and scrapped over provinces, he looked to the unification of Japan. His first acts as regent, in 1586, were to start shipbuilding and to build a base on the northern coast of Kyushu from which to launch an invasion force.

Like many leaders since, Hideyoshi saw war abroad as a way of securing peace at home: his title to power was disputed, and Japan was full of samurai. Without an external enemy, they might direct their aggression at each other or turn on him. So he began negotiations with Korea's Choson regime about an

answer to the skill and prowess of Hideyoshi's soldiers. Though they had some heavy cannon, they relied mainly on bows and arrows, which could not compete with the Japanese arquebuses for range or penetrating power. Korea's capital, Hanseong (present-day Seoul), was taken in mid-June and, by the end of August, the country was all but conquered.

It was a different story at sea, however. Here, the Japanese navy suffered heavy blows in a series of engagements with Yi Sun-sin's Korean fleet, complete with turtle ships, which culminated in a savage encounter at

Korean weaponry
Crucial to the Korean victory at Haengju fortress, the Korean *hwacha* used gunpowder charges to fire a hundred arrows or more at once. A 45-degree angle allowed a range of 500m (550yd).

> ## "Men and women, **even cats and dogs were beheaded**."
> JAPANESE COMMANDER'S REPORT ON THE CAPTURE OF BUSAN, 1592

alliance against China. It was not long, however, before he realized that Korea itself was virtually defenceless.

So it seemed to a ruler with half a million men under arms – samurai with years of experience in the arts of war. On 24 May 1592, within one day of landing on the Korean coast, his men captured the strategic fortress-city of Busan and killed some 30,000 of its inhabitants in cold blood.

Ill-armed and inadequately equipped, the Koreans' regular troops and their "Righteous Army" of volunteers had no

Hansando on 13 August. What was left of the Japanese fleet had to be confined to port. All of a sudden, their supply line seemed very long and desperately exposed. Inevitably, they were plagued by difficulties ashore: the morale of Korea's defenders soared while that of their invaders slumped, and Korea's troops maintained a dogged guerrilla struggle. In October they successfully defended the fortress of Jinju and, in February 1593, with just 2,000 soldiers to Hideyoshi's 30,000, the Korean army also held Haengju fortress.

A second attempt
Hideyoshi gave up and agreed to a truce, although he did not renounce his imperial ambitions in Korea. In January 1597, he launched another invasion, sending hundreds of ships and over 100,000 troops. This time, however, they lacked the advantage of surprise; their enemy had been making preparations. Boosting both their land forces and their navy, the Koreans had also armed themselves with backing from Ming China, which sent 75,000 men as well as ships. The Japanese took the city of Namwon and the strategic fortress of Hwangseoksan, but these victories did not prove to be substantial breakthroughs.

At sea Yi Sun-sin had been forced to relinquish his command after a dispute with his superiors, and his replacement managed to lose almost his entire fleet

in a single battle. Back in charge, Yi had just 12 ships left, but his supremacy was unabated: his fleet sank 133 Japanese vessels at the battle of Myeongnyang. Meanwhile, on land, Japan's army was now in retreat. By the autumn of 1598 Hideyoshi's health was fading. On his deathbed, he ordered a withdrawal.

AFTER

Hideyoshi's dream of a Japanese empire had turned out to be a fantasy. His successors would henceforth concentrate on maintaining stability at home.

A NEW ERA FOR JAPAN
Conspicuous by his absence in Korea was **Tokugawa Ieyasu**, Hideyoshi's sometime ally and long-term rival. That he came through this episode **untouched by failure** did no harm to his prestige, however: by 1603 he had seized the **shogunate**. Now, far from pursuing Hideyoshi's imperial project, the **Tokugawa shoguns** pulled down the shutters on Japan, excluding foreign merchants and missionaries.

KOREA'S NEW-FOUND CONFIDENCE
Korea had been through terrible traumas, but it had gained much in **military capability** and **confidence**. Both of these factors would help Korea resist the **Chinese Manchu invasions of the 17th century 132–33 ≫**.

TECHNOLOGY

TURTLE SHIPS

Turtle ships were so-called because they had completely enclosed decks beneath a curved cover that resembled the shell of a turtle. The cover was shaped so that cannon- and small-arms fire glanced off, and iron spikes protruded from the surface to discourage enemy boarders. In some accounts, the cover also had iron plates by way of armour. Oars and as many as five different types of cannon protruded from protected ports along the sides of the ship; there were additional cannon at the bow and stern. Traditionally the bow cannon fired directly out of the dragon's mouth. The dragon had another significant role, however, in providing a spout for the thick, sulphurous smoke that was emitted by the crew to help conceal a vessel's movements at sea. A typical turtle ship measured 35m (115ft), was operated by 60 oarsmen, and could carry 70 armed marines.

Samurai Armourer

Japan's Samurai tradition combined a code of honour and self-sacrifice with an aesthetic of war, and the craftsmen who furnished the warriors with weapons and armour shared this aesthetic. One of the greatest Japanese armourers of all time was the 16th-century Myochin Nobuiye, creator of this magnificent helmet.

Heroic headgear
A thing of beauty, but also immensely functional, this *kabuto* (helmet) was created by Myoshin Nobuiye in about 1535 and is signed on the inside of the front plate. It is made in the *heichozan* shape: high-sided, but with a flattened crown.

In 1563, as he charged into battle with the Ikko warrior-monks, Tokugawa Ieyasu (see pp.126–27) heard the sound of shots being fired and sensed the thump on his chest as bullets hit him. The shock was no sooner felt than forgotten. Charged up with a warrior's frenzy and swept along in the confusion, he fought on, eventually leading his warriors to victory. Only afterwards when, back in camp, he unfastened his armour and two small leaden balls fell out, did he appreciate quite how close he had come to death.

Like that of generations of Samurai before and after, Ieyasu's armour would have been made of narrow metal plates, bound together in a way that was both flexible and strong. His helmet was also made of metal strips, riveted together for rigidity, then lacquered over. More metal strips, laced together, protected the back of the neck. Arching forward in a wing- or horn-like shape, the *fukigayeshi* covered the ears. Despite their compound construction, such helmets could be strong. In the *Heike Monogatari*, the

Myochin tsubas, 19th century
Myochin Nobuiye made the *tsuba*, the guard that protects the hand on Samurai swords, the ultimate expression of the armourer's art.

epic of the Gempei Wars (see pp.80–81), we hear how, at the battle of Uji, in 1180, the warrior-monk Tsutsui Jomyo Meishu brought his sword down on an opponent's helmet so hard that the blade "snapped at the hilt".

The Myochin mystique

Just as the honour of a Samurai warrior was a quality that transcended his effectiveness in the field of battle, so the worth of armour far exceeded its functionality. Beautiful and exquisitely wrought, it embodied the values of the Samurai *bushido* code and announced the heroic valour of its wearer. Not surprisingly, the armourer's trade was revered – indeed, it was not so much a trade as a vocation. Its secrets were carefully guarded and its skills were handed down from father to son over generations – nowhere more so than in the Myochin family. This dynasty of court armourers was at the centre of Japanese military life from the medieval era right up until the 20th century. A certain Myochin Munesuke is said to have created the

famous helmet that saw the great Minamoto warlord Yoshitsune safely through so many campaigns before his betrayal and suicide in 1189. But it was with his descendant, Myochin Nobuiye, in the early part of the 16th century, that the skills of the Samurai armourer finally left behind the realms of artisanship for those of art.

Artistic genius

Nobuiye's skills were legendary, winning him the sort of renown that was outshone only by that of a great warrior. For all his fame, the details of his life are obscure. We know that he lived and worked in the town of Shirai, in the Kozuke district of central Honshu, and that his armour and swords were much admired by the great warlord Takeda Shingen. He died aged 79, but whether in 1554 or 1564 remains uncertain. So avidly did others imitate his work, that relatively few of his pieces have been reliably authenticated, and many craftsmen have set out to make deliberate forgeries. His signature piece was the *tsuba*, or sword-guard. From this time on, indeed, the *tsuba* became the part of the sword on which Japanese swordsmiths lavished their most dazzling skills.

"Carefully forged, using a divine method of forging against arrows and guns …"

INSCRIPTION ON SUIT OF SAMURAI ARMOUR, 1681

Fighting to the finish
The Toyotomi clan made their last stand against the forces of the Tokugawa shogunate in the fortress at Osaka in 1615. Their defeat brought the wars of the Sengoku era to an end.

Sixty-two plates radiate downwards from the ornate *tehen* at the top. The entire helmet has been lacquered to a russet finish.

The *fukigayeshi* – forward projections of the *shikoro*, or neckguard – are richly decorated with embossed and gilded clouds and dragons.

Manchu Conquests

The Manchu sauntered into Beijing, seizing power as the Ming administration imploded. They faced a tougher challenge than they had expected: more than 25 million may have been killed in their fight to enforce their authority across the empire. This task was to take them over 40 years.

Force of the Manchu
Brandishing spears, bows, and guns, Manchu warriors send a Chinese force into retreat. Some soldiers ride on armoured wheelbarrows propelled by their comrades – the wheelbarrows also functioning as shields.

BEFORE

The Ming emperors had come to power in 1368 at the expense of the Mongols. But Kublai Khan's successors had shown little of his wisdom or – increasingly – his strength.

THE GREAT PROTECTOR
The Ming had hardly established themselves when, in the early 15th century, a new surge of Mongol attacks were launched under the leadership of **Esen Tayisi**. The menace was eventually lifted, but the Ming emperors, ever mindful of the threat, ploughed resources into **renewing the Great Wall of China**.

FALLING BEHIND
The 16th century brought the Portuguese to China, along with their modern cannon. Europe now led the way in a field the Chinese had pioneered. Under the Wanli emperor, China fell into decline, drained by **its support for Korea against Japanese aggression ‹‹ 128–29**. The Jurchen (Manchu) nomads to the north were also unnerving the Chinese. Their **Jin dynasty** had been in power once before, taking up swathes of the north in the 12th century until **Genghis Khan swept it away ‹‹ 82–83**.

Manchu history is said to have started with Nurhaci, a Jurchen warlord, at the end of the 16th century. Not only did Nurhaci encourage the creation of a written script of the Manchu language, but he brought together the warring nomad groups of the eastern steppe. In 1616 he had himself elected "Great Khan".

There are many similarities with the reign of Genghis Khan. Four centuries before, the Mongol ruler had trampled the Jurchen's last bid for ascendancy. Their Jin dynasty had extended its dominion across swathes of northern China, but Genghis Khan had reduced it to dust and smoke. Forced since then into vassal status, the Jurchen people pledged their duty to China's Ming emperors. However, Nurhaci's unifying efforts gave them the strength to assert

EAST ASIA

Manchu conquest of China
Dates 1618–83
Location Manchuria, China, Korea, and Taiwan

have met. As it was, they faced many other difficulties – floods and famines, economic chaos, and political corruption – and rebellion in the empire was rife. Agrarian dissension and military mutiny were endemic. Li Zicheng's revolt during the 1630s in Shaanxi, north-central China, began as a simple uprising by soldiers who felt they had been left unpaid and unfed for far too

> # "Those who have **not yet surrendered** will note this … and **grow cold at heart**."
>
> THE KANGXI EMPEROR ON THE EXECUTION OF REBEL LEADERS, 1680

themselves and – from 1618 – their independence. They attacked the northern provinces of China, setting up a capital for their leader's "Later Jin dynasty" on land taken from the Ming, at Mukden (present-day Shenyang). From here, the Jurchen continued their raids and expansion into both China and the Choson dynasty's Korea.

A raft of rebellions

However, Nurhaci was among those killed at Ningyuan in 1626. Just 10,000 Ming soldiers, under the inspirational leader, Yuan Chonghuan, defeated a Manchu army 120,000 strong. Yuan's study of modern Western artillery weapons and techniques was crucial – Nurhaci was wounded by a cannonball from which he never recovered. The shock of their leader's death distressed the Manchu, but the late Khan's sons, Dodo and Dorgon, quickly took control. By 1638 they had captured Korea, an important conquest in its own right but crucial too as an ally of the Ming.

In another era, the rise of the Manchu might have represented a crisis for the Ming rulers, but one that they could

long. A heavy-handed crackdown by the Ming only fanned the flames. A mutiny led by Zhang Xiangzhong broke out in the 1640s in Sichuan; hundreds of thousands of people were killed in this self-proclaimed emperor's reign of terror. The whole empire seemed to be spiralling into anarchy. Desperate times brought desperate measures: in 1642 Ming forces trying to head off Li Zicheng's rebels diverted the Huang He (Yellow river) in order to flood the city

of Kaifeng. Over 300,000 people died. By 1644 the situation was growing increasingly hopeless and, on 26 May, Li Zicheng's troops entered Beijing.

Zhu Youjian, the Chongzhen emperor and the Ming dynasty's last, committed suicide. His military commander, General Wu Sangui, fought on but was soon cornered by Li Zicheng's advancing forces. Turning to the Manchu (his old arch-enemy), Wu Sangui enlisted their help. With their assistance, the general

CHINESE RULER (1654–1722)

THE KANGXI EMPEROR

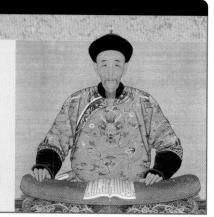

Only seven when he ascended the throne in 1661, the Kangxi emperor was the third ruler of the Manchu dynasty. He was also the longest-reigning – his rule lasted for an impressive 61 years – and he is noted for the prosperity and peace he brought to China. The Kangxi emperor was a military man who led his armies from the front. His empire saw vital victories over the Russians and the Dzunghar Mongols. He orchestrated the standard Kangxi dictionary in 1710.

China was now united under the Qing dynasty but this unification came at a dreadful price – up to 25 million lives are believed to have been lost.

EXPANDING EMPIRE

Peace was not forthcoming under the Qing regime. The Kangxi emperor extended his empire and **strengthened his hold** at home by undertaking military campaigns beyond his frontiers. To the west, against the Tibetans; to the north, against the Dzunghars; and, in the far east of Siberia, Russian colonists. From 1736, when his grandson, the **Qianlong emperor**, ascended the throne, the Chinese empire realized its greatest extent.

MOUNTING PRESSURES

Resistance still flared up from time to time – the end of the 18th century brought the **White Lotus Rebellion**, and the 19th century witnessed the extensive **Taiping Rebellion 240–41 »**.

Like the ruling powers of Japan, the Qing had fostered a splendid isolation. However, the outside world soon pressed in. The colonial period brought its own battles, such as the devastating **Opium Wars** of 1839–42 and 1856–60. The Qing regime was finally removed from power during the **Nationalist Revolution** of 1911.

THE QIANLONG EMPEROR'S MILITARY DRESS

Charismatic leader
Zheng Chenggong leads his army out against the Manchu. This popular general remained loyal to the Ming and went on to expel the Dutch from Taiwan, concluding 38 years of foreign rule on the island.

won a crushing victory over the rebels at Shanhaiguan. But he had effectively invited an invasion by the Manchu. Their forces fanned out through China, extending their dominions far to the south under the pretence of mopping up the rebels and re-establishing order.

A new dynasty
Wu Sangui's hopes that the Chongzhen emperor's son would succeed to the throne were soon dashed. Dorgon proclaimed his young nephew, Shunzhi, emperor, with himself as regent. The Jin dynasty, now renamed the Qing, henceforth governed China. The country's new rulers took control with no compassion; Ming supporters and rebels melded into one. The Manchu felt little sympathy for a Han Chinese population whose agricultural traditions and settled ways they despised. They made their new subjects shave their

hair at the front and wear a long pigtail behind in the Jurchen style – a profound humiliation for the Han. Any resistance was ruthlessly crushed. Over ten days in 1645, the city of Yangzhou in Jiangsu was the scene of a massacre: thousands died at the hands of Prince Dodo's men.

Such atrocities appear only to have encouraged opposition, and fighting continued across the country. In the

8 The number of "banners", or divisions, that the Manchu people were divided into, family by family, for military duty and organization – also later used for political purposes.

south-eastern coastal region of Fujian, General Zheng Chenggong – also known as "Koxinga" – established his own state as a centre of resistance. Starting from Amoy (present-day Xiamen), Koxinga's armies thrust deep into Manchu territory, forming alliances with other nearby powers, including the Portuguese in Macau and the Spanish in the Philippines. Despite a series of victories against the Qing, the general gradually

lost ground and in 1662 was finally forced back to the coast. From there he invaded Taiwan – then a Dutch colony – and made it his offshore base for the continuing campaign against the Qing. The general's death from malaria later that year ended any hope of a Ming restoration, but the Manchu rulers still faced opposition from other quarters.

The Kangxi emperor, who ascended the throne in 1661, faced a revolt by his "Three Feudatories". These Chinese generals, who

included the one-time Ming commander, Wu Sangui, had been charmed by the invaders with the promise of power and wealth, and had been given provinces to govern in southern China. The idea had been to extend the reach of an invasion force that was in danger of spreading itself too thin: it would also afford the Manchu an important source of inside information and advice. For a while this strategy worked. However, the Feudatories became ever more wayward; by 1674 they had risen up against the Qing dynasty. The regime had a scare; but the rebels defeated themselves with their disunity. Confidence was high. The emperor sent an invading fleet of 300 ships to take Taiwan in 1683.

Intricate ensign
The gold, ivory, and coral design on this 17th-century Manchu saddle signify the rider's status and rank.

BEFORE ««

Europe was in a state of upheaval in the 16th century. The Reformation overturned many old certainties, while dynastic power struggles caused widespread destruction.

VALOIS SUPREMACY
The 15th century had treated the **French House of Valois** well. Charles of Valois's **Aragonese Crusade ‹‹ 90–91** of 1284–85 was, by now, a long-forgotten failure: the **Hundred Years War ‹‹ 102–03** had ended in victory for the Valois.

THREAT OF THE HABSBURGS
The growing power and international standing of the Valois was, however, challenged by the **Habsburgs**, whose influence had reached a peak in the great **"universal monarchy"** of

> **HUGUENOT** A Protestant in the context of 17th-century France: the word's origins are unknown, though it appears to have been a term of abuse to begin with.

Charles V (1517–57). But even after he abdicated, the two branches of the family held the thrones of Spain and the Austrian Lands, ensuring they were a natural choice for election as Holy Roman Emperors. Rivalry with the Valois was inevitable and had worked itself out in the second phase of the **Italian Wars of 1517–59 ‹‹ 114–15**.

REFORMING ZEAL
Dissenting fervour was sweeping through France: the protests of Protestant reformer, **John Calvin**, had been heard, despite his enforced exile in Geneva. The Church had hit back with a **"Counter-Reformation"** of its own: society was becoming increasingly polarized.

NORTHWEST EUROPE

The French Wars of Religion
Dates 1562–98
Location France

French Wars of Religion

In the mid-16th century the great French dynasties began to struggle with each other for power. The conflict embroiled the whole nation and became all-consuming; their fervour fuelled by sectarian hatred and the age-old, implacable fear of change.

Italian-born Catherine de' Medici of France was a conciliator. As regent to her young son, Charles IX, in the 1560s she sought peace among the nobility – an accommodation between Catholics and Calvinists. In the vacuum left by her husband Henri II's death in 1559, however, the great houses looked to their own interests, while Catholic France refused to be reconciled with the Protestant "heretics".

This intransigence was encouraged by the House of Guise, self-appointed guardians of Catholicism. In March 1562, Duc Francis de Guise led an attack for two hours. Condé's cavalry could not penetrate the wall of Swiss pikemen facing them, but his own *landsknechts* were not so stalwart. The Catholics won the day. Two months later, the Duc de Guise was killed – allegedly assassinated – at the siege of

Turning wheel

Iron pyrites hammer

Trigger

Wheellock pistol
When the trigger was pulled, the sprung wheel spun, releasing the hammer, which struck sparks. Pistols were prestige items, as this one's elaborate decoration shows.

The pauldron protected the shoulder and armpit area.

Armour
On the brink of obsolescence during these wars, plate armour afforded a degree of protection against the shot from early firearms.

> "Almighty God, how can you allow … such **bloody butchery** of so many **innocent people**?"

CATALOGUE OF CATHOLIC ATROCITIES PRESENTED TO CHARLES IX, 1564

attack on Protestants found worshipping in Vassy, Champagne, killing over 80 men and women. Civil war erupted between the Catholic Crown and the Protestant Huguenots, led by Louis I de Bourbon, Prince de Condé.

Blundering into battle
The battle of Dreux (north of Orléans) was fought in December 1562, and was marked by hapless generalship on both sides. Having not sent any scouts ahead, Condé was caught unawares when his force met the Catholic army face to face. Stunned himself, the Crown's marshal, Anne, duc de Montmorency, failed to

Orléans. Catherine de' Medici arranged a truce. That same year, Charles IX began to rule France in his own right.

Outside interference
Other countries watched. Protestant England, sympathetic to the Huguenots, enjoyed its enemy's difficulties. Spain's Philip II had no love for the House of Valois, but his Catholic piety was real. And he feared Protestantism's capacity to create political unrest, which had already manifested in the Netherlands.

The "Armed Peace" in France gave way to war in 1567. Outnumbered at the Battle of Saint-Denis, near Paris,

KEY MOMENT

ST BARTHOLOMEW'S DAY MASSACRE

In August 1572, France's Huguenot elite had gathered in Paris for the wedding of their co-religionist, Henri of Navarre, to Charles IX's sister, Marguerite of Valois. The match was intended to promote religious harmony, though many Catholics opposed it – including, it was said, the bride. The prominent Catholic, Duc de Guise, was enraged – the more so because among those present was the Huguenot Admiral de Coligny, thought to have ordered Guise's

father's assassination years before. When an agent of Guise tried to shoot Coligny, the admiral survived but the Huguenots were outraged. The fear of Protestant reprisals created a murderous mood in Paris. Guise took the lead, this time succeeding in killing Coligny. Catholic mobs took to the streets; they burst into Huguenot houses murdering men, women, and children in an orgy of slaughter that went on for three days and left over 12,000 dead.

Armoured helmet with a hinged visor, enclosing the entire head and face.

Faulds – segmented metal strips below the breastplate – helped to protect the hips of the mounted knight.

the Huguenots were defeated once again, but the Peace of Longjumeau (1568) made them concessions, which enraged diehard Catholics.

The Huguenots were soon ready to campaign again. Funded by England, they had 14,000 German *reiters*. These "riders", mercenary cavalry, fought with guns and swords. A popular manoeuvre, known as the *caracole*, involved riders advancing in formation, each one with a pistol at the ready in both the right and the left hands. On approaching his enemy, each man turned his mount slightly to one side, firing

from that hand, before half-turning the other way to fire again from the other hand. He then wheeled around, withdrawing to reload.

The Royalists had numbers on their side, with troops from Spain and states in Italy. At Jarnac (Bordeaux), in March 1569, the Huguenots lost not just the battle, but also their commander: in the heat of the encounter, the Prince de Condé was shot. Although the Protestants prevailed nearby, at La Roche-l'Abeille, the Catholics defeated them again at Moncontour in 1570, bringing an end to this round of fighting.

In 1572 the St Bartholomew's Day Massacre sparked another war: it ended with the Edict of Boulogne restricting the Huguenots' rights. Most were restored under the Edict of Beaulieu, which concluded the "Fifth War" of 1574–76. Charles IX died in 1574, and was succeeded by his brother, Henri III – a conciliator, like his mother.

10 PER CENT of France's population adopted Protestantism by 1560.

2 PER CENT of France's population practise Protestantism today.

No compromise
In 1576 Duc Henri de Guise, Francis's heir, established a "Catholic League", its unstated aim to secure the throne for himself. The pope and Philip II of Spain backed it. But Henri III had Henri of Navarre on his side – a Bourbon and a Protestant, already fighting for the Huguenot cause. Henri of Navarre also descended from King Louis IX and, as Henri III was childless, this made him the legitimate heir to the French throne.

Battle of Dreux
Fought in March 1562 this battle marked the beginning of the French Wars of Religion. Family members were killed on the opposing sides as poor planning made for the most brutal of encounters.

The Catholic League was determined to stop him. At Coutras, in 1587, the Catholic forces marched quietly through the night to surprise Henri of Navarre at dawn. But his men, well-trained veterans, held their formations, making every shot tell. The Huguenot *reiters* were deployed to great effect. De Guise's Catholic cavalry, made up of armoured knights with lances, made a stirring sight as they charged towards their enemy, but were cut down easily by Henri of Navarre's arquebusiers. The way was clear for their general to become king of France.

Two years later he did, following the assassination of Henri III by a Catholic extremist. Henri of Navarre, now Henri IV, converted to Catholicism before he was crowned, but did not entirely abandon the Protestant cause. In 1598 the Edict of Nantes confirmed the Huguenots' religious freedoms and gave them security in the form of rights to maintain their own garrisons and troops.

AFTER

Although the coronation of Henri IV appeared to have taken most of the acrimony out of France's religious divisions, not much had been settled.

UNREST IN THE NETHERLANDS
Philip II found his worst fears realized in **the Netherlands**, where Protestant fervour fuelled demands for **political change 138–39 >>**.

RESURGENCE OF HATRED
Peace in France was brought to an abrupt end in 1610, when **Henri IV was assassinated** by a Catholic fanatic. In 1627 Louis XIII besieged the **Huguenot city of La Rochelle**. But France's domestic problems were quickly overshadowed by the wider religious conflict of the **Thirty Years War 142–43 >>**.

The France that emerged from this nightmare was an **autocratic, highly-centralized state** with no room for dissent of any kind. **King Louis XIV** made his own views on religion clear with his **Revocation of the Edict of Nantes** in 1685, which effectively outlawed Protestantism in France once more.

HENRI IV

BATTLE OF MONCONTOUR
This idealized bird's-eye view of the battle of Moncontour, between French Catholics and Huguenots in 1569, shows a typical Renaissance battlefield: an opening artillery barrage, followed by advancing squares of pikemen, flanked by musketeers, with cavalry in support. The battle was a victory for the Catholics (in the foreground) who were supported by troops from Spain, the Papal States, and the Grand Duchy of Tuscany.

The Dutch Revolt

When the Spanish Crown sent troops to quell an uprising in the Netherlands in 1567, no one guessed that they were going to be fighting for 80 years. The Dutch finally won their independence, not just by their bravery but by their resourcefulness and readiness to adapt.

For the Dutch Protestants, sacred images of every kind were false idols. Catholic churches were full of stone and wooden figures, stained glass, and carvings. In 1566 a Protestant spree of pious vandalism commenced.

Philip II had always suspected that Protestantism was associated with the rejection of authority. The doctrines of Calvin and Luther had taken root in northern Europe, among an increasingly affluent merchant class. The ports and industrial cities were home to self-confident communities whose people expected a measure of intellectual independence. When the Spanish general, the Duke of Alba, led an army into Brussels in 1567 to crack down on the rebels and reinstate Catholicism, the population rose up in a patriotic rage.

Resistance coalesced around the figure of William the Silent, Prince of Orange, but the suppression of the dissenters was quick. Hundreds were executed. A rebel army marched out at Rheindalen in April 1568, but its volunteers were no match for the soldiers of the Spanish Crown.

Repression and resistance

The unrest went on. Alba, exasperated at the Dutch defiance, reacted with atrocities. Terrible massacres took place at Zutphen and Naarden, and then in Haarlem in 1573. Far from encouraging other cities to surrender, such conduct strengthened their defiance. Alba found this conflict frustrating. He knew his 60,000 soldiers should be "a sufficient number to conquer many kingdoms", and yet, he lamented, "it does not suffice me here". Alba took a town but, once he had departed, the rebels reappeared. The siege of Leiden in 1573 had to be

Key

- Spanish Netherlands at outbreak of revolt
- Joined Union of Utrecht 1579, 1581
- Union of Arras 1579
- Border of United Provinces agreed by truce of 1609
- — Frontiers 1568
- Dutch victory
- Spanish victory

The Dutch Revolt 1568–1609
Spain's early victories were soon forgotten as, fighting bravely on own home ground, the Dutch turned a quick policing operation into a long-running war.

lifted when William the Silent appeared with a makeshift army. Alba defeated them at Mookerheyde and in September 1574 resumed his siege. The Dutch failed to oust the Spanish, and were unpaid. Angry soldiers went on a rampage in Antwerp in an episode known as the "Spanish Fury", killing 8,000 in three days. Chastened, the Spanish authorities agreed an alliance

> "Bodies of men might have been **seen hovering piecemeal in the air** … "
>
> MAURICE OF NASSAU ON A MINE BLAST AT THE SIEGE OF STEENWIJK, 1592

on the point of starvation when they were relieved by the ships of the *Watergeuzen* ("Sea Beggars"). The *geuzen* were Calvinist privateers who had originally sought religious asylum in English ports. Expelled by Elizabeth I in 1568, they returned to fight for the rebels in the Netherlands. Despite this early rebuff, England gave covert then, from the 1580s, increasingly open support to the Dutch Revolt.

A new approach

Alba was called back to Spain in 1573. His replacement, Luis de Requesens, found it hard to maintain a moderate course in a conflict that was not just exasperating but financially draining. By 1576 Spanish troops were going

of the various regions of the Habsburg Netherlands. The Pacification of Ghent was signed in 1576. Spain, however, reclaimed the initiative when significant funds began to arrive from the American silver mines. In 1579 the Duke of Parma was sent as governor. His "divide and rule" approach played on the tensions he saw between the southern cities and the more militant, aggressively Calvinist northern centres. Parma persuaded the southern states (now Flanders) to form the Union of Arras, loyal to Spain. The north responded with their own Union of Utrecht. The Duke made the southern cities his base for a new campaign of conquest. Spain suffered a setback in 1588 when the Armada, sent to wage war on England, was defeated.

Point

Axe blade

A versatile weapon

The halberd proved one Dutch answer to the fearsome Spanish pike. The point pushed off attackers; the tilted axe blade could cut deep.

William the Silent died in 1584: his son, Maurice of Nassau, was among the greatest generals of the age, creating coherence in what had been an ill-matched assemblage of volunteer militias and mercenaries. While his recognition of the need to make his army into a fighting machine seems modern, his stated aim was to train his troops *more Romano* ("in the Roman way"), and he culled many of his ideas from the ancients. His men performed endless repetitive drills with pikes and muskets, every one broken down into individual movements and each one numbered. He rationalized the army's structures, training new officers to command smaller companies. Maurice of Nassau thereby built a more flexible fighting force.

He then did all he could to keep it safe. In 20 years (while laying siege to cities and attacking fortresses), he contrived to fight just two pitched battles. In 1600, however, his superior tactics were shown when he defeated Spain at Nieuwpoort, near Dunkirk. Less fortunately for Maurice, the brilliant Italian general and financier, Ambrogio Spinola, entered the service of the Crown. But from 1609, hostilities were suspended during the Twelve Years Truce.

Naval mastery

The Thirty Years War began in 1618, and fighting resumed in the Netherlands in 1621. Maurice of Nassau's health was failing and he could not prevent Spinola from taking the crucial city of Breda in 1625. By this point Maurice was gravely ill – he died while the siege of Breda was taking place. His half-brother, Henry Frederick, assumed command.

The Dutch nevertheless made good progress at sea. In 1628 Piet Heyn captured the Spanish treasure fleet. Its ships were bringing silver back from the mines of the New World – their loss was a deep humiliation and a major blow for Spain. Maritime warfare had been changing fast – ships with side-mounted cannon were becoming the norm, and the Dutch had been quick in acquiring mastery. They had shown this as early as 1607 in their audacious attack on the Spanish off Gibraltar. In 1639, at the battle of the Downs, just off the coast of England, Maarten Tromp and his fellow seafarers savaged a Spanish fleet bringing reinforcements for the war effort in Flanders.

Spain was running out of options. It had not been defeated; but neither was there any realistic prospect of its winning – money was running out and lives were being lost. When the Thirty Years War came to its conclusion in 1648, Spain's power was weakened. The country finally acknowledged the independence of the Dutch Republic.

The Surrender of Breda

Diego Velázquez's famous painting underlines the importance of this conflict to the Spanish Crown. The city fell in 1625 after a nine-month siege.

AFTER

The Dutch Revolt claimed many lives and destroyed many cities. The survivors were to witness many changes as their country revelled in its new-found independence.

THE THIRTY YEARS WAR

Those who survived the Dutch Revolt – especially in the northern cities – discovered a new sense of national identity. Though only peripherally involved in the unfolding agonies of the **Thirty Years War 142–43 》**, they felt the turbulence that the conflict caused at the heart of Europe.

RENEWED NAVAL MIGHT

As soon as hostilities ceased and the **Treaty of Westphalia** was signed in 1648, the Netherlands flourished. A new economic and cultural force in Northern Europe, the country became an emergent military power, its growing might at sea setting it against England during **the Anglo-Dutch Wars 148–49 》**.

As intrepid seafarers, the Dutch were soon opening up new areas for colonial exploitation in the **East Indies**. Some of these conquests were to haunt them in much later times, such as when **Indonesia struggled for its independence 318–19 》** in the years after World War II.

The Anglo-Spanish War

Religious conviction and power-politics proved a combustible mix in the escalating conflict between the Spanish and the English. The events of the Anglo-Spanish War were to become fundamental to England's sense of itself as divinely appointed defender of Protestant liberty.

Spanish helmet
The classic "comb morion" was the helmet of choice for Spain's 16th-century soldiers. The "comb", or crest, reinforced the helmet and deflected enemy blows.

WESTERN EUROPE AND ATLANTIC

1 Raids on Cádiz
Dates 1587, 1596
Location Southern Spain

2 The Spanish Armada
Date 1588
Location The English Channel

3 The Counter Armada
Date 1589
Location Coast of Portugal and Spain

4 The Azores
Date 1591
Location Mid-Atlantic

F rancis Drake sighted the *Nuestra Señora de la Concepción* ("Our Lady of the Conception") off the coast of Ecuador on 1 March 1579. Having trailed it discreetly throughout the day, his ship, the *Golden Hind*, finally closed in as darkness fell. Drake's crew opened up with cannon and musket fire, shattering its mast. The shocked crew surrendered, the English taking the Spanish cargo of gold and silver.

However, forays like this were not viewed as piracy. English vessels that stopped Spanish ships on the high seas did so with Her Majesty's blessing. The Crown benefited financially by issuing "letters of marque" (official warrants to inspect, capture, and destroy foreign vessels) to seamen like Francis Drake, Martin Frobisher, and John Hawkins.

Invincible fleet

Inconveniencing Spain – Europe's richest Catholic power – was one thing, but Elizabeth's interference in the Spanish-controlled Netherlands was something more. The Earl of Leicester's 1585 expedition there in support of the Dutch rebels was futile, but for Spain's Philip II it was the final indignity. Open hostilities broke out. Across the Atlantic, Francis Drake stepped up his plundering.

The sinking of the Armada

A relatively minor skirmish in itself, the defeat of the Armada in 1588 did still successfully frustrate Spanish invasion plans. And the encounter was to loom large in the English myth-making of later times.

131

The number of ships sunk by Sir Francis Drake in the raid on Cádiz, 1587. A further six vessels were captured.

In January 1586, with Frobisher, he led a party ashore to sack Santo Domingo; several weeks later he looted Cartagena de las Indias. With rumours growing of a sizable Spanish *armada*, or fleet, that would take the war to England, Drake did to Spain what he had done to its colonies. In April 1587, he sacked Cádiz, sinking ships and looting warehouses. The raid became known as the "Singeing of the King of Spain's Beard": the damage was minor, but the affront to Philip II was outrageous.

By 1588 Spain was ready. Its *Armada Invencible* was to travel up the Channel to Flanders. There, the Duke of Parma would be waiting with an army 30,000

BEFORE

When Queen Mary I ascended the throne she restored Catholicism to England. Despite protests at her betrothal to a Spanish prince she was able to face down her opponents.

THE QUEEN EXERTS HER AUTHORITY

Queen Mary I's marriage to Prince Philip of Spain in 1554 promised to ensure lasting good relations between the two countries – though the wedding prompted violent protests in England. "Bloody Mary" was not to be cowed: she began a programme of harsh repression.

PHILIP II OF SPAIN

A NEW PERIL

Protestant dangers were all too evident. The **French Wars of Religion** started in 1562 **‹‹ 134–35**.

Mary's husband, Philip II (king of Spain from 1556, so ruler of the Spanish Netherlands), had his own problems with the reformers, with **the Dutch Revolt** and the **Eighty Years War ‹‹ 138–39**.

Mary's death in 1558 was not just a personal loss for Philip but a **diplomatic challenge** – her Protestant half-sister, Elizabeth I, took the throne.

Naval armament

Often mounted on the upper deck of warships from this period, the 3m (10ft) long-barrelled culverin could fire a light shot over long distances.

Mounting peg

strong to invade England. His troops would sail in small boats, the Armada escorting. In May the Armada left Iberia: it included 24 warships and 47 armed merchantmen, along with unarmed transport ships (carrying up to 20,000 extra infantrymen), and smaller craft.

Battles abound

Commanded by the Duke of Medina Sidonia, Spain's Armada travelled up the Channel without much trouble. But Parma's army had been held in Flanders by *Watergeuzen* (Dutch privateers who raided foreign ships). On 7 August the Armada, waiting at Calais, proved vulnerable when the English dispatched fireships to float into its lines. Panicked Spanish crews cut their anchor cables and the Armada broke free, its defensive formation quickly lost. Lord Howard of Effingham's English warships fired at will. Four ships were sunk, and several

damaged. Parma's invasion was foiled, and the Armada was forced to push on into the North Sea. The voyage home proved costly, stormy waters claiming some 60 ships and thousands of lives.

Jubilant England sent out its own armada in 1589, but this endured heavy losses. In 1591 Spain reasserted its naval superiority at the battle of the Azores, when an attempt to capture its treasure fleet was thwarted. Lord Howard led a joint attack on Cádiz in 1596 with the Earl of Essex. The treasure ships they were hoping to take were scuttled and

sent to the bottom of Cádiz harbour by their quick-thinking commander, for retrieval later: the English raiders sacked the city, but left empty-handed.

In 1595 Hugh O'Neill, Earl of Tyrone, and "Red" Hugh O'Donnell had fitful Spanish backing when they led an Irish rebellion. In 1601 Spain landed soldiers on the coast of Cork in support, but the groups did not rendezvous successfully. Instead the Spanish were pinned down by the English at the siege of Kinsale. Philip II died in 1598 and Elizabeth I in 1603. By 1604 their successors had made peace with the Treaty of London.

> **"Their fleet is wonderful great and strong; and yet we pluck their feathers, little and little."**
>
> LORD HOWARD OF EFFINGHAM'S DISPATCH OF 9 AUGUST, 1588

QUEEN OF ENGLAND (1533–1603)

ELIZABETH I

"I know I have but the body of a weak and feeble woman, but I have the heart and stomach of a king, and of a king of England too." Elizabeth's famous address to the troops at Tilbury showed there was no doubting her resolution or her strength. Or indeed the Protestant convictions that brought her into conflict with Spain – a 16th-century superpower – and helped shape her country's foreign policy for years to come. By the time she died in 1603, Queen Elizabeth I had made England the most important European counter to the dominance of the world's great Catholic monarchies.

AFTER

The defeat of the Spanish Armada had sent England's confidence soaring. However, its Irish neighbour would prove a problem, as would the Dutch Republic.

THE PLANTATION OF ULSTER

The conflict with Spain had given the English a fright. There was a new **sense of vulnerability**. Given the events of 1601, Ireland was a particular concern. It appeared a susceptible "back door" for invasion, its people Catholic in religion and prone to rebellion. The British clamped down in the north, establishing the **"Plantation of Ulster"**. The settling of loyal Protestant Lowland Scots in the northern Irish lands of the O'Donnells and O'Neills did successfully transform the political culture of the north of Ireland. However, the strategy did not stop France from repeatedly trying to exploit **Irish insurgencies** towards the end of the 18th century.

ANGLO-DUTCH CONFLICT

England's status as Europe's **leading Protestant power** was to be challenged by a buoyant Dutch Republic as the 17th century wore on. Eventually, the two countries would go to war, and in 1652 the **Anglo-Dutch Wars** began **148–49 ≫**.

« BEFORE

Religious faith may begin with the individual conscience, but it seldom ends there. In 16th-century Europe, it was also at the heart of social and cultural existence.

JOSTLING FOR POSITION

Religion was increasingly the centre of political life, especially once the **Protestant Reformation** had opened up the possibility of difference of belief. In 1562 Catholic opposition had plunged France into civil war during **the Wars of Religion** « 134–35, and fuelled the hatreds that resulted in **the Dutch Revolt** « 138–39.

FAITH DIVIDE

Feelings ran high in the home of the Reformation. In 1517 **Martin Luther** had made his famous stand in Wittenberg, Germany, within the

RUDOLF II, HOLY ROMAN EMPEROR

Holy Roman Empire actually a patchwork of principalities, duchies, and other small states, was soon divided along religious lines. Serious conflict was avoided when, at the **Peace of Augsburg** in 1555, the principle of *cuius regio, cuius religio* ("whose region, whose religion") was agreed and regional independence cemented. If the ruler was Catholic, then that was the state's religion; if he was Protestant, then so were his people. As time went on, impatience grew over what appeared to be an unresolved issue. Emperor Rudolf II seemed to be storing up trouble with his tolerant attitude.

The Thirty Years War

Habsburg plans to turn back the clock, reimposing Roman Catholicism as the established religion, turned Central Europe into a cauldron of conflict and suffering. This war for the continent's Christian soul was outstanding in its heartless cynicism and in the staggering extent of its civilian casualties.

One of Europe's most tragic episodes began in farce, when Protestant nobles in Bohemia hurled two imperial governors, accused of violating Protestants' rights, from a high window into a heap of horse manure. The officials in the Town Hall had been acting on behalf of the empire and the Church, and this "Defenestration of Prague" symbolized the Protestants' defiance. Rocked by the Reformation, the empire had drawn strength from the Counter-Reformation and there were fears that Catholicism would again be enforced. While the Habsburg emperor, Matthias, remained ruler of Upper and Lower Austria and Holy Roman Emperor until his death in 1619, in 1617 his nephew, Ferdinand, had been elected king of Bohemia by the Bohemian Diet in a move that was engineered by loyalist Bohemian grandees to ensure a fluid Habsburg succession to the aged Matthias's titles. Ferdinand's aggressive Catholic devotion was well known but the Bohemian elites assumed that he would respect their religious privileges.

The conflict spreads

Instead, Ferdinand instantly sought to change things in Bohemia in favour of the Catholics – the result was the Defenestration and open rebellion against Habsburg authority. The Protestant rebels looked to their religious allies for help, and especially to the Calvinist ruler of the Palatinate, Elector Frederick V. Frederick was leader of the Protestant Union, a military alliance of the radical Protestant States in Germany set up by his father in 1608.

In 1619 Matthias died; Ferdinand inherited his remaining titles and was

Europe engulfed

The Thirty Years War began in Bohemia and the German territories of the Holy Roman Empire. But the war spread beyond these borders, with trouble flaring up from Sicily to Scotland. Europe's structure would be changed irrevocably.

elected as the Holy Roman Emperor, Ferdinand II. Despite this development, the Bohemian rebels declared Ferdinand deposed and elected Frederick V to his place as ruler of Bohemia. Ferdinand responded by preparing his military forces and looking to the support of his Habsburg cousin in Spain, Philip III, and the Catholic League, composed of German states under the leadership of Bavaria, which had been set up in 1609

4 MILLION
The number of people who died during the Thirty Years War, whether killed in the fighting or by associated famine or disease. Some estimates give a figure almost twice as high.

to counter the Protestant Union. In late 1620, at the battle of White Mountain just outside Prague, a united Catholic army crushed Frederick's forces, deposed him, and put down the revolt. Frederick fled into exile, his own territories in Germany held by the victorious Catholic forces, and Habsburg authority and

Catholicism were imposed in Bohemia. But this was just the start, not the end, of hostilities, as with religious principles and political issues at stake both in the Holy Roman Empire and across a wider European stage, a variety of powers and interests were to get involved.

In 1626 Christian IV of Denmark took up the Protestant banner, but he was worsted in successive engagements with the army of the Catholic League led by Count Tilly and by the emperor's army, created, funded, and led by Albrecht Wallenstein. Wallenstein aroused fear and outrage among the rulers of the Holy Roman Empire. Although without a princely title, his virtually private army had carried the emperor's power across Germany and to the Baltic coasts, and had been funded by a wave of transfers and confiscations of territory into his hands. Eventually his power was to

Key

- Austrian Habsburg possessions 1618
- Spanish Habsburg possessions 1618
- States at war with the Imperial forces and Catholic League
- Boundary of Holy Roman Empire 1618
- Frontiers 1618
- → Gustavus Adolphus's intervention 1630–32
- Imperial/Catholic victory
- Imperial/Catholic defeat

Map labels: North Sea, Baltic Sea, SWEDEN, Gothenburg, DENMARK, Copenhagen, ENGLAND, London, UNITED PROVINCES, Amsterdam, PRUSSIA to Brandenburg, POLAND, Warsaw, Antwerp, SPANISH NETHERLANDS, Cologne, Magdeburg, BRANDENBURG, Stettin, Elbe, Oder, Vistula, Lutter 1626, Dessau Bridge 1626, SAXONY, Breitenfeld 1631, 1642, Rocroi 1643, SMALL STATES, Rhine, Mainz, Lützen 1632, Dresden, BOHEMIA, Prague, SILESIA, Cracow, Paris, Rheims, White Mountain 1620, Jankov 1645, MORAVIA, FRANCE, Wimpfen 1622, Nördlingen 1634, Danube, Zusmarshausen 1648, Freiburg 1644, Rain 1632, BAVARIA, Munich, AUSTRIA, Vienna, OTTOMAN EMPIRE, SWISS CONFEDERATION

German burgonet helmet

The burgonet was light despite being reinforced internally. The combed crown deflected an enemy's blows.

unnerve the emperor himself – by the
late 1620s Wallenstein had an army
60,000 strong. But for the moment
though, he was the emperor's greatest
asset. Wallenstein's defeat of Denmark
took that country out of the war, while
Sweden's Gustavus Adolphus stepped
up to lead the Protestants.

The Peace of Prague

Gustavus Adolphus won a resounding
victory at the first battle of Breitenfeld
(pp.144–45) on 17 September 1631. The
following year, Wallenstein's men were
mauled at Lützen
by the Swedes, but
Gustavus Adolphus
was killed. Without
him the Swedes
faltered and were
beaten at Nördlingen in 1634. The
emperor had the upper hand again. He
imposed a truce, followed by a general
German peace at Prague, in 1635.

The German princes, Protestant and
Catholic, were war weary and alienated
by Sweden's military policies. They
accepted a settlement that moderated
the emperor's tough religious demands.
This settlement did not please Catholic
France, however. Cardinal Richelieu,
King Louis XIII's chief minister, had
grown uneasy at the thought of the

> **156** The number of distinct states
> and polities at the negotiations
> leading up to the signing of the Treaty of
> Westphalia, marking the end of the war.

The sack of Magdeburg
The Protestant city of Magdeburg was the scene of one
of the greatest atrocities of European history. In 1631
some 25,000 people were slain and the city destroyed.

Habsburgs being so firmly established in
Germany and Spain. So France declared
war on both Spain and the empire, soon
invading the Spanish Netherlands and
Imperial territories along the Rhine, but
they were repelled. Spanish and German
armies cut through Picardy, Burgundy,
and Champagne. The Habsburgs were
also weakened by Dutch victories at sea
and an uprising in
Portugal in 1640.
Concentrating
its forces in North
Germany, Sweden
regrouped before
winning decisively at the second battle
of Breitenfeld in 1642. Spain's *tercios*
were massacred at Rocroi in France the
year after, by France's Duc d'Enghien
and his use of cavalry and artillery.

Gradually, the fighting eased, and
in 1648 the Treaty of Westphalia was
signed. After 30 years of battle and
the loss of millions of lives, the two
sides had effectively returned to the
accommodation acceded at the Peace
of Augsburg in 1555: both Catholic
and Protestant rulers agreed to differ.

Chequer-board pike and musket formations
Bristling pikes catch the eye in Matthäus Merian's engraving of the battle of Breitenfeld. It was the discipline and tactical flexibility of the Swedish infantry units that won the day for Gustavus's forces.

First Battle of Breitenfeld

Sparked by religious conflict, the Thirty Years War settled down into a struggle for strategic advantage and political power. In time it became a blood-soaked, life-and-death laboratory in which a new science of warfare slowly took shape. Nowhere was this more apparent than at Breitenfeld, where in 1631 Swedish forces gave the world a terrifying taste of things to come.

By 1630 the advantage in a war that had been going on for just over a decade seemed to have swung towards the Catholic powers. Swedish king Gustavus Adolphus's entry into the conflict on the Protestant side occasioned little concern, for the Duke of Friedland had proved all but indomitable in his service to Ferdinand II, the Holy Roman Emperor. However, the emperor himself had become so alarmed by Friedland's growing power that he replaced him in 1630 with another great commander, Count Tilly.

A new way of war

In 1630 Gustavus landed in Pomerania with an army that had learned much from previous combat experience. His infantry were now organized into brigades of 1,200–1,500 men, which combined excellent cohesion and battlefield staying-power with tactical flexibility. The infantry were powerful in defence, could quickly deploy in lines six deep to maximize the impact of musketry, and could combine with artillery and cavalry to deploy a variety of offensive tactics.

The large, deep infantry formations of Gustavus's enemies brought massive weight to bear in an assault on opposing forces, but they offered a limited range of tactical options to a commander, mostly being employed in a single line of battle and operating as

isolated battlefield "fortresses". In contrast, Gustavus's brigades could be broken into smaller "squadrons" of 400–500 men, able to make better use of their muskets in units as little as six men deep, but without sacrificing the capacity to lock together into full brigades that bristled with as many pikes and could put up as stalwart a defence as any of their rivals. Above all the brigades deployed less densely: they could match the enemy's front with a fraction of his units, leaving additional brigades to form second and third lines on the battlefield. It was this tactical flexibility that gave Gustavus victory against Tilly; a victory that was far from assured on the outset of the battle.

From theory to practice

Tilly advanced into Saxony, where Gustavus had linked up with the Elector of Saxony's army. The opposing forces met in open country, at Breitenfeld. The initial assault of Tilly's troops swept away the Saxon army corps on the left flank, and threatened to roll up the Swedes from the flank. The rapidity, skill, and determination with which the second line were swung round to drive back the Catholic forces turned apparently inevitable disaster into crushing victory. Tilly's army resisted bravely, but Adolphus's juggernaut could not be stopped.

LOCATION
Just outside Leipzig, Germany

DATE
17 September 1631

FORCES
Imperial: 35,000;
Swedish and Saxons: 42,000

CASUALTIES
Imperial: c.8,000 killed;
Swedish and Saxons: c.4,000 killed

KEY
- Imperial infantry
- Imperial cavalry
- Swedish infantry
- Swedish cavalry
- Saxon infantry
- Saxon cavalry

The British Civil Wars

"What can warrs, but endlesse warr still breed?" asked the English poet John Milton. Despite this, deep conviction drove him to support the Cromwellian cause. The 17th century saw the British Isles torn by religious and ideological struggles, which were to exact an appalling human cost.

Charles I's attempt to arrest leading Parliamentarians – in parliament itself – precipitated the outbreak of civil war. He raised his standard at Nottingham on 22 August 1642. He had 2,000 cavalry, his aristocratic "cavaliers" (from the French *chevalier* – "knight" or, more literally, "horseman"), but only a few hundred infantrymen (though more rallied round as he marched south). Meanwhile, the Earl of Essex had been assembling a Parliamentarian force, derisively named "Roundheads" by their opponents on account of the radical

Protestant fashion for close-cropped hair. While the war was fought in the defence of sincerely-held principles, a number of soldiers signed up as mercenaries, including leading officers who were veterans of the Thirty Years War.

The two armies met on 23 October at Edgehill, Warwickshire. Led by the king's nephew, Prince Rupert, the

Essex was waiting west of the city at Turnham Green. He had been busy creating volunteer town and village militias, so he also had an ample force; too big for the king to think of tackling. Charles withdrew to Oxford to ponder his next move. Over the following year, the armies criss-crossed southern England, closing occasionally for brief

THE BRITISH ISLES

1 **First Civil War**
Dates 1642–46
Location England and Wales

2 **Second and Third Civil Wars**
Dates 1648, 1649–51
Location Scotland, northwest England, and Wales

3 **Cromwell's campaign in Ireland**
Dates 1649–50
Location Eastern and southern Ireland

> ## "If these times hold, I fear there will be **no men** left for women."
> **ENGLISHWOMAN ELIZABETH ISHAM ON HER NIECE'S WEDDING,** 1645

cavaliers charged with scorching pace and force, scattering the Parliamentarian horses before them. Some infantrymen fled, but the core was disciplined – and apparently forgotten by Charles's Royalists, who seemed to think the battle already won. The Royalists threw away their advantage, chasing plunder while the Parliamentarian infantry pushed forth, their cavalry regrouping. Neither could win a convincing victory. The king's army headed for London, growing as it went.

engagements, most of which were won by the Royalists. But much of this good work was undone in one afternoon at Newbury in September 1643 where, once again, the Royalist cavalry charged to apparently devastating effect against Essex's horsemen. Despite a succession of attempts, however, and dreadful

casualties on both sides, the Royalists could not break the steady resolve of the Parliamentarian pikemen.

A leader emerges
Essex seemed no more able to press his advantage than Charles had been before. Both armies struggled to sustain support among their troops, and both were short of supplies and funding. Men deserted and preyed on the country people, who grew disillusioned with the conflict. Both sides sought help from outside, Charles from the Catholic Irish lords; his enemies from the Presbyterian Scots.

Charles I of England believed in the king's "divine right" to rule unchallenged. This absolutism brought him into a long and bitter conflict with his parliament.

THE ISSUE OF RELIGION
Alongside concern at his despotism, there were suspicions in what was now a proudly Protestant England that the **Stuart dynasty** had Catholic sympathies. Charles certainly had no time for the freedom of individual conscience that Protestants prized. In 1638 Presbyterians in Scotland signed a **National Covenant**, noting their defiance. Charles undertook two **"Bishops' Wars"** for his right to impose his own hierarchy on the **Scottish Kirk**. The failure of this

CHARLES I

enterprise not only damaged his **authority at home**, but saddled England with an enormous **debt for reparations** to the Scots.

LOSING CONTROL
In order to raise taxes, Charles had to recall his parliament, to the alarm of Ireland's **"old English" Catholic nobility**, fearful for their position in a situation in which the **Protestants of Scotland** and England's Parliamentarians were in the ascendant. Their rebellion in 1641 precipitated a **political crisis**: many assumed that Charles had encouraged the Catholic uprising. Such trust as still existed between the king and his critics now broke down.

Falconet
Essentially an outsized musket on wheels, the falconet could fire single-round shot, and tiny "grapeshot" – both devastating against enemy infantry.

Light as it was, the falconet could be hitched up to horses and moved quickly from one place to another – important in the fast-moving action of the British Civil Wars.

Bullet mould and shot
Shot could be made in the field by pouring molten lead into a hinged mould. Troops used pointed "nippers" – or their teeth – to trim the rough edges.

Mould

But the Parliamentarians already had the answer to their problems. Oliver Cromwell had come a long way since the fighting started. Though his political resistance to the king had commanded respect in the years leading up to the war, as a military novice, he had since been sidelined. Nevertheless, he had set

900,000
An estimate of the number of casualties in the British Civil Wars in 1639–51. About a third of the population of Ireland is thought to have been killed or exiled.

about raising his own mounted militia in Cambridgeshire. Learning fast, he had won several victories. By July 1644 he was a Lieutenant-General of the Horse, and served at the head of 3,000 cavalry under Sir Thomas Fairfax at the battle of Marston Moor, near York. Fairfax

was hurt, though only slightly. Many Parliamentarian soldiers fled in panic as night fell. The Scots stood firm, however, and Cromwell called his cavalry back into formation. Seizing the initiative, he led an audacious charge across the breadth of the battlefield to attack the Royalist horse, putting them to flight before turning on the infantry. With Fairfax's foot soldiers pressing forward, Royalist resistance simply collapsed.

The New Model Army
Marston Moor might have given the Parliamentarians mastery in the north, but Essex was being overwhelmed in the south. Fairfax created a "New Model Army", numbering 20,000, a body of professional full-timers who could be deployed at speed wherever needed. With 11 regiments of cavalry, 12 of infantry, and a single regiment of dragoons, they were trained and drilled in the best modern continental style. Its men were well supplied and regularly paid, and the army was scrupulously depoliticized: its officers were expressly barred from sitting as MPs. Above all,

Ornate muzzle

it was centralized and imbued from top to bottom with the Protestant virtue – and military value – of discipline.

Hence the manner in which the army held its shape as Prince Rupert's cavalry squandered another victory at Naseby in Northamptonshire the following June. The defeat was decisive; Charles sued for peace. In 1648 Scots nobles came to Charles's rescue with 20,000 men, but they were halted by Cromwell

Battle of Naseby
The Royalists were heavily outnumbered at the battle of Naseby in 1645, but it was the superior discipline of the Parliamentarian forces – and the crucial contribution of their cavalry – that won the day.

at Preston. This "Second Civil War" was quickly over. Cromwell and his party were now England's rulers. In 1649 they tried and executed Charles I.

Both sides in England's First Civil War had learned from the example of the Thirty Years War in technology and tactics. Cromwell's determination to quash the Irish rebellion in 1649 was shocking in its ferocity. At the siege of Drogheda on 11 September, the entire garrison of 2,800 and some civilians were purposely killed when the city was stormed by Cromwell's troops. He went on to Wexford, slaying 3,500 more.

Scotland's turn
The role of Scotland in the conflict had been changing. While its Presbyterian religious and political establishment had at first supported the Parliamentarian cause in England, rifts over political aims and the more doctrinally-radical Protestantism espoused by much of the New Model Army, including Cromwell himself, had led to rifts, and finally to Scottish support for a Stuart monarchy, which they considered would better maintain their Presbyterian religious settlement. In 1648 the Scots had mounted an invasion of England, and in 1650 they prepared for another. This time they were under the leadership of Charles I's son, Charles II. Cromwell returned from Ireland and marched an army north, besieging Edinburgh. Running short of supplies, he withdrew east as far as Dunbar. There, on 3 September, he trounced the much larger Scottish army that came after him, drawing it down from its superior position on higher ground then deftly outflanking it.

Back in England, at Worcester, exactly a year after his triumph at Dunbar, Cromwell smashed Charles II's Royalist army once and for all. Charles II went into hiding then fled to the continent.

himself led the infantry – 8,000 in all, backed by 14,000 Scots. Some 18,000 Royalists faced them, including dragoons (mounted infantry) and cavalry.

Cromwell led the Parliamentarian attack, striking unexpectedly in the evening. His cavalry came forward in close formation. The attack started well but faltered when Fairfax's infantry was slowed by marshy ground. As the Royalists counterattacked, Cromwell

LORD PROTECTOR (1599–1658)

OLIVER CROMWELL

Cromwell was an astonishing man in both energy and resource. A self-taught soldier, he helped build an army – and a strategy – from scratch, and was indefatigable in the execution of his plans. To the point, at times, of fanaticism: the opposition between the frivolous "Cavalier" (Royalist) and the grim-faced "Roundhead" is often exaggerated, but Cromwell was a desperately driven man. He showed a shockingly implacable side during his campaigns in Ireland.

AFTER »

The execution of Charles I in 1649 – a traumatic event in itself – took England into uncharted waters; it was no longer a "kingdom" but a "commonwealth".

CROMWELL'S LEADERSHIP
Cromwell repressed rebellions in Ireland and Scotland. In Ireland **"Penal Laws"** were passed preventing Catholics from holding public office and restricting their property rights. Priests were persecuted, and mass had to be held in secret.

While Cromwell was away, his **parliament** in England bickered and government eventually ground to a halt. Cromwell suspended parliament in 1653 and took power as **"Lord Protector"** in what amounted to a military coup.

THE MONARCHY RESTORED
Cromwell died in 1658, to be succeeded by his son, Richard – as ineffectual as his father had been strong. **"Tumbledown Dick"** lasted just nine months before he was deposed and the **Protectorate** ended. A reconvened parliament invited **Charles II** to return from exile and take his crown. So in 1660 the Stuart monarchy was restored. The **Commonwealth period** was retrospectively defined as nothing more than an **"Interregnum"** – a break between two reigns.

AIMING FOR SUPREMACY
For all their differences, the **Commonwealth** and the restored monarchy had a continuity of interest in promoting England's commercial advantage and colonial aspirations. Both fought an expansionist **Dutch Republic** for supremacy at sea in the **Anglo-Dutch Wars 148–49** ».

Four Days Battle
What remains the longest-ever naval engagement in history was fought in 1666 at the height of the Second Anglo-Dutch War. The English faced a struggle to rebuild their fleet in the years afterwards.

BEFORE

In the second half of the 17th century, two ambitious, up-and-coming maritime powers came into conflict with each other over the possession of the seas.

MARITIME ADVERSARIES
The Netherlands had won their freedom after **80 years of struggle ⟨⟨ 138–39**, emerging as a major mercantile economy and colonial power. England's rise as **a maritime nation** dated from the 16th century, when its fleet had faced down **the Spanish challenge ⟨⟨ 140–41**. But that rise had been interrupted by domestic difficulties, which ultimately plunged the country **into civil war ⟨⟨ 146–47**.

REGRET
But now that peace had returned to England, the **Commonwealth** was looking to a future it saw as being shaped overseas, in **a growing empire**. War with the Netherlands seemed inevitable, though it was a policy that England was soon to regret.

PIKEMAN'S BREASTPLATE, 17TH CENTURY

The Anglo-Dutch Wars

England and the Dutch Republic had much in common. Two Protestant nations in the north of Europe, they had both recently triumphed over an overbearing Spain. They were also both seagoing powers on the rise. From the 1650s they fought a series of wars over which state was to have supremacy.

The Commonwealth's "General at Sea", George Monck, declared that "the Dutch have too much trade and the English are resolved to take it from them." Under the Navigation Act of 1651, imports to England had to be shipped direct from their source nation – vessels from a third nation could not be involved. There was no doubt as to what the legislation implied by "third nation": the Dutch dominated long-distance trade with Europe. England, just emerging from its civil war, could not possibly compete on a "free trade" basis; why should its shipowners not have this boost? The Dutch disagreed, and the two nations prepared for war.

A portentous start

Both sides were caught out when the fighting started, however. On 29 May 1652, Lieutenant-Admiral Maarten Tromp's fleet and that of England's Robert Blake chanced upon each other in the English Channel. The encounter led to the battle of Goodwin Sands, which lasted five hours and left both fleets badly damaged. It also marked a point of no return.

George Ayscue's English fleet attacked a convoy of Dutch merchantmen that August, taking a battering from Michiel de Ruyter's warships for its efforts. Blake took revenge in October, defeating the Dutch at the battle of Kentish Knock. Differences between Dutch commanders over tactics weakened their overall strategy: Vice-Admiral Witte de With wanted to take the battle to the English, while Vice-Commodore Michiel de Ruyter favoured a more cautious, defensive approach. With their bigger ships and superior cannon, the English won decisively, while the Dutch fled in disarray – scattered, like sheep before wolves, complained a bitter de With.

In the slightly longer term, however, the Dutch were to benefit from this bruising. Taking stock, they set about building bigger, more powerfully armed ships. In the meantime, the English, becoming complacent, sent additional vessels to reinforce the Mediterranean fleet: the result was a shattering defeat by the Dutch off Dungeness. So deflated by failure that he offered his resignation (it was rightly rejected), Admiral Blake could not contain his disgust at what he described as a certain "baseness of spirit" in some sections of his fleet – those ships whose skippers had hung back from the fighting at its height. In more measured mood, he reflected on the inadequacy of merchantmen for use in battle: the

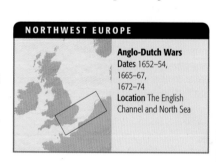

NORTHWEST EUROPE

Anglo-Dutch Wars
Dates 1652–54, 1665–67, 1672–74
Location The English Channel and North Sea

Feather spring

Ramrod pipe

Dutch combination musket
This unusual weapon had matchlock ignition as a fallback: flintlock technology was still very new and, as a consequence, unreliable.

squadron shall endeavour to keep in a line with their chief." (Hence the later expression, a "ship of the line".)

The new tactics paid off in March 1653 at the battle of Portland, in an engagement known as the Three Days Battle. Blake's fleet finally made its superiority in arms and tactics tell against a Dutch fleet of similar size, and the enemy was forced out of the English Channel. After another defeat, off Suffolk at the battle of the Gabbard

into the Thames Estuary, then up the Medway to the Chatham Royal Dockyard. Having burned the buildings and sunk several ships, the Dutch towed away the HMS *Unity* (a captured Dutch vessel they were reclaiming) and – most humiliating of all – the English

> **"That gallant bulwark of the Kingdome, miserably shattered, hardly a vessel intire, but … so many wracks and hulls … "**
> JOHN EVELYN ON THE ENGLISH FLEET AFTER THE FOUR DAYS BATTLE, 1666

in June, the Dutch were confined to their home ports. Their country under siege, they tried to break out in August. They were beaten back, but the English had to withdraw as well. The hostilities ended in mutual exhaustion, though the underlying issues remained unresolved.

Fighting began again in 1665: with the monarchy restored to England, King Charles II was trying to interfere in the politics of the Dutch Republic. The real cause of the conflict, however, was continuing competition for trade.

The Dutch had built up their fleet since the first conflict and felt confident of a victory, so the battle of Lowestoft, on 13 June, proved a rude awakening. They lost 17 ships and 2,000 men; a further 2,500 men were captured. The English casualties were negligible, and yet they did not build on this victory. Instead, the Dutch were able to recover and went on to triumph at the Four Days Battle, which was fought off the east coast of Kent from 1–4 June 1666.

A year later, Michiel de Ruyter led a task force

flagship, the *Royal Charles*. This was the final straw for an enemy reeling from the impact of both the Great Plague of 1665–66 and the Great Fire of London of 1666. England, desperate, agreed to terms: under the Peace of Breda it acquired New England (the former New Netherlands) in North America, but was forced to give way on the Navigation Act of 1651.

The French connection
England no longer had the stamina for further fighting, but King Charles had committed his support to Louis XIV of France, so when the latter attacked the Dutch in 1672, he was compelled to help. Louis's invasion was halted when the Dutch opened up their dykes to flood the countryside, and the English fleet was summoned to assist. The worst fears of the (by now) demoralized English public were confirmed when

need for specialized men-of-war was becoming clear. To add insult to injury, England's Mediterranean fleet – despite its recent additions – was badly beaten at the battle of Leghorn (Livorno). It was clear that something had to be done.

A new directive
The English Admiralty issued fresh "Instructions", schematizing a new approach to war at sea. Until now, ships had simply closed with enemy vessels as quickly as possible, hoping to get men aboard in a general free-for-all. But the advent of artillery had made this approach obsolete. Ships not only risked being destroyed by enemy gunfire but also endangered comrade-vessels with their own.

Fighting at sea was now to be an orderly, arm's-length affair. The fleet would file past the enemy, firing as it went. As such, the broadsides inflicted the greatest possible losses, while avoiding damage by "friendly fire". "Each squadron shall take the best advantage they can to engage with the enemy next unto them," the Instructions said, and "All ships of every

Dutch flagship
The *Zeelandia* was richly decorated, with elaborate designs: naval warfare was still conducted in some style.

The Dutch and the French remained at war after Charles II retired from the conflict in 1674. Further battles occurred both on land and at sea.

FIGHTING THE FRENCH
Michiel de Ruyter died in 1674 at the battle of Augusta, though his fleet was victorious. By 1678 the Dutch had forced King Louis XIV to give up his idea of conquering their country.

AN UNEASY PEACE
It would not be too long before England had a Dutchman as its ruler. **William of Orange** was called to take the place of the Catholic Stuart king, James II, in 1688. This **"Glorious Revolution"** was not welcomed quite so eagerly by Irish Catholics, many of whom now flocked to **James's banner 152–53 »**. But it did bring almost a century of peace with the Netherlands before a **Fourth Anglo-Dutch War** flared up in 1780. Again, trade was the underlying issue, although the immediate trigger for the conflict was Dutch support for the rebels in the **American Revolution 178–79 »**.

A NEW ERA FOR NAVAL WARFARE
No longer could **naval combat** be seen as a continuation of land warfare by other means. Later editions of the **Admiralty Instructions** developed new theories of naval warfare – just as the reforms of **Maurice of Nassau** were rationalizing the waging of war on shore.

the Dutch navy easily staved off their fleet's attack. By some good fortune, a sudden change in the wind averted a shattering defeat by the Dutch at the battle of Solebay, off the coast of Suffolk, on 7 June 1672. However, divisions between the French and English navies led to crushing defeats at Schooneveld and Texel, in June and August 1673 respectively, and Charles II was forced to sue for peace.

MICHIEL DE RUYTER

The Dutch admiral who was to win such admiration for his dash and daring was a surprisingly modest man. There was nothing showy about his style. Almost 60 years old when he masterminded the Raid on the Medway in 1667, he had been at sea since boyhood. Scrupulously professional and cautious by nature, the audacity of his most famous victories was that of a consummate seafarer, thoroughly familiar with his men and ships, their limitations and capabilities.

BEFORE

Aged just five when he succeeded to the French throne in 1643, Louis XIV reigned under the guidance of his chief minister, Cardinal Mazarin, until he came of age.

THE SUN KING
The Thirty Years War **<< 142–43** was still under way when Louis XIV's reign began. For France, the war ended in an eruption of civil violence, the *Fronde*. This helped shape the attitudes of Cardinal Mazarin – and of his charge, who grew up to be the "Sun King", Europe's model for the **absolute monarch**.

TRADE WAR
Not too far from the French coast, **war had been raging between England and the Netherlands** over which country would have advantage as a trading power **<< 148–49**. This conflict appeared to have very little to do with France, still very much an **agrarian economy**, with limited involvement in overseas trade.

The Early Wars of Louis XIV

Louis XIV's vision for himself and for France was too grand and heroic to be contained within the frontiers he had inherited from his forebears. Determined to win recognition as the continent's pre-eminent ruler, the "Sun King" plunged Europe into a dark period of permanent conflict.

From 1661 Louis XIV assumed full control of his country, but France was almost bankrupt. The king's dreams of military glory would have to wait. Jean-Baptiste Colbert, the finance minister, inaugurated a programme of economic rearmament, encouraging industry and stimulating trade. France grew richer and tax revenues increased. By 1665 Louis was ready to wage war. He claimed the Duchy of Brabant in the Spanish Netherlands. Louis argued that as the local law of Brabant allowed equal rights of female succession to property, he could claim that the duchy had "devolved" to his Habsburg-descended queen, Marie-Thérèse, and the elder sister of Spain's new king, Carlos II. The War of Devolution began in 1667, the Vicomte de Turenne leading the French army into the southern Netherlands.

Turenne picked off the main towns in a series of rapid sieges. The Spanish garrisons were undermanned and the defensive infrastructure neglected. In an attempt to halt the French king, the Dutch allied with England and Sweden to form a "Triple Alliance".

Louis backed down, but discreetly set to work undermining the Alliance. He bribed Charles II of England to sign the secret Treaty of Dover in 1670. Two

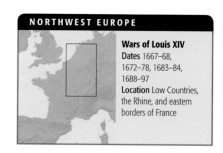

NORTHWEST EUROPE

Wars of Louis XIV
Dates 1667–68, 1672–78, 1683–84, 1688–97
Location Low Countries, the Rhine, and eastern borders of France

The siege of Maastricht
Military engineering entered the modern era at Maastricht. Vauban deployed heavy cannon above the ground and carefully-directed miners below; he dug zigzag trenches running parallel to the walls to protect his infantry.

years later, as if out of the blue, France and England declared war on the Dutch Republic. Louis's cavalry swam across the Rhine to take the enemy by surprise. Sweden sided with the aggressors, but Spain, the elector of Brandenburg, and Leopold I, ruler of the Austrian Lands and Holy Roman Emperor, allied with the Dutch, who opened the dykes to flood their countryside – impeding the French infantrymen. Unable to defeat them, Louis turned his attention back to the Spanish Netherlands. Drawn into a further six years of war against an able coalition of enemies, Louis's armies were successful on the battlefield and gained him more territory at the expense of the Spanish monarchy.

Building success

The conflict saw advances in siegecraft and fortification – in particular after the capture of Maastricht by Sébastien Le Prestre de Vauban. Vauban, a military engineer, convinced Louis that he could build a Fortress France. Utilizing Vauban's "systems of fortifications", the king erected a chain of ramparts and fortresses along his northeastern frontier. He substantially modified 83 towns; eight new strategic centres were built from scratch.

The king was also building an overseas empire. Pioneers opened up the Mississippi basin in the American colonies, and Canada; missionaries and merchants set up contacts in southern Asia and the Far East. But Louis sowed suspicion in 1685 when he outlawed Protestantism by revoking the Edict of Nantes (an order of 1598 that gave French Protestants rights and religious freedoms). The year after, his enemies – not just the Dutch Republic, Sweden, and the Protestant principalities in Germany, but Catholic

Louis XIV, king of France
L'État, c'est Moi ("The state, it is I"), Louis XIV reputedly said. The "Sun King" became the despotic ruler of a wealthy and powerful France.

had married William of Orange in 1677 – his concerns proved well-founded when the Dutchman was crowned King William III of England. Although France's navy triumphed in 1690 at Beachy Head, it was unable to prevent William's landing in Ireland to contend with James's fightback. "King Billy" defeated James at the battle of the Boyne in 1690 – now part of Ireland's sectarian folk-history.

Inconclusive conflict

Louis XIV, meanwhile, was finding things extremely frustrating. A man who ruled by diktat, he was horrified by the indecisiveness of war. Generals might

AFTER

The 17th century came to an end, but Louis XIV still had business that needed attending to – both with Europe and with his country's military strength.

A STRONGER FORCE
Unfazed, the Sun King simply **built up his military** all the more. The French army reached a size – some 350,000 men by the mid-1690s – not seen in Europe since the fall of the Roman

2 PER CENT The proportion of France's population serving in the army by 1700.

76 PER CENT The proportion of France's overall budget going towards military expenditure.

17 PER CENT The proportion of military spending going towards Vauban's fortifications.

empire. Although the army, and an impressive navy, imposed a **huge financial burden** on the population of France, it had the enthusiastic support of the nobility, who served, en masse, as the **officer corps**.

But the king's enemies were stronger too. Not only did Louis have to face the financial and military might of the Anglo-Dutch alliance, but in 1683, the Austrians repulsed the Ottomans at Vienna. He was to face a bigger challenge with **the War of the Spanish Succession 154–55 ≫**.

"I never saw a more obstinate fight. Those old regiments of the Emperor's did mighty well."

VICOMTE DE TURENNE, AFTER THE BATTLE OF SINSHEIM, JUNE 1674

states like Spain and the Austrian Habsburg monarchy – united in "The Grand Alliance". This coalition, founded by Emperor Leopold I in 1686, had the primary aim of challenging the French king's expansionist plans.

The War of the Grand Alliance

In 1688, in anticipation of an Imperial invasion, Louis sent an army to lay waste the Palatinate of the Rhine. The empire was beset by the Ottomans in the east, though Louis had problems of his own when Protestants deposed his ally, James II, in England's "Glorious Revolution". Louis had been dismayed when James's daughter, Princess Mary,

study their maps and plan tactical manoeuvres and feints, but these invariably foundered on the muddy ground of Europe. The huge infantry armies of the 17th century seemed to

12 MILLION Annual spending in French livres on Louis XIV's defensive fortifications by 1689; by 1705 the total spent amounted to 220 million livres.

be outgrowing their own sustainable size – they were too big and hungry to live off the land, as soldiers had done previously. They moved sluggishly – and, frequently, fought to no effect.

At Fleurus in 1690, for example, Louis's army, led by the Duc de Luxembourg, won what appeared to be a victory over Prince Waldeck's allied army (William III had entrusted his forces to the prince while he was away) – yet the battle had no strategic gain. Before the battle at Leuze in 1691, the king told France's Marshal Luxembourg to use his cavalry "rather than engaging … in an infantry battle … which never decides anything".

The War of the Grand Alliance ended with the Treaty of Rijswijk in 1697, but no resolution was reached. Louis XIV was militarily the war's victor (he had modernized warfare in many ways), but the Sun King had gained very little else.

TECHNOLOGY

VAUBAN'S STAR-SHAPED FORT

The fortresses of the medieval period, still used up until this point, had presented flat walls to the enemy gunner – an open target, and structurally weak. Vauban's star-shaped fortress was a brilliant response to the challenges of the gunpowder age. The angled bastions were brick-built, for resilience, and cannonballs glanced off the walls. Defenders could shoot at their besiegers from a range of positions on the fort while also providing covering fire for their comrades.

The War of the Spanish Succession

Frustrated in his efforts to gain pre-eminence in Europe, Louis XIV was delighted when a dynastic quirk gave him a legitimate stake in Spain. But other nations came together in opposition. They feared the rise of a Franco-Spanish superpower and were prepared to fight to make sure this did not come about.

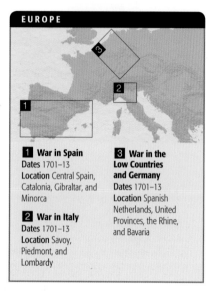

EUROPE

1 War in Spain
Dates 1701–13
Location Central Spain, Catalonia, Gibraltar, and Minorca

2 War in Italy
Dates 1701–13
Location Savoy, Piedmont, and Lombardy

3 War in the Low Countries and Germany
Dates 1701–13
Location Spanish Netherlands, United Provinces, the Rhine, and Bavaria

«

BEFORE

The reign of the "Sun King" was at its zenith by the start of the 18th century, but Louis XIV had not managed to impose his authority on the continent at large.

UNPOPULAR IN EUROPE
Despite **a series of successful wars**, France's international status had not been much advanced **« 152–53**. In 1700 King Charles II of Spain died, and Louis's great-grandson, Philip, Duc d'Anjou, succeeded the throne. The Habsburg emperor, Leopold I, objected, as did England, Portugal, Prussia, and the Netherlands.

KEY MOMENT

THE BATTLE OF BLENHEIM

The Duke of Marlborough's conduct of the battle of Blenheim on 13 August 1704 was masterly. On a battlefield spanning almost 6km (4 miles), Marlborough threw his enemy off-guard with a series of feints, before smashing his way through their centre. The brilliance of his thinking and the fluent ease with which his forces executed his instructions on the ground were something quite new in military history.

The Habsburgs did not like the idea of the Duc d'Anjou inheriting the Spanish crown; neither did other European nations. The fighting began in Italy, where Austria's Prince Eugène of Savoy invaded the Spanish-held duchy of Milan. After beating off a French attack at Chiari in September 1701, Eugène captured Cremona the following February; he was said to possess a bloodthirsty ire during battle.

England's John Churchill, the Duke of Marlborough, could not have been more different in his style, though like Eugène he led his soldiers from the front. An inspired organizer and tactician, he played the long game. At the head of English, Dutch, and allied German forces in the Low Countries – the "Grand Alliance" – had been renewed – he seized a series of fortresses along the river Meuse.

In October 1702, Prince Louis William of Baden-Baden faced a French force at Friedlingen, Bavaria. He lost the battle, but it was a strange defeat: he stopped the French joining their Bavarian allies and, having inflicted heavy casualties, extricated his army almost intact.

Battle had been joined at sea as well: days later, in Vigo Bay, Galicia, George Rooke's Anglo-Dutch expedition took the Spanish treasure fleet and sank its French escort – 15 warships strong. Yet France was holding fast: Marlborough captured Bonn in 1703, but could not

30,000 The number of men killed, wounded, and taken prisoner on the Franco-Bavarian side at Blenheim. Just 250 out of 4,500 emerged unscathed. English casualties were only slightly lower: 13,000 killed or wounded.

take Antwerp. In September Marshal Villars defeated an Imperial army at Höchstädt in Bavaria, opening the road to Vienna.

False hope for France
In the summer of 1704, Marlborough transformed the war, duping the French by marching 40,000 men from the Low Countries to the Danube – 400km (250 miles) – in just five weeks.

On 2 July he took the "impregnable" Schellenberg fortress. Prince Eugène had, in the meantime, brought his army up from Italy and together, at Blenheim in Bavaria, they engaged with Franco-Bavarian forces. Marlborough began by encircling Blenheim village – with much of the enemy inside. He tricked the remaining troops with dummy attacks, prompting them to commit their reserves too soon. On the right, although outnumbered, Prince Eugène's forces pressed forward. Marlborough had his artillery moved at speed across the battlefield to where it could be most advantageously deployed. Cavalry charges delivered precise thrusts at a weakened enemy before a final and devastating advance of the infantry.

Marlborough's victories
The campaign had seen great daring underpinned by supreme efficiency. The modern idea of the army as a "military machine" had been gaining ground for some time, with increased regimentation and standardization of uniforms and weapons. The flintlock was replacing the unreliable matchlock musket, while lightweight and easily movable cannon could be deployed more imaginatively on the battlefield.

Marlborough used the same tactics at the battle of Ramillies, in present-day Belgium, in May 1706. With a feint to one side, followed by a shattering frontal attack, the French and Bavarians were defeated,

with 22,000 casualties to the Alliance's 2,500. Having lost half the Spanish Netherlands as a result of this crushing defeat, France attempted to recover the territory. Marlborough, once more linked up with Eugène, ordered, in 1708, an overnight march to ambush the invading French, whom they

Double cock

Frizzen spring

Trigger

attacked across the River Scheldt to win a third great victory at the battle of Oudenarde.

Queen Anne's War

All this time, a subsidiary struggle had been unfolding across the Atlantic. The French, Spanish, and Native American allies had been fighting Britain and its American colonists, allied with the tribes

Double-barrelled flintlock pistol
This ornate weapon, made around 1700, was routinely used in combat by the cavalry. During this period flintlocks were gradually replacing matchlocks, which tended to be less reliable.

Battle of Malplaquet
Eugène urged the Alliance to fight at Malplaquet in 1709. Almost 40,000 were killed and wounded in a battle that critics claimed need not have been fought.

of the Iroquois Confederacy. While attacks on South Carolina by Spanish forces from Florida were easily rebuffed, the French became a real threat when they struck south from Canada into New England. "Queen Anne's War" (named after Britain's monarch from 1707) was to end badly for the French, however. Britain captured the colony of Acadia, renaming it Nova Scotia. Peace came in 1713 with the signing of the Treaty of Utrecht. It would be an exaggeration to claim that the Grand Alliance had won this most mutually draining of wars; but it was clear that Louis XIV had lost.

The outcome of the War of the Spanish Succession was less conclusive than it at first appeared. Much in European politics remained to be contested.

BRITAIN'S MONARCHY
Though ousted in the "Glorious Revolution" of 1688, **James II** still considered himself king of England. He lived until his death, in 1701, as a guest of Louis XIV who continued to treat him as rightful king. In 1701 Louis recognized James's son as James III of England, one of the factors that determined the British on war. James the "Old Pretender" was expelled from France under the terms of the **Treaty of Utrecht**, but following Queen Anne's death and the succession of the Hanoverian George I, he made a fresh attempt

to win back the British throne. The **Jacobites** (as supporters of James – in Latin, *Jacobus* – were called) mounted an **uprising in 1715**, but James's Catholicism was a stumbling block for most of the conservative groups in English society. The failure of James, the **Old Pretender**, in the Fifteen Rebellion, led eventually to the **"Young Pretender"**, Charles Edward Stuart, who launched **his own rebellion in 1745–46 162–63 »**.

FRANCE STILL STRONG
Louis XIV's death in 1715 did not mean his country was weakened. France appeared to be – **in European eyes** – as threatening as ever. In a long but ineffectual reign, however, his successor – his great-grandson, Louis XV – was to preside over **the gradual erosion of France's foreign-policy prestige**.

1 FLINT DAGGER (c.10,000 BCE)

2 AZTEC FLINT DAGGER (c.1500)

3 EUROPEAN QUILLON DAGGER (c.1600)

6 INDIAN KATAR (c.1760)

9 ITALIAN GUNNER'S STILETTO (c.1760)

12 NORTH AFRICAN DAGGER (c.1890)

13 CONGOLESE THROWING KNIFE (c.1900)

Daggers

The dagger is designed for use in close combat: for assassinations, duels, last stands, even heroic suicides. The intimacy of the warrior's relationship with this weapon helps explain why it is so often ornamented. The dagger is not just a weapon but a boast and a warning: a declaration of dangerous intent.

1 **Paleolithic flint dagger blades** were probably mounted on wooden handles, as shown here. 2 **Aztec daggers in the 16th century** were made of flint or obsidian (volcanic glass). Priests used them to cut out sacrificial human victims' hearts. 3 **Quillons, or crossguards,** were designed in Medieval Europe to stop the blade sinking in too far, and to protect the hand. 4 **A sword-breaker** was a dagger wielded instead of a shield by fencers. Toothed notches helped to snag an opponent's blade. 5 **The Highland dirk** was often used in conjunction with the broadsword, the fighter wielding one weapon in each hand. 6 **A Rajput warrior's *katar*** was held horizontally, and used with a "punching" action. 7 **The Indian *bichwa*** is curved like a buffalo horn. It has a decorated cast-brass hilt. 8 **This 18th-century Sri Lankan warrior's dagger** was exquisitely ornamented to reflect the owner's elite status. 9 **This is an 18th-century Italian gunner's stiletto** with a numbered

scale on the blade for quickly measuring the bores of guns. 10 **Native American daggers** in the 19th century had iron blades and traditional decorated handles. 11 **This late 19th-century East African finger-knife** belonged to a Turkana herder from Uganda. 12 **The North African *koummya* dagger** was curved like the slashing tusk of the wild boar, an animal that also shielded against the evil eye. 13 **The Congolese throwing knife** was lethal whichever way it struck. 14 **The *kukri*** is still the weapon of choice of the British Army's Gurkhas. 15 **Papuan obsidian blades** are razor sharp. 16 **The Sudanese sickle knife** has a sickle-shaped blade. 17 **The bayonet** fits on the end of a rifle and is still in use today. This one is from World War I. 18 **This knuckle-duster knife** could be used for punching as well as stabbing. 19 **The Fairbairn-Sykes fighting knife** was first carried and used by British commandos on raids in German-occupied Norway in World War II.

4 ITALIAN SWORD-BREAKER (c.1600)

5 SCOTTISH DIRK (c.1710)

7 INDIAN BICHWA (c.1750)

8 SRI LANKAN SILVER DAGGER (c.1750)

10 NATIVE AMERICAN DAGGER (c.1800)

14 NEPALI KUKRI (c.1900)

11 UGANDAN FINGER-KNIFE (c.1890)

15 PAPUAN OBSIDIAN DAGGER (c.1900)

19 BRITISH FAIRBAIRN-SYKES FIGHTING KNIFE (1941)

18 US KNUCKLE-DUSTER KNIFE (1918)

16 SUDANESE SICKLE KNIFE (c.1910)

U.S.1918
L.F&C-1918

The **Great Northern War**

BEFORE

The Baltic, long a backwater, was by the 17th century one of Europe's most prosperous regions. Sweden was influential but Russia too was on the ascent.

SWEDISH EXPANSIONISM

The year 1655 saw the start of the *Stormakstiden*, or **"Age of Great Power"**, in Sweden. In what outsiders call the **Northern Wars**, an expansionist Sweden attacked Russia, Denmark, Brandenburg, the Polish-Lithuanian Commonwealth, and the Netherlands. The French and Dutch were drawn in when **Norway-Denmark** invaded the island of Scania in 1675. The war that resulted ended indecisively, but Sweden's influence was growing.

RUSSIA IN THE ASCENDANT

Peter the Great of Russia, tsar since 1682, was resolved to build a modern and militarily powerful state. He constructed his own highly centralized administration and **reformed the army** at the expense of the old officer elite, the *streltsy*. He had already **expanded his empire** in the south, taking the Ottoman naval base of Azov in 1696. Now he aimed to expand it in the north.

STRELTSY (RUSSIAN GUARDSMEN)

The steady growth of Sweden's Baltic empire sparked all-out war in 1700. An alliance of neighbouring rulers fought back. After more than 20 years of conflict, Swedish supremacy was finally brought to an end. In subsequent years, though, Russia emerged as an aggressor in the region.

Sweden's neighbours were jubilant when, in 1697, its king, Charles XI, died. The whole area had lived in fear of the king's imperial ambitions. Now they had to deal, not with this despot, but with his son, Charles XII, not yet 15. Rival rulers united to plan Sweden's ruin. Peter I (the Great) of Russia was making reforms that he hoped would bring his country major power. Augustus II, was both the king of Poland-Lithuania and elector of Saxony. Christian V of Denmark-Norway completed the coalition, although he was soon succeeded by Frederick IV. In 1696 the death of his half-brother left Peter I as sole ruler of Russia, and he was able to give greater priority to a series of military and naval reforms with which he planned to assert Russian power over his neighbours.

Born to fight

The rivals had underestimated their opponent, however, whose upbringing and education had prepared him for

Baltic supremacy

During the 17th century, the Baltic Sea became both a highway and battlefield for the powers competing for authority around its shores.

ruling and for waging war. They also failed to see the advantages Charles XII had inherited. Sweden's army had 30,000 infantry and 11,000 cavalry at home and 25,000 mercenaries around the empire. Superbly organized and trained, it was constantly replenished by a system of conscription, which allotted men both to the military and – in peacetime – to agricultural work, ensuring supplies.

Still, Sweden's enemies were soon disabused. They launched a crushing combined attack in early 1700, only to be brought up short almost instantly. Denmark was defeated in a matter of days, Charles personally leading the expedition that took Copenhagen

COSSACK A member of one of several warlike, formerly nomadic communities of the southern steppe, generations of whom served the Russian tsars as cavalry.

in July. Augustus II was severely weakened when, with Riga surrounded, an expected uprising of local nobles failed to materialize. He had to lift his siege and retire. By now the Russians were besieging Narva,

Coin showing the Narva battle

Peter the Great of Russia badly underestimated Sweden's young king, Charles XII, at the battle of Narva in 1700. The Swedish army smashed a Russian force four times its size.

Key

- Sweden and possessions 1700
- Russia 1700
- Denmark-Norway 1700
- Other enemies of Sweden
- Russian gains from Sweden by 1721
- — Frontiers 1700
- Swedish victory
- Swedish defeat

in present-day Estonia. Charles appeared with his Swedes. They defeated the Russians, capturing just about all the weaponry Peter's army had.

All that remained was for Charles to name his conditions for his enemies' surrender; no one was in a position to object. Yet Charles fought on, and won

Battle of Poltava
Brought low by a ghastly winter in the field, Charles XII's all-conquering army was savaged by the Russians. Charles fled south, seeking sanctuary with the Ottomans.

a string of victories against Augustus's increasingly desperate forces in Poland and Lithuania. The most glittering came in July 1702, at Kliszów, Poland: Charles braved overwhelming odds to deliver the decisive blow.

A campaign too far
But now it was the Swedish king's turn to underestimate an enemy. Profoundly affected by the shock of Narva, Peter had ordered a root-and-branch reform of his forces. The country Charles invaded in the autumn of 1708 was not the same as before. Winter was

"The final stone has been laid in the **foundations** of St Petersburg."
PETER THE GREAT AFTER TRIUMPHING AT POLTAVA, 1709

on its way – the coldest anyone could remember – and Charles's force of 40,000 was advancing ever further from its food supplies. Striking south into grain-rich Ukraine as Peter's forces retreated might have seemed sensible, but the Russians' scorched-earth tactics left the Swedes starving.

Disease was rife, and the army that surrounded the fortress of Poltava in spring 1709 was reduced to 14,000 men. The Russians had 30,000 infantry, well dug-in, 9,000 cavalry, and 3,000 highly mobile Cossacks, also more than 100 heavy guns. Yet Charles was optimistic, and his plan to "punch through" in an audacious frontal attack might well have worked against the Russian troops of old. Though rocked by the shock of his assault, Peter's soldiers hit back with devastating force. Charles was captured, but escaped, fleeing for the safety of the Ottoman realms: it took him five years to make it home.

Peter's sense that Poltava had been a turning-point was borne out in the years that followed. Sweden's enemies were closing in and Charles continued the struggle on his return, building up his navy. But Peter's Baltic fleet was prepared for battle. Charles, ever-proactive, invaded Norway, but died at the siege of Frederiksten in 1718. Sweden was also

losing the war at sea, suffering defeats by Peter's new navy at Ösel Island in 1719 and Grengam in 1720. Russia now ruled the Baltic waves and a large area of dry land as well. The year after, the Treaty of Nystad gave the tsar authority over much of the Baltic coast.

AFTER

Sweden was a power no more. Russia had risen to replace it. Peter, who had desired to secure a "window on Europe", proclaimed his kingdom an "empire" in 1721.

A PERIOD OF INACTIVITY
Peter died in 1725 and his immediate successors struggled to stay in charge of what was still an unruly nation. But **Empress Elizabeth** showed that she was prepared to fight, taking Russia into the **War of the Austrian Succession** in 1741 **162–63 》**, and later engaging in the **Seven Years War** in 1756 **172–73 》**.

95 The percentage of Russia's population who were serfs – peasants, bound to their landlords' fields – on the accession of the Empress Catherine the Great in 1762.

A GREATER POWER
Not until 1762 would Russia have a ruler who could match Peter for resolve or ruthlessness. **Catherine II ("the Great")** was another modernizer, keen to shake up an obdurately conservative nation. She too cast expansionist eyes towards the east, and made Russia one of **Europe's greatest powers 182–83 》**.

Russian military uniform
Peter the Great founded the Preobrazhensky Lifeguard Regiment as part of his military reforms, and it fought with distinction in the Great Northern War. The tsar himself wore this uniform in the course of the conflict.

Supplies

However dramatic the events on the front line in any war, much of the most important action takes place behind the scenes. Ensuring those fighting have the food, tools, weapons, ammunition, and other supplies they need is vital to the success of any military campaign.

Ancient armies lived off the land, so summer was the best season for a campaign. Even where food was readily available, organizing its collection and managing its distribution to a large body of men were constant headaches. Enormous quantities of water were also needed. An army of 40,000 required 80,000 litres (17,500 gallons) a day just for the men. Each horse or mule needed 50 litres (11 gallons) or more each day – not just the cavalry mounts, but also the pack animals, of which there were often thousands. Obtaining so many animals in the first place was a major challenge. The Assyrians (see pp.18–19) had dedicated officials who could procure and train 3,000 horses a month. Feeding them posed further problems. That number of horses or mules needed some 30 hectares (75 acres) of good grazing a day, so huge quantities of fodder had to be carried where fresh grass was scarce.

Weighted down

According to Livy, writing in the reign of the first emperor, Augustus (reigned 27 BCE–14 CE), a Roman army of 40,000 men needed 1,600 smiths and other craftsmen to maintain its armour and weapons. Roman legionaries carried not only their weapons and food and water rations, but also basic cooking utensils, spades or pickaxes for digging, baskets for moving earth or gathering fresh produce, stakes for palisades, and much more. Even so, Roman armies increasingly required pack animals and ox-drawn wagons for especially heavy or bulky equipment.

The organization of Peter the Great
Peter's military reforms at the beginning of the 18th century made the Russian army a force to be feared. His attention to detail in matters of supply played a major part in his victory over Sweden in the Great Northern War.

A big army was reliant on a baggage train keeping it well supplied. This slowed it down, however, and was a weak point that an enemy could exploit. The Gallic chieftain Vercingetorix's attempt to detach Caesar's legions from their baggage train outside Gergovia in 53 BCE (see pp.34–35) failed only because of the discipline of the Roman soldiers.

Problems with gunpowder
The advent of artillery brought new problems. Not only were big cannon cumbersome themselves – it took 50 pairs of oxen to shift the enormous Orban gun used by the Ottoman army at the Siege of Constantinople in 1453 (see pp.106–07) – but the barrels of powder were heavy, hard to keep dry, and dangerous to move. As the complexity and size of siege engines, guns, and other hardware increased in the 16th century, a paradoxical problem arose. The better equipped an army, the bigger and slower its baggage train became.

Roman legionary's basic kit
A campaigning legionary's essential kit included a pickaxe, food bag, water flask, cooking pan, blanket, woollen cloak, and leather satchel.

The art of supply
The 17th and 18th centuries were an age of centralization: under Louis XIV the French state negotiated all contracts for the provisioning of armies. This change markedly enhanced the performance of France's armed forces in the field.

Of the many factors contributing to Russia's epoch-making victory over Sweden at the battle of Poltava (see pp.158–59), Peter the Great's civil service reforms are easily overlooked. But it was largely thanks to the tsar's centralization of military administration that Russia's army had been in a position to fight at all. Conversely, Charles XII's Swedish troops would have better endured the ravages of the Russian winter had they been properly supplied with warm clothes and sufficient food; nor would they have fared so poorly in the field had they been adequately equipped with guns and powder. "The hungry dog bites best," Charles had snapped before the battle, when his army's problems were pointed out; Napoleon knew better when he claimed that an army "marches on its stomach".

Despotic rulers were not the only ones to reorganize army supplies. Field commanders such as England's John Churchill, 1st Duke of Marlborough, did so too. During the War of the Spanish Succession (see pp.154–55), Marlborough saw how the tedious business of organizing and supplying an army could open up possibilities for flamboyant exploits in the field. His march from the Netherlands to the Danube with 40,000 men in the weeks before the battle of Blenheim in 1704 (see pp.154–55) would not have been possible without the efficient flow of food, weapons, and ammunition. Marlborough also sent advance parties to set up camps and make sure hot food was waiting at the end of each day's march. When his army arrived in Frankfurt, each man was issued with a new pair of boots.

US Army Quartermaster badge
The US Army Quartermaster Corps was set up in 1775. The US Army's other logistics branches are the Ordnance and Transportation corps.

Possibilities and problems
The 18th and 19th centuries brought an industrial revolution in warfare, affecting everything from guns and ammunition to uniforms and rations. These could now be mass produced, and as technology improved, so did the art of organizing it all; entire quartermaster corps were set up for the task of moving supplies.

Stubborn suppliers
Tough and reliable, mules have kept armies supplied for centuries, and can still prove their worth in terrain inaccessible to vehicles.

Another revolution came with the modernization of transportation systems such as railways. For military purposes, railways came of age in the American Civil War (see pp.232–37) and were of vital importance to both the Union and Confederate armies. In Europe they were essential for the movement of men and materiel during the Franco-Prussian War (see pp.228–29); almost one million Prussian and German troops were moved to the front, and then supplied and equipped. However, timetabling so many trains and ensuring that rolling-stock was in place when they were needed was no easy task.

Infrastructure is key
The absence of railways or adequate roads lost the Crimean War for Russia before the fighting even started (see pp.220–21). It took the Russians three months to move their supplies to the front. And yet it took only three weeks for Britain and France to ship their own materiel much further by sea.

Ironically, the lack of infrastructure in Russia later worked in the Soviet Union's favour, when the Germans invaded Russia in 1941. Hitler's whole *blitzkrieg* philosophy depended on the use of motor vehicles and planes, but these had to be taken to the war zone (be it in France, North Africa, or the

Caucasus), and then maintained and kept in fuel. The Germans struggled to supply their army across inadequate Russian roads. Simply obtaining fuel can be difficult, and moving such a volatile substance as petrol is extremely dangerous; not only can an attack on the fuel supply cause terrible loss of life, any transports dependent on the fuel will be rendered useless. In the first weeks of Operation Iraqi Freedom in 2003 (see pp.348–49), US military engineers built a record 354-km (220-mile) long fuel pipeline from Kuwait into Iraq to avoid just such a disaster.

The challenges keep growing. A major problem for a superpower like the United States lies in maintaining a supply-line that may stretch halfway around the world. Troops must be moved over huge distances and their high-tech equipment must be serviced in a range of usually inhospitable environments.

Resupplying troops in Afghanistan
A Chinook helicopter hovers while troops attach slingloads of supplies to its underbelly for transport to remote US military encampments in the mountains of Afghanistan.

c.2000 BCE Egyptians in Nubia build the island fortress of Askut, a fortified granary to supply military campaigns in the region.

c.1250 BCE Ramesses II transforms Egyptian logistics, introducing the ox-cart in place of pack-donkeys and donkey-carts.

9th century BCE The Assyrians' *musarkisus* – a special military office – takes charge of the procurement and training of horses.

6th century BCE Persian armies use teams of oxen 16-strong to haul gigantic siege engines.

4th century BCE The Persians introduce the horse-drawn cart to military logistics.

312 BCE The Romans complete the first section of the Appian Way in Italy, the start of an extensive network of roads built primarily for the rapid movement of soldiers and their supplies.

218 BCE The Carthaginian general, Hannibal, crosses the Alps on his way to Rome – not just with elephants, but with 2,000 cattle for meat.

2nd century CE The office of *Logista* – keeper of accounts – is created in the Roman army.

1147 Thousands of French soldiers and their supplies are shipped to the Holy Land for the Second Crusade.

15th century The Incas set up storage depots and rest-stations for troops along roads across their Andean empire.

1402 Turko-Mongol warlord Timur Lenk diverts a stream to deprive the Ottoman army of water in the run-up to the battle of Ankara.

1540 For the battle of Kanauj, Emperor Humayun's Mogul army needs over 3,000 oxen to haul 700 guns and 21 heavy cannon.

1668–72 Louis XIV's Secretary of State for War, the Marquis de Louvois, overhauls military administration. He establishes a network of pre-stocked magazines.

1807 Napoleon sets up a specialist Transport Corps for moving artillery and supplies.

BRITISH ARMY TINNED TREATS ISSUED TO TROOPS IN WORLD WAR II

1812 Logistical failures hobble Napoleon's invasion of Russia. Supplies stockpiled in Prussia cannot be brought quickly enough to his troops.

1861–65 Troops and supplies are transported by train in the American Civil War.

1914–18 The introduction of trucks transforms logistics in World War I.

1942 At the second battle at El Alamein, both sides' supply-lines are overstretched in the North African desert. Rommel's snaps first.

1959–75 In the Vietnam War, supplies for the Vietcong are brought by bicycle and on foot down the Ho Chi Minh Trail through Laos.

1962 The CH-47 Chinook helicopter becomes a vital logistical workhorse for US forces.

1990 The US moves 2,000 tanks, 1,990 aircraft, 100 warships, and 550,000 personnel to Saudi Arabia in a few weeks, ready to liberate Kuwait.

BEFORE «

By the 1730s Western and Central Europe had not seen a large-scale war for decades. There had not, however, been peace – minor skirmishes were a regular occurrence.

POWER STRUGGLES

Earlier European conflicts had stemmed from dynastic disputes. Notably, during **the War of the Spanish Succession** « 154–55, these familial arguments had provided the pretext for a tussle for supremacy.

It seemed that any excuse for conflict would suffice. In 1739 Britain and Spain had fought in the Caribbean in the **"War of Jenkins' Ear"**,

4 PER CENT The proportion of Britain's capital spent on the Royal Navy in the 18th century.

80 PER CENT The proportion of the British governments' military expenditure in the 18th century.

15 PER CENT The proportion of British MPs who were either naval or army officers.

sparked after a Spanish coastguard allegedly cut off the ear of Robert Jenkins, an English merchant sea captain he accused of piracy.

In the interim, Prussia's Frederick William I had been modernizing his forces, ready to stake his own **claim to military ascendancy**.

The War of the Austrian Succession

Dynastic disputes loomed large in an age when Europe's great royal families held absolute dominion over vast and wealthy empires. The disagreement over who should succeed to the Austrian throne in 1740 ignited a protracted and far-reaching series of interlocking conflicts.

The "Pragmatic Sanction", pushed through by Emperor Charles VI in 1713, stated that, in the absence of a male heir, a daughter might succeed to the Habsburg monarchy. It was no coincidence that the emperor had just such a daughter. When he died in 1739, the Habsburgs' allies accepted Maria Theresa as ruler of Austria, Bohemia, and Hungary without demur, but their enemies found a deep and principled objection to the idea that royal power might be imparted down the female line.

Frederick II promptly dispatched his Prussian forces into Habsburg Silesia, in present-day southwestern Poland. His father, Frederick William I, had drilled his soldiers relentlessly for years, inculcating iron discipline to produce a powerful military machine that was ready for action at any time. Marginal till now, Prussia was to gain respect and fear, not just as a military power, but as a militaristic one. Its army was ready to march onto the European stage.

16 The number of combatant countries in the War of the Austrian Succession. It was fought on three continents: Europe, North America (as "King George's War"), and Asia.

Widening war

Crossing the Oder in December 1740, Prussian armies took the area almost unopposed. Caught unawares, Austrian forces retreated into fortresses or withdrew into Bohemia (present-day Czech Republic). Europe looked on, amazed at the speed and efficiency of the Prussian conquest. But slowly Austria marshalled its resistance,

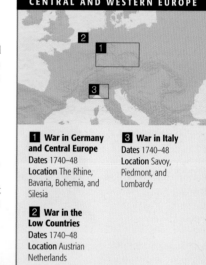

CENTRAL AND WESTERN EUROPE

1 War in Germany and Central Europe
Dates 1740–48
Location The Rhine, Bavaria, Bohemia, and Silesia

2 War in the Low Countries
Dates 1740–48
Location Austrian Netherlands

3 War in Italy
Dates 1740–48
Location Savoy, Piedmont, and Lombardy

Hand-protected hilt

Slender steel blade

Residual quillon (crossguard)

Prussian infantry sword
The "smallsword" was light and thin, its blade fairly short – sometimes only 60cm (24in) in length. Though soon overtaken by the socket bayonet, the smallsword was still used for fencing and thrusting.

Maria Theresa turning out to be an adept war leader. In April 1741, the battle of Mollwitz, in present-day Poland, was a close Prussian victory. That December, still undefeated, but feeling the pressure, Frederick II allied with France, agreeing to support the Bavarian elector, Charles Albert, as the next emperor. The War of the Austrian Succession was under way.

The fighting moved to Bohemia, with Frederick's forces pushing southwards, while the French marched into Prague from the west. The city fell in November 1741, and Charles Albert was placed on the Bohemian throne by his allies. In February 1742, he was elected the Holy Roman Emperor Charles VII. He had

Battle of Fontenoy
The Duke of Cumberland's English soldiers prepare to attack the French at Fontenoy in 1745, the troops lining up in a deep column numbering 15,000. Fighting was fierce, and English regiments lost half their infantry.

hardly been crowned, though, when Bohemia was overwhelmed by Maria Theresa's men, and the new emperor fled. The conflict escalated. Any enemy of France being Britain's friend, King George II had enlisted in the "Pragmatic Army" (a league of states who supported the Pragmatic Sanction). Battle rejoined in New England and Canada between France and Britain and their Native American allies; there was war in India too, where Britain and France had colonies. Britain was also at war with Spain in the Caribbean, and in the Mediterranean the widening war was taking in the little states and duchies of Italy. But although Maria Theresa had ceded most of Silesia to Prussia in 1742 as part of the Peace of Breslau, the situation deteriorated for the anti-Habsburg allies.

Flag fragment
The remains of a Prussian military ensign from the War of the Austrian Succession when Prussia became a military power.

Prussian tactics
King George II led the British attack at the battle of Dettingen, Germany, in June 1743. The allies were victorious despite having their line of retreat cut off during the "Mousetrap" – a trap laid by the Duc de Noailles. Both France and Prussia rallied in 1744. Frederick II reopened hostilities in Silesia after Austria had tried to reclaim the region.

> **WILD GEESE** Young male Catholics from Ireland, dispossessed by the Penal Laws introduced by the English, who took flight to seek advancement as soldiers of fortune in the armies of France, Spain, Sweden, Austria, and even Russia.

In June 1745, he won a tactical victory at the battle of Hohenfriedberg, in present-day Poland, approaching the enemy in "oblique order" – focusing his attack on one flank while at the same time presenting a solid front. This left the enemy with no room to adjust their positions or regroup. Frederick not only won his reputation here for tactical genius, but also the title, "Frederick the Great". Another triumph followed at Soor, in the present-day Czech Republic, in September. In December Leopold II won at Kesselsdorf in Germany.

With events swinging against the Pragmatic cause, Britain's growing difficulties were seen as opportunities by longstanding foes. Ireland's soldiers

of fortune, the "Wild Geese", led the vital cavalry charge when the French triumphed at Fontenoy, in present-day Belgium, in May 1745. That same year, supporters of Charles Edward Stuart, or "Bonnie Prince Charlie", tried to place him on the throne. In July he landed in the Outer Hebrides in Scotland, and marched south with an army from the Highlands. The troops made it as far as Derby before turning back, disillusioned at the lack of English support. Prince Charlie fled to France after the defeat at Culloden, Scotland, in April 1746.

French occupation
From France's perspective, 1745 had been successful in distracting Britain from the "real" war. Marshal Saxe's French forces won at the battle of Rocoux, outside Liège, in October 1746, triumphing again at Lauffeld in July 1747. France now occupied the whole of the Austrian Netherlands, threatening the United Provinces to the north. With the Dutch town of Maastricht besieged by French troops for the second time in less than a century, negotiations began, leading to the Treaty of Aix-la-Chapelle.

For all the years of bloodshed, not a great deal had changed. Prussia gained the most: its possession of Silesia – and its status as a military power – were confirmed.

THE SEVEN YEARS WAR
Frederick the Great felt that his father's past efforts – and his own – in rebuilding Prussia as a soldier-state had been amply vindicated. He continued his reforms with renewed zeal. Prussia was ruled as though it were an **arm of the military**, becoming a byword for regimentation and discipline.

FREDERICK THE GREAT

The **surrender of Silesia** apart, Austria had emerged unscathed, and Maria Theresa held on to her throne. That left unfinished business at the heart of Europe. Austria and Prussia were to be at the centre of another far-reaching conflict with the start of **the Seven Years War 172–73 »**.

THE END OF A DREAM
In the months after Culloden, the Duke of Cumberland exacted cruel retribution in the Highlands, using terror tactics to **quell the population**. The traditional rights of the chiefs were formally rescinded. Weapons had to be handed in and the trappings of the **clan system** were outlawed; wearing tartan plaids or kilts became a crime. Having escaped from Scotland in disguise, Charles Edward Stuart spent the rest of his life in embittered exile. When he died in 1788, the **Jacobite dream died** with him.

KEY MOMENT

THE BATTLE OF CULLODEN

The incompetence of Bonnie Prince Charlie, and the heroism of his Highland army, were both exhibited on 16 April 1746 at Culloden – the brutal climax of the "Forty-Five" rebellion. The night before, the army had marched cross-country to Nairn so it could attack the Duke of Cumberland's government forces as they slept. Arriving too late, with dawn rapidly approaching, the army was compelled to retrace its steps to Culloden Moor, where Cumberland's army happened upon the tired troops. While he pondered his next move, Prince Charlie left his infantry lined up – steadfastly holding their positions – within range of Cumberland's cannon as they fired at will. Only after half an hour did he order the charge. His men obeyed, their pistols and broadswords useless as they ran across the boggy ground, cut down by heavy fire. The government artillery was by now no longer firing regular cannonballs but tiny "grapeshot" that scattered as they flew. Those who reached the redcoat lines found themselves facing the Duke's resolute troops with bayonets fixed. As many as 2,000 were killed or wounded in the battle.

THE CULLODEN BATTLEFIELD TODAY

4

THE AGE OF REVOLUTION

1750 – 1830

The French Revolution of 1789 failed to create a radical new political system. Instead, it gave power to an emperor who set out to conquer Europe. More successful revolutions took place in the Americas, where colonists won their independence from Britain and Spain.

THE AGE OF REVOLUTION
1750 – 1830

The period 1750 to 1830 was a time of revolutionary upheaval in politics and society: the American Revolution founded the United States in 1776; the French Revolution of 1789 promoted "liberty, equality, and fraternity"; the Industrial Revolution initiated a rapid development of the productive power of Western societies. But it was not a time of revolution in the technology of war. The principal battlefield weapons were the flintlock musket, bayonet, sword, and muzzle-loaded smoothbore cannon, as they had been since around 1700. There were improvements in weapon design, but genuine innovations such as the semaphore telegraph and the Congreve rocket had only a marginal impact on warfare. The fundamental changes lay elsewhere: in the mobilization of the resources of European states on an unprecedented scale, the organization of mass armies, the adoption of more aggressive strategy and tactics, and the growth of new ideological bases for war.

Organizational revolution

The growing power of European states was evident in sheer numbers – the French army of over 600,000 men that invaded Russia in 1812 was of a size unprecedented in European warfare.

French victory at Austerlitz
French general Jean Rapp presents the defeated Russian prince Repnin and enemy prisoners to Napoleon after the battle of Austerlitz in 1805.

States were able not only to mobilize such large forces, but also to equip them. Nelson had more than 2,000 cannon at Trafalgar in 1805, and there were some 1,200 artillery pieces deployed at Borodino in 1812. The most fervent attempt to mobilize a whole society for war was made by the French revolutionaries of 1793, who decreed a *levée en masse* (mass conscription) for the defence of France. But other states could equal the French commitment to war – militant patriotism grew just as decisively in Britain and Russia.

The key innovative commanders of the revolutionary era – Napoleon on land and Nelson at sea – expressed the progressive spirit of the age. Their predecessors had appreciated the merits of a well-conducted land campaign, with meticulously organized supplies and immaculately drilled troops, or at sea the conduct of a battle in a well-formed line. Nelson preferred to break up the line in search of decisive victory in an unpredictable mêlée. Napoleon abandoned dependence on a formal supply system in favour of

British 5.5 inch howitzer, 1782
Howitzers evolved to provide a high-angle counterpart to standard low-trajectory cannon. This Royal Artillery howitzer was a companion to the 9-pounder field gun.

living off the land, allowing his large army corps to advance at speed. His aim was to bring the enemy forces to battle and destroy them. Battlefield tactics became more flexible and less formal. Skirmishers and sharpshooters armed with rifles became an essential element of armed forces, supplementing the ultra-disciplined musket-and-bayonet infantry. Napoleon, a former artillery officer, turned artillery into an offensive force on the battlefield, concentrated in batteries to maximize firepower and used to soften up the enemy in preparation for an infantry and cavalry attack. Napoleonic infantry often attacked in column, rather then deploying into a line on the battlefield, and the full force of the cavalry charge was restored by the French armoured cuirassier.

European states went to war across the world, fighting in India, the Caribbean, and North America. They demonstrated a clear supremacy over opponents from outside Europe, and the process of non-European countries adopting Western-style military organization and technology began to gather pace.

1755	**1760**	**1765**	**1770**	**1775**

1756
The Seven Years War begins in Europe. Prussia invades Saxony and the French take Minorca from Britain. ■ The nawab of Bengal, a French ally, seizes the British East India Company fort at Calcutta.

1760
The Russian and Austrian armies briefly occupy Berlin; Frederick II fights back with victories at Liegnitz and Torgau. ■ In North America, Montreal surrenders to the British.

1765
French minister the Duc de Choiseul introduces new naval regulations while building a powerful new fleet. Jean-Baptiste Gribeauval begins a major transformation of French artillery.

1775
The American Revolutionary War begins. After initial clashes at Lexington and Concord, the British are besieged in Boston. Congress establishes the Continental Army under Washington.

❯❯ 18th-century British blunderbuss pistol

≪ American militiamen fighting British troops at Lexington

1757
Prussian king Frederick II defeats the French at Rossbach and the Austrians at Leuthen. ■ The British defeat the nawab of Bengal at Plassey.

1761
In northern India an Afghan army led by Ahmad Shah Durrani fights the French-trained Indian Marathas at Panipat. ■ In southern India the British capture the port of Pondicherry from the French.

1767
Start of the First Anglo-Mysore War between the British East India Company and Hyder Ali, ruler of Mysore in southern India. ■ The British parliament passes the Townshend Acts, imposing duties on imports to the North American colonies.

1762
After the death of Empress Elizabeth, Russia makes peace with Prussia. Spain enters the Seven Years War as an ally of France. ■ The British seize Havana and Manila from Spain and Martinique from France.

1768
The Bar Confederation of Polish nobles rebels against Russian dominance of their country. This conflict leads to the Russo-Turkish War.

1770
The Ottoman navy is destroyed by the Russians at Chesma. The Russian army defeats the Ottomans in Bessarabia at Kagul.

1776
The 13 North American colonies declare independence. The British abandon Boston but take New York.

1771
Russian forces capture the Crimea from the Ottomans.

❯❯ Ottoman cavalry sabre

1773
In Massachusetts American protesters against customs duties defy British authority in the Boston Tea Party.

1777
A British and Hessian army surrenders to the Americans under Horatio Gates at Saratoga. General William Howe defeats the Americans at Brandywine and occupies Philadelphia.

≪ British mortar c.1770

⌃ Prussian king Frederick II

1758
The British capture the French fortress of Louisbourg, Nova Scotia. ■ The Russians and Prussians suffer heavy losses at the battle of Zorndorf.

1763
The Seven Years War ends. North American Indian tribes take part in Pontiac's Rebellion. The French army adopts the Charleville musket.

1774
Britain imposes military government on colony of Massachusetts. ■ Russians inflict decisive defeat on the Ottomans at Kozludzha. End of the Russo-Turkish War. ■ Pugachev's Cossack Rebellion is defeated by Russian forces at Kazan.

1778
Washington's Continental Army survives a winter at Valley Forge. France declares war on Britain in support of the American colonists. ■ Prussia and Austria begin the War of the Bavarian Succession.

1759
A Prussian-Hanoverian-British army beats the French at Minden. Prussia is defeated by the Russians and Austrians at Kunersdorf. ■ At sea, the British defeat the French at Quiberon Bay. ■ Victory at the Plains of Abraham gives Britain Quebec.

1764
The British East India Company defeats an Indian alliance including the forces of the nawab of Bengal and the Mogul emperor at Buxar.

1769
The First Anglo-Mysore War ends inconclusively. ■ France conquers Corsica, driving the Corsican national leader Pascal Paoli into exile.

1779
Taking advantage of the problems facing the British in the American Revolutionary War, Spain declares war on Britain. ■ The Royal Navy adopts the carronade, a powerful, short cannon for fighting at close range.

≪ Battle of Quiberon Bay

1780
The British take Charleston and win a victory at the battle of Camden. ■ The Royal Navy defeats a Spanish fleet at Cape St Vincent. ■ Tipu sultan of Mysore fights the British in India as an ally of France – the Second Anglo-Mysore War.

1784
Britain and Mysore make peace in the Treaty of Mangalore.

1785
The Northwest Indian War begins between the US and a confederation of Indian tribes.

≪ Battle of Ochakov

1788
Austria joins the war against the Ottomans as an ally of Russia. The Russians take Ochakov and win a naval victory at Fidonisi. ■ Sweden declares war on Russia, opening naval operations in the Baltic.

1792
French Revolutionary Wars begin. France defeats the Prussians at Valmy and the Austrians at Jemappes.

1796
Napoleon defeats the Austrians at Arcole. Spain allies with France.

1797
Napoleon defeats the Austrians at Rivoli. Austria makes peace with the treaty of Campo Formio.

≪ Knapsack of the Queen's Rangers, a regiment of American colonists loyal to Britain

1781
A French fleet defeats the British at Chesapeake Bay. British general Cornwallis surrenders at Yorktown.

1787
Ottoman Sultan Abdulhamid declares war on Russia – the second Russo-Turkish War begins.

1789
Beginning of the French Revolution. ■ The Russians and Austrians defeat the Ottomans at Focsani. ■ In India, Mysore goes to war with Britain for the third time.

1793
In the French Revolutionary Wars, France declares war on Britain, Spain, and the United Provinces. Napoleon Bonaparte commands French artillery at the siege of Toulon.

1782
A British fleet defeats the French at the battle of the Saints in the Caribbean, successfully employing the tactic of breaking the line. ■ French admiral Suffren fights the Royal Navy off India at Providien and Trincomalee.

1794
The French defeat the Austrians at Fleurus. First military use of a balloon.

1798
Napoleon leads an army to Egypt and defeats the Mameluks at the battle of the Pyramids. British under Nelson destroy the French fleet in Aboukir Bay. ■ US begins an undeclared naval war with France.

≪ 18th-century Swedish cannon

1783
By the Treaty of Paris the US gains independence from Britain.

≫ Treaty of Paris document

1790
The Russo-Swedish War ends. ■ Austria makes peace with the Ottomans, but the Russo-Turkish War continues.

1791
Ottoman sultan Selim III makes peace with Russia and starts modernizing his empire's forces.

1795
France makes peace with Spain and Prussia. Napoleon defeats an attempted coup by turning cannon on insurgents in Paris. In western France, Republican forces crush the royalist uprising in the Vendée region.

≫ The Vendée uprising

1799
Russia and Austria declare war on France; Russian General Suvorov campaigns in Italy and Switzerland. After defeating the Ottomans at Aboukir, Napoleon returns to France and takes power in a coup d'état. ■ In India, the British capture Seringapatam, the capital of Mysore.

1805

1805
War of the Triple Alliance. Austria and Russia ally with Britain against France. Nelson defeats the French and Spanish at Trafalgar. Napoleon defeats the Austrians at Ulm and the Russians and Austrians at Austerlitz.

1806
The French crush the Prussians at Jena and Auerstedt. ■ War breaks out between Ottoman Turkey and Russia.

1807
Napoleon and Tsar Alexander become allies. The British bombard Copenhagen and seize the Danish fleet. France invades Portugal. The French defeat the Prussians at the battle of Friedland.

1808
Janissaries overthrow Ottoman sultan Selim III to stop his army reforms. ■ Start of the Peninsular War. The British land in Portugal and defeat the French at Vimeiro.

1809
Austria is crushed by Napoleon at Wagram.

≫ Model of a British first-rate ship of the line

1810

1810
In Portugal the French are halted by the defensive line of Torres Vedras. ■ Wars of independence begin in Argentina and Mexico.

1811
War of independence begins in Venezuela. ■ Russia wins war with Turkey.

1812
Napoleon's invasion of Russia ends in the disastrous retreat from Moscow. ■ In the Peninsular War, Wellington defeats the French at Salamanca. ■ The US declares war on Britain – the War of 1812.

1813
Prussia, Austria, and Sweden join Russia in the war against France, defeating Napoleon at Leipzig. ■ An American naval squadron defeats the British on Lake Erie in the War of 1812.

≫ Congreve rockets, used by the British throughout the Napoleonic wars

≪ Zulu chief Shaka

1814

1814
Napoleon abdicates and is exiled to Elba. ■ In North America the British burn Washington, DC and bombard Baltimore. The first steam gunboat, *Demologos*, defends New York's harbour.

1815
The British lose the battle of New Orleans to the Americans. ■ Napoleon returns to France, gathers an army, and invades Belgium. He is beaten by the British and Prussians at Waterloo.

≫ French chasseur's shako

1816
A Spanish force retakes New Granada (Colombia, Venezuela and Ecuador). ■ The British and Dutch bombard Algiers, demanding an end to piracy. ■ In southern Africa the Zulu begin a period of expansion under Shaka.

1817
An army of liberation led by José de San Martín crosses the Andes from Argentina to attack royalist forces in Chile. ■ Russia begins a series of wars to conquer the peoples of the Caucasus.

1818

1818
In India the British defeat the Maratha Confederacy. ■ San Martín wins battles in Chile at Chacabuco and Maipu. ■ US forces invade Florida in the First Seminole War.

1819
In New Granada the liberator Simón Bolívar wins a great victory at the battle of Boyaca.

1820
Civil war breaks out in Spain between liberals and royalists.

1821
The Greek War of Independence against Ottoman rule begins. Simón Bolívar defeats the royalists and liberates Venezuela.

1822

1823
The French intervene in the Spanish Civil War. They invade Spain to reinstate King Ferdinand VII. ■ French artillery officer Henri-Joseph Paixans develops a naval gun firing explosive shells.

≫ Simón Bolívar

1824
Victories for Bolívar and Sucre in Peru end Spanish rule in South America. ■ Britain's Royal Navy uses a steam ship, *Lightning*, on a mission to bombard Algiers.

1825
An Egyptian army led by Ibrahim Pasha lands in the Peloponnese to assist the Ottomans in suppressing the Greek revolt. ■ Brazil goes to war with Uruguay and Argentina.

1826

1826
Missolonghi and Athens fall to Ottoman and Egyptian forces in Greece. Ottoman sultan Mahmud suppresses the janissaries who are blocking military reforms. ■ Burma is defeated by the British in the first Anglo-Burmese War.

≫ The battle of Navarino

1827
At Navarino, off the west coast of Greece, British, French, and Russian warships destroy an Egyptian and Ottoman fleet.

1828
Russian armies launch offensives against the Ottoman empire in the Balkans and eastern Anatolia.

1829
Russian forces advance to Edirne. The Ottomans are forced to accept a peace agreement granting autonomy to Greece, Serbia, Moldavia, and Wallachia.

‹‹ BEFORE

Conflicting colonial ambitions of age-old enemies, Britain and France, led repeatedly to warfare in North America, with Native Americans becoming involved on both sides.

SPARRING PARTNERS

In 1682 the French laid claim to a vast swathe of territory from their sparsely populated colonies in Canada, down the Mississippi to the Gulf of Mexico, as **"New France"**. The claim was a direct challenge to the territorial ambitions of the British colonies on the eastern seaboard of North America, which had no defined western borders. Whenever Britain and France went to war, which was often, fighting flared in North America. The British colonists, with the **Iroquois Indians**, attacked

BRITISH 60TH ROYAL AMERICAN REGIMENT BUTTON

New France in **King William's War** of 1689 to 1697. This was followed by **Queen Anne's War ‹‹ 154–55** from 1702 to 1713, through which Britain gained Newfoundland and part of Acadia.

CONTINUED FIGHTING

From 1744 **King George's War** – the North American offshoot of the **War of the Austrian Succession ‹‹ 162–63** – brought very heavy fighting between British colonial militias, the French colonial Troupes de la Marine, and their respective Indian allies. Colonial militia and the Royal Navy captured the French fortress of Louisbourg in 1745, but this was returned to France by the **Treaty of Aix-la-Chapelle** in 1748, which restored pre-war borders.

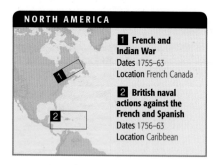

NORTH AMERICA

1 French and Indian War
Dates 1755–63
Location French Canada

2 British naval actions against the French and Spanish
Dates 1756–63
Location Caribbean

Mortar shell

This 10-inch shell was found near the site of Fort Ticonderoga. Mortar shells proved highly effective during siege operations.

Lifting handle

Hollow iron sphere

French and Indian War

Involving relatively small forces, the French and Indian War was fought for high stakes. The outcome of battles for isolated forts and settlements would determine the future shape of North America. Had the war gone differently, Canada and the United States would not exist as we know them today.

Generally seen as a North American offshoot of the Seven Years War of 1756 to 1763, the French and Indian War in fact started before the related European conflict. Britain and France were still at peace when the first significant clashes occurred in 1754. The area under dispute was the Ohio Valley. For France, this was an essential link between its colony in Canada and the lands it claimed along the Mississippi. The British government, however, was busy awarding land grants in the region to the Ohio Company, founded by its Virginian colonists.

In 1752 Marquis Duquesne was made governor of New France with specific instructions to assert control of the Ohio territory. He set about establishing a

186 The number of men led by Virginian Major George Washington on his expedition to Fort Duquesne in spring 1754. The forces engaged in the French and Indian War were often surprisingly small.

string of forts southward from the Great Lakes, winning the support of many of the traditionally pro-British Algonquin Indians. Virginia governor and leading participant in the Ohio Company, Robert Dinwiddie was determined to resist the French advance. In spring 1754 he sent a body of Virginia militia, under Lieutenant-Colonel George Washington, to face the French at Fort Duquesne, on the site of present-day Pittsburgh.

A skirmish between Washington's force and a French patrol on 28 May left a French officer dead. Washington's men were too weak to resist a French and Indian force sent to punish them. On 4 July, Washington surrendered at Fort Necessity. He was released only after signing a document admitting to the "murder" of the French officer.

The British falter

The Virginians appealed to the British government for support, and received it in the form of two regiments of troops under Major General Edward Braddock. With Washington as his aide-de-camp, Braddock marched 2,000 men to attack Fort Duquesne. On 9 July 1755, they were ambushed by a predominantly Indian force under French leadership at the Monongahela river. About 500 were killed, including Braddock. After this disaster the French were in the

ascendant. The British had successes, taking Nova Scotia and holding the Hudson Valley. But when the situation in Europe brought Britain and France to a declaration of war in May 1756, it was the French who were in a position to take the offensive in North America.

General Louis-Joseph de Montcalm was sent to take command in Quebec. He captured and destroyed Fort Oswego, a key British outpost on the southern shore of Lake Ontario, in August 1756, and a year later forced the British to surrender at Fort William Henry on

ELITE TROOPS

ROGER'S RANGERS

Formed in 1755 during the French and Indian War, Roger's Rangers were a company of colonial militia that specialized in special operations deep inside hostile territory and intelligence gathering. Their leader, Major Robert Rogers, trained his men to move undetected through the wilderness, track down the enemy, and carry out ambushes. His precepts included: "See the enemy first"; "Half the party stays awake while the other half sleeps"; and "Don't ever march home the same way [you came]". Rogers later led Loyalist Rangers during the American Revolution.

"The **groans and cries** along the road of the wounded for help … **were enough to pierce a heart of adamant**."

GEORGE WASHINGTON DESCRIBING THE RETREAT FROM MONONGAHELA, 1755

George Washington at Monongahela
When the British were ambushed at Monongahela in 1755, their commander, General Braddock, was mortally wounded, leaving his aide-de-camp, George Washington, to ride around the battlefield rallying the troops.

Lake George. The fall of Fort William Henry became notorious because of the behaviour of Montcalm's Indian allies, who tortured and massacred hundreds of British men following their surrender.

The balance of power shifts
By 1757 the shape of the war was changing. Now engaged in a general war with France, Britain began to devote more substantial military resources to the North American conflict. The British Royal Navy's command of the Atlantic Ocean made it difficult for France to reinforce its troops in Canada, so the British enjoyed a growing numerical advantage. As they began to score victories, the Indians tended to switch sides, further shifting the balance against

the French. While the struggle for the Ohio territory continued, the war increasingly became a British campaign of conquest directed at Canada.

An outstanding general, Montcalm ensured that his opponents enjoyed no easy successes. In summer 1758 General James Abercrombie led a British army of more than 15,000 men – a huge force by the standards of this conflict – in an advance through New York state to the Canadian border at Fort Ticonderoga (also known as Fort Carillon). With less than 4,000 men under him, Montcalm prepared field fortifications that Abercrombie disastrously attempted to take by frontal assault.

Tomahawk blade
Tomahawks were general-purpose axes used in warfare by both the Indians and the colonists. This tomahawk was found at Fort Miller.

The British suffered 2,000 casualties and were obliged to withdraw. In the same month of July 1758, however, the French fortress of Louisbourg on Cape Breton Island, commanding the Gulf of St Lawrence, was taken by British troops under General Jeffery Amherst, brought from Halifax, Nova Scotia, by sea.

The British take Canada
The following year, the Louisbourg fortress provided the base for a thrust into the heart of Canada. While other British and colonial forces captured Forts Ticonderoga and Niagara from the French, a British fleet carried 8,000 troops under the command of General James Wolfe up the St Lawrence River to attack Quebec. The city was ably defended by Montcalm. An initial

15,000 This estimated number of deaths in seven years' fighting during the French and Indian War. Some 11,000 soldiers were killed in one day at the battle of Kunersdorf, in 1759, during the Seven Years War in Europe.

British landing was repulsed and a bombardment of the city from the opposite riverbank had little effect. Feeling unable to maintain a lengthy siege, Wolfe adopted a risky plan that required a night landing upriver from Quebec, and the scaling of the cliffs of the Heights of Abraham. This was achieved on 12 September, forcing Montcalm to give battle on the Plains of Abraham, a plateau outside the city walls, the following day. The British were victorious in a brief but savage encounter in which both commanders lost their lives. The French made one last effort to retake Quebec in spring 1760, but their attacks were held off. Their position became increasingly untenable. Vastly outnumbered, the French surrendered Canada to the British at Montreal in September 1760.

The European war between Britain and France continued until 1763, but the contest in North America was over at last. The peace agreement of 1763 confirmed the British in possession of Canada. The Spanish ceded Florida to the British and, in return, took Louisiana from the French, leaving France with no substantial territory in North America.

AFTER »

The aftermath of the war was far more painful for the Indians than for the French Canadians. It set Britain on the path to conflict with its North American colonies.

CIVIL DISQUIET
By the **Quebec Act of 1774**, Britain allowed its new Canadian subjects the free practice of the Catholic faith and the use of **French civil law**, reconciling many of them to British rule. The Indian tribes found that treaties agreed by the

PONTIAC was an Ottawan leader who played a significant role in the Indian uprising of 1763. His name was later appropriated for a city in Michigan and a brand of automobile.

British during the war to win their support were not respected after the war ended. An Indian uprising known as **Pontiac's Rebellion** flared in 1763, but this petered out after a few years of massacre and counter-massacre.

UNPOPULAR POLICY
The British government tried to prevent trouble by **banning the westward expansion** of its colonies into Indian territory. This limitation, like the **tolerance of Canadian Catholics**, was deeply unpopular in the British colonies. British attempts to make colonists pay the cost of their defence through various duties led directly to the **American Revolution 178–79** » and Britain's loss of its colonies south of Canada.

KEY MOMENT

DEATH OF GENERAL WOLFE

General James Wolfe was just 32 years old when he led the British expedition against Quebec in the summer of 1759. He was killed after being hit by several musket balls, at the climax of the battle of the Plains of Abraham on 13 September. Reportedly he died content in the knowledge that the battle had been won. The famous painting of his death by Benjamin West was first exhibited in 1771.

Seven Years War in Europe
Dates 1756–63
Location Germany, especially Silesia and Saxony

The Seven Years War

Between 1756 and 1763 Europe was immersed in a general conflict between the major powers. Prussia, having precipitated the war, fought for survival against a coalition of Austria, Russia, and France. The French and British fought an almost separate war, chiefly at sea, linked to colonial conflicts.

« BEFORE

Both a land war between Europe's major powers and a worldwide colonial conflict between Britain and France, the Seven Years War had two separate points of origin.

THE WAR BEGINS

The first shots of the conflict were fired in North America. Lieutenant colonel **George Washington** of the Virginia militia ambushed a party of French Canadian scouts at Fort Duquesne in 1754. This initiated **the French and Indian War, a colonial war between Britain and France «« 170–71**.

In Central Europe the Seven Years War was a follow-up to the indecisive **War of the Austrian Succession**, which ended in 1748 **«« 162–63**.

60,000 The number of men in the **Prussian Army in 1740, at the accession of King Frederick II.**

In that war Prussia had proved itself a **major military power** and, by annexing the wealthy province of Silesia, had greatly enhanced its resources. Austria felt threatened by this and sought to regain Silesia. In May 1756, Austrian Empress Maria Theresa formed a **defensive alliance** with the Habsburg's enemy, France. Austria was also allied to Russia, another rising military power, having defeated Sweden in **the Great Northern War** of 1700–20 **«« 158–59**.

AGREED ALLIANCE

For Britain, a big concern was to defend Hanover, the German state from which the **British ruling dynasty** had come, against the French. The British government made an agreement to back Prussia in a war over Silesia, in return for their promise to defend Hanover against France – a promise the Prussians proved incapable of fulfilling.

Prussian firepower

This flintlock carbine, which has a rifled barrel, was manufactured by the Prussian state arsenal at Potsdam. It was a cavalry weapon issued to one in ten Prussian cuirassiers (cavalry soldiers).

The diplomatic revolution effected by the alliance between Habsburg Austria and Bourbon France in 1756 was seen by Frederick II of Prussia as a preparation for war. Expecting to be attacked by the Austrians the following year, Frederick seized the initiative and launched his own preemptive assault against Saxony, a state closely aligned with Austria and the obvious starting point for an invasion of Prussia. Saxony was overrun by Prussia's efficient army, but in response to Prussian aggression both France and Russia agreed to enter the war in support of Austria. Frederick faced a coalition – soon to be joined by Sweden – vastly superior in aggregate manpower and resources. Britain was already at war with France at sea and in the colonies, and only committed to a limited intervention in the European land war to defend the German state of Hanover, ruled by King George II, against the French.

British support

Through the summer of 1757, the war went badly for the British and Prussians. Britain's attempted defence of Hanover failed with the comprehensive defeat of the Duke of Cumberland by the French at the battle of Hastenbeck in July. Frederick was meanwhile in a desperate situation as the Russians overwhelmed East Prussia and French and Austrian armies approached from the west and south. In November and December the Prussian king achieved victories over the French at Rossbach and the Austrians at Leuthen – both skirmishes fought against odds of almost two to one. Exploiting the ability of Prussia's disciplined infantry, cavalry, and artillery to carry out swift marches and complicated battlefield manoeuvres, these encounters were the superlative exhibition of Frederick's military talent.

Rossbach and Leuthen did little more than buy Frederick some time. They did encourage the British, under a coalition government dominated by William Pitt, to provide ample financial aid to Prussia, and the deployment of a British and

Battle of Quiberon Bay
Fought in choppy waters off the coast of Brittany in 1759, Admiral Edward Hawke's victory shattered French naval power and ended plans for an invasion of Britain.

Hanoverian Army of Observation on Prussia's western front was sufficient to hold off the discouraged French. But Austria and Russia continued to attack

34,000 The number of men killed or wounded in a day's fighting between Prussia and the Russians and Austrians at Kunersdorf, 12 August 1759. Around 100,000 troops took part in the battle.

Prussia with the advantage of having far more men. In August 1758, Russia advanced to within 100km (62 miles) of Berlin. A desperate drawn battle was fought at Zorndorf – both the Russians and the Prussians suffered more than 30 per cent casualties.

Winners and losers

For Britain and France, the conflict reached crisis point in 1759. Their war was always mainly naval and colonial. After an initial setback in Minorca at the outset of the war, the Royal Navy had reasserted its superiority, blockading French ports and raiding coastal areas. France planned a seaborne invasion of England and Scotland. This required their Mediterranean squadron to sail

from Toulon to Brittany, where it would join the Atlantic fleet and escort troop transports to Britain. The Mediterranean squadron was intercepted and destroyed by Admiral Edward Boscawen off Lagos, southern Portugal, in August. France continued its invasion preparations, but in November its Atlantic fleet was trailed and shattered by Admiral Edward Hawke in an extraordinary battle fought in an Atlantic storm amid the perilous rocks and reefs of Quiberon Bay. Spain was later induced to join France's naval war against Britain, but there was never another serious challenge to the Royal Navy's command of the sea. Coupled

KEY MOMENT

LOSS OF MINORCA

For Britain, the Seven Years War in Europe began with the dispossession of the island of Minorca to the French. The blame for this setback was laid upon Admiral John Byng. Sent with a naval force from Gibraltar to relieve besieged British forces on the island, he had withdrawn after a bloody encounter with a French squadron. Byng was court-martialled for failing to do his utmost to engage the enemy and, despite a plea for mercy, was executed by firing squad on the deck of HMS *Monarch* at Portsmouth on 14 March 1757.

Flintlock mechanism   Rifled barrel   Ramrod

with victories in Canada and India, Quiberon Bay made 1759 a triumphant year for the British.

British and Hanoverian forces also defeated the French on land, at Minden, but still Frederick of Prussia fought the Austrians and Russians unaided. Though his triumphs were many, so were his defeats. At Kunersdorf, in August 1759,

and went on to defeat the Austrians at Liegnitz in August 1760 and at Torgau the following November.

In 1761 British support for Prussia faltered; Pitt, the force behind Britain's war effort, resigned. As losses mounted, Prussia's administration struggled to find fresh men and money to keep the war going. By the year's end Frederick was

" It's easier to **kill these Russians** than to defeat them."

FREDERICK THE GREAT AFTER THE BATTLE OF ZORNDORF, 25 AUGUST 1758

the Russian commander-in-chief, Count Pyotr Saltykov, inflicted a defeat so bad that Frederick contemplated suicide, writing: "I will not survive the doom of my fatherland." Out of 50,000 Prussian troops involved, 19,000 were killed or wounded. In October 1760, the Russians and Austrians briefly took Berlin. In fact, Frederick did not lose the will to fight

again suicidal, attempting to "preserve for my nephew, by way of negotiation, whatever fragments of territory we can save from the avidity of my enemies". The Empress Elizabeth of Russia died and the pro-Prussian Peter III crowned. Peter was assassinated after six months, but he had time to make peace with Prussia, letting Frederick retake Silesia from Austria. After almost seven years of war, money and willpower were running out. Peace was signed in February 1763 between Prussia and Austria and between Britain and France.

Battle of Minden, 1759
British and Hanoverian infantry put the French cavalry to flight in a rare example of successful offensive action by foot soldiers against mounted troops.

Frederick the Great's coat
Frederick II of Prussia was admired both as a military commander and an enlightened despot. His coat is preserved in the German Historical Museum in Berlin.

The Seven Years War left the map of Europe broadly unchanged, but it had important consequences that were not confined to the European colonies.

THE AFTERMATH
The war confirmed the rise of both Prussia and Russia. France's power was diminished, while Britain was the great beneficiary. The British became the **world's leading colonial and commercial nation**, having evicted the French from North America and from most of India in its **wars in India 176–77 »**. France built a new navy, funded by the patriotic French public. The army was also reformed, and soon defeated Britain in the **American Revolution 178–79 »**.

900,000 **The lowest estimate of the death toll in the Seven Years War. Some sources give a figure of 1.4 million dead.**

This was followed by a reassertion of French military might in Europe after the 1789 revolution, both in the **French Revolutionary Wars 186–87 »** and throughout **Napoleon's imperial triumphs** on the continent **194–95 »**.

Leuthen

Leuthen was the second of King Frederick II of Prussia's two great victories of 1757. A month after crushing the French at Rossbach, on 5 December he encountered a Austrian army twice the size of his own and defeated it through bold manoeuvre and the aggressive use of combined arms – infantry, field artillery, and cavalry. The victory confirmed his reputation as Europe's finest military commander.

Under Prince Charles of Lorraine, the 80,000-strong Austrian army had invaded the valuable province of Silesia. Determined to keep it, Charles ordered his army to take up a defensive position on a four-mile line between two reaches of marshland, centred on the village of Leuthen. Frederick's army numbered only 36,000 men but he chose to attack against the odds rather than leave Charles in possession of Silesia.

Cunning manoeuvres

Frederick's plan of attack depended on the ability of the rigorously disciplined Prussian infantry to stay disciplined and faultlessly transfer parade-ground drill to the field of battle. First he used his cavalry to drive back the Austrian pickets who were observing his forces, knowing that his army's subsequent manoeuvres would largely be masked from the enemy by low hills. Frederick then marched his infantry in perfect order to the left of the Austrian line, while his cavalry rode about showily opposite the right of the Austrian line. The Austrians were utterly confused by what little they could see of the Prussian infantry's movements. Interpreting their redeployment as a withdrawal, Charles reinforced the right of his line. When the marching Prussian infantry columns emerged

unexpectedly on the Austrian left, they reformed with precision into their conventional two-line attacking formation, at right-angles to the end of the enemy line. With 12-pounder guns positioned on a knoll to support them, the Prussian infantry attacked.

The Austrians in disarray

Battered by cannon from the knoll and by volleys of musket fire from the advancing infantry, the Austrian left was rolled up as Charles struggled to bring across reinforcements from the distant right wing of his position. The chaos of pitched battle took over from organized manoeuvre, the Prussians taking the fortified village of Leuthen after a furious fight lasting 40 minutes.

Beyond Leuthen the Austrian forces managed to form a new defensive line that stalled the Prussian advance, and the Austrian cavalry assembled for a charge to sweep the Prussian infantry from the field. But Frederick ordered his own cavalry into action to counter the Austrian horse. The rival bodies of men on horseback clashed head-on in a swirling mêlée. Eventually Charles's cavalry was driven back, and Austrian resistance crumbled. The battle had lasted three hours. Frederick had won back control of Silesia for Prussia and the disgraced Charles was forced to resign in the wake of his defeat.

[1] Prussians initially deploy in front of Borne

[2] Austrians send left flank reserves to bolster their right

[3] Prussians use subterfuge of a cavalry attack to draw Austrians southwards

[4] Prussians redeploy to south of Lobetinz

[5] Austrians reform to south of Leuthen

[6] Austrian counter-attack repulsed by Prussian cavalry

[7] Austrian counterattack on Prussian right defeated

Borne

FREDERICK

Frobelwitz

CHARLES

Radaxdorf

Leuthen

Lobetinz

NÁDASTI

Schriegwitz

KEY
- Prussian infantry
- Prussian cavalry
- Austrian infantry
- Austrian cavalry

LOCATION
Around the village of Leuthen (now Lutynia) in Silesia, in present-day southwestern Poland

DATE
5 December 1757

FORCES
Prussians: 36,000;
Austrians: 80,000

CASUALTIES
Prussians: 1,000 killed;
Austrians: 3,000 killed

The Leuthen chorale
In a moving moment after the battle, a soldier leads the singing of Martin Luther's well-known hymn, "Now Thank We All Our God". The surviving soldiers of the Prussian army struggle to sing with him.

Britain's Wars in India

The disunity of India made the country ripe for exploitation in the 18th century. Britain, represented by the East India Company, and often in alliance with Indian states, extended its rule over ever larger areas of the subcontinent through a series of military campaigns fought using mostly Indian troops.

« BEFORE

The decline of the Mogul empire gave European powers the chance to expand their influence in India by intervening in the affairs of rival Indian princedoms.

A SHIFT OF POWER
After the death of Emperor Aurangzeb in 1707, Mogul rule was soon restricted to the area around Delhi. The new dominant power was the **Maratha Confederacy**, but smaller states such as Hyderabad, Mysore, and Bengal also flourished.

TRADING POSTS
The **British East India Company** established its first trading post (or "factory") on the Indian coast at Surat in 1612. By the 18th century its factories included Bombay (Mumbai), Calcutta (Kolkat) in Bengal, and Madras. Other European countries also had trading companies, including France.

BRITISH EAST INDIA COIN

ANGLO-FRENCH RIVALRY
From 1742, under governor-general **Joseph François Dupleix**, the French attempted to drive out the British and extend their influence over India. In 1746 they captured Madras, but it was returned to the British in the peace settlement at the end of the **War of the Austrian Succession « 162–63**. Anglo-French rivalry was given fresh impetus by the outbreak of the **Seven Years War « 172–73** in 1756.

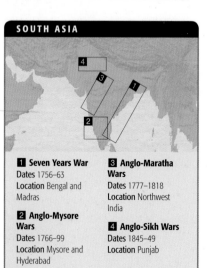

SOUTH ASIA

1 **Seven Years War**
Dates 1756–63
Location Bengal and Madras

2 **Anglo-Mysore Wars**
Dates 1766–99
Location Mysore and Hyderabad

3 **Anglo-Maratha Wars**
Dates 1777–1818
Location Northwest India

4 **Anglo-Sikh Wars**
Dates 1845–49
Location Punjab

The British takeover of India began in Bengal at the start of the Seven Years War. The British and French East India Companies had trading posts, permitted by the Nawab of Bengal (Siraj ud-Daulah). At war with France from May 1756, the British bolstered their defences in Calcutta in case of a French attack. But the Nawab saw this as a snub to his authority. His forces seized the fort, allegedly causing the deaths of many British soldiers and *sepoys* (Indian troops) by interning them in the "Black Hole of Calcutta" (a small cell within the fort).

Britain on the offensive
The British sent a small force by sea from Madras, commanded by Colonel Robert Clive, which retook Calcutta at the start of 1757. Supported by French artillery men with heavy cannon, the Nawab led an army more than 50,000 strong to confront Clive, who had less than a thousand

> ## "It is better to **die as a tiger** than to **live as a sheep**."
> ### TIPU SULTAN, RULER OF MYSORE AND ENEMY OF THE BRITISH

European troops and around 2,000 *sepoys*. However, British leaders had undermined the Nawab's position by intrigue. They had promised the throne to a rival claimant, Mir Jafar, and bribed most of Siraj's commanders. In the battle at Plassey (Palashi), on 23 June, barely one tenth of the Nawab's forces actually fought. The British won what appeared, by numbers alone, an impossible victory and took control of Bengal, with Jafar as a puppet Nawab.

The British victory at Plassey was a setback for French policy in India, and worse followed. The major French settlement was at Pondicherry, which rivalled British Madras on the Carnatic coast. Britain shipped a newly raised infantry regiment, the 84th Regiment of Foot, to India in 1759 and, led by Sir Eyre Coote, it defeated the French under Count de Lally at Wandiwash (Vandavasi) in January of the following

The fall of Seringapatam
In 1799 British forces, led by General David Baird, stormed the city of Seringapatam, capital of Mysore. Mysore's ruler, Tipu Sultan, was killed by the British while defending his palace.

year. Pondicherry was placed under siege and surrendered a year later. The French ended the Seven Years War with only a nominal presence in India. They failed to restore their position when war broke out with Britain again in 1778, during the American Revolution, and Napoleon's later ambitions to rule India remained in the realm of fantasy.

The East India Company's army, consisting of Indian *sepoys* under Indian NCOs and British officers, often aided by elements of the British Army paid for by the Company, was undoubtedly effective. The Company confirmed its control of Bengal with a victory over numerically superior forces, including the Mogul emperor's army, at Buxar in 1764. But it would be a mistake to exaggerate the impact of the European presence at this time or its military superiority. The largest battle fought in India in the mid-18th century was at Panipat in 1761, a conflict between an invading Muslim Afghan army led by Ahmad Shah Durrani and the Hindu Marathas. There may have been over 100,000 troops involved in this costly but ultimately inconclusive encounter.

A formidable foe
One result of the battle of Panipat was to facilitate the rise of Hyder Ali, ruler of Mysore, who took advantage of the temporary weakness of the Maratha Confederacy to extend his power in southern India. Between 1767 and 1799, first under Hyder Ali and then under his son, Tipu Sultan, Mysore engaged in a series of hard-fought wars against the British, urged on by the French, who provided arms and training. Mysore fielded armies that fought with discipline, incorporating much of the best of contemporary European tactics, including cannon. It also deployed rocket brigades – units of several hundred soldiers armed with explosive rockets fired in salvos from iron tubes – which so impressed the

Battle of Pollilur
The Mysore ruler, Tipu Sultan, defeats the British East India Company forces, at Pollilur in 1780. Indian armies combined traditional dashing cavalry with cannon and muskets.

British that they developed Congreve rockets of their own. Tipu Sultan scored impressive victories, notably at Pollilur in 1780 and Tanjore in 1782. It was not until 1799, when Napoleon's invasion of Egypt awoke British fears of a revival of French influence in India, that Tipu Sultan was defeated. As France's ally, he had to be. The British invaded Mysore with a force that included Maratha *sepoys* from Bombay, British infantry under Arthur Wellesley (he later became the Duke of Wellington), and the army of the Nizam of Hyderabad. Mysore's capital, Seringapatam (Srirangapatna), was taken and Tipu killed.

The British turned their attention to the Maratha Confederacy, a potential enemy weakened by divisions in its constituent semi-independent states. The Marathas traditionally fought as skirmishing light cavalry, but under French influence they also had a musket infantry and field artillery. In 1803 the British defeated Maratha armies in the north, while Wellesley campaigned in central India. In September Wellesley blundered into a Maratha force at Assaye that was stronger than his own in cavalry and artillery, as well as in overall numbers. He chose to attack across a river and carried the day despite heavy losses.

These victories brought the British large territorial gains, but over the next two years they suffered reverses, and peace in 1805 left the Marathas still independent. It took more fighting, in 1817–18, to break up the Confederacy, leaving Britain in control of the Indian subcontinent up to the Punjab.

Company rule extended to northern India after two fiercely fought wars against the Sikhs in the 1840s. The Sikh state had been rapidly expanding in the early decades of the 19th century, and its army, the *khalsa*, was a highly motivated force that had European-trained artillery and uniformed infantry. The key British victory at Sobraon in 1846 cost more than 2,000 British and *sepoy* casualties. Yet again the British were not militarily superior, but they had an edge that was enough.

Setluj gun and carriage
This fine, bronze artillery piece was manufactured in Lahore for the Sikh army. It was captured by the British Army during the wars with the Sikhs in the 1840s.

AFTER ≫≫

The Indian Mutiny of 1857 marked the end of an era. The last Mogul was exiled, the East India Company was abolished and India became a possession of the British Crown.

BRITISH RULE
Bengali *sepoys* mutinied, attempting to reinstate the **Mogul emperor** as ruler of India. Sufficient *sepoys* remained loyal for the British to crush the rebellion, which included notable military actions at the **siege of Delhi** and the **relief of Lucknow**. Massacres of some British civilians were used as justification for the extreme brutality used when suppressing the revolt.

INVASION OF AFGHANISTAN
Afghanistan remained outside the borders of **Britain's Indian Raj**. In 1839 British forces invaded the country and installed a pro-British ruler, but they were driven out by an uprising in 1842. A **second British invasion** in 1878 was militarily more successful, but could not subdue the Afghans, who remained independent.

The American Revolution

Between 1775 and 1783 rebels in 13 American colonies, supported by France, fought a conflict for independence from British rule. A civil war between American loyalists and rebels as well as a war between Britain and America, the fighting ended in a humiliating British surrender at Yorktown.

In 1775 General Thomas Gage had orders to suppress the rebellion in Massachusetts. In practice, his British army Redcoats only controlled Boston. On the night of 18–19 April almost 700 Redcoats marched out of the city to seize rebel weapons stored at the nearby town of Concord. They clashed with local militia first at the village of Lexington and then at Concord's North Bridge. The Redcoats were forced to retreat. The rebel militia, strengthened by soldiers recruited by the American Congress, besieged the British in Boston. Britain sailed 4,500 troops across the Atlantic to reinforce the garrison, which sortied to attack fortified militia positions on Breed's Hill and Bunker Hill on 16 June. The disciplined British infantry took the rebel positions, but at heavy cost – it eventually abandoned the garrison at Boston in March 1776.

King George III's government hoped that American loyalists would play the leading role in restoring royal authority

Colonial territories

The 13 colonies that rebelled against British rule stretched down the eastern seaboard of North America between Canada (which remained British-ruled) and Florida. The decisive battle was at Yorktown in 1781.

in the colonies. There were indeed many Americans who fought for the British, including black slaves who saw Britain as offering hope of freedom, but the rebels controlled the militias in most of the colonies. Despite recruiting 30,000 "Hessian" German mercenaries, the British faced an insoluble manpower problem. They had insufficient forces to campaign across the broad spaces of North America and garrison areas under

> ## "They are the **most accurate marksmen** in the world."
>
> FUTURE US PRESIDENT, JOHN ADAMS, ON AMERICAN SHARPSHOOTERS, 1775

HUDSON'S BAY COMPANY · NOVA SCOTIA

Lake Superior · Lexington Apr 1775 · NEW HAMPSHIRE · QUEBEC former French and Indian territory under British rule · Lake Huron · Lake Michigan · Lake Erie · Lake Ontario · Saratoga Oct 1777 · Boston · Bunker Hill Jun 1775 · MASSACHUSETTS · RHODE ISLAND · NEW YORK · CONNECTICUT · New York · PENNSYLVANIA · Philadelphia · NEW JERSEY · Germantown Oct 1777 · MARYLAND · DELAWARE · VIRGINIA · Yorktown Oct 1781 · Jamestown Jul 1781 · NORTH CAROLINA · LOUISIANA to Spain 1763–1800 · INDIAN RESERVE · SOUTH CAROLINA · Camden Aug 1780 · GEORGIA · ATLANTIC OCEAN

1763–83: Florida under British rule · Gulf of Mexico

0 500km
0 500 mil

Key

- The Thirteen Colonies
- Western frontier of Thirteen Colonies by British proclamation of 1763
- Quebec under Quebec Act 1774
- — Other British possessions
- ······ Approximate frontiers 1775
- NEW YORK State of the new USA
- American victory
- British victory

« BEFORE

The North American British colonies entered into confrontation with the British government over taxation to finance defence and their right to run their own affairs.

COLONIAL DISCONTENT

The **French and Indian War of 1754–63** **« 170–71** led Britain to station an army in North America permanently, which the British government expected the colonists to pay for. But most resented the army presence and none wanted to pay taxes imposed by the British nor the customs duties to support it.

BADGE OF THE BRITISH 4TH REGIMENT, WHICH FOUGHT AT LEXINGTON

RETALIATION

Trouble flared up in Boston, Massachusetts, where British troops killed five people in suppressing a riot in 1770. The famous **"Boston Tea Party"** of 1773, a protest against customs duties, was a more thorough-going defiance of British authority. In 1774 **Massachusetts was placed under the military rule** of General Thomas Gage. The Massachusetts legislature refused to recognize his authority and the other colonies (initially excepting Georgia) rallied to its support, meeting in the **Continental Congress**. Radical "patriots" began attacks on pro-British Americans, and local militias prepared to resist the British soldiers.

their control. Keeping large numbers of soldiers supplied across the Atlantic was a formidable task. Moreover, Britain needed to reconcile the colonies to its rule, yet the conflict caused a bitterness that made this almost impossible.

The American political leaders in the Congress were more conservative than revolutionaries – lawyers and landowners predominated – and their views on the prosecution of war were conventional. In June 1775, they voted to form a Continental Army, recruited from all the colonies, to fight the war under George Washington. This was to be a traditional European-style army, which was to be disciplined and drilled into an efficient fighting machine. Washington, assisted from 1778 by his Prussian inspector-general, Baron Friedrich von Steuben, had a hard task creating and maintaining such a force. It was short of money and supplies and desertion was a constant problem. Yet in the end the army fought effectively.

French support
Congress took the decisive and irrevocable measure of declaring independence in July 1776; however, it was the British who went on the offensive. General William Howe seized New York after an amphibious landing and used it as a base from which to attack the rebel capital, Philadelphia, which he occupied in 1777. Meanwhile, after the repulse of an initial American attack on Canada, General John Burgoyne led a British army south from the Canadian border to the Hudson river. By October 1777, Burgoyne's force was surrounded at Saratoga and had to surrender.

The American victory at Saratoga was the turning point of the conflict; it persuaded France that the newly founded United States was worth

Lexington Green
On 19 April 1775, about 700 British Redcoats exchanged fire with a small body of local militiamen at the village of Lexington outside Boston. These were the opening shots of the American Revolution.

Washington at Valley Forge
The Continental Army underwent great hardship encamped at Valley Forge in the winter of 1777–78. Here, Washington rides past the Marquis de Lafayette, a French lord who served with the army as a volunteer.

backing. The French allied themselves with the Americans in February 1778 and went to war with the British the following June. By 1780 Britain was also at war with the Spanish and the Dutch. For the British, the conflict in North America was less important than the wider war with these European enemies, who threatened other more valuable British interests, including the colonies in the West Indies. British strength in North America declined, while a French army under the Comte de Rochambeau arrived in July 1780 to support Washington. Still, for a long time, it was unclear how the Americans could win control of the new country they had founded.

The rebels fight back
The Continental Army barely survived a gruelling winter camped at Valley Forge in 1777–78. Then the British used their naval power to spread the fighting to the south. Under their new commander-in-chief, General Sir Henry Clinton, they seized Charleston in South Carolina and Savannah in Georgia. This triggered a vicious war in the back country of the Carolinas – a virtual civil war between rebel and loyalist militias. American rebels such as South Carolina's militia leader, Francis Marion, and Continental Army general, Nathanael Greene, turned to guerrilla warfare, but the loyalists also practised irregular warfare ruthlessly and to good effect.

General Charles Cornwallis was the commander of British forces in the southern theatre. He scored a striking

David Bushnell's Turtle
The *Turtle*, propelled by hand, was the first submarine used in war. In 1776 it was used to attack a British ship in New York harbour.

victory over General Horatio Gates at Camden in South Carolina in August 1780 but was less successful in following battles. Cornwallis decided to end his campaign and marched north through North Carolina into Virginia.

In summer 1781, Cornwallis dug in to a position on Chesapeake Bay, where he could be supplied from the sea. But British command of the sea could no longer be relied upon in the face of a French Navy reinvigorated since the seaborne disasters during the Seven Years War. While Washington and Rochambeau brought their armies south to besiege Cornwallis's force on land, on 5 September, Admiral de Grasse defeated a British fleet off Chesapeake Bay. Trapped, heavily outnumbered, and without hope of relief, General Cornwallis surrendered his army at Yorktown on 19 October 1781.

AFTER

After the humiliation of the surrender at Yorktown, Britain gave up trying to win the war in North America, although peace was not signed for another two years.

BRITAIN STEPS BACK
The British **recognized the independence** of the United States in the Treaty of Paris (1783). A **naval victory over the French** in the West Indies in 1782 limited Britain's losses in the wider war, although **Florida**, held by Britain since 1763, was **returned to Spanish rule**.

100,000 The approximate number of North American loyalists who quit the United States during or after the war.

CONSTITUTIONAL LAWS
In the United States the role of armed citizens in the initial resistance to Britain ensured that a **right to bear arms would be written into the Constitution**. There was a fierce dispute in the post-independence period over whether the **US required a standing army**, but a small permanent force was maintained. **The US fought Britain again in the War of 1812 208–09 ≫**.

US GENERAL (1732–1799)
GEORGE WASHINGTON

A wealthy plantation owner, George Washington fought as an officer in the Virginia militia during the French and Indian War. As commander of the Continental Army throughout the Revolutionary War, he patiently husbanded his limited resources, aware that keeping the army in being was more important than controlling territory or winning battles. After the war he retired into private life, reluctantly emerging to become the first president of the USA in 1789.

BRITISH SURRENDER AT YORKTOWN
French and American troops (in yellow and blue respectively) guard the defeated British army at Yorktown, Virginia, on 21 October 1781. French ships fill the harbour. The surrender of over 8,000 British troops marked the end of the fighting in the American Revolutionary War. The two commanders, the British general Charles Cornwallis and the American general George Washington, conducted the surrender via their deputies.

The Wars of Catherine the Great

Catherine II – "the Great" – ruled Russia from 1762 to 1796, impressing the most advanced thinkers in Europe as an example of an "enlightened despot". Wars fought during this period substantially extended the territory of the Russian empire, mostly at the expense of the Turkish Ottoman empire and Poland.

EASTERN AND NORTHERN EUROPE

1 First Russo-Turkish War
Dates 1768–74
Location Ukraine, Moldavia, Aegean

2 Second Russo-Turkish War
Dates 1787–92
Location Ukraine, Moldavia, Black Sea

3 Russo-Swedish War
Dates 1788–90
Location Gulf of Finland

The strategic position of Russia at this time was uniquely favourable to an expansionist policy. Ottoman Turkey, standing in Russia's path to the south, was a once-great state in military and political decline. Its sultans had failed to modernize their armed forces and were also vulnerable to pressure from Christian subject nations within their borders. Russia coveted control of the Black Sea as an outlet into the Mediterranean, and could envisage even wider ambitions to liberate the Christians of the Balkans from Muslim rule, capturing Constantinople (Istanbul) and restoring the Byzantine empire. The Polish-Lithuanian Commonwealth, dominant in Central Europe as recently as the 17th century, had entered an even steeper decline than the Ottomans. All that stood in the way of a Russian takeover of Poland was the hostility of Prussia and Austria to a westward thrust of Russian territory and power.

While pursuing these territorial ambitions, Catherine's Russia had to keep a watchful eye on the balance of power in the Baltic region, where the dominance the Russians had gained through the Great Northern War was still open to challenge from Sweden. These areas of ambition and concern interacted, with the engagement of Russian forces in one zone presenting an opportunity for the country's enemies in another area to initiate combat.

partly on the optimistic predictions of court astrologers. The Russian army was, indeed, initially preoccupied with operations in Poland, but the Ottomans proved unable to take any advantage of this. Despite support from the French, the Confederation failed to oust the Polish king; its forces were worn down through campaigns in which Russian General Alexander Suvorov

Cock

Striking stee[l]

GRECKE

Trigger

Ivory stock

Trigger guard

Catherine's pistol
This ornate flintlock pistol was produced by St Petersburg gunmaker, John Adolph Grecke, for Empress Catherine the Great in 1786. Muskets with the same flintlock mechanism armed her infantry.

BEFORE

By the time Catherine II came to the throne in 1762, Russia had already grown into an impressive military power with a tradition of expansion through victory in warfare.

EARLY EXPANSIONISM
Peter the Great, who reigned from 1682 to 1725, transformed Russia from a backward state into a **dynamic power** with a modernized army and navy. Territorial expansionism led to conflict with the **Ottoman empire** when Peter seized the fortress of Azov in 1696. He ended Sweden's reign over the Baltic in the **Great Northern War** ≪ **158–59** in 1770, and reduced Poland to, in effect, a **dependency of Russia**.

CATHERINE THE GREAT

Under Empress Elizabeth, who reigned from 1741 to 1762, troops were sent as far west as the Rhine in the **War of the Austrian Succession** ≪ **162–63**. A Russian army briefly occupied the Prussian capital, Berlin during the **Seven Years War** ≪ **172–73**. Elizabeth's death in 1762 brought **Peter III** to power. He was **assassinated after six months** by a group of nobles who placed his wife, Catherine, on the throne.

The trigger for the first round of warfare was the revolt of the Bar Confederation in Poland in 1768. This group of Polish nobles rejected Russia's domination of their country, embodied in the occupant of the Polish throne, King Stanislaw August Poniatowski, former lover of Catherine the Great.

Crushing the Ottomans

The Polish uprising encouraged the Ottoman sultan, Mustafa III, to declare war on Russia, an unwise decision based

Siege of Ochakov

Catherine's favourite, Prince Potyomkin, failed to reduce the Turkish fortress of Ochakov by bombardment and blockade in the siege of 1787. It eventually fell to an assault by General Alexander Suvorov in 1789.

> "Deliver **heavy blows**, pass in masses through the gap, attack directly, **hit with speed**."
> GENERAL ALEXANDER SUVOROV, ORDERS TO HIS ARMY, 1790

made his reputation. Meanwhile, the Russians attacked the Ottomans by sea and land. They sent two squadrons of warships to the Mediterranean under the overall command of Count Alexei Orlov, brother of another of Catherine's lovers, Grigory Orlov. Count Orlov's mission was to stimulate the Greeks to revolt against Turkish rule. In this he failed, but the expedition did achieve the destruction of an entire Ottoman fleet at Chesma Bay off the island of Chios in July 1770.

Ottomans defeat on land

The Ottomans fared no better on land. In the same month, Russian general, Count Pyotr Rumyantsev, defeated Ottoman forces and their Crimean Tartar allies twice; first at the river Larga and then at Kagul. In both encounters

Meanwhile, Rumyantsev's boldness at Larga and Kagul appeared to have exhausted his energy and the war with the Ottomans stagnated. The transfer of Suvorov from Poland to the Turkish front in 1774 brought a renewal of the offensive spirit, however. A bold thrust into Bulgaria persuaded the Ottomans to make peace at Kuchuk Kainarji, with humiliating terms that not only gave Russia ports on the Black Sea and the right of passage into the Mediterranean, but also recognized Russia's legitimate interest in the fate of the Ottoman sultan's Christian subjects.

A decade of peace followed, during which Catherine and her favourite, Prince Potyomkin, hatched bold plans for the demise of the Ottoman empire. In 1783 Russia annexed the Crimean Khanate, until 1774 an Ottoman

Barrel   Fore sight

the 38,000-strong Russian army was outnumbered, but triumphed through aggression and speed of movement in the face of inert opponents.

By 1772 Poland had been pacified and the Bar rebels exiled. Russia, Prussia, and Austria took large slices of Polish territory in the First Partition of Poland. Russia was then shaken by an internal revolt, the Pugachev Uprising. In 1773 Emelyan Pugachev, with the support of Cossacks and rebellious peasants in the Volga region, declared himself tsar and proclaimed the liberation of the serfs. After scoring a number of successes against the government forces, Pugachev was eventually defeated at the battle of Kazan, taken prisoner, and executed.

possession, and set up a protectorate over Georgia in the Caucasus. Catherine then allied with the Austrian emperor, Joseph II, envisaging a joint attack on and partition of Ottoman territory. The Ottoman sultan Abdulhamid I responded to these provocations by declaring war on Russia in 1787.

A war on two fronts

The next year the war widened when Sweden's King Gustav III seized the opportunity offered by the Russo-Turkish War to attack Russia in the Baltic. This war on two fronts placed Catherine's forces under considerable strain. If Sweden had succeeded in achieving naval superiority in the Baltic, it could have attacked the Russian

capital, St Petersburg. A series of hard-fought naval engagements, contested by oared galleys in shallow coastal waters and sailing ships out to sea, frustrated Swedish efforts to land troops but ended with a costly Russian defeat at Svenskund. Both sides accepted a compromise peace in 1790. The Russo-Turkish War also had an important naval aspect, with a series of battles fought on the Black Sea. Many of the officers in Russia's navy were foreigners – they included American Revolutionary war hero John Paul Jones – but the Russians found their own inspired leader in Admiral Fyodor Ushakov, whose victories from Fidonisi in 1788 to Tendra in 1790 gave the Russians command of the sea.

518,000 The amount of territory, in square kilometres (200,000 square miles), added to the Russian empire during Catherine the Great's reign. This is an area that equates roughly to the size of France.

On land, campaigning on both sides was predominantly pedestrian, Suvorov providing the striking exception. When Russia besieged the Turkish fortress at Ochakov in 1788, their commander, Prince Potyomkin, settled for a sedate blockade, provoking Suvorov to make the comment: "You don't take a fortress by looking at it." Only after a six-month siege, during which the Russians lost many troops to disease, was Suvorov allowed to storm the fortress. He then defeated the Ottomans at Focsani in 1789 and, the year after, attacked the supposedly secure fortress of Izmail, which controlled the mouth of the river Danube. This victory ended the serious fighting of the Russo-Turkish War, but peace was not agreed until 1792.

The final campaigns in the reign of Catherine the Great were fought against the Poles. In 1792 and again in 1794,

Cossack cavalry

The fiercely independent Cossack settlers of the frontier areas of the Russian empire provided the Russian Army with excellent skirmishing light cavalry.

Russian armies crushed Polish resistance to impose two further – and final – partitions of the country. By 1795 Poland had ceased to exist as an independent entity, its territories having been absorbed into Russia, Austria, and Prussia.

AFTER

Catherine the Great died in 1796, having achieved a dominant position for Russia on the Black Sea with a western border that had advanced to what is now Belarus.

FIGHTING THE FRENCH
Under Catherine's successor, **Paul I**, Russia participated in the Second Coalition against France in the **French Revolutionary Wars 186–87 »** from 1798 to 1799, Suvorov scoring **notable victories** against the French in Italy. Under Paul's successor, **Alexander I**, Russia again fought France in the **Napoleonic Wars 194–95 »**. Russian forces were defeated by **Napoleon** from Austerlitz in 1805 to Friedland in 1807, but redeemed themselves in later campaigns that started with the repulse of a massive French invasion in 1812 and ended with Russian forces in occupation of Paris in 1814.

SETTLING OLD SCORES
Russian conflict with the **Ottomans** continued. There were other **Russo-Turkish Wars** – from 1806–12; from 1828–29 (an offshoot of the **Greek War of Independence 212–13 »**); and again from 1877–78. The **Crimean War 220–21 »** in the 1850s also originated as a Russo-Turkish war. The two empires last fought during **World War I**, when the Russian empire had the **annexation of Constantinople** as one of its secret war aims.

186–87 »; 194–95 »; 212–13 »; 220–21 »

MILITARY COMMANDER (1730–1800)

GENERAL SUVOROV

Russia's most admired military commander, General Alexander Suvorov joined the army at the age of 12. His campaigns against the Poles and Ottomans exhibited the principle of maximum application of force in pursuit of a decisive victory. He was exceptional among Russian officers in his rapport with the rank and file. In 1799 he led an army on a sweeping campaign against the French in Italy and Switzerland, but he died in St Petersburg the next year.

The King's Right Arm

In spring 1789, Count Gustav Wachtmeister, a Swedish army officer, was wounded in the arm by a musket ball while fighting the Russians at Valkeala in Finland. His tunic, preserved to this day with its torn sleeve, is a silent witness to an era when European monarchs fought one another for limited objectives in wars that cost lives and limbs, often to little discernible purpose.

The wounded aide-de-camp
King Gustav rides up to inquire after Wachtmeister. The aide-de-camp calmly leans his wounded arm on a rock as he explains to the king how he came to be shot.

Wachtmeister was an aristocrat, whose career depended as much upon his skills of a courtier as upon military prowess. He was born in 1757 and, as was common for sons of Swedish noble families, embarked on military life at a young age, receiving a commission as an ensign in 1772. Sweden was a country with a formidable military tradition, but it had declined into a second-rate power during the 18th century. Its army was a hybrid force, with a kernel of professional soldiers supported by a larger number of provincial reserves.

The king whom Wachtmeister served, Gustav III, was determined to reassert royal authority over parliament and suppress aristocratic privileges. His policies were resented by many of the Swedish aristocracy as an offence to their liberties. Wachtmeister kept

Positive propaganda
Swedish King Gustav III, here shown inviting an old soldier to join him sitting on a log, liked to be represented as a benign ruler and friend to the common man.

clear of the conspiracies that multiplied among his fellow officers. In 1778 he went abroad to gain experience on campaign, joining the Prussian army fighting Austria in the War of the Bavarian Succession in 1778–79.

Initiation in the arts of war
Instead of executing bold manoeuvres and fighting set-piece battles, the opposing armies devoted their energies to a desperate search for food that earned the conflict the nickname "the potato war". Returning to Sweden, Wachtmeister's career flourished. In the 1780s he had a posting as lieutenant-colonel commanding a battalion in the provincial Dalecarlia regiment, but he was also a court officer serving as aide-de-camp to Gustav III.

In 1788 Gustav declared war on Russia, cynically hoping to silence domestic opposition with a victorious campaign in Finland while the Russians were preoccupied with a war against the Turks. The encounter at Valkeala was hardly a major battle,

with around 3,000 troops on each side, but the Swedes had the better of it and Wachtmeister, with his wounded arm, was made the hero of the hour by a king desperate for good publicity. The war ended in 1790 with no gain for Sweden or Russia, but promotion to major-general for Wachtmeister.

In 1792 Gustav III was assassinated by a conspiracy of army officers at a masked ball at the Royal Opera House. His successor, Gustav IV Adolf, was as hostile to ideas of liberty as his father, but Wachtmeister suffered no interruption to his career.

Subsequent service
With the French Revolution and the rise of Napoleon, however, times were changing. Sweden's participation in a coalition against Napoleon in 1805, during which Wachtmeister fought in Pomerania, revealed how outdated the Swedish army had become. Gustav IV then found himself involved in another war with Russia. He was deposed in a

military coup in 1809 as a Russian army advanced into Sweden. The new king, Karl XIII, ordered Wachtmeister to land his troops behind Russian lines. Meeting the Russians at Sävar, his troops performed well, mounting a counterattack uphill into enemy fire, but Wachtmeister then withdrew to the coast, where his forces were sheltered by naval guns. Peace was made soon after. Wachtmeister was considered not to have acted with sufficient boldness and soon retired to his estates, a man whose time was past.

Russian flintlock
The standard weapon of 18th-century warfare in Europe, a flintlock rifle like this was probably responsible for wounding Wachtmeister at the battle of Valkeala.

"If you **follow me** … then I will **risk my life and blood** for you and the salvation of the fatherland!"

GUSTAV III, FACED BY AN ATTEMPTED COUP, 1772

Battle tunic

This is the tunic worn by Count Gustav Wachtmeister at the battle of Valkeala in Finland in 1789. Although wounded in the arm, Wachtmeister suffered no permanent disability and continued to serve in the Swedish army for another two decades.

The tunic sleeve was presumably cut by a surgeon preparing to remove the musket ball from Wachtmeister's arm after he was shot. The lining still bears faint traces of blood stains.

French Revolutionary Wars

The revolution that broke out in France in 1789 was progressively radicalized, leading to the declaration of a republic in 1792 and the subsequent execution of King Louis XVI. A mix of aggressive nationalism and revolutionary enthusiasm propelled the French into a series of wars against most of the rest of Europe.

WESTERN EUROPE

1 **War of the First Coalition**
Dates 1792–97
Location France's eastern borders

2 **War in the Vendée**
Dates 1793–96
Location Western France

« **BEFORE**

In the period leading up to the French Revolution, France made determined efforts to reform its armed forces and regain military ascendancy in Europe.

A NEW AGE OF WARFARE

The setbacks France experienced in the **Seven Years War** « 172–73 led to a drive for reform of the army and navy. Army officer Jean-Baptiste de Gribeauval was responsible for **a new artillery system**, with an improved range of standardized guns for aggressive deployment on the battlefield.

Another influential figure was the **Comte de Guibert**, who prophesied a new age of warfare in which **fast-moving armies** would seek to annihilate the enemy in decisive battles: "The hegemony over Europe," he wrote, "will fall to that nation which ... becomes possessed of manly virtues and creates a national army."

MILITARY ACADEMIES

Reformers such as Guibert and Gribeauval met resistance from the **French nobility**, however, who defended their monopoly of the higher officer ranks. New **military academies** were created for the sons of the poorer nobility – Napoleon Bonaparte was one beneficiary – but even they could mostly progress only in the artillery or engineers.

TRICORN, c.1790

NEW RECRUITS

After the **revolution of 1789**, large numbers of aristocratic officers emigrated – about 5,500 out of 9,500 by 1792. It was thus out of necessity as well as principle that the **officer corps** was opened to all classes in 1790, with **NCOs and junior officers** soon promoted to high rank. New infantry regulations adopted in 1791 embraced Guibert's theories on **aggressive tactics and strategy**.

The French declaration of war on Austria that came in April 1792 was motivated by little more than a desire to maintain popular enthusiasm for the revolution. It took little account of the state of the French army, which since 1789 had lost the majority of its officers as well as many regular soldiers. An appeal for volunteers partly made up the numbers of infantry, but there was almost no cavalry and the supply system was in chaos. An initial French advance into the Austrian Netherlands (now Belgium) was a fiasco, with most of the volunteers fleeing the moment they came under fire. Undaunted by this, the revolutionary government declared war on Prussia that summer.

Initial victories for France

The Austrians and Prussians were preoccupied with Poland, which they were preparing to partition with Russia. Despite a bold declaration of support for Louis XVI in 1791, they had little interest in restoring his monarchical powers. But a prostrate France was a tempting target and, after lengthy preparations, an army led by Duke Ferdinand of Brunswick crossed the French frontier in August 1792. It advanced as far as Valmy, where on 20 September the artillery of the old French royal army put up stiff enough resistance to persuade Brunswick to withdraw. The elated French army now returned to the offensive, again invading the Austrian Netherlands and defeating a smaller Austrian force at Jemappes.

Despite these victories, France plunged deeper into political and military crisis. It increased its number of enemies by declaring war on the Dutch, British, and Spanish in 1793. The introduction of conscription in February sparked uprisings in parts of the country that were already alienated by revolutionary policies, notably the Vendée. Royalists handed the naval port of Toulon to the British and a French army was driven out of the Austrian Netherlands by the Austrians – its commander, General Charles Dumouriez, defecting to the

other side. The French revolutionary government responded to this boldly. Lazare Carnot, a military engineer, became Minister of War in August 1793. He oversaw the *levée en masse*, not only an extension of conscription to all men aged 18 to 25, but a general mobilization of the masses in aid of the war effort.

Turning the tide of war

Carnot ensured that all new conscripts were integrated with the regular army and that arms supplies were expanded to equip them. Talented and aggressive

" **Every citizen must be a soldier and every soldier a citizen.** "

REPORT TO THE FRENCH CONSTITUENT ASSEMBLY, DECEMBER 1789

War in the Vendée
The rag-tag army of royalist rebels in the Vendée region of France flees government troops at Cholet in October 1793. The pacification of the Vendée was utterly ruthless, with mass killing of women and children.

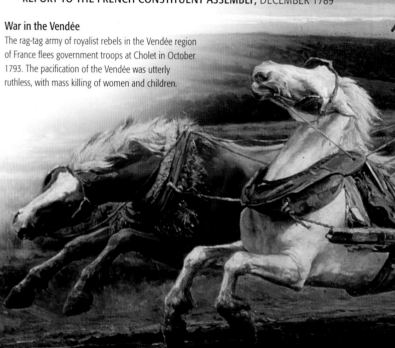

French cavalry sword

This long-bladed thrusting sword equipped French heavy cavalry from 1794. The cavalry was the part of the army worst hit by the revolution, which left it short of both horses and experienced riders.

young soldiers won rapid promotion; for instance, Louis Hoche, a corporal in 1789, was a general by autumn 1793. Life for senior officers was precarious; the revolutionary government ruled by terror, and a general could easily lose his head to the guillotine for political or military failings. But a combination of bold, ambitious commanders and armies swollen with fresh conscripts turned the tide of the war.

In the second half of 1793, Toulon was retaken – partly through the efforts of artillery captain Napoleon Bonaparte – and the Vendée was retaken, although the ruthless "pacification" of rebel areas would take another three years. The French Army of the North defeated the British and Austrians at Tourcoing in May 1794, and General Jean-Baptiste Jourdan's Army of the Sambre-Meuse defeated the Austrians at the battle of Fleurus in June, finally driving France's foes out of the Austrian Netherlands. (Incidentally, this battle marked the first military use of aviation in the form of an observation balloon.)

84
French generals were executed in 1793–94 when the reign of terror in France was at its peak. Deputies were sent by the revolutionary government to keep watch on all officers on campaign.

By 1795 the French had annexed the Austrian Netherlands, occupied the Rhineland, turned the Dutch Netherlands into the satellite Batavian Republic, and made peace with Prussia and Spain. There was no longer any military threat to France and the revolution had passed its virulent phase, with the end of the terror and the installation of the more moderate government of the Directory.

The glory of war

The French lost none of their lust for war, however, which had turned into a self-sustaining system. In response to supply problems, as well as Guibert's theories of mobile warfare, their armies had taken to living off the land. As long as they campaigned on foreign territory, they cost little to maintain and brought in great wealth through plundering conquered lands. As well as exporting revolutionary principles, successful warfare brought glory to the regime, satisfied ambitious officers, and kept soldiers paid and fed. In 1796 the French embarked on fresh campaigns against Austria, giving Napoleon Bonaparte the chance to show his military genius and begin the transition from the Revolutionary to the Napoleonic Wars.

Napoleon's campaigns in Italy in 1796–97 brought the first phase of the Revolutionary Wars to a close, but left France still at war with Great Britain.

CONQUERING MAINLAND EUROPE

In 1796 French armies advanced against Austria on the Rhine and in northern Italy, where they won a string of victories against the **Austrians and their Sardinian allies 188–89 »**. The following year Austria was forced to **make peace** on French terms, leaving France temporarily at peace on the European continent.

WAR WITH BRITAIN

Britain remained at war with France, defeating the Spanish (now allied with the French) in **a naval battle at Cape St Vincent 190–91 »**, in February 1797. France had failed to land an army under General Hoche in Ireland in December 1796, but supported the **United Irishmen uprising** in 1798. The French were only able to land a small force in County Mayo, however, and could not prevent the British from **crushing the Irish rebellion**.

BEFORE

The French Revolutionary Wars gave eager young troops an unparalleled opportunity to rise to high command. None was more ambitious and talented than Napoleon.

THE SIEGE OF TOULON

Born in Corsica in 1769, Napoleon Bonaparte was sent to military college and then **entered the artillery**, where promotion was less dependent on high birth. During the **French Revolutionary Wars ≪ 186–87**, he marked himself out at the **siege of Toulon** in 1793, **earning promotion** to brigadier-general at the age of 24.

RISING UP IN THE RANKS

In 1795, when the **Directory government was threatened by a coup**, Napoleon led loyalist forces in Paris and was rewarded by promotion to full general. In 1796 France launched an **assault against Austria** on two fronts – on the river Rhine and in northern Italy, where the Austrians fought in alliance with the Piedmontese Kingdom of Sardinia. As a result, Napoleon was given **command of the Army of Italy**.

The **Rise** of Napoleon

Between 1796 and 1800 Napoleon Bonaparte led two invasions of Italy and a spectacular expedition to Egypt. A continuation of the French Revolutionary Wars, these campaigns made him a hero to the French army and people, and cleared the way for his rise to absolute political power in France.

When Napoleon Bonaparte took command of the soldiers of the French Army of Italy in spring 1796, they were short of pay, food, boots, and muskets. Napoleon's solution was to supply the needs of his army by defeating the enemy and living off occupied territory. He faced Austrian and Sardinian armies (the Kingdom of Sardinia included Piedmont in Italy's north) that together outnumbered his forces. By attacking them separately, however, he swiftly drove Sardinia out of the war and forced the Austrians to retreat, allowing the French to occupy Milan. Throughout the rest of the year Napoleon fought a series of campaigns against Austrian counter-offensives that showed his skill at concentrating his forces at the point of combat. A decisive victory at the battle of Rivoli, in January 1797, further highlighted his tactical skill and paved the way for the Army of Italy to threaten an attack over the Alps into the south of Austria. Austria had won

various battles in the south of Germany in 1796 but now, rapidly losing their nerve, the Austrians sought an armistice. The action in Italy brought rich plunder for the Republic and glory for Napoleon, who was presented in popular prints as a romantic figure leading his soldiers from the front.

Cairo taken

The peace with Austria meant Napoleon was briefly unoccupied. Though France was still at war with Britain, an invasion across the English Channel was rejected as unfeasible, given the strength of the Royal Navy. Instead, a plan was hatched for a military expedition to Egypt. The motives for this were never entirely clear. Egypt was officially a province of the Ottoman empire, though in effect ruled by the Mamelukes, descendants of Turkish slave soldiers. If Egypt fell into French hands, it might give France

Austrian musket

In 1798 Austria introduced a new flintlock musket to match the latest French model. The basic flintlock design did not change from the 17th to the 19th century, but improvements were made in reliability and rate of fire.

Flint

MEDITERRANEAN

1 Italian campaigns
Dates 1796–1800
Location Northern and central Italy

2 Egyptian campaign
Dates 1798–1801
Location Egypt and Palestine

control of the eastern Mediterranean and even threaten British interests in India. The project pleased the leaders of the Directory because it would take a dangerously popular general and political rival away from Paris.

Sailing from Toulon in May 1798, the French Army of the Orient had the good fortune to evade Admiral Horatio Nelson's British Mediterranean fleet, landing in Egypt in July. At the battle of the Pyramids the charges of the armoured Mameluke cavalry proved powerless against French infantry squares and Napoleon was able to occupy Cairo. However, this success was immediately negated by Admiral Nelson's destruction of the French fleet in Aboukir Bay at the battle of the Nile.

The French are routed

With his communications cut and the Ottoman sultan declaring war, Napoleon's long-term prospects were poor. He took the offensive nevertheless, heading north over Palestine to Acre in spring 1799. Ably defended by Ottoman

29

French soldiers were killed at the battle of the Pyramids in 1798, under attack from 6,000 Mameluke cavalry. The Mamelukes lost around one-third of their mounted troops.

troops and British naval gunners, Acre resisted a series of attacks by Napoleon, until he retreated to Egypt with his army struck down by plague. The Ottomans took the offensive, landing at Aboukir Bay in July. The French advanced from Cairo and, though inferior in number, drove the Turks back with aggressive tactics. By August 1799, however, France's successes in Egypt were overshadowed by defeats in Europe. France faced a new coalition of hostile states, which this time included Russia as well as Austria and Britain. The Russian general, Alexander Suvorov, routed French armies in a series of victories in Italy ending at Novi in August, while Archduke Charles of Austria drove the French back over the Rhine. Napoleon returned to France to play his part in the political and military crisis. At Christmas, in a military coup, he took power as First Consul.

By then France's military prospects had revived. After the failure of an Anglo-Russian invasion of France's ally, the Batavian Republic (the Netherlands),

Battle of Marengo

The meeting between the Austrians and French in northern Italy on 14 June 1800 was close-fought. This painting by Louis Lejeune, who fought in the battle and who appears on horseback, depicts the surrender of Austrian soldiers.

and a shattering loss in Switzerland for Russian forces – which obliged Suvorov to stage a desperate winter retreat across the Alps – Tsar Paul I pulled his country out of the war. Austria was left to fight Napoleon's French armies alone.

In May 1800, Napoleon took a force through the Alps from Switzerland and descended into Italy behind Austrian General Michael von Melas, who was besieging Genoa. The Austrians turned and attacked Napoleon at the battle of Marengo in northern Italy, on 14 June. Napoleon had unwisely divided his army and was almost overwhelmed by superior numbers before General Louis Desaix, marching to the sound of the guns, brought back a division to support him. Desaix was killed, but a cavalry charge commanded by François

Kellermann won the battle for France. Another notable French triumph was won by Jean-Victor Moreau's Army of the Rhine at Hohenlinden in southern Germany, on 3 December 1800. This decisive victory concluded the war. Austria, now threatened from the west as well as from Italy in the south, made peace in February 1801. A war-weary Britain eventually followed suit, signing the Treaty of Amiens in March 1802.

AFTER

The French army left in Egypt by Napoleon was defeated by Britain in 1801. Muhammad Ali, an officer in the Ottoman forces, set himself up as Egypt's governor in 1805.

EGYPTIAN POWER

Muhammad Ali crushed the Mamelukes and embarked on a modernization drive that made Egypt the most **progressive economic and military power** in the Muslim world. Meanwhile, the work of the scholars and scientists whom Napoleon had brought with him on his expedition gave a boost to **Egyptology**. The Rosetta Stone, the key to reading **ancient Egyptian hieroglyphics**, was discovered in 1799 by a French army engineer, Captain Pierre-François Bouchard.

THE ROSETTA STONE

ITALY UNDER NAPOLEON

Meanwhile, the western half of northern and central Italy was absorbed by France, while in the eastern half **an Italian Republic was formed** in 1802, with Napoleon as its president. After he was crowned Emperor of the French in 1804, Napoleon was also proclaimed **King of Italy** and Italian troops served in many of his armies. The Kingdom of Italy lasted until 1814.

Forward sling swivel

Battle of Aboukir

The French attack the Ottoman army in its prepared defensive positions on Egypt's Mediterranean coast in 1799. In a one-sided battle several thousand Ottomans were killed.

Triumph of the Royal Navy

From Britain's entry into the French Revolutionary Wars in 1793 to the end of the Napoleonic Wars in 1815, the Royal Navy achieved and maintained command of the seas through victory in major fleet battles and a gruelling commitment to the blockade of hostile ports, while defending merchant shipping.

The French Revolution had a disastrous impact on France's navy. By 1793 it had lost most of its experienced officers and had fallen into a state of indiscipline and demoralization. The French Navy was also at an extreme numerical disadvantage, since its enemies in the early stages of the war included not only Britain – which itself had 115 ships of the line to France's 76 – but also the Dutch United Provinces and Spain, both significant naval powers. The French suffered substantial losses of warships during a British occupation of the Mediterranean naval base, Toulon, in August 1793. They also suffered losses during the Glorious First of June, in 1794. Admiral Vilaret de Joyeuse succeeded in defending a crucial grain convoy, but went on to lose seven ships of the line.

23 MILLION Britain's annual naval budget in 1815 in pounds sterling. The British naval budget had stood at £2.4 million in 1793, so this represents an almost tenfold increase in funds.

Mounting pressure

By 1796, however, the Spanish and the Dutch had allied with France and the Royal Navy was coming under severe pressure. It was not able to prevent French general General Hoche sailing troops over to Ireland that December, although they failed to land. French privateers and frigates had begun to take their toll on merchant shipping – 11,000 British merchant ships were lost to enemy action between 1793 and 1815.

Under the strain of prolonged war, seamen pressed into the Royal Navy rebelled against their harsh conditions of service, staging mutinies at Spithead and the Nore in the spring of 1797. With a mixture of stern punishments and placating concessions, the crisis

Boarding encounters

Many battles were fought between single ships; the exchange of broadsides was often followed by boarding and hand-to-hand fighting. Here the British frigate *Ambush* and the French corvette *La Bayonnaise* engage in 1798.

was overcome, however. Britain won victories over the Spanish at Cape St Vincent in February 1797 and the Dutch at Camperdown the following October. Admiral John Jervis, the victor at Cape St Vincent, was the major influence in a restoration of discipline and improved standards among naval commanders.

Horatio Nelson emerged as a British national hero with his stunning victory at the battle of the Nile in 1798. Having failed to prevent Napoleon landing an army in Egypt, Nelson led his 14 ships of the line into Aboukir Bay, where the French fleet was at anchor. He destroyed or captured 11 enemy ships of the line plus two frigates. Nelson reinforced his reputation for boldness at Copenhagen in 1801. A British fleet was sent to pressure Denmark into quitting a league of Armed Neutrality, led by Russia, which threatened to deny Britain access to vital naval supplies

British cutlass

A short-bladed sword, ideal for use in combat at close-quarters in the restricted space of a ship's deck. Sailors used them to support musket-armed marines in boarding encounters.

BEFORE

For Britain, the Royal Navy was the key to national defence and to prosperity as a commercial and colonial power. Only France posed any challenge to its naval superiority.

THE THREAT OF FRANCE

Britain humiliated France during the **Seven Years War ≪ 172–73**, but a **rebuilding programme** masterminded by the Duc de Choiseul made the French Navy a **far better match** for the British during the **American Revolution ≪ 178–79**. Although the French generally had ships that were better designed than the British, the Royal Navy remained **superior in gunnery**.

BATTLE TACTICS

Fleet actions in the 18th century were fought by two- or three-deck ships of the line, exchanging broadsides and closed to board. **Fast-sailing frigates** acted as scouts and commerce raiders. Innovations in the late-18th century included the **British carronades** – powerful and lightweight short-range, upper-deck guns – and **copper sheathing hulls**, which allowed ships to stay at sea for longer periods of time.

CARRONADE

Key

- French territory ruled directly from France 1812
- Dependent states 1812
- Britain
- Territory occupied by Britain 1812
- Frontiers 1812
- British naval blockade
- Territories refusing to trade with Britain under Continental System
- Movement of British fleet
- Movement of French fleet
- British victory
- British defeat

British strategy

The main French naval bases at Brest, Rochefort, and Toulon were kept under constant blockade by the Royal Navy. Copenhagen was strategically vital to the British as it controlled trade with the Baltic, which was a source of essential naval supplies.

1809: Walcheren expedition. British make disastrous attempt to invade continental Europe

Camperdown 1797 British defeat Dutch

1798: French invasion force defeated at Killala Bay

1796: Unsuccessful French invasion attempt at Bantry Bay

NORWAY
Stockholm
North Sea
SWEDEN
DENMARK
Dublin
ATLANTIC OCEAN
BRITAIN
Copenhagen 1801, 1807
Glorious First of June 1794
Bristol London
Hamburg
Portsmouth
PRUSSIA
RUSSIAN EMPIRE
Brest Boulogne
Berlin
Warsaw
Lorient
Brussels
Paris
GRAND DUCHY OF WARSAW
Bay of Biscay
Basque Roads 1809
CONFEDERATION OF THE RHINE
FRANCE
Ferrol
Rochefort
HELVETIA
Vienna
HABSBURG EMPIRE
PORTUGAL
KINGDOM OF ITALY
Marseille
Genoa
Black Sea
Lisbon
Madrid
SPAIN
Toulon
Rome
Cape St Vincent 1797
Barcelona
Iles d'Hyères 1795
Corsica
Naples
OTTOMAN EMPIRE
Constantinople
Seville
Balearic Is.
Minorca 1798–1800 to Britain
KINGDOM OF SARDINIA
Cádiz
Gibraltar to Britain
KINGDOM OF NAPLES
Trafalgar 1805
Algeciras Bay 1801
Palermo
Mediterranean Sea
MOROCCO
ALGIERS
Tunis
KINGDOM OF SICILY
Malta
Crete
Cyprus
Jun 1798: occupied by Napoleon. Sep 1800: retaken by British
AFRICA
Jun 1798 Battle of the Nile 1798
Alexandria
EGYPT
Cairo

0   500km
0   500 miles

Britain emerged from the Napoleonic Wars as the world's uncontested naval power, a position underpinned by its industrial, commercial, and financial strength.

BRITAIN'S TERRITORIAL GAINS
British **command of the sea** brought far-flung territorial gains in the peace settlement at the end of the war, ranging from **Malta** in the Mediterranean, to **Cape Town** at the southern tip of Africa, to **Tobago** in the West Indies, and **Mauritius** in the Indian Ocean.

A MUCH-REDUCED FORCE
After the war, the Royal Navy was shrunk by **an economy drive**, falling from a total of over 700 to around 120 warships. But **no other navy** compared with even this much-reduced force. The US Navy performed well during the **War of 1812 208–09 »**, but was a minnow compared to the Royal Navy. France remained the world's **second largest naval power**, but had neither the will nor the resources to tackle Britain at sea.

A NEW ERA LOOMS
The 19th century brought major technological changes. **Steam-driven ironclads** supplanted wooden sailing ships and **explosive shells** began to replace solid shot. But British naval dominance was not seriously contested until the rise of **American, Japanese, and German** naval power in the late 19th and early 20th centuries.

HORATIO NELSON

Horatio Nelson began his naval career aged 12 and rose to the rank of admiral in 1797. Always exposing himself to danger, the Admiral lost an arm and the sight of an eye in combat during the 1790s. Resistant to discipline and a bold risk taker, he liked to break up the enemy line to create a "pell-mell" battle, as in his victories at the Nile and Trafalgar. He was shot dead at Trafalgar by a sniper while standing on the deck of HMS *Victory*.

---

from the Baltic. Nelson sailed into Copenhagen harbour and, ignoring an order to withdraw, battered the Danish fleet and bombarded the city.

The British mainland under threat
Nelson's final triumph over a combined French and Spanish fleet at Trafalgar in October 1805 was decisive. Napoleon planned to invade Britain, but needed temporary naval superiority in the Channel in order to ferry his army safely across from Boulogne to southern England. Admiral Villeneuve, commander of the French Mediterranean squadron, needed to join up with their Atlantic squadron, then under British blockade in Brest. Together with their Spanish allies, the French would then have the concentration of naval strength required. Villeneuve succeeded in luring Nelson into a pursuit to the West Indies, then dashed back across the Atlantic. But instead of freeing the Brest fleet from blockade, he joined the Spanish in Cádiz. Nelson's victory at Trafalgar did

not avert the French invasion of Britain – Napoleon had already abandoned the project, as he needed to fight the Austrians and Russians. But Trafalgar did ensure that there would be no further attempt to organize a cross-Channel invasion.

Britain retains naval superiority
Napoleon never lost hope of overcoming British naval superiority, pumping vast resources into shipbuilding right up to the end of the conflict. The long war continued to demand an exceptional effort from the Royal Navy. In 1807, the British had to take prompt action against Denmark, attacking Copenhagen for a second time, in order to stop the substantial Danish fleet fighting as an ally of France. The policy of keeping a permanent, close blockade of French

ports placed a heavy burden on men and resources. The Royal Navy's insatiable manpower requirements led to abuse of the press-gang system – a form of selective conscription – and to enlisting too many landsmen, often from jails and courthouses. On the other hand, by giving constant exercise at sea to British crews and denying the same to French crews bottled up in port, the policy increased the gap in teamwork and skills between the two navies.

The overall impact of sea power on the course of the war was significant but limited. Naval superiority kept Britain safe from invasion and broadly secured its trade routes. It also allowed Britain to sustain an army in Portugal and Spain during the Peninsular War of 1808-14. However, the amphibious operations on mainland Europe, most notably the landings at Walcheren in the Netherlands in 1809, were not a success. Ultimately, Napoleon had to be beaten on land.

> "We have only one great object in view, that of **annihilating** our enemies."
>
> HORATIO NELSON, DISPATCH BEFORE TRAFALGAR, 9 OCTOBER 1805

Trafalgar

The largest sea battle of the Napoleonic Wars, Trafalgar confirmed Britain as the world's supreme naval power and Admiral Horatio Nelson as the foremost naval commander in the age of sail. Despite the scale of the eventual British victory over a combined French and Spanish fleet, this was a desperately hard-fought battle and Nelson's high-risk tactics could easily have gone awry.

The combined Franco-Spanish fleet had ended up under blockade in Cádiz, in southwest Spain, after a failed attempt to organize naval cover for a French invasion of England. Admiral Pierre-Charles Villeneuve led 33 ships of the line out of port on 19 October 1805 and sailed towards Gibraltar. Nelson's blockade force was on paper inferior – he had 27 ships of the line when battle was joined – but he saw this as an opportunity to deliver a mortal blow to the seapower of Britain's enemies.

The British attacked on the morning of 21 October, when the two fleets were off Cape Trafalgar, south of Cádiz. Nelson arranged his ships in two columns sailing at right-angles to the Franco-Spanish line, which was conventionally organized into vanguard or van (front), centre, and rear squadrons. Nelson planned for his columns to break through the enemy line in the centre and rear, creating a "pell-mell" (disordered) fight in which his superior gunnery would prevail. The enemy van would find itself left out of the battle until later as Nelson feigned to head towards the van, but checked back to attack the centre. The drawback of Nelson's scheme was that his fleet had to make their approach with the forward part of their ships (their prows) exposed to enemy broadsides, the simultaneous firing of all guns on one side of a ship. As his ships could not return fire across the bow or stern of the enemy, this meant that Nelson's fleet would come under fire without being able to defend itself.

Breaking the line

With only a light wind the approach was agonizingly slow. Nelson led one column on board HMS *Victory*, Admiral Collingwood the other on HMS *Royal Sovereign*. Both succeeded in sailing through the Franco-Spanish line, raking (firing through the length of the enemy's ships with broadsides) as they went. The battle resolved, as was Nelson's intention, into a series of close-quarters engagements in which British broadsides prevailed over an enemy who fought with the utmost courage and determination. The exception was the Franco-Spanish van, which was slow to beat back against the wind towards the fighting and then unaccountably failed to fully engage the British fleet.

Early in the afternoon Nelson was shot by a marksman in the rigging of the French ship *Redoutable*. He died three hours later. By the evening 17 Franco-Spanish ships had been captured; one had exploded and sunk. Half of the British ships were badly damaged but none had been lost.

LOCATION
Off Cape Trafalgar, south of Cadiz, Spain

DATE
21 October 1805

FORCES
British: 27 ships of the line; French and Spanish: 33 ships of the line

CASUALTIES
British: 449 killed; French and Spanish: 4,408 killed

KEY
- British ship of the line
- French ship of the line
- Spanish ship of the line
- Flagship

Napoleon's Imperial Triumphs in Europe

NAPOLEON'S BATTLE FORCE
Land warfare in Europe ended with the **Treaty of Lunéville**, signed by France and Austria in 1801. Britain was a more tenacious enemy of France, peace between the two only lasting from March 1802 to May 1803. But the British Army was too weak to seriously challenge the French on the European mainland, while the **French could not attack Britain without at least temporary command of the sea ‹‹ 190–91**. Nonetheless, having crowned himself emperor in December 1804, Napoleon had his Grande Armée camped at Boulogne ready for a cross-Channel invasion. It was a formidable force, its numbers swelled by **annual conscription** and its conscripts highly trained, with experienced commanders bearing the newly created rank of marshal.

Between 1805 and 1809 Napoleon defeated Austria, Prussia, and Russia in a series of campaigns that amply demonstrated his mastery of offensive warfare. Bringing the enemy to battle on his own terms, he deployed artillery, heavy cavalry, and infantry columns aggressively on the field in search of victory.

In August 1805, Austria joined Russia and the lesser powers of Sweden and Naples in an anti-French coalition financed by Britain. Emperor Napoleon thus abandoned his plans for a British invasion, instead marching his Grande Armée from Boulogne across Germany to strike at Austria. His aim was to defeat the Austrians before they could combine with the Russian army under General Kutuzov, which was advancing west to join its ally. Napoleon's Grande Armée numbered almost 200,000 troops, and was organized into seven all-arms corps, each capable of independent manoeuvre under the orders of one of the emperor's marshals. The rapid movement this vast army achieved was peerless, a result of forced marches, self-sufficiency without the encumbrance of a supply train, and skilful organization by the general staff. The Austrian General Mack, who had crossed Bavaria to Ulm, was encircled by the French sweeping around to the east and surrendered a 25,000-strong force without a major battle. In November Napoleon occupied Vienna, 11 weeks after leaving Boulogne.

The unstoppable army
But as the emperor pursued the enemy eastward, the Grande Armée's position became increasingly precarious. Living off the land was hard on the troops and their horses in winter. The Austrian and Russian armies had combined and more

Triumphant campaigns

Between 1796 and 1809 Napoleon repeatedly defeated his three major enemies in Europe: the Habsburg Austrian empire, Prussia, and the Russian empire.

Napoleon at Eylau
Napoleon as a compassionate leader visiting the wounded after the hard-fought winter battle at Eylau, in February 1807. The assault, lasting for an exhausting 14 hours, did not see a decisive result.

away when the emperor attacked in October. The Grande Armée's capacity to fight independently was shown at the simultaneous battles of Jena and Auerstädt. With both sides unsure of their enemy's dispositions, Napoleon sent most of his army – almost 100,000 men – to fight a small Prussian force at Jena, while Marshal Davout's corps of 26,000 confronted the 64,000-strong principal Prussian army at Auerstädt, and Marshal Bernadotte's soldiers hovered unused between the two. Despite his numerical inferiority, Davout drove the Prussian army from the field. Pursued by French cavalry, they dissolved in a general rout and Napoleon occupied Berlin.

The cost of war

The Russians and winter weather were Napoleon's enemies. Dispersal enabled his army to survive the winter in Poland, but at Eylau, in February 1807, the men were required to focus for a battle with Russia and Prussia. This was a savage clash in a snowstorm with both sides calling up reinforcements. The day was won by a French cavalry charge, 10,000 strong, which crushed the Russian infantry and overran their cannon. With the French suffering some 25,000 casualties, Eylau was far from a decisive victory. However, after their defeat at Friedland in the

Austrian forces were arriving. Napoleon gambled on bringing his enemies to battle quickly and deciding the war with a single crushing victory. On 2 December at Austerlitz this was achieved – despite Emperor Francis of Austria and Tsar Alexander of Russia combining their armies. Their generals taking the offensive, Napoleon defeated them in a desperately contested battle, holding their initial attack and then delivering counterblows. After this loss the Austrians sued for peace, while the Russians withdrew into Poland.

Throughout this campaign Prussia had remained on the sidelines, unsure where its advantage lay. With Austria defeated, the Prussians went to war with France in 1806. Prussia's army, once the envy of Europe, was no longer a match for the French. Prussia had Russia as an ally, but the Russian armies were far

3,926,000 The number of muskets and other small arms manufactured in France during the period of Napoleon's empire, 1804–14.

summer, the Russians were forced to make peace at Tilsit. Two years of battle had given him mastery of Europe.

In 1809 the Austrians tried to throw off this domination by declaring war on the French again. With Prussia failing to assist and Russia hostile, Austria had little hope. But at Aspern-Essling in May, Archduke Charles inflicted a rare reverse upon Napoleon, catching his army halfway through a river crossing and forcing him to abandon the bridgehead. At Wagram in July, Napoleon got revenge but not without heavy losses. Austria sought an armistice. For Napoleon the price paid for European control was rising.

Key

- France 1797
- Under French control by 1805
- Members of the Third Coalition 1805–07
- Frontiers 1797
- Napoleon's campaign of 1805–07
- French victory

French 12-pounder cannon
Napoleon's favourite field artillery weapon was the 12-pounder, first introduced before the French Revolution by Gribeauval. Originally an artillery officer, Napoleon held that: "It is with artillery alone that battles are won."

AFTER

Napoleon never succeeded in stabilizing his command of Europe, partly because Britain remained at war, but also because his policies bred opposition and resistance.

QUEST FOR DOMINANCE

Napoleonic France had absorbed the southern Netherlands, the west bank of the Rhine, and a large part of Italy into its territory. Napoleon also created **client states** that were under French control. He placed family members on thrones and made a marriage alliance by wedding Marie Louise of Austria. His Marshal of France, Jean-Baptiste Jules Bernadotte, became crown prince of Sweden in 1810.

From 1806 the emperor installed the **Continental System** to destroy British commerce, banning all trade between Europe and Britain. In Spain **the Peninsular War** raged from 1808 **198–99 ≫**.

MARSHAL BERNADOTTE

From 1807 France's army underwent changes that lessened its fighting efficiency. Conscripts no longer had proper training, and a decreasing percentage of its troops were ethnic French.

The Peninsular War

Although a sideshow in the overall context of the Napoleonic Wars, the Peninsular War of 1808–14 contributed substantially to Napoleon's downfall. For the Spanish and Portuguese, it was a struggle for freedom. For the British, it was a chance to mount a sustained campaign on mainland Europe.

SOUTHWEST EUROPE

Peninsular War
Dates 1808–14
Location Spain and Portugal, later southern France

BRITISH GENERAL (1769–1852)

THE DUKE OF WELLINGTON

Irish-born Arthur Wellesley, later the Duke of Wellington, first distinguished himself fighting the Kingdom of Mysore and the Marathas (people from Maharashtra state) in India. His success in the Peninsular War made him a British national hero, a status enhanced by his leading role in the defeat of Napoleon at Waterloo in 1815. Usually a cautious general, he was also capable of bold attacking strokes, as at Salamanca in 1812. He was never careless of his men's lives and took only necessary risks.

« BEFORE

The Peninsular War was a result of Napoleon's interference in Iberia, with an initial French invasion of Portugal followed by an attempt to grab the Spanish throne.

SPAIN AT NAPOLEON'S MERCY

In 1804 the Spanish Bourbon monarchy allied itself with France against the British. Two years later Napoleon initiated his **Continental System**, placing an embargo on all trade between Europe and Britain. To **enforce this blockade**, a French army, helped by the Spanish, **occupied Portugal** in 1807, obliging the Portuguese royal family to flee to Brazil. The presence of French forces in the Iberian peninsula left **Spain at France's mercy**. By May 1808, French soldiers had seized control of key Spanish fortresses and occupied Madrid. Napoleon bullied the Bourbons into abdicating, but his attempt to **place his brother, Joseph, on the Spanish throne** provoked an uprising.

On 2 May 1808, the population of Madrid rebelled against the French garrison occupying their city. The uprising in the Spanish capital was swiftly and brutally suppressed, but the insurrection spread across Spain as provincial councils organized military resistance. In mid-July a 20,000-strong French army corps surrendered after being encircled by forces of the Spanish regular army at the battle of Bailen.

Meanwhile, Britain landed an army under Arthur Wellesley in Portugal and defeated Marshal Junot's French forces at Vimeiro. Junot was isolated by the uprising in Spain, and felt his situation was untenable. He sought an accord with more senior British generals who had replaced Wellesley for the time being. Junot's army was generously but foolishly repatriated to France, with its arms and booty, on board British ships.

Napoleon responded to these setbacks with customary vigour. He led a large army into Spain, scattered the Spanish armies, retook Madrid, and turned upon

340,000 The number of French soldiers fighting the Peninsular War in August 1810. In the same period the British Army in Portugal numbered 30,000 men.

a British column under Sir John Moore that had advanced from Portugal but was now forced to flee towards the northern Spanish coast – the survivors were evacuated by the Royal Navy from La Coruña in January 1809. By then the emperor's lightning intervention in Spain was at an end. Napoleon left the Iberian peninsula for Germany, where Austria was presenting a fresh challenge to his dominance of the continent. He was never to return.

Allied counterattacks

The prospect of a swift French victory in the peninsula soon evaporated. The Spanish army sustained a stubborn resistance, while a British army – again under Wellesley, with Portuguese troops in support – denied the French control of Portugal. A combined push towards Madrid by the British and Spanish in the summer of 1809 resulted in a costly victory over the French at Talavera, but then had to be abandoned as further French forces approached. Wellington (as Wellesley now became, ennobled for Talavera) retired back across the

Portuguese border and prepared to face French efforts to evict him. But the French armies, although large, were stretched far too thinly.

France needed to devote ample forces to garrisoning territory it occupied. Its armies were harassed constantly by guerrilla bands, while campaigning against the tenacious Spanish regular armies in Spain as well as the British and Portuguese in Portugal. The French marshals found the rapid, decisive movement of army corps, in the established Napoleonic manner,

Battle of Salamanca

Wellington's victory at Salamanca, on 22 July 1812, was a turning point. Like all battles of the period, it was fought in an obscuring fog of gunpowder smoke.

impossible in countryside increasingly denuded of food and fodder. Napoleon's troops were required to get much of their food by "living off the land". But soldiers foraging for supplies were vulnerable to ambush by guerrillas and had to seize what they needed from hostile villagers by brute force. Wellington coped better, able to depend on supply by sea through Lisbon and cautiously and thoroughly organizing his supply and communication routes when advancing with his men away from the coastal regions.

In 1810 a French army commanded by Marshal Masséna invaded Portugal, but in September came up against the strong defensive lines of Torres Vedras that Wellington had prepared in front of Lisbon. The following spring, supply problems forced Masséna to withdraw towards the Spanish border. Wellington's pursuit was cautious, for the French always had the potential to assemble forces large enough to shatter him. Indecisive battles with heavy casualties on both sides were fought at Fuentes de Oñoro and Albuera in May 1811. The British then concentrated on reducing the pivotal fortresses of Badajoz and

TECHNOLOGY
SHRAPNEL SHELL

British artillery officer Henry Shrapnel's eponymous invention was a hollow iron sphere packed with explosive powder and musket balls. A time fuse was designed to ignite the explosive when the sphere, fired from an ordinary cannon, was above the heads of enemy soldiers. The airburst hurled the musket balls into their ranks to deadly effect. Shrapnel had far greater range than canister, until then the standard way of firing multiple projectiles from a cannon. Described by Wellington as "a great benefit", it was first used by the British Army in 1808 during the Peninsular War.

HOLLOW SHELL

MUSKET BALLS

The war left Spain and Portugal devastated, economically backward and politically unstable. The conflict also deeply affected their colonies in the Americas.

COLONIAL WARS

Many Spanish and Portuguese who fought in the Peninsula War embraced liberalism and **resisted the reimposition of absolutist monarchy**. In Spain King Ferdinand VII, restored in 1814, faced a **liberal revolt in 1820** that started the first of a series of civil wars that was to plague Spain throughout the 19th century. In Portugal liberals **imposed a constitution** on the king, who had fled to Brazil during the war. The **Portuguese liberals won a civil war** against a conservative reaction in 1828–34.

The **Spanish colonies** in the Americas were thrown into turmoil by the weakening of Spanish rule during the war and the conflicting political currents after it. The Spanish monarchy never fully recovered control of its colonies and soon **lost them entirely 210–11 »**. In Brazil the son of the Portuguese monarch refused to return from exile and became ruler of an **independent Brazil** as Emperor Pedro I from 1822.

> " General Pakenham said: '**Advance**,' adding, 'There they are, my lads, just let them feel the **temper of your bayonets**.'"
>
> BRITISH SERGEANT MORLEY, DESCRIBING THE BATTLE OF SALAMANCA, 22 JULY 1812

Ciudad Rodrigo, controlling the portals from Portugal into Spain. Wellington was ill-equipped for siege operations – which were a rarity in the Napoleonic Wars – but succeeded in taking Ciudad Rodrigo by storm in January 1812 and Badajoz in April. The assault on the walls showed British soldiers at their best; the aftermath of the capture of the fortresses did not, degenerating into orgies of plunder and massacre that proved Wellington's oft-expressed view of his soldiers as "the scum of the earth".

The British enter France

After the fall of Badajoz, Wellington advanced northwards through Spain. In July 1812, at Salamanca, he decisively defeated Marshal Marmont in a battle that revealed an unexpected flair for bold opportunistic attack. The French withdrew from southern Spain and abandoned Madrid to concentrate their forces against Wellington. Even with Portuguese and Spanish regulars now attached to his army, Wellington was, in theory, outnumbered two to one. But Spanish guerrillas were increasingly active, and French morale was low.

In spring 1813, Wellington resumed the offensive, pressing towards the French border. He attacked an army under King Joseph (Napoleon's brother) at Vitoria in June. The following October the British forces crossed the Pyrenees into southwest France and by the time Napoleon abdicated, in April 1814, they were fighting for the city of Toulouse.

The Peninsular War had been a drain upon French manpower, tying down troops who otherwise might have been available for the struggle against Prussia, Russia, and Austria.

Communications

At one time communication on the battlefield was limited to what soldiers could directly see and hear of each other while fighting. The telephone and the radio transformed communications in the 20th century, and on today's hi-tech battlefield, electronic communication systems have reached astonishing levels of sophistication.

Before the 20th century, command on the battlefield was mostly exercised by a variety of visual and auditory signals. For small units, agreed and understood hand gestures were effective when operating with stealth, changing to shouted commands once fighting was out in the open. Such simple and effective methods are still used today. For fighting on an extended battlefield, brass instruments such as trumpets or bugles and, of course, drums were widely used to signal simple commands such as "advance" or "retreat."

Flags and banners provided an effective means of visually communicating commands. Originally these were quite simple, but flag codes were substantially improved in the mid-18th century when the French navy introduced number flags. This allowed many more increasingly complex messages to be transmitted.

Battlefield communication
This detail from the Bayeux tapestry shows a young boy delivering a message to William the Conqueror during the battle of Hastings.

Long-range signals

Developments in optics, such as high-quality telescopes and binoculars, greatly increased the distance over which visual signals could be sent. However, all visual communication suffered from the fact that poor weather conditions and smoke often obscured the battlefield. This difficulty proved to be especially acute in the gunpowder era, when battlefields were blanketed in smoke as soon as the firing started. The Mongols had used smoke signals to transmit commands that would be seen through the clean air of the medieval battlefield, but this system would not have worked at Waterloo (see pp.206–07).

Napoleonic drummer boy

This painting depicts soldiers marching into the battle of Waterloo in 1815. In the British Army, drummer boys and band boys (often soldiers' orphans) accompanied their regiments into battle.

By World War I (see pp.268–77), the replacement of gunpowder by smokeless propellant and explosive had improved visibility, but the sheer scale of the 20th-century battlefield made it difficult to make use of visual signalling. Colour-coded signal rockets, however, were effectively used in World War I trench warfare; for example, by infantry calling for artillery support. At sea, messages transmitted by Aldis lamps (which had shutters for making pulses of light) largely took over from flags as a visual means of communication.

Regardless of the advances in military communication, however, the role of the messenger – whether travelling on foot, on horseback, or on a motorbike – has remained prominent. Even at sea in the era of sail, small boats flitted from ship to ship in the heat of battle delivering orders and messages. Carrying messages on the battlefield was notoriously dangerous work, never more so than for the "trench runners" of World War I. In the thick of battle, commanders often sent a series of soldiers with the same message, hoping that at least one would make it through.

Pre-electric communication

Communication over longer distances developed in ingenious ways. By applying the principle of a chain of communication, it was possible to transmit messages with remarkable speed over long distances with quite limited technology. The system of fire beacons built around the English coast, for example, gave rapid warning of the approach of the Spanish Armada in 1588. A widely spaced line of warships, each stationed within telescope range of its neighbour on each side, could transmit a flag-coded message over long distances in a few minutes. The same principle can be applied to smoke and light signals; a heliograph, for

Crimean war bugle

This copper bugle was used by Trumpet-Major Henry Joy of the 17th Light Dragoons at the battle of Balaclava during the Crimean War. On 25 October 1854, Joy sounded the Charge for the Heavy Brigade.

example, is essentially a mirror that can be used to flash sunlight over great distances. Using heliographs to flash signals in Morse code became popular in the second half of the 19th century; for example, during the Boer War in southern Africa (see pp.248–49).

The most effective form of pre-electric long-range communication was probably the semaphore system (an alphabet signalling system) developed by the French inventor Claude Chappe in the early 1790s. Semaphore stations, which used paddles mounted on large pivoting arms as visual signals, were built during the French Revolutionary (see pp.186–87) and Napoleonic wars (see pp.188–203), primarily by France but also by Britain, linking the Admiralty in London to the main naval ports. The chief disadvantage of the system was its inflexibility – it could convey messages only where lines of linked stations had been built.

For all the ingenuity of these systems, long-distance communication continued mostly to be conveyed no faster than a ship could sail, a horse could run, or a pigeon could fly – carrier pigeons being an important means of communication in armies into World War I and beyond.

Increased range

The electric age brought inventions that revolutionized civilian and military communications. The electric telegraph, perfected by Samuel Morse in 1837, was first put to military use in the Crimean War (see pp.220–21) and the American Civil War (see pp.232–37). Although the telegraph was extremely useful for long-distance transmitting, it did not serve on battlefields, which at that point in time were not extensive enough for such a technology to be appropriate. Far more important for command in battle was the field telephone, developed in the 1880s and first used in action during the Spanish-American War of 1898 (see pp.252–53). The field telephone was in principle a flexible mobile system allowing units engaging the enemy to keep in contact with commanders in the rear on the ever-expanding modern battlefield. As such it was an essential item of equipment for all armies in World War I. Unfortunately, telephone cables are vulnerable to artillery shells, and advancing troops usually found their communications severed. The field

telephone nonetheless remained a useful communication tool through World War II (see pp.288–305) into the contemporary age.

Modern times

Developed in the early 20th century, wireless communication was primarily used by navies. Wireless telegraphy made an influential naval debut in contributing to the Japanese victory at the battle of Tsushima in 1905 (see pp.254–55). It also played an important part in the naval war in World War I, though the opportunity it presented for admiralties to interfere with the command of operations at sea was not always beneficial. Air-ground radio communications first developed in World War I to allow spotter aircraft to communicate with artillery, and ground stations to communicate with bomber aircraft and airships. Once improvements in radio allowed reliable

mobile voice communication, for example, between tanks and aircraft, the basis was laid for a new era of fast-moving warfare in which aircraft provided close air support for ground forces. Airmen could also be guided to targets by ground controllers, as well as receiving orders from their squadron commander and sharing what information they could see from the air. In World War II, radios coordinated everything from U-boat operations to fighter interception of incoming bomber aircraft.

The main drawback of radio was the ease with which signals could be intercepted by the enemy. Encoding machines were devised in an effort to make radio communications secure, but codes proved thoroughly breakable, as many armed services on both sides found in the course of World War II. And assumptions about enemy movements can be made from the volume of radio traffic alone – a sudden cluster of radio signals, for example, might indicate a squadron of bombers taking off, or a fleet setting to sea.

In the post-World War II era, global communication systems using satellites and computers have brought the potential for coordination and control of large-scale military operations to a new level. Control centres use many computers to sort through and analyse a vast input of information and generate precise commands. Any soldier can potentially be in contact with a commander, anywhere in the world.

Satellite communications

Although map and compass reading are still required skills, the modern soldier also has access to the latest GPS (Global Positioning System) technology to plot his exact location.

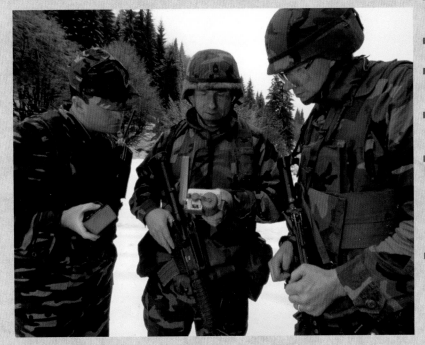

TIMELINE

405 BCE The ancient Greeks use flashing shields to send messages in battle.

c.100 CE On parts of the border of the Roman empire, messages are transmitted along lines of watchtowers by simple semaphore.

c.1250 The Mongols have the ability to convey messages up to 483km (300 miles) a day by an organized system of post horses.

1653 During the First Anglo-Dutch War (see p.148), Britain's Royal Navy establishes a basic system of communication by flag signals for use in fleet actions.

1792 French inventor Claude Chappe (1763–1805) demonstrates the transmission of a message by semaphore telegraph from Paris to Lille.

1795 Britain begins construction of a semaphore system between major ports and London.

1837 Samuel Morse and Alfred Vail invent the first electric telegraph; the Morse code is developed in the following decade to send messages through the telegraph system.

1860 The US Army Signal Corps is founded by Alfred James Myer.

1867–68 Royal Navy officer Philip Colomb introduces a system of naval communication using a signal lamp.

1876 American inventor Alexander Graham Bell patents the telephone. The Bell Telephone Company is created in 1877, and stock in the company soars from $50 to over $1,000 a share within three years.

WORLD WAR I FIELD TELEPHONE

1898 Field telephones are employed by the US Army for the first time in military operations during the Spanish-American War.

1905 The Japanese navy uses radio in tracking down the Russian Baltic Fleet, which is then destroyed at the battle of Tsushima.

1914–18 In World War I, radio is used for military communications, especially at sea and in the air.

1942 The hand-held portable two-way radio receiver – the walkie-talkie – comes into military use during World War II.

1964 The first satellite navigation system, TRANSIT, is adopted by the US Navy.

1969 The US Department of Defense begins development of the ARPA Net (Advanced Research Projects Agency Network), the forerunner of the World Wide Web and the internet.

SMARTPHONE, A MODERN-DAY WALKIE-TALKIE

1991 In Iraq, the success of Operation Desert Storm demonstrates the effectiveness of JSTARS (Joint Surveillance Target Attack Radar System), an airborne command and control system.

Napoleon's Downfall

From the catastrophic invasion of Russia in 1812 to defeat by the British and Prussians at Waterloo in 1815, Napoleon's downfall was warfare on an epic scale, unmatched in Europe before the 20th century. Armies numbering hundreds of thousands battled to subdue him and end two decades of conflict.

Imperial eagle
A symbol of Napoleon's regime, the imperial eagle was carried into battle on a staff. It became prized plunder for foreign troops invading France in 1814. This example was removed by the British from the arsenal at Toulouse.

‹‹ BEFORE

Tsar Alexander I of Russia had negotiated peace with France's Emperor Napoleon at Tilsit in July 1807, but the position of subordinate ally to France soon rankled.

TRADE EMBARGO
Napoleon's imperial triumphs in Europe
‹‹ 194–95 increasingly endangered Russian interests. The Russian economy suffered from the French-imposed embargo on trade with Britain, known as the **Continental System**. Moreover, Napoleon's creation of the Grand Duchy of Warsaw in 1807 and his expansion of the state in 1809 provided a threat to **Russian control of Polish lands** on its western frontier. By 1811 Tsar Alexander had withdrawn from his agreements with France and Napoleon had decided to subdue Russia by force.

By the summer of 1812, Napoleon had assembled an army of around 600,000 soldiers for an invasion of Russia. About a half of them were from France, although even these included numerous men from recently annexed regions that were not ethnically French. The rest were troops exacted from client states such as the German Confederation of the Rhine, the Kingdom of Italy, and the Polish Duchy of Warsaw. France's reluctant allies, Prussia and Austria, also provided contingents that advanced on the flanks of Napoleon's army. As well as the men, there were some 200,000 horses. Napoleon knew that such a host would find it impossible to survive off the land in Russia and so made complex supply arrangements, but these were adequate only for a short campaign. He envisaged crossing the border, bringing the Russians to battle, defeating them, and imposing a humiliating peace.

The invasion was launched in June. Nothing went to plan. The cautious Russian generals withdrew ahead of Napoleon, drawing him deeper into Russia. By the time the first battle was fought, at Smolensk in August, the French supply line had broken down and thousands of soldiers were dropping out through hunger, fatigue, and disease. The battle was indecisive, although the Russian army again fell back, ceding Smolensk.

A costly victory
Napoleon continued his advance towards Moscow, reasoning correctly that the Russians would feel bound to defend the city. The veteran general, Kutuzov, newly appointed to command the country's forces, took a stand at the village of Borodino. What came next on 7 September was mass slaughter – some 70,000 from both sides were killed or wounded in a single day – as France overcame the Russian defensive position by frontal assault.

Napoleon had his victory, but it did not produce the result he expected. The Russian general kept his army in being, and even when the French occupied Moscow, Tsar Alexander refused to make peace. Napoleon could not provide for his army in Moscow, especially after part of the city burned down. Shadowed by the Russian army, the French began a withdrawal in mid-October. The retreat from Moscow was an epic of suffering. Driven by hunger to eat their remaining horses, harassed by Cossack skirmishers, frozen once the winter snows set in, the surviving French troops became ragged, skeletal figures. Despite this, they still managed to flee Russian encirclement with a crossing of the Berezina river in late November, but only a few thousand of Napoleon's men who had made it as far as Moscow

Napoleon's cut-throat razor
The emperor's razor fell into British hands after his defeat at Waterloo. It is now in the Army Medical Services Museum in England.

> "The French will leave their **bones strewn over the soil of Russia**."
> RUSSIAN GENERAL KUTUZOV, ORDER TO HIS ARMY, 10 NOVEMBER 1812

Key
- France
- Britain
- Prussia
- Habsburg empire
- Russian empire
- Frontiers 1797
- War with Russia 1812
- Napoleon's Hundred Days 1815
- Wellington's campaigns 1812–14
- French victory
- French defeat

The defeat of France

After the catastrophic invasion of Russia in 1812, Napoleon could no longer resist his enemies in Spain and Central Europe. France was invaded and occupied. Napoleon returned from Elba in 1815 to be beaten at Waterloo.

Following defeat at Waterloo, Napoleon's military and political career was at an end; but the world emerged much changed from the wars the emperor had fought.

POWER SHIFT

At the **Congress of Vienna** in 1814–15, the victorious powers returned Europe to the rule of the old dynasties. Overall, the Napoleonic Wars had left France greatly diminished as a **European power** and Britain unchallenged as the world's most prominent naval power.

For Napoleon, there was no hope of another return to power. **Surrendering to a British naval squadron** on board HMS *Bellerophon* in July 1815, he was interned for three weeks before being sent to the remote Atlantic island of **St Helena**. He passed the time dictating his memoirs, and died in 1821. In his will Napoleon had written: "I wish my ashes to rest on the banks of the Seine, among the people of France I loved so much."

NAPOLEON IN EXILE

completed the return journey. Yet this disaster did not crush Napoleon. In 1813 he built a new army of fresh French conscripts, Poles, and Germans, ready to battle as Prussia, Austria, and Sweden allied with Russia and Britain.

A ruler on the wane

At first Napoleon looked set to defeat his enemies again despite the odds, but in October's three-day battle of Leipzig, the weight of forces against him proved set. Outnumbered almost two to one, his army withdrew with heavy losses. In December the anti-French coalition

agreed to pursue the total defeat of Napoleon and invaded France, already penetrated by the British from Spain during the Peninsular War. Napoleon

560,000 The number of troops engaged at Leipzig in October 1813, the largest battle in European history before World War I.

once more rebuilt his army, calling up Frenchmen from the age of 16 to 60, but there was scant enthusiasm for the draft and he could field little more than 100,000. He fought a brilliant series of

defensive battles against the invading armies, but at the end of March 1814, Paris was occupied by the Allies. The following month Napoleon abdicated. The victors allowed him an honourable exile as ruler of the small Mediterranean island of Elba.

However, the reinstatement of the Bourbon monarchy in France did not go smoothly, and Napoleon returned to French soil in March 1815 to begin what is now known as his "Hundred Days". Gathering an army of young and old, Napoleon seized the offensive, hoping to repulse his enemies before they

united. In June he invaded Belgium, attacking the armies of the Duke of Wellington and the Prussian general, Gebhard Blücher. After repulsing them separately on 16 June at Quatre-Bras and Ligny, he was beaten by the two together at Waterloo two days later.

The retreat from Moscow

Napoleon's French army had to travel almost 900km (560 miles) from Moscow back to French-controlled territory. The majority of his soldiers died, either through hardship or enemy action.

1 GREEK BRONZE CUIRASS
(5TH CENTURY BCE)

3 RUSSIAN SUIT
OF ARMOUR
(14TH CENTURY)

2 ROMAN LORICA
SEGMENTATA
(1ST–3RD CENTURY CE)

4 ITALIAN BRIGANDINE
(14TH–15TH CENTURY)

Armour

Nowhere are the complexities of war's history so clearly displayed as they are in armour. Changing times have not simply brought technological advance. Trends have depended as much on the materials and the fabricating skills available, on tactical factors, and on the type of weapons likely to be deployed against the wearer.

1 This 5th-century BCE **Greek bronze cuirass** gave good protection against spear thrusts and would have been worn by a wealthy hoplite. **2** A **Roman legionary's** *lorica segmentata* was made of iron strips laced together with leather cords for flexibility as well as strength. **3** This **medieval Russian armour** shows clearly the influence of the Mongols in its overlapping scales and conical helmet. **4** The **brigandine** was a canvas or leather doublet with small plates of steel riveted inside. A lighter, cheaper alternative to plate armour, it was worn by medieval European foot soldiers, often over chain mail. **5** The **plate armour worn by a European knight** in the 15th century was made of steel, fashioned by skilled metalworkers. Although heavy, it offered superb protection, allowing the mobility to fight in the saddle

or on foot. **6** A **Japanese samurai's armour** from the 16th century onwards was made of small iron plates sewn together with leather cord. The helmet had flaps to protect the neck, and sweeping horns in front. **7** This **early-modern infantry armour** was used by an elite *landsknecht* mercenary, who would lead an attack on the pike-and-musket battlefield. It was often worn over chain mail. **8** A late 15th-century **Ottoman warrior's chain mail coat** was reinforced in the most vulnerable places with plates of steel. **9** **Napoleon's heavy cavalry wore iron cuirasses**, both for protection and for show. The plate would stop a sword thrust or cut and might deflect a musket ball. **10** **Flak jackets** became standard issue for US troops in Korea and Vietnam. The pads of tightly woven fabric or ceramic plates gave some defence against bullets or shrapnel

5 ENGLISH KNIGHT'S
ARMOUR
(15TH CENTURY)

6 JAPANESE
SAMURAI ARMOUR
(16TH CENTURY
ONWARDS)

7 GERMAN
FOOTSOLDIER'S ARMOUR
(LATE 16TH CENTURY)

8 OTTOMAN WARRIOR'S ARMOUR
(LATE 15TH CENTURY)

10 US MARINE'S FLAK
JACKET (c.1970)

9 FRENCH CUIRASS
(19TH CENTURY)

Waterloo

The last battle of the Napoleonic Wars was fought south of Brussels on 18 June 1815. Napoleon sought to destroy an army of British and Netherlands troops, commanded by the Duke of Wellington, before it could be joined by the Prussians under Marshal Blücher. The gamble failed but it was, according to Wellington, "the nearest run thing you ever saw in your life".

Having withdrawn from an encounter with the French two days earlier at the battle of Quatre Bras, Wellington's army had taken up a strong defensive position on the Mont St Jean ridge, just south of the village of Waterloo. Napoleon prepared to attack with 72,000 men to Wellington's combined British, German, and Dutch force of 68,000. The disparity in force was of more significant than the numbers suggest, for Napoleon had a greater number of experienced soldiers and twice as many cannon at his disposal.

During the French preliminary bombardment Wellington kept the bulk of his army hidden from view on the reverse slope of fthe ridge. He had fortified local farm buildings to form strongpoints in front of the ridge and these were first to come under attack. Then the mass of the French infantry advanced in broad columns. Wellington's infantry formed up in line and their musket fire, along with the grapeshot and canister of the field artillery, sowed carnage through the French ranks. Despite this, the French infantry still looked set to overwhelm the British line until Wellington's heavy cavalry drove them back with a forceful charge. Encouraged by their success the British horsemen unwisely continued their charge towards the French batteries and were cut down by a cavalry counterattack.

Believing that the British and their allies were ready to break, Marshal Ney threw his cavalry forward in repeated charges. The red-coated British infantry formed squares bristling with bayonets, the horsemen surging around them. Sometimes a square was ripped apart by cannon fire, but otherwise the cavalry could not break in and were decimated by volleys of musketry at close range.

Turning the tide

The crucial fortified farm of La Haye Sainte eventually fell to the French after long resistance, but too late for Napoleon – Blücher's Prussians, a force of more than 50,000 men, were drawing near. As part of his army struggled to hold the Prussians at bay, Napoleon threw his Imperial Guard forward in a last bid to break Wellington's battle-worn soldiers. But confronted with steady musket fire, it was the Imperial Guard that wavered and then broke. The French were driven from the field, and the Prussian cavalry mounted a savage pursuit. Napoleon's army had suffered 25,000 casualties and 8,000 had been taken prisoner. His career was over.

- Brussels
- ■ WELLINGTON
- [4] 18 Jun: Wellington draws up his army south of Waterloo
- [6] Blücher's forces advance on La Belle Alliance, taking Napoleon by surprise
- (N)
- Halle
- Waterloo
- Wavre
- [7] Grouchy arrives too late to intercept Blücher
- La Belle Alliance
- ■ BLÜCHER
- ■ NAPOLEON
- [5] Imperial Guard launch attack, repulsed by British
- Mont St Guibert
- Nivelles
- Walhain
- [2] 16 Jun: French under Ney defeated, but force tactical withdrawal of British forces
- Quatre Bras
- Gembloux
- NEY ■
- ■ GROUCHY
- [3] 17 Jun: Prussians withdraw, following defeat at Ligny
- 0 10km
- 0 10 miles
- [1] 16 June: Napoleon defeats Prussians
- Ligny

LOCATION
Waterloo, south of Brussels, Belgium

DATE
18 June 1815

FORCES
British, Dutch, German, and Belgian: 68,000; Prussian: 50,000; French: 72,000

CASUALTIES
British, Dutch, German, and Belgian: 15,000; Prussian: 7,000; French: 25,000

KEY
■ French infantry
◢ French cavalry
■ British-led forces
■ Prussian forces

The victorious duke
Wellington directs his multinational force at Waterloo. In front of him are the British heavy cavalry. For most of the day his troops were outnumbered, but resolutely withstood the furious French attacks.

The War of 1812

Between 1812 and 1815 the United States fought what has sometimes been called a "second war of independence" against Britain. It was a war Britain did not want and, on the American side, was fought for unclear goals – whether the United States intended to annex part or all of Canada was never clear.

NORTH AMERICA

1 Operations in the north
Dates 1812–14
Location Great Lakes region

2 British coastal raids
Dates 1814
Location Washington, DC, and Baltimore

3 Operations in the south
Date 1814–15
Location Around New Orleans

« BEFORE

The background to the war between Britain and the United States lay in Britain's war with France, which had raged since 1793, and in the conflict with Native Americans.

TRANSATLANTIC WARS
The United States had **declared itself neutral in the European war**, a stance that angered the French, who felt it was poor recompense for supporting the Americans during **the American Revolution « 178–79**. Between 1798 and 1800 an undeclared naval war (the **Quasi War**) was fought between the US and France, with battles between warships and attacks on merchant shipping. British and US relations became strained in the following years – the US objecting to the Royal Navy **blocking their trade** with France and **forcibly recruiting sailors** from US ships intercepted at sea.

TECUMSEH, LEADER OF THE SHAWNEE

TRIBAL STRIFE
Americans also alleged that the British in Canada were stirring up trouble among the country's Indian tribes, accusing them of supporting **the tribal confederation led by the Shawnee leader, Tecumseh**, which was opposing the expansion of the United States in the northwest.

The United States declared war on Britain on 18 June 1812. It was a controversial decision, pushed through by President James Madison and the "war hawks", many of whom were aggressive advocates of American expansion. However, the United States was ill-prepared to fight. While the small standing army was supplemented by short-term volunteers, the Americans relied heavily on state militias. Madison was convinced that these forces would be adequate enough to occupy Canada. This was possible in principle, as Britain's greater resources were concentrated on its war with France, leaving minimal forces in Canada. Yet a US invasion of Canada launched in August 1812 degenerated into a debacle. The three-pronged attack was defeated by only handfuls of British soldiers, Canadian militia, and Indian tribal warriors.

These setbacks for the United States on land were offset by stirring naval victories. Overall the US Navy was no

5,000 The total strength of the British regular army in Canada in 1812. The number of British troops engaged in the war with France at the same time was around 250,000.

given command of a small squadron of warships that were built on the spot to contest British control of the lake. On 10 September 1813, Perry took on and defeated a roughly equal British force. By controlling the lake waters, the US retook Detroit, which it had lost the previous year, thus securing Ohio.

The death of Tecumseh
This defeat also sealed the fate of Tecumseh, leader of the Shawnee tribe, who was fighting alongside the British. When his allies retreated from Detroit, he had no option but to follow, pursued by the Americans under William Henry Harrison. In 1813, at the battle of the Thames, the British and Indians were crushed; Tecumseh was slaughtered.

With the pressure of conflict and the passage of time, the United States' army developed greater discipline and found better leadership. General Winfield Scott ("Old Fuss and Feathers") emerged as an American hero in summer 1814

> **"Shall this harbour of Yankee democracy be burned? All for it will say Aye!"**
>
> BRITISH ADMIRAL COCKBURN IN WASHINGTON, DC, 24 AUGUST 1814

match for the Royal Navy. The British had more than 700 warships. America possessed 17 warships, none larger than a frigate. The Royal Navy's main force, however, was committed to blockading French ports and could not be spared for the American war. US frigates, more heavily armed than the British ones and manned by determined and skilful officers and crew, were well suited to solo raids. It was a shock to British pride when the USS *Constitution* triumphed in successive single combats with the British frigates *Guerriere* and *Java*, and the USS *United States* captured the frigate *Macedonian*. American warships and privateers also took a heavy toll of British merchant shipping.

The most important American naval victory, however, was won on Lake Erie. Commandant Oliver Perry was

when the US mounted a second and more competent invasion of Canada. He led his men to victory against the British in a sharp battle at Chippewa and was then badly injured in a fierce encounter at Lundy's Lane (present-day Niagara Falls) in July.

Far to the south another American made his mark fighting Native Americans: Colonel Andrew Jackson, in charge of the Tennessee

Battle of New Orleans
General Andrew Jackson directs the defence of New Orleans in January 1815. Success in the battle made Jackson a popular hero in the United States.

militia. A Creek faction known as the Red Sticks had begun fighting against the United States. In 1814 Jackson's militia, supported by other Creek and Cherokee Indians, fought a campaign against the Red Sticks, defeating and massacring them at the battle of Horseshoe Bend in March. In spite of these successes, by 1814 the war was turning against the United States. In

Burning of Washington, DC
In August 1814, the British raided the American capital and set fire to many buildings, including the White House. This avenged the American firing of buildings in York (present-day Toronto) the previous year.

Europe Napoleon was deposed in April, freeing up British troops and warships. Despite the feats of American sailors, the power of the Royal Navy was making itself felt. The American frigates USS *Chesapeake* and *Essex* had been defeated and captured, salvaging British naval pride. An ever-tightening blockade of the United States' coast impacted severely upon the American economy and government finances.

Burning the capital

Free to attack the eastern seaboard at will, the British sent troops recently arrived from Europe to raid Washington, DC, in August 1814. Commanded by General Robert Ross, they brushed aside militia defending the city and burned down public buildings. The

following month the British moved on to Baltimore, but despite landing troops and a naval bombardment with mortars and rockets, they were unable to take the stoutly defended Fort McHenry guarding the port.

In the same month the British took eastern Maine, but an invasion of New York state from Canada failed. Sir George Prevost escorted an army as far as Plattsburgh city on Lake Champlain, but Prevost's accompanying naval force was defeated by an American lake squadron and he was forced to withdraw.

By this stage both sides were tired of the conflict. The only point in continued fighting was to manoeuvre for potential advantage in the peace negotiations that had opened at Ghent in Belgium.

The British decided to grab New Orleans, Admiral Sir Alexander Cochrane leading a body of soldiers across from Jamaica. On 8 January 1815, under the cover of darkness, an army commanded by Sir Edward Pakenham attempted a frontal assault on fortifications defended by the American general, Andrew Jackson, and his 5,000 determined men. Pakenham was among those struck down by American fire before the whole operation was finally abandoned. The troops were unaware that a peace treaty – the Treaty of Ghent – had been signed two weeks earlier. News would not arrive until February.

Peace treaty
The treaty ending the war was signed at Ghent in Belgium on 24 December 1814.

TECHNOLOGY
CONGREVE ROCKETS

Inspired by missiles used against the British by the Mysore Army in India, these rockets were developed by William Congreve at Britain's Royal Arsenal. Although not very accurate, they carried an explosive or incendiary warhead to a range of 3km (2 miles). The rockets were used with some success by the British during their 1807 bombardment of Copenhagen in the Napoleonic Wars and during their 1814 assault on Baltimore in the War of 1812. Smaller, more mobile versions were also deployed, usually less successfully, in various major battles, including the battle of Waterloo against the French in 1815.

AFTER

The only territorial change resulting from the War of 1812 was the US gain of Mobile from Spain, and they were not even fighting. But there were also other consequences.

AMERICAN PRIDE
The war stimulated an upsurge of national consciousness both in the United States and Canada. The **"Star-Spangled Banner"**, written by Francis Scott Key during the assault on Baltimore, was later to become the US national anthem. It was to prove **America's last war with Britain**, however. Further disputes over the US-Canadian border were determined by agreement in the course of the 19th century.

THE TRAIL OF TEARS
The war brought **freedom to thousands of black slaves**, who escaped their American owners by joining the British. For Native

3,900 The number of US and British military personnel killed in action in the war. Around 20,000 died of disease.

Americans, the war brought further subjugation. Andrew Jackson led attacks on Native Americans and escaped slaves in Florida in the **Seminole War** in 1817–18; Florida was ceded by Spain to the US in 1819, becoming an area where slave-owning was legal. After Jackson became president in 1829, an **Indian Removal Act** was passed, ensuring the eviction of Cherokee, Creek, Chickasaw, and Choctaw from their tribal lands. They were forced along the **"Trail of Tears"** to the Indian Territory (mainly in present-day Oklahoma) in the 1830s.

BEFORE

The movements for independence in Spanish America were precipitated by the collapse of royal authority in Spain rather than by any resentment of Spanish rule.

REVOLUTIONARY WARNING

The ideas of liberty and equality spread by the **American Revolution ‹‹ 178–79** and the **French Revolution ‹‹ 186–87** had limited impact on Central and South America, where Spanish administrators ruled in alliance with privileged Creoles (American-born whites). **The Haitian rebellion** in the 1790s, which set up the first black-ruled state in the Americas, was seen by most Creoles as a warning against revolutionary upheaval, which might end their domination of the *pardo* (mixed race) and black majority in the Spanish colonies.

THE PENINSULAR WAR

When Spain allied itself with France against Britain in the **Napoleonic Wars**, links between the colonies and Spain were disrupted by British naval control of the Atlantic. In 1806 Creole republican, Francisco de Miranda, tried to invade Venezuela with British support, but was repulsed by a people still loyal to Spain. Things changed after 1808, when Napoleon deposed Spain's Bourbon dynasty, sparking **the Peninsular War ‹‹ 198–99**. By 1810 Latin-American Creoles decided to take government into their own hands.

South America's Wars of Liberation

The wars that resulted in the independence of Spain's colonies in South America were a complex series of conflicts, primarily fought between opposing groups of colonists and only secondarily against Spanish forces. From the confusion, a few individuals stand out as exceptional military leaders.

The colonial independence struggles in South America started in 1810, with uprisings from New Granada (present-day Colombia) and Venezuela to Chile and the Viceroyalty of Río de la Plata (including what is now Argentina). Those engaged in assertions of varying degrees of autonomy from Spain were by no means united. They included many royalists, loyal to the recently deposed Spanish Bourbon king Ferdinand VII. Nor did they generally enjoy the support of the population as a whole. The poverty-stricken and the enslaved, mostly mixed race or black, hated the rich Creoles more than the Spanish authorities. In many regions civil war raged and central government collapsed as *caudillos* (military leaders) ran their own localities. Only in Peru

did the Spanish authorities maintain control virtually unchallenged, but in other areas those people asserting independence at first achieved at best a tenuous hold on power.

Bolívar's war

In Venezuela a republic declared in 1811 was overwhelmed the following year in a royalist reaction led by Domingo de Monteverde. Simón Bolívar was among

10 PER CENT of the royalist soldiers in South America that were fighting for the continuation of Spanish rule were Spanish. Most were American royalists fighting other Americans.

the republicans who fled to nearby New Granada. From there, Bolívar launched an invasion in 1813 that trounced the royalists, occupied the city of Caracas, and re-established a republic. Victory was short-lived: an army of *llaneros*, the tough outlaws of the Venezuelan plains, under Jose Bovés counterattacked and drove Bolívar out again. The fighting saw horrific massacres on both sides. Those among the defeated who did not escape the country established guerrilla forces in remote areas.

The end of the Peninsular War and the return of Ferdinand to the Spanish throne in 1814 heralded a determined

Venezuelan llaneros

The horsemen of the Venezuelan plains were a mix of bandits and fugitives from slavery and poverty. Initially they supported the royalists, but later *llaneros* became a vital component in Bolívar's liberation army.

attempt to reassert Spanish rule in the colonies. A 10,000-strong expeditionary force under General Pablo Morillo was shipped across the Atlantic to occupy Venezuela and New Granada. Morillo took control of the major settlements along the coasts but armed groups, with Bolívar's supporters, kept up resistance in the interior. Bolívar found an ally in José Antonio Páez, the new leader of the *llaneros*, and attracted the support of a British Legion – British and Irish troops left unemployed by the conclusion of the Napoleonic Wars. In 1819, with

Wars of independence

The series of Wars of Liberation in South America from 1812 to 1824 were conducted over a vast expanse of often daunting terrain, including mountains, swamps, and jungles.

*Map labels:*

Caribbean Sea
Tenerife Dec 1812
Carabobo Jun 1821
Maracaibo
Caracas
Cartagena
Mérida
La Puerta Jun 1814
Panama
Cúcuta Feb 1813
Calabozo Feb 1818
Gamarra Mar 1819
BRITISH GUIANA
FRENCH GUIANA
CAPTAINCY-GENERAL OF VENEZUELA
Bogotá
GRAN COLOMBIA
SURINAM (Dutch)
Buenaventura
Boyacá Aug 1819
1819
VICEROYALTY OF NEW GRANADA
Pichincha May 1822
Bomboná Apr 1822
Quito
Guayaquil
Amazon
BRAZIL 1822
Andes
Trujillo
PERU 1821
Junín Aug 1824
Huacho
Callao
Lima
VICEROYALTY OF PERU
Ayacucho Dec 1824
Puno
La Paz
PACIFIC OCEAN
Tacna
Arica
BOLIVIA 1825
Chuquisaca (La Plata)
Potosí
VICEROYALTY OF RÍO DE LA PLATA
PARAGUAY 1811
Asunción
Andes
CAPTAINCY-GENERAL OF CHILE
Tucumán
CHILE 1818
Chacabuco Feb 1817
Córdoba
Valparaíso
Mendoza
Maipú May 1818
Santiago
UNITED PROVINCES OF LA PLATA 1815
URUGUAY 1828
Montevideo
Talca
Talcahuano Dec 1817
Cancha Rayada Mar 1818
Bueno Aires
Concepción May 1817
Patagonia
ATLANTIC OCEAN

Key

- Spanish possessions 1810
- *VICEROYALTY OF PERU* Spanish administrative division
- **CHILE 1818** New state with date of independence
- Victory of armies of liberation
- Defeat of armies of liberation

0 ——— 1000km
0 ——— 1000 miles
N

INDEPENDENCE LEADER (1783–1830)

SIMÓN BOLÍVAR

Known as "the Liberator", Simón Bolívar was born in Caracas in 1783. As a young man he imbibed revolutionary ideas in Europe. Returning to Venezuela he became the most prominent leader of the independence fight. The founding of Gran Colombia in 1819, with himself as president, seemed a step towards his goal of a federal state embracing all Latin America. Instead, even the state of Gran Colombia dissolved in disunity and Simón Bolívar died, disillusioned, in 1830.

these hard-bitten veterans and *llaneros*, Bolívar advanced into New Granada and routed the Spanish at Boyacá, occupying Bogotá. A victory in 1821 at Carabobo in

"Our native land is America …
Our ensign is liberty."

SIMÓN BOLÍVAR, OCTOBER 1814

Venezuela gave him effective control of almost all New Granada and Venezuela, which were united as Gran Colombia.

In Argentina a *junta*, a government of military leaders, was established in 1810. It fought the Spanish and royalists with

The battle of Chacabuco
On 12 February 1817, José de San Martín's Argentines and Bernardo O'Higgins' Chileans defeated the royalists at Chacabuco after an epic crossing of the Andes.

mixed success until the arrival of José de San Martín, an Argentine-born officer who had fought for Spain in the Peninsular War in 1812. San Martín

improved the organization of the *junta's* forces, securing them against a royalist reaction. In nearby Chile a civil war left the Spanish and royalists in control in 1814, forcing their leading opponent, Bernardo O'Higgins, to escape to Argentina with the remnants of his forces. San Martín conceived a plan to ally with O'Higgins for an invasion of Chile as a prelude to an assault on Peru, the stronghold of

Spanish authority. In January 1817, San Martín and O'Higgins led some 5,000 soldiers across the Andes. It cost them heavy losses – but their surprise arrival in Chile allowed them to defeat outnumbered royalists at Chacabuco.

An end to Spanish rule
The Spanish sent an army to Chile from Peru under General Mariano Osorio that at first had considerable success, but in April 1818, at Maipú in the Andes, Osorio was defeated by San Martín, guaranteeing Chilean independence.

Politics in Chile remained complex, but in 1820 San Martín launched an invasion of Peru, aided by a Chilean navy commanded by British Admiral Lord Thomas Cochrane. He declared Peruvian independence in the capital, Lima, in 1821. Under circumstances still not fully understood, after talks with Bolívar in 1822, San Martín withdrew to private life. It was thus Bolívar who led the final campaign against surviving royalist strongholds in Peru. He won a cavalry skirmish at Junín in August 1824 before his second-in-command, Antonio José de Sucre, conclusively defeated the Peruvians at the battle of Ayacucho in December 1824. This ended Spanish rule in South America.

The former Spanish colonies found neither peace nor stability. The legacy of the wars included disputed frontiers and a tradition of power based on military force.

THE SKIRMISHES CONTINUE
In the wake of independence, there were **border wars** between Gran Colombia and Peru, and between Argentina and Brazil. The republic of Gran Colombia soon split up into Colombia, Venezuela, and Ecuador. Later, Paraguay fought Argentina, Brazil, and Uruguay in **the War of the Triple Alliance** (1864–70), which cost around 400,000 lives. Chile fought Bolivia and Peru in **the War of the Pacific** (1879–83). Even more damaging for South America was the tradition of the *caudillo*, founded in the liberation wars. These local warlords with their armed supporters **undermined the authority of governments** and at times seized political control in military coups.

SPANISH AMERICAN CAVALRY PISTOL

The **Greek War** of **Independence**

Launched in 1821, the Greek uprising against Ottoman rule led to the creation of an independent Greek state nine years later. The course of the war was determined by the intervention of European powers who, by the 19th century, enjoyed a comfortable military superiority over the Ottoman empire.

EASTERN MEDITERRANEAN

Greek War of Independence
Dates 1821–29
Location Greece, Crete, and the Aegean

« BEFORE

By the early 19th century the Ottoman empire was in decline, neither able to exercise effective rule over its territories nor defend itself against external enemies.

A FRAGILE EMPIRE
The Ottoman sultans governed domains stretching from Mesopotamia (Iraq) to Algeria, and from the Balkans to Egypt. Most of their **provinces** were controlled by **local rulers**, however, with little reference to Ottoman government. The Ottoman army fared poorly in **a series of wars with Russia «« 182–83**. Pressure from both **Russia and Austria** threatened Ottoman rule in southeastern Europe, encouraging resistance from the empire's **Christian subjects**. A revolt led by **Karadjordje Petrovic** broke out in Serbia in 1804. Ottoman rule in the Balkans was also contested by Muslim

KARADJORDJE PETROVIC

Albanian warlord **Ali Pasha**, based in Ioannina, who ruled over much of what is now Greece.

ATTEMPTS AT SURVIVAL
Sultan Selim III, who reigned from 1789 to 1807, tried to modernize his state but was overthrown by the **janissaries**, the traditionalist elite corps of the army. **Mahmud II**, his successor, was similarly committed to reform, but pursued it with more caution. He suppressed the Serbian revolt in 1813, and in 1820 campaigned against Ali Pasha, whom he defeated in 1822.

About one in four subjects of the Ottoman empire spoke Greek. They constituted a socially and ethnically diverse population, ranging from the wealthy Phanariot families of Constantinople, who were part of the ruling elite of the empire, to the *klephts* (bandits) and peasants of the mountain country of the Peloponnese. Some were what we would now call Romanians or Albanians. Through the centuries of Ottoman rule, a sense of Greek identity had been maintained chiefly through allegiance to the Greek

dragged from church in Constantinople and hanged from a city gate. On the Aegean island of Chios in 1822 most of the population was either massacred or deported. The defeat of Ali Pasha that same year freed the best elements of the Ottoman army to focus on suppressing the Greek revolt, but the Peloponnesian *klephts* under leaders such as Markos Botsaris were fierce fighters who defied the sultan's forces. A kernel of resistance was also maintained at Missolonghi, in present-day western Greece, under the Phanariot Alexandros Mavrokordatos.

"**Fair Greece!** Sad relic of departed worth … "

BRITISH POET LORD BYRON, "CHILDE HAROLD", CANTO 2, 1812

Orthodox Church. In the early 19th century the tide of nationalism that swept through Europe in the wake of the French Revolution encouraged Greeks to aspire to national self-rule. In 1814 a secret Greek organization, the *Philiki Eteria* (Society of Friends), was founded. It sought support from Russia, which claimed to be a natural protector of Orthodox Christians and had many Greeks in its service. Alexander Ypsilantis, a Phanariot general in the Russian army, assumed the leadership.

Ottoman strength prevails
In February 1821, Ypsilantis attempted to begin a Greek revolt in the Ottoman principalities of Moldavia and Wallachia (now part of Romania). Russia refused to back him, and his forces were swiftly crushed by the Ottoman army. Scattered uprisings broke out in the Peloponnese and other parts of the empire. The Ottomans responded with ferocity. At Easter 1821, the Greek Orthodox Patriarch, Gregory V, was

Well-publicized Turkish atrocities won widespread sympathy in Europe for the Greek cause. The British poet Lord Byron travelled to Missolonghi, aiming to join in the fighting, and died there amid a blaze of publicity in April 1824. Other military idealists followed Byron's example, including British Admiral Sir Thomas Cochrane, later commander of the Greek naval forces.

A more effective foreign intervention came from elsewhere, however. Egypt, officially part of the Ottoman empire, was, in practice, an independent state under Mohammed Ali, a modernizing ruler who had succeeded in improving his armed forces in a way the Ottoman sultans had singularly failed to do. At Sultan Mahmud's request, Mohammed Ali sent his son, Ibrahim Pasha, with a large naval force and 10,000 drilled and disciplined soldiers to reduce the Greeks to submission. The forces landed in the southern Peloponnese in February 1825.

Battle of Navarino
The encounter between British, French, and Russian warships and the Ottomans and Egyptians in Navarino Bay on 20 October 1827 was the last major naval battle of the sailing ship era.

The Greek rebels had been weakened by internecine struggles between rival factions and were in poor shape to resist Ibrahim Pasha's onslaught. They were simultaneously attacked by a less efficient but still formidable Ottoman army under Reshid Pasha from the north. The Ottomans and Egyptians

2,000 **The number of Greeks left on the island of Chios after the massacres and deportations by Ottoman forces in 1822. The population of the island had originally been 50,000.**

together took Missolonghi in 1826, and Athens fell the following year after a ten-month siege of the Acropolis.

Meanwhile, Sultan Mahmud took on the power of the janissaries, who had for so long blocked his military reforms. On resisting the imposition of Western-style drill and uniforms, in June 1826, the janissary corps was abolished and thousands of them killed to prevent a

Ottoman pistol
The flintlock muskets and pistols employed by Ottoman forces were generally copies of European weapons, often inferior in performance but finely decorated.

Barrel

Trigger guard

reaction. With the Greek revolt doomed and the path open for modernization, by 1827 the Ottoman empire looked in better shape than it had for many years.

Europe acts at last

European public opinion had been horrified, by the depredations visited upon the Greeks by the Egyptian forces in response to the guerrilla warfare of the *klephts*. Governments were reluctant to intervene but felt under pressure to take some action. In July 1827, in the

Treaty of London, Britain, France, and Russia agreed to support the creation of an autonomous Greek state and to send a fleet to the war zone to persuade the sultan to agree to a ceasefire.

In September an Egyptian fleet sent from Alexandria joined Ottoman ships at anchor in the bay at Navarino (Pylos) on the west coast of the Peloponnese. They found themselves blockaded by the British under Admiral Sir Edward Codrington, subsequently joined by Russian and French squadrons. The

Allied naval commanders did not have instructions to engage the enemy but decided to provoke a confrontation, rather than face a long winter blockade. On 20 October, the Allied fleet sailed into Navarino harbour. Firing started almost immediately and many Ottoman and Egyptian vessels were destroyed.

The battle of Navarino did not end the warfare. The sultan was defiant, so, in April 1828, the Russians seized the opportunity to pursue territorial gains by attacking the Ottomans in both the Balkans and eastern Anatolia. By the

70 The number of Egyptian and Ottoman ships sunk at Navarino in October 1827, almost 90 per cent of their fleet of 78 vessels. Not a single British, French, or Russian ship was lost.

following September, Russian armies had reached Edirne (Adrianople), only 240km (150 miles) from Constantinople. Reluctant to see Russia gain too much advantage, other Europeans intervened diplomatically to bring the fighting to an end. Meanwhile, a French expeditionary force landed in Greece to oversee the repatriation of Ibrahim Pasha's forces, and John Capodistrias, a former Russian foreign minister born in Corfu, arrived to head a Greek government.

Massacre at Chios

This famous painting by French artist Eugène Delacroix represents the Ottoman atrocities on the island of Chios in the Aegean. Exhibited in Paris in 1824, it expressed popular support for the suffering of the Greeks.

AFTER

In the aftermath of the war, the European powers dictated a settlement to the Ottoman empire, which entered a period of decline and would not survive another century.

GREEK AUTONOMY

Under the terms of the 1829 **Treaty of Edirne**, the Ottomans were finally forced to accept the **autonomy of Greece** as well as that of Serbia, Moldavia, and Wallachia. In 1830 Britain, France, and Russia went a step further and decided that Greece should now be **fully independent**. The quarrelsome Greeks, however, continued to fight among themselves. In 1831 their head of state, **John Capodistrias**, was assassinated. The allied powers insisted that Greece become a **monarchy** and Prince Otto of Bavaria became king.

48 THOUSAND The area of Greece in sq km (18,532 square miles) in 1830.

132 THOUSAND The area of Greece in sq km (51,000 square miles) in 2009.

INTERCEDING FOR THE EMPIRE

The European powers saw a need to keep the **Ottoman empire** in existence, fearing the chaos its dissolution would bring. They intervened in 1833 and 1839 to defend the Ottomans against **Egypt**, which threatened to take over much of the empire. Britain and France defended the Ottomans once more, this time against Russia in the **Crimean War** of 1854–56 **220–21** ≫.

5

THE DAWN OF MECHANIZED WARFARE

1830 – 1914

Trains, steamships, powerful new artillery, and machine-guns gave the US and the industrialized countries of Europe an enormous military advantage over the rest of the world. Britain and other European powers rapidly expanded their empires in Africa and Asia.

PRUSSIAN DREYSE NEEDLE GUN, 1841

THE DAWN OF MECHANIZED WARFARE 1830 – 1914

Between 1830 and 1914 developments in technology transformed warfare from the era of flintlock muskets, cannonballs, and wooden sailing ships to the age of machine-guns, high-explosive shells, and steam-powered steel battleships. The capacity of the world's leading industrialized states to mobilize military resources and productive power was formidable, bringing vast areas of Africa, parts of Asia, and all of North America under their rule. A wide gap opened up between the leading European powers, the US and latterly Japan, and those states struggling to modernize, such as Spain, China, and the Ottoman empire. The gap was even more extreme with tribal peoples encountered in the course of colonial expansion.

Citizen armies and modern war

One-sided imperial conflicts, such as the Sino-French War in which the Chinese navy was utterly destroyed at Foochow by the French, were not a rigorous testing ground for new technologies, which found their full expression in wars between similarly armed powers. A series of wars fought from the 1850s to the 1870s – the Crimean War, the American Civil War, and the wars that unified Italy and Germany – saw the first use of railways for the movement of troops; the replacement of the flintlock musket by the rifle-musket and then by breech-loading rifles; and the introduction of ironclad steamships. An armed peace in Europe from 1871 did nothing to slow the pace of technological development. New high explosives and smokeless propellant ended the reign of gunpowder. On land and sea rifled big guns could fire shells to a range measured in kilometres rather than metres. Rapid-fire rifles with metal cartridges became the standard infantry weapon. Machine-guns were widely adopted late in the 19th century. Warships combined steam propulsion and steel construction with large breech-loading guns. Torpedo boats and mines complicated battles at sea. The fruits of these developments were seen in the Russo-Japanese War of 1904–05. This deserves more than any other the title of "the first modern war", with artillery firing beyond line of sight, machine-guns mowing down infantry, and telephone and radio used for communications.

On the brink of global war

The major powers in Europe pursued military expansion at an accelerating rate through the first decade of the 20th century. The system of universal military training pioneered by the Prussians meant that, in the

Armstrong breech-loading field gun
Designed by William Armstrong, this wrought-iron 12-pounder was the first rifled breech-loading gun. It was adopted by the British Army in 1859 and saw use in the American Civil War.

event of the great war for which they constantly planned, France, Germany, Russia, and Austria would be able to field citizen armies numbered in millions. Britain did not have a mass army, but it increased the size of its armaments industry and its world-beating navy. The modernization of armed forces, however, should not be exaggerated. Horses were still the fastest means of transportation for men and supplies once they left a railhead. Submarines, aeroplanes, and airships were military novelties with barely explored potential. But as European powers approached 1914, they had greater military force at their disposal than any previous societies in history.

German army in China
German soldiers march into battle in China in 1900. They arrived as part of a multinational force sent to quell the Boxer Rebellion – a Chinese nationalist uprising that sanctioned the murder of all foreigners living in the country.

1830
1835
1840
1845
1850
1855

1840
British start the First Opium War against China. ■ The Maoris accept British rule in New Zealand.

1846
The US-Mexican War begins. The Americans occupy California and invade Mexico.

1850
The Taiping Rebellion breaks out in China.

1855
The French capture of the Malakoff stronghold ends the siege of Sevastopol.

⌄ Capture of Malakoff

⌃ French Revolution of 1830

1830
Revolution in France topples the monarchy. ■ France begins its occupation of Algeria. ■ Belgium wins a war of independence against Dutch rule.

1842
The First Opium War ends. Britain gains Hong Kong and five treaty ports. ■ The US-Canadian frontier is settled. ■ Britain withdraws from Afghanistan.

⌃ US artilleryman's sword c.1840s

1847
US troops seize Veracruz and Mexico City.

≪ 19th-century Chinese bannerman

1831
Liberal revolts are crushed in Poland and Italy.

1832
Britain claims the Falkland Islands. ■ Greece gains independence from the Ottoman empire.

1848
Revolutions break out across Europe. The *Communist Manifesto* is published. The US war with Mexico ends with the US making massive territorial gains.

1853
The Russian navy destroys the Turkish fleet at Sinope at the start of the Crimean War.

1856
The Treaty of Paris ends the Crimean War.

1857
Mutiny in India against British rule. ■ The Second Opium War begins between Britain and China.

≪ 19th-century Indian gun

1834
Abolition of slavery throughout the British empire. ■ In southern Africa the Boers start the Great Trek out of the British-ruled Cape Colony.

1835
Texans revolt against Mexican rule. ■ Second Seminole War starts between US troops and the Seminole nation in Florida.

1858
Treaty of Tientsin ends the Second Opium War and opens ten new treaty ports.

1859
The French move troops by railway to defeat the Austrians at Magenta and Solferino, driving them out of Italy.

⌄ Battle of Solferino

⌃ 19th-century Ottoman musket

1836
Mexicans besiege the Alamo, killing its Texan defenders. The Texans defeat the Mexican army at San Jacinto river and win independence.

1854
British and French troops land in the Crimea and besiege Sevastopol. The battle of Balaclava is noted for the futile British light cavalry charge. ■ The French fight the Tukulor empire in Senegal. ■ Japan opens up to Western trade.

≪ Boer trekkers

1838
Boers defeat the Zulus at the battle of Blood river.

1843
Britain acquires Natal in South Africa and Sind in India.

1849
Austrians crush uprisings in Italy. ■ The short-lived Roman Republic is ended by French military intervention.

1839
British invade Afghanistan on the pretext of securing the northwest frontier of India. First Anglo-Afghan War.

1860	1864	1868	1872	1876	1880

1860
Italian patriot Giuseppe Garibaldi conquers Sicily and Naples.

1864
Austria and Prussia seize Schleswig-Holstein from Denmark. ▪ International Red Cross founded in Geneva. First Geneva Convention is signed. ▪ Sherman's March to the Sea lays the Confederacy to waste. ▪ At Sand Creek, Cheyenne and Arapaho Indians are massacred by Colorado territorial militia.

« Victor Emmanuel II of Savoy, first king of a unified Italy

1868
The Lakota Sioux sign a treaty with US government. ▪ The Meiji Restoration in Japan.

1869
Suez Canal opens.

⌃ French Reffye Mitrailleuse volley gun c.1870

1872
Austria-Hungary, Germany, and Russia form the Three Emperors League.

⌃ Battle of Little Bighorn

1876
Lakota Sioux defeat US Army at the battles of Rosebud and Little Bighorn. ▪ Bulgarian uprising against Ottoman rule.

1861
Proclamation of the Kingdom of Italy. ▪ Secession of Southern states to form the Confederacy provokes the US Civil War. Fighting begins with the Confederate attack on Fort Sumter. ▪ Gatling gun patented in US.

1865
The Union wins the US Civil War. President Lincoln is assassinated.

1870
Franco-Prussian War begins; major French defeats at Metz and Sedan. ▪ The withdrawal of the French garrison from Rome allows Italian forces to take the city and complete the unification of Italy.

1877
In southern Africa Britain annexes Transvaal. ▪ Russo-Turkish War begins.

1880
Second Anglo-Afghan War ends in British withdrawal.

1881
In the First Boer War, the Boers of Transvaal defeat the British at Laing's Neck and Majuba Hill to regain independence. ▪ The British occupy Egypt.

1862
Ironclad warships clash for first time at Hampton Roads in US Civil War.

1863
Emancipation Proclamation promises to free slaves in the US Confederacy. Union victories at Gettysburg and Vicksburg.

⌄ Battle of Vicksburg

1866
Prussia defeats Austria at Königgrätz in the Seven Weeks War. ▪ Italy acquires Venetia from Austria. ▪ The French adopt the Mitrailleuse machine-gun, with the Gatling gun the first rapid-firing weapon to be used in combat.

» Prussian Pickelhaube helmet

1873–74
British expeditionary force defeats the Asante on the Gold Coast of West Africa.

1878
End of the Russo-Turkish War. Treaty of San Stefano creating Greater Bulgaria is revised at Berlin. Serbia, Romania, and Montenegro all gain independence. ▪ Second Anglo-Afghan War breaks out.

» Battle of Isandhlwana

1867
French intervention in Mexico ends with the execution of Emperor Maximilian. ▪ The Austro-Hungarian dual monarchy established.

1875
Uprising against Ottoman rule by Christian populations of Bosnia and Herzegovina. Unrest spreads to other parts of the Balkans.

1879
The British invade Zululand and are humiliated at the battle of Isandhlwana, but withstand a siege at Rorke's Drift. The Zulus are defeated at Ulindi. ▪ Austro-German Dual Alliance agreed.

1884
European powers begin the "Scramble for Africa". ▪ Start of the Tonkin War. The French destroy the Chinese fleet at Fuzhou. ▪ The Maxim machine-gun is developed.

⌄ Mountain gun used in Britain's colonial wars

1871
Prussians bombard Paris to win the Franco-Prussian war. The German empire is proclaimed at Versailles. The French Republic fights the Paris Commune.

1885	1890	1895	1900	1905	1910

1895
Japan gains Taiwan, and Korea gains independence at the end of the Sino-Japanese War. ■ Cuba revolts against Spanish rule.

1900
The British relieve the Boer sieges of Mafeking, Ladysmith, and Kimberley, then occupy the Boer republics of Transvaal and Orange Free State. The Boers start guerrilla warfare.

1905
Japan defeats the Russian army at Mukden and the navy at Tsushima. ■ Revolution breaks out in Russia.

≫ Battle of Tsushima

⌃ Naval Gatling gun c.1885

1885
In the Mahdist War, the Mahdi's army captures Khartoum and evicts the British from Sudan. ■ The Tonkin War ends with France gaining Vietnam. ■ Bulgarians win the Serbo-Bulgarian War.

1890
Some 300 Sioux – men, women, and children – are massacred at Wounded Knee.

1896
Italians are defeated by the Ethiopian army at Adowa in the First Italo-Ethiopian War.

1902
The Treaty of Vereeniging ends the Boer War.

1888
Wilhelm II becomes German kaiser.

1898
The British overwhelm the Khalifa's forces at Omdurman in Sudan. ■ The Spanish-American War. The US seizes Guam, the Philippines, and Puerto Rico from Spain.

≪ Plate commemorating the USS *Maine*, sunk in the run-up to the Spanish-American War

1906
The British launch HMS *Dreadnought*, a new battleship, more heavily armed than any previous warship. This accelerates the naval arms race between Britain and Germany.

1910
Japan annexes Korea. ■ The foundation of the Union of South Africa. ■ Start of the Mexican revolution.

1894
Sino-Japanese War breaks out. Japanese defeat Chinese fleet at Yalu river.

1907
Britain signs an entente with Russia, thus forming a loose alliance between France, Russia, and Britain. In World War I these three Entente Powers oppose the Central Powers – Germany and Austria-Hungary.

1911
Italy invades Ottoman Libya and seizes the coastal regions. The Italians are the first to use aircraft for reconnaissance and bombing. ■ Revolution begins in China.

1912
In the First Balkan War, the Ottomans lose almost all their remaining European territories.

1889
Brazil overthrows its emperor to become a republic.

1899
Start of the Second Boer War. In southern Africa the Boers declare war on Britain and besiege Kimberley, Ladysmith, and Mafeking. ■ The Hague Peace Conference sets up a Permanent Court of Arbitration. ■ The Boxer Rebellion begins in China.

⌃ News of the British relief of Mafeking in 1900

1903
The US acquires a lease on Guantánamo Bay in Cuba for use as a naval base.

1908
Austria-Hungary annexes Bosnia-Herzegovina. ■ The Young Turks come to power in the Ottoman empire.

1913
In the Second Balkan War, Bulgaria attacks its former allies from the first war. In less than a year the volatile situation in the Balkans will spark off World War I.

≫ Bulgarian gun crew, Second Balkan War

1904
Britain signs the Entente Cordiale with France. ■ The Russo-Japanese War starts as Japan attacks the Russian base at Port Arthur.

≪ Execution of a Boxer rebel

219

The Crimean War

The war fought between Russia and the fading Ottoman empire in 1853 was the latest in a long-running series of disputes between the two empires. It was a war marked by bad planning and incompetence on both sides. Its causes were minor, but its political implications affected the whole of Europe.

T he first shots of the war were fired in November 1853 when the Russian navy, making good use of its new Paixhans naval guns firing explosive shells, sailed across the Black Sea and destroyed the Ottoman fleet at Sinope, northern Turkey. Faced with this threat to the Ottoman empire and alarmed by possible Russian expansion towards the Mediterranean, Britain and France declared war in March 1854. They were joined by the Italian state of Piedmont, which was anxious to gain French support for its campaign to unite Italy. (See pp.224–25.)

Fighting far from home

The British and French forces faced considerable logistical problems in marshalling troops and supplies so far from home. Assembling at Varna

A hussar's hackle
The hackle was attached to a military cap. This example belonged to a British assistant surgeon who served in the Crimea during the battle of Sevastopol.

on the Bulgarian coast, the Allies ferried troops across the Black Sea to the Crimea with the aim of capturing the naval fortress of Sevastopol and nullifying Russian naval power in the region. The French army included many troops hardened in campaigns in North Africa and was generally better organized than the British, who were fighting their first European war since 1815. The British commander-in-chief, Lord Raglan, had never commanded a unit larger than a battalion and had no experience of modern warfare despite being 66 years old. To make matters worse, his troops had been ravaged by cholera, and were poorly trained and badly equipped.

The Allies landed in the west of the Crimea and advanced south towards Sevastopol. They first encountered the Russian army dug in on the Alma river. On 20 September 1854 the Allies crossed the river but the British then faced the Russians at the top of a steep slope. British casualties were high, but poor leadership and inferior firearms forced the Russians to retreat. The

Allies then advanced to within sight of Sevastopol. The Russians had blocked the entrance to the harbour, forcing the Allies to besiege the port from the land. Had the Allies arrived sooner, they might have taken their target at once, as the Russians had only just completed its defences. But by the date of the attack, on 17 October 1854, the Russians were securely fortified against the Allied bombardment.

In an attempt to break the siege, Russian forces advanced towards the Allied base at Balaclava. A battle took place on the hills above the port on 25

October, a contest distinguished only by its cavalry charges (see KEY MOMENT). In the third major battle of the campaign, the Allies managed to occupy an undefended ridge at the town of Inkerman, which commanded the approaches to Sevastopol, and from here held off repeated Russian attacks on 5 November. Casualties were high on both sides and the result of the battle was inconclusive. British and French troops were forced to dig in as the siege was set to continue through the winter. The Allies were unprepared for the freezing conditions, with inadequate food, fuel, and clothing supplies. British troops suffered the worst. Without proper shelter and provisions they were soon impaired by malnutrition and cholera. Conditions became so desperate that they were reduced to only 12,000 fit men. Critical reports of the situation were sent back to London by The

A British officer's hat
This bicorne hat is typical of the style of headgear that was popular in Europe in the 18th and 19th centuries, in imitation of Napoleon Bonaparte.

EUROPE

1 **Crimean War**
Dates 1853–56
Location Crimea and the Black Sea

2 **Baltic Campaign**
Dates 1854–56
Location Baltic Sea, coast of Russia and Finland

Times correspondent William Howard Russell, considered to be one of the first war correspondents. These led to the fall of the government and a swift improvement in supply. After the war the British introduced wartime censorship of the press to prevent such stories appearing again.

> ## "For all I can observe, these **men die** without the **least effort** being made to **save** them."
> **WILLIAM HOWARD RUSSELL, REPORTER FOR "THE TIMES"**, 1855

Spring brought a renewal of the bombardment of Sevastopol. By July the Russians were suffering daily losses of almost 350 men, but held out until 8 September when the French, in the one perfectly planned and executed operation of the war, captured the vital bastion of Malakoff, which overlooked the city. That night the Russians destroyed Sevastopol's defences before evacuating the southern part of the city.

Fighting also took place in the Baltic Sea, where a Franco-British fleet bombarded Russian positions, and threatened St Petersburg, the Russian capital. But this theatre of operations reached a stalemate early on in the war as the Russian fleet was too small to be effective, while the British and French believed that the Russian coastal fortifications were too strong to take on.

Peace and consequences

By the time Sevastopol fell, in September 1855, Russia's new tsar, Alexander II, was anxious to make peace. By the 1856 Treaty of Paris, Russia recognized the territorial integrity of the Ottoman empire, and gave up its guardianship of Orthodox Christians in the empire, but ultimately its dominant role in the Balkans was only temporarily reduced. The Ottoman empire, while remaining intact, continued to decline.

«

BEFORE

The Ottoman empire was in decline by the mid-18th century, and the rise of Russian power in the region increasingly worried the major powers of Europe.

LOSS OF THE CRIMEA

The **Russo-Turkish War in 1768–74** led to Crimean independence and Russian gains at the expense of the Ottomans along the Black Sea. Under the peace treaty the tsar became protector of Orthodox Christians within the Ottoman empire. Russia annexed the Crimea in 1783.

EUROPEAN LOSSES

Further wars between Russians and Ottomans in 1787–92 and 1806–12 saw more territory ceded to Russia. **Serbia gained autonomy from Ottoman rule** in 1817, as did the Danubian provinces of **Moldavia and Wallachia** in 1829 after Russian intervention.

CAUSES OF WAR

Since 1774 Russia had regarded itself as the protector of Christian Orthodoxy in the Ottoman empire. In 1852 the **Ottoman sultan allowed French Catholic monks to protect the holy places in Jerusalem**, which was under Ottoman control. The Russians objected and occupied the **Danubian provinces** in 1853.

Capture of Malakoff
Led by General MacMahon, the French *zouave* troops distinguished themselves during the battle of Malakoff on 8 September 1855. The victory brought about the end to the Siege of Sevastopol.

AFTER ≫

The Crimean War neither ended Russian expansion nor halted the decline of the Ottoman empire.

THE RUSSIAN EMPIRE

Despite defeat in the Crimea, **Russia continued to expand its empire**, conquering the northern Caucasus by 1864 and gaining control over the central Asian Muslim khanates (chieftains) by 1884.

BULGARIANS

War between the Ottoman and Russian empires broke out again after the Ottomans suppressed a rebellion in Bulgaria in 1876. Russia supported Bulgaria and declared war in 1877. The sultan made peace in March 1878: the **Treaty of San Stefano** established the independence of Serbia and Romania, and set up a Bulgarian state. Alarmed by the creation of this large, pro-Russian state, the other European powers met in Berlin in July, cutting Bulgaria down in size and returning Macedonia to Ottoman rule. **Balkan dissatisfaction** with this deal led to further wars in 1912–13.

HOSPITAL LAMP

MILITARY REFORMS

In Britain Edward Cardwell, Secretary of State for War, abolished the **purchase of commissions**, introduced short service as the basis of enlistment, and set up an army reserve force. **Under Florence Nightingale's 222–23 ≫ direction, army military medical care** was properly organized.

222–23 ≫

KEY MOMENT

CAVALRY CHARGES

The battle of Balaclava was distinguished by three cavalry charges. A Russian charge towards Balaclava was met by the "Thin Red Line", two rows of British infantry from the 93rd (Highland) Regiment who stopped the charge with three volleys. Another Russian cavalry advance was repelled by the British Heavy Cavalry Brigade, charging uphill against advised military practice. The British Light Cavalry Brigade then misunderstood its instructions and charged down a valley towards a Russian field battery while coming under fire from Russian guns on either side. This charge of the Light Brigade (below), up and back down the valley, is seen as one of the most futile actions in military history.

Medicine

Throughout history, millions of combatants have died in wars, most of them killed not so much by the severity of their wounds as by subsequent infections and diseases, and through lack of immediate or effective medical care. Only with the medical advances of the 19th century did the care of wounded troops really begin to improve.

For a great many centuries, wounded or sick soldiers – in the West, at least – did not receive special treatment. Roman *valetudinaria* hospitals treated slaves and gladiators as well as soldiers. In Jerusalem in the 12th and 13th centuries, wounded or sick crusading knights were treated by monks called the Knights Hospitallers at the hospital of St John, which was originally set up for pilgrims. When Isabella of Spain pioneered the use of wagon ambulances at the siege of Malaga in 1487, the wounded were taken to local civilian hospitals. (These *ambulancias* were of limited use as they went into action after a battle, by which time many of the wounded were already dead.)

The first specifically military hospital in Europe was not built until the late 16th century, when the Spanish, fighting a lengthy campaign against Dutch independence, established one at Mechelen in Brabant, in what is now Belgium. The hospital had 330 beds and a staff of up to 100, treating everything from combat injuries to battle trauma, as well as diseases such as malaria and dysentery. Spain, however, was unusual in caring for its wounded troops. After the defeat of the Spanish Armada in

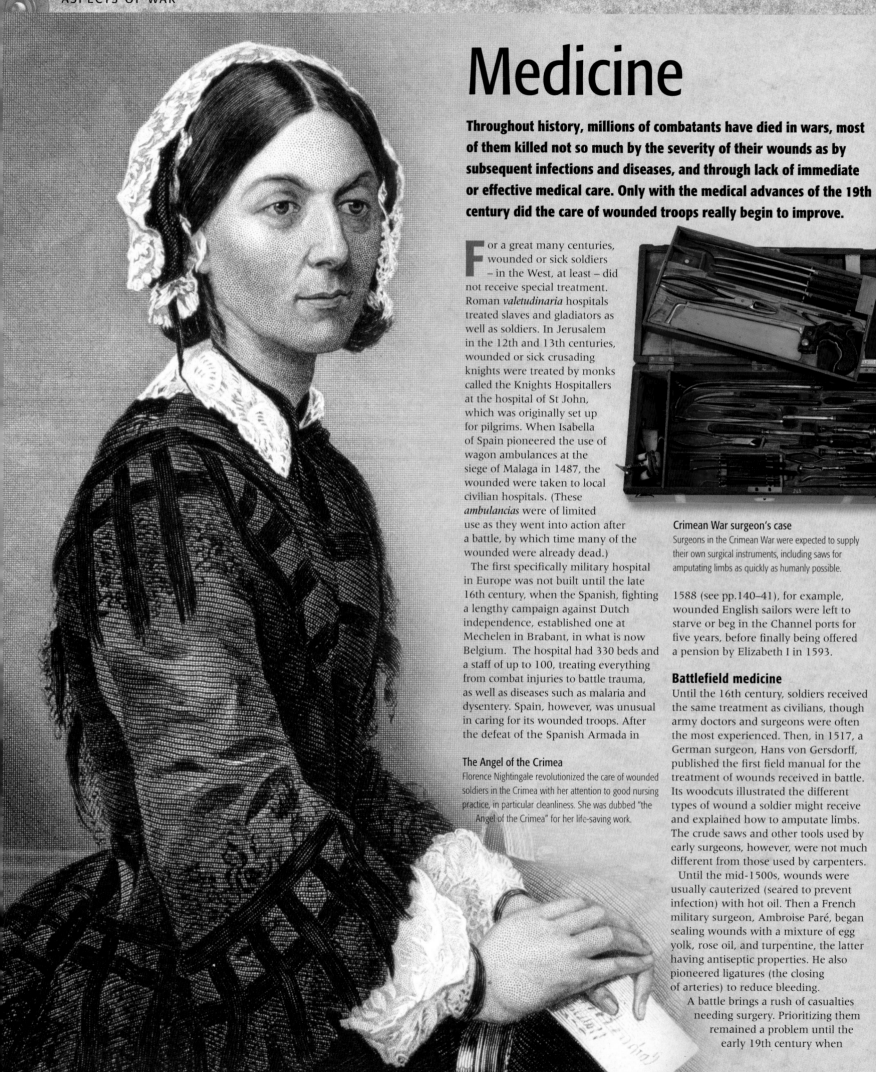

Crimean War surgeon's case
Surgeons in the Crimean War were expected to supply their own surgical instruments, including saws for amputating limbs as quickly as humanly possible.

1588 (see pp.140–41), for example, wounded English sailors were left to starve or beg in the Channel ports for five years, before finally being offered a pension by Elizabeth I in 1593.

Battlefield medicine
Until the 16th century, soldiers received the same treatment as civilians, though army doctors and surgeons were often the most experienced. Then, in 1517, a German surgeon, Hans von Gersdorff, published the first field manual for the treatment of wounds received in battle. Its woodcuts illustrated the different types of wound a soldier might receive and explained how to amputate limbs. The crude saws and other tools used by early surgeons, however, were not much different from those used by carpenters.

Until the mid-1500s, wounds were usually cauterized (seared to prevent infection) with hot oil. Then a French military surgeon, Ambroise Paré, began sealing wounds with a mixture of egg yolk, rose oil, and turpentine, the latter having antiseptic properties. He also pioneered ligatures (the closing of arteries) to reduce bleeding.

A battle brings a rush of casualties needing surgery. Prioritizing them remained a problem until the early 19th century when

The Angel of the Crimea
Florence Nightingale revolutionized the care of wounded soldiers in the Crimea with her attention to good nursing practice, in particular cleanliness. She was dubbed "the Angel of the Crimea" for her life-saving work.

Dressing station on the Somme

British soldiers wounded in the Somme Offensive in France in 1916 had their wounds bandaged at field dressing stations just behind the front line.

Dominique Jean Larrey, Napoleon's chief physician and surgeon-in-chief of his armies, introduced the practice of triage, or sorting.

Triage prioritized patients according to the severity of their condition, dividing them into those who were likely to live regardless of their care, those who were likely to die regardless of their care, and those for whom immediate medical intervention might be life-saving. Distressed that the ambulances Napoleon had ordered to be stationed around the battlefield did not pick up the wounded until the battle had ended, Larrey also devised a system of *ambulance volantes*, or "flying ambulances". These were horse-drawn wagons that removed wounded soldiers (enemy soldiers included) during the battle after they had received early treatment on the field, and took them to centralized field hospitals well away from the action.

Nurses and anaesthetics

In 1847 the Russian surgeon Nikolay Ivanovich Pirogov became the first surgeon to use ether as an anaesthetic in a field operation, a procedure he deployed during the Crimean War (see pp.220–21). He was also the first to treat large numbers of broken bones using plaster-of-Paris dressings, and introduced female nurses into Russian military hospitals, just as Florence Nightingale was doing in British military hospitals. Also, the introduction of morphine and of antiseptics (both civilian inventions) to the battlefield in the mid-1800s greatly reduced suffering and infection.

In the US Civil War (see pp.232–37), the Union doctors Jonathan Letterman and Joseph Barnes ensured that every regiment had at least one two-wheeled ambulance cart capable of carrying three men. They also pressed steamboats into use as mobile hospitals and, for the first time, transported wounded soldiers to hospital by the relatively fast means of the railroad.

Letterman used triage to good effect in forward regimental first-aid stations. The effectiveness of his methods was shown after Gettysburg, when 14,000 wounded Union soldiers and 6,800 wounded Confederate soldiers (the latter left behind by their retreating army) were treated in a vast medical encampment nicknamed Camp Letterman.

Although such actions were effective, the lack of really fast transport to take soldiers to hospital remained a problem until

Early penicillin vial
Mass production of penicillin began following vital research breakthroughs made in 1943.

motor ambulances were introduced in World War I. Most wounded soldiers then had a fair chance of survival if orderlies could reach them quickly.

Modern developments

Three developments between the two World Wars revolutionized medical treatment for soldiers. First was the discovery of penicillin in 1928, which opened the way for the proper treatment of bacterial infections. Second (also in 1928) was the setting up of the precursor of the civilian Flying Doctor Service, which flew doctors to patients and patients to hospitals. Originating in Australia, the idea was taken up by the armies of various countries. The US Army first used helicopters to evacuate troops to field hospitals towards the end of World War II. At the same time, the US Army introduced the Mobile Army Surgical Hospital (MASH), a unit designed to get medical personnel close to the front line. The third development came in 1936 when Canadian doctor Norman Bethune developed the first mobile blood-transfusion service, administering life-saving transfusions on the spot to soldiers who might otherwise have died.

Thanks to these developments, soldiers today are less at risk of dying from their wounds. But the sheer carnage caused by war and the side-effects of using certain weapons, such as depleted-uranium-treated projectiles, still pose a huge challenge for medical teams.

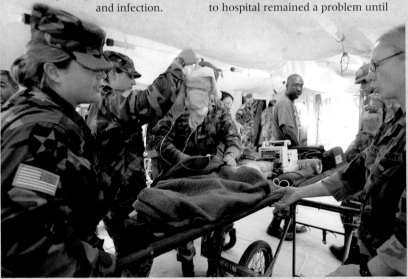

MASH unit in earthquake relief

In 2005 a MASH unit helped save earthquake victims in Pakistan. The last MASH unit was deactivated in 2006. Since then, MASH units have been replaced in the field by Combat Support Hospitals (CSH, or "CASH").

« BEFORE

Since the fall of the Roman empire in the 5th century CE, Italy had consisted of a series of rival kingdoms and city-states, fought over and often controlled by foreign powers, notably Spain and Austria.

NAPOLEONIC ITALY
In 1796 Napoleon Bonaparte's French army invaded northern Italy to drive out the Austrians. French rule was established over the northwest and centre of the country while the rest was rearranged into the **kingdoms of Italy in the north and Sicily in the south**. Napoleon's failure to reunite Italy led patriots to form secret societies, such as the Carbonari, to fight for unity.

RESTORATION
After Napoleon's defeat in 1815, the pre-war rulers and borders of Italy were restored, but with Austria now ruling a combined **Lombardy-Venetia** kingdom in the north and controlling three small duchies in the centre. The restoration

15 separate Italian states had their independence restored after the defeat of Napoleon in 1815.

led to uprisings in Naples in 1820, Piedmont and Palermo in 1821, and Modena and the Papal States in 1831 – all were crushed.

RISORGIMENTO
These setbacks sparked a *Risorgimento* ("resurrection") of Italian nationalism. Radicals led by **Giuseppe Mazzini** and other exiles in France set up the Young Italy movement to replace earlier secret societies and campaign for Italian unity. It was encouraged by Charles Albert, the new king of Piedmont and Sardinia.

Victor Emmanuel II
Although respected and well liked, the king angered many by retaining his dynastic designation, rather than renaming himself Victor Emmanuel I of Italy.

Wars of Italian Unification

Two short wars in 1848–49 and then in 1859–61 transformed Italy from a collection of rival and largely foreign-controlled states into a single unified nation, a process completed over the next decade when foreign powers were finally driven from the peninsula.

In February 1848 a revolution broke out in France that had a knock-on effect across Europe. Protests spread to Austria in March, with uprisings against Austrian rule breaking out in Milan, Lombardy, and in Venice. Taking advantage of Austrian weakness, King Charles Albert of Piedmont declared war on Austria to evict it from Lombardy, and Venice declared its independence.

The Austrian Marshall, Josef Radetzky, withdrew his troops from Milan to the Quadrilateral: the fortress towns of Verona, Mantua, Peschiera, and Legnano. The Piedmontese army besieged and took Peschiera then set out to occupy the hill town of Custoza. But they were faced and defeated by Radetzky in July 1848. He then went on to re-occupy Milan and drive the Piedmontese out of Lombardy. A truce was declared but when war broke out once more in March 1849, the Austrian forces again inflicted a defeat on the Piedmontese, at Novara, and ended the independence of Venice after a siege in August. A brief revolt in Florence was also crushed by Austrian troops. All hopes of driving the Austrians out of northern Italy were now lost, causing Charles Albert to abdicate in favour of his son, Victor Emmanuel II. To the south, Italian nationalists declared a republic in Rome in February 1849 and drove out Pope Pius IX. In response, the King of Naples and

the new French president, Louis Napoleon, sent troops to reinstate him. The Romans, helped by the arrival of the celebrated Italian nationalist, Giuseppe Garibaldi, from South America, defended the city, but by the night of 30 June the French had crushed the new republic.

Second Italian war for unity
Nationalist hopes for Italian unity seemed doomed. The only product of the recent upheavals was the granting of a liberal constitution in Piedmont. Yet events soon favoured the Italians. In 1859 the Piedmontese prime minister, Count Cavour, signed a secret treaty with Emperor Napoleon III, to gain his support against Austria. The Austrians were then manipulated into declaring war on Piedmont, prompting the French to intervene. This they did in style, swiftly moving 130,000 men and the same number of horses to the war zone by train – the first mass military movement by rail in history. The two sides met at Magenta in Lombardy on 4 June. A small French contingent attacked across a canal from the west, while a larger force under

KEY
- Kingdom of Sardinia 1815
- Territory annexed 1859
- Territory annexed 1860
- Territory annexed 1866–70
- Kingdom of Italy 1861
- Frontiers 1815
- Garibaldi and the Redshirts 1860
- Sardinian army 1860
- Battle

The battle for Italy between 1815 and 1860
Early in the 19th century Italy was a collection of small states, whose rulers included the Austrian emperor. The most successful Italian campaigns in the struggle for unification took place between 1859 and 1860.

General MacMahon attacked from the north. Their progress was slow, however, allowing the far greater Austrian force to hold the French at the canal. MacMahon's troops eventually entered the town in the late afternoon, expelling the Austrians in house-to-house fighting. Austrian forces retreated eastwards, losing control of Milan, but on 24 June French forces unexpectedly caught up with them at Solferino. The ensuing battle was chaotic and bloody. Both sides used rifle muskets firing Minié bullets, but the 400 French rifled cannon proved more effective than the Austrian smoothbore artillery. The Austrians were eventually dislodged, largely thanks to the skills of the French *zouave* (see p.238) infantry and foreign legionaries. Horrified by the carnage, Napoleon III hastily made peace with Austria. Piedmont gained Lombardy from Austria while losing some of its own French-speaking areas to France in

ITALIAN PATRIOT (1807–82)

GIUSEPPE GARIBALDI

A 19th-century revolutionary, Garibaldi's military daring and fervent support for Italian nationalism inspired people the world over. Fleeing Piedmont after an unsuccessful uprising in Genoa in 1834, he spent 14 years fighting guerrilla wars in South America. He returned to Europe in 1848 and played a major role in the defence of the Roman Republic. After another exile he returned to Europe, commanding Piedmontese troops against the Austrians in 1859 and then leading his Redshirts to conquer Sicily and Naples in 1860–61. Having given up his conquests to the king of Piedmont he continued to fight for Italian unity.

return for its help. Austria lost control of three central Italian duchies, which voted for union with Piedmont.

The partial union of northern Italy prompted change in the south. In May 1860 Giuseppe Garibaldi and around 1,000 of his Redshirts sailed from Genoa in Piedmont to Sicily, ruled jointly with the rest of southern Italy by Francis II.

Marching inland, where volunteers flocked to his cause, Garibaldi defeated a Neapolitan army at Calatafimi and occupied Palermo. Under the gaze of the British Royal Navy, Garibaldi crossed to the mainland in August. He took Naples with barely a fight, defeated the Neapolitans again at Volturno

in October, and then joined up with a Piedmontese army marching south to besiege the rest of the Neapolitan army at Gaeta, which surrendered in February 1861. In March Victor Emmanuel II became king of Italy, although the new kingdom still lacked Venetia and the Papal States surrounding Rome.

Venice and Rome

In a further attempt at unification, Italy joined Prussia in the war against Austria in June 1866 (see pp.226–27) and invaded Venetia. The two armies met at Custoza where the Austrians were victorious, as they were at Lissa. But as Prussia won the war, Venetia was ceded to Italy in August 1866.

The Franco-Prussian War (see pp.228–29) enabled Italy to seize Rome when the French legion protecting the pope was withdrawn in 1870. Italian troops occupied the Papal States and entered Rome, which became the new national capital.

After Italy was united, the kingdom continued to expand and to add Italian-speaking Austrian territory into its borders.

ITALIAN CONSOLIDATION

Further Italian-speaking Austrian territory in the Alps was obtained in 1919 after Austria's defeat in **World War I 266–77 ≫**. South Tyrol, Trieste, and Istria were ceded to Italy under the terms of the Treaty of St Germain, and **the Lateran Treaty of 1929 set up the Vatican City as an independent state**.

THE RED CROSS

After the battle of Solferino, Swiss humanitarian, Henri Dunant, was horrified to see the wounded lying untended all over the battlefield. His proposals to help war victims led to the **establishment of the International Red Cross in 1863** and the signing by **12 nations in 1864 of the Geneva Convention concerning the treatment of the wounded** and the protection of medical personnel.

MEDICAL RED CROSS PACK

The horror of war
The battle of Solferino was the definitive engagement of the second Italian war of Independence. The French cannons proved more effective than the Austrian artillery over the course of the nine-hour battle.

The **Rise** of **Prussia**

In the 1860s Germany consisted of numerous small, independent states dominated by Prussia and Austria and bound together inside the German Confederation. Prussia and Austria contested the leadership of the Confederation, and so control of Germany itself. Three wars in the 1860s ensured Prussian dominance and ended Austrian involvement in German affairs.

WESTERN EUROPE

1 Second Schleswig War
Dates 1864
Location Schleswig, northern Germany

2 Seven Weeks War
Dates 1866
Location Bohemia, Saxony

3 Third Italian War of Independence
Dates 1866
Location Northeastern Italy and the Adriatic

« BEFORE

After the defeat of Napoleon in 1815 a confederation of 39 German states was created out of the remains of the Holy Roman empire. Like the empire before it, this German Confederation was dominated by Austria, a state of affairs that was contested by Prussia, the Confederation's second-largest state after Austria.

PRUSSIAN ARMY REFORMS
The vast **army of Frederich the Great was outdated by the Napoleonic period** « 188–203, which saw a need for smaller, more versatile forces. **Reform of the Prussian army began under Gerhard von Scharnhorst**, who was hired by King Frederich Wilhelm III in 1801. **It continued later in the century under Count Helmuth von Moltke**, whose understanding of logistics and technology gave Prussia a truly modern fighting force.

BISMARCK
Otto von Bismarck became minister-president of Prussia in 1862. He took power at a time of conflict between a conservative government and a liberal parliament, but **forced through controversial army reforms (including three-year universal conscription)** while gaining liberal support for his foreign policies. Convinced that Austria had no part to play in German politics, he **directed the policies that led to the confrontation with Austria in 1866**.

The Prussian chief minister, Otto von Bismarck, set out to unify Germany under Prussian rule. His first opportunity came in a short war with Denmark in 1864. Ownership of the two duchies of Schleswig and Holstein was contested by Denmark and Prussia, the southerly Holstein having a German majority with a Danish minority and the northerly Schleswig the reverse. In 1863 King Frederick VII of Denmark announced a new constitution for Denmark that incorporated Schleswig into the Danish Kingdom. In response, the German Confederation sent troops to occupy Holstein. Bismarck made an alliance with Austria, and the two armies invaded Schleswig in February 1864.

Second Schleswig War
The war lasted eight months, the Allies following a battleplan devised by their chief-of-staff, Count Helmuth von Moltke. The plan was sound, but it was mismanaged until Moltke himself left Berlin and joined the battlefield. His appearance changed the war; the Danes withdrew and soon agreed peace terms.

The Treaty of Vienna in October 1864 saw Denmark surrender the two duchies to Austria and Prussia, but Austria's refusal to accept Prussian dominance in northern Germany soon led to hostilities between the victors. Austria allied itself with some smaller German states, while Italy joined Prussia in return for Austrian-ruled Venetia – a province it required to complete Italian unification. The Italian dimension of the conflict was therefore part of the Third Italian War of Unification.

Prussian army Pickelhaube
The Prussian spiked helmet, or Pickelhaube, was designed in 1842 by King Frederich Wilhelm IV of Prussia. It was made of boiled leather with a metal trim.

> "All the sources of support of a **hostile government** must be considered; its finances, railroads ... **even its prestige**."
>
> COUNT HELMUTH VON MOLTKE, WRITING IN DECEMBER 1880

Battle of Königgrätz
The Prussians under Crown Prince Friedrich Wilhelm overrun the Austrian defences. In the foreground, the defeated Austrian commander, Ludwig von Benedek, sits with his captured troops.

Austrian victory at Lissa
In a revival of the classical tactic of ramming, the Austrian armoured frigate *Erzherzog Ferdinand Max* (centre) holes the Italian ship *Re d'Italia* (left).

The Seven Weeks War

On the outbreak of war on 14 June 1866, von Moltke had two armies to face: 270,000 Austrian and Saxon troops in the southeast, and 120,000 Hanoverian and southern German troops to the northwest and south. Total Prussian forces were smaller by around 64,000 men. Von Moltke sent 278,000 troops against Austria and Saxony, leaving just 48,000 to face the various other German armies. This small force captured the Hanoverian army in just two weeks and then drove off the remaining southern German troops.

The larger Prussian force moved south on railway lines and split into three separate armies – the Army of the Elbe and the First and Second Armies – to march into Saxony and Austria. The Saxon army withdrew into Austrian Bohemia, pursued by the Prussians, but the Austrians, commanded by Ludwig Benedek, were unsure which Prussian army to face. The Prussians took the advantage, attacking the Austrians with breech-loading Dreyse needle guns, which fired four times as quickly as the Austrians' muzzle-loaders. Benedek withdrew his shattered troops to high ground in front of Königgrätz fortress.

Moltke's plan was for the Elbe and First armies to restrain the Austrians while the Second Army hit its right flank. The day of the battle (3 July) brought driving rain and near disaster, for a breakdown in communications meant that the Second Army did not receive the order to attack. The other two armies attacked at dawn, but their advance stalled and they were driven back. Luckily for the Prussians, Benedek did not press his advantage and the Prussians still had their superiority in rifles and firepower. In the early afternoon the Second Army at last received its order to attack, and its onslaught on the Austrian flank

forced Benedek to withdraw. The Prussians had won the battle of Königgrätz and within three weeks the Austrian emperor sought a ceasefire.

The Italian front

The Austrians had more success in their battles against Italy, Prussia's ally. The Austrian and Italian armies met at Custoza, south of the Italian lakes. The Austrians tried to attack the rear of the advancing Italian army but failed. The confused battle was resolved by the Austrian rifled artillery outperforming the Italian smoothbore guns and by an improvised charge by

15 The number of railway lines used to transport Prussian troops to the Saxon border.

Dreyse needle gun
Made by Johann Nikolaus von Dreyse, this Prussian bolt-action rifle features a needle that detonates the cartridge in the barrel when fired.

Austrian lancers that endured heavy losses but unsettled the Italians. A second battle, this time at sea off the Croatian island of Lissa in the Adriatic, was also won by the Austrians. Occurring at a transitional time in naval technology, it saw the engagement of a variety of wooden sailing ships and ironclad steamships, the latter armed with battering rams. However, the two victories were to no avail, as the main battle against Prussia was already lost.

The Treaty of Prague ended Austrian influence in Germany and created a Prussian-dominated country.

POSTWAR AUSTRIA
The peace treaty **evicted Austria from Germany**. To ensure good relations in the future, Prussia **did not demand compensation from Austria**. Austria did, however, lose Venetia to Italy. The **Dual Monarchy of Austria-Hungary** was created out of the Austrian empire in 1867.

POSTWAR GERMANY
Prussia gained Holstein, Hanover, Hesse-Kassel, Nassau, and the city of Frankfurt. **The German Confederation collapsed** and a new North German Confederation controlling all states north of the river Maine was established under Prussian control. The Prussian king became its president and controlled its foreign policy and army. Three southern states (Baden, Bavaria, and Württemberg) remained outside the Confederation but were forced to sign an alliance with Prussia against France. This new German structure lasted until the defeat of France and **the creation of the German empire under Prussian rule in 1871 228–29 »**.

PRUSSIAN STRATEGIST (1800–1891)

COUNT HELMUTH VON MOLTKE

Chief of general staff of the Prussian army from 1857 to 1881, von Moltke was a skilled strategist and leader. In his view, military strategy should be open to revision, since only the start of a campaign could be planned in detail. He therefore ensured that military leaders were trained for all options. "No battle plan survives contact with the enemy," he noted. "War is a matter of expedients." He also pioneered the use of railways to move troops at speed.

The defeat of Austria in the Seven Weeks War ‹‹ 227 saw the removal of a major impediment to German unification. Another obstacle was the growing power of France.

PRETEXT FOR WAR

In 1870 the vacant throne of Spain was offered to Prince Leopold von Hohenzollern-Sigmaringen, a member of the Catholic branch of the ruling house of Prussia. The French objected, Leopold withdrew, but Wilhelm I of Prussia refused to give assurances that the offer would not be made again, recording the events of his meeting with the French ambassador in a telegram he sent to Bismarck. The latter then edited the telegram to suggest that insults had been exchanged and released it to the press. A huge furore followed, causing France to declare war on 19 July.

PRUSSIAN CHIEF MINISTER OTTO VON BISMARCK

NORTHWEST EUROPE

Franco-Prussian War
Dates 1870–71
Location Eastern France

Von Bredow's "Death Ride"

Prussian cavalry under Major-General Friedrich von Bredow overrun French artillery at Mars-la-Tour in one of the few successful cavalry charges in modern history. Von Bredow used gun smoke to obscure his attack.

Franco-Prussian War

The war between Prussia and France in 1870–71 transformed Western Europe, creating a unified German empire under Prussian leadership, and replacing the Second French empire under Napoleon III with a republic. It also saw Germany taking over two French provinces (Alsace and Lorraine), a cause of massive French resentment that itself became one of the causes of World War I.

Within two weeks of the French declaration of war, Prussia and her German allies had moved 300,000 troops in three armies along the French border. The French mobilized in disarray, but had the advantage of the Reffye Mitrailleuse, an early machine-gun, and the Chassepot rifle that had a range over twice that of the Prussian Dreyse needle gun. The Prussian breech-loading artillery, however, was superior to the French muzzle-loaders.

Early Prussian victories

The first encounters between the two sides in eastern France saw heavy Prussian casualties, but the French were forced to withdraw by Prussian outflanking moves. Marshal Bazaine, in command of the French left wing in Lorraine, withdrew from Metz towards Verdun to avoid encirclement. His troops then ran into a Prussian army corps at Mars-la-Tour. The Prussians were heavily outnumbered and risked defeat if the French attacked. But the cavalry under Friedrich von Bredow launched a charge that disrupted French artillery and deterred the French from taking any initiatives until the main Prussian army could arrive. The Prussians then cut the main road to Verdun, forcing Bazaine to withdraw towards Metz and take up a defensive position between Gravelotte and St Privat. On 18 August the Prussians attacked in force, but suffered huge losses as they advanced over open ground into heavy Reffye Mitrailleuse fire. Bazaine, however, failed to launch a counterattack, allowing Prussia's Saxon army to take St Privat and forcing the French to retreat into Metz. Here, they were besieged, removing them from the war and giving a strategic victory to the Prussians despite their terrible loss of over 21,000 troops.

French defeat at Sedan

To the northwest, the French Army of Châlons under Marshal MacMahon, accompanied by Napoleon III, set out to relieve Bazaine in Metz but was driven into a loop of the river Meuse at Sedan and encircled by the Prussian army led by Helmuth von Moltke. On 1 September Prussian artillery on the hills overlooking the city opened fire and for two days pounded the French, whose own guns were too far away to respond. The French cavalry bravely charged the Prussian lines, but the gesture was futile. Faced with this ongoing slaughter, Napoleon III surrendered, meeting Bismarck the next day to agree peace terms. He and his entire army were then taken into captivity.

The French Republic at war

The surrender of Napoleon III, however, did not end the war. The news from Sedan led to a bloodless revolution in Paris. The emperor was formally deposed and a provisional republican government of national defence was created under General Trochu. As the

> ## 5 BILLION
> **The number of francs France had to pay Germany within three years in compensation for the war.**

Prussians made for Paris, to besiege it on 19 September, Trochu rapidly organized the city's defences. He was greatly assisted by his Interior Minister, Léon Gambetta, who in early October left Paris by hot-air balloon, flying over the enemy lines to organize the new Armies of National Defence in the provinces. The Prussians fought hard against these forces and engaged guerillas who attacked their lines of communication. Prussian reprisals for these attacks and Trochu's unsuccessful sorties from Paris added to the mayhem.

On 5 January 1871 the Prussians began a bombardment of Paris, an attack that saw the first use of anti-aircraft

Lefaucheux pinfire revolver

This French cavalry revolver features one of the first designs of brass cartridge. The hammer strikes a pin on the side of the cartridge, which fires the bullet.

artillery – a steel Krupp piece designed to shoot down the balloons being used by French couriers. At first the attack stiffened Parisian morale, but over four months famine took hold and a final, major breakout failed on 18 January, with heavy losses. In the provinces the Prussians were also routing the national defence armies. On 28 January, recognizing their inevitable defeat, the French signed an armistice with Bismarck, bringing the war to an end.

AFTER

The Treaty of Frankfurt signed in May 1871 transformed the political map of Europe.

FRANCE

France ceded **Alsace and northern Lorraine** to Germany. Its desire for revenge was one of the causes of **World War I 266–77 ››. The Third Republic was created**, but Paris rejected the new government and established the **independent Paris Commune**. French troops besieged the city, recapturing it on 21 May.

GERMANY

On 18 January 1871 **King Wilhelm I of Prussia was proclaimed Emperor of Germany** in the Hall of Mirrors in Versailles. The new empire included all 25 states in north and south Germany, plus the new territory of Alsace-Lorraine.

ITALY

The withdrawal of French troops from Rome in 1870 **completed Italy's unification ‹‹ 224–25**.

Flying over enemy lines
French Interior Minister, Léon Gambetta, escapes
Paris in a balloon to rally his troops in northern
France. Although targeted by Prussian artillery
fire, his flight is successful.

« BEFORE

Mexico had been part of the Viceroyalty of New Spain ever since it was colonized by Spain in the early 16th century.

INDEPENDENCE
The **independence of the United States** « 178–79 and the outbreak of the **French Revolution** « 186–87 had a great impact in Mexico. After Emperor Napoleon of France **occupied Spain in 1808** « 198–99, liberal Mexicans seized their opportunity and in 1810 **rose in revolt**. They were supported mainly by **Amerindians and mestizos**, people of mixed race, but opposed by wealthier mestizos and conservative Spaniards, who feared for their privileges. War against the colonial authorities continued for ten years, but after liberals came to power in Spain in 1820, conservatives declared Mexico **an independent republic** in order to preserve the status quo. In 1822 the country was proclaimed **an empire**.

A MILITARY STRONG MAN
Regional differences, conflicts over the form of government and the role of the church, and acute economic problems made the independent state almost ungovernable. In 1823 **the empire was overthrown** and replaced by a republic. From then on, politics was dominated by powerful individuals, often army officers, seeking power for their own ends. In 1832 **General Antonio López de Santa Anna seized power** to become president for the first of 11 times.

SANTA ANNA

THE SIEGE OF THE ALAMO

In December 1835 a group of Texan volunteers drove the Mexicans out of San Antonio and occupied the old San Antonio de Válero mission, known as the Alamo. On hearing of the approach of Santa Anna's army, Texan commander, Sam Houston, urged them to leave but they refused. The siege began on 23 February. The 183 defenders, including frontiersmen Davy Crockett and James Bowie, held out for 13 days until the Mexicans finally overwhelmed them on 6 March 1836. No prisoners were taken, with only a few women and children emerging.

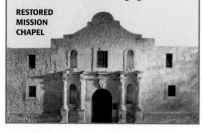

RESTORED MISSION CHAPEL

Mexican Wars

At independence in 1821, Mexico consisted of not just the present-day country but also what are now the southwestern states of the US, stretching from Texas in the east across to California on the Pacific coast. Tensions with the increasingly expansionist United States of America soon led to problems.

In 1821 the first 300 American families seeking new lands to farm settled in the empty plains of Texas. By the end of the decade there were more than 30,000 US settlers, who outnumbered native Mexicans three to one. The Mexican government perceived these settlers as a threat and in 1830 its troops occupied Texan towns and policed its borders, levying heavy duties on imported goods. The troops were withdrawn in 1832 but when the Texan leader, Stephen Austin, went to Mexico City the following year to petition the government to make Texas an autonomous province, he was arrested and imprisoned for 18 months.

War with Texas
Mexican troops then returned and tension rose, until, in September 1835, they tried to disarm a group of Texans in the town of Gonzales. The Texans rose in revolt and by the end of the year had evicted all Mexican troops from their state in a series of surprise attacks. But the Mexican government was already preparing its response, assembling an army led by President Santa Anna to recapture the state. It crossed the Rio Grande in February 1836 and advanced to San Antonio. One of the first clashes was at the Alamo (see KEY MOMENT).

With the arrival of the Mexican army the prospects for an independent Texas looked bleak, but a convention was summoned to prepare a declaration of independence. This was quickly drafted and signed on 3 March, while the defenders of the Alamo were still holding out. Prospects became even worse when, after gaining a victory at Coleto, the Mexicans massacred over 300 Texans at Goliad on 27 March. The victims had all surrendered and given up their arms, expecting to be treated as prisoners of war.

Santa Anna then spread out his forces to cover as much territory as possible, while Sam Houston, commanding the small Texan army, at first made a strategic retreat. When the Texans switched to the offensive, they came face to face with the part of the Mexican army commanded by Santa Anna himself, near the San Jacinto river (in the modern-day city of

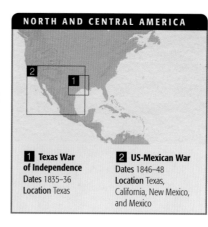

1 Texas War of Independence
Dates 1835–36
Location Texas

2 US-Mexican War
Dates 1846–48
Location Texas, California, New Mexico, and Mexico

Houston). In a remarkable battle fought on 21 April the Texans took the much larger Mexican force completely by surprise, achieving victory in the space of 18 minutes. Over 600 Mexicans lost their lives, many of them drowning in the marshland beside the river as they tried to flee. Santa Anna was captured during the mopping-up operations the following day.

In May he signed two documents, known as the Treaties of Velasco, bringing the war to an end; but with Santa Anna now out of office, the government of Mexico refused to recognize Texas as independent.

2,400 Mexican soldiers are thought to have fought against the 183 defenders at the siege of the Alamo, although some estimates put the number as high as 4,000.

An independent state
Many Texans, including the new president, Sam Houston, hoped to join the USA, but this idea was rejected by anti-slavery states fearful of slave-

Texas Rangers to keep out marauding bands of Mexican troops. Agitation grew both in Texas and across the southern US states for Texas to join the USA.

War with the United States
In 1845 Congress voted to admit Texas to the Union. James Polk had won the recent presidential election because he supported Texas's admission and also wanted to acquire California. He sent a delegation to Mexico City to negotiate a border settlement and the purchase of New Mexico and California for $30 million. But the Mexicans snubbed the US delegation, causing Polk to send troops to the disputed mouth of the Rio Grande on the Gulf of Mexico. The Mexicans counterattacked, and war broke out in April 1846.

In the west General Stephen Kearny and 1,600 troops, including a group of Missouri volunteers led by Alexander Doniphan, easily captured Santa Fe in New Mexico. Kearny then advanced into California, only to find it had already been seized by a small group of armed men under the command of the

> **"I have sustained a continuous bombardment** and cannonade **for 24 hours** … I shall **never surrender** or retreat."**
>
> WILLIAM BARRAT TRAVIS, A DEFENDER OF THE ALAMO, 1836

owning Texas disrupting the balance of free and slave states in the Union. For the next nine years Texas remained an independent state, although its border with Mexico was a matter of debate. The new republic, however, was poor. Large sums were needed to maintain the

explorer and surveyor John Frémont. Doniphan and his men meanwhile headed south from Santa Fe to take El Paso and then cross the border to seize Chihuahua in northern Mexico. In Texas US commander, Zachary Taylor, quickly defeated the Mexicans at Palo

Crossed cannons, the insignia of the US Army field artillery

Leather sheath

Brass hilt with embossed eagle on the pommel

Short, stabbing, 48-cm (19-in) blade

Swordbelt

US gunner's sword
US army artillerymen were issued with a short sword in case their batteries were overrun by the enemy, but it was of little practical use as a weapon.

AFTER »

6 THOUSAND regular soldiers made up the US army before the outbreak of war in 1846.

115 THOUSAND fighting men and staff were employed by the army by the end of the war.

The war with the United States left Mexico with a weak central government and the country was dominated by regional *caudillos* (leaders). Santa Anna returned as president in 1853 but he and the conservatives were ousted in a revolution in 1855.

FRENCH INTERVENTION
The liberals introduced a new constitution in 1857, causing a **civil war with the conservatives** that ended in a **liberal victory in 1861**. With the country bankrupt, the new president, **Benito Juárez,** suspended interest payments on foreign loans. In January 1862 the three main creditors, Britain, Spain, and France, sent fleets to Veracuz to **enforce payment of the debts**. It emerged that France had a secret agenda and

EXECUTION OF MAXIMILIAN

intended to conquer the country, so the British and Spanish withdrew. The French advance on Mexico City was halted at **Puebla, where a Mexican army drove them back** in May. The French had to await reinforcements and did not take Puebla until the following year, eventually entering Mexico City in June 1863. They then installed the **Habsburg Archduke Maximilian as emperor**, but he was unable to rally support for his rule. A **guerrilla war against France** ensued until the French emperor, Napoleon III, withdrew his troops in 1867. Juárez retook Mexico City and Maximilian was captured and executed.

TRAINING FOR THE WAR TO COME
For many of the Americans who fought against Mexico, it was their first experience of war. In 1861–65 officers such as **Robert E. Lee and William T. Sherman** would meet again fighting on opposite sides of the much longer and bloodier conflict of the **US Civil War 232–37** »

Alto and Resaca de la Palma and crossed the Rio Grande, capturing Matamoros and then heading inland to link up with Doniphan's force and take Monterrey after a five-day siege in September. At this point, Santa Anna came back from exile in Cuba, where he had been since losing the presidency in 1844, to resume leadership of his country. He raised an army and in February 1847 came close to defeating Taylor at Buena Vista outside Monterrey.

In order to break the deadlock, Polk ordered General Winfield Scott to lead a 12,000-strong army by sea to capture the Mexican port of Veracruz on the Caribbean coast. The city surrendered in March after a three-day bombardment and US troops then headed inland to seize Mexico City. Santa Anna suffered three heavy defeats before he asked for an armistice in August. After two weeks of futile negotiations, US troops resumed fighting and entered the city in September 1847, remaining there until peace terms were agreed.

The spoils of war
The US had won largely because Mexico had been unable to present a united front. The presidency had changed hands several times during the war and some provinces had refused to fight. By the Treaty of Guadalupe Hidalgo, signed in February 1848,

21 PER CENT was the amount by which US national territory was increased following the war of 1846–48.

40 PER CENT of Mexico's national territory was sold to the US. (This figure does not include Texas.)

Mexico recognized the independence of Texas and its subsequent entry into the Union. It also agreed to sell what are now the US states of New Mexico, Arizona, half of Colorado, Utah, Nevada, and California to the United States for $15 million. The border was fixed along the Rio Grande and then west to the Pacific. In 1853, in return for a further $10 million, the impoverished Santa Anna government agreed another boundary adjustment in southern New Mexico and Arizona. The land purchased would provide suitable terrain for the US Southern Pacific Railroad to reach the Pacific. By this time the discovery of gold in California in 1848 had transformed the previously poor rural state into one of the richest regions on the continent.

Battle of Buena Vista
Future US president, Zachary Taylor, shown here on the right, repels an attack by far superior Mexican forces. He was perhaps fortunate that Santa Anna was summoned back to Mexico City to put down a revolt

« BEFORE

The US Civil War arose from a deep divide between North and South over slavery.

THE STATES BALANCED

The convention of 1787 that drew up the US Constitution allowed each of the 13 states to decide for itself whether to allow slavery. **The seven northern states abolished slavery**, while the six southern states kept it, as **slaves provided cheap labour** on their lucrative cotton, tobacco, and sugar plantations. But as new states were admitted to the Union, **the southern states grew increasingly concerned** that the balance would shift against slavery, leading to its abolition and **massively damaging their plantation-based economy**.

5.5 MILLION The free population of the southern states in 1860.

3.5 MILLION The slave population of the southern states in 1860.

THE STATES DIVIDED

For a while the Missouri Compromise of 1820 balanced the admission of free and slave states to the Union. In 1857, however, **the US Supreme Court overturned the Missouri Compromise as unconstitutional**. Then in 1860 Abraham Lincoln won the presidential election. **Lincoln was already a figure of hate in the southern states**, having promised that he would refuse to extend slavery to new territories in the west if elected. **The stage was set for war**.

ROBERT E. LEE

Robert E. Lee could have commanded either side in the war, as Lincoln offered him command of the Union forces when the war broke out and he was opposed to the 11 states leaving the Union. But as the son of a former governor of Virginia and the owner of 196 slaves, he chose to serve the Confederacy. Tactical skill against numerically larger forces won him major victories at the Seven Days Battles, Fredericksburg, and Chancellorsville, but strategically he was less successful, failing to invade the North in 1862 and 1863, and losing at Antietam and Gettysburg.

Start of the US Civil War

The four-year civil war that divided North and South in the US was the most destructive war ever fought on the North American continent. The outcome of its battles was often finely balanced, and in the first two years both sides tried but failed to achieve the outright victory they so desperately sought.

Before Abraham Lincoln was even inaugurated as the new president, southern leaders withdrew their states from the Union. South Carolina left first, on 20 December 1860, and ten more followed early the next year. Together they set up the Confederacy, choosing Jefferson Davis as president and establishing a capital at Richmond, Virginia. On 12 April 1861 Confederate forces bombarded the Union-held Fort Sumter in South Carolina, marking the start of the civil war.

The two sides were by no means evenly matched. The Union's population of 23 million dwarfed the Confederacy's 9 million, more than a third of whom were slaves. The Union held most of the country's industry and railroads, while the Confederacy lacked most essential supplies other than food. Neither side, however, had an army, for the regular US army was only 16,000 strong and had divided with the states. Both sides therefore started to recruit new armies staffed with volunteers and state militia members. Holding the naval advantage, the Union soon blockaded Confederate ports to prevent supplies getting in, and began amphibious operations, the most successful of which was the capture of New Orleans in April 1862.

1 MILLION people are thought to have died on both sides in the US Civil War, including some 618,000 soldiers, two-thirds of whom died from disease.

First battles

The Union's first aim was to capture the Confederate capital, Richmond, only 160km (100 miles) south of the old national, now Union, capital of Washington, DC. Inexperienced troops under General Irvin McDowell headed south into Virginia, but in July 1861 faced a hastily assembled Confederate army, reinforced by troops moved in by train, between Bull Run stream and Manassas rail junction. Initially the Union troops had the advantage of surprise, but soon ran into Colonel Thomas J. Jackson's brigade standing before them "like a stone wall", as Confederate General Barnard E. Bee put it. A counterattack saw off the Union troops at this first battle of Bull Run, earning "Stonewall" Jackson promotion to general.

Further battles in Virginia in 1862 showed the Union that the war would be hard won. A new front opened to the west when Union general, Ulysses S. Grant, captured forts in Tennessee and forced the Confederates to abandon Nashville. Grant then advanced down the Tennessee river and waited near Shiloh Church for the Army of the Ohio to join him. Before the two armies

Popular pistol
An unprecedented demand for firearms saw sales of the Colt .44 revolver soar during the US Civil War.

Star-spangled banners
After Kansas became the 34th state of the Union in January 1861, the Union flag had 34 stars (above left). The Confederate battle flag (above) has 13 stars – one for each breakaway state plus Kentucky and Missouri.

could meet, Confederate general, Albert S. Johnston, launched a surprise attack on 6 April 1862. Grant was forced back, but with the overnight arrival of the Ohio army he was able to launch his own attack at dawn the next day, and force the Confederates to withdraw.

New technology

Union victory at Shiloh weakened the Confederate hold of the west and opened the way to Union seizure and control of the Mississippi. A range of naval craft took part in this campaign, including ironclad gunboats, often

> ## "A **house divided against itself** cannot stand."
>
> **ABRAHAM LINCOLN**, JUNE 1858

converted from paddle steamers. These revolutionary craft were first seen on 8 March 1862, at the battle of Hampton Roads. In an effort to break the Union blockade of the coast of Virginia, the Confederates clad the half-burned hull of the captured USS *Merrimack* with thick iron plates from the waterline up. Renamed the CSS *Virginia*, it rammed and sank one Union ship, and drove two more aground. The next day the Union navy responded

with another revolutionary ship, the semi-submerged armoured iron raft the USS *Monitor*. The two met in the first-ever clash of iron warships, although neither caused sufficient damage to decide the contest.

Modern technology made an impact throughout the war. Railways and the telegraph eased communications over long distances, despite being vulnerable to enemy disruption. Photographers and reporters brought the war home to people via newspapers. But weaponry advanced little. The muzzle-loading rifle-musket used Minié bullets that could be loaded quickly and fired accurately, but still only from a standing position. Modern breech-loading repeater rifles were restricted to cavalry and sniper use, while cannon were little improved from Napoleonic times.

Stalemate

Throughout 1862 the war in Virginia swung from side to side. A Union army advanced towards Richmond but was met by a bold counterattack by General Robert E. Lee at the end of June at the series of encounters known as the Seven Days Battles. Although the Union forces outnumbered their opponents and were better equipped, the offensive unnerved their commander, General George B. McClellan, who withdrew to

the coast. The Confederates then won a second battle at Bull Run in August and decided to invade the North.

McClellan learned of the invasion plan but was too slow to act, allowing Lee to regroup behind Antietam Creek in Maryland. The one-day battle that followed on 17 September 1862 was unevenly matched, as Lee's army was greatly outnumbered. But McClellan was too cautious. Holding too many troops back, he failed to overwhelm his

23 THOUSAND **The total number of casualties at Antietam, the costliest one-day battle of the whole war.**

20 THOUSAND **The number of reserve Union troops fatally held back by General McClellan at Antietam.**

enemy, and suffered 12,000 casualties – the Confederates suffered almost as many. Worse still, he allowed Lee to withdraw the next day. But the battle ended Lee's invasion plans for good.

A last Union effort to take Richmond failed in December that year when Union troops heading south to the city crossed the Rappahannock river in an attempt to seize Fredericksburg, but were repelled by superior firepower.

Step by bloody step

Although the North had far greater resources than the South, as well as command of the sea, Union forces had to conquer Confederate territory to secure victory, so the conflict was always going to be a long war of attrition.

AFTER »

The stalemate reached between the two sides by the end of 1862 was not broken until July of the following year.

TURNING POINTS
Two decisive victories in July 1863, at **Gettysburg 234–35** » and **Vicksburg 236–37** », swung the war the Union's way. While mourning the loss of Jackson at Chancellorsville in May, **the Confederates continued to rely on Lee's tactical genius.** But McClellan lost his job for failing to pursue Lee after the battle at Antietam, and **the promotion of Grant to commander-in-chief in 1864 gave the Union the military leader it needed to win the war.**

DECISIVE RE-ELECTION
Lincoln won the 1860 election against a divided, pro-slavery opposition, taking less than half of the popular vote but winning all the free states except one. **In 1864 he stood for re-election.** No longer able to vote as they had left the Union, **the Confederates hoped he would be defeated by an anti-war candidate** who would bring the war to an end. **Many in the Union were tired of the war** and wanted it over as well. But in the end **Lincoln was re-elected quite comfortably**.

LINCOLN ELECTION CAMPAIGN PIN

KEY

- Union states 1861
- Confederate states 1861
- — State border
- - - - Union front line Dec 1861
- ····· Union front line Dec 1863
- Union blockade
- → Union campaign/landing
- Union victory
- Confederate victory
- Inconclusive battle

Pickett's Charge
Brigardier-General Lewis Armistead, with his hat skewered on the tip of his sword, leads Virginian troops in Pickett's Charge against the Union Army on Cemetery Ridge on 3 July 1863.

Gettysburg

The crucial battle of the US Civil War occurred at the small Pennsylvania town of Gettysburg in early July 1863. The battle itself was not planned and for three days its outcome was unclear, but the result was overwhelming. The Confederate invasion of the North was stopped and the tide of war turned inexorably in the Union's favour.

In late June the Confederate Army of Northern Virginia, led by General Robert E. Lee, advanced north up the Shenandoah Valley into Union-held Pennsylvania. The plan was to invade the North and bring the civil war to an end. In response, the Union Army of the Potomac, led by General George Meade, had instructions to seek out and destroy Lee's army. When Lee heard that the Union Army was nearby, he ordered his scattered troops to gather at Gettysburg. A division led by A.P. Hill arrived first and on 1 July entered the town in search of much-needed shoes. A small, dismounted Union cavalry troop opened fire on them, the sound of gunfire drawing in large numbers of troops from both sides. Confederate infantry then swept forwards through the town, but the Union infantry and artillery established and held an inverted, U-shaped, defensive line on the high ground of Cemetery Ridge to the south of the town.

The Confederates halted

On 2 July Lee launched an attack on the now reinforced Union lines. Confederate infantry drove Union troops out of a low-lying wheatfield and peach orchard west of the ridge, but were held by concentrated fire in Plum Run Valley, the "Valley of Death". At the north end of the ridge they failed to capture Cemetery Hill and other Union-held positions. Crucially, they also failed to capture Little Round Top at the south end, from where their artillery could have dominated the battlefield.

Lee ordered another assault the following day. At around 1:00 pm a lengthy Confederate bombardment softened up Union positions in the centre. Two hours later, Confederate infantry, including a division under Major-General George Pickett, advanced through open fields but were met by heavy Union artillery fire. When they got to within 200m (220yd) range, Union infantry opened up with volleys of Minié bullets fired from behind earthworks and stone walls. The Confederates were stopped in their tracks and within an hour the battle was over.

The next day, 4 July, sporadic fighting continued until it petered out in the afternoon. Both sides collected their wounded and began to bury their dead, although Lee's proposal for a prisoner exchange was rejected by Meade. Gettysburg had been (and still remains) the largest battle ever fought on American soil. About 85,000 Union troops faced 75,000 Confederates with both sides suffering heavy casualties. On 5 July Lee gave the order to head back south to Virginia. The Confederate invasion of the North had failed.

LOCATION
Gettysburg, southern Pennsylvania

DATE
1–3 July 1863

FORCES
Union: 85,000;
Confederate: 75,000

CASUALTIES
Union: 23,000 killed, wounded, missing, or taken prisoner;
Confederate: 28,000 killed, wounded, missing, or taken prisoner

KEY
▬ Union forces on the morning of 3 July
▬ Confederate forces on the morning of 3 July

235

« BEFORE

Civil war broke out in the US in April 1861 after 11 southern states left the Union.

CONTRASTING ECONOMIES
The Union states had a large industrial and agricultural economy capable of sustaining a long war. **The breakaway Confederate states were mainly agricultural**, needing to export their produce to pay for the import of war goods.

1.5 MILLION The total number of Springfield rifle-muskets manufactured at various different factories across the states of the Union in the four years of the war.

INITIAL STALEMATE
Early defeats of Union armies « 232–33 by inspired Confederate commanders such as General Robert E. Lee and Colonel "Stonewall" Jackson proved that the Confederacy would not easily be crushed. **But the Union was too slow to bring its superior resources to bear** – despite its ongoing naval blockade and its successes in the west, **in the main arena in and around Virginia there was stalemate**.

End of the US Civil War

Two years into the US Civil War, neither Union nor Confederacy had gained a decisive military advantage. A total commitment to win – at whatever cost – would now be required for either side to achieve an outright victory. Leadership and strategy would prove crucial.

The issue of slavery had caused the war, and it was a resolution of this issue that President Lincoln used to break the deadlock. On 1 January 1863 he issued the Emancipation Proclamation, declaring free all slaves residing in states still in rebellion against the Union. Its immediate effect was limited, as it did not free slaves in the Union and could not yet be enforced in the Confederacy. But it gave the Union the moral high ground and ended Confederate hopes of recognition and support from Europe – particularly Britain, a major customer for its cotton and tobacco exports. The proclamation also helped recruit large numbers of black soldiers. Some 200,000 joined up, although they were paid less than white soldiers and could not become officers. Conscription, which the Confederacy

had introduced in 1862, was enforced in the Union in 1863. By the end of the war around 50 per cent of eligible Union men and some 75 per cent of Confederate men had been mobilized.

The tide turns
In both Ulysses S. Grant and William T. Sherman, Lincoln found the generals he needed to achieve victory. Superior manpower, greater resources, and the industrial production of weapons and other supplies did the rest. The genius of General Lee, however, still had a part to play. Boldly taking the war into Union territory, he advanced towards Pennsylvania, his tactical skills winning a superb victory at Chancellorsville in May 1863. But two months later his offensive was turned back at the fiercely contested three-day battle

of Gettysburg (see pp.234–35) and he was forced to retreat south. On the same day Union forces finally took the city of Vicksburg on the Mississippi after a lengthy siege, cutting off the states of Arkansas, Louisiana, and Texas from the rest of the Confederacy.

The Confederacy was now on the defensive. As the Union naval blockade slowly throttled the economy of the South, the Confederate army was denied extra manpower by Lincoln's decision in April 1864 to end prisoner exchanges between the two sides – to the much greater detriment of the resource-starved South than the North. Any hope that the Confederacy might have had of holding out until the Union

Enfield bullet mould
Commonly used on both sides in the US Civil War, this simple hand-held device made one bullet at a time out of carefully poured molten lead.

A trail of devastation
In late 1864 General Sherman's troops marched east through Georgia, ripping up railway tracks, burning crops, and destroying farms in an effort to "make Georgia howl", as Sherman himself described it.

"Napoleon" gun-howitzer
The most common field gun used by both sides in the war, the smoothbore "Napoleon" fired spherical solid shot, shell, or case rounds at ranges greater than about 550m (600yds), and canister rounds at closer range.

Leather cover to keep 1.13kg (2.5lb) powder charge dry

Cascabel, for moving barrel up and down

Prolonge, a thick rope for manoeuvring the gun

Hitch

Rammer

Detachable sight

Wooden wheel with metal rim

AFTER »

The effects of the US Civil War were felt for years, as the Union struggled to reunite its divided people and put slavery behind it.

ASSASSINATION OF LINCOLN
On 14 April 1865, five days after the Confederate surrender, Abraham Lincoln attended Ford's Theatre in Washington, where **he was shot in**

BOOTH SHOOTS LINCOLN

the head with a .44 Derringer pistol by the actor John Wilkes Booth, a Confederate sympathizer. Lincoln died the next day.

THE EMANCIPATION OF SLAVES
All US slaves were freed in 1865 when the Emancipation Proclamation of 1863 became law as the 13th Amendment to the US constitution. **The 14th Amendment of 1868 granted them US citizenship**, and the 15th Amendment of 1870 guaranteed their right to vote.

RECONSTRUCTION LAWS
The defeated Confederate states were occupied by Union troops. "Reconstruction" laws prohibited Confederates from holding public office and required ex-soldiers to pledge allegiance to the Union. **Defeated states were allowed to rejoin the Union only after they approved the 14th Amendment.** All did so by 1871, but **white Southerners manipulated laws to disenfranchise black people again**.

FURTHER CONFLICT
In 1864, near the end of the US Civil War, conflict broke out in the west as **Native Americans of the Great Plains fought the US Cavalry 242–43 »** to protect their ancestral hunting grounds from encroaching white settlers.

wearied of fighting would disappear once and for all as Lincoln headed for re-election as president in late 1864.

The character of the war changed, the skirmishes and pitched battles of the first two or so years replaced by a brutal war of attrition that was designed to attack the Confederate economy and intimidate its population. Lincoln and Grant did not seek such a war, preferring to win quickly on the battlefield, but they were prepared to achieve victory at any cost. They agreed with Sherman, who in 1864 wrote bluntly: "War is cruelty, and you cannot refine it."

In March 1864 Grant planned to end the war with a giant pincer movement. The Army of the Potomac would head south into Virginia to engage General Lee's Army of Northern Virginia and

> **"No terms, except unconditional and immediate surrender, can be accepted."**
> GENERAL ULYSSES S. GRANT, FEBRUARY 1862

ULYSSES S. GRANT

Grant had resigned from the US army in 1854 and then lost his Missouri farm during the 1857 depression. The war revived his fortunes. Back in the army in the rank of colonel, he fought aggressively in Tennessee, notably at Shiloh, and was soon promoted. In March 1864 Lincoln appointed him commander-in-chief as the man he believed would best achieve victory. "He fights," said the president. In 1868 Grant himself was elected to the presidency.

finally capture the Confederate capital, Richmond, while further to the west, Sherman's army would sweep from Tennessee southeast into Georgia.

The final months
The war in Virginia was bloody and initially inconclusive. Union attacks at Wilderness and Spotsylvania in May 1864 and at Cold Harbor in early June failed to break through Confederate defences. In June Grant crossed the James river to attack Richmond from the south, but the town of Petersburg lay in his path. There developed a nine-month siege, both sides digging defensive trenches and earthworks. Tied down, the

42 THOUSAND **Union troops were killed or wounded at Petersburg.**

28 THOUSAND **Confederates were killed or wounded during the siege.**

Confederates grew increasingly hungry and demoralized as well-supplied Union reinforcements kept arriving.

In May 1864 Sherman and his troops swept into Georgia, taking Atlanta by the end of August. His troops then cut an 80-km (50-mile) wide swathe of destruction as they headed east through Georgia. At the

"Dictator" railway mortar at Petersburg
At Petersburg the Union army employed a variety of siege tactics. This mortar mounted on a railway flatcar was one; another was detonating 320 kegs of gunpowder in a tunnel under the Confederate lines.

coast he headed north to complete the Union encirclement. With the Confederate army now down to barely 60,000 men, Lee decided to withdraw from Petersburg, abandon Richmond, and try to link up with troops still fighting Sherman in North Carolina. But he had left it too late.

On 2 April 1865 Union troops broke through and finally captured Petersburg. A day later Richmond fell at last. Lee managed to withdraw, but was blocked at Appomattox Court House on 8 April. The next day, he surrendered.

The Union had been saved, but at huge cost. The economy and towns of the South were in ruins. Some 360,000 Union soldiers were dead and 275,000 wounded. Confederate deaths totalled 258,000, with 100,000 wounded.

« BEFORE

In the early 1800s Africa consisted of European trading posts and a few colonies around the coast and African-led empires and kingdoms in the interior.

EUROPEAN COLONIES

In the 15th century the **Portuguese** set up a number of trading stations down the west coast of Africa as they made their way south round the tip of Africa to India. The **French, Dutch, and English** followed in the 1600s, setting up **trading** and **slaving stations** on the **West African coast**. The only substantial settlements were those established by the Portuguese after 1505 in what is now Mozambique, and after 1652, by the Dutch in the Cape Colony.

AFRICAN EMPIRES AND KINGDOMS

Powerful African peoples that opposed European incursions on their territory included the **Asante** in the **gold-producing region of West Africa** and the **Zulus in the south 246–47** ». There were also a number of powerful Islamic states that emerged in sub-Saharan West Africa during the 19th century. The most important were the **Sokoto caliphate**, established in northern Nigeria in 1820, and the **Tukulor empire** in the Niger Valley, founded in 1863.

ASANTE WARRIOR

Imperial Wars in Africa

At the beginning of the 19th century European contact with Africa was limited to trading stations around the coast, those on the west coast playing a major role in the shipping of African slaves to the Americas. By the end of the century almost the entire continent was under European control.

The first major European invasion of Africa took place in 1830, when the French drove out the Dey, the ruler of Algiers, a vassal of the Ottoman empire, and began the occupation of Algeria. The coastal regions were swiftly subdued, but a determined resistance movement grew up around the figure of Abd al-Qadir. As France continued its conquests he proclaimed a holy war against the invading infidels. The French retaliated with a brutal scorched earth policy and eventually occupied his headquarters at Mascara. In 1844 the Sultan of Morocco intervened but was defeated by the French. Al-Qadir eventually surrendered in 1847. Algeria soon became an important source of troops for the French army, notably the *zouaves*, who served as light infantry.

Further European incursions

In West Africa British trading posts on the Gold Coast came into conflict with the gold-rich Asante kingdom. Asante efforts to regain their coastline led to war in 1823–31 and then again in

Landing in Algeria
On 14 June 1830 a large French invasion fleet anchored off Sidi Ferruch to the west of Algiers. An army of 34,000 men was landed, which swiftly defeated the troops sent to oppose them and occupied Algiers on 5 July.

protectorate over Tunisia, while the Germans grabbed Namibia, Cameroon, and Togo in 1884. A "Scramble for Africa" broke out, in which European powers competed for African resources, markets, investments, peoples, and territories. Otto von Bismarck, the German chancellor, convened a conference in Berlin in 1884–85 to control the situation. It established a framework for expansion that largely avoided conflicts between the powers, opening the way for the total European colonization of Africa.

1873–74. A British expedition led by Sir Garnet Wolseley halted an Asante advance in November 1873 and then moved into the interior, armed with artillery. Wolseley defeated the Asante in January at Amoafu and then burned down their capital, Kumasi, forcing their king, Kofi Karikari, to make peace. Further wars in the 1890s led to the establishment of a British protectorate in 1897.

Elsewhere, the establishment of a colony at Lagos in 1861 brought the British into conflict with the Sokoto caliphate, while the French establishment of a protectorate in Senegal in 1854 led to conflict with the Tukulor empire. In southern Africa Boer colonists came into conflict with Bantu tribes in 1834 and then the Zulus in 1838, defeating them at the battle of Blood river (see pp.246–47).

In 1879 King Leopold II of Belgium and his International African Association began to set up trading stations on the Congo river, establishing a personal empire in the region. In 1881 France established a

The Scramble for Africa

The race to colonize the whole of Africa accelerated dramatically after 1885. Urged on by public opinion back home, European explorers, adventurers, traders, and missionaries led the race into the interior of the continent.

Map labels

Algiers 1830: occupied by French
Oran 1831: French rule
Tunis
Casablanca 1907: French occupation
Revolt of Abd el-Qadir 1832–47
ALGERIA
TUNIS
Tripoli
TRIPOLITANIA
Laghouat
Benghazi
Derna 1912: Italian occupation
CYRENAICA
Alexandria
Cairo
Tel el-Kebir 1882
Canary Islands
Sahara
Ghat
Murzuk
EGYPT
Tushki
Wadi Halfa 1895–98: Anglo-Egyptian army HQ
Taoudenni 1906: French occupation
Tamanrasset 1902
Dongola 1885–96: Mahdist Revolt
Red Sea
Timbuktu 1894: captured by French
Agadez
Bilma
SUDAN 1885–98: Mahdist state
Suakin
Kaédi
Gao
Zinder
Lake Chad
Khartoum
Massawa
SENEGAL
Nioro
DARFUR
Omdurman 1898
GAMBIA
Kayes
Bamako 1883: French occupation
Say
Sokoto
Kano 1903
Adowa 1896
Gulf of Aden
PORTUGUESE GUINEA
Nikki 1894
Lokoja 1859
Fashoda 1898
Djibouti 1888
SIERRA LEONE
Kumasi 1896: British occupation
Lomé
Lagos
Addis Ababa
Accra 1850: ceded to British
Porto Novo
Douala 1884: German occupation 1896
Congo
Kampala 1890
Mogadishu
ATLANTIC OCEAN
Takoradi
São Tomé
Kisumu
INDIAN OCEAN
1 GOLD COAST COLONY
2 ASANTE
Brazzaville
Entebbe 1893
Nairobi 1899
Mombasa 1881
Leopoldville
1885: to Germany
Zanzibar — 1890: to Britain
Luanda
Dar es Salaam 1887: German occupation
ANGOLA
Benguela
Lusaka 1905
Tete
Mozambique 1505: to Portugal
Majunga 1895: French occupation
Livingstone 1888
Salisbury
MOZAMBIQUE
Beira 1891
Tananarive
Windhoek
Bulawayo
Walvis Bay
SOUTH AFRICAN REPUBLIC (TRANSVAAL) 1876–81: to Britain
Mafeking 1885
Lourenço Marques
Fort Dauphin 1642
Lüderitz
Johannesburg 1886
ORANGE FREE STATE
Kimberley 1871
NATAL
Durban 1824: colonization
CAPE COLONY
Cape Town
Port Elizabeth

Key

Colonial territory by 1880 and expansion after 1880

- Ottoman suzerainty
- British
- Portuguese
- French
- Spanish
- Boer republics
- German
- Belgian
- Italian
- Battle

Sudanese arrowheads

These weapons were used by the Mahdi's army when it overran Khartoum, killing General Gordon, in 1885. In a pitched battle, however, traditional African weaponry was of little use against modern rifles and machine-guns.

The British in Egypt and Sudan

Although technically part of the Ottoman empire, Egypt had been autonomous since 1807. Ismail Pasha, who had permitted the construction of the Suez Canal in 1869, had modernized the country, but had run up huge debts in the process. Demands by creditors for repayment in 1881 led to riots in Alexandria that killed several British citizens. In July 1882 British gunboats bombarded the port while a

British army under Wolseley defeated a 38,000-strong Egyptian force at Tel el-Kebir in a 30-minute battle in September. Britain then occupied Egypt and established a protectorate.

Control of Egypt brought with it Sudan, which the Egyptians had conquered. In 1881 Muhammad Ahmad declared himself the Mahdi ("Expected One") and waged a holy war against Egyptian rule, annihilating a British-led Egyptian army of 10,000 men in 1883. The British government dispatched General Charles Gordon to evacuate citizens from the capital, Khartoum, but he chose to stay and after a lengthy siege was killed by the Mahdi's troops on 26 January 1885. Gordon's death was avenged in 1898,

when an Anglo-Egyptian army led by General Kitchener set out to reconquer Sudan. On 2 September his 26,000-strong army met 50,000 men under the command of the Mahdi's successor at Omdurman. The battle was one-sided, the British artillery

Charge of the 21st Lancers at Omdurman, Sudan

As they advanced, the British encountered a concealed force of 2,500 determined Mahdists. These were driven off by a cavalry charge – one of the last by the British army – in which a young Winston Churchill took part.

decimating the Mahdists even before they came within range of the deadly Maxim guns or the British trenches.

European superiority

The technological gap between well-armed, well-trained European armies and primitively armed native peoples mostly ensured European victory, although the invaders often needed to enlist local allies and recruit large numbers of local troops to win. Technological superiority did not, however, always guarantee peace.

Fore sight

Crank handle to turn barrels

Gatling gun

The most successful of the early rapid-fire guns, the Gatling was developed in the US in the 1860s. This ten-barrelled model was used by the British army in Africa and India in the 1870s and 80s.

Each of the ten revolving barrels had its own breech, chamber, and firing pin mechanism. One cartridge at a time was fed into the breech by gravity from a magazine attached to the top of the gun.

The gun was cradled on a yoke fixed to the centre of the axle. This allowed the elevation of the gun to be adjusted. The barrels moved from side to side automatically with the turning of the crank.

Trail, the projecting beam at the back for balancing and towing the gun

Trail spade for anchoring gun to the ground

Early Gatlings were mounted on a carriage with two large wheels, like conventional field artillery. Not until it was made lighter and mounted on a tripod was the gun's full potential as an infantry weapon realized.

AFTER

The colonization of Africa continued in the 20th century, with the French and Spanish takeover of Morocco in 1912 and the Italian invasions of Libya and Ethiopia.

ITALIAN CONQUESTS

Of the European colonial powers, the only one to suffer a lasting military setback was Italy, **defeated by Ethiopia at Adowa in 1896**. In 1935–36 Italy finally conquered the country, uniting it with its other East African colonies of Eritrea and Italian Somaliland. In 1911 Italy had also **seized Libya** from the Ottoman empire.

OPPOSITION TO COLONIAL RULE

Many parts of Africa saw years of **fierce resistance to European rule**. In 1926 it took a combined Franco-Spanish force of 250,000 men to put an end to the successful **guerrilla campaigns of Abd el-Krim in Morocco**.

After World War II **independence movements** gained strength all over Africa. In some countries the European colonizers relinquished power relatively peacefully; in others, such as **French Algeria** and **Portugal's various colonies**, long **brutal wars of independence** were fought **328–29 ≫**.

« BEFORE

The Qing dynasty brought stability to China and expanded its territory throughout the 18th century.

MANCHU EXPANSION

The Manchus of northern China **seized power from the Ming dynasty in 1644, establishing the new Qing dynasty « 132–33**. They slowly expanded their control of the region, taking Taiwan in 1683, Amur in Siberia in 1689, Mongolia in 1697, Tibet in 1720, and eastern Turkestan in 1760. Korea, Annam (Vietnam), Laos, and Mian (Burma) all became vassal states by 1769.

CHINESE INSULARITY

By the late 18th century Qing insularity brought China into conflict with European powers. Like his predecessors, Emperor Qianlong (1736–96) ruled "an empire with no boundary", and recognized no equal. In 1793, at the height of European expansion, he was met by a **British trade delegation led by Lord Macartney, who sailed to China aboard HMS *Lion***, a 64-gun man-of-war. The emperor received the delegation, but declined to offer any trading concessions to Britain. He stated that the British king, George III, was welcome to pay him homage, but that **no European manufactured goods could be exchanged for Chinese exports** (mainly tea, porcelain, and silk), which could only be paid for in silver. A further British mission was expelled in 1816 under the rule of Emperor Jiaqing (1796–1820). As a result, a crisis grew in Europe; **the demand for Chinese imports increased, while supplies of silver became ever scarcer**.

CHINESE RULER (1835–1908)
EMPRESS DOWAGER CIXI

The Empress Cixi became ruler of China during the regencies of her son, Tongzhi, and her nephew, Guangxu. When Guangxu announced plans to modernize China she overthrew him and consigned him to house arrest until he died. She opposed all reforms and supported the violently xenophobic Boxer rebels. She is held largely responsible for China's failure to modernize and for the Revolution of 1911.

Wars in China

In the 19th century the Chinese empire declined as foreign powers intervened in its internal affairs and slowly acquired parts of its territory. This erosion of Chinese power was accelerated by the highly conservative nature of the Qing government, which led to civil wars and finally to revolution in 1911.

China's ban on European imports and the increasing demand for Chinese tea, porcelain, and silk in Europe caused a huge trade imbalance between the regions. The British East India Company redressed this by illegally selling Bengali opium to China. As the number of addicts rose, the Chinese tried to suppress the trade, confiscating stocks of opium in Guangzhou and besieging the British merchants.

First Opium War

In June 1840 a fleet of 44 British ships with some 4,000 marines was sent from Singapore to demand compensation. The expedition blockaded the mouth of the Pearl river, then defeated the Chinese at the mouth of the Yangtze river. Coastal towns were bombarded, Guangzhou was taken, and tax barges were seized, drastically cutting the imperial income. Due to lack of modernization, China's defences were no match for ironclad steamships and European cannon and muskets; the chief weapon of the Manchu soldier (or bannerman) was still the composite bow.

In 1842 the Chinese sued for peace and signed the Treaty of Nanjing, ceding Hong Kong to Britain and opening up five so-called "treaty ports" to British merchants, who remained exempt from the jurisdiction of local law. The emperor also recognized Britain as equal to China. The US and France gained similar rights in 1844.

Second Opium War

Although trade restrictions were lifted after the war, opium remained illegal. In 1856 Chinese officials boarded the *Arrow*, a British-registered Chinese ship it suspected of smuggling opium. The British retaliated by seizing Guangzhou and attacking other Chinese ports, this time joined by the French who used the murder of a French missionary in China as a pretext. In 1858, with the British close to Beijing, the Chinese signed the Treaty of Tientsin, giving the British diplomatic representation at the imperial

court for the first time, and opening up ten new treaty ports. Merchants from all foreign powers were allowed to use all 15 treaty ports, and Christian missionaries and other foreigners were given leave to travel throughout China. The Chinese failed to ratify the treaty immediately, only doing so after an Anglo-French force captured Beijing and burnt the Summer Palace.

Taiping Rebellion

While European powers were attacking China from without, the country was assailed from within. In 1851, after a year of insurrections in Guangxi province, Hong Xiuquan, a failed scholar who had studied under a Baptist minister, established the God Worshippers' Society and proclaimed a new dynasty – the Taiping Kien-kuo ("Heavenly Kingdom of Great Peace"). His aim was to overthrow what he saw as the "foreign" Qing regime, to take the land into common ownership, and to ban the use of opium, tobacco, and alcohol. Exploiting people's fears about China's failing economy, the rebels rapidly grew in numbers and determination. Within two years, a million-strong army swept

Taiping currency

When Hong Xiuquan established the Taiping dynasty he minted coins such as these as a way of legitimizing his rule.

down the Yangtze valley and took Nanjing, killing thousands of civilians and over 30,000 imperial soldiers. With Nanjing as its capital, the Heavenly Kingdom expanded to encompass much of south and central China, totalling some 30 million people at its height. However, its power began to wane in 1861 when Hong was repulsed at Shanghai by the European-trained "Ever-Victorious Army", led by American general, Frederick Ward. On Ward's

EAST ASIA

1 **Opium Wars**
Dates 1839–42, 1856–60
Location Coastal China

2 **Taiping Rebellion**
Dates 1850–64
Location Eastern China

3 **Tonkin War**
Dates 1893–95
Location Northern Vietnam

4 **Sino-Japanese War**
Dates 1894–95
Location Korea and Manchuria

5 **Boxer Rebellion**
Dates 1899–1900
Location Area around Beijing

death, command passed to the British general, Charles Gordon, who, with the aid of modern artillery, retook Nanjing in 1864. During the siege over 100,000 rebels committed suicide, including Hong, who took poison. Fighting ended with the rebels' defeat in 1871.

Wars against France and Japan

With southern and central Vietnam under its control by 1883, France began to invade the Chinese-held north Vietnamese province of Tonkin. Captain Henri Rivière marched into Hanoi and evicted the Chinese troops occupying the city,

> "The government [prohibits] ... under pain of **death** membership in any **anti-foreign society**."
>
> FROM THE PEACE AGREEMENT FOLLOWING THE BOXER REBELLION, 1901

but was killed in a counterattack. French reinforcements then won a series of victories, forcing the Chinese viceroy to concede a joint protectorate over the province. When the French government rejected this agreement China declared war. Its army held off French attacks on southern China, but any idea that China could match European power was cruelly disabused when, in just half an hour in August 1884, French naval guns and torpedo ships destroyed its entire fleet of six new cruisers at Fuzhou. By the peace terms, China surrendered Vietnam to France.

Even worse was to come in the next decade when Japan and China clashed over the Chinese protectorate of Korea. Although vastly outnumbered, Japan's armed forces won major victories. In August 1894 their two navies met on the Yalu river, on the border between Korea and China. Japan's superior tactics and weaponry, combined with Chinese ineptitude (two of their ships were destroyed when their own paint and varnish caught fire), gave Japan an easy victory and ownership of Taiwan. Korea gained independence, but rivalry between Russia and Japan over Korea led to war in 1904–05, and Japan's annexation of the country in 1910.

Boxer Rebellion

Resentment of foreign involvement in China reached its peak in the Boxer Rebellion of 1899. Encouraged by the Empress Dowager Cixi in return for their support of the Qing dynasty, the I-ho-chuan ("Righteous and Harmonious Fists") society had the professed aim of ridding China of all its foreigners, particularly the Christian missionaries. In 1899 bands of these Boxers (so called because of their belief that certain boxing rituals made them immune to bullets) attacked Christians and burned their churches around Beijing. A multinational force tried to quell the uprising but was repelled by imperial forces. Cixi then ordered the killing of all foreigners, the resulting dead including a German minister and Japanese diplomat. A far larger force entered Beijing in August

Execution of Ketteler's murderer
One of the foreigners killed in the Boxer Rebellion was German minister Clemens von Ketteler; here, his killer is executed.

Qing dynasty matchlock wall gun
Dating from 1830, this simple gun, which could only be fired from a rest, illustrates the conservative nature of China at the time. Matchlocks had been replaced by flintlocks in much of Europe over 200 years earlier.

1900 and finally crushed the rebels. In the aftermath China was fined some $6.5 billion (in today's terms), her coastal forts were razed, and all anti-foreign societies were banned. Foreign troops were also stationed along the railway from Beijing to Shanghai.

AFTER

The collapse of Qing power led to revolution in 1911 and a long period of instability and war that only ended with the Communist takeover of 1949.

THE CHINESE REVOLUTION
In 1911 Sun Yat-Sen's Revolutionary Alliance Party (or Guomindang) exploited an army mutiny in Wuhan in central China to **overthrow the Qing dynasty and seize power**. Sun Zhongshan proclaimed the **Three Principles of Revolution (nationalism, democracy, and socialism)** but gave way to **General Yuan Shikai, who became president**.

CIVIL WAR AND INVASION
Shikai failed to unite the country, and by the time of his death in 1916 China was under the control of regional warlords. Shikai's eventual successor, **Jian Jieshi (Chiang Kai-shek), re-established central power from the new capital of Nanjing**. Meanwhile, **Japan took advantage of China's weakness to invade Manchuria** in northern China to acquire its raw materials and **extend its empire 282–83 ≫**.

Sioux horsemen
The horse was adopted by the Sioux on its introduction to the Americas by the Spanish in the 17th century.

Plains Indian Wars

Expansion west across the Mississippi to the Pacific coast brought US settlers into conflict with Native American tribes who lived on the Great Plains. Settler encroachment into their hunting grounds led to massacres and wars that would last until the end of the 19th century.

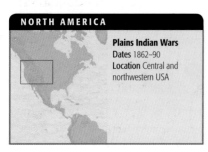

NORTH AMERICA

Plains Indian Wars
Dates 1862–90
Location Central and northwestern USA

« **BEFORE**

The expansion of the US westwards from its original 13 colonies on the Atlantic coast to the Mississippi river brought settlers into conflict with Native Americans.

DRIVING OUT THE NATIVES
The **Indian Removal Act of 1830** allowed for the **forced expulsion of native tribes to the unsettled Indian Territory west of the Mississippi river**. Resistance from the Sac and Fox tribes of Illinois and Wisconsin led to the Black Hawk War of 1832, and the Creeks of Georgia and Alabama were crushed in 1836. The Seminole of Florida were defeated in 1837, and the Cherokees were evicted during the winter of 1838–39; on their "**Trail of Tears**" to the Indian Territory more than 4,000 lost their lives. By the 1860s **the land west of the Mississippi was itself being encroached on by the settlers**.

The Great Plains west of the Mississippi river were peopled mainly by Sioux, Comanche, Cheyenne, Kiowa, and Arapaho tribes, whose age-old way of life was disturbed when the settlers appeared in the 18th and early 19th centuries. But the settlers had legal backing; Congress had passed a series of bills that offered supposedly free or unowned land on the plains in return for minimal investment.

The first wars
Conflicts between tribes and settlers were inevitable, but war broke out in 1862 when bands of eastern Sioux, or Dakota, took up arms against settlers living along the Minnesota river. Sparked by the US government's failure to ratify its own treaty agreements (by which land was ceded by the Sioux in return for money and goods), the war lasted three months and led to the hanging of 38 Dakota on 26 December 1862 – the largest

US cavalryman's sabre
Issued in 1860, this light cavalry sabre saw action throughout the US Civil War and the Plains Indian wars. It was an effective thrusting weapon and replaced the heavier model of 1840.

number of hangings in a single day in US history. The rest of the Dakota were expelled from Minnesota and sent to Nebraska and South Dakota, and their reservations were abolished by Congress.

The next major outbreak took place less than two years later, as the US Civil War was ending. Some 600 Cheyenne and Arapaho were camped on a bend of Sand Creek in Colorado, flying the American flag and a white flag of truce. Their chief, Black Kettle, had come to seek peace with the Americans after hostilities had flared between militant Cheyenne Dog Soldiers and white immigrants who had entered their lands in search of gold. He met with the Americans at Fort Lyon to ensure peace, but was later attacked in his camp by 700 Colorado militia led by Colonel John Chivington. Though Kettle himself survived, 150 Indians, many of them women and children, were killed in the attack.

The atrocity led to over a year of war in Colorado, the two sides using tactics that were replicated across the plains for nearly 40 years. Very often they fought on even terms; both sides largely fought on horseback, and the musket-rifles and pistols of the US troops regularly found their way into

native hands. The Native American Indians were skilled at guerrilla warfare and knew the land intimately, but natives from hostile tribes often provided scouts and information to US troops. Tragically, each side also inflicted massacres on the other.

The Bozeman Trail
At the same time as the Colorado War, a similar war was being fought in Montana, where the Bozeman Trail was established on Sioux lands in the early

Sioux warrior headdress
Though often considered a feature of all Native American dress, the feathered bonnet was only worn by the Sioux warriors of the Midwest.

lured off the trail and massacred. Two years later Red Cloud became the first (and remained the only) Indian leader to sign a peace treaty with the US government as a victor. By the Treaty of Fort Laramie the white settlers were banned from using the Bozeman Trail and the US army forts were abandoned. The Great Sioux Reservation was also established, encompassing all of modern "West River", South Dakota, including the Black Hills, and parts of Nebraska.

Broken promises
The US government honoured the treaty for just six years, until gold was discovered in the Black Hills in 1874. As gold miners and traders poured in, Sioux and Cheyenne warriors fought back under the leadership of chiefs Sitting Bull and Crazy Horse. The US government sent three armies to force the tribes back to their homes in the spring of 1876, one of which was defeated by the Lakota at the battle of Rosebud. On 25 June came the Sioux's finest hour; Lieutenant-Colonel George Custer and 225 US cavalry attacked a Sioux camp by the Little Bighorn river, only to be surrounded by Crazy Horse's warriors and massacred. The Sioux victory was decisive, but short-lived; the arrival of increasing numbers of US troops forced them to surrender in 1881.

The end of the conflict
By the late 1880s most tribes were settled on reservations and officially the war was over, but their suffering continued. Not only had they lost their traditional lands, but their means of subsistence had been destroyed by the slaughter of the buffalo, driven almost to extinction by the settlers' indiscriminate hunting. Furthermore, the Sioux reservation was now so small that it could no longer support the population. The half-starved Sioux turned to mysticism and the rites of the "Ghost Dance", a religious ceremony associated with the ending of white rule and the rebirth of

Custer's last stand
Lieutenant-Colonel George Custer's 7th Cavalry Regiment is surrounded by Lakota and Northern Cheyenne warriors near the Little Bighorn river on 25 June 1876. Custer's entire force is soon annihilated.

1860s following the discovery of gold in the region. After numerous Sioux attacks on the trail, the US army built three forts along its route. The Lakota Sioux leader, Red Cloud, attacked the forts, at one point holding a wagon train hostage on the trail. On 21 December 1866 Captain William Fetterman and 80 US cavalry rode to rescue the hostages but were

---

The removal of the Plains Indians to reservations from the 1860s onwards precipitated a similar fate for Native Americans across the continent.

THE NEZ PERCÉ
Gold was the cause of a war waged in 1877 between US troops and the Nez Percé peoples of Idaho. In 1863 **their reservation was reduced to a quarter of its size to allow for mining**, but after raids by both sides, their chief, Joseph, decided in 1877 that their future lay in Canada. They trekked north for five months, but were **encircled at Bear Paw mountain**, just 65km (40 miles) from the border. The two sides fought for five days, but the Nez Percé gave up when they realized US reinforcements were on their way. They were **banished to the Indian Territory**.

THE APACHE WAR
Conflict also raged in the southwest. The **Apache were gradually confined to**

APACHE CHIEF GERONIMO

reservations after 1870, but pressure from white settlers led the government to consolidate them in the arid San Carlos Reservation. One Apache chief, Geronimo, repeatedly broke out of the reservation, fleeing to Mexico and **raiding settlements on both sides of the border**, until he surrendered in 1886. Imprisoned in Florida and Alabama, he died in Fort Sill in the Indian Territory in 1909.

NATIVE LANDS
The **Indian Territory changed soon after it was set up in the 1830s**. It shrank in size in 1854 and again in 1890, and was finally **abolished in 1907**, when, as Oklahoma, it became the 46th state to join the Union. By then, almost all native tribes had signed treaties with the US government and moved into reservations. Some tribes received US citizenship from 1855, a right that was extended to all in the Indian Territory in 1901. **Full US citizenship was granted in 1924 to all Native Americans born in the country**.

---

the former world of the Sioux. Though the ceremony was banned, the Lakota of Pine Ridge and Rosebud performed it in October 1890, provoking the US government to send troops to arrest the leaders. While under arrest, Chief Sitting Bull was killed, provoking some 200 Sioux to leave their reservation. On the night of 28 December 1890, they surrendered quietly to the 7th Cavalry

> **250,000** The approximate Native American **population in 1900, down from ten million when Europeans first arrived in 1492.**

at Wounded Knee Creek. The following morning, however, a scuffle broke out as the natives were being disarmed and a trooper was shot. The soldiers moved in with machine-guns and massacred the largely unarmed natives. The war with the Sioux was finally over, leaving the white man master of the plains.

Native American knife
A common weapon among the Plains Indian tribes was a simple knife made from the head of a spear or lance attached to a wooden handle. A leather wrist loop prevented it from being dropped in battle.

Muskets and Rifles

The first matchlock muskets were fired by holding a slow-burning match above a pan of gunpowder primer to ignite it and propel the bullet out of the barrel. Later rifles contained a percussion cap that burst into flame when struck. Bolt-action rifles used a simple bolt to detonate the primer. Today's guns use gas as a propellant.

1 The German arquebus was an early type of matchlock musket invented around 1475. Though largely superseded by the wheel-lock in the 16th century, it continued in use until the late 17th century because of its simplicity. **2** This British matchlock musket dates from the 17th century. Pulling the trigger plunged a smouldering match into a pan containing a small primer of gunpowder. This ignited, sending a flash through a touch hole into the barrel to set off the main charge. Early models were heavy, clumsy, and unreliable – the match often went out – but later ones were lighter, and much more effective. **3** This Indian matchlock musket was made in Mysore (Karnataka) in the 18th century to a design first introduced to India by the Portuguese two centuries earlier. The design was much copied, adapted, and decorated by Indian gunsmiths. **4** The British Baker rifle of 1800 was the first rifle officially adopted for use by the British Army, and only superseded in 1838. Its slow or shallow rifling – a groove of just a quarter turn along the length of the barrel to spin the bullet – kept the barrel clean and usable for longer than weapons with unrifled barrels. **5** The Spencer rifle was developed in the US by Christopher Spencer in his spare time. When it appeared in 1863, it was the world's first practical, manually loaded repeater rifle, holding seven

rounds in a tubular magazine in the stock. **6** The Italian Cavalry Carbine of 1891, often known as the Mannlicher-Carcano, used a modified version of the bolt-action used in the German Mauser M1889 rifle. It continued in service in Italy until after World War II. US dealers bought many of them, one of which Lee Harvey Oswald used to assassinate President John F. Kennedy in 1963. **7** The German Mauser Infanteriegewehr 98 of 1898 was one of the best bolt-action rifles, with improved gas sealing, a refined magazine, and a third rear-locking lug to reinforce the two forward-mounted lugs. Its one flaw was that its bolt handle stuck out to the side. **8** The AK-47 assault rifle, designed by Russian tank commander, Mikhail Kalashnikov, was adopted by the Soviet Red Army in 1949. Its rugged simplicity, good handling, and ability to operate in almost any conditions made the rifle the most popular gun in the world. This version has been adapted to carry a grenade launcher. **9** The American Stoner M16A1 self-loading rifle of 1982 was capable of fully automatic fire, one of many such automatic rifles that replaced the earlier bolt-action weapons. **10** The Walther WA 2000 sniper rifle was made for German police marksmen in 1978. The model shown here is the experimental Series 1 version, with a fluted barrel.

1 GERMAN ARQUEBUS (c.1500)

3 INDIAN MATCHLOCK (18TH CENTURY)

7 GERMAN MAUSER INFANTERIEGEWEHR 98 (1898)

8 RUSSIAN AK-47 (1978 MODEL)

9 AMERICAN STONER M16A1 (1982)

2 BRITISH MATCHLOCK
(17TH CENTURY)

4 BRITISH BAKER RIFLE (1800)

CARTRIDGE CONTAINING
ROUND AND CHARGE

5 AMERICAN SPENCER RIFLE (1863)

6 ITALIAN CAVALRY CARBINE (1891)

7.62MM ROUND

GP25 GRENADE

5.56MM ROUND

10 GERMAN WALTHER WA 2000 (1978)

The Zulu Wars

In the 19th century the Zulus were the most aggressive and disciplined fighting force in southern Africa, a proud people whose battles with the Boers and British earned them legendary status. In the end, modern weapons and tactics defeated them – but not until they had dealt British prestige a major blow.

W hen on 6 February 1838 a party of about 100 Boer trekkers led by Piet Retief approached the Zulu chief, Dingane, in Natal to discuss the cession of land, they were taken to Kwa Matiwane Hill and clubbed to death on the spot. Eleven days later Dingane's warriors massacred hundreds of men, women, and children at various trekker camp sites along the Bushman river.

The trekkers fought back in the following months under their new leader, Andries Pretorius. Then on 15 December, when the trekkers crossed the Mzinyathi, or Buffalo river, a scouting party reported the approach of a large Zulu force. Pretorius suspected that the Zulus were hoping to lure the trekkers into rocky terrain where the trekkers'

20,000 The estimated number of Zulu warriors who surrounded, attacked, and massacred the 1,700 British troops who were encamped at Isandhlwana on January 22 1879.

The battlegrounds of the Zulu Wars

The key battles between the Zulus and the Boers, and between the Zulus and the British, were fought in the northeast of what is now KwaZulu-Natal Province in the Indian Ocean coastal region of South Africa.

rifles would be least effective, so instead of moving into the attack he decided to pitch camp on open ground by the Ncome, or Blood river, with wagons drawn up in a protective circle, or laager.

At dawn the next day the Zulus launched a mass attack with some 10,000 men. But armed mainly with clubs and short stabbing spears – Shaka had ruled that the traditional Zulu throwing spears were cowards' weapons – they faced a hail of rifle fire. For two hours the Zulus charged repeatedly, then Pretorius launched a counter-offensive with a group of horsemen. After suffering heavy losses, the Zulus fled, with the trekkers in pursuit. By nightfall Zulu casualties totalled 3,000. Three trekkers had been wounded. The battle of Blood River, as it became known, was over.

Although the Boers established an independent Republic of Natalia in 1838, they continued to fight the Zulus in Natal for another two years, until Dingane's brother, Mpande, joined forces with the Boers, bringing with him a large number of men. Dingane was finally defeated in January 1840, and was assassinated later in the year.

Massacre at Isandhlwana

The Republic of Natalia lasted only five years before the British took it over, forcing the Boers to move west and north. To the west they established the independent Orange Free State, to the north the Transvaal republic.

But the British had not finished expanding their southern African territories. Anxious to claim territory before the Germans or Portuguese, in 1877 they annexed the Transvaal. The British government in London was anxious to avoid war with the Zulus, but in southern Africa the British High Commissioner, Henry Bartle Frere, and

the commander of the British forces, Lieutenant-General Frederic Thesiger – soon to be Lord Chelmsford – knew that sooner or later war would come: so it might as well be sooner. Gambling on a quick victory, and taking advantage of the slow communications between London and southern Africa, they took the initiative. Using a minor border incident as an excuse, they demanded that Zulu Chief Cetshwayo disband his army, knowing full well he would not.

Cetshwayo duly refused, and in January 1879 the British marched across the Buffalo river into Zululand at Rorke's Drift, confident of success – far too confident, indeed, because Lord

IKLWA The Zulu term for the short stabbing spear they used in close combat, after the squelching sound its blade made on being pulled out of a person's body.

Chelmsford took only 4,000 or so men with him. After pitching a small camp at Rorke's Drift, Chelmsford established a second, larger camp at Isandhlwana on 20 January, but did nothing to fortify it.

Slaughter at Isandhlwana

Armed with single shot, breech-loading Martini-Henry rifles and bayonets, the British troops inflicted heavy casualties on the Zulus at Isandhlwana before finally being overcome by sheer weight of numbers.

BEFORE

Boer homeland aspirations and British imperial ambitions in southern Africa in the 19th century faced a major obstacle – the mighty Zulus.

A WARRIOR PEOPLE

The Zulu heartland – Zululand – neighboured Natal in what is now eastern South Africa. Once a small, peaceful tribe, **the Zulus became a large warring force after Chief Shaka (left) seized power in 1816.** In a series of brutal campaigns he massacred other tribes or forced them to join him. **On his death in 1828, his empire reached almost as far north as Swaziland.**

IN SEARCH OF NEW TERRITORY

In 1814 the British took over the Cape Colony, home to the Boers – white farmers of Dutch descent. Alienated by British rule, **in 1835 some 12,000 Boers – the trekkers – moved northwards** in search of a new homeland. They headed for Natal, **hoping to negotiate the peaceful cession of some land from Chief Shaka's successor, Chief Dingane.**

AFRICA

The Zulu Wars
Dates
Boers/Zulus 1838–40
British/Zulus 1879
Location
Zululand and Natal
in southern Africa

KEY

Shaka's Zulu kingdom 1817
Mzilikazi's Ndebele kingdom 1826
Boer Republic with date of establishment
Zulu victory
Boer victory
British victory
Main Boer trek routes 1836–54
Frontiers 1895

Kalahari Desert

Pietersburg
Nylstroom
TRANSVAAL 1852 1877–88: annexed by British
Rustenburg
Pretoria
Johannesburg
Potchefstroom *Vaal*
Rorke's Drift 1879
Lourenço Marques
ORANGE FREE STATE 1854
Winburg
Vegkop 1836
Isandhlwana 1879
Thaba Nchu
Thaba Bosiu
Blood River 1838
Bloemfontein
BASUTOLAND British protectorate
Weenen
Pietermaritzburg
Boomplaats 1848
Orange River
Tugela
Drakensberg
Durban (Port Natal)
CAPE COLONY
Colesberg
Fish
Kei
NATAL 1838 1843: annexed by British
Graaff-Reinet
Tarka
Slagtersnek
Uitenhage
Grahamstown
Port Elizabeth
INDIAN OCEAN

N

0   300km
0   300 miles

Worse, he let himself be lured away with 2,500 troops by Zulu scouts, leaving 1,700 men behind, including most of the 1st Battalion of the 24th regiment, with Lieutenant-Colonel Henry Pulleine in command. Chelmsford fatally underestimated the military abilities of the Zulu forces, 20,000 of whom on 22 January launched a typically disciplined attack on the British camp at Isandhlwana in their traditional encircling buffalo-horns-and-chest formation, under the command of generals Ntshingwayo and Mavumengwana. Although armed with a few rifles of their own, the Zulus still relied on the stabbing spear and club as their main weapons, and despite suffering 2,000 casualties to both rifle and bayonet, by sheer weight of numbers they eventually overwhelmed the camp and slaughtered the British forces to a man.

Defiance at Rorke's Drift

If Isandhlwana represented one of the worst defeats in British military history, what followed later the same day and all the following night at Rorke's Drift has entered British military folklore. There, at the mission station, from behind hastily constructed ramparts made from wagons and grain bags, a small garrison of 139 men, led by Lieutenant John Chard of the Royal Engineers, held off 3,000 Zulus led by Prince Dabulamanzi. At one point the two sides engaged in quite desperate hand-to-hand combat. The fighting lasted for ten hours, the Zulus finally withdrawing at dawn when they saw Lord Chelmsford's relief column approaching in the distance.

Cetshwayo's last stand

News of Isandhlwana outraged London. The British government sent reinforcements and Sir Garnet Wolseley was ordered to take over command from Chelmsford. Cetshwayo, meanwhile, was anxious to cease hostilities and end the slaughter. He knew that there would be no more Isandhlwanas for the Zulu nation.

A Zulu warrior's weapons

Each warrior carried a shield made of hide, decorated with his regiment's colours. His traditional weapons included a heavy ironwood club, 1m (3ft) long, and a short, broad-pointed stabbing spear.

British medal tally

Eleven Victoria Crosses were awarded for gallantry at Rorke's Drift – the most ever awarded for a single action.

Chelmsford, though, rejected all peace overtures from Cetshwayo and was anxious to crush the Zulus before Wolseley could arrive and steal his thunder.

The showdown took place on 4 July 1879, at the Zulu capital of Ulindi. Here, a British force of some 4,200 men armed this time with two Gatling guns and artillery, as well as the usual rifles, formed a hollow square formation, mounted troops covering the sides and rear, and awaited the Zulu attack. At least 15,000 Zulus soon surrounded the British in typical horn formation, stamping their feet and banging their shields as one. But this time when they attacked, none got close enough to use a club or stabbing spear. Hundreds were killed by rifle and machine-gun fire, or by canister shot. Many were then chased down by British cavalry, who exacted revenge for Isandhlwana by systematically butchering the wounded. The Zulus were routed, their chief was taken prisoner, and their nation was defeated.

AFTER

Following the defeat of the Zulus, the British took control of all southern Africa.

BRITISH IMPERIAL RULE

After the battle of Ulindi, **Cetshwayo was exiled to Cape Town and later visited Britain**. The British allowed him to return home in 1883 as a client-king. Arguments between rivals for the throne led to civil war the same year. Cetshwayo was defeated once again at Ulundi and died in 1884. **In 1897 Zululand became part of Natal, which joined the independent Union of South Africa in 1910**.

THE BOER STATES

In 1880 Transvaal rebelled against British rule and defeated the British in 1881 at Laing's Neck and Majuba Hill before Britain recognized its independence. Britain, however, continued to pressurize Transvaal and the Orange Free State and **in 1899 both republics declared war on Britain 248–49 »**. After defeat in 1902, they eventually joined the Union of South Africa. In 1905 neighbouring Swaziland, under Transvaal's control since 1895, became a British protectorate.

The Second Boer War

Between 1899 and 1902 the war between Britain and the Boers in South Africa pitted the world's largest empire against two small and poorly armed republics. What should have been a routine imperial victory became a drawn-out affair that revealed the limits of British military power.

The failure of the Jameson raid in 1895 poisoned relations between the Transvaal and Britain. The British, however, continued to put pressure on the governments of both the Transvaal and the Orange Free State, who felt threatened by Britain's support of the Uitlanders ("foreigners") and by its perceived imperialism. In response, both states declared war on Britain in October 1899 with the aim of forcing a negotiated settlement.

The two sides were far from evenly matched. The British had close to 25,000 soldiers in the region when war broke out, but quickly called on a large standing army stationed elsewhere in the empire. They were well armed and

AFRICA

Second Boer War
Dates 1899–1902
Location South Africa

trained, although not familiar with the territory. Their experience of close-formation fighting in wars around the world since 1815 was not, however, that relevant or useful when faced with the highly mobile and well-armed Boers. In contrast, the Boers avoided set-piece

> The British stretcher-bearer at Spion Kop was Mohandas Gandhi, the future leader of India who had organized the Indian Ambulance Corps in South Africa during the war to care for the wounded.

battles, preferring hit-and-run tactics. They could call on around 83,000 men of fighting age, of whom around 40,000 were fighting at any one time, but they had no trained army. Instead, they had a local militia system grouped into mounted commando units that varied in strength according to the population from which they were recruited. All were skilled, mounted marksmen, their skills learned from hunting on the veldt (wide, treeless grasslands).

Although it was a legal requirement that all adult men own a rifle, many Boers did not, or at least not a modern

A nation relieved

The relief of Mafeking caused ecstatic joy in Britain, out of all proportion to its significance. For a time the expression "to Maffick" embodied celebrating extravagantly.

one, so President Paul Kruger of the Transvaal ordered 37,000 rifles and ten million cartridges from Krupps, the German manufacturer. The Mauser model 1895 rifle was extremely accurate at long range and superior to the British Lee-Metford magazine rifle. The Boers also had a small quantity of modern French and German field artillery.

Under siege

At the start of the war fast-moving Boer columns advanced out of the two republics, besieging Colonel Robert Baden-Powell and his troops at Mafeking and the garrison at Kimberley, while a 15,000-strong Transvaal force invaded British-run Natal and besieged Ladysmith. The British, commanded by Sir Redvers Buller, sent out three columns to relieve the sieges. The first column, a force of around 10,000 men with 16 guns, advanced northwest from the Cape towards Kimberley and overcame Boer resistance at the Modder river at the end of November 1899. However, it was then defeated by the Boers, led by Piet Cronjé, at Magersfontein outside Kimberley on 10–11 December. On the 9th the second column, which headed north from the eastern Cape to relieve Mafeking, had been defeated at Stormberg. On 15 December the third column heading from Durban in Natal and led by Buller himself, encountered the Boers, led by Louis Botha, at Colenso. The British third column numbered around 21,000

BEFORE

Relations between the Boers and Britain had been tense ever since the British took over the Afrikaans-speaking Cape Colony in South Africa in 1814.

THE BOER REPUBLICS
In response to the Emancipation Act and attacks by local tribes, Boers began to leave the **Cape Colony** in 1835 and set up the independent republics of the Orange Free State and Transvaal. The British had recognized both states by 1854.

THE FIRST BOER WAR
The Transvaal was bankrupt by 1877 and threatened by the Zulus. Britain, worried about German colonial expansion into the region, annexed the Transvaal in return for defending it against the Zulus. With the **Zulus defeated << 246–47** by 1879, the Boers rebelled against British rule, defeating them at Laing's Neck in January 1881 and then at Majuba Hill in February. The **Treaty of Pretoria**, signed in April, restored the state's independence.

THE JAMESON RAID
The **discovery of gold** in the Transvaal in 1886 attracted thousands of Uitlanders (foreigners) to the region. The Transvaal government refused to give them voting and other rights, which led to unrest. In 1895 Cecil Rhodes, owner of a Transvaal mining company, sent an armed party of 500 men commanded by **Leander Starr Jameson** to support an Uitlander uprising. The uprising, however, never materialized.

BURGERWACHT

Boer armband
The Boers were not professional soldiers and did not have uniforms. The militiamen (burgerwacht) who fought the British wore armbands such as this one so that they could be identified on the battlefield.

RELI...
OF
MAF...
LATES...
THE 'SCOR...
TH...
½d

Boer riflemen in a trench
Although the British were superior in number, trench warfare and modern weaponry reduced their effectiveness. This type of warfare was a prelude to what would happen in the Great War of 1914–18.

men but was driven back by the 6,500 Boers concealed in difficult terrain. The British had all of its artillery captured, and sustained losses of 143 men killed, 756 men wounded, and 220 men captured. Boer casualties, at around 50, were negligible, as they had been in the previous two encounters.

The three defeats suffered by the British during this "Black Week" led to a rapid change in command. Buller, who retained his local command, was replaced by Field Marshal Viscount Roberts, with General Kitchener as his chief-of-staff. The two rapidly reorganized the British forces to counter Boer mobility, and Buller made another attempt to finally relieve Ladysmith. He divided his force into two; one, led by General Warren, attempted to take control of the commanding heights of Spion Kop to the west of Ladysmith, the balance being held in

Magazine clip

Detachable stock

allowed Buller to retreat. Buller eventually managed to relieve Ladysmith on 28 February.

The long war
Meanwhile, Roberts had helped free Kimberley in mid-February and then decided to strike at the Boer capitals. A 6,000-strong British force led by Kitchener trapped a slightly smaller Boer force on Paardeberg hill and attacked it directly, suffering more

Boer weapons
The Mauser C-96 (above) and the Mauser 95 rifle were both used by the Boers. Transvaal president, Paul Kruger, ordered thousands of the rifles when it became clear that war with Britain could not be averted.

policy that burned farms to deny the rebels food and moved the displaced civilians into concentration camps (see KEY MOMENT). Faced with such harsh measures, the Boers capitulated, signing a peace treaty in May 1902.

The Boer War had a huge impact on those on both sides of the conflict.

AGREEING THE PEACE
The treaty signed at Vereeniging on the Transvaal-Orange Free State border was lenient on the Boers. **The two Boer republics accepted British sovereignty** and the promise of future self-government, which both republics gained in 1907. The Boers were also compensated £3 million for restocking and repairing their farms. Both Boer republics eventually joined with Cape Colony and Natal to become part of the **Union of South Africa**, founded in 1910.

MILITARY REFORMS
It had taken the British more than 500,000 troops to defeat a far smaller number of Boers. Army reforms were desperately needed. Richard Haldane, Secretary of State for War from 1905 to 1912, created a **British Expeditionary Force ready to fight overseas at any time**, and a Territorial Force that amalgamated all voluntary local militia forces into a single home defence force. The wisdom of these reforms was proved in the opening months of **World War I 266–67 »**.

SOUTH AFRICAN WAR MEDAL

INTERNATIONAL DIPLOMACY
The war had revealed Britain to be isolated diplomatically, with most nations supporting the Boers. What had once been a deliberate policy of **"Splendid Isolation"** from European affairs now became a liability. Britain therefore moved to secure an alliance with Japan in 1902 and an entente, or **understanding, with France** in 1904 that settled outstanding colonial differences between the two nations. In 1906 the first in a series of confidential military conversations took place between their military staff in order to determine a common strategy in the event of a war against Germany. An **entente with Russia**, similar to that with France, was signed in 1907.

> "The **patience** of everybody in Mafeking in **making the best of things** under the long strain of **anxiety, hardship, and privation** is beyond all praise … "
> COLONEL BADEN-POWELL, IN A DESPATCH SENT TO FIELD MARSHAL VISCOUNT ROBERTS, 1900

reserve. On the night of 24 January, 1900 2,000 men scaled the hill but discovered in daylight that they could not dig in, had no sandbags, and, worse, were overlooked by Boer artillery. The British came under heavy fire, which they could not return, but reinforcements allowed them to keep the hill despite a Boer attempt to scale the hill and engage them at close quarters. By the evening both sides were exhausted and withdrew, the Boers then regrouped taking the abandoned summit and

than 1,000 casualties before Kitchener withdrew. Roberts then took command and subjected the Boers to an eight-day artillery barrage before they submitted. He then marched on Bloemfontein, the Orange Free State capital, which he took on 13 March before heading north to Transvaal to take Johannesburg on 31 May and Pretoria on 5 June. As Roberts forged ahead, the siege of Mafeking, which had been in progress since the start of the war, was over. Defended by Colonel Baden-Powell, the town was relieved on 17 May 1900.

The Boers, having all but lost the war, turned to guerrilla tactics. They sabotaged railway communications, attacked isolated outposts, and ambushed British troops. The British responded by starting a scorched earth

THE FIRST CONCENTRATION CAMPS

After the British had burned Boer farms and destroyed their crops to deny Boer fighters food and shelter, General Kitchener set up a series of refugee camps to accommodate Boer civilians who had become displaced. Known as concentration camps – the first time this term had been used anywhere in the world – the 45 camps housed in the region of 100,000 Boers, mainly women and children. A similar number of Black Africans who lived in Boer areas were placed in another 64 camps. Conditions were appalling and food rations meagre, leading to the deaths from starvation, disease, and exposure of 27,927 Boers, of whom 24,074 were under 16 – half the Boer child population. An estimated 15,000 Africans died, although these deaths were never properly recorded.

Veldt Diary

In 1899 a young British soldier set sail to fight in the Boer War in South Africa. Almost every day he kept a diary recording the battles, marches, and hardships he endured. The diary, which lay unread until it was rediscovered by his great-grandson almost a century later, gives a fascinating personal view of what it was like to fight in the war.

Frederick Roseblade was born in Northampton, England, in 1869 and worked in the local shoe trade as a clicker, someone who chooses and cuts the leather pieces used in the upper part of a shoe. On 16 January 1891, aged 21, he signed up for 12 years in the British Army, serving in the Oxfordshire Light Infantry. In 1899 he sailed from Southampton to join the British, Australian, and other imperial troops fighting in the Boer War and was promoted to sergeant while on board ship.

The diary starts on 21 December 1899, the day before Frederick Roseblade sailed to war, and records in great detail his actions and thoughts from when he arrived in Cape Town on 14 January 1900 through to September 1900.

Devastating defeats

The Boer War had started in October 1899, when the Orange Free State and Transvaal declared war on Britain. Events went badly for the British, the Boers besieging Mafeking, Kimberley, and Ladysmith and, in "Black Week"

The retiring sergeant

This card is possibly from the men of Roseblade's regiment, wishing him good luck in civilian life. In the photograph Roseblade is wearing the Queen's South Africa Medal and the King's South Africa Medal.

The Queen's South Africa Medal
Roseblade's own medal is lost, but would have had three of the clasps on this example, showing he had fought at Paardeberg, Driefontein, and in Transvaal. His also had a Kimberley clasp.

in December 1899, defeating three columns of troops sent to lift the sieges. The British commander, General Sir Redvers Buller, was relieved of his command and replaced by Field Marshal Viscount Roberts, with General Kitchener as his chief-of-staff. Roberts advanced towards Kimberley and then headed east to capture the Orange Free State capital, Bloemfontein. Roseblade took part in this advance.

Into action

On 12 February, Roberts' columns left Enslin in the Northern Cape to march to Bloemfontein. Each day started early, around 5:00am, the troops covering around 10 miles by mid-morning before it became too hot to march. Water was scarce, as was food, and many got sunstroke. On 15 February, Roseblade records meeting Kitchener, who was encouraging his men as they moved heavy guns to the top of a koppie, a small hill rising out of the veldt, in order to shell Boer positions. On 18 February, Roseblade

took part in the bloody battle of Paardeberg. The Boer army led by General Piet Cronje was attempting to retreat across the Modder river but had found its way blocked by British cavalry led by Brigadier General John French, who had raced back after successfully lifting the siege of Kimberley. Cronje ordered his men to dig in beside the

river. Kitchener ordered a frontal attack on the Boer positions on Paardeberg Hill, in which Roseblade took part. He got to within 275m (250yd) of the river, but could advance no further. As the casualties mounted, Roseblade held his position as the British pounded the enemy with heavy guns. He was "very lucky in having plenty of cover", but

> **" … it seemed almost a miracle how any man could live as the bullets were flying around us just like hail stones."**
>
> FREDERICK ROSEBLADE'S DIARY, 18 FEBRUARY 1900

Their were some men who had been laying ...re for over a week, it was a very nasty ...b, for us, but still we had to do it, how ... enemy got rid of a good many of their ...en, was throwing them in the river, ...hich you could almost walk across, on ...e cattle and men that were thrown in ... had to drink this water, which was ...t very nice I can assure you, but still ... did not think about what was in it, ... can tell you it was a common thing ... see dead horses, and men floating ...own the river, we had this night to ...rselves, and very glad we was to of ...aving what we call a night in bed ...t if you can call a night in bed on ...e veldt, with one blanket, and the dew ...lling all through the night, I dont, but ...t is what we call a night in bed

1·3·00

...he regiment marched away to a place ...lled Roebuck Farm Hosfontein, a distance

> " … we had to **drink this water**, which was not very nice … I can tell you it was a common thing to see **dead horses and men floating down the river**."

ROSEBLADE ON THE AFTERMATH OF PAARDEBERG, 28 FEBRUARY 1900

Day-by-day account of the war

Frederick Roseblade kept his war diary in a small notebook, writing his neat entries on every page. These pages record the events of 28 February and 1 March 1900, the days following the battle of Paardeberg.

others were not so fortunate, the British suffering 320 dead and 942 injured before the Boers finally repulsed their attack. Roseblade ends his diary entry for the day by recording that "we slept on the field that night without blankets or covering of any sort, alongside our arms and very glad every man was to lay down and sleep being utterly worn out … Very cold night."

A different kind of war

That day at Paardeberg was the fiercest fighting Roseblade and his regiment experienced on their tour of duty in South Africa. On 27 February, Cronje and his army of 4,000 were finally forced to surrender to the vastly superior British force. Thereafter, Roseblade played a less dramatic role in the war as the Boers avoided pitched battle and waged a guerrilla campaign against Lord Roberts' troops. The diary continues to record various skirmishes with the enemy, but it is dominated by descriptions of long marches, cold, hunger, and thirst.

Roseblade got back to England in August 1902, just after the war had ended. He was discharged on 15 January 1903, having completed exactly 12 years' service, and went back to his trade in Northampton, where he married in February 1908.

Deadly waters

British troops wade across a river on the veldt. Rivers were frequently polluted by the bodies of dead men, horses, and mules from earlier battles. Dysentery killed many British troops on Lord Roberts' march to Bloemfontein.

Spanish-American War

Although known to history as the Spanish-American War of 1898, the conflict could, more appropriately, be called the Spanish-American-Cuban-Filipino War, as four different parties were involved in a conflict that occurred in two places on opposite sides of the world.

The Cuban rebellion of 1895 was caused by growing discontent with incompetent Spanish rule and resentment against restrictions placed by Spain on Cuban trade. The revolt, led by José Martí and his Cuban Revolutionary Party, began on the east of the island, but by 1896 it had reached the outskirts of Havana in the west. The response of Cuba's governor, General Valeriano Weyler, was brutal. Aiming to isolate the rebels from the rest of the population and to cut off their supplies, he set up a series of fortified towns (*reconcentrados*), protected by Spanish troops, in which to intern the rural population.

Intended as havens, these towns were effectively concentration camps in which, within a year, some 300,000 Cubans died of starvation and disease, an atrocity that caused an outcry in the US, where Cuban emigrés were agitating for intervention.

For the Americans, there were many reasons to support military action. Some politicians believed that Cuban independence would increase trade between the two nations and thought it their duty as democrats to support the island's struggle for independence.

TO HELL WITH SPAIN

> "A vote is like a **rifle**; its usefulness depends upon the character of the **user**."
>
> SAYING ATTRIBUTED TO THEODORE ROOSEVELT

Teddy Roosevelt's Rough Riders
The Rough Riders were one of three voluntary cavalry regiments raised in 1898 during the Spanish-American War. They were also called the Weary Walkers as they invariably fought on foot.

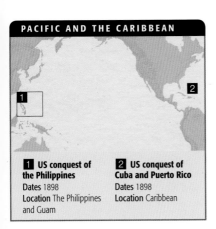

PACIFIC AND THE CARIBBEAN

1 US conquest of
the Philippines
Dates 1898
Location The Philippines
and Guam

2 US conquest of
Cuba and Puerto Rico
Dates 1898
Location Caribbean

Others saw it as an opportunity for the US to extend its sphere of influence and to evict a major colonial power from the Caribbean – and to reap new colonies for the US as a result.

Military action became inevitable on 15 February 1898, when the USS *Maine* exploded and sank in Havana harbour with the loss of 266 men. The ship had arrived uninvited at the end of January, allegedly to offer protection to the 8,000 American citizens in Cuba. A US naval enquiry was unable to pin responsibility on anyone in particular, but Spanish culpability was assumed, which gave the Americans the justification for military action that they required. The US Congress called for war against Spain, which began on 21 April.

The Pacific

The first battles took place in the Pacific. The US Asiatic Squadron, which lacked a base of its own in the Far East, was ordered to proceed from its anchorage off China to engage the Spanish in the Philippines. Commanded by Commodore George Dewey, the six warships and three support vessels entered Manila Bay on the night of 30 April, opening fire on the moored Spanish fleet at dawn the next day. Despite concerns about lack of ammunition, and facing attack from shore batteries, the US made swift work of the Spanish, destroying six of their seven ships by midday; the seventh was scuttled by its captain. With the Spanish navy neutralized, US and Filipino troops overran the Philippines, but collaboration between the two allies ended on 13 August when the US took the Philippine capital, Manila. Determined to keep the port as a base for their fleet, the Americans prevented Filipino troops from entering the city, an event that outraged the Filipinos and led to the Philippine-American War (1899–1913).

9 The number of US casualties during the naval attack on the Spanish fleet in Manila Bay. The Spanish suffered 381 losses.

In the western Pacific Captain Henry Glass on board the cruiser USS *Charleston* was ordered to capture the island of Guam. When he arrived on 20 April, he fired a few cannon rounds at Forta Santa Cruz, and a Spanish officer, not knowing that war had been declared, came out to ask for some gunpowder so that he could return the American salute. Captain Glass informed the officer that they were at war, then took him prisoner and sent him back to the island under escort to discuss surrender terms. The next day the 54 Spanish infantry stationed on the island were disarmed and Guam was taken.

The Caribbean

In Cuba the US planned to capture the city of Santiago de Cuba, in the far southeast, and to destroy the main Spanish army and fleet stationed there. On 1 July some 15,000 US troops and 4,000 rebel Cuban forces attacked Spanish positions at El Caney and San Juan Hill in the hills overlooking Santiago. The US force included regular infantry and cavalry regiments, African-American regiments (notably the Buffalo Soldiers), and the 1st Volunteer Cavalry, known as the Rough Riders. The latter were recruited, trained, and led by Theodore Roosevelt, who had recently resigned as Assistant Secretary to the Navy in the US government to fight in the war. At El Caney some 500 Spanish troops held up more than 8,000 US troops for nearly 12 hours, preventing them from joining in the main attack on San Juan Hill. That main attack was difficult, as the heat was intense and the Spanish, secure in their trenches on the hill, were excellent marksmen. The Rough Riders took the first target, the smaller Kettle Hill, during the day, and eventually US infantry managed to cut through the barbed wire surrounding the Spanish positions and take San Juan Hill.

USS Maine commemorative plate
The sinking of the USS *Maine* in Havana harbour in 1898 became a rallying call for Americans to support the war against Spain.

The Treaty of Paris that ended the war in December 1898 gave the US control of the Philippines, Guam, and Puerto Rico, and temporary command of Cuba.

THE AMERICAN PHILIPPINES
In August 1898 11,000 US troops arrived in the Philippines to replace the departing Spanish. The ensuing **war with Filipino rebels left 1 million Filipino civilians dead**. The US won the war in 1902, but **resistance continued until 1913**.

CUBA
The end of the war saw Cuba under US military control. **The island became independent in 1902, the US gaining a perpetual lease on the naval base at Guantánamo Bay**. The new Cuban constitution gave the US the right to supervise Cuban affairs, but the Americans relinquished this in return for a trade deal in 1934.

THE EXPANDING EMPIRE
The year after the war ended, the US gained control of the eastern Samoan islands in the south Pacific. US support for Panama in 1903 secured Panama's independence from Colombia, and the new government gave the US **ownership of a thin strip of land across the isthmus on which to build the Panama Canal**.

At sea the US navy and marines secured Guantánamo Bay as a base in early June, and the US fleet sailed on to blockade the main Spanish fleet anchored at Santiago de Cuba. On 3 July the six ships of the Spanish fleet tried to evade the blockade but were caught and either destroyed or grounded by US firepower. To the east, on Puerto Rico, a squadron of 12 US ships bombarded the capital, San Juan, on 12 May and blockaded its harbour. Approximately 3,300 US troops landed in July and encountered some resistance, but military actions were suspended when peace was agreed on 12 August.

The battle of Manila Bay

George Dewey's US Asiatic Squadron destroyed the Spanish fleet at Cavite naval yard in Manila Bay. The Spanish commander, Patricio Montojo, anchored his ships at harbour to give his men a better chance of escape.

Night-time attack at Port Arthur
Japanese destroyers launched a surprise attack on Russia's Pacific Squadron at Port Arthur shortly after midnight on 8 February 1904, starting a war that would cost many thousands of lives on both sides.

« **BEFORE**

Following civil war in 1863–68, Japan's restored imperial regime built a powerful navy and modern army, and pursued an aggressive foreign policy.

NEW LANDS
Between 1871 and 1900 Japan acquired an empire in east Asia, gaining the Ryukyu and Bonin islands in the Pacific, and the Kuril Islands to the northeast of Japan. **War with China in 1894–95 « 240–41 gained Taiwan for Japan** and secured independence for Korea, over which Japan exerted huge influence.

GROWING TENSION
Russia viewed Japan's influence over Korea with great concern, while Japan was alarmed when **Russia secured a lease from China on the Liaotung Peninsula of Manchuria** in 1898 and built a naval base there at Port Arthur. When **Russia stationed troops throughout Manchuria** in 1900 and built a railway linking Port Arthur to Siberia, the tension heightened.

LATE 19TH-CENTURY JAPANESE TELESCOPE

The Russo-Japanese War

The first major war of the 20th century, this 1904–05 conflict propelled Japan to the front rank of modern world powers. Japan employed tactics and weapons that were next seen in World War I, and its victory was the first, in modern times, of a non-Western nation over a European one.

In 1903 armed conflict between Russia and Japan became inevitable when Russia refused to carry out an agreement undertaken in the Boxer Rebellion of 1900 (see p.241) to withdraw from Manchuria. Russia sought a warm-water port with access to the Pacific for its navy and maritime trade – Russia's recently built port of Vladivostok on the Sea of Japan was ice-bound in winter – so Russia had no intention of leaving Port Arthur.

Port Arthur and the war at sea
Japan decided to act. In February 1904 Admiral Togo Heihachiro launched a surprise night-time attack on Russia's First Pacific Squadron at Port Arthur. Ten Japanese destroyers fired their Whitehead torpedoes at the Russian ships, but no ships were actually sunk.
With Russian searchlights sweeping the sea, the attack had to be called off. Another attack the following

morning also failed, the Russians keeping the Japanese at bay with shore guns. Japan blockaded the port, but had no choice now but to plan a long land siege of Port Arthur.
The siege of Port Arthur started in August 1904. There followed four months of bloody fighting in a new

form of mechanized, trench warfare. The Japanese launched mass infantry attacks against Russian troops dug in on hilltop positions heavily fortified with barbed wire, after first pounding the Russian positions with heavy guns. The key hill was the highest one – 203 Meter Hill – overlooking the harbour.

Thousands of Japanese died in a hail of Maxim machine-gun fire in repeated attempts to take this strategic hill. But eventually, after fierce hand-to-hand fighting, the Japanese succeeded in taking 203 Meter Hill on 5 December. A month later, on 2 January 1905, the Russian garrison surrendered.

> **"You may wish to compare me to Lord Nelson, but … "**
> ADMIRAL TOGO HEIHACHIRO

Meanwhile, on 10 August 1904, the Russian First Pacific Squadron had boldly steamed out of Port Arthur into the Yellow Sea to join the rest of the Russian fleet at Vladivostok. Heihachiro was unprepared and let the squadron escape. The six Russian battleships were slower than the Japanese, however,

End of an era
Japan's victory over Russia in the 1904–05 war ended centuries of European assumption of racial superiority. It was gained largely because the Japanese forces were better led, trained, and motivated than the Russians.

KEY

- Japan and Korea
- Russia
- To Russia 1898, to Japan 1905
- Frontiers 1895
- → Japanese advance/landing
- → Route of Russian Baltic Fleet 1905
- ┅ Railway line
- ✸ Japanese victory

Harbin
Changchun
Liaoyang Aug–Sep 1904
1898: China leases Port Arthur to Russia
Beijing
Mukden 1–10 Mar 1905
1900: Russian troops occupy Manchuria
MANCHURIA
RUSSIA
Yingkou
Fushan
Vladivostok
8 Feb 1904: Japanese bombard Russian fleet in Port Arthur harbour
Yalu River 27 Apr–1 May 1905
Hoeryong
Port Arthur
Dairen
QING CHINA
Siege of Port Arthur Feb 1904–Jan 1905
Pyongyang
Sea of Japan
Yellow Sea 10 Aug 1904
Wonsan
Seoul
KOREA
1905: Japanese protectorate 1910: Japanese crown colony
Japanese Sea 14 Aug 1904
Yellow Sea
Pusan
Honshu
Tsushima 15 May 1905
Shimonoseki
Hiroshima
JAPAN
Tokyo
Yokohama
Kyushu

N
0   200km
0   200 miles

and later that day four Japanese battleships and two cruisers caught up and attacked. In the rapid exchange of fire that followed, Togo's flagship, the *Mikasa*, one of the most advanced battleships in the world, was struck many times, but greater damage was done to the Russian flagship, the *Tsesarevich*, when two shells hit her bridge, killing Rear Admiral Vitgeft and all his senior officers. Eventually, with night falling and no hope of escaping the Japanese ships, most of the Russian ships returned to Port Arthur. Japan's fleet was almost unscathed, while the

Admiral Togo Heihachiro
Nicknamed "the Nelson of the East", Togo himself revered the great 16th-century Korean naval commander, Yi Sun-sin, often calling on his spirit for guidance.

Russians had lost a battleship and two cruisers. Four of their ships, including the *Tsesarevich*, found sanctuary in neutral ports, where they were held for the rest of the war. The squadron would play no further part in the war. Neither would the small Russian fleet that was stationed at Vladivostok. This fleet had steamed into the Sea of Japan to meet the squadron but was chased back by the Japanese with the loss of a cruiser.

The war on land

While the siege of Port Arthur was taking place, Japanese troops overran Korea, then, pushing aside a Russian force on the Yalu river, moved into Manchuria in May 1904. At Liaoyang in August, 125,000 Japanese faced 158,000 Russians reinforced with a corps that had come in on the Trans-Siberian Railway.

The Japanese aggressively repulsed two Russian assaults, but the results were indecisive, as the Japanese lost some 23,000 men and the Russians around 18,000. Believing he had been defeated, the Russian commander, General Kuropatkin, retreated north to the Manchurian capital of Mukden. Here, in February–March 1905, the major land battle of the war took place. The forces involved were vast, with

89 THOUSAND Russians were killed at the battle of Mukden.

71 THOUSAND Japanese were killed at the battle of Mukden.

270,000 Japanese troops attacking 333,000 Russian troops. The Japanese Fifth Army crossed the mountains to the west of the city and attacked the Russian left flank before the main Japanese assault began against the Russian centre and right flank.

The ensuing bloody battle raged for 19 days, with the Japanese held back by withering Russian machine-gun fire. Both sides used forward observers linked by telephone to rear gunners, so they could direct them to fire on targets out of their sight. At last the stalemate broke as the Russian troops, unable to resist the flanking Japanese, withdrew to the north. With all Manchuria now in its hands, Japan had won the land war decisively, despite great losses.

The war seriously weakened Russia and strengthened Japan's influence in East Asia.

PEACE TREATY

US mediation led to the signing in September 1905 of the Treaty of Portsmouth, by which **Japan and Russia both agreed to leave Manchuria**, while **Russia handed over the Liaotung Peninsula to Japan**, as well as the southern half of the island of Sakhalin, north of Japan. Russia's ambitions in East Asia were at an end, **Japan now dominated the region**, and the **US had emerged as a world power** prepared to intervene and mediate in the affairs of other countries around the world.

JAPAN AND KOREA

After the war Japan assumed responsibility for Korea's foreign policy and dominated Korea's economy. **In 1910 Japan formally annexed Korea**. Korea remained Japanese until Japan's defeat at the end of **World War II 304–05 »**.

UNREST IN RUSSIA

Russia's failure led directly to revolt at home, as discontent with the war – combined with Tsar Nicholas II's refusal to allow reforms, the increasing distress among industrial workers, and the over-taxed rural peasantry – saw protests break out in January 1905. **The tsar made some concessions after a general strike**, but the revolt went on into 1906.

IMPERIAL RUSSIAN CREST

Two months later Togo inflicted a crushing defeat on the Russian fleet in the Tsushima Strait between Japan and Korea (see pp.256–57) – a defeat that forced Russia's government, now facing a workers' revolt at home, to seek a humiliating peace treaty.

The bloody battle of Mukden, 1905

Of the hand grenades used by the Japanese cavalry at Mukden, one horrified war correspondent wrote of "the ghastly injuries which they inflicted, killing men by the score and blowing them to fragments of flesh".

255

Tsushima

The war between Russia and Japan reached an epic climax at the end of May 1905 with the two-day naval battle in the Tsushima Strait between Japan and Korea. The battle of Tsushima was the greatest and most costly encounter at sea since Trafalgar on the other side of the world almost exactly a century earlier. It was also the first, and last, great naval action of the ironclad, pre-dreadnought era.

The outbreak of war between Russia and Japan saw most of the Russian fleet stationed over 32,000km (20,000 miles) away, in the Baltic Sea. The decision was taken to send most of these ships halfway round the world to engage the Japanese. They left port on 15 October 1904 under the command of Admiral Rozhdestvenski and headed out across the Baltic.

After seven months Rozhdestvenski's fleet crossed the Indian Ocean to reach Van Fong Bay in French Indochina, and prepared for battle. It consisted of eight battleships, eight cruisers, nine destroyers, and three smaller craft. This was an impressive number but their quality was dubious, with most vessels obsolete in design and suffering from inferior leadership and gunnery when compared with Admiral Togo Heihachiro's Japanese fleet of 4 battleships, 27 cruisers, 21 destroyers, and 16 torpedo boats.

Ready and waiting

By the time Rozhdestvenski reached Van Fong Bay, Port Arthur had fallen to the Japanese and the Russian fleet trapped there had been captured. His only available destination was Vladivostok. Running short of coal, Rozhdestvenski opted for the most direct and risky route there, through the Tsushima Strait, where Togo and his fleet lay in wait.

The night of 26–27 May was foggy and the Russian fleet might have slipped through unseen had not a Japanese cruiser spotted the Russian hospital ship *Orel* lit up as international law demanded. Immediately informed by the new wireless technology, Togo prepared his attack. Using his greater speed and tactical awareness, he manoeuvred his fleet into a line while the Russians, suffering from confused orders and poor seamanship, remained huddled in a group.

Togo rules the waves

The Japanese used their better speed, training, and range-finding technology to deadly effect. Their high-explosive shells smashed into the Russian ships, with devastating effect. Four Russian battleships were sunk, Rozhdestvenski's flagship *Knyaz Suvorov* was hit, and the Russian admiral himself was seriously wounded, yielding command to the inexperienced Admiral Nebogatov. Japanese destroyers and torpedo boats continued the assault through the night and at 10:30am on 28 May, Nebogatov surrendered those ships under his immediate command while the Japanese continued to hunt down the rest. Twenty-eight Russian ships had entered the strait, but only three made it to Vladivostok. Of the rest, 17 were sunk, 5 were captured, and 3 headed south for the Philippines.

7 Japanese pursuit continues through night

6 Japanese inflict more damage on disorganized Russian fleet

5 Russian line reforms and heads north

1 Togo turns fleet to bring it parallel with the Russians

4 In fog and smoke the two fleets lose sight of each other

Borodino

Alexander III

Knyaz Suvorov

Ural

TOGO

Oslyabya

3 Japanese turn to avoid torpedoes

2 Russian battleship *Oslyabya* sunk. Flagship *Knyaz Suvorov* is set on fire and loses control

ROZHDESTVENSKI

0 5km
0 5 miles

LOCATION
Tsushima Strait between Japan and Korea

DATE
27–28 May 1905

FORCES
Japanese: 4 battleships, 64 other ships; Russians: 8 battleships, 20 other ships

CASUALTIES
Japanese: 117 dead; three torpedo boats sunk;
Russian: 4,380 dead; 17 ships sunk

KEY
— Japanese battleship/armoured cruiser
— Russian battleship
✎ Sunk Russian ship

In the heat of battle
The chaos of the battle is vividly conveyed in this Japanese woodblock print; Russian crews desperately row away from their burning ships, while shell splashes all around almost swamp them.

« **BEFORE**

The decline of the Ottoman empire accelerated during the 19th century as its peoples struggled for independence and Russian influence rose across the Balkans.

EUROPEAN LOSSES

The Ottoman empire lost its first European domains in 1817, when Serbia gained autonomy. Then in 1821 **the Greeks revolted « 212–13**. Pro-Ottoman Egyptian forces retook the country in 1825, but when the Ottomans rejected mediation with Russia in 1827, Britain and France, sent **a combined fleet that destroyed the Egyptian navy at Navarino**. The Greeks gained their independence in 1832.

THE CRIMEAN WAR

Tension between an expansionist Russia and the Ottoman empire led to the **outbreak of war in 1853 « 220–21**. Britain and France supported the Ottomans and attacked Russian-held Crimea. The war ended in 1856 with an Ottoman victory, but it was only a temporary reprieve.

War in the Balkans

The war that broke out between Russia and the Ottoman empire in 1877 was the twelfth such conflict in 200 years. Within a few decades, further wars stripped the empire of almost all its European and African territories and caused great instability throughout the region.

G rowing nationalism and a desire for independence led to uprisings against Ottoman rule in Bosnia and Herzegovina in 1875 and Bulgaria in 1876. The Ottoman response in Bulgaria was brutal. Its "Bulgarian atrocities" outraged European opinion and gave Russia the excuse to declare war on behalf of its fellow Orthodox Christians in July 1877. Russian and Romanian armies marched south to besiege Nicopol. A Turkish force led by General Osman Pasha marched north to reinforce and defend the town, but

on learning that the town had been bombed into submission before it could be relieved, he occupied the Bulgarian town of Plevna in July and quickly increased its fortifications by setting up gun emplacements for his modern Krupp artillery. General Schuldner's Russian army was unaware of what Pasha was doing and when the Russians were ordered to occupy the city, they were not in a position to do so. A lengthy siege began, during which the 400,000-strong Ottoman army were surrounded by 100,000 Russians. After

many unsuccessful assaults, Russian reinforcements eventually tipped the balance, and Pasha surrendered in December. Russian forces then headed for Constantinople, causing the Ottoman sultan to sue for peace.

Greater Bulgaria

The peace treaty was signed at San Stefano, outside the Ottoman capital, in March 1878. Its terms created a large, autonomous Bulgaria, although the country was to be occupied by Russian troops for two years, with an outlet

Siege of Adrianople
This series of battles, led primarily by the Bulgarians and aided by Serbia, proved to be the decisive actions of the First Balkan War. However, tensions among the victors resulted in a second Balkan war.

EUROPE AND NORTH AFRICA

1 **Russo-Turkish War**
Dates 1877–78
Location Romania, Bulgaria

2 **Italo-Turkish War**
Dates 1911–12
Location Libya

3 **First and Second Balkan Wars**
Dates 1912–13
Location Macedonia, Greece, Albania, Bulgaria, Aegean Sea

Massacre at Montkrik

The Ottoman empire dealt severely with its enemies, as this depiction of the massacre at Montkirk in Serbia illustrates. Both sides carried out similar atrocities.

through Macedonia to the Aegean Sea. Serbia, Montenegro, and Romania received their independence, while Bosnia-Herzegovina was granted self-rule, and Russia gained territory on both sides of the Black Sea. The Ottoman empire was all but expelled from Europe. News of this treaty caused concern among the major European powers, as it created a large pro-Russian state at the heart of the Balkans, giving Russia huge influence throughout the region. European diplomats hurriedly met in Berlin and in July enforced a new settlement. Under the revised agreement Bulgaria was reduced in size and divided into three separate regions, Austria-Hungary occupied Bosnia-Herzegovina, Russia handed over its gains on the western shore of the Black Sea to Romania, and in a secret clause Britain occupied Cyprus. The Ottoman empire retained control over Macedonia and Albania.

constitution of 1876 and convene parliament. With the empire in turmoil as liberal reformers and traditional Islamic leaders tussled for power, its enemies pounced. Austria-Hungary annexed Bosnia-Herzegovina, while Bulgaria, having already recovered part of its lost San Stefano lands, now declared full independence.

> ## "From now on, **all the citizens**, **Muslim or non-Muslim**, work hand in hand and make our **fatherland rise**."
> YOUNG TURK ENVER BEY, AT A RALLY IN SALONICA, MACEDONIA, 23 JULY 1908

The outcome was to have long-lasting effects, for the Ottoman empire was severely weakened and Bulgaria was embittered at losing so much territory. Slowly but surely, Ottoman power and influence began to evaporate. Greece took the province of Thessaly in 1881, while the island of Crete, though effectively under Greek control, became self-ruled in 1898. In 1908 the Young Turks reform movement – a group of exiled liberals – took power in the Ottoman empire after widespread army mutinies and forced the sultan to reintroduce the liberal

The final decline

In 1909 hardline Islamic elements staged a coup in support of the sultan. It was crushed by the Young Turks, who then deposed the sultan. When Albania rose up in revolt in 1911, Italy took the opportunity to seize Libya in North Africa, bombarding Tripoli and other coastal ports and defeating Ottoman armies at Derna and Sidi Bilal in 1912. Targets were also bombed from the air for the first time when an Italian pilot dropped grenades from his aircraft onto the Ottoman camp near the Taguira oasis. The Italian navy then

Mosaic signature of Abdul Hamid

Abdul Hamid II was the 34th Sultan of the Ottoman empire but he inherited a power in decline. The Young Turks revolutionaries deposed him in 1909.

threatened Constantinople before withdrawing to seize the Dodecanese Islands, including Rhodes, in the Aegean.

The war with Italy gave Serbia, Montenegro, Bulgaria, and Greece the opportunity to form an alliance and, in October 1912, attack Ottoman-controlled Macedonia. The Allies were able to muster approximately 340,000 troops, with a similar number in reserve, and had the advantage of Greek naval control in the Aegean Sea, which prevented the movement of Ottoman soldiers to the Balkans. They also had the benefit of superior leadership, although 240,000 Ottoman troops matched them in courage and stamina.

As the Greek army moved north, defeating the Turks at Venije in November, the Serbs moved south, forcing the Ottomans to evacuate the Macedon capital of Skopje and retreat to the heights of Monastir. Here, on 5 November, the Serbs attacked the recently reinforced Ottoman army but were repelled with great losses. However, the Turkish centre was so weak that a renewed Serbian frontal attack broke through. As the Greeks approached from the south, Ottoman resistance collapsed and nearly 20,000 soldiers were killed or captured. Four days later the strategic Ottoman garrison of Salonika surrendered to the Greeks. To the east the Bulgarians moved into Thrace and besieged Constantinople, while a joint Bulgarian and Serbia force seized Adrianople. By the provisional Treaty of London, signed in May 1913, the Ottoman empire lost all its European possessions to the four victors except for a narrow strip of land alongside the Turkish Straits, and Albania, which was declared an independent state.

> **Italians bombed the Turkish railway station of Karaagac in October 1912 and then used bombs with x-shaped tails and impact detonators during the siege of Adrianople in 1913. This type of bombing, from the air, was a military first.**

Bulgaria, however, felt aggrieved about its limited gains in Macedonia and in July attacked Serbia and Greece. To its surprise, it was then attacked by Romania and the Ottomans. The Romanians advanced towards Sofia, the Bulgarian capital, while the Ottomans regained Adrianople in Thrace, thus preserving a foothold in Europe. Bulgarian resistance quickly collapsed, and by the Treaty of Bucharest, signed in August, it had lost most of its Macedonian gains of the first war as well as some territory to Romania.

The effect of the first and second Balkan Wars was felt almost immediately, as the wars soon turned global.

SARAJEVO

Serb nationalists had opposed the Austrian takeover of Bosnia-Herzegovina in 1878 and sought to incorporate the province into a greater Serbia. On 28 June 1914 **Serb nationalist Gavrilo Princip assassinated the heir to the Austrian throne** in the Bosnian capital, Sarajevo. The Austrians blamed the Serb government and declared war at the end of July. The third Balkan War soon became global, as European alliances came to their allies' support, which resulted in **World War I 266–67 »**.

GAVRILO PRINCIP'S PISTOL

THE OTTOMANS AT WAR

The Ottoman empire entered World War I alongside Germany and Austria against Russia, in the hope of regaining some of its lost territories. Bulgaria, too, joined on the same side with the same hope. Although successful in repelling an Anglo-French attack at Gallipoli in 1915, **the Ottomans were weakened by the Arab revolt in 1916** and by British advances through Mesopotamia and Palestine, finally asking for peace in the last weeks of the war. The **Ottoman empire collapsed in 1922** and a Turkish republic was established in 1923.

THE RED CRESCENT

After witnessing the aftermath of the battle of Solferino in 1859, Henri Dunant founded the Red Cross movement. His aim was to provide neutral and impartial help to relieve suffering in times of war.

While the red cross emblem has no religious meaning, the symbol reminded soldiers from the Ottoman empire of the crusaders of the Middle Ages and so, in 1876, in countries where the population was largely Muslim, the emblem of the red crescent was adopted as an alternative.

6

ERA OF THE WORLD WARS

1914 – 1945

World War I and World War II had their origins in the mistrust between Germany and its rivals in Europe. Both wars spread to involve other theatres of war beyond Europe, and World War II became an even wider conflict when Japan launched an attack on the US and its allies in the Pacific.

BRITISH TORPEDO, WORLD WAR II

ERA OF THE WORLD WARS

1914 – 1945

Between 1914 and 1945 the world's major powers twice clashed in total war. The entire resources of modern states were devoted to the destruction of their enemies with little or no moral limit on the means employed. Together, World War I and World War II probably cost at least 70 million lives.

World War I

The war that broke out in 1914 was one that European states had long anticipated. Yet nothing went according to plan. The principal combatants – France, Britain, Russia, and Germany – soon found themselves in an attritional stalemate. Once trenches were dug, the defence held the advantage over the offence. Industrialized Europe was able to supply its millions of soldiers with unprecedented firepower, and massive casualties were inevitable. The deadlock extended to the sea, where submarines and mines unexpectedly inhibited the operations of the mighty battle fleets. The strategic situation changed when the US entered the war in 1917, bringing the stalemate to an end. New offensive tactics were developed with better coordination between advancing infantry and artillery. Tanks and aircraft, though still primitive, provided a glimpse of a more mobile form of warfare to come.

Although Europe was the crucial battlefield, war spread to other theatres, notably the Middle East where Ottoman Turkey fought as Germany's ally. Both Europe and the Middle East were radically reshaped after 1918. Hopes that this might have been the "war to end wars", however, soon proved vain. In the postwar chaos, movements arose in Europe embracing aggressive, nationalist militarism – Fascism in Italy, Nazism in Germany.

Conflict renewed

In Asia in the 1930s Japan began a campaign of expansion at the expense of China. The end of World War I proved to have been merely a truce in an ongoing global conflict. World War II began in 1937 in China, 1939 in Europe, and 1941 in the Pacific. Tanks and motorized infantry provided the mobility that World War I armies had lacked, with improved aircraft supporting them as aerial artillery. Both sides used strategic bombing to disrupt the enemy's industrial production and demoralize civilian populations. Aircraft carriers revolutionized naval warfare, ending the reign of the battleship, and amphibious operations were developed on an unprecedented scale.

The changing face of war

Germany and Japan won stunning early victories, but in the long run they had no answer to the superior productive power and human resources of the US and the Soviet Union. World War II was fought with equipment more advanced than, but not radically different from, that used in World War I. But, as the conflict drew to a close, technological developments were transforming the military scene. The first jet aircraft, experiments with guided weapons, ballistic missiles such as the German V2, and above all the dropping of atomic bombs on Japanese cities, marked the start of a new era in warfare.

German Jagdpanzer, World War II
The Jagdpanzer, or tank destroyer, was an anti-tank gun mounted on a tank chassis with heavy sloping armour at the front.

B-17 bombers en route to Germany
The US 8th Airforce, stationed in Britain from 1942, flew daylight raids, targeting factories, oil refineries, airfields, and other strategic installations in Nazi Germany. Until long-range fighter escorts were introduced in late 1943, the missions suffered heavy losses.

1914	**1915**	**1916**	**1917**	**1918**	**1919–1920**	»»

❥ Pistol used by Gavrilo Princip to shoot Archduke Franz Ferdinand at Sarajevo in Bosnia

MARCH
German airships bomb Paris.

FEBRUARY
German offensive at Verdun.

APRIL
Anglo-Indian troops surrender to Turkish forces at Kut in Mesopotamia. ■ Easter Rising in Dublin against British rule in Ireland ends in failure.

MARCH
Following the "February Revolution" in Russia, Tsar Nicholas II abdicates. A provisional government of liberals and socialists assumes power.

JUNE
Assassination of Austrian archduke Franz Ferdinand by a Serbian militant.

JULY
Austria-Hungary declares war on Serbia.

AUGUST
Germany declares war on Russia and France; German troops enter Belgium; Britain declares war on Germany. Germans drive British and French out of Belgium and defeat Russians at Tannenberg.

APRIL
Germany makes first effective use of poison gas at second battle of Ypres. Allied troops, including ANZAC forces, land at Gallipoli.

APRIL
Failure of the French Nivelle offensive on the Aisne is followed by mutinies in the French army. US president Woodrow Wilson declares war on Germany.

1919
Civil war between the Bolsheviks and their enemies rages in Russia. ■ Irish republicans start a war of independence against Britain.

JUNE 1919
Treaty of Versailles imposes territorial losses, arms limitations, and financial reparations on Germany.

»» Turkish army uniform

❮ US recruiting poster

SEPTEMBER
French and British forces halt German advance at the Marne.

MAY
German airships bomb London. Italy declares war on Austria-Hungary.

AUGUST
German offensives drive Russians out of Poland. Allied landings at Gallipoli fail to overcome Turkish defences.

MAY
British and German fleets meet in the North Sea in the indecisive battle of Jutland.

⌃ German offensive 1918

MARCH
Treaty of Brest-Litovsk gives Germany control of large area of former Russian empire. German *Kaiserschlacht* offensive opens in the West.

JUNE
German offensive on the Aisne front is stopped.

❮ French 75mm field gun

JUNE
Russia makes substantial gains in Galicia on the Eastern Front. Sherif Hussein of Mecca proclaims Arab revolt against Turkey.

JULY
Britain and France launch offensive on the Somme. The British use tanks in battle for the first time.

JUNE
German Gotha aircraft make their first raids on London.

OCTOBER
British troops begin an attack on German forces at Passchendaele. A German and Austrian offensive at Caporetto drives the Italian army into flight.

JULY
Germans are turned back at the Marne. Number of American troops in Europe reaches one million.

AUGUST
British-led offensive on the Amiens front initiates final phase of the war on the Western Front.

OCTOBER
Allied and German forces collide in Flanders. Turkey enters the war on the side of the Central Powers.

NOVEMBER
First battle of Ypres ends in stalemate. Army from British India invades Turkish-ruled Mesopotamia.

OCTOBER
Germany, Austria-Hungary, and Bulgaria invade Serbia.

⌃ White Russian cavalry in the Russian Civil War

1920
Bolshevik Red Army is victorious in the Russian Civil War, but is defeated by the Poles at Warsaw.

⌃ British Mark IV tank

NOVEMBER
Battle of the Somme ends, with over half a million casualties.

DECEMBER
Battle of Verdun ends in stalemate. Start of withdrawal of Allied troops from Gallipoli.

NOVEMBER
Bolsheviks seize power in Russia in the "October Revolution". ■ The British stage a massed tank attack on the German lines at Cambrai.

DECEMBER
The Bolsheviks open peace negotiations with Germany at Brest-Litovsk. ■ British forces take Jerusalem.

SEPTEMBER
US troops take the leading role in the St Mihiel and Meuse-Argonne offensives. In Palestine, the Turks are defeated at Megiddo.

NOVEMBER
Germany signs an armistice and fighting stops on the Western Front.

1920
Berbers led by Abd-el Krim start a rebellion in the Rif region of Spanish Morocco.

JULY 1920
Iraqis rebel against British occupation of Mesopotamia.

❮❮ British troops at the Somme

1921–1924

1921
General Giulio Douhet's book *The Command of the Air* advocates winning wars by bombing cities.

NOVEMBER 1921
The Washington Naval Conference opens; the major naval powers agree limitations to fleet sizes.

» USS *Texas*, a World War I battleship

1922
Mustafa Kemal declares a Turkish republic and fights to establish Turkey's borders.

JUNE 1922
In Ireland civil war follows an agreement between Britain and Irish republicans that ends the Irish War of Independence.

OCTOBER 1922
Mussolini takes power in Italy.

1925–1929

MAY 1925
In Morocco, Abd el-Krim's Rif rebellion is crushed by the Spanish and French Foreign Legions.

JUNE 1925
Geneva Protocol bans use of gas and other chemical weapons.

» World War I gas shell

1927
In China, Jiang Jieshi, leader of the Kuomintang Nationalists, enters into conflict with the Chinese Communists; he establishes his rule over most of China.

AUGUST 1928
Kellogg-Briand Pact, calling for the "renunciation of war", is agreed; it is eventually signed by 63 nations, including all the major powers.

1930–1932

APRIL 1930
The London Naval Treaty, agreed by the major naval powers, sets new limits on naval forces.

JUNE 1930
French troops leave the Rhineland. France begins construction of the Maginot Line on its border with Germany.

☆ Japanese type 96 light machine-gun

SEPTEMBER 1931
The Japanese army seizes Manchuria from China.

JANUARY 1932
Japanese bombard Shanghai.

FEBRUARY 1932
Japan establishes puppet state of Manchukuo in Manchuria.

1933–1935

JANUARY 1933
Adolf Hitler becomes chancellor of Germany.

❯ Hitler at Nazi rally

MAY 1933
Japan and the Chinese Nationalists agree ceasefire. Japan leaves the League of Nations.

OCTOBER 1933
Germany leaves the League of Nations.

AUGUST 1934
German army swears oath of allegiance to Hitler. German rearmament gathers pace.

OCTOBER 1934
Chinese Communists begin the Long March from Jiangxi province to Shaanxi.

OCTOBER 1935
Italy invades Abyssinia.

« Italian ammunition column in Abyssinia

1936–1938

MARCH 1936
German troops march into the demilitarized Rhineland.

JULY 1936
Spanish Civil War begins; German transport aircraft airlift rebel Nationalist troops from North Africa to Spain.

NOVEMBER 1936
Germany and Japan sign Anti-Comintern Pact.

» Spanish Civil War poster

JULY 1937
Start of Sino-Japanese War.

NOVEMBER 1937
Italy joins Germany and Japan in Anti-Comintern Pact.

MARCH 1938
Germany annexes Austria.

SEPTEMBER 1938
German claims on the Sudetenland bring Europe to the brink of war, but agreement is reached at the Munich Conference.

❯ Scuttling of the *Graf Spee*

1939

MARCH
Nationalists win the Spanish Civil War. ■ German forces occupy Prague; Czechoslovakia ceases to exist. ■ Britain and France guarantee Poland against German aggression.

APRIL
Italy invades Albania.

GANAR la GUERRA
¡MENOS PALABRAS VANA

SEPTEMBER
German forces invade Poland. Britain and France declare war on Germany. The Soviet Union joins the attack on Poland, which is defeated within four weeks.

OCTOBER
The British battleship *Royal Oak* is sunk by a German U-boat in Scapa Flow.

NOVEMBER
Soviet forces attack Finland.

DECEMBER
The German battlecruiser *Graf Spee* is scuttled after battle of the River Plate.

APRIL
German forces invade Norway and Denmark.

MAY
Germans invade the Low Countries and France.

JUNE
Allied forces evacuate from Dunkirk. France surrenders. Italy enters the war.

FEBRUARY
The German Afrika Korps under Erwin Rommel arrives in North Africa. British forces land in Greece.

APRIL
German troops overrun Yugoslavia and Greece. Rommel launches a German offensive in North Africa.

⌃ Japanese poster celebrating victory over Western powers

FEBRUARY
Germans surrender at Stalingrad. Japanese abandon Guadalcanal. Rommel halts US forces in North Africa.

MAY
Axis forces in Tunisia surrender to the Allies. In the Atlantic the U-boat offensive is defeated. RAF bombers destroy two Ruhr dams.

JULY
Soviet T-34 tanks defeat the German panzers at Kursk. Following the battle, German armies are gradually driven westwards out of the USSR. Allied forces land in Sicily.

JANUARY
Allied forces land at Anzio in Italy. Soviet forces lift the 872-day siege of Leningrad.

MAY
In Italy the German Gustav Line is finally broken with an assault on Monte Cassino.

JANUARY
German Ardennes offensive is defeated. Soviet army advances through Poland into eastern Germany.

FEBRUARY
Allied bombers destroy Dresden in Germany. In the Pacific, US Marines land on Iwo Jima.

MARCH
Western Allies cross the Rhine. US bombing raid destroys much of Tokyo.

⌄ Stuka dive-bomber, a key element of German *Blitzkrieg*

FEBRUARY
Singapore Island falls to the Japanese.

MAY
Japanese complete conquest of the Philippines.

≫ T-34 tank

⌄ Soviet troops celebrate with US forces on the Elbe

JULY
Battle of Britain begins.

SEPTEMBER
Battle of Britain ends in British victory. Germany changes strategy and starts bombing campaign against London and other British cities – the Blitz.

⌄ Unexploded bomb, London

JUNE
Germany launches invasion of the Soviet Union.

JULY
Japanese forces occupy French Indochina.

≫ German invasion of USSR

JUNE
Allied D-day landings in Normandy. German V-1 flying bombs hit London.

JULY
Soviets advance into Poland.

AUGUST
Allied armies sweep across France and liberate Paris.

SEPTEMBER
Siege of Leningrad begins.

NOVEMBER
Counterattack by Soviet forces around Moscow.

DECEMBER
Japanese attack Pearl Harbor, then invade Southeast Asia.

JUNE
Americans defeat Japanese in carrier battle of Midway.

AUGUST
US troops land on Guadalcanal. Montgomery takes command of the British Eighth Army in North Africa. German forces begin the battle for Stalingrad.

SEPTEMBER
German V-2 rockets fired at London.

OCTOBER
US forces invade the Philippines. The Japanese navy is defeated at Leyte Gulf. Warsaw uprising is crushed by German troops.

OCTOBER
Montgomery launches major offensive at El Alamein.

NOVEMBER
Allied landings in French Northwest Africa. Soviet Union mounts counter-offensive outside Stalingrad.

⌃ Mustang, US fighter escort on bombing raids

NOVEMBER
US bombers begin daylight raids on Japan from bases in the Marianas.

DECEMBER
German counterattack in the Ardennes. Start of the battle of the Bulge.

APRIL
US and Soviet troops meet on the Elbe river. Soviet forces take Berlin. Hitler commits suicide. Mussolini is executed by partisans.

MAY
Germany surrenders. War ends in Europe. Japanese pilots carry out mass *kamikaze* attacks on Allied fleet.

NOVEMBER
British torpedo aircraft attack the Italian fleet in harbour at Taranto.

DECEMBER
British score major victories over Italians in North Africa.

⌄ Soviet sniper's rifle

AUGUST
Sicily falls to the Allies.

SEPTEMBER
Italy surrenders.

OCTOBER
Italy declares war on Germany.

JUNE
Battle for Okinawa ends in American victory.

AUGUST
Atom bombs are dropped on Hiroshima and Nagasaki. The Soviet Union declares war on Japan and invades Manchuria. Japan surrenders.

≪ Ruins of Hiroshima

« BEFORE

The war had long been coming. For 20 years European powers had divided into hostile alliances. Engaged in an arms' race, the two blocs drew up plans for fighting one another.

EUROPE'S ALLIANCES

France and Russia had **allied with each other** in 1894. **Germany was allied to Austria-Hungary and Italy.** Britain formed a **Triple Entente** with France and Russia from 1907, and developed military co-operation with France.

ASSASSINATION IN SARAJEVO

On 28 June 1914, Bosnian Serbs opposed to Austro-Hungarian rule **assassinated** the heir to the throne of Austria-Hungary, Archduke Franz Ferdinand **« 258–59**, in the Bosnian capital city, Sarajevo. Keen to strike the **rising force of Slav nationalism**, the Austro-Hungarian government blamed Serbia for the archduke's assassination and declared war on 28 July. This triggered the wider conflict.

EUROPE

1 **Western Front**
Date 1914
Location Belgium and northeastern France

2 **Eastern Front**
Date 1914
Location East Prussia, Poland, and the Carpathian Mountains

Outbreak of World War I

All the major European powers went to war in the summer of 1914 with plans for rapid offensives in pursuit of swift victory. Generals were convinced that all-out attack would triumph over defence. They were proved wrong, although Germany came close to striking a decisive blow in France.

Within just one week, Austria-Hungary's attack on Serbia became a general European conflict. All the continental powers were caught up in an arms' race with elaborate hopes to expand their armies whenever war threatened. Hundreds of thousands of reservists (men who had previously been given military training) were called up from civilian life. This process of mobilization took time and was complicated; but no nation wanted to be left behind when its enemies sent their troops into the field.

On 30 July Russia announced plans to mobilize its army in support of Serbia. Interpreting this mobilization as a threat, the German military leadership set in motion their long-established Schlieffen Plan for winning a war against Russia and France. The Germans anticipated that Russia would be the slowest nation to mobilize its massive armies. Faced with a war on two fronts, Germany planned to overpower France in a lightning offensive mounted through neutral Belgium, while fighting a holding action in the east. It would then turn its forces to Russia.

Committed to this plan, German leaders brushed aside last-minute peace moves that might have interfered with their military deployment. The country declared war on Russia on 1 August and on France on 3 August. The next day Germany invaded Belgium. Despite having a secret agreement to aid France in a war with Germany, Britain's Liberal government would have had difficulty leading the country into the war had it not been for the German invasion of Belgium. It was as a treaty guarantor of Belgian neutrality that Britain declared war on Germany on 4 August.

Flag-waving crowds greeted the declarations of war in all the combatant capital cities. Although many people did

12 MILLION The number of reservists at hand to the French, Germans, Russians, and Austro-Hungarians in 1914.

not share this enthusiasm, few opposed the war at its outset. Political divisions were set aside for the moment – in Germany, for example, the Russian threat drove most opposition Social Democrats to support the war effort. On the whole, the rapid mobilization of mass armies was achieved with great efficiency. Civilian reservists everywhere reported for duty when called up. In Britain 750,000 men volunteered for military service within two months of the outbreak of war.

Thousands of trains – 11,000 in Germany alone by mid-August – working to precise timetables, carried about six million men to railheads near the frontiers. The British Expeditionary

German occupation of Belgium
German soldiers occupy Brussels on 20 August 1914. The people of neutral Belgium were unaware of the troops arrival. The invasion ensured Britain's entry into the war.

Leaving for the front
French reservists leave Paris in August 1914. Efficient rail networks allowed countries to move troops rapidly to assembly points near the frontiers.

Germany's attack on France and Belgium
To avoid striking France's border defences head on, the Schlieffen Plan provided for France to be attacked via neutral Belgium. In the event, German troops overran much of northern France but failed to reach Paris.

East Prussia, Germany hastily transferred two army corps from the Western Front – a contributory factor in the failure of the Schlieffen Plan.

General Paul von Hindenburg and his chief-of-staff, General Erich Ludendorff, achieved an overwhelming victory at Tannenberg in East Prussia at the end of August. They killed or injured some 40,000 Russian troops, and took some 100,000 prisoner. The Russian commander, General Alexander Samsonov, killed himself. Meanwhile, Germany's Austro-Hungarian allies suffered reverses against the Russians in the Austrian province of Galicia, and also failed to overcome the Serbs.

Race to the Sea

On the Western Front in September 1914, there was still clear space for manoeuvre between the Aisne and the northern coast of France. The opposing armies now engaged in a "Race to the Sea". This involved a series of attempted outflanking movements, each of which was blocked in turn as infantry on both

Scarlet and blue – France's army in 1914
French troops went to war in 1914 in colourful and all-too-visible uniforms and soft hats. Soon they and all armies would be wearing duller shades of camouflage clothing, topped with protective steel helmets.

Force (BEF) – a small professional force in contrast to the mass conscript armies on the Continent – shifted 100,000 men across the Channel and deployed them near the Franco-Belgian border.

At first the German offensive in the west, based as it was on optimistic assumptions, came surprisingly close to success. Implementing their Schlieffen Plan, German forces advanced swiftly over Belgium, overcoming the resistance of forts at Liège and Namur with heavy Krupp guns. The BEF, finding itself in the line of the German advance at Mons, was forced to retreat alongside its French allies. Meanwhile, large-scale French offensives in Alsace and Lorraine were hugely costly failures, the supposed *élan* ("fighting spirit") of France's soldiers proving no match for heavy machine-gun and artillery fire.

Failure of the Schlieffen Plan

Helmuth Johann Ludwig von Moltke, Germany's chief of general staff, now began to advance his forces south from Belgium, intending to surround the French armies engaged in eastern France. Days of marching exhausted his footsore infantry, and his supply lines, dependent upon horse-drawn transport, became overextended. The line of advance also exposed his right flank to the Paris garrison. French chief-of-staff, General Joseph Joffre, pulled forces back from the eastern frontier to confront the invading soldiers, while General Joseph Gallieni, in charge of the defence of Paris, sent an army to attack the German flank. The combined counter-offensive,

> ## "Of course none of us could foresee the **four terrible years** that lay ahead of us."
> BANDSMAN H.V. SHAWYER OF THE RIFLE BRIGADE, AUGUST 1914

known as the First Battle of the Marne, drove the Germans back to the River Aisne in northeastern France. Here, they entrenched in a strong defensive position. Believing that the collapse of the Schlieffen Plan meant that the war was lost, von Moltke suffered a nervous breakdown and was replaced as Germany's principal commander by Erich von Falkenhayn.

Meanwhile, on the Eastern Front, German calculations had been upset by the unexpected speed of Russian mobilization. Faced with the Russian forces advancing into its province of

sides clashed and then dug themselves into defensive positions to protect themselves from each other.

Stalemate

The Germans fought successfully to overcome remaining Belgian resistance around Antwerp, but ran into French and British forces in Flanders in October. There followed a series of vicious battles, known collectively as the First Battle of Ypres, which lasted into mid-November. The sheer desperation and savagery of the fighting was typified by the deaths of 25,000 German student volunteers. Having received hasty training, the men had been thrown into the fighting, only to be mown down at Langemarck in what Germans call the *Kindermord*, or "Slaughter of the Innocents". The outcome of the battle was stalemate.

The onset of winter towards the end of 1914 brought a lull in the fighting on all fronts, with hopes of a rapid end to the war utterly dashed. However, both sides still intended to fight until victory was won; few considered trying to make a compromise peace.

The taxis of the Marne
During the battle of the Marne in September 1914, 600 Paris taxis were commandeered to carry reserve troops to join the Sixth Army defending France's capital.

AFTER »

The fighting left German troops in control of almost all of Belgium and a swathe of northern France. The Allies' offensive strategy sought to regain this territory.

THE COST OF FIGHTING
Casualties by the end of 1914 were **tragically high**. France had lost some 300,000 dead and Germany 240,000. Around **one-third of the British** soldiers sent to France had been killed. Russia and Austria-Hungary each counted more than **a million dead, wounded, or taken as prisoners of war**.

ADAPTING TO MODERN WEAPONRY
A contributory factor to the very high casualties in 1914 was the **lack of adequate head protection** for soldiers. None of the combatants wore metal helmets. In 1915–16 steel helmets such as the **British Brodie** and the **German Stahlhelm** were universally adopted.

BRITISH STEEL HELMET WITH SHRAPNEL DAMAGE

POLICY OF FEAR
Ideas about civilized behaviour in war had been disregarded. The actions of German forces in Belgium **outraged world opinion**, and influenced the future policy of the United States. Although atrocities were exaggerated by Allied propaganda, the Germans did pursue a **policy of *Schrecklichkeit*** ("fearfulness") to cow popular resistance. Massacres included the **execution of more than 600** civilians in the Belgian town of Dinant.

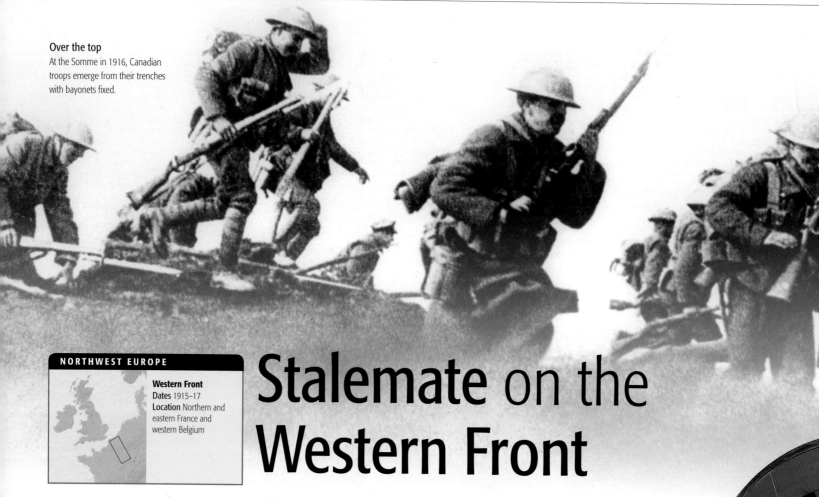

Over the top
At the Somme in 1916, Canadian troops emerge from their trenches with bayonets fixed.

NORTHWEST EUROPE

Western Front
Dates 1915–17
Location Northern and eastern France and western Belgium

Stalemate on the Western Front

Millions of men fought and died on the Western Front between 1915 and 1917, with no apparent, decisive result. The front line in late 1917 had moved little from its position three years before.

BEFORE

The failure of either side to achieve a decisive advantage by the end of 1914 left opposing forces dug into trenches on the Western Front.

IMPERIAL TROOPS

By 1915 the British and French empires were becoming an important **source of manpower** on the Western Front – now virtually a continuous line from the north coast of France to neutral Switzerland – and elsewhere. British Indian and French North African troops fought in the key battles of 1914. A Canadian Expeditionary Force was sent to the front in February 1915. Troops from Australia, New Zealand, and South Africa were initially used in **Africa and the Middle East**, but from 1916 became a highly respected presence on the Western Front.

ADVENT OF CHEMICAL WARFARE

Although the land battles were dominated by the **ever-increasing artillery** forces on both sides, **new weapons** were also coming into use. Chemical warfare began on a small scale in 1914, when France **experimented with tear gas** and Germany fired shells containing a chemical irritant. The **first lethal gas** used was chlorine, released by the Germans at the Second Battle of Ypres in April 1915. Other gases, including **phosgene and mustard gas**, followed and were eventually employed on a wide scale by both sides, causing large numbers of casualties.

At the start of 1915 the opposing armies recognized the urgent need to mobilize maximum military and industrial resources for a long conflict. Already France was struggling to find sufficient manpower for both factories and the front. Britain created mass armies out of volunteers before resorting to conscription in the spring of 1916. It also vastly expanded its war production – British output of shells, for instance, rose from 6 million in 1915 to 76 million in 1917. German manpower had to be split between the Eastern and Western fronts.

Despite their new resources, the generals puzzled over how to win a war in which both sides were entrenched and manoeuvre had become impossible. Through 1915 the French launched offensives in Artois and Champagne, the British at Neuve Chapelle and Loos, and the Germans at Ypres, to little effect.

A war of attrition

In 1916 more troops, guns, and shells only served to increase the slaughter. The year began with a German attack at Verdun. In the summer Britain's volunteer New Armies were blooded in a vast Allied offensive on the Somme. The fighting here continued into November; at Verdun the battle lasted from February to December. The Germans probably lost at least 800,000 dead and wounded, but British and French casualties in the two battles totalled over a million. There were mistakes of generalship on all sides but the immensity of the losses was directly related to the size of the armies engaged, the duration of the battles, and the quantity of munitions.

Trench troops
German soldiers wearing gas masks defend a trench in 1916. They are wielding stick grenades, a distinctively German weapon nicknamed the "potato masher". The handle allowed the grenade to be thrown further.

Howitzer
The British 6-inch howitzer gun was first used in the Boer War (1899–1902). It was utilized in France until the end of 1915.

"Among the living lay **the dead**. As we dug ourselves in **we found them in layers** …"

GERMAN LIEUTENANT ERNST JÜNGER, WRITING OF THE SOMME, SEPTEMBER 1916

Howitzers had shorter barrels than other artillery guns. They were ideal for trench warfare because their shells flew in a high trajectory, dropping on top of a concealed enemy.

Aftermath of combat at Passchendaele
Through 1917 persistent rain and the effects of artillery bombardment turned the Flanders battlefield into a wasteland of mud. Here, soldiers attend to the dead.

Despite the evolution of the war into brute attrition, a decisive breakthrough was still the ultimate goal. General Robert Nivelle was given command of the French Army in December 1916, promising an offensive that would win the war. But when he launched his attack the following April it failed completely. Elements of the war-weary French infantry mutinied. Nivelle was succeeded by Philippe Pétain, the hero of Verdun, who focused on rebuilding morale. Meanwhile, German forces, now under Hindenburg and his deputy, Ludendorff, settled for the defensive, even sacrificing territory in withdrawing to the Hindenburg Line. Only Field Marshal Douglas Haig, the commander of the BEF, remained committed to a breakthrough, launching the Third Battle of Ypres in June 1917. His forces made some progress but became bogged down in the Flanders mud, finally taking Passchendaele in November at immense cost and to no decisive effect.

A test of endurance

Despite the repeated failure of offensives, warfare on the Western Front was not simply futile mass slaughter. Armies strove to improve their fighting methods in search of a decisive advantage and experimented with new techniques and tactics. The use of artillery in support of infantry improved, as did co-operation between air and land forces. The infantry grew in fighting skill and tactical flexibility. But the chief quality required of a soldier was endurance under near-intolerable conditions. Remarkably, although the French did waver, none of the armies broke.

AFTER

The stalemate on the Western Front led to a search both for new tactics that might deliver the elusive breakthrough and for alternative strategies for winning the war.

TANK WARFARE
Tanks were first fielded by Britain at the Somme, but they were too slow and vulnerable to be effective. At **Cambrai in November 1917 274–75 ≫** the British launched the first offensive led by a **mass formation of tanks** – 476 in total. More than one-third were lost in the first day's fighting and it proved impossible to exploit the initial breakthrough. Nevertheless, Cambrai did point to the **effective use of tanks by the Allies in 1918**.

ALTERNATIVE STRATEGIES
The Allies sought alternatives to the Western Front stalemate in fighting elsewhere, but only reproduced static trench warfare in new locations. Neither **the Allied strategy of naval blockade** nor **the U-boat attacks of the Germans** proved decisive **272–73 ≫**. In 1918 the outcome of the war would be decided – as generals like Haig had always said – by great land battles in France.

BRITISH MARK IV TANK

Mounted on wheels, the howitzer was towed by horses or, later in the war, by a tractor or truck. In trench warfare, however, howitzers were often mounted on siege platforms for firing.

BEFORE

When war broke out in Europe in 1914, it also ignited conflicts in the Pacific, Africa, and the Middle East, although much of the fighting was on a relatively small scale.

WAR IN THE FAR EAST

Britain's ally since 1902, **Japan declared war on Germany** on 23 August 1914. It occupied German-ruled Pacific islands and fought a brief campaign to seize the German stronghold of Tsingtao (Qingdao) on the Chinese coast. **China declared war on Germany** in August 1917.

GERMANY'S AFRICAN COLONIES

Germany had four colonies in Africa. **Togo** fell to the Allies at the start of the war and **German Southwest Africa** (Namibia) was invaded and occupied by South African forces by mid-1915. Any German resistance in **Kamerun** ended in 1916, but in **German East Africa** (present-day Tanzania) General Paul von Lettow-Vorbeck fought an inspired guerrilla campaign and **remained undefeated** at the end of the war.

THE MIDDLE EAST

The **Ottoman empire** **《258–59**, including modern Turkey and the whole Middle East as far as Arabia and Iraq, entered the war on 28 October 1914 by **attacking Russian ports**. The Turkish military government of Enver Pasha had **aligned itself with Germany** before the war.

Britain **had military control** of Egypt, nominally part of the Ottoman empire, and deposed its pro-Turkish khedive, Abbas Hilmi, in December 1914. Egypt served as **a base for Allied operations** in the eastern Mediterranean and its Suez Canal was a vital imperial lifeline.

EUROPE AND SOUTHWEST ASIA

1 Italian Front
Dates 1915–18
Location Northeastern Italy

2 Serbia
Dates 1914–15
Location Serbia

3 Gallipoli
Dates 1915–16
Location Gallipoli Peninsula, Turkey

4 Caucasus Front
Dates 1915–18
Location Eastern Turkey

5 Mesopotamia
Dates 1915–18
Location Present-day Iraq

6 Arab Revolt
Dates 1915–18
Location Arabia and Palestine

The Wider War

While stalemate prevailed on the Western Front, warfare raged across Southern and Eastern Europe, from the Italian Alps to the Baltic, and around the Ottoman empire from Gallipoli to Iraq. Less advanced states with a doubtful hold on their people's loyalty began to collapse under the strain of modern war.

The entry of the Ottoman empire into the war as an ally of Germany opened up new arenas for British, French, and Russian forces, in which political and military gains might offset lack of success in Europe. But the Turks at first proved anything but easy opponents. A seemingly simple plan was conceived for British and French warships to force a passage through the Dardanelles and bombard the capital, Constantinople (Istanbul), to bring about an Ottoman surrender. But the warships came to grief on a combination of Turkish mines and land guns, forcing the Allies to change their plans.

Attacking the Ottoman empire

A force of 75,000 soldiers, including Australian and New Zealand volunteers in the ANZAC Corps, was landed on the Gallipoli Peninsula on 25 April 1915. The landings were almost a success, but confusion and hesitation allowed the Turkish defenders to corner the Allied troops in narrow beachheads. Fresh landings at Suvla Bay in August momentarily revived the campaign, but Turkish commander, Mustafa Kemal (who would later rule Turkey as Kemal Ataturk), determinedly resisted all Allied efforts. The stalemated Allied force was evacuated in January 1916.

60 The approximate percentage of casualties suffered by both sides in the Gallipoli campaign – a soldier had roughly a one in three chance of escaping unscathed.

A seaborne invasion of Ottoman-ruled Iraq by British and Indian troops in 1915 also led to initial disaster when the force was besieged at Kut and obliged to surrender in April 1916. But in the Caucasus, Turkish forces were defeated by the Russians, who then invaded Anatolia. A number of Armenians

Stab in the back
A French magazine depicts Serbia attacked from behind as it resists Austria-Hungary and Germany. Bulgaria's attack completed Serbia's defeat.

Sailing to Gallipoli
Young Australians and New Zealanders are packed on board a troop ship destined for the landings at Gallipoli in April 1915. About one in three ANZAC soldiers died in the campaign.

FINLAND
6 Dec 1917: declared
independence from
Russian empire

SWEDEN

Petrograd
(St Petersburg)

Pskov

Riga
1917

Moscow

**RUSSIAN
EMPIRE**

Gumbinnen 1914

Danzig

Smolensk

Lake
Naroch
1916

GERMANY

Masurian Lakes
1914, 1915

Minsk

Tannenberg 1914

Baranovichi 1916

POLAND

Berlin

Warsaw
1914

Brest-Litovsk

Lodz
1914

Lutsk 1916

Krasnik 1914

Komarow
1914

Kiev

Tarnow 1915

Lemberg

Jul 1917: failed
Russian offensive

Gorlice 1915

1915

GALICIA

Rostov

Przemysl

UKRAINE

Budapest

Odessa

Sea
of
Azov

AUSTRIA-HUNGARY

Belgrade

ROMANIA
1916: conquered by Germany

Sevastopol

SERBIA
1915: conquered by Germany

Black Sea

KEY

- Russian empire and allies
- Central Powers
- Neutral states
- —— Frontiers 1914
- --- Furthest extent of Russian advance 1914
- —— Front line at armistice 1917
- --- Extent of territory occupied by Germany
  following Treaty of Brest-Litovsk 1918
- ⇨ Brusilov Offensive 1916
- ✼ Major battle or siege

The Eastern Front
Although pressed back by the Germans, Russia did not concede any decisive amount of territory until the Bolshevik revolution of October 1917 definitively undermined its war effort.

ADVENTURER (1888–1935)

T.E. LAWRENCE

An archaeologist before the war, in 1915 Thomas Edward Lawrence was recruited as a British intelligence officer, based in Cairo. Adopting Arab dress and customs, he fought alongside Feisal ibn Hussein, the future king of Iraq, in the Arab revolt of 1916–18 against Ottoman rule. Lawrence and the Arab irregulars proved exceptionally gifted at guerrilla warfare and contributed to the defeat of the Turks in Palestine and Syria in 1918. Lawrence felt that promises made to the Arabs in the war were not kept by the Allies in the postwar settlement.

joined the Russians in fighting the Ottomans. The Turkish response was to launch a massacre of Armenians under the cloak of brutal deportations, costing more than one million men, women, and children their lives.

The Ottomans' Arab subjects revolted in 1916, aiding a British advance from Egypt into Palestine the following year. The Turks suffered severe setbacks in 1917, Baghdad falling to the British in March and Jerusalem in December. Ottoman forces were weakened by disease and desertion. Defeated again by the British at the battle of Megiddo in September 1918, the Turks sought an armistice.

New theatres
The Serbians had held out in 1914, but in the autumn of 1915 they faced a joint offensive by German and Austro-Hungarian forces, while also being invaded by Bulgaria; Serbia was inevitably overrun.

Italy entered the war in 1915 on the Allied side and fought a border war against Austria-Hungary at the foot of the Alps. A series of failed offensives produced nothing but casualties until six divisions of experienced German troops effected a breakthrough at Caporetto in October 1917. Italy had to be rescued by British and French forces.

The Eastern Front
Although Russia's opening attack on Germany was defeated at Tannenberg in September 1914, initial advances

further south against the Austrians were more successful. Both sides were badly trained, ill-equipped, and often incompetently commanded, yet the Russians captured much of Austria's province of Galicia later in 1914.

The Eastern Front was never as static as the Western Front, because the armies were spread out over a much larger area. The Russians suffered heavy casualties in a series of battles against the Germans in 1915, losing large areas of territory in what are now Poland, Belarus and Lithuania. However, the Russian armies still fought on and achieved by far their greatest success of the entire war with an offensive mounted by General Alexei Brusilov against the Austro-Hungarians in Galicia in the summer of 1916. Brusilov's forces advanced some 100km (60 miles) before German troops arrived to halt their progress. Romania, tempted to enter the war on the Allied side by the prospect of imminent victory, was also crushed by German forces in late 1916.

Revolution in Russia
Brusilov's offensive had entailed huge casualties – probably half a million men killed or wounded. The strain of war was now too much for the Russian state. A revolution in Petrograd (present-day St Petersburg) in February 1917 resulted in the abdication of Tsar Nicholas II. The new Provisional Government tried to keep fighting, but in July the disastrous failure of the Kerensky offensive left the army in disarray. Mutiny and desertion were rife as revolutionary soldiers' committees challenged the authority of officers.

In October 1917 the Bolshevik Party seized power under the leadership of Vladimir Ilyich Lenin. The Bolsheviks signed an armistice with Germany at Brest-Litovsk in December and the following March reluctantly agreed to a punitive peace treaty giving up large areas of the former Russian empire.

Ottoman Turkish uniform
Ottoman troops wore German-style uniforms, apart from the distinctive *kabalak* helmet.

AFTER

The war resulted in the collapse of the Russian, Ottoman, and Austro-Hungarian empires and the creation of new states in Europe and the Middle East.

NEW NATIONS
Most of the territory of the former Russian empire was reassembled as the Communist-ruled **Soviet Union** after Lenin's Bolsheviks won **a bitter civil war 280–81 ≫**. The last Ottoman sultan was deposed in 1922 and **Turkey became a republic**. Britain and France took control of the former Ottoman territories of **Palestine** and **Syria**.

V.I. LENIN, THE PRINCIPAL LEADER OF RUSSIA'S BOLSHEVIKS, ADDRESSING A RALLY IN 1918

Air and Sea Battles

Primarily fought between Britain and Germany, the naval war disappointed the expectations of the British public who longed for a repeat of Trafalgar. Yet the Royal Navy never lost its command of the sea. Meanwhile, air warfare developed in all aspects, from fighter combat to strategic bombing.

1 Actions involving main British and German fleets
Dates 1914–18
Location North Sea

2 U-boat activity in the Atlantic
Dates 1915–18
Location Western approaches to Britain

3 Mediterranean
Dates 1914–18
Location U-boat activity throughout the Mediterranean. Clashes between Italy and Austria in the Adriatic and between Turkey and Russia in the Black Sea

BEFORE

In the years before World War I a naval race between Britain and Germany raised international tension. All states explored the potential of newly invented aircraft.

DREADNOUGHTS

Germany's drive to challenge **British dominance at sea** began under Admiral Alfred von Tirpitz in 1898. This provoked Britain to build ever **bigger and more powerful** battleships, beginning with HMS *Dreadnought*, launched in 1906. The ship so outclassed all earlier battleships that these were dismissively referred to as pre-dreadnoughts. The naval arms race now became so intense that by the outbreak of war in 1914, **Germany** had **24 modern dreadnoughts and battlecruisers to Britain's 34.**

USE OF AIRCRAFT

The **first ever air attack** was carried out in 1911 by an Italian plane in Libya. In August 1914 the flimsy flying machines of all the combatants totalled just 500.

In 1914 the world's greatest naval power, Britain, entered a war that it had to win on land. The Royal Navy was able to maintain a trade blockade of Germany, but although this severely weakened the Germans in the long run, it could not be decisive. Alternatively, a naval catastrophe could have driven Britain out of the war. Germany knew that if it could win command of the sea through the defeat of the British fleet, Britain would be unable to supply its army in France and might even be open to invasion by German land forces. The Kriegsmarine sought opportunities to wear down the British fleet, in the hope of one day meeting it on equal terms and contesting maritime superiority. The stance of the Royal Navy was essentially defensive. It had to maintain its superiority over the Kriegsmarine, while also keeping vital British trade routes open. If it failed to do this, Britain's war industries would soon collapse and its people starve.

Although the Royal Navy easily stopped merchant shipping from reaching German ports, it could not maintain a close blockade to prevent

The most serious problem for the Royal Navy was the existence of new weapons that undermined the value of its large surface warships. From early in the war, German submarines (U-boats) were impressively effective. British naval losses to German torpedoes and mines were high. Fear of these hidden hazards severely limited Jellicoe's ability to manoeuvre. U-boats also proved a menace to British merchant shipping.

The submarine menace

Britain soon disposed of any German surface warships that threatened its ocean trade, but when U-boats began unrestricted attacks on merchant ships in February 1915, their success was alarming. Fear of bringing the United States into the war, as a result of American civilian deaths on passenger ships, led to the reining in of U-boat attacks in 1916, but Germany resumed full-scale submarine warfare in February 1917. Over the next six

Bristol F-2B Fighter

The Bristol Fighter was a two-seater introduced by Britain's Royal Flying Corps on the Western Front in 1917. As well as operating in the fighter role, the F-2B served as a reconnaissance, bomber, and ground-attack aircraft.

The observer in the rear cockpit had a Lewis gun to defend against an enemy attack from above and behind. The main offensive weapon was a fixed, forward-firing Vickers machine-gun operated by the pilot.

KEY MOMENT

SINKING OF THE LUSITANIA

The Cunard liner, the *Lusitania*, was carrying passengers from New York to Liverpool on 7 May 1915. As the ship approached Ireland, it was struck by a torpedo fired by German submarine *U-20*. The ship sank in 18 minutes, drowning 1,198 of the passengers and crew, among them 128 American citizens. The sinking of the *Lusitania* turned public opinion in the neutral United States decisively against Germany. There were anti-German riots in British cities. Germany claimed that the liner had been transporting war material; there was in fact some small-arms ammunition in the ship's hold.

> **"** ... the only man ... who could **lose the war** in an afternoon. **"**

WINSTON CHURCHILL ON ADMIRAL SIR JOHN JELLICOE

German warships making sorties into the North Sea. The east coast of Britain was bombarded by German surface raiders in December 1914. However, the Royal Navy had excellent signals intelligence, which gave warning of later German sorties.

As a result, the main British force, Admiral John Jellicoe's Grand Fleet, was able to surprise its considerably smaller German equivalent, the High Seas Fleet, when it made a rare venture out to sea at the end of May 1916. The resulting encounter, now known as the battle of Jutland, revealed deficiencies in the Royal Navy – for example, in ship and shell design, fire control, and night fighting. Yet although British losses of men and ships were heavier than their opponents' at Jutland, the battle was to confirm the Royal Navy's command of the sea, for the Germans could only fight a holding action, fleeing once in contact with the Grand Fleet's battleships.

months hundreds of Allied merchant ships were sunk, before the belated adoption of a convoy system decisively turned the tide.

War in the air

Aircraft were primarily an adjunct to armies on the ground. They quickly proved their worth for reconnaissance in the mobile fighting of 1914 and became even more vital in that role

Biplane construction with two pairs of wings braced by wires and struts became almost universal because, although creating drag, it was far more robust than contemporary monoplane designs.

once the trenches were dug. Flying over enemy lines, the airmen photographed trench systems, "spotted" for artillery – observing where their shells fell – and reported on troop movements. They also dropped small bombs on targets such as stations and marshalling yards. A number of aircraft were fitted with guns so that they could shoot down enemy reconnaissance aircraft and bombers, and soon these aircraft were fighting one another.

31,500 The number of aircraft built by British factories in 1918. Germany produced less than half this number in the same year.

Civilians desperate for an alternative to the grim industrial warfare of the trenches were gripped by the idea of war in the air. The most successful fighter pilots, such as the German Baron Manfred von Richthofen or France's Georges Guynemer, were hailed as "aces" and celebrated as "knights of the air". In reality, the air war was mass slaughter

Battle of Jutland
This Nassau-class battleship, one of Germany's first dreadnoughts, fires its 11-inch guns during the indecisive battle of Jutland on 31 May 1916.

just like the ground war. Hastily trained airmen had, at times, a life expectancy measured in weeks rather than months. Tens of thousands of aircraft were rapidly put into service; the construction of aircraft moved from craft workshops to mass production in factories.

Targeting cities from above
In addition to ongoing land campaigns, aircraft were used for strategic bombing. German Zeppelin airships bombed the city of London for the first time in May 1915. These huge machines inspired terror in the civilian population, but soon proved hopelessly vulnerable to British aeroplanes using

incendiary ammunition. Forced to fly at high altitudes to escape interception, the airships had lost their effectiveness by the end of 1916. The development of ever larger multi-engined aeroplanes allowed the German strategic bombing campaign to continue. From June 1917 both London and Paris were raided by German Gothas and R-planes. British, French, and Italian aeroplanes also launched raids against enemy cities late in the war. Although small-scale by later standards, these air attacks were by no means entirely ineffectual – in Britain more than 5,000 people were casualties of air raids in World War I.

Lessons learned from the course of the air and sea wars between 1914 and 1918 led to important strategic and technological developments in the postwar period.

AIRCRAFT CARRIERS
Seaplanes operated from warships throughout World War I, and the first true **aircraft carriers**, with a flat deck for take-off and landing, emerged in 1918. The first purpose-built aircraft carriers, Britain's *Hermes* and Japan's *Hosho*, were built in the early 1920s. Such vessels were to play a pivotal role in **the Atlantic 294–95 »** and in **the Pacific 302–03 »** during World War II.

AIR FORCE POWER
In April 1918 Britain created the **Royal Air Force**. Part of the RAF's rationale was to conduct strategic **bombing campaigns** against Germany. After the war, Italian General Giulio Douhet argued that **air power** could win a future war on its own. Relegating armies and navies to a minor defensive function, fleets of heavy bombers would destroy cities and industries until the enemy surrendered. This view was adopted in the 1920s by air commanders such as the American General Billy Mitchell and Britain's Sir Hugh Trenchard.

The two-bladed propeller was driven by a Rolls Royce Falcon V12 engine, cooled by a radiator in the nose. The fighter's top speed was around 200kph (125 mph).

The two-wheel main undercarriage was not retractable so it created a great deal of drag that slowed the aircraft down.

Bombs could be carried on racks fitted underneath its lower wing. Despite its name, the Bristol Fighter was a multi-purpose aircraft, as suitable for reconnaissance and ground attack as for air combat.

THE WESTERN FRONT BY NIGHT
Nights in the trenches were usually quiet, a time for bringing fresh troops, ammunition, and supplies up to the front line under cover of darkness. In some sectors, however, there were regular raids aimed at disrupting the enemy's movements. This painting by Paul Nash, Britain's official war artist during World War I, shows a mule train trying to cross a shattered landscape of burned trees and flooded trenches lit up by an artillery barrage.

« BEFORE

BEFORE

Events in 1917 radically altered the shape of the war, bringing both the entry of the United States into the European conflict and the exit of Russia.

RUSSIA DEFEATED
The Bolsheviks came to power in October 1917 and withdrew Russia from the war. The **peace treaty of Brest-Litovsk** was imposed on Russia by the Germans in March 1918. The treaty confirmed **German control** of vast swathes of Central and Eastern Europe formerly part of the Russian empire. The **Russian defeat** released large numbers of German soldiers for transfer to the **Western Front**, but also undercut popular support for the war in Germany, which had been motivated largely by fear of Russia. Many German workers were also attracted by the **ideals of the Russian Revolution**.

AMERICA ENTERS THE WAR
Woodrow Wilson won re-election as president in 1916 with the slogan: "He kept us out of the war". But neutral America was already a major **source of supplies and finance** for Britain and France. In February 1917 Germany resumed its **unrestricted submarine warfare** « 272–73 and British intelligence revealed the **Zimmermann telegram**, in which Germany secretly encouraged Mexico to attack the US. On 6 April Wilson asked Congress to **declare war on Germany**, which it quickly did. In January 1918 Wilson issued his **Fourteen Points**, war aims based on freeing territories won by Germany and self-determination for subject nationalities of European empires.

GERMAN GENERAL 1847–1934

PAUL VON HINDENBURG

Born in 1847, Prussian General Paul von Hindenburg led the 1914 defeat of the Russians at Tannenberg, a victory that made him a national hero. Appointed German chief-of-staff in August 1916, he supplanted the civilian government as director of the country's war effort. With Ludendorff, his principal assistant, he led Germany's futile offensives in 1918. Von Hindenburg then oversaw the Armistice, yet later fostered the myth that the German army had not been defeated but "stabbed in the back". President from 1925 until 1934, he did nothing to prevent Hitler from rising to power.

The Defeat of Germany

In 1918 the stalemate on the Western Front was broken. The Germans advanced menacingly towards Paris, then were relentlessly driven back towards their own frontier. With its armies retreating, its allies collapsing, and revolution brewing at home, Germany signed an armistice on its enemies' terms.

During 1917 Germany's chief of general staff, Field Marshal Paul von Hindenburg, and his deputy, General Erich Ludendorff – in practice the dominant figure – took control of their country, subordinating Germany's economy and society to the needs of war production. But their gamble on unrestricted U-boat attacks only resulted in the United States now joining the war. Despite the collapse of Russia, Germany was bound to lose the war once US resources of manpower and industrial production were brought to bear on the Western Front. It was, however, a slow process. The US had to recruit, train, and equip a mass conscript army virtually from scratch. The commander of the American Expeditionary Force, General John Pershing, refused to allow troops arriving in Europe to join the British and French armies at the front, instead methodically building up an independent army. In spring 1918 Hindenburg and Ludendorff staked everything upon a last titanic offensive that might win the war before General Pershing's men were ready to join the battle.

Germany's spring offensive
Germany's *Kaiserschlacht*, or Michael Offensive, was launched on the Somme on 21 March 1918. As always in World War I, sheer numbers were absolutely vital. Germany had increased its troop strength on the Western Front by 30 per cent before the offensive, mostly through transfers from the now quiet Eastern Front. But the Germans had also developed new tactics to achieve a breakthrough in depth. The army's best infantry were grouped into units of "stormtroopers" or entire "storm battalions". Their role was to punch holes in the enemy lines and infiltrate in depth, bypassing strongpoints to maintain momentum and wreak havoc in the enemy's rear.

The initial German offensive was an overwhelming success. British defences were shattered by a hurricane artillery barrage as the stormtroopers attacked.

The Germans advanced 60km (40 miles) within the first week. When a follow-up offensive in Flanders opened in early April, there were fears the Allied armies might crack. For the first time the British and French forces were brought under a single Supreme Commander, France's Marshal Ferdinand Foch. By early June the German advance was within 100km (60 miles) of Paris.

America needs you
The image of Uncle Sam in James M. Flagg's now famous poster captivated the American public.

But this progress was costly. As German casualties in successive offensives rose towards a million, the fresh American troops began to arrive, first blooded in June at the battle of Belleau Wood. As

3,728 The number of poison gas cylinders fired at the Germans by British artillery on a single day, at Lens on 31 March 1918.

in 1914, the German advance came to an end at the Marne. On 15 July a German offensive was held and then thrown back in the second battle of the Marne. Then, on 8 August, Canadian and Australian infantry spearheaded a large-scale Allied offensive at Amiens.

Supported by 350 tanks and some 2,000 aircraft, they broke through the German lines. Ludendorff called it "the black day of the German army" and declared that there was no further hope of Germany winning the war.

Germany accepts defeat

Over the next three months the Allies attacked and advanced steadily, taking back all the lost ground and breaking through Germany's Hindenburg Line (a defence system in northeastern France) into territory the country had held since 1914. In September Pershing led half a

million US troops in the battle of St Mihiel and even more in the Meuse-Argonne Offensive in the last weeks of the war. Many German soldiers resisted, but there were signs of war-weariness and low morale – many surrendered.

Meanwhile, Austria-Hungary was on its knees, its army retreating in Italy and threatened from the Balkans by

German prisoners of war

From the summer of 1918 German soldiers surrendered in ever-increasing numbers. Some 350,000 were taken prisoner in the last three months of the war, decisive evidence of demoralization.

German stormtroopers

German shock troops advance during the spring offensive of 1918. The stormtroopers were used to break through the weak points in the Allied line and penetrate in depth, forcing the enemy to withdraw.

Allied forces advancing north from Greece through Bulgaria. Both Austria-Hungary and Bulgaria would soon seek an armistice, as would Ottoman Turkey after heavy defeats inflicted by British empire forces in Iraq and Palestine.

On 4 October Germany's leaders appealed directly to President Wilson. They declared their acceptance of his Fourteen Points as a basis for peace.

6,250,000 The number of German military casualties in the war, of whom about two million died.

Britain and France insisted that any armistice must be based on tough terms; Pershing argued against negotiating an armistice at all, believing that the war should continue until the Germans were totally defeated.

In the event, Germany was told that it had to cede much of its military arsenal and allow Allied troops to occupy the Rhineland in return for an end to the war. General Ludendorff wanted the terms to be rejected, but he was sacked. Germany was in no position to continue the war. Sailors of the High Seas Fleet mutinied, triggering revolutionary outbreaks in several German cities. A nation reduced to starvation by the Allied blockade had lost faith in its leaders. The country was declared a republic on 9 November; Kaiser Wilhelm abdicated and fled the country. An armistice was signed on 11 November.

The war destroyed the German, Russian, Ottoman, and Austrian empires. Europe's borders were redrawn, resulting in the creation of a number of new states.

GERMAN RESENTMENT

The **Versailles Treaty**, imposed on Germany after its signing in France on 28 June 1919, forced the country to disarm and was harsh in territorial terms. France took back Alsace-Lorraine, lost in the **Franco-Prussian War ‹‹ 228–29**, and other German land was taken to form part of Poland. But Germans resented the **"war guilt"** clause declaring them responsible for the war and the victors' demand for the payment of huge **financial reparations** as well as coal, agricultural products, and even horses and cows to replace those people killed.

THE PRICE OF WAR

Some **9 million troops** had died, including 2 million Germans, 1.8 million Russians, 1.4 million French, and some 900,000 from Britain and its empire. Of 116,000 US troops who lost their lives, thousands died in the **"Spanish flu"** epidemic at the war's end. Civilian losses are impossible to estimate, but a figure of **6 million** is credible.

THE LEGION OF HONOUR MEDAL OF FRANCE

Final battles

A German offensive in spring 1918 made substantial gains, but in July and August Allied counter-offensives on the Marne and Amiens fronts reversed the tide. The war ended with Allied troops advancing into Belgium.

Key

▨ Germany	--- Furthest extent of German advance Jul 1918
▨ Allied states	····· Front line at Armistice 11 Nov 1918
▨ Neutral states	→ German offensives Mar–Jul 1918
— Frontiers 1914	→ Allied offensives Jul–Nov 1918
— Front line Mar 1918	⚔ Major battle

Artillery

Artillery has made extraordinary progress in range, accuracy, rate of fire, mobility, and destructive power. A late-medieval siege gun was immobile and could only be fired a few times a day. Today, self-propelled guns firing every few seconds can hit precision targets far beyond the line of sight with explosive munitions.

1 This early 15th-century European culverin is a small muzzle-loading gun. There were smaller, hand-held versions of the gun which were really muskets. 2 This mid-15th-century veuglaire is a breechloader made in Burgundy, France. Veuglaires usually had a removable chamber, so spare chambers could be readied for firing. 3 Mons Meg was a bombard made by the Duke of Burgundy's artillery artificer, Jean Cambier, in the 1450s for King James II of Scotland. Like other bombards of its day, it was massive, weighing almost 7,000kg (7 tonnes) and having a calibre of 510mm (20in). Used in sieges, it fired a stone ball weighing about 200kg (440lb). 4 This Swedish three-pounder cannon was a typical light artillery piece of the mid-17th century. On the battlefield such guns were placed in gaps in the infantry line. 5 The French 12-pounder cannon was introduced by Jean-Baptiste de Gribeauval in the 1770s and used until the end of the Napoleonic Wars. A smoothbore cannon firing mostly round iron shot, it was more accurate and mobile than earlier field guns, with a maximum range of about 1,200m (4,000ft). 6 The soixante-quinze field gun – a French 75mm (3in) – was revolutionary when introduced in 1898. With hydraulic recoil, it could fire up to 30 high-explosive or shrapnel rounds a minute. But it was ill-adapted to trench warfare. 7 The Skoda 149mm (5.9in) howitzer was a Czech-made gun used by the Central Powers in World War I. Firing explosive shells in a high trajectory, howitzers were ideal for trench warfare. 8 This Russian 152mm (6in) gun from 1904 was much less successful than light artillery models and obsolete by 1914. 9 The German 88mm flak gun proved to be just as effective against tanks as it was against aircraft. 10 The American-made M109A6 self-propelled howitzer is a state-of-the-art 155mm (6.1in) artillery piece.

1 EUROPEAN CULVERIN (EARLY 15TH CENTURY)

5 FRENCH 12-POUNDER (19TH CENTURY)

4 SWEDISH THREE-POUNDER (MID-17TH CENTURY)

9 GERMAN 88MM FLAK GUN (WORLD WAR II)

8 RUSSIAN 152MM GUN (1904)

2 FRENCH VEUGLAIRE
(MID-15TH CENTURY)

3 FRENCH MONS MEG BOMBARD
(MID-15TH CENTURY)

7 CZECHOSLOVAKIAN SKODA
149MM HOWITZER (WORLD WAR I)

6 FRENCH SOIXANTE-QUINZE
FIELD GUN (WORLD WAR I)

10 AMERICAN M109A6 PALADIN SELF-
PROPELLED HOWITZER (1991)

« BEFORE

In October 1917 the Bolshevik Party seized power in the Russian capital, Petrograd. The new revolutionary government was engaged in armed struggle from the very start.

THE END OF AN ERA

The uprising of February 1917 that overthrew Tsar Nicholas II set up a Provisional Government. The **Bolshevik Party**, led by Vladimir Ilyich Lenin, **staged a coup** on the night of 24 October 1917. The coup was masterminded by Leon Trotsky, leader of the Petrograd Soviet (revolutionary committee), and armed workers and revolutionary former soldiers (Red Guards) played a prominent role. Alexander Kerensky, head of the Provisional Government, called on the army to regain control, but it failed, confirming Lenin's grip on power.

In March 1918 the Bolsheviks signed the **Brest-Litovsk peace treaty « 276–77** with Germany, which deprived Russia of one-third of the people and territory of its empire. Now Azerbaijan, Poland, Belarus, Ukraine, Lithuania, Latvia, Estonia, Georgia, Armenia, and Finland became nominally independent German satellites.

EASTERN EUROPE AND ASIA

1 Russian Civil War
Dates 1917–21
Location Mainly European Russia

2 Russo-Polish War
Dates 1919–21
Location Ukraine and Poland

3 Japanese Invasion
Dates 1918–22
Location Region around Vladivostok

The Russian Civil War

The collapse of the Russian empire in 1917 triggered a complex series of interlocking conflicts that lasted into the 1920s and are estimated to have cost 13 million lives, mostly civilian victims of famine and of the massacre and depredation practised by all sides in the Civil War.

At the time of the Brest-Litovsk Treaty that took Russia out of World War I, Lenin's Bolshevik revolutionary government controlled the cities of Petrograd and Moscow, but its hold on the rest of Russia was fragile or non-existent. The Bolshevik People's Commissar for War, Leon Trotsky, founded the Worker's and Peasant's Red Army in February 1918, initially based on the Red Guards who had helped bring the Bolsheviks to power. Enemies of the regime began to assemble forces of their own: the Cossacks of the Kuban and Don regions of southern Russia revolted against Bolshevik rule, while former tsarist General Anton Denikin formed an army in southern Ukraine. Such groups were known as "Whites", in contrast to the Bolshevik "Reds".

Foreign involvement

The situation was complicated by the presence of foreign troops. In spring 1918 some 30,000 Czechs, who had been taken prisoner by the Russians while soldiers in the Austro-Hungarian Army, were travelling along the Trans-Siberian Railway towards the Pacific port of Vladivostok, from where they intended to join the Allied forces in France. Local clashes with the Bolshevik authorities en route flared into full-scale fighting. The Czechs soon controlled a swathe of Siberian territory, allowing Admiral Alexander Kolchak to establish himself as head of a Siberian-based anti-Bolshevik Russian government.

Other foreign troops also arrived in Russia. The northern ports of Murmansk and Arkhangelsk were occupied primarily by the British; Japanese and American troops took control of Vladivostok; and the French landed forces at Odessa on the Black Sea. These interventions were in part motivated by a desire to prevent weapons and munitions sent to Russia for use against Germany falling into the wrong hands. But Allied governments also wished for the overthrow of the Bolshevik regime in order to prevent its ideas of revolution spreading to their own countries.

In practice, foreign troops played little part in the civil war. The intervention was in fact deeply unpopular with working-class movements in Britain and France, and with many of the military personnel sent to Russia. A mutiny by

Soviet commemorative poster
Celebrating the third anniversary of the Bolshevik Revolution, this poster underlines how power was won and held, gun in hand.

French sailors at Odessa in April 1919 underlined the severity of the problem and most of the foreign troops had left by the end of that year. But Britain and France continued to supply and encourage the White armies.

Factionalism and terror

Unopposed intervention by foreign forces was possible because of the chaos that dominated Russia in 1919. As well as the Cossacks and the White armies – which included not only the combined forces of Kolchak and Denikin, but also armies formed by General Pyotr Wrangel in the Caucasus and General Nikolai Yudenich in Estonia – there was a peasant "Black Army" led by anarchist Nestor Makhno that established a formidable presence in Ukraine.

The war was conducted with almost inconceivable savagery, crude terror serving as a weapon on all sides. Much of the strategy focused on extracting grain from peasants to feed men and horses – the side that got the grain would win, the peasants always lost. Fought over wide distances with few

White Army
The cavalry of anti-Bolshevik White forces ride with sabres drawn in Siberia in 1919. This was the last of the world's major conflicts in which horsemen played an important offensive role.

Starving peasant children
The Russian people suffered untold hardships during the Civil War and its aftermath. The famine in the Volga region in 1921–22, partly caused by war and revolution, killed five million people.

tanks or aircraft involved, it was the last major war in which the cavalry was an offensive force.

Creation of the Red Army
The survival of the Bolshevik regime depended upon Leon Trotsky's ruthless organizational genius, which forged the Red Army into an effective instrument of war. The ranks were filled by peasants conscripted at gunpoint, and thousands of former tsarist officers were recruited as "military experts" to lead the forces. Discipline was enforced by terror, with the families of officers held as hostages to ensure their loyalty. Although they were surrounded by enemies, the Reds

were able to exploit the disunity of the enemy, and defeated various groups one by one over the next two years.

Commanded by 26-year-old Mikhail Tukhachevsky, the Red forces won back Siberia from Kolchak in the course of 1919 – the admiral was captured and shot in February 1920. The Reds also triumphed over General Denikin in southern Ukraine, after his army had been weakened through clashes with Makhno's Blacks. In October, however, the Bolsheviks almost lost Petrograd to Yudenich's 20,000-strong army. Trotsky prepared a desperate defence of the city and Yudenich halted in the outskirts, withdrawing the following month.

The Red Army faced a new challenge in April 1920. Marshal Josef Pilsudski, leader of the Polish forces, was keen to establish his country's borders as far east as possible. Aided by anti-Bolshevik Ukrainian Nationalists, Polish forces

200,000 The number of foreign soldiers present at some time in Russia during the Civil War. The men came from 13 different countries.

invaded Belarus and the Ukraine, occupying Kiev and Minsk with ease. The Red Army launched a counterattack in June, spearheaded by Semyon Budyonny's First Cavalry Army. The Russians managed to sweep the Poles back across the border, and had pursued them to the gates of Warsaw by August. Aided by a French military mission, the Polish forces regrouped, fought back,

and claimed a historic victory. The exhausted Red Army retreated, after which an armistice was agreed.

Meanwhile, the last of the White generals, Wrangel, had launched an offensive from the Crimea. However, once the fighting in Poland ended, he was doomed and had to retreat to the coast. His followers were evacuated on British ships in November 1920. The Red Army then turned on Makhno's forces, which were brutally crushed.

This marked the end of the Civil War as a serious contest for power, although scattered fighting – some of it savage – continued until Vladivostok fell to the Red Army in October 1922.

Foreign intervention
Allied troops, including Japanese, American, and British, parade through the Russian Pacific port of Vladivostok. Intervention forces did little fighting in the Civil War.

AFTER

Victory in the Russian Civil War allowed the Bolsheviks – renamed the Communist Party – to found the Union of Soviet Socialist Republics (USSR) in December 1922.

RUSSIA STARVES
The Civil War brought huge devastation. By 1920 cities were depopulated and **typhus** raged freely. Preyed upon by soldiers, who conscripted their sons and stole their grain, peasants ceased to grow crops. Worsened by drought, the collapse of the harvest led to a **famine** in 1921 that killed millions.

REVOLUTIONARY RULE
Russia's new government established its rule over much of the **pre-war Russian empire**, regaining most of the territory lost under the Brest-Litovsk Treaty. However, it had to accept the loss of land to Poland and the independence of the Baltic states and Finland. Except for most of Finland, these areas were **retaken by the USSR** in 1939–40 **288–89 》**.

7 MILLION The number of orphaned or abandoned children thought to be living rough in Russia in 1922.

DECLINE OF THE RED ARMY
Civil War hero Tukhachevsky played a leading role in **modernizing the Red Army** in the 1930s. He was an advocate of **"deep operations"**, which involved the combined use of tanks and aircraft. In 1937 he was one of a number of men arrested and shot as part of Stalin's **Great Purge** of likely opponents. In the process, the Red Army was weakened in the run-up to World War II.

Mosin-Nagant rifle
The 1891 Mosin-Nagant rifle equipped the Russian Army during World War I and was used by both sides in the Civil War. It remained in use during World War II.

820mm barrel

Magazine holding five 7.62mm rounds

BEFORE ◀◀

The origins of the war lay in the rise of Japan as an aggressive militarist power, and the efforts of Chinese Nationalists to revive their country's fortunes.

JAPAN THE AGGRESSOR

Japanese encroachment began with the First Sino-Japanese War of 1894–95, giving Japan control of Taiwan and Korea. After the **Russo-Japanese War ◀◀ 254–55** Japan took over the formerly Russian-owned railway through Manchuria, stationing troops along its length. During World War I Japan gained the German concession in China's Shandong province.

UNREST IN CHINA

China became a republic in 1912, but authority was fragmented until the **Kuomintang Nationalist government** of Jiang Jieshi (Chiang Kai-shek) extended its rule over much of the country in 1926–28. It failed, however, to crush the **Chinese Communists** in 1927, who survived as rural guerrillas at war with the **Nationalists**.

PLANS FOR A JAPANESE EMPIRE

From 1932 the government of Japan effectively came under military control as ultranationalist army officers pushed for an **aggressive foreign policy**, seeking to turn China into a subordinate part of a Japanese empire in Asia.

JAPANESE SOLDIERS IN TRAINING

The Sino-Japanese War

Simmering conflict between Japan and China flared into full-scale war in 1937. The Japanese invasion of China can be seen as the beginning of World War II in Asia, for the war it started was only ended through the defeat of Japan by the Allies in 1945.

On 18 September 1931 Japanese army officers arranged for part of the track on the Japanese-owned South Manchurian Railway to be blown up. Claiming the explosion to have been the work of the Chinese, Japanese forces seized control of the city of Mukden. Within five months they had subjugated the whole region of Manchuria. Fighting spread south to the port-city of Shanghai with its various foreign enclaves. Here, clashes between Chinese troops and Japanese marines guarding the city's foreign settlement became the pretext for a Japanese aerial and naval attack on

of Manchuria. There, the Japanese installed Pu Yi, China's deposed last emperor, as ruler of the new puppet state of Manchukuo.

Nationalists and Communists

Jiang Jieshi's Chinese Nationalist government used the truce with Japan to strengthen its forces with the aid of military advisers from Nazi Germany. It also exploited the opportunity to launch a crushing offensive against the Chinese Communists. In 1934 the Communist Red armies were forced to retreat to Shaanxi province to avoid annihilation, with Mao Zedong leading

> ### EAST ASIA
>
> **1** Occupation of Manchuria
> Dates 1931–33
> Location Northern Chinese province of Manchuria
>
> **2** Sino-Japanese War
> Dates 1937–45
> Location Northern, central, and coastal China

"Kill all, burn all, **destroy all!**"

JAPANESE "THREE ALLS" ORDER TO ARMY UNITS IN CHINA, 1940

the Chapei residential area – an action that brought widespread international criticism and condemnation.

From January to May 1933 Japanese land forces from Manchuria started to push south of the Great Wall, scattering Chinese armies and threatening Beijing. But the drift to war was then paused by a truce that left Japan securely in control

Battle of Wuhan

Entrenched Japanese infantry look on as their artillery bombards the defences of Wuhan during the fighting in October 1938. The Chinese Nationalists lost the battle but refused to accept defeat in the war.

the now famous Long March of some 12,800km (8,000 miles) from Jiangxi. Chinese patriotic sentiment and hostility towards Japan was still strong, however, and in late 1936 both Nationalists and Communists tentatively formed a "united front" against the Japanese.

War resumed

A contingent of Japanese troops was stationed in Beijing under the terms of the treaty imposed on China by the foreign powers after the Boxer Uprising in 1901. On 7 July 1937 there was a confused outbreak of fighting between these Japanese forces and local Chinese soldiers at the Marco Polo Bridge to the southwest of Beijing.

The incident could easily have been contained, but both sides reinforced their troops and the fighting spread. The Japanese Kwantung Army had been spoiling for a fight and now occupied the entire region around Beijing and Tianjin. Jiang Jieshi replied by ordering an attack on the Japanese garrison in Shanghai. The city

now became the focus for the rapid escalation of the conflict into a full-scale Sino-Japanese war.

The Chinese attack in Shanghai had not succeeded in overrunning the Japanese defensive perimeter. Japan countered with amphibious landings of troops supported by naval and air bombardment. Air raids killed large numbers of the city's civilian population. By the beginning of October 200,000 Japanese soldiers were engaged in

Front sight

Japanese type 96 light machine-gun

This model entered service in time for the invasion of China in 1937. It had a 30-round box magazine and a rate of fire of 550 rounds per minute.

Folding bipod

fighting in or around the city. The combined firepower of Japanese aircraft, warships, and artillery inflicted heavy casualties – around a quarter of a million Chinese soldiers were killed or wounded – yet the Chinese fought a determined defensive battle. Japanese commanders had expected an easy victory and were shocked by the ferocity of the resistance they encountered. In early November they landed fresh forces at Hangzhou Bay, south of Shanghai. Threatened

Part of the global conflict from December 1941, the outcome of the Sino-Japanese War was decided by the victory of the United States in the Pacific.

AMERICAN SUPPORT FOR CHINA
As relations between the United States and Japan worsened through 1940–41, the US increasingly backed the Chinese Nationalists. US pilots were authorized to join the **American Volunteer Group**, which provided air cover for the Chinese in Chongqing. In the diplomatic talks that preceded the Japanese **attack on Pearl Harbor 302–03 ≫**, President Roosevelt demanded a Japanese withdrawal from China.

CHINA'S ROLE IN WORLD WAR II
From December 1941 to the end of World War II, China fought as **one of the Allied powers**. The United States provided the Chinese Nationalists with large-scale military aid and was annoyed

15 MILLION
A low estimate of the number of Chinese who died as a result of the war in 1937–45.

when Jiang Jieshi proved **reluctant to attack** the Japanese. When Japan launched its major **Ichi-go offensive 304–05 ≫** in 1944, it easily rolled back the Nationalist forces. Japan

JAPANESE GOVERNMENT 10 CENT NOTE USED IN POW CAMPS

treated the Chinese with great brutality, employing **biological weapons** to spread cholera, typhus, anthrax, bubonic plague, and typhoid dysentery.

CHINA AFTER THE WAR
The end of the war in August 1945 was followed by **renewed hostilities 314–15 ≫** between the Chinese Nationalists and Communists, ending in a complete Communist victory in 1949.

---

with Japanese encirclement, Chinese forces withdrew from Shanghai and retreated to the relative safety of the Nationalist capital, Nanking.

Rape of Nanking
Exhausted, disorganized, and short of ammunition, Chinese soldiers failed to hold fortified strongpoints between Shanghai and Nanking. The capital was attacked by the Japanese on 9 December and occupied four days later. Japanese troops ran amok, killing at least 40,000 civilians and fleeing soldiers, and raping 20,000 of the city's female population.

Carrying handle

Barrel

diplomatic shift, for Nazi Germany had dropped relations with Nationalist China in favour of a rapprochement with Japan, while Stalin feared Japan's ambitions on the Soviet Union's eastern border. Despite this aerial assistance, the Chinese were again forced to withdraw westward, this time to Chongqing in the mountains of Szechuan. This remote city would be Jiang Jieshi's provisional capital for the rest of the war.

By the end of 1938 Japan had won control of the whole of eastern China, which it proceeded to form into various puppet entities under the nominal rule of a range of Chinese collaborators. The Nationalists consolidated their position by building a supply road linking Chongqing through daunting terrain to British-ruled Burma. But Jiang Jieshi

Air attacks on Chongqing
Chongqing, the provisional Nationalist capital, was attacked by Japan in 1939. The sight of Chinese civilian suffering helped turn American opinion against Japan.

through the countryside, destroying entire villages and killing every living being – human and animal – in sight.

Japan held all the regions of China that, from its point of view, were worth having. But the Japanese could not bring the war to an end. Since neither the Communists nor the Chinese Nationalists were ready to give in, Japan found itself committed to a draining long-term struggle that tied up around 40 per cent of its armed forces. Following the outbreak of the Pacific War in December 1941, the Sino-Japanese War became a theatre of World War II.

Box magazine fits here

Rear sight

Wooden butt

This ruthless "Rape of Nanking", along with the earlier bombing of Shanghai, helped turn world opinion sharply against the Japanese.

Jiang Jieshi's armies retreated westward along the Yangtze River and on to Wuhan. A large and complex series of battles was fought here in late summer of 1938. Chinese ground troops were supported by elements of the Soviet air force sent by Josef Stalin. This intervention marked an important

was not in a position to mount a serious offensive. In fact, he was not even able to protect his provisional capital against repeated Japanese bombing raids. A number of Communist armies based at Yanan in Shaanxi, carried out a series of attacks on Japanese positions in 1940, known as the Hundred Regiments Offensive, but these brought terrible retribution upon peasants in areas of Communist military activity. The Japanese moved

Wooden pistol grip

The Spanish Civil War

The Spanish Civil War began with a revolt of right-wing army officers against a left-wing government elected in 1936. From the outset, German and Italian forces supported the rebel Nationalists, while the Soviets backed the Republic, giving the war an international dimension that prefigured World War II.

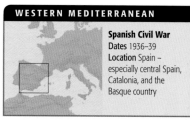

WESTERN MEDITERRANEAN

Spanish Civil War
Dates 1936–39
Location Spain – especially central Spain, Catalonia, and the Basque country

Elections in Spain in February 1936 brought to power a Popular Front government – a coalition of liberal and left-wing parties. Over the next few months there were many outbreaks of violent disorder promoted by both the right and left wing. On 17 July a group of Spanish generals, including Francisco Franco, attempted to seize power in a military coup. They controlled the Army of Africa in Spanish Morocco, but were less successful in mainland Spain, where the coup failed in the face of resistance by loyal paramilitary forces and workers' militias. The Nationalist revolt was saved from defeat by Nazi Germany and Fascist Italy. Luftwaffe Junkers Ju-52 transport aircraft were sent to ferry troops from North Africa to southern Spain – the first military airlift in history.

The division of Spain between the Popular Front's Loyalist Republicans and Nationalist rebels was complex, both politically and geographically.

The Republicans included Basque and Catalan separatists, and every shade of left-wing group from the moderate socialists to communists, anarchists, and Trotskyists, all often bitterly hostile to one another. The Nationalist side ranged from Catholic conservatives to fascists and monarchists, but was held together by the dominant personality of General Franco, who gradually imposed himself as undisputed leader. From the outset, the war was marked by massacres and atrocities on both

German medal
The Spanish Cross was awarded to the Germans who served on the Nationalist side in Spain. The war gave German forces invaluable combat experience.

sides, but the killings carried out by the Nationalists were more systematic and claimed a far heavier toll in lives. Despite Republican forces being made up primarily of irregular militias, there was little guerrilla warfare.

The style of combat was conventional and often static in the manner of World War I, with entrenched infantry confronting one another for long periods on immobile fronts. The "modern" element in the fighting – aircraft and tanks – mostly came from foreign forces. Some 50,000 Italians and 12,000 Germans, as well as contingents from Portugal, were

sent to fight for the Nationalists. A much smaller number of military personnel sent by the Soviet Union made a vital contribution to the Republican cause, organizing air and armoured forces. Some 40,000 foreign volunteers fought for the Republic in the International Brigades, organized by the communists. Britain, France, and the US followed a policy of non-intervention, imposing an arms embargo that, in practice, favoured the Nationalists.

In 1936 a swift end to the war looked likely. The Nationalist forces advanced rapidly on Madrid from two directions. An army pressing towards the capital from its northern headquarters at Burgos was halted by Republicans in the Guadarrama mountains, but Franco's Army of Africa, marching up from the south, looked unstoppable. After relieving a Nationalist garrison that

« BEFORE

In the 1920s and 30s Spain was prey to chronic political instability and social unrest. The Spanish also fought a brutal colonial war in Morocco.

MOROCCAN REBELLION
In 1920 Berbers in the Rif region of Spanish Morocco rebelled against colonial rule. Led by **Abd el-Krim**, they inflicted a severe defeat on the Spanish at Annual in 1921. Partly in response to setbacks in Morocco, in 1923 General Miguel Primo de Rivera formed a government under King Alfonso XIII. Over the following two years, Spanish and French forces **crushed the Rif revolt**. The Spanish **Army of Africa**, comprising Spanish Foreign Legion and Moroccan troops, emerged as a **battle-hardened** force under officers such as General Francisco Franco.

POLITICAL UNREST IN SPAIN
In 1930–31 mounting unrest in Spain led first to the **deposition of Primo de Rivera** and then the overthrow of the monarchy. However, the **democratic republic** born of this peaceful revolution degenerated into a **fierce political battleground**, with fascist, anarchist, socialist, and monarchist movements in contention. A full-scale workers' revolt in the northern province of Asturias was crushed by the army in 1934.

had been besieged by Republican militias in Toledo, in November it pushed into the suburbs of Madrid.

The Republic fights back

The Republican government fled to Valencia, but makeshift militia forces and International Brigade volunteers, backed by Soviet tanks and aircraft, held firm. Madrid was battered by a heavy air and artillery bombardment, but it did not fall. Republican morale was further lifted when, early in 1937, the International Brigades fought the Army of Africa to a standstill in the Jarama valley east of Madrid. In March a Nationalist offensive was beaten at Guadalajara by Republican forces that included anti-fascist Italians of the Garibaldi Battalion.

Divided Republic
This communist poster calls on the Republicans to stop their war of words and unite in the armed struggle. In fact, under orders from the Soviet Union, the communists put a high priority on crushing rival political factions on their own side.

500 THOUSAND The approximate number of people who died during the Spanish Civil War.

150 THOUSAND were victims of massacres, the majority carried out by the Nationalist rebels.

In response to the Nationalist failure to win a quick victory, Nazi Germany strengthened its predominantly aerial forces in Spain. Now known as the Condor Legion, it was equipped with the latest Luftwaffe aircraft, including the Messerschmitt Bf 109 fighter and the Junkers Ju-87 Stuka dive-bomber. These high-performance machines outclassed the Soviet aircraft on the Republican side. In the spring of 1937 German and Italian air support enabled the Nationalist armies to take control of northern Spain, including the Basque country – it was during this campaign that the infamous bombing of Guernica took place.

The Republicans made an offensive at Brunete outside Madrid in July, but it was a costly failure – Republican forces made an initial breakthrough but were unable to exploit it quickly enough and were hammered by a Nationalist counter-offensive. The same thing happened at Teruel in Aragon from December 1937 to February 1938. In a battle fought in harsh winter weather, Republicans first seized the city, then lost it to a Nationalist counter-offensive, in which the superiority of both manpower and materiel was decisive.

Losing no time, Franco followed up the victory at Teruel with a drive east to the Mediterranean, cutting off Catalonia from the rest of the Republican-held areas. Although severely weakened by in-fighting, the Republicans launched their final offensive on the Ebro in July 1938. As the fighting dragged on over the following months, their forces, inferior on the ground and in the air, suffered heavy losses. By 1939 there was little fight left in the Republican ranks. The Nationalists occupied Barcelona in February and Madrid in March, bringing the war to an end.

KEY MOMENT

BOMBING OF GUERNICA

In spring 1937 aircraft of the German Condor Legion were supporting the Nationalist offensive in the Basque country, bombing targets behind the enemy front line. German airmen had orders to drop their bombs "without regard for the civilian population". On 26 April they attacked Guernica, known as the "cradle of Basque culture". Waves of bombers dropping incendiary and high-explosive devices devastated the defenceless town, killing at least 300 civilians. Publicized worldwide, the attack became a symbol of the destructive power of aircraft and, more specifically, of the Luftwaffe.

Republican soldiers
Militiamen prepare for action in Andalucía in September 1936. The Republicans were often short of war supplies, including bullets for their World War I-vintage bolt-action rifles.

AFTER »

The defeat of the Republicans allowed General Franco to install a right-wing dictatorship in Spain that ended only after his death in 1975.

FATE OF THE DEFEATED
For those fighting for the Republic, defeat was a catastrophe. Some **50,000 were executed**; many more were held prisoner for years and used as slave labour. A few escaped capture and maintained a low-level guerrilla campaign into the 1950s. About **half a million Republicans fled** across the border into France when the war ended. Many thousands were still being held in French internment camps when **France was defeated 288–89 »** in 1940. Handed over to the Nazis, many **died in concentration camps**.

SPAIN IN WORLD WAR II
Despite support from Germany and Italy in the Civil War, Franco **kept Spain neutral** during World War II. He entered into **negotiations with the Nazis**, meeting Hitler at Hendaye in October 1940, but the two sides failed to agree terms for Spain's entry into the war. Germany nonetheless reaped **invaluable experience** from the war in Spain, which allowed its armed forces to practise **close air support**, the operation of **tanks** in coordination with aircraft, and **tactical bombing 296–97 »**.

Red Army recruitment
During the Russian Civil War, the Bolsheviks (Communists) used powerful images on their boldly designed posters to encourage men to volunteer to fight in the Red Army.

Propaganda

The main purposes of propaganda in warfare are to persuade one's own men to fight, to demoralize the enemy, and to generate support for the war effort on the home front. Mass media from the printing press to television and the internet have expanded the distribution of propaganda, but it is as old as warfare itself.

The oldest form of war propaganda is the glorification of the heroic leader. Paintings and reliefs on the palaces of Ancient Egyptian pharaohs and Assyrian kings celebrate their glorious victories, representing the ruler and his army in triumph and the humiliated enemy either slain or enslaved. Victorious Roman generals and emperors staged highly dramatic triumphs – victory celebrations and marches during the course of which a defeated enemy was executed. These ancient celebrations of victory in war confirmed not only the prestige and power of the individual leader but also of the entire system – the empire, its army, and its gods. In modern times, depiction of the enemy killed or humiliated is no longer seen as good propaganda. The Court artists who glorified Napoleon Bonaparte (see pp.186–203) on canvas emphasized the sympathy he had for his soldiers and his sharing of their sufferings, as well as his military triumphs. In general, more democratic times have seen the ordinary soldier celebrated as much as the leaders, and sacrifice stressed as much as, or more than, glory.

Fighting for a cause

Going to war in the name of religion or some secular ideal has often justified warfare (see pp.344–45). Propaganda circulates these ideas, making them known to friend and foe. In the 4th century BCE, Alexander of Macedon (see pp.24–25) presented his campaign against the Persians (see pp.18–29) as advancing Greek civilization against barbarians, stage-managing a visit to Troy to identify himself with the Greek heroes of the Homeric age.

In medieval times, religious war was preached by Christian popes and Muslim caliphs. The pulpit as well as the mosque provided platforms for the statement of war aims. In the 18th century, American and French revolutionaries fought in the name of freedom and human rights, their beliefs proclaimed in speeches in assemblies and published in newspapers and tracts. In the 20th century, fascism, communism, and democracy became major subjects of propaganda, each promising liberation from the others, and modern technology provided the means of reaching a larger audience than ever.

Vilifying the enemy

Slandering the enemy is as established a function of propaganda as glorifying one's own cause. Publicizing the enemy's crimes and massacres or ridiculing their cultural and racial characteristics are also standard aspects of propaganda. During the religious wars of early modern Europe, when Protestant fought Catholic, the use of the printing press made it possible to distribute to a wide public images of a vicious enemy. Protestants, for example, depicted the Catholic Spanish as extremely cruel and superstitious and lingered upon gory details of their alleged massacres.

Pope Urban preaches crusade

Pope Urban II (centre) promised wealth and salvation to those who fought to avenge the alleged atrocities perpetrated by the Muslims in Jerusalem.

During the French Revolutionary Wars (see pp.186–87) and the Napoleonic Wars (see pp.188–209), the British cartoonists portrayed the French as covetous and malnourished. Both the real and the imagined horrors inflicted by Germany on "gallant little Belgium" allowed the Allies to demonize the Germans in World War I (see pp.266–77), producing images of "the Hun" as a blood-crazed gorilla. Japan's attack on Pearl Harbor in December 1941 provoked a similiar response in World War II (see pp.288–99) when American propagandists' representation of the Japanese was clearly racist. Nazi cartoonists depicted Allied leaders as puppets of the Jews (who themselves were utterly dehumanized by Nazi propaganda), and emphasized the presence of caricatured African Americans among the Allied forces.

Recruitment posters

A major function of propaganda has always been to recruit men to fight. The appeal by Pope Urban II for the First Crusade in the late 11th century was a striking example of successful voluntary enlistment. The World War I recruitment poster is a good example of the propagandist's art. The images of Lord Kitchener saying "Your Country Needs You" in Britain, and of Uncle Sam with "I Want You for the US Army" in America, are simple, direct, and aimed at the most basic instinct of national solidarity. The posters of Stalinist Russia in World War II drew

on a mix of nationalist and communist themes: people were to fight for the homeland and the worker's revolution. A poster of Che Guevara in the 1960s had the same function of enlisting troops for a global Marxist revolution.

Managing information

From the mid-19th century, liberal states had to contend with the war journalist and photographer. It was above all the bad press that the British received for their war against the Boers (see pp.248–49) at the start of the 20th century that persuaded European governments of the need to focus on information management. Since that time, keeping control of what people see and hear has become increasingly important, as has broadcasting a biased version of events to the enemy. Specific government departments or agencies devoted to propaganda, such as the British Ministry of Information and the US Committee on Public Information, were an innovation of World War I.

Napoleon as Caesar

Napoleon carefully controlled his image. On this coin he is represented in the style of a Roman emperor.

Communist Russia, Nazi Germany, and the Fascist Party in Italy, carried on the development of modern propaganda in the 1920s and 30s, when radio and sound films became key media. World War II was perhaps the conflict in which propaganda was at its most effective, playing a large role in the success of states in mobilizing their populations for total war.

In contrast to the situation in World War II, during the Vietnam War in the 1960s, the United States suffered an almost total loss of official control, and even influence over how the war was presented to its people back home. This was not so much the direct effect of television – even though it was the first televised war – as a consequence of a mistaken belief by those in power that the media would voluntarily support a national war effort. After Vietnam, military authorities effectively clawed back control over war coverage. No television images from the Falklands (see pp.336–37) were broadcast during Britain's war with Argentina in 1982, and throughout Operation Desert Storm in 1991 (see pp.342–43) the American authorities' control of information was flawless. Today, in the age of digital photography and the internet, it has become even more difficult to suppress unwanted coverage of events, yet spin-doctors show little sign of losing the battle to keep official views in the forefront. At the same time, terrorist movements are devoted to the idea of "propaganda by the deed", carrying out military actions with the sole purpose of publicizing a cause and influencing world opinion.

Joseph Goebbels and radio propaganda

Nazi propaganda minister, Joseph Goebbels, was a master of radio broadcasting, which was one of the key propaganda mediums of the 1930s and 40s.

TIMELINE

c.1275 BCE Egyptian Pharaoh Ramesses II's war with the Hittites is celebrated as a great victory by his artists and scribes at Thebes.

113 CE Trajan's Column in Rome presents an official version of Emperor Trajan's defeat of the Dacians.

1095 Pope Urban II calls on Christian knights to volunteer for a crusade against the Muslims, graphically detailing the atrocities that the Muslims had allegedly committed.

1568–1648 During the Eighty Years War, Dutch pamphleteers highlight and exaggerate Spanish Catholic atrocities and repressive ambitions.

c.1800 French artists such as David and Gros create heroic images of Napoleon Bonaparte.

1854–56 During the Crimean War, the reports of journalist William Russell and the photographs of Roger Fenton present a realistic, anti-heroic view of warfare.

1914–18 During World War I, Germany and the Western Allies fight a propaganda war in which newspaper articles and posters play the leading part.

1916 A documentary film of the battle of the Somme is shown in British cinemas. Sponsored by the War Office, it fosters British patriotism and graphically portrays the horrors of trench warfare.

1917 On entering World War I, the United States government establishes the Committee of Public Information as an agency to influence public attitudes to the war.

1918 The British government creates its first Ministry of Information.

1933 Joseph Goebbels is appointed Propaganda Minister in Hitler's Nazi government in Germany.

1937 Pablo Picasso's painting depicting the bombing of the city of Guernica is exhibited by the Spanish Republic protesting at German military action during the Spanish Civil War.

1939–45 In World War II, radio and cinema are the prime propaganda media. Information about the progress of the war is controlled by government agencies.

US ANTI-GERMAN POSTER

1947–89 During the Cold War, the United States and the Soviet Union engage in an unremitting propaganda war using all available media.

1965–72 Television camera crews with lightweight equipment provide graphic, and often critical, visual coverage of American military operations and casualties in Vietnam.

1991 During Operation Desert Storm, the Americans show great skill in manipulating news media; for example, releasing television footage of accurate Smart bombs hitting their targets.

2001 During military operations in Afghanistan and Iraq, photos and videos taken by military personnel and civilians are potentially available instantly worldwide via the internet.

BEFORE «

The rise to power of Nazi Party leader Adolf Hitler in Germany in 1933 led directly to the outbreak of war in Europe six years later.

GERMANY THE AGGRESSOR

Overturning the **Versailles Treaty**, Hitler expanded German armed forces and marched troops into the demilitarized Rhineland in 1936. He formed the **Axis alliance** with Italian Fascist dictator, Benito Mussolini, and both sent forces to the **Spanish Civil War « 284–85**.

Germany annexed Austria in March 1938 in **the "Anschluss"**. When a last-minute deal at September's Munich Conference averted war, Hitler occupied **Czechoslovakia's Sudetenland**

HITLER AT A NAZI PARTY NUREMBERG RALLY

region. Britain and France rapidly rearmed but hoped that Hitler would be "appeased" by these territorial gains. By March 1939, though, German forces had occupied Prague, and Czechoslovakia ceased to exist.

THE GERMAN-SOVIET PACT

Britain and France responded by **guaranteeing Poland** against German aggression. Hitler wanted a return of Danzig to Germany and adjustments in the border territories, but the Poles refused to accept any of these demands. While **Germany prepared to invade Poland**, the Western democracies tardily sought to make an agreement with the Soviet Union. But the Soviets instead chose to do a **deal with Hitler's Nazis**, their ideological enemies. The signature of the German-Soviet Pact on 23 August 1939 inevitably cleared the path to war.

KEY MOMENT

DUNKIRK

In May 1940 the British Expeditionary Force was cut off by the rapid German advance from the Ardennes, and troops fell back on the port of Dunkirk. While French and British troops held a defensive perimeter, evacuation of the British troops by sea began on 25 May. While under constant air attack, men were taken off from the port itself and the beaches outside the town. Royal Navy warships bore the brunt of the operation, although hundreds of volunteer civilian vessels joined in – small local boats ferrying men from the beaches to larger vessels offshore. French and Belgian troops joined the British in the last few days of the evacuation, which ended on the night of 3–4 June. Almost 340,000 soldiers were evacuated in total, 220,000 of them British, but they were forced to leave most of their weapons behind.

World War II Begins

The lightning victories of the German armies in the first two years of World War II, won by a combination of rapid manoeuvre and air power, gave Hitler control over most of Europe. But Britain remained undefeated and the Soviet Union refused to succumb to the shock of *Blitzkrieg*.

German forces invaded Poland on 1 September 1939. Two days later Britain and France declared war on Germany. Despite the Axis alliance, Italy stayed neutral, as it had in 1914. In theory, the declaration of war by the Western Allies placed Hitler in a perilous situation. With the majority of German armed forces thrown into the invasion of Poland, Germany's western border was weakly defended. But France was committed to a defensive strategy based upon the supposed impregnability of the Maginot Line border fortifications built in the 1930s, and Britain's army was very small. The British and French planned a three-year war of attrition and blockade, but failed to provide the Poles with military assistance of any kind. In mid-September, with the Germans already at the gates of Warsaw, the Soviet army invaded Poland from the east. On 28 September Germany and the Soviet Union divided the defeated country between them.

Western Front and Scandinavia

Exhilarated by this victory, Hitler now instructed his commanders to prepare immediately for an attack on France and Belgium. An offensive in the west was, however, twice postponed – much to the relief of the German generals – and resulted in a period of inactivity known as the "phoney war". Although a British Expeditionary Force (BEF) took up its

The occupation of Europe

At its height, German command of Europe stretched from the Atlantic to the Caucasus. Despite talk of creating a "New Order" in Europe, Germany never advanced beyond the crudest exploitation of the countries under its control.

position on the left of the French line, the Allied armies were content to stay on the defensive.

Throughout the winter of 1939–40 the only war that raged was in Finland; invaded by the Soviets on 30 November, the Finns held out fiercely until March. An armistice was finally agreed on 12 March and Finland avoided occupation or being turned into a communist vassal state. The war did, however, attract attention to Scandinavia. The Allies prepared naval and land forces for an intervention in neutral Norway, aiming to cut off supplies of Swedish iron ore shipped to Germany from Norwegian ports. The Germans moved faster. On 9 April 1940 they occupied Denmark and began landings in Norway by sea and air, quickly capturing airfields in both countries. The Allies countered with their own landings on Norway's coast and inflicted considerable losses on the German Navy. But on land the Germans were superior in leadership, organization, and equipment, and they also gained command of the air. The last Allied forces were evacuated from Norway on 8 June.

Key

▨	Greater Germany
▨	Axis powers and satellites of Germany
▨	Vichy France and colonies
▨	Territory occupied by Germany and satellites Dec 1941
▨	Allied states
▨	Neutral states
—	Frontiers Dec 1941

Fall of France

On 10 May the Germans launched their offensive in France and the Low Countries. Hitler had adopted a plan, proposed by General Erich von Mannstein, for a swift thrust through the Ardennes region of southern Belgium. The tanks would break the Allied line and head westwards, encircling the Allied forces in Belgium. The plan was bold, risky, and utterly successful. The German invasions of the Netherlands and Belgium held the attention of the Allied commanders, while General Heinz Guderian's tanks surged out of the Ardennes, pressing on to the Channel coast. The Allied armies had plenty of tanks, but they were poorly deployed. The Luftwaffe established command of the air, and Stuka dive-bombers wreaked havoc among retreating infantry and civilian refugees.

TECHNOLOGY

BLITZKRIEG

Blitzkrieg, literally "lightning war", was the name given to the technique used by the German forces in their great successes of 1939–41. The aim was to achieve rapid victory through shock and mobility. Tanks and mechanized infantry broke through weak points in the enemy's defences and advanced at speed to cut communication lines. Aircraft, notably Stuka dive-bombers, acted as aerial artillery in support of the tanks. *Blitzkrieg* depended heavily on causing the collapse of enemy morale and, subsequently, a total breakdown of command and control.

After the evacuation of Allied troops from Dunkirk, Britain's prime minister, Winston Churchill, urged his country to fight on. Mussolini only just had time to bring Italy into the war before France surrendered to the Germans on 21 June. Northern and western France came under German military occupation, with a collaborationist government led by Marshal Pétain operating from Vichy.

Hitler's hopes that the British would make peace were in vain. He toyed with plans to invade Britain while, over the south of England, his Luftwaffe fought the Royal Air Force. But by autumn 1940, the Germans were bombing British cities and Hitler was looking east to the Soviet Union for new conquests.

Detailed planning for the invasion of the USSR began in September 1940. But German forces were distracted the following spring by problems in the Balkans; the Italians had invaded Greece from Albania in October and required assistance. In April Germany overran both Yugoslavia and Greece.

The Eastern Front

The German invasion of the USSR, known as Operation Barbarossa, began on 22 June 1941. Hitler expected another swift victory and his troops were not equipped for winter warfare. On a far larger scale than any operation Hitler's forces had previously attempted, it involved three million German troops and a further million from Germany's allies. Stalin had refused to believe the reports of German military preparations and his forces were caught off-guard.

Once again German armies rapidly out-fought and outmaneuvered their enemies. Hundreds of thousands of

340 THOUSAND The number of German soldiers killed in the campaigns of 1941.

5.7 MILLION The number of Soviet soldiers taken prisoner by the Germans in World War II.

Soviet troops were taken prisoner. But the Soviets did not cave in. The autumn rains, followed by a bitterly cold winter, exposed serious supply problems in German armies still dependent on horse-drawn transport. Thrown forward in suicidal counter-offensives, the Soviets suffered appalling casualties but still managed to push the Germans back from the outskirts of Moscow. By the end of 1941 the period of lightning victories was over, and Germany now faced a long war of attrition in the east.

Germany was now supreme in Europe but overstretched strategically. Exploiting its conquered territories was essential to sustaining the war effort.

GERMAN RULE IN EUROPE

The Nazi leadership saw its country as short of food and manpower. Both could be **extracted from conquered peoples**. Millions of forced labourers worked in German factories and fields. The Germans used **prisoners of war** and civilian workers from all over Europe, treating many with appalling brutality. In addition to **killing Europe's Jews**, the Nazis planned to leave 30 million "surplus" people in Poland and the Soviet Union to starve to death or die of disease in order to release food supplies for Germany.

GERMANY ON THE RETREAT

By the end of 1941 Germany was also at **war with the United States 290–91 »**. German armies continued to advance in the Soviet Union through 1942, until meeting catastrophe **at the battle of Stalingrad 292–93 »**. By 1943 Germany was on the **retreat on all fronts**.

VICHY POSTER RECRUITING WORKERS FOR GERMANY

> "We must forget the idea of comradeship between soldiers … **This is a war of annihilation.**"
>
> HITLER SPEAKING TO SENIOR OFFICERS BEFORE OPERATION BARBAROSSA, 30 MARCH 1941

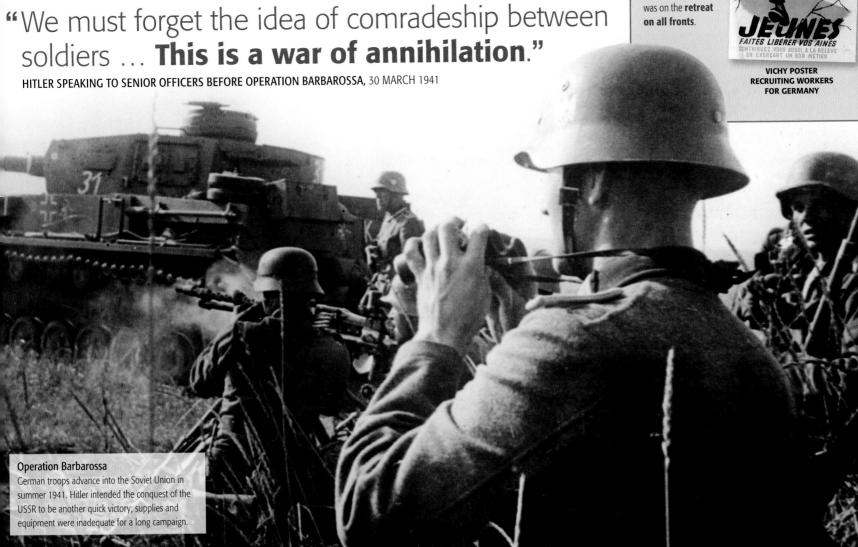

Operation Barbarossa

German troops advance into the Soviet Union in summer 1941. Hitler intended the conquest of the USSR to be another quick victory; supplies and equipment were inadequate for a long campaign.

« BEFORE

Well before the entry of the United States into the war in December 1941, President Franklin D. Roosevelt had made his country an ally of Britain in all but name.

MUNITIONS AND WAR MATERIALS

Roosevelt declared the United States neutral at the start of the war, but changes to US neutrality laws soon allowed American factories to begin **supplying munitions** to Britain and France. The United States also began a limited build-up of its

45 BILLION
The amount in dollars of US Lend-Lease aid to all of its allies during the war. Reverse Lend-Lease from the Allies to the US amounted to some $8 billion.

armed forces, **introducing conscription** in 1940. The **Lend-Lease programme**, initiated in March 1941, supplied Britain and other allies with war materials they did not have the money to pay for.

AMERICA ENTERS THE WAR

The United States remained officially at peace until the **Japanese attack on Pearl Harbor** on 7 December 1941. Conveniently for Roosevelt, Hitler promptly **declared war** on the United States in support of Japan, an Axis ally.

EUROPE AND NORTH AFRICA

1 **Eastern Front**
Dates 1941–43
Location Western USSR

2 **North Africa**
Dates 1940–43
Location Egypt, Libya, Algeria, and Tunisia

3 **Italian Campaign**
Dates 1943
Location Sicily and southern Italy

The Turning Tide

By 1942 Germany was at war with the United States, the Soviet Union, and the British Empire, who were vastly superior in manpower and resources. Yet the Germans kept the upper hand at first, threatening to establish an unassailable hold on Europe before American strength was brought to bear.

In 1942 the Soviet Union could fairly claim to be sustaining the brunt of the land war against Germany with only limited help from its Western allies. Although the British were engaged against both Germany and Italy in the North African desert, there was no comparison with the scale and ferocity of the battles on the Soviet front. Both dictators, Hitler and Stalin, took over supreme command of their armed forces and mercilessly drove them into a combat to the death.

Russia's "Great Patriotic War"

Stalin rallied the Soviet people after the great defeats of 1941 during Germany's Operation Barbarossa, appealing more to traditional Russian patriotism rather than Communist ideology. Discipline in the army and on the home front was also brutally enforced by the secret police. Germany had overrun most of the USSR's industrial areas, but new factories were improvised beyond the Urals and began turning out large quantities of simple but highly effective weapons, notably the superb T-34 tank.

A series of attacks ordered by Stalin in the first half of 1942 failed disastrously, leaving the Soviet armies exposed to a renewed German advance. Hitler directed his main thrust south towards the Caucasus, aiming to cripple the Soviet war machine by capturing the oil fields at Baku. But he was distracted by another objective, the city of Stalingrad on the Volga. The German Sixth Army entered Stalingrad but failed to subdue its defenders in the ferocious battle that ensued. Meanwhile, General Georgi Zhukov organized a

"Beat the German beast!"
A Soviet poster calls for the extermination of Hitler's invading armies. The Soviet state mobilized its people for the war effort with a mix of exhortation and terror.

vast encirclement from late November that trapped and destroyed the German forces inside the city. The battle of Stalingrad (pp.292–293) was one of the bloodiest encounters of World War II.

By the time the German Sixth Army surrendered at Stalingrad in January 1943, American troops were facing a

24 THOUSAND
The number of tanks and armoured vehicles made in the USSR in 1942.

93 HUNDRED
The number of tanks and armoured vehicles made in Germany in 1942.

baptism of fire in North Africa. The fighting in the Mediterranean theatre had begun with Italy's entry into the war in June 1940. British Empire forces based in Egypt defeated the Italians in East Africa and Libya, but the arrival of the German Afrika Korps under

Americans in the desert
An M4 Sherman tank rolls through the North African desert in 1943. Although outclassed by German tanks in armour and firepower, the Sherman was produced in large numbers for the British and American forces.

Cocking handle

Box magazine

Folded stock

Soviet PPS 43 submachine gun
Introduced in the middle of the war, the PPS 43 was highly effective, sturdy, and, above all, easy to manufacture in large quantities.

General Erwin Rommel in February 1941 presented an altogether stiffer challenge. While the Royal Navy battled to keep the sea route from Gibraltar to Malta and Alexandria open, Britain's Eighth Army struggled to stop Rommel's tanks overrunning Egypt and threatening the Suez Canal. To Hitler the desert war was always a sideshow, and the Americans took a similar view. But the British, deeply pessimistic about their chances of a successful seaborne invasion of France, persuaded the United States to land forces in North Africa as offering an immediate prospect of engaging an enemy army.

On 23 October 1942 British general Bernard Montgomery began an offensive at El Alamein, which drove Rommel's forces out of Egypt. On 8 November Allied forces under the US general, Dwight D. Eisenhower, landed in French North Africa in Operation Torch. The German and Italian forces were soon trapped in Tunisia between those of Eisenhower and Montgomery. In May 1943 the Axis forces in North Africa surrendered; some 200,000 Germans and Italians were captured.

Germany's last attacks in Russia
The titanic struggle on the Eastern Front raged unabated. In February 1943 the Germans fought back in fierce battles for the city of Kharkov. By July they were ready for a major offensive at the Kursk salient. With some 2,000 tanks engaged, the battle at Kursk was the largest armoured encounter in history. Despite heavy losses, the Soviet forces repulsed the Germans and followed up with a counter-offensive that drove the enemy back into Ukraine and Belarus by winter.

The Western Allies were now under pressure from Stalin to open a "Second Front". The Americans wanted to invade France as soon as possible, but British leaders persuaded them that this was not feasible in 1943. Instead, victory in Tunisia was succeeded by an invasion of Sicily in July. Churchill fondly imagined that the Allies were striking into "the soft underbelly of Europe". Certainly, the Italians had no appetite to continue the fight. Mussolini was overthrown and his successor, Marshal Pietro Badoglio, signed an armistice when Allied troops landed in mainland Italy in September. But the Germans swiftly took over the defence of the Italian peninsula. By the year's end Allied forces were stuck in front of the Gustav Line, the strong defensive position passing through the ancient abbey at Monte Cassino.

The contrast between the fighting in 1942–43 and the earlier *Blitzkrieg* phase of the war was pronounced. The offensive power of armoured troops had been subdued by anti-tank guns and tank-busting aircraft. Whether at El Alamein, Kursk, or Monte Cassino, massed artillery firepower and dogged foot soldiers were as crucial as tanks in battles that resolved into attritional trials of strength. The tide of war had turned, but the Allies would find no easy route to victory.

BRITISH COMMANDER (1887–1976)

BERNARD MONTGOMERY

Bernard Law Montgomery was the most successful British commander of World War II, always popular with his troops because of his care not to throw away their lives. Commanding the Eighth Army in the Western Desert in August 1942, he raised troop morale with his flamboyant presence and resisted pressure from Churchill to begin a premature offensive. He commanded the land forces at D-Day but was downgraded as American generals came to the fore. Montgomery demonstrated an unusual boldness in planning Operation Market Garden in September 1944, the airborne assault that failed at Arnhem.

AFTER

Allied armies ground forward on the Eastern and Italian fronts in the first half of 1944, enjoying an increasing advantage over the Germans in men and materiel.

DEADLOCK ENSUES
On 22 January 1944 Allied forces were put ashore at Anzio, between the **Gustav Line** and Rome. They were held by a German counterattack. The destruction of the monastery at Monte Cassino by Allied bombers in February also achieved nothing. The Gustav Line was breached in late May. Allied forces, led by General Mark Clark, at last entered Rome on 4 June, two days before **the D-Day landings in Normandy 298–99 »**.

US GENERAL MARK CLARK ENTERS ROME, JUNE 1944

On the Eastern Front in 1944 Soviet forces outnumbered the Germans by two to one. Pushing the Germans back in a series of large-scale offensives, their advance ran out of steam just short of Warsaw in late July.

THE STALEMATE CONTINUES
The **U-boat offensive 294–95 »** in the Atlantic was tamed by the Allies in the spring of 1943. The Allied **strategic bombing offensive 296–97 »** against Germany inflicted substantial damage, but showed no signs of forcing a German surrender.

House-to-house fighting
Red Army troops launch a counterattack through the rubble of Stalingrad. The Soviets never allowed the Germans to consolidate their positions and individual buildings changed hands many times.

Stalingrad

In 1942 German forces advancing across the Soviet Union were ordered to capture Stalingrad, an industrial centre on the river Volga. Defended to the death by Soviet soldiers, the city turned into a trap in which an entire German army was caught and crushed. Stalingrad was the first major defeat for Hitler's forces on the Eastern Front, one from which they never fully recovered.

The city had already been reduced to ruins by Luftwaffe air attacks before the German Sixth Army under General Friedrich Paulus began fighting its way into Stalingrad in September 1942. General Vasilii Chuikov, in command of the Soviet 62nd Army, had orders to hold the city at any cost. His troops fought the advancing Germans street by street and building by building with the river Volga at their backs. Supplies were ferried across the river by night to the Soviet soldiers who turned ruined factories and apartment blocks into fortresses, each of which had to be taken at a heavy cost in time and lives. To prevent the Germans exploiting their superiority in artillery and aircraft, Chuikov had his men "hug" the enemy, the two sides sometimes fighting inside the same building. Snipers racked up impressive scores. Even though German forces reached the River Volga in November they could not dislodge Red Army resistance.

The trap is sprung

Meanwhile, Soviet commander Georgi Zhukov had prepared a masterly counterstroke, Operation Uranus. On 19 November Soviet forces to the south and north of Stalingrad broke through a defensive perimeter weakly held by Romanians and other Axis allies. Within four days they had closed their pincers behind Paulus's army, leaving him encircled. Hitler ordered Paulus to stay put and fight on, supplied by air, but the Luftwaffe did not have sufficient transport aircraft. In December the Soviet forces around the city fought off a German attempt to break through and relieve the trapped army. The air link became more precarious as winter weather worsened. The German troops ran short of food, ammunition, and fuel, as Zhukov tightened the noose.

All hope gone

By the third week of January the German Sixth Army was doomed. Suffering from frostbite and malnutrition, the Germans could barely fight on. Paulus appealed to Hitler for permission to surrender but it was refused. Instead, Hitler promoted Paulus to field marshal, to instil resolve, but on 31 January Paulus surrendered. The last German resistance ceased on 2 February. Of the 110,000 German soldiers taken prisoner at Stalingrad, only 5,000 survived captivity.

LOCATION
Stalingrad (modern-day Volgograd, Russia)

DATE
September 1942–
2 February 1943

FORCES
Axis: 500,000 (290,000 inside Stalingrad);
Soviets: more than 1 million

CASUALTIES
Axis: 500,000;
Soviets: 750,000

KEY
German front line, 19 Nov 1942
Romanian front line, 19 Nov 1942
German front line, 2 Jan 1943
Soviet advance

1. 19 Nov 1942: Soviet offensive is launched from Serafimovich against Romanian 3rd Army

5. 10 Jan 1943: Soviet attack on German 6th Army at Stalingrad begins. 6th Army surrenders by the 31st

3. 23 Nov 1942: The two Soviet attacking forces meet up south of Kalach, trapping German 6th Army in Stalingrad

4. 12 Dec 1942: Start of Operation Winter Storm. German relief column advances to within 55km (35 miles) of Stalingrad by the 19th

2. 20 Nov 1942: Soviet offensive is launched south of Stalingrad, forcing part of 4th Panzer Army into city

VATUTIN
Serafimovich
ROKOSSOVSKI
DUMITRESCU
PAULUS CHUIKOV
Kalach Stalingrad
Morozovsk
River Donets
MANSTEIN
Kotelnikovski
River Don
River Volga

BEFORE

German U-boats had preyed effectively on Allied merchant ships in World War I, but the Nazi leadership was slow to funnel resources into submarine warfare.

HITLER'S KRIEGSMARINE
When Hitler began **rearming in the 1930s** **<< 288–89**, the Kriegsmarine was given low priority. Within the service, factions argued over whether to devote resources to **submarines or surface warships**. Admiral Karl Dönitz, head of the U-boat arm, wanted a force of 300 boats, but by September 1939 he had only 65. Admiral Erich Raeder, navy commander-in-chief until late 1942, instead backed **Plan Z** to build a fleet of battleships and aircraft carriers. However, Plan Z was barely under way when World War II began.

SONAR DETECTION
The Royal Navy believed that it had found the way to **overcome the U-boat threat**. By 1939 it had a sonar device known as ASDIC to track **submerged U-boats** and depth charges to sink them. However, the reliance on ASDIC ignored the fact that German U-boats spent as much as **90 per cent of their time on the surface** – and for surface detection, sonar was useless.

BRITISH NAVAL MINE WITH SINKER

The Battle of the Atlantic

As a country utterly dependent upon imported food and raw materials – including all of its oil – Britain was uniquely vulnerable to naval blockade. Had the Germans succeeded in closing the Atlantic trade routes, the British would have been defeated and the United States shut out of the war in Europe.

A t the outset of the war, Germany had the same disadvantages as in 1914–18: all its naval forces were hemmed in, needing to pass through the Channel or the North Sea to reach the open ocean. The German conquests of 1940 transformed this situation. Not only did they deprive the Royal Navy of French support, but they also gave Germany bases on the Atlantic coasts of Norway and France, from which the Germans could launch sorties into the Atlantic and, following the entry of the Soviet Union into the war, threaten convoys bound for Russia's Arctic ports. From June 1940 the Royal Navy also had to fight the Italian Navy in the Mediterranean.

The threat to Allied shipping
German surface warships suffered huge losses off Norway in spring 1940, but in the early war years they had given Britain some scares. The heavy cruisers known as "pocket battleships", *Admiral Graf Spee* and *Admiral Scheer*, were both deployed with some success raiding commerce ships. However, *Graf Spee* was put out of action following the battle of the River Plate in the South Atlantic in December 1939. The breakout of the powerful battleship *Bismarck* into the North Atlantic in May 1941 threatened Allied shipping, but after sinking the battle cruiser HMS *Hood*, the *Bismarck* was tracked and sunk by a group of Allied battleships, aircraft carriers, and cruisers. The battleships *Scharnhorst* and *Gneisenau* were both out of action by the end of 1943.

However, Dönitz's U-boat fleet came close to victory in the battle of the Atlantic. Several major British vessels were sunk in 1939, but it was only after the U-boat bases moved to Brittany from June 1940 that the Germans mounted a full-scale campaign against Allied shipping. The British adopted a convoy system for merchant ships in 1939, yet did not have enough escort ships to protect them properly. Dönitz deployed his U-boats in groups known

> **15 MILLION** The total tonnage of Allied shipping sunk in the course of the battle of the Atlantic.

NORTH ATLANTIC

1 U-boat campaign	**3** Attacks on Arctic convoys
Dates 1940–41	Dates 1942–43
Location Western approaches to Britain	Location Arctic Ocean

2 U-boat campaign	**4** Wolf pack attacks on convoys
Date 1942	Dates 1942–43
Location Eastern seaboard of US	Location Mid-Atlantic

The sinking of the *Graf Spee*
The German surface raider *Graf Spee* on fire. The pocket battleship was scuttled outside Montevideo harbour, Uruguay, on 17 December 1939, after sustaining damage in the battle of the River Plate.

as "wolf packs", coordinated by radio. In one five-day period in October 1940, a wolf pack sank 32 ships in two convoys. The Royal Navy responded by increasing the number of escorts and improving the training of its men and equipment. By March 1941 these incremental changes reached the point where they tipped the balance. U-boat losses rose sharply. This set the pattern for the U-boat war: one side or the other would gain the upper hand, sometimes quite suddenly, through shifts in relative numbers, tactics, or technology.

Defending the convoys
A Royal Navy destroyer on convoy escort duty attacks a submerged German U-boat with a depth charge during the battle of the Atlantic.

The Allied situation improved through 1941. The Canadian Navy expanded and the United States, officially neutral, helped to protect the convoys in the western Atlantic. Unexpectedly, the US entry into the war in late 1941 gave the German U-boats a new opening. In the first half of 1942, the U-boats operated off the US east coast, where there was no convoy system. Some 600 merchant vessels were sunk before the Americans adopted effective defence measures.

From summer 1942 German U-boats again concentrated in the mid-Atlantic, exploiting the "air gap" beyond the range of Allied shore-based patrol aircraft. The climax came in March 1943, when

In World War II all forces had to encipher radio messages, since these were easily intercepted by the enemy. The Enigma machine was used by German forces as an encryption device; every U-boat, for example, had its own machine on board. The machine automatically encrypted a message typed on the keyboard and its settings were changed daily. An operator could also use his own Enigma machine and the daily settings to decode messages that had been received. During the war cryptologists at Bletchley Park in eastern England often succeeded in decrypting Enigma messages, generating a flow of intelligence known as "Ultra". The reading of German naval messages is credited as a major contribution to the defeat of the U-boats, although Germany's intelligence was at times equally successful at cracking British naval ciphers.

> "The only thing that … frightened me was the **U-boat peril**."
>
> WINSTON CHURCHILL, IN HIS MEMOIR, "THE SECOND WORLD WAR"

U-boats sank 480,000 tons of Allied ships in the Atlantic, raising real fears that Britain's lifeline would be severed. Yet in the next two months, 49 U-boats were sunk. There was no one reason for this dramatic turnabout. The Allies had steadily improved their equipment for the detection of U-boats, and their codebreakers intermittently succeeded in reading the transmissions of German navy Enigma machines. The Americans produced more escort vessels, while escort aircraft carriers and long-range shore-based aircraft closed the "air gap". These developments were enough to win the battle. Dönitz briefly withdrew his U-boats from the Atlantic; when their operations resumed later in the year, the U-boats were no longer a threat to the Allied war effort.

AFTER

The outcome of the battle of the Atlantic appeared to show the failure of the U-boat, but by the war's end the submarine was evolving into a far more effective weapon.

U-BOAT FAILURE
The degree of Allied triumph over the U-boats was amply demonstrated during **the Normandy landings 298–99 »** in June 1944. All German submarines were ordered into the Channel to combat the invasion fleet, yet their impact was negligible. In return for the sinking of a handful of Allied vessels, **26 U-boats** were lost.

28 THOUSAND U-boat crew members were killed in the war.

32 THOUSAND British merchant seamen were killed in the war.

NEW, IMPROVED VESSELS
The types of U-boat employed in the battle of the Atlantic were **"submersibles"**, rather than true submarines, and could not operate for long periods under the sea. In 1943 Germany developed the **Type XXI submarine**, which was capable of operating submerged for days. It had a better top speed undersea than most surface warships. Owing to production problems, however, only two Type XXIs saw active service, but the design was the precursor of modern submarines.

Ruins of Cologne
Cologne was devastated by Allied bombing, as were most other German cities. It was the target of the RAF's first thousand-bomber raid in May 1942.

‹‹ BEFORE

Of the many possible uses of air power, the bombing of cities was the focus of most attention in the run-up to World War II – both as strategy and moral conundrum.

FEARS OF AERIAL ATTACK
During the **Spanish Civil War ‹‹ 284–85** the **bombing of Guernica** on 26 April 1937 had a great impact on international opinion. Heavy **Japanese bombing of Chinese cities ‹‹ 282–83** was also widely condemned. In both cases, air raids conducted against defenceless targets led to exaggerated expectations of destruction in a war between major powers.

THE ALLIES PREPARE DEFENCES
Fear of German air power led Britain in particular to concentrate **planning and resources** on air defence. Britain's Royal Air Force developed a radar **early warning system** and produced new high-performance fighters. Despite the denunciation of the bombing of cities and their **civilian populations** by political leaders in Britain and the United States, both countries were keen to develop **strategic bombing forces**.

The **War** in the **Air**

Throughout World War II aircraft played a vital role in the land and sea war, but they also fought autonomous air campaigns, carrying out strategic bombing and contesting air superiority. Germany, Britain, and the United States all sought decisive advantage through air power alone.

Contrary to most expectations, the German and Allied air forces did not attempt to bomb each other's cities at the outset of World War II. To help the German Army's *Blitzkrieg* ground offensives of 1939 and 1940, the Luftwaffe bombed Warsaw and Rotterdam, but an exclusively aerial campaign only began with the Battle of Britain in the summer of 1940.

Battle of Britain
Hermann Göring, commander-in-chief of the Luftwaffe, was ordered by Hitler to drive the RAF from the skies "in the shortest possible time" as a prelude to an invasion of Britain. Fleets of German bombers with Messerschmitt fighter escorts, flying in daylight from bases in northern France, attacked a range of targets, including airfields and factories.

Alerted by radar, ground controllers scrambled RAF fighters to meet the intruders. The head of RAF Fighter Command, Hugh Dowding, had a clear concept of the battle as an attritional struggle, in which the goal was to keep his aircraft and pilots in being as an effective fighting force. The Luftwaffe had more experienced air crews and numerical superiority, but even the largest raids – almost 500 aircraft on 15 September – failed to overwhelm Britain's air defences. Their objective was to crush the RAF and degrade Britain's military and economic capacity to make war; only later did Hitler hope that attacks on cities would also produce demoralization among the population.

The first German daylight bombing raids on the city of London were made on 7 September 1940, and in later raids

Bomb disposal
In the aftermath of a German air raid on London during the Blitz in 1940, a bomb disposal squad gingerly prise an unexploded device from its crater.

Mustang fighter
Later versions of the North American P-51 Mustang had the range to escort Allied bombers to Germany and back.

yet seen. For its part, the RAF initially had few resources to combat night bombing but soon began putting radar-equipped night fighters into service. The RAF also began night bombing raids on Germany in 1940, but at first ineffectually. British RAF commanders were keen advocates of strategic bombing, but were singularly ill-prepared for it. Early raids showed that daylight attacks were suicidal, yet Bomber Command was not equipped for night fighting. At first its bombers could not even locate cities in the dark, let alone the specific factories or railway yards that were their targets.

Changing tactics

From February 1942 Bomber Command generally gave up its attempts at precision attacks and adopted an "area bombing" strategy that aimed to lay waste whole cities and kill or demoralize their civilian inhabitants. The policy was implemented under the leadership of Air Chief Marshal Sir Arthur Harris. Four-engine Lancaster and Halifax bombers entered service, carrying heavier bomb loads, and various navigational devices that allowed bombs to be dropped with some accuracy.

The Germans responded by developing effective night defences, their anti-aircraft guns and night fighters taking a heavy toll of British bomber crews. But with hundreds of RAF bombers taking part in a single raid, German cities suffered grievously. Raids on Hamburg in July 1943, for example, started a firestorm that killed 40,000 people.

Bomber poster
A British poster encourages citizens to save their money in government bonds to fund the building of bombers.

During 1942 the US Army Air Force started its own bombing campaign, first from bases in eastern England and later also from North Africa and Italy. The Americans believed that their B-17 and B-24 bombers were fast enough and had enough defensive firepower to carry out mass daylight raids without prohibitive losses. They also had the Norden bombsight, a proto-computer that was meant to allow them to hit specific industrial targets – although accuracy proved hard to achieve under combat conditions. German fighters and AA guns savaged the massed bomber formations; the US lost 60 bombers on a single day in August 1943. What was needed was a fighter aircraft with sufficient range to escort the bombers deep into Germany. Once long-range variants of the P-51 Mustang arrived in late 1943, the balance of the air war over Germany was transformed.

Air victory

In mid-1944 the Allies established almost total air superiority over the Germans. Factories were flattened and transport systems wrecked. Although Hitler's war production minister, Albert Speer, achieved little less than miracles, relocating industrial plant underground and cruelly coercing maximum productivity from forced labour, the

the German bomber force took heavy casualties. By October the Luftwaffe had abandoned their attempts to win daylight command of the air in favour of the night bombing of cities. Known as the Blitz, this campaign continued throughout the winter, until intensive bombing ended in May 1941 when the majority of German aircraft were shifted to support the invasion of the Soviet Union in Operation Barbarossa.

The Luftwaffe had not been as well prepared for strategic bombing as for tactical air strikes in support of an army

> **66,000** The number of bomber crew from US 8th Air Force based in England killed, wounded, or captured in 1942–45 – one in three of all the aircrew of the "Mighty Eighth".

campaign, and did not possess a four-engine heavy bomber. But the Germans had developed effective techniques for night navigation, using radio signals to guide bombers to their targets. A single raid on Coventry in November 1940 destroyed a third of the city's housing.

Some 43,000 civilians were killed during the Blitz, by far the heaviest losses to air attack that the world had

Technological developments late in World War II – such as jet aircraft and the atom bomb – ensured no air war of quite the same kind would ever be fought again.

NEW TECHNOLOGIES

The **first atom bomb**, developed in the United States in the Manhattan Project, was dropped on **Hiroshima** on 6 August 1945. Nuclear bombs and warheads gave an apocalyptic destructive power to bomber aircraft and missiles.

The first jet aircraft went into combat towards the end of World War II. The most successful was the **Messerschmitt Me 262**, used to intercept bombers attacking Germany from July 1944. The

> **12,500** The explosive power, in tons of TNT, of the atomic bomb dropped on Hiroshima on 6 August 1945.

first operational Allied jet, the **British Gloster Meteor**, was used chiefly to intercept V1 flying bombs over southern England. The **first air combat between jet fighters** did not occur until the **Korean War 316–17 »**.

THE COST OF STRATEGIC BOMBING

Disputes about the **morality and effectiveness** of strategic bombing have continued ever since the war. Current estimates calculate that 420,000 German civilians and 70,000 non-Germans (such as forced workers and POWs) were killed. British and US bomber crews suffered among the **highest percentage casualties** of any Allied armed forces in the war.

German war effort suffered. Aircraft and artillery desperately needed at the fronts were diverted to air defence. Supplies of fuel, successfully targeted by the Allied air campaign, were also much reduced.

The devastation of German cities in the final months of the war – including the horrific destruction of Dresden in February 1945 – reached a point where no further obvious strategic purpose was being served. The morality of such attacks has increasingly been questioned in the years since the end of the war.

TECHNOLOGY

GERMANY'S "VENGEANCE WEAPONS"

Germany responded to the devastation of its cities with the "vengeance weapons" – the V1 flying bomb and the V2 rocket. The V1s were unpiloted jet aircraft, packed with explosives and controlled by a primitive guidance system. Beginning in June 1944, thousands of these simple but effective devices were fired at London and later also at Antwerp. Arriving by day and night in all weathers, they caused substantial damage and casualties, although anti-aircraft guns

and fighter aircraft soon became skilled in shooting them down. However, there was no defence against the V2 ballistic missiles, first used in September 1944, again primarily against London and Antwerp. Striking without warning, the V2 was potentially terrifying – a single hit on a cinema in Antwerp caused 567 deaths. Fortunately for the Allies, large numbers of these missiles went astray, missing urban areas altogether; their launch sites were also priority targets for Allied air attacks.

BEFORE «

While Soviet forces pressed west towards Germany, the Allies were planning a second front. Operation Overlord was to be a seaborne invasion of Normandy.

THE TEHRAN CONFERENCE
The "Big Three" Allied leaders – Roosevelt, Stalin, and Churchill – met for a conference at Tehran in November–December 1943. Here, Churchill and Roosevelt agreed to mount an invasion of France in spring 1944, satisfying the Soviet demand for

3 MILLION
The number of military personnel assembled in the UK under Eisenhower's command for the invasion of Europe.

a "second front" in Western Europe. British leaders were worried about possible heavy losses but the Allies had experience in amphibious operations, through landings in **Sicily and Italy** «**290–91** in 1943, and in assaults on Japanese-held islands **in the Pacific 302–03** ».

PLANS FOR DECEPTION
The Germans prepared for a **seaborne invasion**, strengthening their coastal fortifications in 1944. However, a successful Allied deception plan led the Germans to believe that **Calais** was more likely to be the invasion point than **Normandy**.

Victory celebrations
Soviet and American troops meet at Torgau on the river Elbe in central Germany on 25 April 1945 to celebrate their victory over the Nazis.

The Fall of Hitler

By summer 1944 Germany was battling against overwhelming odds, but the Nazi regime did not collapse and the German armies kept on fighting. The war in Europe only ended when Soviet soldiers raised their flag in the heart of Berlin, where Adolf Hitler had killed himself a few days before.

American, British, and Canadian forces under General Dwight D. Eisenhower landed on beaches in Normandy, northern France, on 6 June 1944. Operation Overlord was the largest seaborne invasion ever carried out: more than 150,000 soldiers were supported by more than 1,000 warships and some 13,000 aircraft. The D-Day landings clearly showed the material superiority of the Allies – in industrial output, manpower, and organizational ability. Yet the operation was far from being a foregone conclusion. American forces suffered heavy losses on one of the five landing beaches, codenamed Omaha. Having established beachheads, the troops made slow progress inland. The breakout from Normandy was not achieved until the end of July.

The failure of an attempt by German officers and bureaucrats to assassinate Hitler in July ensured the survival of Nazi rule and a fight to the death. But in August 1944 hopes were still high for a quick Allied victory. The first Normandy breakout was to be followed by swift advances. Paris was freed on 25 August, by which time the Allies had landed in southern France, thus opening up a new front. By mid-September Allied troops were nearing the German border.

The Germans still had to keep the largest part of their forces on the Eastern Front to face the Soviet's huge army. From late June into August, the Soviets won a crushing series of victories in Belarus and the Ukraine. With these and the concurrent defeats in France, Germany appeared to be on the verge of collapse. But at this critical point the Allied advances stalled. Their forces were outrunning their supply lines and had to slow down.

Liberating Europe
As the end of the war approached and occupied countries were liberated, a number of political disputes surfaced.

Most countries had governments-in-exile but not all of them commanded popular support. General de Gaulle's London-based Free French forces succeeded in establishing control of France at the liberation, despite the substantial Communist element in the internal French resistance movement. In Yugoslavia various monarchist and communist resistance groups vied for Allied support, the Communist Josip Broz Tito winning out. In Greece a monarchist government-in-exile was only able to regain control with the support of the British Army. Italians were split three ways, some fighting with the Allies on behalf of the Italian government, others joining Mussolini as support to the German forces, and partisans fighting

Allied advances into Germany in 1945
German forces were overwhelmed by a simultaneous onslaught from east and west. The Soviets and the Western Allies did not race one another to occupy territory but followed an agreed strategy.

Key
- Territory held by Germany Dec 1944
- Territory held by Allies Dec 1944
- Neutral states
- — Frontiers 1939
- — German front line Dec 1944
- ⇒ Western Allied advance
- ⇒ Soviet advance
- 9 May Date taken by Allies

[Map of Europe showing Allied advances into Germany in 1945, with labels including SWEDEN, DENMARK, Copenhagen, Flensburg, Hamburg, Bremen, NETHERLANDS, Rotterdam, Arnhem, Brussels, BELGIUM, Aachen, Cologne, Düsseldorf, Frankfurt, Mannheim, LUX., Metz, Stuttgart, FRANCE, SWITZERLAND, Milan, Genoa, ITALY, Bologna, Lübeck, Stettin, Hanover, Berlin, Torgau, Dresden, Prague, Linz, Munich, Vienna, GERMANY, AUSTRIA, Riga, LATVIA, Memel, LITHUANIA, Kaunas, Königsberg, EAST PRUSSIA, Bialystok, Warsaw, POLAND, USSR, Lemberg (Lvov), SLOVAKIA, HUNGARY, Budapest, Trieste, Zagreb, Belgrade, YUGOSLAVIA, and various army fronts. Scale 300km / 300 miles]

Sten gun and Tokarev pistol
The Sten gun was a cheap, but effective, British 9mm submachine gun, much used by resistance fighters in Europe. The 7.62mm Tokarev TT-33 was the standard Soviet army semi-automatic pistol used in World War II.

Wooden stock; most had a simpler metal type

Trigger housing; most Sten components were easily manufactured

Butt holds 8-round magazine

under Communist leadership for the liberation of northern Italy. Poland had two governments-in-exile – in London and Moscow. In August 1944 the Polish Home Army, loyal to the London-based government, staged an uprising in Warsaw. Soviet forces, within sight of the city, dropped supplies and allowed a Polish division to fight its way in. Despite their best efforts, the uprising was soon crushed by German troops.

Last great battles

In December 1944 Hitler gambled on a last attack. Attempting to repeat the success of May 1940, he launched an offensive through the Ardennes region of Belgium. The Allies were caught off-guard and desperate winter fighting ensued. But by February 1945 this so-called Battle of the Bulge was over and the scene was set for the final act. Soviet forces entered Germany from the east, closing in on Berlin, and in March the Western Allies crossed the Rhine. Hitler threw all available men into a desperate last defence. The German

Fallen eagle

Russian soldiers observe a fallen Nazi symbol in the ruins of Berlin after the fall of the city to the Soviet army in May 1945. The Soviet flag would soon be displayed from the Reichstag.

people suffered desperately, especially at the hands of Russian soldiers, but sympathy was in short supply as the overrunning of camps such as Auschwitz revealed the mass murder practised by the Nazi regime under the cloak of war.

Advancing American and Soviet troops met amicably on the River Elbe on 25 April. By agreement between the Allies, the costly honour of taking Berlin fell to the Soviets. On 30 April, as Soviet forces fought their way into the German capital, Hitler committed suicide in his bunker in the city centre. Mussolini was shot by Italian partisans. On 2 May German commanders surrendered in Italy, and in Germany on 4 May. A final surrender took place on 7 May.

AFTER

The Allied victory in Europe resulted in the division of Europe – and of Germany – by the "Iron Curtain" between Communist and non-Communist states.

THE AFTERMATH

Some of the most prominent Nazi leaders were tried for war crimes at the Nuremberg trials from 1945–46 by the International Military Tribunal.
Changes to European borders were far slighter than after World War I. The Soviet Union kept the Baltic states and eastern Poland, while Poland took over a vast area of pre-war Germany.

THE COLD WAR

During 1945–48 Communist-led governments ruled all **Soviet-occupied areas** in Eastern Europe, while democratic governments **aligned with the US** returned in Western Europe. This became known as the **Cold War 312–13 ≫**.

12 NAZI LEADERS AWAITING TRIAL IN NUREMBERG, 1946.

Wartime Odyssey

As well as Red Cross food parcels, British POWs in Germany received personal parcels from relatives and friends. It was in one of these that Lance-Corporal Les Kerswill was sent a pair of well-made boots by his mother. When he escaped in 1944, they carried him on an extraordinary journey of an estimated 2,000km (1,300 miles).

Les in his uniform before the war
Many of Les Kerswill's memories of his wartime escape are still astonishingly vivid, although he is sometimes uncertain about the exact order in which the events happened.

Twenty-year-old Les was one of the tens of thousands of young men sent to France in late 1939 to join the British Expeditionary Force. Early one morning, just after Christmas, the men of his battalion – 4th Battalion the Royal Berkshire Regiment, stationed in Reading – were woken up and given orders to prepare to leave immediately. From Reading they travelled by train to Southampton, where they embarked on a crowded troopship to Cherbourg. Les would not return to England until the very last day of the war in Europe, in May 1945.

In northeastern France, the Berkshires lived under canvas, in farm buildings, and even in an empty chateau as they prepared to counter the threat of German invasion. On 10 May 1940, they were ordered forward in the attempt to stop the German advance through Belgium. Constantly on the move, plugging gaps in the line, they were bombed and strafed by Stukas and fought a number of short, bloody actions with the enemy.

Captured

Outmanoeuvred and outgunned, the British retreated to the beaches of Dunkirk. Les was among those detailed to make a last-ditch stand against the Germans to give the rest of the British forces time to make their escape. In this he and other men like him succeeded. Some 340,000 troops – British and French – were shipped back to safety in England. As the German bombing intensified, Les, who had been wounded by a piece of spent shrapnel, could see Dunkirk burning behind him. He and his few remaining comrades had been in action now for three weeks and, exhausted by their efforts, fell asleep in a ditch. The following morning, they were rounded up and taken prisoner.

Les was imprisoned in a series of camps in Germany, where he worked in a variety of jobs, ranging from digging ditches to working in a schnapps distillery. He ended up in a coalmine at Bytom on the River Oder (now in Poland). It was there that he received the Red Cross parcel with new boots from his mother. His own army boots had long since fallen to pieces and he was making do with wooden clogs. As the Soviets advanced westwards into Poland, the opportunity arose to put the boots to good use. The Germans often had to transfer prisoners away from battle zones and on one such occasion Les and a friend managed to escape.

Royal Berkshires cap badge
The Chinese dragon commemorates the exploits of the regiment in the First Opium War of 1839–42.

March to freedom

In the winter of 1944–45, Poland's roads were filled with all kinds of people on the move. Keeping out of the way of the retreating Germans were refugees, deserters, and escaped prisoners of war. Almost all were moving west or south ahead of the advancing Soviet armies. Germans detailed to escort prisoners were more concerned with saving their own skins. Even so, Les was recaptured twice, but each time escaped again. Scrounging food from farmers and sleeping in barns and cowsheds, he and his companion, "Lofty" Harris, had to rely on their wits and the kindness of local people. Les remembers that boiled potatoes with sour milk was a luxury.

From Poland they eventually found their way into Bohemia – the part of Czechoslovakia annexed by Hitler in 1939. By the time they reached Bavaria in southern Germany, the Russians were close behind, while the Americans were advancing rapidly from the west. At Regensburg the two men were taken in by the US 3rd Army and treated to huge meals of frankfurters and beans. After helping the Americans to interrogate German prisoners, Les was flown to Reims in France, then back to England – just in time for VE Day, 8 May 1945.

A mark on the leather upper is a souvenir of a night spent on a Czech farm. When Les tried to put his boots on again in the morning, they were frozen solid. The leather was burned when the farmer's wife put them on her stove to thaw.

Original eyelets, all still in place

The original hobnails on the soles of the boots survived the journey more or less intact. Les's mother had chosen well when she bought these military-style boots to send to her son.

> "We **never had any socks**, so we did what the Germans did and used **Fusslappen**, **squares of cloth** that you **wrapped round your feet**."
>
> LES KERSWILL, DESCRIBING HOW HE SURVIVED ON HIS WALK FROM POLAND

British prisoners after Dunkirk
German soldiers march their captives off to camps in Germany. Some 34,000 British troops were captured in France in 1940. Of Les's battalion only 47 men got off the beaches. The rest were all killed or taken prisoner.

Well-travelled boots
Les Kerswill has kept the boots in which he made his long, circuitous journey through occupied territory after escaping from the Germans in 1944. They show obvious signs of wear and tear, but are remarkably well preserved.

The heels of the boots wore out and needed a few repairs on Les's long journey across Europe. He used odd scraps of leather and, failing that, wood, to rebuild them.

The War with Japan

Japan attacked the United States and its allies in December 1941. Initial lightning victories failed to give the Japanese the impregnable strategic situation they sought, and a vigorous American reaction gradually turned the war around, until Japan was fighting a desperate defence against mounting odds.

Japan's war plan was to capture the British and Dutch Southeast Asian colonies – Malaya, Singapore, and the Dutch East Indies (Indonesia) – and the American-controlled Philippines. These were to be seized in a series of seaborne invasions. At the outset the main threat to Japan's plans, the US Pacific Fleet, would be crippled by a huge surprise attack on the naval base at Pearl Harbor in Hawaii, buying the Japanese time to establish a far-flung defensive perimeter in the Pacific. The Japanese leaders hoped that the US – which they saw as a nation lacking in martial spirit – would be daunted by Japan's strong position and, instead of marshalling their superior resources, make peace on terms favouring Japan.

Pearl Harbor

Although the Americans knew that war with Japan was imminent, they were utterly unprepared when the Japanese aircraft carriers struck the naval base early on 7 December 1941. Eight US battleships were sunk or disabled and

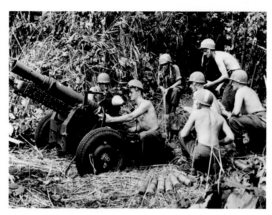

Jungle war in New Guinea
Allied troops in New Guinea had to fight in intolerable conditions, although survival was often even harder for their poorly supplied Japanese enemies.

2,400 Americans were killed. Such an attack, delivered before a declaration of war, was a blow the Americans would never forget or forgive.

Japan's attacks in Southeast Asia were synchronized with the Pearl Harbor raid, with troop landings in

Malaya and air strikes on US bases in the Philippines. Japan's troops were well trained and equipped for fighting in jungle terrain, and were ably supported by aircraft. They advanced rapidly through Malaya and in mid-February 1942 forced the surrender of the British base at Singapore – a mortal blow to British prestige in Asia. Japanese landings in the Philippines were equally successful, trapping American and Filipino troops in the Bataan peninsula. The American commander, General MacArthur, was ordered to leave before the majority of the soldiers surrendered in April.

The Japanese Navy brushed aside Allied warships attempting to defend the Dutch East Indies, which were then

90 per cent of the torpedoes launched by Japanese aircraft in the attack on Pearl Harbor in Hawaii struck an American ship.

easily occupied. By the end of May 1942 the Japanese had also taken most of Burma from the British.

These successes were exhilarating for the Japanese, but there were soon signs that their strategy was failing. The raid on Pearl Harbor had not destroyed the US Navy's aircraft carriers, which were fortuitously at sea at the time. American cryptographers had also managed to break Japanese naval codes, giving the US command an inestimable advantage.

Japan's first defeats

As the Japanese moved to extend their defensive perimeter to include the Solomon Islands and New Guinea in May 1942, they were met by the US carriers in the Coral Sea. This battle ended in a draw but was followed by a more decisive encounter at Midway in June. Four Japanese carriers were sunk, a defeat from which Japan's naval aviation never recovered. From August 1942 Japanese and American forces fought a ferocious series of battles for control of Guadalcanal in the Solomons.

Samurai poster

A samurai scatters the Allied fleet, the flags of Japan's Axis allies behind him. Despite their alliance, the Japanese and Germans made no real effort to coordinate their strategy.

◀◀ BEFORE

Japan's military-dominated government was convinced that only the creation of an empire in Asia would give it the resources to be one of the world's major powers.

INVASION OF MANCHURIA

Japan's encroachments upon China, from the occupation of Manchuria in 1931 to **full-scale invasion in 1937 ◀◀ 282–83**, showed their imperial ambitions in Asia. The Japanese Army leadership favoured further expansion from Manchuria into **Mongolia and Siberia**, but a short border war with the Soviet Union in 1938–39 ended in defeat at the Battle of Khalkin Gol. Japan signed a non-aggression pact with the Soviet Union in April 1941. Stalin, facing a potential German attack, needed security in the East, while Japan redirected its attention towards Southeast Asia.

JAPAN JOINS THE AXIS

Germany's victories in Europe in April to June 1940 had a profound impact on Japanese

policy. With France and the Netherlands defeated and Britain under siege, Japan saw an opportunity to take over European colonies in Southeast Asia, **rich in oil, rubber, and other strategic materials**. Japan signed the Tripartite Pact with Germany and Italy in September 1940.

PREPARATIONS FOR WAR

The United States stood as a **major obstacle** to Japanese expansionism, backing China against Japan and protesting vehemently in August 1940 when **Vichy France** allowed Japanese troops to establish bases in northern French Indochina. Japanese troops moved into the rest of Indochina in July 1941. The United States responded by **imposing an oil blockade** on Japan and demanding Japan's withdrawal from Indochina and China. In October 1941 General Tojo Hideki became prime minister of Japan and began to **prepare for a war** in Southeast Asia and the Pacific.

GENERAL TOJO HIDEKI

At the same time, Australian and American troops were successful in countering Japanese landings in the hostile jungle terrain of Papua.

By 1943 the United States had taken the initiative. General MacArthur led an Australian and American thrust through New Guinea and the Solomon Islands, aiming eventually to return to the Philippines. Admiral Chester Nimitz began an "island-hopping" campaign by the US Navy and Marines across the Central Pacific. This offensive relied on the largest shipbuilding programme in history, providing the United States with

130,000
The number of US, Dutch, and British Empire prisoners of war taken by the Japanese from 1941–42. About one-third of them died in captivity.

an overwhelming superiority in aircraft carriers and a vast fleet of landing craft for amphibious operations.

The Japanese knew that they lacked the industrial and manpower resources to match the United States. Instead, they fell back upon a belief in the warrior spirit. The readiness of Japanese troops to fight to the death ensured that the war would be fought at mounting cost. At Tarawa in the Gilbert Islands, in November 1943, US Marines had more than 1,000 men killed taking a small coral atoll defended by some 3,000 Japanese, only 17 of whom survived to be taken prisoner.

AFTER

The Japanese never had time to consolidate their rapidly won Southeast Asian empire, although they managed to hold onto most of it until the end of the war.

SUPPORT FOR JAPAN
The Japanese referred to their conquests in Asia as a **"Co-Prosperity Sphere"**, styling themselves as leaders of an Asian liberation from European colonial rule. This idea won some followers – the Indian National Army and Burmese nationalists fought on Japan's side – but mostly Asians suffered **brutal oppression and exploitation**.

LOSS OF MERCHANT SHIPPING
From 1943 Allied submarines began to take a heavy toll of Japanese merchant shipping, making it impossible to transport essential materials to Japan. **Eighty per cent** of Japanese merchant shipping was sunk by the war's end.

THE WAR CONTINUES
Allied forces fought in New Guinea and the Solomons into 1945, and invaded the Philippines from 1944. The Allies also made landings on the **Marshall and Mariana Islands 304–05 ❯❯** in 1944.

JAPANESE AIRMAN DOLL

Key
- ■ Japanese Empire 1937
- ■ Allies in war against Japan 1941
- — Frontiers 1937
- ➡ Japanese offensives 1941–42
- ▥ Japanese perimeter Jun 1942
- ⦿ Japanese base 1942
- ⦿ Allied base 1942
- ✹ Japanese victory
- ✹ Japanese defeat
- ✹ Inconclusive battle

Expansion of the Japanese Empire
Initial victories gave Japan control of Southeast Asia and the western Pacific. The Allies bypassed these gains, heading directly for Japan in 1944–45.

The Defeat of Japan

The absolute dedication of the United States to the defeat of Japan and the determination of the Japanese to defend their homeland at any cost gave the final battles of the Pacific war an awesome intensity. The war ended with the apocalyptic destruction of Japanese cities from the air.

In spring 1944, the Japanese Army was still able to mount offensives in Asia. Lasting from April through to December, Operation Ichi-Go was the largest-scale Japanese campaign against China's National Revolutionary Army since 1938. Japanese forces also invaded British India from Burma. In China the Japanese troops carried all before them; in Burma their soldiers were defeated and driven back southward. But neither outcome was strategically significant, for growing naval and aerial superiority in the Pacific allowed the Americans to thrust directly towards Japan.

America's Pacific advance

In June 1944 the US Navy and Marines opened a campaign to seize the Mariana Islands with landings on Saipan. The Japanese Navy attacked the supporting US fleet with hundreds of carrier-based and land-based aircraft, but their pilots and machines were no longer a match for the Americans; they lost over 300 aircraft in the "Marianas Turkey Shoot". Japan's carrier fleet was finished as an effective fighting force. In desperation, Japanese admirals sought to bring their still powerful battleships and cruisers into play for a final epic showdown. In October, when US naval forces massed to support landings in the Philippines at Leyte Gulf, every available Japanese warship was sent to attack them. The result was the largest naval battle ever. There was some desperate fighting, but the Japanese gamble failed. The United States sank 25 warships and won total control of the sea.

After the defeat at Leyte Gulf, Japan's position was objectively hopeless, but the determination of its soldiers never wavered as the US pressed island by

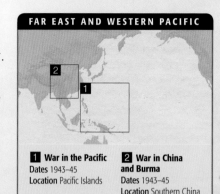

FAR EAST AND WESTERN PACIFIC

1 War in the Pacific
Dates 1943–45
Location Pacific Islands

2 War in China and Burma
Dates 1943–45
Location Southern China and Burma

« **BEFORE**

At the start of 1944 Japan still held large areas of Asia, but its position in the Pacific was desperate and a powerful American secret weapon was nearing completion.

ALLIED SUPERIORITY
The balance of naval forces in the Pacific was turning against Japan by 1944 – **the US launched 90 aircraft carriers** in 1943–44, while Japan launched seven. The new **American naval aircraft were superior** to their Japanese counterparts and their pilots were better trained.

Early on in the war the Japanese mainland was protected from Allied air attack by sheer distance. United States bomber aircraft launched from carriers attacked the capital, Tokyo, in April 1942 (**the Doolittle Raid**), but this was a one-off. A sustained bombing campaign had to wait for the introduction of the very long-range **B-29 Superfortress** in the summer of 1944.

ATOMIC WARFARE
In the early war years Britain, Germany, Japan, and the US were all aware of the possibility of creating an **atom bomb**. Only the US devoted the necessary resources to nuclear research and development in its **Manhattan Project**. The bomb was originally intended for use against Germany, but at a meeting between Roosevelt and Churchill in September 1944, it was agreed that if Germany had surrendered by the time the device was ready, it might be used against Japan.

Hiroshima destroyed
The atom bomb dropped on Hiroshima laid waste an area of more than 11 sq km (4 sq miles). Up to 90 per cent of the buildings in the city were destroyed or badly damaged.

island closer to mainland Japan. The US Marines became more experienced at carrying out opposed landings, utilizing a range of new amphibious vehicles and tactics, but even when backed up by naval and air bombardments, they found Japanese resistance harder and harder to overcome.

The taking of the islands
The US taking of Saipan saw some 13,000 casualties. Iwo Jima, an island of volcanic rock, was taken in February–March 1945 at a cost of 26,000 casualties. The next target was Okinawa, one of the Ryukyu Islands and officially part of Japan itself. The island's capture in April–June 1945 saw some 50,000 casualties. These intense battles, fought in confined spaces with no possible retreat, ended in the near annihilation of the Japanese defenders. On both Saipan and Iwo Jima more

21,700 The number of Japanese soldiers and sailors killed in the battle for Iwo Jima in February–March 1945.

than 95 per cent of enemy troops died. Japanese commanders adopted a policy of no surrender, instructing their troops to launch suicidal *banzai* charges; US soldiers were not able to take prisoners.

A massive Allied naval force was assembled to support the assault on Okinawa, with a significant Royal Navy contingent joining the US Fifth Fleet. Stationed within range of airbases on the Japanese mainland, the Allied warships were assaulted by aircraft – used by the Japanese to mount suicide attacks. Although these inflicted some losses, they failed to disrupt the plans.

One of the fundamental objectives of the Allied forces in the seizure of the islands was to bring Japan under aerial bombardment. In July 1944 American B-29 bombers began raiding Japan from Nationalist-controlled China, but the extreme range of Japan's mainland limited the B-29s'

effectiveness. It was not until October 1944 that a sustained campaign of bombing would become possible, when airbases were built on the Marianas. But the results were disappointing at first. Attacking by daylight at high altitude, the bombers had difficulty locating their targets. In March 1945, under General Curtis LeMay, the B-29s adopted new tactics, assaulting Japanese cities at low altitude by night and mostly dropping incendiary bombs. A raid on Tokyo on 9 March ignited a massive firestorm, killing up to 80,000 people. The defeat of Germany in May 1945 and the fall of Okinawa the following month left Japan facing certain defeat.

The high cost of peace
The B-29 bombers were devastating Japan's virtually defenceless cities while an Allied naval blockade threatened the Japanese people with starvation. The Japanese did not appear to be close to surrender, however. The US Army was preparing for an invasion of Japan, with landings on Kyushu planned for November. The Japanese government

100,000 The approximate number of Japanese soldiers killed in the battle for the island of Okinawa in April–June 1945.

was split, though. The "war party" believed a suicidal fight to the death would salvage Japan's spirit; the "peace party" wanted an armistice that would keep the enemy off Japanese soil – a deal the US would never have conceded.

At the Allied Potsdam Conference in July 1945, the Soviet Union agreed to join in the war against the Japanese. Meanwhile, atom bombs, tested in New Mexico on 16 July, were sent to the

Raising the flag on Iwo Jima
US Marines raise the Stars and Stripes on Mount Suribachi, Iwo Jima, 23 February 1945. Subduing Japanese resistance on the island took five weeks.

Marianas. The Potsdam Declaration was issued on the 26 July. It called on Japan to surrender absolutely; the Japanese government rejected it. On 6 August an atom bomb was dropped on Hiroshima. Three days later the city of Nagasaki was hit and Soviet forces invaded Manchuria. On 14 August Emperor Hirohito of Japan told his government that they must "bear the unbearable" and consent to Allied terms. The Japanese surrender was announced the following day.

The Japanese air forces started using suicide tactics to attack Allied warships in October 1944. Outnumbered and outclassed, the Japanese pilots were no longer able to cause significant damage with bombs and torpedoes. *Kamikaze* ("divine wind") units were an elite at first, but during the battle for Okinawa in 1945, suicide tactics became a cynical form of warfare. Hundreds of young, barely trained men were presented with headbands that depicted the rising sun before being flung into battle. Few would penetrate the US fleet defences and succeed in crashing their aircraft onto an enemy warship. The *kamikaze* sank some 50 Allied ships, but at the cost of around 4,000 pilots' lives.

> "The war situation has developed **not necessarily to Japan's advantage**."
> EMPEROR HIROHITO, SURRENDER BROADCAST, 15 AUGUST 1945

AFTER ≫

Japan formally surrendered on board USS *Missouri* in Tokyo Bay on 2 September 1945. The conquered country was then occupied by Allied troops.

and Nagasaki, either instantly or from the **short- or long-term effects of radiation**. Estimates vary widely from 80,000 to 140,000 for Hiroshima and 35,000 to 70,000 for Nagasaki.

THE AFTERMATH
After the war Japan was controlled by General Douglas MacArthur. Some Japanese leaders, including General Tojo Hideki, were tried as war criminals, but Emperor Hirohito was left on the throne. Japan became a liberal democracy with a constitutional monarch. By 1951, when a peace treaty was signed, **Japan had become an ally of the US in the Cold War 312–13** ≫.

It is impossible to establish how many people were killed by the atom bombs dropped on Hiroshima

WAR LOSSES
Total Japanese deaths are estimated at 2.7 million. This is dwarfed by more than 20 million dead in the Soviet Union, 15–20 million in China, 5.3 million in Germany, and 6 million in Poland. The **Nazis murdered millions of their own** and other countries' citizens. Both Italy and France lost around half a million. Roughly 292,000 American service personnel died in all theatres. The British death toll was around 350,000, including more than 60,000 civilians.

GENERAL DOUGLAS MACARTHUR

British Royal Marines of 45 Commando land from a
Chinook helicopter near Now Zad in Helmand province,
Afghanistan, in 2006. Their task was to reinforce other
British troops and the Afghan police in the ongoing
battle against Taliban forces active in the region.

7

CONFLICTS AFTER WORLD WAR II

1945 – PRESENT

The period was dominated by the Cold War
between the two superpowers, the US and the
USSR. This never came to nuclear conflict, but
conventional wars continue across the globe,
especially in Africa and the Middle East.

SPANISH CETME AMELI LIGHT MACHINE-GUN, 1982

CONFLICTS AFTER WORLD WAR II
1945 – PRESENT

After World War II, the US and the Soviet Union emerged as the world's two superpowers, and instead of disarming they embarked on a headlong arms race that saw the development of awesomely powerful nuclear arsenals. These arsenals and other high-tech equipment were developed for use in a third world war that never happened. The US intervened militarily on a large scale against communist movements in North Korea and later in Vietnam, but the practice of "limited war" prevented escalation to a superpower conflict. Although nuclear weapons remained unused, smaller wars proliferated across the world.

Guerrilla wars
Mao Zedong's victory over the Kuomintang in the Chinese Civil War, won largely by the use of guerrilla tactics, led to a popularization of guerrilla warfare. This mode of warfare, widely adopted by anti-colonial movements, used advanced infantry weapons such as the AK47 and the RPG7 rocket launcher. Against guerrillas the major powers' arsenals proved largely ineffectual, although the helicopter gave mobility and firepower to counter-insurgency forces. Decolonization left a range of festering regional disputes in its wake. In particular, the creation of the state of Israel gave rise to a series of Israeli-Arab wars that were testing-grounds for state-of-the-art conventional weaponry mostly supplied by the superpowers, who inevitably backed rival sides in any regional conflict.

By the 1980s cumulative changes in military technology had transformed the battlefield. Missiles were ubiquitous, computers and sensors made guidance systems ever more effective, and stealth technology (which renders aircraft, ships, and submarines invisible to radar, infrared, and sonar detection systems) made some attack forces all but invulnerable to less sophisticated defences. When the ending of the Cold War changed the rules of the strategic game, the US was able to demonstrate the superiority of its arsenal of cruise missiles and smart bombs in the demolition of the Iraqi army in 1991. The post-Cold-War world proved to be no more peaceful than the old one. Wars continued to proliferate, although they did not escalate into conflicts between the major powers. The collapse of the Soviet Union was followed by widespread nationalist conflicts, the Middle East remained chronically unstable and warfare in Africa was endemic.

The electronic battlefield
Interventions in Iraq and Afghanistan in the 21st century showed again that, once war descended to the guerrilla and terrorist level, major powers had little advantage on the ground over enemies equipped with up-to-date infantry weapons. In response to public dismay at even light casualties, the US sought to increase the distance between killer and killed by deploying unmanned drone aircraft to attack enemy targets, their operators sitting hundreds of miles away in perfect safety. Meanwhile, international terrorists, only too ready to die for their cause, used suicide tactics to target soldiers and civilians.

SAS desert combat vehicle
Named the Pinked Panther after its camouflage, this vehicle is used by the SAS in desert operations.

Mujahideen victory in Afghanistan
Ahmed Shah Massoud's *mujahideen* capture Bagram from the Taliban on 20 October 1996. The town is a key junction between the Panjshir Valley and Kabul, the capital of Afghanistan.

1945
World War II ends. US and Soviet troops occupy Europe and divide Korea. ▪ Vietnam and Indonesia declare independence. ▪ Chinese Civil War resumes. ▪ Founding of the United Nations. ▪ Start of the Nuremberg War Trials.

1957
USSR launches the first intercontinental ballistic missile and the first space satellite, Sputnik. ▪ Malaya gains independence from Britain. ▪ Ghana becomes the first black state to gain independence in Africa.

⌃ Soviet Mig fighter, used in Korean War

» Poster announcing the launch of Sputnik

1946
Churchill describes the division of Europe as an "Iron Curtain". ▪ The French Indochinese War begins in Vietnam. ▪ The Dutch fight Indonesian nationalists.

1948
Pro-Soviet governments are established in Eastern Europe. The Berlin airlift begins. ▪ The Communists take Manchuria in the Chinese Civil War. ▪ UN Declaration of Human Rights is agreed. ▪ Israel proclaims its independence, but is then invaded by armies from neighbouring Arab states.

1951
After fierce fighting the Korean War reaches stalemate as UN troops establish positions along the pre-war border.

1954
The French defeat at Dien Bien Phu ends the war in Indochina. Vietnam becomes an independent, but divided state. ▪ Start of revolt against French rule in Algeria. ▪ The CIA backs a coup against the elected government in Guatemala. ▪ In Kenya the Mau Mau revolt against the British is crushed.

1958
French army coup over Algerian policy causes the collapse of the French Fourth Republic. General de Gaulle takes power.

1960
Growing differences between China and the USSR over the direction Communism should take result in a Sino-Soviet split. ▪ The Belgian Congo receives its independence; the province of Katanga secedes.

1949
The Western Allies form NATO; the Eastern Bloc forms Comecon. ▪ The USSR tests its first atomic bomb. ▪ Mao Zedong's Communists take power in China. ▪ Indonesia gains independence from the Netherlands.

« Mao Zedong, leader of the People's Republic of China

⌃ Interned Mau Mau rebels

1961
The Berlin Wall is built to prevent East Germans fleeing to the West. ▪ US troops arrive in Vietnam. ▪ Bay of Pigs an unsuccessful, US-backed invasion of Cuba by anti-Castro Cuban exiles. ▪ Revolts in the Portuguese colonies begin. ▪ Indian army seizes Portugal's colonies in India.

1950
Korean War begins as Communist North Korea invades South Korea. Predominantly American UN forces drive the invaders back, but then China intervenes on the side of the North. ▪ China begins occupation of Tibet.

1952
The Mau Mau uprising against British colonial rule begins in Kenya. ▪ The US tests its first hydrogen bomb.

1955
Eastern Bloc forms the Warsaw Pact. ▪ Fearing the spread of Communism in Southeast Asia, the US sends military advisers to South Vietnam.

⌃ Viet Cong hand grenades

1947
US president Truman announces his anti-Communist Doctrine. ▪ The Marshall Plan provides money for rebuilding Europe. ▪ The AK47 Kalashnikov assault rifle is first used by the Red Army. ▪ The first Indo-Pakistani War is fought over Kashmir.

⌄ Soviet Kalashnikov assault rifle

1956
Uprising in Hungary against Communist rule. ▪ The Suez Crisis. British and French connive at Israeli invasion of Egypt. ▪ Castro starts a second uprising against Cuban government. ▪ Algerian nationalists battle the French in Algiers.

1962
Cuban missile crisis. Threat of war between the US and the USSR is averted when the Soviets withdraw their missiles from Cuba. ▪ Algeria gains independence. ▪ Brief war between China and India over disputed frontier regions.

1953
Stalin dies in the USSR. ▪ An armistice ends the Korean War. ▪ Fidel Castro fails in his first attempt to overthrow the Cuban government. ▪ USSR tests its first hydrogen bomb.

1959
War begins between Communist North Vietnam and South Vietnam. ▪ Castro takes power in Cuba. ▪ The Chinese crush a rebellion in Tibet. The Dalai Lama flees into exile in India.

» Fidel Castro, the leader of Communist Cuba from 1959

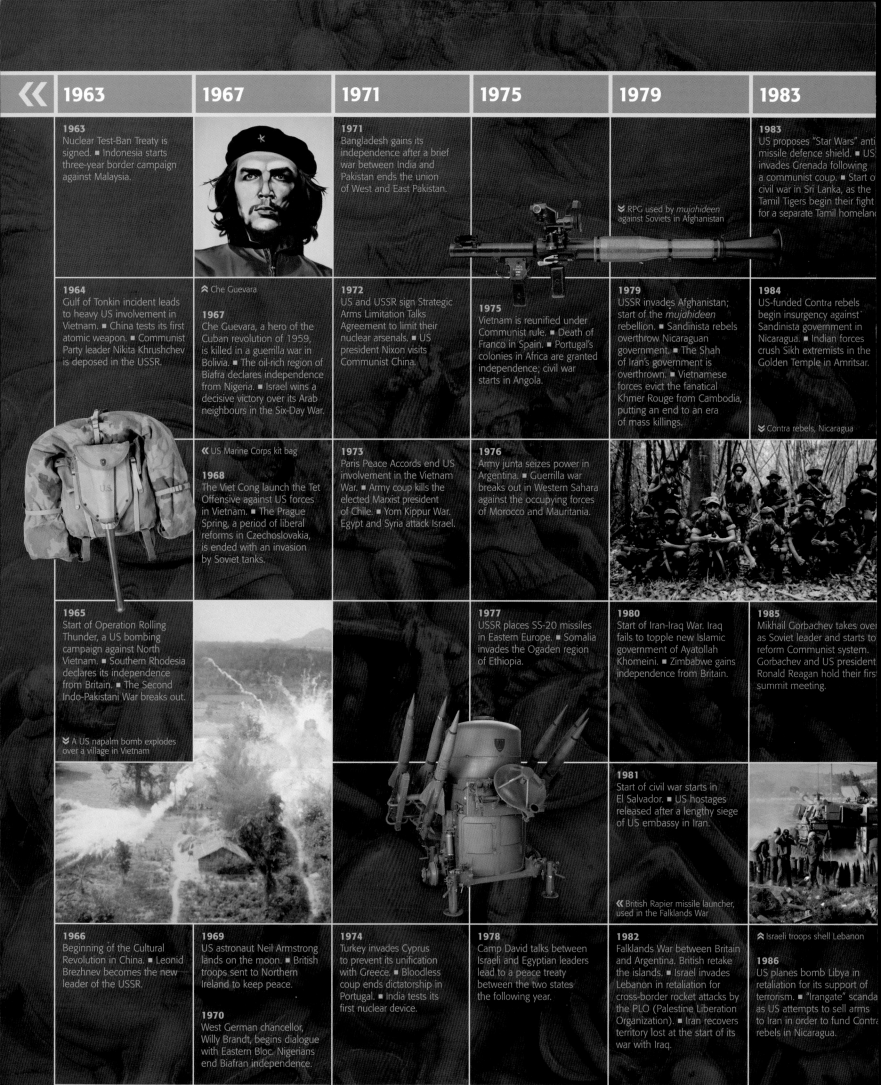

1963
Nuclear Test-Ban Treaty is signed. ■ Indonesia starts three-year border campaign against Malaysia.

❯❯ RPG used by *mujahideen* against Soviets in Afghanistan

1983
US proposes "Star Wars" anti missile defence shield. ■ US invades Grenada following a communist coup. ■ Start of civil war in Sri Lanka, as the Tamil Tigers begin their fight for a separate Tamil homeland.

1964
Gulf of Tonkin incident leads to heavy US involvement in Vietnam. ■ China tests its first atomic weapon. ■ Communist Party leader Nikita Khrushchev is deposed in the USSR.

❯ Che Guevara

1967
Che Guevara, a hero of the Cuban revolution of 1959, is killed in a guerrilla war in Bolivia. ■ The oil-rich region of Biafra declares independence from Nigeria. ■ Israel wins a decisive victory over its Arab neighbours in the Six-Day War.

1972
US and USSR sign Strategic Arms Limitation Talks Agreement to limit their nuclear arsenals. ■ US president Nixon visits Communist China.

1975
Vietnam is reunified under Communist rule. ■ Death of Franco in Spain. ■ Portugal's colonies in Africa are granted independence; civil war starts in Angola.

1979
USSR invades Afghanistan; start of the *mujahideen* rebellion. ■ Sandinista rebels overthrow Nicaraguan government. ■ The Shah of Iran's government is overthrown. ■ Vietnamese forces evict the fanatical Khmer Rouge from Cambodia, putting an end to an era of mass killings.

1984
US-funded Contra rebels begin insurgency against Sandinista government in Nicaragua. ■ Indian forces crush Sikh extremists in the Golden Temple in Amritsar.

❯ Contra rebels, Nicaragua

« US Marine Corps kit bag

1968
The Viet Cong launch the Tet Offensive against US forces in Vietnam. ■ The Prague Spring, a period of liberal reforms in Czechoslovakia, is ended with an invasion by Soviet tanks.

1973
Paris Peace Accords end US involvement in the Vietnam War. ■ Army coup kills the elected Marxist president of Chile. ■ Yom Kippur War. Egypt and Syria attack Israel.

1976
Army junta seizes power in Argentina. ■ Guerrilla war breaks out in Western Sahara against the occupying forces of Morocco and Mauritania.

1965
Start of Operation Rolling Thunder, a US bombing campaign against North Vietnam. ■ Southern Rhodesia declares its independence from Britain. ■ The Second Indo-Pakistani War breaks out.

❯❯ A US napalm bomb explodes over a village in Vietnam

1977
USSR places SS-20 missiles in Eastern Europe. ■ Somalia invades the Ogaden region of Ethiopia.

1980
Start of Iran-Iraq War. Iraq fails to topple new Islamic government of Ayatollah Khomeini. ■ Zimbabwe gains independence from Britain.

1985
Mikhail Gorbachev takes over as Soviet leader and starts to reform Communist system. Gorbachev and US president Ronald Reagan hold their first summit meeting.

1981
Start of civil war starts in El Salvador. ■ US hostages released after a lengthy siege of US embassy in Iran.

« British Rapier missile launcher, used in the Falklands War

1966
Beginning of the Cultural Revolution in China. ■ Leonid Brezhnev becomes the new leader of the USSR.

1969
US astronaut Neil Armstrong lands on the moon. ■ British troops sent to Northern Ireland to keep peace.

1970
West German chancellor, Willy Brandt, begins dialogue with Eastern Bloc. Nigerians end Biafran independence.

1974
Turkey invades Cyprus to prevent its unification with Greece. ■ Bloodless coup ends dictatorship in Portugal. ■ India tests its first nuclear device.

1978
Camp David talks between Israeli and Egyptian leaders lead to a peace treaty between the two states the following year.

1982
Falklands War between Britain and Argentina. British retake the islands. ■ Israel invades Lebanon in retaliation for cross-border rocket attacks by the PLO (Palestine Liberation Organization). ■ Iran recovers territory lost at the start of its war with Iraq.

❯ Israeli troops shell Lebanon

1986
US planes bomb Libya in retaliation for its support of terrorism. ■ "Irangate" scandal as US attempts to sell arms to Iran in order to fund Contra rebels in Nicaragua.

| **1987** | **1991** | **1995** | **1999** | **2003** | **2007** |

1987
Palestinian Intifada (rebellion) against Israeli occupation begins. ▪ US and USSR agree to dispose of all intermediate-range nuclear missiles.

⌄ Soviet military parade in Red Square, 1987

1995
Dayton Peace Accords end Bosnian civil war and set up separate Bosnian-Muslim and Serb states within Bosnian Federation.

1999
US hands over Canal Zone to Panama. ▪ Brief conflict between India and Pakistan in Kashmir. ▪ War in Chechnya begins again. Russian troops flatten the capital, Grozny.

⌃ US bombing of Baghdad, 2003

2000
George W. Bush is elected president of the United States.

2001
9/11 attacks by al-Qaeda on targets in New York and Washington. US-led invasion of Afghanistan overthrows the Taliban government.

2003
US, British, and other allied troops invade Iraq and overthrow the government of Saddam Hussein. Sunni supporters of Hussein resist subsequent occupation.

⌄ British SA80 assault rifle used in both Gulf wars

1988
Gorbachev pulls Soviet troops out of Eastern Europe. ▪ Iraq and Iran agree a ceasefire to end their war. ▪ Ethnic violence erupts in Armenia and Azerbaijan over disputed enclave of Nagorno-Karabakh.

1991
US-led coalition liberates Kuwait from Iraqi occupation. Separatist rebellions by Shi'as and Kurds are crushed by Iraq. ▪ USSR collapses and is replaced by 15 independent republics. ▪ Civil war ends in El Salvador. ▪ Somalia collapses into permanent state of anarchy and civil war.

1996
End of Burmese separatist campaigns. ▪ Lengthy guerrilla war ends in Guatemala. ▪ Russia agrees to a ceasefire in the war in Chechnya. ▪ The Taliban seize power in Afghanistan.

2007
US sends 20,000 additional troops to Iraq in "surge" to suppress insurrection.

1989
Revolutions against Communist rule across Eastern Europe; Berlin Wall comes down. ▪ Soviet troops leave Afghanistan.

1992
Communist government is overthrown by *mujahideen* in Afghanistan. ▪ Bosnian civil war begins.

1993
Georgian troops expelled from Abkhazia. ▪ Oslo Accords lead to peace treaty between Israel and the Palestine Liberation Organization.

≫ Chechen guerrilla

2004
Insurgency against occupation of Iraq spreads to Shi'a community. Two bitter battles take place in Fallujah.

2005
Peace deal ends 22 years of civil war in southern Sudan, but conflict intensifies in the western province of Darfur.

2008
Russia clashes with Georgia over the latter's breakaway regions of South Ossetia and Abkhazia. ▪ Communists take power in Nepal after a lengthy insurrection. ▪ Kosovo declares its independence from Serbia. ▪ US agrees to withdraw its troops from Iraq by 2010.

1997
Ottawa Treaty outlaws the use of landmines. ▪ Joseph Mobutu is overthrown in the Congo. Country is sucked into conflict on its eastern border between Rwanda and Hutu refugees. ▪ British colony of Hong Kong reverts to Chinese rule.

2006
NATO troops reinforce US and British troops in Afghanistan.

2009
Sri Lankan army crushes Tamil Tigers. ▪ British troops leave Iraq. ▪ Israeli troops leave Gaza strip after campaign to end Hamas attacks on Israel.

⌄ Hamas militants

⌃ A-7E Corsair used by US in First Gulf War

1990
East and West Germany are unified. ▪ Nicaraguan civil war ends with defeat of Sandinistas. ▪ Civil war in Liberia soon spreads to neighbouring states. ▪ Iraq invades Kuwait to seize oil. First Gulf War begins.

1994
Genocide in Rwanda as extreme Hutus massacre Tutsis. ▪ Chechen War begins between separatists and the Russian army.

1998
Border war between Ethiopia and Eritrea. ▪ NATO intervenes to end Serb ethnic cleansing of Kosovo. ▪ Good Friday Agreement brings peace to Northern Ireland. ▪ Pakistan tests its first nuclear device.

2002
International Criminal Court is set up in The Hague to try war crimes. ▪ Angolan civil war ends. ▪ UN and British forces end civil war in Sierra Leone.

The **Cold War**

After the hot war of World War II, a Cold War of ideas and propaganda broke out between the former allies of the Communist East and capitalist West. The Cold War kept the peace in Europe for 50 years but sparked conflict in other continents and threatened an annihilating nuclear exchange.

Submarine-launched missiles
Because submarines are difficult to detect, submarine-launched nuclear missiles, like this US Trident, gave nations the ability to retaliate quickly to a surprise attack, deterring such an attack being made in the first place.

« **BEFORE**

The German invasion of the USSR in June 1941 created an alliance between the USSR, Britain, and later the US. This alliance went on to defeat Germany and Japan in 1945.

PLANNING FOR PEACE
In 1945 the three main **Allied wartime leaders** – Churchill, Roosevelt – and Stalin met, first at Yalta in the Crimea, and then at Potsdam outside Berlin to **plan the postwar world**. Between them, they agreed a four-way division, with France, of Germany and Austria, settled the new eastern and western borders of Poland, and **allowed the USSR a free hand in Central Europe**. Korea was to be divided between the Soviet and American zones.

160 The distance in kilometres (100 miles), across Soviet-dominated East Germany, between West Berlin and West Germany.

BERLIN DIVIDED
Although the German capital, Berlin, fell to Soviet troops in 1945, and was within the Soviet zone of occupied Germany, it was agreed that **the city would be divided** between the four Allies. The Western Allies would be able to reach Berlin from West Germany along road, rail, and air **corridors through the Soviet zone**.

The end of World War II in Europe brought peace but not security. Soviet troops had freed the east from Nazi rule, while American and other Allied troops had liberated the west. The two sides faced each other along a frontier nicknamed the Iron

> **MUTUALLY ASSURED DESTRUCTION**
> **The form of nuclear stalemate in which each side has the ability to destroy the other, even after being attacked first. In theory this deters each side from considering making a "first strike".**

Curtain. The USSR helped to set up Communist states in the east by 1948, while democratic governments resumed control of the liberated countries in the west. However, many in the West feared that Communism would spread.

The Marshall Plan
In 1947 US President Truman promised to help any country being threatened by a Communist takeover. He pledged immediate aid to Greece, then enduring a bitter civil war between royalists and Communists. The Truman Doctrine, as it became known, was supported by the Marshall Plan, a vast programme of economic aid named after US Secretary of State, George Marshall, "to restore the confidence of the European peoples in the economic future of their own countries and of Europe as a whole."

The Marshall Plan was open to any country in Europe, but only those in the West accepted. The Communist bloc

formed Comecon, the Council for Mutual Economic Assistance, in 1949, tying their economies to the Soviet Union. The main issue for both sides concerned Germany. The USSR feared a reunited Germany, while the US and its Allies wanted to rebuild the country as a peaceful, pro-Western state. Their differences came to a head in 1948, when the Western Allies merged their zones and introduced a new currency for West Berlin. The USSR responded by cutting road and rail links between the city and the West. With the city facing starvation, the Western Allies began to airlift up to 13,000 tonnes

in the western North Atlantic Treaty Organization (set up in 1949) and the eastern Warsaw Pact (1955).

Nuclear weapons
The Soviets exploded their first nuclear bomb in 1949, ending the US nuclear monopoly. Both sides then developed increasingly powerful thermonuclear weapons ("hydrogen bombs") in the 1950s. Nuclear weapons were initially designed to be dropped from aircraft but in 1957 the USSR tested the first intercontinental ballistic missile; unlike bombers, these missiles were impossible to intercept. Both the US and the USSR

> **" … it must be the policy of the United States to support free peoples who are resisting … outside pressures."**
> **PRESIDENT HARRY TRUMAN, ADDRESSING CONGRESS,** 12 MARCH 1947

of supplies into the city every day. The airlift lasted almost a year, until the USSR ended the blockade in May 1949.

The Berlin blockade showed that, while both sides would stand their ground, neither wanted to face armed confrontation. In Europe at least, the Cold War would be fought with ideas and propaganda, not guns, despite the creation of rival defence organizations

deployed numbers of these weapons and, from the 1960s, versions launched from submarines. A system of deterrence gradually developed; neither side could use its nuclear weapons for fear of a devastating counter-strike.

The Cold War nearly became a hot war when the USSR placed nuclear missiles on Cuba, but survived crises in Europe when the Soviets put down an

KEY MOMENT
THE CUBAN MISSILE CRISIS

On 14 October 1962, a US U-2 spy plane photographed a Soviet missile site under construction in Cuba, just 145km (90 miles) from the United States. President John Kennedy imposed a naval blockade on Cuba and demanded the removal of the missiles. The world waited anxiously as the two sides faced each other down, the USSR refusing to comply unless the US removed missiles from Turkey. A deal was reached on 28 October that saw the Soviet missiles removed in return for a US promise not to invade Cuba. US missiles were removed from Turkey the next year.

US SPY PLANE IMAGE, AS RELEASED FOR PUBLICATION

Reel-to-reel tape

STASI MINIATURE RECORDER

Modified shaft containing camera

Screw mechanism

KGB CAMERA CONCEALED IN A GLUE STICK

4.5mm barrel

Hidden camera

Secret services

Spies on both sides of the Cold War were equipped with disguised, concealed, and miniaturized equipment with which to take photographs, record voices, and eavesdrop on their opponents without their knowledge.

STASI PEN CONTAINING HIDDEN MICROPHONE

KGB LIPSTICK PISTOL

AFTER

uprising in Hungary in 1956, built a wall to seal East Berlin from the West in 1961, and crushed new reforms in Czechoslovakia in 1968.

Outside Europe, the Cold War saw clashes in Korea and Vietnam. Alliance systems tied countries everywhere to one side or another, despite the growth of a non-aligned movement headed by, among others, India and Yugoslavia.

Aware that deterrence might fail catastrophically, both sides tried to reduce tension. Treaties made during the 1960s limited nuclear testing and sought to prevent the spread of nuclear weapons to new countries. (By then Britain, France, and China were also nuclear powers.) The US and the Soviet Union agreed to limit their nuclear arsenals in 1972, the first stage in a process known as détente.

Tension between the two sides over human rights abuses in the East, the placing of a new generation of shorter-range Soviet and US missiles in Europe,

and the Soviet invasion of Afghanistan in 1979 turned détente into deep freeze during the 1980s.

A new era

The US response under President Ronald Reagan was to raise military spending by 50 per cent. The Soviet economy was unable to compete with the new level of American military developments, but the resulting confrontation continued until Mikhail Gorbachev came to power in the USSR in 1985. Committed to a reform of his country through policies of *glasnost* ("openness") and *perestroika* ("reconstruction"), he began a series of summit meetings with Reagan that removed all intermediate-range missiles from Europe, relaxing military tensions across the continent.

However, Gorbachev's reforms also meant that Communism weakened its hold in the USSR and across Eastern Europe. With the collapse of the USSR in 1991, the Cold War came to an end.

The Cold War ended as Communism collapsed across Europe and the Soviet Union itself began to disintegrate.

THE EASTERN BLOC

In 1988 Mikhail Gorbachev signalled the **end of Soviet control** over Eastern Europe by saying he would withdraw 500,000 troops and give its countries "freedom of choice". No longer could **unpopular Communist regimes** rely on Soviet power. Protests soon broke out in most countries. Opposition parties were legalized in Hungary, while the Polish elected the first **non-Communist government** in Eastern Europe since 1948.

A PIECE OF THE BERLIN WALL

Hungary opened up its borders to the West, thus tearing the Iron Curtain open. The **Berlin Wall** – the hated symbol of the divided city – was torn down in 1989, and **East and West Germany were reunified** in October 1990.

THE USSR

Gorbachev's attempts to reform the USSR led to **growing unrest and demands for independence** from the country's 15 individual republics. Hardline Communists staged a coup in August 1991, but were defeated by Russia's new leader, Boris Yeltsin. Gorbachev tried to hold the USSR together, but had little support. One by one, the republics **declared independence**, forcing him to resign as president on Christmas Day 1991, **bringing the USSR itself to an end.**

The Chinese Civil War

The civil war between the Nationalists and Communists that ended in 1949 was the culmination of a lengthy struggle for control of China. Huge armies fought massive battles in a war little known in the West but which has continued to have a huge impact right up to the present day.

Left hand grasps stock to shoulder

The renewal of the Chinese Civil War after Japan's surrender at the end of World War II saw the Communists begin with most of the advantages. The Communists had led popular resistance to the Japanese occupation and had gained expertise in guerrilla warfare. Their arsenal was now increased with enough weapons for 600,000 troops, seized from the Japanese by the Soviet forces that had occupied the province of Manchuria at the very end of the war, before handing the arms and, in effect, the province over to the Communists.

In contrast, the Nationalist army had mainly held the rural south and west and increasingly lacked the support of the people. The army quickly seized the coastal cities from the Japanese as they departed, helped by a US sea and air lift that transported 500,000 Nationalist troops into central and northern China.

165
The number of days it took the Communists to defeat the Nationalists at the battle of Xuzhou.

The Nationalists had been allies of the US during the war and expected that alliance to continue in peace.

In October 1945, as both sides tried to consolidate their territory, peace talks sponsored by the US ambassador failed to find any agreement. The Nationalist army then moved north, only to find, in January 1946, that its progress into Manchuria was blocked by a US-negotiated ceasefire. The rival armies now regrouped before hostilities were renewed in earnest in spring.

The five-million-strong Nationalist army lined up across northern China, cutting Manchuria off from the rest of the country, while other divisions attacked Communist strongholds to their south and west. The Nationalists eventually took 165 Communist-held towns, including their capital, Yan'an, in March 1947.

Communist successes
Although the Nationalists won the major battles, the Communists gained ground relentlessly through many

Chairman Mao
Propaganda posters greeted Communist Party chairman, Mao Zedong, as victor of the Civil War and leader of the new People's Republic of China.

Nationalist army enters Kweilin
Continued fighting between Nationalists and Communists, and then Chinese and Japanese, left many towns and cities in the populous east of China in ruins.

<< **BEFORE**

War had raged almost continuously in China since the 1920s, as first rival warlords fought for power, and then Mao Zedong's Communists challenged the Nationalists.

CIVIL UNREST
In 1911 Sun Zhongshan's Nationalist party overthrew the Qing dynasty and **declared China a republic**. Rival warlords fought for power until his eventual successor, General Jiang Jieshi, **established a national government** with its capital at Nanjing in 1928. His rule was **challenged by the Chinese Communists** led by Mao Zedong, who set up a Soviet republic in Jiangxi province, but after Nationalist pressure forced them to abandon it in 1934, their troops and their families set out on the **Long March** to a new base in the northern Shaanxi province.

JAPANESE INVASION
In 1931 Japan occupied the northern Chinese province of **Manchuria**, invading the rest of the country in 1937 << **282–83**. The Japanese soon captured China's east coast and occupied it until defeated at the end of World War II. Nationalists and Communists **collaborated** to some extent in fighting the Japanese, but both also **prepared for a later struggle** over the control of China.

Rear sight

14.5 mm calibre

Bipod

Foresight

PTRD anti-tank rifle

Manufactured in the USSR during World War II, the PTRD was supplied in large quantities to Chinese Communist forces during the Civil War. It was most effective when used against light armoured vehicles.

smaller offensives, killing or capturing some 400,000 Nationalist troops during 1947 and obtaining some useful heavy guns. In late 1947 the Communist Fourth Field Army under Lin Biao took the offensive in Manchuria. His troops split the Nationalists into distinct pockets and picked them off one by one until they captured Mukden in November 1948, the last Nationalist garrison in the province of Manchuria.

The decisive battle

The biggest formal battle of the war began in September 1948. Led by Ch'en Yi, the Communists' Third Army moved east, out of Shaanxi province, and into Shandong province south of Beijing, pushing the Nationalist's Seventh Army, led by Du Yuming, south towards the Huai He river. Du Yuming halted at Xuzhou, a major rail junction. In theory, he had some 500,000 men available, but many Nationalist troops were disloyal

and at least four divisions in the centre of Du's line changed allegiance to the Communists, joining the total of 800,000 troops who defected during the course of the war. With the enemy centre now disintegrating, the Communists attacked the two wings during November and December, cutting their communications, surrounding their troops, and bombarding them into surrender. The battle was won on 10 January 1949, when the Communists at last took Xuzhou. The situation was so bad for the Nationalists that Jiang Jieshi ordered his air force to bomb his own lines, killing many of his own troops, to prevent arms and equipment from falling into Communist hands.

Mauser automatic pistol

Many unlicensed copies of the German Mauser C96 pistol were manufactured in China in the first half of the 20th century and were used by both sides in the Civil War.

The defeat was disastrous for the Nationalists, who lost 250,000 men, among them the commanders of two army groups.

The Communists were now on the offensive, with far greater firepower, mobility, numbers, and popular support than the Nationalists, who were ill equipped and poorly led. On 15 January, Lin Biao's Fourth Field Army took Tianjin and then, seven days later, marched unopposed into Beijing, where it was welcomed as the one force

that could bring the long years of war and occupation to an end. The fall of Beijing brought the Communists control of all north and east China.

Communist victory

The end came swiftly in 1949. In April Communist troops began to move south, taking the Nationalist capital, Nanjing, without a fight, on 24 April and then the commercial city of Shanghai on 27 May. Faced with defeat and mass desertions, in July the Nationalist leaders decided to flee to the offshore island of Taiwan, taking the nation's art and treasure collection and gold reserves.

On 1 October 1949, Mao Zedong stood on the Gate of Heavenly Peace in Beijing and announced the formation of the People's Republic of China. The Communists had triumphed.

China's Civil War

Communist strength was initially confined to the northeast of the country, spreading south as the Nationalists withdrew south of the Yangtze river and then, eventually, to Taiwan.

Key
- Under Communist control 1946
- Under Communist control mid-1949
- Under Communist control 1950
- Frontiers 1945
- Long March Oct 1934–Oct 1935
- Major Communist offensive
- Major battle or siege
- Jun 1948 Date taken by Communists

AFTER

Since 1949 Communist China has exercised growing power and influence in the world. Mao Zedong's revolutionary zeal inspired revolutionaries in other countries.

TAIWAN

At the end of the **Chinese Civil War**, Nationalist forces **controlled only Taiwan** and a few small offshore islands. Neither Nationalist Taiwan nor Communist China recognized the other, Taiwan claiming to be the legitimate government of all China and holding China's seat in the United Nations until expelled in 1971. A **defence treaty with the US** in 1954 guaranteed Taiwan's independence. Relations with China remain tense to this day, although **direct air and shipping routes** were established in 2008.

COMMUNIST CHINA

Communist troops **occupied Tibet** in 1950–51, crushing an uprising for independence in 1959. China supported the Communists in North Korea during the **Korean War 316–17 »** and in North Vietnam during the **Vietnam War 320–21 »**. Other than that, China has rarely intervened directly in the affairs of other nations. China exploded an **atom bomb** in 1964, becoming the world's fifth **nuclear power**.

«

BEFORE

Korea has been controlled or divided by outside powers for much of its history. Both Japan and China have intervened in Korea at various times.

FOREIGN RULE

Following the **First Sino-Japanese War** of 1894–95, Korea gained **independence from China**, but soon became the subject of intense economic and political rivalry between Russia and Japan. Following the **Russo-Japanese War** of 1904–05 **« 254–55**, Japan took over responsibility for Korea's foreign policy and dominated the country's economy. In 1910 **Japan formally annexed Korea**, ruling it until Japan's defeat in World War II in 1945.

DIVISION

At the end of the war, the US and USSR agreed that Soviet troops would occupy Korea north of the **38°N parallel**, while American troops occupied the south, pending the establishment of a unified, independent, democratic Korea. **Soviet troops remained** in place until the establishment in Pyongyang in September 1948 of the Soviet-backed **Korean People's Democratic Republic**. US troops remained until June 1949 to support the newly formed **Republic of Korea**, set up in Seoul in August 1948. UN **attempts to reunite the country failed** when the USSR did not support all-Korean elections. Border incursions by the rival sides increased tension on the peninsula.

The Korean War

The North Korean invasion of South Korea to reunite the divided peninsula was the first major open battle of the Cold War, pitting former allies – the US, USSR, and China – on opposite sides. The war lasted for three years and ended in stalemate, the unity of the divided country still not achieved today.

Equipped with arms from the USSR and with a tacit agreement from Communist China to send military support if required, North Korea made a surprise dawn attack on South Korea on 25 June 1950. Statements made by senior American figures suggesting that the United States might not defend South Korea against such an invasion may have played a part in inspiring the move. Seven infantry divisions and one armoured division headed south, capturing the South Korean capital, Seoul, within three days. Many of the North Korean troops had fought in the recent Chinese Civil War; they were skilled and experienced fighters and had the advantage of operating on home territory.

The South was ill prepared for the attack and appealed for international support. The United States pushed a resolution through the United Nations (UN) Security Council – the USSR was boycotting the council (and was thus unable to use its veto power), while the pro-US Chinese Nationalist government of Taiwan occupied China's UN seat – and gained approval to lead an international force to stop the attack. US general, Douglas MacArthur, then commander of the post-World War II occupation forces in Japan (the closest sizable body of US troops), was appointed commander. The first UN troops arrived on 1 July but were immediately pushed back by

EAST ASIA

Korean War
Dates 1950–53
Location North and South Korea

Maximum range 23.5km (25,700yd)

Ammunition load 20 rounds

Barrel 7.06m (23ft) long

BIG SHOT

Tracks 58cm (23in) wide

M40 gun motor carriage
The US M40 self-propelled 155-mm gun first entered service at the end of World War II and was extensively used during the Korean War to provide long-range fire support for UN forces. The vehicle had a crew of eight.

Searching North Koreans
Soldiers from the United Nations forces search capture North Korean troops during the very successful September 1950 landings at Inchon.

North Korean forces. Throughout July and August the UN and South Korean troops retreated to a defensive perimeter line around the port of Pusan in the far southeast. The US ground commander, General Walton Walker, did not at first have enough troops to defend this line but made good use of intelligence to warn him of North Korean attacks and concentrate his forces against them. The arrival of reinforcements, British troops included, by the end of August helped to stabilize the situation, while bombing raids and naval bombardment against the North Korean supply lines restricted their army's effectiveness.

By early September MacArthur was confident he could hold Pusan and therefore went over to the offensive.

On 15 September, the US Marines X Corps began a daring amphibious landing at Inchon, 320km (200 miles) northwest of Pusan on the western side of the peninsula, to recapture Seoul and cut the enemy's forces in two. The assault was instantly successful, with only light casualties.

The battle for Seoul proved to be more intense, as the North Koreans fought to the death despite having fewer numbers. On 26 September, X Corps met up with the forces driving up from Pusan and soon cleared South Korea of its northern invaders.

Chinese intervention

General MacArthur now asked for permission to invade the North. US President Harry Truman worried about provoking a Chinese response but gave his approval. He was right to have fears, for as UN troops began to head up the

had to fight their way south, suffering heavy losses of men and equipment. In the east, meanwhile, an attacking force of US Marines also found itself under pressure and made a fraught retreat.

In January 1951, a new surge of Chinese and North Korean troops pushed the UN forces south of Seoul. Faced with a possible re-run of the opening weeks of the war, a new US ground

155-mm M2 gun fired 43.1-kg (96-lb) shells

Hull design based on the M4 Sherman tank

"If we **lose the war** to Communism in Asia the **fall of Europe** is **inevitable**."

GENERAL DOUGLAS MACARTHUR, 20 MARCH 1951

aterpillar tracks roduced a top road beed of 38kph (24mph)

peninsula, taking the northern capital of Pyongyang on 12 October, clashes began with Chinese soldiers who had crossed the frontier. From this time on, MacArthur regularly disobeyed orders and publicly disagreed with the less aggressive policies of the Truman administration. This would lead to his dismissal. MacArthur did not take the first reports of Chinese involvement too seriously, because he assumed they were not part of a major armed incursion, and on 24 November ordered a final assault up to the Yalu river border with China in an attempt to bring an end to the war.

Two days later his Eighth Army came under attack from massed Chinese infantry units that were hidden in the mountains. MacArthur gave the order for the troops to retreat but they found their way blocked by Chinese forces who had closed in behind them. They

commander, General Matthew Ridgway (who assumed supreme command in 1951), stopped the retreat. He drew up his forces on a line across the peninsula and slowly pushed north, using artillery and air firepower as the means to take North Korean and Chinese positions. The Chinese responded to "Ridgway's meatgrinder" (as the process became known) with wave after wave of human attacks, beaten back at huge cost.

After three months of heavy fighting, UN troops stabilized the front along the pre-war border. The previously mobile war settled down to a static stalemate, with the sides exchanging artillery fire and initiating a small number of infantry engagements. Peace talks were started in July 1951 and dragged on for another two years, until an armistice ending the war and setting up a demilitarized zone between the two sides was eventually agreed on 27 July 1953.

Decolonization in Southeast Asia

The Japanese invasion of Southeast Asia in 1941–42 swept away the European colonial empires. In 1945 the European powers expected to resume their rule, but faced nationalist revolts in almost every country. In little over a decade, the nationalists had won and the region was free from European rule.

The declaration of independence by the Indonesian Nationalist Party (PNI) in Jakarta allowed them to fill a power vacuum before the Dutch colonial authorities returned from exile following the defeat of Japan. Fighting soon broke out between the two sides, notably in Java. The British arranged a truce in November 1946 that provided for a United States of Indonesia linked to the Dutch crown. But it was not long before the two fell out again, causing the Dutch powers to launch punitive police raids in July 1947. A US-brokered ceasefire began in December 1947, but collapsed in September 1948, when the Dutch launched powerful attacks against the nationalists. The Dutch bombed Jakarta heavily in December 1948, but worldwide protests forced them to agree to convene a conference in The Hague in August

1949 to settle the colony's future. On 27 December 1949, the Dutch handed over power to Achmad Sukarno as president of the new republic.

Vietnam

As in Indonesia, Viet Minh nationalists in Vietnam took advantage of the brief lapse of power that arose following the defeat of Japan in 1945 to declare an

Drum magazine

Rear sight

Laminated wooden stock

Flash hider

Degtyarev 7.62mm light machine gun
Soviet-manufactured weapons, such as this World War II-era light machine-gun, were supplied to North Vietnam and then passed on to the Viet Cong guerrilla fighters operating in the South.

independent republic in the northern city of Hanoi. In March 1946, the French signed an agreement with Ho Chi Minh that recognized Vietnam as a free state within an Indochinese federation and allowed French troops to return to the north of the country.

However, this agreement soon broke down when the French decided to keep control of Cochin China in southern Vietnam. In November 1946, French soldiers attacked the Viet Minh-held port of Haiphong, killing 6,000 people. In December the Viet Minh attacked the French garrison in Hanoi. France had better weaponry and naval support, and called on troops from the Foreign Legion and from the French army in Europe. The Viet Minh army, led by General Giap, drew on considerable local support in the north and received military supplies first from the Chinese Nationalists and then, after their victory in 1949 in the civil war, China's new Communist government. The USSR also sent weapons and other supplies.

In the early years of the war, the French quickly took control of all the major northern cities, sending assault teams to attack Viet Minh bases. In response, the Viet Minh fought a classic guerrilla war, attacking French targets but avoiding set-piece battles. In 1949 the French installed Bao Dai, local emperor of the French Vietnamese province of Annam, as emperor of an independent Vietnam. Bao Dai's government was recognized by France,

the US, and other Western countries, but failed to gain widespread support in Vietnam or among its neighbours, as Bao Dai was felt to be a French puppet.

Faced with increasingly successful Viet Minh attacks in 1950, the French turned to the United States for financial aid (by 1954 the US were paying about 80 per cent of France's military budget in Vietnam). The war soon turned into a stalemate, with the French holding the northern cities and a few outposts, while the Viet Minh held control of the northern countryside. French successes in late 1950 and January 1951 – when

a Viet Minh force was trapped on open ground at Vinh Yen, north of Hanoi, and annihilated – were then reversed by Viet Minh victories in 1952–53. In an effort to break the stalemate, the French attempted to engage the Viet Minh at Dien Bien Phu. The French defeat there, in May 1954, effectively brought an end to the war.

Malaya

Although the Japanese occupation stimulated nationalist opposition to British rule in Malaya, the British returned unopposed to power in 1945. In 1948 Britain set up a federation of Malay states, but resentment by ethnic Chinese at Malay dominance fuelled a Communist guerrilla campaign waged by the Malayan Races Liberation Army that broke out the same year. The

<< BEFORE

Nationalist groups campaigned against European colonial rule in Southeast Asia after the 1920s. The region was then occupied by Japan during World War II.

VIETNAM

In 1925 **Vietnamese nationalists seeking independence** from French Indochina founded the Vietnamese Nationalist Party. In July 1941, **Japan occupied French Indochina**, including Laos and Cambodia. Vietnamese nationalists and Communists **formed the Viet Minh** resistance movement under **Ho Chi Minh** in order to fight the occupation, receiving help from the United States. When Japan surrendered in 1945, the Viet Minh **declared Vietnam independent** under Ho Chi Minh's leadership.

SOUTHEAST ASIA

Resistance to **Dutch rule in Indonesia** was led from 1927 by the Indonesian Nationalist Party (PNI) of **Achmad Sukarno**. In 1942 **Japan invaded Southeast Asia**, taking the British and Dutch colonies. The Japanese were largely welcomed as **liberators from colonial rule** and many nationalists collaborated with them. In August 1945, the PNI seized power and on the 17th **declared Indonesia independent**.

SOUTHEAST ASIA

1 **Indonesia**
Dates 1946–49
Location Chiefly Java and Sumatra

2 **French Indochina**
Dates 1946–54
Location Vietnam and Laos

3 **Malaya**
Dates 1948–60

4 **Burma**
Dates 1948–96

VIETNAMESE GENERAL (1912–)

VO NGUYEN GIAP

General Giap was the pre-eminent expert in guerrilla warfare in the 20th century, his expertise enabling him to defeat three technologically superior armies, those of Japan, France, and the US. A member of the Vietnamese Communist Party since 1933, Giap was a key figure in resistance to the Japanese after 1941. After World War II he took command of the Viet Minh army and led it to victory against the French at Dien Bien Phu in 1954. He remained in charge against the Americans and their allies in the Vietnam War and achieved the unification of the country under Communist rule in 1975.

"[Dien Bien Phu] was **the first great victory** for a weak, **colonized people** struggling against the full strength of **modern Western forces**."

VIETNAMESE GENERAL VO NGUYEN GIAP, INTERVIEW, 1999

British imposed a state of emergency and began a jungle war. British use of helicopters and specially trained jungle warfare troops, their establishment of protected villages to guard local people, their close supervision of foodstuffs to cut off guerrilla supplies, and the failure of the guerrillas to convince the mainly Malay population that communism would benefit them, all contributed to a British victory. In 1957

Britain accelerated plans to give Malaya independence, denying the guerrillas an anti-colonial platform. The "Malayan Emergency" ended officially in 1960.

Burma
Opposition to British rule in Burma led some Burmese people to welcome the Japanese as liberators in 1942. Leading nationalists Aung San and U Nu set up a puppet government, but both later helped British and Indian forces to evict the Japanese. In 1946 the British agreed to grant Burma

independence, which was achieved under U Nu in January 1948. The new republic faced an immediate rebellion by Karen and other separatist groups, followed by a Communist insurrection. The army under Ne Win took power in 1962 and set up a dictatorship, cracking down on dissent. Separatist groups had seized two-fifths of the country by 1976 but a government offensive effectively ended the rebellions by 1996. Aung San Suu Kyi (Aung San's daughter) led political opposition to military rule, which continued into the 21st century.

Independence from colonial rule did not bring peace to the region. Nationalist and anti-Communist struggles led to bitter conflicts in Vietnam and elsewhere.

INDONESIA
The army under General Suharto brutally **crushed a Communist revolt** in 1965. Sukarno was then deposed in favour of Suharto in 1967. Indonesia also fought a **repressive campaign in East Timor** until the island gained its independence under supervision of the United Nations in 2002.

AUNG SAN SUU KYI

VIETNAM
France **recognized the independence of Vietnam** in the Geneva Accords of 1954. Conflict continued, leading to direct **US involvement 322–23 »**.

MALAYSIA
In 1963 Malaya, Singapore, and the British colonies on Borneo formed the Federation of Malaysia. Britain helped Malaysia fight a **border war with Indonesia** on Borneo until 1966.

British troops of the Special Air Service
The use of helicopters to carry troops specially trained in jungle warfare to remote areas helped the British defeat the Communist insurgency in Malaya in the 1950s.

Dien Bien Phu

The French colonial rulers of Vietnam planned the crucial battle of Dien Bien Phu to break the stalemate in their war with the Viet Minh guerrillas seeking independence. Their intent was to entice what they thought was a largely peasant army to join a battle in which French firepower would win the day. The result was exactly the reverse.

The airstrip of Dien Bien Phu lay in a remote valley surrounded by forested hills 300km (186 miles) west of Hanoi near the border with Laos. The only way in was by air. On 20 November 1953, the first of 16,000 French regulars, Foreign Legionnaires, and loyal Vietnamese troops parachuted in, driving out the defending Viet Minh and fortifying a series of outposts up to 6.4 km (4 miles) away from the airstrip. The Viet Minh commander, General Giap, reacted by quickly surrounding the strip and building up his strength. On the surrounding hills he placed more than 200 anti-aircraft artillery and rocket launchers to prevent the French from resupplying their base.

On 13 March 1954, the main Viet Minh assault began, quickly taking the outlying Gabrielle and Béatrice outposts. The northern outpost of Anne-Marie fell when its previously loyal T'ai tribal defenders melted away or defected on 17 March. Viet Minh artillery on the hills and machine guns nearer the base now covered the airstrip so that all French supplies had to be parachuted in and were vulnerable to attack or capture. The Viet Minh artillery proved to be highly effective, shooting down 62 French planes and damaging another 107.

After a lull in the fighting, the Viet Minh renewed their assault at the end of March. One by one the French outposts were overrun, the result of

effective mining, artillery fire, and finally direct assault. The French did have some successes, setting their 105mm howitzers to zero elevation (i.e. horizontally) and firing into Viet Minh troops attacking Dominique on 30 March while another French force near the airstrip opened fire with anti-aircraft guns, forcing a Viet Minh retreat. Lone planes flying high above the base dropped in reinforcements.

The final days

The French success in recapturing part of the Eliane outpost on 11 April undermined Viet Minh morale, for they had suffered high casualties – up to 6,000 dead, 10,000 wounded, and 2,500 captured by that point – and had no adequate medical services for the wounded. General Giap called in reinforcements from Laos. On 22 April the Viet Minh took the initiative again, overrunning Huguette and now commanding almost all of the airstrip. Accurate parachute drops now became impossible. The final assault began on 1 May, with Soviet Katyusha rockets used for the first time. On 6 May the Viet Minh detonated a mineshaft dug under Eliane and blew away its defenders. The next day, the remaining French positions were captured, the Viet Minh taking 11,721 French soldiers prisoner. Only 73 men of the original French garrison managed to escape to Laos; the rest of the garrison was dead.

LOCATION
North Vietnam, 300km (186 miles) west of Hanoi

DATE
13 March–7 May 1954

FORCES
Viet Minh: 80,000;
French: 16,000

CASUALTIES
Viet Minh: 23,000 killed and wounded;
French: 7,488 killed and wounded

---

**Map labels:**

3 17 Mar: T'ai soldiers abandon positions, forcing French withdrawal

2 13 Mar: Viet Minh infantry launch night attack on French positions

Gabrielle

Béatrice

artillery

Anne-Marie

Airstrip

Huguette

Dominique

1 13 Mar: Viet Minh launch daytime artillery attack to weaken French position

Claudine

Eliane

GIAP

DE CASTRIES

Nam Yum

4 30 Mar: Fierce fighting begins for Elaine and Dominique

6 7 May: Their supplies exhausted, French abandon Isabelle at night

7 1 May: Giap launches an all-out attack on remaining French positions

5 30 Mar: Isabelle is isolated by artillery fire, stopping reinforcements from heading north

Isabelle

0   1km
0   1 mile

KEY
Viet Minh forces
French defensive position

French paratroopers on patrol
French troops patrol the area surrounding the airstrip at Dien Bien Phu, which they captured in November 1953. Their enemy, the Viet Minh, continually harrassed them from the dense vegetation.

❮❮ BEFORE

The division of Vietnam in 1954 led to open conflict by the end of the decade as the northern Communists sought to reunify the country under their leadership.

DIVIDED VIETNAM

The Geneva Agreements of July 1954 **ended French rule over Vietnam** ❮❮ **318–19** and divided the country. **Ho Chi Minh** led the Communist-controlled Democratic Republic of Vietnam in the north; **Ngo Dinh Diem** led South Vietnam.

NORTH VIETNAM

Diem's government was repressive and corrupt. In 1956 North Vietnam authorized southern Communists to **begin an insurgency**, sending cadres to the south to organize **guerrilla war** in 1959. These guerrillas were named the **Viet Cong**.

SOUTH VIETNAM

In November 1955, US president, Dwight D. Eisenhower, sent 740 men of the **Military Assistance Advisory Group** to train the South Vietnamese Army. Their arrival marked the official **start of US military involvement** in Vietnam.

TECHNOLOGY

AGENT ORANGE

Agent Orange was a defoliant used by the Americans to destroy vegetation in Vietnam, its name deriving from the orange-striped barrels in which it was shipped. Agent Orange induced rapid growth that killed plants, stripping all vegetation from the land, denying cover to enemy soldiers. Some 80,000 cubic metres (17 million gallons) were sprayed on Vietnam. However, the spray included chemical compounds that were poisonous to humans. Of the 4.8 million Vietnamese exposed to Agent Orange, 400,000 died or suffered disabilities, while 500,000 children were born with birth defects. Many US troops were also harmed.

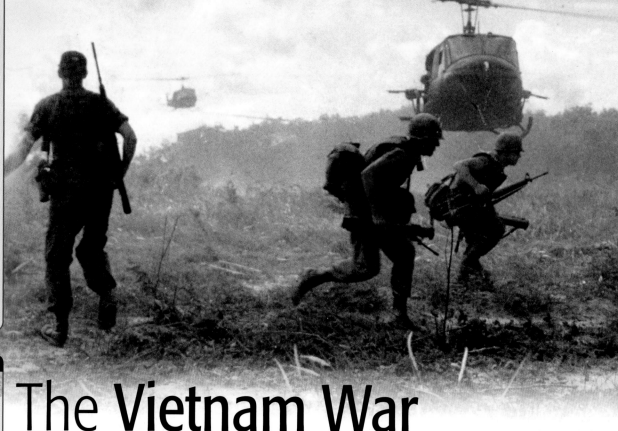

Indispensable air power
The helicopter was used extensively in Vietnam for the first time in the history of warfare, carrying out attack missions, transporting large numbers of troops, and flying the wounded to aid stations.

The Vietnam War

The US sent troops to South Vietnam in order to prevent the country falling under Communist control. The war was the lengthiest, most brutal, and most unpopular war American troops had ever fought, and ended in their withdrawal and the eventual defeat of their objectives.

In May 1961, President John Kennedy sent the first American troops – 400 US Army special forces (the Green Berets) – to South Vietnam to train its army in guerrilla tactics. Kennedy was concerned about rising Communist strength across Southeast Asia and saw South Vietnam as an important bulwark against this. By the time of his death, in November 1963, Kennedy had increased troop numbers to 16,300.

By mid-1964 the Communists were clearly gaining ground in South Vietnam and they seemed set to take control of the country unless the US massively increased its military support. On 2 August, USS *Maddox* clashed with North Vietnamese torpedo boats in the Gulf of Tonkin near North Vietnam's coast. President Lyndon Johnson used the incident to gain Congressional authorization "to take all necessary steps, including the use of armed forces" to assist South Vietnam.

306,183 **The number of US air attack sorties against North Vietnam flown during Operation Rolling Thunder.**

Immediate retaliatory air strikes against North Vietnamese ports and their naval facilities led in March 1965 to Operation Rolling Thunder, a bombing campaign that aimed to destroy North Vietnam's will to fight, by attacking its transport network, air defences, and industrial base. The first US Marines came ashore in South Vietnam in March to protect the airbases used in Rolling Thunder. The first army ground troops – 173rd Airborne Brigade – arrived in May. Troop numbers steadily rose to a peak of 530,000 in 1969. Further units – from Australia, New Zealand, the Philippines, South Korea, and Thailand – joined them.

Ruling out an invasion of North Vietnam as too costly and risking a confrontation with China and the Soviet Union, the US preferred to use its massive firepower to mount search-and-destroy missions against Communist-controlled areas in South Vietnam, while bombing the North.

South Vietnamese troops were sidelined in this conflict, as their morale was low and leadership poor. In contrast, both the North Vietnamese Army and the Viet Cong were disciplined fighters, supplied with weapons brought down

Viet Cong booby traps
The Viet Cong made simple weapons for attacking US soldiers. Among them were a spike plate that broke in two to penetrate the lower leg, and a grenade detonated with a trip wire.

The war in Vietnam

CHINA

LAOS

NORTH VIETNAM

THAILAND

CAMBODIA

SOUTH VIETNAM

Red River
Black River
PHONG SALY
Dien Bien Phu
Vinh Yen
Hanoi
Hoa Binh
SAM NEUA
Haiphong
Gulf of Tonkin
Hainan
Plain of Jars
1965–69: Communist-controlled areas bombed by US
Vientiane
1954: North-South Demarcation Line agreed at Geneva Conference
Aug 1964: North Vietnamese attacks reported on US destroyers. Gulf of Tonkin Resolution, commits US forces to war
Con Thien Sep 1966
Dai Do Apr–May 1968
Quang Tri
Khe Sanh Jan–Apr 1965
Hue
Hamburger Hill May 1969
A Shau Mar 1966
Da Nang
Mar 1965: First US ground forces arrive in Vietnam, ostensibly to protect air base
Mar 1968: Notorious massacre of 300–400 South Vietnamese civilians by US soldiers in My Lai
Dak To Nov 1967
Kontum
Pleiku
Qui Nhon
Ia Drang Nov 1965
Kompong Thom
Tonle Sap
Mekong
Ban Me Thuot
Bu Gia Map May 1966
Phuoc Long
South China Sea
Loc Ninh Oct–Nov 1967
An Loc
Xuan Loc
Phnom Penh
Kompong Som
Bien Hoa
Saigon
Phan Thiet
Apr 1975: North Vietnamese Army encircles city. US civilians are evacuated by helicopter from embassy rooftop. Final surrender
Gulf of Thailand
Can Tho
Ca Mau

Key
- North Vietnam
- South Vietnam
- Frontiers 1964
- Ho Chi Minh Trail
- Sihanouk Trail
- Major battle with US involvement
- Tet offensive 1968
- Final offensive 1974–75

0 300km
0 300 miles

The war in Vietnam
The war to unify Vietnam under Communist leadership was mainly fought in the south, with the Communists supplying their troops along jungle trails in neutral Laos and Cambodia. US planes bombed targets in the north.

the Ho Chi Minh and Sihanouk trails through neutral Cambodia and Laos. They used local knowledge and support to surprise the Americans, before melting away into the jungle. Their sniping skills and use of booby traps proved effective against the US troops, unused to guerrilla warfare.

The Tet Offensive

In mid-1967 General William Westmoreland, US commander in Vietnam, saw "light at the end of the tunnel" and hoped American soldiers could withdraw within two years. Events proved him wrong in January 1968, when the Viet Cong launched the Tet Offensive. The offensive struck targets across South Vietnam, aiming to incite a popular uprising. The Viet Cong even managed to attack the US embassy in the South's capital, Saigon.

Although, in the end, the Communist forces suffered severe casualties, the offensive had a huge psychological impact in the US. Public opinion that once supported the war now believed it unwinnable. Protests grew across the United States demanding that the troops

Mapping the war
The Chinese supplied the Viet Cong with cases to hold maps. This map shows the details of transport routes and the location of enemy bases.

come home. The rising death toll – more than 14,000 in 1968 alone – added to the anger. In March the increasingly unpopular Johnson announced that he would not seek re-election and sought peace talks with North Vietnam. Talks opened in Paris in May.

The US administration of Richard Nixon, elected in November 1968, introduced a policy of "Vietnamization", aimed at building up the strength and effectiveness of South Vietnamese forces while the US troops pulled out

with some dignity intact. At the same time, Nixon expanded the bombing campaign against Viet Cong bases and supply trails in Laos and Cambodia. This was kept secret from Americans back home. US and South Vietnamese forces then briefly invaded Cambodia in 1970, hoping to block the supply routes. None of these measures were successful, for at Easter 1972, the North Vietnamese Army launched a full-scale

58,336 The number of US troops killed during the war, while more than one million Vietnamese troops and civilians died.

invasion of the south with Soviet-supplied tanks and heavy artillery.

The attack was initially successful, giving North Vietnam control of large areas of the south, but was turned back by July. The following month, the last American combat division left Vietnam. Bombing raids against the north ceased in late December. In January 1973, the United States and North Vietnam signed the Paris Peace Accords and agreed a ceasefire. The US troops left the country a fortnight later.

AFTER

The Paris ceasefire agreement provided for talks between North and South Vietnam on the future of the country, but the hostilities continued after the Americans had left.

UNITED VIETNAM

In March 1975, the North Vietnamese finally overwhelmed the south, capturing Saigon in April and bringing an **end to the war**.

CAMBODIA

In 1975 **Khmer Rouge guerrillas** seized control of Cambodia and implemented a revolutionary restructuring of its society; over **one million Cambodians were murdered** in the process. Frontier disputes with Vietnam led to conflict in 1978. **Vietnam invaded Cambodia** in 1979 and installed a pro-Vietnamese government.

WAR WITH CHINA

North Vietnam had **support from both the Soviet Union and China** during its war with the United States, but turned more towards the USSR in 1978. The Vietnamese invasion of Cambodia led the **Chinese to invade** Vietnam briefly in February 1979.

The bare necessities
When Paul Schulz was first imprisoned, he was issued with a spoon, a cup, soap, toothpaste, and a toothbrush. Prisoners were allowed matches and pencils only towards the end of their captivity.

The soap provided by the guards was for personal hygiene and for washing clothes. It was a precious commodity and small fragments were carefully pressed together to form a larger piece.

Home-made bamboo clothes pegs

Matches were banned for most of the time Schulz was in prison. Prisoners were allowed to smoke but had to wait for a guard to light their cigarettes for them.

" … subjected him to **extreme mental and physical cruelties** … Through his resistance to those brutalities, **he contributed significantly** toward the eventual **abandonment of harsh treatment** by the North Vietnamese.**"**

FROM COMMANDER SCHULZ'S SILVER STAR CITATION, 1973

The Silver Star
On his return from captivity in 1973, Paul Schulz was awarded the Silver Star "for conspicuous gallantry and intrepidity while a prisoner of war in North Vietnam".

Prisoner in Vietnam

US naval pilot Paul Schulz was held captive for 1,945 days. After interrogation and torture, his treatment improved, but conditions were basic as is evident from the few possessions that a prisoner was allowed.

Paul Schulz was born in Erie, Pennsylvania, in 1934. After college, he joined the Naval Aviation Cadet Program in January 1956. He was commissioned as an Ensign in the US Navy in April 1957. In 1966 he flew the first of 150 combat missions against North Vietnam, flying an F-4 Phantom II fighter escorting strike aircraft to and from their targets.

Shot down and captured
On 16 November 1967, while on his second tour of duty operating off USS *Coral Sea*, Schulz flew a mission to a target near Hanoi, the capital of North Vietnam. The mission came under surface-to-air missile attack and his plane was hit. He and his fellow crew member ejected and landed safely in North Vietnam. They were captured and taken separately to Hanoi.

Schulz was first interrogated on 17 November 1967. As required by the Geneva Convention governing the treatment of prisoners of war, Schulz gave his name, rank, serial number,

Homecoming
This is how Lieutenant Commander Schulz looked on his first day back in the US, 16 March 1973, when he was reunited with his family at an airbase in California.

and date of birth. His interrogators wanted more, asking for information about the target his mission was attacking. When he refused to answer, he was subjected to the first of three sessions of torture. Forced to sit on the floor with his legs straight out in front of him, his head was pushed down so that his nose touched his knees while his arms were pulled up behind him. The pain was excruciating, as if the ligaments in the backs of his legs were being ripped out of his body. This method of torture was specifically designed to leave no scars, unless the interrogators made a mistake.

Learning to lie
When eventually forced to answer, Schulz named old targets. When his interrogators asked from which carrier he had flown from, he again gave false

information. They then started asking about his family and life in the US. When Schulz refused to answer, he was tortured again, this time suffering a dislocated jaw and shoulders.

Schulz spent his first six months of captivity in solitary confinement, then five years in various camps, including the notorious "Hanoi Hilton" and the "Zoo". He was eventually released on 13 March 1973 and returned home to continue his naval career, retiring from the US Navy in 1987.

Non-cooperation
US prisoners at the "Zoo" prison camp turn their backs on a North Vietnamese photographer, refusing to be photographed for propaganda purposes. The room they are in is nothing like their normal cells.

Revolutionary Wars in Latin America

The United States' fear of communism in its "backyard" led it to intervene in the internal affairs of Latin American and Caribbean nations throughout the Cold War, supporting right-wing and military governments against left-wing opponents. Its main focus was the revolutionary government of Fidel Castro in Cuba.

On 2 December 1956, Fidel Castro landed in Cuba with 81 men. His aim was to overthrow the dictatorial president, Fulgencio Batista. Castro had previously tried to depose Batista in 1953 when he launched an attack against the Moncado Barracks, but he was arrested and sent to prison. Released in an amnesty two years later, he fled to Mexico, where he founded the 26th of July Movement, named after the date of the failed attack. In Mexico he met other Cuban exiles, as well as Ernesto "Che" Guevara, a revolutionary from Argentina who shaped Castro's political beliefs.

Castro's second attempt at seizing power started disastrously, when most of his small band was quickly killed or taken prisoner. The few survivors,

including Castro and Guevara, began a guerrilla war, linking up with other resistance groups on the island. A government offensive launched in May 1958 was unsuccessful, Castro's forces winning victories against Batista's far larger army, which suffered mass desertions among its poorly trained conscripts. Castro now took advantage of the situation, invading central Cuba

81 The number of revolutionaries who landed with Fidel Castro in eastern Cuba on 2 December 1956. No more than 20 survived initial clashes with government troops.

and seizing many towns, including Santa Clara, which was taken after bloody house-to-house fighting.

Among the Cubans, discontent with Batista's corrupt regime was growing. Urban insurrection, including strikes and terrorism, weakened his grasp on power. Above all, Batista lacked the support of the American government, which was not prepared to intervene to keep him in office. On 1 January 1959, President Batista fled into exile in the Dominican Republic. Seven days later,

Young Sandinista soldiers
The Sandinista Liberation Front – named after Augusto Sandino, who fought the US occupation of Nicaragua in 1927–33 – was founded in 1961 and overthrew the Somoza dictatorship in 1979.

Castro's troops entered the Cuban capital, Havana. Castro was sworn in as prime minister on 16 February.

Castro was initially opposed to communism and wooed the United States, hiring a public relations firm to organize a charm offensive when he visited the US in April. However,

CENTRAL AMERICA

1 Cuba Dates 1953–59

2 Dominican Republic Dates 1965–66

3 Guatemala Dates 1966–84

4 Nicaragua Dates 1978–88

5 El Salvador Dates 1981–91

6 Grenada Date 1983

his restrictions on foreign land ownership, his expropriation of US companies' assets, notably those of the United Fruit Company, and his decision to buy oil from the USSR, caused the US to break diplomatic relations. Castro increasingly turned to the Soviet Union as the US steadily withdrew its support from Cuba.

In response, the new US government under President Kennedy organized an invasion of Cuba by 1,400 CIA-trained exiles. Kennedy hoped that discontent with Castro was substantial enough for Cubans to welcome a US invasion, but he was wrong. When the force landed at the Bay of Pigs, on 17 April 1961, it was met by the Cuban armed forces, and was crushed within just three days.

Castro's response was to embrace communism, prompting the US to impose a trade and travel embargo against Cuba that continued into the start of the 21st century. A further flashpoint arose in 1962, when Cuba allowed the Soviets to install nuclear missiles on the island. The result, the Cuban Missile Crisis, brought the world close to nuclear war. The crisis was resolved by an agreement that the missiles would be removed in exchange for a US pledge not to invade the island.

Exporting the revolution
Castro and Guevara were committed to world revolution, believing that small groups of dedicated fighters, as in Cuba,

Viva Cuba
Posters praising the revolution have done much to inspire the Cuban population and increase support for Castro's government. Many of the posters reflect the armed struggle that first overthrew Batista's government.

could be the focus for popular discontent leading to dramatic, profound change. Guevara also suggested that the power of the United States could be negated by a number of "Vietnams" occurring simultaneously. His belief proved fatal when he was killed leading a guerrilla

≪ BEFORE

The Americans have regularly intervened in the politics of the Caribbean and Central America to protect their own investments and prop up friendly governments.

AMERICAN INTERVENTION
The **Mexican Revolution** that began in 1910 destabilized the country, causing the US to send military missions in 1914 and again in 1916–17 in support of the moderate Venustiano Carranza. Further south, **instability in Nicaragua** caused the US to station marines in the country from 1916–33, while US ownership of the Panama Canal Zone led it to send troops to Panama City in 1914 to keep the order. In 1954 the Central Intelligence Agency **backed a coup** against President Jacobo Arbenz Guzmán's **socialist government of Guatemala**. In the Caribbean political upheavals saw **US Marines occupy Haiti** from 1915–34 **and the Dominican Republic** from 1914–24.

CUBA
The US took control of Cuba at the end of the **Spanish-American War ≪ 252–53** of 1898. The island became independent in 1902, but the new constitution gave the US the **right to intervene** in Cuban affairs. The US gave up this right in return for a trade deal in 1934.

Combating dissent

Repressive military governments in both El Salvador and Guatemala faced popular insurrections from left-wing guerrilla groups. Here, an El Salvador government unit prepares for an anti-guerrilla operation in 1984.

uprising in Bolivia in 1967. America's response to this revolutionary activity was to back anti-Communist groups, governments, and individuals with military aid and technical assistance.

Overt US military intervention was rare: troops occupied the Dominican Republic in 1965 and the Caribbean island of Grenada in 1983. However, from 1946 to 2001 the US military trained more than 61,000 Latin American soldiers and policemen in counter-insurgency tactics at the School of the Americas in Panama, including future military dictators Leopoldo Galtieri of Argentina and Manuel Noriega of Panama.

Social unrest, poverty, and repressive military governments led to a surge of discontent across the Americas during the 1960s and 70s. Guerrilla groups formed in Uruguay, Argentina, Peru, El Salvador, Guatemala, and Brazil. A left-wing government was elected in Chile but was then overthrown in a bloody CIA-backed military coup.

Only in Nicaragua was the Cuban model more fully replicated, when the Sandinista rebels overthrew the Somoza dictatorship in 1979. The US channelled covert aid to the "Contra" rebels, a process that was continued by US officials after the Sandinistas won re-election in 1984 and Congress cut off the Contras' funding. A secret plan to sell arms to Iran and hand the revenue over to the Contras caused a major political scandal in 1986. The United States continued to support the Contras until the Sandinistas lost power in the elections of 1990.

The vicious civil war that raged in Nicaragua during the 1980s was seen elsewhere, in Guatemala and El Salvador, where the US-backed

governments used death squads against opponents. Murders were common, one paramilitary unit killing human rights campaigner Archbishop Oscar Romero in his cathedral in San Salvador, capital of El Salvador, in 1984.

The end of the Cold War in the 1990s, together with US support for human rights and the acceptance of elected left-wing governments, ended many of the insurrections. On the other side, many groups abandoned their belief in revolutionary struggle and embraced democracy as a path to power.

AFTER

Cuba has exported its revolution around the world, sending its well-trained armed forces to support a number of friendly, like-minded governments abroad.

CUBA
Cuban troops fought in **Angola's civil war 330–31 »** from 1976–91, and in Ethiopia in 1977. Cuba also supported the socialist government of **Maurice Bishop** in Grenada after 1979. More recently, Cuban doctors have worked in Venezuela in return for **much-needed oil imports**. Cuban reliance on Soviet support ended with the collapse of the USSR in 1991, causing widespread economic hardship on the island. In 2006, in poor health, Fidel Castro passed power to his brother, Raúl.

BADGE OF THE FARC GUERRILLAS

COLOMBIA
Colombia has the **longest-running armed conflict** in the Americas. Government troops, left-wing guerrillas (e.g. FARC), and right-wing paramilitaries have fought for power since the mid-1960s. The hostilities have been fuelled by the profits from the **cocaine trade**.

"But my voice will not be stifled ... Condemn me. It does not matter. **History will absolve me.**"

FIDEL CASTRO, FACING TRIAL FOR ARMED REVOLT, 1953

African Wars of Independence

At the end of World War II, European rule was still entrenched across most of Africa. The colonial powers ruthlessly suppressed uprisings against their rule, yet within 30 years almost the entire continent had received its independence, although not always in peaceful circumstances.

White settlement in the British East African colony of Kenya was opposed by many of the Kikuyu people. In 1948 they organized secret groups, soon known as Mau Mau, to drive white farmers off Kikuyu land. The planned killings and arson attacks began in October 1952, prompting the British to proclaim a state of emergency and deploy troops. Many Kikuyu were interned or deported to reserves in the highlands. The British also arrested Jomo Kenyatta, a future president of independent Kenya, on suspicion of leading the revolt, even though he had denounced the movement.

A Mau Mau massacre of more than 80 Africans at Lari in the Rift Valley, in March 1953, led to widespread revulsion among the Kikuyu themselves, as well as from other Kenyan tribes. The Mau Mau revolt was eventually crushed in 1954, although the state of emergency

Mau Mau prison camp
The British interned around 150,000 Kikuyu in concentration camps during the Mau Mau rising. Conditions in the camps were grim and many people died of cholera and other diseases.

remained until 1960. The revolt was marked by great brutality on both sides. Reports vary, but it is thought that as many as 12,000 to 20,000 Kikuyu lost their lives, while being responsible for the deaths of 2,000 African civilians themselves. Some 68 European farmers and 167 British troops were killed or died before the conflict ended in late 1954. Many of the Kikuyu sent to detention camps also perished.

Algeria

A far more dangerous revolt against European rule erupted in Algeria when the Algerian National Liberation Front

> "The **Algerian departments** are part of the **French Republic**."
> FRENCH PRIME MINISTER PIERRE MENDÈS-FRANCE, 12 NOVEMBER 1954

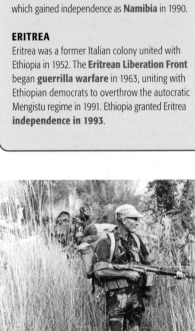

Folding stock

30-round magazine

The AK47
The Soviet-designed AK47 assault rifle has become the most popular gun in the world, with more than 70 million produced. It has been the weapon of choice for guerrilla movements around the world.

(FLN) rose in revolt against the French in 1954. Algeria had been a French colony since 1830 and many of its inhabitants were white French settlers who wished to remain part of France. The FLN's 800 or so guerrilla fighters concentrated first on terrorist attacks on isolated rural targets but met a violent response from the 20,000-strong French army: 12,000 Algerians

1 MILLION
An estimate of the number of French settlers and pro-French Algerians – around 10 per cent of the country's population – who fled Algeria for France once independence was granted in 1962.

were killed in retaliation for the deaths of 123 settlers at Philippeville, on 20 August 1955. However, FLN attacks boosted the group's standing in the country and increasingly united Arabs and Berbers behind its campaign.

In 1956 the FLN was strong enough to switch its campaign to the capital, Algiers, planting bombs at the offices of Air France and two other sites on 30 September. The campaign swiftly gained momentum, with more than 8,000 bombings or shootings a month and a general strike in 1957. France's 10th Parachute Division under General Jacques Massu gained police powers in Algiers, which it deployed savagely against alleged FLN members and their supporters. The army's tactics alienated many ordinary Algerians. Taking, in effect, the settlers' side, the army was seen to be strongly against proposals made by the French government to negotiate a deal with the FLN.

On 13 May 1958, Massu seized power from the French authorities in Algeria with support from elements in the

French army, which in turn plotted a coup against the French home government. A constitutional crisis erupted in France that led to the collapse of the Fourth Republic and the return to power of the wartime Free French leader, General Charles de Gaulle. It was assumed that de Gaulle would support continued French rule in Algeria, but when he came out in favour of a limited settlement in 1959, the settlers turned against him. An insurrection broke out in January 1960 and de Gaulle was greeted with riots when he later visited Algiers. Under the leadership of General Raoul Salan, former leader of the army in Algeria, the terrorist Organization de l'Armée Secrète (OAS) began its own campaign against the FLN, staging a second coup in April 1961. Events led to the introduction of a state of emergency being declared in both Algeria and France.

By now the French army had lost control of all Algeria except the major cities, while the conflict was tearing French society apart. De Gaulle began secret negotiations with the FLN in Switzerland, in December 1961, and eventually offered Algeria the choice of integration into France, self-rule, or full independence. When a referendum

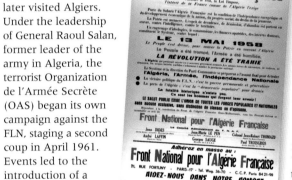

"Algeria is French"
Algerian settlers wishing to remain part of France had wide support in mainland France itself.

overwhelmingly backed independence, the French government handed power over to the FLN and Algeria became independent in July 1962.

Independence
By this time, all but one of the remaining French colonies in Africa had received their independence, most in 1960. That same year, Belgium gave independence to its vast Congo colony, with Rwanda and Burundi following in 1962. Britain had also started to relinquish control, giving independence to Ghana in 1957, making it the first independent black state in Africa. Nigeria and Somalia followed in 1960, with Sierra Leone and Tanzania (Tanganyika) joining them in 1961. The rest of British Africa was independent by 1968. The only exception to this was Southern Rhodesia, where the white settlers refused to accept black majority rule, illegally declaring independence in 1965. A lengthy guerrilla war broke out, and it was 15 years before majority rule was finally accepted, in 1980, when the country became independent as Zimbabwe.

ZIMBABWE The name of the country means "great house built of stone boulders" in the Shona language and is used in tribute to Great Zimbabwe, the 11th–15th-century stone-built capital of the Great Zimbabwe trading empire.

While most European countries gave up their African colonies, Portugal tried to maintain its empire. Resistance to colonial rule began in Guinea-Bissau, the Cape Verde Islands, and Angola in 1961, and Mozambique in 1964. The cost of the colonial wars that resulted almost bankrupted Portugal and led to a revolution in 1974 that overthrew the authoritarian government in Lisbon and established democratic rule. All four colonies, as well as Sao Tomé & Principe, were independent by 1975.

Three colonies now remained in Africa – Western Sahara, Namibia, and Eritrea – each of them having to fight for their independence from other African nations.

WESTERN SAHARA
Spain's withdrawal from its colony of Western Sahara in 1976 led Morocco and Mauritania to occupy and partition the country. **Polisario Liberation Front** guerrillas waged war against both occupying nations, forcing Mauritania to withdraw its claim in 1979, whereupon Morocco occupied the whole country. Guerrilla warfare continued until a **UN ceasefire in 1991**; the future status of the country remains contested.

NAMIBIA
Former German South-West Africa was mandated to South Africa in 1920. SWAPO (South West Africa People's Organization) fighters seeking independence started a **guerrilla war against South African rule** after racist apartheid laws were introduced in 1966. The end of South Africa's involvement in **Angola's civil war 330–31 »** to the north led to its withdrawal from the territory, which gained independence as **Namibia** in 1990.

ERITREA
Eritrea was a former Italian colony united with Ethiopia in 1952. The **Eritrean Liberation Front** began **guerrilla warfare** in 1963, uniting with Ethiopian democrats to overthrow the autocratic Mengistu regime in 1991. Ethiopia granted Eritrea **independence in 1993**.

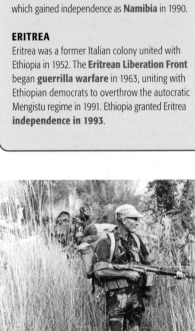

Rhodesian army patrol
Rhodesian security forces fought a vicious 14-year bush war against guerrillas of the Patriotic Front, led by Robert Mugabe among others, before black majority rule was achieved in 1980 with Mugabe as prime minister.

KEY MOMENT

THE SUEZ CRISIS

In July 1956 President Gamal Abdel Nasser of Egypt nationalized the Suez Canal. Britain resented loss of control over the canal, while France objected to Nasser's support of FLN guerrillas in Algeria. The two nations colluded with Israel to attack Egypt, invading the canal zone in October supposedly to keep warring Egyptian and Israeli forces separate from each other. International pressure forced Britain and France to withdraw, a fiasco that ended their imperial pretensions in Africa.

Post-colonial Africa

Africa has been plagued by war ever since its nations gained independence. Civil wars, often based on ethnic divisions, military coups, border disputes, and interference from the two superpowers or former colonial rulers, have cost millions of lives and blighted the development of this poor continent.

The somewhat hasty independence of the Belgian Congo in June 1960 created chaos. Within days, the army mutinied and thousands of white Belgian citizens became refugees. The former colonial power sent paratroopers in to help them. That July, the southern copper-rich state of Katanga declared its independence and employed European mercenaries to protect it. The United Nations intervened to restore peace. UN secretary general, Dag Hammarskjöld, was killed in an accidental plane crash on a peace mission to Katanga in 1961. Earlier in the year the prime minister, Patrice Lumumba, had been assassinated.

By now the country had broken into four virtually independent states, which were eventually reunited under central rule through the use of US arms, UN and Belgian troops, and white mercenaries. In 1965 Joseph Mobutu seized power. He ruled the renamed state of Zaire as a ruthless dictator, draining the national treasury for his own use until his overthrow in 1997.

Biafra
In Nigeria, independent from Britain since 1960, the Ibo of the southeast dominated both the military and the central government, but felt threatened when moves to strengthen the central government led to anti-Ibo massacres in 1966. The next year, the Ibo governor, Odumegwu Ojukwu, declared the oil-rich eastern region independent as Biafra. Britain and the Soviet Union supported the central government, while France and Rhodesia backed the rebels. Biafra held out until a naval blockade, Soviet arms, and starvation led to its surrender in 1970. More than a million Biafrans died in the conflict.

Angola
One of Africa's longest civil wars took place in Angola, after its independence from Portugal in 1975. The Marxist Popular Movement for the Liberation of Angola (MPLA) seized power and, with Cuban and Soviet aid, attacked the US- and Zaire-backed National Liberation Front of Angola (FNLA) and the South African-backed National Union for the Total Independence of Angola (UNITA). The MPLA defeated the FNLA. Alarmed by this, and by the presence of Cuban troops, the United States switched its support to UNITA.

The civil war raged into the 1980s. In 1987 South Africa invaded Angola to support UNITA. Fighting continued until 1991, when the UN brokered a peace deal that led to elections won by the MPLA. Jonas Savimbi, UNITA's founder, rejected this and resumed guerrilla war. A further agreement created a new government of both MPLA and UNITA, but this collapsed in 1997 and fighting resumed in 1998. In 2002 government troops assassinated Savimbi, which put an end to the war.

South African interventions
South Africa's racist policy of apartheid, or separate development, in place since 1949, had a huge impact throughout the region. The country mounted an invasion of Angola from Namibia, where its soldiers were fighting against the South West Africa People's Organization (SWAPO). South Africa and white Rhodesia also fomented a civil war in Mozambique to prevent Somora Machel's government supporting the struggle for majority rule in their countries. War raged in Mozambique during the whole of the 1980s until the ending of apartheid in South Africa led to peace in 1992.

The Horn of Africa
Border disputes and civil war have frequently destabilized the Horn of Africa. In 1977 war broke out when Somalia invaded the ethnic-Somali Ogaden region of Ethiopia.

The US supported Somalia, while Soviet and Cuban troops backed Ethiopia. Border disputes between Ethiopia and its former colony, Eritrea, also erupted into war in 1998. In 1991 Somalia collapsed into civil war as rival clans and warlords struggled for supremacy. Two of its northern regions splintered off, while the country's central government disintegrated.

Tensions in Sudan between the Muslim north and the animist and Christian southern region led to a lengthy war of independence in the south as soon as the country gained independence in 1956. A peace deal was signed in 1972 but fighting resumed in 1983 when Sharia, or Islamic law, was introduced across the whole country – including the non-Muslim southern region. A comprehensive peace agreement came into force in 2005, establishing a power-sharing government. Since then, ethnic violence in the western region of Darfur between government-backed Arab militia forces

> ## "But in the end, **the ballot must decide, not bullets**."
> JONAS SAVIMBI, LEADER OF UNITA IN ANGOLA, 1975

BEFORE

Europe's African colonies often had to struggle for their independence, and their colonial masters did little to prepare them for self-rule when the time came.

INDEPENDENCE
From the 1950s, the European powers began giving their **African colonies independence ‹‹ 328–29**. The handover of power was usually peaceful, although major **guerrilla wars** broke out in Kenya, Algeria, and four Portuguese colonies against their colonial ruling powers. Most African countries had **no experience of self-rule** or any form of **multi-party democracy**. The Belgian Congo, for example, held its inaugural, local elections in 1957 and was then given only six months to prepare for full independence

BELGIAN TROOPS LEAVE THE CONGO, 1960

in 1960. Almost all the Belgian civil servants who ran the country left in the weeks leading up to independence, **without training the local people to take over** in their place.

THE COLD WAR
The **Cold War confrontation** during the latter part of the 20th century **‹‹ 312–13** between the USSR and the US had a major impact in Africa. The rival superpowers sought to **extend their influence and power** by involvement with the new African states.

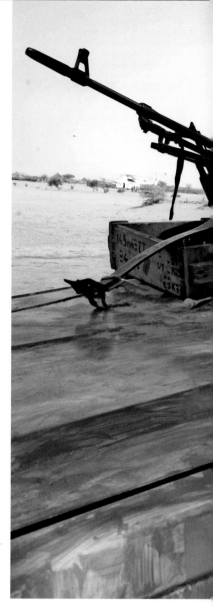

Milkor MGL Mk 1
South Africa developed this six-shot revolver grenade launcher for its campaigns in Angola and elsewhere.

Stock can be folded forwards

Cylinder holds six 40mm grenades

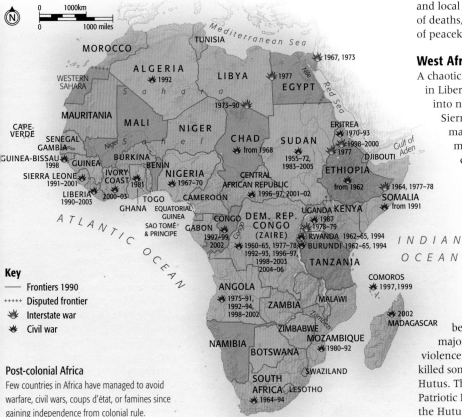

Darfur
Fighters throughout the Horn of Africa, like these in Darfur in Sudan, have converted pickup trucks into "technicals" armed with heavy machine-guns.

Africa remains a war-torn continent, with many long-running conflicts unresolved. In the wake of war, abject poverty, disease, and oppression are all too widespread.

SOMALIA

Somalia has been without a stable government since **civil war broke out in 1991**. Rival warlords ignored a limited UN peacekeeping intervention in 1992, while a US attempt in 1993 to create a base for humanitarian relief ended in disaster with US and Somali casualties. Attempts to set up a **new government in 2004** failed when it was overthrown by militias allied to the Islamic Courts Union (ICU) that sought to institute Sharia law. Fearful of

US TROOPS IN SOMALIA, 1992

an Islamic state on its borders, Ethiopian forces attacked the ICU in 2006. Today, Somalia remains a "failed state", with international intervention limited to attempts to prevent **Somali pirates holding ships for ransom** in the Indian Ocean.

SUDAN

The peace agreement that ended the civil war in 2005 set up a **power-sharing government** uniting the north and south of the country. A six-year period of transition will lead to a **referendum** in the south on secession in 2011.

---

and local tribes has caused thousands of deaths, despite the constant presence of peacekeeping forces.

West Africa

A chaotic and complex civil war erupted in Liberia in 1990 that spilled over into neighbouring Ivory Coast and Sierra Leone. The three wars were marked by great brutality, with many of the rebel groups using child soldiers to mutilate their opponents. The war in Sierra Leone finally ended in 2001 when a large UN and British force restored order. War crimes courts were set up in Sierra Leone in 2002 and Liberia in 2007 to try the rebel leaders.

Rwanda, Congo, and Zaire

Ethnic tensions in Rwanda between the minority Tutsi and majority Hutu erupted in genocidal violence in 1994 when extreme Hutus killed some 800,000 Tutsis and moderate Hutus. The Tutsi-dominated Rwandan Patriotic Front subsequently defeated the Hutu government, prompting some

two million Hutus to flee to refugee camps in neighbouring Burundi, Zaire, Tanzania, and Uganda.

In 1996 clashes broke out in eastern Zaire as Hutu militia forces launched raids against Rwanda and attacked local Tutsis. The Tutsis fought off the Hutu militias and then allied themselves with rebel Zaire leader, Laurent Kabila, to end

5.4 MILLION
The estimated number of people who have died in the Democratic Republic of the Congo's civil war since 1996.

Mobutu's rule. But Kabila failed to bring peace to Zaire, causing the Tutsis to rebel against him in 1998. Rwanda and Uganda backed the rebellion, while Angola, Zimbabwe, Chad, Namibia, and Sudan sent troops to support Kabila. A peace deal was reached in 2002 and all but the Rwandan troops withdrew from the by now-renamed Democratic Republic of the Congo. A further coup against the new Congolese leader, Kabila's son, Joseph, in 2004 brought renewed war. A fragile peace was restored in 2006, yet violence continues.

Post-colonial Africa

Few countries in Africa have managed to avoid warfare, civil wars, coups d'état, or famines since gaining independence from colonial rule.

Key
- — Frontiers 1990
- ++++ Disputed frontier
- ⚜ Interstate war
- ⚜ Civil war

Map labels:
TUNISIA
MOROCCO
ALGERIA 1992
LIBYA 1977
EGYPT 1967, 1973
1973–90
WESTERN SAHARA
MAURITANIA
MALI
NIGER
CHAD from 1968
SUDAN 1955–72, 1983–2005
ERITREA 1970–93
1998–2000
1977
DJIBOUTI
CAPE VERDE
SENEGAL
GAMBIA
GUINEA-BISSAU 1998
GUINEA
SIERRA LEONE 1991–2001
LIBERIA 1990–2003
IVORY COAST 1981
BURKINA
BENIN
NIGERIA 1967–70
GHANA
TOGO
EQUATORIAL GUINEA
CAMEROON
CENTRAL AFRICAN REPUBLIC 1996–97, 2001–02
ETHIOPIA from 1962
SOMALIA from 1991
UGANDA 1987, 1978–79
KENYA
SAO TOMÉ & PRINCIPE
GABON
CONGO 1997–99, 2002
DEM. REP. CONGO (ZAIRE) 1960–65, 1977–78, 1992–93, 1996–97, 1998–2003, 2004–06
RWANDA 1962–65, 1994
BURUNDI 1962–65, 1994
TANZANIA
COMOROS 1997,1999
ANGOLA 1975–91, 1992–94, 1998–2002
ZAMBIA
MALAWI
MADAGASCAR 2002
ZIMBABWE
MOZAMBIQUE 1980–92
NAMIBIA
BOTSWANA
SWAZILAND
SOUTH AFRICA 1964–94
LESOTHO
2000–03

Mediterranean Sea
ATLANTIC OCEAN
INDIAN OCEAN
Gulf of Aden
Red Sea

0 1000km
0 1000 miles

« BEFORE

The British withdrawal from India saw the subcontinent divided roughly on religious grounds, creating two rival states and a number of other territories.

PARTITION

The British announcement in 1945 that it supported the early **independence of India as a united state** divided Muslims from Hindus. Many **Muslims feared Hindu domination** of the new state and wished to set up their own independent, Muslim nation of Pakistan. Lord Mountbatten, the last British viceroy, decided in June 1947 to partition the empire between the **two new states of India and Pakistan** and to bring independence forward from June 1948 to 15 August 1947. **Burma and Ceylon** (now Sri Lanka) were to become independent in 1948. **Millions lost their lives** during the massacres that accompanied India and Pakistan's transition to independence, and **millions more became refugees** as Hindus and Muslims fled to safety in their respective states.

KASHMIR

British India included a number of **semi-independent princely states**, which were allowed to decide which new country to join. The **Hindu Maharajah of Kashmir** hesitated before deciding to join India in October 1947, despite the fact that more than **three-quarters of his people were Muslim** and wanted to join Pakistan.

FLAG OF PAKISTAN

South Asian Wars

Since independence from Britain, a number of South Asian states have fought a series of wars. The conflict between India and Pakistan has been by far the lengthiest, and has become potentially the most dangerous, as both states are now in possession of nuclear weapons.

The decision of the Maharajah of Kashmir to join India in 1947 provoked conflict between the region's Muslim tribesmen, fighting to join Pakistan, and Hindus from around Jammu in the south, who wanted to stay in India. Both India and Pakistan moved armies into the province, India denouncing Pakistan as the aggressor and appealing to the United Nations for support. In January 1949, the UN established a demarcation line between the two sides that left Kashmir divided.

The end of British rule left many of India's borders and territories unclear. The Muslim Nizam of Hyderabad (its sovereign – from the Urdu *Nizam-ul-Mulk*, literally "administrator of the realm") wished to keep his largely Hindu state independent. The Indian Army invaded in 1948 and forced the state to join the Indian Union. Five French territories joined the Union in 1954, and the Portuguese colonies of Goa, Daman, and Diu were later annexed by force in 1961.

New Kashmir conflict

In 1962 Chinese troops crossed over India's mountainous northern borders. The Indians were ill prepared but, after brief fighting, the Chinese forces left the northeastern region but remained in occupation in the Aksai Chin area.

India's defeat by China encouraged Pakistan to renew its Kashmir conflict. In 1965 troops from both sides poured over their common borders in Kashmir, Punjab, and the Rann of Kutch in the far south. Fighting with tanks, artillery, and jet fighters continued for most of the year until a truce was negotiated by the Soviet Union in Tashkent in 1966.

The birth of Bangladesh

When originally created in 1947, Pakistan consisted of western and eastern parts separated by 1,760km (1,100 miles) of India. The Bengalis of East Pakistan had little in common with the Pakistanis of the west – other than their religion – and felt economically exploited by the government in West Pakistan. From 1954 the Awami League, led by Sheikh Mujibur Rahman, pressed for autonomy, winning a major electoral victory in December 1971. Pakistan's government twice postponed calling a new assembly and imprisoned Rahman, which prompted a general strike in East Pakistan. Then, on 26 March, Rahman declared East Pakistan independent as Bangladesh, and set up a government-in-exile in Calcutta, India. This secession led to civil war, as Mukti Bahini

> **PAKISTAN** literally means "land of the pure". It comes from the Urdu words *pak* ("pure") and *stan* ("land").

guerrillas fought the Pakistan Army. Possibly 1 million Bengalis were killed in the war, with another 10 million fleeing to safety in India.

Indian support for the rebels led the Pakistan Air Force to launch a pre-emptive strike against Indian airfields on 3 December. The war that followed was short. The Indian Army invaded Bengal, while tank battles broke out along the border with West Pakistan. Pakistan's army was quickly defeated, surrendering unconditionally on 16 December. Rahman was released from prison and returned to lead his country to independence. Pakistan finally recognized Bangladesh in 1974.

Further tensions

Elsewhere in the Indian subcontinent, Maoist guerrillas carried out a lengthy insurgency against the royal government of Nepal that led to a takeover by the Maoist Communist Party in 2008, who

SOUTH ASIA

1 **First and Second Indo-Pakistani Wars**
Dates 1947–48, 1965
Location Kashmir and the India-Pakistan border

2 **Sino-Indian War**
Date 1962
Location Points on border between China and India

3 **Third Indo-Pakistani War**
Date 1971
Location Chiefly Bangladesh

4 **Tamil Separatist Movement**
Dates 1983–present
Location Sri Lanka

M24 Chaffee

This US-made tank from 1944 was used in the 1971 Indo-Pakistan War, when Pakistani Chaffees fared badly against more modern Soviet-made Indian T-55s.

On top of the world
Part of the war between Indian and Pakistani troops over Kashmir has been conducted high among the mountain peaks and glaciers of the Himalayas.

Caterpillar tracks faced with rubber track blocks

Armour plate 25-mm (1-in) thick

Sri Lankan soldiers on patrol
Sri Lankan troops patrol outside their capital, Colombo, after Tamil Tiger rebels sent light aircraft on suicide missions against government targets in early 2009.

declared it a republic. Sikh Nationalists seeking an autonomous state in the Punjab, and separatist movements in the eastern provinces of Nagaland and Mizoram have all threatened the unity of India.

The biggest conflict in the region took place in Sri Lanka between the majority, mainly Buddhist, Sinhalese and the minority Hindu Tamils of the north and east who have been striving to establish an independent homeland. A civil war began in 1983, with the Liberation

Tigers of Tamil Eelam (Tamil Tigers) seizing territory in the north of Sri Lanka and conducting attacks against several government targets. India's government tried to arbitrate in 1984 and intervened militarily in 1987, as it feared the war might involve its own Tamil population in Tamil Nadu state. Indian troops left in 1990, but the violence continued throughout the 1990s. A ceasefire was agreed in 2001 but did not last long, as residual mutual suspicions caused the government of Sri Lanka to resume hostilities. The final Tamil-held towns fell to the Sri Lankan army in early 2009. Up to 100,000 people, including many civilians, have died in this war to date.

GOLDEN TEMPLE SIEGE

During 1984 Sikh extremists demanding an autonomous Sikh state in the Indian province of Punjab took over the Golden Temple in Amritsar – Sikhism's holiest shrine – and used it to store weapons. The threat of civil war in the Punjab led the Indian prime minister, Indira Gandhi, to send in troops to the temple and to 37 other Sikh shrines, on 5 June, to expel the militants. At least 300 Sikhs were killed in the operation. Four months later, two of Gandhi's Sikh bodyguards assassinated her in revenge. Anti-Sikh riots across India killed 3,000 Sikhs in retaliatory attacks.

AFTER

Relations between India and Pakistan have remained strained up to the present day. Existing tensions have been worsened by Pakistan-based Islamic extremist groups.

NUCLEAR CONTEST

India conducted a **nuclear test** in 1974, which was later followed by Pakistan in 1998. The ownership of nuclear weapons by the two nations, **hostile to each other,** makes any discord hold implications for the world. The first war following the feat of nuclear status by both states took place in the Kargil district of Kashmir in 1999, when Pakistani soldiers and **Kashmiri militants** entered Indian Kashmir. The Pakistani government blamed the fighting on independent Kashmiri insurgents, but **Pakistani paramilitary forces** were involved.

EXTREMIST ATTACKS

Islamic extremists operating out of Pakistan have **targeted several cities in India,** most notably Mumbai, where attacks in 2006 and 2008 each killed some 200 people. **India has blamed Pakistan** for not cracking down on extremist groups based in the country.

« **BEFORE**

Both the Zionists and Arab nationalists were disappointed that World War I did not lead to the independence that they thought had been promised by the Allies.

ZIONISM AND THE ARAB REVOLT

During World War I, British leaders encouraged the Ottoman empire's Arab subjects to rise in revolt in the hope of winning **independence after the war**. However, in 1917 British Foreign Secretary, **Arthur Balfour, promised support** for the establishment of a **Jewish national home** in Palestine. The World Zionist Congress had called for this in 1897, partly in response to anti-Semitism in Russia, where many Jews lived.

650,000 Approximate number of Jews living in Palestine at independence in 1948, ten times as many as in 1918.

THE BRITISH MANDATE

After World War I, Britain ruled Palestine under a **League of Nations mandate**. Tension between Jews and Palestinians rose as Jewish immigration increased. Britain suppressed a major **Palestinian revolt** in 1936–39, but also restricted Jewish immigration, a move resisted by militant Jewish groups. The **experience of the Holocaust** meant that Jewish immigration and support for a Jewish state greatly increased after World War II. In November 1947, the United Nations decided to partition Palestine into Jewish and Arab states. The **Arab League rejected this plan** as contrary to the wishes of the majority of the local population. However, **Israel proclaimed its independence** on 14 May 1948.

The **Arab-Israeli Conflict**

The state of Israel was born in warfare in 1948 when the neighbouring Arab countries attempted to create a single state of Palestine. Israel has remained embroiled in conflict ever since, fighting three subsequent major wars and engaging in an increasingly bitter struggle with the Palestinian people.

1974: Demilitarized zone held by UN

1982: Israeli invasion of southern Lebanon to drive out PLO and Syrian troops

1975: Demilitarized zone held by UN after 2nd Sinai agreement

1979–82: returned to Egypt

Key
- ▪ Israel 1949
- ▪ Occupied by Israel after 1967 war
- ▪ Occupied by Israel after 1973 war
- — Frontiers 1949
- +++++ Disputed frontier
- ▪ Demilitarized zone held by UN after 2nd Sinai agreement 1975
- ➡ Israeli invasion of Lebanon 1982

Arab-Israeli wars 1967–82
In the aftermath of the Six-Day War and the Yom Kippur War, Israel gained control of formerly Arab- or Palestinian-held territory. Sinai was returned to Egypt in 1982. The Golan Heights remains under Israeli control, while parts of the West Bank are governed by the Palestinian Authority.

O n 14 May 1948, as the British mandate over Palestine ended, David Ben-Gurion, the first prime minister of Israel, proclaimed the establishment of the State of Israel. The next day, troops from the armies of Egypt, Transjordan (to be renamed Jordan in 1949), Syria, Lebanon, and Iraq attacked. The Arabs claimed that they were seeking to establish a unified, religiously neutral state of Palestine in accordance with the wishes of the non-Jewish majority of the population; Jews took note of anti-Semitic statements by some Arab leaders.

Although they were initially probably better-equipped, the Arab forces had no common strategy or command. The Israelis, meanwhile, felt they were fighting for their lives and had a strong and unified command. The Jewish militia, Haganah, was well trained and disciplined, and had bought arms from Europe, as well as receiving enough aid to equip itself with artillery, ammunition, and a small navy and air force. By the end of the war, the Israeli forces also greatly outnumbered those of their Arab opponents.

Two weeks of bitter fighting saw the Israelis halt the Arab offensives and gain ground. In further periods of fighting, interspersed with truces, the newly established Israel Defence Force enlarged Israel's land corridor east to Jerusalem and captured new territory in Galilee in the north and the Negev in the south. The war ended in January 1949 with Israel occupying all of the old British Palestine mandate except the Gaza Strip, taken over by Egypt, and the West Bank, taken over by Jordan. Israel now held a substantially larger area than in the 1947 UN partition plan.

The approach to war and the war itself were marked by atrocities on both sides. Many Palestinians were forced from their homes during the conflict, mostly settling as refugees in Gaza and the West Bank. In subsequent years a similarly large number of Jews migrated

750,000 The approximate number of **Palestinians forced out of their homes and made refugees during fighting for the creation of Israel in 1948–49.**

Jerusalem conflict

The ancient Jewish capital of Jerusalem was the scene of heavy fighting during the first Arab-Israeli War of 1948 and was partitioned between Israel and Jordan in 1949. The city was reunited under Israeli control in 1967.

Canal – owned mainly by the British government and French investors – provoked Britain and France to collude secretly with Israel. The plan was for Israel to invade Sinai, supposedly to forestall an Egyptian attack, giving Britain and France the pretext to seize the canal, while keeping the warring Israelis and Egyptians apart.

Israel duly attacked Egypt on 29 October and, following Nasser's refusal to accept a ceasefire, British and French forces attacked Egyptian bases. Then, on 5 November, they occupied Port Said at the entrance of the canal. Widespread condemnation of the attack from the United States and other nations, and a collapse in the value of the British pound, forced both the French and the British governments to suspend operations on 7 November.

This squalid event marked the end of any major British or French imperial role in the region. Israeli forces were successful in lifting the blockade of Eilat and reducing attacks from Gaza. UN peacekeepers then arrived in the region to keep the peace.

The Six-Day War

The Suez crisis of 1956 made the Egyptian president an Arab hero for successfully standing up to British and French forces. Nasser bolstered his armed forces with Soviet arms, while Israel bought state-of-the art aircraft from France and tanks from Britain and the United States. Through the mid-1960s Israel and Syria also clashed

especially fiercely along their border. Claiming that Israel was preparing an invasion of Syria, Nasser forced the UN Sinai peacekeepers to withdraw in May 1967 and, along with Jordan, Iraq, and Syria, massed troops along Israel's borders. Once again, Israel struck first.

On 5 June 1967, the Israeli air force launched a series of devastating raids against its enemies, virtually destroying the Egyptian, Syrian, and Jordanian air forces. Israeli troops invaded Sinai and reached the Suez Canal on 8 June. Its troops also occupied the entire West Bank, gaining control of the whole of Jerusalem for the first time, and seized the Golan Heights from Syria, advancing 48km (30 miles) towards Damascus, the Syrian capital. When the fighting stopped on 10 June, Israel had doubled the size of its territory, gained new defensible borders along the Suez Canal, the Jordan river, and the Golan Heights, and had removed the threat of enemy guns bombarding its cities.

600,000 The number of Palestinians Israel brought under its control after gaining territory during the Six-Day War in 1967.

Yom Kippur

The Six-Day War brought Israel military success but no better security, as none of the neighbouring states would trade peace in return for lost territory. Egypt, in particular, was humiliated by the outcome of the war and its loss of Sinai, and waged a three-year campaign of raids and artillery fire across the Suez Canal. On 6 October 1973, its new leader, Anwar Sadat, planned a surprise attack against Israel in alliance with Syria to coincide with the Jewish holy day of Yom Kippur. Egyptian troops crossed the canal and headed into Sinai, supported by surface-to-air missile batteries and portable anti-tank missiles that limited the traditional Israeli strengths of air and tank power. More than 100 Israeli planes were shot down by the Soviet-supplied missile launchers in the first days of the war.

By 9 October, the Egyptians had overstretched their lines of supply and outreached their defensive air cover and so ground to a halt. Supplied with new US equipment, the Israelis went on the offensive on 16 October. The Israelis broke through between two Egyptian armies and crossed to the west bank of the Suez Canal, encircling the Egyptian Third Army on the east bank.

To the north, Israel fought off a Syrian offensive against the Golan Heights and destroyed around 900 Syrian tanks in a massive battle. Its forces then advanced to within 40km (25 miles) of Damascus.

A UN ceasefire on 24 October ended the Yom Kippur War, the fourth and, to date, final attempt by the Arab states to invade and overthrow Israel.

willingly and unwillingly to Israel from their homes in Arab countries. All these events have left a legacy of bitterness that persists in the 21st century.

The Suez Crisis

Following the 1948–49 war, border clashes and terrorist and counter-terrorist operations continued. The new Egyptian government under President Gamal Abdel Nasser was also seeking to end the long-standing Anglo-French involvement in his country. In 1955 Egypt closed the Gulf of Aqaba, thereby blockading Eilat, Israel's only outlet to the Red Sea. The subsequent Egyptian nationalization, in 1956, of the Suez

MIRAGE FIGHTER

The Mirage IIIC supersonic fighter aircraft was manufactured by Dassault Aviation in France and sold to the Israelis, for whom it played a major role in the Six-Day War of 1967. The single-seater, medium-weight interceptor was armed with twin 30mm cannon capable of firing air-to-air missiles. It proved particularly effective fighting against the Soviet-made Mikoyan-Gurevich MiG-17s and MiG-21s of the Syrian air force, as well as providing cover for attacks on Egyptian and Syrian aircraft on the ground.

Later Mirage variants were designed both as multi-role fighters and as reconnaissance aircraft. Those in Israeli service included some aircraft bought from France and others designed and built in Israel.

Israel and Egypt made peace, but conflict in the region continued. Israel kept much of the land it had captured and Palestinians fought to create a nation of their own.

PEACE TALKS

President Anwar Sadat of Egypt visited Jerusalem in 1977, marking the first **recognition of Israel** by an Arab head of state. Talks led to a **peace agreement**, signed in Washington, DC, in 1979. **Israel handed back the Sinai**, but not Gaza, to Egypt by 1982.

LEBANON

Palestinian exiles set up the **Palestine Liberation Organization (PLO)** in Jordan in 1964 to bring together Palestinian political parties. In 1970 the PLO moved its headquarters to Beirut, in Lebanon, which was home to more than 300,000 Palestinian refugees. The PLO used the country as a base from which to **fire rockets at northern Israel**. In retaliation, **Israel invaded Lebanon** in June 1982. Israeli tanks attacked targets in the Palestinian stronghold of West Beirut, while Christian militias allied to the Israelis attacked the **Sabra and**

INVASION OF LEBANON, 1982

Chatila refugee camps, killing 800 people. International outrage forced Israel to withdraw from the city, leaving a residual force in the buffer zone that eventually withdrew in 2000.

INTIFADA

From the 1980s Israel established **Jewish settlements in the West Bank**, and extended its **control of Jerusalem**. Palestinians living in Israeli-occupied territories launched an uprising, the first "Intifada", against Israeli rule in 1987. **Israel and the PLO recognized each other** in the 1993 Oslo Accords and began moves towards **Palestinian self-rule** in Gaza and the West Bank. Political changes on both sides and

INTIFADA Arabic word literally meaning "shaking off", but usually translated as "rebellion" or "uprising" and commonly used to refer to the Palestinian crisis that started in 1987.

continuing terrorist attacks and military clashes meant that progress was slow. **A renewed intifada from 2000** saw tensions rise again. **Israeli attacks** on **Lebanon in 2006 and Gaza in 2008–09** brought worldwide condemnation, although Israel cited **continuing Palestinian terrorism** as its justification.

The Falklands War

In 1982 Britain and Argentina fought each other over a group of rocky, windswept, sparsely inhabited islands in the South Atlantic. The war was the biggest air-naval contest since World War II and went on to have an enormous impact on both countries, and on the Falklands themselves.

SOUTH AMERICA

Falklands War
Date 1982
Location Falkland
Islands, South Georgia,
and surrounding waters

On 19 March 1982, an Argentinian navy transport landed a group of scrap-metal merchants on the remote island of South Georgia, a British dependency 1,280km (800 miles) to the southeast of the Falkland Islands. These included a group of marines, who raised the Argentinian flag. On 2 April, forces from Argentina landed on the Falkland Islands themselves – the first invasion of British territory since World War II.

The two sides in this war were badly matched, for the Argentinians were within 480km (300 miles) range of the islands. Britain, though, was 12,000km (7,440 miles) away to the north and had only a detachment of 68 marines on the islands – which was prompt to surrender – and an ice patrol ship armed with two 20mm guns to protect its territories. The US gave its support to Britain, but the US

Navy considered a successful British invasion to be "a military impossibility". In Britain the foray created a political crisis, as the Conservative government of Margaret Thatcher was accused of having neglected the islands and of sending out the wrong signals to Argentina about their future.

The task force
The British government responded by organizing a task force of 30 warships plus auxiliary and transport vessels, including the converted cruise liner SS *Canberra*, and 6,000 troops to recover the islands. An air base was set up on the mid-Atlantic island of Ascension, while a 370-km (200-nautical mile) exclusion zone was set up around the Falklands, in which all Argentinian ships and planes would be attacked.

Argentinian air attack
The British troop transport ship *Sir Galahad* blazes in Bluff Cove, 8 June 1982, following an air attack by Argentinian Skyhawk aircraft.

The arrival of British troops
The bleak Falklands landscape provided little cover for British troops, who were forced to walk for miles across open moorland and roads.

As the task force headed south across the Atlantic, a team of marines and special forces troops from the Special Air Service (SAS) and Special Boat Service (SBS) recaptured the island of South Georgia on 25 April. British Westland Wasp helicopters attacked and hit an Argentinian submarine, ARA *Santa Fe*, with AS-12 anti-ship missiles, forcing it ashore on the island.

RAF Avro Vulcan bombers began to attack Stanley airport on 1 May. The 16-hour round trip from Ascension Island required the bombers to be refuelled mid-flight by RAF tanker planes. Although a remarkable achievement, the attacks proved to be of limited effectiveness. Closer-range sorties by Sea Harrier jets launched from HMS *Hermes* dropped cluster bombs on Stanley and the airstrip at Goose Green. None of the Falkland airports could support jets, so Argentinian fighters and attack aircraft had to operate from the mainland, targeting the incoming task force with bombs and missiles. The task force defended itself with anti-missile weapons, anti-aircraft guns, and Sea Harrier fighters.

Missile weight 45kg (99lb)

Wheels removed for firing

Launcher jack

The ownership of the Falkland Islands (also known as the Malvinas) in the South Atlantic Ocean has long been contested between Argentina and Britain.

DISPUTED OWNERSHIP
The two countries' claims date back to the late 17th and early 18th centuries. Argentina sent a ship to the islands to **proclaim its sovereignty in 1820** and established a settlement in 1828. The British objected to this and **expelled the Argentinians in 1831–32**, establishing their own sovereignty in 1833.

THE ARGENTINIAN JUNTA
In 1976 the Argentine army overthrew the elected government of Maria Perón and established a three-man **military junta**. It brutally **suppressed human rights**, but inflation soon crippled the economy. In **1981 General Leopoldo Galtieri became president**, but his economic policies met little success. He turned to war to divert the attention of his people.

BRITISH WEAKNESS
British **proposals for a negotiated settlement** on the future of the islands were scrapped after parliamentary criticism in 1980, but Britain then announced the **withdrawal of its only naval presence** in the South Atlantic and refused the islanders full British citizenship. Argentina saw these moves as signalling a **lack of British interest** in the Falklands.

> "The **Falklands thing** was a fight between two bald men over a comb."

JORGE LUIS BORGES, ARGENTINIAN NOBEL LITERATURE LAUREATE, FEBRUARY 1983

The missiles each carried a 1.4kg (3lb) warhead detonated by a contact fuse. This meant that the missile had to hit the target to explode. Later versions were fitted with a more effective laser-controlled proximity fuse.

Single-stage rocket

The parabolic antenna transmitted guidance commands to the missile to correct its course. A TV camera tracked each missile after it had been fired and the system's computer calculated the necessary adjustments.

British Rapier surface-to-air missile launcher
In service since 1971, the Rapier provided air defence for British forces at San Carlos Water. The batteries enjoyed some success, but launchers often failed.

Meanwhile, at sea, the British nuclear-powered submarine HMS *Conqueror* torpedoed and sank the Argentinian light cruiser ARA *Belgrano* on 2 May with the loss of 323 men: another 700

649 Argentinians were killed in the conflict, including 143 conscripted privates. A further 1,188 Argentinians were wounded.

were rescued, the losses accounting for just under half of all Argentinian deaths in the conflict. The attack was later much criticized, as the ship was outside the exclusion zone and sailing away from the Falklands at the time. An Argentinian patrol boat was hit and damaged on the same day. These losses convinced the Argentinian naval commanders to return their remaining vessels to port for the rest of the conflict. Two days later an Argentinian Dassault Super Etendard aircraft sank HMS *Sheffield* with an Exocet missile.

Landings
The first British landings on the islands took place on 14 May, when the SAS raided Pebble Island, and destroyed Argentinian ground-attack aircraft at the airstrip. A week later, 4,000 men of 3 Commando Brigade landed around San Carlos Water on the opposite side of East Falkland island from the main Argentinian base at Stanley. British troops were now vulnerable to nightly bombing raids, while air raids sank four British ships in the area.

British troops first headed south to attack the Argentinian Twelfth Infantry Regiment holding Goose Green. The two-day struggle ended in a British success on 28 May, enabling troops to march on Stanley. A lengthy battle at the end of May gave British troops control of the strategic Mount Kent,

255 British were killed: 88 in the Royal Navy; 27 in the Royal Marines; 16 in the Royal Fleet Auxiliary; 123 in the Army; 1 in the Royal Air Force.

overlooking the town. To their south, British forces moving towards Stanley came under sustained Argentinian air assaults, incurring casualties from hits on two landing ships, RFA *Sir Galahad* and *Sir Tristram*, on 8 June.

Despite this setback, British forces were in a position on the night of 11 June to launch an attack against the defended ring of high ground around Stanley. Two days later they captured Mount Tumbledown, the last defence line around the town. The following morning, 14 June, the Argentinian garrison surrendered, their poorly motivated conscripts no match for the highly trained British troops.

After the conflict, Argentina saw an end to military rule, while Britain's international reputation grew. The islands remain British, despite continuing claims from Argentina.

GALTIERI AND THATCHER
Failure in the Falklands caused **Galtieri to resign** in June 1982. Democratic **elections ended eight years of military rule** in 1983 and Argentina has been a democracy ever since. Margaret Thatcher's Conservatives had first been elected in 1979, but had lost popularity over economic issues. **Victory in the Falklands War** helped her easily **win re-election** in 1983 and again in 1987. **The prestige of Britain rose around the world** as a result of its recapture of the Falkland Islands.

MARGARET THATCHER

THE FALKLANDS
Since the war, Britain has **maintained a sizable military garrison** on the islands and has invested in their economy. Revenue from fishing licences and tourism, as well as military expenditure, has boosted local income. Britain and Argentina **restored diplomatic relations** in 1992 but continue to disagree about the islands' future – Britain supporting the **islanders' wish to remain British** while Argentina **continues to claim the islands**.

TECHNOLOGY

EXOCET MISSILE
The Exocet is a French-built anti-ship missile that can be fired from ships, submarines, or aircraft. In 1982 the Argentinians had many ship-launched MM.38 Exocets but these were unsuited for aircraft operation. They only had five air-launched AM.39s, but used them effectively to sink the destroyer HMS *Sheffield* and the transport ship *Atlantic Conveyor*. Most warships of the period were not well equipped to fend off such attacks. Although the Exocet that hit HMS *Sheffield* did not actually detonate, the energy of the missile on impact and its unused fuel that then exploded, caused enough damage to destroy the ship.

Machine-guns

Rapid-fire machine-guns have dominated warfare since the second half of the 19th century. The first versions employed multiple barrels that were pre-loaded with bullets and rotated into place by hand. Later versions featured a single barrel and used the recoil force of each shot to expel the spent cartridge and insert a new one.

1 The Gatling Gun, patented in the US in 1861, was the precursor of all modern machine-guns. The brass bullet cartridges dropped down into six, later ten, barrels arranged around a cylindrical shaft that were revolved by hand-operated crank. **2** The Mitrailleuse ("grapeshot shooter") was first developed in Belgium in 1851. During the Franco-Prussian War (1870–71) the French version of the gun (shown here), became the first rapid-firing weapon to be deployed by an army in combat. **3** The Maxim machine-gun of 1884 was the first self-powered, single-barrelled machine-gun, using energy from the recoil force to expel each spent cartridge and insert the next one. **4** This Browning M1917 machine-gun of 1912 adopted a simpler method to the Maxim for harnessing the gun's recoil to eject and reload bullets. Its water jacket was later replaced by an air-cooling system. **5** The design for the Hotchkiss MLE was bought from Baron von Augezd in 1893 and modified many times to correct an overheating fault. This 1914 version used metallic strips to hold 24 rounds. **6** This US-designed 1912 Lewis gun was adopted by the British Army in 1915. Air-cooled and gas-operated, this gun remained the main light-support weapon until superseded by the Bren. **7** The Bren was named because it was developed in 1937 in Brno, Czechoslovakia, and modified at Enfield, London. It served as the British Army's principal light-support weapon until the 1970s. **8** The M60, the US Army's 1960s replacement for the Brownings, was a general-purpose, gas-operated machine-gun. **9** This FN Minimi was designed to accept both a fixed magazine or disintegrating-link belts. **10** The L86A1 light-support weapon was developed in the UK in 1986 and used the same calibre ammunition as the L85A1 assault rifle. **11** This MG43, developed in Germany in 2001, is a conventional light machine-gun with an action based on a rotating rather than a roller-locked bolt.

1 AMERICAN GATLING GUN (1862)

7 CZECHOSLOVAKIAN BREN (1937)

10 BRITISH L86A1 (1986)

9 BELGIAN FN MINIMI (1975)

2 FRENCH
MITRAILLEUSE (1870)

3 BRITISH MAXIM
MK 3 (1912)

4 AMERICAN BROWNING (1912)

5 FRENCH
HOTCHKISS MLE
(1914)

6 AMERICAN LEWIS (1912)

8 AMERICAN M60 (1963)

11 GERMAN MG43 (2001)

BEFORE

Rival world powers, primarily Britain and Russia, have struggled to dominate Afghanistan ever since it became an independent nation in the mid-1700s.

THE BIRTH OF AFGHANISTAN

In the mid-19th century, Afghanistan found itself caught up in the **"Great Game"** – the struggle between Britain and Russia for control of Central Asia and India. **Britain unsuccessfully invaded** in 1839–42 and again in 1878–81, before agreeing with Russia in 1895 to make Afghanistan **a neutral buffer state** between them. After a third war in 1919, Britain recognized **Afghan independence**.

COMMUNIST CONTROL

Following the **British withdrawal from India** in 1947 **<< 332–33**, Afghanistan called for Pashtuns in the new Pakistan to be given the right to decide if they wanted to set up an independent Pashtun nation, which it hoped would eventually unite with Afghanistan. Pakistan refused, with support from the **United States**. Afghanistan therefore **turned to the USSR**. The Soviets built roads and irrigation projects and trained the army but their influence waned after **a republic was declared in 1973** and the new reforming government moved the country away from the USSR. The pro-Soviet Afghan force resisted this move, overthrowing the president in 1978, and setting up a **Communist government**.

TECHNOLOGY

STINGER MISSILE

One of the most important weapons the *mujahideen* used against the Soviets was the US-supplied FIM-92 Stinger infrared-homing, surface-to-air missile. The missile, which first entered service in 1981, is small, and light enough to be fired from the shoulder of a single operator and can hit helicopters and aircraft up to 4,800m (15,750ft) away. The American Central Intelligence Agency (CIA) supplied around 500 missiles to the *mujahideen* during the 1980s, although some sources say nearer 2,000. The missiles proved highly effective against Soviet transport planes and helicopter gunships, restricting the Soviets' ability to move around the country or reinforce their troops.

Wars in Afghanistan

The Soviet occupation of Afghanistan in 1979 marked the start of war and insurgency in the country that continues 30 years later. What was once a backwater has now become the focus of much international attention and the scene of a bitterly contested ongoing conventional conflict and anti-terrorist struggle.

In late 1979, the Communist Afghan government had introduced reforms that brought turmoil to the country. The USSR could not allow Communism to fail in Afghanistan nor could it risk civil war on its borders. It therefore staged a coup to install a new leader, who then "invited" Soviet help. On 25 December 1979, Soviet troops moved in.

Opposition to the Soviet occupation of Afghanistan was led by the *mujahideen* ("holy warriors"), an Islamic group that had been established in 1975. After the Communist government was set up, in 1978, they had received weaponry and training from the United States. The *mujahideen* also had the advantage of a friendly local population and knowledge of the mountainous terrain. The Soviets, however, had little local support. They held the main towns but were unable to subdue the countryside despite their deployment of aerial bombardments and heavy artillery. At least 1.5 million civilians perished in the fighting.

By 1985 the *mujahideen* were waging successful guerrilla campaigns in every province. In 1988 the Soviet leader, Mikhail Gorbachev, concluded Soviet involvement in the war and withdrew his 175,000 troops the next year, leaving President Mohammad Najibullah's Communist government to fend for itself. To everyone's surprise, it managed to hold on until the *mujahideen* finally entered the capital, Kabul, in April 1992 and overthrew the Communists.

The Taliban

The *mujahideen*, however, were united only by their opposition to the Soviets. Civil war broke out in December 1992, causing at least 50,000 deaths. Anxious about tribal conflict crossing its border, Pakistan began to support the Taliban ("seekers" of religious knowledge), a fundamentalist Islamic group that wanted to see a return to the original teachings of the Koran. Led by Mullah Mohammed Omar, the Taliban swept through the country in 1994–95 before seizing power in Kabul in September 1996. Many Afghans welcomed the Taliban, because they brought peace and stability, but as the Taliban were mainly Pashtun, they were unsuccessful in uniting the country, especially those

areas that remained controlled by the *mujahideen* Northern Alliance of Tajiks, Uzbeks, and Hazaras, among others.

Afghanistan became home to a large number of foreign-born Muslim fighters under the Taliban, and groups who wished to wage *jihad* (holy war) against supposed enemies of Islam. The most important of these groups was al-Qaeda, set up by Osama bin Laden some time after 1988. The group attracted volunteers from across the Arab world as well as Europe and set up training camps along the border with Pakistan. Its militants launched attacks against US embassies in East Africa in 1998 and against the USS *Cole* in Aden in 2000. Their most audacious attack was made on 11 September 2001, when suicide bombers hijacked planes to destroy the World Trade Center in New York.

The US demanded that the Afghan government close down all al-Qaeda training camps and hand over bin Laden and other Talibans for trial. When the Afghans refused, US and British Special Forces linked up with Northern Alliance troops fighting in the north in October 2001, while US and British aircraft launched bombing missions from air bases in Uzbekistan, Pakistan, and Tajikistan. The areas they targeted most were in the Tora Bora Mountains east of Kabul, where B-52 bombers pounded the caves and underground bunkers known to be in use by the Taliban and al-Qaeda. Small numbers of US Marines arrived in late November

> ## 3.5 MILLION
> **The total number of Afghan civilians who sought refuge in Pakistan during the Soviet occupation. Another 1.5 million fled west, to Iran.**

War with the USSR
Soviet armoured vehicles struggled in the rough and mountainous terrain of Afghanistan and made easy targets for the well-armed *mujahideen* guerrilla fighters.

to help with the capture of Kandahar in early December. This seemingly ended the conflict in a rapid American victory. The brief campaign was notable in US military history for its use of special forces and air power without the need to deploy a large force of ground troops.

AFTER

The eventual fall of the Taliban government in 2001 did not bring an end to conflict in Afghanistan, where the new government has never gained full control of the country.

THE KARZAI GOVERNMENT

In December 2001, an interim government led by **Hamid Karzai**, a moderate Pashtun, took power and drafted a new constitution that was agreed upon in January 2004. Karzai won the subsequent presidential election but his government **failed to win control over the whole country** and became increasingly ineffectual and corrupt.

THE TALIBAN REVIVAL

Neither Mullah Omar nor Osama bin Laden were captured in the war. The Taliban regrouped and started a new campaign in 2003, funded with money from the annual opium harvest, the raw material of heroin. After January 2006, **NATO troops arrived** to help US forces but the Taliban continued to expand its control over most of the country outside Kabul and the north. Al-Qaeda and other militant Islamic groups consolidated in the mountainous **border regions of Pakistan**, from where they mounted **terrorist attacks** against regional and international targets. The **Obama administration** announced plans to **strengthen US forces** in the region in 2009.

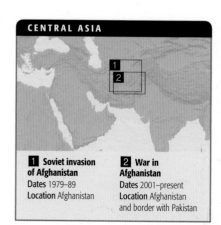

CENTRAL ASIA

1 Soviet invasion of Afghanistan	2 War in Afghanistan
Dates 1979–89	Dates 2001–present
Location Afghanistan	Location Afghanistan and border with Pakistan

US Marine operations
A CH-47 Chinook helicopter arrives with medical supplies for the US forces fighting in Afghanistan's Hindu Kush mountains in 2001. A Marine machine-gunner is ready to give covering fire.

Gulf Wars

The Iraqi government faced strong opposition from Shi'a Muslims and Kurds. Saddam Hussein decided to invade Iran – in the throes of its Islamic revolution – to unite his country behind him. He expected a quick victory, but the Iran-Iraq War and subsequent Gulf War severely weakened his power.

The pretext for Iraq's war against Iran, which began in 1980, was the disputed ownership of the Shatt al-Arab waterway between the two countries that leads into the Gulf. Iran and Iraq had clashed over the waterway in the early 1970s but reached an agreement in 1975. Now, the fall of the Shah, the new Islamic government's antagonism to the US, and its subsequent purges of Iran's armed forces all suggested that Iran might be weak. The result was an opportunistic attack on 22 September 1980 that Saddam hoped would topple the Iranian government, enlarge Iraq's oil reserves, and establish his leadership in the Gulf and wider Arab world.

The Iraqi air force attacked ten airfields but failed to destroy the Iranian air force on the ground. The next day, Iraq launched a ground invasion along a 650-km (400-mile) front, with four divisions crossing Iran's southern border, to besiege Khorramshahr and Abadan, one division invading in the centre to block a potential Iranian invasion route, and another division in the north to protect the Iraqi oil complex at Kirkuk.

Stalemate

The Iraqi invasion soon stalled in the face of vigorous, if disorganized, Iranian resistance. Iran retaliated with air strikes against targets in Iraq, including oil installations and the capital, Baghdad. Its air force quickly gained air superiority, while the Iraqis did not have enough bombers to be effective against a country the size of Iran. Saddam's hopes that opponents of the Ayatollah's government would rise against it were dashed, as Iranian nationalism led people to rally round their government and resist the Iraqis, not welcome them.

An Iranian counterattack in March 1982 recovered lost territory, and Iraq withdrew its forces in June, agreeing to a Saudi Arabian plan to end the war. Iran refused to compromise, however, insisting on the removal of Saddam from power. In July its forces crossed the Iraqi border and headed for Basra. They were met by a vastly increased Iraqi army – approaching one million strong – and entrenched in formidable border defences, who repelled the attack with coordinated small arms and artillery fire and by the use of gas, a regular feature of the Iraqi war effort. In 1984 Iraq launched an air bombardment of 11 Iranian cities to force the country's government into peace talks. The Iranian response against selected Iraqi cities began the first of five "wars of the cities" that took place during the conflict.

Offensives by both sides in 1985 and 1986 failed to break the stalemate, as neither side had sufficient artillery or air power to support large-scale ground advances. The rest of the war consisted of both sides bombing each other's cities and exchanging Scud missile attacks. Iraqi chemical attacks in 1988 against Kurdish targets in both Iran and Iraq enraged the Iranians but they did not have the means to continue the war and agreed a ceasefire on 20 August.

The pre-war territorial status quo was restored, although at the cost of perhaps a million lives and two much-weakened economies. Crucially, however, Iraq had received support from many Western and Arab countries, including funding

> ## "The great duel, the **mother of all battles** has begun. The dawn of **victory nears** as this great showdown begins."
>
> SADDAM HUSSEIN, BROADCAST ON BAGHDAD STATE RADIO, 17 JANUARY 1991

BEFORE

From the 1960s onwards, rival territorial claims, differences between Islamic sects, and the impact of outside influences created political tensions between the Gulf states.

KUWAIT
When Kuwait received its independence from Britain in 1961, Iraq renewed its historic **claim to the country as its 19th province**; Britain sent troops to guard the border. **Kuwait later sided with Iraq in its war with Iran**, as it too feared Iranian intentions in the region.

IRAQ
In 1968 the **nationalist Ba'ath Party took power** in a coup. **Saddam Hussein** overthrew a Ba'ath predecessor to become president in 1979. Saddam brutally ruled this mainly Shi'a country through its governing Sunni minority. He also **persecuted its Kurdish minority**. He viewed the Iranian revolution with concern, as he feared it might spread to Iraq. **Border disputes with Iran** and Iraqi support for Iranian separatist groups increased the tension between them.

IRAN
In 1979 the corrupt pro-Western **Shah of Iran** was overthrown in a popular Islamic uprising that **brought Ayatollah Khomeini to power**. Iran became the world's largest theocracy and a leading centre of Shi'a Islam, threatening not only Iraq, but the other Sunni kingdoms around the Gulf.

SUPPORTERS OF AYATOLLAH KHOMEINI

Operation Desert Storm

The coalition attack on Saddam Hussein's Iraq combined air and missile attacks with a devastating ground advance mounted from Saudi Arabia.

Key

- ▨ Iraq
- ▨ Main Kurdish region
- ▨ Members of US-led coalition
- — Frontiers 1990
- ┉┉┉ Disputed frontier
- ⟶ Iraqi invasion of Kuwait
- ⟶ Coalition land campaign
- ⟶ Coalition airstrike
- ⊕ Iraqi airbase
- ⌦ Scud missile installation
- ⊕ Allied airbase
- ⟶ US aircraft carrier

AFTER >>

Although defeated, Saddam Hussein continued to rule Iraq. Suspicions about Iraq's supposed weapons of mass destruction led to his downfall in 2003.

REBELLIONS

At the conclusion of the First Gulf War, **Shi'as** in the south of Iraq and **Kurdish separatists** in the north both launched **rebellions against Saddam**, hoping they would receive support from the US. With no help forthcoming, both **revolts were brutally crushed**, resulting in hundreds of thousands of Kurds fleeing to Iran and Turkey. The United States, France, and Britain established **no-fly zones** over the north and south of the country to protect the rebel areas from possible Iraqi bombing or chemical attacks.

SADDAM HUSSEIN

POSTWAR IRAQ

UN economic sanctions imposed at the start of the First Gulf War remained in place, as Iraq was deemed to have **failed to comply with UN resolutions** forbidding it from developing or possessing **chemical, biological, or nuclear weapons**. Weapons inspectors managed to destroy some weapons, but alleged obstruction over the issue was one of the main causes of the **US-British invasion of Iraq** in 2003 **348–49 >>**.

As in the First Gulf War, an air campaign was followed by a brief ground offensive. This time coalition forces went all the way to Baghdad to achieve **"regime change"**, but many aspects of the campaign were controversial and the US had **fewer coalition partners** than in 1990–91.

Burning oil installations

Control of oil resources was a major factor in each war. Both sides attacked oil refineries during the Iran-Iraq War, and in the Gulf War Saddam's troops destroyed Kuwaiti installations when forced to retreat.

from oil-rich Kuwait, one of its biggest creditors. In its impoverished state, Iraq looked to Kuwait to solve its problems and cancel its debts. Unwisely confident that the West would not intervene, Saddam Hussein sent his troops to invade and occupy Kuwait on 2 August 1990.

The Gulf War

The UN imposed economic sanctions on Iraq, while the United States put together a coalition of 31 nations, including Saudi Arabia and the Gulf States, to liberate Kuwait. The combined ground and air forces assembled in Saudi Arabia and naval units were deployed in the Gulf. A

five-week aerial bombing campaign began on 17 January 1991, when eight US AH-64 Apache and two MH-53 Pave Low helicopters destroyed Iraqi radar sites near the Saudi Arabian border.

Into combat

An A-7E Corsair aircraft heads for its target in Iraq with eight Mark 82 500-lb bombs.

These were just the first of more than 100,000 sorties flown over Iraq, with little loss, in which some 88,500 tons of bombs were dropped, devastating the military and civilian infrastructure of Iraq. Most of the bombs were of the traditional gravity type, but smart

bombs and cruise missiles were also used effectively against selected targets. More than 2,000 tons of smart bombs were dropped on Baghdad and other targets by US F-117 Stealth bombers. Iraq responded by launching a number of Scud missiles against Israel in the hope of provoking Israel to retaliate – an action that Saddam trusted would peel Arab support away from the Allied coalition. Armed with supplies of American defensive missiles, however, Israel did not respond to these attacks and the coalition remained intact.

The coalition's ground campaign began on 24 February when American troops from the 2nd Armored Cavalry Regiment entered Iraq just to the west of Kuwait. To their north, the US XVIII Airborne Corps thrust into the sparsely defended desert of southern Iraq, their left flank protected by the French Sixth Light Armoured Division, their right by the British 1st Armoured Division. The

advance was swifter than anticipated. Two days later Iraqi troops began to leave Kuwait, setting fire to its oil fields as they left. The long convoy retreating along the main highway to Baghdad came under intense fire in what many

190 The number of coalition troops killed by enemy action during the First Gulf War.

44 The number of coalition troops killed by friendly fire in the First Gulf War.

20 THOUSAND An estimate of the number of Iraqi soldiers killed during the First Gulf War.

described as a "turkey shoot". French, British, and US troops pursued Iraqi forces out of Kuwait to within 240km (150 miles) of Baghdad. The retreat turned into a rout, and on 28 February, after 100 hours of fighting, President George Bush declared a ceasefire.

Ethics of War

War is always barbaric, but throughout history attempts have been made to control its excesses. These attempts range from religious restrictions and codes of chivalry to the criminalization of certain acts in war. Today, in an era that has seen global war and systematic genocide, the ethics of war have never been more closely scrutinized.

The earliest known attempts to regulate warfare appear in religious texts. The Book of Deuteronomy in the Jewish Bible, compiled around 700 BCE, set limits on the amount of environmental damage that was acceptable during war and ruled on the treatment of female captives. In the early 7th century CE, Abu Bakr, the first Muslim caliph, laid down ten rules for the conduct of his army on the battlefield, including injunctions not to kill children, women, or old men, nor the enemy's livestock unless for food. These rules were expanded from the 9th century onwards to include the treatment of diplomats, hostages, and prisoners of war, the protection of women, children, and civilians, and the right of asylum.

Despite religious instructions, conduct in war was (and still is) much more a matter of custom than the result of adhering to written laws. The use of the white flag of surrender, for example, appeared in Han China (23–220 CE) and in the Roman empire around 100 CE, but did not become law until the First Geneva Convention in 1864. There was also no actual law among the ancient Greek city-states

Respect for prisoners
Saladin's troops take Christians prisoner in the Holy Land during the Third Crusade. Saladin treated his prisoners humanely in accordance with Islamic law.

implying that all wars should be settled in a single battle, but that was how their wars tended to be fought, since neither side could afford heavy casualties or the attrition of a sustained campaign. This custom changed during the Greco-Persian wars when far larger armies than those available to a single city-state were needed to fight the armies of the Persian empire (see pp.20–21).

Justification of war
In the Christian era, theologians, notably Augustine of Hippo and later Thomas Aquinas, developed the theory of the just war – a war that can be justified according to certain philosophical or religious criteria of justice. Those criteria are set out in two main laws: *jus ad bellum*, the right to go to war, and *jus in bello*, the right conduct of soldiers in a war. More recently, a third law, *jus post bellum*, has been added concerning the end of a war, including the prosecution of war criminals. These laws seek to define, for example, a just cause for war, its military necessity, the probability of its success, and the proportionality of waging a war – that is, the anticipated benefits against the expected evils. Such laws are of course highly contested, not least by pacifists who believe that no war can ever be just.

Attempts have also been made to control warfare through spiritual sanction.

Child soldiers
The use of children to fight wars, particularly widespread in Africa, was outlawed by a UN protocol of 2000. Nevertheless, perhaps as many as 300,000 children are currently fighting in wars around the world.

Founded in 989 CE, the French *Pax Dei* (Peace of God) movement tried to control violent nobles through their fear of spiritual retribution or excommunication from the Church. Immunity from violence was given to non-combatants who could not defend themselves. This idea, and the later adoption of truce days, slowly spread across Western Europe and survived until the 13th century. Christian values of right conduct and charity also informed European knights, who were meant to fight according to unwritten codes of chivalry that governed their conduct and behaviour, although such codes were often abandoned in the heat of battle.

The first work dedicated specifically to the justification of war appeared in Poland in the early 15th century. The scholar and jurist Stanisław of Skarbimierz's sermons, *De bellis justis* (About Just Wars), put forward a theory to justify Poland's war against the Teutonic Knights. In the early 1500s, the Spanish theologian Francisco de Vitoria justified the Spanish conquest of the Americas. His views had a major influence on Hugo Grotius, the 17th-century Dutch lawyer whose three volumes on the conduct of war are the first legal code of warfare and form the basis of modern international law. Grotius claimed that wars are justifiable if based on self-defence, reparation of injury, or punishment, and that once

Landmark in the history of war
The Geneva Convention of 1864 was the first of four such conventions covering the care of the wounded and the treatment of prisoners of war and civilians.

a war has begun both sides are bound by certain rules regardless of whether their cause is just or not.

International treaties

The laws put forward by medieval and Renaissance thinkers were entirely theoretical, and there was no effective means of enforcing them. That changed in the mid-19th century when the heavy casualties caused by increasingly mechanized warfare prompted tentative steps towards enforceable laws. In 1856 delegates at the Congress of Paris that ended the Crimean War (see pp.220–21) agreed a "declaration respecting maritime law" that abolished privateering (the use of private warships by national governments). Of greater importance was the First Geneva Convention of 1864 "for the amelioration of the condition of the wounded and sick in armed forces in the field", prompted by Henri Dunant witnessing the bloody aftermath of the battle of Solferino in 1859 (see pp.224–25). His concern gave birth to the International Red Cross, which drafted the First Geneva Convention, and then enforced it and three later conventions covering casualties of war at sea (in 1906), prisoners of war (in 1929), and civilians during wartime (in 1949).

Two peace conferences at The Hague, in 1899 and 1907, produced conventions that broke new ground in setting out not only the rules of war but also some methods of resolution and enforcement. The first convention banned the

Battle of Solferino
The lack of medical attention given to the wounded at the battle of Solferino in 1859 inspired Henri Dunant to found the International Red Cross.

use of certain modern technologies, such as hollow-point bullets that expanded on entering the human body. It also supported the peaceful settlement of international disputes through the use of international commissions of inquiry, and set up the Permanent Court of Arbitration in The Hague, the world's first institution for resolving international disputes. The Second Hague Convention concentrated on naval warfare.

A brave, if over-ambitious, attempt to outlaw war altogether was made by the Paris Peace Pact of 1928, better known as the Kellogg-Briand Pact after the US secretary of state and the French foreign minister who drafted it. The treaty provided "for the renunciation of war as an instrument of national policy". It failed in that aim, but was significant for later developments in international law and was used against Nazi leaders charged with war crimes at Nuremberg in 1945.

The horrors of World War II provided the impetus for the establishment of the United Nations in 1945. Its founding charter dedicated the organization to the maintenance of international peace and security, a role it has interpreted by introducing a number of conventions and agreements that, among other things, limit certain types of weapon, define war crimes, and seek to prevent and punish acts of genocide. These agreements carry considerable weight and are, in theory, enforceable in national and international courts of law.

TIMELINE

- **700s BCE** Book of Deuteronomy sets out the first religious restrictions on the conduct of war.

- **100s CE** The white flag is used for surrender in both Han China and the Roman empire.

- **632** Abu Bakr becomes the first caliph of the Muslim world and instructs his army on conduct.

- **1139** Pope Innocent II bans the use of the crossbow against Christians.

- **1207** The Council of Toulouges proclaims the Truce of God by prohibiting violence initially on Sundays and holy days.

- **1400** Stanisław of Skarbimierz justifies the use of war by Poland against the Teutonic Knights.

- **1625** Hugo Grotius publishes *On the Law of War and Peace: Three Books*.

- **1856** The Paris Declaration Respecting Maritime Law abolishes privateering.

- **1863** The International Red Cross founded in Geneva.

- **1864** The First Geneva Convention governs the care of wounded soldiers on the battlefield; the red cross becomes a symbol to identify people and equipment governed by the convention.

MEDIEVAL CROSSBOW

- **1888** The St Petersburg Convention renounces the use of fragmentary, explosive, or incendiary ammunition.

- **1899** The First Hague Convention agreed.

- **1907** The Second Hague Convention agreed.

- **1925** The Geneva Protocol to the Hague Convention bans all forms of chemical and biological warfare.

- **1928** The Kellogg-Briand Pact attempts to outlaw war.

- **1945** The United Nations is founded after World War II.

- **1945–46** The International Military Tribunal tries Nazi war criminals at Nuremberg.

- **1947** The UN agrees Nuremberg Principles defining war crimes.

- **1948** The UN Convention on the Prevention and Punishment of the Crime of Genocide.

WWI GAS SHELL

- **1972** A Biological Weapons Convention agreed.

- **1984** The UN Convention Against Torture.

- **1993** The Chemical Weapons Convention.

- **1997** Ottawa Treaty bans the use of land mines.

- **2000** The UN General Assembly amends the UN Convention on the Rights of the Child to outlaw the use of child soldiers.

- **2002** The International Criminal Court is set up in The Hague, Netherlands, to try cases of genocide, war crimes, and crimes against humanity.

MODERN LAND MINE

Post-Communist Wars

The collapse of Communism in Eastern Europe and the break-up of the USSR and Yugoslavia released nationalist and ethnic rivalries in each country as age-old antagonisms and divisions re-emerged. Bloody wars broke out in the Caucasus and Yugoslavia that are still a source of trouble today.

The nations of the Caucasus were incorporated into Russia's empire during the 19th century but were never fully reconciled to, first Russian, and then Soviet, domination.

Modern conflict in the region began in Armenia and Azerbaijan. The enclave of Nagorno-Karabakh was officially part of, and totally surrounded by, Azerbaijan but was historically part of Armenia and was almost entirely Armenian in terms of population. Its regional parliament voted to join Armenia in February 1988, prompting widespread ethnic violence as Azeris were expelled from Armenia and Armenians forced out of Azerbaijan. In January 1990, the Azeri Popular Front won an election held in Azerbaijan and declared not only its independence from the USSR but also war on Armenia. Soviet tanks crushed the revolt, killing more than 100 people in the capital, Baku. But as the USSR broke up, both Armenia and Azerbaijan declared their independence. In 1992 Armenian Nagorno-Karabakh irregulars occupied the narrow border region between Armenia and the province, linking the two together. Despite peace talks being held in 2001, the future of the enclave remains unsettled today.

Georgia

Georgia declared independence in 1991 but immediately faced ethnic separatist movements in three provinces. South Ossetians wishing to remain Russian by joining the republic of North Ossetia fought Georgian troops in November 1991 until a ceasefire was arranged in July 1992. Russian peacekeeping forces occupied a buffer zone between Georgia and South Ossetia. Abkhazia, to the west, also declared its independence in 1992. The Georgians invaded but were driven out in 1993 after savage fighting. Again, Russian troops then kept the two sides apart. Adzharia, the third province, was reconquered by Georgia in 2004.

Chechnya

The present-day Russian Federation consists of 83 republics, districts, and other regions. The Chechen republic in the northern Caucasus has always been fiercely independent and has resented Russian rule since it was conquered in 1859. In the chaos surrounding the USSR's break-up, Chechnya declared its independence. Russia ignored the move and tried to agree a settlement. In 1994 fighting broke out when

BALKANS AND THE CAUCASUS

1 Former Yugoslavia
Dates 1991–99
Location Croatia, Serbia, Bosnia, Kosovo, and Macedonia

2 Georgia
Dates 1991–93, 2008
Location Caucasus

3 Armenia and Azerbaijan
Dates 1992–94
Location South Caucasus

4 Chechnya
Dates 1994–96, 1999–2004
Location North Caucasus

Chechen capital in ruins
Intense Russian shelling of Grozny, the capital of Chechnya, in 1994–95, and again in 1999–2000, reduced much of the city to rubble.

« BEFORE

Both the USSR and Yugoslavia consisted of federations of partly autonomous republics with many peoples held together in a single state under Communist rule.

THE SOVIET UNION

The Union of Soviet Socialist Republics (USSR) consisted of **15 separate republics**, the largest of which was the **Russian Federation**. In 1985 **Mikhail Gorbachev** became leader and began to reform its Communist economy and political system through **perestroika** ("reconstruction") and **glasnost** ("openness"). He tried to **hold the USSR together** as a Communist nation by giving greater power to the individual republics, but in 1991 they **declared their independence**, so bringing an end to Communist rule and **dissolving the USSR**.

YUGOSLAVIA

At the end of World War II, the Communists under **Yosip Broz Tito** took power in Yugoslavia. Tito reorganized the multi-ethnic country into a **federation of six republics** held together by his strong leadership. After his death in 1980, tensions rose between the republics. Slovenia and Croatia both elected non-Communist governments, while the Serbian government of **Slobodan Milosevic** became **increasingly nationalist**. In 1991 Milosevic refused to accept a Croat as federal president, causing **Slovenia, Croatia, and Macedonia to declare their independence** from Yugoslavia.

Chechens opposing independence tried to take the capital, Grozny. Russia sent troops to intervene, who shelled the city and seized it in early 1995. The Chechen rebels fighting for independence then took to the mountains and conducted guerrilla warfare against Russian targets. In 1996 Russia agreed a ceasefire and withdrew its troops.

Chechen separatists renewed their campaign in 1999. A series of bomb attacks across Russia killed 300 people, although many suspected the Russian Secret Service of planting the bombs in order to provide a pretext for a renewal of the war, as neither the Secret Service

KEY MOMENT

SIEGE OF SARAJEVO

Serb forces from the Republika Srpska and the Yugoslav Army besieged Bosnia's capital, Sarajevo, from April 1992 to February 1996. The siege, one of the longest in modern times, killed 12,000 people and wounded 50,000, 85 per cent of them civilians. Food, electricity, and water supplies were cut off, while Serb snipers picked off residents in the streets. The siege attracted worldwide humanitarian attention, and was only lifted when peace talks ended the Bosnian war.

The conflicts in the former Soviet republics and Yugoslavia have yet to be resolved. Ethnic rivalries remain intense and fears of Russian empire-building persist.

SERBIA AND KOSOVO
After the war, Kosovo came under United Nations administration. **Up to 280,000 Serbs left**, as they feared retaliation from Albanians. In 2008 the **Assembly of Kosovo** declared the province independent, but it was **not recognized by Serbia or Russia**. Many prominent Serbs have been indicted for war crimes, including **Slobodan Milosevic**, who died during his trial in 2006, and **Radovan Karadzic**, former president of Republika Srpska.

RADOVAN KARADZIC, FACING HIS ACCUSERS IN THE HAGUE

GEORGIA
In August 2008, fighting broke out again between Russia and Georgia over **South Ossetia**. Georgian troops attempted to retake the breakaway province, but **Russia sent in tanks and bombed targets inside Georgia**. At the same time, Russian troops stationed in Abkhazia invaded western Georgia. A precarious **ceasefire** was **arranged by the European Union**.

"Six centuries later, now, we are being again engaged in battles and are facing battles ... "

SLOBODAN MILOSEVIC, ON ENDING KOSOVO'S AUTONOMY, 28 JUNE 1989

nor the Russian Army had been willing to accept defeat in Chechnya. Russian troops invaded the republic again in October 1999 and heavily bombed Grozny, causing many casualties and forcing some 200,000 citizens to flee. The majority of them headed for the region of Ingushetia. In response, Chechens seized hostages in a Moscow theatre and subsequently fought an increasingly bitter battle in the province itself with Russian troops. A new constitution was agreed in 2003 that gave Chechnya greater autonomy within Russia and a pro-Russian president installed in what was widely seen as a rigged election.

Yugoslav soldier's cap
The Serb-led Yugoslav Army fought during the 1990s to keep the former Yugoslavia united under Serb control.

Yugoslavia
The break-up of Yugoslavia in June 1991 was contested by Serbia, whose people were the dominant ethnic group in the country. The Serb-controlled Yugoslav Army fought a one-week battle to stop Slovenia leaving the union before a ceasefire was declared. Fighting with Croatia lasted until January of the following year, when the Yugoslav Army withdrew, although its troops remained in Serb-majority areas of Croatia until they were evicted by the Croat army in 1998. The successful departure from Yugoslavia of Croatia and Slovenia led multi-ethnic Bosnia-Herzegovina to fear for its future, for in March 1991, Serb and Croat leaders had secretly agreed to divide Bosnia between them. In March 1992, Bosnia

declared independence, prompting its Serb population to set up their own independent Republika Srpska.

A three-way civil war then broke out: an uneasy coalition of Muslims and Croats fought the Serbs, while elsewhere Muslims defended themselves against separate Serb and Croat forces. By mid-1993 Serbs controlled about 70 per cent of Bosnia, killing or expelling non-Serbs in a brutal campaign of "ethnic cleansing". The United Nations imposed sanctions against Serbia and established six safe havens for Muslims in Bosnia. But the UN failed to protect these areas, allowing Serbs to overrun them in 1995, killing some 8,000 Muslims at Srebrenica. NATO then bombed Serb positions, forcing Serbia to agree a peace treaty with Bosnia and Croatia that divided the region between Serb and Muslim-Croat states.

Kosovo
In the former Yugoslavia, Kosovo was a southern Serbian province inhabited mainly by Kosovar Albanians. Slobodan Milosevic's Serb government decided to end the province's autonomy in 1989 and fiercely suppressed all dissent, claiming that Kosovo was a historic part of Serbia: 600 years previously, in 1389, the Ottoman Turks had ended Serbian independence at the battle of Kosovo Polje.

Albanian fighters in the Kosovo Liberation Army (KLA) first confronted Serb forces in January 1998, prompting the

Kosovan refugees
Around 600,000 Kosovans fled for safety in Macedonia and Albania after Serbia began a policy of murderous "ethnic cleansing" against them in 1999.

Serbian government to send in troops to crush the rebels. Many hundreds of thousands of Albanians fled their homes as Serbs conducted widespread ethnic cleansing in the province. When Serbia subsequently refused to accept peace terms, NATO planes bombed the region in an 11-week campaign. It was only after this prolonged bombardment that Serbia ended its attacks on Kosovo and began to withdraw its troops.

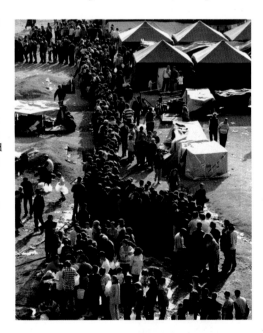

« BEFORE

BEFORE

The Iraqi regime of Saddam Hussein had threatened its neighbours and challenged the wider world ever since 1980.

CONFRONTATON

The **Gulf War of 1990–91** « **340–341** left Saddam Hussein in charge in Iraq, but opposition to his rule led to **uprisings from Kurds and Sh'ia Arabs**, which were savagely repressed. The US, UK, and France enforced **"no-fly zones"** in the north and south of the country to protect these minorities. The UN also imposed a **trade embargo** on Iraq, leading to as many as 500,000 deaths from malnutrition and disease.

WAR ON TERROR

The **attacks of 9 September 2001** led the US to launch a "war on terror", starting with the **invasion of Afghanistan** « **338–339**. In 2002 President George W. Bush identified Iraq, along with Iran and North Korea, as part of an "axis of evil" that aided terrorism. There were, however, no known links between Iraq and Al-Qaida.

WEAPONS OF MASS DESTRUCTION

After 9/11 the US government accused Iraq of hiding **weapons of mass destruction** (nuclear, chemical, or biological weapons) from UN inspectors. The UN's own experts were unable to find any evidence of weapons of mass destruction, stating that Iraq was complying with UN resolutions.

A UN INSPECTION

TECHNOLOGY

TALON ROBOT

The Talon is used to move and dispose of live grenades and bombs. Small, light, easily transported, it is instantly ready for operation. A soldier uses a digital control unit to direct its movements from a safe distance. US troops have used the Talon since 2000, first in Afghanistan, then working for ground troops in Iraq. Talon also played an important search and recovery role at Ground Zero in New York after the 9/11 attacks.

TALON

The Occupation of Iraq

The invasion of Iraq by US, UK, and other forces in March 2003 to overthrow Saddam Hussein produced a quick military victory. While the invasion itself was well planned and executed and its aims were clear, the political and security implications of a lengthy occupation presented more complex problems.

The invasion force consisted of around 248,000 US soldiers and marines, 45,000 British soldiers, 2,000 Australians, 1,300 Spaniards, 500 Danes, and 194 Poles. The force, which assembled in Kuwait and the Gulf, was supported by at least 70,000 Kurds from the north of the country. US President Bush termed those that supported the invasion a "coalition of the willing". The Iraqi army numbered around 300,000.

The invasion

The war began on 20 March 2003 with explosions in Baghdad detonated by Coalition special forces already in the capital. They also targeted installations for guided-precision air strikes. Troops then invaded from the south, with amphibious forces seizing oil installations around Basra and the Al-Faw peninsula to prevent them being destroyed or used in environmental warfare. The first major battle took place on

SOUTHWEST ASIA

Invasion and occupation of Iraq
Dates 2003–present
Location Iraq

captured on 15 April, the last major city to fall to Coalition forces. Saddam was captured on 13 December and later put on trial for crimes against humanity. He was hanged on 30 December 2006. Senior members of his government were also tried and executed.

Insurgency and sectarian killings

The invasion was declared over at the end of April, 2003. It had been well planned and had been carried out with great professionalism despite the difficult

triangle" in the centre of the country. The insurgents were mainly Saddam loyalists and Iraqi nationalists upset at their loss of power, but dissent soon spread to Sunni clerics and their followers. In 2004 the insurgency spread to Sh'ia clerics and radicals who, inspired by neighbouring Iran, saw US troops in particular as an anti-Islamic force. As the security situation deteriorated, foreign fighters and the newly created al-Qaida group in Iraq contributed to the violence as a way of attacking the USA.

> ## "A regime that has something to hide from the civilized world."
>
> PRESIDENT GEORGE W. BUSH ON SADDAM'S GOVERNMENT, 29 JANUARY 2002

23 March for the city of Nasiriyah, strategically situated near bridges over the Euphrates River. A firefight with pro-Saddam elements broke out before US troops took the city. To the south, after two weeks of heavy fighting, British troops fought their way into Iraq's second city, Basra, on 6 April. In the north, coalition special forces and US airborne brigades supported the Kurdish capture of Kirkuk and other towns.

On 5 April US troops raided Baghdad airport to test the city's defences. They were met by heavy resistance but secured the airport. The next day, troops entered the city itself, crushing resistance with attack helicopters and aerial bombardment. The city was occupied fully by Coalition forces on 9 April, with statues of Saddam Hussein toppled throughout the city and his image removed from all public buildings. Tikrit, birthplace of Saddam Hussein and his main powerbase, was

conditions caused by sandstorms and the increasing heat. Casualties were low on both sides. Little thought, however, had been given to Iraq's post-war administration. The country had no history of democratic politics and was split between a Muslim Sh'ia majority previously persecuted by Saddam, a Sunni minority he had used to control the country, and Kurdish separatists in the north. The country's infrastructure lay in ruins. With little or no power or water, cities were barely functioning. The one institution that had united the country – the pro-Saddam army – was immediately dismantled. The Coalition therefore had to set up a provisional authority to govern the country until democratic elections could be held and a new government formed.

The shift from liberator to unwanted occupier was swift, as Iraqis turned against Coalition forces. Much of the dissent came initially from the "Sunni

139 US and 33 British troops were killed in the invasion.

16 THOUSAND Iraqi combatants and civilians were killed.

2.2 MILLION Iraqi refugees later fled to neighbouring countries.

AFTER

Rocket-propelled grenade-launcher
This Al-Nasirah RPG7 is the Iraqi version of the famous Soviet RPG7. Widely used by the insurgents in Iraq, it fires a variety of warheads, the most powerful of which can easily penetrate the armour of a tank.

The main areas of conflict were in the poor Sh'ia sections of Baghdad and other cities and around Fallujah in the centre of the Sunni triangle. Two bitter battles for Fallujah took place in 2004, the second, in November, lasting 46 days. The US military described the battle as the heaviest urban combat it had been involved in since Vietnam. While US troops and installations were the main targets, Sunni suicide and car bombers also targeted Sh'ia mosques and other civilian meeting places in an attempt to stir up sectarian hatred. By 2006, 33 people a day on average were being killed in Baghdad alone. The violence resulted in the ethnic cleansing of many cities, the Sh'ia majority driving Sunnis out of their homes and establishing control at their expense.

In order to suppress the rising violence, 20,000 additional US troops were sent to Iraq in early 2007 to contain the situation. This "troop surge" appeared to work, reducing violence across the country, although Sh'ia dominance over their rival Sunnis probably contributed more. The reduction in violence allowed the US to start withdrawing troops, slowly handing over security duties to the reconstituted and re-equipped Iraqi army and the government of Iraq's 18 provinces to locally elected politicians.

The occupation of Iraq by Allied troops was scheduled to end in 2009, although the security situation in the country was far from secure and its future uncertain.

WITHDRAWAL
In 2008 US and Iraqi governments approved a **Status of Forces agreement**, agreeing that US forces would leave Iraqi cities by 30 June 2009 and that all US forces would **leave the country by the end of 2011**. On 1 January 2009 the US handed over the Green Zone security region in the centre of Baghdad to Iraqi security forces. Britain announced that its troops would all **withdraw by the end of July 2009**. Other Allied troops had been withdrawn by the end of 2008. However, doubts remained that all US troops would leave the country by the required date, with some possibly remaining as a residual force, by agreement with the Iraqi government.

THE COST OF OCCUPATION
The death toll during the invasion and occupation of Iraq is hard to estimate, as many deaths went unreported. The Iraqi death toll between March 2003 and 2009 may have been around **1.2 million people**, almost five per cent of the population. Half were killed in shootings, a fifth by car bombs. **One in five Iraqi families** lost at least one member. The occupation also led to a **deterioration in relations** and increasing animosity between the US and Islamic states, notably Iran, and **undermined the US's status** as the "global policeman". In Afghanistan, the Taliban regained strength as the US concentrated its military efforts in Iraq.

Blazing the trail to Basra
A Royal Marine fires a Milan guided missile at an Iraqi position after British troops, along with US Marines, had landed on the Al-Faw peninsula in southern Iraq on the night of 20/21 March 2003.

SURVIVORS OF GENOCIDE
Rwandan refugees carry water to their huts at the refugee camp in Benaco, Tanzania, in 1995. The crisis was caused by the mass extermination of Rwanda's Tutsi minority by the ruling Hutu tribe; within approximately 100 days, up to 800,000 Tutsis and moderate Hutus were killed, and hundreds of thousands were forced to flee their homes. At the time, the Benaco camp was the largest refugee camp in the world.

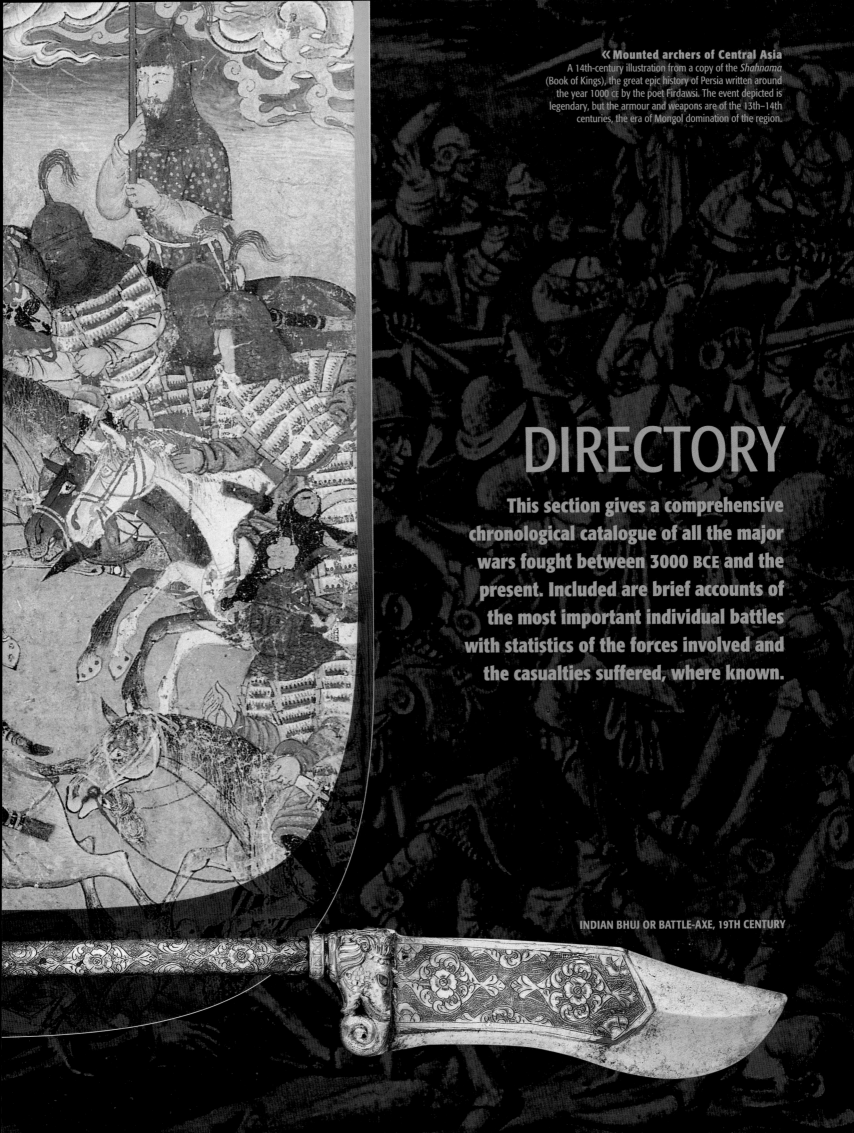

DIRECTORY

This section gives a comprehensive chronological catalogue of all the major wars fought between 3000 BCE and the present. Included are brief accounts of the most important individual battles with statistics of the forces involved and the casualties suffered, where known.

INDIAN BHUJ OR BATTLE-AXE, 19TH CENTURY

War in the Ancient World
3000 BCE–500 CE

HAMMURABI

Our knowledge of the earliest battles of humanity is incomplete and reliant on the surviving accounts available. Many conflicts between ancient peoples have certainly gone unrecorded by history. In many cases, little more than the names of wars, battles, and generals, have survived the passing of centuries. This was the era of such legendary commanders as Ramesses, Darius, Alexander, Constantine, Hannibal, Pompey and Caesar. Even today students of military history begin with the campaigns of their famous ancient forebears.

LAGASH DEFEATS UMMA C. 2450 BCE

Forces Lagash: unknown; Umma: unknown. **Casualties** No reliable estimates. **Location** Sumer, southern Mesopotamia (modern Iraq and eastern Syria).

Eannatum, ruler of the city-state of Lagash, led his forces against the neighbouring city of Umma to resolve a border dispute. Chariots were used as transport but the battle was fought on foot by dense masses of spearmen.

Ramesses II

Egyptian pharaoh Ramesses II (reigned c.1279–1213 BCE) strikes one of his foes. Known as Ramesses the Great, he negotiated the first recorded peace treaty, with the Hittite king Hattusili III.

CONQUESTS OF SARGON OF AKKADE C. 2300–2215 BCE

Forces Sargon: 5,400; Uruk, Ebla, and other Mesopotamian city-states: unknown. **Casualties** No reliable estimates. **Location** Mesopotamia (modern Iraq).

Sargon of Akkade rose from humble origins to carve out an empire. He led an army over 5,000 strong, armed with bronze hand weapons and composite bows.

CAMPAIGNS OF SENUSRET III C.1850 BCE

Forces Senusret III: unknown; Nubian: unknown. **Casualties** No reliable estimates. **Location** Nubia (modern southern Egypt and northern Sudan) and Egypt.

Senusret III campaigned against the Nubians and established Egypt's borders. He then went on to build a chain of fortresses to secure Egypt against raids and invasions.

CAMPAIGNS OF HAMMURABI C.1760–C.1758 BCE

Forces Babylonian: unknown; Neighbouring kingdoms: unknown. **Casualties** No reliable estimates. **Location** Mesopotamia (modern Iraq).

Hammurabi increased the power of Babylon through cleverly making and breaking alliances. Having gained control of much of southern Mesopotamia, he turned on his former allies. He controlled all of Mesopotamia at the time of his death.

HYKSOS INVASION OF EGYPT C.1710–1600 BCE

Forces Hyksos: unknown; Egyptians: unknown. **Casualties** Unknown. **Location** Egypt.

A people of unknown origin entered and overran Egypt, becoming known as Hyksos, or "shepherd-kings". They pioneered advanced military technology, such as horse-drawn chariots and composite bows.

EGYPTIAN 17TH DYNASTY CONFLICTS WITH THE HYKSOS C.1560 BCE

Forces Theban: unknown; Hyksos: unknown. **Casualties** No reliable estimates. **Location** Egypt.

In the last years of the Egyptian 17th dynasty, disputes between the kings of Thebes and the Hyksos rulers of northern Egypt expanded into open conflict. A series of skirmishes was interspersed with diplomacy. By the end of the 17th dynasty, the Hyksos were beginning to suffer their first real reverses.

EGYPTIAN 18TH DYNASTY WARS AGAINST THE HYKSOS C.1550 BCE

Forces Theban: unknown; Hyksos: unknown. **Casualties** No reliable estimates. **Location** Egypt.

Conflict with the Hyksos resumed in the early years of the 18th dynasty. Repeated Theban campaigns finally drove the Hyksos from their capital at Avaris. The first documented use of chariots by the Egyptians was recorded during this conflict.

MYCENAEAN RAIDS
1550–1150 BCE

Forces Varied. **Casualties** Unknown. **Location**: Eastern Mediterranean and surrounding region.

The Mycenaeans were a warrior people who built fortress cities from which they launched trading and raiding expeditions. Mycenaean forces raided Egyptian and Hittite cities (in modern Syria and Turkey), and conquered Crete.

MEGIDDO c.1460 BCE

Forces Egyptian: 10,000–20,000; Palestinian: unknown. **Casualties** Egyptian: unknown; Palestinian: 83 killed, 340 captured. **Location** Near Haifa, northern Israel.

The Egyptian pharaoh Thutmosis III took a huge gamble, leading his forces through a narrow pass where they could easily have been trapped. But he was able to surprise the Palestinians and rout them in battle.

EARLY ISRAELITE CAMPAIGNS
c.1400 BCE

After the Exodus from Egypt (thought by some scholars to have been c.1450 BCE), the surviving Israelites wandered into Canaan, seeking a home that they could make their own.

AI c.1400 BCE

Forces Canaanite: 12,000; Israelite: 10,000–11,000. **Casualties** No reliable estimates. **Location** Between Gibeon and Jericho (modern Palestinian territories).

The ruin of Ai was an outpost garrisoned by a small Canaanite force. Anticipating an easy victory, the Israelites attacked. They were repulsed, but drew out the defenders and defeated them in the field with light infantry.

WATERS OF MEROM c.1400 BCE

Forces Canaanite: no reliable estimates; Israelite: no reliable estimates. **Casualties** No reliable estimates. **Location** Galilee, northern Israel.

An alliance of city-states in northern Canaan sent a force to halt the Israelite invasion. The Israelites counterattacked, catching their foes unawares and routing them with a fearsome head-on assault.

MAHABHARATA WAR c.1300 BCE

Forces Kaurava: unknown; Pandava: unknown. **Casualties** Kaurava: all killed; Pandava: only five survivors. **Location** Kurukshetra, Haryana state, northwest India.

The battles detailed in the Sanskrit epic known as the *Mahabharata* are thought to represent the conflicts of the time rather than describe actual events. They do indicate how Indian wars were fought in the period, that being mainly on foot with some chariots for the nobility.

KADESH c.1275 BCE

Forces Egyptian: 20,000 men and 2,000 chariots; Hittite: 15,000 men and 3,500 chariots. **Casualties** No reliable estimates. **Location** By the Orontes river, western Syria.

One of the largest chariot battles ever recorded, the outcome at Kadesh is unclear, with both sides claiming victory.

Murder of King Priam and his son Polites
This detail from an Athenian vase (c.480–475 BCE) shows Neoptolemos, Achilles' son, killing King Priam during the sack of Troy. On the King's lap is his dead son, Polites. The warrior is armed with a *kopis*, a single-edged sword.

TROY c.1250 BCE

Forces Greek: 100,000; Trojan: unknown. **Casualties** No reliable estimates. **Location** Hisarlik, northwest Turkey.

According to legend, the Greeks ended their ten-year siege of Troy by means of a trick, the famous "Trojan Horse". There is some archaeological evidence to suggest that the siege did, in fact, take place.

SEA PEOPLES' RAIDS
1176 BCE

Forces Sea People: unknown; Egyptian: unknown. **Casualties** No reliable estimates. **Location** Nile Delta, northern Egypt.

The origin of the Sea Peoples remains unclear, but they raided the shores of Egypt's Mediterranean coast. This led to the world's first recorded sea battle, between the Sea Peoples and an Egyptian fleet. According to Egyptian accounts, the Sea Peoples were decisively defeated.

BATTLE OF MUYE 1046 BCE

Forces Shang: 530,000; Zhou: 222,000. **Casualties** Shang: extremely high; Zhou: unknown, but light. **Location** Modern Henan province, China.

Many Shang dynasty troops refused to fight and 170,000 Shang slaves, who had unwisely been armed, decided to fight for the Zhou dynasty instead. The more disciplined Zhou overran their enemies and massacred loyal Shang troops afterwards. The battle marked the transition from the Shang to the Zhou dynasty.

LATER ISRAELITE CAMPAIGNS
c.1240–874 BCE

Once the Israelites became established in their Promised Land, their fortunes fluctuated considerably. After finally defeating the Canaanites, they were forced to defend their new lands against a succession of external threats.

MOUNT TABOR 1240 BCE

Forces Canaanite: probably more than 10,000; Israelite: around 10,000. **Casualties** No reliable estimates. **Location** 17km (11 miles) west of the Sea of Galilee, Israel.

"they were dashed **all in pieces** to the **ground**."
PHARAOH RAMESSES II ON HIS VICTORY OVER THE HITTITES, 1275 BCE

The Canaanites were better equipped than the Israelites, but their chariots were bogged down. A resolute Israelite attack turned this setback into a rout.

SPRING OF HAROD 1194 BCE

Forces Midianite: probably more than 10,000; Israelite: around 10,000. **Casualties** Midianite: no reliable estimates, but high; Israelite: no reliable estimates. **Location** Mount Gilboa, northern Israel.

Having been invaded by Midianite people from the east, the Israelites sent a small elite force to startle the sleeping Midianite army in its camp. The main Israelite army then won a decisive victory.

MOUNT GILBOA c.1100 BCE

Forces Israelite: unknown; Philistine: unknown. **Casualties** No reliable estimates. **Location** Plain of Esdraelon, Israel.

After a campaign against the Philistines, the Israelites were brought to battle at Mount Gilboa. The Philistine army stormed Israelite positions, and Israel's King Saul committed suicide.

MICHMASH 1040 BCE

Forces Israelite: 600; Philistine: unknown. **Casualties** No reliable estimates. **Location** Plain of Esdraelon, Israel.

The Israelite leader Jonathan discovered a secret path that outflanked the Philistine position. The ensuing Israelite attack caused panic among the Philistines, who were either massacred or forced to flee the battlefield.

JEBUS 1000 BCE

Forces Israelite: unknown; Jebusite: unknown. **Casualties** No reliable estimates. **Location** Modern Jerusalem, Israel.

Besieging the city of Jebus (modern-day Jerusalem), the Israelites gained access by a surprise assault. Jebus became the capital of Israel, now a united kingdom.

SAMARIA 890 BCE

Forces Israelite: 8,000; Syrian: unknown. **Casualties** No reliable estimates. **Location** Israel.

Syrian forces advanced on Samaria and laid siege before an Israelite field force could be mustered. Subsequently, the Israelites attacked the siege camp while the Syrian leaders were drunk and routed their army.

GOLAN HEIGHTS
874 BCE

Forces Israelite: unknown; Syrian: unknown. **Casualties** No reliable estimates, but some sources put Syrian casualties as high as 127,000. **Location** Northwest of Samaria, Israel.

As the Syrians prepared for a renewed invasion of Israel, the Israelites launched a pre-emptive campaign. After a standoff, the Israelites attacked and routed the Syrians.

IMPORTANT WAR DEITIES

Name	Gender	Culture
Ankt	Goddess	Asia Minor/Egyptian
Ares	God	Greek
Astarte	Goddess	Semitic
Athena	Goddess	Greek
Chi You	God	Chinese/Korean
Camulus	God	Celtic
Hachiman	God	Japanese
Hadúr	God	Hungarian
Huitzilopochtli	God	Aztec
Indra	God	Hindu
Kali	Goddess	Hindu
Mars	God	Roman
Nike	Goddess	Greek
Odin	God	Germanic/Norse
Sekhmet	Goddess	Egyptian
Set	God	Egyptian
Skanda	God	Hindu
Teoyaomicqui	God	Aztec
Tezcatlipoca	God	Aztec
Thor	God	Germanic/Norse
Tumatauenga	God	Maori
Tyr	God	Germanic/Norse

Egyptian war goddess
This statue (c.1390–1353 BCE) depicts Sekhmet, the war goddess of Upper Egypt. She has the head of a lioness, an animal admired by the ancient Egyptians as a fierce hunter.

CRITICAL MILITARY INVENTIONS IN NAVAL WARFARE

Naval ram (c.1000 BCE)
Introduced by the ancient Greek and Roman navies, a bronze ram enabled a vessel to puncture an enemy ship below the waterline, providing the means to sink another ship in the days before naval firepower.

Trireme
Warships such as this trireme, with its great bronze ram projecting from its bow, were characteristic of ancient Greek and Persian navies.

Naval mines (c.15th century CE)
Possibly first invented by medieval Chinese naval officers, naval mines became a great threat during the 20th century, enabling a navy to control enemy shipping lanes.

Armour plating (15th century)
Korean Panokseon-class "turtle ships" had iron protection on the upper deck and hull. Armour became standard only in the 19th century.

Carronade (late 18th century)
For roughly 100 years, short smoothbore cannon, known as carronades, provided devastating short-range firepower in European ship-to-ship engagements, acquiring the nickname "smashers".

Self-propelled torpedoes (c.1866)
Arguably an Austrian invention, the self-propelled torpedo offered a largely silent and almost invisible anti-ship weapon, and later gave the submarine its principal firepower.

Naval radar (c.1930)
Maritime radar not only revolutionized navigation, but also led to the development of radar-controlled naval gunnery, dramatically improving the accuracy of fire over long ranges.

Steam catapult (c.1912)
The US Navy's development of the steam catapult was the breakthrough that enabled aircraft carriers to develop into the influential fighting systems they are today.

Satellite navigation (1964)
First developed for the US Navy, satellite navigation gave naval forces superb navigational accuracy and eventually led to true precision-guided missile technologies.

"By **force of arms** … I took 46 of his strong-fenced **cities**."

ASSYRIAN KING SENNACHERIB'S ACCOUNT OF DEFEAT OF KING HEZEKIAH, 701 BCE

WARS OF ASSYRIA
c.900–600 BCE

The Assyrians were the first known society to introduce compulsory military service for all male citizens. Its armies were well trained and often considered unbeatable in the field. The Assyrians therefore had to become adept at siege warfare to overcome the defences of enemies who would not come out to fight.

QARQAR 853 BCE

Forces Assyrian: up to 100,000; Syrian-led alliance: c.70,000. **Casualties** Assyrian: unknown; Syrian alliance: allegedly 14,000. **Location** Northwest of Hamath (modern Hama), Syria.

As Assyria grew in power, an alliance of 12 states was formed to counter its expansion. The two sides met in the largest battle the world had yet seen, involving chariots, cavalry and infantry.

Assyrian bow and arrow
This is a reproduction of the type of bow and arrow that may have been used by Assyrian warriors c.1350 BCE.

DAMASCUS 842 BCE

Forces Assyrian: unknown; Syrian: unknown. **Casualties** No reliable estimates. **Location** Western Syria.

While the Assyrian forces under Shalmaneser III ravaged the countryside all around, the Syrians held out in their capital. Damascus was not taken, but several other cities were obliged to offer tribute to the Assyrian empire.

INVASION OF PALESTINE
734–732 BCE

Forces Assyrian: 34,000; Allied garrisons: usually 1,000–5000. **Casualties** No reliable estimates. **Location** Between the Mediterranean Sea and the Jordan river.

Seeking access to the Mediterranean, Assyrian forces pushed westwards. A coalition of states was formed to resist the expansion, including Israel and Damascus. Unwilling to fight in the field, the allies took refuge in their fortresses and cities, which were assaulted one by one.

SIEGE OF JERUSALEM 721 BCE

Forces Assyrian: unknown; Judaean: unknown. **Casualties** No reliable estimates. **Location** Judaean mountains between Mediterranean Sea and Dead Sea, Israel.

After all the other cities of Judah were taken, Jerusalem came under siege by the Assyrian army. The city was not taken, for reasons that remain unclear. Some accounts claim a plague weakened the Assyrian army; others suggest the city was relieved by allies from Africa.

SIEGE OF LACHISH 701 BCE

Forces Assyrian: unknown; Judaean: unknown. **Casualties** No reliable estimates. **Location** Modern Tel Lakhish, Israel.

The Assyrian army took Lachish using sophisticated siege techniques. A tower carrying archers and fitted with battering rams was transported to the wall up a specially built ramp. Other wall sections were undermined. The inhabitants of the city were massacred.

DIYALA RIVER C.693 BCE

Forces Assyrian: unknown; Elamite: unknown. **Casualties** No reliable estimates. **Location** Nippur, central Mesopotamia (modern Iraq).

While campaigning against the Elamites, the Assyrians were attacked by a coalition of Elamite and Chaldean forces. The resulting battle at the Diyala river must have been very costly, as the Assyrians suspended offensive operations for a year.

SUSA 647 BCE

Forces Assyrian: unknown; Elamite: unknown. **Casualties** No reliable estimates. **Location** 250km (150 miles) east of the Tigris river (in modern Iran).

In order to punish the people of Susa for joining an alliance against them, Ashurbanipal's Assyrian armies utterly destroyed Susa, pulling down buildings, looting, and sowing the land with salt. This was standard practice, and induced many other cities to surrender without a fight.

FALL OF ELAM 639 BCE

Forces Assyrian: unknown; Elamite: unknown. **Casualties** No reliable estimates. **Location** Modern southwestern Iran.

After years of conflict with Assyria, the Elamites were weakened by an Assyrian attack on Babylon, which failed, and by civil war. The Assyrian army advanced into Elam and laid waste to the country, eliminating the Elamite threat for good.

ASHDOD 635 BCE

Forces Assyrian: unknown, but smaller than the opposition; Egyptian: unknown. **Casualties** No reliable estimates. **Location** Southern Palestine.

With the Assyrian empire in decline, and its forces facing constant harassment from tribes along its frontiers, Egyptian forces besieged Ashdod, finally capturing it from Assyria after a 29-year siege.

FALL OF ASSUR 614 BCE

Forces Assyrian: unknown; Babylonian and Mede: unknown. **Casualties** No reliable estimates. **Location** Modern northern Iraq.

Taking advantage of the weakness of Assyria, which was dealing with revolts as well as Egyptian incursions, the Medes and Babylonians tried unsuccessfully to attack the Assyrian capital, Nineveh. While most of the Assyrian force were defending Nineveh, the Babylonian and Medean armies moved to quickly capture Assur, the original capital of the empire.

FALL OF NINEVEH 612 BCE

Forces Assyrian: unknown; Babylonian and Mede: unknown. **Casualties** No reliable estimates. **Location** Near modern-day Mosul, Iraq.

As Assyrian military power waned, the allied forces of Babylon and the Medes moved against them. Despite setbacks, the allies were able to capture the Assyrian capital, Nineveh, after a three-month siege.

CHENGPU 632 BCE

Forces Chu army: unknown; Jin army: unknown. **Casualties** No reliable estimates. **Location** Possibly Henan or Shandong Province, China.

The battle of Chengpu was a massive clash between chariot armies. The Jin right wing feigned a retreat, then launched a counterattack. Meanwhile their left wing had smashed its opponents, forcing the Chu to make a hasty retreat.

WARS OF EGYPT AND BABYLON
c.600–586 BCE

As Assyrian power diminished, Babylon and Egypt began to vie for control of Mesopotamia. The Assyrians were caught in the middle of the conflict and were gradually crushed into insignificance.

MEGIDDO 605 BCE

Forces Egyptian: unknown but far larger than the opposition; Judah: unknown. **Casualties** No reliable estimates. **Location** Near Haifa, northern Israel.

Marching through Palestine to bring relief to their Assyrian allies, the Egyptians were confronted at Megiddo by an army from Judah under King Josiah. The Egyptians were victorious and continued their march.

CARCHEMISH C.605 BCE

Forces Egyptian and Assyrian: unknown; Babylonian: unknown. **Casualties** No reliable estimates. **Location** On the frontier of modern Turkey and Syria.

After the fall of Nineveh, the Assyrian capital moved to Carchemish, which was taken by Babylonian forces. A joint Egyptian-Assyrian operation to recapture the city was totally defeated.

HAMA
C.605 BCE

Forces Egyptian: unknown; Babylonian: unknown.
Casualties No reliable estimates, but extremely high on the Egyptian side. **Location** Hama, Syria.

Exploiting the victory at Carchemish, the Babylonians pursued the fleeing Egyptians. The resulting battle inflicted massive casualties on the disorganized Egyptians, ensuring total Babylonian victory.

FALL OF JERUSALEM
586 BCE

Forces Babylonian: unknown; Judaean: unknown.
Casualties No reliable estimates. **Location** Judaean hills between Mediterranean Sea and Dead Sea, Israel.

Abandoned by its Egyptian allies, Jerusalem suffered a siege for 18 months. With his people starving, Zedekiah, king of Judah, confronted the Babylonians near Jericho but was utterly defeated.

WARS OF THE PERSIAN EMPIRE
552–c.500 BCE

The Achaemenid Persian empire grew to become the largest the world had ever seen. It assembled multi-ethnic forces composed of conscripts and mercenaries with varying skills, and welded them into effective and disciplined armies.

PERSIAN REVOLT
552–550 BCE

Forces Persian: over 350,000; Median empire: over 1,000,000. **Casualties** No reliable estimates. **Location** Province of Persis (in modern Iran).

After a long period of rule by Assyria and Media, the province of Persis revolted, starting a war that lasted two years. Led by Cyrus the Great, the Persians became independent and founded an empire.

SARDIS 546 BCE

Forces Persian: c.50,000; Lydian alliance: unknown (but greater). **Casualties** No reliable estimates. **Location** Plain of Thymbra, Anatolia (modern Sart, Turkey).

Outnumbered, Cyrus the Great formed his force into a defensive square. After disrupting the Lydians with archery, the Persians successfully counterattacked.

FALL OF BABYLON 539 BCE

Forces Persian: unknown; Babylonian: unknown.
Casualties No reliable estimates. **Location** Babylon, southern Mesopotamia (modern Iraq).

Cyrus of Persia invaded Babylonia, defeating its forces at Opis. The native Babylonians revolted against their unpopular King Nabonidus, and Cyrus took Babylon without further fighting.

PELUSIUM
525 BCE

Forces Persian: unknown; Egyptian and mercenary: unknown, but weaker than the Persian force. **Casualties** Persian: 7,000; Egyptian and mercenary: 50,000. **Location** East of modern Port Said, Egypt.

Taking advantage of the death of the pharaoh, Persian forces invaded Egypt. The much weaker Egyptian army, bolstered by mercenaries, made a stand at Pelusium but was comprehensively defeated. Egypt was annexed by the Persian empire.

EARLY ROMAN WARS
C.509–C.458 BCE

Early in its existence, Rome used a military system heavily influenced by that of the Greek city-states, as it fought against neighbouring tribes for survival and against rival cities for dominance.

Detail from the Ishtar gate, Babylon
Constructed in about 575 BCE by order of King Nebuchadnezzar II, the Ishtar gate failed to protect the city from the forces of Cyrus the Great in 539 BCE.

LAKE REGILLUS
C.499–493 BCE

Forces Roman: unknown; Latin: unknown. **Casualties** No reliable estimates. **Location** Near Frascati, north of Rome.

This semi-legendary Roman battle cannot be precisely dated due to the lack of records from this time. Both Rome and its Latin neighbours used Greek tactics, with a phalanx supported by lighter troops. Roman cavalry dismounted and joined the fighting on foot, resulting in victory.

MONS ALGIDUS
C.458 BCE

Forces Roman: unknown; Aequi: unknown. **Casualties** No reliable estimates. **Location** 20km (12 miles) southeast of Rome.

A force from the Aequi tribe was camped near Mons Algidus, threatening Roman territory. An army sent to remove the threat became surrounded, but after rescue by another Roman force they crushed the Aequi.

HISTORY'S LONGEST WARS

Conflict	Background	Duration
The Hundred Years War	Dynastic war between English and French monarchs over claims to the French throne and French territory	116 years (1337–1453)
The Dutch Revolt	War of Dutch independence from Spanish rule, fought in Europe and in Spanish colonies	80 years (1568–1648)
Arab-Israeli Conflict	An ongoing conflict between Israel and surrounding Arab nations	60+ years (1948–)
Sudanese Civil War	Protracted conflict between Arab and non-Arab groups, costing nearly three million lives	50 years (1955–2005)
Aceh War	The Dutch empire declared war on the separatists of Aceh, Indonesia in 1873; fighting continued until 1904.	31 years (1873–1904)
The Thirty Years War	Hugely destructive war involving many European states, fought over various religious and territorial issues	30 years (1618–48)
Peloponnesian War	War between rival city states of Athens and the Peloponnesian League, in ancient Greece	27 years (431–404 BCE)

Greek hoplite
A hoplite's basic defensive kit included a crested helmet and a large shield, called a *hoplon*.

IONIAN REVOLT
499–493 BCE

Ionia and other parts of Asia Minor revolted against Persian rule. Troops from Greece took part in the fighting, paving the way for the Greco-Persian wars, which began soon afterwards.

SIEGE OF NAXOS 500–499 BCE

Forces Naxian: 27,800; Persian: 40,000. **Casualties** No reliable estimates, but heavy on the Persian side. **Location** Cyclades Islands in the Aegean Sea.

An attempt by the Persian-backed tyrant of Miletus to capture Naxos led to a long siege, which was broken off when Persian supplies and money ran out.

LADE 494 BCE

Forces Ionian: 353 ships; Persian: 600 ships. **Casualties** Ionian: 234 ships; Persian: 57 ships. **Location** Near the island of Lade, off Miletus, Aegean Sea.

The Ionian rebels were assisted by ships from several islands, creating a large fleet under a weak command. One of the allied factions accepted a Persian bribe not to fight, causing others to drop out as well. The Persian fleet won a decisive victory over those that elected to fight.

GRECO–PERSIAN WARS
499–448 BCE

The Persian empire attempted to expand its influence into Greece with a series of invasions. Resistance by the Greek city-states was countered by the Persians in stages. Some city-states repelled the invaders while others allied themselves with Persia. The result was a drawn-out struggle that resulted in the Greek city-states remaining outside the Persian empire.

FIRST PERSIAN INVASION 492 BCE

Forces Persian: no reliable estimates; Greek, Macedonian, and Thracian: no reliable estimates. **Casualties** No reliable estimates. **Location** Thrace and Macedonia (modern southeastern Europe).

The Persians launched an expedition that gained control of Thrace and forced Macedonia to accept Persian domination. Storm damage to the Persian fleet then curtailed the campaign.

ERETRIA 490 BCE

Forces Persian: 25,000; Greek: no reliable estimates. **Casualties** No reliable estimates. **Location** 60km (37 miles) north of Athens, Greece.

A renewed invasion of Greece began with landings at Eretria. Rather than resist, the Eretrians took refuge within their city walls and were besieged. The city fell by treachery after a few days.

MARATHON SEPTEMBER 490 BCE

Forces Persian: 20,000–25,000; Greek: 10,000. **Casualties** Persian: 6,400; Greek: 192. **Location** 40km (25 miles) northeast of Athens, Greece.

Responding to a Persian landing, Greek forces met the Persians on the coast at

Hemp and linen body armour
This reproduction composite body armour is called a *linothorax*, meaning linen torso. It reflects a style that may have been used in 5th-century Greece.

Marathon. Rather than wait for their reinforcements, the outnumbered Greeks charged and forced the Persians to make a hurried re-embarkation.

THERMOPYLAE AUGUST 480 BCE

Forces Greek: 7,000; Persian: 200,000. **Casualties** Greek: 2,500 (including 300 Spartan); Persian: 20,000. **Location** Thessaly, northern Greece.

While naval forces from Athens confronted the Persian invaders at sea, a small force of 300 Spartans attempted to hold the pass at Thermopylae. Finally outflanked and surrounded, the heroic Spartans fought to the death.

ARTEMISIUM AUGUST 480 BCE

Forces Greek: 271 ships; Persian: possibly 800 ships. **Casualties** Greek: about 100 ships; Persian: about 200 ships. **Location** Off the coast of Euboea, Greece.

Storms destroyed part of the Persian fleet and gave the Greeks a fighting chance to hold the straits of Artemisium. After three days of piecemeal actions the Greeks were forced to withdraw to Salamis.

SALAMIS SEPTEMBER 480 BCE

Forces Greek: c.300 ships; Persian: c.700 ships. **Casualties** Greek: 40 ships; Persian: 200–300 ships. **Location** Saronic Gulf, 27km (17 miles) from Athens, Greece.

Luring the Persian fleet into the narrow channel between the island of Salamis and the mainland, the Greeks attacked and defeated the Persians in a seven-hour battle.

BATTLE OF PLATAEA JULY 479 BCE

Forces Persian: 100,000; Greek: 80,000. **Casualties** Persian: 50,000; Greek: 1,500. **Location** Southeastern Boeotia, south of Thebes, Greek mainland.

Taking advantage of a bungled Greek withdrawal, the Persian army attacked the Spartans on the Greek right wing. The Spartans were able to hold out long enough for their allies to return to the field. Defeat at Plataea ended the Persian invasion of Greece.

MYCALE 27 AUGUST 479 BCE

Forces Persian: 60,000; Greek: 40,000. **Casualties** No reliable estimates. **Location** Anatolia, modern Turkey.

After suffering heavy losses the Persian fleet fled to the island of Samos. The Greek fleet followed, seeking to annihilate it. The Persians would not fight at sea, so the Greeks came ashore and defeated them in a land battle, burning the Persian ships afterwards.

SIEGE OF BYZANTIUM 478 BCE

Forces Persian: unknown; Greek: unknown. **Casualties** No reliable estimates. **Location** Modern Istanbul, Turkey.

A Spartan-led Greek coalition defeated the Persians, depriving them of their last stronghold in Thrace. However, tyrannical conduct by the Spartan leader led the allies to realign themselves with Athens. Thus was formed an alliance known as the Delian League, which became the basis for the Athenian empire.

"The Persians considered the Greeks as **mad**, and rushing on **certain destruction**."

HERODOTUS ON THE BATTLE OF MARATHON, 490 BCE

Running into battle
The Greek hoplite shown in this 4th-century fresco runs into battle with his shield held in his right hand and his spear grasped firmly at his side.

HISTORY'S MOST INFLUENTIAL BATTLES

Battle	Location	Date	Significance
Marathon	Greece	September 490 BCE	Along with subsequent Greek victories, Marathon stopped the Persian takeover of Greece, allowing Greek political and cultural ideas to flourish and subsequently influence the Western world.
Vienna	Austria	October 1529 CE	The Austrian garrison prevented the Muslim army of Suleiman the Magnificent from capturing Vienna, halting the spread of the Ottoman empire into central Europe.
Cajamarca	Peru	16 November 1532	Francisco Pizarro defeated the Incas and opened the way for Spanish hegemony in South America.
Waterloo	Belgium	18 June 1815	Napoleon's defeat brought the French domination of Europe to an end.
Stalingrad	Russia	July 1942–February 1943	The capture and bloody seige of the city saw the beginnings of defeat for Nazi Germany in World War II.
Huai-Hai	China	November 1948–January 1949	Mao Zedong's Communists defeated the Nationalist Army in a massive land engagment, enabling the final Communist take-over of China.

EGYPTIAN CAMPAIGN 462–454 BCE

Forces Persian: 400,000; Egyptian: 200,000–300,00; Athenian 200 ships. **Casualties** No reliable estimates. **Location** Nile Delta, northern Egypt.

Egypt revolted against Persian rule and was granted Athenian assistance. The Persians were defeated on land at Pampremis and at sea near Memphis. The eventual defeat of the Egyptians allowed the Athenian force to return home.

PELOPONNESIAN WAR 431–404 BCE

With Athens dominant at sea and Sparta in the ascendant on land, the Peloponnesian War pitted the two greatest powers in Greece and their allies against each other. Athenian influence was greatly diminished as a result of the conflict.

PYLOS 425 BCE

Forces Athenian: 800 hoplites, 2,000 other troops; Spartan: 420 hoplites. **Casualties** Athenian: unknown; Spartan: 128 killed, the rest captured. **Location** West coast of Peloponnese, southern Greece.

In an attempt to retake Pylos from the Athenians by land and sea, a Spartan force was cut off on Sphacteria. Athenian troops captured those not killed in the fighting.

DELIUM NOVEMBER 424 BCE

Forces Athenian: 7,000 hoplites; Boeotian: 7,000 hoplites; 1,000 cavalry, 10,000 light troops. **Casualties** Athenian: c.1,000 hoplites. Boetian: unknown. **Location** Boeotia, Greece.

Ambushed by a Boeotian army allied to Sparta, the Athenians were hard pressed but had gained the upper hand until Boeotian cavalry appeared on the Athenian flank. Panic spread and the Athenians were routed.

MANTINEA 418 BCE

Forces Athenian and Allied: 8,000; Spartan and Allied: 9,000. **Casualties** Athenian and Allied: 1,100; Spartan and Allied: 300. **Location** The Peloponnese, north of Sparta.

In classic hoplite style, both armies began trying to envelop the left flank of the other. Although the Spartan line was broken, the Spartans defeated the enemy left flank before turning to attack their centre, inflicting a general collapse and rout.

SIEGE OF SYRACUSE 415–413 BCE

Forces Athenian 30,000; Spartan: 3,000; Syracusan: unknown. **Casualties** Athenian: 30,000 killed or captured; Spartan: unknown. **Location** Southeastern coast of Sicily.

Athenian forces besieging Syracuse were themselves blockaded by a Spartan fleet reponding to the Syracusans' request for help. The trapped Athenians were gradually worn down and surrendered.

CYZICUS 410 BCE

Forces Athenian and Allied: 86 ships; Spartan: 80 ships. **Casualties** Athenian and Allied: very low; Spartan: entire fleet lost. **Location** Northwest Anatolia, modern Turkey.

Drawing out the Spartan fleet, the Athenians launched an ambush that resulted in the total destruction of the Spartan force. Sparta offered peace as a result but Athens decided to fight on. The Spartan fleet was quickly rebuilt and Athens' advantage was lost.

AEGOSPOTAMI 405 BCE

Forces Athenian: 200 warships; Spartan: unknown. **Casualties** Athenian: more than 190 ships; Spartan: unknown. **Location** Near Sea of Marmara, modern Turkey.

The Spartans made a surprise attack while their enemies were ashore. The powerful Athenian fleet was almost totally destroyed, and Athens was finally forced to sue for peace.

ALLIA 18 JULY 390 BCE

Forces Celtic: 30,000; Roman: 10,000–15,000. **Casualties** No reliable estimates. **Location** 18km (11 miles) outside Rome.

Outnumbered and outfought by the more flexible Celtic warriors, the Roman phalanx broke and was massacred. Rome was then sacked as a result. Subsequently, the rigid phalanx formation was abandoned in favour of the tactically more flexible legion.

HISTORY'S MOST SUCCESSFUL COMMANDERS

Commanders	Nationality	Life dates	Achievements
Cyrus the Great	Persian	c.590/580–529 BCE	Conquered numerous foreign empires, including the Median, Lydian, and Neo-Babylonian empires, and forged an empire over three continents.
Alexander the Great	Greek/Macedonian	356–323 BCE	Undefeated in battle, Alexander humbled the entire Persian empire and brought most of Asia and the Middle East under his authority.
Hannibal Barca	Carthaginian	247–182 BCE	Defeated the mighty Romans in three major engagements, and brought much of Italy under his power or into his alliance.
Julius Caesar	Roman	100–44 BCE	Caesar secured power over Rome through numerous victories against the Gauls, and went on to deliver crushing defeats in the Civil War.
Attila the Hun	Hun	406–453 CE	Created the Hunnic empire through his conquests and conducted deep raids into Gaul.
William the Conqueror	Norman	1027–1087	Defeated the English army and became king of England in 1066.
Genghis Khan	Mongol	c.1162–1227	Founded the Mongol empire and defeated his enemies in an imperial campaign that stretched from China to Eastern Europe.
Napoleon Bonaparte	Corsican/French	1769–1821	Revolutionized the nature of warfare itself, and inflicted major defeats on most opposing European powers and alliances for more than a decade.
Adolf Hitler	Austrian/German	1889–1945	Although he led his nation to eventual ruin, in 1939–42 he conquered most of western and southern Europe, parts of North Africa, and Soviet territories up to Moscow and deep into Ukraine.
Georgy Zhukov	Russian	1896–1974	A key figure in Germany's defeat in World War II, Zhukov helped stop the German capture of Moscow, crushed the Sixth Army at Stalingrad, and then drove a Soviet advance to Berlin itself.

Alexander the Great
Like other Macedonian kings, Alexander the Great (356–323 BCE) is often depicted wearing a lion skin as a symbol of his strength and royal lineage.

heavily equipped force of Spartan hoplites with missile fire. Unable to get close enough to use their weapons, the Spartans eventually broke and fled.

CNIDUS 394 BCE

Forces Athenian and Persian: 90 ships; Spartan: 85 ships. **Casualties** Athenian and Persian: very low; Spartan: Almost total. **Location** near modern Datça, Turkey.

Despite the inexperience of its crews, the Spartan fleet achieved some success at first, but was then rapidly overpowered by the Athenian-Persian force. Those ships not sunk were captured.

LEUCTRA JULY 371 BCE

Forces Spartan: 11,000; Theban: 6,000. **Casualties** Spartan: 2,000 killed; Theban: negligible. **Location** Boeotia, central Greece.

By massively reinforcing his left flank and holding back forces from his weak right, the Theban leader Epaminondas broke the Spartan right. His force then wheeled and pushed back the Spartan line.

MANTINEA 362 BCE

Forces Athenian–Spartan alliance: 25,000; Theban: 25,000. **Casualties** Athenian–Spartan alliance: 1,000 killed, 2,000 captured; Theban: similar losses. **Location** Peloponnese, north of Sparta.

Again using a powerful left-flank phalanx, Epaminondas broke the right of the enemy line. However, he was killed in the fighting and little was made of the victory.

GUAI LING 341 BCE

Forces Wei: unknown; Qi: unknown. **Casualties** No reliable estimates. **Location** Northeast central China.

During China's warring states period, the state of Qi sent a force into Wei, forcing the Wei to break off the siege of Handan and march homeward in haste. This drew the Wei into an ambush, which resulted in their utter defeat.

TRIFANUM 338 BCE

Forces Roman and Samnite: unknown; Campanian and Latin: unknown. **Casualties** No reliable estimates. **Location** Campania, southern Italy.

Roman forces and their Samnite allies clashed with rebel Campanians and Latins. The Roman force was able to inflict a defeat that ended the rebellion.

CHAERONEA 338 BCE

Forces Athenian and Theban: 50,000; Macedonian: 32,000. **Casualties** Athenian and Theban: 20,000; Macedonian: no reliable estimates. **Location** 50km (30 miles) north of Thebes, Boeotia

The Macedonian army drew out the opposing hoplites and broke them with a counterattack. A charge by Macedonian cavalry completed the victory.

CONQUESTS OF ALEXANDER 336–323 BCE

In 336 BCE Alexander of Macedon inherited a formidable army from his father, Philip, who had brought the city-states of southern Greece under his control. Alexander extended his father's conquests as far afield as Egypt and even India.

GRANICUS MAY 334 BCE

Forces Macedonian: 40,000; Persian: 35,000. **Casualties** Macedonian: unknown; Persian: more than 15,000. **Location** Northwestern modern Turkey.

Alexander opted for a reckless head-on attack against a Persian army on the far bank of the Granicus river. His cavalry forced a crossing, followed by his infantry, and surrounded the Persian forces.

ISSUS NOVEMBER 333 BCE

Forces Macedonian: 35,000; Persian: 110,000. **Casualties** Macedonian: 450; Persian: 50,000 (allegedly). **Location** Plain on the Gulf of Iskenderun (in modern Turkey).

The battle of Hydaspes
Alexander's conquests took him far into South Asia. The battle of the Hydaspes river in 326 BCE saw his forces defeat the war elephants of the Indian king Porus.

CORINTHIAN WAR AND ITS AFTERMATH 395–362 BCE

At the end of the Peloponnesian War, Sparta was supreme among the Greek city-states. However, domineering Spartan policies led the city of Thebes to end its alliance with Sparta. Theban opposition to Sparta led to a war between the two city-states and their allies.

HALIARTUS 395 BCE

Forces Spartan: unknown; Theban: unknown. **Casualties** No reliable estimates. **Location** Boeotia, central Greece.

A Spartan force attacking Haliartus was repulsed, then driven off by a Theban army marching to relieve the city. The Spartan army counterattacked but eventually had to disband and return home.

NEMEA 394 BCE

Forces Spartan: 18,000; Theban and Allied: 24,000. **Casualties** Spartan: 1,100; Theban and Allied: 2,800. **Location** Peloponnese.

Chinese spearhead
This cast-bronze spearhead was made in China during the "Spring and Autumn" period (770–475 BCE).

The right wings of both armies defeated their opponents. The Spartan phalanx then outfought those of the Thebans and allies, driving them from the field.

CORONEA 394 BCE

Forces Spartan: 15,000; Theban and Allied: 20,000. **Casualties** Spartan: 350; Theban and Allied: 600. **Location** Nemea, in the Peleponnese.

A Theban force penetrated the Spartan line and began to ransack their camp. Other Spartan forces defeated the Thebans' allies, who retreated. The Thebans tried to break out to rejoin their allies but met the Spartan phalanx head-on and were defeated.

LECHEUM 391 BCE

Forces Athenian: unknown; Spartan: 600. **Casualties** Athenian: very low; Spartan: 250. **Location** Lechaeum, near Corinth.

A force consisting of light Athenian troops harassed a much more

"No country **benefited** from **prolonged warfare**."
CHINESE MILITARY STRATEGIST SUN TZU, "THE ART OF WAR", C.400–320 BCE

While attacking the main Persian army, which was holding a fortified position behind a river, Alexander's infantry was fought to a standstill, but his Companion cavalry broke through and put the Persian emperor Darius III to flight.

SIEGE OF TYRE 332 BCE

Forces Macedonian: unknown; Persian and citizens of Tyre: unknown. **Casualties** Macedonian: 400; Persian: no reliable estimates. **Location** Phoenicia (south of modern Beirut, Lebanon).

Alexander's forces built a causeway out to the island city, allowing their siege engines to get into effective range. Battering rams mounted on galleys were used to attack the walls, and the city was stormed.

SIEGE OF GAZA 332 BCE

Forces Macedonian: unknown; Defenders of Gaza: unknown. **Casualties** Macedonian: no reliable estimates; Defenders: no reliable estimates. **Location** Palestine.

Using the siege engines employed at Tyre, Alexander's troops were able to gain access to the city. It took several assaults to finally overwhelm the defenders, but once the city was taken the way to Egypt lay open.

GAUGAMELA
OCTOBER 331 BCE

Forces Macedonian: 40,000 infantry, 7,000 cavalry; Persian: 200,000. **Casualties** Macedonian: 500 killed, 3,000 wounded; Persian: 50,000 killed. **Location** West of Arbela (modern Irbil, northern Iraq).

Outnumbered four to one, the Macedonians staked all on a strike at the Persian emperor, Darius. As light forces struggled to hold the flanks, the main body pushed forwards and put Darius to flight. Alexander then routed the remnants of the Persian army.

PERSIAN GATES 330 BCE

Forces Macedonian: c.15,000; Persian: c.500–700. **Casualties** Macedonian: heavy; Persian: very heavy. **Location** Modern Yasuj, Iran.

Persian forces held a narrow pass against Alexander's army for a month, inflicting heavy losses. Led to an alternative route through the mountains, Alexander's army then advanced on the city of Persepolis.

HYDASPES MAY 326 BCE

Forces Macedonian: 6,000 infantry, 5,000 cavalry; Indian: 30,000. **Casualties** Macedonian: 310 killed; Indian: 23,000 killed (allegedly). **Location** Modern Jhelum river, Pakistan.

After a stealthy crossing of the Hydaspes river, the Macedonians advanced along the banks against the surprised Indian army. Outflanked by cavalry, and under heavy attack, the Indian army broke and fled.

TOUGHEST MILITARY TRAINING – ANCIENT AND MODERN

Military training has always had the same goals: to develop physical and mental toughness, impart tactical and technological skills, and prepare the soldier for the realities of battle.

Spartan (1st millennium BCE)

Period of basic training:	13 years (from five years old to 20)
Endurance exercises:	Running, throwing, wrestling
Survival exercises:	The 12-year-old Spartan spent one year living rough, without shoes or fixed shelter, and wearing only one outer garment.
Weapons training:	Taught to handle sword and spear
Combat training:	War games that often resulted in fatalities. The teenage Spartan would participate in combat raids against the helots (the slave class).
Academic study:	Learned poetry and song; read war theory

British SAS (present day):

Period of basic training:	c.30 weeks
Endurance exercises:	The one-month selection phase involves extreme endurance marches, culminating in a 64-km (40-mile) mountain trek carrying a 25-kg (55-lb) bergen rucksack, plus rifle and webbing, to be completed in under 24 hours.
Survival exercises:	Mountain and wilderness survival training plus a six-week jungle survival course. Four-week parachute course
Weapons training:	Trained to handle full range of British, and most popular foreign, infantry weapon systems
Combat training:	Trained in elite infantry tactics, plus later opportunities to specialize in counter-terrorist, amphibious, mountain, and other operations
Academic study:	Opportunities to learn foreign languages Taught theory and practice of warfare

SAMNITE WARS
343–290 BCE

Although at times Rome allied with the nearby Samnites against other foes, conflicts of interest resulted in three major wars. Victory over the Samnites was critical to the expansion of the Roman republic from a city-state to the dominant power in Italy.

MONS GAURUS 342 BCE

Forces Roman: unknown; Samnite: unknown. **Casualties** No reliable estimates. **Location** Apennine mountains, southeastern Italy.

The First Samnite War took the form of a series of relatively minor engagements between 343–341 BCE. The battle of Mons Gaurus was the most significant of these actions, though there was no long-term decisive outcome.

CAUDINE FORKS 321 BCE

Forces Roman: unknown; Samnite: unknown. **Casualties** No reliable estimates. **Location** Apennine mountains, southeastern Italy.

A Roman army was ambushed in an Apennine pass. Sealing both ends of the pass with felled trees, the Samnites rained missiles on the trapped Romans from above until they surrendered.

BOVIANUM 305 BCE

Forces Roman: unknown; Samnite: unknown. **Casualties** No reliable estimates. **Location** Apennine mountains, southeastern Italy.

In the Second Samnite War the Romans established the practice of taking territory after crushing their enemies. Having captured much of the Samnites' territory, the Romans won a decisive victory at Bovianum, forcing the Samnites to seek peace on whatever terms they could get.

CAMERINUM 298 BCE

Forces Roman: unknown; Samnite: unknown. **Casualties** No reliable estimates. **Location** Modern Camerino, Italy.

After a few years of peace, a third war broke out between the Romans and Samnites. The first action, fought at Camerinum, was a defeat for Rome. The Samnites were seeking to retain territory near Naples and prevent total domination by Rome.

TIFERNUM 297 BCE

Forces Roman: 20,000; Samnite: 25,000. **Casualties** Roman: 2,000; Samnite: 3,400 plus 840 prisoners. **Location** Modern Perugia, Italy.

By attacking one of two Roman forces, the Samnites hoped to defeat it before the other arrived. The battle was going well for the Samnites when a flanking Roman detachment was mistaken for the second Roman army. Believing all was lost, the Samnites withdrew in disorder.

SENTINUM 295 BCE

Forces Roman: 38,000; Samnite and Gaul: c. 60,000. **Casualties** Roman: 8,500; Samnite and Gaul: 25,000. **Location** Umbria, central Italy.

The Roman force's right was successful against the Samnites, but on the left the cavalry was broken by a chariot attack. In the centre, the Roman infantry fought on doggedly to ensure ultimate victory.

AQUILONIA 293 BCE

Forces Roman: unknown; Samnite: unknown. **Casualties** No reliable estimates. **Location** Campania, southern Italy.

As the Romans pushed into Aquilonia, the Samnites scraped together an army by conscripting every available man of fighting age. After a determined stand this force disintegrated, with the survivors seeking refuge in Aquilonia itself. The city was stormed soon afterwards, ending Samnite resistance in the region.

CHANDRAGUPTA'S WARS
C. 310–303 BCE

Forces Mauryan: 600,000 infantry; 30,000 cavalry; 9,000 elephants. Defenders: unknown. **Casualties** No reliable estimates. **Location** Northern and central India and Afghanistan.

Chandragupta Maurya raised a powerful professional army, which he used to carve out an empire in northern and central

Tribal warriors

The tribes of Samnium, a region of southern Italy, were opponents of Rome. This 4th-century fresco from Paestum illustrates the weapons and equipment used by Samnite warriors.

India while in his 20s, in the manner of Alexander the Great, whom Chandragupta had supposedly met in India. Chandragupta attacked and conquered the Macedonian satrapies left behind by Alexander when he had returned westwards.

IPSOS
301 BCE

Forces Antigonid: 70,000 infantry, 10,000 cavalry, 75 elephants; Seleucid: 64,000 infantry, c.500 cavalry, c.500 elephants. **Casualties** No reliable estimates. **Location** Phrygia (modern west-central Turkey).

Battling for control of Alexander the Great's former empire, his former generals Antigonus and Seleucus clashed at Ipsos. The Selucid left was broken but elephants were used to fill the gap. Antigonus was killed in the fighting and his entire army collapsed.

> "With an **army** of 600,000 men, Chandragupta **overran** all India."
>
> PLUTARCH, GRECO-ROMAN HISTORIAN, ON THE CONQUESTS OF CHANDRAGUPTA

PYRRHIC WARS
280–275 BCE

Initially a conflict between Rome and other Italian states, the Pyrrhic Wars widened into a complex series of battles between Rome and various Italian, Greek, and Carthaginian peoples. The wars are named after Pyrrhus, king of Epirus in Greece, who gave his name to a "Pyrrhic victory", which is one gained at too great a cost.

HERACLEA 280 BCE

Forces Roman: 35,000; Greek: 30,000. **Casualties** Roman: 7,000–15,000; Greek: 4,000–11,000. **Location** Apulia, southeastern Italy.

Encountering war elephants for the first time, the Roman cavalry was driven off in panic and the Greek phalanx pushed the Roman infantry back across the Siris river with heavy losses on both sides.

ASCULUM 279 BCE

Forces Roman: 40,000; Greek: 40,000. **Casualties** Roman: 6,000; Greek: 3,500. **Location** Apulia, southeastern Italy.

Hurriedly devising anti-elephant tactics, the Romans clashed with a force of Greeks and their Italian allies under King Pyrrhus. The first day of battle was costly but inconclusive. On the second day elephants broke the Roman line, though the high casualties led King Pyrrhus to exclaim: "One more such victory and I am lost!"

BENEVENTUM 275 BCE

Forces Roman: unknown; Greek: unknown. **Casualties** No reliable estimates. **Location** Campania, southern Italy.

The Romans were pushed back into their camp by Pyrrhus's elephants. Succeeding in driving the beasts back into their own phalanx, the Romans took advantage of the confusion and counterattacked, forcing Pyrrhus's army to retreat. From then on, Rome dominated southern Italy.

FIRST PUNIC WAR
264–261 BCE

Although Carthage had been an ally of Rome, competition for dominance in the Mediterranean resulted in a 23-year war, the first of three.

AGRIGENTUM 261 BCE

Forces Roman: 40,000; Carthaginian: 56,000. **Casualties** Roman: 1,000; Carthaginian: 3,000. **Location** Modern Agrigento, on the southern coast of Sicily.

In their first overseas campaign, the Romans laid siege to Agrigentum. A Carthaginian army was sent to break the siege, bringing on a pitched battle, which the Romans won. The city was taken and the population was sold into slavery.

MYLAE 260 BCE

Forces Roman: 110 warships; Carthaginian: 130 warships. **Casualties** Roman: unknown; Carthaginian: 31 warships captured, 14 sunk. **Location** Off the north coast of Sicily.

The Romans made up for their naval inexperience by the use of the *corvus*, a ramp that allowed legionaries to board enemy craft and fight a land action at sea.

PERSONAL ARMOUR THROUGH THE AGES

Roman armour
This is a reproduction of a *lorica segmentata*, a type of armour made of fitted strips of iron, worn by Roman legionaries of the 1st century CE.

Worn by	Date	Typical armour
Sumerian infantryman	c.2000 BCE	Padded linen cuirass
Roman legionary	mid-1st century CE	Body armour made of mail or riveted metal strips; metal helmet with neck and cheek protection; greaves for leg protection; arm-guards
Seljuk warrior	12th century	One-piece metal helmet; mail coif face-covering; iron segmented cuirass
English knight	14th century	Mail vest and neck protector; visored basinet helmet covering the entire face and skull; full-body articulated metal plate armour
Samurai warrior	17th century	Body armour made of laquered metal strips: cuirass, skirt, arm-guards, thigh-guards; metal helmet with broad neck-protecting rim
French cuirassier	Early 19th century	Metal cuirass for either full-torso or just frontal-torso protection; metal, crested helmet
German infantryman	World War I	Steel helmet; occasionally metal vest for trench combat
US infantryman	Present day	Protective vest made from ballistic fibre and/or ballistic ceramic plates; high-impact ballistic helmet

ECNOMUS 256 BCE

Forces Roman: 330 ships; Carthaginian: 350 ships. **Casualties** Roman: 24 ships sunk; Carthaginian: 30 ships sunk, 64 captured. **Location** Off the southeast coast of Sicily.

While the main forces clashed, transports in the Roman rear were attacked by the Carthaginian wings. The victorious Roman battle squadrons returned to drive off the attack. The way was now clear for Rome to attack Carthaginian North Africa.

TUNIS 255 BCE

Forces Roman: 15,500; Carthaginian: 16,000. **Casualties** Roman: 12,000 plus 500 prisoners; Carthaginian: 800. **Location**: North Africa.

The main Roman force was fought to a standstill by elephants while the cavalry of the Carthaginians drove off its opposite numbers. The Roman infantry was then overwhelmed by cavalry assault. No further Roman expeditions were made into North Africa during the war.

PANORMUS 251 BCE

Forces Roman: unknown; Carthaginian: unknown. **Casualties**: No reliable estimates. **Location**: Modern Palermo, southern Italy.

Drawing out the Carthaginian elephants with an advance force of light infantry, the Romans routed them with javelins, following up with an infantry charge in the ensuing confusion. Victory gave the Romans total control of Sicily.

DREPANA 249 BCE

Forces Roman: 130 warships; Carthaginian: 130 warships. **Casualties** Roman: 93 ships lost. Carthaginian: unknown. **Location** Off the western coast of Sicily.

The Roman fleet was ambushed by a Carthaginian force hidden behind a headland. Most of the Roman ships were rammed and boarded, resulting in a heavy defeat.

AEGATES ISLANDS 241 BCE

Forces Roman: 200 ships; Carthaginian: 250 ships. **Casualties** Roman: 30 ships lost; Carthaginian: 50 ships lost, 70 ships captured. **Location** Off west coast of Sicily.

After the disaster at Drepana, the Romans rebuilt their fleet with better vessels and conducted extensive training. Drawing out the Carthaginian fleet by blockading Lilybaeum (modern Marsala), the Romans shattered the opposing fleet by using ramming tactics. Cut off from Sicily by Roman sea power, the Carthaginians agreed a peace settlement.

KALINGA WARS
C. 262 BCE

Forces Mauryan: unknown; Kalingan: unknown. **Casualties** Mauryan: 10,000 killed; Kalingan: 100,000 killed. **Location** East-central India.

After failing to conquer the kingdom of Kalinga, Emperor Asoka launched a second campaign and inflicted brutal reprisals, before renouncing war and converting to Buddhism.

CHANGPING 260 BCE

Forces Qin army: unknown; Zhao army: unknown. **Casualties** Qin: unknown; Zhao: 400,000 (reportedly). **Location** northeast China.

During a period of almost continuous conflict between China's feudal kingdoms, known as the Warring States period, a desperate attempt by Zhao forces to escape a two-month Qin siege ended in massacre. Zhao troops who were not killed in the battle surrendered, and were executed in their thousands.

Seleucus I
Seleucus I (305–281 BCE), one of Alexander's generals, also called Nicator, founded the Seleucid empire, which rivalled that of Rome.

WEIRD WEAPONS

Weapon	Period	Description
Battle pigs	4th century BCE	The Romans and the Greeks are both said to have used pigs, coated in incendiary fuel and set alight, to alarm and disrupt attacks by war elephants.
Solar artillery	3rd century BCE	Archimedes is reputed to have used sunlight, reflected by lenses and mirrors, to set fire to the Roman fleet that laid siege to Syracuse from 213 to 211 BCE.
Ninja claws	From 7th century BCE	The Japanese *neko-te* consisted of claw-like metal fingernails attached to leather bands that were worn on the fingers or as a clawed glove. The "nails" were sometimes dipped in poison for performing silent assassinations.
Iron fan	From medieval period	The Japanese *tetsu-sen* was configured like a standard hand fan but made of sharp-edged rigid iron blades. It could be used as defensive armour or as an offensive weapon.
Bat bombs	1942–45	During World War II the US government funded a plan to fit bats with tiny incendiary devices, then release them over Japan to start massive fires. It was never used.
Balloon bombs	1944–45	This Japanese weapon consisted of a bomb fitted to a balloon, the whole device carried across the Pacific Ocean on prevailing winds. Some made the trip across harmlessly.
Love gas	1990s	The US Air Force Research Laboratory at Wright-Patterson Air Base in Ohio attempted to develop a gas that would fill enemy soldiers with uncontrollable lust. Other gases sought to induce halitosis and flatulence.

Solar firepower
According to the 2nd-century CE writer Lucian, Archimedes (c.287–c.212 BCE) focused the sun's rays with mirrors and lenses to set Roman ships alight at the great sea battle of Syracuse. This 17th-century illustration imagines how Archimedes' solar reflection weapon would have looked in action.

LIBYAN WAR 240–238 BCE

Forces Carthage: unknown; Mercenaries: possibly 100,000
Casualties Carthage: unknown; Mercenaries: over 50,000.
Location Utica and Carthage (near modern Tunis, Tunisia).

At the end of the First Punic War, mercenary forces hired by Carthage could not be paid. The dispute escalated into a revolt, with the mercenaries capturing Tunis. The war went badly for Carthage at first, but eventually those mercenaries who did not defect to the Carthaginian side were defeated.

SECOND PUNIC WAR
219–201 BCE

After storming Saguntum, Carthaginian general Hannibal Barca crossed the Alps into Italy and inflicted massive defeats on Rome, forcing the Romans to adopt a strategy of harassment and delay until they could achieve a decisive advantage.

SAGUNTUM 219 BCE

Forces Saguntum: unknown; Carthaginian: unknown but greater than their opponents. **Casualties** Saguntum: almost total; Carthaginian: very low. **Location** Modern Sagunto, Spain.

Violating the treaty that ended the First Punic War, Hannibal besieged Saguntum, a fortified city allied with Rome. The city asked Rome for help but none came by the time the walls were finally stormed. Saguntum provided a base for Hannibal's invasion of Italy via the Alps.

"The sight of the **admiral's ship** i enemy hands **created a panic**."
LIVY (59 BCE–17 CE), ROMAN HISTORIAN, ON A SECOND PUNIC WAR NAVAL BATTLE

TREBIA 218 BCE

Forces Roman: 20 ships; Carthaginian: 35 ships.
Casualties Roman: unknown; Carthaginian: 7 ships captured. **Location** Modern Marsala, Sicily.

A smaller but well-prepared Roman force met a Carthaginian fleet sent to attack Lilybaeum. Carthaginian ramming tactics were countered by boarding actions by the Romans. Defeat meant that the Carthaginians were prevented from gaining a base in Sicily.

TREBIA 218 BCE

Forces Roman: 40,000; Carthaginian: 30,000. **Casualties** Roman: 30,000 killed; Carthaginian: 5,000 killed. **Location** South of modern Milan, northern Italy.

Hannibal's Carthaginian army marched across Gaul and over the Alps into Italy, taking the Romans completely by surprise. A Carthaginian force lured the Romans into attacking across the Trebia river, placing them at a severe disadvantage. Meanwhile a concealed force attacked the Roman rear. Most of the Roman force was destroyed.

CISSA 218 BCE

Forces Roman: 11,000; Carthaginian: 22,200. **Casualties** Roman: 500; Carthaginian: 6,000 plus 2,000 captured. **Location** Northeastern Spain.

Roman forces entered Iberia to engage the Carthaginians there, resulting in a straightforward clash near Cissa. The Roman force outfought its opponents and defeated them with heavy losses.

EBRO RIVER 217 BCE

Forces Roman: 55 ships; Carthaginian: 40 ships. **Casualties** Roman: no ships lost; Carthaginian: 4 ships lost, 25 captured. **Location** Spain.

The Carthaginian fleet moored off the mouth of the Ebro river, unaware of the Roman fleet nearby. While Carthaginian crews were foraging ashore, the Romans attacked, causing the Carthaginians to scramble to re-man their ships. Defeated, the Carthaginians beached their ships and fled to join their land forces.

LAKE TRASIMENE JUNE 217 BCE

Forces Roman: 40,000; Carthaginian: 40,000. **Casualties** Roman: c. 30,000 killed; Carthaginian: unknown. **Location** Near modern Perugia, central Italy.

The Carthaginians set up an ambush on the road past Lake Trasimene. Light forces and cavalry attacked the Roman flanks and rear as the main body engaged. Thousands of Romans were either killed or captured in what was a giant ambush.

GERONIUM 217 BCE

Forces Roman: Possibly 34,000; Carthaginian: 50,000. **Casualties** No reliable estimates, but very heavy on the Roman side. **Location** Apulia, Italy.

The Carthaginians managed to draw part of the Roman army into a trap. Worse disaster was averted when Fabius, better known for his tactic of avoiding battle, launched an attack to rescue the embattled legions. The Carthaginians chose not to continue the engagement against the reinforced Romans.

CANNAE 2 AUGUST 216 BCE

Forces Roman: 80,000 infantry, 6,000 cavalry; Carthaginian: 40,000 infantry, 10,000 cavalry. **Casualties** Roman: 48,000 killed; Carthaginian: 6,000 killed. **Location** Apulia, southeastern Italy.

Drawing the Romans into a reckless frontal attack, the Carthaginian centre deliberately gave way while the flanking forces drove off their opposite numbers. The Roman infantry was then surrounded and killed, in this greatest of Carthaginian victories.

SIEGE OF SYRACUSE 213–211 BCE

Forces Roman: unknown; Syracusan: unknown. **Casualties** No reliable estimates. **Location** East coast of Sicily.

The siege of Syracuse was largely a competition between Roman ingenuity and the genius of the inventor Archimedes, who orchestrated the Syracusan defences. The outer walls were eventually stormed in a surprise attack, and eight months later the inner citadel fell to the Romans.

SILARUS 212 BCE

Forces Roman: 16,000; Carthaginian: 30,000. **Casualties** Roman: 15,000 plus 1,000 prisoners; Carthaginian: 6,000. **Location** Modern Sele river, southwestern Italy.

Poor scouting caused the Romans to blunder into an ambush, at which point their allies fled the field. The Roman force was surrounded and almost entirely annihilated.

TARENTUM 212 BCE

Forces Roman: unknown; Carthaginian: 10,000. **Casualties** Roman: Almost total; Carthaginian: Very low. **Location** Puglia, southern Italy.

Unhappy with Roman rule, the people of Tarentum conspired to let the Carthaginian army into their city. Much of the Roman garrison was eliminated but some troops were able to hold out in the citadel.

UPPER BAETIS 211 BCE

Forces Roman: 53,000; Carthaginian: 48,500. **Casualties** Roman: 22,000; Carthaginian: 4,000. **Location** Southern Spain.

The Roman force split to attack two Carthaginian armies. The result was two severe defeats for the Romans within days of each other. The survivors were eventually reinforced and, if nothing else, they drew away Carthaginian forces that might have assisted Hannibal in his main campaign in Italy.

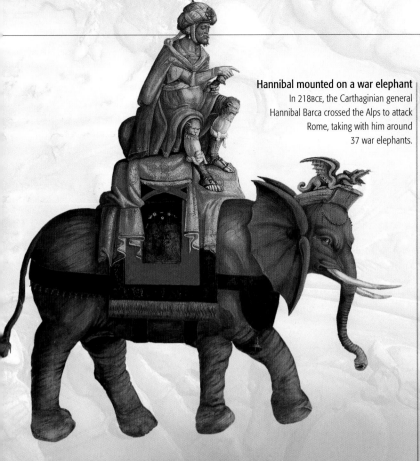

Hannibal mounted on a war elephant
In 218BCE, the Carthaginian general Hannibal Barca crossed the Alps to attack Rome, taking with him around 37 war elephants.

BAECULA 208 BCE

Forces Roman: 35,000; Carthaginian: 25,000 plus unknown number of Allied. **Casualties** Roman: 1,000 or less; Carthaginian: 6,000 plus 10,000 prisoners. **Location** modern Jaén, south-central Spain.

Thinking the Roman army was only engaging in skirmishing, the Carthaginians did not deploy for a full-scale battle until too late, but most of the Carthaginians got away as the Romans stopped for plunder.

GRUMENTUM 207 BCE

Forces Roman: unknown; Carthaginian: unknown. **Casualties** Roman: 500; Carthaginian: 8,000 plus 700 prisoners. **Location** South of Potenza, southern Italy.

The battle of Grumentum was a prelude to the greater Roman victory at Metarus. Although the Carthaginians suffered heavy casualties and were forced to retire from the battlefield, Hannibal ensured an orderly retreat to conserve his troops.

METAURUS 22 JUNE 207 BCE

Forces Roman: 40,000; Carthaginian: 30,000. **Casualties** Roman: 2,000; Carthaginian: 10,000. **Location** Marche region, central Italy.

Caught on the wrong side of the Metaurus river, the Carthaginians attempted to withdraw but were forced to fight. A Roman flanking attack caused the Carthaginian force to disintegrate.

ILIPA 206 BCE

Forces Roman: 43,000; Carthaginian: 70,000. **Casualties** Roman: 2,000; Carthaginian: 20,000 plus 6,000 prisoners. **Location** North of modern Seville, Spain.

The Romans used the Carthaginians' own enveloping tactics at Cannae against them, pulling the centre of their line back while the legions on the wings crushed the enemy flanks. The Carthaginans collapsed under pressure from the Roman flanks and centre.

GREAT PLAINS 203 BCE

Forces Roman: unknown; Carthaginian: 30,000. **Casualties** Roman: unknown; Carthaginian: unknown, but probably heavy. **Location** Near Utica, North Africa.

As the Romans advanced on Carthage, a hastily formed army made a stand near Utica. It was quickly put to rout, forcing the Carthaginians to sue for peace. They then decided to recall Hannibal's army from Italy, bringing about the battle of Zama.

ZAMA 202 BCE

Forces Roman: 35,000; Carthaginian: 45,000. **Casualties** Roman: 1,500 killed; Carthaginian: 20,000 killed, 15,000 captured. **Location** Modern Tunisia, North Africa.

After allowing Carthaginian elephants to pass between their units, the Roman infantry became involved in a tough fight with Hannibal's veterans. Roman cavalry attacked the Carthaginian rear and caused a rout. The Carthaginians were forced to accept a humiliating peace.

CANUSIUM 209 BCE

Forces Roman: 20,000; Carthaginian: 25,000. **Casualties** Roman: 8,000; Carthaginian: 6,000. **Location** Southern Italy.

The battle took place over three days. On the first, skirmishing escalated into an indecisive but bloody fight. On the second, the Romans were badly beaten and forced to take refuge in their camp. On the third day, Hannibal was forced onto the defensive, although the battle itself was not decisive.

CARTAGENA 209 BCE

Forces Roman: unknown; Carthaginian: unknown. **Casualties** Unknown. **Location** Murcia region of southeastern Spain.

Cartagena, also called New Carthage, was blockaded by the Roman fleet while the army made preparations for an assault. Beating off the first attempt, the city was successfully stormed from both the landward and seaward sides by a second assault.

Roman ruins
After its destruction by the Romans in 146 CE (p. 367), Carthage was rebuilt as an affluent Roman colony. This ruined baths complex is a remarkable example of Roman opulence.

WARS OF THE SELEUCID EMPIRE
219–168 BCE

After his death, Alexander the Great's empire was divided among his generals: Seleucus, founder of the Seleucid dynasty, took control of Syria and Iran; Antigonus carved out a kingdom in Anatolia; and Ptolemy founded a dynasty in Egypt.

FOURTH SYRIAN WAR 219–217 BCE

Forces Seleucid: unknown; Egyptian: unknown. **Casualties** No reliable estimates. **Location** Palestine.

Ascending to the Seleucid throne, Antiochus III set about pacifying his eastern possessions and then turned against an Egypt weakened by internal conflict. The Egyptians under Ptolemy IV raised an army to resist the invasion.

RAPHIA 22 JUNE 217 BCE

Forces Seleucid: 62,000 infantry, 6,000 cavalry, 102 elephants; Egyptian: 70,000 infantry, 5,000 cavalry, 73 elephants. **Casualties** No reliable estimates. **Location** Southwest of Gaza, southern Palestine.

The battle was decided by the clash of infantry. Although both sides' elephants and cavalry were evenly matched, the Egyptian infantry, trained and led by Ptolemy IV, carried the day.

FIFTH SYRIAN WAR 202–195 BCE

Forces Seleucid: unknown; Egyptian: unknown. **Casualties** No reliable estimates. **Location** Palestine.

With Egypt in turmoil over who would be regent to the young Ptolemy V, the Seleucids launched a new campaign into Ptolemaic territories in Syria. Victories in the field gave the Seleucids possession of the port of Sidon, but partly in response to Roman demands, there was no invasion of Egypt itself.

PANIUM 198 BCE

Forces Seleucid: unknown; Egyptian: unknown. **Casualties** No reliable estimates. **Location** Palestine.

The battle of Panium, part of the Fifth Syrian War, was decided primarily by cavalry action. Seleucid heavy cavalry (cataphracts) defeated the lighter Egyptian cavalry on the flanks and then fell on the enemy infantry rear. The resulting rout drove the Egyptians from Palestine.

ROMAN–SYRIAN WAR 192–188 BCE

Forces Seleucid and Allied: unknown; Roman and Allied: unknown. **Casualties** No reliable estimates. **Location** Greece and Asia Minor.

Joined by the Carthaginian general Hannibal, the Seleucid empire took advantage of anti-Roman sentiment in Greece to launch a military expedition. The Seleucids were, however, defeated on land and at sea, and were forced to relinquish their Greek interests.

MAGNESIA DECEMBER 190 CE

Forces Rome and Pergamum: 40,000; Seleucid: 72,000. **Casualties** Rome and Pergamum: 350; Seleucid: 53,000. **Location** East of Smyrna (modern Izmir, Turkey).

Han dynasty funerary figures
Painted terracotta warriors, made for the funerary furnishings of a Han dynasty tomb (c.206 BCE–9 CE), illustrate the style of armour and weapons used by the warriors of ancient China.

Although the Roman left was broken by a cavalry charge, the Seleucid phalanx was disrupted by panicking elephants and flanked by cavalry. The formation broke up and the Seleucid army was massacred.

SIXTH SYRIAN WAR 170–168 BCE

Forces Seleucid: unknown; Egyptian: unknown. **Casualties** No reliable estimates. **Location** Palestine.

After declaring war on the Seleucids, the Egyptians quickly ran into difficulties. They appealed to Rome for help, which demanded that the Seleucids withdraw from their conquests, bringing the war to an end.

WARS IN GREECE AND ASIA MINOR
214–148 BCE

For many years Rome had little interest in becoming involved in the affairs of the eastern Mediterranean. A challenge from Macedonia, siding with Carthage, prompted a change in this policy.

FIRST MACEDONIAN WAR
214–205 BCE

Forces Macedonian: unknown; Roman: unknown. **Casualties** Unknown. **Location** Macedonia and Mediterranean Sea.

Taking advantage of Roman reverses during the Second Punic War, Macedonia gathered allies and launched a campaign to gain territory in Illyria and Greece. Naval raiding was also carried out. From the Roman perspective the war was a sideshow to the struggle with Carthage, and ended without any major territorial changes.

CHIOS 201 BCE

Forces Macedonian: 53 heavy warships; Rhodes and Pergamum: 65 heavy warships. **Casualties** Macedonian: 9,000; Rhodes and Pergamum: 130. **Location** The Aegean Sea, just off the coast of western Turkey.

The Macedonians possessed large and capable ships, forcing their opponents to use a cautious strategy. Despite losing their own flagship, the Macedonians captured that of Pergamum before heavy losses brought about their defeat. The forces of Rhodes and Pergamum did not exploit their advantage, however, and the bulk of the Macedonian fleet survived the battle.

SECOND MACEDONIAN WAR
200–197 BCE

Forces Macedonian: unknown; Roman: unknown. **Casualties** Unknown. **Location** Greece and the Mediterranean Sea.

Rome's intervention transformed the wars between Macedonia and other eastern European powers. After some indecisive manoeuvring, the Romans advanced aggressively against Philip V of Macedonia, leading to the decisive encounter at Cynoscephalae.

NOTORIOUS WAR CRIMES

War crimes are violations of the commonly accepted laws of war, including such acts as murdering and imprisoning civilians; the torture, ill-treatment or murder of prisoners of war; taking or killing hostages; and attacking enemy combatants carrying a flag of truce.

Modern location	Date	Details
Orissa, India	261 BCE	Warriors of the Mauryan empire under Ashoka massacred up to 100,000 civilians in a campaign of conquest.
Tunis, Tunisia	146 BCE	Some 150,000 citizens of Carthage died when the city was besieged and destroyed by Roman legions.
Thessalonika, Greece	390 CE	The Romans killed c.7,000 of Thessalonika's population in revenge for a rebellion.
Milan, Italy	March 539	A vengeful army of Goths and Franks massacred most of Milan's population, killing up to 300,000 people.
Jerusalem, Israel	15 July 1099	Having taken Jerusalem from the Muslims, the Crusaders massacred up to 40,000 Muslims and Jews.
Drogheda, Ireland	11 September 1649	Troops of Oliver Cromwell put the city of Drogheda to the sword, murdering some 4,000 men, women, and children.
Ismail, Ukraine	22–24 December 1790	40,000 Turks, mostly civilians were massacred by a rampaging Russian army.
Batak, Bulgaria	30 April 1876	Ottoman troops murdered 5,000 people in Batak, beheading many of them.
Nanking, China	December 1937–February 1938	Following the fall of Nanking, the Japanese occupiers killed at least 40,000 fleeing citizens and soldiers.
Various sites in occupied Poland	June 1941–April 1945	Approximately 2,700,000 people were systematically killed by the Nazis in six extermination camps during World War II.
Babi Yar, Ukraine	29–30 September 1941	A Nazi death squad executed more than 30,000 Jews in the Babi Yar ravine.
Katyn, Russia	April 1943	Russian forces executed some 22,000 Poles, many of them army officers.
My Lai, Vietnam	16 March 1968	US infantry killed almost the entire population of a Vietnamese village, executing up to 504 people.

Siege of Carthage
Chaos ensued following the siege of Carthage at the climax of the Third Punic War (149–146 BCE). The defenders of the city, surrounded by 32km (20 miles) of walls, held out for two years before being overwhelmed by Roman soldiers, who massacred the population.

> **"... the city perishing amidst the flames, Scipio burst into tears."**
>
> POLYBIUS, HISTORIAN, ON SCIPIO AEMILIANUS' DESTRUCTION OF CARTHAGE, 146 BCE

CYNOSCEPHALAE 197 BCE

Forces Macedonian: 26,000; Roman: 26,000. **Casualties** Macedonian: 8,000 killed, 5,000 captured; Roman: 700 killed. **Location** Thessaly, northern Greece.

In an unexpected encounter, the more flexible Roman force drew out the Macedonian phalanx and used the terrain to break it up before closing to attack from the front and from both flanks.

THIRD MACEDONIAN WAR 171–168 BCE

Forces Macedonian: unknown; Roman: unknown. **Casualties** Unknown. **Location** Greece and the Mediterranean Sea.

Macedonian attempts to reduce Roman influence in Greece and to increase their own led to a renewed war.

PYDNA 22 JUNE 168 BCE

Forces Roman: 37,000; Macedonian: 42,000. **Casualties** Roman: fewer than 1,000 killed; Macedonian: 20,000 killed, 11,000 captured. **Location** Near Mount Olympus, northern Greece.

The Macedonian phalanx initially met with success but gradually lost cohesion as it drove forward. Small units of Romans penetrated the phalanx where their short swords gave them a huge advantage over the Macedonian pikemen.

XIONGNU INVASION 201–200 BCE

Forces Xiongnu: 300,000; Chinese: unknown. **Casualties** No reliable estimates. **Location** Mongolia and northwest China.

Having recently been unified under Han rule, China came under attack by Xiongu nomads. The Han army, attempting to drive off the invaders, was defeated by their skilled mounted archers. The Han were forced to sue for peace.

THIRD PUNIC WAR 149–146 BCE

The power of Carthage had been broken in the Second Punic War, but elements within the Roman senate maintained that Carthage must be totally destroyed – "carthago delenda est". War was declared in 149 BCE. Carthage, with no allies, was doomed from the outset.

SIEGE OF CARTHAGE 149–146 BCE

Forces Roman: unknown; Carthaginian: unknown. **Casualties** No reliable estimates. **Location** Carthage (in modern Tunis, Tunisia).

Despite breaching the walls, the Romans were held up for months by a vigorous defence. Finally disease and starvation weakened the defenders and the Romans could make a successful assault. The survivors were killed or sold into slavery, and Carthage was razed to the ground.

AQUAE SEXTIAE 102 BCE

Forces Roman: 30,000–35,000; Teutone and Ambrone: up to 150,000. **Casualties** Teutone: Up to 100,000 killed or captured. **Location** Modern Aix-en-Provence, France.

As Rome's enemies laboured uphill toward them, the legionaries used their standard tactics, hurling javelins (*pila*) at close range before charging. A concealed Roman force made a flanking attack, finishing the rout.

MITHRIDATIC WARS 88–63 BCE

Three wars were fought between 88 and 63 BCE between the Roman republic and the kingdom of Pontus (a region running along the eastern Black Sea coast of modern Turkey) under King Mithridates. Pontus was destroyed and the region came under Roman control.

LARGEST EMPIRES FORGED THROUGH MILITARY CONQUEST		
Empire	**Era**	**Greatest extent**
British	Late 16th–mid 20th century	36.6 million km² (14.1 million sq miles)
Mongol	1206–1368	33 million km² (12.7 million sq miles)
Russian	1721–1917	22.4 million km² (8.6 million sq miles)
Spanish	15th–late 19th century	19.4 million km² (7.5 million sq miles)
Arab caliphate	7th–8th century	13.2 million km² (5.1 million sq miles)
French	17th century–1960s	12.5 million km² (4.8 million sq miles)
Portuguese	15th–late 20th century	12.4 million km² (4.8 million sq miles)
Ottoman	1299–1923	11.5 million km² (4.4 million sq miles)
Japanese	1867–1945	7.4 million km² (2.8 million sq miles)
Persian	8th century BCE–7th century CE	6.2 million km² (2.4 million sq miles)
Roman	27 BCE–5th century CE	5.7 million km² (2.2 million sq miles)

CHAERONEA 86 BCE

Forces Roman: 40,000; Mithridatic: 120,000. **Casualties** Roman: minimal; Mithridatic: 110,000. **Location** Northwest of Thebes, Greece.

The outnumbered Roman forces used the advantage of high ground to dominate the Mithridatic forces, who were routed and fled for the safety of their camp, but were denied entry and overrun with great loss. Some sources claim that only 12 Roman soldiers were lost in the battle.

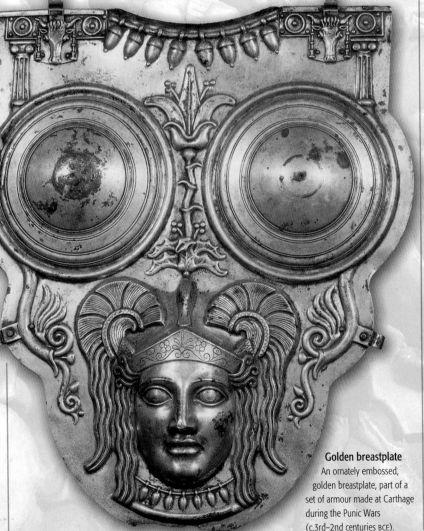

Golden breastplate
An ornately embossed, golden breastplate, part of a set of armour made at Carthage during the Punic Wars (c.3rd–2nd centuries BCE).

SLAVE WAR 73–71 BCE

Forces Roman: unknown; Slave: unknown. **Casualties** No reliable estimates. **Location** Various locations across southern Italy.

Formed around a band of escaped slave gladiators, Spartacus's army fought a successful guerrilla campaign and trounced two Roman armies before finally being defeated. Spartacus and most of his followers were killed during the fighting. The remaining 6,000 were crucified.

JERUSALEM 63 BCE

Forces Roman: unknown; Jewish: unknown. **Casualties** Roman unknown; Jewish: c.12,000. **Location** Modern Israel.

Intervening in a dispute between Jewish princes, the Romans besieged Jerusalem. After methodical preparations the city was stormed and captured. Jerusalem and all of Palestine then came under Roman control.

GALLIC WARS 58–51 BCE

Forces Roman: 120,000; Gallic: claims of up to 3,000,000. **Casualties** No reliable estimates. **Location** Modern France, Switzerland and Belgium.

Julius Caesar campaigned against the Gallic and Germanic tribes (in modern-day France), and even raided Britain. His exploits enriched him and increased his political standing. His greatest victory was over a large Gallic army at Alesia.

CARRHAE 53 BCE

Forces Roman: 39,000; Parthian: 7,000. **Casualties** Roman: 24,000 killed; 10,000 captured. Parthian: unknown. **Location** Syrian desert, east of Euphrates river.

The Romans were forced into a defensive square by the more mobile Parthians, who shot arrows into the formation then retired in the face of counterattacks.

ALESIA JULY–OCTOBER 52 BCE

Forces Roman: 45,000; Gallic: unknown. **Casualties** No reliable estimates. **Location** Near Dijon, France.

The Romans built a double set of siege lines around the Gauls trapped in Alesia. This enabled them to repulse Gallic attempts at relief and breakout. The Gauls were eventually starved into surrender.

ROMAN CIVIL WAR
63–43 BCE

Internal conflict was nothing new in the Roman republic, and few clashes caused long-term changes in the nature of Roman society. But Caesar's crossing of the Rubicon triggered a civil war that changed all that. By the time the upheaval was over the Roman republic had become an empire.

CATILINE CONSPIRACY 63 BCE

Forces Catiline: 10,000; Senatorial: unknown. **Casualties** No reliable estimates. **Location** Near Pistoria (modern Pistoia, Tuscany, Italy).

Lucius Sergius Catilina (Catiline) had conspired with others to overthrow the Roman senate. When the conspiracy was revealed, Catiline assembled a poorly trained and ill-equipped army, which was destroyed by forces loyal to the senate.

CAESAR'S MARCH ON ROME 49 BCE

Forces Caesar's army: 1 legion; Pompey's army: 2 legions plus supporting troops. **Casualties** Unknown. **Location** Northern Italy.

Although outnumbered by loyalist forces under their commander Pompey, Caesar advanced towards Rome. Convinced that Rome could not be defended, Pompey eventually fled Italy, landing in Greece. There he continued his opposition to Caesar, who pursued Pompey after eliminating his allies.

ILERDA 49 BCE

Forces Caesar's army: 6 legions and supporting troops; Pompey's army: 5 legions. **Casualties** Caesar's army: 70; Pompey's army: 800 plus several legions surrendered. **Location** Catalonia, western Spain.

Rapidly marching into Hispania, Caesar defeated an army loyal to Pompey. Finding its retreat blocked, Pompey's army became besieged in its camp and surrendered to Caesar.

BAGRADAS RIVER 49 BCE

Forces Caesar's army: unknown; Varus's army: unknown. **Casualties** Unknown. **Location** North Africa.

A force sent by Caesar to secure Roman holdings in North Africa from the governor, Varus, made good initial progress. However, a reckless advance resulted in an ambush that killed or captured almost all of Caesar's forces.

DYRRACHIUM JULY 48 BCE

Forces Caesar's army: 40,000; Pompey's army: 90,000. **Casualties** Caesar's army: 1,000; Pompey's army: fewer than 1,000. **Location** Modern Durrës, Albania.

Caesar made a daring crossing of the Adriatic and besieged Pompey in his camp. Caesar's force was eventually driven off and retreated.

PHARSALUS 9 AUGUST 48 BCE

Forces Caesar: 22,000 infantry, 1,000 cavalry; Pompey: 45,000 infantry, 7,000 cavalry. **Casualties** Caesar: 230 killed, 2,000 wounded; Pompey: 15,000 killed or wounded. **Location** Thessaly, Greece.

Caesar deployed a fourth line of battle rather than the usual three, enabling his force to drive off a flanking cavalry attack. The fourth line then carried out a flanking action of its own, combined with a renewed frontal attack. Pompey's infantry fled.

ZELA 48 BCE

Forces Caesar's army: unknown; Pharnaces's army: unknown. **Casualties** Unknown. **Location** Modern Zile, Turkey.

Taking advantage of the civil war in Rome, King Pharnaces of Pontus overran Roman and allied holdings in Lesser Armenia. A Roman army was defeated at Nicopolis. Caesar responded

Roman shield
Roman legionaries carried a rectangular *scutum* (shield). These could be interlocked to protect groups of soldiers from arrows or other missiles.

aggressively, defeating Pharnaces at Zela. It was of this conflict that Caesar is quoted as saying *"Veni, Vidi, Vici."* ("I came, I saw, I conquered.")

THAPSUS 6 APRIL 46 BCE

Forces Metellus Scipio's army: 10 or more legions plus supporting troops; Caesar's army: 10 or more legions plus supporting troops. **Casualties** Metellus Scipio's army: 30,000; Caesar's army: 1,000. **Location** Modern-day Tunisia, North Africa.

Caesar besieged Thapsus, forcing his Republican enemies under Metellus Scipio to attempt a relief. Caesar's archers drove off the Republican elephants, after which the Republican army was outfought and put to flight.

MUNDA 45 BCE

Forces Republican: 70,000; Caesar's army: 40,000. **Casualties** Republican: 30,000; Caesar's army: 1,000. **Location** Near Osuna, modern southern Spain.

After the battle of Thapsus, the only significant Republican threat to Caesar was in Hispania. Caesar's army marched to confront the Republicans, bringing about a head-on battle. After a hard fight the Republican force collapsed, suffering very heavy casualties.

MUTINA 43 BCE

Forces Republican: unknown; Mark Antony's army: unknown. **Casualties** Unknown. **Location** Modern Modena, northern Italy.

Forces under Mark Antony, an ally of the murdered Caesar, clashed with Republican troops under Brutus, Octavian, and Hirtius. Antony's force was defeated and Octavian distinguished himself as a commander. The battle led to a truce between Octavian and Antony and their alliance against the assassins of Caesar.

PHILIPPI 3 AND 23 OCTOBER 43 BCE

Forces Republican: 80,000 infantry, 20,000 cavalry; Antony and Octavian: 85,000 infantry, 13,000 cavalry. **Casualties** No reliable estimates. **Location** East Macedonia, modern Greece.

With their supply chain blocked by Antony and Octavian's forces, the Republicans under Brutus launched an attack. While they were occupied to the front they were flanked by troops under Antony and routed.

OCTAVIAN VERSUS MARK ANTONY – CAESAR'S HEIRS
32–30 BCE

After defeating Caesar's assassins, Octavian ruled in the west while Mark Antony dealt with Roman affairs in the east. Antony's alliance with Cleopatra of Egypt led to a clash with Octavian, which saw Mark Anthony's defeat. Afterwards the senate named Octavian "Augustus", and he became the first emperor of Rome.

ACTIUM 2 SEPTEMBER 31 BCE

Forces Octavian: 400 ships; Antony and Cleopatra: 230 ships. **Casualties** Octavian: unknown; Antony and Cleopatra: 150 ships. **Location** Off coast of Acarnania, western Greece.

Mark Antony
Mark Antony, Roman military commander and friend of Julius Caesar, battled Octavian in the last wars of the Roman republic (31 BCE). Allied with Cleopatra of Egypt, he was defeated at Actium and Alexandria.

Blockaded at Actium by Octavian's navy, Antony's ships forced a passage through Octavian's fleet through which Cleopatra's force escaped. Antony lost his flagship in the defeat, but escaped aboard another vessel with what remained of his fleet.

EARLY WARS OF THE ROMAN EMPIRE
1–60 CE

Roman domination of Europe and the lands around the Mediterranean created stability and relative peace for many years. Troubles on the border were often dealt with by conquest and annexation, pushing the frontiers of Rome ever further out.

TEUTOBERG FOREST SEPTEMBER 9 CE

Forces Roman: 15,000; Germanic: unknown. **Casualties** Romans: most of the entire force; Germanic: unknown. **Location** Near modern Osnabrück, northwest Germany.

Lured into the Teutoberg forest and abandoned by their allies, three Roman legions were harassed for several days before the scattered and weakened Roman survivors were overrun by assault.

WESER RIVER 16 CE

Forces Roman: unknown; Germanic: unknown. **Casualties** Roman: unknown but heavy; Germanic: unknown but heavy. **Location** Northwestern Germany.

Attempts to establish a Roman frontier resulted in a long series of skirmishes with Germanic tribes, with few decisive victories. There were no further serious efforts to push the frontier beyond the Rhine.

CONQUEST OF BRITAIN 43 CE

Forces Roman: unknown; British: unknown. **Casualties** Unknown. **Location**: Britain.

The conquest of Britain began in earnest in 43 CE. The Druidic holy island of Anglesey fell in 60 and fortifications were built on the Tay river in 80. The northern frontier was established in 122 with the building of Hadrian's Wall.

"Up my Britons, on my chariot, trample them under us!"

ALFRED LORD TENNYSON, BRITISH POET, "BOADICEA", 1859

RIVER MEDWAY 43 CE

Forces Roman: 40,000; British: Probably more than 40,000. **Casualties** Roman: unknown but not heavy; British: unknown but probably heavy. **Location** Kent, England.

While attempting to prevent a Roman crossing of the Medway river, tribal forces attacked the Roman bridgeheads repeatedly but without success. Eventually enough Roman troops crossed the river to break out of the bridgeheads and repel the Britons.

REVOLT OF THE ICENI 60 CE

Forces Roman: 10,000; British: unknown. **Casualties** Roman: 400 killed; British: unknown. **Location** Central and southern England.

The Iceni, under the leadership of Queen Boudicca, sacked several Roman towns before being overwhelmed by the might of two Roman legions.

YEAR OF THE FOUR EMPERORS 69 CE

Forces Varied. **Casualties** Unknown. **Location** Roman empire

The politics of the Roman empire resulted in internal conflicts. In 69 CE, four emperors were crowned. The Praetorian Guard and the army became the arbiters of power, both in battle and due to their ability to do away with a candidate who did not live up to his promises. The conflict ended when Vespasian ascended the throne, beginning a new period of stability.

JERUSALEM 70 CE

Forces Roman: 30,000–40,000; Judaean: 23,000–24,000. **Casualties** Unknown. **Location** Judaea, modern Israel.

The Roman province of Judaea revolted in 66 CE. The rebels were initially successful, but were soon pushed back to strongholds such as Jerusalem and Masada. The Roman army conducted a methodical siege of Jerusalem, storming a series of defensive positions before taking the Old City. This essentially ended the revolt in Judaea.

SIEGE OF MASADA 72–73 CE

Forces Roman: 5,000; Judaean: 960. **Casualties** Roman: unknown; Judaean: 953. **Location** Near the southwestern coast of the Dead Sea, modern Israel.

In an attempt to remove Jewish rebels from the formidable mountain-top fortress of Masada, the Romans built an enormous ramp up to the walls, and breached them using rams. The defenders committed suicide to escape capture.

MONS GRAUPIUS 84 CE

Forces Caledonian: 30,000; Roman and auxiliary: 25,000. **Casualties**. Caledonian: 10,000; Roman and auxiliary: 360. **Location** Modern northeast Scotland.

Encountering the Caledonian army, the Roman commander Agricola initially employed his auxiliaries. The Caledonian chariots were dispersed by Roman cavalry, which then fell on the enemy rear.

DACIAN CAMPAIGNS 101–106 CE

Forces Roman: unknown; Dacian: unknown. **Casualties** No reliable estimates. **Location** Modern Romania.

Raids by the Dacians prompted a Roman punitive expedition that resulted in a peace settlement. When the Dacians resumed raiding, a new expedition was launched and the region was conquered.

SECOND TAPAE 101 CE

Forces Roman: possibly around 10 legions; Parthian: unknown. **Casualties** No reliable estimates. **Location** Modern Romania.

The decisive battle of the Dacian campaign occurred at Tapae, site of an earlier action against the Dacians. The Dacians proved to be stubborn opponents, but interpreted a storm as an omen and withdrew, conceding victory to the Romans.

FAMOUS FEMALE WARRIORS

Although the fierce Amazons of classical times are almost certainly mythical, a number of remarkable and fearsome female warriors have won their place in military history.

Warrior	Dates	Achievements
Boudicca	d. c.60 CE	Queen of the Iceni tribe, Boudicca led a revolt against the Romans in Britain in c.60, destroying several Roman cities and crushing the Ninth legion before she was finally defeated.
Joan of Arc	c.1412–30 May 1431	A peasant girl who eventually led the French army against the English, Joan of Arc won notable victories before being captured and burnt at the stake at the age of 19.
Isabella I of Castile	1451–1504	As the queen of Castile, Isabella led her soldiers into battle against the Moors, fighting alongside Ferdinand of Aragon.
Graine Ni Maille (Grace O'Malley)	c.1530–c.1603	This piratical Irish princess attacked English ships and and shores until she was granted her territorial demands by the English queen Elizabeth I in 1593.
Hannah Snell	1723–92	A British woman who disguised herself as a man, Snell joined the Royal Marines and fought in many foreign battles, being wounded 12 times.
Margaret Corbin	1751–1800	Margaret Corbin fought alongside her husband John in the American Revolutionary War, crewing cannon at the battle of Fort Washington in 1776 even after John had been killed at her side. She herself was wounded, and received a disabled soldier pension from Congress.
Émilienne Moreau-Evrard	1898–1971	Moreau-Evrard assisted British troops during World War I, shooting two German soldiers dead, and fought in the French resistance in World War II. In the process she won the Croix de Guerre twice (once in each war), the British Military Medal and Royal Red Cross, and the Légion d'honneur.
Ludmilla Pavlichenko	1916–74	A dead-eye Russian female sniper who, during World War II, killed 309 German soldiers.

Boudicca and her daughters
Boudicca was the warrior queen of the British Iceni tribe who rose against Rome during the 1st century CE. Her forces burned the Roman settlement of Londinium (modern London) to the ground in c.60 CE.

"Many a time…**warlike preparations** have ended in total **ruin and defeat**."

CONSTANTINE I, ROMAN EMPEROR, IN AN EDICT TO PALESTINE, 323 CE

RED CLIFFS 208 CE

Forces Cao Cao: 220,000; Liu Bei and Sun Quan: 50,000. **Casualties** No reliable estimates. **Location** central China.

Drawn into a naval engagement on the Yangtze river, the forces of Cao Cao chained their ships together for greater stability at the cost of manoeuvrability. This made them an easy target for the arrows and fireships of their opponents and they retreated in disarray.

NISIBIS 217 CE

Forces Roman: unknown; Parthian: unknown. **Casualties** No reliable estimates, but heavy on both sides. **Location** Modern southeastern Turkey.

The battle of Nisibis pitted the infantry army of Rome against Parthian mounted archers and cataphracts. After three days of heavy fighting the Parthians failed to break the Roman formation. This was the last major conflict between Rome and Parthia.

SASANID PERSIA VERSUS ROME 224–363 CE

The Sasanid dynasty came to power in Persia in 224CE, creating a huge and powerful empire whose influence extended through much of the civilized world. Rome dealt with the Sasanids as equals, though this did not prevent a number of wars between the two empires.

MISICHE 244 CE

Forces Roman: unknown; Sasanid: unknown. **Casualties** Roman: very heavy; Sasanid: no reliable estimates. **Location** Near modern Fallujah, Iraq.

Roman forces under Emperor Gordian invaded Persia in 243. The decisive battle of the campaign took place at Misiche the following year, where the Romans were heavily defeated and the emperor killed.

BARBALISSOS 253 CE

Forces Roman: 70,000; Sasanid: unknown. **Casualties** No reliable estimates. **Location** Modern northeastern Syria.

Tension between Rome and Persia over Roman ambitions in the region led to a renewal of conflict in 253. A large Roman force was defeated at Barbalissos, which permitted the Persians to take the key cities of Antioch and Dura Europos.

EDESSA 259 CE

Forces Roman: 70,000; Sasanid: 40,000. **Casualties** Roman: almost total; Sasanid: very low. **Location** Modern southeastern Turkey.

Sasanid incursions into Roman territory resulted in a Roman campaign to redress the situation. Initially successful, the Roman army was completely defeated at Edessa, with the capture and death of the emperor Valerian.

Battle of the Milvian Bridge, 312 CE
A victory for the Roman emperor Constantine the Great over his rival Maxentius, the battle of the Milvian Bridge was seen by later Christians as the beginning of Constantine's conversion to Christianity.

CAMPAIGNS OF SHAPUR II
344–363 CE

Forces Roman: unknown; Sasanid: unknown. **Casualties** Unknown. **Location** Persian–Roman border region.

Sasanid emperor Shapur II attempted to regain lands lost to Rome and initially met with success. While besieging Singara he received word of nomadic raids on his provinces and a robust Roman response, and so abandoned the campaign.

SIEGE OF AMIDA 359 CE

Forces Roman: unknown; Sasanid: unknown. **Casualties** Unknown. **Location** Modern Diyarbakır, Turkey.

Renewing hostilities with Rome, Shapur II received the surrender of several Roman cities. Amida withstood siege for 73 days before finally succumbing to the Sasanid army, which used siege towers and flaming arrows to overcome the defenders.

CTESIPHON 363 CE

Forces Roman: 83,000; Sasanid: unknown. **Casualties** No reliable estimates. **Location** Near Baghdad, modern Iraq.

In response to the loss of territory to the Sasanid Persians, a Roman army advanced more or less unopposed to the Sasanid capital at Ctesiphon. Despite a total victory over the Sasanid army, the Romans were unable to take the fortified city before Persian reinforcements arrived and the Romans had to retire.

SAMARRA 363 CE

Forces Roman: 35,000; Sasanid probably about equal to the Roman force. **Casualties** Unknown. **Location** Samarra, north of Baghdad, modern Iraq.

Retreating from the Persian capital, the Roman army was harassed by Persian skirmishers. At Samarra a major attack on the Roman rearguard resulted in the death of the Roman emperor Julian. His successor made peace with Persia, ceding several provinces.

WARS OF CONSTANTINE I
312–324 CE

Constantine was the first Christian Roman emperor, and was also responsible for moving the capital to what became Constantinople. Rival emperors Maxentius and (later) Licinius challenged his rule, bringing about a civil war.

AUGUSTA TAURINORUM 312 CE

Forces Constantine: unknown; Maxentius: unknown. **Casualties** No reliable estimates. **Location** Modern Turin, Italy.

As Constantine's army advanced on Rome it was attacked by a cavalry force loyal to Maxentius. The Maxentian army was then outflanked and decisively beaten. Several major cities made demonstrations of loyalty to Constantine soon after.

VERONA 312 CE

Forces Constantine: unknown; Maxentius: unknown. **Casualties** No reliable estimates. **Location** Northern Italy.

A diversionary Constantinian force drew some of the Maxentian troops out of the city, and a siege began. Constantine's army beat off an attempt to raise the siege in a close-fought battle. Once Verona surrendered, Constantine was free to march on Rome itself.

MILVIAN BRIDGE 28 OCTOBER 312 CE

Forces Constantine: 50,000; Maxentius: 75,000. **Casualties** No reliable estimates. **Location** Near Rome, Italy.

Having demolished the stone Milvian bridge over the Tiber river, Maxentius, ruler of Rome, advanced across a pontoon bridge to confront Constantine. Defeated, he retreated by the same route and was drowned when the bridge collapsed.

HELLESPONT 324 CE

Forces Constantine: 200 ships; Licinian: 350 ships. **Casualties** No reliable estimates. **Location** Strait of the Dardanelles, modern northwestern Turkey.

As Constantine was besieging Byzantium, a fleet loyal to Licinius attempted to contest control of the Hellespont. An initial clash went badly for Licinius's fleet, which was outmanoeuvred in the narrow waters. As reinforcements arrived, the Licinian fleet was shattered by a storm, granting victory to Constantine.

CAMPAIGNS OF SAMUDRAGUPTA
C. 330–375 CE

Forces Gupta: unknown. Rival kingdoms: unknown. **Casualties** No reliable estimates. **Location** Southern, central, and northern India.

The Gupta dynasty rulers Chandragupta I and his son Samudragupta attempted to recreate the Mauryan empire. They succeeded in bringing large areas of India under their control. Samudragupta defeated the kingdoms of Kota and Andhra.

ARGENTORATUM 357 CE

Forces Roman: 13,000; Alemanni: 35,000. **Casualties** Roman: 243; Alemanni: 6,000. **Location** Modern Strasbourg, eastern France.

The Alemanni came close to achieving victory over the outnumbered Romans. Assisted by heavy missile support, the Roman infantry were eventually able to rout their foes after a hard fight.

ADRIANOPLE 9 AUGUST 378 CE

Forces Roman: 60,000; Goth: 100,000–200,000. **Casualties** Roman: 40,000; Goth: no reliable estimates. **Location** Modern Edirne, western Turkey.

During an attempt at negotiations with Ostrogothic and Visigothic armies, fighting broke out with the forces of Valens, the Roman emperor in the east. The Goths routed the Roman cavalry

Gold dinar coins
Three of these coins depict Indian kings of the Indian Gupta empire: Samudragupta (335–375); Kumaragupta I (415–454); and the great general, Chandragupta I (320–335).

and then attacked their infantry from the rear. The battle is often seen as the first step in the fall of the Roman empire to the barbarians.

FRIGIDUS 5 SEPTEMBER 394 CE

Forces Roman: unknown; Frankish: unknown. **Casualties** No reliable estimates. **Location** Modern Slovenia.

Having killed the western Roman emperor Valentinian II, the Frankish king Arbogast found himself under attack from eastern Roman emperor Theodosius I's forces. Assisted by gale-force winds along the Frigidus river valley, the Romans managed to defeat the Franks.

WHITE HUNS C.450–530 CE

Forces White Hun: unknown; Persian and Indian: unknown. **Casualties** No reliable estimates. **Location** Modern Punjab and Bihar, India.

The White Huns carved out a kingdom in Persia and India, expanding it in the early 6th century before being defeated and fading into obscurity. Their eventual fate is uncertain.

CHÂLONS
JUNE OR JULY 451 CE

Forces Roman: unknown; Hun: unknown. **Casualties** No reliable estimates. **Location** Near modern Châlons-en-Champagne, northeastern France.

The Hun invasions of the Roman empire struck terror into its settled populations. At Châlons, Attila's Hun forces met the Roman forces. Attila was forced to retreat.

GREAT ROMAN DEFEATS

Defeats	Date	Location	Enemy	Roman losses
Allia	390 BCE	Italy	Gauls	Unknown, tens of thousands
Cannae	2 August 216 BCE	Italy	Carthage	48,000
Arausio	6 October 105 BCE	France	Cimbri, Teutones	70,000–120,000 casualties
Carrhae	53 BCE	Turkey	Parthia	20,000 dead, 10,000 captured
Teutoburg Forest	9–11 September, 9 CE	Germany	Germanic tribes	Up to 20,000 killed
Adrianople	9 August 378	Turkey	Goths	40,000 casualties

PARTHIAN WARRIOR

War in the Medieval World 500–1500

10TH-CENTURY VIKING HELMET

The traditional view of warfare from 500 to 1500 CE is that the dominance of cavalry was slowly eroded by the development of disciplined infantry. Throughout the period, infantry demonstrated its ability to fight off even elite cavalry, for example, at the battle of Poitiers in 732. The period also produced a number of innovative commanders, including William the Conqueror and Jan Zizka, who brought together infantry and cavalry in a variety of battle-winning combinations.

The remnants of the Western Roman empire finally collapsed when the last emperor, Romulus Augustulus, abdicated in 476. In the following centuries peoples such as the Franks and Visigoths fought for supremacy within the former empire.

VOUILLÉ SPRING 507

Forces Frankish: unknown; Visigoth: unknown. **Casualties** No reliable estimates. **Location** Near Poitiers, central France.

Using religious differences as a pretext, King Clovis of the Franks attacked the Visigoths. Clovis slew King Alaric II of the the Visigoths in battle and added most of southwest Gaul to his territory.

BYZANTIUM, PERSIA, AND ISLAM AT WAR 530–732

A wave of Islamic Arab conquests had destroyed the Sasanid Persian empire by 652 and seriously weakened the Byzantine (Eastern Roman) empire. This era of

Danish battle axe
Weapons similar to this axe featured widely in European battles from the 8th to the 13th century.

Muslim expansion ended with the Frankish victory at Poitiers in 732.

DARA 530

Forces Byzantine: 25,000; Persian: 40,000–50,000. **Casualties** Byzantine: unknown; Persian: 8,000. **Location** Dara, Armenia.

After a lengthy archery duel, the Persians drove back the Byzantine heavy cavalry, but were then flanked by Hun horse archers and driven off. The Persians lost heart and retired.

TRICAMARUM 15 DECEMBER 533

Forces Byzantine: 5,000 cavalry, 10,000 infantry, 20,000 sailors; Vandal: up to 50,000. **Casualties** No reliable estimates. **Location** West of Carthage (in modern-day Tunisia).

Although their allied light cavalry was unreliable, the Byzantine heavy cavalry charged as soon as the Vandals came into sight. Seeing that victory was likely, the allied cavalry then joined the fight.

SIEGE OF ROME 537–538

Forces Byzantine: 5,000 and 7,000 reinforcements; Ostrogoth: up to 50,000. **Casualties** No reliable estimates. **Location** Rome, central Italy.

Having taken Rome, the Byzantines were besieged by the Goths. An aggressive defence using cavalry raids eventually forced the Goths to withdraw, at which point the Byzantines counterattacked.

SENA GALLICA 551

Forces Byzantine: 50 warships; Ostrogoth: 47 warships. **Casualties** Byzantine: minimal; Ostrogoth: 36 ships lost, the remainder beached and burned shortly afterwards. **Location** Off Sena Gallica (modern Senigallia), Italy.

Most of the 400-strong Ostrogothic fleet was sent to raid the Greek coast, giving the Byzantines a slight numerical superiority in the Adriatic. The veteran Byzantine crews out-manoeuvred their inexperienced opponents.

TAGINAE JUNE 552

Forces Byzantine: 20,000; Ostrogoth: 15,000. **Casualties** Byzantine: unknown; Ostrogoth: 6,000 killed. **Location** Umbria, central Italy.

As the Ostrogoths launched a head-on cavalry attack, they ran into flanking crossfire from archers and fell back in disorder. The Byzantine cavalry then charged to complete the victory.

VOLTURNUS OCTOBER 554

Forces Byzantine: 18,000; Frankish and Alemanni: 20,000. **Casualties** Byzantine: minimal; Frankish and Alemanni: very heavy. **Location** Volturno river, Italy.

In 553, an army of 75,000 Franks and Alemanni tribesmen invaded Italy in support of the Ostrogoth campaign for control of the area. Much of this force dispersed, and the remainder suffered an epidemic of dysentery, leaving barely 20,000 men to face the Byzantines. The Franks attacked fiercely, but were defeated by repeated cavalry charges into the flanks and rear of their unwieldy infantry. The battle marked the completion of the Byzantine conquest of Italy.

VIMINACIUM 601

Forces Byzantine: unknown; Avar: unknown. **Casualties** Byzantine: minimal; Avar: 28,000. **Location** Viminacium, Dacia (modern Kostolac, Serbia).

In 601, the Byzantines fought a series of actions against the Avars, who had been raiding the Balkan provinces for 20 years. In each case, Byzantine infantry withstood repeated charges from Avar cavalry who were beaten off with heavy losses.

NINEVEH 12 DECEMBER 627

Forces Byzantine: unknown; Persian: unknown. **Casualties** No reliable estimates. **Location** Near modern Mosul, Iraq.

Byzantine and Persian forces clashed near the ruins of Nineveh, fighting for 11 hours. The Byzantine emperor killed the Persian leader in personal combat; the Persian army was then routed.

YARMUK 20 AUGUST 636

Forces Byzantine: up to 80,000; Arab: up to 40,000. **Casualties** Byzantine: possibly 70,000; Arab: unknown. **Location** Yarmuk river, south of Galilee, Israel.

After a period of skirmishing, the Arabs took advantage of a sandstorm to charge the enemy camp. Blinded by sand, the Byzantines were unable to fight effectively and were slaughtered.

QADISIYYA 1 JUNE 637

Forces Arab: 30,000; Persian: 50,000. **Casualties** No reliable estimates. **Location** Near al-Hillah, south of Baghdad, Iraq.

Although outnumbered, the Arab force attacked aggressively and broke the Persian army. As a result the Arabs were able to overrun Mesopotamia.

HISTORY'S BLOODIEST BATTLES

While almost all battles incur some loss of life on each side, the battles listed below are remarkable for the sheer scale of the casualties.

Battle	Description	Dates	Location	Casualties
Jerusalem	Roman capture and destruction of Jerusalem	70 CE	Jerusalem	Anywhere from 60,000 to 1,100,000 dead (mainly civilians)
Salsu	Engagement during the second Goguryeo-Sui War between China and Korea	612	Salsu river, North Korea	302,000 dead
Baghdad	Mongol forces capture and sack Baghdad	1258	Baghdad, modern Iraq	200,000 to 1,000,000 casualties estimated
Tenochtitlán	Small Spanish army supported by indigenous allies conquers the Aztec capital	May–August 1521	Near modern Mexico City	c.200,000 soldiers and civilians killed, almost all Aztecs
Verdun	French resist a major German offensive around Verdun	February–December 1916	Northeastern France	c.700,000 casualties
Brusilov Offensive	Major Russian offensive against the Central Powers in World War I	June–September 1916	Western Russia, Eastern Front	500,000 to 1,000,000 dead and wounded
Somme	Allied offensive around the river Somme in World War I	July–November 1916	Northern France	1,070,000 dead, wounded, and missing
Stalingrad	Soviet defence of the city of Stalingrad	July 1942–February 1943	Southern Russia	1,250,000 casualties
Xuzhou	Battle between Nationalists and Communist People's Liberation Army	November 1948–January 1949	Territories north of the Yangtze river	c.250,000 casualties

NIHAWAND 642

Forces Arab: 16,000–30,000; Persian: 60,000–120,000.
Casualties Arab: 7,500; Persian: 40,000. **Location** Nihawand, near Hamadan, Iran.

A large but ill-trained Persian army was defeated by the Arabs in a three-day battle, which led to the Arab conquest of virtually the entire Persian empire.

SYLLAEUM 677

Forces Byzantine: unknown; Arab: unknown. **Casualties** Byzantine: minimal; Arab: heavy. **Location** Off Syllaeum (near modern Antalya), southwestern Turkey.

This naval battle saw the first major use of "Greek Fire", an extremely effective incendiary weapon that was catapulted at the Arab warships. (Later variants were fired from hand-pumped flame-throwers.) The few Arab vessels that survived the battle were destroyed in a storm.

KARBALA 10 OCTOBER 680

Forces Umayyad: 4,000; Husain: 70. **Casualties** Husain: 70. **Location** 88km (55 miles) southwest of Baghdad, Iraq.

Travelling to Kufah to join a rising against the Umayyad caliphate, Husain ibn Ali was cornered by Umayyad forces at Karbala and killed along with his small retinue.

TRANSDUCTINE PROMONTORIES 711

Forces Visigoth: 15,000; Arab and Berber: 12,000. **Casualties** Visigoth: heavy; Arab and Berber: moderate. **Location** Guadalete river, southern Spain.

A force of 12,000 Berbers and 300 Arab cavalry crossed the Straits of Gibraltar. They were opposed by a larger Visigoth army led by King Roderic. As battle began, much of his army, weakened by feuds within the royal family, deserted, leading to a Berber victory and the rapid Muslim conquest of most of Spain.

SIEGE OF CONSTANTINOPLE 717–718

Forces Arab: 160,000–200,000; Byzantine: unknown. **Casualties** Arab: possibly 130,000–170,000. **Location** Constantinople (modern Istanbul, Turkey).

Held at bay by the Byzantine army's vigorous defence of the city walls, the Arab force finally gave siege. But the Arabs were not able to gain entry or to cut off supplies entirely. The siege was eventually abandoned.

POITIERS 25 OCTOBER 732

Forces Frankish: 15,000–75,000; Muslim: possibly 50,000. **Casualties** No reliable estimates. **Location** Between Poitiers and Tours, west-central France.

After a standoff that lasted for six days, a force of Muslim cavalry attacked an army of Franks, which was under the command of their ruler Charles Martel. The Franks fought dismounted, arranging themselves in a defensive square formation, and were eventually successful in driving back the Muslim troops, forcing them to retire.

" Have ye no **fear** of this multitude. If God be with us, who shall be **against us**?"

EL-SAMEH, ARAB CHIEFTAIN, SHORTLY BEFORE HIS ARMY WAS WIPED OUT AT TOULOUSE, 721

Arabs defeated at Poitiers

The Frankish leader Charles Martel (centre) repelled a Muslim raiding force under 'Abd ar-Rahman al Ghafiqi, near Poitiers on 25 October 732. Martel's victory led to the total annihilation of the Arab army.

Emperor Charlemagne
This reliquary bust of Charlemagne, the first Holy Roman emperor (800–814), was made in the 14th century. It contains the emperor's skull and is housed in the treasury at Aachen Cathedral, western Germany.

TALAS 751
Forces Arab: unknown; Chinese: unknown. **Casualties** No reliable estimates. **Location** Modern-day Kyrgystan, Central Asia.

The Chinese force, composed largely of infantry, was abandoned by its allied cavalry, which defected to the other side. As a result, the Arab horsemen were able to encircle the Chinese force.

MARCELLAE 756
Forces Bulgar: unknown; Byzantine: unknown. **Casualties** No reliable estimates. **Location** Near Karnobat, Bulgaria.

The Bulgars posed the greatest threat to the Balkan provinces of the Byzantine empire throughout the 8th century. In 756, the emperor Constantine V invaded Bulgar territory, supported by a fleet operating in the Black Sea and Danube delta, and won a decisive victory at Marcellae.

THE WARS OF CHARLEMAGNE AND HIS SUCCESSORS
772–851

Charlemagne's exceptional military and political skills helped to create an empire in northwestern Europe. In 800, the pope formally crowned him as "Emperor of the Romans" and, 12 years later, his status was formally recognized by the Byzantine emperor. Charlemagne's death in 814 and the lack of a successor of similar ability led to the rapid break-up of the empire.

THE SAXON CAMPAIGNS
772–799
Forces Frankish: unknown; Saxon: unknown. **Casualties** No reliable estimates. **Location** Saxony and Westphalia, Germany.

Charlemagne's attempts to subdue Saxon rebellions against his rule were met with fierce resistance. However, the size, strength, and skills of Charlemagne's forces eventually prevailed, enabling him to win a glorious victory.

RONCESVALLES 15 AUGUST 778
Forces Frankish: unknown; Basque: unknown. **Casualties** No reliable estimates. **Location** Navarre, northeast Spain.

Returning from an expedition against the Muslims in Spain, Charlemagne's army was attacked by lightly armed Basque troops in the Pyrenees. The rearguard action was the inspiration for the Old French epic poem "The Song of Roland".

FONTENOY 841
Forces Rebel: unknown; Imperialist: unknown. **Casualties** 40,000 (both sides). **Location** Yonne, eastern France.

By 840, Charlemagne's grandsons were quarrelling over the future of the increasingly unstable empire he had founded. The eldest, Lothair I, attempted to impose his authority on his brothers, Louis the German and Charles the Bald, who rebelled. Their army defeated Lothair's forces at Fontenoy, leading to the fragmentation of the empire.

JENGLAND AUGUST 851
Forces Breton: 1,000; Frankish: 4,000. **Casualties** No reliable estimates. **Location** Grand-Fougeray, Ille-et-Vilaine, Brittany, France.

Border disputes between Brittany and the Franks had erupted into open warfare in 845, when the Franks were defeated at Ballon. In 851, the Bretons

Muslim power in Spain quelled
Charlemagne's campaign in Spain (778–801) saw the Franks besiege Barcelona and eventually reconquer Catalonia, checking the Umayyad caliphate at the Ebro river.

won a futher decisive victory at Jengland, which was instrumental in securing virtual independence for Brittany throughout most of the medieval period.

LINDISFARNE 793
Forces Viking: unknown; Anglo-Saxon: unknown. **Casualties** No reliable estimates. **Location** Northeast coast of England.

Up until 793, the Anglo-Saxon kingdoms of England had enjoyed a comfortable sense of security from attack by outside invaders; however, the monastery of Lindisfarne, which was sited on an island off the coast of Northumbria, proved to be vulnerable to Viking raiders. The monastery's considerable treasures were plundered by the Vikings, who also murdered the monks.

PLISKA 26 JULY 811

Forces Byzantine: unknown; Bulgar: unknown. **Casualties** No reliable estimates. **Location** Near modern-day Shumen, northeast Bulgaria.

Attempting to reassert the power of Byzantium, Emperor Nicephorus captured the stronghold of the Bulgar leader Khan Krum. Nicephorus was slain soon after, when his forces were ambushed on a mountain pass.

SIEGE OF PALERMO 831

Forces Arab: 10,000 (before reinforcements); Byzantine: unknown. **Casualties** No reliable estimates. **Location** North coast of Sicily, Italy.

Having raided Sicily for decades, Arab forces launched a full-scale invasion in 831. Initially repulsed, the invaders received reinforcements from Spain and besieged and eventually captured Palermo, which became the capital of an Arab emirate for more than a century.

RAID ON CONSTANTINOPLE
SUMMER 860

Forces Viking: 200 ships; Byzantine: unknown. **Casualties** No reliable estimates. **Location** Constantinople (modern Istanbul, Turkey).

The Vikings sailed down the Bosphorus, burning and pillaging every town and monastery in their way, before besieging the Byzantine city of Constantinople. They did not take control of the city, however, but simply plundered it and left.

LALAKAON 3 SEPTEMBER 863

Forces Arab: 20,000; Byzantine: 40,000. **Casualties** No reliable estimates. **Location** Anatolia, Turkey.

In an attempt to end years of damaging Arab raids, the emperor Michael III assembled three large forces that trapped the Arab army at the Lalakaon river. The outnumbered Arabs attempted to escape, but the vast majority were annihilated. This victory enabled the Byzantine empire to re-establish control of Anatolia.

EDINGTON MAY 878

Forces Viking: c.5,000; Anglo-Saxons: c.5,000. **Casualties** No reliable estimates. **Location** Near Chippenham, southwest England.

With much of England under his rule, the Viking leader Guthrum led his forces against the remaining Anglo-Saxon stronghold of Wessex. Alfred, king of Wessex, summoned a substantial army to fight the Vikings at Edington, defeating Guthrum and forcing his withdrawal.

SIEGE OF PARIS
NOVEMBER 885–SEPTEMBER 886

Forces Viking: c.700 ships, c.30,000 men; Frankish: unknown. **Casualties**: No reliable estimates. **Location** France.

When the Viking assault on Paris failed to seize the city, the Vikings settled in to besiege it. Ultimately, the Frankish emperor Charles the Fat arrived with a larger army, paid the Vikings a large indemnity, and gave them permission to ravage Burgundy, which was refusing to acknowledge his imperial authority.

> "Never before has such **an atrocity** been seen in Britain as we have now **suffered**."
>
> ALCUIN OF YORK ON A VIKING RAID, 793

THE CREATION OF HUNGARY— THE MAGYAR WARS
899–933

In the closing years of the 9th century, intertribal warfare on the steppes of southern Russia drove the Magyars westwards into the area that was to become Hungary. From their newly created homeland, the Magyars launched a series of raids deep into western Europe.

BRENTA 899

Forces Lombard: 15,000; Magyar: 5,000. **Casualties** Lombard: 15,000; Magyar: minimal. **Location** Brenta river, northeastern Italy.

A Lombard force under King Berengar of Italy pursued a Magyar army, which had been raiding the Po valley, as far as the Brenta river. The Magyars initially attempted to negotiate with Berengar and his troops; however, when the talks eventually broke down, they launched a surprise attack on the Lombard camp and routed Berengar's army.

AUGSBURG 910

Forces German: unknown; Magyar: unknown. **Casualties** No reliable estimates. **Location** Augsburg, Bavaria, Germany.

King Ludwig divided his German army into three separate detachments in an attempt to entrap the Magyar raiders who had been devastating large parts of southern Germany. The first two detachments to be sent out were themselves trapped and destroyed by the Magyars. The Magyars then turned on the third force, commanded by Ludwig himself, and completely routed it in a seven-hour battle.

RIADE 933

Forces German: unknown; Magyar: unknown. **Casualties** No reliable estimates. **Location** northern Thuringia, Germany.

The Magyars again invaded Germany when King Henry I ceased to pay them tribute. Henry then deployed a weak decoy force in order to lure the Magyars into attacking, at which point his hidden Bavarian and Franconian cavalry ambushed them. The German troops pursued the Magyar army as far as the Unstrut river, where they effectively destroyed it.

MOST GEOGRAPHICALLY EXTENSIVE CONFLICTS

Conflict	Dates	Territories involved
Conquests of Alexander the Great	334–323 BCE	Almost all states in southeast Europe and Central Asia from Macedonia in the west to northern India in the east, and including Libya, Egypt, Palestine, Syria, and Phoenicia
Islamic conquests	7th–9th centuries CE	All of the Middle East and Persia, Central Asia as far as the Punjab, the Byzantine empire, North African coastal states, Spain, and France
Mongol invasions	13th century	From Mongolia eastwards to the Chinese coast, and west through Central Asia and southern Russia as far as Hungary in Eastern Europe; also invasions in Southeast Asia and the Indian subcontinent
Thirty Years War	1618–48	Europe-wide conflict, involving France, England, the Holy Roman empire, the Spanish empire, Scandinavia, and territories as far east as Hungary and Transylvania
War of the Spanish Succession	1702–14	Almost the whole of Europe, including the Holy Roman empire, Spain, Portugal, France, Britain, and Prussia
Seven Years War	1756–63	Almost the whole of Europe, including the Russian empire, the Holy Roman Empire, Spain, Portugal, Naples, and Sardinia. France and Britain, two other major combatants, also fought in their overseas colonies, resulting in actions in India, North America, Africa, and the Caribbean.
Revolutionary and Napoleonic Wars	1791–1815	The French, Russian, British, and Ottoman empires, plus most other European states from Denmark-Norway in the north to Spain in the south. Fighting also spread out to North Africa and North America.
World War I	1914–18	Europe, Africa, and the Middle East, with fighting also spreading out to China and the Pacific Islands. Combatant nations, however, included the United States, Canada, India, Australia, and Brazil.
World War II	1939–45	With the exception of a number of African and South American states, along with European countries such as the Republic of Ireland, Spain, Portugal, Switzerland, and Sweden, World War II engulfed the entire planet.

Merciless invader
Any soldier or civilian who was unfortunate enough to be captured by the invading forces of the Mongol ruler Genghis Khan was unlikely to be shown any mercy. The barbarity and cruelty of Genghis Khan and his army are legendary.

BRUNANBURGH 937

Forces Anglo-Saxon: 18,000; Scot and Norse/Irish: 18,000. **Casualties** No reliable estimates. **Location** near Rotherham, Yorkshire, northern England.

Constantine III of Scotland organized an invasion of England in alliance with Welsh, Norse/Irish, and Viking chieftains. King Athelstan deployed the Anglo-Saxon army in a strong defensive position, beating off several assaults, before counterattacking and breaking the allied army. The battle resulted in England becoming the dominant power in the British Isles.

BACH DANG 938

Forces Chinese: unknown; Annamese: unknown. **Casualties** No reliable estimates. **Location** Near Haiphong, northern Vietnam.

After driving iron-tipped stakes into the bed of the tidal Bach Dang river, the Vietnamese sent out shallow-draught vessels to lure the seagoing Chinese fleet onto them. The Chinese took the bait, and the trapped ships were then successfully assaulted.

LECHFELD 10 AUGUST 955

Forces German: unknown; Magyar: unknown. **Casualties** No reliable estimates. **Location** Near Augsburg, Germany.

During an attempt to relieve Augsburg, then under siege by the Magyars, the outnumbered Germans were presented with a golden opportunity when the previously elusive Magyar horsemen dismounted to loot the German camp. The horseless Magyars were routed and, as a consequence, their power was permanently diminished.

SILISTRIA 972

Forces Kievan Rus: 60,000; Byzantine: 30,000. **Casualties** Kievan Rus: 38,000; Byzantine: possibly as few as 350. **Location** Silistria, northeastern Bulgaria.

The Byzantine army, commanded by the emperor John I Tzimisces, forced the Rus to withdraw to their fortress of Silistria on the Danube, and began a 65-day siege. A number of sorties were defeated before the Rus surrendered and agreed to evacuate Bulgaria, which became a province of the Byzantine empire.

STILO 14 JULY 982

Forces Arab: unknown; German: unknown. **Casualties** Arab: unknown; German: 4,000. **Location** Capo Colonna, near Crotone, Italy.

The Arab Emirate of Sicily had been established in 965 and was soon launching extensive raids into southern Italy. The Holy Roman emperor Otto II's forces intercepted the Arab army in Calabria and killed the Emir of Sicily, Abu al-Qasim. However, the imperial forces were defeated when a hidden Arab reserve charged into their flank.

MALDON AUGUST 991

Forces Viking: 3,000; Anglo-Saxon: possibly a similar number. **Casualties** No reliable estimates. **Location** Essex, southeast England.

The Anglo-Saxons unwisely agreed to permit the invading Vikings to come inland from their island camp for a formal battle. Although the Vikings lost many men in the battle, it was a defeat for the Anglo-Saxons – their leader was beheaded and the army defeated in the ensuing fight.

PESHAWAR 1009

Forces Afghan Ghaznavid: unknown; Indian: unknown. **Casualties** No reliable estimates. **Location** Modern northwest Pakistan.

Facing an Indian army that relied heavily on the shock effect of massed elephants, the Ghaznavid troops managed turn this to their advantage and panic the beasts, causing them to stampede through their own side. The Ghaznavids then annexed the Punjab.

THESSALONIKA 996

Forces Bulgar: unknown; Byzantine: unknown. **Casualties** No reliable estimates. **Location** Near Thessalonika, Greece.

A Bulgar army commanded by Tsar Samuil invaded the Byzantine Balkan provinces and besieged Thessalonika. Instead of carrying out conventional siege operations, the tsar concealed most of the army in a carefully selected ambush site that was protected by ditches and traps. He then ordered a feint assault on the city by a small force, which provoked a counterattack. The Bulgars staged a fake retreat to draw the garrison into the ambush, where it was annihilated.

SPERCHEIOS 16 JULY 997

Forces Bulgar: unknown; Byzantine: unknown. **Casualties** No reliable estimates. **Location** Spercheios river, Greece.

Tsar Samuil failed to follow up his victory at Thessalonika by taking the city, preferring to loot southern Greece. Returning from raiding as far south as Corinth, he was intercepted by another Byzantine army at the Spercheios river. The two armies were camped on opposite banks of the river, which was in full flood; even after several days, it seemed unlikely that either side could cross. Byzantine scouts eventually found a usable ford, however, and the entire army crossed to launch a devastating surprise attack on the Bulgar camp.

CLONTARF 23 APRIL 1014

Forces Irish c.7,000; Viking and Leinstermen: c.7,000. **Casualties** Irish: 1,600–4,000 killed; Viking and Leinstermen: up to 6,000 killed. **Location** North of Dublin, Republic of Ireland.

An alliance of Vikings and native Leinstermen was defeated in battle by Brian Boru's Irish forces. Unable to return to their boats or retire across the Liffey river, the Vikings were slaughtered.

KLEIDION 29 JULY 1014

Forces Byzantine: unknown; Bulgar: 20,000. **Casualties** Byzantine: unknown; Bulgar: 14,000 blinded. **Location** North of Thessalonika, northeastern Greece.

Lured from their fortifications by a diversionary force in the rear, the Bulgars were surrounded and trapped. Most were captured. The prisoners were blinded and sent back to their ruler.

ASHINGDON 18 OCTOBER 1016

Forces Danish: unknown; Anglo-Saxon: unknown. **Casualties** No reliable estimates. **Location** Ashingdon, Essex, southeast England.

Anglo-Saxon sword
This is a reproduction of an Anglo-Saxon sword found near Abingdon, England, in 1874. It has with a silver-inlaid pommel and an iron double-edged blade.

After several inconclusive engagements, the Danish and Anglo-Saxons clashed at Ashingdon. King Edmund's Mercian contingent fled, causing the Anglo-Saxon army to collapse. As a result, England fell under Danish rule.

DURRACHIUM 1018

Forces Bulgar: unknown; Byzantine: unknown. **Casualties** No reliable estimates. **Location** Durrës, Albania.

After the death of Tsar Samuil in 1014, the Bulgarian empire became increasingly unstable. His successor, Ivan Vladislav, continued the war against the Byzantine empire with an attack on Durrachium, but was killed when the garrison made a sudden sortie. The Byzantines took advantage of the chaos following his death to annex most of the Bulgarian empire.

DANDANQAN 1040

Forces Seljuk: unknown; Ghaznavid: unknown. **Casualties** No reliable estimates. **Location** Near Merv, Turkmenistan.

The Seljuk Turks wore down their opponents by using mounted archers, before closing to a decisive range. Despite the heroic example of their emperor Masud, the Ghaznavids were defeated after a battle lasting three days. The Seljuk victory marked the birth of their great empire in Asia.

CIVITATE 18 JUNE 1053

Forces Norman: 3,000 cavalry; Imperial and papal forces: unknown, mainly infantry. **Casualties** No reliable estimates. **Location** Apulia, southern Italy.

INFLUENTIAL MILITARY BOOKS

Title	Author	Nationality	Date
History of the Peloponnesian War	Thucydides	Greek	5th century BCE
Arthashastra	Chanakya	Indian	c.300 BCE
Strategikos	Onasander	Greek	1st century BCE
Strategemata	Sextus Julius Frontinus	Roman	c.80 CE
History of the Parthian Wars and Order of Battle against the Alans	Arrian	Roman/Greek	2nd century CE
De Rei Militari	Flavius Vegetius	Roman	c.390 CE
The Prince	Niccolò Machiavelli	Italian	1532
Hagakure	Yamamoto Tsunetomo	Japanese	1706–16
The Science of Victory	Alexander Vasilyevich Suvorov	Russian	1806
The Influence of Sea Power upon History	Alfred Thayer Mahan	American	1890
The Command of the Air	Guilio Douhet	Italian	1921
Guerrilla Warfare	Heinz Guderian	German	1937
Achtung Panzer!	Mao Zedong	Chinese	1937
Infantry Attacks	Erwin Rommel	German	1937

Βασιλειε Τζιμισκη самонла цр̃ъ блгарω· и ослѣпинѣ сι· χηλιαдъ блъгарь

Attempting to dislodge the Normans from southern Italy, imperial and papal forces met heavy defeat. The pope was taken prisoner, and the Normans went on to increase their power in southern Italy and the Mediterranean.

King Harald I "Bluetooth"
This 11th-century relief shows King Harald I "Bluetooth" (c.935–986). He famously united and brought Christianity to the Danes.

THE DEFENCE OF NORMANDY
1054–57

The Duchy of Normandy was created in 911 when Charles the Simple, king of France, granted the territory to the Viking chieftain Rollo. Later French kings tried to reclaim it, especially during the early years of William the Conqueror's dukedom (1035–87).

MORTEMER 1054

Forces Norman: unknown; French: unknown. **Casualties** No reliable estimates. **Location** Mortemer-en-Bray, Pays de Caux, Normandy, France.

Two French armies invaded Normandy, advancing on Rouen along both banks of the Seine river. One of the forces occupied Mortemer-en-Braye, and was in the midst of thoroughly looting the town when it was caught by a surprise attack, launched by a Norman army that had been shadowing its advance. It was annihilated. On hearing of the disaster, the second French army hastily withdrew from Normandy.

VARAVILLE 1057

Forces Norman: unknown; French: unknown. **Casualties** No reliable estimates. **Location** Varaville ford, Dives river, Pays d'Auge, Normandy, France.

A French army invading Normandy attempted to cross the Dives river at the Varaville ford, but barely half the force

succeeded before the rising tide made the ford impassable. The shadowing Norman army then attacked, defeating the remaining French troops who had failed to cross the river. The battle was the last serious French attempt to overrun Normandy in the lifetime of William, Duke of Normandy.

KAWASAKI 1057

Forces Abe Sadato: 4,000; Minamoto: unknown. **Casualties** Unknown. **Location** Northern Japan .

While attacking a strongly defended position in a snowstorm, the Minamoto forces were defeated and pursued by the Abe Sadato forces, in this first major battle of the Early Nine Years War (1051–63).

NISSA 1057

Forces Danish: 300 ships; Norwegian: 150 ships. **Casualties** Danish: c.70 ships; Norwegian: unknown. **Location** Nissa fjord, Norway.

One of the largest naval battles of the period was fought between a Danish fleet commanded by Svein Ulfsson and the Norwegian fleet under Harald Hardrada. The Danish flagship and its escorting vessels were roped together to form a large fighting platform. Despite being outnumbered, the Norwegians won a major victory, taking more than 70 Danish ships.

Byzantine knights
Byzantine emperor Basil II's cavalry, from the *Chronicle of Manasses* (c.1081), shows the typical armament of 11th-century knights: conical iron helmets, hooded mail hauberks, triangular shields, and lances.

THE NORMAN CONQUEST
1066

Edward the Confessor's death without a clear successor at the beginning of 1066 signalled a power struggle for the English throne. The strongest claimant was the Earl of Wessex, Harold Godwinson, who had been elected king by the Witangemot (royal council). His rivals were King Harald Hardrada of Norway and William, Duke of Normandy, who became known as William the Conqueror.

FULFORD
20 SEPTEMBER 1066

Forces Saxon: unknown; Viking: unknown. **Casualties** No reliable estimates. **Location** Fulford, near York, northern England.

Norwegian king Harald Hardrada's invasion of England was initially opposed by a force commanded by earls Edwin of Mercia and Morkere of Northumbria. The Anglo-Saxons took up a strong defensive position near the Ouse river in Yorkshire, but were defeated by the more experienced Viking army.

A Norman victory
The late 10th-century Bayeux Tapestry commemorates the Norman victory at Hastings in 1066. In this detail, King Harold Godwinson's Anglo-Saxon infantry confronts a cavalry charge by Duke William of Normandy's troops.

IMPORTANT ADVANCES IN BATTLEFIELD MEDICINE

Period/date	Advance
16th century	Frenchman Ambroise Paré (1510–90) wrote influential treatises on battlefield surgery and the treatment of wounds. He also introduced the tying of severed arteries to military medicine, moving away from cauterization as the favoured surgical technique.
1674	First military use of a tourniquet to control blood at Siege of Besançon.
18th–19th centuries	Frenchman Dominique Jean Larrey (1766–1842) introduced the first battlefield ambulance service, adapting gun carriages for the purpose, crewed by drivers, medically trained corpsmen, and litter-bearers.
1854–56	During the Crimean War, Russian Nikolay Ivanovich Pirogov (1810–81) pioneered the use of ether as an anaesthetic for battlefield surgery. By this time chloroform was another major anaesthethic.
19th century	American Jonathan Letterman (1824–72) introduced a modern three-stage system of battlefield triage and treatment – field dressing (aid) station, field hospital, and large hospital.
World War I (1914–18)	Blood transfusion developed as a form of treatment, with intravenous rehydration. Novocaine used a local anaesthetic. Pioneering developments in plastic surgery and reductions in limb amputations.
1936	During the Spanish Civil War, Canadian Henry Norman Bethune (1890–1939) developed the first mobile blood transfusion service.
World War II (1939–45)	Major improvements in anaesthesia, and the treatment of wounds using antibiotics. Advances in the prevention and treatment of tropical diseases. Pre-packaged sterile intravenous fluids provided to frontline medics.
Korean War (1950–53)	Helicopters were used for rapid medical evacuation (medevac).
Post-World War II	New forms of antibiotics to counter penicillin-resistant strains of bacteria. Vaccines developed against chem-bio weapons. Mobile ventilators in medevac aircraft. Remote imaging and diagnostic tools aid effective treatments.

STAMFORD BRIDGE
25 SEPTEMBER 1066

Forces Anglo-Saxon: 7,000; Viking: 8,000–10,000. **Casualties** No reliable estimates. **Location** Near York, north Yorkshire, England.

On hearing of the Viking invasion by Harald Hardrada, King Harold made an exceptionally rapid forced march from London to Stamford Bridge. He surprised the Viking army, which was encamped along both banks of the Derwent river. The Anglo-Saxons exploited their local numerical superiority and quickly destroyed the Viking troops on the river's west bank, before fighting their way across a bridge and a nearby ford. Harald Hardrada formed his remaining men into a circular shield wall, hoping to hold out until he could be reinforced by the troops that had been detached to guard his ships at Riccall. Repeated Anglo-Saxon charges finally broke the shield wall, and Harald Hardrada was killed just as the reinforcements arrived. These troops were exhausted, and were defeated rapidly.

HASTINGS 14 OCTOBER 1066

Forces Norman: 7,000–15,000; Anglo-Saxon: 9,000. **Casualties** Norman: 2,000; Anglo-Saxon: 4,000. **Location** Near Battle, north of Hastings, southeast England.

William, Duke of Normandy, invaded England to claim the English throne. King Harold deployed the Saxon forces in a strong defensive position on Caldbec Hill, to block the Norman army's route to London. The Saxon shield wall beat off a succession of attacks launched by Norman cavalry and infantry, with the use of two-handed axes proving highly effective even against well-armoured knights. After several futile attacks, part of the Norman force collapsed, and the panic threatened to affect the army. The crisis was worsened by a rumour that William had been killed, but he rode through the ranks to rally his troops. He destroyed the Saxon army with a series of feigned retreats, cavalry charges, and archery. King Harold was killed, and England became subject to Norman rule.

MANZIKERT 19 OR 26 AUGUST 1071

Forces Byzantine: c.50,000; Seljuk: c.40,000. **Casualties** Unknown. **Location** Modern Malazgirt, Armenia.

Although the Byzantine army's centre managed to advance as far as the enemy camp, the flanks collapsed under pressure and the reserves withdrew, abandoning the main body to its fate. This defeat marked the beginning of the decline of the Byzantine empire.

THE SPANISH RECONQUISTA
1084–94

The Reconquista (reconquest) of the Muslim states of the Iberian peninsula was a slow process with many setbacks. The capture of Toledo and Valencia marked key stages in an exceptionally long campaign, one that was only finally completed in 1492.

SIEGE OF TOLEDO
AUTUMN 1084–25 MAY 1085

Forces Unknown. **Casualties** Unknown. **Location** Toledo, central Spain.

Taking advantage of disunity among the Muslims, King Alfonso VI of León and Castile laid siege to the Islamic city of Toledo. Eventually, the city was starved into surrender, giving Alfonso a important strategic base in central Spain.

SAGRAJAS
23 OCTOBER 1086

Forces Muslim: 30,000; Castilian: unknown. **Casualties** No reliable estimates. **Location** North of Badajoz, Spain.

A Castilian surprise attack inflicted heavy casualties, but the larger Muslim army rallied and routed much of the Castilian force. King Alfonso VI of León and Castile was wounded and only just managed to escape.

SIEGE OF VALENCIA
JULY 1093–16 JUNE 1094

Forces Christian: unknown; Muslim: unknown. **Casualties** Unknown, 30,000 prisoners. **Location** Mediterranean coast of southern Spain.

Valencia was taken from a Muslim faction after a long and very bitter siege. Even after the Christian forces razed the suburbs, the inner city held out until starvation forced a surrender.

THE FIRST CRUSADE AND THE DEFENCE OF THE CRUSADER KINGDOMS
1096–1104

In 1095, the Byzantine emperor Alexius I Comnenus appealed to the pope for aid against the Seljuk Turks, who had overrun much of Anatolia following the disastrous Byzantine defeat at Manzikert in 1071. Instead of raising mercenaries, the pope proclaimed a crusade, with the objective of taking Jerusalem.

DORYLAEUM 1 JULY, 1097

Forces Turkish: 3,000; Crusader: 4,000. **Casualties** No reliable estimates. **Location** Modern Eskisehir, Anatolia, Turkey.

Ambushed on the march, the crusaders' heavy cavalry was unable to come to grips with the elusive mounted archers it faced. The arrival of an additional crusader force forced the Turks to retreat.

ANTIOCH
21 OCTOBER 1097–28 JUNE 1098

Forces (June 1098) Turkish: 75,000; Crusader: 15,000. **Casualties** No reliable estimates. **Location** Coast of ancient Syria (now in southern Turkey).

After a long siege, the crusaders captured Antioch, only to be besieged themselves. The discovery of a holy relic (the Holy Lance) inspired the crusaders to launch a sortie that drove off the Turkish army.

SIEGE OF JERUSALEM
7 JUNE–18 JULY, 1099

Forces Crusader: 1,300 knights and 12,000 foot soldiers. **Casualties** No reliable estimates. **Location** Israel.

Although worn down on the march, the crusader army was able to undertake a successful assault on the city. Siege towers, catapults, and "Greek Fire" were employed to support the assault troops. The city was then sacked and its Muslim and Jewish inhabitants massacred.

BATTLE OF ASCALON
12 AUGUST 1099

Forces Crusader: 10,200; Egyptian: 50,000. **Casualties** No reliable estimates. **Location** South of modern Ashkelon, Israel.

An Egyptian army attempting to raise the siege of Jerusalem halted at the port of Ascalon, on hearing of the fall of the city. At dawn, the crusaders attacked the Egyptians, destroying them.

FIRST BATTLE OF RAMLEH
6 SEPTEMBER 1101

Forces Crusader: 1,160; Egyptian: 10,000. **Casualties** No reliable estimates. **Location** Near modern Ramla, between Tel Aviv and Jerusalem, Israel.

A far smaller force commanded by King Baldwin I of Jerusalem attacked a

10,000-strong Egyptian army invading the newly established crusader states. The veteran crusader cavalry launched four successive charges, which finally broke the Egyptian force.

HARRAN MAY 1104

Forces Crusader: 3,000 knights, 9,000 infantry; Muslim: unknown. **Casualties** No reliable estimates. **Location** Modern southeast Turkey.

Both sides attempted to lure the other into an ambush, but it was the reckless crusaders who took the bait. They charged into the hands of the main Muslim force and were decisively defeated.

TINCHEBRAI 28 SEPTEMBER 1106

Forces Anglo-Norman: 7,400; Norman: 5,700. **Casualties** Anglo-Norman: probably fewer than 100; Norman: 300, plus 400 knights captured. **Location:** Tinchebray, Orne, Normandy, France.

The Norman cavalry achieved some initial success, but was held by the second Anglo-Norman line, which was reinforced with a contingent of dismounted knights. A hidden detachment of Anglo-Norman cavalry then charged, and the Norman army broke. The battle gave England control of Normandy for almost 100 years.

SIEGE OF ZARAGOZA WINTER 1118

Forces Christian: unknown; Muslim: unknown. **Casualties** No reliable estimates. **Location** Zaragoza, northeastern Spain.

The campaign of Alfonso I, the "Battler" of Aragon, to capture Zaragoza from the Muslims benefited from siege expertise gained in the Holy Land. After a relief attempt failed, the city surrendered.

> "The **infidel cavalry** waited to make the charges for which it is famous …"

IBN AL-QALANISI, SYRIAN HISTORIAN, DESCRIBING THE CRUSADERS, 12TH CENTURY

BREMULE 20 AUGUST 1119

Forces Anglo-Norman: 500; French: 400. **Casualties** No reliable estimates. **Location** Near Noyon, Picardy, France.

Henry I intercepted a French force under Louis VI that had invaded Normandy. The bulk of the Anglo-Norman knights dismounted behind a front line of about 100 cavalry. This screening force was broken by the first French charge, which plunged on into the dismounted knights, who easily repulsed the attack. Almost 150 French knights were captured, and Louis himself just managed to escape.

BOURGTHEROULDE 26 MARCH 1124

Forces Norman: 200; Royalist: 300. **Casualties** No reliable estimates. **Location** Bourgtheroulde, Normandy, France.

The royalist commander Ralph de Bayeux dismounted some of his men-at-arms to block the road along which the rebels under Waleran, Comte de Mellent, were advancing, but kept a mounted reserve. He also deployed his

PRIMARY INFANTRY WEAPONS BY PERIOD

Ancient 3000 BCE – 500 CE	**Hand-held contact weapons:** Throwing sticks and clubs, swords and daggers (flint, bronze, iron) **Hand-held projectile weapons:** Slingshots and javelins; bows (pellet and arrow) **Artillery:** Mounted crossbows (ballista); catapult and torsion artillery (onager) **Position weapons:** Caltrops, spiked pits, wooden obstacles
Medieval 500–1500	**Hand-held contact weapons:** Swords and daggers (steel), clubs, maces, pole-arms, axes, war hammers, staffs, flails **Hand-held projectile weapons:** Longbow, crossbow, hand cannon, matchlock gun **Artillery:** Breech- and muzzle-loading cannon (static and wheeled); torsion artillery (e.g. magonel) **Position weapons:** Caltrops, spiked pits, wooden obstacles
Early Modern 1500–1750	**Hand-held contact weapons:** Swords and daggers (steel), maces, pole-arms, lances **Hand-held projectile weapons:** Smoothbore musket (matchlock, wheel lock, flintlock muzzle-loaders), bows, crossbows **Artillery:** Muzzle-loading wheeled cannon, mortars, rockets, gunpowder grenades **Position weapons:** Caltrops, spiked pits
Age of Revolution 1750–1830	**Hand-held contact weapons:** Swords and daggers (steel), pole-arms, lances, bayonets **Hand-held projectile weapons:** Muzzle-loading smoothbore musket; muzzle-loading rifles; early revolvers **Artillery:** Muzzle-loading wheeled cannon, mortars, rockets, gunpowder grenades **Position weapons:** Spiked obstacles
Dawn of Modern Warfare 1830–1914	**Hand-held contact weapons:** Swords and daggers, bayonets **Hand-held projectile weapons:** Muzzle-loading smoothbore and rifled muskets, bolt- and lever-action repeating rifles, revolvers, manual then automatic machine guns **Artillery:** Muzzle-loading (smoothbore) then breech-loading (rifled) artillery, mortars, rockets, gunpowder grenades **Position weapons:** Spiked obstacles, land mines
Era of World Wars 1914–45	**Hand-held contact weapons:** Daggers and bayonets **Hand-held projectile weapons:** Bolt-action and self-loading rifles, machine guns, submachine guns, handguns (revolvers and automatic pistols), antitank rifles, antitank rocket launchers; antipersonnel, incendiary and antivehicle grenades, flamethrowers **Artillery:** Antitank, anti-aircraft, and field artillery, infantry mortars, vehicle-mounted rocket launchers **Position weapons:** Antipersonnel and antivehicle land mines
1945–present	**Hand-held contact weapons:** Bayonets **Hand-held projectile weapons:** Assault rifles, machine-guns, automatic pistols, anti-personnel, incendiary and antivehicle grenades **Artillery:** Antitank, anti-aircraft and field artillery, recoilless rifles and antitank guns, infantry mortars, antitank guided missile launchers (personnel and vehicle mounted) **Position weapons:** Antipersonnel and antivehicle land mines, claymore-type mines

40 archers in a concealed flanking position, whose fire broke up the rebels' charge. A royalist counterattack captured Waleran and 80 of his knights.

KAIFENG
SEPTEMBER 1126–JANUARY 1127

Forces Jurchen: unknown; Chinese: more than 500,000. **Casualties** No reliable estimates. **Location** North China.

Despite opposition from a standing army half a million strong, which was assisted by local militias and explosive weapons, the Jurchen captured the city of Kaifeng in a four-month siege and went on to establish the Jin dynasty.

THE STANDARD 22 AUGUST 1138

Forces English: 8,000; Scottish: 10,000. **Casualties** No reliable estimates. **Location** 5km (3 miles) north of Northallerton, Yorkshire, England.

Scots invaded England early in 1138, taking advantage of increasing unrest after Henry I's death in 1135. The English army drew up on a ridge, with a line of dismounted knights supported by archers. They shot down most of the unarmoured Scots, who then broke after several attacks and took heavy losses.

Mace heads

These three types of medieval mace were all designed to effectively bludgeon an opponent to death. They are Polish round or bulbous head (left), western European flanged head (centre), and Indian spiked head (right).

Samurai attack

In this fan painting of the battle at Uji-gawa in 1180, two Minamoto clan samurai, Kagesue and Takatsuna, race across the Uji river. The warriors wear lamellar armour, made of iron strips bound with rawhide and silk cords.

EDESSA 1144

Forces Muslim: unknown; Christian: unknown. **Casualties** No reliable estimates. **Location** Modern Sanliurfa, southeastern Turkey.

A Muslim army out of Aleppo arrived with engines for a siege, but found neglected defences. A breach was opened in the walls, and the city was stormed.

THE SECOND CRUSADE AND AFTERMATH
1147–53

The Muslim conquest of Edessa prompted Pope Eugene III to declare a Second Crusade, the main forces of which were French and German, under the leadership of Louis VII and Conrad III. Their operations in the Middle East ended in a fiasco at Damascus. A significant achievement was the capture of the Moorish city of Lisbon by a mixed force of English, German, and Flemish crusaders, after storms drove their ships into Portuguese harbours.

SIEGE OF LISBON
28 JUNE–24 OCTOBER 1147

Forces Crusader: 13,000 men, 164 ships; Muslim: unknown. **Casualties** No reliable estimates. **Location** Portugal.

Despite early setbacks, when a siege tower became stuck in waterlogged ground and several large catapults were destroyed, renewed efforts breached the walls. The garrison was massacred, despite promises made in surrender negotiations.

DAMASCUS 23–28 JULY 1148

Forces Crusader: unknown; Muslim: unknown. **Casualties** No reliable estimates. **Location** Syria.

Stalled in the face of a stout defence, the commanders of the largest crusader army in history fell to bickering and were forced to retreat by a relief force.

SIEGE OF ASCALON
25 JANUARY–19 AUGUST 1153

Forces Christian: unknown; Egyptian: unknown. **Casualties** No reliable estimates. **Location** Modern Ashkelon, Israel.

At first the Christian troops were unable to breach the defences, but a section of wall collapsed when a siege tower fell against it. The defenders then surrendered in return for safe passage.

COED EULO (COLESHILL)
JULY OR AUGUST 1157

Forces Welsh: unknown; English: unknown. **Casualties** No reliable estimates. **Location** Basingwerk, Clwyd, north Wales.

A Welsh army resisting Henry II's invasion of Gwynedd prepared an elaborate earthwork roadblock in a thickly wooded pass at Basingwerk. Henry ordered feint attacks against the defences, while he led a detachment to outflank the position. Despite inflicting heavy casualties, the Welsh were forced to retreat.

SIEGE OF CREMA
JUNE 1159–FEBRUARY 1160

Forces Frederick Barbarossa's forces: unknown; Cremese: unknown. **Casualties** No reliable estimates. **Location** Crema, near Milan, northern Italy.

Both sides made use of atrocities to reduce enemy morale and undertook extensive engineering works, leading to a campaign of tunnelling and countertunnelling. Eventually the Cremese defenders were starved into surrender.

SIRMIUM 8 JULY 1167

Forces Hungarian: unknown; Byzantine: unknown. **Casualties** No reliable estimates. **Location** Near modern Sremska Mitrovica, Serbia.

A Byzantine army under Andronikos Kontostephanos, the nephew of Emperor Manuel I, intercepted a large Hungarian army near Sirmium. The Hungarians were routed when Andronikos committed his reserve. The victory re-established Byzantine power in the Balkans.

CLAIS AN CHRO MAY 1169

Forces Irish: 5,000; Anglo-Norman: 3,000. **Casualties** No reliable estimates. **Location** Near Freshford, County Kilkenny, Ireland.

The Anglo-Norman army supporting Dermot MacMurrough, the deposed King of Leinster, defeated the Irish after fighting its way through a succession of woodland barricades. The battle marked the beginning of the Anglo–Norman conquest of Ireland.

DUBLIN JUNE 1171

Forces Anglo-Norman: 1,000; Irish: 4,500. **Casualties** Anglo-Norman: minimal; Irish: 2,000. **Location** Dublin, Ireland.

The last Norse king of Dublin, Haskulf Thorgilsson, returned from exile with a largely mercenary army in an attempt to recapture the city, but the garrison made a sudden sortie and broke his forces. Haskulf was captured and executed. Dublin now became the centre of Anglo-Norman power in Ireland.

FORNHAM
17 OCTOBER 1173

Forces Rebel: 3,800; Royalist: 5,000. **Casualties** No reliable estimates. **Location** Fornham All Saints, near Bury St Edmunds, Suffolk, England.

This was the only major battle fought during the Revolt of 1173–74 against Henry II. The rebel army, largely comprising French and Flemish mercenaries, was caught and destroyed by the royalists while fording the Lark river.

LEGNANO 29 MAY 1176

Forces Imperial: 3,500 cavalry; Lombard League: 4,000 cavalry, infantry: unknown. **Casualties** Unknown. **Location** 30km (20 miles) from Milan, northern Italy.

After driving the enemy cavalry from the field, the imperial forces, which included no infantry, were unable to penetrate the pike wall of the Lombard foot soldiers. The returning Lombard cavalry then launched a successful counterattack.

Japanese pole-arm

This fearsome weapon is a samurai *naginata*, a typical Japanese pole-arm, with a wooden handle and a long, curved sabrelike blade.

ISHIBASHI-YAMA 14 SEPTEMBER 1180

Forces Taira: unknown; Minamoto: unknown. **Casualties** No reliable estimates. **Location** In Hakone mountains, near Mount Fuji, Japan.

The Minamoto army, which included a contingent from the Miura clan, was commanded by Minamoto Yorimoto, who was to become shogun less than 10 years later. The Taira general Oba Kagechika won a decisive victory by launching a night attack.

SUNOMATAGAWA 25 APRIL 1181

Forces Taira: unknown; Minamoto: unknown. **Casualties** No reliable estimates. **Location** Near modern Sunamoto, Gifu prefecture, Japan.

The Minamoto forces forded the Sunomata river to make a night attack against the Taira army deployed on the far bank, but were defeated and pursued back across the river.

YAHAGIGAWA 1181

Forces Taira: unknown; Minamoto: unknown. **Casualties** No reliable estimates. **Location** Owari province (in modern Aichi prefecture), Japan.

Shortly after they were defeated at Sunomatagawa, the Minamoto attempted to check the Taira pursuit at the Yahagi river by destroying the bridge and forming a shield wall. Despite this, the Taira were able to force a crossing and continued to attack the retreating Minamoto army.

KURIKARA JUNE 1183

Forces Taira: 100,000; Minamoto: 50,000. **Casualties** No reliable estimates. **Location** Central Japan, north of Kyoto.

The Minamoto clan stalled its enemies for hours with clever ruses and an archery duel, buying time for a detachment to circle into the Taira rear and attack. A vigorous pursuit completed the rout.

MIZUSHIMA 17 NOVEMBER 1183

Forces Taira: unknown; Minamoto: unknown. **Casualties** No reliable estimates. **Location** Modern-day Okayama prefecture, Japan.

A Minamoto army was being ferried across the Inland Sea to attack the Taira stronghold of Yashima when it was intercepted and defeated by a Taira fleet. Many of the Taira ships were lashed together to form large "fighting platforms", from which their archers laid down a heavy bombardment, before boarding the Minamoto vessels.

SACK OF ANGKOR 1177

Forces Cham: unknown; Khmer: unknown. **Casualties** No reliable estimates. **Location** North of Tonle Sap lake, north-central Cambodia.

The 12th century saw prolonged warfare in Southeast Asia. No kingdom was able to make a victory permanent. Although Angkor was sacked by the kingdom of Cham in 1177, by 1181 it was once again a powerful state.

THE GEMPEI WARS
1180–85

The Gempei Wars for control of Japan were fought between the powerful Minamoto and Taira families. The conflicts did much to form samurai culture and allowed the victorious Minamoto to establish the office of shogun, or military dictator, which existed until 1867.

UJI-GAWA 1180

Forces Taira: unknown; Minamoto: unknown. **Casualties** No reliable estimates. **Location** Near Kyoto, Japan.

Defeated by the Taira clan, the Minamoto forces and their warrior-monk allies attempted to hold a broken bridge over the Uji river. Despite a determined resistance, the Taira forced a crossing.

> ## "Using my **armour** and **helmet** as a pillow, I aimed only to fulfil the wish of the Minamoto, to **destroy** the Taira clan."

MINAMOTO NO YOSHITSUNE IN "THE TALE OF THE HEIKE", 12TH-CENTURY POEM

FEATS OF MILITARY ENGINEERING

Pontoon across the Hellespont
In 480 BCE, the engineers of Xerxes' invading Persian army are said to have constructed a pontoon bridge 1,242m (4,077ft) long, using 676 ships lashed together in a double column.

Roman roads
Roman military roads, essential for supplying outlying garrisons, eventually laced the Roman world. The total road network measured 85,004km (53,819 miles) and extended from the coasts of northern Europe to the plains of Central Asia.

The Great Wall of China
The Great Wall was not a single piece of construction, but a series of fortifications that were built and improved from the 5th century BCE up to the 16th century CE. The total network ultimately measured 6,700km (4,160 miles). Some 2 million people died in its construction.

Ledo Road in World War II
In 1942–45, 17,000 Allied engineers built a supply road through the mountainous jungles of northern Burma, reaching 770km (478 miles) from Ledo in India to Kunming in China, at a total cost of US $148 million.

Manhattan Project
The aim of this World War II project, conducted mainly by the United States, was to facilitate the production of atomic weaponry. It was the largest military engineering project in history, employing 130,000 people and costing the modern equivalent of more than US $24 billion.

Ho Chi Minh Trail
In 1959–75, North Vietnamese soldiers and labourers created and maintained an elaborate road system stretching for hundreds of kilometres from North Vietnam through the jungles of Laos and Cambodia. They used these roads to supply the war effort against South Vietnam and to infiltrate troops. Despite massive bombing of the trail by the US Air Force, up to 20,000 Vietnamese troops a month moved along the trail, which featured supply hubs, barracks, and medical facilities.

The Great Wall of China
The Great Wall is a series of fortifications that were erected to protect the northern border of the Chinese empire from invasion. Most of what still stands today was constructed under the Ming dynasty (1368–1644), when around 1 million men where stationed as guards along the entire length of the wall.

SIEGE OF FUKURYUJI 1183

Forces Taira: unknown; Minamoto: unknown. **Casualties** No reliable estimates. **Location** Fukuryuji, Okayama prefecture, Japan.

The Taira fortress of Fukuryuji was stormed by Imai Kanehira's Minamoto forces, in a daring assault across rice paddies while under heavy fire from the garrison's archers.

AWAZU 1184

Forces Yoshinaka: unknown; Noriyori and Yoshitsune: unknown. **Casualties** No reliable estimates. **Location** Awazu, Tokushima prefecture, Japan.

Minamoto Yoshinaka's rule was so vicious that his own clan took up arms against him. He met defeat after a hard fight at Awazu. Yoshinaka himself was killed by an arrow.

ICHI-NO-TANI MARCH 1184

Forces Minamoto: 10,000; Taira: unknown. **Casualties** No reliable estimates. **Location** West of Kobe, western Honshu, Japan.

The cunning Minamoto stalled their opponents with traditional challenges to single combat, while a detachment attacked from the rear. The routed Taira clan lost its last major stronghold.

YASHIMA 22 MARCH 1185

Forces Taira: unknown; Minamoto: unknown. **Casualties** No reliable estimates. **Location** Modern Takamatsu, Shikoku, Japan.

The small Minamoto force panicked the Taira into abandoning their fortress at Yashima by lighting large numbers of fires.

DAN-NO-URA 5 APRIL 1185

Forces Minamoto: 800 ships; Taira: 500 ships. **Casualties** No reliable estimates. **Location** Between Honshu and Kyushu, Japan.

After an archery exchange, the ships closed for boarding actions. The treachery of a Taira admiral and an opportune turn of the tide sealed the fate of the Taira clan, with the Minamoto gaining control of the country.

SIGNIFICANT FORTIFICATIONS AND DEFENCES

Name of fortification	Date built	Location	Type
Hattusas	c.1800 BCE	Near modern Bogazkoy, Turkey	Walled hilltop fortress
Great Wall of China	476 BCE –16th century	From Shanhaiguan to Lop Nur, China	Wall defences
Maiden Castle	c.600–300 BCE	Dorset, England	Iron Age hill fort
Red Fort	c.1st–17th century	Agra, India	Walled city
Constantinople	1st–15th century	Modern Istanbul, Turkey	Fortified city
Great Zimbabwe	c.10th–15th century	South of Harare, Zimbabwe	Fortress city
Krak des Chevaliers	11th–13th century	Near Hims, Syria	Crusader castle
Mehrangarh Fort	1459–19th century	Jodhpur city, Rajasthan, India	Fortress hilltop palace
Deal Castle	1539–40	Deal, Kent, England	Artillery fortress
Fort St George	1639–c.1795	Madras, India	Coastal defence fort
Sevastopol	From 1783	Crimea	Fortified city with coastal defences
Fort Sumter	1827–98	Charleston Harbor, South Carolina, USA	Coastal fortification
Maginot Line	1930–40	French borders with Italy and Germany (lighter defences along Belgian border)	Border defence network

THE DEFENCE OF THE CRUSADER STATES
1177–87

After the failure of the Second Crusade, the crusader states came under increasing pressure from their newly unified Muslim neighbours.

MONTGISARD
25 NOVEMBER 1177

Forces Muslim: 26,000; Crusader: 5,500. **Casualties** Muslim: 20,000; Crusader: 2,000. **Location** Israel.

Saladin's overconfident Muslim army spread out to loot and forage, while advancing on Jerusalem. The crusaders were hugely outnumbered and led by the 16-year-old King Baldwin IV, known as the "Leprous". A sudden crusader attack smashed the disorganized Muslim force and inflicted heavy casualties during a long pursuit.

MARJ AYYUN
10 JUNE 1179

Forces Muslim: unknown; Crusader: unknown. **Casualties** No reliable estimates. **Location** Near Marjayoun, Lebanon.

The crusaders launched an attack on the Muslim camp and were successful in annihilating several groups of raiders. However, they were in turn surprised and comprehensively defeated by the main Muslim force. King Baldwin IV narrowly escaped capture in the rout.

AL-FULE
SEPTEMBER 1183

Forces Muslim: unknown; Crusader: 16,300. **Casualties** No reliable estimates. **Location** Near Alfula, Israel.

A Muslim army invaded the kingdom of Jerusalem, advancing towards Al-Fule and raiding the surrounding areas. The sizable crusader force drove off the raiders and repelled repeated attacks, before the Muslims withdrew.

HATTIN
30 JUNE–4 JULY 1187

Forces Muslim: 30,000; Crusader: 15,000–20,000. **Casualties** Unknown. **Location** Near Sea of Galilee, northern Israel.

Rashly advancing across waterless terrain, the crusaders became encircled on the twin hills known as the Horns of Hattin. Tortured by thirst and under attack, they were compelled to surrender. This was the prelude to the Muslim recapture of Jerusalem by Saladin.

THE THIRD CRUSADE
1189–92

The Muslim recapture of Jerusalem in 1187 prompted the Holy Roman emperor, Frederick I "Barbarossa", Richard I of England, and Philip II of France to launch a new crusade. While it failed to retake Jerusalem, it ensured the temporary survival of the small crusader states.

SIEGE OF ACRE
28 AUGUST 1189–12 JULY 1191

Forces Crusader: unknown; Muslim: unknown. **Casualties** No reliable estimates. **Location** Acre (in modern Israel).

Beating off relief attempts, a small force of crusaders led by Guy de Lusignan managed to breach the walls of Acre. The garrison surrendered, returning the city to Christian control.

Breaching the walls of Acre
In 1191, the crusaders, led by Guy de Lusignan, retook control of the city of Acre – the capital of what was left of the kingdom of Jerusalem. It remained in Christian hands for another 100 years.

ARSUF
7 SEPTEMBER 1191

Forces Crusader: c.20,000; Muslim: unknown. **Casualties** Crusader: 700 killed; Muslim: 7,000 killed. **Location** Israel.

Marching south from Acre, the crusader army led by Richard I of England (the "Lionheart") beat off a near-constant barrage of harassing attacks from Muslim forces, before finally launching a decisive, victorious charge just outside Arsuf.

JAFFA
JULY–AUGUST 1192

Forces Muslim: 7,000; Crusader: 2,000. **Casualties** No reliable estimates. **Location** Israel.

Following the Battle of Arsuf, the crusaders took Jaffa to act as a base for an attack on Jerusalem. In July 1192, a Muslim army stormed the city, but the citadel held out until a crusader relief force arrived.

Syrian "castle of the knights"
Built by the emir of Aleppo in the 11th century, the Krak des Chevaliers was captured by the Christians during the First Crusade (1099). It was expanded as the headquarters of the Knights Hospitaller, until April 1271.

SECOND BATTLE OF TARAIN
1192

Forces Ghurid: unknown; Raiput: unknown. **Casualties** No reliable estimates. **Location** Near Thanesar, northwest India.

After being defeated at Tarain in 1191, Muhammad of Ghur returned for a second attempt on the same battlefield. This time, his Turkish skirmishing mounted archers proved decisive, and the Hindu Raiput army was routed. This battle was a first stage in the expansion of Muslim rule into northern India.

ALARCOS 19 JULY 1195

Forces Muslim: unknown; Castilian: unknown. **Casualties** No reliable estimates. **Location** Ciudad Real, Spain.

The Castilian knights broke through the centre of the Muslim army, but were surrounded and annihilated when their supporting infantry failed to keep up with them. The remainder of the Castilian force was routed, with heavy losses.

THE FOURTH CRUSADE AND ITS AFTERMATH
1199–1212

The Fourth Crusade was intended to take Egypt, before launching an attack on Jerusalem. However, the ill-led campaign was hijacked by the Venetians and became an operation against the Byzantine empire.

CONSTANTINOPLE
JULY 1203–APRIL 1204

Forces Crusader: unknown; Muslim: unknown. **Casualties** No reliable estimates. **Location** Constantinople (modern Istanbul, Turkey).

Sidetracked from its mission to the Holy Land, the crusader army was bribed into joining a Byzantine power struggle. The situation dissolved into chaos, and led to Constantinople being sacked and occupied by the crusaders.

ALASEHIR 1211

Forces Nicaea: unknown; Turkish: unknown. **Casualties** No reliable estimates. **Location** Western Anatolia, Turkey.

After the sack of Constantinople, the Byzantine successor state of Nicaea was formed in western Anatolia. A Seljuk Turkish army commanded by Sultan Kaykhusraw I invaded the territory, but was defeated by the Nicaean emperor Theodore I.

LAS NAVAS DE TOLOSA
16–17 JULY 1212

Forces Crusader: 60,000–80,000; Muslim: 100,000. **Casualties** Crusader: unknown; Muslim: c.60,000 dead. **Location** Sierra Morena, southern Spain.

Surprised by the crusaders' sudden appearance from an unexpected direction, the lightly equipped Muslim force tried to wear down the crusaders, but was broken by their cavalry reserve.

BAD COMMAND DECISIONS

Carrhae (53 BCE)
The motivation behind the elderly Roman leader Marcus Crassus's invasion of Parthia has been variously suggested as greed, envy, and rivalry. Whatever his reasons for marching 44,000 soldiers against the Parthians across the scorching Mesopotamian desert, thousands of Romans died from heat there. Many more were killed in Parthian attacks before Crassus committed his cavalry, which was taken in by a feigned Parthian withdrawal. The jaws of the trap closed, and only 10,000 of the Roman force survived. Crassus was captured and beheaded. The Parthians suffered only very light casualties.

Hattin (1187)
King Guy of Jerusalem ordered 20,000 crusader infantry and 1,200 cavalrymen to attack the Muslim forces of Saladin besieging Tiberias. He did so against the recommendations of one of his commanders, Raymond III of Tripoli, who argued that the Muslims fought best in the open terrain around the city. Raymond was right, and the dehydrated crusader force was virtually massacred around the Horns of Hattin.

Stirling Bridge (1297)
John de Warenne, 7th Earl of Surrey, led an English expedition to crush the rebellious Scots. He chose Stirling Bridge, the worst possible place to cross the Forth river, despite many of his experienced soldiers recommending a wider ford 1.5km (1 mile) away. Crammed onto the narrow bridge, the English soldiers lost all advantage of numerical superiority; when only half the English army had crossed, William Wallace's Scots attacked. The result was an utter rout of the English.

Tumu (1449)
The Chinese Zhengtong emperor Zhu Zhen (1427–64) ordered a half-million-strong army under court official Wang Cheng to go out and destroy invading Mongol forces. The Chinese army marched for an exhausting two weeks, while the Mongols made a tactical withdrawal. At Datong, Chen decided to turn around and march his army back along an exposed northern route, rather than taking a longer but more protected one. As they did so, the Mongols turned and went on the attack, which resulted in up to 250,000 Chinese soldiers being killed or captured.

Little Bighorn (1876)
Lieutenant Colonel George Custer attacked a large Indian encampment in Little Bighorn valley on 25 June 1876. Rather than wait for approaching reinforcements, Custer, who had a reputation for taking personal risks, decided to launch 225 men at 2,000 Cheyenne and Lakota warriors led by Sitting Bull. Custer's command was subsequently slaughtered. The battle has come to be known popularly as "Custer's Last Stand".

Dien Bien Phu (1953–54)
General Henri Navarre, the French commander in chief in Indochina, deployed French airborne forces to the outpost of Dien Bien Phu, in an attempt to interdict Viet Minh operations. Dien Bien Phu is completely isolated and ringed by jungle-covered mountains, and the industrious Viet Minh soon had the base encircled and under siege. In an epic defence, the French held out from November 1953 until 7 May 1954, when they were forced to surrender. More than 7,000 French soldiers were killed and 12,000 captured.

European sword, 14th century
This sword, similar to those used by the crusaders, has a disc-shaped pommel, gently curved quillons (cross guard), and a diamond cross-section blade that tapers acutely to a thrusting point.

THE ALBIGENSIAN CRUSADE 1209–29

This 20-year-long campaign was initiated by the papacy to suppress the Cathar heresy in the Languedoc region of southern France. Much of the fighting was confined to sieges of Cathar strongholds.

BÉZIERS
21–22 JULY 1209

Forces Crusader: unknown; Cathar unknown **Casualties** Crusader: no reliable estimates, but minimal; Cathar: 7,000–20,000 civilians. **Location** Béziers, southwest France.

The crusaders besieged Béziers and demanded that the Cathars surrender. Instead they attempted to break out. The entire city was burned to the ground and the population slaughtered.

MURET
12 SEPTEMBER 1213

Forces Crusader: 900 cavalry, 1,200 infantry; Cathar and Aragonese: 4,000 cavalry, 30,000 infantry. **Casualties** Crusader: unknown; Cathar and Aragonese: at least 7,000 killed. **Location** Southwest France.

Besieged by superior forces, the crusaders staked all on a sortie, crushing the enemy cavalry, before using infantry to break the siege.

TOULOUSE
8 OCTOBER 1217–1 JULY 1218

Forces Crusader: unknown; Cathar: unknown. **Casualties** No reliable estimates. **Location** Southwest France.

" The Turks have surrounded the city. In the fighting they have pierced the walls. Send help at once or we shall be taken. "
MESSAGE FROM THE BESIEGED CITADEL OF TIBERIAS AFTER THE BATTLE OF HATTIN, 1187

After a long siege, the defenders of Toulouse sortied to destroy a massive siege tower. A counterattack drove the sortie off, but the crusader leader, Simon IV de Montfort was killed, effectively ending the campaign.

STEPPES 13 OCTOBER 1213

Forces Liège: unknown; Brabant: unknown. **Casualties** Liège: 3,000 dead and 4,000 prisoners; Brabant: no reliable estimates. **Location** Belgium.

Duke Henry of Brabant was returning from raiding the bishopric of Liège when he was intercepted by a force led by the bishop himself, Hugh of Pierrepoint. Although Duke Henry's initial attacks were successful, the bishop's forces rallied and won a decisive victory.

BOUVINES 26 JULY 1214

Forces French: 1,450 cavalry, 6,000 infantry; German and Flemish: 1,500 cavalry, 7,500 infantry. **Casualties** French: unknown; German and Flemish: 300 captured or killed. **Location** South of Tournai, northeastern France.

In this battle over English possessions in modern-day northern France, one flank of the battle was dominated by cavalry, while the infantry fought their own savage action elsewhere. Despite almost being killed, Philip of France emerged victorious.

THE FIRST BARONS' WAR
1215–17

The war began with a rebellion by a group of English barons against the chaotic rule of King John, but the civil war became a wider conflict when they invited Prince Louis of France to invade, in an unsuccessful attempt to replace John as king of England.

LINCOLN 20 MAY 1217

Forces Royalist: 900; Rebel: 1,600. **Casualties** No reliable estimates. **Location** Lincoln, England.

The death of King John and the accession of his nine-year-old son to the throne, as Henry III, undermined support for the French-backed rebellion known as the First Barons' War. A rebel force besieging Lincoln castle was trapped, and eventually destroyed in fierce street fighting by a royalist relief force.

DOVER 24 AUGUST 1217

Forces Royalist: 36 vessels; French: 10 warships and 70 transport vessels. **Casualties** No reliable estimates. **Location** English Channel, off Dover, southeast England.

The French fleet was intercepted by a royalist squadron off Dover, while carrying reinforcements for the rebel forces in the First Barons' War. The royalists attacked from windward, defeating the French with a barrage of crossbow fire and powdered quicklime.

MOST DESTRUCTIVE WARS IN HISTORY (BY ESTIMATED DEATH TOLL)

War	Dates	Location	Lowest estimates of military and civilian deaths
World War II	1939–45	Global	c.56 million
An Shi rebellion	753–73	China	c.36 million
Mongol conquests	13th–15th century	Asia, Europe, Middle East	c.30 million
Manchu conquest, Ming dynasty	1618–83	China	c.25 million
Taiping rebellion	1850–64	China	c.20 million
World War I	1914–18	Global	c.15 million

The might of the Mongol army
Genghis Khan's soldiers fought with swords, maces, and bows. They wore Chinese-style brigandine armour (embroidered silk coats reinforced with metal plates), bracers on their forearms, and peaked helmets.

THE MONGOL CONQUESTS
1214–41

The disparate Mongol tribes were unified by Genghis Khan in the early 13th century and began to establish an enormous empire, the expansion of which continued well after Genghis's death in 1227.

FALL OF ZHONGDU
FEBRUARY 1214–MAY 1215

Forces Mongol: unknown; Chinese: unknown. **Casualties** No reliable estimates. **Location** Modern Beijing.

After failing to capture cities for lack of a siege train, Genghis Khan finally obtained one, along with Chinese experts in its use. Despite this, it took a year of siege to take Zhongdu, which was burned to the ground.

SAMARKAND JUNE 1220

Forces Mongol: 120,000; Kwarezmian: 100,000. **Casualties** No reliable estimates. **Location** Samarkand, Uzbekistan.

Samarkand, capital of the Kwarezmian empire, was besieged and captured by Genghis Khan's forces, which massacred most of the city's inhabitants and its garrison.

PARWAN 1221

Forces Mongol: 10,000; Kwarezmian: 60,000. **Casualties** No reliable estimates. **Location** Parwan village, near Ghazni, modern Afghanistan.

A large but poorly trained and ill-equipped Kwarezmian army inflicted a surprising defeat on the Mongols. This provoked Genghis Khan into launching the campaign that led to the Mongol victory at the Indus.

THE INDUS 1221

Forces Mongol: 50,000; Kwarezmian: 30,000. **Casualties** Mongol: 8,000; Kwarezmian: 19,000. **Location** Indus river, northern Punjab.

After the Mongol defeat near Ghazni, Genghis Khan led a punitive expedition into the Punjab against the Kwarezmians. The Mongols destroyed the Kwarezmian army and thoroughly looted the region.

KALKA RIVER 1222

Forces Mongol: 40,000; Russian and Cuman: 80,000. **Casualties** No reliable estimates. **Location** Ukraine, north of Black Sea.

The Mongols sent peace envoys to the joint Russian-Cuman army, but they were murdered. The Mongols then proceeded to drive off the Cuman force and all but annihilated the Russians.

YELLOW RIVER 1226

Forces Mongol: 180,000; Xi Xia empire: 300,000. **Casualties** No reliable estimates. **Location** Yellow river near Yingchwan, northwest China.

The Xi Xia empire had risen in rebellion against its Mongol overlords. Genghis Khan personally led the Mongol army, which ruthlessly suppressed the revolt and destroyed the Xi Xia empire.

SIEGE OF KAIFENG
1232–33

Forces Mongol: unknown; Chinese: unknown. **Casualties** No reliable estimates. **Location** Northern China.

Both the attacking Mongols and the Chinese Jin defenders employed classic siege techniques and gunpowder weapons, including the "Heaven-shaking Thunder-Crash Bomb". The city held out for a year, before falling to assault.

VLADIMIR 1238

Forces Mongol: 150,000 horsemen; Russian: unknown. **Casualties** No reliable estimates. **Location** East of Moscow, Russia.

After sacking Ryazan and Moscow, the Mongols encountered an army led by Yuri II, the grand prince of Vladimir. This force was overwhelmed and annihilated, and Vladimir sacked, before the Mongols headed south into the Ukraine.

LIEGNITZ 9 APRIL 1241

Forces Mongol: 20,000; German and Polish: 40,000. **Casualties** Mongol: unknown; German and Polish: 30,000. **Location** Modern Legnica, southwest Poland.

After chasing off part of the Christian German-Polish army with a hail of arrows, the Mongol horsemen lured the Christian knights into charging deep into the Mongol force, where they were surrounded and killed.

MOHI 11 APRIL 1241

Forces Mongol: 90,000; Hungarian: 100,000. **Casualties** Mongol: no reliable estimates; Hungarian: at least 40,000. **Location** Near Miskolc, 145km (90 miles) northeast of Budapest, Hungary.

The Mongols attacked a fortified bridge across the Sajo river, drawing the Hungarians into defending the crossing. Under cover of this attack, a strong force forded the river and broke the Hungarians with flank and rear charges.

ANE 11 APRIL 1227

Forces Utrecht: unknown; Drenthe: unknown. **Casualties** No reliable estimates. **Location** Ane (in modern Overijssel, Netherlands).

The province of Drenthe was in revolt against its ruler, Otto II of Lippe, the Bishop of Utrecht. Otto raised an army to crush the uprising, but allowed his force to be drawn into a marshy area near the village of Ane, where his cavalry could not operate effectively. This was ideal terrain for the armed peasants who made up most of the rebel force, which attacked and destroyed the bishop's army.

SAULE 22 SEPTEMBER 1236

Forces Livonian: unknown; Lithuanian: unknown. **Casualties** Livonian: around 50 killed. **Location** Saule (Siauliai), Lithuania.

The haubergeon
Short-sleeved mail shirts, like this one, were commonly worn by infantry, from ancient Rome through to the Renaissance in Europe, Africa, and Asia. Western examples such as this were made from interlinked iron rings.

> "The **greatest pleasure** is to vanquish your enemies … to **rob them of their wealth** and see their loved ones bathed in **tears**."
>
> ATTRIBUTED TO GENGHIS KHAN, MONGOL EMPEROR, C.1162–1227

Launching an expedition into pagan territory, the Livonian Brethren of the Sword encountered Lithuanian light cavalry equipped with javelins. These proved extremely effective against the unwieldy Livonian horsemen.

NEVA 15 JULY 1240

Forces Swedish; unknown; Novgoroder: unknown. **Casualties** No reliable estimates. **Location** Meeting of Neva and Izhora rivers, Russia.

The Swedish army, attempting to gain control of an important trade route, camped before the city of Novgorod. Before the attack could begin, a Russian army approached the camp under cover of thick fog and launched a successful surprise assault.

LAKE PEIPUS 5 APRIL 1242

Forces Livonian Teutonic: unknown; Russian: unknown. **Casualties** No reliable estimates. **Location** Near Lake Peipus, Russian-Estonian border.

As the Teutonic Knights advanced on Pskov, they encountered a Russian force under Alexander Nevski, victor at the Neva. Nevski's lighter force used its superior numbers and a flanking attack to defeat the heavily armoured knights.

TAILLEBOURG 20 JULY 1242

Forces English: 22,000; French: 24,000. **Casualties** No reliable estimates. **Location** Taillebourg, France.

The English army commanded by Henry III was attempting to recapture the province of Poitou, which had been seized by France, and had taken up position covering the bridge across the Charente river. However, the army was outflanked and defeated by a French attack launched from a flotilla of small river craft.

THE FIFTH, SIXTH, AND SEVENTH CRUSADES 1217–54

An equally unsuccessful Fifth Crusade followed the disastrous Fourth Crusade. In 1229, Emperor Frederick II used the Sixth Crusade as a threat to negotiate the recovery of Jerusalem. Muslim forces retook the city in 1244, provoking the final major crusade in the region.

HARBIYAH 17 OCTOBER 1244

Forces Crusader plus Muslim allied: 1,500; Egyptian and Khwarezmian: 5,000. **Casualties** Crusader: 5,000, plus 800 prisoners; Egyptian and Khwarezmian: unknown. **Location** Near Gaza, Palestine.

A joint crusader-Muslim army engaged a force of Khwarezmian cavalry and Egyptian Mameluks. The Muslim contingent was driven off, and the crusaders were surrounded. Few survived.

MANSURAH 8 FEBRUARY 1250

Forces Crusader: 20,000 cavalry, 40,000 infantry; Egyptian: 70,000 soldiers. **Casualties** Heavy on both sides. **Location** Nile Delta, northern Egypt.

After a successful surprise attack on the Egyptian camp, the crusaders unwisely pursued the survivors into the town of Mansurah, where they were ambushed, suffering heavy losses. The battle, however, was inconclusive.

FARISKUR 6 APRIL 1250

Forces Crusader: unknown; Egyptian: unknown. **Casualties** No reliable estimates. **Location** Nile Delta, northern Egypt.

After Mansurah, the crusaders retreated to their fortified camp, which was soon besieged by Egyptian forces. The crusaders attempted to retreat to their main base at Damietta, but were decisively defeated.

THE SPANISH RECONQUISTA 1229–48

The mid-13th century saw the balance of power in the Iberian peninsula swing decisively in favour of the kingdoms of León, Aragón, and Castile. Only Granada in southeastern Spain would remain under Muslim rule, until 1492.

SIEGE OF PALMA
15 SEPTEMBER–31 DECEMBER 1229

Forces Muslim: unknown; Aragonese: 16,500. **Casualties** No reliable estimates. **Location** Palma, Majorca, Spain.

In September 1229, James I of Aragon invaded Majorca and quickly drove the local Muslim forces into Palma, which was stormed after a three-month siege. The conquest of the rest of the island was not completed until 1232.

SIEGE OF CÓRDOBA 1236

Forces Muslim: unknown; Castilian: unknown. **Casualties** No reliable estimates. **Location** Córdoba, Spain.

Civil unrest in the petty states of al-Andalus (Muslim Spain) provided opportunities for the expansion of Castile. In 1235, a faction in Córdoba opened the gates to a Castilian force that took control of the city, but was unable to take the citadel. King Ferdinand III brought up the main Castilian field army, but the citadel surrendered only on 29 June, after a bitter six-month siege.

SIEGE OF VALENCIA
APRIL–SEPTEMBER 1238

Forces Muslim: unknown; Aragonese: unknown. **Casualties** No reliable estimates. **Location** Valencia, Spain.

King James I of Aragon opened his campaign against Valencia by capturing a hill near the city Pueyo de la Cebolla, in 1237. This was fortified to act as a base for future siege operations, despite repeated attacks by the city's garrison. Not until April 1238 was the king able to assemble a force strong enough to begin assaults on Valencia's defences, which held out for almost six months.

SIEGE OF SEVILLE
1247–48

Forces Muslim: unknown; Castilian: unknown. **Casualties** No reliable estimates. **Location** Seville, Spain.

In the summer of 1247, a powerful Castilian army supported by a fleet on the Guadalquivir river began siege operations against Seville. The city was one of the great strongholds of Muslim Spain and was finally starved into surrender on 23 November 1248, after a 15-month siege.

The Teutonic Knights
This Polish mural shows three leaders of the Teutonic Knights from the 14th and early 15th centuries. At the height of it power, the order fought pagan tribes in the Baltic lands of Prussia and Lithuania.

FALL OF BAGHDAD
11 JANUARY–10 FEBRUARY 1258

Forces Mongol: 150,000. **Casualties** Baghdadi: 80,000–500,000. **Location** Baghdad, Persia (modern central Iraq).

After destroying an army sent to intercept them, the Mongols, led by Hulegu Khan, a grandson of Genghis Khan, surrounded Baghdad using bridges of boats to block access via the Tigris river. The walls were breached with a formidable siege train. This great Islamic city was destroyed by the Mongols.

RESTORATION OF THE BYZANTINE EMPIRE
1204–61

By the mid-13th century, the empire of Nicaea had established itself as a powerful Greek successor state to the former Byzantine empire. It had the ability to challenge the Latin empire of Constantinople that had been established after the Fourth crusade saw the sacking of the city in 1204. The empire lasted from 1204 until 1261.

PELAGONIA SEPTEMBER 1259

Forces: Achaean/Epirote: unknown; Nicaean: unknown. **Casualties** No reliable estimates. **Location** Pelagonia, Greece.

The Nicaean commander Theodore Dukas gathered all the local peasants and their flocks on hillsides behind his forces to give the impression of a huge army, and part of the Epirote contingent deserted to join the Nicaeans. The Nicaean archers concentrated their fire on the horses of the Achaean knights. Once most of their horses were killed, the knights were almost defenceless and surrendered, at which point the Achaean infantry broke and fled.

CONSTANTINOPLE 25 JULY 1261

Forces: Nicaean: 800; Latin: unknown. **Casualties** No reliable estimates. **Location** Constantinople (modern Istanbul, Turkey).

The defeat at Pelagonia had weakened the shaky Latin empire of Constantinople. In July 1261, Nicaean emperor Michael VIII Palaiologos sent a scouting force to reconnoitre the city's defences. Locals reported that the Latin army and its Venetian fleet were raiding the Nicaean island of Daphnousia. Seizing his chance, the leader of the scouts infiltrated a small detachment into the city, who opened one of the gates to let in the rest of the force. The surprise attack thoroughly demoralized the Latin emperor Baldwin II, who fled to the harbour with the remnants of the weak garrison. On 15 August, Michael VIII entered the city to be crowned as emperor of the restored Byzantine empire.

MONTAPERTI 4 SEPTEMBER 1260

Forces Florentine: 33,000; Sienese: unknown. **Casualties** Florentine: 5,000 plus 3,000 captured; Sienese: unknown. **Location** Arbia river near Siena, Italy.

During internecine warfare between two rival Italian factions, the outnumbered Sienese Ghibellines launched a surprise attack that routed the Florentine Guelph cavalry, although the Florentine infantry re-formed and held out until a hidden Sienese detachment broke cover and charged into their rear, ensuring victory.

AIN JALUT 23 SEPTEMBER 1260

Forces Mongol: 20,000; Egyptian: possibly 30,000. **Casualties** No reliable estimates. **Location** Eastern Galilee, Palestine, Middle East.

Part of the Egyptian force waited in ambush as the remainder drew the Mongols into the trap. Despite this ploy, the battle was very closely fought, but ended in a decisive Egyptian victory.

LARGS 14 OCTOBER 1263

Forces Norse: 800; Scottish: 8,000. **Casualties** No reliable estimates. **Location** Largs, North Ayrshire, Scotland.

The kings of Scotland had tried to buy Kintyre, the Hebrides, and the Isle of Man from Norway. Believing that Scottish raids in 1262 were a prelude to an invasion, the Norwegians mobilized a large fleet and army to protect the islands. Landing on the mainland, they were attacked by a larger Scottish army, which almost prevailed before reinforcements arrived.

THE SECOND BARONS' WAR
1264–65

Rebellious landowners led by Simon de Montfort, 6th Earl of Leicester, attempted to force King Henry III of England to surrender more power to a parliament of barons. Despite early successes, including the capture of the king, the barons eventually failed, and de Montfort was killed at Evesham.

CRITICAL MILITARY INVENTIONS – LAND WARFARE

Chariot (c.2,000 BCE)
The classic two-wheel fighting chariot manned by a driver and an archer (or several archers) combined battlefield mobility with firepower.

Cannon (c.14th century CE)
Cannon transformed both warfare and society, making once impregnable castles – typically the centre of feudal power – vulnerable to destruction, and giving the means to inflict casualties at extended ranges. Although there are mentions of a primitive cannon as early as the 3rd century BCE, metal cannons saw their first military use in Europe in the Hundred Years War (1337–1453). Cannon design remained largely constant for more than 300 years.

Flintlock mechanism (late 17th century)
The flintlock mechanism did away with the matchlock's smouldering match and provided a faster lock time (the time from when the trigger is pulled to the moment the main charge detonates), which in turn made the gun more accurate. Flintlocks were also cheaper than expensive wheel locks, paving the way for the mass production of firearms.

Bayonet (late 17th century)
The bayonet enabled the soldier to transform his musket or rifle into a form of short pike, through a simple muzzle-fitted blade. In the flintlock age, this was critical because it enabled the soldier to defend or attack at times when his gun was not loaded (which was often).

Breech-loading mechanisms (19th century)
Breech-loading artillery mechanisms were first seen as early as the 15th century, but it was not until the 19th century that they finally replaced muzzle-loading mechanisms in both artillery and firearms. They offered faster reloading rates, greater dependability, and safer firing processes, as well as the ability to achieve higher firing pressures, and hence greater range and accuracy.

Unitary cartridge (c.1808)
The Swiss gunsmith Jean Samuel Pauly and French gunsmith François Prélat invented the unitary cartridge – a firearms cartridge containing primer, powder, and ball in one unit – in 1808, although it was not introduced in the military until the mid-19th century. Unitary cartridges made efficient breech-loading mechanisms possible and were also essential for future innovations, such as bolt- and auto-loading firearms.

Maxim gun (1884)
Hiram Maxim's machine-gun used the force of recoil to load a cartridge and eject the spent shell, repeating the process as long as the trigger was held down. His invention ushered in the machine-gun age.

Tank (c.1916)
The world's first combat tank, the British Mk I, demonstrated the combination of heavy firepower, mobility, and armoured protection in one vehicle. By the 1940s, the tank, alongside artillery, had become the most influential tool of land warfare.

Bronze cannon
This mid-16th-century bronze cannon is called a "bastard culverin". It could fire iron shot more than 1.6km (1 mile).

LEWES 14 MAY 1264

Forces Royalist: 10,000; Rebel: 5,000. **Casualties** Royalist: 2,500; Rebel: 1,500. **Location** Offham Hill north of Lewes, Sussex, England.

The royalist army commanded by Henry III and Prince Edward was attacked by Simon de Montfort's rebels. Although the rebel's left wing was defeated, the bulk of the royalist force was driven into Lewes, where the king and Prince Edward were captured.

EVESHAM 4 AUGUST 1265

Forces Royalist: 8,000; Rebels: 5,300. **Casualties** Royalist: 2,000; Rebels: 3,000. **Location** Green Hill, near Evesham, Worcestershire, England.

In May 1265, Prince Edward escaped from Hereford Castle, where he had been imprisoned after the battle of Lewes. He quickly raised an army and trapped de Montfort's rebels at Evesham. A royalist detachment blocked Bengeworth bridge, preventing any escape across the Avon river, forcing de Montfort into a frontal attack on Prince Edward's main army. Most of the remaining rebels fled when the royalists counterattacked, killing de Montfort and annihilating his army.

BENEVENTO 26 FEBRUARY 1266

Forces Angevin: 3,000 knights; Manfred: 3,500 knights, several thousand archers. **Casualties** Angevin: unknown, but heavy; Manfred: unknown, but heavier. **Location** East of Naples, southern Italy.

Continuing the conflict between Guelph and Ghibelline factions, this battle degenerated into a huge mêlée. The Angevins, allied with the Guelphs, won, capturing the Kingdom of Sicily.

XIANGYANG 1268–73

Forces Mongol: 100,000; Chinese: unknown. **Casualties** No reliable estimates. **Location** Hebei, southern China.

The pivotal struggle in the Mongol conquest of the Song took place around Fancheng and Xiangyang. The Mongols fielded a riverine fleet as well as a powerful siege train for the campaign, demonstrating their great adaptability.

FIRST MONGOL INVASION OF JAPAN NOVEMBER 1274

Forces Mongol: 40,000; Japanese: 10,000. **Casualties** No reliable estimates. **Location** Hakata Bay, Japan.

The Japanese were unprepared for the savage and effective fighting style of the Mongols, and all opposition crumbled.

Samurai warriors ride into battle
Mongol emperor Kublai Khan attempted to invade Japan in 1274 and 1281. In both campaigns, his armies were driven back with the help of violent weather.

However, this first invasion was simply a reconnaissance in force, and the Mongols soon re-embarked.

NGASAUNGGYAN 1277

Forces Burmese: 60,000 infantry and cavalry, 2,000 elephants; Mongol: 12,000 cavalry. **Casualties** Unknown. **Location** Northern Myanmar (Burma).

The Mongols' horses shied away from Burmese war elephants, so the Mongols dismounted and chased the elephants back into their own ranks with archery. They then remounted and charged the disordered Burmese, who fled.

MARCHFELD 26 AUGUST 1278

Forces Bohemian: 30,000; Imperial (Austrian and Hungarian) 40,000. **Casualties** No reliable estimates. **Location** Between Durnkrut and Jedespeigen, Austria.

Fighting for the throne of the Holy Roman empire, the Bohemian army's formation under King Premysl Ottokar II was disorganized by fire from Hungarian mounted archers, then charged by the imperial heavy cavalry. After a fierce fight, the Bohemian reserves broke, followed by the rest of the army.

SECOND MONGOL INVASION OF JAPAN JUNE–AUGUST 1281

Forces Mongol: 150,000; Japanese: 40,000. **Casualties** Mongol: allegedly 100,000; Japanese: unknown. **Location** Hakata Bay, Japan.

Attempting to invade Japan, the Mongols encountered well-prepared and determined defenders. The Mongol fleet was then scattered by a typhoon, the now legendary *kamikaze*, or "divine wind".

OREWIN BRIDGE 11 DECEMBER 1282

Forces Welsh: 7,000; English: 6,300. **Casualties** Welsh; 3,000; English: No reliable estimates. **Location** Cilmeri, Powys, mid Wales.

Llywelyn ap Gruffydd deployed the Welsh army in a strong defensive position commanding a bridge, but the position was outflanked by an English detachment upstream. The English archers inflicted heavy casualties, allowing their cavalry to break the Welsh army. Ap Gruffydd was killed by an English man-at-arms.

> " He advanced and though his elbow was **shot** through with an **arrow** he still advanced … "

FROM A JAPANESE ACCOUNT OF THE SECOND MONGOL INVASION, 1281

BAY OF NAPLES 5 JUNE 1284

Forces Aragonese: 40 galleys; Angevin: 30–40 galleys. **Casualties** Aragonese: unknown; Angevin: at least 10 galleys captured. **Location** Southern Italy.

Luring the Angevin fleet away from its safe port, the Aragonese turned to fight and were joined by reinforcements. The Angevin fleet was heavily defeated.

WORRINGEN 5 JUNE 1288

Forces Brabant: 4,700; Luxembourg: 5,500. **Casualties** Brabant: minimal; Luxembourg: 1,100. **Location** Worringen, near Cologne, Germany.

This battle was the culmination of a war of succession for the Duchy of Limburg. Duke John I of Brabant was opposed by Count Henry of Luxembourg and the Archbishop of Cologne. The count's cavalry nearly won the battle with its first charge, but the count was killed, and after eight hours of fighting, his men broke. The archbishop's division was also routed, when it was attacked by a force that included rebels from Cologne.

THE FALL OF ACRE
6 APRIL–28 MAY 1291

Forces Muslim: cavalry: 60,000, infantry: 160,000; Christian knights: 1,000, infantry: 16,000. **Casualties** No reliable estimates. **Location** Acre (in modern Israel).

The last crusader stronghold in the Holy Land was besieged by a huge Muslim army. Siege engines and mining prepared the way for a massive and successful assault, and the garrison could not prevent the walls being breached.

Mongol warrior armour
A helmet and armour such as this would have been worn by a Mongol warrior. Made of leather or metal plates stitched to a silk coat, this armour provided lightweight protection for mounted combat.

MAES MOYDOG 5 MARCH 1295

Forces Welsh: unknown; English: 2,500. **Casualties** Welsh: 700; English: 100. **Location** Llanfair Caereinion, Powys, Wales.

The Welsh army was prevented from retreating into nearby woods by English cavalry. An "arrow storm" from the English archers disordered the Welsh formation, which was then broken by cavalry charges. The battle played an important role in breaking Welsh resistance to English rule.

MOST DESTRUCTIVE DISEASES IN WAR

Disease	Transmission	Effect	Example
Cholera	Via contaminated food and water	Chronic diarrhoea and vomiting, muscle cramps; death can occur by dehydration within a day	In 1817–24 more than 10,000 British soldiers in India died during the first cholera pandemic, along with hundreds of thousands of Indian civilians.
Smallpox	Viral infection transmitted through body fluids	Chronic skin abnormalities, fever, vomiting, and haemorrhagic conditions	In 48–49 CE half of a 40,000-strong Chinese army under Ma-Yuan was killed by smallpox during an expedition in Hunan province.
Malaria	Parasite spread through mosquito bite	Chronic fever and fatigue, vomiting and diarrhoea, coma, paralysis, organ failure	In 1895, a French campaign in Madagascar resulted in 13 combat deaths and 4,000 deaths from malaria.
Typhus	Bacteria spread via body lice	High fever, chills, delirium, severe headache, stupor, low blood pressure, skin rash	In 1914, one in six people in Serbia contracted typhus, which also killed 70,000 Serbian soldiers.
Bubonic plague (Black Death)	Bacterial disease spread via flea bites or contact with infected tissue	Swellings at lymph node sites, vomiting blood, systemic organ failure	From c.1320 to 1340 soldiers helped to carry the plague from Central Asia to Eastern Europe. The plague eventually killed over 75 million people worldwide and destroyed entire armies.
Spanish flu	Viral infection spread by body fluids (airborne or on contaminated objects)	Pneumonia, internal bleeding, organ failure	From 1918 to 1919 Spanish flu killed 50 million people worldwide, of these 43,000 were US soldiers in France (half the total number of US casualties in World War I).

WARS OF SCOTTISH INDEPENDENCE
1296–1326, 1333–1357

The Scottish struggles for independence pitted the courageous but lightly equipped Scottish pikemen, backed up by small numbers of knights, against the more diverse forces of England, which included spearmen and bowmen from England and Wales. The wars ended through diplomacy rather than military action.

STIRLING BRIDGE 11 SEPTEMBER 1297

Forces Scottish: 10,000; English: 50,000–60,000. **Casualties** No reliable estimates. **Location** North of Stirling, Scotland.

As the far larger English army tried to cross the Forth river, the Scots attacked and caught many English knights trapped in a marsh. Much of the English army fled.

FALKIRK 22 JULY 1298

Forces Scottish: 12,200; English: 10,000 infantry, 2,000 knights. **Casualties** Scottish: 5,000; English: 200. **Location** 3km (2 miles) south of Falkirk, Stirlingshire, Scotland.

The English knights broke the small force of Scottish archers and cavalry, but were held by the "schiltrons" (defensive circles of spearmen). These were bombarded by fire from English archers, until sufficiently weakened to be broken by cavalry charges.

LOUDON HILL
10 MAY 1307

Forces Scottish: 600; English: 3,000. **Casualties** Scottish: unknown; English: more than 100 knights and men-at-arms. **Location** Loudon Hill, Ayrshire, Scotland.

Robert the Bruce deployed his small Scottish force on a hillside, blocking the road at a point where it ran between marshes. The Scots also dug triple lines of trenches from the edges of the road to the marshes, to prevent any attempts to outflank their

The Black Prince
Edward the "Black Prince" (1330–76) earned his reputation for valour at the battle of Crécy in 1346, where his force, heavily outnumbered, still gained victory.

position. The English army was unable to exploit its numerical superiority and was forced into frontal attacks along the road. At least two cavalry charges were bloodily repulsed by the Scottish spearmen, before the English army hastily retreated.

BANNOCKBURN 24 JUNE 1314

Forces Scottish: 9,000; English: 16,000. **Casualties** Scottish: 4,000 killed; English: up to 15,000 killed. **Location** South of Stirling, Scotland.

As the English men-at-arms laboured to cross the marshy terrain around the Bannockburn stream, the Scots charged down at them in massed pike formations. The English king fled, hastening the disintegration of his force. This was the decisive battle of the First War of Scottish Independence.

HALIDON HILL 19 JULY 1333

Forces Scottish: 14,500; English: 10,000. **Casualties** Scottish: 4,000; English: fewer than 50. **Location** 5km (3 miles) northwest of Berwick-upon-Tweed, Scotland.

Four dense formations of Scottish spearmen advanced uphill into an "arrow storm" from English longbows. The Scottish survivors were routed in a counterattack.

COURTRAI 11 JULY 1302

Forces Flemish: 8,000–10,500 foot soldiers; French: 2,500 knights/squires, plus infantry. **Casualties** Flemish: several hundred dead; French: 1,000 knights killed. **Location** Kortrijk, Belgium.

During the French invasion of Flanders, the French knights rashly advanced through their own infantry and charged at the emplaced pikes of the Flemish infantry. They were then overwhelmed in the ensuing mêlée.

MORGARTEN 15 NOVEMBER 1315

Forces Austrian: 8,000 with 2,500 armoured cavalry; Swiss: 1,500 infantry and archers. **Casualties** Austrian: most killed; Swiss: unknown. **Location** By the Aegerisee, Switzerland.

During the formation of the Swiss Confederacy, soldiers of Duke Leopold I of Austria were ambushed on a mountain pass by Swiss infantry, who hurled boulders and tree trunks down the slope, before charging in with their halberds.

SIEGE OF NICOMEDIA
1333–37

Forces Ottoman: unknown; Byzantine: unknown. **Casualties** No reliable estimates. **Location** Modern Izmit, Turkey.

"William Wallace was dragged to a very **high gallows**, where he was hanged with a halter, then taken down **half-dead** …"

ACCOUNT OF THE EXECUTION OF WILLIAM WALLACE, SCOTTISH PATRIOT, 1305

Nicomedia, the last Byzantine stronghold in Anatolia, came under siege by the Ottoman Turks in 1333. Despite an attempt to buy off the Turks with tribute, the city was taken in 1337, a defeat from which the Byzantine empire did not recover.

MINATOGAWA 5 JUNE 1336

Forces Imperial: 2,700; Ashikaga: unknown. **Casualties** No reliable estimates. **Location** Minato river, near Kobe, Japan.

Attempting to halt the advance of the Ashikaga clan against the capital, the imperial army was outflanked by naval manoeuvres, while other forces engaged it to the front. The imperial army was forced to retreat, suffering heavy casualties.

LAUPEN 21 JUNE 1339

Forces Swiss: 5,000; Burgundian: 15,000. **Casualties** Swiss: no reliable estimates; Burgundian: 4,000. **Location** Laupen, Berne, Switzerland.

The Burgundian army besieging Laupen was attacked by a Swiss relief force largely composed of pikemen and halberdiers. Two of the three Swiss divisions quickly defeated the opposing infantry, while the third held off the Burgundian cavalry, which was then broken by charges against its flanks and rear.

THE HUNDRED YEARS WAR
1337–1453

The death of Charles IV of France with no direct male heir provoked a succession crisis. The war was begun by Edward III of England, in an attempt to enforce his claim to the French crown, but it was to drag on for 116 years, involving English, French, and Spanish forces. At the war's close, England had lost its territories on mainland Europe.

CADSAND 10 NOVEMBER 1337

Forces English: 2,500; Flemish: 5,000. **Casualties** English: no reliable estimates; Flemish: 3,500. **Location** Cadzand, Zeeland, Netherlands.

During an amphibious operation against the pro-French garrison of Cadsand, the Flemish forces formed up on the beach to oppose the landing, but were decimated by longbow fire from the ships and broke when the main force came ashore.

SLUYS 24 JUNE 1340

Forces English: 150–250 ships; French and Genoese: around 190 ships. **Casualties** French and Genoese: 166 ships captured or sunk; English: unknown. **Location** Sluys, Zeeland, southern Netherlands.

The French-Genoese fleet unwisely took up defensive positions with its ships chained together. The more manoeuvrable English fleet was able to bring intense archery to bear to assist the men-at-arms in their boarding actions, resulting in the destruction of most of France's fleet.

CRÉCY 26 AUGUST 1346

Forces English: 10,000–20,000, including 10,000 longbowmen; French 25,000–60,000. **Casualties** English: 200 dead; French: probably 4,000 dead. **Location** Near Abbeville, Picardy, northern France.

Arriving tired and disorganized at the battlefield, the French launched several uphill charges at the English lines. Having already suffered heavily from longbow attacks, the French knights were then repulsed in hand-to-hand fighting. The campaign was led by Edward, Prince of Wales (popularly known as the "Black Prince"). Although he was an exceptional military leader, he died a year before his father, King Edward III of England, and thus never ruled.

SIEGE OF CALAIS
4 AUGUST 1346–4 SEPTEMBER 1347

Forces English: possibly 30,000; French: unknown. **Casualties** No reliable estimates. **Location** Calais, northern France.

Stirling Bridge

In 1297, 15,000 Scots under William Wallace defeated a huge English army led by John, Earl of Warenne and Surrey. The Scottish attacked when the English force was most vulnerable, halfway across the narrow bridge on the Forth river.

TYPES OF CANNON SHOT AND AMMUNITION

Name of shot	Design	Purpose
Roundshot	Solid sphere of stone, then iron	Punching through walls, ship hulls/decks etc; anti-personnel fire
Chain shot	Two sub-calibre balls joined by a length of chain	Naval shot used to cut down masts, yards, rigging, sails etc
Bar shot	Two sub-calibre balls joined by an iron bar	Naval shot used to cut down masts, yards, rigging, sails etc
Shell	Hollow iron sphere filled with gunpowder; timed fuse lit when cannon fired	Incendiary and signal shots; anti-personnel fire
Case	Like shell shot, but also containing shrapnel in the form of metal balls	Anti-personnel fire
Grape	Stack of metal balls contained in a cloth bag, creating a shotgun effect on firing	Anti-personnel fire
Canister	Lead or iron balls contained within a metal case; the case ruptured when the gun was fired, creating a shotgun effect	Anti-personnel fire

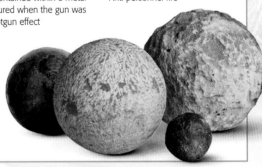

Gun stones
During the 14th century, European artillery fired hand-carved stone shot, such as these examples. Between the 15th and 16th centuries, cast-iron cannonballs gradually replaced these "gun stones".

The English deployed 20 primitive cannon against the walls of Calais, but these proved ineffective. The city was eventually starved into submission and became an English possession.

NEVILLE'S CROSS 17 OCTOBER 1346

Forces English: 15,000; Scottish: 20,000. **Casualties** No reliable estimates. **Location** Durham, England.

King David II invaded England to support France following Crécy and the fall of Calais. The Scottish army took up a defensive position, but was stung into attacking by longbow fire. The English archery and the broken ground resulted in decisive defeat for the Scottish army.

SAINTES 8 APRIL 1351

Forces English: unknown; French: unknown. **Casualties** No reliable estimates. **Location** Saintes, France.

A French army that had invaded Poitou was besieging Saintes when it was confronted by a small English relief force commanded by Sir John Beauchamp, the governor of Calais. The English took up a defensive formation similar to that used at Crécy. The bulk of the French army formed up on foot, with cavalry detachments on each flank, but as it deployed it was routed by a flank-and-rear attack that was launched by a detachment from the English garrison of Taillebourg.

HISTORY'S LARGEST WARSHIPS – SAIL

Ship	Nationality	Launched	Length/weight	Armament
War junks	Chinese	15th–17th centuries	Some war junks were reputed to be more than 121m (400ft) long and weighing in the region of 2,000 tonnes (1,968 tons)	Dozens of cannon
Mary Rose	British	c.1510	38.5m (126ft 3in) / 711 tonnes (700 tons)	91 guns
Henri Grâce à Dieu	British	1514	50m (165ft) / up to 1,524 tonnes (1,500 tons)	184 guns (43 heavy)
Vasa	Swedish	1627	69m (230ft) / 1,200 tonnes (1,181 tons)	64 guns
Santisima Trinidad y Nuestra Señora del Buen Fin	Spanish	1769	61.3m (201ft 1in) / 4,950 tonnes (4,871 tons)	140 guns
Mahmudiye	Ottoman	1829	62m (203ft 4in) / c.5,000 tonnes (4,921 tons)	128 guns
USS Pennsylvania	American	1837	64m (210ft) / 2,817 tonnes (2,773 tons)	120 guns
Valmy	French	1847	64.05m (210ft 2in) / 5,826 tonnes (5,734 tons)	120 guns

Model of a Chinese fighting junk
Warships based on the *sha chuan* (literally "sand ship") design, dating back to the Spring and Autumn Period (770–446 BCE), were built in a variety of sizes.

MAURON 14 AUGUST 1352

Forces Anglo-Breton: 3,000; French: 6,000. **Casualties** Anglo-Breton: 600; French: 2,000. **Location** Near Mauron castle, St Lery, Brittany, France.

A French army marching on Brest was intercepted by Sir Walter Bentley's Anglo-Breton force, which deployed along a ridge, with dismounted men-at-arms in the centre of the line flanked by archers. Most French knights also dismounted, apart from a detachment tasked with attacking the Anglo-Breton right flank. This detachment scattered the archers facing them, but failed to attack the rest of Bentley's force. The main French advance was slowed by bramble thickets in front of the Anglo-Breton position and took heavy casualties from the English archers, before breaking when Bentley counterattacked.

POITIERS 19 SEPTEMBER 1356

Forces English: 12,000, including 4,000 men-at-arms; French: 20,000–40,000. **Casualties** English: 1,000; French: 2,500 plus 2,600 prisoners. **Location** 3km (2 miles) east of Poitiers, central France.

Outnumbered, the English took up a defensive position protected by a hedge. After barely managing to repulse French attacks, the English charged and routed the French force after savage fighting. This battle was one of the three great English victories of the war, the other two being Crécy and Agincourt.

MELLO 10 JUNE 1358

Forces Noble: 2,000; Peasant: 4,500. **Casualties** No reliable estimates. **Location** Mello, near Beauvais, France.

In 1358, the chaos and devastation of the Hundred Years War sparked off a series of French peasant revolts, known as the Jacquerie. The main peasant army drew up in a strong position on a hillside near Mello, but its commander, Guillaume Cale, was tricked into negotiations and killed by the nobles' commander, Charles of Navarre. The nobles' forces then attacked and routed the leaderless peasants, after which the rebellion was ruthlessly crushed in several months of bloody reprisals.

AURAY 29 SEPTEMBER 1364

Forces English: 2,800; Franco-Breton: 4,000. **Casualties** No reliable estimates. **Location** Auray, Britanny, France.

The English force drew up on a hillside overlooking the Loch river to await the French army commanded by Charles de Blois. The French crossed the river and attacked in four divisions, which charged into the English men-at-arms despite taking heavy losses from the fire of English supporting archers. After the entire French force was committed, it was broken by a charge by the English reserve of no more than 200 men, which had been carefully held back from the action.

NAJERA 3 APRIL 1367

Forces French and Castilian: probably 30,000; English: perhaps 20,000. **Casualties** French and Castilian: 7,000 killed; English: 100 killed. **Location** South of the Ebro river, northern Spain.

English longbow archery dominated the battle, causing the Castilian cavalry to retreat and abandon their allies. The French mercenaries fought on, but without support their defeat was inevitable.

LANCASTER'S RAID
JULY–DECEMBER 1373

Forces English: 5,000–10,000 men; French: unknown. **Casualties** English: roughly half of force lost; French: unknown. **Location** France.

John of Gaunt, Duke of Lancaster, launched a five-month raid into France. The French took refuge in their fortresses and harassed the invaders. By the end of the raid, Lancaster had lost half his force.

MERCQ MAY 1405

Forces English: 700; French: 2,000. **Casualties** No reliable estimates. **Location** Mercq (in modern Belgium)

A French force besieging the town of Mercq was surprised by an English relief force from Calais. The French

French defeat at Agincourt
At the battle of Agincourt (25 October 1415), English king Henry V defeated a French army led by Constable Charles d'Albret. English longbowmen and knights wreaked havoc on the French forces.

> "The **piles of the dead** grew so much that men climbed on these heaps and **slew** those below."
>
> AN ENGLISH SOLDIER AT AGINCOURT, 1415

crossbowmen were almost out of ammunition after their earlier attacks on the town and were quickly shot down by the English archers, whose fire then routed the remaining French troops.

AGINCOURT 25 OCTOBER 1415

Forces English: 6,000; French 20,000–30,000. **Casualties** English: 300–400; French: 3,000–5,000. **Location** Near Hesdin in the Pas-de-Calais, northeastern France.

Led by King Henry V, the English army deployed between two woods with archers on the flanks and dismounted men-at-arms in the centre. (Longbowmen formed the vast majority of the English army in the battle.) Struggling over wet ground, the French suffered heavy casualties from archery, before the English counterattacked and drove the French from the battlefield.

VALMONT 11–13 MARCH 1416

Forces English: 1,100; French: 4,000. **Casualties** English: 300; French: 1,000. **Location** Valmont, Normandy, France.

An English raiding party commanded by Thomas Beaufort, Earl of Dorset, was intercepted by a French army at Valmont. The heavily outnumbered English were forced to overextend their line to protect their flanks and, as a result, repeated French charges finally broke through. The attackers then began looting the English baggage train, giving time for Beaufort to rally his men in a thickly hedged garden, before slipping away after dark. The English force then headed along the coast for Harfleur, but were again attacked by the French, who were routed after a fierce battle on the beach.

CRAVANT 31 JULY 1423

Forces Anglo-Burgundian: 5,000; Franco-Scottish: 8,000. **Casualties**: Anglo-Burgundian: 600; Franco-Scottish: 5,000. **Location** Cravant, Loire, France.

Sir John Stuart's Franco-Scottish army besieging Cravant redeployed along the line of the Yonne river, to block the advance of an Anglo-Burgundian relief force commanded by the Earl of Salisbury. The English men-at-arms attacked across the river under covering fire from their supporting archers, while a further attack was made across a narrow bridge. Seeing that Stuart's men were fully committed, the garrison of Cravant broke out and charged into the rear of his force, which was routed with heavy casualties.

VERNEUIL 17 AUGUST 1424

Forces English: 9,000; Franco-Scottish: 15,000. **Casualties** English: 1,000; Franco-Scottish: 7,000. **Location** Verneuil, Normandy, France.

After a successful charge against the English right flank, the French cavalry were repulsed when they attacked the baggage train. On the other flank, the English broke the opposing cavalry, before surrounding and destroying the Scottish contingent.

ROUVRAY 12 FEBRUARY 1429

Forces English: 1,000; Franco-Scottish: 3,000. **Casualties** English: no reliable estimates; Franco-Scottish: 600. **Location** Rouvray, near Orléans, France.

An English supply convoy was attacked by a Franco-Scottish force. The convoy's wagons were formed into a defensive circle that was bombarded by the French artillery. Before the gunfire could take effect, the Scottish contingent attacked and was repulsed with heavy losses. A counterattack then routed the entire Franco-Scottish army.

SIEGE OF ORLÉANS
12 OCTOBER 1428–7 MAY 1429

Forces English: 5,000; Franco-Scottish: variable. **Casualties** No reliable estimates. **Location** Loire valley, central France.

Inspired by the arrival of Joan of Arc, the French defenders began capturing strong points by sortie. The English tried to draw the defenders out into open battle, and abandoned the siege when this failed.

FORMIGNY 15 APRIL 1450

Forces English: 4,000; French: 5,000. **Casualties** English: 3,200; French: 1,000. **Location** 16km (10 miles) west of Bayeaux, Normandy, France.

A French army intercepted an English force attempting to raise the siege of Caen. French artillery fire provoked an English attack that captured the cannon. The attackers were charged by French men-at-arms, who recaptured the guns, at which point a flank charge by French reinforcements broke the English army.

CASTILLON 17 JULY 1453

Forces English: 6,000 men; French: 7,000–10,000 with 300 cannon. **Casualties** No reliable estimates. **Location** Western France.

Attempting to relieve the besieged city of Castillon, the English advanced into the fire of archers to reposition siege cannon. They were repulsed with heavy losses. The French use of cannon was key to the English defeat in this final battle of the Hundred Years War.

RED TURBAN REBELLION
1356–68

Forces Mongol: unknown; Chinese: unknown. **Casualties** Unknown. **Location** Eastern China.

The group known as the Red Turbans were part of a revolt against the Mongol Yuan rulers, one which gradually expanded into a formal military campaign. The Ming dynasty was founded by the Red Turban leader Zhu Yuangzhang.

KULIKOVO 8 SEPTEMBER 1380

Forces Russian: 30,000–80,000; Mongol: 30,000–125,000. **Casualties** No reliable estimates. **Location** On Kulikova Pole (Snipe's Field) by Don river, Russia.

As an invading Mongol army marched on Moscow to punish the city's cessation of tribute, it was intercepted at Kulikovo. After hard fighting, the day was won by a Russian flanking counterattack.

SEMPACH 9 JULY 1386

Forces Swiss: 1,600; Austrian: 4,000. **Casualties** Swiss: 200; Austrian: 700. **Location** Sempach, near Lucerne, Switzerland.

In the ongoing power struggles in the Alps, the Austrian commander Duke Leopold III dismounted his men-at-arms in order to counter the Swiss halberdiers

and pikemen. They pushed back the Swiss vanguard, but were attacked at the flank and overwhelmed.

NAEFELS 9 APRIL 1388

Forces Swiss: 750; Austrian: 6,000. **Casualties** Swiss: no reliable estimates; Austrian: 2,200. **Location** Naefels, Glarus, Switzerland.

The Swiss initially defended "letzinen"– barricades of loose stones blocking the Austrian advance along an alpine valley. When these were breached, the Swiss withdrew up the mountainside and sent avalanches of boulders rolling down into the enemy lines, before counterattacking and routing the Austrians.

THE CONQUESTS OF TIMUR
1379–1405

Timur claimed that Genghis Khan was his direct ancestor and led a ferocious Central Asian people who were the descendants of the Mongols. His campaigns in Arabia, India, Persia, and against his rivals were characterized by great brutality, as well as clever planning and sound strategy. Timur made good use of spies and agents, as well as terror tactics, to persuade his enemies to submit without a fight.

SACK OF ISFAHAN 1387

Forces Timurid: 70,000; Persian: unknown. **Casualties** 70,000 civilians. **Location** Southern Persia (in modern Iran).

When the people of Isfahan revolted rather than pay tribute to Timur, he ordered his army to storm the city and required each soldier to bring him the severed head of one of its citizens.

TEREK 1395

Forces Timurid: 100,000; Golden Horde: unknown. **Casualties** Possibly 100,000 dead. **Location** Central Asia.

Four years after they had met in an incredibly bloody but inconclusive clash at Kondurcha, Timur's forces fought the Mongol Golden Horde under Batu. This time Timur was victorious, and merciless in the subsequent pursuit.

ALEPPO
30 OCTOBER 1399

Forces Timurid: unknown; Mameluk: unknown. **Casualties** No reliable estimates. **Location** Aleppo, Syria.

Brutally putting down rebellions in western Asia, Timur advanced against Syria and shattered a Mameluk army at Aleppo. The city was then sacked, opening the way for him to advance on Damascus.

PANIPAT 16 DECEMBER 1399

Forces Indian: 10,000 cavalry, 40,000 infantry; Timurid: unknown. **Casualties** Possibly 100,000 dead. **Location** North of Delhi, India.

Pillaging its way across northern India, Timur's army became so overencumbered with plunder that all Hindu captives, of which there were perhaps 100,000, were slaughtered. This freed Timur's men to concentrate on capturing and sacking Delhi.

Late-medieval plate armour
By the 15th century, plate armour, called "white harness", provided total protection and was surprisingly well articulated and easy to wear. This German "Gothic" style armour shows the supreme skill of late-medieval European metalworkers.

The advance of the Timurid empire

The Mongol-Turkic armies of Timur (reigned 1370 – 1405) cut a swathe across central Asia. From his capital, Samarkand, Timur founded an empire that stretched from the Caucasus to India.

ANKARA
20 JULY 1402

Forces Timurid: unknown; Ottoman: unknown. **Casualties** Timurid: unknown; Ottoman: at least 15,000 killed. **Location** Near Ankara, Central Turkey.

After failing to contact the forces of Timur, the tired and thirsty Ottomans found their enemies besieging Ankara. Desperate for water, the Ottomans had to attack, and were also assaulted from the rear.

KOSOVO 15 JUNE 1389

Forces Ottoman: 30,000; Serb and allies: 15,000–20,000. **Casualties** No reliable estimates. **Location** Kosovo Polje, near Pristina, Kosovo.

The Ottomans invaded the Balkans. The Serbian-led army met the enemy at Kosovo and a confused battle ensued. The outcome owed much to the Serbs who defected to the Ottoman side.

NICOPOLIS 25 SEPTEMBER 1396

Forces Christian: 16,000; Ottoman: 20,000. **Casualties** Christian: unknown; Ottoman: heavier Christian losses. **Location** Nikopol, Bulgaria.

Attempting to repel the Ottoman invaders, an initial charge by the Christians was defeated by sharpened stakes and archery. Nevertheless, the Christians came close to victory, before the Ottomans' Serbian allies joined the fight and tipped the balance.

OWAIN GLYNDWR'S REBELLION
1400-09

Forces Glyndwr: unknown; English: unknown. **Casualties** No reliable estimates. **Location** Wales.

Led by Owain Glyndwr, the Welsh were able to drive out the English in a protracted guerrilla war. A sortie into England, with French assistance, failed, and the rebellion was gradually defeated.

SHREWSBURY
21 JULY 1403

Forces Royalist: 14,000; Rebel: 10,000. **Casualties** Royalist: 3,000; Rebel: 5,000. **Location** 5km (3 miles) north of Shrewsbury, Shropshire, England.

A rebellion against the English king Henry IV, led by Harry "Hotspur" Percy, almost succeeded, but collapsed when he was killed. Nevertheless, the rebel archers inflicted heavy casualties on the Royalists.

GRUNWALD 15 JULY 1410

Forces Polish-Lithuanian: 39,000; Teutonic Knights: 27,000. **Casualties** Teutonic Knights: 8,000 killed, 14,000 prisoners; Polish-Lithuanian: unknown. **Location** Grunwald (Tannenberg), East Prussia.

The Kingdom of Poland and Duchy of Lithuania took on the expansionist Teutonic Order. The forces met at dawn. The Polish-Lithuanians attacked first and drove off the enemy infantry. The Teutonic Knights counterattacked with some success until flanked by a reserve enemy force.

THE HUSSITE WARS
1419-34

The Hussites were a sect inspired by the teachings of Jan Huss, a Czech religious reformer executed for heresy in 1415. The Hussite general, Jan Zizka, was a military pioneer, developing a battle-winning combination of light field artillery, war-wagons, and light cavalry, in order to fight off a crusade against them.

VYSEHRAD 1 NOVEMBER 1420

Forces Hussite: 12,000; Catholic crusader: 18,000. **Casualties** No reliable estimates. **Location** Vysehrad, Prague (in modern Czech Republic).

The Hussite army besieging the castle at Vysehrad bloodily repulsed a crusader

---

HISTORY'S WORST FIREARMS

Matchlock musket
Although matchlocks laid the foundations of infantry firearms, there was no doubt that they were terrible guns: accuracy was pot luck with anything more than 50m (164ft) away; keeping the match lit and the powder dry was extremely difficult (particularly in wet weather); and the rate of fire was about two shots a minute.

Chauchat
Widely viewed as the worst machine-gun ever built, the French Chauchat entered service in 1916 and was plagued by jamming problems, shocking recoil, poor layout, terrible build quality, misaligned sights, and erratic spent-cartridge ejection. It nevertheless remained in French service until 1944.

Nambu pistol
The Japanese Type 94 pistol entered production in 1935. The build quality was terrible, but the worst "feature" of all was the exposed workings along the side of the gun frame, which meant that the gun could go off if the frame was accidentally squeezed.

Liberator
Manufactured in the US between 1942 and 1945, the Liberator was an unbelievably cheap pressed-steel single-shot handgun. Designed to be dropped to insurgents in occupied countries, it had an inaccurate effective range from its unrifled barrel of about 7.6m (25ft). Poking about in the mechanism with a stick was the only way to extract a spent cartridge.

SA80A1
Although subsequent modifications have turned the SA80 assault rifle into a decent weapon (in its SA80A2 variant), the initial production batch suffered from parts falling off (such as selector switches), constant jamming, an easily knocked magazine-release catch, and awkward arrangement of features.

Rondel dagger
The rondel dagger, with its round pommel and disc-like guard, was popular with the aristocracy and gentry in 15th-century England.

relief force that had attempted a frontal attack on its heavily defended wagons.

KUTNA HORA
21–22 DECEMBER 1421

Forces Hussite: unknown; Catholic crusader: unknown. **Casualties** No reliable estimates. **Location** Kutna Hora, Bohemia (in modern Czech Republic)

The surrounded Hussites formed their wagons into a column that advanced, hand guns and artillery firing, through the enemy line. Having escaped encirclement, the Hussites then counterattacked and drove the crusader forces out of Bohemia.

AUSSIG 16 JUNE 1426

Forces Hussite: 8,000; Catholic crusader: 13,000. **Casualties** Hussite: 100 or fewer; Catholic crusader: 4,000. **Location** Ústí nad Labem (in modern Czech Republic).

The Hussite army was attacked while besieging the town of Ústí, but formed its customary *wagenburg* (a circle of reinforced "war-wagons" armed with light guns). The crusader cavalry unsuccessfully charged the *wagenburg*, and were routed when Hussite cavalry counterattacked.

DOMAZLICE (TAUS) 14 AUGUST 1431

Forces Hussite: unknown; Catholic crusader: unknown. **Casualties** No reliable estimates. **Location** Domazlice, Plzen (in modern Czech Republic).

A large crusader army was routed by the Hussites. It seems likely the crusaders mistook the withdrawal of their baggage train for the start of a general retreat, and panicked when the Hussites attacked. The Hussite Wars petered out gradually.

VARNA
10 NOVEMBER 1444

Forces Hungarian and Allied: 30,000; Ottoman: c.60,000. **Casualties** Hungarian and Allied: probably half killed; Ottoman: unknown. **Location** Black Sea coast of Bulgaria.

In the Ottoman-Hungarian War, the Hungarian and allied Christians used wagons to form a defensive line, offsetting the superior Ottoman numbers, but the Christians lost when their leader was killed.

CONSTANTINOPLE
6 APRIL–29 MAY 1453

Forces Ottoman: 80,000; Byzantine: 7,000. **Casualties** No reliable estimates. **Location** Constantinople (modern Istanbul), Turkey.

After battering the walls with cannon and making several assaults, the Ottomans had stretched the defenders thinly. Access was finally gained through an undefended gate. The loss of Constantinople marked the end of the Byzantine empire.

CHOJNICE (CONITZ)
18 SEPTEMBER 1454

Forces Polish: 20,000; Teutonic Knights: 15,000. **Casualties** Polish: 3,000 plus 300 knights taken prisoner; Teutonic Knights: 100 killed. **Location** Northern Poland

An initial cavalry charge by the Poles was successful until a force of Teutonic Knights broke out of the besieged city and attacked their rear. The Poles retreated. This conflict was part of the Thirteen Years War.

THE WARS OF THE ROSES
1455–87

A challenge by Richard, Duke of York, to the weak rule of Henry VI of England resulted in a series of wars between the houses of York and Lancaster, both of whose members were direct descendants of Edward III. The conflict was known as the Wars of the Roses because of the badges used by each side. Even after the defeat of Richard at the battle of Bosworth in 1485, Yorkist revolts went on until the end of the century.

TOWTON 29 MARCH 1461

Forces Lancastrian: 25,000; Yorkist: 20,000. **Casualties** Lancastrian: 8,000; Yorkist: 5,000. **Location** South of Towton village, between Pontefract and Tadcaster, north Yorkshire, England.

Much of the battle – the bloodiest of the War of the Roses – was fought in a snowstorm. The Yorkist archers' fire was so effective that the Lancastrians were provoked into a charge leading to an extended mêlée. The arrival of Yorkist reinforcements finally broke the Lancastrian army.

BOSWORTH FIELD 22 AUGUST 1485

Forces Lancastrian: 5,000; Yorkist: 8,000. **Casualties** No reliable estimates. **Location** Near Market Bosworth, Leicestershire, England.

During the battle, elements of King Richard's Yorkist army remained unengaged or even switched sides. The king led a charge at Henry Tudor, hoping to kill him and thereby end the campaign, but became surrounded and was himself slain.

STOKE 16 JUNE 1487

Forces Rebel: 8,000; Royalist: 12,000. **Casualties** Rebel: 4,000; Royalist: 2,000. **Location** East Stoke, near Newark, Nottinghamshire, England

The rebels rejected Henry VII as king of England. The rebel army, largely composed of Irish and German mercenaries, attacked Royalist forces immediately to minimize losses from

HISTORY'S LARGEST LAND BATTLES

Thermopylae (480 BCE)
In this famous clash between Greeks and Persians, Greek historian Herodotus (born c.484 BCE) claims that the Persians numbered more than two million men. This is almost certainly an exaggeration: modern estimates suggest a figure of c.200,000 Persians and some 7,000 opposing Greeks.

Battle of Red Cliffs (208–209 CE)
A clash between Chinese warlords pitted the forces of Liu Bei and Sun Quan against those of Cao Cao. The latter was defeated in a battle involving more than half a million men.

Salsu (612)
More than 315,000 Korean and Chinese troops clashed around the Salsu (Chongchon) river in Korea after Sui emperor Yangdi invaded Goguryeo with a million men.

Tenochtitlán (1521)
Spanish commander Hernán Cortés, commander of up to 80,000 troops (mostly Indian Allies), defeated up to 300,000 warriors to take the Aztec capital.

Panipat (1761)
This epic conflict between the Maratha and Afghan armies in what is now Haryana state, India, involved more than 150,000 soldiers, 300 cannon, and an additional 300,000 civilians.

Leipzig (1813)
The biggest European land battle before World War I, this engagement pitted Napoleon's forces against nine states or nations, and involved more than half a million men.

Somme (1916)
More than 3 million troops fought on the Western Front between July and November 1916, with 1 million casualties. This was the largest battle of World War I and one of the bloodiest of all time.

Moscow (1941–42)
It is estimated that 248,000–400,000 Germans and 650,000–1,280,000 Russians were killed in the fighting that took place along a 600-km (373-mile) stretch of the Eastern Front between 2 October 1941 and 7 January 1942.

Kursk (1943)
In the largest tank battle in history, the combined German–Soviet opposing forces included over 6,000 tanks, 2.2 million soldiers, and 5,000 aircraft.

Operation Ichi-Go (1944)
More than 400,000 Japanese troops launched an offensive into southern China in World War II, resisted by equal numbers of Chinese soldiers.

Yom Kippur (1973)
A three-week battle between Israel and surrounding Arab armies pitted more than 400,000 Israeli troops and 2,300 tanks against combined Arab forces of about 200,000 men and more than 3,000 tanks.

Operation Desert Storm (1991)
A million Coalition soldiers took on a similar number of Iraqi troops – but with overwhelming air and armour superiority – in the battle to eject Saddam's invasion force from Kuwait.

their archers. This charge pushed the Royalist vanguard back, but the rebels broke after three hours of hard fighting. This is considered the last battle of the war.

BELGRADE 22 JULY 1456

Forces Ottoman: 80,000; Hungarian: 57,000. **Casualties** Ottoman: 24,000; Hungarian: 10,000. **Location** Belgrade (in modern Serbia).

The Ottomans had broken into the city the previous day, but were pushed back in fierce fighting, which lasted throughout the night. At dawn, scattered Hungarian units pursued the retreating Ottoman forces and began attacking the besiegers' camp. As more Hungarians joined in, the demoralized Ottoman army broke and ran.

THE NIGHT OF TERROR
16–17 JUNE 1462

Forces Ottoman: 50,000; Wallachian: 24,000. **Casualties** Ottoman: 15,000; Wallachian: 5,000. **Location** Targoviste (in modern Romania).

A detachment of the Wallachian army led by Voivode Vlad Tepes (Vlad the Impaler) made a night attack on the

Ottoman camp with the aim of killing Sultan Mehmed II. Although the sultan narrowly escaped, the assault inflicted heavy losses, and the shaken Ottoman force withdrew to Adrianople.

MURTEN 22 JUNE 1476

Forces Swiss: 25,000; Burgundian: 15,000–20,000. **Casualties** Swiss: losses small; Burgundian: 7,000–10,000 killed. **Location** Murten (Morat), west of Bern, Switzerland.

Although the Burgundians had constructed extensive field fortifications, they were surprised by the sudden attack of the Swiss. The defensive works were only lightly held and quickly overrun.

THE FALL OF GRANADA
FEBRUARY 1482–2 JANUARY 1492

Forces Spanish: 26,000 rising to 60,000; Granada Moors: 53,000 at start of siege. **Casualties** No reliable estimates. **Location** Southern Spain.

After a systematic campaign to eliminate Moorish strongholds in the region, the Spanish army besieged the city of Granada until it was forced to surrender. The battle marked the end of Moorish rule in the Iberian peninsula.

Early Modern Warfare 1500–1750

The availability of firearms that were easily portable, as well as field artillery, changed the nature of warfare considerably in the early 16th century. The change was slow and it took many years for the new weapons to achieve their full potential. Given the advantage of increased range that muskets offered over swords and pikes, the move from hand weaponry to firearms as the primary weapon for infantry was as inevitable as it was gradual.

AZTEC FEATHER SHIELD

Ottoman shield
The Turkish *kalkan* is a type of small shield. Such shields were made of iron, brass, or wood and provided lightweight protection for a swordsman's free hand, as well as helping him to parry during fencing.

ITALIAN WAR OF 1494–98

This was the first in a series of conflicts known as the Italian Wars, taking place between 1494 and 1559. The wars arose out of disputes over the Duchy of Milan and the Kingdom of Naples, and drew in a number of states. In the first war, a French force invaded Italy in 1494 deploying siege cannon for what was probably the first time, and took possession of Naples in 1495. The "League of Venice", formed mainly from Italian states, was also an historical first.

Aztec warrior
Shown wearing a feathered battledress, holding a tasselled shield, and carrying an obsidian-bladed wooden sword on his back, an Aztec warrior takes hold of a captive's hair in this image from the mid-16th century *Codex Mendoza*.

FORNOVO
6 JULY 1495

Forces French 12,000; League of Venice: 20,000. **Casualties** French 1,200; League of Venice: 2,000. **Location** 30km (18 miles) southwest of Parma, Italy.

The French cannon had little effect due to damp powder, and the action was bloody but indecisive. The French withdrew to France afterwards, ending the campaign.

ITALIAN WAR OF 1499–1505

Continued French claims to the thrones of Naples and Milan led to a joint French-Spanish expedition to take the cities by force. Disputes over the division of spoils then led to war between France and Spain, in which the Italian states played a lesser role on each side.

RUVO
23 FEBRUARY 1503

Forces French: 600; Spanish: 2,300. **Casualties** French: 600, including prisoners; Spanish: unknown. **Location** Puglia, Italy.

After a preliminary bombardment that breached the walls, the Spanish assaulted the town of Ruvo. Street fighting went on for several hours even after the walls were taken, but eventually the French force was overwhelmed.

CERIGNOLA
28 APRIL 1503

Forces French 32,000; Spanish: 8,000. **Casualties** French: 4,000; Spanish 100. **Location** Ruvo, Puglia, Italy.

The Spanish forces were deployed in a new way, as mixed units of swordsmen, pikemen, and arquebusiers, enabling them to beat off attacks by the French heavy cavalry. Cerignola was the first major battle to be won primarily by infantry firearms.

GARIGLIANO
29 DECEMBER 1503

Forces French: 23,000; Spanish: 15,000. **Casualties** French: 4,000 plus about the same number captured; Spanish: 900. **Location** Gaeta, central Italy.

After manoeuvring on either side of the Garigliano river, the Spanish crossed by means of an improvised bridge, catching the French by surprise. A hurried retreat to Gaeta resulted in the French becoming besieged. Upon their surrender, Spain gained dominance over Naples.

WAR OF THE LEAGUE OF CAMBRAI
1508–16

The League of Cambrai was formed to counter the growing power of the Republic of Venice. Shifting alliances and conflicting interests drew virtually every major power in Europe into a complex conflict that formed the next phase of the wider Italian Wars. The eventual result was gains for Venice and France, which ended the war as allies despite starting on opposite sides.

RAVENNA
11 APRIL 1512

Forces Spanish: 16,000; French: 21,000. **Casualties** Spanish: 9,000 killed; French: 4,500 killed. **Location** Emilia-Romagna, northern Italy.

After a two-hour artillery duel the Spanish launched a charge. This was shattered by French heavy cavalry, who then attacked the Spanish positions from the flank, while pikemen assaulted the front. The Spanish fled the field.

NOVARA
6 JUNE 1513

Forces French: 12,000; Swiss: 5,000. **Casualties** No reliable estimates. **Location** 38km (23 miles) west of Milan, northern Italy.

After a night march, the Swiss were in position to attack the French camp at dawn. Catching the French totally unprepared, the Swiss pikemen overran the camp, killing infantry and chasing off cavalry.

MARIGNANO 13–14 SEPTEMBER 1515

Forces French: 30,000; Swiss: 20,000. **Casualties** French: 5,000–10,000; Swiss: 6,000–10,000. **Location** Modern Melegnano, 15km (9 miles) southeast of Milan, Italy.

The Swiss had expected the shock of their pike charge to overwhelm the enemy, but unexpectedly tough resistance resulted in a long and indecisive battle. The arrival of French reinforcements forced the Swiss forces to withdraw.

MILITARY AND NAVAL PUNISHMENT THROUGH THE AGES

Armed force (period)	Offence	Punishment
Dutch navy, 16th–19th centuries	Various	"Keelhauling", which involved fixing blocks to yardarms on either side of the ship. The offender was bound to a line passing through the blocks and beneath the ship. Lead weights were attached to his feet and he was dropped into the water, hauled under the keel and raised on the other side, where the process was repeated.
Various armies, 17th–19th centuries	Misdemeanour; breaches of the code of conduct	A basic form of punishment in many armies was flogging, or the judicial whipping of a man who had committed an offence against the regiment's rules and regulations. Often flogging was administered by non-commissioned officers, with the offender paraded before the formed company, to serve as a lesson to others.
British East India Company army, mid-19th century	Mutiny	In 1858, after the Sepoy Mutiny had been crushed, the British revived a punishment for high treason from the time of the Mogul emperors. Many native conspirators were lashed to wooden stocks and their bodies placed at the muzzles of artillery pieces in a punishment known as being "blown from cannon". When the gunners fired their guns, the mutineers were literally blown apart.
US Army, 20th century	Various serious offences (e.g. assault, murder)	As part of the punishment of a soldier found guilty of felony crimes by court martial, the convict would often be given a dishonourable discharge from the army. In addition to incurring a prison sentence and other penalties, this form of discharge could impact on the felon's right to own firearms, his eligibility to vote, and his ability to find employment.

Punishments meted out at sea
In this 16th-century woodcut, miscreant sailors receive a variety of punishments: one is lashed to the bowsprit, one has his hand nailed to the mast with a knife, while another is keelhauled, and a fourth is thrown overboard.

defeated the Safavids' cavalry army using a combination of janissaries and artillery.

RAYDANIYA 22 JANUARY 1517

Forces Ottoman: 40,000; Mameluk: c.40,000. **Casualties** Ottoman: 6,000 killed; Mameluk: 7,000 killed. **Location** Sinai desert, east of Cairo, Egypt.

The Mameluks attempted to halt the Ottoman advance using a fortified position equipped with cannon. The Ottomans outshot the Mameluk gunners while their arquebusiers repelled the Mameluk cavalry assaults.

CHALDIRAN 23 AUGUST 1514

Forces Ottoman: 60,000; Safavid: up to 50,000. **Casualties** Probably fairly even. **Location** Between Tabriz and Lake Van (in modern northwestern Iran).

After suffering hardship as a result of a "scorched-earth" policy implemented by the retreating Safavids, the Ottoman army

" [The Italian] custom was to **fight** squadron after squadron … the battle … **lasted a whole day**."

PHILIPPE DE COMMINES, FRENCH KNIGHT AT THE BATTLE OF FORNOVO, 1495

SPANISH CONQUEST OF MEXICO 1519–21

A small number of European troops, assisted by local allies, carried out the Spanish conquest of what is now Mexico. The Aztec capital, Tenochtitlán, was initially occupied without a fight. Ousted by a revolt, the Spanish had to fight a campaign in the field before retaking the city by siege.

NIGHT OF SORROWS 30 JUNE–1 JULY 1520

Forces Spanish: c.1,000; Tlaxcalan and Aztec: unknown. **Casualties** Spanish: c.600 killed or captured; Tlaxcalan and Aztec: unknown. **Location** Modern Mexico City.

Intercepted as they tried to escape a revolt in Tenochtitlán by breaking out of the city

in the night, the Spanish were caught on one of the causeways and unable to use their horses or artillery. Only a few of the Spanish and their allies were able to make their way over the causeway and escape.

SIEGE OF TENOCHTITLÁN 31 MAY–13 AUGUST 1521

Forces Spanish and allies: 900–1,000; Aztec and allies: c.100,000. **Casualties** Spanish and allies: unknown; Aztec and allies: 100,000. **Location** Modern Mexico City.

The Spanish ground down resistance in Tenochtitlán by razing each street as they captured it. Every night they retired out of the city, pushing in again the next day. Much of the surviving population was slaughtered.

ITALIAN WAR OF 1521–26

The election in 1519 of Charles I of Spain as Holy Roman Emperor triggered another round of fighting in the Italian Wars. This time fighting took place all over Europe, although the decisive action was fought at Pavia in northern Italy, south of Milan.

BICOCCA 27 APRIL 1522

Forces French and Allied: possibly 30,000; Imperial: 6,400. **Casualties** French and Allied: 3,000 or more; Imperial: unknown, but light. **Location** North of Milan, Italy.

The Swiss mercenaries in French service in Lombardy were disgruntled because they had received no pay and threatened to return home unless the French commander Lautrec attacked the imperial forces at once. The Swiss used a head-on advance with their pikes levelled, their standard tactic. However, they were halted by obstacles and artillery fire, and then driven off by arquebusiers. Bicocca is sometimes considered the first engagement in which firearms were decisive.

Battle of Pavia, 1525

At the battle of Pavia on 24 February 1525, the pikemen and arquebusiers of the Spanish Holy Roman emperor Charles V destroyed the army of Francis I, king of France.

PAVIA 24 FEBRUARY 1525

Forces French: 20,000; Imperial: 23,000. **Casualties** French: 10,000; Imperial: 1,500. **Location** Around Pavia, south of Milan, Italy.

In autumn 1524 the French king, Francis I, had marched an army over the Alps and occupied Milan. His troops then besieged Pavia, but an imperial force was sent to relieve the garrison there. The imperial forces used a night march to get on the French flank, resulting in a confused battle, in which the French were outfought in a series of small local actions. Francis was captured and taken to Spain. The following year he signed the Treaty of Madrid, renouncing his territorial claims in Italy.

WAR OF THE LEAGUE OF COGNAC
1526–30

The League of Cognac, led by France and the Papal States, was formed to attempt the removal of Spanish and Holy Roman empire interests from Italy. Much use was made of mercenaries. Mutiny and desertion resulted when troops were not paid afterwards.

SACK OF ROME 6 MAY 1527

Forces Papal States: 5,500; Imperial: 20,000. **Casualties** Papal States: 500; Imperial: no reliable estimates. **Location** Central-western Italy.

BATTLEFIELD MUSICAL INSTRUMENTS

Musical instruments have for centuries formed part of the basic equipment of an army going to war. In the confusion after a battle began, loud notes from horns or pipes, or drumbeats could communicate commands more clearly than other kinds of signalling, such as flags. Aboard naval warships, drums and specialized whistles, known as boatswain's pipes, were traditionally used to indicate the arrival of visitors or senior officers, to signal the hours of the watch, and to direct sailors to their action stations in combat.

Horns

During his conquest of Gaul in 58–51 BCE, Julius Caesar used trumpets and other horns to direct Roman troops in battle. Soldiers were trained to respond to certain notes or combinations of notes blown loudly on copper or iron trumpets. The notes would indicate attacks, retreats, and other manoeuvres around the battlefield. In the 19th century, a small horn called a bugle became one of the most important signalling devices on American and many European battlefields, helping command the movements of infantry and cavalry alike.

Drums

Drums may be among the most ancient of martial musical instruments, appearing in combat almost everywhere, from tribal warfare in Mesoamerica and Africa, to Asia and Europe. In naval service, the phrase "beat to quarters" indicated a particular kind of drum roll that ordered sailors to their posts for a fight where some would load and prepare to fire the ship's guns and others would arm with muskets and ascend the rigging as sharpshooters in preparation for combat. On land, drums were used to command manoeuvres in most European-style armies throughout the 19th century. Because for several centuries armies relied on musket-armed infantry, the drum was essential to ensure that very large formations of men moved accurately and held ranks as they closed with the enemy.

Fifes

Developed from medieval folk instruments, small, high-pitched flutes played an important role (along with the drum) in signalling infantry manoeuvres. The shrill notes of the fife, coupled with various drumbeats, could deliver complex commands to infantry units that were engaged in combat and were otherwise unreachable through the smoke and terrible noise of battle. Fifes usually had just six finger holes and typically played in the key of B flat.

Bagpipes

Various cultures around the world have developed and still play forms of bagpipes in their folk music. In some cultures, the bagpipes were pressed into military service in much the same way that the medieval flute became the martial fife. The bagpipes evolved into a sophisticated signalling device in Scotland in particular, where the instrument became almost a national symbol. However, unlike the fifes and trumpets of other armies, the Highland bagpipes also served a psychological purpose: sounding the approach of fearsome regiments whose battlefield prowess was well known, especially during the Napoleonic Wars.

Wooden fife

Developed from the 15th century, the fife, such as this wooden example below, became an important battlefield musical instrument.

"Empire and conquest could not exist without the material and means of war…"

ZAHIR-UD-DIN MUHAMMAD BABUR ON HIS 16TH-CENTURY CONQUEST OF HINDUSTAN

Mercenaries in imperial service mutinied due to lack of pay and forced their commanders to lead a march on Rome. The city was stormed and sacked.

SIEGE OF FLORENCE
24 OCTOBER 1529–10 AUGUST 1530

Forces Republic of Florence: unknown; Imperial: unknown. **Casualties** No reliable estimates. **Location** Italy.

Florence became an independent republic after the sack of Rome, fighting against the imperial faction. An imperial army besieged the city for ten months, and Florence finally surrendered when it became apparent that outside assistance would not be arriving.

ITALIAN WAR OF 1536–38

Forces French: unknown; Imperial: unknown. **Casualties** Unknown. **Location** Italy.

The death of the Duke of Milan triggered another round of conflict over the duchy. French troops captured Turin, but were unable to take Milan, while an imperial incursion into France ended inconclusively.

ITALIAN WAR OF 1542–46

Forces French and Allied: unknown; Imperial: unknown. **Casualties** Unknown. **Location** Much of Europe.

Further disputes over Milan brought about war between France, now allied with the Ottoman empire, and Spain, the Holy Roman empire, and various allies. The outcome was inconclusive despite the vast expense of the war.

ITALIAN WAR OF 1551–59

Forces French and Allied: unknown; Imperial: unknown. **Casualties** Unknown. **Location** France, Flanders (in modern Belgium), and Italy.

The final round of the Italian Wars saw fighting in several corners of Europe, before bankruptcy and internal problems forced both France and Spain to accept a settlement. Despite this, Spain remained the dominant power in Italy at the end of the wars.

WARS OF THE OTTOMAN EMPIRE
1522–26

The removal of the Knights of St John from their stronghold on Rhodes was a priority for the Ottoman sultan Suleiman the Magnificent. After a failed attempt in 1480, the Ottomans besieged the island again in 1522. Due to the situation in Italy, appeals from Rhodes for help from other European states went largely unheeded.

Ottoman expansion into Europe via the Balkans also met with vigorous resistance, primarily from Austria.

RHODES JUNE–DECEMBER 1522

Forces Ottoman: 100,000; Knights Hospitaller: 7,000. **Casualties** Ottoman: 50,000 killed; Knights Hospitaller: 5,200 killed. **Location** Island of Rhodes, Aegean Sea.

The walls had been breached with mining, cannon, and explosive charges, yet the defenders were able to repel many assaults. They eventually agreed to surrender the fortress in return for safe conduct.

MOHÁCS 29 AUGUST 1526

Forces Hungarian: 12,000 cavalry, 13,000 infantry; Ottoman: 70,000–100,000. **Casualties** Hungarian: 15,000 killed; Ottoman: probably similar. **Location** Baranya, south of Budapest, Hungary.

Crashing through the Turkish horsemen, the Hungarian cavalry came up against a line of cannon chained together to make a barricade. Flanked as they tried to break through, the Hungarians were routed.

FIRST PANIPAT 21 APRIL 1526

Forces Mogul: 12,000; Lodi: 100,000 and 1,000 elephants. **Casualties** Mogul: unknown; Lodi: 20,000–50,000 killed. **Location** 90km (55 miles) north of Delhi, northern India.

Goaded into attacking on a narrow front against well-prepared positions, the forces of Sultan Ibrahim Lodi ran into heavy fire from Babur's Mogul army. Mounted archers completed the rout.

Dagger and sheath
This highly decorated dagger, called a *khanjar*, comes from Mogul-era Rajasthan, India. Its pommel is shaped like a ram's head and, like the sheath, it is decorated with semiprecious stones.

SPANISH CONQUEST OF PERU
1526–72

Arriving as the Inca empire was divided by civil war, the Spanish conquistadores were able to capitalize on the situation. Their horses and advanced European weapons helped to intimidate the Inca, many of whom joined forces with the newcomers.

CAJAMARCA 16 NOVEMBER 1532

Forces Spanish: 150–200; Inca: 40,000. **Casualties** No reliable estimates. **Location** Cuzco, northern Peru.

A small band of Spanish troops marched across Peru and confronted the Incan emperor. Treacherously launching an attack during a formal meeting, the Spanish eliminated the Incan leadership.

MANQO QAPAC'S REBELLION
1536–44

Forces (at Cuzco in 1536) Inca: 40,000; Spanish: 200. **Casualties** No reliable estimates. **Location** Peru.

Installed as a puppet emperor by the Spanish, Manqo Qapac led an initially successful revolt. Eventually driven away from the capital, he fought a guerrilla war against the conquistadors until his death in 1544.

TUNIS JUNE–JULY 1535

Forces Imperial: 60,000; Ottoman: unknown. **Casualties** No reliable estimates. **Location** Tunisia, North Africa.

Protected by a Genoese fleet, which had already decisively defeated the Ottomans at sea, the imperial army landed in Tunisia. After taking the port of La Goleta, the imperial forces then advanced on the city of Tunis.

CLASSIC MILITARY MANUALS AND PRACTICAL TREATISES

Title and author	Nationality	Date published	Description
The Art of War by Sun Tzu	Chinese	476–221 BCE	Composed in 13 chapters written on strips of bamboo, the book includes both strategic and tactical advice for commanders planning and waging war, manoeuvring forces, calculating supply and other logistics matters, and developing military intelligence.
The Art of War by Niccolò Machiavelli	Italian	1519–20 CE	*The Art of War* is a series of dialogues discussing how an army should be trained and deployed. Machiavelli suggests to his Florentine rulers that Roman practices should be emulated.
Über die Fechtkunst und den Ringkampf (On Fighting Arts and Tournament) by Hans Czynner	German	1538	This was one of many 15th- and 16th-century manuals that helped to codify Renaissance European fighting styles and schools of fencing and other martial arts, for both sport and war.
The Manual Exercise, as Ordered by His Majesty, in 1764. Together with Plans and Explanations of the Method Generally Practis'd, &c.	English	1764	This was a standard drill book for English King George III's forces during the American Revolution. The manual included musket practice and manoeuvre exercises to train large groups of men how to move and fight as a cohesive unit.
On War by Carl von Clausewitz	Prussian	1816–30	Von Clausewitz's treatise explained the organization, equipment, and use of armies and fortifications, and emphasized the role of military strength in achieving political goals.
The 1863 US Infantry Tactics for the Instruction, Exercise, and Manoeuvres of the United States Infantry	American	1863	This manual of arms for the US Army included revised drill and fighting tactics for line infantry, light infantry, and rifle infantry serving during the US Civil War (1861–65).

BOW VERSUS EARLY FIREARM

When gunpowder first appeared on the battlefields of China, and centuries later in Europe, the science and technology of firearms could not approach that of the bow, a weapon with literally thousands of years of development and evaluation behind it

(dating perhaps to 9,000 or 8,000 BCE). Firearms had some advantages, however: a bullet could penetrate most light steel body armour at relatively long range and artillery could knock down fortress walls.

Bow vs firearm
A 16th-century longbowman (left) and an arquebusier (below).

Weapon	Dimensions	Lethal range/rate	Pros	Cons
English longbow, c.1545 as exemplified by those found aboard the wreck of the English ship *Mary Rose*	Stave length 184–191cm (72–75in); girth 11cm (4.5in); weight approx 1kg (2lb); draw weight 29–41kg (65–90lb)	183m (600ft) with a skilled man shooting 12–15 arrows per minute	High-volume attack with massed archers; inexpensive to produce, maintain, and resupply	While the bow weighed about 1kg (2lb), it required archers to train to build and maintain the strength to draw it efficiently in battle.
Short land pattern musket, c.1750 as carried into battle during the Seven Years War and subsequent conflicts	Length overall 147cm (58in); barrel length 107cm (42in); calibre less than 20mm (.75in); weight 4kg (9lb)	91m (300ft) with a skilled man shooting 3–4 balls per minute	Less time needed in training to master compared with the longbow; industrial production outfitted large regiments	Costly to produce; the musket required maintenance to reduce the effects of carbon fouling and corrosion of mechanical parts.

WARS OF SULEIMAN THE MAGNIFICENT
1552–71

In his last years, Sultan Suleiman the Magnificent of the Ottoman empire continued to push into the Balkans and to seek naval supremacy in the Mediterranean.

SIEGE OF EGER 1552

Forces Ottoman: around 80,000; Hungarian: 2,000 or fewer. **Casualties** No reliable estimates. **Location** Northwestern Hungary, east of the Mátra Mountains.

Despite being massively outnumbered, the defenders of Eger put up a determined defence against the well-equipped but weary Ottoman army. Both sides dug mines and countermines under the walls. After 39 days, the siege was abandoned.

Jean de la Valette's tomb

Grandmaster of the Knights Hospitallers, Jean de la Valette (c.1494–1568) successfully resisted Turkish forces during the siege of Malta in 1565. His tomb is beneath St John's cathedral, Malta.

SIEGE OF MALTA
18 MAY–7 SEPTEMBER 1565

Forces Defender: 13,000–14,000; Ottoman: 30,000–60,000. **Casualties** Defender: 5,000 killed; Ottoman: 24,000 killed. **Location** 93km (58 miles) off the coast of Sicily, Mediterranean Sea.

Having relocated from Rhodes, the Knights of St John set up a new fortified base on Malta, which Ottoman forces attacked in 1565. Despite intense bombardment and repeated assaults, the Knights of St John held out until relief arrived and prevailed. The battle for Malta was an epic of siegecraft and courage on both sides, with the fort of St Elmo fought over with particular ferocity.

SIEGE OF SZIGETVÁR
6 AUGUST 1566– 8 SEPTEMBER 1566

Forces Ottoman: around 100,000; Hungarian and Croatian: 2,300. **Casualties** Ottoman: unknown, but heavy; Hungarian and Croatian: almost total. **Location** Modern Baranya county, southern Hungary.

The outnumbered Hungarian and Croatian defenders held out until 7 September 1566, the day on which Sultan Suleiman died (probably of natural causes). A massive assault that day overran the defenders – almost all were killed. Seven men managed to break out and escape, and four more were captured and later released.

FIFTH OTTOMAN–VENETIAN WAR
1570–73

Selim II, successor to Suleiman, launched a campaign to take Cyprus. The land campaign went well, resulting in Venice ceding Cyprus. The naval battle at Lepanto resulted in a major Ottoman defeat, but this did not change the course of the war.

LEPANTO 7 OCTOBER 1571

Forces Ottoman: 88,000 (16,000 soldiers); Holy League: 84,000 (20,000 soldiers). **Casualties** Ottoman: 15,000–20,000 killed; Holy League: 7,566 killed. **Location** Gulf of Patras, Greece.

The Christian forces enjoyed a considerable advantage in terms of the number and power of their cannon and firearms, which proved decisive in a hard-fought action. The Ottoman fleet suffered heavy losses, but these were soon replaced.

SECOND PANIPAT 5 NOVEMBER 1556

Forces Mogul: 20,000; Afghan/Hindu: 100,000 and 1,500 elephants. **Casualties** Moguls captured 1,500 elephants. **Location** 90km (55 miles) north of Delhi, north India.

At first the war elephants of the combined Afghan/Hindu force were highly successful. The balance tipped in the favour of the Moguls when a lucky arrow struck and wounded the Hindu general Hemu, who was later beheaded.

WARS OF THE SENGOKU PERIOD 1560–82

For a period of about 150 years, Japan was splintered into many states whose clans vied for supremacy. More than once a warlord came close to unifiying Japan through force. Oda Nobunaga was one such, although he was betrayed in 1582.

OKEHAZAMA JUNE 1560

Forces Yoshimoto: 25,000; Nobunaga: 1,800. **Casualties** Unknown. **Location** Owari province, south-central Japan.

Learning the location of his enemy's camp, Oda Nobunaga used woods to cover his approach and attacked from an unexpected direction. Caught totally unawares, Yoshimoto's force was routed.

ANEGAWA 1570

Forces Tokugawa and Nobunaga: 200,000 or more; Azai and Asakura: 140,000 or more. **Casualties** Unknown. **Location** Omi province, Japan.

The battle was fought largely in a shallow river, with a force of arquebusiers taking part on the side of Nobunaga. The Tokugawa force defeated its opponents, then flanked those facing Nobunaga.

MIKATAGAHARA 25 JANUARY 1573

Forces Takeda: 30,000; Tokugawa and Allied: 11,000. **Casualties** Unknown. **Location** Mikawa province, Japan.

The Tokugawa clan hoped to win by use of arquebusiers, but it was overrun by a cavalry charge. The Tokugawa, however, were able to retreat in reasonable order, reducing the severity of the defeat.

FRENCH WARS OF RELIGION, EARLY BATTLES
1562–73

The rise of Protestantism in France led to a period of conflict known as the French Wars of Religion. Periods of open war were interspersed with uneasy peace.

DREUX 19 DECEMBER 1562

Forces Huguenot: 15,000; Royalist: 19,000. **Casualties** Huguenot: 4,000; Royalist: 4,000. **Location** Northwest France, 80km (50 miles) east of Paris.

The Protestant Huguenot cavalry achieved initial success, throwing the Catholic Royalists into confusion. Royalist reserves tipped the balance, though a majority of the Huguenot force was able to retire from the field, resulting in a Royalist victory.

SURPRISE OF MEAUX
28 SEPTEMBER 1567

Forces Huguenot: unknown; Royalist: unknown, but few. **Casualties** No reliable estimates. **Location** Brie, 54km (34 miles) east of Paris, France.

Amidst fears of a Catholic re-mobilisation against them, Huguenot forces made an unsuccessful attempt to capture the king. This event led to new outbreaks of violence in which Catholic priests were massacred.

JARNAC 13 MARCH 1569

Forces Huguenot: unknown; Royalist: unknown. **Casualties** No reliable estimates. **Location** Bassac, western France.

The Huguenot force was defeated as a result of a surprise cavalry attack from an unexpected direction. A portion of the Huguenot army managed to withdraw.

LA ROCHE–L'ABEILLE
25 JUNE 1569

Forces Huguenot: 25,000; Royalist: 29,500. **Casualties** No reliable estimates. **Location** West-central France.

Catching the Royalist force by surprise, the Huguenot attack initially went well. A determined stand by Royalist infantry redressed the balance for a time, until a flanking movement forced a Royalist withdrawal.

SIEGE OF LA ROCHELLE
NOVEMBER 1572–6 JULY 1573

Forces Huguenot: unknown; Royalist: initially 28,000. **Casualties** No reliable estimates. **Location** Western France, on the Bay of Biscay.

The predominantly Protestant city of La Rochelle refused to accept a royal governor and came under siege. Eight

Mogul warriors
In this 16th-century image, the Mogul emperor Babur leads his cavalry in a charge against a Rajput coalition army. Both Babur and his grandson Akbar won decisive victories at Panipat, near Delhi, India.

...ssaults were made, with heavy losses, ...efore a settlement permitting Protestantism in La Rochelle was signed.

TALIKOT 23 JANUARY 1565

Forces Hindu: up to 600,000; Muslim: up to 700,000. **Casualties** Hindus: hundreds of thousands allegedly lost. **Location** 130km (80 miles) north of Vijayanager, India.

Managing to offend several rival sultans enough that they allied against him, the Hindu king Rama Raja was overwhelmed by their forces. Hindu political power was broken in southern India as a result.

THE DUTCH REVOLT
1568–1609

The Dutch Revolt began as an uprising against Spanish rule in the Low Countries, resulting in the formation of the Dutch Republic. The first stages of the war ended with a 12-year truce beginning in 1609.

JEMMINGEN 21 JULY 1568

Forces Spanish: c. 15,000; Dutch: c.15,000. **Casualties** Spanish: c.100 killed; Dutch: 6,000–7,000 killed. **Location** Ems estuary, Friesland in modern Netherlands.

Caught on the peninsula of Jemmingen with the river at their backs, the Dutch rebel army was outmatched in terms of firepower and discipline. Thousands were killed trying to swim to safety.

BRILL 1 APRIL 1572

Forces Spanish: unknown; Dutch: 600. **Casualties** None. **Location** 33km (20 miles) west of Rotterdam, Netherlands.

Part of a rebel Dutch fleet seized the town of Brill as a base. As their numbers grew, these so-called "Sea-Beggars" defeated Spanish naval forces in coastal waters.

SIEGE OF HAARLEM
1572 –13 JULY 1573

Forces Spanish: 17,000; Dutch: 2,800. **Casualties** Spanish: 1,700; Dutch: 2,000, including prisoners. **Location** 20km (12 miles) west of Amsterdam (in modern Netherlands).

After much deliberation, the city of Haarlem declared for the rebels and was subsequently besieged by the Spanish army. A relief army was defeated in July 1573, and with supplies exhausted the city surrendered on 13 July 1573.

ZUIDERZEE 11 OCTOBER 1573

Forces Spanish: 30 ships; Dutch: 24 ships. **Casualties** Spanish: 6 ships captured; Dutch: unknown. **Location** Modern Ijsselmeer, Netherlands.

Unable to survive a conventional gunnery engagement against the heavier Spanish ships, the rebel Dutch force tried to board. A Dutch attack on 5 October was beaten off with heavy losses, but six days later favourable winds helped the Dutch to gain a victory.

GEMBLOUX 31 JANUARY 1578

Forces Spanish: 17,000; Dutch: 25,000. **Casualties** Spanish: 20; Dutch: 10,000. **Location** 43km (26 miles) southeast of Brussels (in modern Belgium).

Catching the demoralized rebel Dutch army in retreat, a force of Spanish cavalry launched a charge that triggered a general panic. The Dutch army was overrun and largely destroyed.

RIJMENAM 31 JULY 1578

Forces Spanish: 17,000; Dutch: 20,000. **Casualties** Spanish: estimates vary; probably 400–1,000; Dutch: approximately equal. **Location** Province of Antwerp (in modern Belgium).

The Spanish attacked a Dutch force composed mainly of foreign mercenaries, who were awaiting reinforcements and had entrenched themselves. After some skirmishing, a general Spanish assault was launched, which was beaten off, although the Dutch were not able to exploit the victory.

SIEGE OF MAASTRICHT
12 MARCH–1 JULY 1579

Forces Spanish: 20,000; Dutch: 2,000. **Casualties** Spanish: 4,000; Dutch: 960, plus several thousand citizens. **Location** Near the Belgian and German borders, Netherlands.

A campaign of mining and counter-mining under the walls gradually wore down the defenders, although the cost to the Spanish was heavy. Eventually the city was stormed at night.

SIEGE OF ANTWERP
SEPTEMBER 1584–AUGUST 1585

Forces Spanish: unknown; Dutch: unknown. **Casualties** No reliable estimates. **Location** Flanders (in modern Belgium).

Dutch rebels opened the dykes to flood the Spanish siege lines around Antwerp. The Spanish responded by building a bridge across the flooded area and establishing strongpoints on the dyke tops. Antwerp surrendered.

BOKSUM 17 JANUARY 1586

Forces Spanish: 3,700; Dutch: unknown. **Casualties** Spanish: very low; Dutch: possibly 1,000. **Location** Friesland (in modern Netherlands).

Caught by surprise in an unfinished defensive position, the Dutch

Renaissance rapier
This Spanish swept-hilt sword (late 16th–early 17th centuries) has an unsharpened section of blade called the *ricasso* (below the hilt), for precise handling.

rebel army was quickly routed. The spring thaw, however, made many roads impassable because of mud, which forced the Spanish to abandon some of their artillery as they withdrew.

ZUTPHEN
22 SEPTEMBER 1586

Forces Spanish: 25,500; Dutch: 17,000. **Casualties** Spanish 4,500; Dutch: 6,000. **Location** West-central Netherlands.

Poor leadership of the Dutch force, which contained numerous foreign mercenaries under an English commander, led to a costly defeat and the loss of the city to the Spanish.

BREDA 1590

Forces Spanish: unknown; Dutch: 70. **Casualties** No reliable estimates, but very low on the Dutch side. **Location** Southern Netherlands.

Held by a strong Spanish force, the city of Breda was taken by stratagem. A force of 70 Dutch troops hid in a peat boat, which they had been informed was never searched, thus gaining entry to the city and taking the garrison by surprise.

NIEUWPOORT 22 JULY 1600

Forces Spanish: 9,900; Dutch: 11,400. **Casualties** Spanish 2,500, plus 600 prisoners; Dutch: 2,000. **Location** West Flanders (in modern Belgium).

While preparing to besiege Nieuwpoort, the Dutch were attacked by a Spanish force. After the initial Spanish attack had been repulsed from their strong position, the Dutch launched a cavalry charge, which drove off part of the Spanish army. Spanish successes elsewhere on the field were also countered by the cavalry, resulting in a Spanish collapse.

Breakout from Nagashino
At the battle of Nagashino (28 June 1575), future shogun Tokugawa Ieyasu's arquebusiers defeated the rival samurai Takeda clan. Here, Tokugawa's ally Katsutaka Torii tries to break out from the besieged castle.

SIEGE OF OSTEND
5 JULY 1601–16 SEPTEMBER 1604

Forces Spanish: 80,500; Dutch: 49,400. **Casualties** Spanish 55,000; Dutch: 45,000. **Location** West Flanders (in modern Belgium).

Ostend was the site of one of the longest sieges in history. After two years of bloody but indecisive fighting, new Spanish leadership undertook the gradual reduction of the outer defences. Once Spanish artillery was established close to the remaining defences, the Dutch surrendered.

NAGASHINO 28 JUNE 1575

Forces Takeda: 15,000 Nobunaga: 38,000. **Casualties** Takeda: around 10,000 killed; Nobunaga: unknown. **Location** Mikawa province, south-central Japan.

Deploying arquebusiers in front of his main force, Oda Nobunaga used their fire to break up the Takeda charge. Once the attack had stalled, Nobunaga's force counterattacked and broke the Takeda force.

GREAT NAVAL EXPEDITIONS

Era	Nation	Commander	Achievements
31 BCE Actium	Rome	Marcus Vipsanius Agrippa (63–12 BCE)	At the battle of Actium, Agrippa's fleet of 400 vessels defeated the combined fleets of Mark Antony and Cleopatra of Egypt, ending the Republican Wars and helping to establish the dominance of Imperial Rome under Caesar Augustus.
11th century CE Chola empire expeditions	Chola empire, southern India (modern Sri Lanka)	Rajendra Chola I (ruled 1012–44 CE)	At its height (c.1030), the Tamil-speaking Chola empire used its sea power (including large fleets of warships and armies of naval infantry) to conquer and hold territories from India's Ganges river to the islands of modern Indonesia.
1405–33 Zheng He voyages	Imperial China, Ming dynasty	Zheng He (1371–1433)	Zheng's first of seven voyages involved a fleet of 300 large ships that visited Southeast Asia, India, Arabia, and Africa. Their goals were diplomatic and naval, securing tribute for the emperor, while suppressing piracy and otherwise showing force.
1588 Spanish Armada	Spanish empire	Don Alonso Pérez de Guzmán El Bueno y Zúñiga-Sotomayor (1549–1615)	The Spanish Armada of 22 warships and 108 converted merchantmen, on a mission to conquer England, foundered and was defeated by the English at Gravelines; 63 ships were lost in the expedition.
1904–05 Tsushima	Imperial (Meiji) Japan	Admiral Togo Heihachiro (1848–1934)	At the battle of Tsushima (1905), a Japanese fleet under Admiral Heihachiro (aboard the battleship *Mikasa*) sortied to demonstrate the effectiveness of Japanese naval gunnery, explosive shell technology, and superior seamanship by destroying 17 Russian warships.
1941 Hunting the Bismarck	Germany, Third Reich	Captain Ernst Lindemann (1894–1941)	The sortie of the 50,900-ton battleship *Bismarck*, during which she sank the British Royal Navy's battlecruiser HMS *Hood* ended on 27 May in one of the greatest gun duels in naval history. It resulted in *Bismarck* being sunk in deep water off the Atlantic coast of France.
1982 Falkland Islands	Great Britain	Rear Admiral Sir John Forster Woodward (1932–)	The expedition of Britain's South Atlantic Task Group reconquered the Falkland Islands from Argentina; this long-distance expedition of 12,000km (7456 miles) also included the only modern sinking of an enemy naval combatant (ARA *Belgrano*) by a nuclear-powered fast-attack submarine (HMS *Conqueror*).

Route of the Armada
This detailed map, made in 1588, shows the route travelled by Spain's "Invincible" Armada during its ill-fated 16th-century expedition to conquer England.

HALDIGHATI 18 JUNE 1576

Forces Mogul: 80,000; Mewari: 20,000. **Casualties** Unknown, but heavier on Mewari side. **Location** 45km (30 miles) north of Udaipur, India.

Seeking to subjugate the last of the Rajputs (Hindu warrior princes), the Moguls launched a campaign against Mewar. The battle was indecisive and Mewar did not accept defeat until 1614.

ALCAZARQUIVIR 4 AUGUST 1578

Forces Portuguese: 16,500–18,000; Moroccan: unknown. **Casualties** Portuguese: 7,000 killed, 8,000 taken prisoner; Moroccan: unknown. **Location** Ksar el Kebir, northwest Morocco.

Leading a mixed force of Portuguese troops and European mercenaries seeking to conquer Morocco, King Sebastian of Portugal was met by an Ottoman-style army as he pushed inland. Almost all of Sebastian's force was killed or captured.

YAMAZAKI 2 JULY 1582

Forces Hideyoshi: 36,500; Mitsuhide: 16,000. **Casualties** Unknown. **Location** Southwest of Kyoto, Japan.

Occupying a hill with his arquebusiers, Toytomi Hideyoshi faced the army of Akechi Mitsuhide, a self-appointed shogun. As Hideyoshi's arquebusiers

drove off attempts to storm their position, the forces of Hideyoshi enveloped the enemy's flanks.

SHIZUGATAKE 21 APRIL 1583

Forces Katsuie: 11,000; Hideyoshi: 30,000. **Casualties** Katsuie: many thousands killed. **Location** On the northern shore of Lake Biwa.

Marching rapidly to the relief of Shizugatake, whose forces were then under siege by forces loyal to Shibata Katsuie, Hideyoshi's army arrived much sooner than expected. The surprised besiegers were routed and pursued.

ANGLO-SPANISH WAR 1587–1604

From 1587 to 1604, England and Spain were involved in an undeclared war fought largely at sea. The conflict was a heavy drain on both treasuries, forcing a negotiated settlement.

RAID ON CÁDIZ 29 APRIL–1 MAY 1587

Forces Spanish: unknown; English: 23 ships. **Casualties** 33 Spanish ships lost. English: none. **Location** southwest Spain.

Sir Francis Drake led an English fleet into Cádiz harbour and attacked the ships

there. The damage inflicted on Spain was not great, but the exploit was an impressive feat of seamanship and daring.

SPANISH ARMADA MAY–OCTOBER 1588

Forces Spanish: 130 ships; English: c.170 ships. **Casualties** Spanish: 63 ships. **Location** Most battles fought in the English Channel.

After a running engagement in the English Channel, the Spanish fleet anchored off Calais. An attack by fireships forced the Spanish to sea in disarray and allowed the English fleet to make a decisive attack.

ENGLISH ARMADA 1589

Forces Spanish: 4 galleons, plus an unknown number of armed merchant ships; English: 6 warships, 60 armed merchant ships. **Casualties** Spanish: No ships lost; English: 30 ships lost. **Location** Off the coast of Spain and Portugal.

Hoping to take advantage of heavy losses sustained by the Spanish fleet, an English expedition was launched against Corunna and Lisbon, with a view to taking the Azores as well. Bad weather and stubborn Spanish resistance caused the operation to fail, with heavy losses.

FRENCH WARS OF RELIGION, LATER BATTLES
1587–98

The French Wars of Religion continued, as attempts at finding a settlement collapsed into more violence. On his deathbed, King Henry III urged his successor, Henry IV, to become a Catholic. Henry IV instead tried to end the conflict by force, but eventually realized that conversion to Catholicism represented his only real chance to rule a united country. War with Spain followed, also with religious overtones. The wars of religion ended with the Edict of Nantes in 1598, which granted tolerance to Protestants.

COUTRAS 20 OCTOBER 1587

Forces Royalist: 10,000; Huguenot: 6,500. **Casualties** Royalist: 3,000 killed; Huguenot: up to 200 killed. **Location** Western France, northeast of Bordeaux.

The Royalist cavalry attempted to charge home with lances. Weakened by arquebus fire from the infantry, the charge fell apart on contact with the Huguenot cavalry. The Royalist army was routed.

VIMORY 26 OCTOBER 1587

Forces Royalist: unknown; Huguenot plus mercenaries: 25,000. **Casualties** No reliable estimates. **Location** North-central France.

The Huguenot army included many mercenaries funded with English and Danish money. After pillaging in Lorraine, the Protestant force became divided. A Catholic force defeated part of the army, and some mercenaries entered into negotiations with the Catholics.

ARQUES
15–18 SEPTEMBER 1589

Forces Royalist: 13,250; Catholic League: 35,000. **Casualties** No reliable estimates, but very high on both sides. **Location** Arques-la-Bataille, northern France.

> "Our ships **dashed forward** with the **roar of cannons** … the other enemy vessels **scattered and fled**."
>
> YI SUN-SIN, KOREAN ADMIRAL, ON THE BATTLE OF HANSANDO, 1592

Badly outnumbered, the Royalist army retired into Arques and fortified itself. After beating off several assaults in very bloody fighting, the Royalists were relieved by a force sent from Britain, forcing a Catholic retreat.

FONTAINE-FRANÇAISE 5 JUNE 1595

Forces Royalist: 3,000; Spanish and Catholic: 12,000. **Casualties** Royalist: unknown; Spanish and Catholic: unknown. **Location** Eastern France.

Rushing to counter a Spanish incursion into France, the small Royalist army caught its opponents by surprise and inflicted a temporary defeat. This was exploited by a deception, where local peasants simulated reinforcements moving up. Believing they were outnumbered, the Spanish retreated.

MOROCCANS DEFEAT SONGHAI EMPIRE MARCH 1591

Forces Moroccan: 5,000–25,000, including 2,000–4,000 musketeers; Songhai: 10,000–18,000 cavalry, 30,000–100,000 infantry. **Casualties** Unknown. **Location** Niger river, West Africa.

Advancing on the city of Gao, the Moroccan force was met by a much larger Songhai army. The Moroccans' muskets proved decisive; most of the Songhai fled when fired upon.

Edo period castle, Japan
Matsumoto-Jo is a well-preserved castle located at Hagano prefecture, in Japan. Completed in the late 6th century, the castle controlled a strategically important area during the Edo period (1603–1868).

JAPANESE INVASION OF KOREA
1592–98

Having succeeded in unifying Japan, Toyotomi Hideyoshi launched an invasion of Korea in 1592. This was initially conceived as part of a larger campaign of conquest, but came to an end in 1593. A second invasion was launched the following year, resulting in a war that continued until 1598.

SIEGE OF BUSAN 24 MAY 1592

Forces Korean: 8,000 or more; Japanese: 15,000 or more. **Casualties** Korean: estimates vary from 8,500 more than 30,000; Japanese: unknown. **Location** Busanjin-gu, Korea.

Simultaneously attacking the castle at Busan and the harbour forts, the Japanese launched an assault covered by arquebus fire. After the collapse of the defence, all surviving troops and civilians were massacred.

DADAEJIN 24 MAY 1592

Forces Korean: 3,000; Japanese: 5,000. **Casualties** Korean: total force; Japanese: 500–700. **Location** Korean peninsula.

With no effective counter to the fire of Japanese arquebuses, the Korean garrison could not prevent an assault. A vigorous Korean counterattack failed, despite heavy hand-to-hand fighting. Once the fort was taken, the garrison and civilian population were massacred.

DONGNAE 24 MAY 1592

Forces Korean: 3,000 or more; Japanese: 18,000. **Casualties** Korean: total force; Japanese: unknown. **Location** Korean peninsula.

The fortress of Dongnae threatened the Japanese bridgehead in Korea and was attacked quickly after their initial landings. The outmatched garrison put up a stout defence, but lacked the equipment and training to withstand the Japanese assault.

CHUNGJU JUNE 1592

Forces Korean: 16,000; Japanese: 19,000. **Casualties** Korean: more than 3,000 killed. Japanese: unknown. **Location** Southeast of Seoul, South Korea.

Seeking to halt the Japanese advance on Seoul, the Koreans offered battle

Kato Kiyomasa (1562–1611)
This 19th-century print shows one of Japan's most famous samurai, Kato Kiyomasa, a warrior whose accomplishments included the capture of Seoul during Japan's 16th-century invasions of Korea.

...on an open plain. Their cavalry charge was halted by arquebus fire, at which point the Japanese counterattacked.

OKPO JUNE 1592
Forces Korean: 54 ships; Japanese: 70 ships. **Casualties** Korean: minimal; Japanese: 50 or more ships lost. **Location** Okpo Bay, Geoje Island, southwest Korea.

Catching the Japanese fleet in the harbour at Okpo, the Koreans launched an attack and sank several ships. They then drew off, attacking again the next day to inflict further heavy losses on Japanese shipping.

SACHEON JUNE 1592
Forces Korean: 1 turtle ship, 25 other vessels; Japanese: 70 or more ships in harbour, possibly 20–30 in action. **Casualties** Korean: minimal; Japanese: 20–30 ships lost. **Location** South Gyeongsang province, South Korea.

Deploying a type of large armoured warship called a "turtle ship" for the first time, the Korean fleet drew part of the opposing fleet out of harbour by feigning a retreat. All of the Japanese ships that came out to fight were sunk.

IMJIN RIVER JUNE 1592
Forces Korean: 13,000; Japanese: unknown. **Casualties** No reliable estimates. **Location** South Korea.

Drawing out the Korean cavalry with a feigned retreat, the Japanese broke their charge with concentrated arquebus fire. Infantry then dashed out from concealed positions to complete the victory.

DANGPO JUNE 1592
Forces Korean: 1 turtle ship, plus 25 other vessels; Japanese: 90 ships. **Casualties** Korean: minimal; Japanese: unknown, but heavy. **Location** Sacheon, South Korea.

Catching another Japanese fleet in harbour, the Koreans launched an attack. The turtle ship proved impervious to Japanese fire and quickly sank the enemy flagship. A second Japanese force approached from seaward, but was chased off.

CHONJU 10 JULY 1592
Forces Korean: unknown; Japanese: unknown. **Casualties** No reliable estimates. **Location** West of southern Korea.

After their armies were beaten in the field, the Koreans fought a guerrilla war against the Japanese invaders. At Chonju a Korean force defeated a Japanese army, gaining additional support for the guerrillas' cause.

HANSANDO 15 AUGUST 1592
Forces Korean: unknown; Japanese: unknown. **Casualties** Japanese: 59 or 73 ships destroyed. **Location** Near Hansan Island, off southern Korea.

After luring the Japanese fleet out into open water, the Korean force turned and attacked. Korean accounts claim the enemy fleet was annihilated. In the Japanese version, some vessels escaped.

SIEGE OF CHINJU 4–10 OCTOBER 1592
Forces Korean: 3,800; Japanese: 20,000. **Casualties** No reliable estimates. **Location** West of Pusan, Southern Korea.

As the garrison and citizens of Chinju beat off a Japanese attempt to storm the fortress a large force of Korean guerrillas attacked the besiegers. This forced the Japanese army to withdraw.

HAENGJU FORTRESS 12 FEBRUARY 1593
Forces Korean: 2,000; Japanese 30,000. **Casualties** Korean: unknown: Japanese: 10,000. **Location** Goyan, Gyeonggi province, South Korea.

Desperately short of supplies, the Japanese launched a hasty, ill-prepared assault up steep slopes with the Koreans' fortified positions above them. After suffering massive casualties in the disorganized attack, the Japanese withdrew.

CHILCHEOLLYANG 28 AUGUST 1597
Forces Korean: 169 ships; Japanese: more than 500 ships. **Casualties** Koreans: 157 ships lost: Japanese: minimal. **Location** Strait near Geoje Island, Korean peninsula.

Rightly suspecting a trap, Korean admiral Yi refused to act on information obtained about the Japanese fleet's movements. He was relieved, and his replacement blundered into a massive Japanese fleet, resulting in the only Japanese naval victory of the war.

MYEONGYANG 16 SEPTEMBER 1597
Forces Korean: 12 ships; Japanese: 133 ships. **Casualties** Korean: unknown; Japanese: many ships sunk. **Location** Off the southwest coast of Korea.

Despite being reduced to a dozen ships by the disaster at Chilcheollyang, reinstated Korean admiral Yi attacked the Japanese fleet at Myeongyang, destroying the flagship and inflicting serious losses before breaking off the action.

SIEGE OF ULSAN 1597–98
Forces Korean and Chinese: 40,000–80,000; Japanese: 5,000. **Casualties** No reliable estimates. **Location** 60km (37 miles) north of Pusan, South Korea.

Korean forces, assisted by troops from China, were able to drive the invading Japanese into a number of coastal forces. At Ulsan, the Japanese withstood siege and repeated assaults until an army arrived to relieve them.

NORYANG 16 DECEMBER 1598
Forces Korean and Chinese: 145 ships; Japanese: 500 ships. **Casualties** Korean and Chinese: low; Japanese: 200 ships sunk, plus 100 ships captured. **Location** Noryang Strait, off Namhae Island, off the south coast of Korea.

When ordered to withdraw from Korea, the Japanese forces were unable to do so because of the Korean naval blockade. An attempted break-out resulted in the Japanese fleet being overwhelmed by Korean and Chinese cannon fire.

SEKIGAHARA 21 OCTOBER 1600
Forces Tokugawa Ieyasu: 80,000; Ishida Mitsunari: 80,000. **Casualties** Ishida Mitsunari: up to 60,000 killed. **Location** Northeast of Kyoto, Japan.

Ishida Mitsunari positioned one of his allies, Kobayakawa Hideaki, on the flank, not realizing that Hideaki had arranged to betray his ally. Attacked in front by Ieyasu and on the flank by Hideyaki, Mistunari's force collapsed.

TENNOJI 7 MAY 1615
Forces Toyotomi Hideyori: 55,000 Tokugawa Ieyasu: 150,000. **Casualties** Unknown. **Location** Outside Osaka, Honshu, Japan.

Toyotomi Hideyori's bold plan went awry when part of his army attacked too soon and his flanking force was intercepted before it could attack. Tokugawa's forces broke through into Osaka Castle, forcing Hideyori into the keep, which they fired on with cannon. With all hope lost, Hideyori committed suicide.

COMBAT LOADS CARRIED BY SOLDIERS, 17TH – 21ST CENTURIES

Infantry all over the world have faced the same basic challenge: they must carry on their backs everything that will sustain them until they are resupplied. Although clothing and equipment have become increasingly lighter in weight, the burden on the modern soldier has increased. Logisticians refer to different kinds of loads that soldiers carry. The Combat Load refers to the total minimum amount of equipment required for a soldier to fight and survive in immediate combat. The Fighting Load refers only to the equipment that is worn on the soldier's body (including weapons, ammunition, and hand grenades). The Approach Load refers to the maximum equipment the soldier carries while on the march (including the rucksack, shelter, etc.). The Approach Load can total up to 45 per cent of a soldier's body weight.

Armoured mask
A samurai's *menpo* (armoured mask), defended the warrior's face and throat. It was worn with a *kabuto* (helmet), which protected his head and neck.

Soldier/army	Period	Weight/load carried
Samurai, Tokugawa shogunate, mounted and fully caparisoned at the battle of Sekigahara	1600	27–45kg (60–100lb): the "six pieces" (*roku gu*) of the samurai's full armour included the helmet (*kabuto*), face mask (*menpo*), neck guard (*yodarekake*), shoulder guards (*sode*), and arm guards (*kote*), the breastplate (*do*), upper leg guards (*haidate*), and lower leg guards (*suneate*). The samurai's weapons included a sword (*katana*) and, often, a lance (*yari*) or other pole-arm.
French infantryman, Napoleonic Wars	1806	18–36kg (40–80lb): the typical infantryman of the period carried into battle his musket, bayonet, 50–100 rounds of ammunition (in a large cartridge pouch slung over his shoulder), and a short cutlass (*briquet*) at his left side.
American paratrooper, 82nd Airborne Division, in France during Operation Overlord, World War II	1944	36–54kg (80–120lb): to the World War II US light infantry kit (steel helmet, rifle, bayonet), the airborne trooper's field equipment added a main parachute and a reserve parachute, gas mask, two bandoliers (48 rounds of .30 calibre ammunition each), four blocks of TNT, three fragmentation hand grenades, and smoke grenades. Some troopers would carry parts of crew-built weapons as well, such as a Browning .30 calibre machine gun or a 60mm light mortar.
British Army soldier in Afghanistan	2009	27–54kg (60–120lb): the modern warrior's equipment load is every bit as heavy as that of his or her forebears. In combat, he or she must wear a bulky ballistic protective helmet and an adjustable system of fabric, metal, and ceramic body armour, as well as 180 rounds of 5.56mm ball ammunition for the SA80 assault rifle, a bayonet, hand grenades, and water.

GREAT WARS MOTIVATED BY RELIGION

Conflict	Period	Belligerents	Outcome
Muslim conquests	632–732 CE	Various tribes and states from the Arabian Peninsula, east to the Indonesian Archipelago, and west to the Iberian Peninsula	The first major expansionist period in Islamic histor came about when the foundations for a nearly global caliphate were laid from Spain to China, and north to the doorstep of the Byzantine empire.
Spanish Reconquista	721–1492	Medieval Roman Catholic kingdoms of France, Spain, and Portugal and the papacy; the caliphate of Cordoba, and later, the Almohad dynasty and its allies	By the middle of the 13th century, the Catholic kingdoms had won back most of the land of the Visigoth kingdom of Hispania, which had been conquered by the Umayyad Caliphate in the 8th century; after the Siege of Granada in 1492, the last Muslim kingdom on the Iberian Peninsula had been defeated.
The Crusades	11th–13th centuries	The papacy and kingdoms of Western Europe and their allies (including Christian Ethiopia); the Byzantine empire; the Seljuk empire; Arabs, Kurds, and other Muslims	A legacy of European colonialism in the Levant was established that has cultural and political reverberations into the 21st century; it became a key front in the millennium-long medieval confrontation between militant Christianity and militant Islam.
War of the Three Henrys	1584–89	The Catholic League, under Henry of Guise, Henry of Navarre and the Huguenots, and Henry III, king of France	During the so-called French Wars of Religion, after Henry III executed Henry of Guise, the king was himself assassinated, leaving Henry of Navarre the victor; Navarre later renounced his Protestant faith and converted to Catholicism to take the crown of France.
Thirty Years War	1618–48	Roman Catholics and Calvinist protestants in the Holy Roman empire and other nations of Europe	Fighting and disease killed off as much as one-third of the population of certain areas of the empire; with the Treaty of Westphalia, Protestants and Catholics were granted rights under law; also, each state had sovereignty over its religious self-determination.

THIRTY YEARS WAR
1618–48

Arising largely out of religious disputes between Catholic and Protestant powers within the Holy Roman empire, the Thirty Years War gradually drew in most of the states of Europe. Not all the combatants' motives were religious; territorial and political issues also influenced a number of states to take sides, and to make and break alliances. The war eventually ended with the Treaty of Westphalia in 1648, which also ended the Dutch Revolt.

PILSEN
19 SEPTEMBER–21 NOVEMBER 1618

Forces Imperial (Catholic): 158 cavalry plus civilian volunteers; Bohemian (Protestant): 20,000. **Casualties** No reliable estimates. **Location** Western Bohemia, 90km (56 miles) west of Prague, modern Czech Republic.

Fleeing a Protestant uprising in Bohemia, many Catholics took refuge in Pilsen (modern Plzen). The small force of defenders was able to withstand siege and bombardment until 21 November, when the walls were breached and the city was stormed.

Weak supply chain

Forces depend upon a logistics network, which may become vulnerable as the army advances. Here, in this scene from the Thirty Years War (1618–48), soldiers attack an enemy supply column.

WHITE MOUNTAIN 8 NOVEMBER 1620

Forces Catholic League: 20,000; Protestant: 24,000. **Casualties** No reliable estimates. **Location** Bilá Hora, near Prague (in modern Czech Republic).

Deployed on high ground, the Bohemian army was not expecting a frontal attack. The centre of their line was quickly overrun and the rest of the army disintegrated.

WIMPFEN 6 MAY 1622

Forces Imperial and Catholic League: 25,000; Protestant: 14,000. **Casualties** Imperial and Catholic League: no reliable estimates; Protestant: almost total. **Location** Near Heidelberg, southwest Germany.

The outnumbered Protestant force deployed on a hill and fought a stubborn defensive battle. A lucky hit on the Protestant powder store caused an enormous explosion, permitting an assault to take the hill and pursue the Protestant army to destruction.

HOCHST 22 JUNE 1622

Forces Imperial and Catholic League: 25,000; Protestant: 12,000. **Casualties** Imperial and Catholic League: very low; Protestant: 2,000. **Location** Near Frankfurt, Germany.

While attempting to rendezvous with their allies, the Protestant force was brought to action at Hochst on the Main river. Cornered and outnumbered, the Protestants forced a crossing of the river and linked up with their allies, though at significant cost.

> "No wonder, then, if these **wandering nations** exhausted every territory in which they encamped, and by their **immense consumption** raised the necessaries of life to an **exorbitant** price."
>
> FRIEDRICH VON SCHILLER (1759–1805), GERMAN HISTORIAN, ON THE THIRTY YEARS WAR

FLEURUS 29 AUGUST 1622

Forces Spanish: 8,000; Protestant: 14,000. **Casualties** Spanish: 1,200; Protestant: 5,000 including prisoners. **Location** Province of Hainault (in eastern modern Belgium).

The Protestant force launched a frontal attack that exposed deficiencies in training and became disordered. Repeated Protestant cavalry charges achieved some success but were eventually driven off. The Protestant infantry was largely overrun by cavalry while retreating the following day.

DESSAU BRIDGE 25 APRIL 1626

Forces Imperial: 20,000; Protestant: 12,000. **Casualties** Imperial: unknown; Protestant: 4,000 dead. **Location** 50km (30 miles) north of Leipzig (in modern Germany).

Correctly predicting that the Protestant army would cross into Silesia at the Dessau Bridge, the Imperial army laid an ambush by covering the bridge with concealed artillery, which turned it into a death trap for the Protestant forces.

STADTLOHN 6 AUGUST 1626

Forces Catholic League: 25,000; Protestant: 15,000. **Casualties** Catholic League: unknown; Protestant: 13,000. **Location** North Rhine-Westphalia (in western modern Germany).

A Protestant advance placed the army deep in hostile territory and without support. On retreating, it was caught and attempted to fight a defensive battle. When the cavalry wings were broken, the Protestant infantry attempted to fall back but were overrun.

LUTTER 27 AUGUST 1626

Forces Catholic League: 20,000; Danish: 20,000. **Casualties** Catholic League: unknown, but slight; Danish: 6,000 plus 2,500 prisoners. **Location** Lower Saxony, Germany.

After advancing to assist Protestant forces defeated at Dessau, the Danish were brought to action at Lutter. Repeatedly battered by infantry attack, the Danish were eventually forced to abandon their artillery and retreat.

MAGDEBURG 20 MAY 1631

Forces Imperial: unknown; Swedish: unknown. **Casualties** 20,000–25,000 Magdeburg citizens massacred. **Location** Central Germany, 130km (80 miles) west of Berlin.

The Protestant stronghold of Magdeburg fell to Imperial forces after artillery breached the walls in two places. The city was so thoroughly sacked that "Magdeburg Quarter" became a slang term for atrocity.

WERBEN 22 JULY 1631

Forces Imperial: 23,000; Swedish: 16,000. **Casualties** Imperial: unknown; Swedish: 6,000. **Location** Modern-day Elbe, 57km (35 miles) southeast of Hanover, Germany.

Entrenched in front of Werben, the Swedish army under Gustavus Adolphus drove off an initial assault, with cavalry and artillery proving decisive. A second assault broke the Swedish position and forced a retreat.

FIRST BREITENFELD 17 SEPTEMBER 1631

Forces Imperial: 35,000; Swedish/Saxon: 42,000; **Casualties** Imperial: 20,000 (of which 7,000–8,000 killed); Swedish/Saxon: c.4,000 killed. **Location** Just outside Leipzig, modern Germany.

Although the disciplined Swedish forces drove off several cavalry attacks, their Saxon allies were overrun. At this desperate juncture the Swedish reserves attacked the Imperial flank in conjunction with artillery fire and delivered a decisive victory.

LÜTZEN 16 NOVEMBER 1632

Forces Imperial: 13,000 infantry, 6,000 cavalry; Swedish: 12,800 infantry, 6,200 cavalry. **Casualties** Imperial 6,000–8,000 dead; Swedish: 5,000–6,000 dead. **Location** Saxony, Germany.

Catching the Imperial army marching as two columns, the Swedish fell on one but were then attacked by the other. The Swedish king, Gustavus Adolphus, was killed leading a cavalry charge to restore the situation. The Swedish held the field.

BATTLE OF THE LECH 15 APRIL 1632

Forces Imperial and Spanish: 25,000; Swedish: 40,000. **Casualties** Imperial and Spanish: 3,000; Swedish: 2,000. **Location** Near Rain, Bavaria, modern Germany.

Crossing the Lech river on a bridge of boats, the Swedish army stormed Catholic positions. Imperial general Count Tilly was mortally wounded, causing his army to lose heart and fall back. This saved the Catholics from being trapped by Swedish cavalry sent on a flanking movement.

NÖRDLINGEN 6 SEPTEMBER 1634

Forces Spanish: 20,000 infantry, 13,000 cavalry; Protestant: 16,000 infantry, 9,000 cavalry. **Casualties** Spanish: 3,500 killed or wounded; Protestant: 17,000 killed, 4,000 prisoners. **Location** Northwest of Munich (in modern Germany).

The Swedish army planned a coordinated attack, which became disorganized due to the terrain. As the battle degenerated into a series of isolated engagements the Swedish forces were overwhelmed.

WORLD'S OLDEST MILITARY AND NAVAL FORCES

While today's military and naval forces continually reorganize, modernize, and change, some active units have been in service for many centuries. For example, the company of Swiss Guards, currently serving as the personal protection force for the pope, is the last remnant of a proud tradition that stretches back to the halberdiers and pikemen of the Renaissance.

Unit	Year formed	Service
British Royal Navy	12th–13th centuries	England, Great Britain
Swiss Guard	1497	Vatican, Pontifical Guard
Life Guards (Livgardet)	1521	Swedish Army
Scots Guards	1642	British Army
Royal Marines	1664	British Royal Navy
US Army	1775	United States
Gurkha Rifles	1815 (although belonging to a warrior tradition that may date to the 8th century or earlier)	British Army

SWISS GUARD

ALTENDORF
31 AUGUST –4 SEPTEMBER 1632

Forces Imperial: 40,000; Swedish: 50,000. **Casualties** Imperial: 2,300; Swedish 2,700. **Location** West of Nuremberg, Bavaria (in modern Germany).

The Swedish launched repeated attacks on the well-positioned Imperial army, but rough terrain prevented them from making the best use of their artillery and cavalry. Unable to break through and desperately short of supplies, the Swedish withdrew to the north.

WITTSTOCK
4 OCTOBER 1636

Forces Imperial and Saxon: 18,600; Swedish: 18,000. **Casualties** Imperial and Saxon: 5,000; Swedish: 3,100. **Location** 95km (59 miles) northwest of Berlin, Germany.

Having set up a fortified position, the Imperial force was flanked by the Swedish and had to make a hurried redeployment. It was then attacked from another direction by a detached Swedish force and had to abandon its artillery as it retreated.

RHEINFELDEN 28 FEBRUARY 1638 AND 3 MARCH 1638

Forces Imperial and Bavarian: unknown; French and Allied: unknown. **Casualties** Imperial and Bavarian: unknown; French and Allied: unknown. **Location** (February) Northeast of Rheinfelden near Basel (in modern Germany); (March) South of Rheinfelden (in modern Switzerland).

After an inconclusive action on 28 February, the French pulled back to regroup their forces. The complacent Imperials were caught by surprise when the French attacked on 3 March, inflicting a major defeat.

SECOND BREITENFELD
2 NOVEMBER 1642

Forces Imperial: 20,000; Swedish: 22,000. **Casualties** Imperial: 15,000 plus 5,000 taken prisoner; Swedish: unknown. **Location** Outside Leipzig (in modern Germany).

Falling back after a failed attempt to take Vienna, the outnumbered Swedish forces regrouped at Breitenfeld and launched a sudden attack on the unprepared Imperials. A cavalry charge broke the Imperial left wing before it was properly deployed, permitting the centre in turn to be defeated. The Imperial right wing fought on for a time but was overwhelmed. This was the first occasion where cannon fired chain shot on land.

ROCROI 19 MAY 1643

Forces Spanish: 8,000 cavalry, 19,000 infantry; French: 7,000 cavalry, 15,000 infantry. **Casualties** Spanish: 8,000 killed, 7,000 prisoners; French: unknown. **Location** 90km (56 miles) northeast of Reims, France.

The cavalry of each side attacked successfully on their respective right wings. The French cavalry then charged through the centre and chased off the Spanish cavalry, who abandoned their infantry to encirclement.

JANKOV 5 MARCH 1645

Forces Imperial: 15,000; Swedish: 15,000. **Casualties** No reliable estimates. **Location** Near Prague (in modern Czech Republic).

The Swedish easily overpowered the Imperial infantry in a series of skirmishes in hilly and wooded terrain. The Imperial cavalry put up more resistance but suffered heavily as a result.

HERBSTHAUSEN 2 MAY 1645

Forces Bavarian: unknown; French: unknown. **Casualties** No reliable estimates. **Location** In modern Mergentheim, Germany.

After pursuing the Bavarian army into Württemburg, the French concluded that they were no longer a threat and entered their camp. The subsequent Bavarian attack caught the French unprepared and shattered their force.

SECOND NÖRDLINGEN
3 AUGUST 1645

Forces Imperial and Bavarian: 12,000. French and Allied: 12,000. **Casualties** Both forces: 5,000 each. **Location** Northwest of Munich (in modern Germany).

Repeated frontal attacks by the French eventually broke the Imperial positions, though at high cost on both sides. Strategically the battle was indecisive as the French were unable to follow up.

ZUSMARSHAUSEN 17 MAY 1648

Forces Imperial: unknown; Franco–Swedish: unknown. **Casualties** No reliable estimates. **Location** Near Munich (in modern southern Germany).

Badly outnumbered, the Imperial army attempted to fight a rearguard action with cavalry while the infantry and artillery disengaged. This was successful for a time but the Imperials were eventually forced to seek shelter in Landsberg.

LENS 20 AUGUST 1648

Forces Spanish: 18,000; French and Swedish: 16,000 . **Casualties** Spanish: 3,000 plus 5,000 prisoners; French and Swedish: 3,500. **Location** Pas-de-Calais, France.

The Spanish advanced towards Lens and were met by a French army, bringing about a series of skirmishes that escalated

IMPORTANT PEACE TREATIES

Date	Antagonists	Treaty	Outcome
1274 BCE	Egyptian kingdom of Ramesses II vs the Hittite kingdom of Hattusili III	Treaty of Kadesh	Established peace and set terms for the empires' coexistence in the Middle East.
445 BCE	Athens vs Sparta	Thirty Years Peace	Ended the First Peloponnesian War, although the peace actually lasted only 13 years, when in 432 BCE Athens attacked a colony that was allied to Corinth, one of Sparta's friends.
1215 CE	King John of England and his vassals	Magna Carta	Established the English legal principle that the king was bound by rights and responsibilities under law, as were his subjects.
1479	Republic of Venice vs the Ottoman empire	Treaty of Constantinople	Ended a 15-year war and compelled the Venetians to pay tribute to the Turkish Sultan in order to trade on the Black Sea.
1492	Catholic Spain vs the Moorish kingdom of Granada	Treaty of Granada	Ended the siege of Granada and established the supremacy of Isabella and Ferdinand of Castile, Aragon, Leon, and Sicily over all of Spain; also, the treaty guaranteed certain rights to religious freedom for Muslims living within the Catholic kingdom.
1639	Persia vs the Ottoman empire	Treaty of Zuhab	Helped shape the territorial boundaries of the Middle East, including the borders of the present-day states of Iran, Turkey, and Iraq.
1648	Roman Catholics vs Protestant factions in the Holy Roman empire, and allies of both sides, including France, Sweden, and England; the Spanish empire vs rebels in the Netherlands	Treaty of Westphalia	One of the treaties that ended the Thirty Years War (a conflict primarily among religious factions within the German states of the Holy Roman empire); the treaty limited the Holy Roman Empire's power in Europe and established the modern principle of state sovereignty, particularly over the issue of religious freedom; also, the treaty helped end the Eighty Years War (a revolt of the Netherlands against Spanish rule).
1701	France, the Huron, the Algonquian, vs the Iroquois Confederation	Great Peace of Montreal	Ended the war between France, her native allies, and the Iroquois Confederation (allied to the British).
1783	United States of America vs Great Britain	Second Treaty of Paris	Ended the American War of Independence, with King George III recognizing the independence of the United States.
1815	France vs Austria, Great Britain, Prussia and Russia.	Fourth Treaty of Paris	Ended Napoleon's Hundred Days campaign and compelled France to repay 700 million francs to the coalition.
1840	Great Britain and Maori chiefs	Treaty of Waitangi	Established New Zealand as a Crown Colony, considered the founding document of that nation today.
1854	United States and the empire of Japan	Convention of Kanegawa	Ended two centuries of Japanese isolationism and opened two ports to US trade after Commodore Matthew Perry negotiated with officials from the government of Tokugawa Ieyasu.
1919	Great Britain, France, and their Allies vs Imperial Germany allies including Austria-Hungary and the Ottoman empire	Treaty of Versailles	Formally ended World War I, including controversial provisions for Germany to accept responsibility for the war, disarm, and pay reparations to the nations allied against her.

17th-century Dutch musket
This unusual Dutch musket fires percussion caps but is fitted with redundant flint-and-match firing mechanisms, possibly as a failsafe against mechanical failure in either type of lock.

into a general engagement between two armies composed mainly of cavalry. The superior French cavalry won the day.

PRAGUE 1648

Forces Defenders: unknown; Swedish: unknown. **Casualties** No reliable estimates. **Location** Western bank of the Vltava river (in modern Czech Republic).

A Swedish independent unit attempted to take Prague but was fought to a standstill before entering the Old Town. Prague Castle was captured and looted by the Swedish. This was the final action of the Thirty Years War.

DUTCH REVOLT, LATER ACTIONS
1607–48

After a period of truce, the Dutch Revolt against Spanish rule flared up again. Political and military events of the later war became enmeshed with those of the Thirty Years War (1618–48). Both wars were ended in 1648.

GIBRALTAR 25 APRIL 1607

Forces Dutch: 30 ships; Spanish: 21 ships. **Casualties** Dutch: no ships lost; Spanish: 21 ships lost. **Location** Bay of Gibraltar, Spain.

Catching the Spanish fleet in Gibraltar Bay, the Dutch force doubled up on their opponents, attacking from both sides at once. Having smashed the fleet, the Dutch massacred many survivors in the water.

Pequot War
English colonial musketeers and swordsmen confront Native American warriors armed with bows and lances. in the Pequot War in Connecticut, USA.

SIEGE OF BREDA
28 AUGUST 1624–5 JUNE 1625

Forces Dutch: unknown; Spanish: unknown. **Casualties** No reliable estimates. **Location** North Brabant, The Netherlands.

The siege of Breda, a key Dutch border fortress, was carried out using a chain of defended strongpoints rather than trench lines. The starving defenders eventually accepted generous surrender terms.

BAY OF MATANZAS 1628

Forces Dutch: unknown; Spanish: 16 ships. **Casualties** Spanish: 16 ships captured. **Location** Caribbean Sea.

A Dutch naval force, sent to intercept the Spanish "treasure fleets" bringing silver from the Americas, laid an ambush in Matanzas Bay in the Caribbean. Part of the Spanish fleet was forewarned and avoided the trap, but 16 vessels were taken by the Dutch for virtually no loss. The captured funds were used to pay the Dutch army for several months.

THE DOWNS 31 OCTOBER 1639

Forces Dutch: 117 ships; Spanish: 77 ships. **Casualties** Dutch: unknown; Spanish: 70 ships destroyed or captured. **Location** Off the southern coast of England, east of Dover.

As the Spanish fleet approached Dunkirk in France it was ferociously attacked by the Dutch and driven into neutral English waters. The Dutch then brought up more vessels and most of the Spanish ships, trapped close to the English coast, were destroyed or captured.

LA MARFÉE 6 JULY 1641

Forces French: 13,000; Sedan and Allied: 11,000. **Casualties** French: 3,000 plus 5,500 prisoners; Sedan and Allied: unknown, but low. **Location** Sedan, northern France.

In a battle that was part of the Thirty Years War, the Sedanese, assisted by allied forces from Spain, the Papacy, and the Holy Roman empire, were able to resist a frontal attack by the French. The French were then hit in the flank by Sedanese cavalry and routed.

FAMOUS MILITARY MOTTOES

FREIBURG 3–10 AUGUST 1644

Forces French: 16,000; Imperial: 15,000. **Casualties** French: 8,000; Imperial: 5,000. **Location** Württemberg, southern Germany.

As part of the Thirty Years War conflict, the Imperials fought a determined defensive battle in an attempt to prevent the French from reducing Imperial fortresses along the Rhine. Outflanked, the Imperials withdrew and abandoned Freiburg.

HULST 1645

Forces Dutch: 15,000; Spanish: 2,750. **Casualties** Dutch: 1,600; Spanish: 2,500 including prisoners. **Location** Southwestern Netherlands.

An initial Dutch attack on the eastern side of the city went well despite a Spanish counterattack. Once established, the Dutch cannonaded the defenders into surrender. Hulst was the last major siege operation of the conflict.

MANILA 1645

Forces Dutch: 18 ships; Spanish: 4 ships. **Casualties** No reliable estimates. **Location** Philippines.

The Dutch sent a number of ships to attack Spanish possessions in the Philippines, bringing about a series of small-scale naval actions. The Spanish inflicted heavy losses on the Dutch, making an invasion of the Philippines impracticable.

PUERTO DE CAVITE 10 JUNE 1647

Forces Dutch: 12 ships; Spanish: unknown. **Casualties** Dutch: 2 ships; Spanish: unknown. **Location** Manila Bay, Philippines.

While attempting to blockade the Spanish in their port, the Dutch force came under artillery fire from shore batteries. Although a coastal fort was wrecked the Dutch were driven off. As a result, the blockade was lifted although the Dutch continued to harass shipping until the end of the war.

THE POWHATAN ATTACK IN VIRGINIA 22 MARCH 1622

Forces Powhatan: about 3,000 warriors; English: about 1,000 settlers. **Casualties** English: 347 killed; Powhatan: unknown. **Location** Coastal Virginia, USA.

Upon becoming leader of the Powatan Confederacy, Chief Opechancanough decided to eliminate Jamestown, a small English settlement in the Virginia Colony, which had previously been ignored. A surprise attack caused the deaths of 347 men, women and children, but the settlement survived.

SIEGE OF LA ROCHELLE
27 JUNE 1627–28 OCTOBER 1628

Forces Royalist: c.25,000; French: unknown. **Casualties** 18,600 die in La Rochelle; 2,000 English killed. **Location** Western France on the Bay of Biscay.

Continued religious conflict in France resulted in the renewed siege of La Rochelle, a city that tolerated Protestantism. After English troops sent to assist the Huguenot rebels were forced to retreat, the Royalist siege of the city tightened until most of the population starved to death. The survivors were forced to surrender.

PEQUOT WAR
AUGUST 1636–SEPTEMBER 1637

Forces Pequot: unknown; English settlers: 110; Mohicans and Narragansetts: 300. **Casualties** Over 500 Pequots killed; 2 English killed. **Location** Connecticut, USA.

After a series of raids and punitive expeditions, the Connecticut Militia with North American allies from the Narragansett and Mohican tribes attacked the Pequot village of Mystic, massacring the population. Any survivors were sold into slavery. The remainder of the Pequot tribe broke up.

IROQUOIS WARS 1640-98

Forces Iroquois: varied **Casualties** Unknown.
Location Eastern North America.

Beginning with attacks on Huron settlements, the Iroquois expanded their campaign to include attacks against French settlers. Punitive action brought a few years' peace, but fighting flared up again in 1693.

FALL OF BEIJING APRIL–JUNE 1644

Forces Manchu: c.170,000; Rebel: unknown. **Casualties** No reliable estimates. **Location** Northeast China.

With rebels in control of several provinces and the Ming dynasty under attack by the Manchu from the north, the dynasty fell and the rebels took Beijing unopposed. They were then defeated, and Beijing was taken by the Manchu.

BRITISH CIVIL WARS 1642–51

The conflict known as the British Civil Wars can be split into three English civil wars, all of which were fought between supporters of Parliament and those of the king, and Scottish and Irish rebellions. Royalist forces in the First Civil War, which ran 1642–46, and the Second, 1648–51, were led by King Charles I, who was executed in 1649; his son (later Charles II) led the Royalist forces in the Third Civil War, 1649–51. After Parliamentary victory in 1651, Britain had no king until 1661, when Charles II returned from exile.

POWICK BRIDGE 23 SEPTEMBER 1642

Forces Royalist: 1,000; Parliamentarian: 1,000.
Casualties Royalist: minimal; Parliamentarian: 140.
Location Worcester, West Midlands, England

In the early stages of the First Civil War, Parliamentary and Royalist cavalry unexpectedly came across each other near Worcester. The Royalists routed their opponents, establishing a superiority that lasted for some time.

EDGEHILL 23 OCTOBER 1642

Forces Royalist: 12,400; Parliamentarian: 15,000.
Casualties Royalist: 2,000; Parliamentarian: 2,000.
Location Warwickshire, England.

The first major battle of the First Civil War took place at Edgehill, between poorly trained, recently raised forces that in many cases lacked proper arms and equipment. As darkness fell, the Parliamentarians broke off the inconclusive encounter.

> " ... our men **pressing heavily** upon them, they could not bear it, but all their body **ran away.**"
>
> PARLIAMENTARIAN GENERAL, OLIVER CROMWELL ON A BRITISH CIVIL WAR BATTLE, JULY 1643

Musketeer's bandolier
Hollow wooden cartridges, each containing a measured powder charge, are suspended from this 17th-century musketeer's bandolier. The leather pouch holds lead balls for the matchlock arquebus.

BRENTFORD 12 NOVEMBER 1642

Forces Royalist: 12,000; Parliamentarian: 1,300.
Casualties Royalist: no reliable estimates; Parliamentarian: 170, and 400 prisoners. **Location** Middlesex, England.

The Royalist force launched a cavalry attack under cover of morning mist, surprising the Parliamentarians and putting much of their cavalry to flight.

STRATTON 16 MAY 1643

Forces Royalist: 2,900; Parliamentarian: 5,600. **Casualties** Royalist: no reliable estimates; Parliamentarian: 300 plus 1,700 prisoners. **Location** Cornwall, England.

The Royalists hoped, but failed, to achieve surprise. The resulting close-quarters action went on for eight hours before Royalist cavalry finally broke the opposition.

ROUNDWAY DOWN 13 JULY 1643

Forces Royalist: 3,800; Parliamentarian: 4,300. **Casualties** Royalist: no reliable estimates; Parliamentarian: 600 plus 1,000 prisoners. **Location** Wiltshire, England.

Royalist forces marching to the relief of troops besieged in Devizes were confronted by a Parliamentarian force on Roundway Down near the town. The Royalist cavalry swiftly broke the Parliamentarian wings, but their centre fought on until it was attacked in the rear by a force coming out of Devizes.

RELIEF OF NEWARK 21 MARCH 1644

Forces Royalist: 7,500; Parliamentarian: 7,000. **Casualties** Royalist: no reliable estimates; Parliamentarian: no reliable estimates. **Location** Newark-on-Trent, Nottinghamshire, England.

CHERITON 29 MARCH 1644

Forces Royalist: 6,000; Parliamentarian: 10,000. **Casualties** Royalist: 300; Parliamentarian: 60. **Location** Hampshire, England.

Outmanoeuvred, the Parliamentarian force decided to attack, bringing about a fight for Cheriton Wood. A disorganized Royalist cavalry attack was beaten off, after which the Royalist force retreated.

SIEGE OF YORK 22 APRIL–16 JULY 1644

Forces Royalist: 5,800; Parliamentarian: 14,000. **Casualties** Royalist: 1,000 plus 1,000 prisoners; Parliamentarian: no reliable estimates. **Location** North Yorkshire, England.

Gradually tightening the siege, the Parliamentarians pushed the defenders back to the medieval walls. After a failed relief attempt, which resulted in the battle of Marston Moor, the situation became hopeless and the city was surrendered.

CROPREDY BRIDGE 29 JUNE 1644

Forces Royalist: 9,000; Parliamentarian: 9,000. **Casualties** Royalist: no reliable estimates; Parliamentarian: 700. **Location** Near Banbury, Oxfordshire, England.

Learning that the Royalist army was strung out on the march, the Parliamentarians crossed the Cherwell river at Cropredy Bridge and attacked. After the Royalists fought to gain control of the bridge, the Parliamentarians were pushed back and broke contact that evening.

MARSTON MOOR 2 JULY 1644

Forces Royalist: 18,000; Parliamentarian and Scottish: 25,000. **Casualties** Royalist: 4,150 killed; Scottish and Parliamentarian: c.2,000 killed. **Location** 6km (4 miles) west of York, northern England.

A rapid Royalist approach and cavalry attack forced the Parliamentarian force besieging this important garrison to retire into an untenable position.

The Royalists were caught by surprise when the Parliamentarians attacked very late in the day. Breaking the Royalist right flank, the Parliamentarian cavalry then attacked the enemy rear and won a decisive victory.

NASEBY 14 JUNE 1645

Forces Royalist: 9,000; Parliamentarian: 14,000. **Casualties** Royalist: 400–1,000 killed; Parliamentarian: 150 killed. **Location** South of Leicester, England.

The Royalist cavalry smashed through the Parliamentarian left, but did not return to contribute further to the battle. The Parliamentarian cavalry broke the opposite flank and then fell on the Royalist centre, destroying the king's main army.

STOW-ON-THE-WOLD 21 MARCH 1646

Forces Royalist: 3,500; Parliamentarian: 3,100. **Casualties** Royalist: 1,000 prisoners; Parliamentarian: unknown. **Location** Gloucestershire, England.

Forced to stand and fight, the Royalist infantry won some initial successes, but its cavalry was broken. The infantry fought a rearguard action as it retired from this, the last major action of the First Civil War.

ST FAGANS 8 MAY 1648

Forces Royalist: 8,000; Parliamentarian: 2,700. **Casualties** Royalist: 200 plus 3,000 prisoners; Parliamentarian: unknown. **Location** West of Cardiff, Wales.

Unpaid Parliamentarian troops in Wales defected to the Royalist cause and fought against a force sent to deal with them. The Royalist flank was broken by Parliamentarian cavalry, causing the Royalist ranks to panic and collapse.

PRESTON 17–19 AUGUST 1648

Forces Scottish: 17,600; Parliamentarian: 8,600. **Casualties** Scottish: 1,000 killed; Parliamentarian: unknown. **Location** Northwest England.

Advancing through Lancashire, the Scottish forces were surprised by Parliamentarian forces that overran their road guards and secured Preston. The Parliamentarians then began a pursuit of the disorganized Scottish army.

DROGHEDA 11 SEPTEMBER 1649

Forces Royalist: 2,300; Parliamentarian: 12,000. **Casualties** Royalist and civilian: 3,500 killed; Parliamentarian: 150 killed. **Location** 45km (28 miles) north of Dublin, Ireland.

Despite the Royalist defenders' confidence in their defences, the walls were breached by artillery. Two assaults on the small breach were repelled, but the third was successful. The Parliamentarian army ran wild once inside the town.

DUNBAR 3 SEPTEMBER 1650

Forces Scottish Royalist: 20,000; Parliamentarian: 11,000. **Casualties** Scottish Royalist: 3,000 killed; Parliamentarian: 20–40 killed. **Location** East Lothian, 48km (30 miles) east of Edinburgh, Scotland.

Launching a surprise attack across a ravine, the Parliamentarians met with determined resistance until their reserve cavalry drove in the Scottish flank. The Scottish army broke up and was routed.

INVERKEITHING 20 JULY 1651

Forces Scottish Royalist: 4,500; Parliamentarian: 4,500. **Casualties** Scottish Royalist: 2,000 plus 1,400 taken prisoner; Parliamentarian: low. **Location** Firth of Forth, Scotland.

Outflanking Scottish forts around Stirling with a landing in Fife, the Parliamentarians beat off an attack on their bridgehead and advanced against the Scots army. Victory at Inverkeithing tipped the strategic balance in Scotland in favour of the Parliamentarians.

WORCESTER 3 SEPTEMBER 1651

Forces Royalist: 16,000; Parliamentarian: 31,000. **Casualties** Royalist: 3,000 plus 10,000 or more prisoners; Parliamentarian: 200. **Location** West Midlands, England.

Marston Moor, 2 July 1644
Oliver Cromwell and his New Model Army ride to battle at Marston Moor. Note the distinctive "lobster tail" helmet of one mounted soldier (far left), and the crested burgeonet helmet of an armoured trooper (right).

The final battle of the Civil War was fought on both banks of the Severn river. The Parliamentarians were able to shift troops using pontoon bridges, and eventually gained the upper hand. The Royalist army was almost completely destroyed, but Charles II managed to escape and made his way to France.

SIEGE OF YANGZHOU MAY 1645

Forces Ming: unknown; Manchu: unknown. **Casualties** Hundreds of thousands killed in Yangzhou massacre. **Location** On the Grand Canal, northeast of Nanjing, China.

Surviving members of the Ming dynasty resisted the Manchu invaders, proclaiming an emperor in Nanjing. The Manchu stormed the city after a seven-day siege. The populace was massacred.

CAMPAIGNS OF SHIVAJI MAHARAJ 1646–80

Forces Maratha confederacy: unknown; Mogul: unknown. **Casualties** No reliable estimates. **Location** Central India.

Shivaji Maharaj fought a successful guerrilla campaign against the weakening Mogul empire, increasing his power and influence. His religious tolerance meant that both Hindus and Muslims were willing to serve in his forces.

THE DUNES 3 JUNE 1658

Forces Anglo-French: 15,000; Spanish and Allied: 14,000. **Casualties** Anglo-French: 400; Spanish and Allied: 1,000 plus 5,000 prisoners. **Location** Near Dunkirk, France.

Spanish forces, including a contingent of English Royalists, attempted to break the Anglo-French siege of Dunkirk. The result was a Spanish defeat.

KING PHILIP'S WAR JUNE 1675–76

Forces British: unknown; Wampanoag: unknown. **Casualties** British: 600; Wampanoag: 3,000. **Location** Massachusetts, Connecticut, Rhode Island, and Maine, USA.

"King Philip" was the English name for Metacomet, chief of the Wampanoag. He conducted a campaign of raids against the settlers until British troops arrived and gradually wore down his power.

ACTS OF MUTINY

Most of us are familiar with the term "mutiny" when meaning a rebellion by sailors against their commanding officers. But mutiny may also occur among the ranks of military and police forces on land. In some cases, mutinies have influenced significant changes in the course of history. The laws of most of the world's navies and armies state that those found to have conspired or taken part in an armed rebellion must be severely punished, and execution was a frequent punishment. In 1842, for example, a midshipman and two sailors on the brig USS *Somers* were hanged in the rigging for plotting to murder their officers and hijack their ship for piracy.

Mutinies in England's New Model Army (1647-49)

In the early phase of the Second English Civil War, some soldiers mutinied within Oliver Cromwell's New Model Army. At Corkbush Field, Hertfordshire in 1647, Cromwell's men tried and convicted nine conspirators, one of whom was shot as an example. At Bishopsgate, London in April 1649, after the regicide of Charles I, the army quelled another revolt and hanged its leader. And in May 1649, Cromwell's soldiers put down a final uprising by 400 mutinous troopers near Banbury, Oxfordshire. The army arrested and executed three ringleaders by firing squad.

Mutiny aboard HMS Bounty (1789)

During an expedition to Tahiti, 19 members of HMS *Bounty*'s crew mutinied. They were led by acting Lieutenant Fletcher Christian, who put Captain William Bligh and 18 loyal crewmen adrift in one of *Bounty*'s open boats. Bligh's ordeal became one of the great feats of navigation in British naval history, as he captained his small craft 3,618 nautical miles (about 6,705km) to the Dutch colonial harbour at Timor. Of the mutineers, many were put ashore in Tahiti and later faced courts martial. The admiralty found five guilty, hanged three, and pardoned two. Fletcher Christian and eight other mutineers, along with 17 Tahitian men and women, escaped to settle the Pitcairn Islands, where some of their descendants live today.

The Sepoy mutiny in India (1857)

In 1857, a series of mutinies in regiments of the British East India Company military service pitted some native Sepoys (from a Persian word for soldier) against their European officers. The mutinies were primarily caused by native Indian dissatisfaction with British social policies. When order was restored in 1858, the uprising had effectively ruined the East India Company and marked the beginning of the British Raj, direct imperial rule in India.

The Russian battleship Potemkin (1905)

The crew of the Black Sea Fleet battleship *Potemkin* rose against the Russian Imperial Navy's harsh discipline, killed seven of their officers, and used their ship's guns to support a rebellion in the Ukrainian city, Odessa. The mutiny foreshadowed and became a model for the uprisings of the Russian Revolution in 1917, which overthrew the tsar and laid the foundation for the Soviet Union.

Bangladesh Rifles (2009)

In February 2009, the Bangladesh Rifles, a police force that guards that nation's borders, rebelled demanding greater pay and more autonomy from the army. The mutineers murdered many of the army officers appointed to lead them and held others hostage at their headquarters in Dhaka, and at bases in other towns. The siege ended when the army surrounded the rebels with tanks and artillery and arrested more than 200 mutineers.

DRUMCLOG 1 JUNE 1679

Forces Covenanter: 1,500; Government: 150. **Casualties** Covenanter: very low; Government: 40. **Location** South Lanarkshire, southeast of Glasgow, Scotland.

During his reign, England's King Charles II imposed ever tighter controls over religious non-conformists in his kingdom.

This led to open revolt by the Presbyterian Covenanters of southwest Scotland. Covenanter rebels met government cavalry near Drumclog. After some skirmishing the government troops were driven off. Soon after, the Covenanters then tried to take Glasgow, but failed.

BOTHWELL BRIDGE 22 JUNE 1679

Forces Covenanter: 6,000; Government: 5,500. **Casualties** Covenanter: 400 plus 1,200 prisoners; Government: light. **Location** Near Glasgow, Scotland.

Responding to the defeat at Drumclog, a government force attacked and defeated the Covenanters at Bothwell Bridge, which put an end to the Covenanter rising.

PUEBLO REVOLT
AUGUST–SEPTEMBER 1680

Forces (At Santa Fe) Pueblo: 2,500; Spanish: about 1,000. **Casualties** Pueblo: unknown; Spanish: about 400 killed. **Location** New Mexico, USA.

Provoked into revolt by religious intolerance and demands for labour, the Pueblo forced the Spanish settlers to seek safety in Santa Fe, which was then besieged. The Spanish retired to El Paso.

Siege of Vienna, 1683
Ottoman Grand Vizier Kara-Mustapha Pasha's janissaries clash disastrously with the combined Austrian, Polish, and German armies at the siege of Vienna.

AUSTRO–OTTOMAN CONFLICTS 1683–87

Conflict over the Balkans was unremitting between Austria and the Ottoman empire for many decades. Austria was supported by various Christian states (the "Holy League"), acting as a buffer to prevent further Ottoman advances into Europe.

SIEGE OF VIENNA
16 JULY–12 SEPTEMBER, 1683

Forces Ottoman: 150,000–200,000; Holy League: 12,000, John Sobieski's relief army: 75,000–80,000. **Casualties** No reliable estimates. **Location** Austria.

The siege made slow progress, relying on mining rather than cannon to breach the walls. At the eleventh hour a Polish-Lithuanian force arrived and routed the Ottoman army.

SECOND BATTLE OF MOHÁCS
12 AUGUST 1687

Forces Ottoman: 80,000; Holy League: 60,000. **Casualties** Ottoman: over 10,000; Holy League: around 1,000. **Location** On the Danube river (in modern Hungary).

Attempting to halt Christian expansion into the Balkans, the Ottoman army was decisively defeated at Mohács. Austria gained control over Hungary, and the Ottoman Sultan was deposed.

ZENTA 11 SEPTEMBER 1697

Forces Ottoman: unknown; Holy League: 50,000. **Casualties** Ottoman: 30,000 killed or taken prisoner; Holy League: 300 killed. **Location** Northern Serbia.

The Holy League waited until the Ottoman cavalry had crossed the Tisza

Mogul empire shield
Warriors of the Indian Mogul empire (c.1526–mid-19th century) carried round shields called *dahl*, such as this finely etched and gilded steel example, left.

river before destroying their pontoon bridge. The Ottoman infantry, cut off and unsupported, were then crushed by the Holy League.

ALBAZIN 1685–86

Forces Chinese: possibly 10,000; Russian: a few hundred. **Casualties** Unknown. **Location** On the Amur river, northern Manchuria, China.

Seeking to remove foreign settlers from their territory, the Chinese drove the Russians out of Albazin in 1685. The next year the Russians returned, but were once again defeated, establishing a border more to Chinese liking.

SEDGEMOOR 6 JULY 1685

Forces Government: 2,500; Rebel: 3,700. **Casualties** Government: 300; Rebel: 1,000 plus 500 prisoners. **Location** Somerset, western England.

Rebel forces under Protestant Duke of Monmouth, illegitimate son of Charles

II, who hoped to seize the throne, launched a night attack on the camp of government troops sent to suppress the rebels. A counterattack scattered them. The Duke of Monmouth was captured soon after and executed.

EARLY JACOBITE UPRISINGS
1689–90

The initial Jacobite risings were aimed at restoring Catholic James VII of Scotland and II of England to the throne. Fighting took place in Scotland and Ireland, with Irish troops also sent to assist the Scots. Defeat at the battle of the Boyne ended any realistic chance of success, and the first rising failed.

KILLIEKRANKIE
27 JULY 1689

Forces Government (mainly Lowland Scots): 3,500; Jacobite (mainly Highland Scots and Irish): 2,400. **Casualties** Government: 2,000; Jacobite: 800. **Location** Near Pitlochry, Scotland.

After a lengthy exchange of musketry, the Jacobites advanced downhill from their defensive position, reaching the enemy line before many government soldiers fixed their plug bayonets. The government force was routed, though at heavy cost.

MILITARY AND NAVAL CODES

Type of cryptography	Principle(s)	Characteristics
Substitution cipher	Substitution replaces the letters according to a preselected pattern within the words of a message. Sometimes symbols are substituted for letters. The simplest uses a single alphabet, but some very complex systems use a substitution grid of 26 x 26 letters. One such system dates to the 15th century and was developed by the French diplomat Blaise de Vigenère.	The weakness of substitution systems is that longer messages allow cryptanalysts (those who decipher code systems) more opportunities to see patterns in the substitutions. The American writer Edgar Allen Poe, a talented amateur cryptanalyst, wrote about such a cipher and its unravelling in the story *The Gold Bug*.
Transposition cipher	In its simplest form, transposition involves jumbling the letters of a message according to a mathematical key or algorithm, which only the intended recipient possesses.	Variations of transposition ciphers have often been used in military history. For example, by the US Army during the US Civil War, and by the Imperial German Army during World War I.
Enigma/Ultra	Enigma, developed for the military, naval, and special police forces of the German Third Reich in World War II, used electrical and mechanical means (such as stepped rotors) to encrypt text typed into the machine's keyboard.	The British, Polish, and French cracked the Enigma cipher and collected information undetected by the Germans under the code name "Ultra". These intercepts helped the Allies plan and carry out major operations, including the invasion of Normandy in 1944.
JN25	The Imperial Japanese Navy (IJN) used JN25, which comprised a number of mathematical keys, which had to be selected from a book of key tables, to encode or decipher encrypted text.	Allied naval and military intelligence units broke some versions of JN25 before World War II, but the IJN continued to update the code. A version of this code, which was broken in 1942, helped the Americans anticipate the Japanese attack at Midway Island, where the US Navy caught the IJN in a devastating ambush.
US National Security Agency (NSA) Suite B	The length (in bits, or 1s and zeros) of the key or algorithm used to decipher a coded message is one measure of its strength. US government ciphers currently use 256-bit and 384-bit keys. Internet websites that offer secure transactions use at least 128-bit keys.	NSA Suite B is a published standard for the types of algorithms that are used to secure classified information in US government computer systems. Another set of algorithms, not published, is set aside for essential national security systems, possibly including launch communications for strategic nuclear deterrent forces.

NEWTOWNBUTLER
31 JULY 1689

Forces Williamite: 2,000; Jacobite: 3,000. **Casualties** Williamite: unknown, but few; Jacobite: 2,000 plus 400 prisoners. **Location** Near Enniskillen, Northern Ireland.

Responding to guerrilla raids by Williamite irregulars, a Jacobite force was lured into an ambush and attempted to give battle. The Jacobite force rapidly disintegrated and was pursued.

DUNKELD
21 AUGUST 1689

Forces Government: 1,200; Jacobite: 4,000. **Casualties** Government: no reliable estimates; Jacobite: 300. **Location** 24km (15 miles) north of Perth, Scotland.

Jacobite forces attempted to storm Dunkeld, which was held by government troops. After hours of heavy fighting in the streets, the Jacobites withdrew when their ammunition ran out.

CROMDALE
30 APRIL–1 MAY 1690

Forces Government: unknown, but superior; Jacobite: 1,200. **Casualties** Government: likely fewer than 100; Jacobite: 400 including prisoners. **Location** Speyside, Scotland.

A depleted Jacobite force on the march encountered a government detachment at Cromdale. Severely pressed by government cavalry, the Jacobites slipped away in the fog. Defeat at Cromdale effectively ended the uprising in Scotland.

THE BOYNE
12 JULY 1690

Forces Williamite: 35,000; Jacobite: 21,000. **Casualties** Williamite: 500; Jacobite: 1,500. **Location** Near Drogheda, east coast of modern Republic of Ireland.

Unable to dislodge the Williamite infantry, who had forced a crossing of the Boyne, the Jacobites were then forced to retire when the opposing cavalry crossed the river. Defeat at the Boyne ended any chance of success for the uprising.

WAR OF THE GRAND ALLIANCE
1688–97

Expansionism on the part of Louis XIV of France led to the formation of the Grand Alliance, an opposition coalition consisting primarily of England, the Dutch Republic, the Holy Roman empire, and the Duchy of Savoy. France had few allies other than the Jacobite factions in Ireland. The war continued until all parties were financially exhausted.

BANTRY BAY
11 MAY 1689

Forces French: 24 ships; English: 19 ships. **Casualties** French: no ships lost; English: no ships lost. **Location** County Cork, southwest Ireland.

The English fleet sought to prevent French transports from offloading arms destined for Jacobite forces in Ireland. The resulting action was not conclusive and the transports were able to offload.

> "It **cannot be denied** that they defended themselves **bravely**, especially the **companies of janissaries.**"
>
> KING JOHN III SOBIESKI OF POLAND ON THE OTTOMAN DEFEAT AT VIENNA, 1683

BEACHY HEAD
30 JUNE 1690

Forces French: 70 ships; Anglo-Dutch: 70 ships. **Casualties** Dutch: 13 ships sunk, 1 captured; French: no ships lost. **Location** English Channel, off the coast of East Sussex England.

During this battle for control of the English Channel, the Dutch squadron closed with their opponents before the English were ready, and were mauled by the French in the subsequent one-sided fight. The channel temporarily fell into French hands, and the allied fleet fell back in disorder, fleeing to the Thames river.

FLEURUS
1 JULY 1690

Forces Dutch, Spanish, and Imperial: 38,000; French: 35,000. **Casualties** Dutch, Spanish, and Imperial: 11,000 plus 8,000 prisoners; French: 6,000. **Location** Province of Hainault (in modern Belgium).

The French occupied the allies' interest with a frontal infantry attack, then, hidden by the terrain, divided their forces to carry out a double envelopment with cavalry. The battle was a clear tactical success for the French but was not followed up to create a strategic benefit.

STAFFARDA
18 AUGUST 1690

Forces French: 12,000; Spanish and Savoyard: 18,000. **Casualties** French: 2,000; Spanish and Savoyard: 2,800 plus 1,200 prisoners; **Location** 60km (37 miles) southwest of Turin, Italy.

French demands forced Savoy to join the Grand Alliance, which in turn resulted in a punitive campaign by French forces. In a hard-fought action at Staffarda, the Savoyards with their Spanish allies were defeated and their lands devastated.

LEUZE 18 SEPTEMBER 1691

Forces French: 28 squadrons; Anglo-Dutch: 72 squadrons of cavalry. **Casualties** French: 400; Anglo-Dutch: 1,500–2,000. **Location** Leuze-en-Hainau (in modern Belgium).

A force of Allied cavalry attacked the French rearguard, also composed entirely of cavalry. The French relied on shock action with the sword rather than firearms, and won a decisive victory despite being heavily outnumbered.

STEENKERQUE 3 AUGUST 1692

Forces French: 80,000; Grand Alliance: 80,000. **Casualties** French: 8,000; Grand Alliance: 10,000. **Location** 50km (31 miles) southwest of Brussels (in modern Belgium).

Catching the French by surprise, the Allied force launched an attack on their camp. After initial success the Allied force became disorganized, enabling the French to form a solid line. After a period of confused fighting the Allies withdrew.

LAGOS 27 JUNE 1693

Forces French: 70 warships plus auxiliaries; Anglo-Dutch: 16 warships plus 200 or more merchant vessels. **Casualties** French: no ships lost; Anglo-Dutch: 90 merchant ships destroyed or captured. **Location** Algarve, Portugal.

Intercepted en route to the Mediterranean, the Anglo-Dutch convoy scattered when the French approached. Despite the best efforts of the vastly outnumbered escort, large numbers of Anglo-Dutch merchant ships were lost.

NEERWINDEN (LANDEN)
29 JULY 1693

Forces French: 80,000; Dutch: 50,000; **Casualties** French: 9,000; Dutch: 19,000. **Location** Flemish Brabant, Belgium.

Mounted Ottoman warrior
From the middle of the 15th century, the threat of Turkish invasion inspired popular themes in central and southern European art. This Italian dish depicts a mounted Ottoman warrior bordered by Islamic-style designs.

> "Blessed be those happy ages that were strangers to the dreadful fury of these **devilish instruments of artillery** ... "
>
> MIGUEL DE CERVANTES ON THE USE OF CANNONS IN BATTLE, 1615

The outnumbered Dutch army benefited from better artillery than their opponents and resisted attack for some time. The French cavalry eventually broke through and the Dutch suffered heavy losses.

MARSAGLIA
4 OCTOBER 1693

Forces French: 35,000; Savoyard and Spanish: 30,000. **Casualties** French: 1,800; Savoyard and Spanish: 10,000 including prisoners. **Location** Near Turin, Italy.

The French stood on the defensive, occupying a good position. A frontal attack by Savoyard forces was repulsed with heavy casualties.

TORROELLA
27 MAY 1694

Forces French: 24,000; Spanish: 16,000–24,000. **Casualties** French: 3,000 including prisoners; Spanish 500. **Location** Near Girona, Catalonia, Spain.

French troops crossed the Ter river unobserved, catching the Spanish force by surprise. The Spanish fell back in disorder, retiring on Girona.

SIEGE OF NAMUR
1 SEPTEMBER 1695

Forces French: 13,000; Allied: unknown. **Casualties** French: 8,000; Allied: no reliable estimates. **Location** Southern Belgium.

Namur was the site of one of 90 fortresses designed by the Marquis de Vauban (1633–1707) and based on mathematical principles. Besieged by an army from England, Bavaria, and Brandenburg, Namur held out for three months.

JAO MODO 1696

Forces Chinese: 80,000; Zhungar: unknown. **Casualties** No reliable estimates. **Location** Mongolia, south of Ulan Bator.

Pre-empting the rise of the Zhungar tribes as a new power in Mongolia, the Chinese sent large forces across the Gobi desert. Chinese artillery played an important part in the Zhungar defeat.

GREAT NORTHERN WAR
1700–21

The Great Northern War was fought over control of the Baltic, though combat took place as far away as the Ukraine. Sweden fought an alliance of Denmark, Poland, Lithuania, Russia, and Saxony. By the end of the war Russia dominated the Baltic.

NARVA 30 NOVEMBER 1700

Forces Swedish: 8,000; Russian: 40,000. **Casualties** Swedish: light; Russian: up to 10,000 killed. **Location** Northeastern Estonia.

A small Swedish force sent to relieve the besieged garrison at Narva attacked the Russian camp under cover of a snowstorm. After a long hand-to-hand struggle the Russians were finally driven off.

INFANTRY COMBAT RANGES THROUGHOUT HISTORY

The assumption is that, as weapon technology has improved over time, combat range has increased. However, even on today's high-tech battlefields, the modern infantryman must often close with his enemy in order to defeat him.

Soldiers	Period	Combat range
Egyptian charioteers armed with bows	16th century BCE	Closed quickly to 183–274m (200–300yd), loosed arrows, and then retired out of danger
Chinese armed with repeating crossbows	341–200 BCE	Range of 165–183m (180–200yd), but most effective at close range of 73m (80yd) or less
English longbowmen at battle of Crécy	August 1346	Range 165–330m (180–361yd) for effective mass volleys at a rate of 12–15 arrows per minute, per archer; a range of 80m (90yd) or less was required for accurate target shooting
French knights at Agincourt, mounted and fully caparisoned with lance and sword	October 1415	Range of 3m (10ft) or less, in one-to-one contact
British Army regiment, formed square at the battle of Waterloo, with the Brown Bess .75 calibre musket and bayonet	1815	Range of 73–91m (80–100yd); but also in one-to-one contact, when using the bayonet to defend against charging cavalry
US Marine Corps rifle company with the M16A2 assault rifle	Modern-day	Range of 274–457m (300–500yd)

THE DUNA 9 JULY 1701

Forces Swedish: 7,000; Polish and Saxon: 19,000.
Casualties Swedish: 500; Polish and Saxon: 2,000.
Location Riga, Livonia, modern Latvia.

The Swedish forces made a crossing of the Duna river in boats, surprising the Allied forces on the far bank. Despite a vigorous counterattack, the Swedish held their bridgehead as additional forces were ferried across to reinforce them.

GEMAUERTHOF 16 JULY 1705

Forces Swedish: 7,000; Russian: 12,000. **Casualties** Swedish: 1,000; Russian: 2,000–6,000. **Location** 80km (50 miles) southwest of Riga (in modern Latvia).

Although tired from a forced march, the Swedish launched a series of attacks on the Russians. In the ensuing melée the Swedish outfought their opponents, driving off the Russian cavalry and overrunning the infantry.

WARSAW 31 JULY 1705

Forces Swedish: 2,000; Saxon and Polish: 9,500. **Casualties** Swedish: 300; Saxon and Polish: 1,500. **Location** Polish-Lithuanian Commonwealth (modern Poland).

Although outnumbered, the Swedish launched an aggressive cavalry attack, achieving some success. A counterattack was derailed by the fire of a small detachment of Swedish infantry that had stayed concealed until that point, and the Swedish gradually defeated their remaining opponents.

FRAUSTADT 13 FEBRUARY 1706

Forces Swedish: 9,400; Russian, Saxon, and Polish: 18,000–25,000. **Casualties** Swedish: 1,400; Russian, Saxon, and Polish: 7,377 plus 7,300–7,900 prisoners. **Location** Wschowa in modern Poland.

The Allied force took up a defensive position because the Swedish side had more cavalry. The Allied flanks were defeated by Swedish cavalry, which then fell on the Allied rear. Combined with a frontal attack by infantry, this caused a disintegration of the Allied line.

POLTAVA 8 JULY 1709

Forces Swedish: 14,000; Russian: 42,000. **Casualties** Swedish: 10,000 killed/captured; Russian: 1,300 killed. **Location** Eastern Ukraine.

Ignoring his advisors, Charles XII of Sweden ordered an assault on Poltava. Poor reconnaissance and communications resulted in a badly coordinated and ultimately unsuccessful assault. Swedish military power declined rapidly thereafter.

HELSINGBORG 28 FEBRUARY 1710

Forces Swedish 14,000; Danish: 14,000. **Casualties** Swedish: 2,995; Danish: 5,000 plus 2,677 prisoners. **Location** Southern Sweden.

Re-entering the war, Danish forces invaded Sweden. The Swedish raised a new army and sent it to cut Danish supply lines. The Danish force slowly fell apart.

OSEL AND GRENGAM: OSEL 24 MAY 1719; GRENGAM 27 JULY 1720

Forces Osel: 6 Russian warships; Grengam: 61 Russian ships, 4 Swedish frigates, 1 warship. **Casualties** Osel: 2 Swedish ships sunk; Grengam: 4 Swedish frigates captured. **Location** Off Osel Island, Estonia.

The Russian navy, established in 1700, won its first major victory in 1719 at Osel. A year later the Russian fleet lured Swedish warships into shallow water, where they were overwhelmed.

WAR OF THE SPANISH SUCCESSION 1701–14

The death of Charles II of Spain created a situation in which Spain and France might be united under a single monarch. This was unacceptable to many nations of Europe. The resulting dispute expanded into a general war as various states pursued their own agendas, not all of them directly connected with the fate of the Spanish throne.

CARPI 9 JULY 1701

Forces Austrian: 30,000; French: 25,000. **Casualties** Austrian: no reliable estimates; French: no reliable estimates. **Location** Near Modena, Italy.

After several weeks of manoeuvring, the Austrians crossed the Adige river and drove off the French cavalry encountered at Carpi. This small action was the first battle of the war. Both sides then spent some time concentrating their forces and re-establishing supply lines.

Prince Eugene of Savoy

A brilliant commander in the service of the Austrian Habsburgs, Prince Eugene (1663–1736) fought in the War of the Spanish Succession in partnership with England's Duke of Malborough.

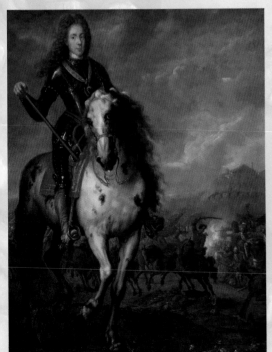

RELIGIOUS WARRIOR GROUPS

Shaolin monks, Henan Province, China, founded c.497

The monks of Shaolin are famous for their development of open hand and armed martial arts styles, which they cultivate in addition to Buddhist asceticism. The many fighting styles developed by Shaolin masters over the centuries may have influenced some other martial arts styles, such as some forms of karate.

Sohei warrior monks, Japan c.900

Some Buddhist monks in Japan chose to follow both a martial and religious lifestyle, with many devoted to the practice of Zen Buddhism. Warrior monks had a role in some of the most turbulent periods in Japanese military history, including the Gempei War in the 12th century. Some Sohei orders grew very powerful, and were able to field armies, especially during the Japanese civil wars of the 16th century.

KHALSA WARRIOR

The Knights Templar 1118

The Knights Templar were among the first military monastic orders founded during the crusades in Palestine. The Templars, having taken their name from the Temple Mount in Jerusalem where they were billeted, swore to protect Christian pilgrims to the Holy Land. As the order gained favour with the papacy, the Templars gradually grew more powerful, eventually becoming bankers to many of Europe's kingdoms. In the 1300s, the order's status as moneylenders led to a dispute with the French crown. In 1314, the French arrested the order's grandmaster, Jacques de Molay, and tried and burned him at the stake for heresy.

Sikh Khalsa, Punjab province, India 1699

The Khalsa began as an elite religious order, with male and female disciples within Sikhism. Members of the Khalsa were expected to follow a strict code of conduct. In addition to their religious devotion and adherence to the principles of the Sikh gurus, the Khalsa also trained as warriors to defend their brethren against oppression. At that time, the Muslim Moguls of India persecuted Sikhs and Hindus who did not convert to Islam.

CÁDIZ 23 AUGUST–3 SEPTEMBER 1702

Forces Spanish: 1,000 plus local militia; Anglo-Dutch: 14,000. **Casualties** Spanish: unknown, but light; Anglo-Dutch: unknown, but light. **Location** The coast of southern Spain.

Early in the war, Anglo-Dutch forces attempted to capture the port of Cádiz in order to obtain a Spanish base and trigger local uprisings. The expedition failed, largely due to looting by the Anglo-Dutch troops, which reduced the force's ability to fight effectively.

VIGO BAY 23 OCTOBER 1702

Forces French and Spanish: 18 warships plus smaller vessels; Anglo-Dutch: 25 warships plus frigates and fireships. **Casualties** French and Spanish: all ships lost; Anglo-Dutch: no ships lost. **Location** Off the coast of Galicia, Spain.

Retiring from the failed expedition at Cádiz, the Anglo-Dutch fleet was able to attack a treasure fleet en route to Spain from the Americas. The attack was a total success, offsetting defeat at Cádiz.

BLENHEIM 13 AUGUST 1704

Forces English and Allies: 52,000; French: 56,000. **Casualties** French: 30,000; English and Allies: 13,000. **Location** 15km (10 miles) west of Donauworth (in modern Germany).

The battle was a turning point in the war. Realizing that the French army was overextended, the English set about defeating isolated sections of it. The French centre, consisting of unsupported cavalry, was routed.

VELEZ-MÁLAGA 24 AUGUST 1704

Forces Anglo-Dutch: 56 ships; French and Spanish: 59 warships, 7 fireships. **Casualties** Anglo-Dutch: 1,600; French and Spanish: 2,700. **Location** Off Málaga, Spain.

In some cases still short of ammunition from the capture of Gibraltar, the Anglo-Dutch force confronted a Franco-Spanish fleet off Málaga. Despite heavy damage and considerable casualties on both sides, the action was inconclusive, benefiting the Anglo-Dutch strategic position.

TURIN 14 MAY–7 SEPTEMBER 1706

Forces French and Spanish: 44,000–47,000; Austrian, Prussian, and Savoyard: 30,000. **Casualties** French and Spanish: no reliable estimates; Austrian, Prussian, and Savoyard: no reliable estimates. **Location** Piedmont region, northern Italy.

In a decisive victory for the Allied forces under Eugene of Savoy, the Franco-Spanish siege of Turin was broken, causing the beginning of the withdrawal of French forces from northern Italy.

RAMILLIES 23 MAY 1706

Forces Anglo-Dutch: 62,000; French: 60,000. **Casualties** Anglo-Dutch: 2,500; French: 22,000, and 6,000 prisoners. **Location** Banks of Mehaigne river, near Namur, Belgium.

Catching the French forces overextended and in vulnerable, swampy positions, the Anglo-Dutch army first attacked the flanks. This pulled troops from the French centre, which was then assaulted. Despite a tough rearguard action, the Anglo-Dutch forces soundly defeated the French army.

DEVELOPMENT OF THE BAYONET

For more than 400 years, one of the infantry soldier's most important weapons was the bayonet. The most basic form was a blade that attached to the muzzle of a long-arm (such as a musket or rifle), allowing the gun to function as a pike, spear, or similar pole weapon in close-quarters battle. This innovation allowed the light infantry tactics of the musketeer to be combined with the heavy infantry tactics of the pikeman and grenadier, within the same troop formation. The European bayonet may have originated in Spain at the end of the 16th century, with the introduction of daggerlike plug bayonets, which fitted into the muzzle. Later, socketed bayonets were developed. These enabled a combatant to load and fire the weapon without having to remove the blade. Despite its antique origin, the bayonet continues to be issued to soldiers of many of the world's most advanced armies.

Era	Innovation	Description
c.1580 CE	Plug-type bayonet	This was the simplest form of bayonet; as its name implies, it fitted into the muzzle and blocked the barrel, so that the gun could be fired only with the bayonet removed.
c.1670	Socket bayonet	The socket, probably introduced by the French, fitted the bayonet over the muzzle, allowing the musket to be fired without removing the bayonet; most European armies quickly adopted the socketed bayonet.
c.1715	Triangular blade	Early experiments taught that, generally speaking, bayonets with long triangular cross-sections were stronger in the charge and thrust than single or double-edged blades; typical 18th-century bayonets were acutely pointed triangular blades of about 55cm (21in).
19th century	Locking socket	In the late 18th century, some armies issued socket bayonets with spring clips to help secure the blade; in the 1800s, a ring was added to the socket to lock the bayonet onto the firearm.
c.1800	Sword bayonet	From the 17th century, armies experimented with many types of long, swordlike bayonets. These allowed the musket or rifle to be used as a slashing pole arm. One form of sabre bayonet popular with rifle-armed troops during the 19th century was the *yataghan* blade. This had a shallow double curve, which improved the weapon's cutting properties on the muzzle, or as a sidearm.
c.1871	Knife bayonet	Modern bayonets are typically shaped like large fighting knives, allowing the bayonet to function as a handy field tool (for opening containers of food, or for various roles in survival woodcraft).

Socket bayonet
This 19th-century bayonet is fitted with a ring latch that locks it securely onto the muzzle of a musket's barrel.

CASTIGLIONE
8 SEPTEMBER 1706

Forces French: unknown; Hesse-Kassel: 23,000. **Casualties** French: 8,000; Hesse-Kassel: no reliable estimates. **Location** 30km (18 miles) northwest of Mantua, Italy.

Part of the French force in northern Italy was drawn off by the Allies' attack at Turin. The remainder marched to attack a Hessian army, which was besieging Castiglione delle Stiviere. The Hessians were defeated and driven off.

ALMANZA 25 APRIL 1707

Forces English, Dutch, and Portuguese: 22,000; French and Spanish: 25,000. **Casualties** English, Dutch, and Portuguese: 5,000, plus 12,000 prisoners; French: 3,500. **Location** Near Albacete, southeastern Spain.

After an artillery duel the English contingent attacked in the centre. Franco-Spanish cavalry counterattacked and broke the Portuguese cavalry, which led to a general collapse. This eliminated the main Allied army in Spain.

OUDENARDE 11 JULY 1708

Forces English, Dutch, Prussian, and Imperial: 105,000; French: 100,000. **Casualties** English, Dutch, Prussian, and Imperial: 3,000; French: 15,000, including prisoners. **Location** East Flanders, Belgium.

Considerable Allied forces were able to cross the Schelde river before they were detected. A French attack to dislodge their bridgeheads was beaten off. The Allied forces then executed a flank attack which routed the French army.

MALPLAQUET
11 SEPTEMBER 1709

Forces Allied: 90,000; French: 90,000. **Casualties** Allied: 40,000; French: 40,000 dead, 30,000 prisoners. **Location** 15km (10 miles) south of Mons (in modern Belgium).

The Allied army sustained heavy casualties in making attacks on the well-positioned French flanks. A powerful frontal attack resulted in a huge mêlée, from which the French were able to retire in good order.

> ## "If you want to be loved by your soldiers … do not lead them into slaughter."
> FREDERICK THE GREAT OF PRUSSIA, IN HIS "INSTRUCTIONS TO HIS GENERALS", 1747

ZARAGOZA
20 AUGUST 1710

Forces English, Dutch, Aragonese, and Imperial: 23,000–30,000; Spanish: 20,000. **Casualties** English, Dutch, Aragonese, and Imperial: 1,500; Spanish: 10,000, plus 5,000 prisoners. **Location** Zaragoza province, Aragón, Spain.

After an artillery exchange that lasted the entire morning, the Spanish launched a frontal assault, which the Allied force resolutely withstood. The Allied force then launched a counterattack, shattering the Spanish army.

SEIGE OF BOUCHAIN
5 AUGUST–12 SEPTEMBER 1711

Forces English, Dutch, and Austrian: 85,000; French: 90,000. **Casualties** English, Dutch, and Austrian: 4,080; French: 6,000, plus 2,500 prisoners. **Location** Northern France.

Five thousand French troops were besieged inside the fortress of Bouchain, with the remainder of the force camped close by. The Allies drove a force between the two and constructed field fortifications to hold the position. The siege carried on until the garrison surrendered.

DENAIN 24 JULY 1712

Forces Dutch and Austrian: 105,000; French: 120,000. **Casualties** Dutch and Austrian: 18,000; French: 5,000. **Location** Denain, northern France.

Deprived of its English component by an independent peace treaty, the Allied army was attacked by the French, who were initially repulsed. After Allied counterattacks failed, the French again advanced, breaking the Allied army.

SIEGE OF BARCELONA
25 JULY 1713–
11 SEPTEMBER 1714

Forces French and Spanish: 40,000; Austrian and Allied: 6,700. **Casualties** French and Spanish: 14,000; Austrian and Allied: 7,000, including civilians. **Location** Catalonia, Spain.

Barcelona was taken by troops landed from an Austrian fleet in 1705. Attempts to retake it did not begin until 1713. Lack of artillery meant that little progress was made until the summer of 1714, after which a series of assaults gradually regained control of the city.

LATER JACOBITE UPRISINGS
1719–46

Repeated attempts were made to restore the Stuart dynasty to the thrones of Scotland and England, backed by foreign powers when French troops were sent in 1708 and a Spanish force the following year. After a failed uprising in 1715, and an aborted French invasion of England in 1744, Charles Edward Stuart ("Bonnie Prince Charlie") led a doomed uprising of Scottish chieftains in 1745.

GLEN SHIEL 10 JUNE 1719

Forces Jacobite and Spanish: 1,000; Government: 970. **Casualties** Jacobite and Spanish: 121 killed; Government: 100 dead, plus an unknown number of wounded. **Location** Northwest Highlands of Scotland.

A planned large-scale Spanish invasion did not occur, and the small force landed in Scotland was abandoned, along with its Jacobite allies. Government forces engaged the rebels at Glen Shiel, driving in the flanks and forcing the Spanish to surrender.

PRESTONPANS 21 SEPTEMBER 1745

Forces Jacobite: 2,500; Government: 2,300. **Casualties** Jacobite: 100; Government: 800, plus around 1,500 prisoners. **Location** Near Edinburgh, Scotland.

Musket drill
In the 17th and 18th centuries musketry was the most important part of infantry training. By 1700 these crude matchlocks had been superseded by more efficient flintlocks.

Battle of Malplaquet, 1709
Prince Eugene of Savoy's imperial troops and the Duke of Marlborough's troops rout the French in one of the main battles of the War of the Spanish Succession.

The Jacobites attacked from an unexpected direction, causing the inexperienced government army to become disordered. The government troops became surrounded, with most of the force taken prisoner.

INVERURIE 23 DECEMBER 1745

Forces Jacobite: 1,100; Government: 500. **Casualties** Jacobite: no reliable estimates; Government: no reliable estimates, about 50 prisoners. **Location** 26km (16 miles) northwest of Aberdeen, Scotland.

Government forces advanced to occupy Inverurie, placing themselves in an exposed position. The Jacobites attacked from two directions, catching the government force by surprise and driving them out of the town.

FALKIRK 17 JANUARY 1746

Forces Jacobite: 5,000; Government: 7,000. **Casualties** Jacobite: 130; Government: 250, plus 300 prisoners. **Location** Central Scotland.

The Jacobite force advanced to attack the complacent and unprepared government troops. The ensuing battle was a confused affair fought in a storm. The government force was routed, but the Jacobites were scattered and unable to pursue.

CULLODEN 16 APRIL 1746

Forces Jacobite: 5,400; Government: 9,000. **Casualties** Jacobite: 1,000 killed; Government: 50 killed. **Location** Just east of Inverness, Scotland.

Against the advice of the Highland chieftains, the Jacobite army made a head-on attack against the well-trained government force. The assault was beaten off by intense fire, and the Jacobites were driven from the field.

NADIR SHAH'S INVASION OF INDIA 1738–39

Forces Nadir Shah: unknown; Indian: unknown. **Casualties** Up to 20,000 in sack of Delhi. **Location** Northern India.

Nadir Shah of Persia brushed aside Indian resistance at Karnal and entered Delhi unopposed. After Indians attacked Persian troops on hearing the false rumour that Nadir Shah had been killed, the city was sacked and more than 20,000 citizens massacred in one day. This gave rise to a new word, *nadirshahi*, or "holocaust".

WAR OF THE AUSTRIAN SUCCESSION 1740–48

Arising out of a dispute over whether Maria Theresa of Austria was, as a woman, eligible to succeed to the throne, the War of the Austrian Succession gave various states an opportunity for expansion and territorial gain. The conflict drew in most of the major states of Europe, but was largely inconclusive.

MOLLWITZ 10 APRIL 1741

Forces Prussian: 23,000; Austrian: 16,600. **Casualties** Prussian: 3,900, plus 700 prisoners; Austrian: 2,500, plus 1,500 prisoners. **Location** Silesia (in modern Poland).

The standing army of Prussia was able to make rapid gains in Silesia before Austria could assemble an army to oppose the invasion. An Austrian attempt to relieve Neisse resulted in a confused action at Mollwitz, which was won by the firepower of the better-drilled Prussians.

DETTINGEN 27 JUNE 1743

Forces Austrian, British, and Hanoverian: 40,000; French: 60,000. **Casualties** Austrian, British, and Hanoverian: 2,400 dead; French: 5,000 dead. **Location** 110km (70 miles) east of Frankfurt (in modern Germany).

Cut off and hemmed in, the Allied force managed to drive off and rout a French attack. This was the last occasion when a British king commanded directly in battle.

PFAFFENHOFEN 15 APRIL 1745

Forces French, Bavarian, and Allied: 7,000; Austrian: 10,000. **Casualties** French, Bavarian, and Allied: 2,400; Austrian: 800. **Location** Modern Bavaria, Germany.

Despite a vigorous defence, the French and their allies were ejected from the town of Pfaffenhofen. A second position outside the town held for a time, but the French were forced to retreat to avoid becoming surrounded.

FONTENOY 11 MAY 1745

Forces Allied: 53,000; French: 70,000. **Casualties** Allied: 9,000; French: 5,000. **Location** 8km (5 miles) southeast of Tournai (in modern Belgium).

The French army occupied excellent positions, with many units hidden by undulating terrain. Despite some successes, the Allied forces were forced to withdraw in the face of fire from these concealed positions.

HOHENFRIEDBERG 4 JUNE 1745

Forces Prussian: 58,500; Austrian and Saxon: 58,700. **Casualties** Prussian: 8,650, plus 5,080 prisoners; Austrian and Saxon: 4,800. **Location** Striegau (in modern Poland).

The Prussians achieved at least partial surprise and were able to overrun the Saxony wing of the enemy force. The Austrian contingent was more resilient but was eventually broken by a cavalry charge. It was largely in honour of this victory that Frederick of Prussia gained the title "the Great".

ROCOUX 11 OCTOBER 1746

Forces Allied: 97,000; French: 80,000. **Casualties** Allied: 4,000–5,000; French: 3,500. **Location** Liège, Belgium.

Austrian, British, Dutch, and Hanoverian troops were attempting to prevent the French, who had invaded Flanders, from advancing into the Dutch Republic. Poor cooperation between different nationalities allowed the French to break the line and drive the Allies into retreat.

FIRST CAPE FINISTERRE 14 MAY 1747

Forces British: 16 warships, 1 fireship; French: 7 warships plus 30 merchant vessels. **Casualties** British: no ships lost; French: 6 warships lost, 7 merchant vessels captured. **Location** Off the northwest coast of Spain.

As French warships tried to keep shipping lanes open and to protect its merchant ships, the British admiral signalled for a "general chase", bringing about a number of successful small actions, rather than a line-of-battle engagement.

SECOND CAPE FINISTERRE 25 OCTOBER 1747

Forces British: 14 warships; French: 8 warships. **Casualties** British: no ships lost; France: 6 warships captured. **Location** Off the northwest coast of Spain.

Although the British ships were individually less powerful than the French, they were able to overwhelm them by taking on one enemy ship at a time. Several French warships were lost, and the battle put an end to French naval operations for the rest of the war.

The Age of Revolution 1750–1830

BRITISH NAPOLEONIC CAMPAIGN MEDAL

As the technology of gunpowder weapons matured and evolved, generals and their armies developed an organizational structure and a system of tactics designed to exploit them fully to their advantage. The classic combined-arms doctrine of "horse, foot, and guns" quickly came to dominate the battlefields of the world, and was brought to a pinnacle during the Napoleonic Wars, in which European states took the field with unprecedented numbers of men, horses, and guns.

THE FRENCH AND INDIAN WAR
1754–62

The French and Indian War was a series of conflicts in North America. Clashes between British colonists and French forces, and their Native American allies, sparked a war in which the fighting raged from the wilds of Canada to Pennsylvania and New York. Britain ultimately took control of Canada from the French, and also captured Guadeloupe in the Caribbean.

JUMONVILLE'S GLEN
8 MAY 1754

Forces Colonial: 52; French: 50. **Casualties** Colonial: 1; French 13. **Location** Allegheny foothills, Pennsylvania.

Reinforcing British claims to the area, George Washington's party of Virginia militia and Iroquois warriors attacked a

The Battle of Quebec
The Canadian city of Quebec was captured by the British in 1759, after a battle lasting less than an hour. This coloured engraving is based on a drawing made by Hervey Smyth, one of the British officers.

French scouting party under Joseph Coulon de Villiers de Jumonville near modern Uniontown, Pennsylvania. The Iroquois leader Tanacharison killed the captured Jumonville after the battle. Washington's attack was a major cause of the French and Indian War.

FALL OF FORT NECESSITY 3 JULY 1754

Forces Colonial: 450; French: 600, Indian 100. **Casualties** Unknown. **Location** Forks of the Ohio river, Pennsylvania.

Captain Louis Coulon de Villiers led a punitive expedition to avenge Jumonville, his brother. Washington's resistance and fortifications crumbled in a rainstorm. The colonials surrendered, but were allowed to withdraw with their weapons.

MONONGAHELA RIVER 9 JULY 1755

Forces British and Colonial: 2,000; French and Indian: 900. **Casualties** British and Colonial: 500; French: 56, Indian: 40. **Location** Near the forks of the Ohio river, Pennsylvania.

Encountering a force of French and Indians on the banks of the Monongahela river, the British advance guard retreated, colliding with the main British force. The British fled, with the French and Indians inflicting heavy casualties on them.

LAKE GEORGE
8 SEPTEMBER 1755

Forces Colonial and Indian: 1,220; French, Indian, and Canadian: 1,520. **Casualties** Colonial and Indian: c.300; French: c.300. **Location** Upper Hudson river valley, New York.

Under Baron Ludwig Dieskau, the French ambushed Colonel William Johnson along the road, and drove the colonials back into their semi-fortified camp. The colonials rallied and drove the French off in disorder, causing heavy French casualties.

FALL OF FORT WILLIAM HENRY
9 AUGUST, 1757

Forces British and Colonial: 2,300; French, Indian, and Canadian: 2,300. **Casualties** British: c.300; French and Indian: unknown. **Location** Upper Hudson river valley, New York.

A British fort on the shores of Lake George withstood General Louis-Joseph Montcalm's superior numbers and siege train for a week before surrendering. Montcalm's Indians butchered many of the survivors after the surrender.

SIEGE OF LOUISBOURG
8 JUNE–26 JULY 1758

Forces British and Colonial: 26,000, including naval personnel; French, Indian, and Canadian: 7,000. **Casualties** British and Colonial: 527; French, Indian, and Canadian: 405. **Location** Nova Scotia, Canada.

In order to gain access to the St Lawrence river, British forces laid siege to the fortress of Louisbourg. A French naval squadron in the harbour was eliminated by the bombardment and by boarding parties in small boats. The fall of Louisbourg gave the British a base for an attack on Quebec.

FORT TICONDEROGA
8 JULY 1758

Forces British: 6,300, Colonial: 9,000; French, 3,400. **Casualties** British: 2,000; French: 372. **Location** Southern end of Lake Champlain, on the borders of northern New York State and Vermont.

British Major General James Abercromby decided to rush the fort before French reinforcements could arrive. The British charged into General Montcalm's intricate defences, but withdrew after severe losses, abandoning a land invasion of Canada.

FORT DUQUESNE
14 SEPTEMBER 1758

Forces British and Colonial: 750; French and Indian: 500. **Casualties** British and Colonial: 324; French and Indian: 16. **Location** Modern Pittsburg, Pennsylvania.

The British force attempted to draw out the defenders of the fort in order to ambush them. The defenders were far more numerous than expected and overwhelmed both the decoy force and the main British body.

CAPTURE OF FORT NIAGARA
26 JULY 1759

Forces British: 2,500, Indian: 1,000; French: 600. **Casualties** British: c.250; Indian: unknown; French: 109. **Location** Mouth of Lake Ontario near Youngstown, New York.

Brigadier General John Prideaux conducted a formal siege of this isolated French garrison, which blocked the British route to Montreal. The French surrendered after William Johnson and his Iroquois ambushed and destroyed a relief column at the island of La Belle Famille.

BEAUPORT 31 JULY 1759

Forces British: 4,000; French: 10,000. **Casualties** British: 440; French: 70. **Location** Quebec, Canada.

A British effort to land forces for an assault on Quebec was only partially successful. After attempting to fight uphill against well-fortified French troops, the British force pulled back.

QUEBEC 13 SEPTEMBER 1759

Forces British: 4,800; French: 4,000. **Casualties** British: 658; French: 644. **Location** Plains of Abraham outside the walls of Quebec City, Quebec, Canada.

Needing to find an alternative to a long siege, the British were able to achieve surprise. Winning a pitched battle near the city, the British received Quebec's surrender a few days later. This was the decisive British victory of the war.

SAINTE-FOY 28 APRIL 1760

Forces British: 3,800; French: 5,000. **Casualties** British: 1,088; French: 833. **Location** Quebec City, Quebec, Canada.

Faced with a French attempt to regain Quebec City by siege, the British garrison elected to come out and offer battle. A close-range firefight ensued, which the French eventually won. The British then withstood siege until reinforced by sea. French naval support failed to make it past the British blockade.

RESTIGOUCHE 23–8 JULY 1760

Forces British: 5 warships; French: 1 warship, 5 merchant ships. **Casualties** No reliable estimates. **Location** Pointe-à-la-Croix, Quebec, Canada.

A French convoy tried to evade the British blockade by anchoring in the Restigouche river and positioning cannon on the banks. After the first position was broken, the French withdrew upriver, but were forced to scuttle their ships.

FALL OF MONTREAL 8 SEPTEMBER 1760

Forces British and Colonials: 17,000; French: 447, Canadian: 1,600. **Casualties** None. **Location** Île de Montréal in the St Lawrence river, Canada.

The French army fled up the St Lawrence river after General Montcalm's death at Quebec. Three British and colonial armies converged in overwhelming force, forcing Governor Pierre de Rigaud de Vaudreuil de Cavagnial's surrender.

SIGNAL HILL 15 SEPTEMBER 1762

Forces British and Colonial: 200; French: 295. **Casualties** British and Colonial: 25; French: 20–40. **Location** St John's, Newfoundland, Canada.

LOGISTICS TRANSPORT THROUGH THE AGES

One variation of an old saying is that "generals win battles while logisticians win wars". It is certainly true that without adequate supplies of food, water, clothing, weapons, ammunition, and other equipment, those on the battlefront could not hope for victory. Today, modern transport aircraft and helicopters, as well as specialized naval cargo vessels, are essential to military logistics.

Horsepower

From its first appearance in ancient warfare (c.4000–3000 BCE), the horse has been used in service to carry warriors and haul their equipment into battle, despite the fact that horses must be provided with stables and fodder while on campaign, generating a major logistics burden for an army. A typical mid-19th-century British artillery battery, for example, required between 160 and 200 horses, including those that hauled the guns and ammunition wagons, and those that bore gun crews and their officers to the front. Other beasts of burden have also served as military transports, including donkeys, oxen, mules, camels, and elephants, notably Hannibal's arrival in Italy with 30 African war elephants in 218 BCE. During World War II, both Allied and Axis armies used animal power to draw wagonloads of ammunition and supplies when motor fuel rations proved inadequate. Even in the 21st century, horses and donkeys have served as transports for special forces soldiers fighting in the remote and rugged highlands of Afghanistan.

Sealift

In addition to their use as naval fighting platforms, boats and ships have served as troop transports and supply vessels for thousands of years. Medieval chroniclers – such as Jean de Joinville (c.1224–1317), who wrote of the Seventh Crusade – frequently mention the dependence of military expeditions upon naval supply. Sometimes the difference between warships and noncombatant transports was blurred. For example, during the Napoleonic Wars (1803–15), armed merchant vessels belonging to the British East India Company sometimes fought alongside the Royal Navy against French warships and pirates. Modern armies sent to fight far from their home countries still depend upon the sea for most of their supplies. Specialized naval cargo vessels, such as the Large Medium Speed Roll-on, Roll-Off (LMSR) ships of the US Military Sealift Command, can carry enough materiel to supply 20,000 troops of a heavy armoured brigade for 15 days.

Railroads

Developed at the beginning of the 19th century, railways soon became an important form of military transport. Generals realized that large tonnages of supplies, horses, artillery, and even whole regiments of infantry and cavalry troops could be moved efficiently by steam locomotive. In the Crimean War (1853–56), rail supply was crucial for British troops at the battle of Balaclava. In the US Civil War (1861–65), during the Petersburg campaign in Virginia, the military railroad system supplied tens of thousands of federal troops and their horses with hundreds of tonnes of food, fodder, ammunition, and other stores. Some historians have pointed out that, by 1914, the military strategies of the European powers had become completely dependent on railroad timetables for the mobilization of their armies.

Airlift

Today, aircraft are essential to military logistics. Building on the rapid development of both airships and load-carrying bombers during World War I, the use of transport planes and airships became commonplace in civilian and military service in the interwar years. During World War II, Allied and Axis nations used air transport to deliver troops and supplies forwards, and retrieve wounded soldiers from the battlefield. On many occasions air transport (or the lack of it) proved to be a decisive factor. One example was in the battle of Stalingrad in the former Soviet Union (1942–43), where more than 300,000 soldiers of the German Sixth Army were encircled and defeated, despite heroic but inadequate attempts by the Luftwaffe to resupply the army by air. One modern transport aircraft, the C-17 Globemaster III, although expensive (more than US$202 million each) is remarkable in that it can haul 77,519kg (170,900lb) of cargo, or 102 paratroopers, and land on just 1,065m (3,500ft) of runway.

Heavy guns in the mud
Horses and British artillerymen toil to roll a bronze 9-pounder cannon into firing position during the Napoleonic Wars.

French troops holding high ground dominating St John's were driven off by a surprise assault. British possession of the hill made the position of the St John's garrison untenable, forcing a surrender.

PLASSEY 23 JUNE 1757

Forces British and East India Company: 3,000; Nawab of Bengal, including French gunners: 55,000. **Casualties** British: 65; Bengali: unknown. **Location** Bengal, India.

Having bribed some of the Bengali commanders, the outnumbered British beat off a cavalry charge and infantry attacks. The Bengali artillery was useless due to damp powder, and resistance crumbled before the British counterattack.

PONTIAC'S REBELLION 1763–66

Forces British/American: unknown; Native peoples: unknown. **Casualties** British/Colonial: c.200; Native peoples: unknown. **Location** The Great Lakes region, North America.

Pontiac, an Ottawa chief, led an uprising against the British that began near Detroit and spread to other regions. Several British forts were captured before superior British numbers forced the Native Americans to negotiate peace terms.

THE SEVEN YEARS WAR IN EUROPE AND INDIA
1756–63

In a complex imperial struggle, Prussia joined Britain and several small German states against France, Spain, Russia, and Austria. Initial French and Austrian success faded against the brilliance of Prussia's Frederick the Great and the might of Britain's Royal Navy.

FALL OF MINORCA 20 MAY 1756

Forces British: 13 ships of the line, 3,000 troops; French and Spanish: 12 ships of the line, 15,000 troops. **Casualties** British: 38; French and Spanish: 45. **Location** Off the Mediterranean coast of Spain.

The British garrison on the island of Minorca was overrun by the French. A British naval relief force commanded by Admiral Byng engaged a French fleet, but after an inconclusive naval action the British withdrew. Byng was later court-martialled and executed for "failure to do his utmost" to relieve the garrison.

MILITARY INVENTIONS IN CIVILIAN USE

Firearms

Firearms, which evolved from Chinese and early European battlefield weapons (c.1100), have long been in civilian use for hunting, sport, and law enforcement. Parallel innovations in military and civilian firearm technologies continued throughout their development. During the 17th and 18th centuries, for example, a great variety of long arms were developed for hunting. Some of these were smoothbore and others rifled for accuracy (meaning that they had longitudinal grooves cut on the inside of the barrel to give the ball or bullet spin). Many weapons, such as the French *fusil de chasse* and the American long rifle, were precisely made and highly prized by the explorers of North America, as well as by the Indians. During the French and Indian War (1754–63) and later conflicts, the use of civilian long rifles by military scouts, sharpshooters, and militia units was crucial. Today, versions of hunting rifles, such as the Remington model 700, are used by military and police snipers.

Canned food

Napoleon Bonaparte is said to have remarked: "an army marches on its stomach." Realizing the complex logistical problem of transporting, storing, and distributing food to a large army, Napoleon offered 12,000 francs for the invention of a better way to preserve and store military rations. In 1809, Nicolas Appert won the prize, using glass bottles and boiling to cook and preserve the contents. In Britain, another inventor, Peter Durand, proposed a method for preserving food in a variety of containers, including tins. By 1813, Durand's method was being used to prepare food for the British Army. The process of "canning" quickly became a major industry in many nations.

Radar

The English word "radar" was originally an acronym that stood for "radio detection and ranging". In the 1930s, several nations and commercial companies were experimenting with range- and direction-finding devices based on the physics of radio frequency transmission, and reception technology. Scottish inventor Sir Robert Watson-Watt was among the first to propose using reflected radio waves to detect thunderstorms, as well as aircraft in flight. Others considered how the technology might be used to detect ships at sea and even direct naval gunfire. In 1939, the US Navy installed its first operational radar aboard the battleship USS *New York*. During World War II, military and naval radar developed quickly and proved decisive. During the battle of Britain, for example, the Luftwaffe used radar to help navigate bombing missions. Building on the successful Home Chain radar system of the 1930s, the Royal Air Force used a sophisticated network to detect and range incoming enemy planes. Today, radar systems are essential for safe commercial air and sea travel, space travel, and vehicle law enforcement.

The Internet and the World Wide Web

During the 1960s and 1970s, the US military sought to build a new communications system that would enable a large number of users to share information, and thus be less vulnerable to attack. The basic concept was of a computer network that exchanged standardized blocks, or "packets", of information. The process of "packet switching" allowed many computers to communicate simultaneously, creating a large network. If some failed or were attacked, others would survive. This became the Internet as we know it today. In Switzerland, during the 1980s, scientists developed the idea of a universal medium where users could share different kinds of information (text, graphics, audio, video, etc.). That concept became the World Wide Web.

Global Positioning System (GPS)

Development of GPS began in the 1960s as a naval timekeeping and navigation system. Orbiting the Earth every 12 hours, a constellation of 24 satellites emits radio signals that GPS receivers on the surface can interpret. In war, the system enables some "smart" weapons to locate targets with precision; however, civilian users worldwide now far outnumber military users.

Sharpshooter rifle

The .625in calibre Baker rifle (c.1800) was issued to the British Army's elite sharpshooters, the 95th Rifles, and other units. The rifle was accurate up to around 137m (450ft).

LEUTHEN 5 DECEMBER 1757

Forces Prussian: 36,000; Austrian: 80,000. **Casualties** Prussian: 1,000 killed; Austrian: 3,000 killed, plus 12,000 taken prisoner. **Location** Modern Lutynia, Poland.

After a feint attack on the Austrian right, the Prussians rapidly redeployed and attacked on the other flank. The Austrians could not react quickly enough and were soundly defeated.

KREFELD 17 JUNE 1758

Forces Prussian and Hanoverian: 32,000; French: 47,000. **Casualties** Prussian and Hanoverian: 1,700; French: 4,000. **Location** Westphalia, Germany.

A large Prussian-Hanoverian army surprised the French, who were drawn up along a canal near the banks of the Rhine. Feint attacks against the French centre and right allowed a successful flank attack on the French left.

ZORNDORF 25 AUGUST 1758

Forces Prussian: 36,000; Russian: 43,500. **Casualties** Prussian: 12,797; Russian: 18,500. **Location** Modern Sarbinowo, Poland.

A Prussian cavalry charge routed part of the Russian army, but the remainder fought on stubbornly. Hand-to-hand fighting was common, as both sides ran out of ammunition. By nightfall, it was not clear who had won, but the Russian army later retreated, satisfying the Prussian strategic objective of keeping the Russians and Austrians apart.

HOCHKIRCH 14 OCTOBER 1758

Forces Prussian: 31,000; Austrian: 80,000. **Casualties** Prussian: more than 9,000; Austrian: 8,300. **Location** Saxony, Germany.

The Austrian force achieved surprise by the use of a night march, and attacked the Prussian right flank. A determined stand by the rearguard enabled the Prussian army to retire in good order.

MINDEN 1 AUGUST 1759

Forces British and Hanoverian: 37,000; French: 44,000. **Casualties** British and Hanoverian: 2,800 killed; French: 7,000, plus 8,000 taken prisoner. **Location** 28km (44 miles) west of Hanover, Westphalia, Germany.

Acting on a mistaken order, a British infantry brigade attacked the French cavalry and managed to defeat it. Artillery pushed rapidly forwards in support and forced the French to withdraw.

KUNERSDORF 12 AUGUST 1759

Forces Prussian: 50,000; Austrian and Russian: 50,000. **Casualties** Prussian: 19,000; Austrian and Russian: 15,000. **Location** 19km (12 miles) west of Swiebodzin, Poland.

Frederick the Great's Prussian army disintegrated with heavy casualties when he attacked an Austrian–Russian army threatening Berlin. Frederick was only barely able to regroup while the Austrians faced delays waiting for supplies.

QUIBERON BAY 20 NOVEMBER 1759

Forces British ships: 23; French ships: 21. **Casualties** British: 2 ships wrecked; French: 8 ships lost or captured. **Location** South coast of Brittany, France.

Boldly following the French fleet into Quiberon bay, the British attacked in bad weather and poor light. Several French ships escaped into the Vilaine river, where they were penned up for some time. The outcome was a brilliant victory for the British navy.

WARBURG 31 JULY 1760

Forces Britain, Hanover, Brunswick, and Hesse-Kassel: 24,000; France: 21,500. **Casualties** Britain, Hanover, Brunswick, and Hesse-Kassel: 1,200; France: 1,500, plus 1,500 prisoners. **Location** Rhine-Westphalia, Germany.

The Allies sought to stop a detached French corps marching to Hanover. The action was decided by an Allied cavalry charge. The French force retreated.

LIEGNITZ 15 AUGUST 1760

Forces Prussian: 30,000; Austrian: 30,000. **Casualties** Prussian: 1,000; Austrian: 4,000, plus 6,000 prisoners. **Location** Southwestern Poland.

New England militia
In Massachusetts, this statue commemorates the "Minutemen" of the New England militias that confronted the British infantry at Lexington and Concord (19 April 1775).

LOBOSITZ 1 OCTOBER 1756

Forces Prussian: 29,000; Austrian: 34,500. **Casualties** Prussian: 2,900; Austrian: 2,900. **Location** Lovosice (in modern Czech Republic).

Austrian forces marching to the assistance of their Saxon allies were attacked by a Prussian army at Lobositz. The situation was confused by fog, resulting in reverses for the Prussians before a bayonet charge drove the Austrians off. The isolated Saxon army near Pima was forced to surrender.

REICHENBERG 21 APRIL 1757

Forces Prussian: 16,000; Austrian: 10,500. **Casualties** No reliable estimates. **Location** Bohemia (in modern Czech Republic).

Prussian forces advancing on Prague were intercepted by part of the Austrian army. Additional Austrian forces were too far away from the battle site to take part in the action. The Prussians pushed their opponents aside, capturing much of their supplies.

HASTENBECK 26 JULY 1757

Forces Britain, Brunswick, Hanover, and Hesse-Kassel: 35,000; France: 60,000. **Casualties** Britain, Brunswick, Hanover, and Hesse-Kassel: 1,211; France: 2,200. **Location** Hamelin, Lower Saxony, Germany.

Attempting to draw Prussian attention away from Bohemia, a French flank attack drew in the Allies' reserves and permitted the main attack in the centre to succeed. Both sides thought that they had lost the battle; both commanders had actually ordered a withdrawal, before the French realized that they had won.

ROSSBACH 5 NOVEMBER 1757

Forces Prussian: 21,000; French and Austrian: 42,000. **Casualties** Prussian: 550; French and Austrian: 7,700. **Location** Near Leipzig, Germany.

Attempting to march one flank around the Prussian left, the Franco-Austrian force was completely unprepared for the ferocity of the Prussian attack. The Prussian infantry followed up with a devastatating cavalry assault, leading to total victory for Prussia.

Attempting to avoid becoming surrounded, the Prussian army tried to retire. It met an Austrian force moving to complete the encirclement and was forced to fight its way out of the box.

KLOSTER KAMPEN
15 OCTOBER 1760

Forces British, Hanoverian, Brunswick, Hesse-Kassel, and Prussian: 20,000; France: 25,000. **Casualties** British, Hanoverian, Brunswick, Hesse-Kassel, and Prussian: 1,615; France: 3,123. **Location** Rhine-Westphalia, Germany.

The Allies attacked at night, gaining possession of Kloster Kampen. In the morning, the French counterattacked and drove the Allied forces back. The Allies were then forced to retreat across the Rhine.

TORGAU 3 NOVEMBER 1760

Forces Prussian: 49,000; Austrian: 53,000. **Casualties** Prussian: 20,000; Austrian: 16,000 prisoners. **Location** Northwestern Saxony, Germany.

After an artillery duel, the Prussians attempted to storm Austrian positions on high ground, and were bloodily repulsed. A renewed assault later in the day took the artillery position, turning the Austrian guns on their own army. Austrian assaults to retake their positions were beaten off.

VILLINGHAUSEN 15–16 JULY 1761

Forces British, Hanoverian, and Prussian: 100,000; Austrian: 80,000. **Casualties** British, Hanoverian, and Prussian: 1,400; Austria: 5,000. **Location** Hamm, western Germany.

On the first day of the battle, the French made some gains but were eventually halted. Both sides were reinforced during the night, and the French attacked again on the Allied left flank. Against the right Allied flank, the French were more passive. The arrival of more Allied reinforcements allowed a successful attack, which forced the French into retreat.

FREIBERG 29 OCTOBER 1762

Forces Prussian: 22,000; Austrian: 27,000–31,000. **Casualties** Prussian: 1,400; Austrian: 7,400. **Location** Saxony, Germany.

At first the Prussians failed to make much headway against determined Austrian opposition, but a fight for a strategic hill drew in Prussian reserves and weakened the Austrian flank. A renewed Prussian assault broke the Austrian flanks and forced a retreat. With states on both sides facing financial ruin, a peace treaty was signed in February 1763.

THE AMERICAN REVOLUTION
1775–83

The British Parliament's reluctance to grant distant colonists the "Rights of Englishmen" led to uproar, antagonism, and finally war. France and Spain moved to avenge losses in the Seven Years War by aiding the Americans in their successful revolt against British rule.

LEXINGTON AND CONCORD
19 APRIL 1775

Forces British: 700; American: 4,000. **Casualties** British: 273; American: 95. **Location** Massachusetts.

After a brief engagement at Lexington, the British marched on Concord, where the rebels ambushed them. The British then fell back to Charlestown, fighting constant skirmishes along the way.

BUNKER HILL 17 JUNE 1775

Forces British: 2,600; American: 1,400. **Casualties** British: 1,053; American: 310, plus 30 prisoners. **Location** Near Boston, Massachusetts.

The battle of Bunker Hill was actually fought on Breed's Hill, which had been fortified instead by mistake. The British took the position but with heavy losses.

QUEBEC 31 DECEMBER 1775

Forces British and Canadian: 1,800; American: 900 **Casualties** British: 20; American: 72. **Location** The gates of Quebec City, Quebec, Canada.

The American invasion of Canada fell apart when its leader Richard Montgomery died attacking the walls of the city. Abandoning captured Montreal, Colonel Benedict Arnold led the surviving Americans back below the St Lawrence river in the spring.

SIEGE OF BOSTON 17 MARCH 1776

Forces British: 7,000, Loyalist: 1,000; American: 17,000. **Casualties** None. **Location** Dorchester Heights overlooking Boston, Massachusetts.

Waking up to find the captured cannon of Fort Ticonderoga bearing down on the besieged city, and able to see British ships in the harbour from Dorchester Heights, General John Thomas agreed to evacuate British and loyalist forces from the city.

SULLIVAN'S ISLAND 28 JUNE 1776

Forces British: 2,900, 9 ships; American: 425. **Casualties** British: 64, 1 ship; American: 20. **Location** Mouth of Charleston harbour, South Carolina.

Fort Sullivan, built of shot-repelling palmetto logs, proved resistant to a British landing party and bombardment by conventional ships, as well as by a bomb ketch. The British retreated, setting fire to HMS *Actaeon*, aground near the fort.

BATTLE OF LONG ISLAND
26 AUGUST 1776

Forces British: 12,000; American: 12,400. **Casualties** British: 400; American: 1,400. **Location** Brooklyn Heights, southern Long Island, New York.

The British army, Hessians, and the Royal Navy repeatedly flanked Washington's army as it tried to defend the colonies' largest city. American resistance finally crumbled, leaving the British in control of Manhattan until 1783.

HARLEM HEIGHTS 16 SEPTEMBER 1776

Forces British: 1,000; American: 2,000 **Casualties** British: 140; American: 90. **Location** Manhattan, New York.

Washington and his generals made a stand to the north after the British took New York City. The British broke contact after American resistance, which gave Washington time to withdraw.

WHITE PLAINS 28 OCTOBER 1776

Forces British: 14,000: American: 14,500; **Casualties** British: 300; American: 300. **Location** Westchester County, New York.

Realizing that their positions had been bypassed by the British using amphibious capability, Washington ordered a retreat to White Plains. The British captured a strategic hill on the American right, compromising the Americans' position and forcing them to retreat further.

TRENTON AND PRINCETON
26 DECEMBER 1776–3 JANUARY 1777

Forces British: 1,200; American: 2,400 at Trenton. **Casualties** British: 106, plus 900 prisoners; American: 4. **Location** New Jersey.

Crossing the Delaware river, American forces seized Trenton. Using supplies captured there, the rebels then routed another British force at Princeton.

BATTLE OF BRANDYWINE
11 SEPTEMBER 1777

Forces British: 15,000; American: 11,000. **Casualties** British: 500; American: 1,300. **Location** Southwest of Philadelphia, Pennsylvania.

In the largest battle of the revolution, Washington and the reformed Continental army failed to defend Philadelphia from the British advance due to British flanking manoeuvres. The Americans retired in good order to the north of the city.

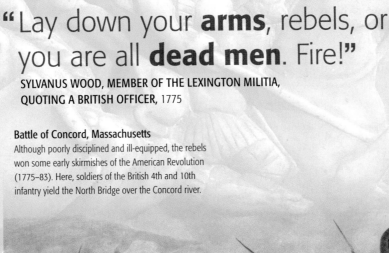

"Lay down your **arms**, rebels, or you are all **dead men**. Fire!"

SYLVANUS WOOD, MEMBER OF THE LEXINGTON MILITIA, QUOTING A BRITISH OFFICER, 1775

Battle of Concord, Massachusetts
Although poorly disciplined and ill-equipped, the rebels won some early skirmishes of the American Revolution (1775–83). Here, soldiers of the British 4th and 10th infantry yield the North Bridge over the Concord river.

GERMANTOWN 4 OCTOBER 1777

Forces British: 8,000; American: 10,000. **Casualties** British: 500; American: 700. **Location** 8km (5 miles) northwest of Philadelphia, Pennsylvania.

Washington sent four converging columns against an isolated part of Howe's British army, achieving surprise. British resistance, fog, and a lack of ammunition resulted in the Americans' withdrawal.

ORISKANY 6 AUGUST 1777

Forces Loyalist: 800, Indian: 400; American: 800. **Casualties** Loyalist and Indian: 150; American: 200. **Location** Mouth of the Oriskany river, upstate New York.

Loyalists and Iroquois ambushed General Herkimer's column while he was en route to relieve a fort under British attack. Suffering heavy casualties, the Americans held a perimeter on a nearby hill while skirmishers destroyed the British supply train.

BENNINGTON 16 AUGUST 1777

Forces Hessian (German auxiliary): 700; American: 2,000 **Casualties** Hessian: 200; American: 80. **Location** Border of New York and New Hampshire.

A Hessian (German auxiliary) column veered off towards New Hampshire in the vanguard of British General Burgoyne's invasion. Swarming colonial militia engulfed and captured the Hessian force.

SARATOGA
19 SEPTEMBER AND 17 OCTOBER 1777

Forces British: 10,000; American: 15,000. **Casualties** British: 800 plus 6,000 prisoners; American: 1,600. **Location** New York State.

The British initially repelled an attack and then counterattacked, suffering heavy losses on both occasions. When reinforcements failed to arrive the British tried to withdraw and were surrounded, which forced them to surrender.

FALL OF FORTS MERCER AND MIFFLIN 22 NOVEMBER 1777

Forces British: 4,000, 5 ships; American: 900. **Casualties** British: 500; 2 ships; American: 200. **Location** Banks of the Delaware river, south of Philadelphia.

In need of supplies, British Major General William Howe moved to open the Delaware river to Philadelphia. The garrisons of the two forts below the city resisted for four weeks, inflicting heavy losses.

MONMOUTH 28 JUNE 1778

Forces British: 11,000; American: 5,000. **Casualties** British: 300; American: 350. **Location** north-central New Jersey.

The British abandoned Philadelphia and made for the sea and New York. While they were en route, the British rear guard was attacked by Washington at Monmouth Court House, which held until relief arrived. The British withdrew unpursued.

STONY POINT 16 JULY 1779

Forces British: 600; American: 1,300. **Casualties** British: 134; American: 100. **Location** Hudson river valley, New York.

American General "Mad Anthony" Wayne suddenly turned the tables on the British advancing up the Hudson river and overwhelmed and captured an entire British garrison. The Americans bypassed strong British defences with a night march along the river.

PAULUS HOOK
19 AUGUST 1779

Forces British and Loyalist: 312; American: 600. **Casualties** British: 12; American: 3. **Location** Modern Jersey City, New Jersey.

Inspired by General Wayne, American Revolutionary War officer "Lighthorse Harry" Lee led a night assault of dismounted US dragoons on a British outpost across the river from Sir Henry Clinton's British stronghold in New York. The Americans took 159 British captive and escaped unscathed.

SAVANNAH 9 OCTOBER 1779

Forces British and Loyalist: 2,500; French: 3,800, 22 ships; American: 2,300. **Casualties** British: 57; French: 521, American: 231. **Location** Coastal Georgia.

The French and Americans attempted to besiege Savannah. However, they failed to coordinate properly and the attack failed, leaving the British in charge.

FALL OF CHARLESTON
12 MAY 1780

Forces British: 11,000; American: 5,500. **Casualties** British: 258; American: 250. **Location** South Carolina.

American general Benjamin Lincoln defended the city from March to May 1780 before surrendering his entire command, as well as ships and a large number of cannon, to surrounding British forces. It was the worst American defeat of the war.

WAXHAWS 29 MAY 1780

Forces British: 270: American: 380; **Casualties** British: 17; American: 263 plus 51 prisoners. **Location** Border of North and South Carolina.

An American force attempting to retreat after the fall of Charleston was caught and brought to action by a combined British and Loyalist column. The American commander deserted his force, which was annihilated.

CAMDEN 16 AUGUST 1780

Forces British: 2,239; American: 4,100. **Casualties** British: 324; American: 723 (including prisoners). **Location** South Carolina.

Inexperienced troops on the American left flank broke when the British advanced against them, leaving the stouter right exposed to the well-executed flanking manoeuvre that followed. The British prevailed.

KING'S MOUNTAIN 7 OCTOBER 1780

Forces Loyalist militia: 1,100; American Patriot: 900. **Casualties** Loyalist militia: 320 plus 698 prisoners; American Patriot: 90. **Location** North Carolina.

Despite having no overall commander, the various groups of American Patriots cooperated well, regrouping when repulsed and attacking again. With casualties mounting and their leader dead, the Loyalists surrendered.

COWPENS 17 JANUARY 1781

Forces British: 1,900; American: 4,400. **Casualties** British: 150 plus 830 prisoners; American: 73. **Location** North of Spartanburg, South Carolina.

British regulars and a scattering of Loyalists attacked American prepared defences of militia and Continentals. The Continental cavalry forestalled British attacks on their flanks and the British were defeated.

GUILFORD COURTHOUSE
15 MARCH 1781

Forces British: 1,900; American: 4,400. **Casualties** British: 532; American: 339. **Location** Greensboro, North Carolina.

Set on destroying an American army commanded by Nathaniel Greene, the British attacked the concentrated American forces and drove them from the battlefield with so many casualties that Greene retreated back into Virginia.

YORKTOWN SEPTEMBER–OCTOBER 1781

Forces British: 7,500; American: 8,845; French: 7,800. **Casualties** British: 482 plus 7,018 taken prisoner; American: 108; French: 186. **Location** Southeastern Virginia.

Pressed by the American armies, the British fortified their position and waited in vain for evacuation by sea. The British surrendered after an American attack forced their outer defensive line.

THE AMERICAN REVOLUTION AT SEA
1775–83

The British navy that had proved so decisive in the Seven Years War found itself challenged by the French who, still smarting from their defeat in the same war, were at their highest level of ship construction and naval expertise. The

---

GREAT NAVAL SHIPYARDS

Shipyard, Location	Years Active	Description
Lothal, Gujarat, India	2400–1900 BCE	One of the earliest known dockyards, capable of berthing and servicing large vessels
Royal Naval Dockyard Portsmouth, United Kingdom	13th century CE–present	One of the royal dockyards that has been active since the Royal Navy's inception; includes the world's oldest drydocks (built by King Henry VII in 1495)
Lagos, Portugal	15th century	The shipyards at Lagos became famous for the caravels they produced under Prince Henry "the Navigator" (1394–1460)
Royal Passaia, Gipuzkoa, Spain	Founded 1597 (shipbuilding activity continues in the port area)	Located in Spain's Basque region, Passaia is one of many yards that historically built ships for the Spanish Royal Navy, including the 1,200–1,500-tonne galleon, *Capitana Real*
Nantes-Indret, France	Founded 1771	Became a centre for naval shipbuilding in France in the 18th and 19th centuries; built ships for the Americans during the American Revolution (1775–83), including the 550-tonne, 24-gun frigate, *Deane*.
Portsmouth Naval Shipyard, Maine, United States	1800–present (although shipbuilding has continued in the area since 1690)	Oldest shipyard of the US Navy, built sail and steam warships and, beginning in 1917, submarines (including nuclear-powered boats during the 1950s and 1960s).
Blohm + Voss, near Hamburg, Germany	1877–present	Privately owned yard that built the World War I-era armoured cruiser SMS *Scharnhorst* and the World War II-era battleship *Bismarck*.

Nelson's flagship
Laid down in 1759, HMS *Victory*, a 100-gun "first rate" ship of the line, is preserved at Portsmouth, in Hampshire. She was Vice Admiral Lord Horatio Nelson's flagship at the battle of Trafalgar, which took place on 21 October, 1805.

Spanish and Dutch also resumed hostilities, with the rebellious Americans making their own attempts to challenge British naval power.

VALCOUR ISLAND 11 OCTOBER 1776

Forces British: 25 ships, galleys, and gunboats, 5,000 troops; American: 15 ships and galleys. **Casualties** British: 3 gunboats; American: 15 ships. **Location** Strait between Valcour Island and mainland New York.

After the retreat from Canada, Benedict Arnold's American "motley crew" of schooners and gunboats sank under overwhelming British firepower. The battle nonetheless delayed the British invasion down the Hudson river valley.

RAID ON WHITEHAVEN 23 APRIL 1778

Forces British harbour sentries: unknown; American: 1 sloop, landing party of 30. **Casualties** British: 3 prisoners; American: 1 deserter. **Location** Cumbria, northwestern England.

In the first hostile landing on British shores since 1667, John Paul Jones sent Britain into an uproar by landing, setting a ship on fire, and sabotaging the guns of the harbour fort, before escaping unscathed.

BATTLE OF USHANT 17 JULY 1778

Forces British: 30 ships of the line; French: 29 ships of the line. **Casualties** Unknown but low. **Location** Bay of Biscay, off northwestern France.

British artillery
Displayed at Saratoga, New York State, this British artillery piece is mounted on a gun carriage that includes two ammunition boxes, so that the weapon could be quickly brought into action.

After four days of manoeuvring, French Admiral d'Orvilliers forced British Admiral Keppel's squadron back into port, leaving the French free in the Atlantic. The result was indecisive, but British control of the sea was shaken badly.

BATTLE OF FLAMBOROUGH HEAD 23 SEPTEMBER 1779

Forces American: frigate *Bonhomme Richard*; French: frigate *Pallas*; British: frigate *Serapis*, sloop *Countess of Scarborough*. **Casualties** Unknown. **Location** North Sea off the coast of Yorkshire, England.

A joint US–French fleet attacked two British escort vessels protecting a large merchant convoy sailing from the Baltic. In a four-hour battle, John Paul Jones in *Bonhomme Richard* took *Serapis*, and *Pallas* captured *Scarborough*. The convoy escaped, and Jones sailed in *Serapis* after *Bonhomme Richard* sank.

BATTLE OF PORTO PRAYA 16 APRIL 1781

Forces British: 5 ships; French: 5 ships. **Casualties** Unknown, but low. **Location** North Atlantic Ocean off the Cape Verde Islands.

French Admiral Bailli de Suffren encountered a British squadron under Commodore George Johnstone en route to seize the Cape of Good Hope from the Dutch. He inflicted enough damage to slow the British and warn the Dutch.

MORE MILITARY AND NAVAL QUOTATIONS

Name, date, nation	Quotation
Thucydides (c.460–395 BCE), Greece	"The nation that makes a great distinction between its scholars and its warriors will have its thinking done by cowards and its fighting done by fools."
Aleksander Vasilyevich Suvorov (1729–1800), Russian empire	"One minute can decide the outcome of the battle, one hour the outcome of the campaign, and one day the fate of the country."
John Paul Jones (1747–92), 1st Lieutenant, American Continental Navy	"I wish to have no connection with any ship that does not sail fast, for I intend to go in harm's way."
Napoleon Bonaparte (1769–1821), emperor of France	"God fights on the side with the best artillery."
Ulysses S. Grant (1822–85), 18th President of the United States, former general of the US Army	"There never was a time when, in my opinion, some way could not be found to prevent the drawing of the sword."
Isoroku Yamamoto (1884–1943), Fleet Admiral of the Imperial Japanese Navy	"In the first six to twelve months of a war with the United States and Great Britain I will run wild and win victory upon victory. But then, if the war continues after that, I have no expectation of success."

JOHN PAUL JONES

> " The Spanish left one brig **on fire**. We made **plunder** out of her."
>
> BRITISH SAILOR ON A SEA BATTLE AGAINST THE SPANISH FLEET, 1780

CURIOUS MILITARY AND NAVAL UNIT NICKNAMES

Army	Unit/regiment/ship	Nickname
Ottoman empire, Turkey	Janissaries	From the 14th century until 1826, these household troops were known as "kapıkulu" (door slaves) because they served as personal bodyguards to the sultan
British Army	17th Lancers	"Death or Glory Boys", from the badge on their caps: a death's-head and the words "Or Glory" beneath
US Navy	USS Constitution	"Old Ironsides", from the legendary toughness of this 50-gun sail frigate's oak timbers
Canadian Forces	48th Highlanders of Canada	"Glamour Boys", from their having been recruited in the city (Toronto), compared with the "cowboys" and "plough jockeys" of regiments from rural areas

Officer of the 17th Lancers
The British 17th Lancers, known as "Death or Glory Boys" because of the insignia on their cap badge, are famous for their participation in the tragic Charge of the Light Brigade in October 1854.

BATTLE OF THE VIRGINIA CAPES
5 SEPTEMBER 1781

Forces British: 19 ships; French: 24 ships. **Casualties** British: 1 ship; French: no ships lost. **Location** Mouth of Chesapeake Bay, Virginia.

The French fleet blocked a British relief fleet as it moved to rescue besieged British forces from Yorktown. The French

Heroic charge
This somewhat fanciful illustration shows Napoleon bearing a tricolour flag as he leads a charge across a bridge at the battle of Arcole, 15–17 November 1796.

warships inflicted considerable damage as the British engaged in an uncoordinated fashion and withdrew.

BATTLE OF FRIGATE BAY
26 JANUARY 1782

Forces British: 22 ships; French: 29 ships, 6,000 troops. **Casualties** Low. **Location** Off St Kitts, West Indies.

The British fleet's brilliant manoeuvring forced the stronger French fleet from its anchorage, but the French forces that had already landed forced the surrender of St Kitts after an exchange of fire.

BATTLE OF THE SAINTES
12 APRIL 1782

Forces British: 36 ships; French: 33 ships. **Casualties** British: no ships lost, 1,059 killed; French: 5 ships captured, 1 sunk, 8,000 killed. **Location** Off Dominica, West Indies.

Calm winds and coppered hulls allowed the British to sail through the line of the French fleet, with devastating results. French power in the Caribbean suffered badly from this defeat.

SIEGE OF GIBRALTAR
24 JUNE 1779–7 FEBRUARY 1783

Forces British: 5,000–7,000; French and Spanish: c.10,000. **Casualties** British: 307; French and Spanish: c.5,000. **Location** Strait of Gibraltar, Mediterranean Sea, and neighbouring Spain.

Gibraltar's British garrison resisted scurvy, starvation, and floating gun batteries with the help of supply fleets and red-hot shot.

CUDDALORE 20 JUNE 1783

Forces British: 15 ships; French: 18 ships. **Casualties** British: 500; French: 500. **Location** Bay of Bengal.

French Admiral Suffren sailed to the Indian Ocean, attacking British shipping and fighting four battles with the British fleet. The last battle saved the French post at Cuddalore from capture by the British.

SECOND RUSSO–TURKISH WAR
1787–92

Turkish anger over Catherine the Great's annexation of the Crimea in 1786 boiled up in a war in which the Russian empress executed yet another drive upon the Bosporus. Fighting Russia and Austria simultaneously, the Turkish were saved only by Prussian intervention.

FIRST BATTLE OF THE LIMAN
17 JUNE 1788

Forces Russian: 18 ships, 19 gunboats; Turkish: 17 ships, 50 gunboats. **Casualties** Russian: 1 ship, 6 gunboats; Turkish: 9 ships, 20 gunboats. **Location** Dnieper river estuary, Black Sea.

The Russian heavy squadron was commanded by American naval hero John Paul Jones, now in the service of Catherine the Great. His ships mauled a Turkish squadron in shallow waters as it attempted to resist the Russian advance on Constantinople.

SECOND BATTLE OF THE LIMAN
29 JUNE 1788

Forces Russian: 17 ships, 36 gunboats; Turkish: 17 ships, 50 gunboats. **Casualties** Russian: 1 ship; Turkish: 10 ships, 5 gunboats. **Location** Dnieper river estuary, Black Sea.

The Turkish brought up their heavier vessels and found John Paul Jones's large warships anchored and ready to receive them. Meanwhile, the smaller ships of the Russians wrought havoc on the damaged or grounded Turkish vessels. The result was a decisive Russian victory.

SIEGE OF OCHAKOV
6 DECEMBER 1789

Forces Russian: 13,000; Turkish: 9,000. **Casualties** Russian: 4,000; Turkish: 8,300. **Location** Dnieper river estuary, Black Sea.

The Turkish fleet had been dispersed by the battles of the Liman. Russian Prince Grigori Potemkin used artillery and patience to reduce Ochakov, a major Turkish fortress. Turkish janissaries

British cavalry sword
The blade of this 1796 light cavalry sword is broadened towards the tip, to give greater power at the point of impact. It was considered among the finest cutting swords available at the turn of the 19th century.

attacked the besieging Russian forces, but Russian sappers broke into and seized the city.

BATTLE OF TENDRA 9 SEPTEMBER 1790

Forces Russian: 16 ships; Turkish: 22 ships. **Casualties** Russian: 50; Turkish: 700. **Location** Black Sea.

The great Russian admiral Fyodor Fyodorovich Ushakov encountered a powerful Turkish fleet already in line of battle. Ushakov manoeuvred from three lines into one, keeping the faster Turks from heading him off. Russian firepower settled the issue, leaving Russia now in control of the Black Sea.

FRENCH REVOLUTIONARY WARS
1792–99

Presuming that the French revolution was a contagion that would spread, the monarchical powers of Europe joined forces to restore the authority of the French monarchy. Despite dissension and disorganization, the revolutionary French, through their *levée en masse* (mass mobilization), successfully resisted.

VALMY 20 SEPTEMBER 1792

Forces French: 30,000; Coalition: 30,000–40,000. **Casualties** French: 300 killed; Coalition: 200 killed. **Location** Northeastern France.

Attempting to dislodge French Rrevolutionary forces from the heights of Valmy, the coalition army tried artillery bombardment, and then began an assault. Seeing that the French were not going to break, the coalition force withdrew.

JEMAPPES
6 NOVEMBER 1792

Forces French: 40,000–45,000; Austrian: 13,000–25,000. **Casualties** French: 2,000–4,000 killed or wounded; Austrian: 4,500 killed or wounded. **Location** North of Mons, eastern Belgium.

After an ineffective artillery barrage, the French launched a series of frontal assaults, which the Austrians drove off.

Eventually the weight of French numbers began to tell, and the Austrians were forced to withdraw.

TOULON
27 AUGUST–19 DECEMBER 1793

Forces Some 18,000 British, Spanish, and Piedmontese inside Toulon; French Republic: 32,000. **Casualties** No reliable estimates. **Location** Southern France.

Royalist forces invited an Anglo-Spanish fleet to occupy Toulon. They were driven out by the enterprise of the young Napoleon Bonaparte, whose force seized high ground from which artillery could command the port.

FLEURUS 26 JUNE 1794

Forces French: 75,000; Austrian and Dutch: 52,000. **Casualties** French: 4,000 killed; Austrian: 2,300 killed. **Location** North of Charleroi, Belgium.

Although his flanks were both driven back, the French commander used reconnaissance data from a hydrogen balloon to coordinate his response. The coalition forces pulled back, although the French were not in a position to pursue.

ARCOLE 15–17 NOVEMBER 1796

Forces French: 20,000; Austrian: 17,000. **Casualties** French: 4,500; Austrian: 6,000. **Location** Southeast of Verona, Italy.

Napoleon's attempts to cross the Alpone river by a bridge at Arcole were repulsed. However, French flanking movements convinced the Austrians that they were in danger of encirclement, so they withdrew.

CAPE ST VINCENT 14 FEBRUARY 1797

Forces Spanish: 27 ships; British: 15 ships. **Casualties** Spanish: 255 killed, 341 wounded, 4 ships captured; British: 73 killed, 227 wounded, no ships lost. **Location** Southwesternmost point of Portugal.

Spain had now entered an alliance with France and declared war on Britain. Intercepting the Spanish fleet on its way to join with French forces, the outnumbered British attacked and split the Spanish line of battle in two, inflicting a serious defeat and reinforcing British naval superiority.

CONSTELLATION TAKES INSURGENTE 9 FEBRUARY 1799

Forces French: 1 ship; American: 1 ship. **Casualties** French: 70; American: 3. **Location** Off the coast of Nevis.

A deterioration in Franco-American relations during the 1790s led the French to seize American shipping. The dispute erupted into military conflict that included a fight between the *Constellation* and the *Insurgente*. After a short, brutal battle, the American *Constellation* took the French frigate *Insurgente*, which had attacked an American flotilla.

THE AMERICANS SUBDUE THE EASTERN TRIBES
1778–1794

As Britain's ban on colonial expansion west of the Appalachians faltered, American settlers crossed the mountains and encountered powerful confederations of native peoples. The Americans prevailed by threatening the large Indian settlements.

SIEGE OF BOONESBOROUGH
17 SEPTEMBER 1778

Forces Indian and French militia: 400; American: 40. **Casualties** Indian: c.37; American: 6. **Location** Kentucky.

For 10 days a Shawnee war party under Chief Blackfish attempted to capture or burn Daniel Boone's settlement at Boonesborough. French-directed attempts failed in a heavy rain, and the Shawnee were forced to withdraw.

BATTLE OF PIQUA 8 AUGUST 1782

Forces Indian: 700; American: 1,050. **Casualties** Indian: c.40; American: 40. **Location** Near Springfield, Ohio.

General George Rogers Clark led a powerful American force against five Shawnee settlements, including the largest at Old Chillicothe in southwestern Ohio. The Indians evacuated the town but retreated after offering battle behind it. The Americans burned Chillicothe and its crops.

BATTLE OF BLUE LICKS
19 OCTOBER 1782

Forces British ranger: 50, Indian: 300; American: 182. **Casualties** British ranger and Indian: 17; American: 97. **Location** Near Mount Olivet, Kentucky.

The British had surrendered at Yorktown 10 months earlier ending the Revolutionary War, but a Shawnee war party and British rangers withdrawing from an attack on a settlement ambushed and destroyed a smaller pursuing force of Kentuckians, before withdrawing across the Ohio river.

"The roar was like **heavy thunder,** and the ship **shook** as if she was inclined to fall to pieces."
BRITISH MIDSHIPMAN GEORGE PARSONS ON THE USE OF NAVAL CANNON AT THE BATTLE OF CAPE ST VINCENT, 1797

BATTLE OF THE WABASH
4 NOVEMBER 1791

Forces Indian: 1,000; American: 900. **Casualties** Indian: 61; American: 600. **Location** Near Fort Recovery, Ohio.

A dawn attack by the Miami tribe on the camp of an American column inflicted the worst defeat ever suffered by the United States in combat against Indians.

BATTLE OF FALLEN TIMBERS
20 AUGUST 1794

Forces Indian: 1,400, Canadian: 70; American 3,000. **Casualties** Indian: heavy, Canadian: unknown; American: 144. **Location** Maumee, near Toledo, Ohio.

General Wayne's "Legion of the United States" brought vengeance on the confederated tribes of the Northwest. Wayne's powerful frontal assault at the battle of Fallen Timbers, flanked by cavalry, crushed Indian resistance and forced a peace settlement that lasted for 15 years.

Nelson's victory at the Nile
During the battle of the Nile on the night of 1 August 1798, the powder magazine of the French flagship *l'Orient* exploded, killing around 900 sailors.

NAPOLEON'S EGYPTIAN CAMPAIGN
1798–99

Seeking new resources and to sever Britain's link with India, Napoleon turned against the decrepit Ottoman empire and took a fleet and army into the eastern Mediterranean. However, Napoleon's prospects in the east withered after Nelson annihilated his fleet, and, despite a victory over the Ottomans at Aboukir, Napoleon was forced to abandon his army.

PYRAMIDS 21 JULY 1798

Forces French: 25,000; Egyptian: 20,000–30,000, including 6,000 Mameluk cavalry. **Casualties** French: 29 killed, 260 wounded; Egyptian: 4,000 killed (2,000 Mameluk). **Location** Embabeh, near Cairo, Egypt.

The French formation consisted of squares whose fire interlocked, augmented by artillery positioned at the corners. The Mameluk cavalry could not penetrate the squares and was eventually driven off.

NILE (ABOUKIR BAY)
1–2 AUGUST 1798

Forces British: 14 ships; French: 13 ships. **Casualties** British: no ships lost; French: 9 ships captured, 2 destroyed. **Location** Mediterranean Sea near Alexandria, Egypt.

Surprising the French fleet in harbour, the British ships anchored alongside their French counterparts and opened fire. The fighting continued through the night, and only two French ships escaped.

ABOUKIR 25 JULY 1799

Forces French: 10,000; Ottoman: 15,000. **Casualties** French: 220 killed, 750 wounded; Ottoman: c.2,000 killed. **Location** Near Alexandria, Egypt

As the French infantry applied pressure, the cavalry delivered a charge that broke the Ottoman force. The Turkish fled to their ships in defeat.

SECOND COALITION
1799–1802

While Napoleon was on expedition in Egypt, European powers united for the second time in an attempt to curtail revolutionary France. Great Britain, Austria, Russia, and Turkey launched attacks on Napoleon, who proved up to the challenge.

Battle for Egypt
At the battle of the Pyramids on 21 July 1798, Napoleon defeated Murad Bey's Mameluk army and conquered Egypt. As this image shows, the pyramids after which the battle is named were barely visible on the horizon.

NOVI
15 AUGUST 1799

Forces Austrian and Russian: 51,547; French: 34,930. **Casualties** Austrian and Russian: 8,200; French: 12,000 plus 4,600 prisoners. **Location** Novi Ligure, Piedmont, Italy.

Although the French commander was killed by skirmisher fire early in the battle, the French army repulsed several Austro-Russian attacks. Late in the day, the Austro-Russians finally managed to break through and forced the French into retreat.

> ## 'We are now preparing for a **march of five days** across the **desert**."
>
> ADJUTANT TO NAPOLEON'S STAFF DURING THE EGYPT CAMPAIGN, 1798

BERGEN 19 SEPTEMBER 1799

Forces British and Russian: 30,000; French and Dutch: 22,000. **Casualties** British and Russian: 3,537; French and Dutch: 3,000 prisoners plus an unknown number of casualties. **Location** North Sea coast of the Netherlands.

The Anglo-Russian force launched a confused attack delayed by bad roads and deficiencies in command. As a result, the Russians found themselves unsupported by the British and their attack was repulsed with considerable losses.

MONTEBELLO 9 JUNE 1800

Forces Austrian: 18,000; French: 14,000. **Casualties** Austrian: 4,275; French: 3,000. **Location** Lombardy, Italy.

Despite being outnumbered, the French launched repeated attacks. In the early afternoon French reinforcements arrived, after which the Austrian position began to crumble, causing them to retreat.

MARENGO 14 JUNE 1800

Forces Austrian: 31,000; French: 32,000. **Casualties** Austrian: 9,400 killed, wounded, or taken prisoner; French: 7,000 killed or wounded. **Location** Northern Italy.

Catching the French army dispersed and unready for battle, the Austrians' initial attacks prevailed. The arrival of detached French forces turned the tide, resulting in a hard-fought victory for Napoleon.

HOHENLINDEN 3 DECEMBER 1800

Forces Austrian: 70,000; French: 60,000. **Casualties** Austrian: 6,000 plus 11,000 prisoners; French: 5,000. **Location** Near Munich, Germany.

The French force invited an Austrian attack, which became disordered because of the close terrain. The French were then able to concentrate fire against each of the dispersed Austrian forces in turn, inflicting a decisive defeat.

COPENHAGEN 2 APRIL 1801

Forces Danish: 18 ships; British: 33 ships (12 committed to battle). **Casualties** Danish: 12 ships captured, 2 ships sunk; 1 ship destroyed; British: no ships lost. **Location** Just off Copenhagen, Denmark.

The Royal Navy was sent to prevent the Danish fleet from enforcing free trade with France. Negotiating natural hazards while engaging enemy warships, armed hulks, and floating gun batteries, the British fleet was ordered to withdraw at the height of the battle. Admiral Horatio Nelson chose not to see the signal and the British prevailed.

ALGECIRAS BAY 8, 12 JULY 1801

Forces British: 7 ships of the line; French: 8 ships of the line. **Casualties** British: 1 ship captured; French: 2 ships lost, 1 ship captured. **Location** Near Gibraltar.

The British squadron attempted to attack a French force that was protected by Spanish coastal forts, but failed. Four days later, reinforced by Spanish ships, the French squadron left port. The British attacked again, this time successfully. The war of the second coalition was ended by the Treaty of Amiens the following March.

ASSAYE 23 SEPTEMBER 1803

Forces British East India Company and Indian: 13,500; Maratha Confederacy: 40,000. **Casualties** British East India Company and Indian: 1,500; Maratha Confederacy: 6,000. **Location** Western India.

French Napoleonic uniform

This uniform of a French *voltigeur* (a member of a French military skirmish unit) of the 21st Regiment of the Line includes a dark blue jacket and white trousers.

Marching to meet a coalition of Maratha princes during the Second Anglo-Maratha War, the British force met the coalition earlier than anticipated. Although outnumbered, the British made an immediate attack, capturing the enemy cannon and their defensive position in the village of Assaye.

THIRD COALITION 1803–06

Britain had stood alone against Napoleon since 1803, until Austria, Prussia, Portugal, and Russia resumed hostilities against him in 1805. Napoleon again succeeded in gradually defeating the coalition, but the Royal Navy preserved Britain.

CAPE FINISTERRE 22 JULY 1805

Forces British: 15 ships of the line; French and Spanish: 20 ships of the line. **Casualties** British: no ships lost; French and Spanish: 2 ships captured. **Location** Off Galicia, Spain.

The Franco-Spanish force intended to enter the English Channel to invade England and Ireland. It was successfully intercepted by a British squadron in a chaotic battle fought in poor visibility.

WERTIGEN 8 OCTOBER 1805

Forces Austrian: 5,500; French: 12,000. **Casualties** Austrian: 4,000 plus 2,900 prisoners; French: 200 or more. **Location** Southern Germany.

The rapid French advance caught the Austrians unawares, and only 5,500 men out of a much larger force took the field. Heavily defeated, the Austrians began to retreat towards Ulm.

ULM 16–19 OCTOBER 1805

Forces Austrian: 45,000; French: 150,000. **Casualties** Austrian: 10,000 killed or wounded, 30,000 taken prisoner; French: 1,500 killed or wounded. **Location** Southern Germany.

As the Austrian army waited at Ulm for its Russian allies to appear, a French army, which had arrived much faster than the Austrians had anticipated, encircled it. After failed breakout attempts, the Austrians surrendered.

MILITARY MASCOTS

Unit/army (date)	Mascot
Alexander the Great, Macedonian empire (c.336–323 BCE)	Bucephalus, Alexander's beloved warhorse, died after the battle of the Hydaspes river (325 BCE) in India.
US Army (1775–present)	General Scott, a mule, is the mascot of the US Military Academy. The first Army mule mascot, adopted in 1936, was called Mr Jackson.
Hans Majestet Kongens Garde (King's Guard), Norway (1856–present)	Nils Olav II, a king penguin living at the Edinburgh Zoo, Scotland, currently holds the honorary rank of colonel in chief of the regiment.
Irish Guards, British Army (1900–present)	Fergal, an Irish wolfhound, is the latest in a long line of wolfhound mascots of the Irish Guards, dating back to 1902.

TRAFALGAR 21 OCTOBER 1805

Forces British: 27 ships of the line; French-Spanish: 33 ships of the line. **Casualties** British: no ships lost; French-Spanish: 21 ships captured, 1 ship destroyed. **Location** South of Cádiz, off Cape Trafalgar.

Cutting through the Franco-Spanish line of battle at two points, the British fleet, boldly led by Admiral Horatio Nelson, brought on a close-quarters action, where its superior gunnery and seamanship overwhelmed the enemy.

AMSTETTEN 5 NOVEMBER 1805

Forces Russian and Austrian: 6,700; French: 10,000. **Casualties** Russian and Austrian: 1,300, plus around 700 prisoners; French: 1,000. **Location** Austria.

After an attack by French cavalry the Austro-Russian force counterattacked, but were defeated by artillery fire. As French reinforcements came up, the allies were slowly pushed out of their positions.

HOLLABRUNN 16 NOVEMBER 1805

Forces Russian: 7,300; French: 20,600. **Casualties** Russian: 2,402; French: 1,200. **Location** Austria.

After capturing an important bridge, the French attacked the next evening. The

Russians withdrew, but delayed the French long enough for the Austrian and Russian armies to make a junction at Brunn.

AUSTERLITZ
2 DECEMBER 1805

Forces French: 73,000; Allied: Russian: 70,000, Austrian: 15,000. **Casualties** French: 1,300 killed, 7,000 wounded; Allied: 16,000 killed or wounded, 11,500 taken prisoner. **Location** Moravia (in modern-day Czech Republic).

As the Austrians and Russians attacked the deliberately weakened French right, the main French attack advanced through morning fog and took the high ground in the allied centre. It was Napoleon's greatest victory.

MAIDA 18 JULY 1806

Forces British: 5,000; French: 6,440. **Casualties** British: 387; French: 1,785. **Location** Calabria, Italy.

A British force landed in support of guerrillas fighting against French rule. This was the first time the British line and French column met in direct combat. The French columns were defeated by British firepower.

WAR OF THE FOURTH COALITION
1806–07

As individual members of the Third Coalition made peace with France, the rest of the alliance collapsed. However, it was replaced by a Fourth Coalition consisting of Prussia, Russia, Sweden, the United Kingdom, and their allies. The conflict in Europe went on unabated.

JENA-AUERSTÄDT 14 OCTOBER 1806

Forces French: 121,000; Prussian: 117,000. **Casualties** French: 12,000 killed or wounded; Prussian: 40,000 killed, wounded, or taken prisoner. **Location** East of Weimar, Germany.

As the main French army under Napoleon engaged the Prussians at Jena, a flanking force encountered a larger

Prussian formation. After a defensive battle the French counterattacked at Auerstädt and routed their opponents.

LÜBECK 6 NOVEMBER 1806

Forces Prussian: 15,000; French: 30,000. **Casualties** Prussian: 2,000, plus 4,000 prisoners; French: around 1,000. **Location** Northern Germany.

Most Prussian field forces and fortresses surrendered in the panic following the defeat at Jena-Auerstädt. One that had not was pursued to Lübeck, where it was forced to fight a superior French force. Having run out of food and ammunition, the Prussian force surrendered the following day.

GOLYMIN 26 DECEMBER 1806

Forces Russian: 16,000; French: 38,000. **Casualties** Russian: 750; French: 700. **Location** Near Warsaw, Poland.

"They **cannot** now **escape us**! I may … lose a leg; but that will be **cheaply purchasing** a **victory**."

ADMIRAL HORATIO NELSON AT TRAFALGAR, 21 OCTOBER 1805

Pitched battle
Admiral Horatio Nelson (standing, right) observes the cannonade at the battle of Trafalgar from HMS *Victory*'s weather deck. The battle was a resounding victory for the British Royal Navy.

Retreating Russian forces were brought to action at Golymin by the French, who could not bring their artillery up along the muddy roads. An inconclusive battle ensued, after which the Russian force continued to pull back.

PULTUSK 26 DECEMBER 1806

Forces Prussian and Russian: 40,000; French: 25,000. **Casualties** Prussian and Russian: 5,000; French: 7,000. **Location** 61km (38 miles) north of Warsaw, Poland.

French attacks met with initial success, but Russian counterattacks restored the situation in most areas. By the afternoon the French were starting to lose, but were reinforced and renewed the attack. The action was inconclusive, but the Russian force pulled back, some elements joining up with units retiring from Golymin.

EYLAU 8 FEBRUARY 1807

Forces French: 71,000; Russian: 76,000. **Casualties** French: 25,000 killed or wounded; Russian: 15,000 killed or wounded. **Location** Modern-day Bagrationovsk, Russia.

Colliding with the Russian army in a snowstorm, the French launched a frontal assault that was repulsed with huge losses.

A huge French cavalry charge restored the situation, and French reinforcements prompted a Russian withdrawal.

DANZIG 19 MARCH–24 MAY 1807

Forces Prussian and Russian: 20,000; French: 27,000. **Casualties** Prussian and Russian: 11,000; French: 400. **Location** Modern-day Gdansk, northern Poland.

French forces encircled the city of Danzig and beat off a Russian attempt to reinforce the garrison. After a period of bombardment and mining, the garrison surrendered on generous terms.

FRIEDLAND 14 JUNE 1807

Forces Russian: 46,000; French: 80,000. **Casualties** Russian: 25,000; French: 8,000. **Location** 40km (25 miles) southeast of Konigsberg, Lithuania.

The Russian army crossed the Alle river and attacked what it thought was an isolated French corps. Additional French forces joined the fighting, inflicting a severe defeat on the Russians. A peace treaty was agreed a few weeks later.

PENINSULAR WAR 1808–14

The tide turned against Napoleon when he thrust his brother onto the vacant throne of Spain. Portugal and Britain supported grim Spanish resistance. During the war, Britain's Arthur Wellesley (later Duke of Wellington) emerged as an adversary capable of meeting Napoleon on his own terms.

BAILEN 19 JULY 1808

Forces Spanish: 35,000; French: 20,000. **Casualties** Spanish: light; French: entire force killed or captured. **Location** Southern Spain.

Isolated by a Spanish rising against French rule, a French corps surrendered in return for safe conduct to France. Instead, many of the prisoners were massacred by Spanish irregulars, and the remainder were mostly confined in prison hulks.

VIMEIRO 21 AUGUST 1808

Forces British and Portuguese: 18,800; French: 13,000. **Casualties** British and Portuguese: 700; French: 2,000. **Location** Portugal.

The British took up a position on a ridge between the village of Vimeiro and the sea. From there, they beat back French infantry columns attacking up the slope.

BURGOS 7 NOVEMBER 1808

Forces Spanish: 9,000; French: 24,000. **Casualties** Spanish: 2,000, including prisoners; French: No reliable estimates. **Location** Northern Spain.

French attacks overwhelmed the heavily outnumbered Spanish, but they were able to retreat thanks to a determined stand by their rearguard, which was almost entirely wiped out by repeated cavalry charges.

Blood relic
At the battle of Jena, on 14 October 1806, a priest at Hassenhausen, Germany, used a church ledger to splint a soldier's injuries. The book, displayed here with a collection of lead musket balls, is still stained with blood.

HISTORY'S LARGEST NAVAL BATTLES

Battle	Location	Fleets	Description
Salamis (480 BCE)	Straits of Salamis, off Greece	1,207 warships of the Persian Achaemenid empire versus 378 vessels of the Greek Alliance	After the famous defeat at the battle of Thermopylae, the Greeks' triremes turned the tables when they destroyed 200 Persian warships (contrasted with a loss of just 40 of their own), and drove Xerxes I's invasion force back into Asia.
Yaman (1279)	South China Sea, off Guangdong Province, China	More than 1,000 warships of the Song dynasty's navy versus approximately 50 vessels in the service of Kublai Khan's Yuan dynasty	Although outnumbered more than 10 to 1, the Mongol force used superior tactics to defeat and destroy the Song's naval power, annihilating the Song dynasty, and securing Yuan dominance in China.
Lepanto (1571)	Gulf of Patras, Ionian Sea	284 warships of the Holy League (including the Papacy, Venice, Spain, Genoa, and the Duchy of Savoy) versus 277 vessels of the Ottoman empire	In the third and greatest battle of this name since 1499, a massive seaborne artillery duel resulted in the destruction and rout of the Ottoman fleet, and the loss of more than 20,000 men.
Trafalgar (1805)	Cape Trafalgar, off the Atlantic Coast of Spain	41 warships of the First French empire and the Spanish fleet versus 33 vessels of the British Royal Navy	Vice Admiral Horatio Nelson attacked a superior force under Pierre de Villeneuve from his flagship, the 100-gun ship-of-the-line HMS *Victory*. By crossing the French line with his own line, Viscount Nelson effectively cut his opponent's forces in half. After a couple of hours' fighting, the French and Spanish withdrew, having lost 22 ships and suffering almost 5,000 men killed and wounded. Nelson himself was mortally wounded by a French musket ball.
Jutland (1916)	Skagerrak Strait, off Norway and Denmark	151 warships, including 28 battleships of the Grand Fleet of Britain's Royal Navy versus 99 vessels, including 16 battleships, of the High Seas Fleet of the German Kaiserliche Marine	Admiral Sir John Jellicoe's Grand Fleet, which included 28 battleships, met the German fleet commanded by Reinhard Scheer off the coast of Denmark. Although outnumbered, the 16 battleships of the German High Seas Fleet had drawn the British into an epic duel. The German fleet inflicted heavy casualties on the British battle cruiser squadron, but it was forced to retreat to harbour, where it remained for the rest of World War I.
Philippine Sea (1944)	Eastern Philippine Sea, off the Marianas Islands	129 warships of the US Navy (including 15 aircraft carriers and seven battleships) versus 57 vessels of the Imperial Japanese Navy (IJN) (including nine carriers and five battleships)	In the largest aircraft-carrier battle in the history of naval warfare, the Americans sank three Japanese carriers and destroyed more than 600 planes. It was a battering from which the IJN never recovered.

Siege of Badajoz
In one of the bloodiest battles of the Napoleonic Wars, British and Portuguese soldiers commanded by Wellington captured the town of Badajoz in Spain.

ZARAGOZA
20 DECEMBER 1808–20 FEBRUARY 1809

Forces Spanish: 32,400; French: 44,000. **Casualties** Spanish: 54,000 including noncombatants; French: 4,000. **Location** Aragón, Spain.

Even though the defences of the city had already been damaged from having to withstand repeated storming in an earlier siege, Zaragoza held out for several weeks. After the walls were breached, savage street fighting went on for some time, and the French were forced to lift the siege and withdraw.

LA CORUÑA
16 JANUARY 1809

Forces British: 15,000; French: 20,000. **Casualties** British: 800 killed or wounded; French: 1,000 killed or wounded. **Location** On the coast of Galicia, northwestern Spain.

After protecting the rest of the British army during its retreat, the rearguard took up defensive positions and beat off French attacks until the force could be evacuated by sea.

TALAVERA
28–29 JULY 1809

Forces British and Spanish: 24,000; French: 47,000. **Casualties** British and Spanish: 6,500 killed or wounded; French: 7,400 killed or wounded. **Location** 94km (58 miles) southwest of Madrid, central Spain.

Retreating towards Madrid, an outnumbered French army turned to fight at Talavera, making a series of attacks that almost broke the Anglo-Spanish line. Both sides then withdrew.

BUSSACO 27 SEPTEMBER 1810

Forces British and Portuguese: 50,000; French: 65,000. **Casualties** British and Portuguese: 1,250; French: 4,500. **Location** Near Luso, Portugal.

Wellington's Anglo-Portuguese force occupied a steep 16-km (10-mile) long ridge on the heights of Bussaco. As the French columns advanced, the allies were able to shift reinforcements along a road built by their engineers right behind British-Portuguese positions. Several French assaults were defeated by firepower and bayonet counterattacks.

FUENTES DE ONORO
3–5 MAY 1811

Forces British and Portuguese: 23,950; French: 46,000. **Casualties** British and Portuguese: 1,550; French: 2,260. **Location** 16km (10 miles) west of Ciudad Rodrigo, western Spain.

The French force marched to the relief of Almeida, which was under siege. Repeated assaults by the French almost succeeded in breaking through the Anglo-Portuguese position. The British right flank was turned, but close cooperation between cavalry and infantry units permitted the situation to be restored.

ALBUERA 16 MAY 1811

Forces British, Spanish, and Portuguese: 35,000; French: 24,600. **Casualties** British, Spanish, and Portuguese: 6,200; French: 8,000. **Location** 22km (14 miles) southeast of Badajoz, Spain.

Feinting at the centre of their force, the French made a flanking attack on the right, driving the Spanish troops there out of position. The first British units to respond were overrun, but the arrival of more reinforcements stabilized the situation.

SIEGE OF BADAJOZ
16 MARCH–6 APRIL 1812

Forces British: 40,000; French garrison: 5,000. **Casualties** British: 5,000 killed or wounded; French: 5,000 killed, wounded, or captured. **Location** Southern Spanish-Portuguese border.

After digging in around the city, the British launched a night assault, which became confused and disjointed. The British eventually fought their way into the town of Badajoz using scaling ladders.

SALAMANCA
22 JULY 1812

Forces British and Portuguese: 52,000; French: 48,000. **Casualties** British and Portuguese: 4,800 killed or wounded; French: 14,000 killed, wounded, or captured. **Location** Western Spain.

Attempting to block a British withdrawal, the French became overextended. An infantry attack broke up French squares for a cavalry assault. The French took heavy casualties and lost Madrid.

VITORIA
21 JUNE 1813

Forces British and Allied: 70,000; French: 50,000. **Casualties** British and Allied: 5,000 men; French: 8,000 men and 150 cannon. **Location** South of Bilbao, northern Spain.

Under Wellington, the British attacked in four columns, turning the French flanks and breaking through the centre. The victors were sidetracked from pursuit by the volume of loot and supplies left behind by the French.

TOULOUSE 10 APRIL 1814

Forces British and Spanish: 50,000; French: 42,000. **Casualties** British and Spanish: 4,500; French: 3,200. **Location** Southernwestern France.

As the Anglo-Spanish army advanced into France, the French Army of Spain made a stand at Toulouse. Neither commander was aware that the war was effectively over and that Napoleon had agreed to surrender. The French were defeated and pulled back from the city, and shortly afterwards a local armistice began.

THE FIFTH COALITION
1809

For the fifth time, a coalition rose up to oppose Napoleonic France. It consisted primarily of the United Kingdom and the Austrian empire, with assistance from Sicily, Sardinia, and Brunswick.

ABENSBERG 19–20 APRIL 1809

Forces Austrian: 90,000; French: 80,000. **Casualties** Austrian: 2,000; French: 2,800 plus 4,000 prisoners. **Location** Southwest of Regensberg, Bavaria, Germany.

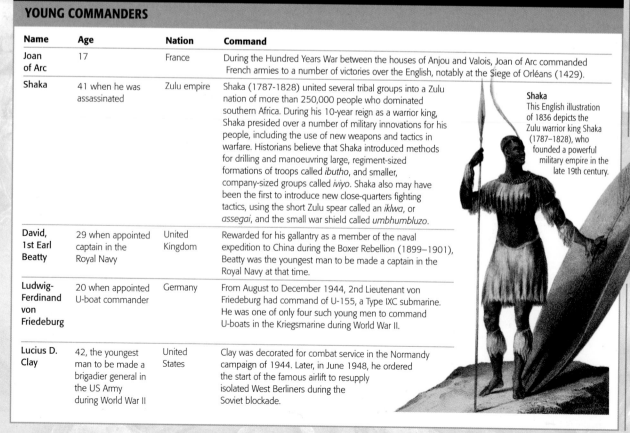

Shaka
This English illustration of 1836 depicts the Zulu warrior king Shaka (1787–1828), who founded a powerful military empire in the late 19th century.

YOUNG COMMANDERS

Name	Age	Nation	Command
Joan of Arc	17	France	During the Hundred Years War between the houses of Anjou and Valois, Joan of Arc commanded French armies to a number of victories over the English, notably at the Siege of Orléans (1429).
Shaka	41 when he was assassinated	Zulu empire	Shaka (1787-1828) united several tribal groups into a Zulu nation of more than 250,000 people who dominated southern Africa. During his 10-year reign as a warrior king, Shaka presided over a number of military innovations for his people, including the use of new weapons and tactics in warfare. Historians believe that Shaka introduced methods for drilling and manoeuvring large, regiment-sized formations of troops called *ibutho*, and smaller, company-sized groups called *iviyo*. Shaka also may have been the first to introduce new close-quarters fighting tactics, using the short Zulu spear called an *iklwa*, or *assegai*, and the small war shield called *umbhumbluzo*.
David, 1st Earl Beatty	29 when appointed captain in the Royal Navy	United Kingdom	Rewarded for his gallantry as a member of the naval expedition to China during the Boxer Rebellion (1899–1901), Beatty was the youngest man to be made a captain in the Royal Navy at that time.
Ludwig-Ferdinand von Friedeburg	20 when appointed U-boat commander	Germany	From August to December 1944, 2nd Lieutenant von Friedeburg had command of U-155, a Type IXC submarine. He was one of only four such young men to command U-boats in the Kriegsmarine during World War II.
Lucius D. Clay	42, the youngest man to be made a brigadier general in the US Army during World War II	United States	Clay was decorated for combat service in the Normandy campaign of 1944. Later, in June 1948, he ordered the start of the famous airlift to resupply isolated West Berliners during the Soviet blockade.

Austrian forces entered Bavaria and attempted to isolate and defeat a corps of the French army. The French concentrated their forces and inflicted a defeat, which broke the Austrian army in two, then pushed the halves apart.

RATISBON
19–23 APRIL 1809

Forces Austrian: 26,000; French: 37,000. **Casualties** Austrian: 6,000; French: 2,000. **Location** Regensberg, Bavaria, Germany.

Austrian forces captured Ratisbon on 20 April, and their presence in the city protected the Austrian retreat after the defeat at Abensberg. The French decided to storm Ratisbon, making two failed attempts before Marshal Lannes rallied his troops for a final, successful, attempt.

LANDSHUT
21 APRIL 1809

Forces Austrian: 36,000; French: 77,000. **Casualties** Austrian: 10,000; French: 3,000. **Location** Bavaria, Germany.

Retiring from the defeat at Abensberg, part of the Austrian army was cornered by a much larger French force. Additional French forces under the command of Napoleon himself arrived to ensure a decisive French victory.

ECKMUHL
21–22 APRIL 1809

Forces Austrian: 35,000; French: 30,000–60,000. **Casualties** Austrian: 12,000 including prisoners; French: 6,000. **Location** Bavaria, Germany.

Even though the Austrian army had been broken in two during the battle of Abensburg, it remained a potent force. The northern segment launched an attack which was countered by the arrival of French reinforcements. After heavy fighting the Austrians were forced to retire.

ASPERN-ESSLING
21–22 MAY 1809

Forces Austrian: 90,000; French: 55,000. **Casualties** Austrian: 23,000; French: 21,000. **Location** Lobau, 8km (5 miles) east of Vienna on the north side of the Danube river.

Seeking to destroy the Austrian army, the French crossed the Danube river using pontoon bridges via the island of Lobau. The Austrians attacked the bridgeheads in an attempt to dislodge them. After heavy fighting the French pulled back to the island.

WAGRAM 5–6 JULY 1809

Forces Austrian: 146,000; French: 170,000. **Casualties** Austrian: 40,000 killed or wounded; French: 37,000 killed or wounded. **Location** Northeast of Vienna, Austria.

After a day of fierce but indecisive fighting the Austrians attacked again, seriously threatening the French left flank. Once this attack was repelled, the French began to advance, winning a costly victory.

WALCHEREN CAMPAIGN
30 JULY–9 DECEMBER 1809

Forces British: 40,000; French and Dutch: 20,000. **Casualties** British: 4,000 including prisoners, plus many more sick; French: 5,000 plus many more sick. **Location** Mouth of the Scheldt estuary, Netherlands.

Hoping to destroy the French fleet at Flushing and create a second front against France, the British landed in the notoriously disease-ridden Walcheren region. The French moved their fleet and contained the British. Casualties from disease were higher than those sustained in combat for both.

NAPOLEON'S INVASION OF RUSSIA
1812

Napoleon's greatest desire at the pinnacle of his success and strength was to destroy Russia, the largest of his enemies. However, half a million French and their allies perished as the Russians used scorched-earth policies, as well as taking advantage of the winter cold, to undermine French military expertise.

KLYASTITSY
30 JULY–1 AUGUST 1812

Forces French: 28,000; Russian: 22,000. **Casualties** French: 5,500 killed, 1,000 taken prisoner; Russian: 3,500. **Location** Belarus.

French troops advancing towards St Petersburg were caught by surprise by Russian forces. Although their initial cavalry attack was successful, the Russians were unable to push their opponents back until the following day. A defeat at Klyastitsy prevented the French from reaching St Petersburg.

SMOLENSK
17 AUGUST 1812

Forces French: 50,000; Russian: 60,000. **Casualties** French: 12,000; Russian: 6,000. **Location** Russia.

Confusion over orders accidentally placed a Russian force in Smolensk where it blocked the French advance for a time. The French reached the walls of the city, but lacked any scaling apparatus to climb them. Eventually they breached the walls, but the Russians abandoned the city in order to save their army, giving the French the victory.

BORODINO
7 SEPTEMBER 1812

Forces French: 130,000; Russian: 120,000. **Casualties** French: 30,000 killed or wounded; Russian: 44,000 killed or wounded. **Location** 120km (75 miles) west of Moscow.

Ignoring advice recommending that he make a flanking attack, Napoleon launched a series of costly frontal assaults on well-fortified positions. Both sides took heavy casualties but, because the Russians withdrew, the French claimed victory.

MALOYAROSLAVETS
24 OCTOBER 1812

Forces French: 15,000; Russian: 20,000. **Casualties** French: 5,000; Russian: 6,000. **Location** 113km (70 miles) west of Moscow, Russia.

The French hoped to retreat from Moscow along a different route, avoiding areas they had stripped bare of fodder and supplies during their advance. The French vanguard was turned aside at Maloyaroslavets and instead had to march west via Smolensk, suffering terribly as a result.

BEREZINA RIVER
26–29 NOVEMBER 1812

Forces French: 85,000; Russian: 65,000. **Casualties** French: 50,000 killed or captured; Russian: 10,000 killed or wounded. **Location** East of Minsk (in modern Belarus).

Napoleon had originally intended to retreat across the frozen Berezina river, but he found it thawed. Trapped between a pursuing Russian army and the icy river, the French fought a defensive action while engineers built two wooden bridges. The French destroyed these after the remnants of their army had passed over them.

Napoleon, Roman god
Exemplary of neoclassical artistic style, this marble bust (c.1806) of Napoleon, by Italian sculptor Antonio Canova (1757–1822), portrays the emperor as a Roman god.

> "The presence of the **general** is **necessary**… It was not the **Roman army** which reduced Gaul, but Caesar."

NAPOLEON BONAPARTE, WRITING IN HIS DIARY, 1801

EPIC FEATS OF LOGISTICS

Napoleon's invasion of Russia (1812)
When Napoleon moved his Grand Armée east, he faced a major challenge provisioning such a large force. However, Napoleon had developed a sophisticated logistics infrastructure. This included 17 battalions of 6,000 vehicles each, which would supply his troops for 40 days. Also, magazine stores were set up in several towns along the march in Poland and Prussia. In the event, the preparations proved inadequate for the long journey to Moscow. The Russian retreat drew Napoleon away from his lines of supply. This, and the terrible Russian winter, proved to be his undoing.

Battle of the Atlantic (1939–45)
At the beginning of World War II, the German navy was able to inflict heavy losses on Allied merchant shipping, almost with impunity. By the end of the war, this longest battle had cost the lives of 30,248 Allied merchant sailors and 28,000 Kriegsmarine sailors. The Germans sank 3,500 Allied ships and lost 783 U-boats. Despite mass attacks on the convoys, the Allies were still able to deliver approximately 165 million tons of supplies to besieged Britain, owing much to good convoy strategies and new technology in place to protect ships. In addition, the massive shipbuilding effort in the US was more than able to replace the vessels lost.

The Berlin Airlift (1948–49)
After World War II, the Soviet Union occupied the eastern area of Germany, which included the capital, Berlin. In June 1948, a dispute arose between the Soviets and the other Allied armies that occupied the western half of Berlin. The Soviets blockaded the city, effectively isolating it from communication with the Americans and British, and also cutting supplies of food and water. An airlift operation was organized to relieve the city. The 15-month campaign involved 278,228 sorties (individual flights) of American and British transport aircraft, delivering more than 2.3 million tons of supplies, at a cost of US$224 million.

The Ho Chi Minh Trail (1959–75)
Using centuries-old footpaths through the highlands of Indochina, the People's Army of Vietnam developed a vast network of about 16,000km (10,000 miles) of tracks and trails along which the Viet Cong and North Vietnamese moved more than 60 tons of materiel every day to support their war effort. Because a significant portion of the trail network passed through other nations such as Laos and Cambodia, which American policy initially forbade as targets for fear of widening the war, the Americans and South Vietnamese were unable to halt its traffic decisively.

BATTLE OF TIPPECANOE
7 NOVEMBER 1811
Forces American Indian confederation: 700; American: 970. **Casualties** American Indian confederation: c.120; American: 194. **Location** Prophetstown (near modern Battle Ground, Indiana).

A tribal confederation threatened the progress of white settlement of the area, by undermining concessions made by other Indian leaders. The Indian confederation attacked US troops before dawn, but was repulsed with a series of charges. The battle was considered a victory for the American troops.

WAR OF 1812
1812–15

The three-year "Second War of Independence", known as the War of 1812, was the child of the Napoleonic Wars, as both the British and the French seized American ships and cargoes in their struggles. British support of allied Indians on the frontier and the British navy's forcible recruitment of American seamen pushed the United States to declare war.

SURRENDER OF DETROIT
16 AUGUST, 1812
Forces British: 730, Indian: 600; American: 2,500. **Casualties** British: 2, Indian: unknown; American: 7. **Location** Michigan.

After an abortive invasion of Canada, a British force and an Indian force, led by the Shawnee leader Tecumseh, convinced the Americans that they were facing greater numbers and likely Indian atrocities. The American force surrendered the city with barely a shot fired.

QUEENSTON HEIGHTS
13 OCTOBER 1812
Forces British: 2,340; American: 6,660. **Casualties** British: 105; American: 370, 9,935 taken prisoner. **Location** Bank of the Niagara river, Upper Canada (near modern Queenston, Ontario).

The British decisively defeated the uncoordinated and ill-prepared American efforts to cross the Niagara river and invade Canada, even though their commander General Brock was killed in the conflict. The British took 9,935 American prisoners in the largest battle of the war so far.

BATTLE OF THE RAISIN RIVER
22 JANUARY 1813
Forces British: 1,300; American: 934. **Casualties** British: 182; American: 397. **Location** Near Lake Erie, Michigan.

British forces intercepted the invading American column, which collapsed after some resistance. Britain's Indian allies butchered around 60 of the 561 Americans they had taken prisoner.

SIEGE OF FORT MEIGS 1 MAY 1813
Forces British: 890, Indian: 1,200; American: 1,100. **Casualties** British: 102, Indian: 19; American: 270. **Location** Near modern-day Toledo, Ohio.

A British force and an Indian force, led by Tecumseh, attacked the largest American post left after the Detroit debacle, only to find the Americans well defended and within range of reinforcements. Artillery and deception failed to take the fort.

CRANEY ISLAND 20 JUNE 1813
Forces British: 8 ships, 3,000 men; American: 150. **Casualties** British: 400; American: low. **Location** Off Norfolk, Virginia.

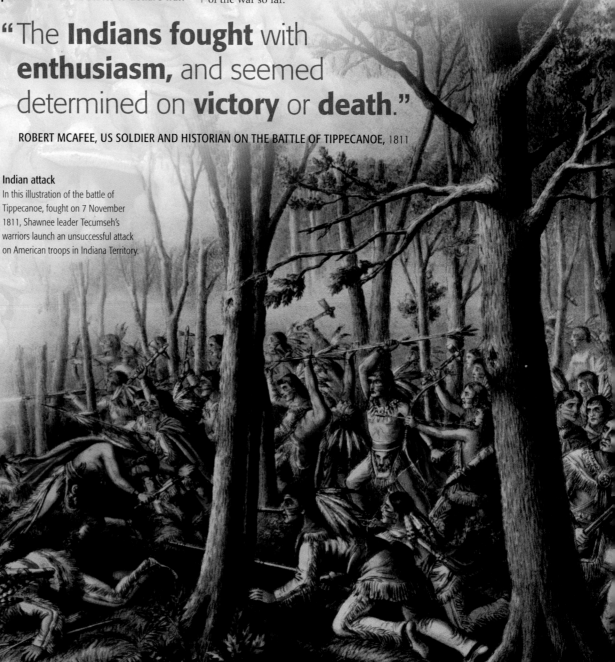

"The **Indians fought** with **enthusiasm,** and seemed determined on **victory** or **death**."

ROBERT MCAFEE, US SOLDIER AND HISTORIAN ON THE BATTLE OF TIPPECANOE, 1811

Indian attack
In this illustration of the battle of Tippecanoe, fought on 7 November 1811, Shawnee leader Tecumseh's warriors launch an unsuccessful attack on American troops in Indiana Territory.

A powerful British fleet landed troops and used Congreve rockets in an attempt to take the Norfolk navy yard and burn the *Constellation*; however, her gunners at the fort and the Virginia militia drove the British back with heavy losses.

BATTLE OF THE THAMES
5 OCTOBER 1813

Forces British: 430, Indian: 500; American: 3,000. **Casualties** British: 80, Indian: 33 or more; American: 45. **Location** Near modern Chatham, Ontario.

Retreating back into Canada, British and Indian forces made a stand on some high ground near Moraviantown. The Americans scattered the British with a cavalry charge, while infantry killed Tecumseh, the Shawnee Indian leader, and repelled a fierce Indian attack.

CHÂTEAUGUAY
26 OCTOBER 1813

Forces Canadian: 1,450, Indian: 180; American: 4,000. **Casualties** Canadian: 21, Indian: unknown; American: 70. **Location** Modern Ormstown, Quebec, Canada.

A force of mostly French-Canadian militia and Mohawk Indians blocked another American column of inexperienced troops from invading Canada. The Americans gave up after failing to turn the French-Canadian position.

BATTLE OF HORSESHOE BEND
27 MARCH 1814

Forces Indian: 1,200; American: 3,000. **Casualties** Indian: 800; American: 131. **Location** Near Dadeville, central Alabama.

The powerful Creek tribe rose in answer to the urgings of Tecumseh, who had spent much of his life rallying various tribes to defend their lands. The Creek attacked isolated American posts and settlements. General Andrew Jackson, wanting to clear Alabama for white settlement, crushed the Creeks' defended camp with artillery and the assistance of allied Indian tribes.

BATTLE OF CHIPPAWA 3 JULY 1814

Forces British: 2,000; American: 4,800. **Casualties** British: 515; American: 318. **Location** West bank of the Niagara river, Niagara Falls, Ontario, Canada.

Fort McHenry, Maryland

With the star-shaped layout of its walls and redoubts, Fort McHenry is an example of Vauban-style fortification. The fort was a centrepiece of the American victory at the battle of Baltimore on 12–15 September 1815.

American forces took Fort Erie from the British, who counterattacked, only to be bloodily repulsed by American artillery. The Americans retained the fort.

LUNDY'S LANE 25 JULY 1814

Forces British: 3,000; American: 3,100. **Casualties** British: 643; American: 744. **Location** Near Niagara Falls, Ontario.

A British force moving towards the border of the United States and Canada encountered an American advance force. The Americans attacked, suffering heavy losses before withdrawing.

BLADENSBURG RACES
24 AUGUST 1814

Forces British: 4,000; American: 6,000. **Casualties** British: 245; American: 52. **Location** Near Washington D.C.

British rockets and veterans routed the inexperienced US militia and cleared the way for the burning of Washington DC. A stand by US sailors and marines allowed most of the American defenders to escape.

BALTIMORE 12–15 SEPTEMBER 1814

Forces American: 10,000 defenders; British: 5,000 troops. **Casualties** British: 82; American: 163. **Location** Maryland, 14km (9 miles) from Washington D.C.

After landing troops, the British fleet bombarded Fort McHenry. American General Ross died during the attack, but the city's defences and the fort still held, inspiring Francis Scott Key to write "The Star-spangled Banner".

BATTLE OF STONINGTON
9 AUGUST 1814

Forces British: 4 ships, 1,800 men; American: unknown number of civilians. **Casualties** British: 18, American: 7. **Location** Long Island Sound between Connecticut and Long Island, New York.

British Captain Thomas Hardy informed the citizens that he would destroy Stonington. The townspeople responded with cannon fire, inflicting many casualties on the British and forcing them to withdraw.

HISTORY'S MOST FAMOUS RETREATS

Retreat, or military withdrawal, is an orderly, armed manoeuvre under fire. Generally speaking, while retreat is necessary for a weaker or damaged force to escape capture or destruction by a stronger one, sometimes retreat is a wise tactical decision, even when on the offensive. Retreating with some, or all, of the force can allow a commander time.

Location, date	Description	Outcome
Fornovo, near Parma, Italy (1495)	In the opening battle of the Italian Wars, 20,000 soldiers of the League of Venice drove King Charles VIII and his army of 12,000 French troops out of Italy.	Charles VIII's bloody campaign to conquer Naples failed, and he was forced to retreat from the Italian peninsula. The result was something of a pyrrhic victory for the Italians: the French abandoned their campaign, but the league of Venice suffered 2,000 casualties, nearly twice those of the French (who lost 1,200 men).
Russia (1812)	After some initial successes, Napoleon's massive invasion force was outmatched on several occasions by Russian armies. During the retreat west, Napoleon endured some of his worst defeats, including at the battle of Berezina, where 50,000 of his men were killed or captured.	Of the approximately 600,000 soldiers of the Grande Armée that began the invasion of Russia in 1812, fewer than 10,000 returned to France. Most of these losses were caused by the extreme cold weather, and critical shortages in supplies of winter clothing, food, and fodder for the army's horses.
Afghanistan (1842)	During the First Anglo-Afghan War, following an uprising of native Afghans, and a subsequent British punitive expedition that laid waste to many Afghan towns, a force of approximately 11,000 British and Punjabi troops withdrew back to India.	The Duke of Wellington famously said, "It is easy to get into Afghanistan. The problem is getting out again." As they retreated, the British and Indian force lost at least 4,500 soldiers as they were harried by Afghan guerrillas along the mountainous route to India.
Galicia and Poland (1915)	During the Great Russian Retreat, Russian Grand Duke Nicholas withdrew his armies to the Pripet Marshes after being outmanoeuvred by a numerically superior German force.	This skilfully conducted retreat prevented an encirclement of three Russian armies and gained time for the nation's industry to improve its soldiers' equipment. But the price was high: more than 1 million Russian soldiers were killed and almost 1 million captured.
Normandy (1944)	In August, during the Allied invasion, a large German armoured and infantry force became encircled by the advancing British, Canadian, and American armies. Eight panzer divisions and 150,000 infantrymen attempted to break out of the "Falaise Pocket" and retreat south across the Seine.	The Allies killed more than 10,000 German soldiers (twice the losses of the Allied side, including 5,500 Canadians), destroyed more than 300 tanks and guns, and captured perhaps 50,000 German soldiers. The battle ended Operation Overlord and put the Germans on the defensive until December 1944.
Basra, Iraq (1991)	As US forces invaded, Iraqi conscripts and a retreating column of Iraqi armour withdrew to Basra on what became known as the "Highway of Death".	US strike aircraft attacked the 1,500 vehicles on the highway. The number of Iraqi casualties is unknown. Photographs of the aftermath show many burnt-out cars, trucks, and tanks.

Retreat from Russia
Napoleon and his beleaguered army retreated from Moscow in mid-November 1812.

COMMUNICATION TECHNOLOGIES THROUGH THE AGES

Despatches

Carried by messenger on horseback, on foot, or by ship, handwritten messages were for many centuries an important method of reporting on the outcome of battles and communicating orders. One long-standing method of carrying written messages over long distances was by carrier pigeon. In his expedition to Gaul, Julius Caesar used pigeons to deliver messages. In 1870–71, in the Franco-Prussian War, the method was revived, and many European armies developed their own variants of the "pigeon post". In World War I, messenger pigeons, and dogs, played an important role in battlefield communication. In 1918, the American Expeditionary Force's famous pigeon, Cher Ami, helped to save the "Lost Battalion".

Radio

In the early 20th century, experiments in practical wireless telegraphy helped to revolutionize field communications. Freed from wires, lines of communication were limited only by line of sight. Improvements in field radio technology allowed frontline units to penetrate even further behind enemy lines while remaining in contact with their commanders. Later in the 20th century, satellite radio communications broadened the scale of tactical communication globally.

Telegraph

Developed in the 1830s, the electric telegraph was a defining feature of 19th-century battlefield communication. One of the tasks regularly assigned to an army's engineer corps was the laying and maintenance of telegraph wires to ensure that command posts in the rear could instantly communicate with their soldiers at the front.

Early telegraphy
Telegraph receivers, such as the 19th-century model shown above, translated electrical impulses into coded messages, which could then be read by trained operators. Using this device greatly improved battlefield communications.

PENSACOLA 7 NOVEMBER 1814

Forces Spanish: 500; British: 200; American: 4,000. **Casualties** Spanish and British: low; American: 15. **Location** Florida panhandle, Florida.

Even as the British pressured their Spanish allies to allow them the use of Florida to threaten the Southern United States, Andrew Jackson arrived and forced the surrender of Pensacola. The British blew up Fort Barrancas, which they had been occupying, and evacuated by sea.

NEW ORLEANS 8 JANUARY 1815

Forces British: 10,000 troops; American: 5,000–7,000 troops. **Casualties** British: 700 killed, 1,400 wounded; American: 8 killed, 13 wounded. **Location** Mouth of the Mississippi river, New Orleans.

While the British assembled their forces, the Americans, led by General Andrew Jackson, fortified their position. The British had to advance across open terrain and were shot down in large numbers, including their commander.

WAR OF 1812 AT SEA
1812–15

After Trafalgar, Britain's command of the sea found only a few challengers, among them superb American ships specifically developed to outfight what they could not outrun. British force was overwhelming, yet still suffered defeats on the Great Lakes and in ship-to-ship duels.

CONSTITUTION TAKES GUERRIÈRE
19 AUGUST 1812

Forces British: 1 frigate; American: 1 frigate. **Casualties** British 1 ship; American: no ships lost. **Location** 966km (600 miles) due east of Boston, Massachusetts.

The British attacked with *Guerrière* immediately upon sighting *Constitution*. The Americans used their ship's heavier construction and armament to devastating effect, leaving *Guerrière* without a mast. The Americans scuttled *Guerrière* after taking her crew prisoner.

UNITED STATES TAKES
MACEDONIAN 25 OCTOBER 1812

Forces British: 1 frigate. American: 1 frigate. **Casualties** British 1 ship; American: no ships lost. **Location** Off the island of Madeira.

Mistaking *United States* for a smaller ship, the British ship sought a long-range engagement, in which she was outmanoeuvred and outgunned by the Americans' heavier vessel. The *Macedonian* was captured and entered the US Navy.

SHANNON TAKES CHESAPEAKE
1 JUNE 1813

Forces British: 1 ship; American: 1 ship. **Casualties** British: no ships lost; American: 1 ship. **Location** Off Boston Harbor, Massachusetts.

The ships opened fire, both making contact, but the British guns on *Shannon* did more damage, causing crippling casualties on *Chesapeake*'s quarterdeck and mortally wounding the US commander. Only 15 minutes after the battle had begun, *Chesapeake* was under British control.

LAKE ERIE 10 SEPTEMBER 1813

Forces American: 9 ships; Britain: 6 warships. **Casualties** American: 27 dead, 96 wounded; British: 41 dead, 94 wounded. **Location** Lake Erie.

With the American flagship disabled early in the action, the American commodore transferred under fire to another ship and led a bold attack, forcing a British surrender.

LAKE CHAMPLAIN
11 SEPTEMBER 1814

Forces British: 4 ships, 12 gunboats; American: 4 ships, 10 gunboats. **Casualties** British: 300; American: 200. **Location** Cumberland Bay, off Plattsburgh, New York State.

The British enjoyed a great advantage in heavier guns and ships, but their attack on the anchored American fleet disintegrated when the Americans winched their ships around to present fresh broadsides to the enemy.

FAYAL
25 SEPTEMBER 1814

Forces British: 4 ships, 2,000 men; American: 1 ship, 90 men. **Casualties** British: 260 men; American: 1 ship, 9 men. **Location** Azores islands, Atlantic Ocean.

An American privateer, the *General Armstrong*, was provisioning in a neutral port when a British fleet carrying troops to New Orleans demanded its surrender. The Americans resisted for three days, which delayed the British from reaching New Orleans for three weeks.

CAPTURE OF USS PRESIDENT
15 JANUARY 1815

Forces British: 3 ships, 1,050 men; American: 1 ship, 475 men. **Casualties** British: 25 men; American: 1 ship, 105 men. **Location** Off Long Island, New York State.

Escaping New York Harbor, the USS *President*'s keel was broken on a sand bar. The damage allowed the British HMS *Endymion* to overhaul and damage the *President* further, while British ships *Pomone*, *Majestic*, and *Tenedos* caught up with the battle and received the Americans' surrender.

CONSTITUTION TAKES CYANE AND
LEVANT 20 FEBRUARY 1815

Forces British: 1 frigate, 1 corvette; American: 1 frigate. **Casualties** British: 2 ships; American: no ships lost. **Location** 290km (180 miles) off Madeira, in the mid-Atlantic Ocean.

Overtaking the rearguard of a British convoy, the American frigate, *Constitution*, defeated two British ships despite their efforts to fight it in concert. Stewart took in his sails to rake *Cyane* twice, bringing her in as a prize.

SIXTH COALITION
1812–14

Napoleon's allies were weakened and disaffected after his disastrous attempt to invade Russia. Austria, Prussia, Sweden, Britain, Spain, Portugal, and the German states joined forces in the hope of finally destroying him. Having remodelled their armies along Napoleonic lines, the Allies succeeded in subduing France and sending Napoleon into exile on Elba.

Battle of Quatre-Bras 16 June 1815
In the foreground of this illustration of the battle of Quatre-Bras, the French 2nd Cavalry Division piles into the British lines, which included the 42nd Highlanders, also known as the "Black Watch".

LÜTZEN 2 MAY 1813

Forces Prussian and Russian: 73,000; French: 120,000. **Casualties** Prussian and Russian: 20,000; French: 22,000. **Location** Southwest of Liepzig.

Using one corps as bait, the French drew the Allied army into a trap. A large concentration of artillery was brought to bear on the Allied centre, while the Imperial Guard attacked the flank. The Allied force was able to break off, mainly due to the exhaustion of the French troops.

BAUTZEN 20–21 MAY 1813

Forces Prussian and Russian: 100,000; French: 199,000. **Casualties** Prussian and Russian: 15,000; French: 13,000. **Location** Eastern Saxony, Germany.

Detaching a large force to make a flank march, the main French army launched a successful frontal assault. The flank attack was less well handled, allowing the Allied army to retire in good order.

KATZBACH 26 AUGUST 1813

Forces Prussian and Russian: 114,000; French: 102,000. **Casualties** Prussian and Russian: 4,000; French: 15,000. **Location** near Liegnitz, Prussia (in modern Poland).

The French and Allied armies made unexpected contact during a heavy thunderstorm, and a confused battle ensued. A French flanking attempt failed, and an Allied counterattack in the centre forced the French to withdraw.

DRESDEN
26–27 AUGUST 1813

Forces Austrian, Prussian, and Russian: 158,000; French: 70,000. **Casualties** Austrian, Prussian, and Russian: 38,000; French: 10,000. **Location** Saxony, Germany.

Believing Dresden to be held by a single corps, the Allies attacked and were halted by the main French army. On the second day, the French launched an attack on the Allied flank and forced them to retreat.

LEIPZIG 16–19 OCTOBER 1813

Forces French: 195,000; Allied: 365,000. **Casualties** French: 70,000; killed, wounded, or captured; Allied: 54,000 killed or wounded. **Location** By the city of Leipzig, Saxony, Germany.

Vastly outnumbered by a coalition of nations, the French army made a stand at Leipzig. The French were eventually forced to withdraw, leaving about 15,000 men trapped on the wrong side of the Elster river.

THE DEFENCE OF FRANCE
29 JANUARY–31 MARCH 1814

Forces French: 110,000; Allied: 345,000. **Casualties** French: 30,000; Allied: 50,000. **Location** Eastern France.

With the allies advancing into France along three separate routes, Napoleon attempted to defeat each force in turn. Despite some brilliant successes, the weight of numbers inevitably resulted in his defeat.

SIX DAYS 10–14 FEBRUARY 1814

Forces Prussian and Russian: 100,000; French: 30,000. **Casualties** Prussian and Russian: 17,500; French: 3,400. **Location** Northeastern France.

Despite being considerably outnumbered, the French army inflicted a series of defeats on the Prussians at Champaubert, Montmirail, Chateau-Thierry, and Vauchamps. The Prussians took heavy casualties, but this was not enough to derail their advance on Paris.

PARIS
30–31 MARCH 1814

Forces Austrian, Prussian, and Russian: 100,000; French: 50,000. **Casualties** Austrian, Prussian, and Russian: 8,000; French: 4,000. **Location** France.

The Allies gradually reduced French defensive positions, despite a counterattack by elements of the Imperial Guard. An assault on the high ground at Montmartre resulted in heavy fighting, which the Allies eventually won. A segment of the French force arranged to be captured, and soon after the remainder of the garrison agreed to surrender.

THE 100 DAYS
1 MARCH–22 JUNE 1815

The "one hundred days" refers to the time between Napoleon's arrival in Paris until the restoration of the French monarchy. After fewer than 10 months in exile on the island of Elba, Napoleon escaped. Seven days before he returned to Paris, however, Napoleon was declared an outlaw, though the veterans of his Grand Armée had rallied to him. A Seventh Coalition was raised against him. He was defeated at the battle of Waterloo and Louis XVIII was restored to the throne.

LIGNY 16 JUNE 1815

Forces Prussian: 84,000; French: 70,000–80,000. **Casualties** Prussian: 16,000 killed or wounded; French: 12,000 killed or wounded. **Location** Northeast of Charleroi, southern Belgium.

Hoping to defeat the Prussians before they joined up with the British, Napoleon threw his main strength at them. The Prussians, while defeated, were not crushed and were able to continue the campaign.

QUATRE-BRAS 16 JUNE 1815

Forces British and Dutch: 32,000; French: 24,000. **Casualties** British and Dutch: 5,400 killed or wounded; French: 4,400. **Location** Northwest of Ligny, Belgium.

French delays in launching their attack allowed reinforcements to reach the weak Dutch force struggling to hold the crossroads at Quatre-Bras. The defence was successful, but the following day the Anglo-Dutch force withdrew.

"Let us be **grateful** to the **god** of battles…"

US MAJOR GENERAL ANDREW JACKSON, AFTER THE BATTLE OF NEW ORLEANS, 1815

General Andrew Jackson (1767–1845)
This bronze equestrian statue of the American general and, later, seventh US President, Andrew Jackson, commemorates the American victory over the British at the battle of New Orleans on 8 January 1815.

WAVRE 18–19 JUNE 1815

Forces Prussian: 17,000; French: 33,000. **Casualties** Prussian: 2,500; French: 2,500. **Location** Walloon Brabant province, Belgium.

The right wing of the French army attempted to prevent the Prussians from regaining contact with their Anglo-Dutch allies via the city of Wavre, which was held by the Prussian rearguard. Although the Prussians eventually retreated, they held off the French long enough for the majority of the Prussian army to march to Waterloo and contribute to the decisive victory there.

WATERLOO 18 JUNE 1815

Forces Allied: Anglo-Dutch 67,000, Prussian: 53,000; French: 74,000. **Casualties** Allied: Anglo-Dutch: 15,000, Prussian: 7,000; French: 25,000. **Location** Outside Waterloo village, south of Brussels, Belgium.

Hoping to break the Anglo-Dutch before the Prussians could assist them, the French attacked throughout the day. The arrival of the Prussians on the French flank made Napoleon's defeat inevitable.

LA SUFFEL 28 JUNE 1815

Forces Austrian: 40,000; French: 20,000. **Casualties** Austrian: 2,125; French: 3,000. **Location** Souffelweyersheim and Hoenheim, near Strasbourg, France.

The V Corps of the French Army was deployed against the Austrians, and so was not involved in the Waterloo campaign. Although the Napoleonic cause was lost by that time, V Corps engaged an Austrian army and inflicted a defeat.

French headgear
In the early 19th century, soldiers of many nations wore headgear called *shakos*, such as this light infantry example. Note the red feather plume, tricolour cockade, and brass imperial eagle plate.

ISSY 3 JULY 1815

Forces Prussian: unknown; French: unknown. **Casualties** Unknown. **Location** Southwest of Paris.

The last action of the Napoleonic Wars was fought at Issy, close to Paris. A strong French force, with artillery in support, launched an attack against an inferior Prussian force, but was beaten off. Thus the final attempt to defend Paris came to an end.

SOUTH AMERICAN WARS OF INDEPENDENCE
1810–24

A witness to Napoleon's campaigns, Simón Bolívar swore to liberate South America, a task aided by Napoleon's overthrow of Spain's government. Other rebels such as José de San Martín and Antonio José de Sucre joined him in the struggle to bring an end to Spanish control.

TUCUMÁN 25 SEPTEMBER 1812

Forces Rebel: 1,100; Royalist: 3,000. **Casualties** Rebel: 280; Royalist: 1,000. **Location** Just north of Santiago, Chile.

With a Royalist army advancing on Buenos Aires, Rebel leader General Manuel Belgrano disobeyed orders to retreat and made a stand against greater numbers and artillery. His cavalry plundered the Royalist supply train and forced a retreat.

BATTLE OF LA PUERTA 15 JUNE 1814

Forces Rebel: 3,000; Royalist: 7,000. **Casualties** Rebel: 3,500; Royalist: unknown. **Location** Central Venezuela.

Simón Bolívar's worst defeat came at the hands of Royalist José Tomás Boves, whose *llanero* light cavalry overwhelmed the Rebel army. Boves destroyed Bolívar's first Venezuelan Republic by killing all wounded and prisoners, and a great many civilians.

BATTLE OF SAN LORENZO
3 FEBRUARY 1813

Forces Rebel: 100; Royalist: 350. **Casualties** Rebel: 42; Royalist: 54. **Location** Bank of the Paraná river, Argentina.

Rebel José San Martín hid his elite cavalry in a monastery, erupting out to defeat a detachment of Royalist cavalry. A Rebel sergeant took a fatal thrust and saved his commander, who had become trapped under his slain horse.

CHACABUCO
12 FEBRUARY 1817

Forces Rebel: 3,000; Royalist: 1,500. **Casualties** Rebel: 12 dead, 120 injured; Royalist: 500 dead, 600 captured. **Location** Just north of Santiago, Chile.

Making a difficult crossing of the Andes, the Rebels were able to surprise the Spanish garrison in Chile. Initially repelled by cavalry, the Rebels attacked again on the flank, this time successfully.

> "The **Duke of Wellington** in **person** led some battalions of infantry against [the French] columns ... They attacked at the **point of the bayonet**."
>
> GENERAL COUNT POZZO DI BORGO, WITH THE RUSSIAN ARMY AT WATERLOO, IN A LETTER TO PRINCE WOLKONSKY, 1815

Napoleon at Waterloo
The view from Napoleon's position, near La Belle Alliance farm, at the battle of Waterloo on 18 June, 1815. The Anglo-Dutch position can be seen on the ridge in the background.

Defeat at Boyacá, 7 August 1819

After the defeat of the Spanish army at Boyacá, General Simón Bolívar (centre right) accepted the surrender of General Rodil. This pivotal battle ended Spanish rule in northern Latin America and made Bolívar a hero.

MILITARY SCANDALS

Location, date	Parties involved	Description
China, November 1839–42	Britain, China's Qing dynasty	As the British East India Company's trade in opium with China increased, Chinese authorities cracked down, demanding a halt to the illegal commerce that had addicted thousands of Chinese to the drug, even as it had enriched European treasuries. The British demanded compensation for opium seized by the Qing authorities. Lord Palmerston demanded compensation for trade losses and ordered British troops and warships to China. In the ensuing conflict, a numerically superior Chinese naval and military force was defeated, and the Qing emperor was forced to continue the opium trade with Britain and other Western powers. The war was a public scandal for the British government because it defended what some pamphleteers and newspapers called an "abominable vice".
France, November 1894	Captain Alfred Dreyfus	Dreyfus, a French artillery officer of Jewish descent, was falsely convicted of espionage and sentenced to life imprisonment on Devil's Island, Guiana, in 1894. Two years later, evidence emerged that implicated another man, but the French military command suppressed this. Newspaper reports of the affair resulted in a public outcry and allegations of anti-Semitism. A military commission exonerated Dreyfus in 1906.
Mogadishu, Somalia, March 1993	Soldiers of the Canadian Airborne Regiment; Shidane Arone, a Somali	Canadian soldiers captured, tortured, and murdered teenage civilian Arone, caught stealing supplies from the Canadian base. An inquiry led to the resignation of the Minister of National Defence and two senior generals. The Airborne Regiment was disbanded due to public revulsion and outcry.
Abu Ghraib Prison, Iraq, 2003	Soldiers of the US Army's 160th Military Police Battalion; Iraqi prisoners	After US newspapers published evidence that soldiers of the US Army had abused prisoners, the US Army filed charges against six soldiers for dereliction of duty and other crimes. In 2005, the prison's former commanding officer, Brigadier General Janice Karpinsky, was punished with suspension from duty and demotion to the rank of colonel.

MAIPU 2 APRIL 1818

Forces Rebel: 5,000; Royalist: 5,500. **Casualties** Rebel: 1,000; Royalist: 4,900. **Location** Near Santiago, Chile.

A Royalist force under Mariano Osorio moved up into the Chilean Highlands, and was shattered by José de San Martín's elite Argentine cavalry and artillery train.

BOYACÁ 7 AUGUST 1819

Forces Royalist: 3,000; Rebel: 3,000. **Casualties**. Rebel: unknown; Royalist: 100 dead, 1,800 captured. **Location** Outskirts of Bogotá, Colombia.

Struck in the flank and by a frontal assault at the same time, the Spanish attempted to make a cavalry attack, which was repelled by the Rebels. The Spanish force collapsed quickly thereafter.

CARABOBO 24 JUNE 1821

Forces Rebel, including British and Irish volunteers: 6,500; Royalist: 5,000. **Casualties** Rebel: 200; Royalist: 3,000. **Location** Plains near Caracas (in modern Venezuela).

The Royalist force was demoralized and suffering badly from desertion when it met the Rebel army at Carabobo. The Rebels attacked on the flank with infantry, and frontally with cavalry, winning a destructive victory.

AYACUCHO
9 DECEMBER 1824

Forces Rebel: 6,000; Royalist: 9,000. **Casualties** Rebel: 900; Royalist: 2,000 killed. **Location** The high plateau near Ayacucho, Peru.

Despite being outnumbered and heavily outgunned by the Royalist forces, the Independentist rebels led by Antonio José de Sucre launched an attack, spearheaded by a cavalry charge. The Royalist surrender secured the independence of Peru, and removed the last remaining Spanish force from South America.

CONQUESTS OF SHAKA
1818-28

Forces Zulu: 150,000; Other: unknown. **Casualties** Unknown, but in tens of thousands. **Location** Natal, South Africa.

After the assassination of the Zulu chief Dingiswayo, Shaka fought for supremacy with the king's assassin, Zwide. A brutal and innovative leader, Shaka added defeated enemies to his army, slowly gaining control of all of Natal. At the time of his assassination, Shaka could command more than 50,000 Zulu fighters.

The Dawn of Mechanized Warfare 1830–1914

By the early decades of the 19th century, small arms were accurate to several hundred metres, and the artillery pieces available were effective at much greater ranges. These innovations meant that it was no longer practical for combatants to fight in the traditional fashion, with armies arrayed in massed ranks, as they would present an easy target for enemy fire. It was not until several decades later, however, that the potential of these new technologies were fully realized.

LEAD RIFLE BULLETS

REVOLT OF ABD EL-QADIR 1832–47

Forces Algerian: around 10,000; French: up to 100,000. **Casualties** No reliable estimates. **Location** Modern Algeria.

Abd el-Qadir, emir of Mascara, proclaimed a holy war against French rule in Algeria. His forces were defeated in a brutal campaign that included the destruction of crops and livestock.

KONYA 21 DECEMBER 1832

Forces Turkish: unknown; Egyptian: unknown. **Casualties** No reliable estimates. **Location** south of Ankara, Turkey.

Supposedly a vassal of the weak Turkish government, Muhammad Ali effectively ruled an independent Egypt. In an attempt to occupy Syria, his army easily defeated Turkish forces at Konya, but was unable to fully capitalize on its victory because of European intervention.

PLAINS INDIAN WARS 1832–1890

The expansion of settlers into the west of North America inevitably resulted in conflict with the native population, who were forced from their ancestral lands.

BLACK HAWK WAR 1832

Forces US: 10,500 plus allied tribes; Black Hawk and allied: 500. **Casualties** US: 60–70; Black Hawk and allied: 450–600 including non-combatants. **Location** Modern Illinois and Wisconsin, USA.

The war, named for the Native American war chief, took the form of many minor skirmishes. Black Hawk and his followers achieved early victories using ambush tactics and surprise attacks, drawing in the US troops. Eventually Black Hawk's band was brought to action and shattered by overwhelming force.

SECOND SEMINOLE WAR 1835–36

Forces Seminole: 4,000 remaining when they surrendered; US: unknown. **Casualties** US: 2,000; Seminole: several thousand. **Location** Florida, USA.

US attempts to remove the Seminole from Florida resulted in a long and bloody guerrilla war, also known as the Florida War. It became the most expensive Indian war fought by the US. It was not until the Seminole leader Osceola had been taken hostage that the Seminole were ejected from their lands.

THE GREAT RAID AUGUST 1840

Forces US: possibly 200; Native American: possibly 1,000. **Casualties** US: at least 40; Native American: no reliable estimates. **Location** Around Linnville, Texas, USA.

In the largest-ever raid on white settlements by Native American forces, a large war party raided Victoria and sacked Linville, whose population took refuge on boats in the harbour. Intervention by Texas Rangers resulted in a running fight as the native force retreated.

DEFEAT OF THE NAVAJO
APRIL 1860–MARCH 1864

Forces US: unknown; Navajo: unknown. **Casualties** No reliable estimates. **Location**: Arizona, USA.

After a Navajo attack on Fort Defiance in 1860, US forces conducted a scorched-earth policy against the Navajo, finally penning them in the Canyon de Chelly.

Trophy scalp
A human scalp was removed, complete with hair, as a trophy of prowess in war by Native American warriors. Scalping was a common wartime practice among many Native American tribes.

When the starving Navajo surrendered, they were marched to Fort Sumner in New Mexico.

THE FETTERMAN FIGHT
21 DECEMBER 1866

Forces US cavalry: 80; Lakota Sioux, Northern Cheyenne, and Arapaho: 1,000. **Casualties** ; US cavalry: all 80 killed; Native American: unknown. **Location** Just outside Fort Kearny, Wyoming, USA.

Sent to the assistance of a wagon train, a US column under Captain Fetterman was lured into following an Indian decoy. His force advanced into an ambush and was totally wiped out.

RED RIVER WAR 1874–75

Forces US: 3,000; Cheyenne, Comanche, Kiowa, Kataka: several thousand. **Casualties** A few hundred dead on each side. **Location** Oklahoma and Texas, USA.

Resisting attempts to clear the region for white settlement, Native Americans fought many large engagements and even pitched battles. They were armed with ex-US Civil War rifles, but nevertheless were ultimately defeated.

ROSEBUD CREEK 17 JUNE 1876

Forces US cavalry: 1,300; Native American: 1,500. **Casualties** US cavalry: 31; Native American: 99. **Location**: Big Horn County, Montana, USA.

Overconfident US cavalry troops were caught in a surprise attack. After several hours of fighting, the Native American force broke off and withdrew. The cavalry also withdrew rather than joining up with Custer's command, a decision that might have altered the outcome at Little Bighorn.

LITTLE BIGHORN 25 JUNE 1876

Forces US cavalry: 600; Cheyenne and Dakota (Eastern Sioux): 900–1800 warriors. **Casualties** US cavalry: 268 killed, 55 wounded; Native American: 136 killed, 160 wounded. **Location** Little Bighorn river, Montana, USA.

Lt Col George Custer foolishly divided his force of 600 cavalrymen into three columns. He led one of these columns into a Native American ambush, and all 212 men were wiped out in the attack. The remaining two columns fought a desperate battle for two days until the arrival of reinforcements forced the Native Americans to retire.

WOLF MOUNTAIN 8 JANUARY 1877

Forces US cavalry: 436; Native American: around 500. **Casualties** US cavalry: 11; Native American: similar numbers. **Location**: Montana, USA.

Superior US firepower and the movement of reserves thwarted Native American attacks before a counterattack forced them to retreat. The action more or less brought the Sioux War to an end.

NEZ PERCÉ WAR JUNE–DECEMBER 1877

Forces US troops: 5,000; Nez Percé warriors: 250. **Casualties** US: 266; Nez Percé: 239, (including women and children). **Location** Idaho, Oregon, and Montana, USA.

After a period of mutual raiding, a band of Nez Percé Indians decided to relocate to Canada. They were pursued by government

---

TRIVIAL CAUSES OF CONFLICT

The War of the Bucket
Claiming booty after their victory over Bologna at the battle of Zappolino in 1325, some Modenan soldiers crept into Bologna's main town square and stole a bucket from the civic well. Feeling humiliated, the authorities of Bologna began what turned out to be a 12-year conflict that resulted in thousands of deaths.

The War of the Pig
In 1859, on San Juan Island, a territory on the disputed British-American boundary between Oregon and Columbia, a pig owned by British settler Charles Griffin of the Hudson Bay

Company wandered onto the land of American Lyman Cutler and was shot dead. Dispute over compensation for the pig expanded into a full-blown military conflict, with 500 American troops facing 2,000 British soldiers and five warships. British marines were ordered to engage the Americans, but refused to escalate the incident any further.

The War of the Stray Dog
In 1925, a Greek soldier on the Macedonian-Bulgarian border chased after his dog, and in doing so inadvertently crossed over to the Bulgarian side. There he was shot by an enthusiastic Bulgarian

sentry, precipitating a Greek invasion of Bulgaria that resulted in 50 deaths before the League of Nations negotiated a ceasefire.

The Soccer War
Political and social hostility between Honduras and El Salvador boiled over in 1969 after a series of acrimonious soccer matches between the two nations as part of the 1970 World Cup qualifiers. After two disputed matches, a third match in Mexico resulted in a 3–2 win for El Salvador, and the level of feeling that this provoked ran so high that it sparked a four-day war, resulting in more than 2,000 casualties.

troops and cornered just short of the border. Forced to surrender, they were dispatched to a reserve in Oklahoma.

WOUNDED KNEE 29 DECEMBER 1890

Forces US cavalry: unknown; Sioux: several hundred.
Casualties US cavalry:
25 killed, 30 wounded; Sioux: c.150 killed, 30 wounded.
Location Wounded Knee Creek, South Dakota, USA.

A band of Sioux Indians had left their reservation, but surrendered quietly to US cavalry. While they were being disarmed, a scuffle broke out that rapidly turned into a massacre.

Late 19th-century rifle
The .45–70-calibre, model 1873, Springfield "trapdoor" rifle was a breech-loading firearm used by the US Army during the Indian Wars of the late 19th century. This converted muzzle-loader used a metallic unitary cartridge and was faster to load than its predecessors, giving the infantryman more firepower.

" It was a **big fight**. I do not know how long it lasted. There were a lot of **dead** soldiers everywhere."

CHIEF EAGLE BEAR, OGALLALA SIOUX, ON THE BATTLE OF LITTLE BIGHORN, 1876

RATES OF FIRE THROUGHOUT HISTORY

Gun	Period	Rate of fire (rpm – rounds per minute)
Matchlock musket	15th century	2 rpm
Flintlock musket	18th century	Average of 3 rpm
Bolt-action rifle	Late 19th century	8–10 aimed rpm
Gatling gun	Late 19th century	400–600 rpm
Maxim machine-gun	Late 19th century	c.600 rpm
Revolver	19th century	1–2 shots per second, from a five- or six-round cylinder
Vickers machine-gun	1910s	450–600 rpm
Thompson submachine gun	1920s	600–800 rpm
M1 Garand semi-auto rifle	1940s	24 rpm
MG42 machine-gun	1940s	900–1500 rpm
M16A1 assault rifle	1960s	800 rpm
M134 Minigun	1960s	4000–6000 rpm
Metal Storm electrical-ignition machine-gun (36-barrel prototype)	Modern-day	One million rounds, cyclical rate

The battle of Little Bighorn
Native American warriors, led by war chiefs Sitting Bull and Crazy Horse, annihilate Lt Col George Custer and more than 200 of his troops in one of the climactic fights of the Plains Indian Wars.

MEXICAN WARS
1835–1920

Originally a Mexican possession, Texas revolted to become independent in 1836, then joined the USA. This led to further conflict, this time between the USA and Mexico, in the mid-19th century. French intervention in Mexico followed (1861–67) and, in the second decade of the 20th century, the country was torn apart by revolution.

TEXAS REVOLUTION
2 OCTOBER 1835–21 APRIL 1836

Forces Mexican: 6,500; Texan: 2,000. **Casualties** Mexican: 1,500; Texan: 700. **Location**: Texas, USA.

After initial successes, the "Texians" suffered several defeats at the hands of superior Mexican forces. They were finally victorious, however, at San Jacinto.

ALAMO 23 FEBRUARY–6 MARCH 1836

Forces Mexican: 2,400–4,000; Texan volunteers: 183. **Casualties** Mexican: 1,000 killed or wounded; Texan volunteers: 183 killed. **Location** San Antonio, Texas, USA.

Having driven a Mexican force from San Antonio, the Texan volunteers ignored advice to pull back and tried to hold on to their gains. They were overwhelmed by weight of numbers; however, for Texans, the Alamo fortress became a symbol of heroic resistance.

SAN JACINTO 21 APRIL 1836

Forces Mexican: 1,360; Texan: 910. **Casualties** Mexican: 830; Texan: 25. **Location**: Texas, USA.

After a long retreat, the Texan force turned and inflicted a spectacular defeat on a column of the Mexican army. Mexican president Santa Anna was captured, and signed a treaty that effectively granted independence to Texas.

US–MEXICAN WAR
25 APRIL 1846– 2 FEBRUARY 1848

Forces US: 78,700; Mexican: 20,000–40,000. **Casualties** US: possibly 17,000; Mexican: at least 5,000. **Location**: Texas and New Mexico, USA, and Mexico.

Dissatisfied with Texan independence, Mexico threatened to declare war if it were annexed into the US. Rising tensions resulted in a bloody conflict.

THE VERACRUZ CAMPAIGN
MARCH–SEPTEMBER 1847

Forces US: 25,000 regulars and 70,000 volunteers; Mexican: 20,000 regulars. **Casualties** US: 6,000; Mexican: tens of thousands. **Location** East coast of Mexico.

Seeking to revitalize a stalled campaign during the US–Mexican War, US forces attacked Veracruz by sea. This was accomplished without difficulty, and the drive on Mexico City began, leading to eventual victory and ending the war.

THE FRENCH EXPEDITION
JANUARY 1862–MARCH 1867

Forces (At the battle of Puebla) Mexican: 2,000–4,000; French: 6,000. **Casualties** (At the battle of Puebla) Mexican: no reliable estimates; French: 1,000 killed. **Location** East coast of Mexico.

French troops, intervening in a civil war in Mexico, encountered well-prepared positions at Puebla and unwisely launched a frontal assault. This was driven off, although the city was taken by the French the following year.

Defenders of the Alamo

At San Antonio, Texas, a monument features the figures of Davy Crockett (right) and other slain defenders of the Alamo fortress. In the battle, more than 2,000 Mexican troops destroyed a garrison of fewer than 200 Texan revolutionaries.

THE MEXICAN REVOLUTION 1910–20

Forces Various armies, including government troops, Zapata's peasant guerrillas, and Villa's guerrilla cavalry. **Casualties** About 1,000,000 soldiers and civilians killed. **Location** Mexico.

During a bloody decade of political turmoil, in which the United States intervened in 1916–17, the existence of many political factions ensured that any revolutionary leader who successfully assumed power was in turn opposed by a new or existing rebellion. The rebel leaders, who could count on huge support from the peasant population, included Pancho Villa and Emiliano Zapata.

ZULU–BOER CONFLICT
1830–1840

Migrating towards the northeast, away from the Cape Colony in South Africa, the pioneering Boers (known as Voortrekkers) came into conflict with the powerful Zulus, who claimed possession of the lands that the Boers had entered.

ITALENI 9 APRIL 1838

Forces Zulu: c.8,000; Boer: 347. **Casualties** Zulu: unknown; Boer: 10. **Location** Natal (in modern South Africa).

In a confused action, two Voortrekker commandos fought an inconclusive series of skirmishes against a large Zulu force. Lessons learned at Italeni, such as using ox wagons for shelter, proved useful at Blood river.

BLOOD RIVER
16 DECEMBER 1838

Forces Zulu: c.10,000; Boer: 470. **Casualties** Zulu: c. 3,000; Boer: 3 wounded. **Location** Natal (in modern South Africa).

Advancing to remove the Voortrekkers from their lands, the Zulu host found their enemies' wagons in a defensive circle or *laager*. After suffering heavy casualties from rifle fire, and under attack by horsemen, the Zulus withdrew.

OPIUM WARS

Arising out of a trade dispute between British merchants and the Chinese government, the Opium Wars were fought over British rights to import goods, which included the banned opium, into China.

FIRST OPIUM WAR
SEPTEMBER 1839–AUGUST 1842

Forces Chinese: 1,000,000; British and Indian: 10,000. **Casualties** Chinese: 30,000; British and Indian: 10,000. **Location** Numerous areas along the Chinese coast.

With little means to counter the gunboats of the British fleet, the Chinese were repeatedly defeated and forced to cease trying to restrict British trade, including the sale of opium.

ARROW WAR (SECOND OPIUM WAR)
OCTOBER 1856–AUGUST 1860

Forces Chinese: 2,000,000; British and French: 50,000. **Casualties** Chinese: 6,000; British and French: 4,000. **Location** Eastern China.

Arising from the boarding of a British-flagged ship by Chinese officials, the "Arrow War" was a one-sided conflict, in which the Chinese were, once again, unable to match the superior firepower of the European forces. In the conflict's aftermath, the Europeans extended their trading influence throughout China.

COLONIAL WARS IN INDIA AND AFGHANISTAN
1839–1842

Having taken control of India and the surrounding regions, British troops undertook several major campaigns in order to maintain their supremacy in these territories. Some of the native peoples had access to modern weaponry.

FIRST AFGHAN WAR
1839–42

Forces Afghan: unknown; British and Indian: unknown. **Casualties** Afghan: possibly 7,000; British: 3,800, plus c.12,000 civilians. **Location**: Modern Afghanistan.

Intending to keep Russian influence out of Afghanistan, British forces annexed the region under the pretext of assisting Shah Shuja in regaining his throne. Resistance proved to be much more fierce than expected, and the British suffered one of their worst setbacks since taking power in the area in the mid-18th century.

GHAZNI
23 JULY 1839

Forces Afghan: 3,500; British: 20,500. **Casualties** Afghan: 500, plus 1,600 prisoners; British: 200. **Location** Ghazni, Afghanistan.

After occupying Kandahar, the British advanced on the fortress of Ghazni. Having driven off a relief attempt, the British stormed the city through a gate that reconnaissance had indicated was lightly held.

SIEGE OF JELLALABAD
12 NOVEMBER 1841–13 APRIL 1842

Forces Afghan: 5,000; British and Indian: 1,500. **Casualties** Afghan: unknown; British and Indian: 62. **Location** Jalalabad (in modern Afghanistan).

After a local uprising in Kabul in 1841, which resulted in the loss of the British mission, British forces were driven from the city (which they had taken in 1839). They fled to Jellalabad (now Jalalabad), where they held out for several months and finally counterattacked, driving off the besiegers.

The Voortrekker monument
This bronze monument commemorates the battle of Blood River, where a commando of around 470 Boers met and defeated a large Zulu force in 1838.

The Sikhs deployed on a ridge with the river Sutlej to their backs. Recognizing the village of Aliwal as the key to the battle, British forces attacked and captured it, triggering a general Sikh retreat that was hindered by the need to cross the river. The battle has been regarded as the turning point of the First Anglo-Sikh War.

SOBRAON 10 FEBRUARY 1846

Forces Sikh (including Muslims and Hindus): 30,000; British: 20,000. **Casualties** Sikh: 10,000; British: 2,293. **Location** Sobraon, northwest India.

This was the decisive battle of the First Anglo-Sikh War. After an ineffective bombardment, the British made a series of attacks that were initially repulsed by counterattacks. Once the Sikh position was finally penetrated, a general collapse resulted, with heavy casualties as the Sikh army was routed.

SECOND ANGLO-SIKH WAR
1848–49

The Sikhs were displeased by the outcome of the recent war and, in 1848, violence flared up, which led to renewed general conflict. Despite setbacks in the field, the British won a decisive victory at Chillianwala and, after also defeating the Sikhs at Gujarat, annexed the Punjab.

RAMNAGAR 22 NOVEMBER 1848

Forces Sikh (including Muslims and Hindus): unknown; British: unknown. **Casualties** Sikh: no reliable estimates; British: 64. **Location** Near Ramnagar, Punjab, India.

The British attempted a surprise crossing of the river Chenab, but found the ford to be strongly held. Sikh cavalry crossed the river and attacked the British force, inflicting a sharp defeat and forcing a retreat. Sikh morale was lifted, although the Sikhs later withdrew from the banks of the Chenab.

> ## "[Pancho] Villa rode over to where Salgado was at work and **shot him** before the **affrighted eyes** of his fellow workmen."
> N.C. ADOSSIDES, JOURNALIST IN MEXICO DURING THE MEXICAN REVOLUTION

RETREAT FROM KABUL
6–13 JANUARY 1842

Forces Afghan: unknown; British and Indian: 4,000. **Casualties** British: 3,800, and c.12,000 civilians. **Location** Between Kabul and Jalalabad (in modern Afghanistan).

Judging their position in Kabul to be untenable as a result of the Anglo-Afghan war, British civilians there were forced to make a long march through harsh country back to India. Despite having been granted safe conduct, they were harassed by Afghan irregulars, and few of the 16,000 individuals in the column survived. It was the greatest British military disaster of the 19th century.

GANDAMAK
13 JANUARY 1842

Forces Afghan: 18,000; British: 65. **Casualties** Afghan: no reliable estimates; British: almost total. **Location:** Near Gandamak, Afghanistan.

During the retreat from Kabul, the last remnants of the British force were cornered near Gandamak and overrun by a massively superior force. Only one British survivor reached Jallalabad.

FIRST ANGLO–SIKH WAR
1845–1846

The Sikh empire was created in the early 1800s and grew to considerable power before internal conflict erupted. Rebellious elements within the empire began to threaten British interests in India, namely the British East India Company, bringing about conflict between what were, at the time, the two greatest powers in India. Eventually, a costly British victory at Sobraon forced the Sikhs to accept the Treaty of Lahore, which granted considerable territory to Britain.

MUDKI
18 DECEMBER 1845

Forces Sikh (including Muslims and Hindus): 10,000; British: 11,000. **Casualties** Sikh: no reliable estimates; British: 872. **Location** Mudki, northwest India.

This battle at the beginning of the First Anglo-Sikh War took place in the evening and through the night. After repulsing a flank attack by Sikh cavalry, the British advanced, becoming disorganized in the process. After confused fighting in the darkness, they eventually drove off the Sikh army.

FEROZESHAH
18 DECEMBER 1845

Forces Sikh (including Muslims and Hindus): 25,000; British: 16,700. **Casualties** Sikh: no reliable estimates; British: 2,415. **Location** Ferozeshah, northwest India.

The British attacked a fortified Sikh encampment, bringing about a two-day action that began to turn in the Sikhs' favour. Misinterpreting a cavalry movement as a flank attack, the Sikhs withdrew, granting a costly victory to the British.

ALIWAL
28 JANUARY 1846

Forces Sikh (including Muslims and Hindus): 12,000; British: 20,000. **Casualties** Sikh: 850; British: 2,000. **Location** Sutlej river, northwest India.

MILITARY USE OF ANIMALS

Horses
No animal has been used and abused in warfare more than the horse. Of course, horses were used in combat, racing into hails of arrows, bolts, or shot with cavalrymen on their backs, and suffered accordingly. But entire armies also depended on horsepower to transport food, bulk ammunition, and major weapons to the battlefront. When Napoleon marched on Moscow in 1812, he took with him some 200,000 horses, almost all of which eventually perished. Victualling the horses created problems of its own. Napoleon took Vienna in 1805, and in one day alone the city was forced to give up 127 tonnes of hay for provisioning horses.
  Reliance upon horses endured well into the 20th century. During Operation Barbarossa in 1941, the German armies took 750,000 horses to draw the bulk of their supplies, and the US and British armies used mules and horses to carry loads through difficult terrains in Southeast Asia, North Africa, and Italy.

Camels, elephants, and oxen
These have all been pressed into service as four-legged supply trucks. There was even a US Army Camel Corps in mid-19th-century America.

Dogs
Attack dogs were used by the ancient Greeks, and remain in service today as guard animals on military bases and installations. Dogs carried messages in World War I and were used as "guided weapons" during World War II, when Russian soldiers strapped explosives to their backs and trained them to run under German tanks. The project was abandoned after Soviet tanks were also destroyed.

Elephants
War elephants were used as battering rams and as shooting platforms throughout the ancient Hellenistic and Persian world, and across into India.

Pigeons
Carrier pigeons have been used for more than 3,000 years to carry messages with unerring accuracy across miles of battlefield.

Bees, pigs, rats, and dolphins
In the present day, bees, pigs and rats are used to perform mine detection in countries such as The Congo and Israel. Dolphins are trained by the US Navy to perform security duties – sabotage detection and anti-diver patrols – beneath US warships.

Villa's guerrilla cavalry
Guerrilla leader Pancho Villa, who commanded the División del Norte during the Mexican Revolution, aimed to supply a horse to each of his infantrymen, as well as the cavalrymen, to increase his army's speed. He also employed horse ambulances.

The battle of Chilianwallah
A Sikh force of perhaps more than 23,000 men fought an army of the British East India Company that included approximately 12,000 infantry and 66 guns.

CHILIANWALLAH 13 JANUARY 1849

Forces Sikh (including Muslims and Hindus): 23,000; British: 16,000. **Casualties** Sikh: 3,600; British: 4,333. **Location** Chilianwallah (in modern Pakistan).

A disorganized British advance was successful in some areas, although in other parts of the field British troops were routed. After an inconclusive action, the Sikhs withdrew and were reinforced.

GUJARAT 21 FEBRUARY 1849

Forces Sikh (including Muslims and Hindus): 66,000; British: 25,000. **Casualties** Sikh: 2,000 or more; British: 674. **Location**: Gujarat (in modern Pakistan).

Following a lengthy bombardment, the British delivered an infantry attack that broke the Sikh line and resulted in a decisive victory.

HUNGARIAN UPRISING
1848–49

Beginning as a series of demonstrations in the capital, the Hungarian Uprising became a revolution against Habsburg rule. An independent Hungary was initially accepted by Austria, but the rising was eventually put down by Austrian and Russian troops.

PÁKOZD 29 SEPTEMBER 1848

Forces Austrian and Croatian: 35,000; Hungarian: 27,000. **Casualties** No reliable estimates. **Location** Pákozd, Hungary.

Loyalties were conflicted on both sides, as all the troops involved were drawn from the army of the Habsburg empire. The battle was indecisive, but this suited the Hungarian strategic position better than that of Austria, as the Hungarians only had to avoid defeat to remain independent.

SEGESVAR 31 JULY 1849

Forces Russian: 12,000; Hungarian: 6,000. **Casualties** Russian: unknown; Hungarian: 1,700. **Location** Segesvar, Hungary.

The Hungarian force launched an attack against the Russian right flank, gradually gaining the upper hand. Counterattacking, the Russians enveloped the Hungarian right flank, forcing a hurried retreat.

TEMESVAR 9 AUGUST 1849

Forces Austrian: unknown; Hungarian: unknown. **Casualties** No reliable estimates. **Location** Temesvar, Hungary.

The far larger Hungarian force was composed of inexperienced fighters and was less well equipped than the Austrians, leading to an Austrian victory.

WARS OF ITALIAN UNIFICATION
1848–66

Beginning as a series of riots against Austrian rule in northern Italy, this conflict involved the Italian kingdoms and their French allies fighting for independence from Austria, eventually resulting in the unification of Italy.

SANTA LUCIA 6 MAY 1848

Forces Sardinian: 41,500; Austrian: 42,000. **Casualties** Sardinian: 886; Austrian: 262, plus 87 prisoners. **Location** Santa Lucia, near Verona, Lombardy, Italy.

Sardinian forces assaulted an Austrian army entrenched around Verona, forcing them from their positions. The victory was not followed up and thus failed to have a decisive effect on the campaign.

FIRST CUSTOZA 24–25 JULY 1848

Forces Austrian: 33,000; Piedmontese: 22,000. **Casualties** No reliable estimates. **Location** Lomabardy, northern Italy.

An uprising in Milan forced the Austrians to pull back to a defended position to await reinforcements. They then defeated the outnumbered Piedmontese at Custoza and reoccupied Milan.

SIEGE OF ROME 9 FEBRUARY–3 JULY 1849

Forces Roman republic: 20,000; French: 8,000. **Casualties** No reliable estimates. **Location** Rome, Lazio, central Italy.

After being sent to put down a revolt that had deposed the pope, French and Neapolitan troops were repelled by the ill-armed but enthusiastic rebels, who had declared the short-lived Roman republic. After a month-long siege, the French launched a final assault and took the city.

MONTEBELLO 20 MAY 1859

Forces French and Sardinian: unknown; Austrian: 30,000. **Casualties** French and Sardinian: 694 including prisoners; Austrian: 1,423 including prisoners. **Location** Montebello, Lombardy, northern Italy.

A force of Sardinian cavalry and French infantry was confronted by a much larger Austrian army, but its subsequent defeat convinced the Austrians that their forces were qualitatively inferior.

MAGENTA 4 JUNE 1859

Forces French and Piedmontese: 59,000; Austrian: 58,000. **Casualties** French and Piedmontese: 4,600 killed, wounded, or missing; Austrian: 5,700 killed and wounded, 4,500 missing. **Location** Lombardy, northern Italy.

Notable as the first large-scale movement of troops by rail, Magenta was a "soldier's battle", arising from an unplanned encounter in which the French troops fought their way to victory with little help from their commanders.

SOLFERINO 24 JUNE 1859

Forces French and Piedmontese: 160,000; Austrian: 160,000. **Casualties** French and Piedmontese: 17,300, of which 2,500 killed; Austrian: 22,000, of which 3,000 killed. **Location** Near Lake Garda, Lombardy, northern Italy.

After accidentally colliding with the Austrian army they were pursuing, the French/Piedmontese force fought a confused but savage action, in which French rifled artillery played an important part in defeating the Austrians. In the ensuing peace treaty, Austria ceded Lombardy to Piedmont.

GARIBALDI'S REDSHIRTS
11 MAY 1860–13 FEBRUARY 1861

Forces Garibaldi: 5,000; Neapolitan: 25,000. **Casualties** No reliable estimates. **Location** Sicily and southern Italy.

Italian nationalist Giuseppe Garibaldi and his followers, known as "Redshirts", were able to take Palermo in Sicily before advancing on Naples. Further victories led to the establishment of the united kingdom of Italy.

THE HIGHEST MILITARY HONOURS

Country	Medal	First awarded
Italy	*Medaglia d'Oro al Valore Militare* (Gold Medal of Military Valour)	1793
France	*Légion d'honneur* (Legion of Honour)	1802
UK and Commonwealth	Victoria Cross	1856
United States	Medal of Honor	1861
India	*Param Vir Chakra* (Bravest of the Brave)	1950
Germany	*Ehrenkreuz der Bundeswehr in Gold* (Bundeswehr Cross of Honor in Gold)	1980
Russia	*Geroy Rossiyskoy Federatsii* (Hero of the Russian Federation)	1992

SECOND CUSTOZA
24 JUNE 1866

Forces Italian: 125,000; Austrian: 75,000. **Casualties** Italian: 8,000 killed, wounded, or missing; Austrian: 5,600 killed, wounded, or missing. **Location** Lombardy, northern Italy.

In this confused engagement, a spirited attack by Austrian cavalry unnerved the Italians, who fell back in disorder. The Austrian victories at Custoza and at Lissa a month later were, however, rendered largely irrelevant, as defeat by Prussia in the Seven Weeks War forced Austria to cede Venetia to the Italians.

US Medal of Honor
Awarded in recognition of exceptional personal valour, the US Medal of Honor was originally created for the US Navy during the US Civil War (1861–65), but was later adopted by other branches of the military.

The battle of Solferino
The battle, in which the Austrian army was defeated by an alliance between France and Sardinia, resulted in almost 40,000 casualties, inspiring the creation of the International Red Cross in 1863.

LISSA 20 JULY 1866

Forces Italian: 12 ironclads, 14 other vessels; Austrian: 7 ironclads, 19 other vessels. **Casualties** Italian: 2 ironclads sunk. **Location** Adriatic Sea, off Lissa (Modern Vis, Croatia).

During this major sea battle the Austrian fleet caught the Italians by surprise and used ramming and short-range gunfire to achieve a decisive result. For several decades afterwards, ramming was considered to be an effective tactic, greatly influencing ship design.

TAIPING REBELLION 1850–64

During this religiously inspired large-scale revolt against the Qing regime in China, the Taiping rebels eventually fielded more than a million soldiers. Although the uprising was successful for a time, Western-trained Chinese forces eventually suppressed it, with enormous bloodshed. More than 20 million people lost their lives during the conflict, including many civilians.

CIXI 20 SEPTEMBER 1862

Forces Taiping army: unknown; Government army: unknown. **Casualties** No reliable estimates. **Location** Cixi, eastern China.

> "The **mortar shell** was always considered to be the most **formidable enemy** that we had to contend against."
>
> BRITISH ARMY MAJOR WHITWORTH PORTER AT THE SIEGE OF SEVASTOPOL, 1854

The government Qing army, led by an American general named Frederick Ward, attacked Cixi and won a decisive victory over rebel forces there. Ward died of wounds received during the battle, so command of the government force passed to British general Charles Gordon, who later became known as "Chinese Gordon".

THIRD NANJING 14 MARCH 1864–19 JULY 1864

Forces Taiping army: 500,000 or more; Government army: 60,000. **Casualties** Taiping army: more than 200,000; Government army: 9,000. **Location** Eastern China.

The Taiping army made what amounted to its last stand at Nanjing. After a failed assault the government force used underground explosions to breach the city walls. Government forces, some of whom were equipped with bolt-action rifles, then overwhelmed the tired and hungry defenders.

WARS IN SOUTH AMERICA 1852–70

The middle of the 19th century was a time of great upheaval in South America as emergent nations fought over disputed territory and formed powerful coalitions to unseat unpopular dictators.

CASEROS 3 FEBRUARY 1852

Forces Rosas: c.25,000; Coalition: c.25,000. **Casualties** Rosas: 1,400 dead, 7,000 captured; Coalition: 600 dead. **Location** Northwest of Buenos Aires, Argentina.

Facing a coalition of opponents to the rule of Juan Manuel de Rosas, many of the latter's troops surrendered before the fighting began. The issue was decided by a coalition cavalry charge that smashed Rosas' right flank.

PARAGUAYAN WAR 1 MAY 1865–1 MARCH 1870

Forces Paraguayan: 50,000; Argentinian, Brazilian, and Uruguayan: 26,000. **Casualties** Paraguayan: 300,000, including civilians; Argentinian, Brazilian, and Uruguayan: unknown. **Location** Paraguay.

In an ill-advised attempt to expand his rule, Paraguayan dictator Francisco López invaded Brazil and Argentina. The result was the bloodiest war in the history of Latin America, which almost destroyed Paraguay.

SECOND ANGLO-BURMESE WAR 1852–53

Forces British: unknown; Burmese: unknown. **Casualties** No reliable estimates. **Location** Burma and India.

Relatively minor disputes between Britain and Burma (now Myanmar) expanded into open warfare as a result of heavy-handed diplomacy. The British then captured Martaban and Rangoon (now Yangon), driving the Burmese army northwards. The British annexed considerable territory and relations gradually normalized, although no treaty was signed to end the war.

Cossack sabre (shashka)
The Cossacks, warrior societies of the Russian steppes, played a key role in the Crimean War. This Cossack sabre has an acutely pointed blade, designed for both cutting and thrusting.

CRIMEAN WAR 1853–56

Arising mainly out of a dispute between the Turkish Ottoman empire and Russia, the Crimean War drew in British and French forces that were committed to preventing Russian influence from expanding.

SINOPE 30 NOVEMBER 1853

Forces Turkish: 2 steam vessels, 10 sail warships; Russian: 6 line-of-battle ships, 2 frigates, 3 steam vessels. **Casualties** Turkish: 11 vessels lost; Russian: no vessels lost. **Location** Sinope, northern Turkey.

Imperial Russian warships attacked a Turkish squadron at Sinope using shell-firing guns to quickly destroy most of the Turkish force. Britain and France declared war on Russia largely as a result of this action.

ALMA 20 SEPTEMBER 1854

Forces Allied: 26,000 British, 37,000 French, 7,000 Turkish; Russian: 35,000. **Casualties** British: 2,000; French: 1,000; Russian: 6,000. **Location** Alma river, Crimea, Ukraine.

Landing north of Sevastopol, the Allied force found the Russians well dug in on the Alma river. Despite heavy casualties, the Allies were able to force the Russians from their positions.

SEVASTOPOL 17 OCTOBER 1854– 9 SEPTEMBER 1855

Forces Allied: 40,000, including 15,000 Sardinians; Russian: 40,000. **Casualties** No reliable estimates. **Location** West coast of Crimea, Ukraine.

The siege of Sevastopol lasted for a year, with the Allies making slow progress against the defences. After Russian relief efforts failed, the key strongpoints were stormed and surrender became inevitable.

BALACLAVA 25 OCTOBER 1854

Forces Allied: 15,000; Russian: 25,000. **Casualties** Allied: 615; Russian: 627. **Location** West coast of Crimea, south of Sevastopol.

Russian forces advanced on the Allied base at Balaclava. In the ensuing battle, the British Heavy (cavalry) Brigade won notable successes. The Light (cavalry) Brigade fared less well. As a result of misinterpreted orders, its famous charge was crushed by Russian artillery – perhaps the most ill-fated event in British military history.

HISTORY'S LARGEST LAND ARTILLERY PIECES

Weapon	Date and nationality	Calibre and shell weight	Points of interest
Cannon of Mehmed	1484, Turkish	1,067mm (42in) 543kg (1,200lb)	Range: 1.6km (1 mile); could fire only seven times a day
Tsar Puchka	1586, Russian	919mm (36in) 800kg (1,760lb)	Total weight: 40.6 tonnes (40 tons)
Mallet's great mortar	1857, British	919mm (36in) 1,091kg (2,400lb)	Built for the siege of Sevastopol
Gamma-Gerät howitzer	1912, German	420mm (16.5in) 821kg (1,807lb)	Total weight: 150 tonnes (147 tons)
Paris-Geschütz	1918, German	210mm (8.3in) 94kg (210lb)	Railway gun with barrel 28m (92ft) long. Range: 193km (120 miles)
BL 14in railway gun	1918, British	356mm (14in) 719kg (1,586lb)	Range: 35km (22 miles)
Schwerer Gustav	1941, German	800mm (31.5in) 7,100kg (15,656lb)	Fired 300 rounds in total before its barrel wore out
Little David Heavy Mortar	1944, United States	914mm (35.9in) 1,678kg (3,692lb)	Tested as a bunker-busting weapon; never reached operational service

Mallet's great mortar
In 1857, Irish engineer Robert Mallet developed a massive mortar capable of throwing a 1,100kg (2,400lb) shell more than 2.4km (1.5 miles). This mortar is on display at the Royal Armouries' museum, Fort Nelson, Portsmouth, England.

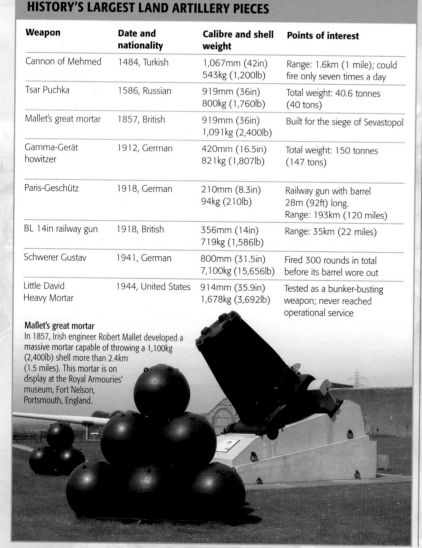

INKERMAN 5 NOVEMBER 1854

Forces Allied: 8,500 British, 7,000 French; Russian: 35,000. **Casualties** British: 2,357; French: 1,700; Russian: 11,800. **Location** Near Inkerman, northeast Crimea, Ukraine.

Attempting to dislodge the British from a strategic ridge, the Russians launched a series of determined assaults supported by artillery. Were it not for the intervention of French troops, heavy casualties would have forced a British retreat.

KARS JUNE–26 NOVEMBER 1855

Forces Allied: possibly 17,000; Russian: 25,000. **Casualties** Allied: unknown; Russian: unknown. **Location** Kars, Eastern Turkey.

Russian forces besieged the Turkish fortress of Kars in the hope of drawing Allied troops away from Sevastopol. Turkish forces sent to its relief became sidetracked elsewhere and the fortress eventually surrendered.

CHERNAYA RIVER 16 AUGUST 1855

Forces Allied (French and Sardinian): 60,000; Russian: 58,000. **Casualties** Allied: 1,260; Russian: 2,239. **Location** Chernaya river, Ukraine.

Hoping to relieve Sevastopol, the Russians launched a determined but disorganized assault that failed to dislodge the Franco-Sardinian army. Count Leo Tolstoy was sufficiently outraged at the incompetence of the Russian commanders to write a satirical song about the battle.

FINAL ASSAULT ON THE MALAKOFF 8 SEPTEMBER 1855

Forces Allied: more than 10,000 in the final assault; Russian: 13,000. **Casualties** No reliable estimates. **Location** Malakoff, Ukraine.

The Malakoff, a great stone tower, was a key feature of the defences of Sevastopol. It was bombarded and assaulted repeatedly during the siege, until 8 September when the fortress was successfully stormed by French troops.

KINBURN 17 OCTOBER 1855

Forces Allied: no reliable estimates; Russian: no reliable estimates. **Casualties** Unknown. **Location** Kinburn Peninsula, Ukraine.

Although not a decisive action, the bombardment of Russian positions at Kinburn established ironclad ships as viable weapons. Allied vessels were hit repeatedly, but it was the Russian forts that were put out of action. The war was concluded with a peace treaty in 1856.

INDIAN MUTINY 1857–58

Beginning as a mutiny among sepoy (Indian troops) in Meerut in May 1857, the conflict spread and became a widespread insurrection against British rule. Although the situation was largely restored by September 1857, some regions remained under rebel control for much of 1858.

BADLI-KI-SERAI 8 JUNE 1857

Forces British officers and loyal *sepoy*: 2,500; Rebel *sepoy*: 3,400. **Casualties** British officers and loyal *sepoy*: 182; Rebel *sepoy*: 1,000. **Location**: 9.6km (6 miles) west of Delhi, India.

British forces advancing on Delhi encountered a rebel *sepoy* force dug in on the Delhi road. After being driven back by rebel artillery, the British made a flanking attack and drove the rebels from their positions. With this obstacle removed, the British force was able to move on to Delhi and begin siege operations.

CHINHAT 30 JUNE 1857

Forces British officers and loyal *sepoy*: 600; Rebel *sepoy*: 5,000. **Casualties** No reliable estimates. **Location**: Near Lucknow, India.

Thinking that they faced a small rebel force, the British attacked and were driven back by heavy fire from well-fortified positions. Many local troops deserted or defected, forcing the British to make a fighting retreat into Lucknow, where they were besieged.

LUCKNOW JUNE–NOVEMBER 1857

Forces British officers and loyal *sepoy*: 1,712; Rebel *sepoy*: 6,000. **Casualties** British officers and loyal *sepoy*: 1,050; Rebel *sepoy*: unknown. **Location** Uttar Pradesh State, north-central India.

Besieged by rebel *sepoy*, the small British garrison was forced to abandon part of the city. After a failed sally against the rebels, the defenders withstood the siege until relief forces arrived.

DELHI JULY–SEPTEMBER 1857

Forces British officers and loyal *sepoy*: 12,000; Rebel *sepoy*: possibly 30,000. **Casualties** British officers and loyal *sepoy*: 5,747; Rebel *sepoy*: no reliable estimates, but very heavy. **Location** Delhi, north-central India.

Restoring the elderly Mogul emperor to power as a figurehead, the rebel forces of the Indian Mutiny occupied Delhi. They held out under British siege for two months until the city was finally stormed.

AONG 15 JULY 1857

Forces British officers and loyal *sepoy*: unknown; Rebel *sepoy*: unknown. **Casualties** No reliable estimates. **Location** Aong, India.

The British were moving forward to the relief of Cawnpore. After pushing aside a force sent to halt its advance on 12 July, the column fought a second successful action at Aong. Prisoners captured there provided intelligence on the positions of rebel forces in the area.

NAJAFGARH 25 AUGUST 1857

Forces British officers and loyal *sepoy*: 2,500; Rebel *sepoy*: 6,000. **Casualties** British officers and loyal *sepoy*: 95; Rebel *sepoy*: 800. **Location** 29km (18 miles) west of Delhi, India.

Attempting to break the siege of Delhi, a force of rebel *sepoy* broke out with the intention of launching an attack on the British positions outside the city. The force was intercepted and attacked as it made camp, forcing a retreat back into Delhi.

FAMOUS WAR CORRESPONDENTS

Name	Dates	Nationality	Wars covered
William Howard Russell	1820–1907	Irish	Crimean War
Richard Harding Davis	1864–1916	American	Spanish-American War, Second Boer War, World War I
Lodewijk Herman Grondijs	1878–1961	Dutch	World War I, Manchuria 1937, Spanish Civil War
Charles Bean	1879–1968	Australian	World War I
Ernie Pyle	1900–45	American	World War II
Martha Gellhorn	1908–98	American	World War II, Vietnam War, Six Day War, Central American conflicts
Chester Wilmot	1911–54	Australian	World War II
Robert Capa	1913–54	Hungarian	Spanish Civil War, the Second Sino-Japanese War, World War II, 1948 Arab-Israeli War, First Indochina War
Richard Dimbleby	1913–65	British	World War II
Dickey Chapelle	1918–65	American	World War II, Vietnam War
David Halberstam	1934–2007	American	Vietnam War
Martin Bell	1938–	British	Vietnam War, numerous Middle Eastern and African conflicts, Northern Ireland, Bosnian War
Kenji Nagai	1957–2007	Japanese	Conflicts in Afghanistan, Cambodia, Palestine, Iraq, Burma
Christiane Amanpour	1958–	British/Iranian	Conflicts in Afghanistan, 1991 Gulf War, Somalian civil war, Rwandan genocide, Bosnian War
Anna Stepanovna Politkovskaya	1958–2006	Russian	Second Chechnyan War
Robert Fisk	1946–	British	Northern Ireland; Portuguese Revolution, multiple conflicts in Middle East and Asia
Ryszard Kapuscinski	1932–2007	Polish	Multiple conflicts in Asia, Europe and Americas

William Howard Russell (1820–1907)
A war correspondent who covered the Crimean War, William Howard Russell reported on the famous, fatal Charge of the Light Brigade, bringing the horrors of modern warfare home to his readers.

AGRA 21 OCTOBER 1857

Forces British officers and loyal *sepoy*: 2,650; Rebel *sepoy*: unknown. **Casualties** No reliable estimates. **Location** Agra, India.

Thousands of British civilians took shelter from the *sepoy* mutiny at Agra, where they were besieged in a half-hearted manner. After the fall of Delhi to the British forces, a large force of rebels gathered near Agra. A relief column was sent to the town but was surprised in camp. The column was able to drive off the attack, and pursued and scattered its opponents. Using forward-deployed artillery aggressively, the British routed the rebel *sepoy* force and pursued it for some distance. The battle thwarted the rebels' final attempt to regain the cities of Cawnpore and Lucknow and was a turning point in the Indian Mutiny.

CAWNPORE 6 DECEMBER 1857

Forces British officers and loyal *sepoy*: c.5,000; Rebel *sepoy*: 25,000. **Casualties** British officers and loyal *sepoy*: 99; Rebel *sepoy*: unknown. **Location**: Kanpur, Uttar Pradesh, India.

BETWA 1 APRIL 1858

Forces British officers and loyal *sepoy*: c.1,500; Rebel *sepoy*: 22,000. **Casualties** British officers and loyal *sepoy*: very light; Rebel *sepoy*: 1,500 killed, number wounded unknown. **Location**: Betwa river, Central India.

The vastly outnumbered British force suddenly charged at the advancing rebel *sepoy* force, triggering a panic and general rout. Large numbers of rebel *sepoys* were drowned trying to cross the river.

LONGEST SIEGES IN HISTORY

Siege	Period	Account
Azotus	7th century BCE	According to Herodotus, Azotus in Israel was besieged for 29 years by the forces of Psammetichus I of Egypt.
Carthage	149–46 BCE	Carthage endured three years of siege under the Romans, who eventually put the city to the sword in 146 BCE.
Constantinople	674–78 BCE	A four-year Arab siege failed to break the city, which was relieved after the Byzantine navy crushed the Umayyad navy in the Sea of Marmara in 678 BCE.
Nicea	1328–31 CE	The Ottoman forces of Osman I put Nicea under a three-year siege; the city fell in 1331, after several failed relief attempts.
Harlech Castle	1461–68	Harlech Castle in Wales endured the longest siege in British history, holding out for seven years against English forces during the Wars of the Roses.
Ishiyama Hongan-ji	1570–80	The fortress of Ishiyima Hongan-ji was besieged by the forces of Oda Nobunaga in Japan's longest siege.
Candia	1648–69	Ottoman forces encircled the city of Candia, now Heraklion in Crete, for 21 years, eventually wresting the fortress from the hands of the Venetians.
Gibraltar	1779–83	Combined French and Spanish fleets blockaded Gibraltar for four years, but the British defenders refused to give in.
Fort Sumter	1863–65	Confederate soldiers held out against massive Union bombardments until the end of the US Civil War.
Leningrad	1941–44	The epic German siege never managed to take the city, but it did kill more than one million of the city's inhabitants.

"A deep chest note… with a savage blood-curdling scream."

EDWARD TREGEAR, NEW ZEALAND WRITER AND SOLDIER, DESCRIBING THE MAORI WAR CRY, LATE 19TH CENTURY

Maori carved wooden club
Before battle, fierce Maori warriors would square off in complex, ritual dances called *haka*. They demonstrated their prowess in athletic displays, often brandishing weapons, such as this ornately carved wooden club.

GWALIOR 17–20 JUNE 1858

Forces British: unknown, but outnumbered by rebels; Rebel *sepoy*: possibly 12,500. **Casualties** No reliable estimates. **Location**: 240km (150 miles) south of Delhi.

The last major action of the Indian Mutiny was fought around the fortress of Gwalior. The rebel army was defeated in the field and the fortress taken. Several rebel leaders were killed or captured.

COLONIAL WARS 1858–85

The mid to late 19th century was characterized by colonial conflicts that often involved well-equipped but small European forces facing much greater numbers of local troops or warriors.

COCHINCHINA 1858–62

Forces French and Spanish: unknown; Vietnamese: unknown. **Casualties** No reliable estimates. **Location** Southern Vietnam.

Landing at Tourane (modern Danang), the French marched on Saigon. Resistance went on for three years, but the modern weapons of the Europeans provided a decisive advantage.

MAORI WARS 1860–72

Forces At Gate Pa: British: 1,700; Maori: c.300. **Casualties** At Gate Pa: British: 120; Maori: fewer than a dozen. **Location** North Island, New Zealand.

The wars consisted mainly of sieges of Maori pas (fortified villages). At the siege of Gate Pa in 1864, the defenders drew the British into an overconfident assault, which was repulsed with heavy casualties. The British then sought peace terms.

CAMARÓN 30 APRIL 1863

Forces Mexican: 2,000–3,000; French Foreign Legion: 65. **Casualties**: Mexican: c.300; French Foreign Legion: entire force killed, wounded, or captured. **Location**: Between Vera Cruz and La Puebla, Mexico.

Attacked by Mexican forces, the vastly outnumbered Foreign Legion took refuge in a farmstead, from which it made a defensive stand until every one of its personnel was killed or incapacitated. The battle of Camarón confirmed the bravery of the Foreign Legion.

CONQUEST OF BOKHARA 20 MAY 1868

Forces Russian: unknown; Bokharan: unknown. **Casualties** No reliable estimates. **Location** 150km (100 miles) west of Samarkand, Uzbekistan.

Raiding by central Asian nomads prompted Russia to subdue the khanates of Bokhara and Khiva. The Bokharans fended off Russian advances for a time but were eventually forced to accept vassal status.

CONQUEST OF KHIVA KHANATE 1873

Forces Russian: 10,000; Khivan: unknown. **Casualties** No reliable estimates. **Location** 37km (25 miles) west of Amu-Darya river, Uzbekistan.

Although some previous campaigns against Khiva had failed, Russia made advances in the region during 1847–65. A large-scale expedition overran the area without much of a fight in 1873, and the city of Khiva became a quasi-independent Russian protectorate.

SECOND ASHANTI WAR JUNE 1873–13 FEBRUARY 1874

Forces British and West African Allied: 4,000; Ashanti: 20,000. **Casualties** British and Allied: 1,700; Ashanti: unknown. **Location** Modern-day Ghana, West Africa.

Attempts by the Ashanti kingdom to take control of the coastal region from the British resulted in a punitive expedition. Lacking artillery, the Ashanti were defeated and their capital razed. This was the second of four Anglo–Ashanti wars between 1823 and 1896.

SECOND AFGHAN WAR SEPTEMBER 1878–80

Forces Afghan: unknown; British: 40,000. **Casualties** unknown. **Location**: Afghanistan.

British forces occupied key points in Afghanistan, leading to a treaty. Hostilities were resumed when the British resident at Kabul was murdered. Afghan forces were defeated and a settlement agreed.

HAMPTON ROADS 8–9 MARCH 1862

Forces: Union: 1 ironclad, 5 other vessels; Confederate: 1 ironclad, 3 other vessels. **Casualties** Union: 2 wooden ships sunk, 368 personnel killed or wounded; Confederate: 24 personnel killed or wounded. **Location** Hampton Roads, Virginia, USA.

This was the most famous naval battle of the US Civil War, also known as the battle of *Monitor* and *Merrimack*. Although the two ironclads were unable to destroy each other, resulting in an indecisive action, the impotence of wooden ships against ironclads was graphically illustrated, and the effects on worldwide ship construction were thus immense.

FIRST KERNSTOWN 23 MARCH 1862

Forces Union: 8,500; Confederate 3,800. **Casualties** Union: 590; Confederate: 710. **Location** Shenandoah Valley, Virginia, USA.

An aggressive march up the Shenandoah Valley by the Confederates caught the Union by surprise, but superior Union numbers forced the Confederates to retreat.

YORKTOWN 5 APRIL–4 MAY 1862

Forces Union: 121,500; Confederate 35,000. **Casualties** Union: 182; Confederate: 300. **Location** Yorktown, Virginia, USA.

Confederate forces deceived the Union into overestimating their numbers to delay a Union attack. After beating off a half-hearted attack, the Confederates withdrew.

Indian Mutiny

Victory in the siege of Delhi in September 1857 was costly for the British East India Company, but it proved a decisive moment of the Indian Mutiny, which did not end until the fall of the fort at Gwalior in June 1858.

SIEGE OF KANDAHAR
1 SEPTEMBER 1880

Forces British and Indian: 10,000; Afghan: 13,000. **Casualties** No reliable estimates. **Location** Kandahar, South-central Afghanistan.

Having occupied Kandahar, the British were besieged there. Relief forces marched from Kabul to break the siege, but found that the Afghan army had already retired. However, it was later brought to battle and defeated. This was the last major conflict of the Second Anglo-Afghan War.

TEL EL-KEBIR 13 SEPTEMBER 1882

Forces British: 11,000 infantry, 2,000 cavalry; Egyptian: 38,000. **Casualties** British: 460; Egyptian: up to 3,000. **Location** About 100km (60 miles) northeast of Cairo, Egypt.

Following a British and French takeover of the government of Egypt, a revolt led by Arabi Pasha erupted. Reacting to protect its financial interests in Egypt, particularly the Suez Canal, the British defeated the Egyptians at Tel el-Kebir in a 30-minute battle.

TONKIN WAR AUGUST 1883–JUNE 1885

Forces French: c.35,000 troops; Chinese and Vietnamese: c.40,000-50,000 including Black Flag irregulars. **Casualties** French: 2,100; Chinese and Vietnamese: unknown. **Location** Northern Vietnam.

Already in possession of Cochin China (southern Vietnam), the French pressed northwards to Tonkin, then under nominal Chinese rule but largely under the control of Vietnamese "Black Flag" irregulars. Despite repeated attempts to drive the French out of Tonkin, the Chinese were eventually forced to cede control of the city to their opponents.

US CIVIL WAR
1861–65

Pitting the Union army of the north against the Confederate army of the south, the US Civil War began after 11 southern states seceded from the Union over the issue of slavery. Huge advantages in numbers and materiel led to a Union victory in a costly war of attrition.

FORT SUMTER 12–14 APRIL 1861

Forces Union: 84; Confederate: 5,000. **Casualties**: none. **Location** Charleston Harbor, South Carolina, USA.

After the Union refused the Confederate demand that the fort be surrendered, the Confederates began a bombardment that forced the tiny garrison to capitulate. It was this action that began open hostilities between Confederacy and Union.

FIRST BULL RUN 21 JULY 1861

Forces Union: 30,000; Confederate: 25,000. **Casualties** Union: 2,700 dead; Confederate: 2,000 dead. **Location** 40km (25 miles) southwest of Washington, DC, USA.

The inexperienced Union army attempted to take the rail junction at Manassas from the equally raw Confederates. The result was a confused action in which the Union attack was eventually beaten off.

FORT DONELSON
12–16 FEBRUARY 1862

Forces Union: 27,000; Confederate: 21,000. **Casualties** Union: 2,832; Confederate: c.2,000 plus 15,000 prisoners. **Location** Cumberland river, Tennessee, USA.

Assisted by river gunboats, Union forces besieged the fort. The garrison attempted a breakout, but only a force of cavalry was actually able to escape. The remainder was forced to surrender.

FIVE MAJOR MYTHS OF MILITARY HISTORY

1. The US Civil War was fought on the issue of the abolition of slavery
President Abraham Lincoln's motivation in launching America's greatest civil conflict was purely based on preserving the Union. Although he openly expressed ideas of white supremacy, Lincoln stated in a letter to the *New York Tribune* in 1862: "My paramount objective in this struggle is to save the Union, and it is not to either save or destroy slavery. If I could save the Union without freeing any slave I would do it, and if I could save it by freeing all the slaves I would do it."

2. The Pacific was the major Asian battleground of World War II
During World War II, China dwarfed the Pacific theatre in terms of casualties and the total numbers of troops involved. The Second Sino-Japanese War (1937–45) had cost the Japanese 186,000 troops even before they went to war with the US, and they subsequently lost well over half a million troops in China. Up to two-thirds of Japan's divisions were tied down in China. China's own death toll from the war was somewhere between 15 and 20 million.

3. Nelson's last words
While dying from a French marksman's bullet at the battle of Trafalgar in 1805, Nelson did not say "Kiss me, Hardy" or "Kismet, Hardy" ("Kismet" being an anglicization of an Arabic word for fate) to Sir Thomas Masterman Hardy while lying on the deck of HMS *Victory*. In fact, once wounded, he was taken below decks and died three hours later, while Hardy remained on deck. In fact, Nelson's most likely last words were "I have then lived long enough".

4. The Indian Mutiny was caused by British ammunition
It is generally believed that the Indian Mutiny (1857–58) was caused by the British having issued musket cartridges that were greased with a mixture of cow and pig fat, making their use taboo to both Hindus and Muslims. An experimental batch was indeed greased in this way, but the standard issue cartridges actually used a beeswax and sheep-tallow grease. The original cartridges did create alarm among the Indian population, but the root causes of the Mutiny were more to do with British social legislation in India.

5. The Spanish conquered the Aztecs and Incas with just a handful of soldiers
The Spanish colonization of modern-day Mexico and Peru in the 16th century was indeed conducted by relatively small numbers of Spanish troops, but they were often backed by thousands of Indian allies. The smallpox disease imported to the Americas by the Spanish also aided the conquest – some three million Aztecs alone were killed by the disease.

Buffalo soldiers
Formed in 1869, the 25th Infantry was an all-black regiment of the then-segregated US Army. Many such African-American regiments were formed during the US Civil War. The "Buffalo Soldiers", as they were known, helped to pacify the western frontier.

SHILOH 6–7 APRIL 1862

Forces Union: 65,000; Confederate: 45,000. **Casualties** Union: 13,000; Confederate: 11,000. **Location** Cumberland-Tennessee rivers, Kentucky and Tennessee, USA.

Caught by surprise, the Union army was reduced to a small perimeter, but received reinforcements and fought on to eventual victory.

NEW ORLEANS
25 APRIL–1 MAY 1862

Forces Union: 43 vessels, 15,000 troops; Confederate: 14 vessels, 4,000 troops. **Casualties** No reliable estimates. **Location** Perryville, Kentucky, USA.

While mortar boats bombarded the river forts, a Union squadron of steam-powered wooden ships ran past the forts and Confederate vessels that were defending the approaches to New Orleans. The city surrendered and was occupied by Union forces.

SEVEN DAYS BATTLES
26 JUNE–2 JULY 1862

Forces Union: 100,000; Confederate: 100,000. **Casualties** Union: 16,000; Confederate: 20,000. **Location** East of Richmond, Virginia, USA.

Seeking to dislodge the Union army from the Jamestown peninsula, Confederate forces launched a series of costly attacks that caused the Union commander, McClellan, to lose his nerve and withdraw.

SECOND BULL RUN
28–30 AUGUST 1862

Forces Union: 62,000; Confederate: 50,000. **Casualties** Union: 10,000; Confederate: 8,300. **Location** Manassas Junction, Kentucky, USA.

Confederate forces captured a Union supply depot and beat off counterattacks until their reinforcements arrived. A massed Confederate attack then drove the Union force from the field.

RICHMOND 29-30 AUGUST 1862

Forces Union: unknown; Confederate: unknown. **Casualties** Union: 5,353 including prisoners; Confederate: 451. **Location** Richmond, Kentucky, USA.

Confederate forces advancing into Kentucky were halted and driven back on the first day. The following day a Confederate advance broke the Union line, resulting in large numbers of prisoners being taken.

Confederacy flag
The short-lived Confederate States of America was extinguished with Lee's surrender at Appomattox, Virginia, in April 1865. Shown here is one of the national flags of the Confederacy (the so-called "Stars and Bars" pattern), folded beneath a drumstick.

ANTIETAM 17 SEPTEMBER 1862

Forces Union: 80,000; Confederate: 40,000. **Casualties** Union: 12,000; Confederate: 11,000. **Location** Sharpsburg, Maryland, USA.

Despite the caution of the Union commander, which prevented a decisive use of superior numbers, the Confederates were hard pressed until a successful flank attack allowed them to break contact.

PERRYVILLE 8 OCTOBER 1862

Forces Union: 36,040 (22,000 directly engaged in the battle); Confederate: 16,000. **Casualties** Union: 3,696; Confederate: 3,145. **Location** Perryville, Kentucky, USA.

Raw Union troops were attacked by a much smaller, but more experienced, Confederate force. Although the Confederates won a tactical victory they were forced to retreat upon discovering the size of the Union army.

FREDERICKSBURG 13 DECEMBER 1862

Forces Union: 120,000; Confederate: 75,000. **Casualties** Union: 12,000; Confederate: 5,300. **Location** Fredericksburg, Virginia, USA.

After a bungled river crossing under fire, the Union army battered fruitlessly at Confederate positions. A flank attack achieved some success but was driven off by a counterattack.

CHANCELLORSVILLE
30 APRIL–6 MAY 1863

Forces Union: 120,000; Confederate: 60,000. **Casualties** Union: 17,000; Confederate: 13,500. **Location** Near Fredericksburg, Virginia, USA.

Bold Confederate manoeuvring and a well-delivered flank attack derailed the Union battle plan. But the death of General "Stonewall" Jackson as a result of wounds sustained at this battle was a severe blow to the Confederacy.

VICKSBURG 19 MAY–4 JULY 1863

Forces Union: 70,000; Confederate: 32,000. **Casualties** Union: 10,000; Confederate: 9,000. **Location** Vicksburg, Mississippi, USA.

After several assaults, the Confederate stronghold of Vicksburg finally surrendered. This opened up the Mississippi to Union navigation and effectively split the Confederacy in two.

Confederacy general Beauregard
General P.G.T. Beauregard was the first prominent Confederacy general of the US Civil War. This commemorative statue of him stands in New Orleans, the city in which he was buried in 1893.

BRANDY STATION 9 JUNE 1863

Forces Union: 11,000; Confederate: 9,500. **Casualties** Union: 907 including prisoners; Confederate: 523. **Location** Culpeper County, Virginia, USA.

Union cavalry caught the Confederates by surprise, bringing about a confused action that demonstrated that Union cavalry could at last take on their opposite numbers on equal terms.

GETTYSBURG 1–3 JULY 1863

Forces Union: 85,000; Confederate: 75,000. **Casualties** Union: 23,000; Confederate: 28,000. **Location** Gettysburg, south Pennsylvania, USA.

Elements of both armies collided in Gettysburg, drawing the rest of the respective armies into a three-day battle. Although close-run at times, the action was a decisive Union victory, but losses were very heavy on both sides.

CHICKAMAUGA
18–20 SEPTEMBER 1863

Forces Union: 62,000; Confederate: 65,000. **Casualties** Union: 16,170; Confederate: 18,472. **Location** South of Chattanooga, Georgia, USA.

Fought in difficult terrain, the action was extremely confused and most of the Union army collapsed after heavy fighting, forcing a retreat into Chattanooga. The Confederates then besieged the town.

WILDERNESS AND SPOTSYLVANIA
5–21 MAY 1864

Forces Union: 120,000; Confederate: 60,000. **Casualties** Union: 32,000; Confederate: 20,000. **Location** Spotsylvania County, Virginia, USA.

A series of confused actions in the dense scrub terrain of the Wilderness resulted in heavy casualties. The Union army then attacked the Confederates at Spotsylvania but was unable to break through.

COLD HARBOR 3 JUNE 1864

Forces Union: 109,000; Confederate: 59,000. **Casualties** Union: 7,000; Confederate: 1,500. **Location** 10km (6 miles) north of Richmond, Virginia, USA.

Failing to make sufficient reconnaissance of the Confederate positions, the Union army launched a frontal assault that suffered heavy casualties.

SIEGE OF PETERSBURG
18 JUNE 1864–2 APRIL 1865

Forces Union: 96,000 (rising to 106,000); Confederate: 55,000 (falling to 47,000). **Casualties** Union: 42,000; Confederate: 28,000. **Location** (40km) 25 miles south of Richmond, Virginia, USA.

The ill-fated "Pickett's Charge"
More than 46,000 men were killed or wounded in the three-day battle of Gettysburg in July 1863. In the disastrous Confederate advance seen here, the division lost more than half of its men.

The town of Petersburg was an obstacle to the Union advance on Richmond. Both armies dug in and a nine-month stalemate began, until increasing Union pressure forced the Confederates to retreat.

KENNESAW MOUNTAIN 27 JUNE 1864

Forces Union: 100,000; Confederate: 74,000. **Casualties** Union: 3,000; Confederate: 1,000. **Location** 10km (6 miles) near Marietta, Georgia, USA

After probing heavily fortified Confederate positions, the Union army launched frontal assaults, which were repulsed. After clinging to positions close to the Confederate line for three days, the Union began an outflanking movement instead.

MOBILE BAY 5 AUGUST 1864

Forces Union: 4 ironclads, 14 other vessels, 5,500 troops; Confederate: 1 ironclad, 3 other vessels, 1,140 troops. **Casualties** Union: 1 ironclad sunk, 328 casualties; Confederate: 2 vessels captured, 1 destroyed, 35 casualties plus 1,587 captured. **Location** Mobile Bay, Alabama, USA.

Rushing past the forts guarding the bay, Union naval forces defeated their Confederate opponents. Deprived of naval support, the forts soon surrendered, making the Union blockade complete in the region.

MARCH TO THE SEA

15 NOVEMBER–21 DECEMBER 1864

Forces Union: 68,000; Confederate: unknown. **Casualties** Union: minimal; Confederate: no reliable estimates. **Location** From Atlanta to Savannah, Georgia, USA.

Advancing through Georgia in the face of little resistance, the Union forces inflicted massive destruction, aiming to reduce Confederate fighting capability. They then seized the port of Savannah.

FAMOUS MILITARY SPEECHES

Abraham Lincoln Gettysburg, Pennsylvania 19 November 1863	"We here highly resolve that these people shall not have died in vain, this nation under God shall have a new birth of freedom, and that government of the people, by the people, for the people shall not perish from this earth."
British prime minister Winston Churchill House of Commons, London World War II, 4 June, 1940	"We shall fight on the beaches. We shall fight on the landing grounds. We shall fight in the fields and in the streets. We shall fight in the hills. We will never surrender ..."
General George Patton Various locations in England World War II, June 1944	"War is a bloody, killing business. You've got to spill their blood, or they will spill yours! Rip them up the belly. Shoot them in the guts. When shells are hitting all around you and you wipe the dirt off your face and realize that instead of dirt it's the blood and guts of what once was your best friend beside you, you'll know what to do!"
Lieutenant-Colonel Tim Collins Eve of coalition invasion of Kuwait, 20 March, 2003	"…Iraq is steeped in history. It is the site of the Garden of Eden, of the Great Flood, and the birth of Abraham. Tread lightly there. … If there are casualties of war, then remember that when they woke up and got dressed in the morning, they did not plan to die this day. "

"With one blow of his **sword** he severed **head** from his **shoulders**."

BRITISH DIPLOMAT ON THE DEATH OF
THE SAMURAI GENERAL SAIGO, 1877

DEFEAT OF LEE
28 MARCH–9 APRIL 1865

Forces Union: 120,000; Confederate: 35,000.
Casualties Union: 6,500; Confederate: 10,000.
Location Richmond, Virginia, USA.

Abandoning Petersburg, the Confederate army made an orderly withdrawal but was pursued. Cornered at Appomattox Court House, General Lee surrendered what remained of his force as Union infantry began to arrive in great numbers.

AUSTRO-PRUSSIAN WAR
1866

The rise of Prussia in the 19th century brought it into conflict with the Austrian empire. Military action broke out in 1866, and in the ensuing Seven Weeks War Austria was decisively beaten.

TRAUTENAU 27 JUNE 1866

Forces Austrian: unknown; Prussian: unknown.
Casualties Austrian: 4,787; Prussian: 1,338. **Location** Trutnov (in modern Czech Republic).

Prussian forces advancing into Bohemia were met by Austrian troops, which were pushed aside. But the subsequent arrival of Austrian reinforcements forced the Prussians into a hasty, disorganised retreat.

Slave shackles
One of the results of the Union victory in the US Civil War was the abolition of slavery in the USA, as laid down in the Thirteenth Amendment to the US Constitution.

NACHOD 27 JUNE 1866

Forces Austrian and allied: unknown; Prussian: 1 corps.
Casualties Austrian and allied: 5,500; Prussian: 1,000.
Location Náchod (in modern Czech Republic).

The Prussians' breech-loading rifles gave them a huge firepower advantage over the Austrians, who relied on bayonet charges. The result was a very one-sided action.

LANGENSALZA
27 JUNE 1866

Forces Prussian: 9,000; Hanoverian and Bavarian: 19,000. **Casualties** Prussian: 830; Hanoverian and Bavarian: 1,492. **Location** Langensalza, Thuringia (in modern Germany).

Surrounded by Prussian forces, the Hanoverian army attacked westward, inflicting a serious defeat on part of the Prussian army. Superior Prussian numbers remaining in the field forced a retreat which led to a surrender two days later.

KÖNIGGRÄTZ 3 JULY 1866

Forces Austrian and allied: 240,000; Prussian: 245,000.
Casualties Austrian and allied: 38,000 killed or wounded; Prussian: 9,500 killed or wounded. **Location** Near Hradec Králové (in modern Czech Republic).

Despite early reverses, the Prussians' superior artillery and rifle fire, coupled with their tactic of using small, flexible units against the dense Austrian masses, forced the Austrians to withdraw.

WARS OF MEIJI RESTORATION
1863–77

The eventual restoration of the emperor of Japan after more than a decade of sporadic fighting, most often between Imperialist forces and the ruling Tokugawa shogunate, unified the country under a strong centralized administration.

BOMBARDMENTS OF SHIMONOSEKI 16 JULY–14 AUGUST 1863, 5–6 SEPTEMBER 1864

Forces Japanese: 6 warships, 40 other vessels; Foreign powers: 28 warships in total. **Casualties** No reliable estimates. **Location** Shimonoseki Strait, Japan.

As Japan began to open up to foreign trade, the Choshu clan, which controlled the Shimonoseki straits, began firing on foreign ships in the straits. Foreign warships retaliated with a series of bombardments, forcing the Choshu to surrender.

The Satsuma rebellion, 1877
General Saigo Takamori (in blue tunic, centre left) rebelled against Japan's Meiji government. The uprising ended with the battle of Shiroyama, the final, and most devastating, of many attacks against the new government.

BOMBARDMENT OF KAGOSHIMA
15–17 AUGUST 1863

Forces British: 7 warships; Satsuma clan: 3 warships and coast defences. **Casualties** British: 63; Satsuma clan: 5 casualties plus 3 warships lost. **Location** Kagoshima, Japan.

The British demanded restitution for attacks on their citizens. This was refused, so a naval squadron made a show of force in Kagoshima harbour. When fired upon, the force bombarded the town.

BOSHIN WAR
JANUARY 1868–MAY 1869

Forces Shogunate: 15,000; Satsuma and Choshu: 5,000. **Casualties** No reliable estimates. **Location** Islands of Honshu and Hokkaido, Japan.

Conflict between the shogunate and those wishing to restore the emperor erupted into full-scale war. The Imperial army advanced steadily eastwards, securing oaths of loyalty from local rulers along the way.

HAKODATE
20 OCTOBER 1868–15 MAY 1869

Forces Imperial: 7,000 plus 10 steam warships; Ezo Republic: 3,000 plus 11 steam warships. **Casualties** Imperial: 770; Ezo Republic: 1,700 plus 1,300 captured. **Location** Hokkaido, Japan.

Defeated by Imperial forces, the army of the shogunate retired to Hokkaido and set up a rebel republic, the Ezo. Both sides made use of steam warships and modern weaponry, including Gatling guns. Defeat by the Imperial forces led to the Ezo surrender in May 1869.

SATSUMA REVOLT
JANUARY–SEPTEMBER 1877

Forces Imperial: 34,000 plus marines and police; Satsuma: 20–40,000. **Casualties** Imperial: unknown; Satsuma: only 400 samurai survived. **Location** Southern Kyushu, Japan.

Angry at the rejection of a proposal to invade Korea, the Satsuma clan rebelled. The Satsuma samurai were opposed by a modern army with artillery and rifles, and were crushed.

FRANCO-PRUSSIAN WAR
19 JULY 1870—10 MAY 1871

The Franco-Prussian war saw these two great European powers clash over a Prussian contender for the vacant Spanish throne. New military technologies – notably breech-loading rifles and early machine-guns – were deployed for the first time on a large scale. The war ended in defeat for France, which lost the territories of Alsace and Lorraine to a newly unified Germany.

WISSEMBOURG 4 AUGUST 1870

Forces Prussian and Allied: 60,000; French: 8,000. **Casualties** Prussian and Allied: 1,551; French: 1,300 plus 900 prisoners. **Location** 60km (37 miles) north of Strasbourg, France.

Wissembourg was garrisoned by the French to secure their line of supply for an attack into German territory. The French garrison was surprised by the Prussian attack and defeated after a stubborn defence.

SPICHEREN 6 AUGUST 1870

Forces Prussian and Allied: 27,000; French: 24,000. **Casualties** Prussian and Allied: 4,500; French: 4,000. **Location** French-German border region.

A somewhat confused German attack suffered heavy casualties due to French Chassepot rifle fire, before reinforcements arrived and forced a French withdrawal.

WORTH 6 AUGUST 1870

Forces Prussian and Allied: 81,000; French: 37,000. **Casualties** Prussian and Allied: c.10,500; French: c.8,000 plus 12,000 prisoners. **Location** French-German border.

Clashes between sentries and foraging parties expanded into a general conflict characterized by great confusion. The Prussians gradually gained the upper hand and pulled back under cover of darkness.

MARS-LA-TOUR
16 AUGUST 1870

Forces Prussian and Allied: 80,000; French: 127,000. **Casualties** Prussian and Allied: 15,780; French: 13,761. **Location** Mars-la-Tour, France.

Retiring towards Verdun, the French were blocked by Prussian forces at Mars-la-Tour and became trapped in the vicinity of Metz.

GRAVELOTTE-ST PRIVAT
18 AUGUST 1870

Forces Prussian and Allied: 188,332; French: 112,800. **Casualties** Prussian and Allied: 20,163; French: 12,800 . **Location** Near Metz, France.

In the biggest battle of the war, the Prussians launched a renewed attack. The French had a chance to break out but were hampered by indecision at high command level. After the battle, the French retired into Metz and were besieged there.

SEDAN 1–2 SEPTEMBER 1870

Forces Prussian and Allied: 200,000; French: 120,000. **Casualties** Prussian and Allied: 9,000; French: 17,000 killed or wounded. **Location** Sedan, on the Meuse river.

Encircled and under bombardment by Prussian guns overlooking their positions, a French force made repeated breakout attempts. None were successful, however, and to avoid further bloodshed, Napoleon III surrendered to the Prussians.

SIEGE OF METZ
3 SEPTEMBER–23 OCTOBER 1870

Forces Prussian and Allied: 134,000; French: 180,000. **Casualties** Prussian and Allied: no reliable estimate; French: entire force surrendered. **Location** Eastern France.

Defeated in the field at Gravelotte, the French army was besieged in Metz. Initial attempts to relieve the city were beaten off, and Metz surrendered on 23 October.

SIEGE OF PARIS
19 SEPTEMBER 1870–28 JANUARY 1871

Forces Prussian and Allied: 700,000; French: 420,000. **Casualties** Prussian and Allied: 12,000; French: 4,000 killed, 24,000 wounded. **Location** Paris, France.

The force holding Paris was poor, but the defences around the city were impressive. After a breakout attempt failed, and armies attempting to relieve the siege were defeated, Paris was starved into surrender.

INTERNATIONAL ARMY RANK SYSTEMS

US ARMY	BRITISH ARMY	FRENCH ARMY	INDIAN ARMY	CHINESE ARMY
Enlisted/NCO ranks				
Private	Private	Soldat de deuxième classe	Sepoy or Sowar (cavalry/armoured corps)	Lie Bing
Private First Class	Lance Corporal	Soldat de première classe	Lance Naik/Acting Lance Daffadar	Shang Deng Bing
Specialist	Corporal	Caporal or Brigadier (cavalry)	Naik/Lance Daffadar	Yi Ji Shi Guan
Corporal	Sergeant	Caporal-chef	Havildar/Daffadar	Er Ji Shi Guan
Sergeant	Staff Sergeant	Elève sous-officier	Company Quarter Master Havildar/ Squadron Quarter Master Daffadar	San Ji Shi Guan
Staff Sergeant	Warrant Officer Class 2	Sergent/ Maréchal des logis	Company Havildar Major/Squadron Daffadar Major	Si Ji Shi Guan
Sergeant First Class	Warrant Officer Class 1	Sergent-chef/ Maréchal des logis-chef	Regimental Quarter Master Havildar/ Regimental Quarter Master Daffadar	Wu Ji Shi Guan
Master Sergeant		Adjudant	Regimental Havildar Major/ Regimental Daffadar Major	Liu Ji Shi Guan
First Sergeant		Adjudant-chef		
Sergeant Major		Major		

NB: The US Army has several NCO ranks above that of Sergeant Major

US ARMY	BRITISH ARMY	FRENCH ARMY	INDIAN ARMY	CHINESE ARMY
Officer ranks				
Warrant Officer ranks (WO1, CW2, CW3, CW4, CW5)	Second Lieutenant	Aspirant	Naib Subedar/ Naib Risaldar	Xue Yuan
Second Lieutenant	Lieutenant	Sous-lieutenant	Subedar/Risaldar	Shao Wei
First Lieutenant	Captain	Lieutenant	Subedar Major/ Risaldar Major	Zhong Wei
Captain	Major	Capitaine	Lieutenant	Shang Wei
Major	Lieutenant Colonel	Commandant or Chef d'escadron(s), Chef de Bataillon	Captain	Shao Xiao
Lieutenant Colonel	Colonel	Lieutenant-colonel	Major	Zhong Xiao
Colonel	Brigadier	Colonel	Lieutenant Colonel	Shang Xiao
Brigadier General	Major General	Général de brigade	Colonel	Da Xiao
Major General	Lieutenant General	Général de division	Brigadier	Shao Jiang
Lieutenant General	General	Général de corps d'armée	Major General	Zhong Jiang
General	Field Marshal	Général d'armée	General	Shang Jiang
General of the Army		Maréchal de France (state honour)	Field Marshal	

US Army colonel's epaulettes
During the 19th century, officers in European-style armies often wore flamboyant decorations of rank. These gold-bullion epaulettes are from a US Army colonel's dress uniform dating from the period of the US Civil War (1861–65).

BATTLES WON AGAINST ALMOST IMPOSSIBLE ODDS

Rorke's Drift (22–23 January 1879)
At this battle from the Anglo-Zulu War, British soldiers of the Royal Engineers and British Army 24th Regiment of Foot successfully fought off an assault by Zulu Prince Dabulamanzi kaMpande.

Thermopylae (480 BCE)
During the second Persian invasion of Greece, 300 Spartans held off several hundred thousand Persians in the narrow pass at Thermopylae.

Shayuan (537 CE)
Some 10,000 Chinese troops commanded by Yuwen Tai beat 200,000 men commanded by Gao Huan.

Kaithal (1367)
A massive Hindu army of 540,000 troops was overwhelmed by 40,000 Muslim soldiers at Kaithal, India.

Agincourt (1415)
Just under 6,000 British troops defeated an army of 20,000 of France's best cavalry and infantry.

Cajamarca (1530)
Francisco Pizarro captured the Inca capital, killing 7,000 with no losses.

Assaye (1803)
At Assaye, Maharashtra, in India, the Duke of Wellington defeated some 75,000 Indian soldiers with just 7,000 men.

Rorke's Drift (1879)
A thin red line of 139 British troops and around 300 native soldiers held off 4,000 Zulus at a mission station in Natal, South Africa.

BALKAN CRISES AND RUSSO–TURKISH WAR
1875–78

In the Balkans, war broke out between Russia and Turkey as Russia attempted to regain territory it had lost during the Crimean War. Struggles also took place as Balkan peoples sought to gain independence from Turkish rule.

BALKAN CRISES 1875–76

Forces Turkish: unknown; Balkan peoples: unknown. **Casualties** Turkish: unknown; Balkan peoples: possibly 12,000 including non-combatants. **Location**: Balkan states, southeast Europe.

Risings in Bosnia and Herzegovina, and Bulgaria led to intervention by irregular forces from Serbia and Montenegro. The Turks also sent irregular forces of their own in an attempt to quell the risings, which resulted in massacres.

SERBO–TURKISH WAR
30 JUNE 1876–FEBRUARY 1877

Forces Turkish: c.93,000; Serb: c.63,000. **Casualties** Unknown. **Location** Balkan states, southeast Europe.

Serbian offensives were beaten back by better-armed Turkish forces. The war ended with a ceasefire, but fighting broke out again during the Russo-Turkish War of 1877–78.

PLEVNA JULY–DECEMBER 1877

Forces Turkish: 400,000; Russian and Allied: 100,000. **Casualties** Turkish: 7,000; Russian: 30,000. **Location** Pleven, northern Bulgaria.

Russian forces advanced on Plevna, expecting to find a garrisoned but unfortified town, only to discover that it had been heavily fortified in secret. A five-month siege resulted, and although the Turks were eventually forced to surrender, Russia's strategic military plans lay in ruins.

IRONCLADS IN THE PACIFIC
1879–83

During the later part of the 19th century, many nations, including Chile and Peru, obtained ironclad warships, by then the most powerful vessels afloat.

WAR OF THE PACIFIC 1879–83

Forces At war start: Peruvian and Bolivian: 7,000 plus naval assets; Chilean 4,000 plus naval assets. **Casualties** (total): Peruvian and Bolivian: 40,000; Chilean: 15,000. **Location**: South American coast.

The war was dominated by sea power as the terrain inland made logistics virtually impossible. Territorial gains by Chile resulted in Bolivia becoming landlocked.

EXPLOITS OF HUÁSCAR
MAY–OCTOBER 1879

Forces Peruvian: 1 ironclad; Chilean: 2 ironclads, several other vessels. **Casualties** No reliable estimates. **Location**: Pacific, off Chilean coast

Having taken part in the Peruvian Civil War of 1879, the ironclad *Huáscar* carried on a campaign of blockade, bombardment, and harassment almost single-handedly against the superior Chilean navy.

ANGAMOS 8 OCTOBER 1879

Forces Peruvian; 1 ironclad; Chilean: 2 ironclads, 3 corvettes. **Casualties** Peruvian: 35 plus 1 ironclad captured; Chilean: 7. **Location** Pacific, off Bolivian coast

Brought to action by the entire Chilean navy, *Huáscar* was eventually pounded into submission. Removal of the naval threat allowed the land campaign to advance.

ANGLO–ZULU WAR
1879

British forces invaded Zululand and were initially repelled by the highly organized Zulu warriors. Despite Zulu bravery, superior firepower made an eventual British victory inevitable.

ISANDHLWANA
22 JANUARY 1879

Forces British: 1,700 regulars, 500 African; Zulu: 20,000. **Casualties** British: 1,640; Zulu: c.2,000. **Location** Natal, South Africa.

Unwisely dispersing while looking for their Zulu enemies, a British column was attacked in camp at Isandhlwana. No prisoners were taken as the Zulus overran British positions.

RORKE'S DRIFT
22–23 JANUARY 1879

Forces British: 139; Zulu: 3,000. **Casualties** British: 32; Zulu: 550. **Location** Buffalo river crossing, west of Isandhlwana, Natal, South Africa.

With no prospect of withdrawal, the British detachment at Rorke's Drift fortified their position and defended it against enormous odds. The Zulus retired after suffering heavy casualties.

ESHOWE 22 JANUARY–3 APRIL 1879

Forces British: 1,300 plus 400 wagoneers; Zulu: no reliable estimates. **Casualties** British: 44; Zulu: 1,300. **Location** Eshowe, KwaZulu Natal, South Africa.

The British advance base at Eshowe became cut off after the disaster at Isandhlwana. A relief column fought through to the position in April and the defenders withdrew.

HLOBANE 28 MARCH 1879

Forces British: 675; Zulu: 25,000. **Casualties** British: 233; Zulu: unknown, but light. **Location** Hlobane, South Africa.

A British advance encountered unexpectedly large numbers of Zulu warriors, which forced a disorganized retreat to Kambula. The operation was originally mounted to tempt the Zulus to attack Kambula, however, and so can be viewed as a strategic success.

KAMBULA 28 MARCH 1879

Forces British: 2,000; Zulu: c.20,000. **Casualties** British: 83; Zulu: 1,000. **Location** Kambula, South Africa.

The British were deployed in a wagon laager reinforced by field fortifications. Rifle fire, artillery using canister rounds, and bayonet charges broke the attack. Afterwards, the Zulus were never quite so aggressive.

Charging the enemy at Omdurman
The 21st Lancers (Empress of India's) won three Victoria Crosses at Omdurman, Sudan, on 2 September 1898. The lancers mistakenly charged into the main body of the Mahdist army, driving it back despite heavy losses.

“The Maxim-Nordenfeldts were **fired so fast** that the barrels must have been well **red-hot**.”

BENNET BURLEIGH, WAR CORRESPONDENT, ON THE BRITISH CAMPAIGNS IN THE SUDAN, 1881–89

GINGINDLOVU 2 APRIL 1879

Forces British: 5,670; Zulu: 12,000. **Casualties** British: 59; Zulu: 1,000. **Location** River Inyezane, Zululand, South Africa.

Advancing to the relief of Eshowe, the British column fortified itself in a wagon laager as the Zulus approached. Although the attack was pressed home, the ferocity of earlier Zulu charges was not evident here and they retreated from the battlefield.

ULUNDI 4 JULY 1879

Forces British and allied: 5,200; Zulu: 15,000, possibly more. **Casualties** British and allied: 98; Zulu: in excess of 1,500. **Location** Ulundi, South Africa.

Advancing in a large square, the British force met the Zulu charge with rifle volleys, Gatling guns, and artillery firing canister. Zulu military power was shattered for good, though odd skirmishes went on for some weeks afterwards.

MAHDIST REVOLT
1883–99

Inspired by the religious leader Muhammad Ahmad, known as the Mahdi, the people of the Sudan revolted against colonial governance. This pitted them against the forces of Egypt and Britain.

EL OBEID 3–5 NOVEMBER 1883

Forces Egyptian: 10,000; Mahdists: possibly 40,000. **Casualties** Egyptians: 7,000; Mahdist: unknown. **Location** Kordofan, Sudan.

Attempting to capture the Mahdi, who was besieging El Obeid, the Egyptian force became lost and desertions began. The expedition was overwhelmed by a massively superior Mahdist force.

TAMAI 13 MARCH 1884

Forces British: 4,500; Mahdist: 10,000. **Casualties** British: 120; Mahdist: 4,000. **Location** Tamai, Sudan

Victory at El Obeid convinced the Hadendoa tribe to join the revolt. Although the Mahdists managed to exploit a gap in the British line, they were driven off with heavy casualties.

SIEGE OF KHARTOUM
13 MARCH 1884–26 JANUARY 1885

Forces Anglo-Egyptian: 2,000; Mahdist: c.50,000. **Casualties** Anglo-Egyptian: 2,000; Sudanese: unknown. **Location** Khartoum, Sudan.

Besieged in Khartoum by the army of the Mahdi, a small Anglo-Egyptian garrison held out in the hope of relief. The city fell just three days before the relief force fought its way through.

ABU KLEA 17 JANUARY 1885

Forces British: 1,100; Mahdist: possibly 12,000. **Casualties** British: 158; Mahdist: 1,100. **Location** Abu Klea, Sudan. As the main relief force for Khartoum advanced up the Nile, another camel-borne relief force crossed the desert towards Khartoum. Attacked near Abu Klea, the British formed a square and repelled the assault.

FERKEH 7 JUNE 1886

Forces British and Egyptian: c.9,000; Mahdist: 3,000–4,000. **Casualties** British and Egyptian: 100; Mahdist: 1,000–2000 plus about 500 prisoners. **Location** Ferkeh, Dongola, Sudan.

Caught by surprise, the Mahdists were forced onto the defensive. Some retired in disorder while others defended the village to the death.

Zululand's last king

Cetshwayo kaMpande (c.1832–84) went to war with the British empire when it demanded that his army disband. Cetshwayo's warriors wiped out the entire British force at Isandlwana.

Native forces and modern weaponry

In colonial wars, small, well-armed European forces were often pitted against much larger native troops equipped with relatively primitive weapons. However, some native forces were able to arm themselves with modern weapons, such as these artillery pieces captured by the British near Kandahar.

TOSKI 3 AUGUST 1889

Forces Egyptian: unknown; Mahdist: 6,000. **Casualties** Egyptian: unknown, but light; Mahdist: 1,200 plus 4,000 prisoners. **Location** Abu Simbel, Egypt.

A Mahdist incursion into Egypt was attacked and overwhelmed by Egyptian troops aided by a handful of British cavalry. Thereafter, the Madhists posed no significant threat to Egypt.

ATBARA 8 APRIL 1898

Forces British and Egyptian: 14,000; Mahdist: 15,000. **Casualties** British and Egyptian: 568; Mahdist: 3,000 plus 2,000 prisoners. **Location** Atbara River, Sudan.

After artillery preparations, British and Egyptian forces attacked the Mahdist camp at Atbara, which was quickly overrun. A portion of the Mahdist force retired southwards. The remainder was captured or became casualties.

OMDURMAN 2 SEPTEMBER 1898

Forces British and allied: 26,000; Mahdist: 50,000. **Casualties** British and allied: 430; Mahdist: 30,000. **Location** About 8km (5 miles) north of Omdurman, Sudan.

The Mahdi had chosen the village of Omdurman as his base of operations in 1884. Although outnumbered, the British force possessed the many advantages of modern technology. Their Maxim machine-guns and artillery broke charges by the Mahdists, and the British cavalry made one of its last charges.

Moisin-Nagant bolt-action rifle
Developed in 1891, the Russian M91/30 7.62-mm (0.3 in) Moisin-Nagant bolt-action rifle was the standard infantry firearm for tsarist, and later Soviet, soldiers and was in production until the end of World War II.

UMM DIWAYKARAT 24 NOVEMBER 1899

Forces British and Egyptian: 8,000; Mahdist: 10,000. **Casualties** British and Egyptian: 26; Mahdist: 4,000. **Location** Kordofan, Sudan.

Approaching the Mahdist camp, the British drove off an attack using Maxim guns. The Madhist army collapsed soon after. There was little further resistance as remnants of the revolt were eliminated.

FOOCHOW 23–26 AUGUST 1884

Forces French: 13 warships; Chinese: 11 warships and 11 junks. **Casualties** French: 2 ships damaged; Chinese: 9 ships lost, 10 ships damaged. **Location** Fuzhou, China.

In the opening conflict of the Sino-French war (August 1884–April 1885), a Chinese fleet was annihilated by French warships.

ADOWA 1 MARCH 1896

Forces Italian: 17,000; Ethiopian: 100,000. **Casualties** Italian: 7,300; Ethiopian: 10,000. **Location** Northern Ethiopia.

In the First Italo-Ethiopian War, the Italians unwisely left their defensive positions and advanced into unfamiliar terrain. They were overwhelmed by the Ethiopian army.

FIRST SINO–JAPANESE WAR 1894–95

A failed pro-Japanese coup in Korea prompted Japanese military intervention and war with Korea's powerful ally China. The Japanese navy prevailed over the outdated Chinese fleet.

PUNGDO 25 JULY 1894

Forces Japanese: 3 cruisers; Chinese: 1 cruiser, 2 gunboats. **Casualties** Japanese: none; Chinese: 1,100. **Location** Asan, Korea.

Rising tensions between Japan and China resulted in an exchange of fire between Japanese cruisers and Chinese vessels. As the engagement ended, a Chinese transport and her escort arrived and were also attacked.

SEONGHWAN 28–29 JULY 1894

Forces Japanese: 4,000; Chinese: 3,500. **Casualties** Japanese: 82; Chinese: 500. **Location** Asan, Korea.

In the first major land battle of the war, the Japanese advanced on the port of Asan and drove the Chinese forces there towards Pyongyang. The Chinese were expecting reinforcements, but these were lost in the naval battle of Pungdo a few days earlier.

PYONGYANG 15 SEPTEMBER 1894

Forces Japanese: 10,000; Chinese: possibly 13,000. **Casualties** Japanese: 535; Chinese: 6,000. **Location** Pyongyang, Korea.

While a frontal attack occupied the Chinese defenders, a Japanese flanking movement forced the garrison of Pyongyang to surrender. The Japanese were then able to advance unopposed to the Yalu river.

YALU RIVER 17 SEPTEMBER 1894

Forces Japanese: 12 warships; Chinese: 14 warships. **Casualties** Japanese: 4 ships damaged; Chinese: 5 ships lost, 3 damaged. **Location** Pyongyang, Korea.

Although the Chinese fleet was superior in numbers and firepower, it was hesitantly handled. Poor-quality shells and a tendency of their vessels to catch fire also hampered the Chinese.

JIULIANGCHENG 24 OCTOBER 1894

Forces Japanese: 10,000; Chinese: 15,000. **Casualties** Japanese: 144; Chinese: 2,000. **Location** Korean-Manchurian Border of China.

Chinese forces were entrenched behind the Yalu river. The Japanese used a pontoon bridge to make a crossing and launched a night assault that routed the Chinese force.

PORT ARTHUR 21 NOVEMBER 1894

Forces Japanese: 15,000; Chinese: 13,000. **Casualties** Japanese: 262; Chinese: 4,500. **Location** Port Arthur, Manchuria (modern Lushunkou, Northeast China).

The Japanese launched a night assault that overran the landward side of the port's defences. Pockets of resistance held out for the next day, after which the remaining positions were abandoned.

WEIHAI 1–12 FEBRUARY 1895

Forces Japanese: unknown; Chinese: unknown. **Casualties** Japanese: 262; Chinese: 4,000. **Location** Weihai, China.

The Chinese fleet fell back to Weihai after the loss of Lushunkou, and assisted in the defence of this port against a Japanese land attack. The town fell early in the month, after which the Japanese navy gradually wore down the remaining Chinese naval strength. The surviving vessels surrendered on 12 February. Although this was the last battle of the war, numerous skirmishes followed.

YINKOU 4 MARCH 1895

Forces Japanese: unknown; Chinese: unknown. **Casualties** No reliable estimates. **Location** Yinkou, Manchuria, China.

As the First Sino-Japanese war drew to a close, Japanese forces stormed the port of Niuzhuang, taking Yinkou unopposed soon after. This was the last action of the war on the mainland.

INVASION OF THE PESCADORES 23–26 MARCH 1895

Forces Japanese: 5,500; Chinese: 5,000. **Casualties** No reliable estimates, but probably heavy. **Location** Pescadores, Taiwan.

The Japanese invasion of the Pescadores Islands was undertaken to provide a base for a campaign into Taiwan. After determined initial resistance, the Chinese defence of the islands collapsed as quickly as the invaders could advance.

INVASION OF TAIWAN 29 MAY–21 OCTOBER 1895

Forces Japanese: 37,000; Chinese: 75,000. **Casualties** Japanese: 679; Chinese: 14,000 including noncombatants. **Location** Taiwan.

Preparing to take Port Arthur
In support of a Japanese infantry advance, the 1st Regiment of Artillery fired on Qing dynasty troops near Port Arthur in Manchuria (modern Lushunkou, Northeast China), during the First Sino-Japanese War.

> "The situation is fatal; **surrender inevitable**; we are only **prolonging the agony**; the sacrifice is useless ..."

SPANISH GENERAL ARSENIO LINARES Y POMBO WRITING ON THE EVE OF THE SURRENDER OF SANTIAGO, CUBA, JULY 13, 1898

Taiwan was ceded to Japan as part of the Chinese surrender. Occupation of the new territory was opposed by forces of the newly created Republic of Formosa, but the defence was disorganised and feeble. An insurgency continued for some time afterwards.

SPANISH–AMERICAN WAR
APRIL–AUGUST 1898

An expansionist United States built on its support for the Cuban independence movement and planned to annex Spain's existing colonies in the Caribbean and Pacific. After military victories in Cuba and the Philippines, the Treaty of Paris also ceded Puerto Rico and Guam to the United States, ending Spain's role as a colonial power.

US VICTORY IN CUBA
JUNE–AUGUST 1898

Forces American: unknown; Spanish: unknown. **Casualties** American: 610 killed; Spanish: unknown. **Location** Cuba.

Seizing on the probably accidental sinking of USS *Maine* in Havana harbour in February, the US intervened in an attempt by the Cuban populace to win independence from Spain. The Spanish forces were easily defeated and Cuba effectively became a US protectorate.

SAN JUAN AND EL CANAY HILL
1 JULY 1898

Forces American: 15,000; Spanish: 1,200. **Casualties** American: 1,572; Spanish: 850. **Location** San Juan and El Canay Hill, Cuba.

Spanish forces occupied two hills protecting the approach to the capital city of Santiago. These were successfully stormed by American forces, opening the way for an advance into Santiago, which surrendered on 17 July.

US CONQUEST OF THE PHILIPPINES
1898

Forces American: unknown; Filipino rebel: unknown. **Casualties** American: 4,234 killed, 2,818 wounded; Filipino: c.20,000 rebels killed. **Location** Philippines.

Having defeated the Spanish squadron based at Manila, the US occupied the islands. Sovereignty was transferred to the US at the end of the Spanish-American war, though local Filipino resistance to American rule went on for some time.

SECOND BOER WAR
11 OCTOBER 1899–31 MAY 1902

The Second Boer War pitted British regulars against mobile, sharpshooting Boers of southern Africa, who were particularly adept at mounted infantry tactics. The causes of the war are complex but this was the culmination of two centuries of conflict between the British empire, which had taken possession of the Cape, and the Boers, who had established two independent Boer republics, the South African Republic (Transvaal Republic) and the Orange Free State in the interior.

BOER OFFENSIVE
OCTOBER 1899–JANUARY 1900

Forces British: unknown; Boer: unknown. **Casualties** unknown, but heavier on British side. **Location** Natal and Cape Colony.

The highly mobile Boer horsemen, equipped with modern rifles and artillery, defeated British forces in the field and besieged them in the cities. However, the Boers were thinly spread and their success was short-lived.

KIMBERLEY
15 OCTOBER 1899–15 FEBRUARY 1900

Forces British: 4,606; Boer: 4,000–5,000. **Casualties** unknown, but moderate on both sides. **Location** Kimberley, Cape Colony, South Africa.

Kimberley was besieged and bombarded, but there was no serious attempt to assault the town. The siege was broken by a force of cavalry and mounted infantry, forcing a retreat, which led to the Boer defeat at Paardberg.

LADYSMITH
2 NOVEMBER 1899–28 FEBRUARY 1900

Forces British: 13,745; Boer: 20,000. **Casualties** British: 894; Boer: 1,600. **Location** Ladysmith, Natal, South Africa.

The British army in the region initially attempted to fight in the field. After actions at Talana Hill, Elandslaagte, and Nicholson's Nek, it was driven into Ladysmith, where it was besieged until relieved by a force under Sir Redvers Henry Buller.

MODDER RIVER
28 NOVEMBER 1899

Forces British: 10,000; Boer: 6,000. **Casualties** British: 468; Boer: 80. **Location** 32 km (20 miles) south of Kimberley, Cape Colony, South Africa.

A British column advancing to the relief of Kimberley encountered a Boer force equipped with machine-guns. After a protracted firefight, the Boers withdrew. The British halted to await reinforcements.

STROMBERG 10 DECEMBER 1899

Forces British: 3,000; Boer: 2,300. **Casualties** British: 135 plus 696 prisoners; Boer: unknown, but very few. **Location** Stromberg, Cape Colony, South Africa.

Seeking to retake the rail junction from the Boers, British troops made a night approach that became disorganized. The attack failed and some British troops were left behind in the subsequent retreat.

MAGERSFONTEIN
10–11 DECEMBER 1899

Forces British: 14,000; Boer: 7,000. **Casualties** British: 810; Boer: 300. **Location** 22km (14 miles) south of Kimberley, Cape Colony, South Africa.

Pushing on from the Modder river, the British were heavily defeated just short of Kimberley. Along with Stromberg and Colenso, Magersfontein was one of three defeats in a week later known as "Black Week". Attempts to relieve Kimberley were postponed as a result of the battle.

COLENSO 15 DECEMBER 1899

Forces British: 21,000; Afrikaner: 6,500. **Casualties** British: 899; Boer: 50. **Location** 22km (14 miles) south of Ladysmith, Natal, South Africa.

Although the British troops had the advantage of numbers, they failed to undertake adequate reconnaissance. As a result, they ran into Boer forces that were well dug in, and who inflicted serious casualties.

SPION KOP 24 JANUARY 1900

Forces British: 30,000; Boer: 5,000. **Casualties** British: 2,000; Boer: 200. **Location** 30km (20 miles) west of Ladysmith, Natal, South Africa.

Having attained the heights of Spion Kop, the British found themselves exposed to heavy fire. After fierce close-range fighting, both sides retired from the hill. The Boers then rallied and reoccupied it.

PAARDEBERG 18–27 FEBRUARY 1900

Forces British and Canadian: 6,000; Boer: 5,000. **Casualties** British and Canadian: 1,100; Boer: 1,000. **Location** 37km (23 miles) southeast of Kimberley, Orange Free State, South Africa.

The Boer force was trapped, but well dug in, on Paardeberg Hill. After an initial frontal assault failed, the British conducted an eight-day artillery bombardment, which eventually compelled the Boers to surrender.

SAANA'S POST 31 MARCH 1900

Forces British: 1,900; Boer: 1,500. **Casualties** British: 155 plus 428 prisoners; Boer: 8. **Location** 37km (23 miles) east of Bloemfontein, Free State Province, South Africa.§

Boer forces mounted a raid to capture a convoy and disrupt the British water supply. Staging a brilliantly executed ambush, they captured part of the British force and more than 100 supply wagons.

RELIEF OF MAFEKING 17 MAY 1900

Forces British: 2,000; Boer: 2,000. **Casualties** Unknown. **Location** Northern Cape, South Africa.

Under siege since the start of the war, the British defenders of Mafeking were in a state of starvation by the time a relief column approached. But they were still able to resist a final assault.

DIAMOND HILL 11-12 JUNE 1900

Forces British: 14,000; Boer: 6,000; **Casualties** British: 162; Boer: 50. **Location** Southeast of Pretoria, Transvaal, South Africa.

The battle at Diamond Hill was one of the last "formal" battles between the British and the Boers, who had begun to adopt guerrilla tactics. The battle was fought to push the Boer army away from Pretoria.

WEAPONS BANNED FROM WARFARE

Weapon/Banned	Description
"Dum-Dum" bullets 1899	These expanding soft-nosed bullets that "mushroom" on impact with the body are so called after their creation by the British at the Dum-Dum arsenal in India in the late-19th century. They were banned from military use at the Hague Convention in 1899.
Chemical weapons 1997	More than 180 nations are signatories to the Chemical Weapons Convention (CWC), effective from 29 April 1997, which prohibits the development, production, stockpiling, and use of chemical weapons. At the top of the prohibited list are the Schedule 1 chemicals that have no use – or negligible use – except as weaponized substances. These include mustard gas and nerve agents.
Anti-personnel mines 1997	By 2008, 156 nations had signed the Ottawa Convention (opened 1997), which prohibits the development, production, stockpiling, retention, or sale of anti-personnel mines. This does not, however, apply to remotely triggered mines, such as Claymores.
White phosphorous and napalm 1997	The Ottawa Convention also prohibits "any weapon or munition which is primarily designed to set fire to objects or to cause burn injury to persons through the action of flame, heat, or combination thereof, produced by a chemical reaction of a substance delivered on the target", particularly the use of such weapons against civilian targets. White phosphorus and napalm fall under this convention, but it has been circumvented by many nations exploiting legal loopholes.

GUERRILLA WAR
NOVEMBER 1900–MAY 1902

Forces Varied throughout campaign. **Casualties** Unknown, but high among Boer civilians. **Location** South Africa.

With the conventional war lost, the Boers resorted to guerrilla warfare. They achieved some success but were gradually worn down by the British. A peace agreement was signed at Vereeniging on 31 May 1902.

BOXER REBELLION
NOVEMBER 1899–SEPTEMBER 1901

The Boxers, more correctly the I-ho-chuan, or "Righteous and Harmonious Fists", attacked Western foreigners around Beijing in reaction against imperialist expansion, Western influence, and Christian missionary evangelisation. A multinational force was sent to deal with them, eventually capturing Beijing and suppressing the rebellion.

PEKING
12 JUNE–14 AUGUST 1900

Forces British: 407 regulars plus 125 civilian volunteers; Boxer rebels: unknown, but at least several thousand. **Casualties** British: 120 combatants plus perhaps 1,000 civilians. Boxer rebels: unknown, but heavy. **Location** Peking (modern Beijing), China.

The Boxers attempted to remove all foreign presence from the Chinese capital. Small numbers of guards from various foreign nations, assisted by civilian vounteeers, defended the "foreign" community until relief forces arrived.

Human bomb carrier
Bulgarian airmen prepare for a mission to drop a bomb by hand on Adrianople (now Edirne, Turkey), from their Bleriot XI aircraft, during the First Balkan War. (1912–13). The Bulgarian Air Force was one of the first to use aircraft for military attacks.

RUSSO-JAPANESE WAR
8 FEBRUARY 1904–5 SEPTEMBER 1905

International tensions led to conflict between the Russian empire and the emerging might of the empire of Japan, both of which had imperialist ambitions regarding Korea and Manchuria (modern Northeast China). The Japanese navy, though newly created, was a thoroughly modern and well-trained force.

PORT ARTHUR 8–9 FEBRUARY 1904

Forces Japanese: 38,500; Russian: 17,000. **Casualties** Japanese: 15 major warships; Russian: 12 major warships. **Location** Port Arthur, Manchuria (modern Lushunkou, Northeast China).

The Japanese attack was led by a force of destroyers which torpedoed Russian battleships and cruisers at anchor. The next night a follow-up attack caused additional damage to the Russian fleet.

NANSHAN 25–26 MAY 1904

Forces Japanese: 38,500; Russian: 17,000. **Casualties** Japanese: 6,198 including prisoners; Russian: 1,618 including missing. **Location** Near Port Arthur, Manchuria (modern Lushunkou, Northeast China).

Assisted by gunboat-fire, Japanese troops assaulted Russian positions. The Russian reserves retired, forcing frontline troops to do likewise.

SIEGE OF PORT ARTHUR
AUGUST 1904–JANUARY 1905

Forces Japanese: 90,000; Russian: 40,000. **Casualties** Japanese: 60,000; Russian: 40,000. **Location** Port Arthur, Manchuria (modern Lushunkou, Northeast China).

Japanese forces surrounded the port by sea and land, gradually encroaching on the defences. Suffering high casualties, the Japanese captured a hill overlooking the port, forcing the Russians to surrender.

YELLOW SEA 10 AUGUST 1904

Forces Japanese: 4 battleships, 10 cruisers; Russian: 6 battleships, 4 cruisers. **Casualties** Japanese: 226; Russian: 444. **Location** Yellow Sea, off the coast of Port Arthur (modern Lushunkou in Northeast China).

The Russian fleet came out of Port Arthur to engage the blockading Japanese. A running fight ensued for several hours before contact was lost in darkness. Several Russian ships were forced to seek safety in neutral harbours and were interned.

MUKDEN 20 FEBRUARY–10 MARCH 1905

Forces Japanese: 270,000; Russian: 330,000. **Casualties** Japanese: 71,000; Russian: 89,000. **Location** Mukden, southern Manchuria (modern Shenyang, Northeast China).

Using large numbers of machine-guns and forward observers linked to the artillery by telephone, the Russians were able to inflict heavy casualties. But under heavy attack on their flanks, they were forced to retire.

Guerrilla fighters of a Boer commando
These soldiers fighting in the Second Boer War are armed with various weapons, including German Mauser bolt-action rifles and a British MkIV calibre .577/450 Martini-Henry rifle.

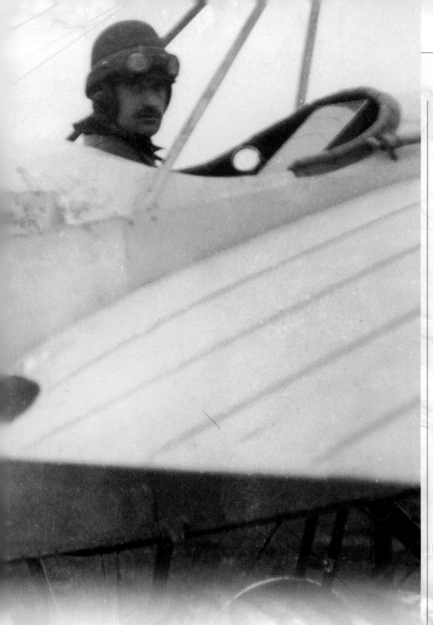

COMBAT STRESS REACTION

Combat stress reaction (CSR), a breakdown in mental health forced by the trauma of war, has affected soldiers on active service throughout all periods of history. The effects of CSR can endure long after the sufferer has left active service.

Early evidence of CSR

Viking chess pieces from as early as the eighth and ninth centuries depict warriors about to go into battle gnawing feverishly on the top edge of their shields. Yet it would be centuries before combat stress became recognized as a genuine and specific medical condition. During the US Civil War, Dr Jacob Mendes da Costa investigated nervous and physical responses to combat among soldiers and noted such symptoms as sweating, breathlessness, racing heartbeat, and acute anxiety.

20th-century understanding of CSR

This condition became known variously as "Da Costa's Syndrome", "Soldier's Heart", or "Nostalgia". However, it was not until observations of the Russo-Japanese War of 1904–05 that doctors began to understand combat stress as a genuine reaction to war. The two world wars brought an explosion of research into CSR based upon tens of thousands of "shell-shock" victims (a label initially applied because it was thought that the detonations of explosives caused the symptoms), and the studies helped refine the methods of prompt battlefield treatment. Although the postwar world recognized CSR as a medical condition, it remains imperfectly handled, largely because of notions of manhood and resilience.

Core symptoms of CSR

Fatigue

Muscular tension

Shaking, tremors, and palpitations

Sweating

Loss of control over urination and digestion

Racing heart and breathlessness

Insomnia

Visual/hearing problems

Partial paralysis

Severe and constant anxiety

Irritability and depression

Substance abuse

Impaired thought processes

The aftermath of siege
Russian prisoners march past the Japanese army after the lengthy siege of Port Arthur (1904–05) during the Russo-Japanese War. Throughout history, soldiers have suffered psychologically from the effects of battle, but it was only after this war that CSR began to be recognized as a medical condition.

TSUSHIMA 27–28 MAY 1905

Forces Japanese: 4 battleships, 64 other ships; Russian: 8 battleships, 20 other ships. **Casualties** Japanese: 117 dead, 3 boats sunk; Russian: 4,380 dead, 17 ships sunk. **Location** Tsushima Strait between Korea and Japan.

After sailing all the way from the Baltic, the Russian fleet was in poor condition. It was met by a modern Japanese force, which out-gunned and outmanoeuvred it to inflict a massive defeat.

BALKAN WARS
1912–13

Two wars were fought in the Balkans in 1912–13. The first pitted Bulgaria, Greece, Montenegro, and Serbia (the Balkan League) against Ottoman forces. The second (1913) was an internal conflict arising from old tensions between the member states of the Balkan League.

KUMANOVO 23–24 OCTOBER 1912

Forces Serbian: 132,000; Ottoman: 65,000. **Casualties** Serbian: 7,844; Ottoman: 4,500 plus 327 prisoners. **Location** Kumanovo, Macedonia.

An Ottoman attack on the first day of the battle made some gains but was pushed back by Serbian counterattacks. A second attempt was made the next day, despite significant desertions during the night. A Serbian counterattack drove in the Ottoman left wing and forced the Ottoman army to withdraw.

EDIRNE (ADRIANOPLE) 22 JULY 1913

Forces Ottoman: unknown; Bulgarian and Serbian: unknown. **Casualties** No reliable estimates. **Location** Edirne, 225km (140 miles) northwest of Istanbul.

The town of Edirne was captured from the Turks by forces from Bulgaria and Serbia. Edirne was, however, retaken by the Turks in 1913.

" The **garrison** of Port Arthur is living on **horseflesh** … the **ammunition** is running short."

BRITISH DIPLOMAT OBSERVING THE RUSSO-JAPANESE WAR, 1904

Era of the World Wars 1914–45

SOVIET RED STAR CAP BADGE

During World War I and World War II, nations engaged in armed conflict on an unprecedented scale. Rapidly advancing technology refined the art of warfare, while the sheer numbers of military personnel involved, and civilians affected, reached staggering proportions. Along with the other brutal conflicts of the early 20th century, the tragedy and scale of modern global war in terms of destruction and human suffering can scarcely be comprehended.

THE CALL TO DUTY
JOIN THE ARMY
FOR HOME AND COUNTRY

PUBLISHED BY RECRUITING COMMITTEE OF THE MAYOR'S COMMITTEE ON NATIONAL DEFENCE

WORLD WAR I
1914–18

Arising out of long-standing tensions between the European powers, World War I was sparked by conflict between Austria-Hungary and Serbia. The alliance structures then in place resulted in a worldwide conflict between the Central Powers (Germany, Austria-Hungary, the Ottoman empire, and Bulgaria) and the Allies (most notably Britain, France, Italy, Russia, Japan, and the USA). The expected war of manoeuvre became an entrenched stalemate in many areas.

GERMAN INVASION OF BELGIUM
4–25 AUGUST 1914

Forces Belgian: 117,000; German: 750,000. **Casualties** Belgian: 30,000; German: 2,000. **Location** Belgium. **Theatre** Western Front.

The Belgian army, though smaller and not as well armed as the German army, inflicted significant delays on the advancing Germans, with some elements holding out around Antwerp until October. Germany carried out a deliberate terror campaign intended to ruthlessly subdue any resistance.

BATTLE OF THE FRONTIERS
7–25 AUGUST 1914

Forces French: 1,000,000; German: 725,000. **Casualties** French: 200,000; German: also heavy. **Location** French-German border. **Theatre** Western Front.

The French plan of war called for an offensive to retake its lost provinces of Alsace and Lorraine. The German army fell back, thereby drawing the French into a trap, and inflicting massive casualties from artillery and machine-gun attacks.

GUMBINNEN
20 AUGUST 1914

Forces German: 9 divisions; Russian: 12 divisions. **Casualties** German: heavy; Russian: 16,000. **Location** Gusev (in modern west Russia). **Theatre** Eastern Front.

On 17 August, First Corps of the German Eighth Army attacked the advancing Russian First Army at Stalluponen, pursuing them east until halted by Russian artillery fire. The German attack at Gumbinnen was halted, counterattacked, and driven back.

MONS AND LE CATEAU
23–26 AUGUST 1914

Forces British: 150,000; German: 320,000. **Casualties** British: 10,000; German: 8,000. **Location** Western Belgium and northeast France. **Theatre** Western Front.

In line with British plans for co-operation with France, the British Expeditionary Force crossed the Channel and advanced into Belgium, where it met the German First Army at Mons. Here the British fought a brief holding action. Retreating, the BEF's II Corps fought a more substantial, day-long rearguard action at Le Cateau. At the expense of heavy casualties, this allowed the British retreat to continue relatively unmolested.

TANNENBERG
22–29 AUGUST 1914

Forces Russian: 150,000; German: 210,000. **Casualties** Russian: 140,000; German: 20,000. **Location** East Prussia (in modern Poland). **Theatre** Eastern Front.

Learning of imminent Russian marching plans by radio intercepts, the Germans quickly transferred reinforcements from the Western Front and laid a trap. The advancing Russians were encircled and pounded with artillery. Fewer than ten per cent escaped.

Poster pressure

During World War I, many nations used propaganda posters, such as this example from the US, featuring evocative imagery to stir young men to join and fight, or others to contribute money and work for the war effort.

HELIGOLAND BIGHT
28 AUGUST 1914

Forces British: 5 battlecruisers, 8 light cruisers, 41 other vessels; German: 5 light cruisers, 31 other vessels. **Casualties** British: 1 light cruiser heavily damaged; German: 3 light cruisers and 3 other vessels sunk, 6 vessels damaged. **Location** North Sea off German coast.

A raid by British forces, intended to draw out the German High Seas Fleet, resulted in a confused action in which the British battlecruisers, assigned at the last minute, proved decisive. As a result, the German High Seas Fleet was instructed to remain in port and to avoid contact with the Royal Navy.

TSINGTAO
2 SEPTEMBER–7 NOVEMBER 1914

Forces German 4,000; Japanese 23,000 plus 1,500 British. **Casualties** Unknown. **Location** Modern Qingdao, China.

Japanese forces, as well as a small British contingent, besieged the German-owned port of Tsingtao in China. The garrison managed to hold out until November in the face of bombardment and night raids.

FIRST MARNE
6–9 SEPTEMBER 1914

Forces French: 1,000,000; British: 125,000; German: 1,275,000. **Casualties** Up to 100,000. **Location** East of Paris, France. **Theatre** Western Front.

As the German advance from Belgium into eastern France became overextended and disorganized, the Allies launched a counter-offensive. Although the fighting was evenly balanced, the German army was ordered to withdraw after suffering severe casualties.

Austrian machine-gun

The machine-gun changed the way wars were fought on land, in the sea, and in the air. This example, a Maschinen Gewehr M07/12, was standard issue for troops of the Austro-Hungarian empire in World War I.

FIRST MASURIAN LAKES
9–14 SEPTEMBER 1914

Forces German: 13 divisions; Russian: 12 divisions.
Casualties: German: 40,000; Russian: 125,000. **Location**
East Prussia (in modern Poland). **Theatre** Eastern Front.

After defeating the Russian Second Army
at Tannenberg in East Prussia, German
forces attempted to encircle the Russian
First Army. The Russians were able to
extricate their army from the trap and
withdraw in reasonable order.

FIRST AISNE
13–18 SEPTEMBER 1914

Forces Allied: unknown; German: unknown. **Casualties**
Unknown. **Location** Northeast of Paris, France. **Theatre**
Western Front.

Crossing the Aisne river under fire,
French and British forces launched a
frontal attack on German positions. As
elsewhere along the front, the assault was
ineffective, and resulted in the Allies
learning how pointless it was to carry out
such strategies.

ALBERT AND FIRST ARRAS
25–29 SEPTEMBER, 1–4 OCTOBER 1914

Forces French: unknown; German: unknown. **Casualties**
Unknown **Location** Northeastern France. **Theatre**
Western Front.

Attempting to outflank fortified German
positions in what became known as the
"Race to the Sea", French forces attacked
near Albert and were subsequently
counterattacked for little gain on either
side. The process was repeated a little to
the north a few days later.

FIRST YPRES
19 OCTOBER–22 NOVEMBER 1914

Forces Allied: unknown; German: unknown. **Casualties**
German: 135,000; British: 55,000; French: 20,000. **Location**
Flanders, northeast France, and Belgium. **Theatre**
Western Front.

In an effort to break through to the
Channel ports, the German army attacked
a salient in front of the town of Ypres,
which was held by the BEF with French
support. Little ground was gained for the
attempt, and casualties were appalling on
both sides.

FALKLAND ISLANDS
8 DECEMBER 1914

Forces German: 2 armoured cruisers, 3 light cruisers;
British: 2 battlecruisers, 1 pre-dreadnought, 5 other
cruisers. **Casualties** British: no ships lost. German:
2 battlecruisers, 2 light cruisers. **Location** South Atlantic
east of Argentine coast.

Brought to battle at Coronel in November
1914, the German Far East squadron
annihilated its opponents, then rounded
Cape Horn to raid the coaling station
at the Falklands. Outgunned by the
force it encountered there and unable
to flee, the squadron fought a gallant
but hopeless action. The only surviving
German warship, the light cruiser
Dresden, remained at large for three
months before surrendering off the Juan
Fernandez Islands.

MILITARY TACTICS

Tactics is both an art and a science. While strategy dictates the
goals of an operation and what resources are available to achieve
them, it is up to the tactician to use those resources effectively in
order to achieve his goals. Through tactical decision-making,
commanders display understanding of their own strengths and
exploit them, while seeking to expose an enemy's weaknesses.

Siege

A siege is a protracted blockade
and armed assault against a city
or fortress and may last for days
or even years.

Masada (72 CE)
Surrounded in their hilltop
fortress near the Dead Sea,
Jewish rebels, outnumbered ten
to one, chose suicide rather than
surrender to the Romans.

The Alamo (1836)
Texans numbering fewer than
200 held off the Mexican Army,
2,400 strong, for 13 days during
the Texas Revolution.

Leningrad (1941–44)
Besieged by the Germans and
Finns, the Russian city was
virtually isolated for 872 days
before the siege was lifted by
the Red Army.

Encirclement

When an enemy force is encircled,
it is prevented from receiving
supplies and reinforcements, and
is open to attack from all sides.

Cannae (216 BCE)
The army of Carthage under Hannibal
formed a deep crescent-shaped
defensive line and executed a double
envelopment to defeat a numerically
superior Roman army, which was
destroyed as a fighting force.

Fraustadt (1706)
During the Great Northern War, the
Swedish army closed a classic pincer
movement to rout an alliance of
Saxony-Poland and Russia.

Tannenberg (1914)
German attacks collapsed both
wings of the Russian Army and
resulted in the loss of 140,000
Russian troops in World War I.

Outflanking

A flanking manoeuvre is an attack
against the exposed sides of an
enemy force.

Chancellorsville (1863)
In a classic flank attack, Confederate
forces routed Union troops during
the American Civil War. The Union
plan was to cross the Rappahannock
river at two points. Hesitant and
defensive Union tactics allowed the
Confederates to redeploy, however,
concentrating against the flank of
one Union force and inflicting a
defeat while keeping the other at bay.

Fall of France (1940)
Advancing through the Ardennes
forest, in terrain considered by the
Allies to be unsuitable for tanks to
drive through, German armoured
forces were able to bypass the
Maginot Line and fight a war of
manoeuvre on their own terms.

Defence in Depth

Layered defences behind a front line
allow an armed force to delay the
advance of an enemy and slow their
momentum, giving an opportunity
to mount counterattacks or await
reinforcements.

Trench warfare (1916–18)
The opposing trenches of the
battlefields of World War I provided
supporting lines and fortifications.
The multiple defences behind the
front lines allowed enemy gains to
be quickly recaptured by each side,
leading to stalemate.

Normandy (1944)
German defenders held back
armoured forces from the D-Day
invasion beaches and instead
fortified the hedgerows in the open
countryside. This was intended to
slow the Allies and allow time for
reinforcements to arrive.

1915

**By the end of 1914, Germany's chance of a
knockout blow against France had passed
and the weight of Russian manpower
made itself felt.**

DOGGER BANK
24 JANUARY 1915

Forces British: 5 battlecruisers, 7
light cruisers, 35 destroyers;
German: 3 battlecruisers, 1
armoured cruiser, 4 light
cruisers, 18 destroyers.
Casualties British: 1

battlecruiser and 1 destroyer seriously damaged; German:
1 armoured cruiser sunk, 1 battlecruiser seriously
damaged. **Location** North Sea.

A clash between battlecruiser forces on
the Dogger Bank resulted in the British
chasing the Germans for several hours,
gradually catching up, and then
exchanging fire with them. The armoured
cruiser *Blücher* could not keep up with her
consorts and was sunk. The rest of the
German squadron escaped.

BOLIMOV
31 JANUARY 1915

Forces German: Estimated 12 divisions; Russian: 11
divisions. **Casualties** German: 20,000; Russian: 40,000.
Location Poland. **Theatre** Eastern Front.

Supported by experimental tear gas shells
the German Ninth Army attacked the
Russian Second Army. The gas failed
and the attack was halted. Russian
counterattacks were beaten off and heavy
losses were sustained by both sides.

Cloth respirators against deadly gas
With the use of poison gas on the battlefield by
1915, European armies began to issue respirators
to their soldiers. The first attempts were merely
cloth filters, as worn by these French soldiers.

CRITICAL MILITARY INVENTIONS IN AIR WARFARE

Invention	Era Developed	Impact
Balloon observation	1700s	Enhanced intelligence gathering
Powered flight	1900–1910	Aerial reconnaissance
Zeppelin airship	World War I	Offensive bombing
Forward-firing machine gun synchronized with propellor	World War I	Made shooting down of enemy aircraft possible
Monoplane fighter	World War I	Improved performance over biplanes
Enclosed cockpit	1920s–30s	Greater pilot control and stability
Wing-mounted guns	1920s–30s	Increased firepower
Heavy bomber aircraft	1920s–30s	Made major air raids possible
Air-to-air refuelling	1920s–30s	Increased aircraft range
Norden bombsight	World War II	Improved accuracy of daylight bombing
RADAR	World War II	Early warning and location of enemy aircraft
Jet engine	World War II	Enhanced speed and performance
Rocket aircraft	World War II	Fast-climbing interceptors and missiles
Supersonic aerodynamics	1950s–80s	Vastly increased speeds
Air-to-air and guided missiles	1950s	Combat at longer ranges
Laser-guided bombs	1960s	Greater bombing accuracy
Stealth technology	1960s–70s	Undetected attacks

As the Western Front settled down into an entrenched stalemate, the Allies attempted to open up a new front against Turkey.

GALLIPOLI CAMPAIGN
19 FEBRUARY 1915–9 JANUARY 1916
Forces Allied: 480,000; Turkish: unknown. **Casualties** British and Imperial: 205,000; French and French colonial: 47,000; Turkish: 300,000. **Location** Gallipoli Peninsula, Turkey. **Theatre** Ottoman Front.

After an attempt to force a passage of the Dardanelles with battleships failed, a land offensive was launched. Turkish resistance forced troops to withdraw.

NEUVE CHAPELLE
10–13 MARCH 1915
Forces British: 40,000; German: unknown. **Casualties** British: 11,200; German: c.11,200. **Location** Artois, France. **Theatre** Western Front.

Launched to eliminate a German salient near Neuve Chapelle, the attack started well. Increasing shortages of supplies and a German counterattack on 12 March prevented greater gains being made.

HELLES AND SUVLA LANDINGS
25 APRIL AND 6–15 AUGUST 1915
Forces Allied: 93,000; Turkish: 84,000. **Casualties** Allied: unknown; Turkish: unknown. **Location** Gallipoli Peninsula, Turkey. **Theatre** Ottoman Front.

After the failure of a naval attempt to force the Dardanelles, Allied troops landed to remove the Turkish forts commanding the Dardanelles straits. The landings were successful in some areas, but a resolute Turkish defence prevented major success.

SECOND YPRES
22 APRIL–25 MAY 1915
Forces Allied: unknown; German: unknown. **Casualties** Allied: 69,000; German: 38,000. **Location** Flanders, northeast France, and Belgium. **Theatre** Western Front.

The use of chlorine gas, against which the Allied troops were powerless, created a large hole in the defensive lines. However, the Germans lacked the reserves to exploit the breakthrough.

FIRST KRITHIA
28 APRIL 1915
Forces Allied: 14,000; Turkish: about equal. **Casualties** Allied: 3,000; Turkish: unknown. **Location** Gallipoli Peninsula, Turkey. **Theatre** Ottoman Front.

After artillery preparation, the Allied forces advanced up the Gallipoli Peninsula towards the town of Krithia. They were met by a stout defence, and their right flank was driven off by a Turkish bayonet charge.

GORLICE–TORNOW
2 MAY–22 JUNE 1915
Forces German: 120,000; Austro-Hungarian: 120,000; Russian: 56,000. **Casualties** German, Austro-Hungarian: 90,000; Russian: heavy. **Location** Southeast of Cracow, Poland. **Theatre** Eastern Front.

A short preparatory bombardment devastated the poorly trained Russian troops, who were crammed into inadequate trenches. They broke and fell back, allowing German and Austro-Hungarian troops to advance rapidly.

FESTUBERT
15–27 MAY 1915
Forces Allied: 6 Divisions; German: 3 Divisions **Casualties** Allied: 16,000; German: unknown. **Location** Artois, 135km (85 miles) north of Paris, France. **Theatre** Western Front.

This offensive, which marked the British army's first attempt at a night attack, was opened by primarily Indian troops. The heavy artillery preparation had been ineffective but significant gains were made early on in the attack nonetheless. Renewed assaults by the Allies succeeded in gaining only a little more ground.

TURKISH COUNTERATTACK AT ANZAC COVE 19 MAY 1915
Forces Allied: 17,000; Turkish: 42,000. **Casualties** Allied: 628; Turkish: 10,000. **Location** Gallipoli Peninsula, Turkey. **Theatre** Ottoman Front.

Turkish preparations for a counterattack intended to dislodge the Allied beachheads were observed. The Turks were forced to advance over open ground against well-prepared defences and suffered heavily.

FIRST ISONZO
23 JUNE–7 JULY 1915
Forces Italian: 225,000; Austro-Hungarian: 115,000. **Casualties** Italian: 16,000; Austro-Hungarian: 10,000. **Location** Northeast Italy. **Theatre** Italian Front.

After attempting a surprise attack, the Italians launched a major frontal offensive across the Isonzo river. Despite some minor gains, the assault failed for lack of artillery support.

ARTOIS–LOOS
25 SEPTEMBER–4 NOVEMBER 1915
Forces British: unknown; German: unknown. **Casualties** British: 50,000; German: 25,000. **Location** 135km (85 miles) north of Paris, France. **Theatre** Western Front.

Using gas to precede the advance, the Allies made good gains on the first day of the offensive, but could not bring up their reserves fast enough to maintain momentum. The result was stalemate.

SERBIA
6 OCTOBER–23 NOVEMBER 1915
Forces German, Austrian, Bulgarian: 300,000; Serbian: 200,000. **Casualties** Serbian: 50,000; Others: unknown. **Location** Serbia. **Theatre** Eastern Front.

After defeating Austro-Hungarian offensives in 1914, Serbia was attacked by the combined forces of the German Eleventh Army, Austria-Hungary, and Bulgaria in the autumn of 1915. Short of supplies, the Serbian army was forced into retreat.

THIRD ISONZO
18 OCTOBER–3 NOVEMBER 1915
Forces Italian: 338 battalions; Austro-Hungarian: 184 battalions. **Casualties** Italian: 67,000; Austro-Hungarian: 40,000. **Location** Northeast Italy. **Theatre** Italian Front.

After trying to batter through the Austrian positions twice using massed infantry attacks, the Italians brought much more

Charity appeal
German charities of World War I supported troops captured while fighting in the trenches. This 1915 poster reads, "Help our prisoners of war in enemy territory."

"We were surprised to see **shells** dropping around us … The sound of a large shell flying overhead is **not a pleasant one.**"

CAPT DR V. BENJAFIELD, AUSTRALIAN ARMY MEDICAL CORPS, GALLIPOLI, 1915

Bersaglieri sharpshooter's crested hat
Stalemated trench warfare inspired European armies to raise highly mobile regiments of light infantry, such as the Bersaglieri, who were the sharpshooters of the Italian army.

artillery to bear. This resulted in even greater gains, but at the cost of heavy casualties.

1916

By 1916 it had become clear that the deployment of reserves would dictate the course of the war. Strategies to draw enemy reserves into or out of critical areas were implemented on all sides.

SIEGE OF KUT-AL-AMARA
7 DECEMBER 1915–30 APRIL 1916

Forces Anglo-Indian: 12,000 in Kut, 30,000 relief; Turkish: 30,000. **Casualties** Anglo-Indian: all in Kut killed or imprisoned; Turkish: 10,000. **Location** Mesopotamia (modern Iraq). **Theatre** Ottoman Front.

British forces advancing on Baghdad were driven into Kut-al-Amara and besieged there. After initially resisting the assault, the British and Indian troops were eventually starved into surrender despite the first ever attempt to supply a besieged garrison by air.

GALLIPOLI EVACUATION
DECEMBER 1915–9 JANUARY 1916

Forces Allied: 105,000; Turkish: 100,000. **Casualties** Allied: 3; Turkish: unknown. **Location** Gallipoli Peninsula, Turkey. **Theatre** Ottoman Front.

Disguising their evacuation by using ruses, such as leaving self-firing rifles behind in the trenches as personnel were thinned, the entire Allied force was withdrawn from Gallipoli. The Allies did not gain access to the Dardanelles until Turkey withdrew from the war in 1918.

VERDUN
21 FEBRUARY–18 DECEMBER 1916

Forces German: 1 million; French: more than 200,000. **Casualties** German: 355,000; French: 400,000. **Location** 195km (120 miles) east of Paris, France. **Theatre** Western Front.

By attacking Verdun, the Germans' plan was to draw the French reserves in and eliminate them. German reserves were also drawn in, however, resulting in

massive loss of life for no territorial gain. The conflict resulted in more than 250,000 battlefield deaths and at least half a million wounded. Verdun was the longest and one of the most devastating battles of World War I.

LAKE NAROCH
18 MARCH–APRIL 1916

Forces Russian: 350,000; German: 75,000. **Casualties** Russian: 70,000; German: 20,000. **Location** Lake Narach in modern northwest Belarus. **Theatre** Eastern Front.

Launched to draw German reinforcements away from Verdun, the offensive suffered from a lack of supplies and muddy thawing ground. Initial attacks made little progress and the operation tailed off with no real gains made.

ASIAGO/TRENTINO OFFENSIVE
15 MAY–10 JUNE 1916

Forces Italian: 172 battalions; Austro-Hungarian: 300 battalions. **Casualties** Italian: 92,000 plus 50,000 prisoners; Austro-Hungarian: 90,000 plus a possible 15,000 prisoners. **Location** Veneto, northern Italy **Theatre** Italian Front.

The Austro-Hungarian army launched a surprise offensive as the Italians were preparing for another assault on the Isonzo river. Slowed by the steep, rugged terrain, and distracted by the Brusilov Offensive, the Austrian offensive was halted by redeployed Italian reserves.

JUTLAND
31 MAY 1916

Forces British: 151 ships; German: 99 ships. **Casualties** British: 14 ships sunk; German: 11 ships sunk. **Location** North Sea, 120km (74 miles) off the Danish coast.

This was the only significant collision between the German High Sea Fleet and the British Grand Fleet in World War I. After a battlecruiser action, the two main fleets clashed twice. The British sustained heavier losses before the German fleet managed to slip away in the dark, but the battle was a strategic victory for Britain, confirming its naval superiority.

BRUSILOV OFFENSIVE
4 JUNE–20 SEPTEMBER 1916

Forces Russian: 573,000; Austro-Hungarian: 448,000. **Casualties** Both sides: 500,000–1 million killed, wounded, or imprisoned. **Location** From the Pripet Marshes, south to Czernowitz (in modern Ukraine) **Theatre** Eastern Front.

LANDMARK AMPHIBIOUS OPERATIONS

Location/War	Date	Action
Island of Malta Ottoman-Habsburg Wars	1565	In the Great Siege of Malta, 5,500 Spanish marines retook the Mediterranean island from the Ottoman invaders and returned it to the control of the Knights Hospitaller.
Quebec French and Indian Wars	1759	British troops crossed the St Lawrence river and defeated the French on the Plains of Abraham.
Gallipoli World War I	1915	Commonwealth troops landed on the shores of Ottoman Turkey during World War I and became locked in a battle of attrition before withdrawing months later.
Tarawa World War II	1943	US Marines assaulted a Japanese-held Pacific atoll and learnt bitter lessons in the art of such operations. Tarawa fell in four days.
Anzio World War II	1944	In an effort to outflank the German positions along the Winter Line during World War II and capture Rome, Allied forces landed near the Italian resort town and become bogged down in a stalemate. After four months, breakout was achieved.
Normandy World War II	1944	In Operation Overlord, the largest amphibious landing ever executed, Allied troops landed on the coast of northwest France on 6 June.
Okinawa World War II	1945	The largest amphibious operation of World War II in the Pacific, the landings were followed by 82 days of fighting before the island was secured by Allied troops.
Inchon Korean War	1950	During the Korean War, United Nations forces landed at Inchon to relieve pressure on the Pusan Perimeter.
San Carlos Water Falklands War	1982	Elements of the Royal Marines' 3 Commando Brigade and the Parachute Regiment of the British Army went ashore during the liberation of the Falkland Islands from Argentine troops.

Gallipoli Campaign, 1915
During the Dardanelles Campaign, Allied forces attempted, unsuccessfully, to conquer a Turkish garrison at Gallipoli and gain control of this strategic peninsula guarding the Black Sea. Here, Australian troops come ashore with a howitzer.

In 1916, Russian General Alexei Brusilov suggested an untried form of assault, which involved attacking at several points instead of just one, and without the normal extensive artillery bombardment beforehand. Using this method, the Russians achieved total surprise over the Austro-Hungarian forces, who were comfortably dug in to deep trenches. They launched with a colossal and accurate, though brief, artillery barrage against the Austrians. The offensive wound down as supply lines lengthened. The final gains were outweighed by the costs, as German reinforcements arrived from the Western Front.

ARAB REVOLT
5 JUNE 1916–OCTOBER 1918

Forces Numbers fluctuated. **Casualties** No reliable estimates. **Location** Arabia, Palestine and Syria. **Theatre** Ottoman Front.

Arab guerrillas, rebelling against Ottoman rule from Constantinople, tied down large numbers of Turkish troops and carried out joint operations with British forces. Arab cavalry and camel-mounted troops working alongside British armoured cars eventually occupied Damascus. Captain T.E. Lawrence rose to fame as the British liaison officer to the Arabs, coordinating their operations with Allied forces in the region.

Desperate to draw German artillery and troops away from the battle for Verdun, the Western Allies launched a large-scale offensive on the Somme. However, they were facing thoroughly prepared defences.

FIRST DAY OF THE SOMME
BRITISH SECTOR, 1 JULY 1916

Forces British: 13 divisions; German: 16 divisions on all sectors. **Casualties** British: 58,000; German: 8,000. **Location** Picardy, northern France. **Theatre** Western Front.

After an eight-day bombardment, the British launched their attack against positions they expected to find shattered by artillery. Instead, the defence was intact and massive casualties resulted. Many British units were only hastily trained volunteer formations.

FIRST DAY OF THE SOMME
FRENCH SECTOR, 1 JULY 1916

Forces French: 11 divisions; German: 16 divisions on all sectors. **Casualties** French: 7,000; German: unknown. **Location** Picardy, northern France. **Theatre** Western Front.

To the south of the British sector, French divisions made their own attack. These suffered fewer casualties due to their use of infiltration tactics and the fact that a French assault was unexpected.

THE SOMME
JULY OFFENSIVES 1916

Forces British: 51 divisions; French: 48 divisions; German: 50 divisions involved throughout the campaign. **Casualties** British: 418,000; French: 194,000; German: 650,000 (overall). **Location** Picardy, northern France. **Theatre** Western Front.

The Allies continued to attack on the Somme throughout July in a frantic bid to draw German reinforcements away from the battle for Verdun. The first German reserves were pulled from Verdun on 11 July, as the Allies gained the first line of German trenches.

ROMANI
3–5 AUGUST 1916

Forces Allied: 2 divisions and supporting troops; Turkish: around 18,000 including German contingent. **Casualties** Allied: 1,130; Turkish 5,000 plus 4,000 prisoners. **Location** Sinai Peninsula, Egypt. **Theatre** Ottoman Front.

Having failed once to gain control of the Suez Canal, the Turks tried again as the British began moving their positions forwards. Initially securing part of Romani, the Turks were driven off by a counterattack, ending the threat to the Suez Canal.

SIXTH ISONZO
6–17 AUGUST 1916

Forces Italian: 22 divisions; Austro-Hungarian: 9 divisions. **Casualties** Italian: 51,000; Austro-Hungarian: 40,000. **Location** Northeast Italy. **Theatre** Italian Front.

Switching from a strategy of broad offensives to a focus on a single point, the Italian army made significant gains. The Austrians pulled back to preserve their forces, which were thinly stretched and having to fight on two fronts.

THE SOMME
SEPTEMBER OFFENSIVES 1916

Forces British: 51 divisions; French: 48 divisions; German: 50 divisions involved throughout the campaign. **Casualties** British: 418,000; French: 194,000; German: 650,000 (overall). **Location** Picardy, northern France. **Theatre** Western Front.

Assisted by a small number of tanks, the Allies made further slow progress against the German lines, relieving the pressure – and permitting the French to go over to the offensive – at Verdun.

THE SOMME
NOVEMBER OFFENSIVE 13–18 NOVEMBER 1916

Forces British: 51 divisions; French: 48 divisions; German: 50 divisions involved throughout the campaign. **Casualties** British: 418,000; French: 194,000; German: 650,000 (overall). **Location** Picardy, northern France. **Theatre** Western Front.

Russian Revolution
Having gained control of the army and overthrown the Provisional Government, Bolshevik troops march through Moscow in October 1917 (November by modern calendar).

The final Allied push on the Somme resulted in further minor gains and assisted the French offensive around Verdun. By the end of the battle the quality of German forces had been reduced by casualties among professional officers and NCOs.

Battling against a sea of mud
Mud was the dominant feature of many World War I battlefields, hindering movement and causing sores on the soldiers' wet feet. Here British stretcher-bearers carry a comrade at Passchendaele in 1917.

1917

New technologies and fighting techniques were introduced in 1917 in an attempt to break the trench deadlock. The Allies deployed tanks while Germany relied upon highly trained infantry. Russia suffered political collapse and left the war, depriving the Allies of manpower.

VIMY RIDGE
9–12 APRIL 1917

Forces British and Canadian: unknown; German: unknown. **Casualties** Canadian: 3,598 killed; German: 20,000 plus 10,000 captured. **Location** 12km (7.5km) northeast of Arras, northern France. **Theatre** Western Front.

A five-day bombardment warned the German defenders of a coming assault, but the use of tunnels to get close to German positions gave an element of surprise. The ridge was secured by 12 April.

NIVELLE OFFENSIVE
16 APRIL–9 MAY 1917

Forces French: 1,200,000; German: unknown. **Casualties** French: 187,000; German: 167,000. **Location** Between Rheims and Soissons, eastern France. **Theatre** Western Front.

Using new tactics and tank support, the French hoped the Nivelle Offensive would provide a breakthrough. Delays allowed the Germans to prepare, and the assault achieved little.

> " …One **officer**… pulled out his **sabre** and slashed the **head** of one working man."
>
> A WITNESS TO THE BOLSHEVIK UPRISING, MAY 1917

LARGEST CONVENTIONAL COMBAT EXPLOSIONS

Location/War	Date	Incident
Siege of Almeida Peninsular War	26 August 1810	At Almeida, Portugal, a French shell detonated 75 tons of powder, 4,000 prepared charges, and a million musket rounds. The British garrison was forced to surrender the next day.
Siege of Multan Second Anglo-Sikh War in India	30 December 1848	A British shell struck a mosque being used as a magazine, igniting 200 tons of black powder.
Battle of the Crater US Civil War	30 July 1864	During the siege of Petersburg, Union engineers packed tunnels beneath Confederate lines with four tons of gunpowder. The ensuing explosion left a crater 52m (170ft) long, 24m (80ft) wide, and 9m (30ft) deep. About 350 Confederate soldiers were killed in the blast.
Battle of the Somme World War I	1 July 1916	At 7:28am, the British detonated 27 tons of explosives, signalling the beginning of the devastating battle of the Somme.
Messines World War I	7 June 1917	Along the Messines-Wytschaete Ridge, 21 mines were placed under German lines. The detonation of 455 tons of explosives killed 10,000 German soldiers.
Daisy Cutter Vietnam War to the present day	1960s–present	From the Vietnam era to combat in Iraq and Afghanistan, US forces have utilized the 7.5-ton Daisy Cutter bomb to clear landing zones.

MESSINES
7–14 JUNE 1917

Forces British and empire: 9 divisions (plus 3 in reserve); German: 5 divisions (plus 4 in reserve). **Casualties** German: 25,000; British and empire: 17,000. **Location** Flanders, Belgium. **Theatre** Western Front.

The detonation of explosives in tunnels under the German positions resulted in a successful assault. German counterattacks were then beaten off with heavy losses.

KERENSKY OFFENSIVE
1 JULY–3 AUGUST 1917

Forces Russian: unknown; German: unknown. **Casualties** Russian: 400,000 killed, wounded, or taken prisoner; German: 60,000. **Location** Galicia (in modern Poland). **Theatre** Eastern Front.

The Russian offensive made good progress at first but rapidly faltered in the face of a German counterattack.

PASSCHENDAELE
31 JULY–10 NOVEMBER 1917

Forces Allied: unknown; German: unknown. **Casualties** Allied: 250,000 (70,000 killed); German: similar. **Location** Ypres, Belgium. **Theatre** Western Front.

Using "bite-and-hold" tactics to make and hold on to small gains, the Allies initially made good progress until well-prepared reinforced positions halted them.

CAPORETTO
27 OCTOBER–12 NOVEMBER 1917

Forces Italian: 41 divisions; Austrian: 29 divisions; German: 7 divisions. **Casualties** Italian: 40,000; German and Austrian: 20,000. **Location** Isonzo river, northeast Italy. **Theatre** Italian Front.

Bolstered by German troops and officers, the Austrian army managed to break the weary Italian line and force a retreat. The Italian army formed a new line along the Piave river.

BOLSHEVIK REVOLUTION
NOVEMBER 1917–MARCH 1918

Forces Bolshevik: unknown; Tsarist: unknown. **Casualties** No reliable estimates. **Location** Russia.

With Russia in turmoil and German armies advancing on Petrograd, Lenin's Red Guards seized control of the capital and set up a revolutionary government. Peace with Germany soon followed.

Electrical detonator
In World War I, explosives set off by detonators were used to dig fortifications, mine enemy approach lines, and destroy infrastructure.

> "... I gripped my gun more firmly and **thrust my bayonet** into his heart ... It was **horrible**."

ATHANASE POIRIER, CANADIAN, ON FIGHTING IN THE BELGIAN TRENCHES, 1915

CAMBRAI
20 NOVEMBER–3 DECEMBER 1917

Forces British: 8 divisions with 476 tanks; German: 20 divisions. **Casualties** British: 45,000; German: 50,000. **Location** Southeast of Arras, northeast France. **Theatre** Western Front.

Making the first massed tank attack, the British achieved great gains on the first day. However, mechanical breakdowns and lack of preparation robbed the British of the chance to exploit the victory.

1918
The collapse of Russia freed up thousands of German troops to be transferred to the Western Front. There, they were committed to a series of offensives intended to win the war before American manpower reached the battlefields.

Canadian Ross bayonet and pocket knife
The stubby Ross bayonet, here shown alongside a standard issue Canadian pocket knife, was designed for the Ross Mk III rifle issued to Canadian troops. Canadian forces reached the Western Front at Ypres in April 1915.

SPRING OFFENSIVES
21 MARCH–3 JUNE 1918

Forces German: 74 divisions; British: 30 divisions. **Casualties** Allied: 500,000; German: 400,000. **Location** Western Front.

Using infiltration tactics backed by massive artillery bombardment, the Germans smashed a hole in the British line. Further offensives exhausted German manpower.

RAID ON ZEEBRUGGE   23 APRIL 1918

Forces Allied: 75 ships; German: unknown. **Casualties** Allied: 500; German: unknown. **Location** North Sea off coast of Belgium.

Attempting to eliminate U-Boat bases, the Allies planned to scuttle old cruisers as blockships, rendering the canals useless. Determined resistance prevented the ships being scuttled in the right place. A similar raid on Ostend also failed.

SECOND VILLIERS–BRETONNEUX
24–27 APRIL 1918

Forces Allied: unknown; German: unknown. **Casualties** Unknown. **Location** East of Amiens, northern France. **Theatre** Western Front.

Supported by 13 tanks, German forces made a successful attack in the direction of Amiens. During the fighting, the first ever engagement between tanks took place. A counterattack reversed the German gains.

THIRD AISNE   27 MAY–6 JUNE 1918

Forces German: 20 divisions; British and French: unknown. **Casualties** German: 130,000; Allied: 127,000. **Location** Near Paris, France. **Theatre** Western Front.

Hoping to win the war before American troops arrived in strength, German High Command launched a surprise offensive. Initially it made large gains but fatigue, the lack of supplies, and Allied counterattacks halted the offensive.

CANTIGNY   28 MAY 1918

Forces American: 3,500; German: unknown. **Casualties**: unknown. **Location** Northern France. **Theatre** Western Front.

American forces in Europe launched their first offensive, albeit on a small scale, against the village of Cantigny. Combined with French tank, artillery, and air support the position was taken and held against counterattacks.

BELLEAU WOOD   6–26 JUNE 1918

Forces American: unknown; German: unknown. **Casualties** American: 9,777; German: unknown; 1,600 taken prisoner. **Location** Between the Aisne and the Marne river, east of Paris. **Theatre** Western Front.

American troops suffered heavy casualties attacking across open ground in the face of machine-gun fire. Belleau Wood was taken and then lost to a counterattack. Subsequent fighting went on for weeks.

PIAVE   15–22 JUNE 1918

Forces Italian: 57 divisions; Austro-Hungarian: 58 divisions. **Casualties** Italian: 85,000; Austro-Hungarian: 70,000. **Location** Northeastern Italy. **Theatre** Italian Front.

Advancing in a pincer movement, the Austrians hoped to crush on the Italian army. But the Italians had recovered from the disaster at Caporetto and, with French and British reinforcements, made a successful counterattack.

LE HAMEL   4 JULY 1918

Forces Allied: Australian: 1 division plus some American troops; German: unknown. **Casualties** Allied: 1,300; German: 2,000 plus 1,600 taken prisoner. **Location** East of Amiens, northern France. **Theatre** Western Front.

Using modern combined-arms tactics with massed machine-guns and heavy tanks, Allied troops quickly overran the German positions. The Allies achieved surprise by omitting a preliminary bombardment.

SECOND MARNE
15 JULY–3 AUGUST 1918

Forces Allied: unknown; German: unknown. **Casualties** French: 95,000; British: 13,000; American: 12,000; German: 168,000. **Location** East of Paris, France. **Theatre** Western France.

Pushing across the Marne river, the German offensive was halted by the Allies, who forced them to fall back to the Aisne.

AMIENS   8–11 AUGUST 1918

Forces Allied: 18 divisions plus tank corps; German: 19 divisions. **Casualties** Allied: 46,232; German: more than 75, 000 including 29,873 prisoners. **Location** East of Amiens, France. **Theatre** Western Front.

The Allied offensive began with a large-scale tank assualt. Surprise was achieved, allowing the Allies to make such dramatic gains that August 8 was described as the "Black Day of the German Army". Although the pace slow after these early successes, the advance continued until the end of the war.

FINAL ALLIED OFFENSIVES
8 AUGUST–11 NOVEMBER 1918

Forces Allied/German: no reliable estimate of numbers. **Casualties** No reliable estimates. **Location** Western Front.

With vast numbers of tanks and aircraft in support, the Allies began making substantial gains against the exhausted Germans. Demoralization and political upheaval ended Germany's ability to resist.

ÉPEHY   18 SEPTEMBER 1918

Forces Allied: 12 divisions; German: 6 or more divisions. **Casualties** Allied: unknown; German: unknown. **Location**, Picardy, northern France. **Theatre** Western Front.

Although the German army was by now on the brink of collapse, the Hindenburg

"Devil dogs" on the attack
In June 1918, at the Battle of Belleau Wood, US Marines earned their German sobriquet *Teufelshunde* ("Devil dogs") for their fierce hand-to-hand fighting in attacks, which helped halt a German offensive.

Line was still formidable. By using a creeping barrage tactic the Allies made good gains, prompting their decision to undertake further offensives against the weakening German army.

VITTORIO VENETO
24 OCTOBER–4 NOVEMBER 1918

Forces Italian: 57 divisions including British and American contingents; Austro-Hungarian: 58 divisions. **Casualties** Italian: 40,000; Austro-Hungarian: 30,000 plus about 300,000 prisoners. **Location** Piave river, northeastern Italy. **Theatre** Italian Front.

Italian advances met with fierce resistance, which suddenly collapsed after hard fighting. The Austrian army ceased to exist as a fighting force and an armistice was agreed as the Austro-Hungarian empire began to disintegrate.

RUSSIAN CIVIL WAR

The Russian Civil War was not an issue between two sides. Within the "Red" (Bolshevik) and "White" (Tsarist) factions there were several groups, many of whom disagreed violently with one another. Furthermore, several foreign forces, including British, Americans, Japanese, Czechs and Poles, intervened to protect their national interests.

RUSSIAN CIVIL WAR
MAY 1918–NOVEMBER 1920

Forces Bolshevik: 800,000; White: c. 300,000; foreign forces: 180,000. **Casualties**: 10 million (mainly civilian). **Location** Former Russian empire.

Threatened by foreign forces, which controlled key ports, nationalist groups in some areas, and by the White (Tsarist) armies, the Bolsheviks built an army and won a bloody war for control of Russia.

RUSSO–POLISH WAR

Both Poland, which had just been re-established as a nation, and the emerging Soviet Union sought to control regions lying between them, because the frontiers between Poland and Soviet Russia had not been clearly laid out in the Treaty of Versailles. Events after World War I also created turmoil. Foreign interests further muddied the waters, and conflict became inevitable. The eventual peace treaty of 1921 divided the disputed territory between Poland and the Soviet Union.

WARSAW 7 MAY–12 OCTOBER 1920

Forces Russian: 200,000; Polish: 200,000. **Casualties** Russian: c. 80,000 killed or wounded, 60,000 taken prisoner; Polish: 50,000 killed or wounded. **Location** Outside Warsaw, Poland.

Polish attempts to secure their nationhood led to an invasion by Soviet Russia, and by the middle of summer the city of Warsaw seemed fated to fall. A surprise Polish counter-offensive threatened the Russians with envelopment before they reached Warsaw. Russia's disorganized retreat led to Polish victory.

TOP FIGHTER ACES IN HISTORY

Perhaps no other military icon so vividly embodies both the idealized romance and risk of warfare than the fighter ace. The phrase originated during World War I, when French newspapers lionized Adolphe Pegoud for shooting down five German aircraft. Comparable with the medieval knights of old, fighter aces often engage in single combat, and thus can take individual credit for kills.

WORLD WAR I

Germany		Kills
Manfred von Richthofen		80
Ernst Udet		62
Erich Loewenhardt		53
Werner Voss		48

France		
René Fonck		75
Georges Guynemer		54
Charles Nungesser		45
Georges Madon		41

Great Britain & Commonwealth		
E. C. Mannock	Britain	73
W. A. Bishop	Canada	72
R. Collishaw	Canada	62
J. T. B. McCudden	Britain	57

United States		
Edward Rickenbacker		26
William Lambert		22
August Iaccaci		18
Frank Luke Jr.		18

WORLD WAR II

Germany		
Erich Hartmann		352
Gerhard Barkhorn		301
Gunther Rall		275
Otto Kittel		267

Great Britain & Commonwealth		
M. T. St. J. Pattle	South Africa	51
J. E. Johnson	Britain	38
B. Finucane	Ireland	32
A. G. Malan	South Africa	32

United States		
Richard Bong		40
Thomas B. McGuire		38
David McCampbell		34
Francis Gabreski	28 (plus 6 more in Korea)	

France		
Marcel Albert		23
Jean Demozay		21
Pierre LeGloan		20
Edmond Marin la Meslee		20

Japan		
Hiroyoshi Nishizawa		87

Combat in the skies
World War I saw the first widespread use of airplanes in combat. German air ace Ernst Udet, pictured here with a Fokker DVII, earned 62 confirmed kills in the war.

Tetsuzo Iwamoto	80
Shoichi Sugita	70
Saburo Sakai	64

Soviet Union	
Ivan N. Kozhedub	62
Aleksandr Pokryshkin	59
Grigori Rechkalov	58
Nikolai Gulayev	57

KOREAN WAR

United States	
Joseph McConnell Jr.	16
James Jabara	15
Manuel Fernandez	14.5
George A. Davis Jr.	14

VIETNAM WAR

United States	
Charles B. DeBellevue (Weapons System Operator)	6
Richard S. Ritchie	5
Jeffrey Feinstein (Weapons System Operator)	5
Randy Cunningham	5

North Vietnam	
Colonel Tomb	13
Nguyen Van Bay	7

ARAB-ISRAEL CONFLICT

Israel	
Giora Aven	18
Oded Marom	17
Abraham Shalmon	17
Yiftah Spector	15

Spanish Civil War Poster
This 1937 propaganda poster extols the strength of the "proletariat" to resist the "military bullying" of the Nationalists (fascist rebels under General Franco), who launched a coup against the government

In 1928 a second expedition took Beijing. Disputes between the Nationalists and the Chinese Communist Party resulted in a split in 1927 leading to years of civil war.

CENTRAL PLAINS WAR
MAY 1930–4 NOVEMBER 1930

Forces Jiang Jieshi: 600,000; Rebel Commanders: 800,000. **Casualties** Jiang Jieshi: roughly 100,000; Rebel Commanders: 150,00. **Location** Central China.

Three warlords, once allied with Jiang Jieshi and the Nationalists, broke away and a civil war began. Chiang Kai-shek's faction benefited from air power, and emerged as the dominant force in China, but the campaign against the Communist Red Army was weakened by this internal conflict.

THE LONG MARCH
16 OCTOBER 1934–20 OCTOBER 1935

Forces 80,000 in initial Communist outbreak from Jiangxi. **Casualties** unknown, but 9,000 arrived at Wuqizhen. **Location** China.

Breaking through Nationalist encirclement in Jiangxi, the Communist forces marched north to find a secure base. Casualties were high from harassing attacks and the hardships of the march, but eventually the survivors reached safety.

THE NEW FOURTH ARMY INCIDENT
7 JANUARY 1941–13 JANUARY 1941

Forces Communist: 9,000; Nationalist: 80,000. **Casualties** Communist: 7,000 including prisoners; Nationalist: unknown. **Location** Maolin, China.

War between Nationalists and Communists had been suspended to fight invading Japanese. But relations broke down when a Communist force including many civilians was encircled and all but annihilated by Nationalists.

LIAOSHEN CAMPAIGN
12 SEPTEMBER 1948–12 NOVEMBER 1948

Forces: Communist: 700,000; Nationalist: 550,000. **Casualties** Communist: 70,000; Nationalist: unknown, but heavy. **Location** Manchuria.

Although the Nationalists controlled the major cities, these were isolated from one another by Communist-held territory. This allowed Communist forces to concentrate against each in turn. The region was brought firmly under Communist control.

HUAIHAI CAMPAIGN
6 NOVEMBER 1948–1 JANUARY 1949

Forces Communist: 600,000; Nationalist: 920,000. **Casualties** Communist: 134,000; Nationalist: 550,000 including prisoners. **Location** Shandong, China.

Concentrating rapidly against different Nationalist forces in turn, the Communists brought heavy artillery firepower to bear and trounced the enemy. Significant Nationalist forces defected to the Communist side.

PINGJIN CAMPAIGN
29 NOVEMBER 1948–31 JANUARY 1949

Forces Communist: 1,000,000; Nationalist: 500,000. **Casualties** Communist: 39,000; Nationalist: 520,000 including prisoners. **Location** North China Plain.

As the balance of the civil war tipped ever further against them, the Nationalists concentrated at Beijing and Tianjin. Victorious Communist forces from the Liaoshen campaign joined local armies to achieve overwhelming superiority. Centres of resistance were crushed one by one. Beijing surrendered and was named capital of the Communist-controlled state.

KUNINGTOU
25–27 OCTOBER 1949

Forces Communist: 19,000; Nationalist: 40,000. **Casualties** Communist: 3,900 plus 5,000 prisoners; Nationalist: 3,250. **Location** Taiwan Straits.

Defeated on the mainland, the Nationalists retreated to Taiwan. Communist forces attacked the island of Quemoy as a prelude to invading Taiwan itself. The level of resistance was underestimated and the attack failed, permitting the Nationalist government to survive on Taiwan.

CHINESE CIVIL WAR
1927–49

Arising out of ideological differences between Nationalists and the Chinese Communist party, both of whom wanted to unify the country, the Chinese Civil War was fought from 1927–49, pausing only during the Japanese occupation of 1937–45.

THE NORTHERN EXPEDITIONS
9 JULY 1926–8 JUNE 1928

Forces Nationalist: 100,000; Warlords: unknown. **Casualties** Unknown. **Location** China.

Seeking to break the power of the warlords in northern China and unify the nation, the National Revolutionary Army won several major victories in 1926–27.

SPANISH CIVIL WAR
1936–39

A complex conflict involving many factions, the combatants in this vicious civil war were loosely grouped into two sides – the rebel Nationalists, led by General Francisco Franco, and the loyalist Republicans. Both sides received military assistance from overseas, notably from Germany and Italy (for the Nationalists) and the Soviet Union (who supported the Republicans). The International Brigades of more than 40,000 anti-fascist foreign volunteers from more than 50 countries joined the Republican side. But Franco triumphed, and exacted harsh reprisals.

FASTEST MILITARY AIRCRAFT BY DECADE

Propeller-driven aircraft gave way to the awesome power of the jet engine during the 20th century. Although the speed record of the US-built SR-71 Blackbird spyplane stands unbroken today, the aircraft was retired in the 1990s. Still in active service, the supersonic MiG-25 interceptor is the fastest military aircraft currently deployed.

Decade	Aircraft	Speed	Used by	Entered Service
1910s	SPAD XIII	218kph (135mph)	French Air Service	1917
1920s	Curtiss P-6 Hawk	328.8kph (204mph)	US Army Air Forces	1927
1930s	Messerschmitt Bf-109	624kph (388mph)	German Luftwaffe	1935
1940s	Messerschmitt Me-163B Komet	1,130kph (702mph)	German Luftwaffe	1944
1950s	Lockheed F-104 Starfighter	2,334kph (1,450mph)	US Air Force; NATO	1958
1960s–1990s	Lockheed SR-71 Blackbird	3,235kph (2,010mph)	US Air Force	1966
2000s	MiG-25 Foxbat	3,521kph (2,188mph)	Russian Air Force	1970

Japanese Nambu Type A/4 pistol
This Japanese 8mm semi-automatic pistol was widely used by the Imperial Japanese army and navy. Its flawed design made it dangerous to use, and its weak cartridge had considerably less stopping power than comparable Western rounds.

> "The bombs **fell short**… Guernica was bombed as a **result**."
>
> LT GEN ADOLPH GALLAND, LUFTWAFFE CONDOR LEGION, APRIL 1937

ADVANCE FROM AFRICA
AUGUST–SEPTEMBER 1936
Forces Army of Africa (Nationalist): 34,000. **Casualties** No reliable estimates. **Location** Morocco and Spain.

Assisted by German and Italian air transport forces, the best troops of the Spanish army, garrisoned in Morocco, crossed into Spain to take part in the war on the mainland. This successful operation was the world's first large-scale military airlift.

DEFENCE OF MADRID
6–23 NOVEMBER 1936
Forces Nationalist: c. 50,000; Republican: unknown. **Casualties** No reliable estimates. **Location** Madrid, Spain.

The arrival of the first volunteer International Brigades on the Republican side enabled the besieged city of Madrid to hold out under attack by the Nationalists. The city remained under siege for the rest of the war.

GUADALAJARA
8–16 MARCH 1937
Forces Republican: 20,000; Italian and Nationalist: 45,000. **Casualties** Republican: 7,000; Italian and Nationalist: 5,000. **Location** Guadalajara, Spain.

Light tanks led the Nationalist attack, which went well initially. Republican reinforcements, led by Soviet T-26 tanks that outgunned those of the Nationalists, arrived in time to drive off the attackers.

GUERNICA
26 APRIL 1937
Forces German (Nationalist): 43 aircraft; Basque: none. **Casualties** German (Nationalist): none; Basque civilians: c. 300. **Location** Guernica, northern Spain.

The air attack on Guernica, ostensibly against military targets, was "without regard for the civilian population", with deliberate attacks on civilians reported. The town's name became synonymous with terror bombing.

BILBAO
11–13 JUNE 1937
Forces Republican and Basque: 50,000; Nationalist and Italian: 75,000. **Casualties** Republican and Basque: unknown; Nationalist and Italian: 530. **Location** Bilbao, northern Spain.

Bilbao became capital of the short-lived Basque autonomous region. The city was defended by extensive, labyrinthine fortifications, including bunkers, tunnels, and fortified trenches in several rings, and all protected by artillery fortifications. Known as the "Iron Belt", the elaborate fortifications were incomplete by the time of the battle and were breached. By then the designer had defected to the Nationalists, along with his plans.

TERUEL
5 DECEMBER 1937–20 FEBRUARY 1938
Forces Republican: unknown; Nationalist: unknown. **Casualties** Republican: 60,000 including prisoners; Nationalist: 50,000 including prisoners. **Location** Teruel, Spain.

Launching a surprise attack against Teruel, the Republicans enticed Nationalist reinforcements away from Madrid. Ultimately the Republicans were forced to withdraw in the face of greater numbers.

EBRO 24 JULY–16 NOVEMBER 1938
Forces Republican: 80,000 in original offensive. **Casualties** Republican: 70,000; Nationalist: 36,500. **Location** Ebro river, Spain.

Facing certain defeat, the Republicans launched a failed offensive across the Ebro river. The retreat from the Ebro effectively decided the final outcome of the war.

Death of the innocent
In April 1937 the bombing of the Basque town of Guernica by German Luftwaffe volunteer squadrons heavily damaged the town's buildings and left around 300 of its civilian population dead.

FAMOUS SPECIAL FORCES UNITS

Special Forces or Special Operations units exist within the military establishments of many nations. A number of these trace their origins to elite guards units. Modern Special Forces units have often been established along the structure of the British Special Air Service (SAS).

Unit	Nation	Founded	In Action
Stormtroopers	Germany	1915	Italian Front, Western Front
Arditi	Italy	1917	Italian Front, Balkans
Brandenburger Regiment	Germany	1939	Low Countries, Eastern Front
Long Range Desert Group (LRDG)	Great Britain	1940	North African Desert
Commandos	Great Britain	1940	Western Europe via combined armed forces organization
Special Boat Service	Great Britain	1940	Mediterranean, China, Burma, India
Special Air Service	Great Britain	1941	North Africa, Western Europe. Actions include Desert Storm and Operation Iraqi Freedom
Chindits	Great Britain	1942	China, Burma, India
Popski's Private Army	Great Britain	1942	North African Desert
Rangers	United States	1942	Mediterranean, Western Europe. Numerous actions as 75th Ranger Regiment including Central America, Persian Gulf
1st Special Service Force	United States–Canada	1942	Mediterranean, Aleutians
SS Commandos	Germany	1943	Western Europe, Italy
Merrill's Marauders	United States	1943	China, Burma, India
Sayeret Matkal	Israel	1957	Six-Day War, Yom Kippur War, Entebbe, Lebanon
5th Special	United States	1961	Lineage to 1st Special Service Force; also known as Green Berets and listed as representative of US Army Special Forces groups
SEALs (US Navy's special operations force for Sea, Air, and Land)	United States	1962	Lineage to UDT Underwater Demolition Teams of World War II; US Navy
Delta Force	United States	1977	Desert Storm; Iraqi Freedom
GROM ("Thunderbolt")	Poland	1990	Representative of numerous special forces units; Afghanistan, Iraqi freedom
KSK (Kommando Spezialkräfte)	Germany	1996	Afghanistan; Balkans

SINO-JAPANESE WAR
1937–38

Taking advantage of the chaos caused by the civil war in China, and as part of its imperialist policy to dominate China militarily and politically, Japan invaded and quickly took Beijing. The ill-equipped and disorganized Chinese warlords were easily overrun.

JAPANESE INVASION OF CHINA
JULY 1937–JANUARY 1938

Forces Chinese: 2,150,000; Japanese/Manchurian: 450,000. **Casualties** Total at Shanghai: c.200,000; Chinese at Rape of Nanking: c.250,000. **Location** China.

The heaviest combat was in Shanghai, with extensive street fighting. Nanking, by contrast, was not ferociously contested but was still sacked by the Japanese.

RUSSO-JAPANESE WAR
1938–39

Having overrun China, Japan now found itself sharing a border with Russia in Manchuria. Mistrust between the two ran deep, and a dispute over the location of the border developed into a brief war.

LAKE KHASAN
29 JULY–11 AUGUST 1938

Forces Japanese: 20,000; Russian: 23,000. **Casualties** Japanese: 3,500; Russian: 1,440. **Location** Eastern Russia.

Taking Manchuria away from the Chinese, the Japanese army came up against Soviet forces in the region. Japan claimed that the Soviet Union had tampered with the border demarcation, and so attacked. This gained the Japanese some ground but they were ultimately dislodged.

NOMONHAN/KHALKHYN GOL
28 MAY–16 SEPTEMBER 1939

Forces Soviet and Mongolian: 65,000; Japanese: 28,000. **Casualties** Soviet: 24,000; Japanese: 18,000. **Location** Border between Manchuria and Outer Mongolia.

As Japanese troops pushed into the Soviet area of influence, the Soviets launched an armoured counterattack supported by mechanized infantry. The Japanese forces were smashed and retreated into Manchuria.

WORLD WAR II
1939–45

The rise of Nazi Germany in Europe, and of Imperial Japan in the Pacific, triggered a widespread conflict between the Axis (primarily composed of Germany, Japan, and Italy at the start of the war) and the Allies (notably Britain, France, the Soviet Union, and the USA). Other nations joined one or sometimes both sides during the conflict. However, none of the nations that fought in World War II was fully prepared for conflict. Some had only recently embarked on rearmament programmes. As a result, although the Allies declared war over the German invasion of Poland, they were not in a position to take much direct action. A "phoney war" ensued, which then gave way to conflict on a massive scale.

TUCHOLA FOREST
1–5 SEPTEMBER 1939

Forces Polish: roughly 2 divisions plus supporting troops; German: 2 army corps. **Casualties** Polish: no reliable estimates; German: no reliable estimates. **Location** Tuchola Forest, northern Poland. **Theatre** Eastern Front.

The speed of the German advance, coupled with the use of tactical air power, weakened the Polish defence. The Polish were driven back or surrounded.

DEFEAT OF POLAND
1 SEPTEMBER–5 OCTOBER 1939

Forces German: 1,250,000; Polish: 800,000. **Casualties** German: 44,000; Polish: 266,000. **Location** Poland. **Theatre** Eastern Front.

Attacked by superior forces along a broad front, the outmatched Polish army fought to the best of its ability. However, Soviet intervention sealed the fate of Poland.

WARSAW 8–18 SEPTEMBER 1939

Forces Polish: 120,000; German: 175,000. **Casualties** Polish: 22,000 plus thousands of civilians; German: 6,500. **Location** Warsaw, Poland. **Theatre** Eastern Front.

A combination of soldiers and civilian volunteers defeated armoured assaults on the city, which then came under siege. When it became apparent that the Western Allies were not going to assist Poland the defenders surrendered.

THE WINTER WAR
30 NOVEMBER 1939–12 MARCH 1940

Forces Finnish: 175,000; Soviet: 1,000,000. **Casualties** Finnish: 25,000; Soviet: 127,000. **Location** Russian–Finnish border region. **Theatre** Eastern Front.

The Soviet forces had far more soldiers, aircraft and tanks than the Finns. Still,

British Supermarine Spitfire Mk VB
It was eventually outclassed by Germany's Focke-Wulf Fw190, but the British Spitfire was one of the most successful fighters of World War II. Shown here is a restored Supermarine Spitfire Mk VB.

overconfidently advancing into Finland, the Soviets suffered heavy casualties and were fought to a standstill at the Mannerheim Line. A second offensive broke through and Finland sued for peace.

RIVER PLATE
13 DECEMBER 1939

Forces Axis: Pocket battleship *Graf Spee*; Allied: 1 heavy cruiser, 2 light cruisers. **Casualties** Axis: *Graf Spee* scuttled; Allied: 1 ship disabled, 2 badly damaged. **Location** South Atlantic off coasts of Argentina and Uruguay.

After an effective raiding cruise the pocket battleship *Graf Spee* was cornered in the Plate river by Allied cruisers. Duped into thinking that a massive Allied force had arrived, the *Graf Spee's* captain ordered her scuttled.

1940

The Axis nations' best chance for victory lay in rapid offensives to overcome their enemies before their war preparations were complete. In 1940 this seemed likely to happen. Denmark, Norway, and France were quickly overrun, and an invasion of Britain might have taken place if air superiority had been obtained. At this point, the United States had not yet entered the wider war.

THE NORWEGIAN CAMPAIGN
8 APRIL–9 JUNE 1940

Forces German: 10,000; Allied: 24,000 (Norwegian: 12,000). **Casualties** German: 5,500; Allied: 7,300 (Norwegian: 1,800). **Location** Norway. **Theatre** Western Front.

Both sides planned to secure Norway, but Germany acted first. Allied landings came too late to prevent the fall of Norway, but resistance continued throughout the war.

FIRST NARVIK
9 APRIL 1940

Forces Allied: 5 destroyers; German: 10 destroyers. **Casualties** Allied: 2 destroyers lost, 1 damaged; German: 2 destroyers and 7 vessels sunk, 4 destroyers damaged. **Location** Coast of Norway. **Theatre** Western Front.

ARRAS COUNTERATTACK
21 MAY 1940

Forces Allied: 1 tank brigade, 2 infantry battalions and supporting troops; German: 1 Panzer division plus supporting troops. **Casualties** Allied: 220; German: 378. **Location**: Northeastern France. **Theatre** Western Front.

As the German armoured spearhead advanced toward the Channel coast, a small force of Allied tanks and supporting infantry launched a counter-strike that overran elements of the German force. The attack was eventually driven off but delayed the Axis advance significantly.

THE BATTLE OF BRITAIN AND THE BLITZ
BATTLE OF BRITAIN JULY–OCTOBER 1940; BLITZ: SEPTEMBER 1940–MAY 1941

Forces German: 1,464 fighters, 1,380 bombers; British: 900 fighters. **Casualties** Battle of Britain: German: 1,887 aircraft; British: 1,023 aircraft; Blitz: 43,000 British civilians. **Location** Britain. **Theatre** Western Front.

Germany's plan to invade Britain required air superiority, which was denied to the Luftwaffe by the hard-pressed RAF. The so-called Battle of Britain was the first major campaign to be fought entirely in the air. Gradually the German policy shifted from attacking fighter bases to the intense bombing of cities. This tactic of *blitzkrieg* ("lightning war"), was intended to demoralize the civilian population of Britain.

Entering Narvik Fjord, the Britsh force attacked German naval assets there and sank two destroyers as well as several merchant vessels carrying ammunition and iron ore. Invasion troops ashore were also bombarded before the destroyer force left.

SECOND NARVIK
13 APRIL 1940

Forces Allied: 1 battleship, 9 destroyers; German: 8 destroyers, 2 submarines. **Casualties** Allied: 3 destroyers damaged; German: 8 destroyers and 1 U-boat lost. **Location** Coast of Norway. **Theatre** Western Front.
A large Allied force sank several ships at Narvik and attacked shore installations. An aircraft from the battleship *Warspite* also sank a U-boat, the first time a submarine had been attacked successfully from the air in the war.

EBEN EMAEL
10–11 MAY 1940

Forces Belgian: 1,000 or more; German: 493. **Casualties** Belgian: 100 plus about 1,000 prisoners; German: 142. **Location** Near Maastricht, The Netherlands. **Theatre** Western Front.
The fort of Eben Emael dominated crucial river crossings with its artillery. German airborne forces took it, helping secure a route for rapid advance into Belgium.

THE BATTLE OF FRANCE
10 MAY–25 JUNE 1940

Forces German: 3,300,000 men, 2,600 tanks; Allied: 2,800,000 men, 3,600 tanks. **Casualties** German: 111,000; Allied: French: 290,000; British: 68,000. **Location** Northeast France. **Theatre** Western Front.

Advancing through the Ardennes forest, German armoured forces broke through the Allied line and headed north for the Channel ports. Other forces advanced on Paris. An Italian incursion was beaten off.

MEUSE BRIDGES
11–14 MAY 1940

Forces Allied: Over 100 aircraft; German: no reliable estimates. **Casualties** Allied: At least 77 aircraft; German: no reliable estimates, but very low. **Location** Meuse river, France. **Theatre** Western Front.

In an attempt to interfere with German crossings of the Meuse, Allied light bombers made repeated but ultimately fruitless attacks on the advancing German columns and on the bridges themselves, where engineers detonated charges as the German were crossing. Casualties were high among the obsolete Fairey Battle aircraft, used for many of the strikes. Later reports claimed that the attacks delayed the German advance by four days.

SEDAN
13–14 MAY 1940

Forces Allied: Roughly 2 divisions; German: 1 army corps plus heavy air support. **Casualties** Allied: no reliable estimates; German: no reliable estimates. **Location** Sedan, France. **Theatre** Western Front.

The French held well-fortified positions and were receiving reinforcements as the German attack began. Massive air attacks stunned the defenders and resulted in a rout among some of them.

LANDMARK SPECIAL FORCES ACTIONS

Elite special forces have conducted numerous operations during wartime. For example, they have been involved in advance attacks, suppression of terrorist activities, and the resolution of hostage situations. Superbly trained and well equipped, special forces deploy from land, sea, and air to conduct hazardous missions, which live on to become famous in both success and failure.

Force	Location	Date	Action
German Stormtroopers	Caporetto	1917	Shock troops overwhelmed Italian defenders in surprise attack.
German Brandenburger Regiment	Gennep, Netherlands	1940	Special forces seized the bridge across the Meuse river intact.
German Airborne	Eben Emael	1940	Elite paratroopers captured Belgian fortress.
British Commandos	Beda Littoria	1941	Raid on German General Erwin Rommel's North Africa headquarters failed.
British Commandos	St Nazaire	1942	Raid destroyed large drydock on coast of occupied France.
French Foreign Legion	Bir Hacheim	1942	Free French and Foreign Legion troops defended the Gazala Line in North Africa.
US Marine Raiders	Makin Atoll	1942	Marines struck Japanese garrison in the Pacific.
First Special Service Force	Monte la Difensa	1943	US-Canadian Commando unit captured enemy position.
US Army Rangers	Cisterna	1944	German ambush near Italian town inflicted heavy casualties.
British Paratroopers	Normandy	1944	Special forces captured Merville Battery overlooking Sword Beach on D-Day.
US Army Rangers	Normandy	1944	Elite troops scaled heights of Pointe du Hoc on D-Day.
French Airborne and Foreign Legion	Dien Bien Phu	1954	Special forces defended outpost against Viet Minh forces.
British, French, Israeli Special Forces	Suez	1956	Joint operation to seize control of the Suez Canal.
US Army Special Forces	Son Tay	1970	Attempt to free POWs ended when Vietnam camp is discovered evacuated.
Israeli Commandos	Entebbe	1976	Raid freed hostages taken to Uganda in airline hijacking.
GSG9	Mogadishu	1977	German special forces rescued 90 hostages from hijacked aircraft.
SAS	Iranian Embassy London	1980	Assault freed 19 hostages and killed five Iranian terrorists.
US Combined Special Forces	Tehran	1980	Attempt to rescue US hostages held in Iran failed.
British SAS and SBS	South Georgia Island	1982	Special forces conducted operations in the Falklands.
US Army Rangers	Mogadishu	1993	Blackhawk Down raid failed to capture Somali warlord.
Russian Special Forces and Army	Beslan	2004	As many as 334 hostages died during standoff and storming of school occupied by Chechen rebels.

HIGHLY DECORATED SOLDIERS OF THE WORLD WARS

Soldier/Nation	War	Decorations
Harry Murray Australia	World War I	Victoria Cross; Order of St Michael and St George; Distinguished Service Order and Bar; 1914–15 Star; British War Medal; Victory Medal; War Medal 1939–45; Australia Service Medal 1939–45; King George VI Coronation Medal; Queen Elizabeth II Coronation Medal; Croix de Guerre
William Barker Canada	World War I	Distinguished Service Order and Bar; Military Cross and Two Bars; Croix de Guerre; Italian Silver Medal for Gallantry (2)
Audie Murphy United States	World War II	Medal of Honor; Distinguished Service Cross; Silver Star with Oakleaf Cluster; Legion of Merit; Bronze Star with Oakleaf Cluster and V device; Purple Heart with two Oakleaf Clusters; US Army Campaign Medals; Good Conduct; Victory Medal; French Legion of Honor; French Croix de Guerre; Belgian Croix de Guerre; numerous others
Douglas MacArthur United States	World War I and II; Korea	Medal of Honor; Distinguished Service Cross; Silver Star; Distinguished Flying Cross; Bronze Star; Purple Heart; Air Medal; French Croix de Guerre; Belgian Croix de Guerre; more than 30 others
Charles Upham New Zealand	World War II	Victoria Cross and Bar; Africa Star; Defence Medal; War Medal with Oakleaf; New Zealand War Service Medal; Queen Elizabeth II Coronation Medal; Queen Elizabeth II Silver Jubilee Medal; New Zealand Commemorative Medal; Order of Honour
Ivan Kozhedub Soviet Union	World War I	Hero of the Soviet Union and Korea (3); Order of Lenin (2); Order of the Red Banner (7); Order of Alexander Nevsky; Order of the Great Patriotic War (2); Order of the Red Star (2)
Hans-Ulrich Rudel Germany	World War II	Knights Cross of the Iron Cross with Golden Oak Leaves, Swords and Diamonds (the only recipient); Iron Cross 1st Class; Iron Cross 2nd Class; Wound Badge in Gold; German Cross in Gold; Hungarian Gold Medal for Bravery; Goblet of the Luftwaffe
Michael Wittmann Germany	World War II	Knights Cross of the Iron Cross with Oak Leaves and Swords; Iron Cross 1st Class; Iron Cross 2nd Class; Panzer Badge in Silver; Wound Badge in Black; Eastern Front Medal; Bulgarian Soldier's Cross; Anschluss Medal

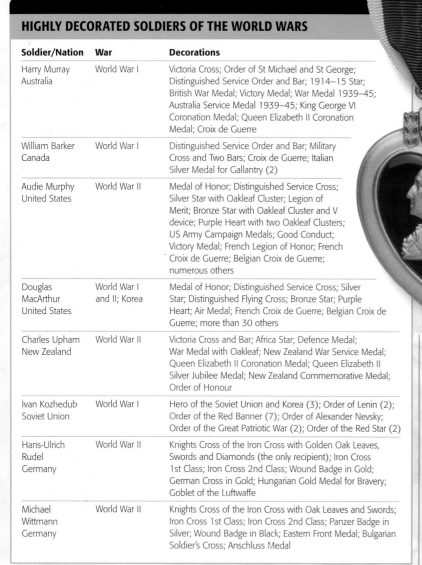

Purple Heart
Beginning in 1917, the US armed forces issued a medal, the "Purple Heart", for soldiers, sailors, and airmen wounded or killed in action against an enemy. It shows a profile of General George Washington.

two planes. The raid forced the Italian fleet to relocate northwards.

1941

With France out of the war and Britain on the defensive, the Axis was able to turn eastward against the Soviet Union. Meanwhile Japanese forces were supreme in the Pacific theatre.

CAPE MATAPAN 27–29 MARCH 1941

Forces Italian: 1 battleship, 8 cruisers, 17 destroyers; British: 1 aircraft carrier, 3 battleships, light cruisers, 17 destroyers. **Casualties** Italian: 3 heavy cruisers and 2 destroyers sunk, 1 battleship damaged; British: 4 cruisers damaged, 1 aircraft lost. **Location** Off southern tip of mainland Greece. **Theatre** Mediterranean.

Having crippled a cruiser and damaged the battleship *Vittorio Veneto* by air attack, the British force caught part of the Italian squadron lying stopped at night. The subsequent point-blank engagement was entirely one-sided.

INVASION OF GREECE 6–30 APRIL 1941

Forces Allied: roughly 500,000; Axis: roughly 1,200,000. **Casualties** Allied: 77,000 plus 14,000 prisoners; Axis: roughly 107,000. **Location** Greece. **Theatre** Mediterranean.

Invaded by Italy in October 1940, Greek forces counterattacked and initially managed drive the Italians back into Albania. German intervention made defeat inevitable despite a transfer of British troops from North Africa, compromising the Allied position there.

SIEGE OF TOBRUK 10 APRIL–7 DECEMBER 1941

Forces Allied: varied during siege; Axis: varied during siege. **Casualties** Allied: 3,000 plus 1,000 prisoners; Axis: 8,000. **Location** Modern Libya. **Theatre** North Africa.

Arriving in North Africa to assist the Italians, German forces pushed the Allies eastwards. Tobruk was left as an isolated outpost under siege, which, in December 1941, Allied forces broke through to lift.

SINKING OF THE BISMARCK 18–28 MAY 1941

Forces Axis: 1 heavy cruiser, 1 battleship; Allied: 2 aircraft carriers, 55 other ships. **Casualties** Axis: *Bismarck*; Allied: 1 battlecruiser. **Location** North Atlantic.

Breaking out into the Atlantic to attack Allied convoys, the *Bismarck* and her consort *Prinz Eugen* were pursued by massive Allied forces. Crippled by air attack, the *Bismarck* fought to the end against overwhelming odds.

CRETE 20 MAY–1 JUNE 1941

Forces Allied: 42,500; Axis: 22,000 men, 600 Ju-52 transports, 80 gliders. **Casualties** Allied: 2,000 plus 12,000 prisoners; Axis: 4,000. **Location** Aegean Sea. **Theatre** Mediterranean.

Despite taking heavy casualties the German airborne forces managed to gain control of the airfield at Maleme, allowing supplies and reinforcements to be flown in. Allied forces were evacuated by sea.

BARBAROSSA 22 JUNE–SEPTEMBER 1941

Forces Axis: 4 million men, 3,600 tanks; Soviet: 2,300,000 men initially, 10,000 tanks. **Casualties** Axis: 400,000; Soviet: 1,000,000 plus 3,000,000 prisoners. **Location** Russian-European border. **Theatre** Eastern Front.

Catching the Soviets by surprise, the initial invasion of the Soviet Union went extremely well. Hundreds of thousands of Soviet troops were taken prisoner. However, Soviet resistance did not collapse as the Germans had predicted and the invasion fell behind schedule.

SIEGE OF ODESSA 8 AUGUST–16 OCTOBER 1941

Forces Axis: 340,000; Soviet: 34,500 initially. **Casualties** Axis: 92,500; Soviet: 41,000. **Location** Southern Ukraine. **Theatre** Eastern Front.

With some assistance from German forces, Romanian troops besieged the city of Odessa, capturing it on the fourth attempt. The remaining Soviet forces evacuated the city on 14 October.

KIEV 9–26 SEPTEMBER 1941

Forces Axis: Around 300,000; Soviet: 676,000. **Casualties** Axis: 100,000; Soviet: 665,000 including prisoners. **Location** North-central Ukraine. **Theatre** Eastern Front.

> "The captain, **badly injured** … went **down** with her."

LT CMDR WALTER EDNEY, ROYAL NAVY, ON THE SINKING OF A U-BOAT, MARCH 1941

THE WAR AT SEA

The convoy routes of the Atlantic Ocean and Mediterranean Sea were severely threatened by German U-boats and surface raiders. Without the ability to move supplies and troops by sea, the Allied war effort would have ground to a halt.

HMS GLORIOUS 8 JUNE 1940

Forces Allied: 1 aircraft carrier, 2 destroyers; German: 2 battlecruisers. **Casualties** Allied: 1 aircraft carrier and 2 destroyers sunk. **Location** North Sea off Norway.

Caught without her aircraft in the air, the aircraft carrier HMS *Glorious* was sunk by gunfire from the German battlecruisers. Her two destroyer escorts met a similar fate, though a torpedo and a number of 4.7-inch shell hits damaged the battlecruiser *Scharnhorst*, whose withdrawal to Trondheim enabled the Allied evacuation convoys from Norway to pass safely through the area later that day.

BATTLE OF THE ATLANTIC
PEAK PERIOD: AUGUST 1940–MAY 1943

Forces August 1940: German: 27 U-boats; 1943: German: more than 400 U-boats. **Casualties** Allied: 3,500 merchant ships, 175 warships; German: 783 submarines. **Location** Atlantic Ocean.

The battle of the Atlantic resulted because of a German attempt to blockade Britain using its submarine forces. The practice of escorting convoys across the Atlantic limited losses somewhat, and gradually the balance tipped in the Allies' favour.

TARANTO
11 NOVEMBER 1940

Forces British: 21 aircraft; Italian: 6 battleships, 9 cruisers, 8 destroyers. **Casualties** British: 2 aircraft; Italian: 2 battleships, 1 cruiser. **Location** Southern Italy. **Theatre** Mediterranean.

Swordfish aircraft from British carriers attacked the Italian fleet in harbour, torpedoing three battleships but losing

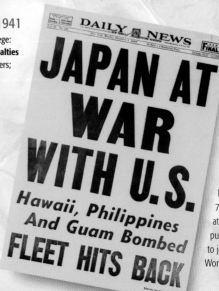

DAILY NEWS FINAL

JAPAN AT WAR WITH U.S.
Hawaii, Philippines And Guam Bombed
FLEET HITS BACK

A rallying cry to war
The New York *Daily News* announces the Japanese attacks on Pearl Harbor, Hawaii, on 7 December 1941. The attacks outraged the US public and spurred them to join the fighting in World War II.

The battle of Kiev was a classic pincer movement, or double-envelopment, which resulted in the largest encirclement in history. Very few Soviets escaped from the pocket before it was reduced.

SIEGE OF LENINGRAD
8 SEPTEMBER 1941–27 JANUARY 1944

Forces Axis: unknown; Soviet: 200,000 plus 3,000,000 civilians. **Casualties** Axis: unknown; Soviet: around 800,000 dead. **Location** Modern St Petersburg, Russia. **Theatre** Eastern Front.

Threatened by the Finns as well as the main Axis advance, Leningrad withstood siege until January 1943. It took a year to drive Axis troops away from the city.

MOSCOW
2 OCTOBER 1941–7 JANUARY 1942

Forces Axis: around 1,500,000; Soviet: around 1,500,000. **Casualties** Axis: 250,000; Soviet: 700,000. **Location** Moscow, Russia. **Theatre** Eastern Front.

Axis troops advancing on Moscow had to contend with stiffening resistance and worsening weather that turned the roads to mud. Freezing conditions restored mobility, but by this time a solid defence was in position.

SIEGE OF SEVASTOPOL
30 OCTOBER 1941–4 JULY 1942

Forces Axis: more than 350,000; Soviet: 106,000. **Casualties** Axis: possibly more than 100,000; Soviet: 106,000. **Location** Modern Southern Ukraine. **Theatre** Eastern Front.

Deploying the world's largest artillery piece, German forces surrounded and gradually reduced the port of Sevastopol. A few senior officers escaped by submarine; the remainder of the garrison stayed and fought to the end.

OPERATION CRUSADER
18 NOVEMBER–7 DECEMBER 1941

Forces Axis: 120,000; Allied: 120,000. **Casualties** Axis: 24,000; Allied 17,700. **Location** Tobruk (in modern Libya). **Theatre** North Africa.

Launched with the objective of relieving the siege of Tobruk, Operation Crusader was the first major Allied victory over Axis forces. Tank losses on both sides were heavy but the Allies were better able to replace theirs.

ROSTOV
21–27 NOVEMBER 1941

Forces Soviet: unknown; Axis: unknown. **Casualties** Soviet: unknown; Axis: unknown. **Location** Western Russia. **Theatre** Eastern Front.

Their resources were limited by commitments elsewhere, but Axis forces captured Rostov as part of an operation intended to secure the industrial centres of the Don basin. The overextended Axis forces were counterattacked and made their first major withdrawal of the war.

WINTER COUNTEROFFENSIVE
5 DECEMBER 1941–7 MAY 1942

Forces Axis: varied; Soviet: varied. **Casualties** Unknown. **Location** Eastern Front.

The Soviets transferred troops from Siberia and, supported by new T-34 tanks, launched a huge counter-offensive intended to drive German forces out of Russia. Although huge gains were made in some areas, Axis forces would remain on Soviet soil for many months to come.

PEARL HARBOR 7 DECEMBER 1941

Forces Japanese: 353 planes; American: 90 ships, 300 planes. **Casualties** Japanese: 130 pilots, 29 planes; American: 2,403 soldiers and civilians, 18 ships, 186 planes. **Location** Oahu, Hawaii. **Theatre** Pacific.

A surprise attack by Japanese air forces caught the US unprepared and caused serious losses. US aircraft carriers, however, were at sea at the time, and survived to become the mainstay of the US Pacific war.

Red army poster
A propaganda poster depicts the Red Army and air force counterattacking against the German invasion in 1941. The Russian Cyrillic text reads: "for the motherland, for honour, for freedom".

ЗА РОДИНУ,
ЗА ЧЕСТЬ, ЗА СВОБОДУ!

HISTORY'S LARGEST WARSHIPS

History's largest warships have been primary projectors of their nations' foreign policy and military power. Naval supremacy has long been a component of empire building, national security, and prestige.

Ship	Nation/type	Laid down	Commissioned	Displacement	Length	Beam
Nimitz	US carrier	22 June 1968	3 May 1975	101,196 tons	340m (1,115ft)	77m (252ft)
Enterprise	US carrier	4 Feb 1958	25 Nov 1961	92,325 tons	342m (1,123ft)	78m (257ft)
Yamato	Japanese battleship	4 Nov 1937	16 Dec 1941	72,000 tons	263m (863ft)	37m (121ft)
Admiral Kuznetsov	Russian carrier	22 Feb 1983	21 Jan 1991	67,000 tons	302m (991ft)	72m (236ft)
Iowa	US battleship	27 June 1940	22 Feb 1943	58,000 tons	271m (890ft)	33m (108ft)
Bismarck	German battleship	1 July 1936	20 Aug 1940	50,900 tons	251m (824ft)	36m (118ft)

Bismarck
Weighing in at 50,900 tons fully loaded, *Bismarck* was one of the largest battleships of World War II. Here she is shown being launched from the Blohm & Voss shipyard, in Hamburg, Germany, in 1939.

LANDMARK WAR MOVIES

Name/Year	Starring	Director	Studio	Synopsis
The Dawn Patrol, 1930	Richard Barthelmess; Douglas Fairbanks, Jr	Howard Hawks	Warner Bros	World War I aerial combat.
All Quiet on the Western Front, 1930	Louis Wolheim; Lew Ayres	Lewis Milestone	Universal	Anti-war film set during World War I and based on the novel by Erich Maria Remarque.
Wake Island, 1942	Brian Donlevy; Macdonald Carey; Robert Preston	John Farrow	Paramount	Heroic defence of a Pacific island against the Japanese during World War II.
The Longest Day, 1962	John Wayne; Henry Fonda; Robert Mitchum; Sean Connery; Richard Burton	Darryl F. Zanuck (uncredited)	20th Century Fox	Hollywood treatment of the D-Day Allied landings and invasion, 6 June 1944, based on the book by Cornelius Ryan.
Zulu, 1964	Stanley Baker; Michael Caine	Cy Endfield	Diamond Films	Outnumbered British soldiers defeat Zulu warriors during the epic battle of Rorke's Drift.
War and Peace, 1968	Sergei Bondarchuk; Vyacheslav Tikhonov; Lyudmila Savelyeva	Sergei Bondarchuk	Mosfilm Studios	Soviet film of the Russian defence against Napoleon based on the classic novel by Leo Tolstoy.
Patton, 1970	George C. Scott; Karl Malden	Frank J. Schaffner	20th Century Fox	The career of the controversial American World War II general, based on the book *Patton: Ordeal and Triumph* by Ladislas Farago.
Breaker Morant, 1980	Edward Woodward	Bruce Beresford	20th Century Fox	Story of an Australian folk hero during the Boer War.
Das Boot, 1981	Jürgen Prochnow	Wolfgang Petersen	Bavaria Film	Harrowing story of U-boat warfare during World War II.
Platoon, 1986	Charlie Sheen; Tom Berenger; Willem Dafoe	Oliver Stone	Orion Pictures	Action in the Vietnam War.
Gettysburg, 1993	Martin Sheen; Tom Berenger; Jeff Daniels	Ronald F. Maxwell	Turner Pictures	The high tide of the Confederacy during the US Civil War.
Schindler's List, 1993	Liam Neeson; Ben Kingsley	Steven Spielberg	Universal	The story of a German businessman saving Jews in Nazi-occupied Poland.
Saving Private Ryan, 1998	Tom Hanks; Matt Damon; Tom Sizemore	Steven Spielberg	DreamWorks	Intense World War II combat during the Normandy campaign.
Downfall, 2004	Bruno Ganz; Alexandra Maria Lara; Juliane Köhler	Oliver Hirschbiegel	Constantin Film	Depiction of the final 12 days of Adolf Hitler in his Berlin bunker.

The Longest Day
The D-Day operations were immortalized in movies. Here, American actor John Wayne portrays Lt. Col. B Vandervoort (1917–90), commander of second battalion, 505th Parachute Infantry Regiment, in the 1962 film, *The Longest Day*.

Battle of Midway June 1942
During the battle of Midway, the US and Japanese navies fought a decisive combat over this strategic atoll in the Pacific Ocean. Here, the carrier USS *Yorktown* lists, mortally wounded by Japanese torpedo bombers.

THE WAR IN THE FAR EAST
After the bombing of Pearl Harbor, Japanese forces moved south to attack British, Dutch, and American colonies in Asia.

HONG KONG 8–25 DECEMBER 1941
Forces Japanese: 40,000; British and Commonwealth: 15,000. **Casualties** Japanese: 3,000; British and Commonwealth: 15,000 including prisoners. **Location** Modern China. **Theatre** Pacific.

It was conceded that Hong Kong was indefensible, but reinforcements were sent anyway. The Allies were driven back to Hong Kong island and held it for a time, but were eventually overwhelmed.

ADVANCE ON SINGAPORE
8 DECEMBER 1941–15 FEBRUARY 1942
Forces Japanese: 55,000; British and Commonwealth: 140,000. **Casualties** Japanese: 3,500; British and Commonwealth: 9,000 killed, 130,000 captured. **Location** Singapore and the Malay Peninsula. **Theatre** Pacific.

Attempting a forward defence on the Malay Peninsula, Allied troops were repeatedly overrun or outflanked by the fast-moving Japanese. The result was a series of defeats as the Allies were pushed back towards Singapore.

THE PHILIPPINES
8 DECEMBER 1941–6 MAY 1942
Forces Japanese: 55,000; American and Filipino: 130,000. **Casualties** Japanese: 12,000; American and Filipino: 100,000 captured. **Location** Philippines and surrounding islands. **Theatre** Pacific.

After the loss of major air assets on the ground, American and Filipino defenders were unable to prevent Japanese landings. Retreating to the Bataan peninsula, US forces held out for a time before being forced to surrender.

HMS REPULSE AND PRINCE OF WALES 10 DECEMBER 1941
Forces Allied: 1 battleship, 1 battlecruiser, 4 destroyers; Japanese: 88 aircraft. **Casualties** Allied: 1 battleship, 1 battlecruiser; Japanese: 6 aircraft. **Location** South China Sea northeast of Singapore. **Theatre** Pacific.

Attempting to interfere with Japanese invasion plans, the Allied vessels came under heavy attack from the air. Both capital ships were sunk for little loss. The action graphically demonstrated the capabilities of air power at sea.

1942
At the start of 1942, the situation looked bleak for the Allies. However, the Axis advance was halted at sea in the Pacific and on land in Europe. The balance would shift back and forth several times during the year before beginning to tip in favour of the Allies.

BURMA
JANUARY 1942– AUGUST 1945
Forces British and Commonwealth: 30,000; Japanese: 30,000. **Casualties** (initial invasion) British: 13,000; Japanese: 4,000. **Location** Burma. **Theatre** Pacific.

The Allies were pushed out of Burma early in the war. Later, the Japanese advanced into India from bases in Burma, but were stopped and ultimately driven back across and out of the country.

FALL OF SINGAPORE
31 JANUARY–15 FEBRUARY 1942
Forces British and Commonwealth: 85,000; Japanese: 36,000. **Casualties** British and Commonwealth: 7,000 plus about 50,000 prisoners; Japanese: 4,500. **Location** Singapore. **Theatre** Pacific.

Demoralized by defeats in Malaya, the Allies made a stand on Singapore island. However, they were unable to prevent Japanese forces from crossing the straits from the mainland. The subsequent loss of Singapore was a severe blow to British morale and prestige in Asia.

"I recalled battles in which hands and legs were **lost** …"
PVT. 1ST CLASS NOMURA SEIKI OF THE JAPANESE IMPERIAL ARMY

JAVA SEA 27 FEBRUARY 1942

Forces Allied: 5 cruisers, 9 destroyers; Japanese: 4 cruisers, 14 destroyers. **Casualties** Allied: 2 cruisers, 3 destroyers sunk; Japanese: 1 destroyer damaged. **Location** Indonesia. **Theatre** Pacific.

In a series of surface actions involving cruisers and destroyers, the last significant Allied naval forces in Southeast Asia were sunk or driven off. The Allies were thus unable to prevent the invasion of Java.

DOOLITTLE RAID 18 APRIL 1942

Forces American: 16 bombers; Japanese: Air defences of the Home Islands. **Casualties** US: 15 bombers and crew; Japanese: around 450. **Location** Tokyo, Japan. **Theatre** Pacific.

The first air raid by American forces against Japan during World War II, the Doolittle Raid was conducted by bombers launched from an aircraft carrier. The raid did little material damage but it influenced Japanese strategic thinking and bolstered Allied hopes during a very bleak period.

CORAL SEA 4–8 MAY 1942

Forces American: 2 carriers, 21 other warships; Japanese: 3 carriers, 13 other warships. **Casualties** American: 1 carrier, 74 aircraft; Japanese: 1 carrier, 80 aircraft. **Location** Coral Sea, near Australia. **Theatre** Pacific.

Aircraft from carriers on both sides inflicted losses, while surface warships acted as floating anti-aircraft batteries.

GAZALA 26 MAY–21 JUNE 1942

Forces Axis: 110,000 men, 560 tanks; Allied: 125,000 men, 850 tanks. **Casualties** Axis: 60,000; Allied: 88,000. **Location** Near Tobruk (in modern Libya). **Theatre** North Africa.

Attempting to cut the British Eighth Army off from the rear, German armoured forces became trapped for a time before a supply line was forced through, enabling the panzers to break through and capture Tobruk.

MIDWAY 4 JUNE 1942

Forces Japanese: 20 ships, 275 planes; US: 26 ships, 321 planes. **Casualties** Japanese: 4 aircraft carriers, 1 cruiser; US: 1 aircraft carrier, 1 destroyer. **Location** Central Pacific Ocean. **Theatre** Pacific.

A Japanese attack on the strategically important US base at Midway resulted in a decisive clash. Heavy losses were taken on both sides, but US carrier aircraft destroyed four Japanese aircraft carriers, decisively altering the balance of naval power in the Pacific.

FALL OF TOBRUK 20–21 JUNE 1942

Forces Allied: 35,000; Axis: possibly 90,000. **Casualties** Allied: 2,000 plus 33,000 prisoners; Axis: 3,360. **Location** Modern Libya. **Theatre** North Africa.

After breaking through at Gazala, Axis armoured forces advanced on Tobruk and attacked. Lacking adequate anti-tank guns and caught unprepared, the previously formidable defences around the city were quickly overrun.

FIRST EL ALAMEIN 1–27 JULY 1942

Forces Allied: 150,000; Axis: 96,000. **Casualties** Allied: 13,250 including prisoners; Axis: 17,000 including prisoners. **Location** Northern Egypt. **Theatre** North Africa.

Retreating eastwards after the defeats at Gazala and Tobruk, the Allies made a stand at El Alamein. The Axis advance was halted after intense fighting, but the Allies failed to make headway.

GUADALCANAL
7 AUGUST 1942–7 FEBRUARY 1943

Forces American: 19,000 rising to 50,000; Japanese: 3,000 rising to 25,000. **Casualties** American: 6,100; Japanese: 25,000. **Location** Solomon Islands. **Theatre** Pacific.

Capturing the Japanese airstrip on Guadalcanal, US forces struggled to retain it against repeated attacks. Naval victories allowed the US to cut off Japanese supplies and reinforcements.

DIEPPE RAID
19 AUGUST 1942

Forces Allied: 6,100; Axis: 1,500. **Casualties** Allied: approximately 3,900 including prisoners; Axis: 600. **Location** Northern France. **Theatre** Western Front.

The operation failed: the port of Dieppe was not captured. The experience gained from the raid, however, was invaluable in planning later amphibious operations including the Normandy landings.

Prayer flag
Soldiers and leaders alike have sought spiritual help during crises. Many Japanese soldiers in World War II carried flags like this one, decorated with Shinto prayers and family names.

WORST FRIENDLY FIRE INCIDENTS

Location/War	Date	Incident
Algeciras Bay Napoleonic Wars	8 and 12 July 1801	Near Gibraltar, Spanish warships fired on one another, killing 1,700.
China World War II	21 February 1942	Fighter planes of the American Volunteer Group, the Flying Tigers attacked a retreating column of Commonwealth troops, believing them to be Japanese. More than 100 were killed.
Sicily World War II	9 July 1943	During Operation Husky, 33 aircraft carrying troops of the US 82nd Division were shot down and damaged by Allied anti-aircraft fire, leaving 318 dead and wounded.
Normandy World War II	25 July 1944	During Operation Cobra, US bombers attacked their own troops, killing 241 and wounding 620, including General Lesley McNair.
Normandy World War II	8 August 1944	The Polish 1st Armoured Division and Canadian 3rd Armoured Division were bombed by US aircraft, killing and wounding hundreds during Operation Totalize.
Lübeck, Germany World War II	3 May 1945	Royal Air Force planes attacked ships carrying concentration camp survivors and Red Army prisoners of war, killing more than 7,000.
Hamburger Hill Vietnam War	11 May 1969	Misdirected fire from helicopter gunships killed two US soldiers and wounded 35.
Persian Gulf Iran-Iraq War	17 May 1987	Two Exocet missiles, fired by an Iraqi fighter struck the frigate USS *Stark* during the Iran-Iraq War, killing 37 and wounding 21.
Iraq Provide Comfort	14 April 1994	US fighters downed two Black Hawk helicopters, mistaking them for enemy aircraft, killing 26.
Afghanistan Enduring Freedom	18 April 2002	A US aircraft dropped a 227kg (500lb) bomb on Canadian troop positions, killing four and wounding eight.

Battle of Stalingrad 1942–43
In one of modern history's bloodiest battles, the Red Army and the German Sixth Army had to fight for every street and building. Here, Soviet soldiers break cover during an assault through the city's ruins.

THE TIDE TURNS

Although it was not yet readily apparent during the summer months of 1942, the tide of victory was finally beginning to turn in favour of the Allies.

OPERATION PEDESTAL
9–15 AUGUST 1942

Forces Allied: 4 aircraft carriers, 2 battleships, 53 other vessels; Axis: 6 cruisers, 26 other vessels, 784 aircraft. **Casualties:** Allied: 1 aircraft carrier and 12 other ships lost; Axis: 2 submarines lost, many aircraft shot down. **Location** Western Mediterranean to Malta. **Theatre** Mediterranean.

Operation Pedestal was the last chance to get desperately needed supplies through to Malta, which had been under siege for many months. Despite heavy losses, part of the convoy got through.

STALINGRAD SEPTEMBER 1942– 2 FEBRUARY 1943

Forces Axis: 500,000 (290,000 inside Stalingrad); Soviet: more than 1 million. **Casualties** Axis: 500,000; Soviet: 750,000. **Location** Modern Volgograd, Russia. **Theatre** Eastern Front.

The battle for Stalingrad degenerated into desperate and chaotic street fighting as the Axis forces pushed slowly forwards. The Axis forces were then encircled and trapped in the ruined city, eventually being forced to surrender.

SECOND EL ALAMEIN
23 OCTOBER–4 NOVEMBER 1942

Forces Axis: 104,000 men, 489 tanks; Allied: 195,000 men, 1,029 tanks. **Casualties** Axis: 25,000 and 30,000 prisoners; Allied: 14,400. **Location** Northern Egypt. **Theatre** North Africa.

The British offensive resulted in bloody, confused fighting. A counter-offensive was repulsed before the British attacked again, driving the Germans back.

Flying Fortress bombers
B-17 Flying Fortress bombers of the Eighth US Air Force attack Nazi Germany by day. Long-range missions such as this one included as many as 600 planes.

OPERATION TORCH
8–10 NOVEMBER 1942

Forces Allied: 107,000; Axis: 60,000. **Casualties** Allied: 1,300; Axis: 3,350. **Location** Algeria and Morocco, North Africa. **Theatre** North Africa.

Joint US-British landings seized ports in Morocco and Algeria, after which the troops advanced eastwards into Tunisia. This led to the action at Kasserine Pass and the eventual removal of Axis forces from North Africa.

1943

At the start of 1943, the Allies were gaining the upper hand. Germany was bogged down in a struggle at Stalingrad and the Japanese had been halted in the Pacific at Guadalcanal. By year end, the Allies had ejected the Axis from North Africa and begun the invasion of Italy.

KASSERINE PASS
14–22 FEBRUARY 1943

Forces Allied: 30,000; Axis: 22,000. **Casualties** Allied: around 5,250 including prisoners; Axis: around 2,000. **Location** Tunisia. **Theatre** North Africa.

Axis forces attacked US formations holding the Kasserine Pass, inflicting a sharp defeat. A US counterattack was repulsed before the Axis force withdrew.

MARETH LINE 20–27 MARCH 1943

Forces Allied: elements of three corps; Axis: 2 Italian corps plus some German armoured troops. **Casualties** Allied: unknown; Axis: unknown. **Location** Southern Tunisia. **Theatre** North Africa.

Allied forces overran the defensive line. A rearguard action by panzer forces enabled a retreat, but remaining Axis forces fell soon after, ending the war in North Africa.

DAMBUSTERS RAID 16–17 MAY 1943

Forces British: 19 Lancaster bombers, 133 aircrew. **Casualties** British: 8 bombers lost, 53 aircrew killed, 3 taken prisoner; German: 1,200 drowned. **Location** Ruhr Valley, Germany. **Theatre** Western Front.

RAF Lancaster bombers breached the Möhne and Eder dams and damaged two others. To defeat anti-torpedo defences they used specially designed "bouncing bombs" that skipped across the water.

KURSK 5–15 JULY 1943

Forces Axis: 900,000 men, 2,700 tanks; Soviet: 1,300,000 men, 3,500 tanks. **Casualties** Axis: 210,000; Soviet: 178,000. **Location** Western Russia. **Theatre** Eastern Front.

Attempting to pinch off a large salient, Axis forces made only slow progress against Soviet defences. Soviet reserves turned the battle and by the middle of July the Soviets were able to advance.

INVASION OF SICILY 10 JULY–17 AUGUST 1943

Forces Allied: 180,000; Axis: 260,000. **Casualties** Allied: 16,000; Axis: 160,000 (including prisoners). **Location** Sicily, Italy. **Theatre** Italian Front.

Bad weather disrupted the airborne component, yet the amphibious landings went well. Considerable Axis forces evacuated from the island before it fell.

HAMBURG 24 JULY–3 AUGUST 1943

Forces Allied: British: 791 bombers; American: 127 bombers. German: fighters and anti-aircraft defences. **Casualties** German: about 40,000 civilians killed; Allied: 108 bombers lost. **Theatre** Western Front.

USAAF bombers attacked by day while RAF aircraft made their raids at night. The bombing killed about 40,000 people.

SCHWEINFURT 17 AUGUST 1943

Forces American: 376 bombers; German: 250 fighters. **Casualties** American: 60 bombers, 552 aircrew; German: 27 aircraft. **Location** Near Frankfurt, Germany. **Theatre** Western Front.

The combined raid on a ball-bearing factory at Schweinfurt and an aircraft plant at Regensburg was the most costly US bombing mission in the war to date.

SALERNO LANDINGS 3–16 SEPTEMBER 1943

Forces Allied: 190,000; Axis: 100,000. **Casualties** Allied: 12,500; Axis: 3,500. **Location** Southwestern Italy. **Theatre** Italian Front.

The Allies met resistance from the start. After failing to dislodge the Allies, Axis forces broke off and withdrew.

BERLIN AND BIG WEEK 18 NOVEMBER 1943–25 MARCH 1944

Forces Allied: 900 RAF bombers (Berlin); 1,000 USAAF bombers (Big Week). **Casualties** No reliable estimates. **Location** Berlin and industrial targets, Germany. **Theatre** Western Front.

The RAF undertook a series of large raids on Berlin to break German morale and to lure the Luftwaffe into a decisive battle by launching attacks on the German aircraft industry. Meanwhile the USAAF attacked industrial targets, culminating in the mass daylight raids of "Big Week". After the Luftwaffe had been severely weakened, the Allied invasion of Europe could proceed.

German 37mm small-calibre gun
Although outclassed by the evolution of armoured vehicles during the early 1940s, small-calibre anti-tank guns such as this PAK 36 were standard issue for many infantry units.

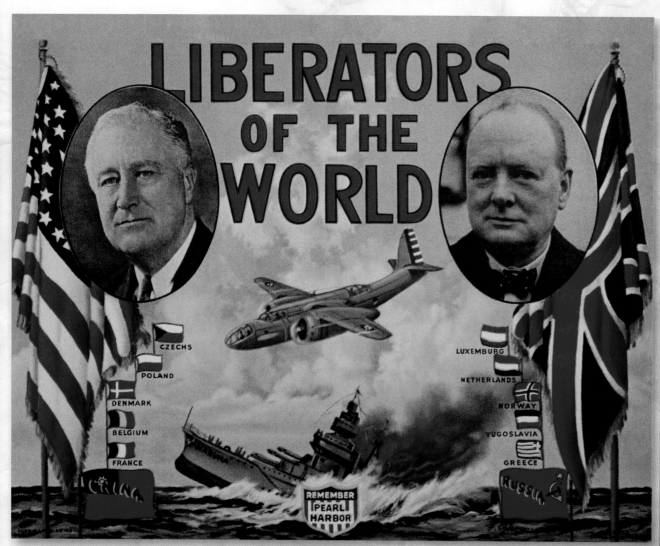

LIBERATORS OF THE WORLD

INDUSTRIAL OUTPUT OF THE UNITED STATES IN WORLD WAR II

During World War II, the United States was a leading producer of arms, military equipment, and raw materials, producing the largest quantities of some materiel in the world and, in others, second only to the Soviet Union.

Equipment	Quantity
Tanks and self-propelled guns	88,410
Artillery	257,390
Machine-guns	2,679,840
Trucks	2,382,311
Mortars	105,055
Fighter aircraft	99,950
Bomber aircraft	97,810
Transport aircraft	23,929
Aircraft carriers	22
Battleships	8
Cruisers	48
Destroyers	349
Convoy escort vessels	420
Submarines	422
Coal	2,149.7 million metric tons
Iron ore	396.9 million metric tons
Crude oil transported	833.2 million metric tons

War industries
This vast American aircraft factory located in Stratford, Connecticut, produced more than 6,000 F-4U Corsair fighters during the war.

CONVOYS UNDER THREAT

Although Germany possessed few major warships, they were a serious threat to Allied convoys. Large naval forces had to be deployed, particularly in the north Atlantic, to watch and contain them.

NORTH CAPE 26 DECEMBER 1943

Forces Allied: 1 battleship, 4 cruisers, 9 destroyers; Axis: 1 battle cruiser. **Casualties** Allied: several vessels damaged; Axis: 1 battle cruiser sunk. **Location** Off Northern Norway. **Theatre** Western Front.

In an attempt to intercept an Allied convoy, the German battle cruiser *Scharnhorst* encountered a powerful Allied force. Deprived of her radar and later slowed by shell hits, she was torpedoed repeatedly by destroyers and sunk.

1944

With the Allied forces finally pushing into Europe from both the south and the west, and inexorably working their way across the Pacific, island by island, the Axis nations now found themselves engaged in a struggle to stave off defeat rather than a battle to win the war.

Allied poster
Roosevelt and Churchill were idealized as liberators of Europe and Asia. This poster marks the destruction of one of the last Japanese battleships, *Haruna*, which Allied aircraft sunk off the Kure naval base in 1945.

MONTE CASSINO
17 JANUARY–18 MAY 1944

Forces Allied: 670,000; Axis: 360,000. **Casualties** Allied: 105,000; Axis: 80,000. **Location** Central Italy. **Theatre** Italian Front.

The monastery of Monte Cassino resisted repeated assaults by the Allies even when reduced to rubble. The garrison held out until May 1944.

ANZIO 22 JANUARY–23 MAY 1944

Forces Allied: initially 50,000; Axis: 90,000. **Casualties** Allied: 40,000; Axis: 35,000. **Location** South of Rome, Italy. **Theatre** Italian Front.

Attempting to outflank Axis defences, the Allies launched an amphibious landing but caution prevented them from exploiting the landing. The beachheads were heavily counterattacked.

IMPHAL 29 MARCH–22 JUNE 1944

Forces Allied: 4 divisions plus supporting troops; Japanese: 3 divisions. **Casualties** Allied: 17,000 including those lost at Kohima; Axis: 53,000 including those lost at Kohima. **Location** Assam, India. **Theatre** Pacific.

Japanese forces attempted to take the Naga Hills and establish a defensive position. After a battle of attrition, a lack of supplies caused the Japanese force to collapse.

KOHIMA 4 APRIL–22 JUNE 1944

Forces Allied: 1 corps; Japanese: 1 division. **Casualties** 17,000 including those lost at Imphal; Axis: 53,000 including those lost at Imphal. **Location** Assam, India. **Theatre** Pacific.

Attempting to prevent resupply and reinforcement of Allied troops at Imphal, Japanese forces clung to a defensive position until starvation and lack of ammunition forced them to retreat.

CRIMEA 8 APRIL–12 MAY 1944

Forces Soviet: 300,000; Axis: no reliable estimate. **Casualties** Soviet: 85,000; Axis: 97,000 including prisoners. **Location** Southern Ukraine. **Theatre** Eastern Front.

The speed of the Soviet advance meant preparations to hold Sevastopol were incomplete. The city was overrun and surviving units were evacuated by sea.

PLOESTI APRIL–AUGUST 1944

Forces Allied: more than 1,000 USAAF bombers. Axis: Luftwaffe **Casualties** Allied: 305 bombers and 3,000 air crew. Axis: unknown. **Location** Romania. **Theatre** Eastern Front.

The Allies sought to cripple German oil production, targeting the Ploesti oilfield. Bomber losses were heavy, but production was halted by the middle of August.

D-DAY 6 JUNE 1944

Forces Invasion force: 154,000 men, 6,500 ships, 13,000 aircraft; German: unknown. **Casualties** Allied: 4,500 killed; (US: 2,500); German: unknown. **Location** Normandy coast. **Theatre** Western Front.

> # "…I had never seen **so many ships** in all my life."
> ### SGT ADOLPH WARNECKE, US PARACHUTE REGIMENT, DESCRIBING D-DAY, 1944

The Allies launched a massive cross-Channel invasion of Europe, the largest single-day amphibious invasion of all time, and caught the defenders by surprise. The heaviest Allied losses were at Omaha beach; elsewhere the landings went according to plan.

NORMANDY 6 JUNE–25 JULY 1944

Forces Allied: 2 million; German: 1 million. **Casualties** Allied: 40,000 killed, 170,000 wounded; German: 240,000 killed or wounded. **Location** Normandy, France. **Theatre** Western Front.

Once ashore, the Allies had to fight their way out of the beachheads. Air power crippled the movement of German supplies and reserves, allowing the Allies to advance into Normandy.

VENGEANCE WEAPONS CAMPAIGN 13 JUNE 1944–29 MARCH 1945

Forces More than 8000 V1 and 3225 V2 weapons launched. **Casualties** Allied: over 10,000. **Location** Britain and the Low Countries. **Theatre** Western Front.

Unmanned flying bombs (V1) and ballistic missiles (V2) were launched in long-range attacks against the Allies. The V3 weapon, a giant artillery battery, was incomplete at the end of the war.

PHILIPPINE SEA 15–20 JUNE 1944

Forces American: 20,000 marines, 15 carriers; Japanese: 32,000 men, 9 carriers. **Casualties** American: 16,500 men, 129 aircraft; Japanese: 31,000 dead, over 500 aircraft, 3 carriers. **Location** Philippine Sea. **Theatre** Pacific.

As a Japanese fleet steamed to intervene in US landings on the Marianas, their air units were shattered by US forces in what became known as the "Marianas Turkey Shoot". The Japanese ships then came under attack from aircraft and submarines.

OPERATION BAGRATION 23 JUNE–28 JULY 1944

Forces Soviet: 1,700,000 men, 2,700 tanks; German: 800,000 men, 450 tanks. **Casualties** Soviet: 178,000; German: 350,000. **Location** Western Russia. **Theatre** Eastern Front.

Operation Bagration aimed to remove German forces from Soviet soil. Attacking along a broad front the Soviets trapped and destroyed German units, which had been given "no retreat" orders by Hitler.

FALAISE 25 JULY–20 AUGUST 1944

Forces German: 250,000; Allied: unknown. **Casualties** German: 100,000 killed or wounded; Allied: 40,000 killed or wounded. **Location** Falaise, France. **Theatre** Western Front.

Following the breakout from Normandy, the Allies succeeded in trapping large numbers of German troops in the "Falaise Pocket". Refusing permission to withdraw, Hitler ordered a counter-offensive that ensured the loss of these forces.

TANNENBERG LINE 25 JULY–19 SEPTEMBER 1944

Forces Soviet: 137,000; Axis: 22,250. **Casualties** Soviet: 170,000 (including reinforcements); Axis: 10,000. **Location** Modern Estonia. **Theatre** Eastern Front.

Assisted by Estonian forces, German units held off the attempted Soviet reoccupation for several weeks but were forced to retreat when outflanked by offensives in other areas.

WARSAW UPRISING 1 AUGUST–2 OCTOBER 1944

Forces Polish Home Army: 20,000–40,000; German garrison in Warsaw: 10,000. **Casualties** Polish Home Army: 50,000; civilians: 220,000. **Location** Warsaw, Poland. **Theatre** Eastern Front.

As the Soviet army approached Warsaw, the Polish Home Army rose up and took control of most of the city. A pause in the Soviet advance allowed the Germans to suppress the uprising.

OPERATION DRAGOON 15 AUGUST 1944

Forces Allied: 200,000; Axis: 100,000. **Casualties** Allied: no reliable estimates. **Location** Southern France. **Theatre** Western Front.

Allied forces landing in southern France encountered little resistance because most of the Axis troops in the region had been transferred north to oppose the D-Day landings.

Allied landings in Normandy

Soldiers from the US Army Quartermaster Corps wade ashore at Normandy, France, on 7 June 1944, the day after D-Day. The landings, known as Operation Overlord, began a campaign of reconquest that helped defeat Nazi Germany.

GOTHIC LINE 30 AUGUST–28 OCTOBER 1944

Forces Allied: 20 divisions; Axis: 22 divisions. **Casualties** Allied: unknown, more than 14,000; Axis: unknown, likely very heavy. **Location** Defensive line across Italy from Massa to north of Pesaro. **Theatre** Italian Front.

A northerly defensive line, the Gothic Line was heavily fortified and bitterly contested. By the time it was breached by the Allies, weather conditions had prevented further offensives in 1944.

ARNHEM 17–26 SEPTEMBER 1944

Forces Allied: 30,000 airborne troops; German: unknown. **Casualties** British: 6,800; American: 4,000; Polish: 400; German: 3,300. **Location** Netherlands and Germany. **Theatre** Western Front.

Attempting to seize vital bridges in Holland to enable the Allied forces to advance rapidly northward and into the German lowlands, the Allies landed paratroops ahead of an advancing armoured force. The operation failed after 10 days of bitter fighting; the Rhine bridges at Arnhem remained in German hands.

Ruins of Monte Cassino monastery, 1944

A sign warns of a minefield in the ruins of the monastery of Monte Cassino, Italy. The Allies eventually dislodged a German force that had moved in and seized the heights after the Allies bombed the abbey.

HÜRTGEN FOREST 19 SEPTEMBER 1944–10 FEBRUARY 1945

Forces Allied: 120,000; Axis: 80,000. **Casualties** Allied: 32,000; Axis: possibly 12,000. **Location** German–Belgian Border. **Theatre** Western Front.

In an action reminiscent of those of World War I, German forces held the Hürtgen Forest region against advancing American troops. This was the longest single battle fought by US forces.

AACHEN 4 OCTOBER–1 DECEMBER 1944

Forces Allied: 300,000; Axis: 250,000. **Casualties** Allied: 85,000. Axis: 70,000. **Location** Franco-German border. **Theatre** Western Front.

During Allied attempts to breach the Siegfried Line, Aachen was taken by the Allies after a week-long battle.

LEYTE GULF 23–26 OCTOBER 1944

Forces Allied: 35 carriers, 177 other ships; Japanese: 4 carriers, 62 other ships. **Casualties** Allied: 3 carriers, 4 other ships; Japanese: 4 carriers, 21 other ships. **Location** Philippines. **Theatre** Pacific.

Attempting to contest US landings in the Philippines, Japanese surface forces were met with massive air attack as well as a gunnery engagement in the Surigao Strait, losing four aircraft carriers and thousands of men. The battle of Leyte Gulf was the most extensive naval battle of World War II, and the largest naval battle in history. It was also the first notable battle in which Japanese aircraft used organized suicidal *kamikaze* attacks. Japan had fewer aircraft than the Allied Forces had sea vessels, which illustrates the contrast in power of the two sides at this time of the war.

THE CLOSING MONTHS

The last months of the war were marked by increasingly desperate resistance on the part of the Axis. Japanese troops defended Pacific islands to the death, while German forces were resolute in the defence of their homeland. Sudden counter-offensives by Axis forces achieved limited success but generally failed for lack of resources.

BOMBING OF JAPAN
JUNE 1944– AUGUST 1945

Forces American: up to 500 bombers per raid. **Casualties** American: up to 512 aircraft lost; Japanese: 500,000 dead. **Location** Japanese Home Islands. **Theatre** Pacific.

With the development of the Boeing B-29 Superfortress bomber, US forces based in China and several Pacific islands could now attack Japan. Starting in June 1944, conventional bombing raids with incendiary munitions proved highly effective, causing huge firestorms.

COURLAND POCKET
15 OCTOBER 1944–4 APRIL 1945

Forces Soviet: varied throughout campaign; Axis: 200,000. **Casualties** Soviet: 400,000 or more; Axis: almost total. **Location** Baltic Coastal region (in modern Latvia). **Theatre** Eastern Front.

Cut off by Soviet offensives, a sizable German force was ordered by Hitler to hold out in the "Courland Pocket". Six major Soviet offensives were launched to reduce the pocket, resulting in heavy losses before the surviving Axis troops surrendered at the end of the war.

"Little Boy"
This is a model of the atomic weapon, nicknamed "Little Boy", that the US B-29 bomber, *Enola Gay*, dropped on Hiroshima on 6 August 1945.

BULGE
16 DECEMBER 1944–15 JANUARY 1945

Forces American: 80,000; German: 200,000. **Casualties** Allied: 80,000 (including prisoners); German: 70,000–100,000 (including prisoners). **Location** Ardennes, Belgium. **Theatre** Western Front.

Launching a surprise attack from the Ardennes, German forces made good gains but were hampered by lack of fuel. This was Germany's last major offensive.

BUDAPEST
26 DECEMBER 1944–14 FEBRUARY 1945

Forces Soviet: unknown; German and Hungarian: unknown. **Casualties** Soviet: 80,000 killed, 240,000 wounded; German and Hungarian: 40,000 killed, 62,000 wounded. **Location** Hungary. **Theatre** Eastern Front.

As the Soviets encircled Budapest, Hitler ordered it held at all costs and sent forces to break the siege. This failed and the city fell to the Allies after bitter fighting.

1945

Neither Germany nor Japan was willing to consider surrender, forcing the Allies to grind their way forward in a series of hard-won battles. The fall of Berlin ended the war in Europe, while the projected invasion of the Japanese Home Islands was expected to be so costly that nuclear weapons were seen as a viable alternative. Japan eventually surrendered on 2 September 1945, after the nuclear bombing of Hiroshima and Nagasaki demonstrated the overwhelming firepower that the USA could bring to bear on its cities.

VISTULA-ODER OFFENSIVE
12 JANUARY–2 FEBRUARY 1945

Forces Soviet: 2.2 million; Axis: 450,000. **Casualties** No reliable estimates. **Location** Poland and eastern Germany. **Theatre** Eastern Front.

The Soviet offensive made good progress despite armoured counterattacks, forcing the defenders into withdrawal. German resistance gradually broke down during the retreat. The offensive halted at the Oder to clear the flanks before the advance on Berlin was resumed.

MANILA 3 FEBRUARY–3 MARCH 1945

Forces Japanese: 14,000; American and Filipino: 38,000. **Casualties** Japanese: 12,000; American and Filipino: 6,575 plus 100,000 civilians. **Location:** Philippines. **Theatre** Pacific.

While part of the Japanese army retreated into the hills, a force fortified Manila and defended it to the death. Thousands of Filipino civilians were killed in the fighting or massacred by the Japanese.

RHINELAND
8 FEBRUARY–28 MARCH 1945

Forces Allied: 1.25 million; German: 150,000. **Casualties** German: 60,000, plus 250,000 prisoners; Allied: 22,000. **Location** Rhine river, Germany. **Theatre** Western Front.

The last great obstacle for the Allies was the Rhine. The bridge at Remargen was captured intact, while other forces crossed elsewhere. Once bridgeheads were established, the German position on the river was untenable.

DRESDEN 13–14 FEBRUARY 1945

Forces Allied: British 796 Lancaster bombers and 9 Mosquitos; American: 311 B-17s. **Casualties** German: 30,000–60,000 (civilians); Allied: 9 Lancaster bombers. **Location** Eastern Germany. **Theatre** Western Front.

As German air defences began to weaken, the Allies launched a massive attack on the historic and previously untargeted city of Dresden. By the time the USAAF attacked on the 14th, a firestorm caused by the night bombing had reduced much of the city to ruins.

IWO JIMA 19 FEBRUARY–24 MARCH 1945

Forces American: 70,000; Japanese: 22,000. **Casualties** American: 26,000; Japanese: 21,700. **Location** Pacific Ocean south of Japan. **Theatre** Pacific.

Correctly expecting the US to use Iwo Jima as a base for the invasion of the Home Islands, the Japanese heavily fortified the island. Rather than contesting the beaches, the Japanese created inland defensive positions that were defended to the death.

LAKE BALATON OFFENSIVE
6–16 MARCH 1945

Forces Soviet: 140,000; Axis: 465,000. **Casualties** Soviet: 33,000; Axis: unknown. **Location** Hungary. **Theatre** Eastern Front.

The Lake Balaton offensive came as a surprise to the Soviets, and the Axis made good gains at first. A counterattack by the Soviets, launched as the offensive wound down, retook all of the ground that had been lost.

TOKYO 9–10 MARCH 1945

Forces American: 334 bombers; Japanese: air defences of the home islands. **Casualties** American: unknown; Japanese: 80,000 (mostly civilians). **Location** Tokyo, Honshu, Japan. **Theatre** Pacific.

Ideal weather conditions were present on the night of 9–10 March 1945 when 334 US Boeing B-29 Superfortress heavy bombers devastated the Japanese capital city of Tokyo with incendiaries and high explosives.

OKINAWA 1 APRIL–2 JULY 1945

Forces Japanese: 130,000; American: 250,000, Allied fleet: 1,300 ships. **Casualties** American: 50,000; Japanese: 100,000. **Location** Pacific Ocean south of Japanese Home Islands. **Theatre** Pacific.

Unable to hold the entire island, Japanese forces contested the southern end, while at sea the invasion fleet was subject to *kamikaze* suicide attacks. A series of fortified positions were held almost to the

last man, with occasional counterattacks. During April the Allies mounted the largest bombardment in the Pacific War before renewing the offensive.

OPERATION TEN-GO 7 APRIL 1945

Forces Japanese: 1 battleship, 1 light cruiser, 8 destroyers; American: 386 aircraft. **Casualties** Japanese: 1 battleship, 1 cruiser and 4 destroyers; American: 10 aircraft. **Location** Between Japan and Ryukyu islands. **Theatre** Pacific.

The Japanese force was directed to attack Allied ships engaged in the invasion of Okinawa but was shattered by air attack before even getting near the target. Among the ships sunk was the battleship *Yamato*, one of the most powerful warships ever built.

BERLIN 16 APRIL–2 MAY 1945

Forces Soviet: 2 million; German: 750,000. **Casualties** Soviet: 305,000 killed or wounded; German: unknown. **Location** Berlin, Germany. **Theatre** Eastern Front.

Two Soviet fronts competed for the honour of reaching Berlin first, even fighting each other. The city was fiercely defended until Hitler committed suicide.

PRAGUE 5 MAY 1945

Forces German: 900,000; Soviet: 2,000,000. **Casualties** German: Entire force became casualties or prisoners; Soviet: 52,498. **Location** Prague, modern Czech Republic. **Theatre** Eastern Front.

The last major resistance to the Allies took place in Prague, after the surrender of Germany. German troops holding the city were able to put down a rising by Czech partisans but were soon overwhelmed by massive Soviet forces.

SINKING OF THE HAGURO 20 JUNE 1945

Forces Japanese: 1 heavy cruiser, 1 destroyer; Allied: 5 destroyers. **Casualties** Japanese: 1 heavy cruiser lost, 1 destroyer damaged; Allied: 5 casualties. **Location** Strait of Malacca between Malaysia and Indonesia. **Theatre** Pacific.

A flotilla of British destroyers attacked the Japanese heavy cruiser *Haguro*. A series of torpedo attacks sank the cruiser, while her escorting destroyer escaped with light damage. This was the last traditional surface action fought with gun and torpedo.

HIROSHIMA 6 AUGUST 1945

Forces American: 3 bombers; Japanese: air defences of the home islands. **Casualties** American: none. Japanese: 80,000 to 140,000 (mostly civilians). **Location** Hiroshima, Honshu, Japan. **Theatre** Pacific.

At 8:15am on 6 August 1945, the US Boeing B-29 Superfortress bomber *Enola Gay* dropped the uranium atomic bomb, nicknamed "Little Boy", on Hiroshima, Japan. Detonating 580m (1,900ft) above the city, the bomb yielded an explosion equal to 15,000 tons of TNT (15 kilotons), levelling or damaging up to 90 per cent of Hiroshima buildings. An estimated 80,000 people were killed immediately. The total number of deaths from radiation exposure continued to mount years afterwards.

NAGASAKI 9 AUGUST 1945

Forces American: 3 bombers; Japanese: air defences of the home islands. **Casualties American:** none; **Japanese:** 35,000 to 70,000 (mostly civilians). **Location** Nagasaki, Kyushu, Japan. **Theatre** Pacific.

The US Boeing B-29 Superfortress *Bockscar* dropped the plutonium atomic bomb, nicknamed "Fat Man", above the Japanese city of Nagasaki on 9 August 1945. Detonating at an altitude of 503m (1,650ft), the bomb's yield was estimated at 21 kilotons, significantly greater than the uranium bomb dropped three days earlier on Hiroshima. The explosion destroyed 52,000 homes. It is impossible to establish exactly how many died, either instantly or from long-term radiation effects.

Conflicts after World War II 1945–Present

ARTILLERY SHELLS

While the dawn of the nuclear age has changed the face of strategic defence since the end of World War II, warfare itself has remained an instrument of ideological, territorial, and nationalistic ambition. The superpowers have asserted their influence through fighting proxy wars in Greece, Korea, Vietnam, and elsewhere. Independence movements have erupted into civil war, the states of the Middle East have renewed centuries-old disputes, and terrorism has triggered intervention in Iraq and Afghanistan.

CHINESE CIVIL WAR
AUGUST 1945–APRIL 1950

Nationalist and Communist factions were focused on fighting the Japanese during World War II, but the defeat of this common enemy signalled the renewal of their rivalry for control of China.

OPENING CAMPAIGN
AUGUST 1945–10 JANUARY 1946

Forces Communist: 100,000; Nationalist: 110,000. **Casualties** Communist: c.45,000; Nationalist: unknown. **Location** Eastern China and Manchuria.

Japan's defeat at the end of World War II left a power vacuum across

large parts of China. Nationalist forces moved in to capture the coastal cities, while the Communists, led by Mao Zedong, managed to occupy Manchuria. As relations between the two opposing factions broke down, the Nationalist forces began to drive the Communists northwards.

TIANMEN 17 AUGUST 1945

Forces Communist: 2,000; Nationalist and Japanese: 400. **Casualties** Communist: dozens; Nationalist and Japanese: 350. **Location** Hubei Province, Central China.

During one of a series of engagements in central China, Communist forces destroyed a contingent of Japanese soldiers and Nationalist troops previously subservient to the rule of the Japanese occupiers.

XIANGSHUIKOU
18 SEPTEMBER 1945

Forces Communist: 4,000; Nationalist: 1,000. **Casualties** Communist: unknown; Nationalist: c.1,000. **Location** Jiangsu Province, Eastern China.

Without popular support, weak Nationalist troops, ordered by leader Jiang Jieshi to stand their ground until reinforced, were virtually annihilated by well-organized Communist forces.

SIPING 15–17 MARCH 1946

Forces Communist: 6,000; Nationalist: 3,000. **Casualties** Communist: 240; Nationalist: c.3,000. **Location** Jilin Province, Northeast China.

A Nationalist offensive to capture Siping City was thwarted by Communist resistance, helped by melting snows which

Victory parade in June 1949
Having defeated the Nationalists in the Chinese Civil War, troops of Mao Zedong's Communist Peoples Liberation Army parade through Shanghai.

Commemorative badges
Enamelled badges, featuring Chairman Mao Zedong, were issued throughout Mao's rule of China (1943–76).

...turned the roads into quagmires. The Nationalist force was virtually wiped out.

MANCHURIA
4 APRIL 1946–NOVEMBER 1948
Forces Communist: c.1,000,000; Nationalist: c.1,000,000. **Casualties** Unknown. **Location** Northeast China.

Nationalist Forces won several large battles in Manchuria, but were defeated in a series of small engagements. The Communists captured large amounts of heavy equipment in this way, notably artillery, before launching a decisive campaign.

RUGAO-HUANGQIAO
25–31 AUGUST 1946
Forces Communist: 16,000; Nationalist: 20,000. **Casualties** Communist: no reliable estimates; Nationalist: 17,000. **Location** Jiangsu Province, Eastern China.

One of seven major battles in the Central Jiangsu Campaign, when Communist forces decisively defeated a larger Nationalist army by dividing their enemy into pockets, then surrounding and eliminating each pocket in turn.

GUANZHONG
31 DECEMBER 1946–30 JANUARY 1947
Forces Communist: 3,800; Nationalist: 8,000. **Casualties** Communist: no reliable estimates; Nationalist: 1,500. **Location** Northeast China.

Communist forces temporarily blocked a Nationalist offensive aiming to occupy the Communist base at Guanzhong. However, renewed effort by the Nationalist troops eventually forced the heavily outnumbered defenders to retreat.

NIANGZIGUAN
24–25 APRIL 1947
Forces Communist: 2,000; Nationalist: 1,000. **Casualties** Communist: unknown; Nationalist: 1,000. **Location** Shanxi Province, Northeast China.

During the Zhengtai Campaign by the Communists, Nationalist forces defending a mountain pass and outnumbered two to one, left their fortified positions and attempted a disastrous counterattack in response to a Communist flanking manoeuvre. The Nationalist defenders were annihilated.

TANG'ERLI
27–28 APRIL 1947
Forces Communist: 2,200; Nationalist: 1,000. **Casualties** Communist: 100; Nationalist: 270. **Location** Hebei Province, Northeast China.

In a series of engagements near the city of Tianjin, Communist forces converged to assault a Nationalist garrison from all sides. The Nationalists held out for several hours before surrendering when reinforcements failed to appear.

PHOENIX PEAK
7–9 DECEMBER 1947
Forces Communist: 300; Nationalist: 1,200. **Casualties** Unknown. **Location** Laiyang, Shandong Province, Eastern China.

Defending their position against Nationalist attacks the outnumbered Communists managed to inflict heavy casualties on the Nationalists, eventually forcing their withdrawal.

SHANGCAI
17–19 JUNE 1948
Forces Communist: 12,000; Nationalist: 20,000. **Casualties** Communist: unknown; Nationalist: 5,000. **Location** Henan Province, Central China.

Communist forces turned back a larger Nationalist army sent to relieve the city of Kaifeng, ensuring the success of the Eastern Henan Campaign.

XUZHOU
SEPTEMBER 1948–10 JANUARY 1949
Forces Communist: 500,000; Nationalist: 500,000. **Casualties** Communist: unknown; Nationalist: 250,000. **Location** Shandong Province, Eastern China.

Xuzhou was the decisive point in the Chinese Civil War. The Nationalist position was compromised when four divisions defected to the Communists. The exposed Nationalist wings were then encircled and bombarded into submission by artillery.

JINZHOU
7–15 OCTOBER 1948
Forces Communist: 250,000; Nationalist: 150,000. **Casualties** Communist: 25,000; Nationalist: 20,000 killed and 80,000 captured. **Location** Liaoning Province, Northeast China.

During this decisive battle of the war Communist forces employed heavy artillery bombardment in a successful attack that drove the Nationalists from the city of Jinzhou and a strategically important road junction.

JIULIANSHAN
15 NOVEMBER 1948–11 JANUARY 1949
Forces Communist: 1,000; Nationalist: 2,500. **Casualties** Communist: unknown; Nationalist: 600. **Location** Guangdong Province, Southeast China.

In an attempt to destroy a Communist base, Nationalist troops failed to take advantage of their superior numbers and arms, employing their troops piecemeal and so dooming their counter-offensive to defeat.

"Their **guerrilla activities** have been especially successful in **disrupting railroads**."
AMERICAN OBSERVER ON DAMAGE DONE IN TSINAN, CHINESE CIVIL WAR, 1947

SEIZURE OF TIANJIN AND BEIJING
15 AND 22 JANUARY 1949
Forces Communist: c.500,000; Nationalist: unknown. **Casualties** No reliable estimates. **Location** Northeast China.

After Xuzhou, the Nationalist forces began to collapse while the Communists continued to gain in strength. Once Tianjin was taken, Beijing fell almost unopposed and the advance on Shanghai could begin.

KININGTOU
25–27 OCTOBER 1949
Forces Communist: 9,500; Nationalist: 40,000. **Casualties** Communist: 3,900 killed and 5,000 captured; Nationalist: 1,267 killed and 1,982 wounded. **Location** Quemoy Island, Taiwan.

Landings by Communist troops on a small island in the Taiwan Strait were defeated by Nationalist forces, putting a stop to the Communist invasion of Taiwan itself.

DENGBU ISLAND
3–5 NOVEMBER 1949
Forces Communist: 20,000; Nationalist: no reliable estimates. **Casualties** Communist: 3,700 killed and 700 captured; Nationalist: 2,200. **Location** Eastern China.

A Communist attempt to take control of a small island off the east coast of China resulted in failure and helped to secure the survival of the Nationalist government and its control of Taiwan.

JIANMENGUAN **14–18 DECEMBER 1949**
Forces Communist: 800; Nationalist: 1,000. **Casualties** Communist: no reliable estimates; Nationalist: 500 killed, 300 captured. **Location** Sichuan Province, Central China.

Outflanked in a narrow mountain pass, Nationalist troops were forced to withdraw from defensive positions and abandon the city of Jiange, opening up Sichuan Province to Communist attack.

YANGTZE INCIDENT **20 APRIL 1949**
Forces British: unknown; Chinese: unknown. **Casualties** British: 117 killed or wounded. **Location** 224km (139 miles) up the Yangtze river, Eastern China.

Fired on by Communist guns on the Yangtze river en route to guard the British embassy in Nanjing, HMS *Amethyst* remained trapped for 14 weeks. A sudden breakout, involving a 224-km (139-mile) dash at high speed down the river, brought the ship to safety.

CONQUEST OF THE SOUTH
APRIL 1949–APRIL 1950
Forces Communist: unknown; Nationalists: unknown. **Casualties** No reliable estimates. **Location** South China.

Nanjing, the Nationalist capital, fell without a fight on 24 April 1949 and, in May that year, Shanghai also fell. Realizing that all was lost, the Nationalists relocated to the island of Taiwan.

FAMOUS SPIES

Name (Dates)	Nationality	Details
Mata Hari born Margaretha Zelle (1876–1917)	Dutch	In October 1917 the French government executed Mata Hari by firing squad for spying for Imperial Germany; she was also alleged to have been a double agent working for the British and their Allies.
Kawashima Yoshiko (1907–48)	Chinese	A Manchu princess, Kawashima spied for the Japanese during the Manchukuo period of the Japanese occupation of China in World War II. After the war, Chinese nationalists tried, convicted, and executed her for treason.
Anthony Blunt (1907–83)	British	During World War II and after, Blunt shared British intelligence information (including Ultra – decrypted German messages) with the Soviet Union. Blunt also famously completed a secret mission on behalf of the Royal Family to retrieve personal letters sent to the Third Reich. Under Prime Minister Margaret Thatcher Blunt's spying was exposed and the Queen subsequently revoked his knighthood.
Vasili Mitrokhin (1922–2004)	Soviet	Mitrokhin, an archivist for the KGB, defected to the West in 1992. During his career he amassed an exhaustive collection of copied Soviet documents, for which he is best known today. The so-called "Mitrokhin Archives" include detailed information on the global activities of the KGB and other Soviet agencies during the height of the Cold War.
Aldrich Ames (1941–)	American	In 1994, the US government convicted Ames (a former Central Intelligence Agency analyst) of spying for the Soviet Union. Ames sold the Kremlin the names of American agents and Russian contacts working inside the Soviet Union.

INDONESIAN REVOLUTION
AUGUST 1945– DECEMBER 1949

Following Japan's defeat in World War II, a movement for independence from the Netherlands gained strength in Indonesia. Dutch colonial authorities finally handed over power in 1949.

SEMARANG
14–19 OCTOBER 1945

Forces Indonesian: unknown; Japanese: unknown. **Casualties** Unknown. **Location** North Java, Indonesia.

Weeks after the Japanese surrendered to Allied forces, occupation troops were ordered to fight an insurgency of Indonesian nationalists, suppressing an uprising of militant Indonesian students.

SURABAYA
27 OCTOBER–20 NOVEMBER 1945

Forces Indonesian: c.20,000; British and Dutch: 30,000. **Casualties** Indonesian: 16,000; British and Dutch: 2,000. **Location** East Java, Indonesia.

This fierce battle resulted in British troops occupying Indonesia's second-largest city. However, the resolve of the Indonesian fighters helped to increase support for the independence movement.

AMBARAWA 12–15 DECEMBER 1945

Forces Indonesian: no reliable estimates; British: unknown. **Casualties** Indonesian: no reliable estimates; British and Dutch: unknown. **Location** Central Java, Indonesia.

British troops evacuating foreign nationals were driven back to Semarang by Indonesian forces commanded by General Sudirman, a leading figure in the Indonesian independence movement.

MARGA 15 NOVEMBER 1946

Forces Indonesian: no reliable estimates; Dutch: unknown. **Casualties** Indonesian: 96 killed; Dutch: unknown. **Location** Bali, Indonesia.

Indonesian national hero I Gusti Ngurah Rai and his small band of guerrilla fighters were wiped out by a much larger Dutch force trying to pacify the island of Bali.

> " It is requested that the **Chinese Army** be ... **mobilized** for us immediately. "
>
> NORTH KOREAN LEADER KIM IL SUNG ON THE UN FORCES' INVASION OF THE NORTH, 1950

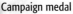

Campaign medal
This United Nations medal was awarded to soldiers fighting the Communists during the Korean War (1950–53).

GREEK CIVIL WAR
MARCH 1946– OCTOBER 1949

Even prior to the defeat of the Nazis, Nationalist and Communist factions were battling for control of Greece. Intervention by the Western Allies helped defeat the Communists.

KONITSA 24 DECEMBER 1947–4 JANUARY 1948

Forces Nationalist: 900; Communist: 2,000. **Casualties** Nationalist: unknown; Communist: 1,200. **Location** Northern Greece.

Greek Communists attempted to seize the city of Konista for use as the capital, but were repulsed by a smaller Nationalist force supported by heavy artillery fire and the city's civilian population.

GRAMMOS 16 JUNE – 21 AUGUST 1948

Forces Nationalist: 100,000; Communist: 12,000. **Casualties** Nationalist: 6,740; Communist: 1,200. **Location** Western Macedonia

During one of the largest battles of the war, Communist troops avoided encirclement by the Nationalists. The following year, with support from US advisors, the Nationalists won a decisive victory, and the Greek Civil War effectively ended.

ISRAELI INDEPENDENCE
MAY 1948–JULY 1949

As soon as Israel declared independence, Arab armies invaded from several directions. But the outnumbered Israeli forces benefited from short supply lines and good training, and were able to reverse the Arab advances.

BATTLES OF LATRUN
24 MAY–18 JULY 1948

Forces Jordanian: 3,500; Israeli: 2,400. **Casualties** Jordanian: fewer than 50; Israeli: 139. **Location** Near Jerusalem, Israel.

Several Israeli attempts to dislodge Jordanian troops blocking a vital road into Jerusalem were unsuccessful. Latrun remained in Jordanian hands until the Six-Day War (5–10 June 1967).

OPERATION HIRAM
29–31 OCTOBER 1948

Forces Arab: 500; Israeli: four brigades. **Casualties** Unknown. **Location** Upper Galilee, Israel.

During a 60-hour offensive, Israeli forces removed Arab troops from Upper Galilee

and the frontier areas of Transjordan. The United Nations had planned for the area to be part of the Arab state of Palestine.

HUK REBELLION
4 JULY 1946–30 SEPTEMBER 1954

Forces Philippine government: 75,000; Huk rebels: 50,000. **Casualties** Philippine government: 3,000; Huk rebels: 5,000. **Location** Primarily Luzon, Philippines.

Following World War II, a Communist insurgency took up arms against the newly independent government of the Philippines. With US assistance, the government forces prevailed.

KOREAN WAR
25 JUNE 1950–27 JULY 1953

After the breakdown of negotiations, North Korean forces invaded South Korea in an attempt to reunify the divided peninsula by force. Hostilities ended with an armistice; however, a formal peace agreement has never been concluded.

UIJEONGBU 25–26 JUNE 1950

Forces North Korean: unknown; South Korean: unknown. **Casualties** North Korean: no reliable estimates; South Korean: no reliable estimates. **Location** North of Seoul, South Korea.

The opening phase of the war saw North Korean troops easily defeat a weaker formation of South Koreans, making way for the Communist advance on Seoul.

OSAN 5 JULY 1950

Forces North Korean: 1,100; American: 540. **Casualties** North Korean: 42 killed and 85 wounded; US: 120 killed and 85 wounded. **Location** Northwest South Korea.

In the first engagement between the Americans and North Koreans, a US task force, commanded by Colonel Charles B. Smith, delayed the Communist invasion of South Korea by about 12 hours.

DAEJEON 13 –20 JULY 1950

Forces North Korean: no reliable estimates; UN: no reliable estimates. **Casualties** Unknown. **Location** South Korea.

In a delaying action, UN forces, mainly from the US 24th Infantry Division,

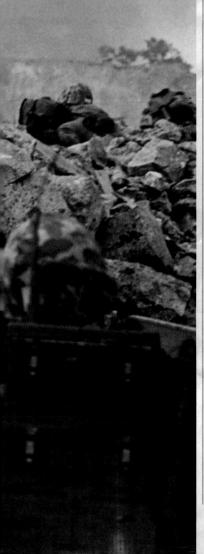

Amphibious assault
US Marines mount scaling ladders as they come ashore at Inchon, Korea in September 1950, during an amphibious assault. This was the last major combat landing undertaken by US forces in the 20th century.

allowed other units to withdraw south and regroup in order to confront the Communists across the 38th Parallel.

THE PUSAN PERIMETER 1 AUGUST–15 SEPTEMBER 1950

Forces North Korean: 98,000; UN and South Korean: 180,000. **Casualties** North Korean: unknown; UN: 3,600 killed. **Location** Southeast Korea.

As North Korean forces invaded South Korea, a UN-backed response prevented the fall of the whole country. At first forced into a pocket around Pusan, UN forces gradually pushed outward.

INCHON 15–27 SEPTEMBER 1950

Forces North Korean: 20,000; UN and South Korean: 40,000. **Casualties** North Korean: 14,000; UN/South Korean: 671 killed, 2,758 wounded. **Location** Northwest South Korea.

An amphibious landing at Inchon involved numerous logistical difficulties. Nonetheless, the surprise assault was successful, with few casualties among the UN/South Korean forces. The taking of Seoul soon afterward was far more costly.

THE INVASION OF THE NORTH 9 OCTOBER–24 DECEMBER 1950

Forces Chinese and North Korean: 300,000–400,000; UN: 250,000. **Casualties** Chinese: 40,000; UN: unknown (US: 718). **Location** North Korea.

UN forces pushed northwards into North Korea, taking the capital, Pyongyang. Chinese forces entering the war forced a UN retreat. Some units had to fight their way southwards toward friendly territory.

PAKCHON 5 NOVEMBER 1950

Forces North Korean and Chinese: unknown; UN: 4,000. **Casualties** North Korean and Chinese: 400 killed, 200 wounded; UN: 12 killed, 70 wounded. **Location** North Korea.

Battles for high ground near Hill 282 resulted in the failure of Communist efforts to occupy a series of nearby ridgelines. UN forces consisted largely of British and Australian troops.

CHOSIN RESERVOIR 26 NOVEMBER–13 DECEMBER 1950

Forces UN: 30,000; Chinese: 150,000. **Casualties** Chinese: 35,000 killed and wounded; UN 7,500 killed and wounded. **Location** East-central North Korea.

Encircled by Chinese troops and facing harsh winter conditions, UN forces, made up primarily of US and British battalions, inflicted heavy casualties on the enemy, and conducted a successful withdrawal south to the port of Hungnam.

RIDGWAY'S MEATGRINDER 25 JANUARY–21 APRIL 1951

Forces Chinese: 542,000; North Korean: 197,000; UN: 270,000. **Casualties** No reliable estimates. **Location** To the north and south of Seoul, Korea.

Under the command of General Matthew Ridgway, UN forces began to advance behind a "meatgrinder" bombardment by aircraft and artillery. Chinese forces responded with "human wave" attacks.

MASS-PRODUCED WEAPONS

Samuel Colt and his mid-19th century contemporaries opened the floodgates on mass-produced small arms at the zenith of the Industrial Revolution. Today, the world's arms markets are awash with more than 200 million light weapons (including assault rifles) and more than 100 million tons of ammunition. These and other mass-produced weapons, including rocket launchers, tanks, and artillery, have changed the character of modern battlefields and other scenes of violence around the globe.

Weapon	Manufacturer, location	Year production began	Number produced
AK47 7.62mm assault rifle , (and derivatives)	Mikhail Kalashnikov, at Izhmash, Soviet Union, and 19 or more nations	1947	90,000,000
RPG-7 40mm anti-tank rocket-propelled grenade launcher (and variants)	Bazalt, at various locations in Soviet Union/ Russia and nine or more nations	1961	9,000,000
M-16 5.56mm (.223 cal.) assault rifle (and derivatives)	Colt, at various locations in United States and other nations	1960	8,000,000
T-54/55 main battle tank (and variants)	Malyshev and Uralvagonzavod, in Soviet Union	1947	100,000
M2A1 (M101) 105mm howitzer	Rock Island Arsenal, in United States	1941	10,000

Under Siege
US Marines fire their M101 howitzer during the siege of Khe Sanh, Vietnam, February 1968.

HOENGSONG 11–13 FEBRUARY 1951

Forces North Korean and Chinese: 120,000; UN: 80,000. **Casualties** North Korean and Chinese: unknown; UN: 11,862. **Location** Northeast South Korea.

A major Communist counterattack resulted in large numbers of UN troops being cut off, forcing an order to withdraw.

CHIPYONG-NI 13–15 FEBRUARY 1951

Forces North Korean and Chinese: no reliable estimates; UN: 5,000. **Casualties** North Korean and Chinese: 2,000 killed, 3,000 wounded; UN: 51 killed, 250 wounded. **Location** Southeast of Seoul, South Korea.

The US 23rd Regimental Combat Team and attached units held onto control of territory near the South Korean capital.

TOMAHAWK 23 MARCH 1951

Forces North Korean and Chinese: unknown; UN: 5,000. **Casualties** North Korean and Chinese: unknown; UN: unknown. **Location** North of Seoul, South Korea.

The airborne phase of Operation Courageous, designed to trap Communist

troops north of Seoul, succeeded in this geographic objective, although enemy troops had already evacuated the area.

IMJIN RIVER 22–25 APRIL 1951

Forces UN: 4,000; Chinese: 70,000. **Casualties** Chinese: 9,000 killed and wounded; UN: 1,078 killed, 2,674 wounded. **Location** Near Seoul, South Korea.

For three days the British 29th Brigade held off a Chinese offensive to recapture Seoul. The Gloucestershire Regiment was surrounded and devastated, but managed to inflict heavy casualties on the Chinese.

KAPYONG 22–25 APRIL 1951

Forces Chinese: no reliable estimates; UN: no reliable estimates. **Casualties** Chinese: 1,000; UN: 43 killed and 87 wounded. **Location** Central South Korea.

Outnumbered UN forces managed to withstand numerous Chinese attacks, helping to halt the Communist spring offensive of 1951.

The US Navy in Korea
Two Grumman F9F-2 Panthers fly past their carrier, the USS *Princeton*, in early 1951. These early jet fighters are dumping excess fuel prior to landing on the carrier after a sortie over Korea.

BLOODY RIDGE
18 AUGUST–5 SEPTEMBER 1951

Forces UN: 25,000; North Korean 30,000. **Casualties** UN: 2,700 killed and wounded; North Korean: 8,000 killed, 7,000 wounded. **Location** South Korea near 38th Parallel.

As both sides sought to exert their influence on the newly initiated peace talks, UN forces decided to launch an attempt to break the stalemate along their line near the 38th Parallel. Superior UN firepower forced the North Koreans to withdraw to nearby Heartbreak Ridge.

HEARTBREAK RIDGE
13 SEPTEMBER–15 OCTOBER 1951

Forces UN: 15,000; North Korean and Chinese: unknown. **Casualties** UN: 3,700; North Korean and Chinese: 25,000. **Location** Northeast South Korea.

The UN forces, which included elements of the US 2nd Division as well as attached French troops, had made repeated attempts to take Heartbreak Ridge, but had failed. A UN victory was only ensured after their troops introduced tanks, which helped to isolate the high ground and made it possible to fire directly onto the enemy positions.

MARYANG SAN
5–8 OCTOBER 1951

Forces Chinese: unknown; UN: 5,000. **Casualties** Chinese: no reliable estimates; UN: 20 killed and 89 wounded. **Location** Near Seoul, South Korea.

This offensive action by Australian forces of the UN led to the capture of Hill 317. However, the area was eventually abandoned to the Communists after the Australian troops were ordered to withdraw.

HILL EERIE
21 MARCH–18 JULY 1952

Forces Chinese: no reliable estimates; UN: no reliable estimates. **Casualties** Chinese: 700 killed and wounded; UN: 250 killed and wounded. **Location** Near Chorwon, South Korea.

After a series of largely inconclusive engagements that involved high ground changing hands numerous times, the UN forces finally managed to retain their control of the area.

SUI-HO DAM
23–24 JUNE 1952

Forces North Korean and Chinese: no reliable estimates; UN: 700 tactical aircraft. **Casualties** Unknown. **Location** North Korea.

Two days of air strikes by UN warplanes against hydroelectric facilities in North Korea resulted in the destruction of around 90 per cent of the Sui-ho dam's capability to generate electricity.

OLD BALDY
26 JUNE–4 AUGUST 1952

Forces UN: 38,000; Chinese: 20,000. **Casualties** UN: 357 killed and wounded; Chinese: 1,100 killed and wounded. **Location** Western South Korea.

Five engagements at Hill 266, nicknamed "Old Baldy" by US forces, began when UN forces captured the crest during heavy fighting and were driven off by a strong Chinese counterattack. Another major UN effort a month later was eventually successful.

WHITE HORSE
6–15 OCTOBER 1952

Forces Chinese: 41,000; UN: 20,000. **Casualties** Chinese: 13,340 killed, 1,000 wounded; UN: 600 killed, 2,500 wounded. **Location** Chorwon, North Korea.

A hill along a UN supply route was repeatedly attacked by Chinese forces. The disputed high ground changed hands 24 times before Communist troops were forced to withdraw from the area.

TRIANGLE HILL
14 OCTOBER –25 NOVEMBER 1952

Forces Chinese: 43,000; UN: 22,000. **Casualties** Chinese: 7,100 killed, 8,500 wounded. UN: 1,500 killed, 4,800 wounded. **Location** Kinwha Province, North Korea.

A series of attempts by US and South Korean troops to dislodge Chinese forces from positions at Triangle Hill and nearby Sniper Ridge were eventually abandoned due to mounting casualties.

PORK CHOP HILL
23 MARCH–11 JULY 1953

Forces UN: 20,000; Chinese: 20,000. **Casualties** UN: 258 killed, 1,036 wounded; Chinese: 1,500 killed, 4,000 wounded. **Location** Border of South and North Korea.

During two controversial engagements, UN troops maintained control of Pork Chop Hill, temporarily losing it in March. In the following weeks renewed Chinese attacks were repelled by reinforcements; however, UN command subsequently abandoned the position.

THE HOOK
28–29 MAY 1953

Forces UN: 1,500; Chinese: 6,500. **Casualties** UN: 24 killed, 150 wounded; Chinese: 1,100. **Location** Kinwha Province, North Korea.

In four separate battles, UN forces repulsed Chinese attempts to capture high ground. Any territory gained would have given the Chinese bargaining power during the impending peace negotiations.

OUTPOST HARRY
10–18 JUNE 1953

Forces Chinese: 15,000; UN: 700. **Casualties** Chinese: 4,500 killed; UN: 114 killed, 419 wounded. **Location** South Korea.

UN forces, primarily Greek and American troops, succeeded in defending an outpost in the so-called Iron Triangle north of Seoul, against repeated assaults by Communist infantry.

> "Weapons, **helmets, wireless sets** all go flying in the **mad scramble** ..."
> **LT P. J. KAVANAGH ON THE FIGHTING IN KOREA,** APRIL 1951

Foreign Legion badges
These French Foreign Legion badge caps include the gold Legionnaires' insignia (*right*) and the silver badge of a qualified paratrooper. Foreign Legion paratroopers formed much of the relief force defending Dien Bien Phu in 1954, suffering heavy casualties.

FIRST INDOCHINA WAR

DECEMBER 1946–AUGUST 1954

With the end of World War II, France made a succession of attempts to reassert its control in the various parts of its widespread colonial empire. In French Indochina, which included Cambodia, Laos, and parts of modern Vietnam, a rebellion was gradually gathering force, driven on by growing Nationalist and Communist sentiment. This would eventually lead to the complete withdrawal of France from Southeast Asia.

OPERATION LÉA

7 OCTOBER–22 DECEMBER 1947

Forces French: 15,000; Viet Minh: 40,000.
Casualties French: no reliable estimates; Viet Minh: 9,000. **Location** North Vietnam.

In an effort to deplete the combat capabilities of the Viet Minh, a combined French airborne and ground offensive managed to inflict heavy casualties on the enemy. However, large numbers of Communist troops were successful in slipping away.

ROUTE COLONIALE 4

30 SEPTEMBER–18 OCTOBER 1950

Forces French and Vietnamese 10,000; Viet Minh: 40,000.
Casualties French and Vietnamese: 4,800; Viet Minh: no reliable estimates. **Location** North Vietnam.

French and Vietnamese troops, including elite paratroopers and members of the Foreign Legion, were almost completely annihilated after being driven into a steep gorge along one of their vital supply routes close to the northeastern border with China.

VINH YEN

13–17 JANUARY 1951

Forces French: 9,000; Viet Minh: 20,000. **Casualties** French: 56 killed, 545 wounded; Viet Minh: 6,000 killed, 8,000 wounded. **Location** North Vietnam.

This offensive by the Viet Minh had been planned as a direct advance on the capital city of Hanoi. However, the Viet Minh had reached about 48km (30 miles) south of the city when they were decisively defeated and driven back by the vastly outnumbered French troops. After this conflict, however, it became clear to the French that the battle for control of Indochina was likely to be much more prolonged than had initially been expected.

MAO KHE

23–28 MARCH 1951

Forces French: 400; Viet Minh: 10,000. **Casualties** French: 40 killed, 150 wounded; Viet Minh: 134 killed, 426 wounded. **Location** North Vietnam.

Supported by naval gunfire from three destroyers, heavily outnumbered French soldiers managed to successfully hold off a Viet Minh attack on the city of Haiphong and its surrounding area. Haiphong was crucial to the success of the French campaign, being the main port through which large quantities of their vital reinforcements and supplies flowed.

HOA BINH

10 NOVEMBER 1951–25 FEBRUARY 1952

Forces French: 6,000; Viet Minh: no reliable estimates.
Casualties French: 436 killed, 2,060 wounded; Viet Minh: 3,455 killed, 7,000 wounded. **Location** North Vietnam.

The French launched an offensive that was designed to lure the enemy into an open, pitched battle. However, this tactic failed and the French troops were finally forced into taking up a defensive position. The French were decisively defeated, despite the Viet Minh forces suffering considerably heavier casualties.

NA SAN

1 OCTOBER–2 DECEMBER 1952

Forces French: unknown; Viet Minh: no reliable estimates.
Casualties French: unknown; Viet Minh: at least 3,000.
Location North Vietnam.

Here the French successfully employed "hedgehog defence" tactics – entrenched positions capable of all-round defence – and used air support for the first time. The use of similar tactics at the later battle of Dien Bien Phu, proved disastrous.

OPERATION LORRAINE

29 OCTOBER–8 NOVEMBER 1952

Forces French: 15,000; Viet Minh: unknown.
Casualties French: 1,200 killed and wounded; Viet Minh: unknown. **Location** Nghia Lo, North Vietnam.

This was one of the numerous French operations that were designed to draw the Viet Minh guerrillas out into the open, where they would become more vulnerable to the vastly superior air power of the French forces. The operation was abandoned after it failed to provide any significant results.

OPERATION CAMARGUE

28 JULY–10 AUGUST 1953

Forces French and Vietnamese: 10,000; Viet Minh: unknown. **Casualties** French and Viethamese: 17 killed, 100 wounded; Viet Minh: 200 killed, 1,200 wounded. **Location** Central Vietnam.

This French offensive had been designed with the hope of engaging substantial numbers of Viet Minh soldiers and thereby limiting the enemy troops that would therefore be available to engage in the regular Viet Minh attacks on the French supply line via Route 1. The operation was eventually seen as a failure and the French troops were ordered to withdraw.

OPERATION CASTOR

20–22 NOVEMBER 1953

Forces French: 4,200; Viet Minh: no reliable estimates.
Casualties French: 16 killed, 47 wounded; Viet Minh: 115 killed, 4 wounded. **Location** North Vietnam.

Having been air-dropped into a remote area in the extreme northwest corner of Vietnam, French troops succeeded in their mission to establish an airbase at Dien Bien Phu. However, just four months later, the Viet Minh forces successfully launched a devastating attack on the French forward base, destroying it completely.

BIGGEST NUCLEAR TESTS

Since 1945, the world has received eight declarations of nuclear capability: the United States, Russia (the former Soviet Union), the United Kingdom, France, China, India, Pakistan, and North Korea. Each has publicized its achievement by exploding weapons during tests. These tests conducted under water, underground, above and in the atmosphere, generate considerable tensions around the world.

Thermonuclear explosion
The characteristic fiery mushroom cloud of a thermonuclear bomb rises above the Marshall Islands in the Pacific Ocean during a test in March 1954.

Location (Date)	Test description
Sukhoy Nos, Novaya Zemlya Test Site, Soviet Union (30 October 1961)	Above a large island test site north of the Arctic Circle, the Soviet Union detonated a thermonuclear device called RDS-220, nicknamed "Tsar Bomba" (King of Bombs). The 27-ton bomb was flown to an altitude of 10,500m (34,449ft) aboard a modified Tupolev Tu-95 "Bar" bomber. Slowed by a drogue parachute (one that deploys from a fast-moving object), the weapon fell to an altitude of 4,200m (13,780ft) before exploding. Tsar Bomba was the largest nuclear weapon ever exploded by any nation, with an estimated yield of more than 50 megatons (mt). The explosion resulted in a fireball 8,000m (26,400ft) in diameter, and a seismic wave that registered more than magnitude five on the Richter scale.
Bikini Atoll, Pacific Proving Ground, US-administered Trust Territory of the Pacific Islands (28 February 1954)	In an atmospheric test dubbed "Castle Bravo", the United States exploded a hydrogen bomb above the Marshall Islands. Differing from the frozen fuel of other early fusion bomb designs, Bravo used a so-called "dry" lithium-hydrogen fuel, which helped the designers create a smaller, lighter weapon that could more easily be transported and delivered. The Castle Bravo device was the most powerful the United States ever tested, resulting in a 15-mt explosion and effects more than 1,200 times the intensity of those of the fission bombs dropped on Japan at the end of World War II. The blast left a crater 2km (1.2 miles) in diameter.
Lop Nor test site, Xinjiang province, Peoples Republic of China (PRC) (17 November 1976)	A Xian H-6 bomber of the Chinese People's Liberation Army Air Force dropped a 4-mt thermonuclear bomb over the Lop Nor test site in western China. The bomb was China's largest atmospheric test, as well as its largest nuclear test overall.
Christmas Island, British Western Pacific Territories (28 April 1958)	In a test codenamed "Grapple Y", a British Royal Air Force Vickers Valiant bomber dropped a 3-mt device, which exploded at 2,438m (8,000ft) above Kiritimati (Christmas Island). One observer, RAF Group Captain Kenneth Hubbard, described the resulting fireball as "a huge red and orange cauldron of fantastic energy, which gave the impression of revolving". It was Britain's largest nuclear weapon test.
Tuamotu Archipelago, French Polynesia (24 August 1968)	Between 1960 and 1996, the French conducted at least 210 nuclear weapons tests. The largest of these, codenamed "Canopus", was a 2.6-mt thermonuclear device detonated above the Pacific Ocean. Suspended from a hydrogen balloon, the device exploded 549m (1,800ft) above the ocean.

DIEN BIEN PHU

13 MARCH–7 MAY 1954

Forces French: 16,000; Viet Minh: 80,000. **Casualties** French: 7,888 killed and wounded; Viet Minh: 23,000. **Location** West of Hanoi, North Vietnam.

Hoping to draw out the Viet Minh for a decisive battle, the French seized Dien Bien Phu, a village surrounded by hills that needed to be supplied by air. The village was shelled from positions in the hills, then besieged and eventually overrun by the Viet Minh, crushing French control in Indochina and forcing their imminent withdrawal.

MANG YANG PASS

24 JUNE–17 JULY 1954

Forces French: 2,500; Viet Minh: 700. **Casualties** French: 500 killed; Viet Minh: 100 killed. **Location** North Vietnam.

During this final major engagement of the war, Viet Minh guerrillas ambushed and savaged the severely depleted French troops that were attempting to withdraw, following their defeat at Dien Bien Phu. This resulted in some of the bloodiest fighting of the entire war. Three days later, on 20 July 1954, a ceasefire was announced, and on 1 August, an armistice was implemented.

CHEMICAL AND BIOLOGICAL WARFARE AGENTS

Mustard gas

The use of sulphur mustard compounds as battlefield weapons dates to July 1917, when the German Imperial Army used "Yellow Cross" gas at Ypres against the British and French armies. The chemical has an extreme blistering effect on the skin, and can destroy sensitive mucous membranes in the eyes, mouth, and lungs. The chemical burn wounds caused by exposure to vesicants, as these blistering chemicals are known, are difficult to heal and may result in septic infections or other serious medical complications.

VX

Organophosphates, such as Sarin, the United Kingdom's VX, Russia's VR, and others, are chemicals similar to those found in industrially produced pesticides. Weapons containing such chemicals distribute toxins that are devastating to humans. Nerve agents affect the central nervous system, blocking neurotransmitters in the brain. Among its effects are loss of involuntary muscle control, causing cramping pain, nausea, uncontrollable defecation, and urination, and difficulty with breathing. These chemicals can cause permanent neurological damage or death through asphyxia, as victims lose consciousness and become unable to breathe.

CS gas

CS or tear gas is classed as a non-lethal agent and is used by police forces and military units around the world for riot control and other law enforcement activities. CS has also been used in military settings, as a teaching tool to demonstrate the effectiveness of chemical warfare protective equipment and procedures during basic training of recruits. CS has additionally been used to obscure movements and deny the enemy access to areas, as was the case when the US used it during some search and rescue missions to recover downed pilots during the Vietnam War.

Anthrax

Military organizations have experimented with the weapons potential of some biological agents, such as the anthrax bacillus. The deadliness of anthrax is shown by the deaths of five people and the severe illness of 17 others during a series of terrorist attacks through the United States postal service in September and October 2001. However, as a rule, biological agents have proved to be more difficult to store, handle, move, and deliver than would be militarily useful. Most developed countries (including the United States and Russia) that formerly amassed stockpiles of biological weapons have isolated and destroyed them under a series of international agreements.

US Air Force chemical warfare training
As part of their basic training, new recruits to the US Air Force are subjected to a simulated chemical and biological warfare attack. These recruits were tested in 1953 at Geneva AFB, New York State.

ALGERIAN WAR OF INDEPENDENCE
1954–62

A campaign of terror waged by Algerian nationalist guerrillas to gain independence drew support from other Arab nations. Eventually, after several peaceful attempts to restore public order, there was an especially savage response from the French forces that were deployed in the country. Although the Algerian guerrilla movement was eventually broken, there were heavy casualties on both sides, including civilians. In March 1962, with increasing anti-colonialism and worldwide opinion going against them, the French government finally made the decision to withdraw completely from Algeria, which was then granted independence.

ALGIERS
30 SEPTEMBER 1956–SEPTEMBER 1957

Forces French: 6,100; FLN: c.1,400.
Casualties No reliable estimates.
Location Algiers, Algeria.

Following the implementation of a general strike and the planting of three bombs at Air France offices by members of the Front de Libération Nationale (FLN) or National Liberation Front, the rebels embarked on a campaign of terror in Algiers, which was brutally defeated by the French army.

HUNGARIAN REVOLUTION
23 OCTOBER–10 NOVEMBER 1956

Forces Soviet: 150,000; Hungarian: unknown.
Casualties Soviet: 722 killed, 1,250 wounded; Hungarian: 2,500 killed, 13,000 wounded, 200,000 refugees. **Location** Budapest, Hungary.

Civil unrest sparked a revolt against the pro-Soviet Hungarian government. A new reformist government was installed, which appealed to the United Nations for support. It declared its intention to withdraw from the Warsaw Pact and set up free elections. However, in early November 1956, Soviet troops and tanks marched into Hungary and crushed the rebellion.

SINAI CAMPAIGN
29 OCTOBER–7 NOVEMBER 1956

Forces Israeli: 40,000; Egyptian: 70,000; Anglo-French: 99,000. **Casualties** No reliable estimates. **Location** Sinai Peninsula between Egypt and Israel.

An Egyptian blockade of the Israeli port of Eilat caused Israel to launch an attack into the Sinai Peninsula. Egypt decided to nationalize the Suez Canal, to gain almost total control of sea trade in the region. When talks failed to persuade Egypt to reverse this decision, a combined Anglo-French force attempted to seize control of the canal and gave their support to Israel in Sinai. UN pressure eventually forced a ceasefire, with more than 3,000 UN troops deployed in the area to keep the peace.

CUBAN REVOLUTION
NOVEMBER 1956–JANUARY 1959

Returning from Mexico, where he had been training and organizing his people, Fidel Castro led an effective guerrilla campaign against the rule of Fulgencio Batista in Cuba. Despite a shaky start, popular support for Castro gradually grew, until he was eventually able to assume power.

SANTA CLARA
28 DECEMBER 1958–1 JANUARY 1959

Forces Communists: 1,000; Cuban government: 3,000.
Casualties Unknown. **Location** Cuba.

While his brother Raul marched on Santiago, Fidel Castro led his Communist force to victory over a government army that was three times its size. Under the command of Che Guevara, the revolutionaries' triumph at Santa Clara helped Castro to consolidate his hold on Cuba.

Victory speech

En route to the Cuban capital, Havana, in 1959, the Cuban revolutionary leader, Fidel Castro, addresses the crowd from the *Palacio Municipal* in Santa Clara, after the city had fallen under Communist control. Within 12 hours of the victory, the former Cuban leader General Fulgencio Batista had fled the country.

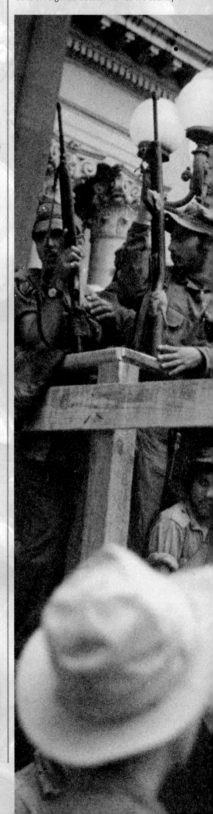

> "In the dim morning light a long **column** of **armoured cars** full of **soldiers in Russian uniforms** was heading for the radio building."
>
> JAN KRCMAR, A CZECH JOURNALIST, ON THE SOVIET ARMY OCCUPATION OF PRAGUE, AUGUST 1968

CONGO CRISIS
30 JUNE 1960–25 NOVEMBER 1965

Forces Congolese and mercenaries: unknown; UN peacekeepers: 19,828. **Casualties** Congolese: unknown; UN peacekeepers: 250. **Location** Mainly in Katanga, Democratic Republic of the Congo.

Independence from Belgium resulted in a series of crises in the Congo. First Katanga province broke away from central government, then other areas of the country began to declare their independence. Mercenaries participated extensively in the prolonged conflict that followed.

BAY OF PIGS
17–19 APRIL 1961

Forces Cuban exiles: 1,300; Castro's troops: unknown. **Casualties** Cuban exiles: 120 killed, 1,180 taken prisoner; Castro's troops: 3,000. **Location** La Playa Giron, Cuba.

An invasion force of Cuban exiles sponsored by the CIA was put ashore at the Bay of Pigs (Bahía de Cochinos) on the south coast of Cuba with the aim of attacking and overthrowing the Communist government, set up and led by Fidel Castro. However, support for the exiles by the United States government had been severely scaled back and they were easily defeated by Castro's troops.

ADEN EMERGENCY
10 DECEMBER 1963–30 NOVEMBER 1967

Forces British: 30,000; Nationalists: unknown. **Casualties** British: 200 killed and wounded; Nationalists: unknown. **Location** Yemen.

Spurred on by an Egyptian-backed wave of Arab nationalism, several factions battled with British forces for control of the crown colony of Aden. The British eventually gained the upper hand. However, after four years of fighting, a decision was made to withdraw all British forces from southern Arabia, including Aden, and the People's Republic of South Yemen was established.

PRAGUE SPRING
5 JANUARY–21 AUGUST 1968

Forces Warsaw Pact: 200,000; Czech opposition: unknown. **Casualties** Warsaw Pact: unknown; Czech opposition: 72 killed, 700 wounded. **Location** Prague, Czechoslovakia.

A burgeoning wave of democratization and increased personal freedom, known as "the Prague Spring", swept over Czechoslovakia under the leadership of the reformist politician Alexander Dubcek, after he was elected as First Secretary of the Communist Party of Czechoslovakia in January 1968. However, hardline Communists, fearing they would lose control of the country, demanded that Dubcek hold back on further reforms. When he refused, they enlisted the help of the Soviet government, which ordered a contingent of Warsaw Pact troops to occupy Czechoslovakia. The occupying forces met with some opposition, but very quickly took control of Prague, the Czech capital. Dubcek and his fellow reformers were arrested, civilian resistance was swiftly quelled, and over a period of several months the reforms of "the Prague Spring" were gradually eroded.

CELEBRITIES WHO SERVED IN THE ARMED FORCES

Name (dates)	Nationality	Famous as	Service
Max Schmeling (1905–2005)	German	Heavyweight boxing champion (1930–32)	Served in a Luftwaffe *Fallschirmjaeger* (paratrooper) unit at the battle of Crete, 1941
Elvis Presley (1935–77)	United States	The "King" of rock 'n roll; numerous film roles in the 1950s–60s	Served in the US Army 3rd Armored Division in Germany, 1958–60
Arnold Schwarzenegger (1947–)	United States (born in Austria)	Six-time Mr Olympia body-building champion; numerous film roles, including *Conan the Barbarian* and *Terminator*; governor of the US State of California	Completed one year of compulsory service in the *Österreichs Bundesheer* (Austrian Army), 1965
Prince Henry of Wales (1984–)	United Kingdom	Younger son of HRH, the Prince of Wales, third in line of succession to the throne of the United Kingdom	2nd Lieutenant, Blues and Royals, Household Cavalry Regiment; served in Afghanistan, February 2008

Serving his country
Elvis Presley at Freiburg in Breisgau, West Germany, in October 1958, during his two-year term of service in the US Army.

VIETNAM WAR
SEPTEMBER 1959–APRIL 1975

Blending Communist philosophy and fervent nationalism, Ho Chi Minh initially led an effort aimed at uniting North and South Vietnam. Following the French withdrawal from the region, and fearing the spread of Communism, the US became increasingly involved, only finally withdrawing after more than a decade of military intervention.

PLEIKU AND QUI NONH
7 FEBRUARY 1964

Forces American: 400; Viet Cong: 200. **Casualties** American: 9 killed, 128 wounded; Viet Cong: unknown. **Location** South Vietnam.

Attacks by Viet Cong guerrillas on the US air base at Pleiku and in the nearby town of Qui Nonh prompted President Lyndon Johnson to order bombing raids on North Vietnam in retaliation. These raids were to serve as a pretext for the widening of US participation in the Vietnam War.

> "Anything that crossed into the **free-fire** zone was fair game – woman, man, boy, girl …"
>
> ANONYMOUS US SOLDIER, VIETNAM

NAM DONG
6 JULY 1964

Forces American and South Vietnamese: 312; Viet Cong: 1,000. **Casualties** American and South Vietnamese: 125 killed and wounded; Viet Cong: 62 killed. **Location** South Vietnam.

Viet Cong guerrillas were repulsed in their attempt to overrun the South Vietnamese camp at Nam Dong under cover of darkness despite the American and South Vietnamese defenders facing an enemy force more than three times larger than they were.

BINH GIA
28 DECEMBER 1964–1 JANUARY 1965

Forces American and South Vietnamese: 4,300; Viet Cong: 1,800. **Casualties** American and South Vietnamese: 201 killed, 192 wounded; Viet Cong: 32 killed. **Location** South Vietnam.

Having been well supplied by the North Vietnamese Communists, Viet Cong guerrilla forces ambushed and inflicted heavy casualties on an elite troop of South Vietnamese Rangers and Marines that was accompanied by a small contingent of US advisors.

OPERATION ROLLING THUNDER
2 MARCH 1965–31 OCTOBER 1968

Forces American: 306,380 sorties. **Casualties** American: 938 aircraft, 1,084 crew lost; North Vietnam: 52,000 killed. **Location** North Vietnam.

Operation Rolling Thunder was a three-year aerial bombing campaign that was intended to apply pressure on the North Vietnamese government to cease promoting the war in the South. The Americans soon learned that low-level raids incurred unacceptable losses of aircraft and crews from anti-aircraft fire, and switched to less accurate but deadly high-altitude bombing.

SONG BE
10–15 MAY 1965

Forces American and South Vietnamese: no reliable estimates; Viet Cong: unknown. **Casualties** American and South Vietnamese: 54 killed; Viet Cong: 85 killed. **Location** South Vietnam.

South Vietnamese and US Special Forces were successful in driving Viet Cong guerrillas, who were occupying the village of Song Be, from the area. This victory helped to boost the flagging morale of the South Vietnamese troops, who had recently experienced a number of setbacks.

Homemade weapon
This crudely made knife with a wooden handle is typical of the small weaponry carried by Communist troops in Vietnam.

IA DRANG VALLEY
14–18 NOVEMBER 1965

Forces American: 1,000; North Vietnamese: 4,000. **Casualties** American: 234 killed, 245 wounded; North Vietnamese: 634 killed. **Location** Central Highlands, South Vietnam.

During the first major battle between US forces and the North Vietnamese Army (NVA), US airborne troops fought successfully to protect their landing zones, and at the same time managed to effectively thwart a planned Communist offensive into South Vietnam.

A SHAU
9–10 MARCH 1966

Forces American and South Vietnamese: 395; North Vietnamese: 2,000. **Casualties** American and South Vietnamese: 55 killed, 12 wounded; North Vietnamese: 800 killed or wounded. **Location** South Vietnam.

Despite being heavily outnumbered, the garrison of the Special Forces base at A Shau fought for hours, sometimes hand-to-hand, with the Communists before being ordered to evacuate. The vicinity later became a staging area for North Vietnamese operations.

HASTINGS
7–25 JULY 1966

Forces American and South Vietnamese: 11,500; North Vietnamese: unknown. **Casualties** American and South Vietnamese: 51 killed, 162 wounded; North Vietnamese: 824 killed. **Location** Demilitarized Zone, Vietnam.

A joint US and South Vietnamese offensive was successful in inflicting heavy casualties on the North Vietnamese. This action prevented the capture of Quang Tri province by the Communists. The North Vietnamese forces quickly withdrew across the Demilitarized Zone.

OPERATION CEDAR FALLS
8–26 JANUARY 1967

Forces American and South Vietnamese: no reliable estimates. Viet Cong: no reliable estimates. **Casualties** American and South Vietnamese: 428; Viet Cong: 750 killed, 280 prisoners. **Location** Northwest of Saigon, South Vietnam.

Operation Cedar Falls involved placing a US cordon around the so-called Iron Triangle area north of Saigon. Helicopter-borne forces then secured and searched the area within the cordon for signs of enemy bases and tunnel complexes.

FAMOUS WAR PHOTOGRAPHERS

Name and dates	Nationality	Subjects
Matthew B. Brady 1822–96	United States	One of the pioneers of modern photojournalism, Brady was most famous for his photographs of the US Civil War, especially portraits of commanders, such as Grant, Sherman, Custer, Lee, and Jackson.
James F. Hurley 1885–1962	Australia	Hurley documented the horrors of World War I, at Ypres and Passchendaele. He also photographed the 1914 Imperial Trans-Antarctic Expedition of HMS *Endurance* under Sir Ernest Shackleton.
Margaret Bourke-White 1904–71	United States	Bourke-White was a photographer and the first female war correspondent, and one of the few female correspondents allowed at the frontlines during World War II.
Joseph J. Rosenthal 1911–2006	United States	Rosenthal famously photographed US Marines and a navy corps man raising an American flag on Mount Suribachi on Iwo Jima in February 1945. US Marine Corps photographer, Louis R. Lowery (1916–87), took the first photograph of the flag raising; the event was repeated for Rosenthal's more famous photograph.
Robert Capa (born Endre Ernö Friedmann) 1913–54	Hungary	One of Capa's best-known photographs is that of a Spanish Republican soldier, captured at the moment he was shot dead during the Spanish Civil War (1936–39).
George Silk 1916–2004	New Zealand	Silk is credited with the first photographs of the Japanese city of Nagasaki after its devastation by an atomic bomb in August 1945.
Yevgeny Khaldei 1917–97	Soviet Union	Khaldei famously photographed the moment a Red Army soldier raised his nation's flag above the Reichstag amid the ruins of Berlin in May 1945.
Dickey Chapelle 1918–65	United States	Chapelle covered World War II and the Vietnam War. While on patrol with US Marines in 1965, she was killed by fragments from an exploding Viet Cong grenade. French photojournalist Henri Huet (1927–71) famously photographed her last moments. Huet himself died in a helicopter crash during Operation Lam Son 719.
Eddie Adams 1933–2004	United States	Adams' most famous shot captured the moment that South Vietnamese Brigadier-General Nguyen Ngoc Loan executed Viet Cong terrorist Nguyen Van Lem with a revolver.
Nick Ut (born Huynh Công Út) 1951–	Republic of Vietnam	Ut's photograph of children fleeing a South Vietnamese napalm strike in 1972 earned him the Pulitzer Prize for Spot News Photography.

In the firing line
War photographers during the Vietnam War faced immense dangers in their quest to capture the full horror of modern warfare.

JUNCTION CITY
22 FEBRUARY–14 MAY 1967

Forces American and South Vietnamese: 30,000; Viet Cong: unknown. **Casualties** American and South Vietnamese: 282 killed, 1,100 wounded; Viet Cong: 2,728 killed and wounded. **Location** South Vietnam.

US and South Vietnamese troops attempted to clear Viet Cong fighters from a stronghold in Tay Ninh Province near Saigon. Large numbers of the Viet Cong evacuated the area while the operation was taking place, but then returned when it was over.

DAK TO
3–22 NOVEMBER 1967

Forces American and South Vietnamese: 16,000; North Vietnamese and Viet Cong: 6,000. **Casualties** American and South Vietnamese: 455 killed, 1,441 wounded; North Vietnamese and Viet Cong: 1,500 killed and wounded. **Location** South Vietnam.

Communist forces failed in their effort to destroy a large US troop formation, but succeeded in drawing many enemy units away from South Vietnam's cities, leaving them under-defended. This was in preparation for the Tet Offensive that took place two months later.

Rooting out insurgents in Saigon
During the Tet Offensive in March 1968, US Army and South Vietnamese troops, in M113 armoured personnel carriers battle Communist insurgents in downtown Saigon.

KHE SANH
21 JANUARY–8 APRIL 1968

Forces American and South Vietnamese: 6,000; North Vietnamese: 20-30,000. **Casualties** American: 730 killed, 2,642 wounded; South Vietnamese: 229 killed, 436 wounded; North Vietnamese: 1,602 killed and verified by body count, actual estimates up to 15,000. **Location** Quang Tri Province, South Vietnam.

The isolated US firebase (camp providing artillery support) at Khe Sanh and nearby positions endured a 77-day siege initiated in conjunction with the Tet Offensive. The outpost at Lang Vei fell to the Communists, although air and ground operations by US and South Vietnamese troops relieved the besieged US Marines' base at Khe Sanh.

TET OFFENSIVE
31 JANUARY–2 MARCH 1968

Forces North Vietnamese and Viet Cong: 84,000; American: 500,000; South Vietnamese: 350,000. **Casualties** North Vietnamese and Viet Cong: 45,000; American: 9,000; South Vietnamese: 11,000. **Location** South Vietnam.

This massive campaign was planned to coincide with the two-day Vietnamese Tet (or new year's day) holiday, when many South Vietnamese soldiers would be on leave. Viet Cong guerrillas and North Vietnamese Army forces seized and took control of a number of urban areas in South Vietnam. Most of these captured areas were retaken by the Americans and their South Vietnamese allies within days.

IMPORTANT ABBREVIATIONS AND ACRONYMS

Military and naval forces around the world use abbreviations and acronyms as shorthand for describing common concepts, actions or equipment. Though each language and culture have their own specific abbreviations, some terms developed in English are common among allied nations, such as those of the North Atlantic Treaty Organization (NATO). The table below lists some of the abbreviations and acronyms developed for use by multinational NATO units operating in the field.

NATO Acronym or Abbreviation	Reference	NATO Acronym or Abbreviation	Reference
AAR	Air-to-air refuelling	MC	Mine countermeasures
AEW	Airborne early warning	NAVAIDS	Navigational aids
BDU	Battle dress uniform	OP	Observation post
CE	Combat engineers	POW	Prisoner of war
CP	Command post	PSYOP	Psychological operations
DMZ	Demilitarized zone	RECCE	Reconnaissance
FAA	Forward assembly area	ROE	Rules of engagement
ILS	Instrument landing system	SOF	Special operations forces
JOC	Joint operations centre	TF	Task force
LP	Light patrol	WPN	Weapon

HUE 31 JANUARY–3 MARCH 1968

Forces: American and South Vietnamese: 2,500; North Vietnamese and Viet Cong: 10,000. **Casualties** American and South Vietnamese: 482 killed, 2,203 wounded; North Vietnamese and Viet Cong: 5,113 killed, 89 captured; Civilian: 5,800 killed and missing. **Location** South Vietnam.

During the Tet Offensive the Communists occupied large portions of the provincial capital of Hue, where they massacred many civilians. They were driven from the city after weeks of bitter fighting.

MY LAI MASSACRE 16 MARCH 1968

Forces American: 200. **Casualties** American: none; Vietnamese civilians: c.300-400. **Location** South Vietnam.

US soldiers entered the South Vietnamese villages of My Lai and My Khe, where they proceeded to massacre civilians. Although 26 US soldiers faced charges for their part in the massacre, only Lieutenant William Calley was ever convicted for the atrocity, which drew worldwide condemnation.

KHAM DUC
10–12 MAY 1968

Forces American and South Vietnamese: 1,750; North Vietnamese and Viet Cong: 7,500. **Casualties** American and South Vietnamese: 270; North Vietnamese and Viet Cong: unknown. **Location** South Vietnam.

A series of heavy attacks by a much larger Communist force eventually compelled the US and South Vietnamese defenders of the Special Forces camp at Kham Duc to abandon their position. However, there was no further infiltration of the Viet Cong guerrillas south into the Central Highlands.

CORAL-BALMORAL
12 MAY–6 JUNE 1968

Forces American and Australian: 2,500; North Vietnamese and Viet Cong: 3,500. **Casualties** American and Australian: 25 killed, 100 wounded; North Vietnamese and Viet Cong: 300. **Location** South Vietnam.

During 26 days of fighting, Australian troops backed by US forces played a major role in disrupting an offensive against the South Vietnamese capital, Saigon, successfully holding on to their operational area and the fire-support bases, from which artillery supported the infantry.

OPERATION SPEEDY EXPRESS
1 DECEMBER 1968–31 MAY 1969

Forces American: 8,000; North Vietnamese and Viet Cong: unknown. **Casualties** American: 40 killed; 312 wounded; North Vietnamese and Viet Cong: 10,889 killed and wounded. **Location** South Vietnam.

This US operation was intended to subdue Communist interference with US stabilization and pacification efforts in the area around the Mekong Delta, and to disrupt enemy communications. It was seen as controversial because attacks were mainly at night and many civilians were killed. US troops involved were later accused of carrying out atrocities.

HAMBURGER HILL
11–20 MAY 1969

Forces American and South Vietnamese: 1,800; North Vietnamese: 1,500. **Casualties** American: 84 killed, 480 wounded; North Vietnamese: 675 killed. **Location** South Vietnam.

Officially designated Hill 937, Hamburger Hill was fortified by the North Vietnamese. In a series of direct assaults, US and South Vietnamese forces captured the higher ground. The battle remains controversial due to the hill's negligible strategic value.

BAN DONG
8 FEBRUARY–20 MARCH 1971

Forces American and South Vietnamese: 8,000; North Vietnamese and Laotian: no reliable estimates. **Casualties** American and South Vietnamese: 1,500 killed; North Vietnamese and Laotian: 300. **Location** Laos.

A series of Communist counterattacks inflicted heavy losses on the US and South Vietnamese forces and succeeded in recapturing the Laotian town of Ban Dong, overrunning two fire-support bases in the process. Fighting was particularly bitter at Hill 723.

Heroes of the revolution
This colourful political poster celebrates the key figures involved in Cuba's socialist revolution, including Fidel Castro and Che Guevara. The latter would meet his end during his less successful campaign to overthrow the Bolivian government in 1966–67.

The strong Communist thrust towards Saigon during the Eastertide Offensive was blunted at An Loc by a single South Vietnamese division supported by massive US air power and a scattering of US advisors and combat troops. The North Vietnamese forces besieged the city for 66 days, before being forced to retreat.

LINEBACKER I
9 MAY–23 OCTOBER 1972

Forces American: 40,000 sorties; North Vietnamese: unknown. **Casualties** American: 134 aircraft; North Vietnamese: 63 aircraft. **Location** North Vietnam.

In response to the North Vietnamese Eastertide Offensive, US air power successfully disrupted enemy resupply efforts and bombed tactical targets inside North Vietnam, thereby halting the Communist operation.

LINEBACKER II
18 DECEMBER–30 DECEMBER 1972

Forces American: 1,100 sorties; North Vietnamese: unknown. **Casualties** American: 8 killed, 33 captured and 25 missing; North Vietnamese: 1,624 killed and 1,216 wounded. **Location** North Vietnam, principally Hanoi and Haiphong.

Popularly known as the Christmas bombing, US air power made a massive assault on the North Vietnamese capital and its major harbour. This action forced the diplomats back to the negotiating table after peace talks that had been held during the autumn of 1972 had faltered.

OPERATION FREQUENT WIND
29–30 APRIL 1975

Forces American and South Vietnamese: unknown; North Vietnamese: unknown. **Casualties** Unknown. **Location** Saigon, South Vietnam.

This major airlift operation evacuated more than 5,000 US and Vietnamese personnel to safety as Communist forces overwhelmed and took control of the South Vietnamese capital, Saigon. The fall of Saigon effectively brought the Vietnam War to a close.

SECOND INDO-PAKISTANI WAR
15 AUGUST–30 SEPTEMBER 1965

Forces Indian: all armed forces; Pakistani: all armed forces. **Casualties** Indian: 3,000; Pakistani: 3,800. **Location** Kashmir.

Fighting over the administration of the disputed state of Kashmir and with each side claiming provocation by the other, India and Pakistan declared war on each other. The war lasted five weeks. It resulted in thousands of casualties on both sides, and ended with a UN-mandated ceasefire.

EASTERTIDE OFFENSIVE
30 MARCH–11 JULY 1972

Forces North Vietnamese: 200,000; South Vietnamese: 500,000. **Casualties** North Vietnamese: 100,000; South Vietnamese: 50,000. **Location** South Vietnam.

Changing their mode of operation from mainly guerrilla tactics to the use of open warfare, the North Vietnamese Army launched this major offensive against South Vietnamese forces. Intervention by US air power helped to bring the offensive to a standstill.

LOC NINH 4–7 APRIL 1972

Forces American and South Vietnamese: 15,000; North Vietnamese and Viet Cong: 30,000. **Casualties** American and South Vietnamese: 6,000 killed and wounded; North Vietnamese and Viet Cong: 7,000 killed and wounded. **Location** South Vietnam.

During their Easterside Offensive, Communist forces initiated a series of heavy attacks on the small town of Loc Ninh close to the border with Cambodia, causing many casualties. The defenders were eventually forced to abandon their positions and retreat. Subsequent airstrikes were ordered by the US command to destroy what remained of the fortifications, in order to prevent them from falling into the hands of the Communists.

AN LOC 13 APRIL–20 JULY 1972

Forces American and South Vietnamese: 7,000; North Vietnamese and Viet Cong: 35,470. **Casualties** American and South Vietnamese: 2,300 killed or missing, 3,100 wounded; North Vietnamese and Viet Cong: 10,000 killed, 15,000 wounded. **Location** South Vietnam.

> "I ask all **servicemen** to stop **firing** and stay where you are… to stop **useless bloodshed.**"
>
> SOUTH VIETNAMESE PRESIDENT DUONG VAN MINH SURRENDERS, SAIGON, 1975

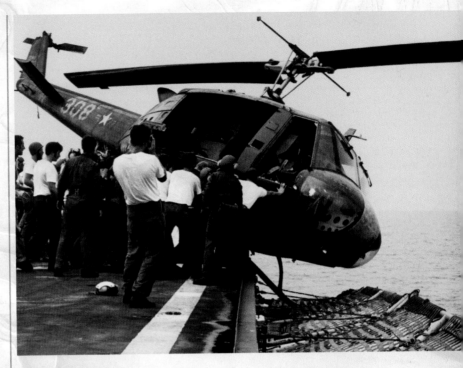

BOLIVIAN CAMPAIGN
3 NOVEMBER 1966–9 OCTOBER 1967

Forces Guevara's guerrillas: 50; Bolivian: 600. **Casualties** All guerrillas killed, captured or dispersed. **Location** Bolivia.

Ernesto "Che" Guevara tried to repeat Castro's success in Cuba. However, lacking the support of the local people, his band of guerrillas was pursued and eventually destroyed by the Bolivian army.

ES SAMU INCIDENT
13 NOVEMBER 1966

Forces Israeli: 400; Jordanian: 100. **Casualties** Israeli: 1 killed, 10 wounded; Jordanian: 16 killed, 54 wounded. **Location** West Bank of Jordan.

An Israeli incursion into Jordanian territory, prompted by repeated attacks from terrorist groups linked to the Palestine Liberation Organization (PLO), was countered by units of the Jordanian Army. The action helped to hasten the start of the Six-Day War.

SOUTH AFRICAN BORDER WAR
26 AUGUST 1966–30 AUGUST 1988

Lengthy wars for Angolan independence from Portugal and the controversial South African influence in Namibia became intertwined, and involved United Nations supervision and military contingents from other African countries and Cuba.

CUITO CUANAVALE
5 DECEMBER 1987–23 MARCH 1988

Forces South African and UNITA: 12,000; Angolan, Cuban and SWAPO: 12,000. **Casualties** South African and UNITA: 3,000 killed and wounded; Angolan, Cuban and SWAPO: 4,800. **Location** Angola.

Both sides claimed victory in this, one of the largest battles to be fought on the African continent since World War II. It influenced not only the outcome of the South African Border War, but also that of the Angolan Civil War.

BIAFRAN WAR
30 MAY 1967–15 JANUARY 1970

Forces Nigerian: 250,000; Biafran: 150,000. **Casualties** Nigerian: 100,000; Biafran: 100,000; civilian: 1,000,000. **Location** Southeast Nigeria.

Seeking independence from Nigeria, the newly declared Republic of Biafra received support from France and Rhodesia. With the assistance of Soviet-supplied weaponry and a naval blockade, however, Nigeria eventually forced the besieged Biafrans to surrender.

SIX-DAY WAR
5–10 JUNE 1967

Facing external threats from several directions, Israel launched a devastating pre-emptive strike. As well as smashing the Egyptian air force and driving through as far as the Suez Canal, Israeli forces also advanced into Syria.

ABU-AGEILA
5–6 JUNE 1967

Forces Israeli: 14,000; Egyptian: 8,000. **Casualties** Israeli: 32 killed; Egyptian: unknown. **Location** Sinai Desert.

During the Israelis' offensive into the Sinai Peninsula, their anti-tank weapons destroyed 40 Egyptian tanks, while they only lost half that number themselves. The Israeli victory facilitated a further advance into the Sinai Desert.

AMMUNITION HILL
6 JUNE 1967

Forces Israeli: 200; Jordanian: 150. **Casualties** Israeli: 37 killed; Jordanian: 71 killed. **Location** East Jerusalem.

Israeli paratroopers launched an attack on the Jordanian troops that were occupying reinforced bunkers near the Police Academy in Jerusalem. But by underestimating the strength of the opposing force, the Israelis suffered a considerable number of casualties in re-establishing their control of the western section of the city.

LIBERTY INCIDENT
8 JUNE 1967

Forces American: 294 crewmen; Israeli: unknown. **Casualties** American: 34 killed, 170 wounded; Israeli: none. **Location** Mediterranean Sea, north of the Sinai Peninsula.

At the height of the Six-Day War Israeli aircraft and torpedo boats launched a surprise combined air and sea attack on the neutral US Navy technical research vessel, USS *Liberty*. The Israelis subsequently claimed that their action had been taken after mistaking the US vessel for an Egyptian cargo ship. However, some sources still claim that the action was premeditated, and the incident is considered to be controversial to this day.

Desperate to escape from Vietnam
A UH-1 "Huey" helicopter is pushed over the side of a US Navy ship to allow more to land during the evacuation of Saigon in April 1975, known as Operation Frequent Wind.

GOLAN HEIGHTS
9–10 JUNE 1967

Forces Israeli: 20,000; Syrian: 75,000. **Casualties** Israeli: 115 killed; Syrian 1,000 killed. **Location** Israeli-Syrian border.

In approximately 27 hours of combat, Israeli forces took control of this strategic high ground from which Syrian artillery had repeatedly bombarded kibbutz settlements along the border and had threatened an invasion of northern Israel.

POSTWAR GENOCIDES

Location and date	Event	Casualties	Group or individuals responsible
Cambodia 1975–79	Mass killings of political dissidents, Muslims, Buddhist monks, and ethnic minorities	Possibly 1,700,000	The Khmer Rouge under the regime of Pol Pot and Ta Mok. Most key figures died before they could be brought to justice but a former leader of the KhmerRouge, Nuon Chea, is still expected to stand trial.
Rwanda April 1994	Massacre of Rwanda's Tutsi minority by members of the Hutu ethnic group	800,000 killed	Interahamwe and Impuzamugambi Hutu militias. The International Criminal Tribunal for Rwanda has convicted 25 of the perpetrators, with several others not yet arrested.
Bosnia-Herzegovina 1992–95	Removal and killing of members of the Bosnian Muslim population by members of the Serb ethnic group, including the Srebrenica massacre in 1995	200,000 killed	Republika Srpska troops and other Serbian military and police units. The International Criminal tribunal for the Former Yugoslavia has indicted former Serbian commanders, Slobodan Milosevic, Radovan Karadžic, and Ratko Mladic.
Darfur, Sudan 2003–	Isolation and killing of black African tribal groups by other ethnic groups that claim Arab identity; a large civilian population is also caught up in the war between factions in Sudan and neighbouring Chad	Possibly 500,000 killed; 2,500,000 displaced	Various militias, including the African-Arab Janjaweed. In March 2008, the International Criminal Court indicted Sudan's president, Omar al-Bashir, for genocide, crimes against humanity, and murder.

INFLUENTIAL TERRORIST GROUPS

Name	Origin/date	Objective	Discussion
Irish Republican Army (IRA)	Ireland 1916	End British rule in Ireland; later, end British rule in Northern Ireland	Although it evolved out of many other groups who opposed British rule, the IRA as it came to be known, emerged after the 1916 Easter Rising. The Easter skirmishes with British Army and police units across Ireland helped lead to independence for three provinces of Ireland, except Ulster in the North. Later, as ideological disputes arose, the IRA split into factions, including the "Original IRA" and the "Provisional IRA." The Provisional IRA attacked British interests in the north for 28 years (1969–97) in a conflict that killed more than 1,700 people in the United Kingdom, Europe, and elsewhere. Today, a group calling itself the "Real IRA" continues to carry out attacks in Northern Ireland. IRA militants have helped train operatives from other terrorist organizations, including Colombia's FARC, and (possibly) nationalist and Islamic groups in North Africa.
Euskadi Ta Askatasuna (ETA; Basque Homeland and Freedom)	Spain, France 1959	Establish an autonomous Marxist Basque homeland on the Bay of Biscay in what today is northern Spain and southwest France	ETA's 50-year campaign of violence has killed more than 850 people, including police, soldiers, judges, politicians, and tourists. Strong public condemnation of ETA's tactics, especially in the wake of the 2004 bombings at Madrid's Atocha station (incorrectly attributed to ETA), have somewhat lowered the organization's profile.
Fuerzas Armadas Revolucionarias de Colombia (FARC)	Colombia 1964	Marxist regime change in Colombia (although the FARC's activities have tended to focus on criminal enterprise, such as narcotics trafficking and kidnapping)	The FARC began as the military arm of Colombia's Communist revolutionary insurgency. Today, the FARC fields 9,000–12,000 fighters in the remote border area between Colombia and Venezuela. The organization is responsible for a number of criminal activities, including murder, drugs trafficking, and extortion.
Liberation Tigers of Tamil Eelam (LTTE)	Sri Lanka 1976	Establish an independent Tamil state in the north of Sri Lanka	The Tamil Tigers are one of the most violent groups in the world. Their Black Tigers unit became infamous for its suicide bombing tactics. The LTTE developed such an extensive fundraising network overseas that it was able to field a limited number of "attack" aircraft, becoming the only terrorist group in history to have its own air force. Following the breakdown of peace talks in 2006, the LTTE retreated before dramatic advances made by government forces. In May 2009 the Sri Lankan government claimed victory over the LTTE.
Hizbollah ("Party of God")	Lebanon, Syria 1982	Eliminate the state of Israel; "liberate" Jerusalem from what Hizbollah perceives to be Jewish occupation	After 30 years of campaigning against Israeli and US interests, Hizbollah enjoyed a public relations victory in 2006 when an Israeli offensive in Lebanon failed to disarm or significantly disrupt the organization.
al-Qaeda ("The Base"; or "The Movement")	Saudi Arabia, Afghanistan 1988	Expel all non-Muslims from Muslim nations; establish a worldwide, pan-Islamic caliphate	In addition to having taken responsibility for the 9/11 attacks against the United States, al-Qaeda and its network of linked or affiliated groups has carried out many other attacks in Afghanistan, Indonesia, Iraq, Kenya, Kuwait, Morocco, Pakistan, Saudi Arabia, Spain, Tanzania, Turkey, the United Kingdom, the United States, and Yemen. Osama bin Laden (the network's ideological leader) has urged Muslims that their duty is to kill US citizens and their friends and allies anywhere in the world.

Rebel militants stand their ground
Tamil Tiger soldiers at the funeral of an assassinated leader at Thandiyady, Batticaloa, Sri Lanka in February 2005. These men are armed with either Russian- or Chinese- and American-made weapons.

PUEBLO INCIDENT
23 JANUARY–23 DECEMBER 1968

Forces American: 83; North Korean: unknown. **Casualties** American: 1; North Korean: none. **Location** Off Korean coast.

North Korean forces seized the crew of a US intelligence vessel operating in international waters and held them for 11 months, before their negotiated release. The vessel remains in Korean hands.

SINO-SOVIET BORDER CONFLICT
2 MARCH–11 SEPTEMBER 1969

Forces Soviet: unknown; Chinese: unknown. **Casualties** No reliable estimates. **Location** Sino-Soviet frontier and Zhenbao Island, Ussuri river on the border.

During the spring and summer of 1969, animosity between the two Communist powers erupted in a series of border clashes and a dispute over an island that both nations claimed. Mutual effort to calm the crisis averted full-scale war.

THE TROUBLES 1966–1998

Forces Paramilitaries: varied. Government: varied. **Casualties** Unknown. **Location** British Isles.

Religious and political friction in Northern Ireland led to a complex conflict involving several paramilitary forces. Government troops and police operated against the paramilitaries until a peace agreement was reached in 1998.

INDO-PAKISTANI WAR
3–16 DECEMBER 1971

Internal troubles in Pakistan led to war with India. East Pakistan was quickly overrun and became independent as Bangladesh. In the west, heavy fighting resulted in relatively little change.

OPERATION CHENGHIZ KHAN
3 DECEMBER 1971

Forces Pakistani: unknown; Indian: unknown. **Casualties** Unknown. **Location** Indian air space.

In the opening act of the war, the Pakistani Air Force, inspired by Israeli success in the Six-Day War, launched preemptive air strikes against targets in India. Retaliation by the Indian Air Force was swift and fighting escalated.

YOM KIPPUR WAR
6–24 OCTOBER 1973

Launching a surprise attack against Israel, Egyptian forces made good use of guided anti-tank and surface-to-air missiles. However, after a desperate period, Israel had begun to make gains by the time the UN established a ceasefire.

FIRST MOUNT HERMON
6–8 OCTOBER 1973

Forces Israeli: 200; Syrian: 300. **Casualties** Israeli: 28 killed, 75 wounded; Syrian: unknown. **Location** Golan Heights, Israel-Syria border.

Syrian troops assaulted an Israeli command post during the opening phase of the war, capturing Mount Hermon and holding it against a determined Israeli counterattack two days later.

> "As **flames shot up** from the T-62, I swung the turret again to face the fourth **tank** …"
>
> ISRAELI TANK COMMANDER AVIGDOR KAHALANI, GOLAN HEIGHTS, 1973

Angolan guerrillas on patrol

Heavily armed fighters of the *União Nacional para a Independência Total de Angola* (UNITA) patrol at Nova Lisboa, Angola in September 1975. Guerrilla groups battled for dominance during Angola's struggle for independence.

VALLEY OF TEARS
6–9 OCTOBER 1973

Forces Israeli: 5,000; Syrian: 10,000. **Casualties** Unknown. **Location** Golan Heights, Israel-Syria border.

In this four-day battle in an isolated valley, strong Syrian forces attacked an Israeli armoured battalion, pushing the Israelis to breaking point. However, for no obvious reason, the Syrians withdrew. They had lost a substantial number of tanks but still had an overwhelming advantage.

SINAI CAMPAIGN
6–24 OCTOBER 1973

Forces Israeli: 20,000; Egyptian: 70,000. **Casualties** Israeli: 3,500 killed and wounded; Egyptian: unknown. **Location** Suez Canal and Sinai Peninsula, Egypt.

Utilizing the cover of surface-to-air missiles, Egyptian troops overwhelmed the small Israeli garrison of the Bar-Lev Line and steadily advanced. However, Israeli forces recovered and encircled the Egyptian Third Army.

GOLAN HEIGHTS CAMPAIGN
6–24 OCTOBER 1973

Forces Israeli: unknown; Syrian: 5 divisions. **Casualties** Unknown. **Location** Israeli-Syrian border.

In concert with the Egyptian offensive in the Sinai, Syrian forces attacked Israeli positions along the Golan Heights. Eventually, the Syrians were halted and the Israelis advanced into Syrian territory.

LATAKIA
7 OCTOBER 1973

Forces Israeli: 6 warships; Syrian: 5 warships. **Casualties** Israeli: none; Syrian: unknown. **Location** Eastern Mediterranean Sea, near Syria.

Guarding the Golan Heights

Israeli soldiers, riding aboard an M113 armoured personnel carrier, backed by a tank, patrol the territory around the Golan Heights in Syria during the Yom Kippur War of October 1973.

Employing surface-to-surface missiles, Israeli naval vessels wiped out an entire Syrian squadron. Unusually, neither side used naval guns.

MARSA TALAMAT 7 OCTOBER 1973

Forces Israeli: 2 patrol boats; Egyptian: unknown. **Casualties** Israeli: 1 killed, 7 wounded; Egyptian: unknown. **Location** Gulf of Suez, Egypt.

Israeli vessels on routine patrol discovered an Egyptian seaborne commando force intent on striking at Israeli positions in the Sinai. The Egyptians were driven off with significant losses and several vessels sunk.

BATTLE OF THE SINAI
14 OCTOBER 1973

Forces Israeli: 60,000; Egyptian: 5,000. **Casualties** Israeli: unknown; Egyptian: 1,000 killed and wounded. **Location** Sinai Peninsula, Egypt.

A renewed Egyptian offensive to relieve pressure on Syrian forces to the north was repelled by entrenched Israeli infantry and armour, causing Egyptian forces to retreat to positions along the Suez Canal.

CHINESE FARM
15–16 OCTOBER 1973

Forces Israeli: c.5,000; Egyptian: c.7,000. **Casualties** Israeli: c.300 killed; Egyptian: unknown. **Location** Suez Canal, Egypt.

In an attempt to isolate a large number of Egyptian troops in the Sinai Peninsula, Israeli forces successfully placed a bridgehead across the Suez Canal, but paid dearly for their victory.

SECOND MOUNT HERMON
21–22 OCTOBER 1973

Forces Israeli: 1,000; Syrian: 400. **Casualties** Israeli: 56 killed, 83 wounded; Syrian: unknown. **Location** Golan Heights.

Determined to retake Mount Hermon, reinforced Israeli troops assaulted the Heights from the east and, despite heavy casualties compelled the Syrians to retreat from positions they had captured two weeks earlier.

SUEZ
24–25 OCTOBER 1973

Forces Israeli: 400; Egyptian: 1,000. **Casualties** Israeli: 80 killed, 120 wounded; Egyptian: unknown. **Location** Egypt.

In the final battle of the Yom Kippur War, Israeli forces attemped to capture the town of Suez. However, they were repulsed by Egyptian troops and militia, who suffered heavy losses during several days of intense urban combat.

TURKISH INVASION OF CYPRUS
20 JULY–16 AUGUST 1974

Forces Turkish: 40,000; Greek/Greek Cypriot: 12,000. **Casualties** Turkish: 3,000 killed and wounded; Greek/Greek Cypriot: thousands of refugees. **Location** Northern Cyprus.

In response to a Greek-sponsored coup on the island of Cyprus, Turkish forces invaded and took control of 37 per cent of the country. Turkish soldiers remain in occupation of the territory to this day.

ANGOLA
10 NOVEMBER 1975–17 FEBRUARY 1976

Forces MPLA: 40,000; UNITA: 30,000; FNLA: 20,000; Cubans: 20,000. **Casualties** Unknown. **Location** West-central Africa.

Independence from Portugal left Angola with three rival groups fighting for power. The Popular Movement for the Liberation of Angola (MPLA) gained control of most of the country, but conflict went on for many years.

RAID ON ENTEBBE
27 JUNE–4 JULY 1976

Forces Terrorist: 6–10; Israeli: over 100. **Casualties** Terrorist: 6–10; Israeli: 1; Ugandan: 45; Hostage: 3. **Location** Uganda.

Jewish passengers from a hijacked Air France airliner were held in the terminal at Entebbe. Israeli Defence Forces (IDF) landed and stormed the terminal, killing the terrorists and some Ugandan troops.

SINO-VIETNAMESE WAR
17 FEBRUARY–16 MARCH 1979

Forces Chinese: 20,000; Vietnamese: 100,000.
Casualties Chinese: 7,000 killed; Vietnamese: 30,000 killed and wounded. **Location** Border between China and Vietnam.

Following the Vietnamese invasion of neighbouring Cambodia and Vietnam's occupation of the long-disputed Spratly Islands in the South China Sea, the Chinese government decided to counter these measures by launching a series of army incursions into Vietnamese territory, in order to reassert China's authority in the region. After some bloody clashes on the border, the campaign eventually ended with both China and Vietnam claiming victory.

> "It wasn't anything like the movies. I'd expected **balls of flame**, but there were just **big bangs** …"
>
> CORPORAL HARRY SIDDAL, FALKLANDS, 1982

SOVIETS IN AFGHANISTAN
25 DECEMBER 1979–FEBRUARY 1989

Responding to US support for rebels fighting the Communist-led government, the Soviet Union sent in 85,000 troops. Although the Soviet army was able to take and keep control of urban centres, a successful insurgency by the mujahideen took place in the Afghani countryside. Eventually, the Soviets decided to cut their losses and ordered their troops to withdraw from Afghanistan.

STORM-333 27 DECEMBER 1979

Forces Soviet: 660; Afghan: 2,500. **Casualties** Soviet: 19 killed, 50 wounded; Afghan: at least 400 killed and wounded. **Location** Kabul, Afghanistan.

Soviet special forces and other troops assaulted the Tajberg Palace in Kabul, taking control of the city and assassinating Afghan President Hafizullah Amin, along with a number of his bodyguards.

MARAVAR PASS
21–22 APRIL 1985

Forces Soviet: 200; Mujahideen: 400. **Casualties** Soviet: 36 killed, 100 wounded; Mujahideen: unknown. **Location** Kunar Province, Afghanistan.

Soviet special forces suffered heavy losses during operations to elminate guerrilla activity in the villages of Sangam and Daridam. The guerrillas employed hit-and-run tactics and Soviet casualties were nearly 75 per cent.

FIRST ZHAWAR
4 SEPTEMBER–12 OCTOBER 1985

Forces Afghan: unknown; Mujahideen: unknown. **Casualties** Afghan: unknown; Mujahideen: 437 killed and wounded. **Location** Afghanistan.

An Afghan army offensive against a *mujahideen* supply base was initially successful. However, guerrilla resistance held out, in spite of Soviet air strikes, and the Afghans withdrew after suffering heavy casualties.

SECOND ZHAWAR
28 FEBRUARY–19 APRIL 1986

Forces Soviet and Afghan: 12,000; Mujahideen: unknown. **Casualties** Soviet and Afghan: no reliable estimates; Mujahideen: 281 killed, 363 wounded. **Location** Afghanistan.

Following heavy fighting, *mujahideen* guerrillas eventually abandoned their base at Zhawar. The price of victory for the

Soviet rifle
Sniper rifles, such as this 7.62x54 *Dragunov* (SVD) from the early 1960s, were part of the standard weaponry issued to Soviet troops fighting in Afghanistan during the late 1970s and the 1980s.

opposition though was high, with Afghan army losses severe and more than 500 Soviet commandos captured.

JAJI
20 MAY–13 JUNE 1987

Forces Soviet and Afghan: unknown; Mujahideen: unknown. **Casualties** Soviet and Afghan: no reliable estimates; Mujahideen: unknown. **Location** Afghan-Pakistani border.

During their withdrawal from Afghanistan, Soviet forces successfully assisted an Afghan army operation to relieve the besieged garrison at Ali Sher. However, the follow-up Soviet-Afghan attack on Jaji failed.

OPERATION MAGISTRAL
19 NOVEMBER 1987–31 JANUARY 1988

Forces Soviet: 20,000; Afghan: 8,000; Mujahideen: 15,000. **Casualties** Soviet and Afghan: 1,100 killed, 56 wounded; Mujahideen: 300 killed. **Location** Afghanistan.

As Soviet forces set their plans for withdrawal from Afghanistan in motion, this operation succeeded in temporarily opening the Satukandav Pass and relieving the embattled city of Khost, which had been surrounded by *mujahideen*.

HILL 3234 7–8 JANUARY 1988

Forces Soviet: 39; Mujahideen: 300. **Casualties** Soviet: 6 killed, 28 wounded; Mujahideen: 90 killed and wounded. **Location** Khost, Afghanistan.

A single company of Soviet paratroopers held high ground against *mujahideen* guerrillas, who outnumbered them 10 to one. Exhausting their ammunition supply, the Soviets repelled at least a dozen assaults by the *mujahideen*.

OPERATION ARROW
23 OCTOBER–7 NOVEMBER 1988

Forces Afghan: unknown; Mujahideen: 2,600. **Casualties** Afghan: 500 killed and wounded; Mujahideen: 18 killed, 53 wounded. **Location** Laghman Province, Afghanistan.

Mujahideen guerrillas launched a successful operation to take control of the Kabul-Jalalabad Highway, capturing large quantities of weapons and ammunition before withdrawing according to their plan.

JALALABAD
5 MARCH–15 JULY 1989

Forces Afghan: unknown; Mujahideen: 10,000. **Casualties** Afghan: unknown; Mujahideen: 3,000 killed and wounded. **Location** Afghanistan.

Afghan army forces supported by air strikes and Soviet missile batteries inflicted heavy casualties on *mujahideen* attempting to capture the city of Jalalabad.

DISASTROUS SPECIAL FORCES OPERATIONS

Unit(s)	Action/objective (Date)	Location	Outcome
Eight US Navy RH-53D Sea Stallion helicopters (with US Marine Corps aircrew); four US Air Force Special Operations MC-130E Combat Talon transports; three EC-130 refuelling tankers; three AC-130 gunships; two C-141 Starlifter transports; elements of US Army Delta Force and the 75th Ranger Regiment	Operation "Eagle Claw" to rescue hostages held by Islamic militants at the American embassy in Tehran (1980)	Iran	At a forward refuelling base, codenamed "Desert One," one of the operation's RH-53Ds crashed into one of the C-130s, killing three Marines and five Air Force air crewmen. The crash and other factors influenced President Carter's decision to cancel the mission. The failure was due to a number of factors, including the poor mechanical readiness of several of the helicopters; poor tactical communications; and poor training coordination. Afterwards, the government established the US Special Operations Command (SOCOM) as an independently-budgeted organization within the Department of Defense. SOCOM's mandate was to coordinate the manning, training, equipment, and readiness for all the military services' special operations units.
US Navy SEAL Team 4; US Air Force Special Operations AC-130U gunship	Operation "Just Cause" to destroy Panamanian General Manuel Noriega's personal aircraft (1989)	Patilla Point Army Airfield, Panama	Senior commanders ignored the SEAL team's tactical plans and pressed forward with one of their own, which involved a conventional assault with 48 SEALs (two platoons). Alerted to their approach, the Panamanian guards at the airfield assumed defensive positions and hit the Americans with automatic weapons fire before they could reach the hangar. Pinned down, the SEALs were unable to call in supporting fire from an AC-130U gunship due to poor communications. The SEAL platoon did destroy Noriega's jet with an AT-4 anti-tank rocket, but four SEALs were killed in the firefight.
Russian *Spetsnaz* (special purpose unit); FSB *Spetsgruppa A* (counter-terrorism) and police	*Nord-Ost* siege, to overpower Chechen separatists holding hostages at a city theatre (2002)	Moscow, Russia	Prior to an assault on the theatre, the Russian forces deployed a chemical agent, most likely an anaesthetic gas, to disable the hostage-takers. The gas also disabled many of the hostages, as well as two members of the FSB assault team. The effects of the gas, perhaps amplified by the enclosed space of the theatre, contributed to the deaths of as many as 170 people.

Special Forces badge
This badge is that of the joint British and American Special Operations Executive (SOE) and the Office of Strategic Services (OSS), two of the specialist intelligence and commando organizations that were formed during World War II.

MOST MINED COUNTRIES

Country	Estimated number of landmines in the field (according to the United Nations)
Afghanistan	10,000,000
Iraq	10,000,000
Angola	9,000,000
Cambodia	7,000,000
Somalia	1,000,000

IRAN-IRAQ WAR
22 SEPTEMBER 1980–8 AUGUST 1988

Iraq invaded Iran in 1980, hoping for a quick and easy victory, as Iran was still in revolutionary turmoil. However, after some initial Iraqi gains, the war degenerated into a bloody stalemate.

KHORRAMSHAHR
NOVEMBER 1980–MAY 1982

Forces Iraqi: 70,000; Iranian: 70,000. **Casualties** Iraqi: 7,000 killed and wounded; Iranian: unknown. **Location** Southwest Iran.

In the spring of 1982, the Iranian army launched an offensive to recapture territory that had been taken by the Iraqis, including Khuzestan Province. The Iranians briefly besieged the port city of Khorramshahr, which fell, following two days of heavy fighting.

OPERATION JERUSALEM WAY
29 NOVEMBER–7 DECEMBER 1981

Forces Iraqi: no reliable estimates; Iranian: no reliable estimates. **Casualties** Iraqi: 3,000 killed; Iranian: 3,000 killed. **Location** Southwest Iran.

Employing their superior manpower in costly "human-wave" attacks, the Iranians succeeded in recapturing the city of Bostan and severing a major Iraqi supply line.

OPERATION UNDENIABLE VICTORY
22–28 MARCH 1982

Forces Iraqi: c.160,000; Iranian: 50,000. **Casualties** Iraqi: unknown; 20,000 captured; Iranian: 30,000 killed and wounded. **Location** Southwest Iran.

In what is considered the turning point of the Iran-Iraq War, the Iranians again made successful use of "human-wave" attacks to wrest the Dazful-Shush region from Iraqi control. Iranian troops then went on to press their advantage into enemy territory.

AL-FAW PENINSULA
11 FEBRUARY 1986

Forces Iraqi: unknown; Iranian: 35,000. **Casualties** Iraqi: 2,500 killed and wounded; Iranian: 2,500 killed and wounded. **Location** Southeast Iraq.

Iranian troops launched a surprise attack on a force of Iraqi conscripts in an attempt to capture the vital Al-Faw Peninsula on the Persian Gulf. However, it was Operation Dawn 8, a later Iranian campaign, that resulted in the capture of the peninsula. The territory was subsequently retaken by the Iraqis near the end of the war, aided by the massive use of chemical weapons.

FALKLANDS WAR
19 MARCH–14 JUNE 1982

Hostilities began when Argentine troops invaded and occupied the long disputed British Overseas Territories of the Falkland Islands and neighbouring South Georgia. At sea, British forces suffered serious losses from air attack, especially from Exocet missiles. On land, the British advanced steadily across the islands, eventually liberating the Falkland Islands' capital, Port Stanley, on 14 June 1982.

GOOSE GREEN
28–29 MAY 1982

Forces British: 500; Argentine: 1,200. **Casualties** British: 17 killed, 64 wounded; Argentine: 55 killed, 145 wounded. **Location** Falkland Islands, South Atlantic.

British troops, primarily of 2 Para, sometimes fighting at night, captured Argentine strongpoints at Goose Green and nearby Darwin, which could have posed a threat to the British landing area at San Carlos.

MOUNT HARRIET
11–12 JUNE 1982

Forces British: 600; Argentine: 400. **Casualties** British: 2 killed, 26 wounded; Argentine 18 killed, 50 wounded, 300 captured. **Location** Falkland Islands, South Atlantic.

Iraqi invaders
Iraqi troops near the Iranian port of Khorramshahr, during the Iran-Iraq War (1980–88).

In one of a series of three assaults on high ground surrounding the capital of the Falklands, Port Stanley, British troops of 3 Commando, supported by naval artillery, defeated Argentine forces that were occupying the high ground.

TWO SISTERS
11–12 JUNE 1982

Forces British: 600; Argentine: 350. **Casualties** British: 4 killed, 17 wounded; Argentine: 20 killed; 66 wounded, 54 captured. **Location** Falkland Islands, South Atlantic.

In order to make sure that their advance on Port Stanley was not going to be threatened from the rear, British troops of 45 Commando attempted to seize the heights of Two Sisters during a daring nocturnal assault. They were successful, despite coming under heavy fire from the Argentine forces.

MOUNT LONGDON
11–12 JUNE 1982

Forces British: 450; Argentine: 278. **Casualties** British: 23 killed, 47 wounded; Argentine: 31 killed, 120 wounded, 50 captured. **Location** Falkland Islands, South Atlantic.

Co-ordinated with the attacks on Mount Harriet and Two Sisters, British troops of 3 Para captured Mount Longdon, which commanded the approaches to Port Stanley. Artillery support played a decisive role in securing the victory.

MOUNT TUMBLEDOWN
13–14 JUNE 1982

Forces British: 900; Argentine: 500. **Casualties** British: 10 killed, 43 wounded; Argentine: 30 killed, 100 wounded, 30 captured. **Location** Falkland Islands, South Atlantic.

Elements from the 2nd Scots Guards, 42 Commando, and Gurkha Rifles, were assisted by tanks of the Blues and Royals and naval gunfire in their capture of high ground, 6.4km (4 miles) from Stanley.

WIRELESS RIDGE
13–14 JUNE 1982

Forces British: 600; Argentine: 500. **Casualties** British 3 killed, 11 wounded; Argentine: 25 killed, 125 wounded, 37 captured. **Location** Falkland Islands, South Atlantic.

Armour of the Blues and Royals and artillery of 29 Commando supported the airlifted 2 Para in its assault on Wireless Ridge, which guarded the approach to Port Stanley. The effective artillery fire demoralized the enemy, which withdrew.

INVASION OF LEBANON
6 JUNE 1982–10 JUNE 1985

Forces Israeli and Christian Phalangist: unknown. PLO, Syrian, and Muslim Lebanese: unknown. **Casualties** Israeli: 675; Arab troops and civilian: 17,825. **Location** South Lebanon.

After invading Lebanon to deny the region to Palestinian guerrillas and to counteract Syrian influence, Israel then withdrew most of its forces. A militia and small Israeli forces were left behind.

GRENADA
25 OCTOBER–15 DECEMBER 1983

Forces American Organization of Eastern Caribbean States: 7,500; Grenadian and Cuban: 2,200. **Casualties** American and Organization of Eastern Caribbean States: 19; Grenadian and Cuban: 78. **Location** Island of Grenada.

With Operation Urgent Fury, US and allied forces ended the influence of Cuba and other Marxist nations in Grenada. They also helped to topple a military government, which had imposed strict martial law on the island's population.

"CONTRAS" IN NICARAGUA
JANUARY 1984–25 FEBRUARY 1990

Forces Contra: 15,000; Nicaraguan: unknown.
Casualties No reliable estimates. **Location** Nicaragua.

When the socialist Sandinista Liberation Front was overwhelmingly elected to power in Nicaragua in 1984, the US government reacted by arming the opposing National Democratic Front, known as the "Contras". American support for the "Contras" continued until the Sandinistas were voted out of power in elections held in 1990.

UNITED STATES IN PANAMA
20 DECEMBER 1989–31 JANUARY 1990

Forces American: 58,000; Panamanian: 46,000.
Casualties American: 24 killed, 325 wounded; Panamanian: 205 killed, 245 wounded. **Location** Panama.

The US government launched Operation Just Cause, sending troops into the central American state of Panama in response to the alarming abuses of that country's leadership. US forces successfully launched attacks on a range of both military and civilian targets, instigating measures to stabilize the nation's government and taking the Panamanian military dictator, General Manuel Noriega into custody. Noriega was transported to the United States to stand trial on a variety of charges, including election rigging and human rights violations.

> " As we get **closer to the target**, I can see **tracers** from the AAA coming **through the clouds** … "
>
> F/A-18 HORNET PILOT STEVE POMEROY ON ANTI-AIRCRAFT FIRE, GULF WAR, 1991

GULF WAR
2 AUGUST 1990–3 MARCH 1991

In response to Iraq's occupation and annexation of neighbouring Kuwait in August 1990, a UN coalition force was sent in to liberate the country. After an air campaign lasting 6 weeks, coalition forces launched a ground offensive that succeeded in driving the Iraqis out of Kuwait. High-technology weapons played a key role in helping the coalition to triumph over an Iraqi army that was largely made up of inexperienced conscripts.

KHAFJI 29 JANUARY–1 FEBRUARY 1991

Forces UN coalition: c.4,000; Iraqi: 2,000. **Casualties** UN coalition: 35 killed, 52 wounded; Iraqi: 300 killed, 400 taken prisoner. **Location** Saudi Arabia.

During the first substantial ground combat of the Gulf War, Iraqi forces crossed the border into Saudi Arabia and occupied the town of Khafji. Fighting continued for two days before the Iraqis were forced to retreat.

HAIL MARY 24–28 FEBRUARY 1991

Forces UN coalition: c.250,000; Iraqi: c.150,000.
Casualties Unknown. **Location** Iraqi desert.

Initiating a 100-hour ground war, US, British, and French airborne troops penetrated deep into the desert, cutting off the retreat of Iraqi forces while the major coalition ground advance into Iraq was undertaken.

War in the desert
An American soldier stands on top of a destroyed Iraqi tank in the Kuwaiti desert in 1991. A line of oil wells, set alight by the retreating troops of Saddam Hussein, blaze away in the distance.

PHASE LINE BULLET
26 FEBRUARY 1991

Forces UN coalition: 30,000; Iraqi: 15,000. **Casualties** UN coalition: 2 killed, 12 wounded; Iraqi: unknown. **Location** Iraqi desert.

The spearheads of the coalition advance, consisting mainly of the US 1st and 3rd Armored Divisions, an infantry division, and the 2nd Armored Cavalry Regiment, were unable to break through prepared Iraqi lines of entrenched infantry defences and tanks placed in dug-in positions. American casualties were not heavy, but among them were a number of victims of "friendly fire" incidents.

AL BUSAYYAH 26 FEBRUARY 1991

Forces UN coalition: c.5,000; Iraqi: c.1,500. **Casualties** UN coalition: none; Iraqi: hundreds captured. **Location** Iraqi desert.

With the approach of the coalition forces – largely the 2nd Brigade, US 1st Armored Division – Iraqi troops surrendered in great numbers. Few shots were actually fired during this coalition advance.

73 EASTING 26–27 FEBRUARY 1991

Forces UN coalition: unknown; Iraqi: unknown. **Casualties** UN coalition: 12 killed, 57 wounded; Iraqi: 600 killed and wounded. **Location** Iraqi desert.

Coalition forces, primarily US and British, demolished the bulk of the Iraqi Republican Guard Tawakalna Division. The US 2nd Armored Cavalry Regiment bore the brunt of the fighting, destroying numerous Iraqi tanks and armoured personnel carriers.

Defending Russian rule
A Russian special forces soldier mans a 7.62x54mm PK machine-gun, defending a landing zone near the border with Dagestan during the ongoing fight against rebels battling for independence in the Chechen Republic.

NORFOLK 27 FEBRUARY 1991

Forces UN coalition: c.12,000; Iraqi: c.10,000. **Casualties** UN coalition: 6 killed, 30 wounded; Iraqi: unknown. **Location** Iraqi desert.

The fighting at Norfolk decimated the remnants of the Tawakalna Division of the Iraqi Republican Guard, which had fought at 73 Easting hours earlier. US heavy tanks destroyed dozens of Iraqi armoured vehicles.

WARS IN THE FORMER YUGOSLAVIA
JUNE 1991–NOVEMBER 2001

The breakup of Yugoslavia resulted in a series of complex and bloody conflicts between factions divided along political, ethnic, and religious lines. Civilian casualties were very high, partially as a result of deliberate polices of genocide and ethnic cleansing on the part of some factions. The conflict eventually drew in an international response, with NATO troops and air forces operating in both a peacekeeping role and directly against some factions.

SIEGE OF SARAJEVO
5 APRIL 1992–29 FEBRUARY 1995

Forces Serbs: varied throughout conflict; Bosnians: varied throughout conflict. **Casualties** Serbs: unknown; Bosnians: unknown. **Location** Sarajevo, Bosnia.

Serbian forces surrounded the Bosnian capital of Sarajevo, bringing about the longest siege in modern history. After initial attempts to assault the city failed, Sarajevo was shelled and subjected to sniper attacks. The siege was eventually lifted in 1995 after UN intervention.

OPERATION STORM
4–8 AUGUST 1995

Forces Serbs: 40,000; Croatians and Bosnians: 130,000. **Casualties** Serbs: c.3,200 plus 5,000 prisoners; Croatians and Bosnians: c.1,500. **Location** Croatia.

Croatian and Bosnian troops attacked the parts of Croatia controlled by separatist Serbs. The offensive was a complete success, resulting in the reintegration of the Serb-held areas, although economic damage was extensive.

OPERATION DELIBERATE FORCE
30 AUGUST–20 SEPTEMBER 1995

Forces Serbs: unknown; NATO: unknown. **Casualties** Serbs: unknown; NATO: 2 aircrew captured. **Location** Croatia.

Undertaken in response to threats to UN-designated safe areas in Bosnia, Operation Deliberate Force was a NATO bombing campaign carried out from land bases and aircraft carriers.

CHECHEN WARS
11 DECEMBER 1994–29 AUGUST 1996; 23 SEPTEMBER 1999–

Fighting between factions for and against independence prompted Russian military intervention in Chechnya. A ceasefire was agreed in 1996, but lasted only until 1999.

DOLINSKOYE
12–26 DECEMBER 1994

Forces Russian: unknown; Chechen: unknown. **Casualties** Russian: 200 killed and wounded; Chechen: unknown. **Location** Chechnya, north Caucasus.

In the first battle of the Chechen War, an advancing Russian convoy was attacked by Chechen rebels. The Russians immediately retaliated with attack helicopters and airstrikes on the Chechen positions. Battle raged for two weeks, with the Chechens managing to hold out against Russian fire.

FIRST GROZNY
31 DECEMBER 1994–8 FEBRUARY 1995

Forces Russian: 38,000; Chechen: 5,000. **Casualties** Russian: 1,784 killed, wounded and missing; Chechen: 1,000 killed. **Location** Chechnya, north Caucasus.

Russian forces won a costly victory in their attempt to capture the Chechen capital, Grozny, during the opening months of the war. The morale of the Russian conscripts suffered and the Chechen civilian population rallied around the rebels.

KIZLYAR-PERVOMAYSKOYE
9–18 JANUARY 1995

Forces Russian: 2,400; Chechen: 400. **Casualties** Russian: 164 killed; Chechen: 120. **Location** Russian Federation.

A major guerrilla raid by Chechen rebels into the Russian Federation resulted in a succession of battles with Russian troops. The Chechens were forced to withdraw, taking with them a number of hostages, including captured Russian servicemen. However, a fierce battle erupted as the retreating Chechens passed through Russian siege lines at Pervomayskoye, completely destroying the village.

SHATOY
16 APRIL 1996

Forces Russian: 200; Chechen: 100. **Casualties** Russian: 53 killed, 52 wounded; Chechen: 3 killed. **Location** Yaryshmardy, Chechnya, north Caucasus.

An ambush by Chechen fighters virtually annihilated a large Russian troop convoy, with only a handful of soldiers escaping what had been a perfectly laid ambush. More than 30 Russian armoured vehicles were destroyed.

SECOND GROZNY
6–20 AUGUST 1996

Forces Russian: 20,000; Chechen: 7,000. **Casualties** Russian: 500 killed, 1,400 wounded; Chechen: 500 killed and wounded. **Location** Chechnya, north Caucasus.

Chechen separatists made a rapid advance into the capital, Grozny, managing to break up the Russian defenders into dozens of small contained pockets of resistance. After the Chechens had repelled several ill-conceived and badly executed Russian attempts to regain control of the city, a ceasefire was called.

THIRD GROZNY
25 DECEMBER 1999–6 FEBRUARY 2000

Forces Russian: 50,000; Chechen: 6,000. **Casualties** Russian: 368 killed, 1,469 wounded; Chechen: 1,500 killed. **Location** Chechnya, north Caucasus.

Russian forces laid siege to and eventually occupied the Chechen capital, inflicting heavy casualties on the rebels and raising many charges of atrocities. A considerable number of rebels chose to flee rather than stay and fight a pitched battle against the superior Russian force.

MOST EXPENSIVE MODERN WEAPON SYSTEMS

While an infantryman from the beginning of the last century would be familiar with the basic elements still present on 21st century battlefields – small arms, tanks, artillery, and close air support by aircraft armed with bombs, rockets and machine guns – the range, power and speeds of today's weapons systems would astonish and amaze a soldier from the trenches of World War I.

Modern warfare increasingly is shaped by advances in technologies such as nuclear reactors, stealth materials, electronics, microprocessors, electro-optical sensors (infrared cameras and lasers) and radio frequency sensors (radar), GPS satellite guidance systems, and explosives chemistry. The capabilities of the weapons developed with these technologies are dramatic, as is their cost.

Weapon	Nation, manufacturer	Function	Cost (in US dollars)
USS *Ronald Reagan* (CVN 76)	United States, Northrop Grumman	97,000-ton Nimitz-class nuclear-powered aircraft carrier	$4,500,000,000
USS *North Carolina* (SSN 777)	United States, General Dynamics, Northrop Grumman	Virginia-class nuclear-powered fast attack submarine	$1,800,000,000
B-2 Spirit	United States, Northrop Grumman	Stealth bomber	$1,157,000,000
F-22 Raptor	United States, Lockheed Martin	Air dominance fighter	$142,000,000
AH-64D Apache Longbow	United States, Boeing; United Kingdom, Agusta-Westland	Attack helicopter	$21,600,000
Tomahawk Block IV	United States, Raytheon	Land attack cruise missile	$1,800,000
AIM-120 Advanced Medium-Range Air-to-Air Missile (AMRAAM)	United States, Raytheon	Radar-guided, air-to-air combat missile	$386,000
AGM-114 Hellfire	United States, Lockheed Martin and Boeing	Radar-guided anti-armour missile	$58,000

High-speed war machine
The Lockheed Martin F-22 Raptor is capable of cruising at speeds of more than one and a half times the speed of sound, and can carry a variety of air-to-air and air-to-ground weapons.

KOSOVO
1 MARCH 1988–10 JUNE 1999

Conflict between Serbian forces and pro-independence guerrillas in Kosovo resulted in massacres and "ethnic cleansing" by both sides. Serbia's continuing refusal to accept a settlement was finally reversed after an intensive and prolonged campaign of bombing by NATO forces.

PREKAZ
5–6 MARCH 1998

Forces Serbian: 100; Kosovan: 38. **Casualties** Serbian: 2 killed, 3 wounded; Kosovan: 38 killed. **Location** Serbia.

The Serbian police responded forcefully to repeated attacks by fighters of the Kosovo Liberation Army (KLA). Several prominent KLA fighters and a number of civilians were killed as police dispersed a hostile crowd in the town of Prekaz.

KOSHARE 9 APRIL–10 JUNE 1999

Forces Yugoslavian: 2,000; Kosovan: 6,000. **Casualties** Yugoslavian: 60 killed, 150 wounded; Kosovan: 150 killed, 300 wounded. **Location** Yugoslavia.

An incursion by Kosovo Liberation Army (KLA) units resulted in a stalemate, following weeks of fighting along the Yugoslav frontier. NATO aircraft bombed Yugoslav positions in support of the KLA.

9/11 11 SEPTEMBER 2001

Forces Terrorist: 19. **Casualties** Terrorist: 19; civilians and other victims: 2,973. **Location** New York City and Washington, DC, USA.

Four airliners were hijacked and used for suicide attacks on buildings important to American financial, military, and political power. The Pentagon was damaged and the World Trade Center was destroyed.

AFGHANISTAN
7 OCTOBER 2001–PRESENT

Accusing the Taliban government in Afghanistan of harbouring terrorists, the US and Britain invaded. Much of the country was pacified, but the Taliban leadership remained at large.

MAZARI SHARIF 9 NOVEMBER 2001

Forces Northern Alliance and American: no reliable estimates; Taliban: c.5,000. **Casualties** Northern Alliance and American: 38 killed; Taliban: at least 300 killed, hundreds captured. **Location** Afghanistan.

Northern Alliance forces, assisted by US troops, mounted an offensive aimed at the occupation of the Taliban stronghold of Mazari Sharif. Surprisingly rapid, the advance caused the Taliban to evacuate thousands of its fighters in order for them to avoid capture.

HERAT
12 NOVEMBER 2001

Forces Northern Alliance, American and Iranian: 5,000. **Casualties** None. **Location** Afghanistan.

Northern Alliance, Iranian, and US Special Forces orchestrated a civil uprising against Taliban rule in Herat and liberated the city without a fight. Taliban forces withdrew and the local population welcomed the Northern Alliance troops.

TORA BORA
1–17 DECEMBER 2001

Forces Northern Alliance, American, British, and German: unknown; Taliban and al-Qaeda: unknown. **Casualties** Northern Alliance, American, British and German: unknown; Taliban and al-Qaeda: c.200. **Location** Eastern Afghanistan.

In an effort to eliminate terrorist resistance, a coalition force, assisted by anti-Taliban tribesmen, rooted enemy fighters from caves, inflicting serious casualties. However, high ranking Taliban and al-Qaeda leaders managed to escape.

OPERATION ANACONDA
1–18 MARCH 2002

Forces American, Canadian, British, German, Australian, New Zealand, Norwegian, Danish, French, and Afghan government: 2,000; Taliban and al-Qaeda: c.1,000. **Casualties** American, Canadian, British, German, Australian, New Zealand, Norwegian, Danish, French and Afghan government: 15 killed, 82 wounded; Taliban and al-Qaeda: c.800. **Location** Paktia Province, Afghanistan.

In a joint coalition and Afghan government operation against an insurgent stronghold in the Shahi Kot Valley, early deployment difficulties at Takur Ghar were overcome and enemy fighters were eventually dislodged from the area. An unknown number of insurgents withdrew.

PANJWALI
1 JULY–30 OCTOBER 2006

Forces Canadian, American, Dutch and Afghan government: 2,000; Taliban: 1,500. **Casualties** Canadian, American, Dutch and Afghan: 18 killed, 50 wounded; Taliban: 1,000 killed. **Location** Southern Afghanistan.

Canadian troops led a coalition, including Afghan forces, in conducting this two-phase operation to flush out and eliminate pockets of Taliban resistance in the rugged countryside of Kandahar Province, utilizing heavy artillery and air support to meet resistance.

OPERATION ACHILLES
6 MARCH–30 MAY 2007

Forces British, American, Canadian, Danish, Dutch, Polish, and Afghan government: 7,200; Taliban: 4,000. **Casualties** British, American, Canadian, Danish, Dutch, Polish, and Afghan government: 35 killed; Taliban: at least 750 killed. **Location** Helmand Province, Afghanistan.

NATO forces, primarily British Royal Marines, engaged in a series of small but sharp battles with Taliban insurgents in an attempt to clear areas of southern Afghanistan from Taliban control. A number of key insurgents were killed, although there were civilian casualties.

WORST TERRORIST ATROCITIES

While conventional military operations are mainly targeted at destroying an enemy's means to wage war, terrorism instead attacks the will of the target to continue the struggle. In the modern age the terrorist has a powerful weapon in the form of mass media, which allows the "message" to reach vast numbers of people. Some attacks are designed to cause economic damage, but the main goal is to provoke fear in as many people as possible, sending a message to the people of the target nation that any of them could be the next victim. Thus terrorist organizations seek to influence the world's great powers by terrorising their populations rather than by fighting their armed forces. This table does not include massacres committed by governments or quasi-governmental organizations, as these may be classified with other violations of international law, such as war crimes and genocides.

Carnage in Madrid Spanish emergency services work amid the wreckage of the bombing of Atocha Station on 11 March 2004. Terrorists claimed that they acted in retaliation to Spain's support of the US-led wars in Iraq and Afghanistan.

Location (Date)	Event	Number Killed	Group or Individuals Responsible
New York, Pennsylvania, and Virginia, US (September 2001)	Nineteen hijackers crashed four airliners into the World Trade Center's twin towers, New York; the Pentagon, Arlington, Va., and a field in Pennsylvania (after the passengers and crew of one plane rose against their attackers).	2,993	al-Qaeda
Beslan, North Ossetia (September 2004).	The terrorists held the children and their teachers hostage by mining the school with explosives wired to "dead man's switches". On the third day of the siege, Russian police and military counter-terrorism units stormed the school.	372	Riyadus-Salikhin Reconnaissance and Sabotage Battalion of Chechen Martyrs
Atlantic Ocean near Ireland; and Tokyo, Japan (June 1985)	A bomb exploded on board Air India Flight 182 during its flight from Montreal to London. The plane crashed in deep water in the North Atlantic. In a related attack, a bomb exploded at Tokyo's Narita airport's baggage terminal.	331	Sikh extremist groups, including Babbar Khalsa
Lockerbie, Scotland, United Kingdom (December 1988)	In 2001, a Scottish court found a Libyan agent guilty of planting a bomb aboard Pan Am Flight 103 in 1988. The bomb caused the huge 747 airliner to break up in mid-air, raining debris and burning fuel onto a Scottish town.	270	Libyan agents, possibly acting on behalf of a terrorist organization called "Guardians of the Islamic Revolution"
Bali, Indonesia (October 2002)	Islamic extremists, acting against what they perceived as corrupt Western influence, bombed nightclubs popular with Australian and other international tourists.	202	Jemaah Islamiyah
Mumbai, India (July 2006)	Terrorists exploded seven bombs aboard crowded commuter trains travelling from Mumbai.	200	Possibly al-Qaeda; possibly other groups, including the Indian *mujahideen*
Madrid, Spain (March 2004)	During a busy rush hour, terrorists exploded a series of backpack bombs aboard trains at the Atocha railway station.	191	Moroccan-Spanish Islamic extremists ideologically linked to al-Qaeda
Mumbai, India (November 2008)	In coordinated assaults, gunmen attacked civilians at a railway station, hotels, and restaurants across Mumbai. The attacks led to a three-day siege between the terrorists and Indian security forces. Only one terrorist was captured alive; he told police he had been ordered to "kill until his last breath".	174	Lashkar-e-Taiba, a Pakistani-Kashmiri militant group
Anuradhapura, Sri Lanka (May 1985)	At Anuradhapura, Tamil Tiger militants fired their automatic rifles into crowds of passengers at a bus station and at a Buddhist temple.	150	Liberation Tigers of Tamil Eelam

"Although the **first ten** times you might survive, all it takes is once and **you're dead**."

US SERGEANT ON THE THREAT OF IMPROVISED EXPLOSIVE DEVICES (IEDS) IN IRAQ

MODERN MILITARY SPENDING

Nation	Military spending In US$, 2008 data from the Center for Arms Control and non-Proliferation
United States	$711,000,000,000
People's Republic of China	$121,900,000,000
Russia	$70,000,000,000
United Kingdom	$55,400,000,000
France	$54,000,000,000
Japan	$41,100,000,000
Germany	$37,800,000,000
Italy	$30,600,000,000

US FUTURE FORCE WARRIOR

KAMIN
26 MAY 2007

Forces Afghan government: unknown; Taliban: unknown. **Casualties** Afghan government: 21 killed, 9 wounded; Taliban: 76 killed. **Location** Kandahar Province, Afghanistan.

An offensive operation launched by Taliban insurgents to inflict casualties on the Afghan army and coalition troops succeeded in detonating a number of car bombs and ambushing several army patrols, before the Taliban survivors managed to slip away.

CHORA
15–19 JUNE 2007

Forces Afghan, Dutch, American and Australian: 800; Taliban: unknown. **Casualties** Afghan, Dutch, American and Australian: 20 killed; Taliban: unknown. **Location** Oruzgan Province, Afghanistan.

In what was to be their largest offensive during 2007, Taliban forces attempted to assert their control over Oruzgan Province in central Afghanistan and were successful in making some initial gains. However, the superior firepower of the coalition forces eventually gained the upper hand, managing to recover their lost strongholds and drive the Taliban back.

MUSA QALA
7–12 DECEMBER 2007

Forces American, British, Danish, and Afghan government: 4,500; Taliban: 2,000. **Casualties** American, British, Danish, and Afghan: 2 killed, 9 wounded; Taliban: no reliable estimates. **Location** Helmand Province, Afghanistan.

During the first battle of the war in which Afghan army soldiers took a prominent role, Taliban insurgents who had been occupying the town of Musa Qala, were eventually compelled to retreat by coalition forces following three days of particularly intensive fighting.

SHAHI TANDAR
7–31 JANUARY 2009

Forces British, Afghan and Canadian: 1,000; Taliban: unknown. **Casualties** British, Afghan, and Canadian: 2 killed; Taliban: several hundred. **Location** Kandahar Province, Afghanistan.

In a series of coordinated raids, the coalition troops, making significant use of armoured vehicles, were successful in uncovering and disrupting a number of Taliban bomb-making facilities, as well as inflicting heavy casualties on the insurgents, causing them to disperse. A large cache of Taliban arms and ammunition was also seized by the coalition forces during this operation.

INVASION AND OCCUPATION OF IRAQ
20 MARCH 2003–PRESENT

Tiring of Iraqi intransigence, a coalition led by the United States invaded the country, removing the dictator Saddam Hussein from power. Iraq continues to be troubled by internal conflict.

NASIRIYAH   23–29 MARCH 2003

Forces American: 7,100; Iraqi: c.12,000. **Casualties** American: 9 killed, 60 wounded; Iraqi: 450 killed, 1,000 wounded, 300 captured. **Location** Southeast Iraq.

The US Marines of Task Force Tarawa captured bridges over the Euphrates river during heavy fighting with elements of the Iraqi Army and Baath Party loyalists.

BASRA   20 MARCH–6 APRIL 2003

Forces British: 10,000; Iraqi: unknown. **Casualties** British: 11 killed; Iraqi: 500 killed. **Location** Southeast Iraq.

British troops captured the second-largest city in Iraq after two weeks of fighting that included a large clash of armoured vehicles.

BAGHDAD   20 MARCH–12 APRIL 2003

Forces American: 30,000; Iraqi: 45,000. **Casualties** American: 34 killed; Iraqi: 2,300 killed. **Location** Iraq.

US forces carried out probing attacks to test the defences of Baghdad and entered the Iraqi capital three days after gaining control of its airport. Iraqi leader, Saddam Hussein fled and managed to elude capture for several months.

UMM QASR
21–25 MARCH 2003

Forces American, British and Polish: 5,000; Iraqi: unknown. **Casualties** American, British and Polish: 14 killed; Iraqi: 40 killed. **Location** Southern Iraq.

Early on in the invasion of Iraq, coalition forces captured the port facilities of

Keeping the peace in Afghanistan
US Marines patrol in Afghanistan aboard a Light Armoured Vehicle (LAV).

Umm Qasr in order to facilitate the arrival of humanitarian aid. Although the port was secured quickly, fighting persisted in the older parts of the city.

DEBECKA PASS   6 APRIL 2003

Forces American and Peshmerga: 100; Iraqi: 100. **Casualties** American and Peshmerga: 17 killed; Iraqi: unknown. **Location** Northern Iraq.

US Special Forces and Peshmerga fighters cut across Highway 2, facilitating further movement into the oil fields of Kirkuk. During the battle, javelin anti-tank missiles destroyed numerous Iraqi armoured vehicles.

IRON HAMMER
11–18 NOVEMBER 2003

Forces American: 15,000; Iraqi: unknown. **Casualties** American: none; Iraqi: 2 killed, 3 wounded. **Location** Baghdad, Iraq.

Responding to mortar and small arms attacks in Baghdad by Iraqi insurgents, US troops launched a massive sweep through the city and captured several large weapon caches, although the insurgency did not wane appreciably.

IRON JUSTICE   7 DECEMBER 2003

Forces American and Iraqi government: 300; Iraqi insurgent: unknown. **Casualties** None. **Location** Baghdad, Iraq.

US forces captured bridges across the Euphrates river during heavy fighting early in the invasion of Iraq. Elements of the Iraqi army and fanatical Baath Party loyalists resisted the US Marines of Task Force Tarawa.

FALLUJAH
7 NOVEMBER–23 DECEMBER 2004

Forces American, British and Iraqi government: 15,000; Iraqi insurgent and al-Qaeda: 5,000. **Casualties** American, British and Iraqi government: 106 killed, 600 wounded; Iraqi insurgent and al-Qaeda: 1,350 killed. **Location** Central Iraq.

Known as Operation Phantom Fury, this resulted in the liberation of the city of Fallujah, previously a hotbed of al-Qaeda activity. The fighting included some of the most intense urban warfare experienced by US troops since Vietnam.

Index

Page numbers in **bold** indicate main entries.

M

Acknowledgments

The publisher would like to thank the following for their kind permission to reproduce their photographs:

Key
a-above; b-below/bottom; c-centre; f-far; l-left; r-right; t-top

1 Dreamstime.com: Jank1000 (c). 2-3 Werner Forman Archive: Kuroda Collection, Japan (b). 4 The Art Archive: Museo Nazionale Terme Rome / Gianni Dagli Orti (br). DK Images: Ermine Street Guard (tc). 5 The Bridgeman Art Library: University of Edinburgh (bl). DK Images: Board of Trustees of The Royal Armouries (tc); Wallace Collection, London (tl). Getty Images: The Bridgeman Art Library (br). 6 Corbis: Philadelphia Museum of Art (br). Getty Images: (cl); Hulton Archive (bl). iStockphoto.com: Andrea Gingerich (tc). 7 Corbis: Bettmann (bl); Bruce Adams / Reuters (br). Dreamstime.com: Argus456 (tc). iStockphoto.com: Graham Heywood (tl). 8-9 The Art Archive: Bibliothèque Nationale Paris. 10-11 The Art Archive: British Museum / Gianni Dagli Orti. 11 akg-images: Erich Lessing (r). DK Images: British Museum (b). 12 Corbis: Christie's Images (b). Werner Forman Archive: Hermitage Museum, St Petersburg (c). 12-13 Getty Images: Jean I Juste/The Bridgeman Art Library (background). 13 akg-images: (tl); John Hios (bc); Archaeological Museum Thasos / Dagli Orti (c). The Art Archive: Archaeological Museum Naples / Dagli Orti (tr). The Bridgeman Art Library: Indian Museum, Calcutta, India / Giraudon (fcrb). DK Images: Hellenic Maritime Museum (clb). Getty Images: The Bridgeman Art Library (crb). 14 akg-images: (tr); Hervé Champollion (c). The Art Archive: Louvre, Paris / Dagli Orti (bl). Corbis: Danny Lehman (tl). V&A Images, Victoria and Albert Museum: (c). 14-15 Getty Images: Jean I Juste/The Bridgeman Art Library (background). 15 Ancient Art & Architecture Collection: (b). The Art Archive: Dagli Orti (cb); National Museum Bucharest / Dagli Orti (cl). Corbis: Asian Art & Archaeology, Inc. (c). DK Images: Ermine Street Guard (tr). Photo Scala, Florence: White Images (cra). 16 DK Images: British Museum (tl). 16-17 The Art Archive: Musée du Louvre Paris / Gianni Dagli Orti (b). 17 The Art Archive: Archaeological Museum Baghdad / Gianni Dagli Orti (t); British Museum / Dagli Orti (cr). Getty Images: The Bridgeman Art Library (br). 18 Werner Forman Archive: Hermitage Museum, St Petersburg (ca). 19 akg-images: Erich Lessing (tc). The Art Archive: British Museum / Dagli Orti (b). Corbis: Chris Hellier (cra). 20 The Art Archive: Musée du Louvre Paris / Gianni Dagli Orti (bl). DK Images: Andy & Elaine Cropper (bc) (br). Getty Images: Antimenes Painter (cl). 21 DK Images: Andy & Elaine Cropper (tr); Hellenic Maritime Museum (bl). 22 akg-images: John Hios (cr). Alamy Images: Peter Horree (cl). 23 The Art Archive: Museo di Villa Giulia Rome / Dagli Orti (tc). DK Images: Andy & Elaine Cropper (cr). 24 The Art Archive: Archaeological Museum Thasos / Dagli Orti (bl); Dagli Orti (ca). 25 akg-images: Erich Lessing (b). 26-27 The Art Archive: Archaeological Museum Istanbul / Gianni Dagli Orti. 28 akg-images: (tl). Alamy Images: INTERFOTO Pressebildagentur (tr). Corbis: Frédéric Soltan / Sygma (b). Getty Images: Persian School (c). 29 The Art Archive: Alfredo Dagli Orti (cr); Musée du Louvre Paris / Gianni Dagli Orti (bl); Museo della Civilta Romana Rome / Gianni Dagli Orti (br). 30 The Art Archive: Musée Archéologique Naples / Alfredo Dagli Orti. 31 Alamy Images: Marco Scataglini (cr). Ancient Art & Architecture Collection: (cr). Getty Images: The Bridgeman Art Library (bc). 32 akg-images: (tr). The Art Archive: Jean Vinchon Numismatist Paris / Gianni Dagli Orti (fcla)

(cla). 33 akg-images: (b). 34 akg-images: (c). Ancient Art & Architecture Collection: (b). 34-35 akg-images: Herve Champollion. 35 akg-images: Herve Champollion (br). 36 The Art Archive: National Museum Bucharest / Dagli Orti (l). DK Images: The Order of the Black Prince (cra). 36-37 Getty Images: Scott Nelson (b). 37 Corbis: Bertrand Rieger / Hemis (cra); Bettmann (tc). Imperial War Museum: (c). Library Of Congress, Washington, D.C.: (br). 38 akg-images: (c) (bl). The Art Archive: (tl); (tc); Erich Lessing (tr). V&A Images, Victoria and Albert Museum: (b). 40 akg-images: Erich Lessing (cla). 40-41 Corbis: Adam Woolfitt (b). 41 The Trustees of the British Museum: (t). 42 DK Images: Ermine Street Guard (tr). Photo Scala, Florence: Courtesy of the Ministero Beni e Att. Culturali (b). 42-43 DK Images: Ermine Street Guard. 43 The Art Archive: Gianni Dagli Orti (cr). DK Images: Ermine Street Guard (ftl) (tc) (tl). 44-45 The Art Archive: Museo della Civilta Romana Rome / Gianni Dagli Orti. 46 Ancient Art & Architecture Collection: (c). The Art Archive: (bl). 47 DK Images: Board of Trustees of The Royal Armouries (cra). Photo Scala, Florence: White Images (b). 48 Corbis: Danny Lehman (c). DK Images: British Museum (b). 49 DK Images: British Museum (t) (cb). 50 Réunion des Musées Nationaux Agence Photographique: Jean-Yves et Nicolas Dubois (c). 50-51 Corbis: Asian Art & Archaeology, Inc.. 51 Réunion des Musées Nationaux Agence Photographique: Thierry Ollivier (crb). Photo Scala, Florence: Museum of East Asian Art, (fcrb). 52 akg-images: Iraq Museum, Baghdad (tl). DK Images: Board of Trustees of The Royal Armouries (c) (cl); Collection of Jean-Pierre Verney (br); Andy & Elaine Cropper (tc). 53 Ancient Art & Architecture Collection: (tl). DK Images: Board of Trustees of The Royal Armouries (fbr) (br) (c) (clb); Wallace Collection, London (cl) (crb); Imperial War Museum (bl). 54 Corbis: Luca Tettoni (t). 55 Ancient Art & Architecture Collection: (cl). The Bridgeman Art Library: Indian Museum, Calcutta, India (bl). The Trustees of the British Museum: (cra). 56-57 The Bridgeman Art Library: Bibliotheque Nationale, Paris, France. DK Images: Wallace Collection, London (b). 57 akg-images: Erich Lessing (r). 58 DK Images: Board of Trustees of The Royal Armouries (c). 58-59 Getty Images: Jean I Juste/The Bridgeman Art Library (background). 59 akg-images: British Library (tc); Musée Saint-Rémi/Gilles Mermet (br). The Bridgeman Art Library: Julian Chichester (c). Corbis: The Gallery Collection (cr). Photo Scala, Florence: Church of San Vitale, Ravenna (cl). 60 akg-images: Musée de la Tapisserie, Bayeaux/Erich Lessing (tr). Ancient Art & Architecture Collection: Museum for Turkish and Islamic Art, Istanbul/Interfoto (br). Corbis: Burstein Collection (c). DK Images: Warwick Castle (br). The Viking Ship Museum, Roskilde, Denmark: (bl). 60-61 Getty Images: Jean I Juste/The Bridgeman Art Library (background). 61 akg-images: Archives Nationales, France (br); Bibliothèque Nationale, Paris/VISIOARS (tr); British Library (bl). Ancient Art & Architecture Collection: (bc). The Art Archive: (tl). The Bridgeman Art Library: Private Collection / Ancient Art and Architecture Collection Ltd. (cl). 62 akg-images: Museo del Prado (bc). 62-63 Photo Scala, Florence: Church of San Vitale, Ravenna (c). 63 The Bridgeman Art Library: Julian Chichester (tr). Réunion des Musées Nationaux Agence Photographique: Hervé Lewandowski (c). 64 Corbis: Kazuyoshi Nomachi (tr). DK Images: British Museum (c). 65 DK Images: British Library. 66-67 Corbis: Brooklyn Museum. 68 akg-images: Musée Saint-Rémi/Gilles Mermet (bl). Ancient Art & Architecture Collection: (tl). The Art Archive:

Stiftbibliotek St Gall/Laurie Platt Winfrey (cr). 69 Corbis: The Gallery Collection (bl). Werner Forman Archive: Universitetets Oldsaksamling, Oslo (c). 70 The Viking Ship Museum, Roskilde, Denmark: (bl). 70-71 DK Images: Danish National Museum. 71 akg-images: Musée de la Tapisserie/Erich Lessing (bl). Alamy Images: Skyscan Photolibrary (br). 72 Corbis: Burstein Collection (tc). DK Images: Board of Trustees of The Royal Armouries (bl). 73 akg-images: Gerard Degeorge (l). Ancient Art & Architecture Collection: Museum for Turkish and Islamic Art, Istanbul/Interfoto (cb). The Bridgeman Art Library: Edinburgh University Library, Scotland (tr). 74 DK Images: Warwick Castle (br). Lebrecht Music and Arts: Rue Des Archives / Tal (br). 75 The Bridgeman Art Library: Centre Historique des Archives Nationales, Paris, France / Lauros / Giraudon (tc). Lebrecht Music and Arts: Rue des Archives/Tal (b). 76 The Bridgeman Art Library: British Library, London (bc). 76-77 Ancient Art & Architecture Collection: (c). 77 akg-images: Bibliothèque Nationale (tr); Cameraphoto (br). 78 The Art Archive: Musée du Louvre Paris / Gianni Dagli Orti (bl). Lebrecht Music and Arts: Leemage (cl). 78-79 Getty Images: Bridgeman Art Library/ Louvre, Paris, France (c). 79 akg-images: Bibliothèque Nationale, Paris (br). 80 akg-images: (tl). V&A Images, Victoria and Albert Museum: (c). 81 akg-images: (br). The Bridgeman Art Library: Tokyo Fuji Art Museum, Tokyo, Japan (cr). Glenbow Museum: (l). 82 The Bridgeman Art Library: Private Collection/Archives Charmet / ADAGP, Paris and DACS, London 2009 (cl). DK Images: Board of Trustees of The Royal Armouries (r). Photo Scala, Florence: BPK, Bildagentur fuer Kunst, Kultur und Geschichte, Berlin (bl); The Metropolitan Museum of Art/ Art Resource (c). 83 Photo Scala, Florence: The Metropolitan Museum of Art/Art Resource (br). TopFoto.co.uk: The Granger Collection (bl). 84-85 The Art Archive: Bibliothèque Nationale Paris. 86 akg-images: Private Collection/François Guénet (tl). Ancient Art & Architecture Collection: UN (bl). DK Images: Royal Artillery Historical Trust (br). 86-87 TopFoto.co.uk: The Granger Collection (c). 87 The Art Archive: (cl). 88 British Library. 89 Ancient Art & Architecture Collection: (crb). Corbis: Ludovic Maisant (cl). DK Images: Board of Trustees of The Royal Armouries (bc). 90 The Art Archive: Bodleian Library Oxford (t). The Bridgeman Art Library: Biblioteca Apostolica Vaticana, The Vatican, Italy / Flammarion (bl). 91 akg-images: British Library (b). The Art Archive: Museo Civico Padua / Gianni Dagli Orti (tl). 92 Alamy Images: Nearby (br). The Bridgeman Art Library: Bernard Cox (r). Getty Images: DEA / M. Carrieri (c). 93 akg-images: (tc). Corbis: Patrick Chauvel / Sygma (bl). DK Images: Board of Trustees of The Royal Armouries (c). 94-95 DK Images: Bibliothèque Nationale Paris (c). 95 akg-images: (cr); Germanisches Nationalmuseum (tl). The Art Archive: (br). 96 Ancient Art & Architecture Collection: (bc). 96-97 The Art Archive: British Library (c). 97 DK Images: Board of Trustees of The Royal Armouries (br); Robin Wigington, Arbour Antiques, Ltd., Stratford-upon-Avon (tr). Getty Images: Purestock (cra). 98 Corbis: Robert Harding World Imagery/Ruth Tomlinson (b). Getty Images: The Bridgeman Art Library (t). 99 akg-images: Armeemuseum Madrid/Gilles Mermet (bl). Mary Evans Picture Library: AISA MEDIA (cr). 100-101 akg-images: Erich Lessing. 102 The Art Archive: Bibliothèque des Arts Décoratifs Paris / Gianni Dagli Orti (br). DK Images: Wallace Collection, London (c). Photo Scala, Florence: British Library (cl). 103 akg-images: Archives Nationales, France (bl); Bibliothèque Nationale, France (t). 104 DK Images: Board of Trustees of The Royal

Armouries (tl) (ca) (cb); Gettysburg National Military Park, PA/Dave King (bc) (c/Indian) (ca/German) (cb/Tulwar) (tc/Italian) (tc/ Scandinavian). 104-105 DK Images: Board of Trustees of The Royal Armouries (ca/Katana) (c/Rapier) (cb/Saber); Wallace Collection, London (bc/Kilu). 105 DK Images: Board of Trustees of The Royal Armouries (c/Broadsword). 106 akg-images: Rainer Hackenberg (cl); Heeresgeschichtliches Museum, Vienna/ Erich Lessing (b). Photo Scala, Florence: The Metropolitan Museum of Art/Art Resource (c). 107 akg-images: Bibliothèque Nationale, Paris/VISIOARS. 108-109 The Art Archive: Private Collection / Eileen Tweedy. DK Images: Wallace Collection, London (b). 109 akg-images: Erich Lessing (r). 110 akg-images: Ulrich Zillmann (b). DK Images: Board of Trustees of The Royal Armouries (t). 110-111 Getty Images: Jean I Juste/The Bridgeman Art Library (background). 111 akg-images: (cl); Bibliothèque Nationale, France/Jérôme da Cunha (bl). The Art Archive: Museo Nacional de Soares dos Reis Porto Portugal / Gianni Dagli Orti (br). Getty Images: Imagno (tc). Photo Scala, Florence: BPK, Bildagentur fuer Kunst, Kultur und Geschichte, Berlin (c); The Metropolitan Museum of Art/Art Resource (br). 112 akg-images: Skokloster Schloß (tr). Ancient Art & Architecture Collection: Europhoto (bl). The Art Archive: Musée des Beaux Arts Lausanne / Gianni Dagli Orti (tl). DK Images: Scottish United Services Museum, Edinburgh Castle/National Museums of Scotland/Geoff Dann (c). Werner Forman Archive: National Museum, Kyoto (tc). 112-113 Getty Images: Jean I Juste/The Bridgeman Art Library (background). 113 The Art Archive: Maritiem Museum Prins Hendrik Rotterdam / Gianni Dagli Orti (cl); Musée des Beaux Arts Dôle / Gianni Dagli Orti (bc); Musée du Château de Versailles / Gianni Dagli Orti (b). China Tourism Photo Library: Fotoe (bl). Getty Images: Imagno (tc). Lebrecht Music and Arts: Interfoto/ Hermann Historica Gmbh (crb). Mary Evans Picture Library: (tr). Réunion des Musées Nationaux Agence Photographique: Paris - Musée de l'Armée/Emilie Cambier / Pascal Segrette (c). 114 akg-images: (cr); Galleria Nazionale di Capodimonte/Erich Lessing (bl). The Art Archive: Alfredo Dagli Orti (c). 114-115 akg-images: Bibliothèque Nationale, France/Jérôme da Cunha. 115 akg-images: Galleria degli Uffizi, Florence/Erich Lessing (tr). 116 akg-images: Ulrich Zillmann (bl). The Bridgeman Art Library: Private Collection (br). 116-117 The Art Archive: Museum für Völkerkunde Vienna / Gianni Dagli Orti (t). 117 DK Images: CONACULTA-INAH-MEX. Authorized reproduction by the Instituto Nacional de Antropologia e Historia. Mary Evans Picture Library: AISA Media (br). 118-119 The Art Archive: © 2009, Banco de Mexico Diego Rivera & Frida Kahlo Museums Trust, Mexico D.F. / DACS / Alfredo Dagli Orti (DETAIL, x). 120 Photo Scala, Florence: Royal Armouries, Leeds (bc) (tl). 120-121 V&A Images, Victoria and Albert Museum: (c). 121 V&A Images, Victoria and Albert Museum: (br). 122 The Art Archive: Topkapi Museum Istanbul / Gianni Dagli Orti (cr). Mary Evans Picture Library: (tl). Photo Scala, Florence: BPK, Bildagentur fuer Kunst, Kultur und Geschichte, Berlin (bl). 123 akg-images: Kunsthistorisches Museum, Vienna. 124-125 Photo Scala, Florence. 126 The Art Archive: Museo Nacional de Soares dos Reis Porto Portugal / Gianni Dagli Orti (bl). Werner Forman Archive: Kuroda Collection, Japan (t). 127 Corbis: Asian Art & Archaeology, Inc (tr). DK Images: Board of Trustees of The Royal Armouries (br). Werner Forman Archive: National Museum, Kyoto (bc). 128 Ancient Art & Architecture Collection: Europhoto. 129 Ancient Art & Architecture Collection: Europhoto (tr) (bl). 130 Courtesy of Sotheby's Picture Library, London: (cl). V&A Images,

Victoria and Albert Museum: (c). 130-131 **Werner Forman Archive:** Kuroda Collection, Japan (b). **131 DK Images:** Board of Trustees of The Royal Armouries (c). **132 British Library:** (tl). **China Tourism Photo Library:** Fotoe (br). **132-133 China Tourism Photo Library.** 133 **Réunion des Musées Nationaux Agence Photographique:** Paris - Musée de l'Armée/Emilie Cambier / Pascal Segrette (tr). **Photo Scala, Florence:** The Metropolitan Museum of Art/Art Resource (br). **134 The Art Archive:** Musée des Beaux Arts Lausanne / Gianni Dagli Orti (br). **DK Images:** Board of Trustees of the Royal Armouries (tr). **134-135 Réunion des Musées Nationaux Agence Photographique:** Musée de l'Armée/Emilie Cambier. 135 **akg-images:** Palazzo Pitti, Gall. Palatina/Nimatallah (br). **The Art Archive:** University Library Geneva / Gianni Dagli Orti (tr). **136-137 The Bridgeman Art Library:** Julian Simon Fine Art Ltd. **138 akg-images:** Sotheby's (bc). **The Art Archive:** Alfredo Dagli Orti (cl). 139 **The Art Archive:** Museo del Prado Madrid / Alfredo Dagli Orti (b). **DK Images:** Board of Trustees of the Royal Armouries. **140 The Art Archive:** San Carlos Museum Mexico City / Gianni Dagli Orti (bl). **DK Images:** Warwick Castle (tr). **140-141 akg-images:** irol Landesmus Ferdinandeum/ Erich Lessing (b). **141 The Art Archive:** Palazzo Pitti Florence / Alfredo Dagli Orti (cr). **The Bridgeman Art Library:** Fitzwilliam Museum, University of Cambridge, UK (r). **142 The Art Archive:** Collection Antonovich / Gianni Dagli Orti (cl). **Lebrecht Music and Arts:** Interfoto/Hermann Historica Gmbh (bl). 143 **akg-images:** Skokloster Schloß (bl). **Photo Scala, Florence:** BPK, Bildagentur fuer Kunst, Kultur und Geschichte, Berlin (t). **144-145 akg-images. 146 akg-images:** Sotheby's (cl). 147 **akg-images:** Coll. Archiv f.Kunst & Geschichte, Berlin (tr). **The Art Archive:** Private Collection / Philip Mould (bc). **DK Images:** Army Medical Services Museum (tl). **148 DK Images:** Scottish United Services Museum, Edinburgh Castle/ National Museums of Scotland/Geoff Dann (bl). **148-149 National Maritime Museum, Greenwich, London:** (r). **149 The Art Archive:** Maritiem Museum Prins Hendrik Rotterdam / Gianni Dagli Orti (bl). **DK Images:** Board of Trustees of the Royal Armouries (tc). **National Maritime Museum, Greenwich, London:** (br). **150-151 National Maritime Museum, Greenwich, London. 152-153 The Art Archive:** Musée du Château de Versailles / Gianni Dagli Orti; Musée des Beaux Arts Dôle / Gianni Dagli Orti (t). **153 The Art Archive:** Musée du Château de Versailles / Gianni Dagli Orti (tc). **154 The Bridgeman Art Library:** National Army Museum, London / Acquired with assistance of National Art Collections Fund (bc). **154-155 DK Images:** Board of Trustees of The Royal Armouries (bc). **Getty Images:** Imagno (t). 155 **akg-images:** (br). **156 DK Images:** Board of Trustees of The Royal Armouries (tl) (bl); CONACULTA-INAH-MEX. Authorized reproduction by the Instituto Nacional de Antropologia e Historia. (tr); Pitt Rivers Museum, University of Oxford/Dave King (br); Robin Wigington, Arbour Antiques, Ltd., Stratford-upon-Avon (c) (ca/Katar). **156-157 DK Images:** Board of Trustees of the Royal Armouries (tc). **157 DK Images:** American Museum of National History (c) (ca/Indian) (ca/Sri Lankan) (cb/Papuan) (cb/Ugandan) (cl/ Nepali); Board of Trustees of The Royal Armouries (cla/Highland) (bc); The Pitt Rivers Museum (clb/Sickle); RAF Museum, Hendon (br); Wallace Collection, London (tc); Imperial War Museum (fbr). **158 akg-images:** Coll. Archiv f.Kunst & Geschichte, Berlin (cl). **Getty Images:** Bridgeman Art Library/Hermitage, St. Petersburg, Russia (cra). **158-159 The State Hermitage Museum, St Petersburg:** Photograph © The State Hermitage Museum (c). 159 **akg-images:** Pushkin Museum, Moscow (tr). **160 akg-images:** Sotheby's (l). **DK Images:** Ermine Street Guard (tr). 161 **Corbis:** David Bathgate (bl). **DK Images:** The Rifles (Berkshire and Wiltshire) Museum (crb). **Mary Evans Picture Library:** Robert Hunt Collection (r). **162-163 The Bridgeman Art Library:** Private Collection (bl). 163 **akg-images:** (tr). **Lebrecht Music and Arts:** Interfoto/Hermann Historica Gmbh (tl) (c). **SCOTLANDSIMAGES.COM:** National Trust

for Scotland/John Sinclair (br). **164-165 The Bridgeman Art Library:** Museo Napoleonico, Rome, Italy / Giraudon. **DK Images:** Board of Trustees of The Royal Armouries (b). **165 akg-images:** Erich Lessing (r). **166 The Art Archive:** Musée du Château de Versailles / Gianni Dagli Orti (b). **166-167 Getty Images:** Jean I Juste/The Bridgeman Art Library (background). **167 The Bridgeman Art Library:** National Army Museum, London (tr); Neues Palais, Potsdam, Germany (cl); Private Collection (b). **DK Images:** Board of Trustees of The Royal Armouries (cla); Museum of Artillery, The Rotunda, Woolwich, London (c); Wallace Collection, London (br). **168 The Art Archive:** Musée d'Histoire et des Guerres de Vendée Cholet / Gianni Dagli Orti (bc). **The Bridgeman Art Library:** Louvre, Paris, France (br). **Corbis:** Bettmann (bl). **DK Images:** Explosion! Museum / Royal Navy Museum (cr); Queen's Rangers/Michael Butterfield (cla). **Mary Evans Picture Library:** (tc). **168-169 Getty Images:** Jean I Juste/The Bridgeman Art Library (background). **169 akg-images:** Château et Trianons, Versailles (crb). **The Bridgeman Art Library:** Look and Learn (cb); Private Collection / Photo © Bonhams, London, UK (cla). **Corbis:** Bettmann (tr). **DK Images:** 1er Chasseurs à Cheval de la Ligne, 2e Compagnie (ca). **Science & Society Picture Library:** Science Museum (bc). **170 www. historicalimagebank.com:** Don Troiani (bl) (br) (tl). **170-171 TopFoto.co.uk:** The Granger Collection. **171 The Bridgeman Art Library:** Private Collection / Phillips, Fine Art Auctioneers, New York, USA (br). **www. historicalimagebank.com:** Don Troiani (bl). **172 DK Images:** Board of Trustees of The Royal Armouries (b). **National Maritime Museum, Greenwich, London:** (tr) (b). **173 akg-images:** Deutsches Historisches Museum, Berlin (tr). **TopFoto.co.uk:** rchiv Gerstenberg / The Granger Collection. **174-175 Photo Scala, Florence:** BPK. **176 Alamy Images:** PjrFoto / studio (cl). **Corbis:** Stapleton Collection (b). **176-177 Mary Evans Picture Library:** Otto Money/ Photography by AIC Photographic Services (t). **177 Photo Scala, Florence:** Royal Armouries, Leeds (bc). **178 www. historicalimagebank.com:** Don Troiani (br). **178-179 The Bridgeman Art Library:** National Army Museum, London (b). 179 **akg-images:** (br). **The Art Archive:** Library of Congress (tl). **Science & Society Picture Library:** Science Museum (r). **180-181 The Bridgeman Art Library:** Bibliotheque Nationale, Paris, France / Lauros / Giraudon. **182 akg-images:** (bl). **Mary Evans Picture Library:** Interfoto (br). **182-183 Photo Scala, Florence:** The Metropolitan Museum of Art/Art Resource. **183 akg-images:** Coll. Archiv f.Kunst & Geschichte, Berlin (tr). **TopFoto.co.uk:** RIA Novosti (bl). **184 DK Images:** Board of Trustees of The Royal Armouries (cb). **Nordiska Museet, Stockholm:** M. Claréus (tr). **184-185 The Bridgeman Art Library:** Nationalmuseum, Stockholm, Sweden (b). **185 DK Images:** Armémuseum, Sweden (r). **186 Lebrecht Music and Arts:** Interfoto/Hermann Historica Gmbh (bl). **186-187 The Art Archive:** Musée d'Histoire et des Guerres de Vendée Cholet / Gianni Dagli Orti. **DK Images:** Board of Trustees of The Royal Armouries (t). **188-189 Corbis:** Historical Picture Archive (b). **DK Images:** Board of Trustees of The Royal Armouries (c). **189 akg-images:** Château et Trianons, Versailles/Erich Lessing (tr). **Corbis:** The Gallery Collection (b). **190 National Maritime Museum, Greenwich, London:** (bl). **190-191 The Art Archive:** Musée du Château de Versailles / Gianni Dagli Orti (t). **191 DK Images:** Board of Trustees of The Royal Armouries (c). **192-193 The Art Archive:** Eileen Tweedy. **194-195 akg-images:** Musée du Louvre, Paris/Erich Lessing (t). **195 The Bridgeman Art Library:** Musee Bernadotte, Pau, France / Lauros / Giraudon (br). **Réunion des Musées Nationaux Agence Photographique:** Paris - Musée de l'Armée/Emilie Cambier / Pascal Segrette (bc). **196-197 The Bridgeman Art Library:** Chateau de Versailles, France. **198 The Art Archive:** Wellington Museum London / Eileen Tweedy (cl). **198-199 The Bridgeman Art Library:** National Army

Museum, London (b). **199 DK Images:** Army Medical Services Museum (t). **200 The Art Archive:** Musée de la Tapisserie Bayeux / Gianni Dagli Orti (b). **The Bridgeman Art Library:** National Army Museum, London (l). **201 The Bridgeman Art Library:** National Army Museum, London (tc). **Corbis:** Leif Skoogfors (bc). **Imperial War Museum:** (cr). **Rex Features:** Paul Melcher (b). **202 DK Images:** Army Medical Services Museum (tr); Royal Artillery Historical Trust (tl). **202-203 akg-images:** Märkisches Museum, Berlin/ Ullstein Bild (b). **203 akg-images:** (tr). **204 DK Images:** Board of Trustees of The Royal Armouries (b); Ermine Street Guard (tc); British Museum (c). **204-205 DK Images:** History Museum, Moscow (c). **205 DK Images:** Board of Trustees of The Royal Armouries (c) (bl); David Edge (bc); Wallace Collection, London (br). **206-207 Corbis:** Gianni Dagli Orti. **208 akg-images:** Ullstein bild (b). **TopFoto.co.uk:** The Granger Collection (br). **208-209 TopFoto.co.uk:** The Granger Collection (tc). **209 Corbis:** Bettmann (bc). **DK Images:** Royal Artillery Historical Trust (tr). **210 Photo Scala, Florence:** BPK, Bildagentur fuer Kunst, Kultur und Geschichte, Berlin (t). **210-211 Mary Evans Picture Library:** AISA Media (b). **211 The Art Archive:** Museo Bolivar Caracas / Gianni Dagli Orti (tc). **www.historicalimagebank. com:** Don Troiani (tr). **212 Lebrecht Music and Arts:** Interfoto/Hermann Historica Gmbh (br). **Photo Scala, Florence:** National Museum Belgrade (bl). **213 akg-images:** Château et Trianons, Versailles (tr). **The Art Archive:** Musée du Louvre Paris (bl). **214-215 Corbis:** Bettmann. **DK Images:** Board of Trustees of The Royal Armouries (b). **215 akg-images:** Erich Lessing (r). **216 akg-images:** (b). **216-217 Getty Images:** Jean I Juste/The Bridgeman Art Library (background). **217 akg-images:** British Library (cl); Erich Lessing (tl). **Alamy Images:** The London Art Archive (cra). **DK Images:** Wallace Collection, London (clb). **Mary Evans Picture Library:** (bl). **Réunion des Musées Nationaux Agence Photographique:** Photo musée de l'Armée (br). **218 The Art Archive:** National Army Museum London (tr). **The Bridgeman Art Library:** Private Collection / Peter Newark Military Pictures (bl). **Corbis:** Bettmann (tr); Elio Ciol (tl). **DK Images:** Collection of Jean-Pierre Verney (cb); Royal Artillery Historical Trust (ca). **218-219 Getty Images:** Jean I Juste/The Bridgeman Art Library (background). **219 akg-images:** (bl). **The Art Archive:** Domenica del Corriere / Alfredo Dagli Orti (tr); Culver Pictures (cl). **Corbis:** Hulton-Deutsch Collection (br). **DK Images:** Explosion! Museum / Royal Navy Museum (tl). **Getty Images:** Time & Life Pictures (cr). **220 DK Images:** Army Medical Services Museum (bc) (cla). **221 Alamy Images:** The London Art Archive (l). **The Bridgeman Art Library:** Florence Nightingale Museum, London, UK (r). **Mary Evans Picture Library:** (br). **222 DK Images:** Army Medical Services Museum/Owned by Surgeon Edward Scott Docker (tr). **Science Photo Library:** Custom Medical Stock Photo (l). **223 Corbis:** Bettmann (b). **DK Images:** Army Medical Services Museum (cra). **Getty Images:** Paul Popper/Popperfoto (tc). **Press Association Images:** AP Photo/Richard Vogel (bl). **224 Corbis:** Elio Ciol (b). **225 The Art Archive:** Private Collection (tl). **DK Images:** Army Medical Services Museum (cr). **Réunion des Musées Nationaux Agence Photographique:** Photo musée de l'Armée (b). **226 DK Images:** Collection of Jean-Pierre Verney (br). **226-227 akg-images:** (b). **227 akg-images:** (br). **The Art Archive:** Library of Congress (bl). **DK Images:** Board of Trustees of The Royal Armouries (c). **Mary Evans Picture Library:** (tc). **228 akg-images:** (bl). **The Bridgeman Art Library:** Schloss Friedrichsruhe, Germany (c). **DK Images:** Gettysburg National Military Park, PA (cr). **229 akg-images. 230 Corbis:** Bettmann (b). **232 The Art Archive:** National History Museum Mexico City / Gianni Dagli Orti (cl). **Corbis:** (bl/1); Joseph Sohm / Visions of America (bl). **DK Images:** US Army Heritage and Education Center - Military History Institute (cb). **Military History, Smithsonian Institution:** (t). **232-233 www.historicalimagebank.com:** Don Troiani (t). **233 DK Images:** Confederate

Memorial Hall, New Orleans (tl). **Getty Images:** Hulton Archive (crb). **www. historicalimagebank.com:** Don Troiani (cr). **234-235 www.historicalimagebank.com:** Don Troiani. **236-237 DK Images:** Confederate Memorial Hall, New Orleans (cr). **237 Corbis:** (cra); Medford Historical Society Collection (br). **DK Images:** Gettysburg National Military Park, PA (c). **Getty Images:** Hulton Archive (bl). **238 akg-images:** (ca). **DK Images:** The Science Museum, London (cla). **239 The Art Archive:** Parker Gallery London / Eileen Tweedy (r). **DK Images:** Royal Artillery Historical Trust (b). **240 akg-images:** (bl). **The Trustees of the British Museum:** (c). **241 akg-images:** (b). **DK Images:** Board of Trustees of The Royal Armouries (t) (c). **242 akg-images:** (tl). **DK Images:** Gettysburg National Military Park, PA (cb). **242-243 DK Images:** American Museum of National History (c). **243 akg-images:** (c). **The Bridgeman Art Library:** (br). **DK Images:** American Museum of National History (crb) (ca/American) (ca/British) (cb/ Russian). **244-245 DK Images:** Board of Trustees of The Royal Armouries (ca/Indian) (bc) (c); Board of Trustees of The Royal Armouries (1/tc) (cb/GP25) (crb/7.62mm). **245 DK Images:** Board of Trustees of The Royal Armouries (tc) (bc) (bl) (c) (cra). **246 The Art Archive:** National Army Museum London (bc). **The Bridgeman Art Library:** Look and Learn (bl). **247 The Art Archive:** Eileen Tweedy (tr). **DK Images:** Board of Trustees of The Royal Armouries (cl) (c). **248 DK Images:** Army Medical Services Museum (bc). **Getty Images:** Time & Life Pictures (t). **249 DK Images:** Army Medical Services Museum (cr); Board of Trustees of The Royal Armouries (ca). **Getty Images:** Time Life Pictures (tc). **Photo Scala, Florence:** Ann Ronan/ HIP (tr). **250 DK Images:** Army Medical Services Museum (cl). **251 Getty Images:** Fox Photos (br). **252 Corbis:** Bettmann (b); David J. & Janice L. Frent Collection (cla). **253 Alamy Images:** Historical Art Collection (br). **The Art Archive:** Culver Pictures (c). **Getty images:** (t). **National Maritime Museum, Greenwich, London:** (bl). **255 Alamy Images:** INTERFOTO Pressebildagentur (br). **Corbis:** (bl); Bettmann (tr). **256-257 The Art Archive. 258 Corbis:** Hulton-Deutsch Collection (br). **259 Alamy Images:** The Print Collector (br). **The Art Archive:** Gianni Dagli Orti (tl). **Corbis:** Chris Hellier (bl). **Getty Images:** Dieter Nagl / AFP (cra). **260-261 Corbis:** Bettmann (tr). **DK Images:** Royal Navy Submarine Museum, Gosport (b). **261 akg-images:** Erich Lessing (r). **262 Getty Images:** Popperfoto (b). **262-263 Getty Images:** Jean I Juste/The Bridgeman Art Library (background). **263 Corbis:** Bettmann (cr) (tr). **DK Images:** Collection of Jean-Pierre Verney (ca); Imperial War Museum (br). **Getty Images:** AFP/Dieter Nagl (tl); MPI (cb); Time Life Pictures/Mansell/Time Life Pictures (bl). **264 The Art Archive:** Marc Charmet (r). **DK Images:** The Rifles (Berkshire and Wiltshire) Museum (cb); USS Texas (t); Imperial War Museum (r). **Getty Images:** Popperfoto (bl); STR/AFP (br). **Mary Evans Picture Library:** Weimar Archive (c). **264-265 Getty Images:** Jean I Juste/The Bridgeman Art Library (background). **265 akg-images:** (cla). **Corbis:** Hulton-Deutsch Collection (c). **DK Images:** Imperial War Museum (cb) (bl). **Getty Images:** FPG/Hulton Archive (c). **Mary Evans Picture Library:** DeAgostini Editore (tl). **TopFoto.co.uk:** (br). **266 The Bridgeman Art Library:** Archives Larousse, Paris, France / Giraudon (b). **Lebrecht Music and Arts:** Rue Des Archives (tr). **267 akg-images:** Erich Lessing (bl). **Lebrecht Music and Arts:** Rue Des Archives (tr). **Réunion des Musées Nationaux Agence Photographique:** Paris - Musée de l'Armée/Emilie Cambier (br). **268 Getty Images:** Popperfoto (c); Time Life Pictures/ Mansell/Time Life Pictures (b). **268-269 DK Images:** Royal Artillery Historical Trust. **269 DK Images:** Imperial War Museum. **Getty Images:** Time Life Pictures/Mansell/Time Life Pictures (tr). **270 The Art Archive:** Imperial War Museum. **271 akg-images:** (br). **Corbis:** Bettmann (cr). **DK Images:** Collection of Jean-Pierre Verney (c). **272 DK Images:** Judith Miller / Auction Team Koln (cl). **Mary Evans Picture Library:** (bl). **272-273 aviation-images.com:** aviation-images.com

ACKNOWLEDGMENTS

Museum, London, UK. **276 akg-images:** Coll. Archiv f.Kunst & Geschichte, Berlin (bl). **Getty Images:** MPI (c). **276-277 Getty Images:** FPG/Hulton Archive (b). **277 Corbis:** Bettmann (tl). **DK Images:** Spink and Son Ltd, London (tr). **278 Réunion des Musées Nationaux Agence Photographique:** Paris - Musée de l'Armée (cr). **278-279 DK Images:** Royal Artillery Historical Trust (bc). **279 DK Images:** Royal Artillery Historical Trust (cl). **US Department of Defense:** SGT Ahner, Rachl M. (br). **280 akg-images:** Lenin Library, Moscow (tr). **280-281 DK Images:** Bettmann. **281 akg-images:** (tl). **Corbis:** Bettmann (tr). **DK Images:** Royal Artillery Historical Trust (c). **282 akg-images:** Ullstein bild (bl). **Getty Images:** Keystone (cl). **282-283 DK Images:** The Rifles (Berkshire and Wiltshire) Museum (b). **283 Corbis:** Hulton-Deutsch Collection (cl). **DK Images:** The Rifles (Berkshire and Wiltshire) Museum (cr). **284 akg-images:** (ca). **Getty Images:** Rolls Press/Popperfoto (b). **284-285 Magnum Photos:** Robert Capa © 2001 By Cornell Capa (b). **285 akg-images:** Ullstein bild (tr). **The Art Archive:** Marc Charmet (tc). **Getty Images:** Erich Lessing (tr). **286 akg-images:** RIA Nowosti (c). **Alamy Images:** Lordprice Collection (crb). **Corbis:** Bettmann (b). **Getty Images:** The Bridgeman Art Library (tc). **287 akg-images:** (bc). **Getty Images:** FPG/Hulton Archive (tr). **Mary Evans Picture Library:** Weimar Archive (cla). **289 akg-images:** (cl). **Lebrecht Music and Arts:** Rue Des Archives (cr). **290 The Art Archive:** Eileen Tweedy (c). **290-291 Getty Images:** Eliot Elisofon/Time & Life Pictures. **291 Getty Images:** Keystone (cra) (crb). **Imperial War Museum:** (t). **292-293 akg-images. 294 DK Images:** Explosion! Museum / Royal Navy Museum (cl). **294-295 Getty Images:** STR/AFP (b). **295 The Art Archive:** Laurie Platt Winfrey (tr). **Getty Images:** Fox Photos (tl). **296 Corbis:** Hulton-Deutsch Collection (b). **296-297 Corbis:** Bettmann (tl). **297 DK Images:** Imperial War Museum (tc) (c). **Lebrecht Music and Arts:** Rue Des Archives (b). **298 DK Images:** Board of Trustees of The Royal Armouries (bc); Imperial War Museum (bl). **TopFoto.co.uk:** Ullstein bild (t). **299 akg-images:** (l). **Alamy Images:** Pictorial Press Ltd (cr). **Getty Images:** Fred Ramage (br). **300 The Rifles (Berkshire and Wiltshire) Museum:** (t). **301 TopFoto.co.uk:** Ullstein Bild (t). **302 Corbis:** Bettmann (tc). **Getty Images:** AFP (bc). **302-303 Mary Evans Picture Library:** DeAgostini Editore (c). **303 DK Images:** Army Medical Services Museum (cr). **304 Getty Images:** Louis R. Lowery/US Marine Corps/Time Life Pictures. **305 Getty Images:** Hulton Archive (br); Time & Life Pictures (cr). **TopFoto.co.uk:** (tc). **306-307 Corbis:** Crown Copyright/MOD /epa. **307 akg-images:** (tl). **308 Corbis:** Patrick Robert/Sygma (b). **DK Images:** Vehicle supplied by Steve Wright, Chatham, Kent/Martin Cameron (c). **308-309 Getty Images:** Jean I Juste/The Bridgeman Art Library (background). **309 aviation-images.com:** Mark Wagner (tc). **Corbis:** Bettmann (br); Michael Nicholson (tr); Swim Ink (cl). **DK Images:** Stuart Beeney (crb); Board of Trustees of The Royal Armouries (bl). **Getty Images:** Bert Hardy (c). **310 Corbis:** Steven Clevenger (cr); Gavin Hellier/Robert Harding World Imagery. **DK Images:** Board of Trustees of The Royal Armouries (tr). **Getty Images:** Hulton Archive (bl); Ya'akov Sa'ar/GPO (br). **310-311 Getty Images:** Jean I Juste/The Bridgeman Art Library (background). **311 Corbis:** (bl); David Brauchli/Sygma (bc); Olivier Coret/In Visu (tr); Peter Turnley (tl). **DK Images:** Board of Trustees of The Royal Armouries (c). **Getty Images:** Mohammed Abed/AFP (br). **312 Cody Images:** (tl) (br). **313 Alamy Images:** John Eccles (br). **DK Images:** H Keith Melton Collection; H Keith Melton Collection (cl) (tc) (tr). **314 The Art Archive:** William Sewell (tr). **314-315 Cody Images. 315 DK Images:** Board of Trustees of The Royal Armouries (t) (tr). **316-317 Chris Streckfus. 317 aviation-images.com:** Mark Wagner (tr). **Corbis:** Bettmann (tl); Bruce Burkhardt (b). **318 Lebrecht Music and Arts:** Rue des Archives (br). **319 Corbis:** Alison Wright (tr). **Getty Images:** Popperfoto (b). **320-321 akg-images. 322 DK Images:**

Stuart Beeney (br). **Getty Images:** Dick Swanson/Time Life Pictures (bl). **322-323 akg-images:** (t). **323 DK Images:** Stuart Beeney (bl). **324 DK Images:** The Rifles (Berkshire and Wiltshire) Museum. **324-325 The Art Archive:** US Naval Museum Washington (t). **325 Corbis:** Bettmann (b). **Paul Schulz:** (t). **326 Getty Images:** Alex Bowie (bc). **326-327 Getty Images:** MPI (c). **327 Corbis:** Claude Urraca/Sygma (tr). **Getty Images:** Robert Nickelsberg/Liaison (br). **328 Getty Images:** Bert Hardy (b). **329 DK Images:** Board of Trustees of The Royal Armouries (tl). **Getty Images:** Grant-Parke/Express (bl). **Lebrecht Music and Arts:** Rue des Archives (c). **Mirrorpix:** (bl). **330 DK Images:** Board of Trustees of The Royal Armouries (br). **330-331 Corbis:** Jehad Nga (t). **331 Corbis:** Les Stone/Sygma (cra). **332 DK Images:** Royal Museum of the Armed Forces and Military History, Brussels (clb). **Getty Images:** William Andrew (clb). **333 Getty Images:** Ishara S. Kodikara/AFP (tl); Robert Nickelsberg (bl). **Rex Features:** Denis Cameron (t). **334 Lebrecht Music and Arts:** Rue des Archives (t). **335 Getty Images:** Abbas Momani/AFP (cr). **Lebrecht Music and Arts:** Rue des Archives (bl). **336 TopFoto.co.uk:** AP (tc) (bc). **337 Getty Images:** Hulton Archive (tr). **MBDA:** Michel Hans (br). **338-339 DK Images:** Royal Artillery Historical Trust (c). **339 DK Images:** Royal Artillery Historical Trust (br); Imperial War Museum (tr). **340 Rex Features:** Alexander Grachtchenkov (tr); Sipa Press (bl). **341 Cody Images. 342 Rex Features:** Sipa Press (bl). **342-343 Corbis:** Henri Bureau/Sygma (t). **343 Corbis:** (bl). **Reuters:** HO Old (tr). **344 Getty Images:** Chris Hondros (l). **Photo Scala, Florence:** British Library, London (tr). **345 Corbis:** Adrees Latif/Reuters (br). **DK Images:** Wallace Collection, London (cra); Imperial War Museum (crb). **Getty Images:** Imagno (tc). **Kevin Quinn, Ohio, US:** On loan to the International Red Cross and Red Crescent Museum in Geneva, Switzerland (bl). **346-347 Corbis:** Yuri Kochetkov/epa (br). **347 Corbis:** Antoine Gyori (tc); Jerry Lampen/Pool/epa (tr). **DK Images:** Army Medical Services Museum (r). **Getty Images:** Ami Vitale (br). **348 Corbis:** Jonathan Montgomery (cl). **Getty Images:** Oleg Nikishin (cl). **348-349 Jon Mills:** (b). **349 DK Images:** Ministry of Defence Pattern Room, Nottingham (tc). **350-351 Karsten Thielker. 354 Corbis:** Jose Fuste Raga (cl). **Getty Images:** The Bridgeman Art Library (tl). **355 Corbis:** Brooklyn Museum (br); Araldo de Luca (tl). **356 DK Images:** Board of Trustees of The Royal Armouries (bl) (fbl). **357 Alamy Images:** Iain Masterton (t). **358 DK Images:** Andy & Elaine Cropper (tr); British Museum (t). **358-359 Corbis:** Gianni Dagli Orti (bc). **360 Corbis:** Asian Art & Archaeology, Inc (bl). **Photos.com:** (tc). **360-361 Getty Images:** National Geographic (br). **362 The Art Archive:** Musée Archéologique Naples (br). **363 Corbis:** Araldo de Luca (br). **DK Images:** University Museum of Newcastle (tl). **364 Corbis:** Bettmann (cl). **365 Alamy Images:** TTL Images (b). **Corbis:** Gianni Dagli Orti (tl). **366 akg-images:** (bc). **The Art Archive:** Galerie Ananda Louvre des Antiquaires (tr). **367 Corbis:** Gianni Dagli Orti (bc). **368 Corbis:** Bettmann (tr). **DK Images:** Ermine Street Guard (bl). **369 Corbis:** Roger Halls / Cordaiy Photo Library Ltd. (br). **370-371 Corbis:** Burstein Collection (bl). **371 The Bridgeman Art Library:** Giraudon (tr) (br). **373 Getty Images:** Charles Auguste Steuben (tl) (br). **374 Corbis:** Gianni Dagli Orti (tl) (br). **375 Getty Images:** Hulton Archive (br). **377 Alamy Images:** Photos 12 (t). **Corbis:** The Art Archive (bl). **378 Corbis:** The Art Archive (t). **379 DK Images:** Wallace Collection, London (fbl) (bc) (bl). **380 DK Images:** Board of Trustees of The Royal Armouries (bl). **380-381 Corbis:** Sakamoto Photo Research Laboratory (tr). **381 Corbis:** Frank Lukassek (cr). **382 The Bridgeman Art Library:** British Library Board (tr). **Getty Images:** De Agostini / G. Dagli Orti (b). **383 DK Images:** Board of Trustees of The Royal Armouries (bl). **384 Getty Images:** The Bridgeman Art Library (bl). **385 Getty Images:** AFP (bl). **386-387 DK Images:** Mary Rose Trust (bl). **387 The Art Archive:** Laurie Platt Winfrey (br). **DK Images:** Board of Trustees of The Royal Armouries (tr). **388**

Corbis: Angelo Hornak (br). **389 DK Images:** Mary Rose Trust (tr). **Getty Images:** Time & Life Pictures (b). **390 DK Images:** The Pitt Rivers Museum (tr). **Getty Images:** The Bridgeman Art Library (bl). **391 DK Images:** Board of Trustees of The Royal Armouries (cl). **392 DK Images:** The Bridgeman Art Library (l). **393 DK Images:** Board of Trustees of The Royal Armouries (tl). **394 DK Images:** CONACULTA-INAH-MEX. Authorized reproduction by the Instituto Nacional de Antropologia e Historia. (tl). **394-395 DK Images:** Board of Trustees of The Royal Armouries (cr). **395 Alamy Images:** Mary Evans Picture Library (r). **396 Getty Images:** Hulton Archive (t). **397 DK Images:** National Museum, New Delhi (tr). **398 Corbis:** Adam Woolfitt (bl). **Getty Images:** Hulton Archive (tr); Time & Life Pictures (ftr). **399 DK Images:** National Museum, New Delhi (r). **400 DK Images:** Board of Trustees of The Royal Armouries (bl). **400-401 Corbis:** Asian Art & Archaeology, Inc (tc). **401 Getty Images:** The Bridgeman Art Library (br). **402 Corbis:** Gavin Hellier / JAI (b). **403 Corbis:** Asian Art & Archaeology, Inc (tl). **DK Images:** Board of Trustees of The Royal Armouries (cr). **404-405 Getty Images:** Hulton Archive (bl). **405 Getty Images:** Tim Graham / The Image Bank (br). **406-407 DK Images:** Board of Trustees of The Royal Armouries (tl). **407 Corbis:** Bettmann (br). **Getty Images:** English Civil War Society (bl). **408 DK Images:** The Pitt Rivers Museum (tr). **409 Getty Images:** Hulton Archive (b). **410 DK Images:** The Pitt Rivers Museum (tr). **410-411 Getty Images:** Hulton Archive (b). **412 DK Images:** Wallace Collection, London (tr). **413 Getty Images:** Hulton Archive (b). **414 DK Images:** Gettysburg National Military Park (tl). **Getty Images:** Hulton Archive (b). **415 Getty Images:** Hulton Archive (tr). **416 The Art Archive:** The British Museum / Eileen Tweedy (tl). **The Bridgeman Art Library:** Private Collection (b). **417 Corbis:** Christie's Images (c). **418 Corbis:** Kevin Fleming (br). **418-419 DK Images:** Board of Trustees of The Royal Armouries (tc). **419 Corbis:** Bettmann (br). **420 Corbis:** Tim Hawkins / Eye Ubiquitous (tl). **421 Corbis:** Richard T. Nowitz (b). **DK Images:** National Maritime Museum, London (tr). **422 Corbis:** Stefano Bianchetti (bl). **Getty Images:** Hulton Archive (tr). **422-423 DK Images:** Board of Trustees of The Royal Armouries (br) (fbr). **423 DK Images:** National Maritime Museum, London (tr). **424 Corbis:** Historical Picture Archive (tr). **424-425 Getty Images:** Robert Dodd (bl). **425 DK Images:** David Edge (tr). **426-427 Corbis:** Fine Art Photographic Library (bl). **427 Corbis:** Gerd Ludwig (tr). **428 The Bridgeman Art Library:** National Army Museum, London (tl). **TopFoto.co.uk:** HIP / William Bagg (br). **429 Corbis:** Araldo de Luca (br). **430 Corbis:** Bettmann (b). **431 Corbis:** Richard T. Nowitz (tl). **Getty Images:** Popperfoto (br). **432 Corbis:** Stapleton Collection (bl). **DK Images:** The Science Museum, London (tl). **433 Corbis:** Jon Hicks (b). **434 DK Images:** Judith Miller / Wallis and Wallis (tc). **434-435 Corbis:** Stapleton Collection (b). **435 Corbis:** Bettmann (b). **436 Alamy Images:** Chris Pondy (tl). **DK Images:** National Maritime Museum, London (cr). **437 DK Images:** Southern Skirmish Association (tr). **Getty Images:** Edgar Samuel Paxson (b). **439 Getty Images:** Time & Life Pictures (br). **440 Getty Images:** Hulton Archive (tl). **440-441 Getty Images:** Hulton Archive (b). **441 Getty Images:** Hulton Archive (tr). **442 DK Images:** Imperial War Museum (r). **Wikipedia, The Free Encyclopedia:** Public Domain (bl). **443 Corbis:** Bettmann (br). **444 DK Images:** British Museum (b). **445 Corbis:** Bettmann (br). **Getty Images:** The Bridgeman Art Library (t); Robert Holmes (bl). **446 Corbis:** Tria Giovan (tr); Robert Holmes (bl). **447 Corbis:** Bettmann (t). **448 Corbis:** Asian Art & Archaeology, Inc (b). **DK Images:** The Royal Geographical Society, London (tc). **449 Corbis:** Tria Giovan (br). **450 Getty Images:** Hulton Archive (tl). **450-451 Getty Images:** William Barnes Wollen (b). **451 Getty Images:** Hulton Archive (t) (bc). **452 Corbis:** Bettmann (b). **DK Images:** Royal Artillery Historical Trust (tr). **454 Corbis:** Hulton-Deutsch Collection (bl). **454-455 Getty Images:** Hulton Archive (tc). **455 Corbis:** The Art Archive (br). **456 Corbis:**

Swim Ink 2, LLC (tr). **DK Images:** Collection of Jean-Pierre Verney (b); Imperial War Museum (tl). **457 Corbis:** Hulton-Deutsch Collection (br). **458 Corbis:** Stapleton Collection (br). **459 Corbis:** Bettmann (cr). **DK Images:** Collection of Jean-Pierre Verney (tl). **460-461 Corbis:** Bettmann (bl). **461 DK Images:** Collection of Jean-Pierre Verney (br). **Getty Images:** Hulton Archive (tl). **462 DK Images:** Collection of Jean-Pierre Verney (cl). **Getty Images:** Hulton Archive (br). **463 Getty Images:** Hulton Archive (tr). **464 Corbis:** (tl). **465 Corbis:** Bettmann (bl). **DK Images:** Imperial War Museum (tl). **466-467 Corbis:** Skyscan (tc). **468 Corbis:** Bettmann (br). **DK Images:** Andrew L. Chernack (tc). **469 Corbis:** Laski Diffusion (tr); Popperfoto (br). **470 Corbis:** Bettmann (tr); CinemaPhoto (bl). **472 Corbis:** Bettmann (tr). **472-473 Getty Images:** Hulton Archive (b). **473 DK Images:** Royal Artillery Historical Trust (cr). **474 Corbis:** Bettmann (bc); David & Janice Frent Collection (tl). **475 Corbis:** Hulton-Deutsch Collection (br). **Getty Images:** Time & Life Pictures (tr). **476 DK Images:** The Bradbury Science Museum, Los Alamos (bl). **476-477 Corbis:** Yevgeny Khaldei (tr). **478 Alamy Images:** Malcolm Fairman (tl). **Getty Images:** Popperfoto (b). **480 Getty Images:** Hulton Archive (tl). **480-481 Corbis:** Bettmann (bc). **481 The Art Archive:** Department of Defense, Washington (cr). **482 Corbis:** Bettmann (tl). **483 Corbis:** (tr). **484 Corbis:** Lake County Museum (cl). **484-485 Getty Images:** Time & Life Pictures (bc). **485 Corbis:** Vittoriano Rastelli (tr). **486 Corbis:** Bettmann (bc). **DK Images:** Andrew L. Chernack (tr). **487 Corbis:** Bettmann (b). **488 Alamy Images:** Lordprice Collection (tc). **489 Getty Images:** Popperfoto (tr). **490 Corbis:** Reuters / Anuruddha Lokuhapuarachchi (bl); Sygma / Henri Bureau (br). **491 Corbis:** Sygma / Patrick Chauvel (tl). **492 DK Images:** Imperial War Museum (bc). **492-493 DK Images:** Ministry of Defence Pattern Room, Nottingham (tc). **493 Corbis:** Françoise de Mulder (bc). **494 Corbis:** Peter Turnley (tr). **Getty Images:** AFP (b). **495 Corbis:** Reuters / Las Vegas Sun / Steve Marcus (br). **496 Corbis:** EPA / Sergio Barrenechea (cr). **497 Getty Images:** Time & Life Pictures (bl). **Wikipedia, The Free Encyclopedia:** U.S. Department of Defense (tr).

Jacket images: *Front and Back:* **David J Colbran.** *Back:* **Alamy Images:** Mary Evans Picture Library fclb; **Corbis:** epa crb; The Gallery Collection fcla; Stapleton Collection fcra; **Getty Images:** cra, fcrb; Purestock clb; **Nick Medrano:** www.ww2incolor.com cb. *Spine:* **David J Colbran** ; Front Endpapers: **The Trustees of the British Museum;** Back Endpapers: **The Trustees of the British Museum.**

Jacket design: Duncan Turner

All other images © Dorling Kindersley

For further information see: **www.dkimages.com**

DK would like to thank the following museums and staff for their kind assistance on the book: Armé Museum, Stockholm; Firepower, The Royal Artillery Museum, Woolwich; Royal Armouries, Leeds; Royal Museum of the Armed Forces of Military History, Brussels; and The Army Medical Services, Aldershot.

DK would also like to thank Helen Peters for the index; Caroline Hunt for proofreading; Betty Jarvis, Les Kerswill, Lloyd Roseblade, and Paul Schulz for providing objects and information for the Aspects of War features; Martin Copeland, Karen Van Ross, and Jenny Baskaya for picture research assistance; and Anna Hall and Todd Webb for design assistance.